BALLENTINE'S LEGAL
DICTIONARY AND THESAURUS

BALLENTINE'S LEGAL DICTIONARY AND THESAURUS

Jonathan S. Lynton, Ph.D., J.D.

WEST PUBLISHING

an International Thomson Publishing company I(T)P®

Albany • Bonn • Boston • Cincinnati • Detroit • London • Madrid
Melbourne • Mexico City • Minneapolis/St. Paul • New York • Pacific Grove
Paris • San Francisco • Singapore • Tokyo • Toronto • Washington

NOTICE TO THE READER

Cover Design: Spiral Design Studio

Delmar Staff

Administrative Editor: Jay Whitney

Developmental Editor: Christopher Anzalone

Project Editor: Theresa M. Bobear

Production Coordinator: Jennifer Gaines

Art & Design Coordinator: Douglas Hyldelund

COPYRIGHT © 1995
By West Publishing
an imprint of Delmar Publishers
a division of International Thomson Publishing
The ITP logo is a trademark under license.

Printed in the United States of America

For more information, contact:

Delmar Publishers
3 Columbia Circle , Box 15015
Albany, New York 12212-5015

International Thomson Editores
Campos Eliseos 385, Piso 7
Col Polanco
11560 Mexico D F Mexico

International Thomson Publishing – Europe
Berkshire House
168-173 High Holborn
London, WC1V 7AA
England

International Thomson Publishing GmbH
Königswinterer Strasse 418
53227 Bonn
Germany

Thomas Nelson Australia
102 Dodds Street
South Melbourne, 3205
Victoria, Australia

International Thomson Publishing – Asia
221 Henderson Road
#05 -10 Henderson Building
Singapore 0315

Nelson Canada
1120 Birchmount Road
Scarborough, Ontario
Canada M1K 5G4

International Thomson Publishing – Japan
Hirakawacho Kyowa Building, 3F
2-2-1 Hirakawacho
Chiyoda-ku, Tokyo 102 Japan

6   7   8   9   10   XXX   03   02   01   00   99   98

Library of Congress Cataloging-in-Publication Data

Lynton, Jonathan S.
   Ballentine's legal dictionary and thesaurus / Jonathan Lynton,
     p.   cm.
   ISBN 0-8273-6526-8
   1. Law—United States—Dictionaries.   2. Law—United States—Terminology.
  3. Law—Dictionaries.   4. Law—Terminology.
   I. Title.
KF156.L95   1995
349.73'03—dc20
   [347.3003]

94-33514
CIP

The West Paralegal Series

Your options keep growing with West Publishing.
Each year our list continues to offer you more options for every course, new or existing, and on-the-job reference materials. We now have over 140 titles from which to choose.

We are pleased to offer books in the following subject areas:

Administrative Law	Family Law
Alternative Dispute Resolution	Federal Taxation
Bankruptcy	Intellectual Property
Business Organizations/Corporations	Introduction to Law
Civil Litigation and Procedure	Introduction to Paralegalism
CLA Exam Preparation	Law Office Management
Client Accounting	Law Office Procedures
Computer in the Law Office	Legal Research, Writing, and Analysis
Constitutional Law	Legal Terminology
Contract Law	Paralegal Employment
Criminal Law and Procedure	Real Estate Law
Document Preparation	Reference Materials
Environmental Law	Torts and Personal Injury Law
Ethics	Will, Trusts, and Estate Administration

You will find unparalleled, practical teaching support.
Each text is enhanced by instructor and student supplements to ensure the best learning experience possible to prepare for this field. We also offer custom publishing and other benefits such as West's Student Achievement Award. In addition, our sales representatives are ready to provide you with needed and dependable service.

We want to hear from you.
The most important factor in improving the quality of our paralegal texts and teaching packages is active feedback from educators in the field. If you have a question, concern, or observation about any of our materials or you have written a proposal or manuscript, we want to hear from you. Please do not hesitate to contact your local representative or write us at the following address:

West Paralegal Series, 3 Columbia Circle, P.O. Box 15015, Albany, NY 12212-5015.
For additional information point your browser to
http://www.westpub.com/Educate and **http://www.delmar.com**

West Publishing — *Your Paralegal Publisher*
an imprint of Delmar Publishers

an International Thomson Publishing company **I(T)P**®

DEDICATION

I dedicate these words
to my sons,
Nick and Aaron,
who, like the flight of birds,
are wonderful beyond words

and to

Michael S. Harper,
through whose vision the magical word
reveals the truth of the sacred ring:

a love supreme

CONTENTS

FOREWORD

As a lawyer who has spent more than six decades striving to communicate with judges, lawyers, and clients, I have developed a slavish reverence for the language of the law, for the punctilious selection of the right words. For those of us who, like me, have spent much of our lives in courts, the search for precision and verbal vigor is unremitting. We must acknowledge our special debt to those scholars who give us their help in that pursuit. We all labor to write well and to speak well. Only the lazy and indifferent fail to understand that there is but one way to write well and to speak well: as one of the greatest writers of our language has put it, "to play the sedulous ape" to the great practitioners of English prose.

No dictionary or thesaurus can equip the indolent, the indifferent, or the ignorant. They will go on stammering and confusing their hearers and readers. But those who approach their tasks with an honest concern and fitting respect for linguistic standards should welcome the appearance of any tool that sharpens the needed skills. *Ballentine's Legal Dictionary and Thesaurus* is such a tool, a new and useful instrument for reaching that objective.

I have often complained that contemporary legal education overemphasizes the need for aspiring lawyers to be familiar with economic, financial, and statistical problems. Generally, those who mold current technologies of legal pedagogy have somewhat neglected the requirement for language skills. An astute lawyer can always use the expertise of others with specialized skills, but for those working in the legal field there is no substitute for possessing and using superb communication and language skills. I think that in earlier times those who came to the bar had a broader experience in and exposure to the substance of human experience, including a familiarity with great literature and especially with the languages from which our native tongue is derived. We need to restore that love of language to the legal profession.

Thus, I persist in the belief that only an exposure to good writing and to the use of words as an art can imbue fledgling legal professionals with an appreciation of the verbal and written skills indispensable to precise and forceful articulation. In my own early time at the New York bar, I was fortunate to see and hear some of the finest advocates of that era. I observed such courtroom artists as Lloyd Paul Stryker, Harold Medina, Joseph Proskauer and others. Plainly, to see and hear such prodigious talent was to recognize them as exemplars of the kind of mastery over words that can come only from the absorption of lofty literature, from studying the work of masters not only in English poetry and prose but also in the other tongues of our civilization. The observation of such masters of persuasion is an object lesson in how vital it is in a learned profession to study, to honor, and to practice the careful use of words.

Because I am a devotee of the use of precise and elevated language in the law, I can appreciate the value of the kind of vade mecum Dr. Lynton provides here. It is simple, easy to use, and unfailing in its scholarship. It should be especially welcome to those of us who are weary of the clichés and bromides, the facile pleonasms, and tortured solecisms that resound in our courtrooms. So, to this new and useful addition to lucidity and accuracy in the language of the law, I give my greeting. To its readers, I say: it will not make you eloquent or erudite unless you already are. But it will help you to speak and write with increased accuracy, dignity, and force.

Milton S. Gould
New York, New York
March 1994

PREFACE

An academic discipline or a profession defines itself, in large part, by the words and phrases—the special use of language—which comprise the working vocabulary of that field. Those who practice a profession are professionals in that they understand and use the vocabulary of their field with fluency; those who are outside a field remain so because they do not understand the ideas and issues, defined through language, which comprise that discipline.

So it is with the law—only more so. Not only has the law spawned its own universe of discourse, with its attendant specialized vocabulary, but the practice of the law—the representation of people and organizations—also requires the facile use of language at every juncture. When a lawyer represents a client, that lawyer is the spokesperson for that client; clients need spokespersons precisely because they cannot fathom the procedures and terminology that constitute the legal process.

It follows, then, that those involved in the legal field can achieve competence and fulfill their professional responsibilities only by being practitioners of language at the highest level, by using words correctly and forcefully in the presentation of ideas. Through words, through language, we do not merely reflect the reality we are describing, but we also create a reality made up of the possible meanings language may have. Law Professor Patricia Williams pointedly articulated the importance of language to the law when she wrote, "Law and life are all about the constant assessment of where on the scale one's words are meant—and by which level of the scale one evaluates the words of others. But I think the game is more complicated than choosing a single level on which to settle for all time. That truth exists on all three levels is the underlying truth I want to pursue here." If the ultimate purpose of the law, then, is to provide access to truth and to justice, it is clear that only through the understanding and mastery of the linguistic universe will we be able to approach those lofty goals.

Ballentine's Legal Dictionary and Thesaurus is a thorough, easy-to-use, logically constructed tool for students and practitioners of the law and their assistants. It is a helpful companion for all phases of legal research and writing, and it provides an accessible, complete, and accurate understanding of over 10,000 definitions of legal terms accompanied by over 25,000 synonyms for those terms. Each entry contains the following information about the word or phrase:

- pronunciation
- part of speech
- definitions: if a word has different definitions, those are denoted by numbers; if a word can be used as different parts of speech, the definition follows the designation for that part of speech
- sample usages of difficult terms
- see and compare references, which show connections between the initial word and other entries in the dictionary/thesaurus
- synonyms for the entry word following the definitions (denoted by ➤): synonyms for different usages of the same part of speech are separated by a semicolon; synonyms for the same work used as different parts of speech are designated by part of speech
- sample usages of the terms
- antonyms for the entry word.

As you can see, each entry contains a great deal of information about the word or term, clearly presented, so that using this reference book is a friendly and helpful rather than frustrating experience.

Whether you are reading legal documents, writing legal documents, performing legal research, or communicating with others in the legal field, it is essential that you have a resource which can help you clarify uncertain terms and use language precisely and confidently. I am confident that *Ballentine's Legal Dictionary and Thesaurus* will be the kind of research tool that you will use again and again to aid in understanding and presenting the language of the law.

ACKNOWLEDGMENTS

Thanks are due to numerous people who assisted and supported me on this project. Jay Whitney, Chris Anzalone, and Glenna Stanfield of Delmar Publishers have been an ideal editorial team. Brooke Graves, of Graves Editorial Service, copy editor extraordinaire, has given this manuscript the benefit of her careful scrutiny, for which I am extremely grateful. Many thanks also to Gwen Peterson for her much appreciated editorial assistance on this project.

I appreciate the loving support of my family: my wife, Kim, my sons, Nick and Aaron, and my parents Joan S. Lynton, William J. Klein, Julian E. Lynton, and Joan L. Lynton. Special thanks also to attorney Milton S. Gould for his friendship and support, and for his outstanding foreword to this book.

Finally, I extend my thanks and gratitude to those who have truly given meaning to the notion that "you get by with a little help from your friends": Rick Klauber, John Richards, Jimmy Stark, Michael Harper, Duncan Smith, Alexander, Phil Lewin, Dennis Grady, Jerry Percifield, Bud Siemon, Terri Lyndall, Michael B. Lyndall, Cory and Alan Begner, Cathy Alterman, Penny Moss Douglass, David Ryback, Hugh Maxwell, Felix Love, Bob Bouwman, Nick Vitterite, Mark Jacobs, and all the other friends, colleagues, clients, and students who have supported, challenged, and assisted me throughout the years.

a [ah] (*Latin*) *prep.* From; after; by; in; on; of; out of; because of; with. "*A*" appears frequently in Latin phrases used in the law. (EXAMPLE: *a fortiori* means "by the stronger reason.") *Ab* is used in place of *a* when the Latin word that follows it begins with a vowel. EXAMPLE: *ab initio*.

a fortiori [for · she · *or* · ee] "By the stronger reason."

a mensa et thoro [*men* · sa et *thore* · oh] "From bed and board." *See* divorce a mensa et thoro.

a posteriori [po · steer · ee · *or* · ee] "From a later point of view." Conveys the idea of reasoning backward from facts or consequences, or inductive reasoning. *Compare a priori.*

a prendre [ah *prawn* · dre] (*French*) To take. *See* profit à prendre.

a priori [ah pree · *or* · ee] "From before"; from the past; from what has gone before. To argue or reason *a priori* is to conclude by deduction that because certain facts exist, certain other facts necessarily follow. *Compare a posteriori.*

a vinculo matrimonii [vin · kyoo · loh mat · ri · *moh* · ni · eye] "From the bonds of marriage." *See* divorce a vinculo matrimonii.

AAA Abbreviation of **American Arbitration Association**, Agricultural Adjustment Act, American Accounting Association, American Automobile Association.

AAfPE Abbreviation of **American Association for Paralegal Education**.

AALS Abbreviation of Association of American Law Schools.

ab [ahb] *prep. See a.*

ab initio [in · *ish* · ee · oh] "From the beginning." USAGE: "The agreement was unenforceable *ab initio.*"

ABA Abbreviation of **American Bar Association**.

abaction [ab · *ak* · shen] *n.* Carrying away by force, especially of animals. *See also* robbery.
➤ carrying away, larceny, robbery, stealing.

abandon [a · *ban* · dcn] *v.* To give up; to surrender; to desert; to remove oneself entirely from a person or a thing, putting aside all care for him or her or it. To abandon a person is to withdraw totally from someone entitled to support. *See* abandonment.
n. A yielding to natural impulses.
➤ *v.* give up, surrender, desert, quit, repudiate, abnegate, forsake, leave ("to abandon an ineffective litigation strategy"). *Ant.* maintain.
n. wantonness, lawlessness ("wanton abandon").

abandoned property [*prop* · er · tee] *n.* Property of which the owner has voluntarily given up possession and control, and which she has no intention of reclaiming. *See* abandonment of property. *Compare* lost property; mislaid property.

abandonment [a · *ban* · den · ment] *n.* The act of voluntarily and totally relinquishing a right or property with no thought of reclaiming it or of giving or selling it to anyone else. *Compare* forfeiture; surrender; waiver.

➤ desertion, relinquishment, disavowal, renunciation, rejection, disownment, forsaking, yielding, withdrawal.

abandonment of action [*ak* · shen] *n.* Failure to file a lawsuit within the time period prescribed by the applicable **statute of limitations** will result in its being dismissed by the court. Additionally, failure to exercise a right in a timely manner during trial may result in its abandonment (EXAMPLE: failure to object to testimony).

abandonment of child *n.* A child is abandoned if a parent deserts her with the intention of casting off all parental obligations. *See* desertion; nonsupport.

abandonment of copyright [*kop* · ee · rite] *n. See* abandonment of property.

abandonment of patent [*pat* · ent] *n. See* abandonment of property.

abandonment of property [*prop* · er · tee] *n.* The act, by an owner of property, of voluntarily giving up possession and control of the property with no intention of reclaiming it. Both real property and personal property may be abandoned. **Copyrights**, **inventions**, and **patents** may be abandoned if the owner permits a **public use** of them. *See* property. *Also see* abandoned property.

abandonment of spouse *n.* Same as **desertion**. It is a ground for divorce.

abandonment of use *n.* The loss of a right to a **nonconforming** use under zoning laws.

abatable [a · bate · ebl] *adj.* That which may be reduced, diminished, discontinued, or ended.

➤ impermanent, modifiable, revocable, destructive.

abatable nuisance [*new* · sense] *n.* A **nuisance** that is not permanent; a nuisance that can be eliminated; a **temporary nuisance**. *Compare* nonabatable nuisance. *See* abatement of nuisance.

abate [a · bate] *v.* To quash, beat down, diminish, or do away with.

➤ quash, decrease, reduce, beat down, diminish, do away with, eliminate, terminate, curtail, modify.

abatement [a · bate · ment] *n.* A lessening or elimination.

➤ termination, eradication, curtailment, extermination, cessation ("abatement of a nuisance"); reduction, lessening, diminution, lowering, mitigation ("tax abatement").

abatement of action [*ak* · shen] *n.* The suspension or termination of **proceedings** in a **legal action**. *See* dismissal. *Also see* plea in abatement.

abatement of bequest [be · *kwest*] *n.* The process of determining the distribution of the **assets** left by a deceased in his will when the assets are insufficient to satisfy all the **bequests** made in the will.

abatement of cause of action [*ak* · shen] *n.* The termination of a right to commence **legal action** because of the death of a necessary party. *See* cause of action. *Compare* dismissal.

abatement of legacy [*leg* · e · see] *n.* Same as **abatement of bequest**.

abatement of nuisance [*new* · sense] *n.* The elimination of a **nuisance**. *See* abatable nuisance.

abatement of rent *n.* The reduction or termination of a tenant's obligation to pay rent.

abbroachment [a · *broach* · ment] *n.* Same as **abbrochment**.

abbrochment [a · *broach* · ment] *n.* Stifling a free market by buying up the goods to be sold and selling them at a considerably higher price. *See* monopoly.

➤ stifling, forestalling, monopolizing.

ABC test *n.* A rule of law that exempts an employer from the obligation to provide unemployment compensation coverage for **independent contractors**.

abdicate [*ab* · di · kate] *v.* To renounce completely, throw off, disown, or relinquish.

➤ forsake, give up, renounce, throw off, disown, relinquish, cede ("The government has abdicated its taxing power").

abdication [ab · di · *kay* · shen] *n.* A person's renunciation or abandonment of an office, trust, or sovereignty to which she is entitled by law. *Compare* resignation. The word is also frequently applied to

the actions of government. USAGE: "The government has abdicated its **police power** in this case."
➤ renunciation, resignation, abandonment, cessation, abjuration, relinquishment.

abduct [ab · *dukt*] *v.* To take away by force.
➤ kidnap, seize, shanghai, capture, steal.

abduction [ab · *duk* · shen] *n.* The illegal carrying away, by force or deception, of a person (EXAMPLES: a spouse; a child; a **ward**; a prisoner) who is in the charge or custody of another. *See* child stealing; kidnapping.
➤ kidnapping, seizure, capture, arrogation.

aberemurder [*ay* · bur · mer · der] *n.* Simple murder.
➤ assassination, killing, homicide, extermination.

abet [a · *bet*] *v.* To encourage another to commit a crime. *Compare* aid. *See* aiding and abetting. *See also* accessory; accomplice.
➤ aid, assist, facilitate, spur, urge, exhort, foment, sustain, conspire.

abettor [a · *bet* · er] *n.* One who **abets**.
➤ accessory, accomplice, advocate, prompter, instigator, partner, collaborator.

abeyance [a · *bay* · ense] *n.* A state of inactivity or suspension.
➤ latency, inaction, deadlock, repose, suspension, remission, quiescence ("held in abeyance").

abide [a · *bide*] *v.* To endure and accept without objection.
➤ obey, comply with, accept, observe, submit to ("abide by the decision of the court"); tolerate, endure, suffer ("He could not abide the new owner").

abide by [a · *bide*] *v.* To obey or comply with; to accept. USAGE: "The parties have no choice but to abide by the order of the court."

abiding *adj.* Certain; unshakeable; enduring; continuing.
  abiding conviction [ken · *vik* · shen] *n.* To be thoroughly convinced of a person's guilt; to believe a person guilty **beyond a reasonable doubt**.

ability [a · *bil* · it · ee] *n.* 1. The state of being able or capable. 2. Skill; competency.
➤ capability, skill, capacity, faculty, acumen, proficiency, talent.
Ant. limitation, incompetency, incompetence, ignorance.
  ability to buy *n.* *See* able buyer.
  ability to pay *n.* A standard used by courts in determining the amount of support to be paid to a spouse or children.

adjudicate [ab · *joo* · di · kate] *v.* 1. To deprive a person of something by court order. 2. To remove by order of court.
➤ deprive, remove, take.

abjuration [ab · joo · *ray* · shen] *n.* A renunciation of one's country, citizenship, or loyalty; a forswearing of the rights that arise from citizenship.
➤ renunciation, forswearing, abandonment, relinquishment, rejection, recantation.

abjure [ab · *joor*] *v.* To disclaim; to renounce; to repudiate.
➤ retract, disclaim, renounce, repudiate.
Ant. assert, inject, put forth.

able [*ay* · bul] *adj.* Capable; proficient; skilled.
➤ competent, proficient, capable, qualified ("an able litigator").
Ant. incompetent.

able buyer [*by* · er] *n.* In the law of contracts, a purchaser who has sufficient money or means with which to fulfill the agreement.

abnegate [*ab* · ne · gate] *v.* To give up; to surrender; to renounce.
➤ give up, surrender, renounce.

abnormal [ab · *nor* · mal] *adj.* Deviating from the norm or average.
➤ uncommon, peculiar, odd, unnatural, idiosyncratic.
Ant. regular, common, normal.

abode [a · *bode*] *n.* A dwelling place; a residence; home. "Abode," or **usual place of abode**, is often but not necessarily synonymous with **domicile** because a person's domicile may be different from his abode, and although a person may have more than one abode he can have

only one domicile. **Permanent abode**, however, is synonymous with domicile.
➤ dwelling, residence, home, domicile, homestead ("usual place of abode").

abolish [a · *bol* · ish] *v.* To repeal; to recall; to revoke; to cancel and eliminate entirely.
➤ repeal, recall, revoke, cancel, eliminate, erase, obliterate, dissolve ("to abolish a tax").
Ant. establish, confirm, legalize.

abolition [ab · o · *lish* · en] *n.* A repeal or elimination. EXAMPLE: the abolition of slavery by the **Thirteenth Amendment** to the Constitution.
➤ negation, nullification, cancellation, rescission, retraction, eradication, disestablishment.
Ant. establishment, confirmation

aboriginal [ab · o · *rij* · in · el] *adj.* Pertaining to the original natives of a place; "of the original."
➤ native, prehistoric, primeval, primal, indigenous, first, original.
Ant. foreign, acquired, alien.
aboriginal title [*ty* · tel] *n. See* Indian title.

abort [a · *bort*] *v.* 1. To terminate a pregnancy. 2. To stop a project in development.
➤ sever, miscarry, stop, terminate.
Ant. continue, save.

abortifacient [a · bore · ti · *fay* · shent] *n.* Anything used to cause an abortion.

abortion [a · *bore* · shen] *n.* The expulsion of a fetus from the womb. An abortion may involve the deliberate destruction of the fetus (an induced abortion) or it may occur naturally (a spontaneous abortion). *See Roe v. Wade,* 410 U.S. 113, 93 S. Ct. 705 (1973).
➤ destruction, miscarriage, aborticide, termination ("Abortion is a woman's choice"); failure, frustration, disaster, blunder ("the committees' work was an abortion").

about [a · *bout*] *prep.; adv.* More or less; approximately; nearly. Because it denotes inexactness, "about" is a word of flexible significance and, therefore, of limited legal meaning. When possible, it is given its common-sense meaning, which,

however, is always imprecise because it depends upon the surrounding circumstances. Generally speaking, "about" is a word to be avoided in legal writing.
➤ *prep.* relating to, concerning, involving.
Ant. exactly, precisely.
adv. approximately, nearly.

above [a · *buv*] *adv.* 1. Higher; superior. EXAMPLE: the "court above" means the **appellate court**. 2. Previously; before. EXAMPLE: "cited above" means previously referred to in a given text, paragraph, or chapter. *See* aforesaid; *supra.*
➤ beyond, superior, on top of, raised, surpassing.

abridge [a · *brij*] *v.* 1. In **copyright** law, to preserve the essence of a work in more succinct language. 2. To reduce; to cut down; to curtail. USAGE: "The Constitution prohibits Congress from enacting any law abridging freedom of speech."
➤ reduce, cut down, curtail, condense, shorten, edit, cut.
Ant. increase, expand, lengthen.

abridgment [a · *brij* · ment] *n.* A shortened version of a work which retains the general sense and unity of the original.
➤ reduction, summary, synopsis, abstract, digest.

abroachment [a · *broach* · ment] *n.* Same as **abbrochment**.

abrogate [*ab* · roh · gate] *v.* To repeal; to render void; to annul. USAGE: "The new statute abrogates the existing laws on this subject."
➤ cancel, repeal, make void, annul, revoke, nullify.
Ant. ratify, establish, invoke, support.

abrogation [ah · roh · *gay* · shen] *n.* The repeal or annulment of a law. *See* abrogate.
➤ repeal, annulment, termination, rescission.

abscond [ab · *skond*] *v.* To leave secretly or furtively; to hide or conceal oneself in order to avoid the law or **legal process**. EXAMPLE: leaving a state or other jurisdiction to avoid one's creditors.
➤ leave, hide, conceal, flee, retreat, escape, vanish, bolt, depart ("abscond with the money").
Ant. remain, stay.

A

absconding debtor [ab · *skond* · ing *det* · er] *n.* A person who leaves the state, or who intentionally conceals herself within the state, in order to put herself beyond the reach of her creditors.

absence [ab · *sense*] *n.* 1. The state of not being present. 2. The state of being in need or deficient.
➤ nonpresence, withdrawal, avoidance, defection, nonappearance; blank, omitted, devoid, lacking, vacant.

absentee ballot [ab · sen · tee *bal* · et] *n.* A vote cast, usually by mail, by a voter who, for legally valid reasons, will not be present at the polls at the time of the election.

absenteeism [ab · sen · *tee* · izm] *n.* An employee's persistent, unexcused absence from work. This term has significance in labor law. An employee's absenteeism may justify his termination by his employer or the denial of unemployment compensation benefits by the state.
➤ absence, nonpresence, nonappearance, truancy ("Management has considered several strategies to deal with increasing absenteeism among the workers").

absentia [ab · *sen* · sha] *See in absentia.*

absolute [ab · so · loot] *adj.* Unrestricted; unconditional; complete. *Compare* qualified; relative.
➤ unrestricted, unconditional, complete, unrestrained, entire, total, unimpeded ("absolute privilege").

absolute conveyance [kon · *vay* · ense] *n.* A transfer of land without restrictions such as a mortgage or an **easement**. *See* conveyance.

absolute deed *n. See* absolute conveyance.

absolute divorce [di · *vorss*] *n.* A total divorce; a **divorce a vinculo matrimonii**. *Compare* divorce a mensa et thoro.

absolute estate [es · *tate*] *n.* An **estate** in real property which is owned unconditionally and which passes to the owner's heirs under the **intestate laws** if the owner fails to leave a will directing otherwise. EXAMPLE: a **fee simple** estate. *See* unconditional ownership. *Compare* conditional estate.

absolute guaranty [*gehr* · en · tee] *n.* An unconditional commitment on the part of a **guarantor** that the debtor will perform his obligation. *See* guaranty.

absolute interest [*in* · trest] *n.* An **interest** that is a person's exclusively and of which she cannot be deprived without her consent. *See* vested interest.

absolute liability [ly · e · *bil* · i · tee] *n.* **Liability** for an **injury** whether or not there is fault or **negligence**. *See* strict liability. *Also see* negligence per se.

absolute nuisance [*new* · sense] *n.* A **nuisance** that is created or maintained intentionally rather than negligently.

absolute right *n.* The exclusive **right** to possess, use, enjoy, and dispose of property. *Compare* qualified right; relative rights.

absolute rule *n.* Same as **rule absolute**.

absolution [ab · so · *loo* · shen] *n.* 1. Exoneration of a crime. *See* acquittal. 2. Release from a debt or other obligation. 3. Forgiveness of sin.
➤ exoneration, discharge, acquittal, release, vindication, liberation, clearance.

absolutism [*ab* · so · loo · tizm] *n.* The principle that a ruler or the government has absolute power. *See* authoritarianism. *Compare* democracy.

absolve [ab · *zolv*] *v.* To free oneself from guilt or become free from an obligation.
➤ acquit, exculpate, exonerate, vindicate, free, liberate.

absorbed [ab · *zorbd*] *adj.* The state of being wholly engaged or involved with something.
➤ engaged, involved, occupied, engulfed, rapt, attentive ("He was so absorbed in his work that he did not hear the telephone ring").

absorbed tax [ab · *zorbd*] *n.* A tax that is included, and sometimes hidden, in the purchase price.

abstain [ab · *stane*] *v.* To refrain, forbear, or hold back.
➤ refrain, forbear, hold back, resist, forgo, refuse, spurn, decline ("to abstain from drinking").

A

abstention [ab · sten · shun] n. The process of holding back from doing something.
➤ avoidance, nonparticipation, evasion, inaction.

abstention doctrine [ab · sten · shen dok · trin] n. A principle often applied by the federal courts, under which the court declines to decide a matter if it can be decided by a state court under state law.

abstract [ab · strakt] adj. Theoretical; hypothetical; unrelated to actuality or reality.
n. [ab · strakt] A summary; a synopsis.
v. 1. To remove or disconnect. 2. To prepare a shorter document from a longer one.
➤ adj. theoretical, impractical, conceptual
n. summary, synopsis, extract, analysis.
v. steal, take away, detach, disengage, purloin; digest, summarize, condense, abridge.

abstract of title [ty · tel] n. A short account of the state of the **title** to real estate, reflecting all past ownership and any **interests** or rights, such as a mortgage or other **liens**, which any person might currently have with respect to the property. An abstract of title is necessary to verify title before purchasing real property. See also chain of title; title insurance; title search.

abstraction [ab · strak · shen] n. The act of abstracting or disengaging. See wrongful abstraction.
➤ taking, removal, larceny, theft ("the abstraction of money"); generalization, theory, concept, notion, hypothesis ("her bizarre abstraction").

abuse [a · byooss] n. Ill treatment, either physical or emotional; improper use; harm; injury. See also battered woman syndrome; child abuse; elder abuse; spousal abuse.
v. [a · byooz] To harm; to use improperly; to treat badly.
➤ n. mistreatment, disrespect, debasement, damage, harm, impairment, crime, molestation, injury.
v. injure, damage, maltreat, molest, debase, misuse, mishandle.
Ant. aid, respect, assist.

abuse of discretion [dis · kresh · en] n. A judicial or administrative decision so grounded in whim or caprice, or against logic, that it amounts to a denial of justice.

abuse of process [pross · ess] n. The use of **legal process** in a manner not contemplated by the law to achieve a purpose not intended by the law. EXAMPLE: causing an ex-husband to be arrested for nonsupport of his child in order to secure his agreement with respect to custody. See malicious abuse of process. Compare malicious use of process.

abut [a · but] v. To end at; to border; to touch against. USAGE: "This is the point at which the lot abuts the highway." "Abut" is most commonly used in connection with matters of real estate. Also see adjoining. Compare adjacent.
➤ end at, border on, adjoin, touch against, neighbor, conjoin.

abutment [a · but · ment] n. The site where abutting occurs; that which borders on something.
➤ connection, attachment, junction; support, buttress, prop.

abutters [a · but · erz] n. Abutting owners.

abutting owners [a · but · ing own · erz] n. Owners whose lands touch.

academic [ak · e · dem · ik] adj.
1. Pertaining to teaching or learning.
2. Without practical significance.
➤ collegiate, learned, scholarly; abstract, theoretical, moot, hypothetical ("an academic question").

academic freedom [free · dem] n. The right to teach what one chooses; similarly, the right to learn. Although not specifically mentioned in the Constitution, academic freedom is secured by the **First Amendment**.

academic question [kwest · shen] n. A theoretical, hypothetical, or speculative question, involving no actual controversy; a question that has no practical significance. Compare hypothetical question; moot question.

accede [ak · seed] v. 1. To give consent; to assent; to concede. 2. To attain a public office, position, or job. See accession.

➤ give consent, assent, concede, concur, acquiesce; attain, succeed to, inherit, assume ("to accede to a position").
Ant. decline.

accelerate [ak · *sel* · e · rayt] *v.* To make something move faster; to speed up.
➤ hasten, rush, quicken, precipitate, stimulate.
Ant. delay.

accelerated depreciation
[ak · *sel* · e · ray · ted
de · pree · shee · *ay* · shen] *n.* Rapid **depreciation** of the value of a **capital asset** in order to produce larger tax deductions during the early years of the life of the asset. *Compare* straight-line depreciation. *See* depreciation.

acceleration [ak · *sel* · er · ray · shun] *n.* A quickening or speeding up.
➤ expedition, quickening, hastening ("acceleration of payment").

acceleration clause *n.* A clause in a **note**, mortgage, or other contract which provides that the entire debt will become due if payment is not made on time or if other conditions of the agreement are not met. *Compare* insecurity clause.

accept [ak · *sept*] *v.* 1. To agree to pay a **draft** when it is due. 2. To take an **offer**. *See* offer and acceptance. 3. To receive with the intent to retain. 4. To agree; to consent. *See* acceptance.
➤ receive, gain, obtain, secure; assent to, admit, welcome, approve, adopt, ratify.
Ant. reject, deny.

acceptance [ak · *sep* · tense] *n.* 1. With respect to **negotiable instruments**, the agreement of the bank or other drawee to **honor** a **draft**, check, or other negotiable instrument. Acceptance, which must be indicated on the instrument, in writing, is an acknowledgment by the **drawee** that the **drawer** has sufficient funds on deposit to cover the draft. *See* certified check. *See* trade acceptance. 2. As applied to the *law of* **contracts**, the assent, by the person to whom an **offer** is made, to the offer as made by the person making it. Acceptance is a fundamental element of a binding contract. *See* offer and acceptance. *Also see* conditional acceptance; implied

acceptance; qualified acceptance. 3. In the *law of* **sales**, the acceptance of the goods which are the subject of the sale has an important bearing upon the passage of **title** from the buyer to the seller, when the contract is **executory**. 4. In general terms, the receipt and retention of that which is offered. *Compare* rejection. 5. Unspoken consent to or concurrence in a transaction by virtue of failure to reject it. *See* silence as assent. 6. Agreement; approval; assent.
➤ acquisition, reception, adoption, compliance, consent, acknowledgment, assent, approval, ("his acceptance of the terms").
Ant. rejection, opposition.

acceptance by mail *n.* Mailed acceptance of an **offer** to enter into a contract is complete upon depositing the letter of acceptance in the mail. *See* mailbox rule.

acceptance of performance
[per · *for* · mense] *n.* The **waiver** of complete performance of the terms of a contract by accepting performance different from that stipulated in the contract. *See* performance.

acceptance of service [*ser* · viss] *n.* Acknowledging **service of process** by dispensing with the formalities normally required of such service. *See* service.

acceptor [ak · *sep* · tor] *n.* A **drawee** who has **accepted** a **draft**. *See* acceptance.

access [*ak* · sess] *n.* 1. Opportunity to come and go; opportunity to approach. EXAMPLES: access to a road; access to a fire hydrant. *See* easement of access. 2. Opportunity to make use of. EXAMPLE: an employee's access to her personnel file. 3. Opportunity to communicate with. EXAMPLE: a student's access to his professor.
➤ opportunity, accessibility, availability ("access to the president"); entry, opening, ingress ("access to the records").

accession [ak · *sesh* · en] *n.* 1. The right of an owner of real property or personal property to any increase that occurs to the property in the course of things. EXAMPLES: the lumber from trees as they mature; acquiring **title** to personal property by **specification** or by **adjunction**.

A

2. Attaining an office or position. 3. A nation's assent to a treaty.
➤ accretion, addition, enlargement; assumption, induction, succession; accedence, assent, concurrence.

accessory [ak · *sess* · e · ree] *n.* 1. A person who is involved with the commission of a crime but who is not present at the time it is committed. *See* accomplice; aiding and abetting. 2. Anything that is a lesser part of a larger undertaking or thing.
➤ accomplice, abettor, conspirator, collaborator, consort, assistant ("accessory after the fact"); supplement, attachment, addition, extension.

accessory after the fact *n.* A person who, after a crime has been committed, assists the person who committed it to escape arrest.

accessory before the fact *n.* A person who helps another person plan or commit a crime but who is not present at the scene of the crime.

accident [*ak* · se · dent] *n.* 1. An occurrence by chance or not as expected; something that happens unexpectedly or that cannot be foreseen. Although "accident," as used in this sense, has no clear-cut meaning which can be applied in every circumstance, it always connotes an occurrence brought about without an **intention** to **injure**. *Compare* negligence. *See* inevitable accident; unavoidable accident. 2. A crash or other mishap involving an automobile. 3. A catastrophe or calamity.
➤ casualty, collision, misadventure, happenstance; mishap, calamity, fortuity.

accident insurance [in · *shoor* · ense] *n.* An insurance policy that **indemnifies** the insured if he suffers a **loss**, is injured, or dies as the result of an accident. *See* insurance.

accident report [re · *port*] *n.* A report of a motor vehicle accident, usually required by law, made to the police by the driver of the car or cars involved.

accidental [*ak* · se · dentl] *adj.* Occurring by accident; unplanned.
➤ fortuitous, coincidental, inadvertent, unexpected, unintended.
Ant. planned, scheduled.

accidental death *n.* Death that occurs by accident. Some insurance policies pay a **double indemnity** benefit in the event of accidental death.

accidental injury [in · joo · ree] *n.* Physical injury which is unintended and unanticipated.

acclamation [ak · la · *may* · shen] *n.* Approval. The spontaneous approval by a legislature or similar assembly of a **resolution**, measure, or candidate by voice vote, without actually counting the yeas and nays.
➤ approval, acclaim, ovation, plaudits, approbation.

accommodate [a · *kom* · o · date] *v.* 1. To do a favor or perform a service. 2. To bring to an agreement; to adjust; to harmonize.
➤ oblige, aid, supply, shelter, assist; adjust, coordinate, integrate, adapt, acclimate.

accommodated party [a · kom · o · *day* · ted par · tee] *n.* *See* accommodation paper.

accommodation [a · kom · o · *day* · shen] *n.* 1. An obligation undertaken, without **consideration,** on behalf of another person; a favor. 2. Lodging.
➤ adaptation, compliance, conformity, modification; lodging, shelter; kindness, assistance.

accommodation loan *n.* A loan made as a favor, without **consideration** or without **adequate consideration**.

accommodation maker [*may* · ker] *n.* *See* accommodation paper.

accommodation paper [*pay* · per] *n.* A **bill** or **note** signed as a favor to another person, known as the *accommodated party*, to enable that person to receive a loan. The person who grants the favor is the *accommodation party* or *accommodation maker*. If the accommodated party and the accommodation party sign jointly, they are known as comakers. If the accommodated party defaults on the note, the accommodation party is fully liable.

accommodation party [*par* · tee] *n.* *See* accommodation paper.

accomplice [a · *kom* · pliss] *n.* A person who knowingly and voluntarily helps another person commit a crime; one who

A

acts as an **accessory**. *See also* aiding and abetting. *Compare* party to a crime.
➤ accessory, abettor, conspirator, collaborator, partner, associate, party.

accord [a · *kord*] *n.* Agreement; an agreement.
v. 1. To coincide with; to conform with; to agree with. USAGE: "That accords with what I have been told." 2. To grant; to confer. USAGE: "We must accord the instructor the respect she is due."
➤ *n.* agreement, settlement, adjustment, concurrence ("her accord with our decision").
v. coincide with, conform with, agree with ("That accords with what I have been told"); grant, confer, give.

accord and satisfaction
[sat · is · *fak* · shen] *n.* An agreement between two persons, one of whom has a **cause of action** against the other, in which the claimant accepts a compromise in full **satisfaction** of his claim. *See* compromise and settlement.

accost [a · *kost*] *v.* 1. To aggressively speak to or approach. 2. To solicit sex.
➤ assail, approach, assault, attack, ambush ("to accost a witness"); lure, prostitute, solicit.

account [a · *kount*] *n.* 1. A claim by one person (the creditor) against another (the debtor), which usually involves a detailed written record or list kept by one or both of them of the transactions between them. *See* charge account; mutual account; open account. 2. A computation of **credits** and **debits**. 3. A bank account. *See* checking account; savings account. 4. An explanation by a person who is under an obligation to make or submit an explanation; a report. EXAMPLE: an **intermediate account** filed by an **executor**. 5. A statement of facts; a narrative.
➤ ledger, register, report, computation ("He audited the firm's accounts"); version, story, chronological explanation, narrative ("an account of the trial").

account book *n.* *See* book of account.

account payable [*pay* · abl] *n.* An account that is owed in the **ordinary course of business**. *See* payable.

account receivable [re · *seev* · abl] *n.* 1. An ordinary business debt that has not been collected. 2. An account set aside for unpaid debts. *See* receivables.

account stated [*stay* · ted] *n.* An agreement between two persons with respect to the balance due on an account.

accountable [a · *kount* · abl] *adj.* Responsible; liable.
➤ responsible, liable, answerable, obligated, beholden, duty-bound ("to be accountable for one's actions").

accountant [a · *kount* · ant] *n.* A person whose profession is the keeping or examination of accounts and who is skilled in maintaining and correcting accounts; a person who is competent to design and control the systems of fiscal records required by the numerous, various, and extensive transactions involved in business and finance. *See* certified public accountant; public accountant.
➤ auditor, bookkeeper, controller, actuary, analyst, CPA.

accounting [a · *kount* · ing] *n.* 1. The act or system of making up accounts; a system of financial records. 2. The act of settling, adjusting, or paying an account. 3. A complete description of a financial transaction or a number of financial transactions. 4. An **equitable action** brought to obtain an **adjudication** of the respective rights and obligations of the members of a partnership.
➤ statement, report, description ("The partner received an accounting from an independent auditor").

accredit [a · *kre* · dit] *v.* 1. To recognize as worthy of merit or rank, for EXAMPLE, to accredit a college or graduate school. 2. To receive an **envoy** of a foreign country and acknowledge her authority; to give **credentials** to an envoy.
➤ license, authorize, certify, sanction ("accredit a school"); attribute, credit, assign, ascribe ("accredit the idea to Alexander").

accretion [a · *kree* · shen] *n.* 1. An increase in land caused by the gradual deposit by flowing water of solid material such as mud, silt, or sediment. *Compare* avulsion. 2. A slow accumulation.

➤ accumulation, augmentation, increase; fusion, conference, consolidation. *Ant.* depletion, erosion.

accrual [a · *krew* · el] *n.* That which accrues; something that grows or develops which is to be added or attached to something else. EXAMPLE: interest added to principal. *See* accrue.

➤ increase, expansion, accumulation, growth, development.

accrual basis [*bay* · sis] *n.* A method of accounting under which income is reported for tax purposes according to the time the right to receive it accrued rather than the time of its actual receipt. *Compare* cash basis.

accrual of cause of action [*ak* · shen] *n.* The point in time when a **cause of action** becomes complete so that the aggrieved party can file a lawsuit. Generally, a cause of action accrues at the moment the wrong occurs. *Compare* statutes of limitations.

accrue [a · *krew*] *v.* To develop and be added to something else; to become complete by growth or development; to accumulate. *See* accrual; accrued.

➤ increase, collect, amass, enlarge, heighten, multiply; flow, follow, proceed, acquire, result from. *Ant.* decrease, stagnate.

accrued [a · *krewd*] *adj.* Accumulated. USAGE: "My accrued wages are the wages I have earned which have not yet been paid to me."

accrued dividend [*div* · i · dend] *n.* A **stock dividend** which has been declared by a corporation but has not yet been paid to its stockholders. Accrued dividends are also referred to as **accumulated dividends**. See dividend.

accrued income [*in* · kum] *n.* Income that a person has earned but has not yet claimed. *See* income. *See also* earned income.

accrued interest [*in* · trest] *n.* Interest that has been earned but has not yet been paid. *See* interest.

accumulate [a · *kyoo* · myoo · late] *v.* To increase by growth or addition. *See* rule against accumulations.

➤ gather, amass, accrue, assemble, combine, increase. *Ant.* separate.

accumulated dividend [a · *kyoo* · myoo · lay · ted *div* · i · dend] *n.* *See* accrued dividend.

accumulated surplus [*ser* · plus] *n.* The property or funds which a corporation has in excess of its **capital stock**, and above all its debts and liabilities. *See* surplus. *Also see* capital surplus; earned surplus.

accumulation trust [a · kyoo · myoo · *lay* · shen] *n.* A **trust** in which the income earned is retained in the trust instead of being disbursed on an ongoing basis to the beneficiaries. *See* rule against accumulations.

accumulative judgment [a · *kyoo* · myoo · la · tiv *juj* · ment] *n.* Another term for **consecutive sentences**.

accumulative sentences [*sen* · tense] *n.* Another term for **consecutive sentences**.

accurate [*ak* · yoo · ret] *adj.* Conforming to standard; free from errors.

➤ precise, correct, reliable, faultless, exact, true.

accusation [ak · yoo · *zay* · shen] *n.* A formal charge that a person has committed a crime. EXAMPLES: a **complaint**; an **information**; an **indictment**.

➤ charge, allegation, gravamen, indictment, complaint, aspersion, arraignment ("the solicitor read the accusation"). *Ant.* exoneration.

accusatory system [e · *kyoo* · ze · toh · ree sis · tem] *n.* The system of criminal justice in the United States. Under the accusatory system, the government must formally accuse a person of having committed a crime and must prove the accusation. *Compare* inquisitorial system. *Also compare* adversary system.

accuse [a · *kuze*] *v.* To charge a person formally.

➤ charge, blame, attack, inculpate, indict, implicate.

accused [a · *kyoozd*] *n.* A person charged with having committed a crime; a defendant in a criminal case.

➤ suspect, defendant, respondent ("they withheld the identity of the accused").

acknowledge [ak · *now* · lej] *v.* To recognize rights or authority.

➤ certify, authenticate, endorse, attest to ("acknowledge the deed"); recognize, respond to, notice ("acknowledge counsel's presence").

acknowledgment [ak · *naw* · lej · ment] *n.* 1. The signing of a document, under oath, whereby the signer certifies that he is, in fact, the person who is named in the document as the signer. 2. The certificate of the person who administered the oath, for EXAMPLE, a **clerk of court**, justice of the peace, or notary. *See* attestation; authentication. 3. An admission of the truth of something asserted to be a fact, for EXAMPLE, the genuineness of a document or the validity of a debt. USAGE: "Would you like my acknowledgment that I owe you twenty dollars to be in writing?"

➤ confirmation, admission, ratification, declaration, endorsement ("acknowledgment of paternity"); recognition, acceptance, assent, acquiescence ("acknowledgment of liability").

acknowledgment of debt *n.* A statement by a debtor admitting to his creditor that he owes the debt and intends to pay it. Such an acknowledgment will revive a **cause of action** arising out of an obligation which has been barred by the **statute of limitations**. Partial payment of the debt serves as an acknowlegment and has the same effect as a verbal acknowledgment. *See* revival of action.

acknowledgment of paternity [pa · *tern* · i · tee] *n.* The admission by a man claimed to be the father of a child that the child is in fact his. *Compare* legitimation.

ACLU Abbreviation of **American Civil Liberties Union.**

acquaintance rape [uh · *kwain* · tense] *n.* A rape in which the victim knows the person who attacked her. *See* date rape; rape.

acquest [a · *kwest*] *n.* Property acquired by purchase.

acquire [a · *kwire*] *v.* To possess; to gain and hold.

➤ derive, gain, reap, assume, attain, obtain, procure, secure.

acquisition [ak · wi · *zish* · en] *n.* Something obtained or acquired.

➤ procurement, attainment, purchase, receipt, takeover.

acquisition charge [ak · wi · *zish* · en] *n.* *See* prepayment penalty.

acquit [a · *kwit*] *v.* 1. To release a criminal defendant by court order from a charge that he is guilty of a crime. 2. To judicially **discharge** a person from a **civil liability** such as a debt.

➤ absolve, exculpate, exonerate, liberate, release ("He was acquitted of the charge"); discharge, exempt, excuse ("acquitted of further responsibility").

acquittal [a · *kwit* · el] *n.* 1. A verdict of not guilty. 2. A **discharge** from **civil liability**. *See* absolution.

➤ exoneration, clearance, dismissal, discharge, release ("He was relieved at his acquittal.").

acquittance [a · *kwit* · ense] *n.* A **release**; a full receipt.

➤ release, discharge.

act *n.* 1. A statute; a **bill** that has been enacted by the legislature. *See* legislative act. 2. A deed or other written instrument evidencing a contract or other obligation. 3. That which is done voluntarily; putting one's will into action. *See* criminal act. *v.* To put a conscious choice into effect; to do.

➤ *n.* law, statute, bill, ordinance, ruling, determination, code, rule ("a legislative act"); pretense, sham, fraud ("We saw through his act"); performance. *v.* perform, do, behave, enact, execute, transact.

act of bankruptcy [*bank* · rupt · see] *n.* A term in use before 1979 when the federal Bankruptcy Act permitted creditors to force a debtor into **involuntary bankruptcy** for acts or reasons other than inability to pay debts as they come due.

act of commission [ko · *mish* · en] *n.* A positive act, as distinguished from an **act of omission** or a failure to act. *Compare* nonfeasance.

act of God *n.* An unusual, extraordinary, and unexpected act caused solely by the forces of nature. EXAMPLES: a storm; a bolt of lightning. A person cannot be held liable for an act of God.

act of omission [o · *mish* · en] *n.* A failure to act, as distinguished from an **act of commission** or an affirmative act.

act of state doctrine [*dok* · trin] *n.* The principle that prevents American courts from inquiring into the validity of the governmental acts of a foreign country.

act of the legislature [*lej* · is · lay · choor] *n.* *See* legislative act.

Act of Congress [*kong* · gress] *n.* A statute enacted by Congress. The **Americans with Disabilities Act** is an EXAMPLE of an Act of Congress.

acting [*ak* · ting] *adj.* Temporarily substituting for or taking the place of another; generally used in reference to an **officer** or **official**. USAGE: "acting chief"; "acting treasurer."
➤ interim, substitute, temporary, transient, provisional ("an acting director").

action [*ak* · shen] *n.* 1. A judicial or administrative **proceeding** for the enforcement or protection of a **right**; a lawsuit. It is important to distinguish a **civil action** from a **criminal action**. 2. The act of doing something.
➤ legal proceeding, lawsuit, dispute, litigation ("an action for divorce"); conduct, behavior, activity, performance, deed ("an unnecessary action").

action at common law [*kom* · en] *n.* A **legal action** governed by the **common law** rather than by a statute.

action at law *n.* A lawsuit brought in a **court of law** as opposed to a **court of equity**. *Compare* equitable action.

action in equity [*ek* · wi · tee] *n.* *See* equitable action.

action in personam [per · *soh* · nam] *n.* Same as **in personam action**.

action in rem *n.* Same as **in rem action**.

action on the case *n.* *See* trespass on the case.

action to quiet title [*kwy* · et *ty* · tel] *n.* *See* quieting title.

actionable [*ak* · shen · abl] *adj.* Conduct is actionable if it furnishes a ground for **legal action**. EXAMPLES of actionable conduct include **defamation**, **negligence**, **nuisance**, and **breach of contract**. *See also* cause of action.
➤ justifiable, suable, litigable, remediable, chargeable.

actionable negligence [*neg* · li · jense] *n.* Same as **negligence in law**.

actionable per quod [per *kwode*] *n.* Refers to spoken or written words which are not presumed to be injurious in and of themselves and with respect to which, therefore, proof of **damages** is required. *Compare* actionable per se. *See per quod. See and compare* libelous per quod; slanderous per quod.

actionable per se [per *say*] *n.* A term in the law of **defamation** that refers to spoken or written words, which are actionable without proof of **actual damages** because it is common knowledge that they are injurious to the reputation of the person about whom they are spoken. *Compare* actionable per quod. *See per se. See* libelous per se; slanderous per se.

actionable wrong *n.* A violation of a **legal right** which provides a basis for a lawsuit. EXAMPLES: a **breach of contract**; a **trespass**; **libel** or **slander**.

active [*ak* · tiv] *adj.* 1. Having the characteristic of action or activity. 2. Functioning; performing. *Compare* passive.
➤ functioning, performing, operational, engaged ("an active manager").
Ant. uninvolved, silent.

active negligence [*neg* · li · jense] *n.* **Negligence** in the doing of an act, as opposed to the failure to do something. *Compare* passive negligence.

active service [*ser* · viss] *n.* Service in the armed forces by a person called to duty, in contrast to readiness to serve or training for duty before being called from civilian life or from the reserve.

active trust *n.* A **trust** in which active duties are to be performed by the **trustee** in administering the **trust estate**. *Compare* passive trust.

actual [*ak* · chew · el] *adj.* Real or verifiable, as opposed to merely possible, **presumptive**, **implied**, or **constructive**.

➤ real, verifiable, objective, legitimate, undeniable.

Ant. indirect, constructive.

actual agency [ay · jen · see] *n.* An **agency** created by an explicit agreement between the **principal** and the **agent**; an **express agency**. *Compare* implied agency.

actual authority [aw · *thaw* · ri · tee] *n.* In the law of **agency**, the power of an agent to bind his principal.

Although such authority must be granted by the principal to his agent, authority will be deemed to have been granted if the principal allows the agent to believe that the agent possesses it. Further, actual authority may be implied from the circumstances and need not be specifically granted. EXAMPLE: A company's purchasing agent has the **implied authority** to make purchases. *Compare* implied authority. *See* authority.

actual cash value [val · yoo] *n.* The fair cash price that something is worth; the cost of replacement less **depreciation**; **fair market value**. *See* fair cash value.

actual damages [dam · e · jez] *n.* Monetary compensation for a **loss** or **injury** which a plaintiff has suffered rather than a sum of money awarded by way of punishing a defendant or to deter others. *Compare* punitive damages. *See* damages.

actual delivery [de · *liv* · e · ree] *n.* Giving the buyer immediate physical possession of the goods she has purchased. *Compare* constructive delivery; symbolic delivery. *See* delivery.

actual fraud *n.* The intentional and successful use of cunning or deception to cheat or deceive. *Compare* constructive fraud. *See* fraud.

actual knowledge [naw · lej] *n.* Real knowledge, as opposed to knowledge **imputed** to a person because he had information that should have caused him to make inquiry which would have led to real knowledge. *See* knowledge; personal knowledge. *Also see* actual notice.

actual loss *n.* The extent of an insurance company's liability; the real **loss**, whether total or partial. *See and compare* partial loss; total loss.

actual malice [mal · iss] *n.* 1. **Malice** that is present in the form of a **specific intent** to kill or to do bodily injury; **malice in fact**. *Compare* constructive malice; implied malice. *See also* express malice. 2. In the law of **defamation**, uttering or publishing a statement one knows to be false or with a reckless disregard for its truth or falsity. For public figures to prove defamed, they must show that the speaker acted with actual malice.

actual notice [no · tiss] *n.* Knowledge of a fact, regardless of how it came to be known. *Compare* constructive notice; implied notice. *See* notice.

actual possession [po · *zesh* · en] *n.* Actual occupancy of property and **dominion** over it; possession **in fact** as opposed to possession **in law**.

actual service [ser · viss] *n. See* actual service of process.

actual service of process [ser · viss] *n.* Also referred to simply as **actual service**, it is **personal service of process**, as distinguished from **service by publication** or some other form of **constructive service of process**. *See* service of process.

actual value [val · yoo] *n.* Same as **fair market value** (FMV).

actuarial tables [ak · choo · ehr · ee · el tay · blz] *n. See* mortality tables.

actuary [ak · choo · ehr · ee] *n.* A person whose profession is calculating insurance **risk** from a statistical point of view as, for EXAMPLE, the appropriate premium cost of a particular fire insurance policy. *See* risk of loss.

actus [ahk · tus] *(Latin) n.* Act. *actus reus* [ree · us] An "answerable act," i.e., an act for which one is answerable; a guilty act. In combination with *mens rea* (a guilty or **criminal intent**), *actus reus* is an essential element of any crime. Thus, for EXAMPLE, the act of killing is the *actus reus* of **murder**.

acute [a · *kyoot*] *adj.* 1. Perceptive; observant. 2. Severe or intense.

A

➤ keen, sharp, penetrating, piercing, fine, discerning; overpowering, overwhelming, severe.

ad [ahd] *(Latin) prep.* To; toward; for; until about. "*Ad*" often appears in Latin phrases used in the law. EXAMPLE: **ad damnum clause**.

ad damnum clause [*dahm* · num] *n.* The clause in a **complaint** which sets forth the plaintiff's demand for **damages** and the amount of the claim.

ad hoc [*hoke*] *adj.* "For this only"; for this situation only; unofficial. USAGE: "This matter should be referred to the ad hoc committee on ozone in the environment."

ad hominem [*hom* · i · nem] *adj.* "To the man"; to the person; personal. *See* ad hominem argument.

ad hominem argument [*ar* · gyu · ment] *n.* An argument challenging the person rather than his point of view. *See* ad hominem.

ad infinitum [in · fin · *ite* · em] *adj.* "To the end"; without end.

ad litem [*ly* · tem] *adj.* "For the suit"; for the purposes of the lawsuit; during the pendency of the **action**. *See* guardian ad litem.

ad testificandum [tes · ti · fi · *kahn* · dum] *adj.* "For testifying." *See* subpoena ad testificandum.

ad valorem [va · *lore* · em] *adj.* "To the value"; according to the value.

ad valorem duty [*dyoo* · tee] *n.* A **customs duty** calculated on the basis of the value of the import. *See* ad valorem.

ad valorem tax *n.* A tax established in proportion to the value of the property to be taxed. EXAMPLE: a tax of $3 on an antique worth $100 and $9 on an antique worth $300, the tax being 3 percent of the value, as distinguished from a $5 tax regardless of the value of the antique. *See* ad valorem.

ADA Abbreviation of **Americans with Disabilities Act**.

add-on clause *n.* A stipulation in an **installment sale contract** which provides, with respect to later-purchased items that no item purchased under the agreement is owned by the buyer until the seller has received payment for all items.

addendum [a · *den* · dum] *n.* An appendix or addition to a document.

➤ supplement, addition, rider.

addict [a · dikt] *n.* 1. An habitual user of narcotics. 2. Any person who has no control over a substance which she uses regularly or a behavior in which she engages repeatedly, if such conduct impairs her ability to function normally. EXAMPLES: an alcoholic; a drug addict; a compulsive gambler. *See* chemical dependency.

addicted [a · dik · ted] *adv.* The state of being dependent.

➤ dependent, habituated, attached, obsessed.

addiction [a · *dikt* · shen] *n.* The state of being an addict.

additional [a · *dish* · en · el] *adj.* Added; more; one more.

➤ extra, supplementary, further, increased.

additional instructions [in · *struk* · shens] *n.* Instructions given to the jury by the judge after the jury has begun its deliberations. *See* jury instructions.

additional insured [in · *shoord*] *n.* A person other than the **named insured** under an automobile liability insurance policy, who uses the automobile with the permission of the named insured.

additur [*ah* · di · toor] *n.* An increase by the judge of the amount of damages awarded by the jury because of the inadequacy of the initial award. *Compare* remittitur.

adduce [a · *dyooss*] *v.* To present, offer, or introduce. Commonly used in connection with evidence offered or introduced in a trial or a hearing. USAGE: "The prosecutor failed to adduce evidence connecting the defendant to the crime."

➤ present, offer, introduce, allege, declare, produce.

ADEA Abbreviation of **Age Discrimination in Employment Act**.

adeem [a · *deem*] *v.* To take away; to make an **ademption**.

➤ take away, revoke, withdraw, cancel, annul.

ademption [a · *demp* · shen] *n.* **Disposition** by a person, during his lifetime, of property

which is the subject of his will. An ademption revokes the **legacy** or **devise**.
➤ retraction, nullification, repudiation, recall, negation.

adequate [ad · e · kwet] *adj.* Sufficient; equal to what is required.
➤ sufficient, suitable, satisfactory, ample, fitting, fair, commensurate ("adequate remedy").

adequate consideration [kon · sid · e · ray · shun] *n.* A fair and reasonable price or value for the subject matter of the contract in question; a sufficient price in law. *See* consideration, peppercorn.

adequate remedy at law [rem · e · dee] *n.* A term meaning that the plaintiff's legal rights are enforceable by an **action** brought in a **law court** (as opposed to a **court of equity**); put another way, the wrong alleged by the plaintiff is more appropriately remedied by an award of **damages** than by an **injunction**. *Compare* inadequate remedy at law.

adhere [ad · *here*] *v.* 1. To hold fast. 2. To maintain loyalty. 3. To be consistent.
➤ attach, cling, secure, join; comply, confirm, follow, espouse; persevere, maintain, sustain.

adhesion [ad · *hee* · zhun] *n.* 1. Firm attachment. 2. An agreement to join or stay joined.
➤ fusion, contact, cohesiveness; allegiance, loyalty, devotion, fealty, support, fidelity.

adhesion contract [ad · *hee* · zhen *kon* · trakt] *n.* A contract prepared by the dominant party (usually a form contract) and presented on a take-it-or-leave-it basis to the weaker party, who has no real opportunity to bargain about its terms. *See* contract. *Also see* overreaching.

adjacent [a · *jay* · sent] *adj.* 1. Near or close to; in the neighborhood. 2. Touching; contiguous. "Adjacent" is an ambiguous word because it can be used in either sense, with the result that its meaning in a given instance is often unclear. *Compare* abut; adjoining.
➤ adjoining, touching, contiguous, bordering, coterminous.

adjective law [a · jek · tiv] *n.* **Procedural law**; law that dictates *how* **rights** are **adjudicated**, as distinguished from **substantive law**, which *creates* legal rights.

adjoin [ad · *join*] *v.* 1. To be next to. 2. To attach.
➤ border, connect, neighbor, meet, touch; add, combine, connect, link, affix.

adjoining [a · *join* · ing] *adj.* Touching or contiguous, as opposed to close or near to. USAGE: "Your lot and mine are not adjoining because they are separated by the highway." *Also see* abut. *Compare* adjacent.
➤ touching, contiguous, abutting, neighboring, joined ("adjoining lots").

adjoining landowners [*land* · own · erz] *n.* The owners of lands that share a common boundary line. *See* abutting owners.

adjourn [a · *jern*] *v.* To postpone or continue to a future time. *See* adjournment.
➤ postpone, suspend, defer, delay, recess, discontinue ("to adjourn for the day").

adjournment [a · *jern* · ment] *n.* The suspension of business, especially by a court, legislature, or administrative agency. Adjournment may be to a definite future time or indefinitely. *See* adjournment sine die. *Compare* recess.
➤ suspension, discontinuation, deferral, postponement, recess, cessation.

adjournment sine die [*see* · nay *dee* · ay] *n.* An adjournment without setting a time for another meeting or session. *See* sine die.

adjudicate [a · *joo* · di · kate] *v.* To decide; to give **judgment**; to render or award judgment; to sentence.
➤ decide, sentence, adjudge, decree, settle, arbitrate, decide, mediate ("to adjudicate a dispute").

adjudicated liability [a · *joo* · di · kay · ted ly · e · *bil* · i · tee] *n.* **Liability** that has been determined by a court. *See* adjudicate.

adjudication [a · joo · di · *kay* · shen] *n.* The final decision of a court, usually made after trial of the case; the court's **final judgment**.
➤ decision, ruling, holding, disposition, pronouncement, verdict, judgment.

A

adjudicatory [a · *joo* · di · ka · tore · ee] *adj.* Refers to the decision-making or **quasi-judicial** functions of an administrative agency, as opposed to the **judicial functions** of a court. Thus, for EXAMPLE, an *adjudicatory hearing* is a hearing before an administrative agency as opposed to a hearing or trial before a court.

adjunct [*ad* · junkt] *adj.* Added in a temporary or subordinate capacity.
➤ corollary, supplemental, auxiliary ("Ms. Neider is an adjunct professor").

adjunction [a · *junk* · shen] *n.* The joining of one article or material with another, as a result of which both form a single item. *See* accession.

adjure [ad · *joor*] *v.* 1. To command or require performance under oath. 2. To entreat.
➤ entreat, command, request, plead, aver.

adjust [a · *just*] *v.* 1. To settle a dispute or difference in a manner agreeable to everyone involved. EXAMPLE: business partners who resolve a disagreement may be said to have adjusted their differences. 2. To correct or to balance. EXAMPLE: the subtraction of $100 from a charge account balance in response to a customer's complaint that she has been overcharged by that amount. 3. To bring into line. *See* adjustment.
➤ correct, rectify, accord ("Our account has been adjusted"); adapt, accommodate, conform ("adjusted to the new circumstances").

adjustable rate mortgage [a · *just* · abl rate *more* · gej] *n.* A **mortgage** in which the rate of interest is not absolute, but is adjusted from time to time based upon conditions in the **money market**. It is often referred to simply as an **ARM**. *Compare* fixed rate mortgage; graduated payment mortgage.

adjusted [a · *just* · ed] *adj.* 1. Settled. 2. Corrected; balanced. 3. Brought into line.
➤ corrected, settled, rectified, aligned, straightened, reset; altered, converted, regulated.

adjusted basis [*bay* · siss] *n.* For the purpose of calculating the amount of income tax due, the original cost of property offset for such things as **casualty losses** and **depreciation**. *Compare* basis.

adjusted gross income [*in* · kum] *n.* An income tax term for **gross income** less the deductions (generally, business expenses) permitted by law. *Compare* taxable income.

adjuster [a · *just* · er] *n.* A person who makes a determination of the value of a claim against an insurance company for the purpose of arriving at an amount for which the claim will be settled. An adjuster may be an **agent** of the insurance company or an **independent adjuster**.
➤ reconciler, arbitrator, intermediary, intervenor, mediator.

adjustment [a · *just* · ment] *n.* 1. A settlement. 2. The act of adjusting.
➤ agreement, compensation, settlement ("acceptable adjustment"); adaptation, orientation, acclimatization ("His adjustment to the higher altitude was quick").

adjutant [*ad* · ju · tant] *n.* An assistant to a superior.
➤ assistant, aide, auxiliary ("The adjutant disobeyed his superior").

admeasurement [ad · *mezh* · er · ment] *n.* The establishment and division of shares.
➤ assignment, apportionment, partition, division.

administer [ad · *min* · is · ter] *v.* 1. To apply or enforce the law. 2. To take charge; to manage. 3. To give, do, or perform. USAGE: "she administered the oath"; "he administered last rites." *See* administration; administrator.
➤ manage, supervise, oversee, steer, operate, take charge; give, supply, furnish, bestow, offer, extend ("administer an oath").

administration [ad · min · is · *tray* · shen] *n.* 1. The application of a law. USAGE: "A judge's primary responsibility is the **administration** of justice." 2. The government or the governing authority. USAGE: "The public does not support the fiscal policies of this administration." 3. The management of anything. *See* administer.
➤ application, supplying ("the administration of justice"); government, governing authority, leadership, regime, presidency, bureaucracy ("The public does not support the fiscal policies of this administration").

administration expenses [eks · *pen* · sez]
n. Payments made by an **administrator**
or **executor** for the preservation of the
property of a **decedent's estate**. Such
expenses include court costs, insurance
premiums, and attorney fees.

administration of estate [es · *tate*] *n.*
The management of a **decedent's estate**
by an **administrator** or **executor** so that
all the decedent's **assets** are collected, all
debts, administration expenses, and taxes
are paid, and all remaining assets are distributed to the persons entitled to receive
them. *See and compare* administrator
CTA; administrator DBN.

Administration for Native Americans
[ad · min · is · *tray* · shen for *nay* · tiv
a · *mare* · i · kenz] *n.* A federal agency
that represents the concerns of Native
Americans in various areas, administers
grant programs, and provides technical assistance. *See also* Bureau of Indian Affairs.

administrative [ad · *min* · is · tra · tiv] *adj.*
Pertaining to administration.
➤ regulatory, organizational, governmental, supervisory, ministerial, supporting.

administrative act *n.* A routine act by a
public official, required by law, as opposed
to an act based upon a decision involving
a degree of choice; a **ministerial act**.
EXAMPLE: the maintaining of court records
by the **clerk of court**. *Compare* judicial act.

administrative agency [*ay* · jen · see]
n. A **board**, **commission**, **bureau**, **office**,
or **department**, of the **executive branch**
of government, that implements the law
which originates with the **legislative
branch**. EXAMPLES: the FBI; a state's
department of motor vehicles; a county
public assistance office. *See* regulatory
agency.

administrative board *n.* *See* board.

administrative discretion [dis · *kresh* · en]
n. The power to choose between courses
of conduct in the administration of a public office or in carrying out a public duty.
Compare judicial discretion; ministerial
act. *See* discretion.

administrative hearing [*heer* · ing] *n.*
A **hearing** before an administrative
agency, as distinguished from a hearing
before a court.

administrative law *n.* 1. The body of
law that controls the way in which administrative agencies operate. 2. Regulations
issued by administrative agencies.

administrative law judge *n.* A person,
generally a civil servant, who conducts
hearings held by an administrative
agency. An administrative law judge is
variously referred to as an **ALJ**, a
hearing examiner, or a **hearing officer**.

administrative notice [*no* · tiss] *n.*
Same as **official notice**.

administrative proceeding
[pro · *see* · ding] *n.* A **proceeding**
before an administrative agency, as
distinguished from a proceeding before
a court. *Compare* judicial proceeding.

administrative remedy [*rem* · e · dee]
n. A **remedy** that the law permits an
administrative agency to grant. *Compare*
judicial remedy.

Administrative Procedure Act
[ad · *min* · is · tra · tiv pro · *see* · jer] *n.*
A statute enacted by Congress that regulates the way in which federal administrative agencies conduct their affairs and
establishes the procedure for **judicial
review** of the actions of federal agencies.
The Act is referred to as the **APA**.

administrator [ad · *min* · is · tray · ter] *n.*
1. A person who is appointed by the court
to manage the **estate** of a person either
who died without a will or whose will
failed to name an **executor** or named an
executor who declined or was ineligible
to serve. The administrator of an estate
is also referred to as a **personal
representative**. 2. A person who
administers anything. *See* administer;
administration.
➤ representative, executor, trustee ("the
estate's administrator"); manager, supervisor, director, facilitator, leader ("the
administrator of the department").

administrator CTA *n.* The court-
appointed administrator of the **estate** of
a **decedent** whose will failed to name an
executor or whose named executor cannot or refuses to serve. The abbreviation
CTA stands for *cum testamento annexo*,
a Latin phrase meaning "with will
attached." *Compare* administrator DBN.

administrator cum testamento annexo [kum tes · ta · *men* · to an · *eks* · o] *n.* *See* administrator CTA.

administrator DBN *n.* The court-appointed administrator of the **estate** of a **decedent** whose **executor** has died or resigned. The abbreviation DBN stands for *de bonis non*, a Latin phrase meaning "goods not administered." *Compare* administrator CTA.

administrator de bonis non [day *bone* · iss non] *n.* *See* administrator DBN.

admiralty [*ad* · mer · el · tee] *n./adj.* The body of law that regulates the conduct of affairs on **navigable waters**. *See* maritime law.

admiralty courts *n.* Federal courts entitled to exercise **admiralty jurisdiction**, specifically, the **District Courts of the United States**.

admiralty jurisdiction [joo · ris · *dik* · shen] *n.* The power of an **admiralty court** to try cases involving admiralty matters. *See* jurisdiction.

admissibility [ad · *mis* · i · bil · i · tee] *n.* The quality of being **admissible**. USAGE: "They argued over the admissibility of the statement at trial."). *See* admissible evidence.

admissible [ad · *mis* · ibl] *adj.* That which should be admitted, allowed, or considered.
➤ allowable, acceptable, just, fair, permissible, sanctioned, unobjectionable, proper. *Ant.* inadmissible.

admissible evidence [*ev* · i · dense] *n.* Evidence that a court may admit and consider in a case before it.

admission [ad · *mish* · en] *n.* 1. A statement of a **party** to an **action** which is inconsistent with his claim or position in the lawsuit and which therefore constitutes proof against him. 2. A voluntary statement that something asserted to be true is true. *Compare* confession. 3. The act of permitting entry. EXAMPLES: the admission of testimony in a trial; general admission at a concert.
➤ confession, acknowledgment, affirmation, declaration, disclosure ("his admission of guilt"); admittance, access, passage ("admission to the bar").

admission against interest [a · *genst* in · trest] *n.* *See* declaration against interest.

admission to bail *n.* The act of a court in permitting a person accused of a crime to be freed until trial, provided that a **surety bond**, called **bail**, is posted.

admission to probate [*proh* · bate] *n.* A determination by a **probate court** that a will offered for **probate** is in fact the will of the **decedent**.

admission to the bar *n.* The certification by a court that a lawyer possesses the required qualifications and is therefore privileged to practice law within the jurisdiction of the court. *See* practice of law. *Compare* disbarment.

admit [ad · *mit*] *v.* 1. To concede as true. 2. To give access to.
➤ accept, affirm, confirm, agree ("admit fault"); allow, induct, open, initiate ("admit into practice").

admonish [ad · *mon* · ish] *v.* 1. To express duties or obligations. 2. To warn or show disapproval.
➤ advise, counsel, enjoin, instruct, recommend; warn, prewarn, forewarn, caution, reprehend.

admonition [add · mo · *nih* · shun] *n.* 1. A warning; the act of advising against something. 2. A reprimand. 3. A scolding; the act of chiding.
➤ warning, advice, forewarning, caveat; scolding, censure, reprimand.

adolescent [*ad* · o · less · ent] *n.* One who is in the state or process of growing up; one who is in a stage of development prior to maturity.
➤ *n.* junior, juvenile, teenager, youth, youngster.
adj. immature, childish, foolish, inconsiderate ("adolescent behavior").

adopt [a · *dopt*] *v.* 1. To take on legal parental responsibility for another's child. 2. To choose or take on something as one's own.
➤ choose, foster, raise ("adopt a child"); accept, affirm, assent, endorse, embrace, assume ("adopt an inconsistent position").

adoption [a · *dop* · shen] *n.* 1. Approving; taking as one's own; **ratifying**. 2. Enacting

a law or publishing a regulation. 3. The act of creating the relationship of parent and child between persons who do not naturally share that relationship.
➤ acceptance, embracement, approval, assumption ("their adoption of a hostile stance"); fostering, fosterage, raising ("adoption of the homeless child").

adoption by reference [*ref* · er · ense] *n. See* incorporation by reference.

adult [a · *dult*] *n.* A grown person; one no longer a child. "Adult" is not a technical legal word. *Compare* **age of majority**, which is the same concept in legal language. *See also* legal age.
adj. Mature; fully grown or developed.
➤ *n.* grownup, person, man, woman.
adj. developed, ripe, mature.

adulteration [a · dul · ter · *ay* · shen] *n.* Combining an impure or cheaper substance with another substance, usually for dishonest purposes. The adulteration of many products, particularly food, is illegal.
➤ alteration, debasement, contamination, impurification, corruption ("adulteration of food products").

adultery [a · *dul* · ter · ee] *n.* Sexual intercourse by a married person with a person not his or her spouse.
➤ infidelity, affair, unfaithfulness, cuckoldry.

advance [ad · *vanse*] *adj.* Before; prior to.
n. 1. A loan. 2. A payment made before it is due. 3. Something supplied before it is paid for.
v. 1. To make a loan. 2. To supply something beforehand. 3. To pay a debt before it is due. 4. To move ahead.
➤ *adj.* early, earlier, leading, previous, prior ("to make advance reservations").
n. loan, deposit, down payment, retainer ("a cash advance"); improvement, progress, development, enrichment ("an advance in the field"); promotion, elevation ("her advance into management").
v. supply, loan, give ("to advance some money to an employee").

advance directive [de · *rekt* · iv] *n.* A term for the various instruments a person can use to insure that her wishes with respect to health care are carried out if she is no longer able to speak for herself.

EXAMPLES: a **healthcare proxy**; a **living will**. *See also* durable power of attorney.

advance sheets *n.* Printed copies of judicial opinions published in loose-leaf form shortly after the opinions are issued. These published opinions are later collected and published in bound form with the other **reported cases** which are issued over a longer period of time. *See* court reports; reporters.

advancement [ad · *vanse* · ment] *n.*
1. Property or money distributed by a parent to a son, daughter, or other heir, which the parent intends to be charged against the heir's share of the parent's **estate** if the parent dies **intestate**. 2. *See* ademption.
➤ improvement, development, progression, evolution.
Ant. deterioration, stagnation.

adventure [ad · *ven* · choor] *n.* 1. A shipment of goods in the care of an agent who is to sell them for the best price possible. 2. A shipment by sea. 3. An enterprise with an element of risk.
➤ challenge, undertaking, experience, happening, event, venture.

adversarial [ad · ver · *sare* · ee · el] *adj.* Contrary; opposing; hostile.

adversarial proceeding [ad · ver · *sare* · ee · el pro · *see* · ding] *n.* Same as **adversary proceeding**.

adversarial system [ad · ver · *sare* · ee · el *sis* · tem] *n.* Same as **adversary system**.

adversary [*ad* · ver · sa · ree] *n.* 1. An opponent; an enemy. 2. The opposite **party** in a lawsuit. *See* adverse party.
➤ opponent, enemy, competitor, foe, challenger; litigant, opposing party, adverse party.

adversary proceeding [pro · *see* · ding] *n.* A trial or other **proceeding** in which all sides have the opportunity to present their contentions; a proceeding involving a contested **action**.

adversary system [*sis* · tem] *n.* The system of justice in the United States. Under the adversary system, the court hears the evidence presented by **adverse parties** and decides the case. *Compare* accusatory system; inquisitorial system.

adverse [*ad* · verse] *adj.* Antagonistic; opposing.
➤ antagonistic, opposing, conflicting, antipathetic, counter, antithetical, contrary ("an adverse party"); unfavorable, destructive, harmful ("adverse circumstances").

adverse witness [*wit* · ness] *n.* A witness who gives testimony which is contrary to the interest of the **party** calling him. The testimony of an adverse witness is subject to **impeachment**. *Compare* hostile witness.

adverse interest [*in* · trest] *n.* An **interest** that is contrary to one's own interest. A witness who has an interest in the outcome of the case which is contrary to the interest of the **party** calling her may be cross-examined by that party.

adverse party [*par* · tee] *n.* A **party** who is on the opposite side in a **legal action**.

adverse possession [po · *zesh* · en] *n.* The act of occupying real property in an "open, notorious, and hostile manner," under a **claim of right**, contrary to the interests of the true owner. Such possession over a period of years is a method for acquiring **title**. *Compare* adverse user. *See* open and notorious; possession.

adverse user *n.* The act of using real property in an "open, notorious, and hostile manner," under a **claim of right**, contrary to the interests of the true owner. (EXAMPLE: walking across land, without permission from the owner, in order to gain access to one's own land.) Such use over a period of years is a method for obtaining the right to continue to do so; that is, it is a method for obtaining an **easement**. *See* user. *Also see* adverse possession; open and notorious; prescriptive easement.

advice [ad · *vice*] *n.* 1. A view or opinion communicated to another. EXAMPLE: a lawyer's advice to her client. 2. In **commercial law**, notification by one person to another of a transaction in which they both have an interest.
➤ view, opinion, suggestion, counsel, guidance, recommendation, input.

advice and consent [kon · *sent*] A term relating to the requirement of the Constitution that the president have the approval of the Senate to appoint certain public officials, including federal judges and the justices of the Supreme Court, and to enter into certain treaties.

advise [ad · *vize*] *v.* To give advice; to offer an opinion; to counsel.
➤ counsel, commend, urge, recommend, encourage, suggest; inform, notify, update.

advisement [ad · *vize* · ment] *n.* Careful consideration; deliberation. USAGE: "The judge said she will take the matter under advisement for now, and won't render a decision for at least two weeks."
➤ consideration, deliberation.

adviser [ad · *vize* · er] *n.* A person who gives advice. EXAMPLES: an attorney; a clergyman; a marriage counselor.
➤ confidante, counselor, consultant, expert, mentor.

advisor [ad · *vize* · or] *n.* Same as **adviser**.

advisory [ad · *vize* · e · ree] *adj.* Informative; by way of suggestion; not binding.
➤ informative, suggestive, recommending, advising ("an advisory opinion").

advisory jury [*joor* · ee] *n.* A jury **impaneled** in a case in which the **parties** are not entitled to a jury trial as a matter of right. The verdict of an advisory jury is not binding on the court.

advisory opinion [o · *pin* · yen] *n.* A judicial interpretation of a legal question requested by the legislative or executive branch of government. Typically, courts prefer not to give advisory opinions. *See* executive branch; legislative branch.

advisory verdict [*ver* · dikt] *n.* A verdict rendered by an **advisory jury**. *See* verdict.

advocacy [*ad* · vo · ke · see] *n.* The act of pleading for, arguing on behalf of, or supporting, especially an idea, cause, organization, or individual. EXAMPLE: forceful persuasion or lobbying on behalf of a client, democracy, women, or the Red Cross.
➤ support, advancement, representation, defense, backing, endorsement, espousal ("the art of advocacy").

advocate [*ad · vo · ket*] *n.* 1. An attorney. 2. Any person who argues or pleads on behalf of another person, organization, or cause.
v. [*ad · vo · kate*] 1. To argue for or plead the case of. 2. To support; propose; encourage.
➤ *n.* attorney, supporter, representative, adviser, counsel ("a fine advocate").
v. argue, plead, espouse, advance, urge ("to advocate a point of view").

AFDC Abbreviation of **Aid to Families with Dependent Children**.

affair [*a · fare*] *n.* A matter; a matter at hand; a matter of concern. "Affair" is a word of broad meaning, including a lawsuit, a business transaction, an illicit sexual relationship, or simply trouble.
➤ matter, concern, activity, transaction, lawsuit, business.

affect [*af · ekt*] *n.* A feeling or mood, influencing behavior. USAGE: "Dr. Jacobs is concerned about his patient's bizarre affect." *Compare* effect.
v. [*a · fekt*] 1. To act upon; to produce an effect. USAGE: "The rain always affects my mood." 2. To change or weaken. USAGE: "Alcohol seriously affects my judgment." 3. To put on airs, imitate, or fake. USAGE: "He always affects an English accent." *Note* that "affect" is not "**effect**."
➤ *n.* feeling, mood.
v. act upon, influence, alter, stir, impact ("The rain always affects my mood"); change, weaken ("Alcohol seriously affects my judgment"); put on airs, imitate, pretend, fake, arrogate ("He always affects an English accent when he visits London").

affected [*a · fek · ted*] *adj.* Feigned or pretended.
➤ fake, feigned, counterfeit, pompous, artificial ("affected mannerisms").
affected class [*a · fek · ted*] *n.* 1. A group of people who have been discriminated against illegally for the same reason, such as gender, age, or race. *See* suspect classification. 2. Individuals who form a **class** for the purpose of a **class action**. *See* class.

affecting commerce [*a · fek · ting kom · erss*] *adj.* Burdening, obstructing, or having an impact upon **interstate commerce**; **in commerce**. "Affecting commerce" is a term with particular application to **constitutional law**. *See* commerce; commerce clause.

affiant [*a · fy · ent*] *n.* A person who makes a sworn written statement or **affidavit**. *See* sworn statement.
➤ deponent, declarer.

affidavit [*a · fi · day · vit*] *n.* Any voluntary statement reduced to writing and **sworn to** or **affirmed** before a person legally authorized to administer an **oath** or **affirmation** (EXAMPLE: a notary public). A **sworn statement**. *Also see* verification.
➤ affirmation, oath, statement, testimony, avowal, averment, declaration, sworn statement.
affidavit of defense [de · *fense*] *n.* An affidavit that states that the defendant has a valid defense to the plaintiff's **action**.
affidavit of merits [*mehr · its*] *n.* In some jurisdictions, the term for an **affidavit of defense**.
affidavit of service [*ser · viss*] *n.* An affidavit that certifies that **process** (EXAMPLES: a **summons**; a **writ**) has been served. *See* service of process.

affiliate [*a · fil · ee · et*] *n.* An organization controlled or directed by another organization. EXAMPLE: a **subsidiary corporation** of a **parent company**.
v. [*a · fil · ee · ate*] To join or to become connected with. USAGE: "she is affiliated with the chamber of commerce"; "he is affiliated with organized crime."
➤ *n.* branch, offshoot, partner ("The Smith Company is an affiliate of the Jones Corporation").
v. join, ally, combine, connect, associate ("affiliate with a lodge").

affiliation [*a · fil · ee · ay · shen*] *n.* 1. Association with an organization. 2. Connection to a family.
➤ association, joining, merging, partnership, relationship ("His affiliation with mobsters hurt his credibility as a witness"); kinship, family, heredity.

affiliation proceeding [*a · fil · ee · ay · shun pro · see · ding*] *n.* A judicial proceeding to establish the paternity of an illegitimate child and to compel the father to contribute to its support. *See also* paternity suit.

affinity [a · *fin* · i · tee] *n.* 1. The relationship existing by virtue of marriage. Affinity is a matter of degree. EXAMPLE: a husband is in a closer degree of affinity with his wife's brother than with his wife's cousin. *Compare* consanguinity; relation by blood. 2. Mutual attraction.
➤ kinship, lineage, propinquity, heritage ("A husband is in a closer degree of affinity with his wife's brother than with his wife's cousin"); attraction, propensity, proclivity, predisposition, penchant ("her affinity for mathematics").

affirm [a · *ferm*] *v.* 1. In the case of an **appellate court**, to uphold the decision or **judgment** of the lower court after an appeal. *See* affirmance. 2. To state formally instead of making a statement **under oath**; to make an **affirmation**. 3. To confirm or ratify a statement, belief, or act. *Compare* disaffirm. 4. To assert or contend.
➤ uphold, validate, confirm, ratify ("The decision was affirmed"); declare, assert, maintain, allege ("He affirmed his innocence").

affirmance [a · *fer* · mense] *n.* 1. The confirmation of a **judgment** or order of a lower court by an **appellate court** after an appeal. 2. The ratification of a **voidable contract**. EXAMPLE: The carrying out by a person, upon reaching his **majority**, of a contract he made during his **minority**. 3. Confirmation; ratification. *Compare* disaffirmance.
➤ confirmation, affirmation, approval, endorsement, substantiation.

affirmant [a · *fer* · ment] *n.* A person who **affirms** in lieu of taking an **oath**. *Compare* affiant.

affirmation [af · er · *may* · shen] *n.* 1. A formal statement or declaration, made as a substitute for a **sworn statement**, by a person whose religious or other beliefs will not permit him to swear. 2. A positive statement.
➤ statement, oath, declaration, assertion, avowal, confirmation ("out-of-court affirmation").

affirmative [a · *fer* · me · tiv] *adj.* Asserting the truth, accuracy, or positive nature of something. *Compare* negative. *n.* 1. Something more than passive tolerance or acceptance. 2. An answer "yes." *Compare* negative.
➤ *adj.* affirming, approving, positive, endorsing.

affirmative action [*ak* · shen] *n.* 1. Positive or constructive action rather than inaction or negative or punitive action. 2. When used in conjunction with "plan," "program," or "guidelines," a term applied to the obligation to remedy discrimination based on sex, race, color, creed, or age with respect to, for EXAMPLE, employment, union membership, or college admission. *See* discrimination. *Also see* Civil Rights Acts.

affirmative charge *n.* A **jury instruction** that removes an issue from the jury's consideration.

affirmative defense [de · *fense*] *n.* A **defense** that amounts to more than simply a denial of the **allegations** the plaintiff's **complaint**. It sets up **new matter** which, if proven, could result in a **judgment** against the plaintiff even if all the allegations of the complaint are true. EXAMPLES of affirmative defenses *in civil cases* include **accord and satisfaction**, **act of God**, **estoppel**, **release**, and **statute of limitations**. EXAMPLES of affirmative defenses *in criminal cases* include **alibi**, **double jeopardy**, **insanity**, and **self-defense**.

affirmative easement [*eez* · ment] *n.* An **easement** whose effect is to compel the owner of the land subject to the easement to permit acts (EXAMPLE: the dripping of water from a neighbor's roof) which he would not permit if there were no easement. *Compare* negative easement.

affirmative proof *n.* Evidence that tends to prove the truth of the matter in question, regardless of the nature of the evidence. *See* proof.

affirmative relief [re · *leef*] *n.* 1. **Relief** granted to a defendant in an **action** over and above dismissing the plaintiff's **complaint**. 2. A court order requiring the losing **party** in a lawsuit to act in a specified manner or to desist from specified conduct. *See* injunction; specific performance.

affix [a · *fiks*] *v.* 1. To attach permanently or to fasten, for EXAMPLE, to attach curtain rods to a window. *See* fixture. 2. To inscribe or sign, for EXAMPLE, to sign one's name to a deed.
➤ attach, unite, append, bond, add ("to affix one's name to a deed").

afforce [a · *forss*] *v.* To increase or add force to.
➤ add, increase, strengthen.

affray [a · *fray*] *n.* Fighting that disturbs the peace in a public place.
➤ fight, brawl, altercation, fracas, mêlée, disorderly conduct, breach of the peace ("the barroom affray").

affreightment [a · *frate* · ment] *n.* A contract for the hiring of a ship to carry a specific cargo. *See* charter of affreightment.

affront [a · *front*] *n.* An insult or discourtesy.
v. To insult another by behavior or language.
➤ *n.* insult, discourtesy, slur.
v. afflict, disturb, grieve, offend, scorn, slight.

AFL-CIO Abbreviation of **American Federation of Labor-Congress of Industrial Organizations**.

aforesaid [a · *fore* · sed] *adj.* Mentioned in an earlier part of the same article or document. USAGE: "the defendant's conduct as aforesaid" means "the conduct of the defendant previously referred to."
➤ preceding, aforementioned, previously described ("the aforesaid conduct").

aforethought [a · *fore* · thawt] *adj.* Previously planned; a thought had before; **premeditation**. *See* malice aforethought.
➤ previously planned, premeditated, preconceived, planned, designed, calculated, deliberate, intended ("malice aforethought").

after [*af* · ter] *adj./adv.* 1. Subsequent to. 2. Later. 3. Behind. 4. Below.

after date A phrase used in some **promissory notes** to indicate when the note matures. EXAMPLE: a note dated January 2, 1998, which states that it is payable 10 days "after date," matures on January 12, 1998.

after sight A **draft** payable within a specified number of days after it is presented for payment. USAGE: "ten days after sight"; "twenty days after sight." *Compare* at sight. *See* sight draft.

after-acquired property [-a · *kwired prop* · er · tee] Property acquired by a debtor after entering into a **secured transaction**. Such property may become additional **security** under the **security agreement**.

after-acquired property clause [-a · *kwired prop* · er · tee] *n.* A clause in a mortgage which has the effect of including in the mortgage anything added to the mortgaged property after the mortgage was entered into.

after-acquired title [-a · *kwired ty* · tel] *n.* The interest (usually ownership) in land that a person acquires after she has **conveyed** the land to another person. In such circumstances, the grantor will not be permitted to revoke the original transaction on the ground that she did not have **title** at the time.

after-born child *n.* A child born after the death of its parent who died leaving a will. Such a child will generally inherit unless it is specifically excluded by the will. *See* posthumous child.

after-discovered evidence [-dis · *kuv* · erd *ev* · i · dense] *n.* Evidence discovered after trial. *See* evidence. *Also see* newly discovered evidence.

against [a · *genst*] *prep.* Compared or contrasted.
➤ versus, counter, facing, in opposition to ("against public policy").

against interest [*in* · trest] *adj.* *See* declaration against interest.

against public policy [*pub* · lik *pol* · i · see] *adj.* *See* public policy.

against the evidence [the *ev* · i · dense] *adj.* *See* verdict against the evidence.

age *n.* 1. The length of time a person has lived or a thing has existed.

A

2. A particular period during one's life.

3. The latter portion of human life.

v. To become older or more mature.

➤ *n.* period, time, epoch, phase, era ("the age of litigation"); seniority, maturity, venerableness, decrepitude ("The senior partner is showing his age").

v. mature, ripen, develop, mellow, decline, deteriorate.

age discrimination
[dis · krim · in · *ay* · shen] *n.*
Discrimination against a person because of his age, particularly an older person. *See* discrimination. *Also see* Age Discrimination in Employment Act.

age of consent [kon · *sent*] *n.* 1. The age at which a man or a woman may marry without parental approval. 2. The age at which a woman may consent to sexual intercourse. The age of consent varies from state to state. A man who has sexual intercourse with a female who is not **of age** commits the crime of **statutory rape**. *See also* legal age.

age of majority [ma · *jaw* · ri · tee] *n.*
The age at which a person may legally engage in conduct in which she could not previously engage because she was a minor. (EXAMPLES: entering into a binding contract; enlisting in the military service; voting; making a valid will; purchasing alcoholic beverages.) The age of majority varies from state to state and differs depending upon the activity in question. *See* majority. *Also see* legal age. *Compare* minority.

age of reason [*ree* · zen] *n.* The age, generally seven, at which the law first holds a person responsible for his conduct. A child who has not yet reached the age of reason is conclusively presumed to be incapable of committing a crime or a **tort**. *See* conclusive presumption.

Age Discrimination in Employment Act (ADEA) [dis · crim · in · *ay* · shen in em · *ploy* · ment] *n.* A federal statute that prohibits discrimination in employment of persons older than 40 on the basis of their age. *See* discrimination.

ageism [*ay* · jizm] *n.* Bias against older people; discrimination against older

people based upon their age. *Compare* age discrimination.

agency [*ay* · jen · see] *n.* 1. A relationship in which one person acts for or on behalf of another person at the other person's request. *See* actual agency; exclusive agency; implied agency; intervening agency; ostensible agency. *Compare* independent contractor. 2. An agent's place of business. An insurance agent, for EXAMPLE, is employed at an insurance agency. 3. Short for **administrative agency**. *Also see* public agency; regulatory agency. 4. A private organization or unit of government organized to provide a particular service or type of service. EXAMPLES: the Red Cross (a relief agency); the **Drug Enforcement Administration** (a law enforcement agency). 5. A means for doing something; an **instrumentality**.

➤ bureau, department, organization ("an administrative agency").

agency by estoppel [es · *top* · el] *n.* An agency created by appearances which lead people to believe that the agency exists. It occurs when the principal, through **negligence**, permits her agent to exercise powers she never gave him, even though she has no knowledge of his conduct. *See* estoppel. *See also* apparent authority; implied agency; implied authority.

agency coupled with an interest
[*cup* · ld with an *in* · trest] *n.* *See* power coupled with an interest.

agency in fact *n.* An agency created by the agreement of the **principal** and the **agent**, as distinguished from an agency created by **operation of law** (EXAMPLE: an **agency by estoppel**).

agency of the United States
[yoo · *ny* · ted] *n.* *See* federal agency.

agency relationship [re · *lay* · shun · ship] *n.* The relationship that exists in law between a **principal** and an **agent**.

agency shop agreement [a · *gree* · ment] *n.* A provision in a **collective bargaining agreement** which states that union membership is optional but that nonmembers must pay the union as much as members pay in dues. Agency shops are prohibited in states with **right to work laws**.

A

Compare closed shop; open shop; preferential shop.

agenda [a · *jen* · da] *n.* An outline of things to be done or matters to be attended to, particularly business to be conducted at a meeting.
➤ schedule, outline, plan, diary, docket, timetable ("not on the agenda").

agent [*ay* · jent] *n.* 1. One of the **parties** to an **agency relationship**, specifically, the one who acts for and represents the other party, who is known as the **principal**. The word implies service as well as authority to do something in the name of or on behalf of the principal. (EXAMPLE: a person who represents a business person in contract negotiations.) Although one can be both an employee and an agent, the usual distinction between the two is that the manner in which an employee does his work is controlled and directed by his employer; in contrast, an agent is free to use independent skill and judgment, his principal's concern being the results he produces, not how he does his work. *See* del credere agent; general agent; managing agent; special agent; universal agent. 2. A power, force, or substance which produces a result; a catalyst.
➤ assistant, delegate, emissary, assignee, deputy, functionary, proxy, representative.

aggravate [*ag* · re · vayt] *v.* 1. To annoy to anger. 2. To make more severe.
➤ annoy, gall, pester, provoke, irritate; increase, deepen, complicate, intensify, worsen.

aggravated [*ag* · re · vay · ted] *adj.* Increased; heightened; more severe; worsened. A criminal act accompanied by violence or a substantial degree of force is an aggravated crime. Aggravated crimes include *aggravated **assault**, aggravated **battery***, and *aggravated **robbery***.
➤ exacerbated, heightened, deepened, intensified, inflamed ("aggravated assault").
Ant. mitigating

aggravated assault [a · *salt*] *n.* A crime of greater gravity than **assault** or **simple assault**, it involves the **intent** to kill or to do **serious bodily harm**. Although the presence of such intent depends upon the circumstances, every state punishes **assault with a deadly weapon**, **assault with intent to rape**, and **assault with intent to commit murder**, among others, as aggravated assault. *See also* assault and battery; criminal assault.

aggravating circumstances [ag · re · *vay* · ting *ser* · kem · stan · sez] *n.* Acts or conduct which increase the seriousness of a criminal act or the gravity of its effect. (EXAMPLE: burglary during which the house is vandalized.) Courts often impose more severe sentences when there are aggravating circumstances. USAGE: "Those previous convictions constitute aggravating circumstances." *Compare* mitigating circumstances.

aggravation [ag · re · *vay* · shen] *n.* 1. That which increases severity or harshness; that which makes something worse. *Compare* mitigation. 2. Annoyance; irritation.
➤ annoyance, bother, irritation; worsening, exacerbation, deepening, intensification, heightening.

aggregate [ag · gre · get] *n.* The total sum or amount.
v. [*ag* · ruh · gate] To bring together.
➤ *n.* assemblage, collection, entirety, whole, sum.
v. accumulate, assemble, collect, gather.

aggressor [a · *gress* · er] *n.* Person who initiates a situation, frequently by force, or who provokes or invites trouble.
➤ attacker, belligerent, initiator, combatant, provocateur, invader.
Ant. victim, respondent.

aggrieved [a · *greevd*] *adj.* The state of having been wronged, injured, or deprived of rights.
➤ distressed, afflicted, harmed, injured, wronged ("an aggrieved party").

aggrieved party [a · *greevd par* · tee] *n.* 1. A person whose legal rights have been infringed by another person. 2. A person whose personal or property rights are adversely affected by a **judgment** or decree of a court.

agio [*ag* · ee · oh] *n.* The **rate of exchange** between the currency of one country and the currency of another.

agree [a · *gree*] *v.* To mutually concur; to unite upon the terms of a contract or agreement; to make an agreement. *See* agreement.
➤ concur, assent, acquiesce, accede, endorse ("agree to new terms"); contract, settle, bargain, compromise.

agreed [a · *greed*] *adj.* Having come to an agreement or settlement.

agreed case *n.* A case in which the parties submit to the court a mutually accepted statement of the facts so that the court will consider and determine only **questions of law**. The term is used interchangeably with other terms, such as "agreed statement of facts," "**case agreed**," and "**case stated**." *See also* amicable action; stipulation.

agreed order [*or* · der] *n.* An order of court which is based upon the agreement of the **parties** rather than an order entered by the court after a trial.

agreement [a · *gree* · ment] *n.* 1. A **contract**. 2. A concurrence of intention; **mutual assent**. *See* meeting of the minds. 3. A coming together of parties with respect to a matter of opinion. *See* articles of agreement; collective bargaining agreement; hold harmless agreement; marital agreement; partnership agreement.
➤ contract, bargain, compact, arrangement, pact; concurrence, compliance, alliance.

agreement against public policy [a · *genst pub* · lik *pol* · i · see] *n.* *See* public policy.

agreement of sale *n.* An *agreement of sale* is an agreement which obligates the seller to sell and the buyer to buy, as distinguished from an **agreement to sell**, which merely obligates the seller to sell. An agreement of sale is also called a **contract of sale**. *See also* contract for sale of goods; sales agreement.

agreement to sell *n.* *See and compare* agreement of sale.

agricultural labor [a · gre · *kul* · choo · rel *lay* · ber] *n.* Work performed on a farm for wages.

agricultural price supports [a · gre · *kul* · choo · rel price sup · *ports*] *n.* *See* parity.

aid *n.* 1. Money received by persons under **public assistance** statutes; welfare. 2. Money or goods given, or labor volunteered, by an individual, an organization, or a government, in order to support or be of assistance.
v. To support by furnishing strength or means. *Compare* abet. *See* aiding and abetting.
➤ *n.* help, support, assistance, encouragement. *v.* support, help, assist, promote, subsidize.

aid and abet [a · *bet*] *v.* *See* aiding and abetting.

aid and comfort [*kum* · fert] *n.* An element of the crime of **treason**. A person gives aid and comfort to the enemy by committing an act which encourages or advances the interests of the enemy.

Aid to Families with Dependent Children [*fam* · i · leez with de · *pen* · dent *chil* · dren] *n.* The largest federally assisted program providing financial assistance to the economically disadvantaged. Also known by its abbreviation, **AFDC**, it provides mothers with funds to purchase basic necessities, such as food and shelter, for their children. *See also* public assistance.

aider by verdict [*ay* · der by ver · *dikt*] *n.* The **cure** of **defects** in **pleading** by virtue of the fact that a **verdict** has been rendered in the case.

aiding and abetting [*ay* · ding and a · *bet* · ing] *n.* Helping or encouraging a person to commit a crime. *See* accessory. *See and compare* accessory after the fact; accessory before the fact. *See also* aid; abet.

AIDS [aidz] *n.* Acquired immunodeficiency syndrome, a virally induced disease that causes severe immune deficiency resulting in infections, malignancies, and, ultimately, death. *See* ARC; HIV.

air carrier [*kar* · i · er] *n.* Anyone in the business of providing air transportation.

air piracy [*pie* · re · see] *n.* The federal crime of seizing or exercising control over an aircraft in flight by force or threat of force. *See* piracy. *Compare* carjacking.

air pollution [po · *loo* · shen] *n.* The contamination of the air as a result, for EXAMPLE, of industrial operations, burning waste and rubbish, and automobile exhausts. Federal, state, and local government are involved in maintaining air quality. *See* pollution; Environmental Protection Agency.

air rights *n.* The **right** to use the airspace above one's land.

airbill [*air* · bil] *n.* An agreement by an air carrier to transport specified goods to a specified location. *See* bill of lading; waybill.

aka Abbreviation of "also known as." *See* alias.

akin [a · *kin*] *adj.* Essentially related; similar to.
➤ alike, analogous, similar, related, connected; fraternal, kindred.

alcoholic [al · ke · *hol* · ik] *adj.* 1. Relating to alcohol. 2. Containing alcohol. *n.* A person addicted to alcoholic liquor. *See also* addict; alcoholism.
➤ *adj.* intoxicating, inebriating, brewed.

alcoholic beverage [al · ke · *hol* · ik *bev* · er · ej] *n.* Any liquor, beer, wine, or other substance which produces intoxication, or which contains alcohol in an amount in excess of the amount set by law, and is used as a beverage. The terms "alcoholic liquor," "alcoholic beverage," "liquor," and "intoxicating liquor" are often used interchangeably.

alcoholism [al · ke · hol · izm] *n.* A **chemical dependency** causing physiological or social impairment, or both, which can result from the consumption of alcohol, generally over an extended period of time. *See also* addict; addiction.

alderman [*all* · der · man] *n.* A title given persons elected to the governing board of some municipalities. The position of alderman is similar to that of councilman in those localities with city councils. Some aldermen also have limited judicial duties similar to those of **magistrates**. *See* board of aldermen.
➤ councilman, legislator.

aleatory [*al* · lee · a · tore · ee] *adj.* Uncertain; dependent upon chance.

aleatory contract [*kon* · trakt] *n.* A **contract** whose performance depends upon an uncertain event. EXAMPLE: a fire insurance policy **indemnifies** the insured only in the event of a **loss** due to fire.

ALI Abbreviation of **American Law Institute**. *See Restatement of the Law.*

alia [*ah* · lee · uh] *n.* (*Latin*) "Other things." "*Alia*" most often occurs as a part of the Latin phrase *inter alia*, meaning "among other things" or "among other matters."

alias [*ay* · li · es] *n.* A false name. *adv.* Otherwise known as; also known as; **aka**.
➤ false name, pseudonym, moniker, stagename.

alias writ *n.* A **writ** issued to take the place of a similar writ which has been lost or for some other reason has not taken effect. "Alias" is also used in conjunction with other writs and judicial orders. Thus, for EXAMPLE, there are *alias executions*, *alias warrants*, *alias summonses*, and *alias subpoenas*.

alibi [*al* · i · by] *n.* The **defense** that the accused was elsewhere at the time the crime was committed. *See* affirmative defense.
➤ defense, excuse, explanation, proof, avowal.

alien [*ale* · yen] *adj.* 1. Foreign. 2. Unfamiliar; strange. *n.* 1. Any person present within the borders of the United States who is not a U.S. citizen. 2. Any foreigner. *See and compare* nonresident alien; resident alien. *v.* To transfer property to another; to **alienate**. *See* alienable.
➤ *adj.* foreign, different, exotic, remote, strange, unfamiliar. *n.* foreigner, immigrant, outsider, stranger, visitor.

alienability [*ale* · yen · a · *bil* · it · ee] *n.* With respect to property, the quality of being transferable. *See* alienable.
➤ transferability, relinquishability, consignability.

alienable [*ale* · yen · abl] *adj.* 1. Lawfully transferable. USAGE: "This property is alienable; I expect to leave it to you in my will." 2. Subject to removal; liable to be taken away. USAGE: "A **privilege** is alienable; a **constitutional right** is not." *Compare* inalienable; inalienable rights.
➤ lawfully transferable, severable, removable.

alienage [*ale* · yen · ej] *n.* The state or condition of an **alien**.

alienate [*ale* · yen · ate] *v.* 1. To transfer ownership of real property, whether by **sale** or **gift**, **deed** or **will**; to **alien**. 2. To cause another to become unfriendly; to remove affection. *See* alienation of affections.
➤ transfer, convey, assign, deed ("alienate property"); estrange, separate ("The attorney's offensive manner alienated the jury").

alienation [ale · ee · e · *nay* · shen] *n.* 1. The act of transferring **title**, particularly to real property. *See* restraint on alienation. 2. The withdrawing of affection.
➤ transfer, exchange, conveyance; separation, hostility.

alienation clause *n.* A provision in an insurance policy which stipulates that the policy will become **void** if the property it insures is sold or otherwise transferred.

alienation of affections [a · *fek* · shenz] *n.* Causing a spouse (other than one's own) to lose affection for the person to whom he or she is married. Such conduct is no longer an **actionable wrong** in many states.

alienee [ale · yen · *ee*] *n.* One to whom ownership of property is transferred.

alienor [ale · yen · *or*] *n.* One who transfers the ownership of property to another.

alimony [*al* · i · moh · nee] *n.* Ongoing court-ordered **support** payments by a divorced spouse, usually payments made by an ex-husband to his former wife. Alimony is not **child support**. *See also* lump-sum alimony; palimony; periodic alimony; permanent alimony; temporary alimony.

➤ support, maintenance, sustenance, allowance, settlement.

alimony in gross *n.* *See* lump-sum alimony.

alimony pendente lite [pen · *den* · tay *lee* · te] *n.* Same as **temporary alimony**.

aliquot [*al* · i · kwot] *adj.* Fractional; a fractional share.

aliunde [ah · *lyun* · day] *(Latin) adj.* "From another place" or another source; independent of. *See* evidence aliunde.

aliunde rule *n.* The rule that jurors' challenges to the verdict of a jury on which they sat, if based upon the misconduct of a member of the jury, will not be allowed unless there is evidence of such misconduct from a source other than the jurors themselves.

alive [a · *live*] *adj.* *See* life. 1. The state of having life. 2. Marked with activity.
➤ living, existing, extant, functioning, viable; animated, eager, energetic, spirited.

ALJ Abbreviation of **administrative law judge**.

all *n.* The whole of anything; the entirety.

all events test [ee · *vents*] *n.* With respect to taxpayers who pay income tax on an **accrual basis**, tax liability accrues when "all events" have occurred which entitle the taxpayer to receive and make use of the income.

all faults *n.* A reference to a sale of an item "with all faults and defects"; a **disclaimer** of **warranty** by making a sale with "all faults," i.e., a sale **as is**.

all fours *n.* *See* on all fours.

all the world *n.* A term meaning everyone who might have an **interest** in a transaction or a claim with respect to the transaction. USAGE: "A **judgment** against real property which is properly **entered** or **recorded** is binding upon all the world."

all-risk insurance [in · *shoor* · ense] *n.* Same as **comprehensive insurance**.

allay [a · lay] *n.* To reduce in severity; to lessen.
➤ calm, lessen, mollify, pacify, decrease.

allegation [al · e · *gay* · shen] *n.* 1. A statement in a **pleading** of a fact that the **party** filing the pleading intends to

prove. *See* material allegation. 2. An assertion.
➤ assertion, accusation, avowal, claim, charge.

allege [a · *lej*] *v.* To make an **allegation**; to assert; to claim; to charge.
➤ declare, state, testify, assert, claim, advance, aver, cite ("I allege that my testimony is true").

alleged [a · *lej* · ed] *adj.* That which is questionably true; that which is asserted.
➤ claimed, announced, asserted, propounded ("the alleged murderer").

allegiance [a · *lee* · jense] *n.* Loyalty and obedience that a person has for a nation, organization, or cause.
➤ dedication, devotion, fealty, fidelity, homage, obedience.

Allen charge [*al* · len] *n.* An instruction to the jury in which the judge tells the jurors that, in reaching their verdict, in addition to considering the evidence, they should carefully consider each other's opinions regarding the evidence. *See* jury instructions.

allocation [al · o · *kay* · shen] *n.* 1. A **distribution**. 2. An allowance, allotment, or designation. USAGE: "In distributing the income which will be earned by your **estate**, it is important that it be appropriately allocated among your heirs."
➤ distribution, allowance, allotment, assignment, share.

allocatur [al · o · *kay* · ter] *(Latin) n.* "Let it be allowed." A court order allowing or granting something. EXAMPLE: an order allowing a **writ of certiorari**.

allocution [al · o · *kyoo* · shen] *n.* A judge's question to a convicted criminal before sentence is passed, inquiring whether he has anything to say or whether there is any reason he should not be sentenced.

allodial [al · *oh* · dee · el] *adj.* A term refering to land which is owned unencumbered, or "free and clear."

allograph [*al* · o · graf] *n.* A signature or other writing made for one person by another. *Compare* autograph.

allonge [a · *lonj*] *n.* A paper attached to a **note** or other negotiable instrument on which an **indorsement** is written.
➤ appendix, rider, addendum.

allotment [a · *lot* · ment] *n.* A division; a distribution; a share; an allowance.
➤ division, distribution, share, portion, quota, part.
   allotment certificate [ser · *tif* · i · ket] *n.* A **certificate** issued to an applicant for **shares** in a corporation stating the number of shares allotted to her and the due dates and payments required of her.
   allotment system [*sis* · tem] *n.* The system under which lands were allotted by **treaty** to Native American tribes for use as hunting grounds and for other purposes.

allow [a · *low*] *v.* 1. To approve. USAGE: "The insurance company is going to allow my claim." 2. To permit. USAGE: "He was allowed to go home on a weekend pass."
➤ approve, authorize, accept, acquiesce; permit, consent to.

allowance [a · *low* · ense] *n.* 1. An allotment; a share; a stipend; a payment. *See also* alimony. 2. A discount; a deduction; an exemption.
➤ allotment, share, stipend, payment, allocation, recompense, pay, remittance.

allowed [a · *lowd*] *adj.* Approved, authorized. USAGE: "This is an allowed extension."
➤ accepted, legal, lawful, rightful, authorized, legitimate, permitted.

alluvion [a · *loo* · vee · en] *n.* The solid material added to land by accretion, that is, by the gradual deposit of mud, silt, and sediment as a result of the water's action. *Compare* diluvion.
➤ accretion, accumulation.
Ant. erosion.

alluvium [a · *loo* · vee · um] *n.* Same as **alluvion**.

alter [*al* · ter] *v.* To change, modify, or conform a document or behavior.
➤ adjust, modify, vary, transform, rearrange, deviate ("The document was altered by an unknown party.").

alter ego [*all* · ter *ee* · go] *n.* The other self; literally, the "other I." USAGE: "An **agent** often acts as the alter ego of his **principal**."
➤ other self, second self, double, stand-in, counterpart, twin.

alter ego rule *n.* Also known as the **instrumentality rule**, a doctrine which allows courts to fix **personal liability** upon a corporation's shareholders when the corporation is used as a sham for conducting personal business under the legal protections given corporate shareholders. *See* piercing the corporate veil.

alteration [all · ter · *ay* · shen] *n.* 1. An erasure, writing, or typing that modifies the content of an instrument or document. EXAMPLE: changing the date on a check (as opposed to securing or writing a new check). Because an instrument can be altered by a person entitled to do so, an alteration is not necessarily a **forgery**. *See* material alteration. 2. A change of a thing from one form to another, i.e., making a thing different from what it was, but without destroying its identity. EXAMPLE: adding a room to a house.
➤ change, modification, conversion, reshaping, shift, switch, correction.

alteration of contract [kon · trakt] *n.* A modification of the terms of a **contract** with the assent of both parties.

alternate [all · ter · net] *adj.* Alternative; another; other.
n. A person appointed to substitute for another.
v. [all · ter · nayt] To go from one to another.
➤ *n.* backup, replacement, surrogate ("alternate juror").
v. rotate, vary, exchange, shift, alter ("to alternate positions").

alternate juror [*joo* · rer] *n.* An extra trial juror selected to attend the trial and to take the place of any member of the jury who becomes ill or is for any other reason unable to serve during the trial.

alternate valuation method [val · yoo · *ay* · shen meth · ed] *n.* The **valuation** of a **decedent's estate** for federal **estate tax** purposes as of six months after the date of death or the date the property is disposed of, whichever comes first. The **administrator** of the estate may choose to use this date as an alternative to using the date of death.

alternative [all · *ter* · ne · tiv] *adj.* Representing or reflecting a choice between two or more things, courses, or options. *See* alternate.
n. A choice.
➤ *adj.* different, alternate, varying ("alternative lifestyle").
n. choice, opportunity, option, selection ("She chose the easier alternative").

alternative contract [kon · trakt] *n.* A **contract** that provides one or more of the parties with more than one way to carry out its provisions.

alternative dispute resolution (ADR) [dis · *pyoot* res · e · *loo* · shen] *n.* A term for speedier and less costly methods for resolving disputes than going to court. EXAMPLES: **arbitration; conciliation; mediation; mini-trial; rent-a-judge; summary jury trial**. *Compare* adversary proceeding; adversary system.

alternative pleading [*plee* · ding] *n.* A form of **pleading** in which the pleader alleges facts that may be inconsistent with each other and contradictory. Such pleading is permissible in most jurisdictions as long as the inconsistent statements, standing alone, are sufficient grounds for a lawsuit.

alternative relief [re · *leef*] *n.* A request in a **pleading** by a plaintiff for several forms of **relief**, so that if the court denies one form of relief it may still grant the others.

alternative writ *n.* A **writ**, issued by a court, that gives the **party** against whom it is directed the choice between performing a certain act or demonstrating why he should not have to perform it. This writ has been replaced in modern practice by the **order to show cause**.

amalgamation [a · mal · ga · *may* · shen] *n.* A joining together of separate things to make one thing; a consolidation.
➤ consolidation, coalescence, commingling, fusion, integration, incorporation.

ambassador [am · *bass* · e · dor] *n.* A country's highest ranking diplomatic representative to another country.
➤ delegate, emissary, consul.

ambiguity [am · bi · *gyoo* · i · tee] *n.* Doubtfulness or uncertainty, especially with respect to a document in which the meaning of words or language is unclear or which is susceptible of more than one interpretation.
➤ uncertainty, equivocation, ambivalence, obscurity, indefiniteness, incertitude, vagueness.
Ant. clarity, lucidity.

ambiguous [am · *big* · yoo · us] *adj.* Able to be interpreted in more than one way.
➤ unclear, enigmatic, vague, uncertain, indefinite.

ambit [*am* · bit] *n.* An enclosing line or limit; a boundary line.
➤ boundary, limit, perimeter, extent, confiner, jurisdiction.

ambulatory [*am* · byoo · le · tore · ee] *adj.* 1. Changeable; capable of alteration; revocable. EXAMPLE: a will is referred to as "ambulatory" because the **testator** can change or revoke it at any time during his life. 2. Pertaining to walking or moving. USAGE: a hospital patient who is not confined to his bed is "ambulatory."
➤ changeable, revocable ("an ambulatory will"); walking, moving, roving, peripatetic ("The hospital patient was ambulatory").

ambush [*am* · bush] *v.* To surprise in an attack.
➤ assail, attack, snare, trap.

ameliorate [a · *meel* · e · orate] *v.* To make better; to improve.
➤ improve, allay, better, enhance, palliate, mitigate.

amenable [a · *men* · ibl] *adj.* Open; billing; cooperative.
➤ pliable, accessible, pliant, flexible, reasonable, yielding, responsive ("to be amenable to negotiations").

amend [a · *mend*] *v.* To improve; to make better by change or modification; to correct; to adjust. Thus, a **motion to amend** is a **motion** by which a **party** seeks the court's permission to correct an error or omission in a pleading or to modify **allegations** and supply new ones. *See* amendment of pleading.
➤ correct, remedy, adjust, change, revise, alter, modify.

amended [a · *mend* · ed] *adj.* Corrected; modified; adjusted. USAGE: "an amended complaint." *See* amend; amendment.

amended return [re · *tern*] *n.* Within the limitations prescribed by law, amended tax returns may be filed to correct inaccuracies and omissions in the original return. *See* return.

amendment [a · *mend* · ment] *n.* A correction or revision, particularly of a document, to correct errors or to better state its intended purpose.
➤ correction, revision, betterment, reworking ("amendment of a document"); statute, act, measure, clause ("the First Amendment to the U.S. Constitution"); attachment, appendix, addendum.

amendment of complaint [kom · *playnt*] *n. See* amendment of pleading.

amendment of constitution [kon · sti · *too* · shen] *n.* A process of proposing, passing, and ratifying amendments to the United States Constitution or a state or other constitution. *See* amendment.

amendment of judgment [*juj* · ment] *n. See* modification of judgment.

amendment of pleading [*plee* · ding] *n.* Although every jurisdiction imposes different restrictions, all jurisdictions permit **pleadings** to be amended for the purpose of correcting errors and omissions and to modify **allegations** and supply new ones. *Compare* supplemental complaint. *See* amend.

amendment of statute [*sta* · choot] *n.* The amendment of a statute by the legislature in the form of a subsequent statute has the effect of modifying the earlier act; the amendment of a **bill** before the legislature has the effect of changing the legislation before it is enacted.

amercement [a · *merse* · ment] *n.* A fine or penalty imposed by a court upon a **public officer** for **official misconduct** or neglect of duty.
➤ fine, penalty, punishment, chastisement.

American Arbitration Association (AAA) [a · *mare* · i · ken ar · bi · *tray* · shen a · so · see · *ay* · shen] *n.* A nonprofit organization that provides **arbitrators** for the **arbitration** of disputes.

A

American Association for Paralegal Education (AAfPE) [a · *mare* · i · ken a · so · see · *ay* · shen for pa · re · *lee* · gal ed · yoo · *kay* · shen] *n.* A national organization of paralegal teachers and educational institutions, which provides technical assistance and supports research in the paralegal field, promotes standards for paralegal instruction, and cooperates with the **American Bar Association** and others in developing an approval process for paralegal education.

American Bar Association [a · *mare* · i · ken bar a · so · see · *ay* · shen] *n.* The country's largest voluntary professional association of attorneys, commonly referred to as the ABA. Its purposes include enhancing professionalism and advancing the administration of justice. *See* bar association.

American Civil Liberties Union [a · *mare* · i · ken *siv* · il *lib* · er · tees yoon · yun] *n.* A nonprofit organization, commonly called the **ACLU**, which is concerned with constitutional rights, particularly individual liberties, and engages in litigation (often as *amicus curiae*) and lobbying.

American clause [a · *mare* · i · ken] *n.* A provision in **marine insurance** policies under which the insurance company is liable no matter how many other policies the insured owns covering the same **loss**.

American Federation of Labor-Congress of Industrial Organizations [a · *mare* · i · ken fed · er · *ay* · shen of *lay* · bor *kong* · gress of in · *dus* · tree · el or · gen · i · *zay* · shens] *n.* The largest federation of labor unions in the United States and Canada, popularly known as the AFL-CIO.

American Law Institute (ALI) [a · *mare* · i · ken law *in* · sti · toot] *n.* A nonprofit organization committed to clarifying legal principles and standardizing them throughout the country. Its best-known works are the **Restatement of the Law** and the **Uniform Commercial Code**, prepared jointly with the National Conference of Commissioners on Uniform State Laws. *See* Commission on Uniform State Laws; Uniform Laws.

Americans with Disabilities Act (ADA) [a · *mare* · i · kenz with dis · e · *bil* · i · tees] *n.* A federal statute that prohibits discrimination against disabled persons in employment, public services, and places of **public accommodation**. *See* disability; discrimination.

amicable [*am* · i · kabl] *adj.* 1. Showing friendliness or peacefulness. 2. Agreed upon by both parties. *Compare* adversaried.
➤ friendly, agreeing, cordial, civil, social, amiable, kind, understanding, like-minded. *Ant.* hostile.

amicable action [*am* · i · kabl] *n.* A lawsuit brought by agreement between the **parties**, for the purpose of resolving a dispute between them, in which the facts are admitted or stipulated. *See* agreed case.

amicus curiae [a · *mee* · kes *koo* · ree · eye] *(Latin) n.* "Friend of the court." A person who is interested in the outcome of the case, but who is not a **party**, whom the court permits to file a brief for the purpose of providing the court with a position or a point of view which it might not otherwise have. An *amicus curiae* is often referred to simply as an *amicus*.

ammunition [am · mu · *nish* · en] *n.* Materials used for attacking or defending.
➤ arms, weapons, munitions, defense.

amnesty [*am* · nes · tee] *n.* An act of the government granting a pardon for a past crime. Amnesty is rarely exercised in favor of individuals, but is usually applied to a group or class of persons who are accountable for crimes for which they have not yet been convicted. *See also* clemency; pardon; reprieve.
➤ clemency, pardon, reprieve, dispensation, absolution.

amortization [am · er · ti · *zay* · shen] *n.* The act of **amortizing**. *See* amortize.

amortize [*am* · er · tize] *v.* 1. To gradually pay off a debt by regular payments in a fixed amount over a fixed period of time. 2. To **depreciate** an **intangible asset** (EXAMPLES: stock; **bills**; **notes**) over the period of its **useful life** (or other acceptable period of time) in order to establish its value at any given point in time. *See* prorate.

➤ pay off, reduce, discharge; depreciate, write off.

amotion [a · *moh* · shen] *n.* Removal from premises or from office. EXAMPLES: the eviction of a tenant; the dismissal of a public official. *See* dispossession; removal from office.

➤ removal, eviction, ouster ("the amotion of a tenant").

amount [a · *mount*] *n.* Quantity; the total of two or more separate sums or quantities; the aggregate.

➤ total, whole, aggregate, bulk, quantity, sum.

amount in controversy
[*kon* · tre · ver · see] *n.* A term relevant to determining a court's **jurisdiction**, when jurisdiction is based upon either a minimum dollar amount with which the court is permitted to concern itself or a maximum amount which represents the upper limit of its jurisdiction. *See* jurisdictional amount. *Also see* diversity jurisdiction.

amount of loss *n.* With respect to insurance, the amount of **loss** suffered by the insured as the result of the **destruction** of or **injury** to her insured property.

amount realized [*real* · ized] *n.* In tax law, the amount of money received by a taxpayer upon the **sale or exchange** of property, plus the **fair market value** of goods or services received in addition to the money.

amphetamine [am · *fet* · e · meen] *n.* A prescription drug that stimulates the central nervous system and has various, although limited, medical uses. Also known as methedrine and methamphetamine, it is a **controlled substance** with a high potential for abuse leading to addiction; its possession, distribution, or sale is a crime.

analogous [a · *nal* · e · gus] *adj.* Similar in some respects; comparable.

➤ similar, corresponding, comparable, akin ("an analogous case").

analogous cases [a · *nal* · e · gus] *n.* Cases which are not **on point** with one another but are closely related so that the reasoning in one may be applied in the other. *See* precedent.

analysis [a · *nal* · uh · sis] *n.* An examination of a complex idea, usually done by breaking it down into its components.

➤ critique, investigation, scrutiny, inquiry, examination.

analytical [an · e · *lit* · i · kel] *adj.* 1. Based on analysis rather than emotion or intuition. 2. Probing, logical; proceeding by investigating the components of an issue or situation.

➤ inquiring, interpretive, critical, judicious, questioning ("She has an analytical mind").

analytical jurisprudence [an · e · *lit* · i · kel joo · ris · *proo* · dense] *n.* A system of law based wholly on analysis and theoretical classification rather than upon principles of right and fairness. *See* jurisprudence.

anarchist [*an* · er · kist] *n.* 1. A person who believes that the best society is one without laws or government. 2. A person who believes in or advocates the overthrow of the government by force or violence. *See* criminal anarchy.

➤ agitator, insurgent, rebel, revolutionary.

anarchy [*an* · er · kee] *n.* 1. The absence of government; a state of society in which there is no law or supreme power; political disorder often coupled with violence. 2. Disarray in any area of activity.

➤ lawlessness, chaos, confusion, disorder, disorganization.

anatomical gift [an · a · *tom* · i · kel] *n.* Under the Uniform Anatomical Gift Act, a donation of all or part of the human body, to take effect on or after death. Anatomical gifts are generally made for purposes of organ transplantation. *See* Uniform Laws.

ancestor [*an* · ses · ter] *n.* A person from whom one is descended. *Compare* descendant. *See* common ancestor.

➤ forerunner, precursor, progenitor, parent, forebear.

ancient [*ane* · shent] *adj.* 1. As used in the law, old but not ancient in the ordinary sense of the word. EXAMPLE: a **judgment**

which is 20 years old is an **ancient judgment**. 2. In ordinary usage, very old; something that has existed for a very long time; pertaining to the ancient world.

➤ old, aged, antiquated, dated, outmoded, venerable ("ancient civilization").

ancient boundaries [*boun* · dreez] *n.* Trees, stones, and other markers that have been in existence since before the memory of living man and therefore may be accepted as legal boundaries by virtue of their history.

ancient document [*dok* · yoo · ment] *n.* A **document** that is at least 30 years old, has been maintained in proper custody, and appears to be authentic. Ancient documents are exempt from the rule that documents cannot be admitted into evidence unless they are **authenticated** by appropriate testimony.

ancient judgment [*juj* · ment] *n.* A **judgment** that is 20 or more years old. There is a strong **presumption** that an ancient judgment is in proper form.

ancient lights *n.* The rule of law that a landowner cannot build anything on his property which blocks the light entering his neighbor's window, if his neighbor had "uninterrupted enjoyment" of the light for 20 years or more.

ancillary [*an* · si · la · ree] *adj.* Subordinate; auxiliary; secondary.

➤ subordinate, auxiliary, secondary, dependent, collateral ("ancillary jurisdiction").

ancillary action [*ak* · shen] *n.* A suit that is secondary to an **action** in another court and aids that action.

ancillary administration [ad · min · is · *tray* · shen] *n.* The **administration** of a **decedent's estate** in a state other than the one in which she lived, for the purpose of disposing of property she owned there. *Compare* principal administration. *Also compare* domiciliary administration.

ancillary jurisdiction [joo · ris · *dik* · shen] *n.* The power of a court to **adjudicate** matters that are only incidentally related to the case before it, which could not have been heard or decided by that court had they arisen on their own. *See* jurisdiction.

ancillary letters [*let* · erz] *n.* **Letters of administration** issued to an ancillary administrator. *See* ancillary administration.

ancillary proceeding [pro · *seed* · ing] *n.* Same as **ancillary action**.

and/or Both or either. This synthetic term is sloppy because it is imprecise; it is best to avoid it in legal writing if possible.

anencephalic [an · en · se · *fal* · ik] *adj.* Having no brain. USAGE: "An anencephalic baby cannot sustain vital functions."

animal [*an* · i · mel] *n.* In law, all animal life other than man.
adj. Having the characteristics of an animal rather than a human being.

➤ *adj.* coarse, vulgar, beastly, brutish.

animal of a base nature [*nay* · cher] *n.* *See* base animal.

animal patent [*pat* · ent] *n.* A **patent** granted on a manmade, nonhuman, multi-cellular, living animal organism that does not exist in nature. *See also* plant patent.

animal rights *n.* A term with no legal significance because animals have no legal rights. Humans, however, have both legal rights and legal obligations. Therefore, the law can regulate human behavior with respect to animals.

annex [*an* · eks] *n.* 1. A smaller building attached to a larger building. 2. That which is attached to something else.
v. [*an* · eks] To attach to; to join on; to affix.

➤ *n.* extension, wing, addition, attachment ("the Police Station annex").
v. attach, join, affix, bind, connect, append ("Please annex the defense to the application"); seize, take, appropriate, arrogate ("to annex the park").

annexation [an · ek · *say* · shen] *n.* 1. The acquisition of territory by a nation, state, city, or town. 2. The attaching of something to a building so that, in law, it becomes a part of the building. *See* fixture.

➤ takeover, appropriation, acquisition ("the annexation of territory"); merger, attachment, joining, addition.

annotate [*an* · o · tayt] *v.* To make an explanation or a comment in writing or in print.

➤ comment, explain, note, elucidate, expound.

A

annotated [an · o · tay · ted] *adj.*
Containing explanatory comments.

annotated codes [an · o · tay · ted] *n.*
Books or volumes that contain both stat-
utes and commentaries upon the statutes.
See annotation.

annotated statutes [an · o · tay · ted
stat · shoots] *n. See* annotated codes.

annotation [an · o · *tay* · shen] *n.* 1. A
notation, appended to any written work,
which explains or comments upon its
meaning. 2. A commentary that appears
immediately following a printed statute
and describes the application of the
statute in actual cases. Such annotations,
with the statutes on which they comment,
are published in volumes known as
annotated statutes or **annotated codes**.
3. A notation that follows an **opinion of
court** printed in a **court report**,
explaining the court's action in detail.
➤ comment, commentary, explanation,
exegesis, explication, footnote.

annoy [a · *noy*] *v.* To irritate or bother.
➤ irritate, offend, displease, grate, harass,
upset, torment.

annual [an · yoo · el] *adj.* Yearly;
happening every year.

annual meeting [*meet* · ing] *n.* A
regular meeting of the stockholders of a
corporation, held once a year.

annual percentage rate (APR)
[per · *sen* · tej] *n.* The rate of interest on
borrowed money, expressed in annual
terms. **Consumer credit protection acts**
require lenders to inform borrowers of
the applicable annual percentage rate so
they will be better able to understand the
actual cost of borrowing money or
financing purchases.

annual report [re · *port*] *n.* A report
issued yearly by a corporation, informing
its stockholders, the government, and the
public, in some detail, of its operations,
particularly its fiscal operations, during
the year. The contents of an annual report
(also called an **annual statement**), as
well as the report itself, are required by
law. *See* 10-K.

annual statement [*state* · ment] *See*
annual report.

annuitant [a · *nyoo* · i · tent] *n.* A person
who receives an **annuity**.

annuity [a · *nyoo* · i · tee] *n.* 1. A yearly
payment of a fixed sum of money for life
or for a stated number of years. 2. A right
to receive fixed periodic payments
(yearly or otherwise), either for life or
for a stated period of time.
   Most annuities are in the form of insurance policies. When payments are made
until the death of the **annuitant**, the
annuity is a **life annuity**. When payments
will be terminated if the annuitant acts in
a specified way (EXAMPLE: accepting full-
time employment), the annuity is a **term
annuity**. A **contingent annuity** is payable upon the occurrence of some stated
event beyond the control of the annuitant
(EXAMPLE: the death of the annuitant's
father). A **joint and survivorship annuity**
is paid to two annuitants and, after one of
them dies, to the survivor. (EXAMPLE:
continued payment to a widow of an
annuity which, prior to her husband's
death, was paid to her and her husband
jointly.) A **retirement annuity** is generally payable upon retirement from
employment. *See* pension; pension plan.
See also deferred compensation.
➤ payment, income, pension, subsidy,
stipend, allotment.

annuity policy [*pol* · i · see] *n.* An
insurance policy that provides for or pays
an annuity.

annul [a · *nul*] *v.* To erase; to nullify; to
wipe out; to make void; to reduce to
nothing. *See* annulment.
➤ erase, nullify, wipe out, make void,
expunge, cancel, revoke, abrogate ("to
annul a marriage").

annulment [a · *nul* · ment] *n.* The act of
annulling or making void.
➤ cancellation, abrogation, voiding, invalidation, repeal, rescission, dissolution,
nullification.

annulment of marriage [*mar* · ej] *n.*
The act of a court in voiding a **marriage**
for causes existing at the time the marriage
was entered into (EXAMPLE: the existing
marriage of one of the parties). Annulment
differs from divorce in that it is not a

A

dissolution of the marriage but a declaration that no marriage ever existed.

annum [an · um] *(Latin) n.* Year. *See per annum.*

anon [a · *non*] *adv.* In a short time; in a while.

anonymous [a · *non* · i · mus] *adj.* Without a name; unnamed.
➤ unnamed, unknown, nameless, unclaimed, unacknowledged ("the anonymous donor").

answer [an · ser] *n.* 1. The reply to a question. 2. A **pleading** in response to a **complaint**. An answer may deny the **allegations** of the complaint, **demur** to them, agree with them, or introduce **affirmative defenses** intended to defeat the plaintiff's lawsuit or delay it. *See* false answer; full answer; unresponsive answer.
v. 1. To reply. 2. In **pleading**, to respond to the plaintiff's **complaint** by denying its **allegations** or by introducing **affirmative defenses** containing **new matter**. 3. To assume liability. USAGE: "I will answer for your debt to the bank."
➤ *n.* defense, reply, denial, rebuttal, refutation, counterclaim ("file an answer to a complaint").
v. reply, respond, defend, controvert ("He answered the plaintiff's complaint by denying the allegations"); assume liability for, be obligated for ("I will answer for your debt to the bank").

answerable [an · ser · abl] *adj.* Liable to pay damages.
➤ liable, accountable.

antagonize [an · *tag* · o · nize] *v.* To act in opposition to; to alienate or make an enemy of. To oppose, frequently in a hostile manner.
➤ offend, embitter, estrange, displease, irritate, insult ("It is best not to antagonize the judge").

ante [an · tay] *(Latin) adv.* Before.

antecedent [an · te · *see* · dent] *adj.* Prior; preceding; preexisting.
➤ previous, preexisting, earlier.
antecedent debt *n.* A previous debt, regardless of whether it is valid. Under certain circumstances, a debt that has

become unenforceable may again become enforceable (EXAMPLE: a debt too old to enforce by a lawsuit may be revived by a current promise to pay; *see* revival of action). Under the **Bankruptcy Code**, an antecedent debt is one incurred before the beginning of the **bankrupcy proceedings**, which will therefore be honored by the **trustee in bankruptcy**.

antedate [an · te · date] *v.* 1. To date a document as of a date prior to the date on which it was actually signed. *Compare* postdate. 2. To precede in point of time.
➤ predate, backdate.

antenuptial [an · te *nup* · shel] *adj.* Before marriage.
➤ prenuptial, premarital.
antenuptial agreement [a · *gree* · ment] *n.* Same as **prenuptial agreement**.
antenuptial settlement [*set* · el · ment] *n.* Same as **prenuptial agreement**.

anti- [an · tie] *pref.* Against; contrary to; in opposition to.

anticipate [an · *tiss* · i · pate] *v.* 1. To think about in advance. 2. To act in expectation.
➤ contemplate, look forward to, await, envision ("anticipate the decision"); foresee, preconceive, augur, predict ("anticipate the problem").

anticipation [an · tiss · i · *pay* · shen] *n.* The act of doing something or considering doing something before its time; expectation; foreknowledge.
Reasonable anticipation is the principle by which **negligence** is determined, its basis being injury which a **reasonably prudent person** would have foreseen. An *anticipation provision* in a **note** or contract allows prepayment without a **prepayment penalty**.
➤ apprehension, anxiety, fear, anguish, dread ("He approached the jury with great anticipation").
anticipation of device [de · *vice*] *n.* In the law of **patents**, an invention cannot be patented if it was anticipated, i.e., if it was preceded by a substantially similar **device** invented by someone else.
anticipation of income [*in* · kum] *n.* Borrowing against income that has not yet accrued. EXAMPLE: a city's issuing of

A

bonds which are to be paid from taxes it expects to levy or to collect in the future.

anticipation provision [pro · *vizh* · en] *n. See* anticipation.

anticipatory breach [an · *tiss* · i · pe · tore · ee] *n.* The announced intention of a party to a contract that she does not intend to perform her obligations under the contract; an announced intention to commit a **breach of contract**. *Compare* repudiation of contract.

antidumping act [an · tie · *dum* · ping] *n. See* dumping.

antilapse statute [an · tie · laps *stat* · shoot] *n.* A statute providing that, if a person named to receive property in a will dies before the person who made the will, her share will not lapse, but will take effect as if she had died immediately after the death of the **testator**. The effect of such a statute is to ensure that a beneficiary's share will go to her heirs and not to others. *See* lapsed devise; lapsed legacy.

antinomy [an · *ti* · no · mee] *n.* A contradiction in a statute or between statutes, principles, or inferences.

antiracketeering acts [an · tie · ra · ke · *teer* · ing] *n.* Federal statutes designed to prevent racketeering through violence and threats. EXAMPLES: the **Racketeer Influenced and Corrupt Organizations Act**; the **Hobbs Act**.

antitrust acts [an · tie · *trust*] *n.* Statutes that prohibit **monopolies** in the production or sale of goods or services which interfere with trade or fair competition. The **Clayton Act** and the **Sherman Act** are EXAMPLES of federal antitrust acts. *See* restraint of trade.

APA Abbreviation of **Administrative Procedure Act**.

apex [*ay* · peks] *n.* Highest point; summit; top.
➤ high point, pinnacle, climax, peak, zenith, summit, apogee, acme, crest, culmination. *Ant.* nadir.

apex rule *n.* A rule of mining law that a person who discovers a mineral vein on **public land** may mine it wherever it

leads from the surface or from its nearest point to the surface.

app. ct. *n.* Abbreviation of **appellate court**.

apparent [a · *par* · ent] *adj.* Clear; plain; evident; obvious; appearing to the eye.
➤ clear, evident, obvious, distinct, likely, discernible.

apparent agent [*ay* · jent] *n.* One who is, in law, an **agent** because she has **apparent authority**.

apparent authority [aw · *thaw* · ri · tee] *n.* **Authority** which, although not actually granted by the **principal**, she permits her **agent** to exercise. *See also* agency by estoppel. *Compare* actual authority.

apparent defect [*dee* · fekt] *n.* 1. Under the **Uniform Commercial Code**, a **defect** ascertainable by reasonable inspection. 2. A defect in **title** that is obvious from the **record**. *See and compare* latent defect; patent defect.

apparent easement [*eez* · ment] *n.* An **easement** that can be seen. EXAMPLE: a pathway; a road. *Compare* discontinuous easement; nonapparent easement.

apparent heir [air] *n. See* heir apparent.

appeal [a · *peel*] *n.* 1. The process by which a higher court is requested by a **party** to a lawsuit to review the decision of a lower court. Such reconsideration is normally confined to a review of the **record** from the lower court, with no new testimony taken nor new issues raised. Review by a higher court may result in **affirmance, reversal, modification**, or **remand** of the lower court's decision. 2. The process by which a court or a higher level administrative body is asked to review the action of an administrative agency. *See* cross-appeal; frivolous appeal; interlocutory appeal. 3. A request for help or assistance.
v. 1. To request that a higher court (court of appeals or Supreme Court, for example) hear a case. 2. To request help or assistance.
➤ *n.* allure, pleasingness, attraction ("The witness had appeal"); petition, review, reexamination ("his appeal to a higher court").

v. petition, review, reexamine ("appeal a case"); implore, beg, beseech, plead ("She appealed for assistance").

appeal bond *n.* **Security** furnished by the **party** appealing a case to guarantee that the appeal is *bona fide*. *See* bond.

appealability [a · peel · e · *bil* · i · tee] *adj.* Able to be appealed. A case before a lower court has appealability when it, or a portion of it, is at a point at which it may be appealed. *See* interlocutory appeal; ripe for review.

appealable judgment [*juj* · ment] *n. See* appealable order.

appealable order [a · *peel* · abl] *n.* An **action** of a lower court which a **party** to the lawsuit has a right to take before a higher court for review. *See* appeal.

appeals court [a · *peelz*] *n. See* appellate court.

appear [a · *peer*] *v.* To enter an **appearance** in a case.
➤ spring, surface, attend, arrive, come in, materialize ("appear in court").

appearance [a · *peer* · ense] *n.* 1. The action of an attorney in declaring to the court that he represents a litigant in a case before the court (also referred to as "entering an appearance"). 2. The act by which a party comes into court. EXAMPLES: The filing of a **complaint** by a plaintiff; the filing of an **answer** by a defendant. *See and compare* general appearance; special appearance.
➤ actualization, entrance, exhibition, materialization, emergence ("The appearance of his attorney was timely"); form, bearing, look, demeanor ("the witness's calm appearance").

appearance docket [*dok* · et] *n.* A **docket** kept by the **clerk of court** in which appearances are entered.

appellant [a · *pel* · ent] *n.* A **party** who appeals from a lower court to a higher court.
➤ appealer, litigant, petitioner, party.

appellate [a · *pel* · et] *adj.* Pertaining to the taking of an appeal.

appellate court *n.* A **higher court** to which an appeal is taken from a lower court.

appellate jurisdiction [joo · ris · *dik* · shen] *n.* The authority of one court to review the **proceedings** of another court or of an administrative agency. USAGE: "In our system, the Supreme Court of the United States has ultimate appellate jurisdiction." *See* jurisdiction.

appellate practice [*prak* · tiss] *n. See* practice.

appellate review [re · *vyoo*] *n.* Review by an **appellate court** of a case appealed to it. *See* review; scope of review. *Also see* Federal Rules of Appellate Procedure.

appellee [a · pel · *ee*] *n.* A **party** against whom a case is appealed from a lower court to a higher court.
➤ respondent, defendant.

append [a · *pend*] *v.* To attach; to add.
➤ adjoin, annex, fasten, stack on, attach ("append the property description to the settlement papers").

appendage [a · *pen* · dej] *n.* A desirable or convenient attachment to a more important thing. EXAMPLES: an arm or leg; a garage adjoining a house.
➤ addition, supplement, extremity, member.

appendix [a · *pen* · diks] *n.* Additional matter inserted at the end of a brief, document, text, or book, for purposes of reference or further explanation.
➤ appendage, codicil, rider, attachment, insertion, pocket part.
Ant. front matter, introduction.

appertain [a · per · *tane*] *v.* To belong to; to pertain to; to refer or relate to.
➤ belong, apply, be proper, refer, pertain.

appertaining [a · per · *tane* · ing] *adj.* Relating to; pertaining to.

applicable [*ap* · lik · ebl] *adj.* Appropriate; pertinent; relevant; that which can be applied.
➤ appropriate, applicative, relevant, befitting, germane, fit, fitting, apt, befitting.

applicant [*ap* · li · kent] *n.* A person who applies for something; a person who files a formal request, usually in writing; a person who files an **application**.
➤ candidate, inquirer, petitioner, aspirer, seeker, suitor.

application [ap · li · *kay* · shen] *n.* 1. A petition or other formal request made to a court or administrative agency. 2. The act of applying. USAGE: "the application of the law to the facts."
➤ proposal, request, submission, bid, motion; relation, interrelation.

apply [a · *ply*] *v.* 1. To put to use. 2. To make a request; to petition.
➤ use, utilize, exercise, employ ("he applied his knowledge to solve the problem"; request, petition, pray, seek ("he applied to the court for relief").

appoint [a · *point*] *v.* 1. To select a person for a specific office, position, duty, or job. 2. To select; to designate.
➤ assign responsibility, furnish, allot, choose, commission.

appointee [a · poin · *tee*] *n.* 1. A person who has been appointed to an office or position. 2. A beneficiary under a **power of appointment**.
➤ beneficiary, deputy, representative, agent, delegate.

appointment [a · *point* · ment] *n.* 1. The selection of a person, other than by election, to occupy an office, generally a public office. 2. The act of exercising a **power of appointment**.
➤ authorization, certification, choice, designation, empowerment.

apportionment [a · *pore* · shen · ment] *n.* 1. **Apportionment of representatives**. 2. The act of dividing and assigning in proportion. EXAMPLE: dividing a water bill between two successive tenants, based upon the number of days each occupied the apartment. *See pro rata*; prorating.
➤ allocation, distribution, parceling out, administration.

apportionment of representatives [rep · re · *zent* · e · tivz] *n.* The computation of the number of representatives each state may have in the House of Representatives, based upon its population, or a county may have in a state legislature. *See* legislative apportionment; reapportionment.

appraisal [a · *pray* · zel] *n.* Valuation; a determination of the worth or value of something, for EXAMPLE, real estate or

antiques. The terms "expert" and "independent" are generally associated with "appraisal" because an assessment of worth by an expert with no financial stake in the result is often required to establish the **fair market value** of property.
➤ estimation, assessment, opinion, valuation, appraisement.

appraisal remedy [*rem* · e · dee] *n.* The right of **dissenting stockholders** in a corporation to be bought out by the corporation before the undertaking of a major corporate action (EXAMPLE: a **merger**) which they oppose. An appraisal is made to establish the **fair value** of their stock.

appraise [a · *praze*] *v.* 1. To estimate value. 2. With respect to insurance, to determine the amount of a **loss**.
➤ value, estimate, examine, review, inspect ("appraise the property at $100,000").

appraiser [a · *pray* · zer] *n.* A person selected to make an appraisal of property. Such a person is usually specially trained or licensed.

appreciable [a · *preesh* · able] *adj.* That which is able to be measured.
➤ measurable, discernable, ascertainable, perceptible, recognizable, substantive ("an appreciable difference between offers"). *Ant.* insignificant, trivial.

appreciate [a · *pree* · she · ate] *v.* 1. To rise in value. 2. To understand; to recognize the worth of a person, thing, or idea.
➤ perceive, comprehend, understand ("I appreciate your point"); enhance, gain, inflate, increase in worth ("The property has appreciated a great deal"); value, respect, adore, savor, treasure ("appreciate the arts").

appreciation [a · *pree* · she · *ay* · shen] *n.* 1. An increase in the value of something. *Compare* depreciation. 2. Recognition of value. 3. Gratitude.
➤ thankfulness, sensitivity, addition, testimonial, gratitude, gain, growth, inflation; recognition, regard, awareness, enjoyment, sensitivity.

apprehend [ap · re · *hend*] *v.* 1. To arrest; to capture; to place in custody; to seize. 2. To have knowledge of something.
➤ arrest, capture, detain, incarcerate, confine ("The prisoner was apprehended earlier

that night"); conceive, fathom, grasp, comprehend ("to apprehend an idea").

apprehension [ap · re · *hen* · shen] *n.* 1. The capture or arrest of a person on a criminal charge. 2. Anxiety. 3. Knowledge of something.
➤ understanding, awareness, knowledge; seizure, arrest, detention, confinement ("the apprehension of the perpetrator").

apprentice [a · *pren* · tiss] *n.* A learner; one who seeks to achieve proficiency in the craft at which she is employed. **Collective bargaining agreements** between **craft unions** and employers generally provide for a lesser wage for apprentices than for more experienced workers (**journeymen**). Formerly, all attorneys served an *apprenticeship,* which was called a **clerkship**.
➤ novice, intern, neophyte, pupil, starter.

apprise [a · *prize*] *v.* 1. To give notice. 2. To teach.
➤ advise, make aware, reveal, disclose.

appropriate [a · *proh* · pree · et] *adj.* Fit; suitable, adapted to; relevant.
v. [a · *proh* · pree · ate] 1. To allot, to assign, to set apart, or to apply to a particular purpose. USAGE: "Do you think the legislature will appropriate enough funds for public education?" *See* appropriation. 2. To take possession of; to take and use for oneself or as one's own.
➤ *adj.* fit, suitable, deserved, apt, belonging, befitting, felicitous, desired, pertinent ("very appropriate phrase").
v. set aside, allot, assign, disburse; steal, lift, pilfer, usurp, embezzle, filch.

appropriation [a · proh · pree · *ay* · shen] *n.* 1. A wrongful taking of anything which deprives another person of his rightful interest. *See* conversion; misappropriation. 2. A governmental **taking** of private property for public use under the power of **eminent domain**. 3. Allocation of funds for a particular purpose by a legislature.
➤ set-aside, apportionment, assignment, stipulation, allocation ("appropriation of funds for education"); conversion, misappropriation, embezzlement ("the appropriation of her savings").

appropriation act *n.* An act of the legislature allocating public funds for particular objects or purposes. *See* act.

appropriation to capital [*kap* · i · tel] *n.* The application of income by a corporation to major undertakings such as plant expansion or permanent improvements. *See* capital; capital budget; capital expenditures.

approval [a · *proov* · el] *n.* 1. Short for **sale on approval**. 2. The act of judging or thinking favorably; the act of confirming or ratifying.
➤ authorization, assent, accord, assurance, endorsement, permit, sanction, confirmation, compliance.

approval sale *n. See* sale on approval.

approximately [a · *prok* · si · met · lee] *adv.* About; more or less; nearly. "Approximately" is an imprecise word whose meaning always depends upon the context in which it appears; should be employed with attention to what is really meant. *Compare* proximate.
➤ nearly, bordering, comparatively, in the vicinity of.

appurtenance [a · *per* · te · nense] *n.* A lesser thing attached to a primary thing. The word appears most commonly in deeds and mortgages, and refers to things attached to the land, ownership of which is transferred when **title** to the land is transferred. A farmhouse, barn, silo, or toolshed located on the land are EXAMPLES of appurtenances to the land.
➤ accessory, auxiliary, extension, addendum, right of way.

appurtenant [a · *per* · te · nent] *adj.* Belonging or attached to something else. *See* appurtenance.
➤ belonging, attached, subsidiary, dependent ("an appurtentant easement").

appurtenant easement [*eez* · ment] *n.* An **easement** that **attaches** to the land, passes with it when it is **conveyed**, and exists for the benefit of the adjoining land. *See and compare* dominant tenement; servient tenement.

appurtenant way *n.* A **right of way** that is one with the land, bears upon its

enjoyment, and is transferred with it. *See* way.

APR Abbreviation of **annual percentage rate**.

arbiter [ar · bi · ter] *n.* A person with power to settle a dispute. Same as **arbitrator**.
➤ referee, umpire, interceder, mediator, moderator, advisor, adjudicator.

arbitrable [ar · bi · trebl] *adj.* Capable of being submitted to **arbitration**.

arbitrage [ar · bi · trahzh] *n.* The simultaneous purchase and sale of identical or equivalent **securities** in two different markets for the purpose of profiting on unequal **rates of exchange** and on the different **market values** of the securities.

arbitrarily [ar · bi · *trare* · i · lee] *adv.* Unreasonably or without justification; in an arbitrary manner.
➤ unreasonably, randomly, whimsically, capriciously.

arbitrary [ar · bi · trare · ee] *adj.* According to notion or whim rather than law; in accordance with personal wishes or one's prejudices, and not on the basis of principles or reason. EXAMPLE: A clerk who refuses to issue a marriage license because he disapproves of the couple's opinions about child-rearing acts in an arbitrary manner. *See also* capricious.
➤ capricious, unreasoned, irrational, fanciful; dictatorial, domineering, bossy.

arbitrary and capricious [ke · *prish* · es] *adj.* 1. A reference to the concept in **administrative law** that permits a court to substitute its judgment for that of an administrative agency if the agency's decision unreasonably ignores the law or the facts of a case. 2. In constitutional law, an action may be deemed impermissible or violate due process if it was done in an arbitrary and capricious manner.

arbitration [ar · bi · *tray* · shen] *n.* A method of settling disputes by submitting a disagreement to a person (an **arbitrator**) or a group of individuals (an **arbitration panel**) for decision instead of going to court. If the parties are required to comply with the decision of the arbitrator, the process is called *binding arbitration;* if there is no such obligation, the arbitration

is referred to as *nonbinding arbitration*.
Compulsory arbitration arbitration required by law, most notably in **labor disputes**. *See* alternative dispute resolution. *Compare* conciliation; mediation.
➤ adjustment, compromise, mediation, determination ("Some courts require that civil litigants go to arbitration before proceeding in court.").

arbitration acts *n.* Statutes that facilitate or require the submission of certain kinds of disputes to arbitration.

arbitration board *n.* *See* arbitration panel.

arbitration clause *n.* A clause in a contract providing for arbitration of controversies that arise out of performance of the contract.

arbitration of exchange [eks · *chaynj*] *n.* The **arbitrage** of a **bill of exchange**.

arbitration panel [*pan* · el] *n.* A number of **arbitrators** who hear and decide a case together. *See* panel.

arbitrator [ar · bi · tray · ter] *n.* A person who conducts an **arbitration**. Generally, the primary considerations in choosing an arbitrator are impartiality and familiarity with the type of matter in dispute. *Compare* mediator.
➤ judge, umpire, mediator, intervenor, adjudicator.

ARC [ark] Acronym for "AIDS-related complex," a group of symptoms exhibited by persons who are infected with the **HIV** virus, but who do not display the typical infections or malignancies of full-blown **AIDS**.

argue [ar · gyoo] *v.* 1. To make an argument to a court. 2. To attempt to convince.
➤ contend, debate, altercate, bicker, wrangle, oppose, challenge.
Ant. concede.

arguendo [ar · gyoo · *en* · doh] *adv.* By way of argument; for purpose of argument. The phrase "assume arguendo" means to assume something is true for the sake of discussion, regardless of whether it is actually true. USAGE: "I believe your facts are incorrect, but I'm willing to assume arguendo that they are accurate."

A

argument [*ar* · gyoo · ment] *n.* 1. An attorney's effort, either by written brief or oral argument, to persuade a court or administrative agency that her client's claim should prevail. 2. A reason put forward in an effort to convince.
➤ disagreement, blow-up, dispute, debate, controversy ("a heated argument"); position, statement, rebuttal ("the attorney's argument to the bench").

argumentative [ar · gyoo · *men* · te · tiv] *adj.* 1. Contentious; combative. 2. Conclusionary.
➤ belligerent, controversial, quarrelsome, litigious ("an argumentative question").

arise [a · *rize*] *v.* To come into being; to originate. A **cause of action** generally arises at the moment the wrong is done. *See* accrual of cause of action.
➤ perceive, commence, derive, emerge, ensure, originate, materialize ("When did the cause of action arise?"); stand up, ascend, rise ("arise from your desk").

arising out of and in the course of employment [a · *rize* · ing . . . em · *ploy* · ment] In some states, double conditions that must be present for an injury to be compensable under **workers' compensation acts**. *See* compensable injury; course of employment.

arising out of or in the course of employment [a · *rize* · ing . . . of em · *ploy* · ment] Conditions, one of which must be present in some states, for an injury to be compensable under **workers' compensation acts**. *See* compensable injury; course of employment.

aristocracy [ar · is · *tok* · re · see] *n.* A government ruled by a class of people, usually based upon inherited wealth and social status.
➤ elite, gentry, nobility, upper class, gentility.

ARM Abbreviation of **adjustable rate mortgage**.

arm's length *adj.* At a distance.
arm's-length transaction [tranz · *ak* · shen] *n.* Dealings or negotiations between parties who are on an equal footing. *Compare* insider trading; sweetheart contract.

armed robbery [*rob* · er · ee] *n.* Taking property from a person by force or threat of force while using or displaying a **deadly weapon**. *See* robbery.

arms *n.* Weapons. *See* right to bear arms.
➤ weapons, firearms, munitions, armament.

arraign [a · *rain*] *v.* To hold or conduct an **arraignment**.
➤ accuse, blame, charge, implicate.

arraignment [a · *rain* · ment] *n.* The act of bringing an accused before a court to answer a criminal charge made against him and calling upon him to enter a plea of guilty or not guilty. *Compare* preliminary hearing.
➤ accusation, incrimination, formal accusal, judicial charge.

arrangement with creditors [a · *raynj* · ment with *kred* · i · terz] *n.* 1. A **proceeding**, also called a *composition*, by which a debtor who is not **insolvent** may have her failing finances rehabilitated by a **bankruptcy court** under an agreement with her creditors. *See* composition with creditors. 2. The plan worked out by the bankruptcy court; also referred to as an *arrangement for the benefit of creditors*. *See* bankruptcy.

array [a · *ray*] *n.* The whole body of men and women called to jury duty, from which juries are chosen (**impaneled**) for individual cases. *See* jury panel.
v. To place in order or position; to arrange.
➤ *n.* collection, arrangement, batch, design ("an array of clothing").
v. align, place, parade, systematize, group.

arrearages [a · *reer* · e · jez] *n.* Same as **arrears**.

arrears [a · *reerz*] *n.* Payments past due. Thus, for EXAMPLE, a person may be in arrears in alimony payments or in arrears on a mortgage.
➤ unpaid debts, obligations, delinquency, overdue payments ("he was $5,000 in arrears in his child support obligations").

arrest [a · *rest*] *n.* 1. Detention of a person on a criminal charge. 2. Any detention of a person, with or without the intent to take him into custody. *See* citizen's arrest; civil arrest; false arrest; lawful arrest; unlawful arrest; warrantless arrest.

A

v. 1. To stop or halt something. 2. To detain a person suspected of a crime; to take a person into custody.

➤ *n.* apprehension, captivity, capture, confinement, detention, incarceration; stoppage, suspension, halt, cessation ("His arrest was of indefinite duration"). *v.* apprehend, catch, capture, block, seize ("The thief was arrested"); stop, block, foil, obstruct, hinder ("arrested development").

arrest of judgment [*juj* · ment] *n.* A judge's order suspending or setting aside a **judgment** when a **defect** in the **proceedings** renders the judgment unenforceable. A **motion in arrest of judgment** is a **motion** that asks the court to **set aside** a judgment.

arrest record [*rek* · erd] *n.* A summary of the dates on which a person has previously been arrested, the law enforcement agencies that made the arrests, and the offenses charged. *See* rap sheet.

arrest warrant [*war* · ent] *n.* **Legal process** issued by a court directing a law enforcement officer to arrest a named person on a specified charge. *Compare* bench warrant.

arrestee [a · rest · *ee*] *n.* A person who has been arrested; a person who is under arrest.
➤ suspect, accused, defendant.

arrogate [*ar* · o · gate] *v.* To assert a claim to something without right; to exercise authority one does not have. USAGE: "Under the Constitution, the president cannot arrogate the **war power** to himself; he must have the approval of Congress."
➤ appropriate, assume, encroach, confiscate.

arson [*ar* · sen] *n.* The **willful** and **malicious** burning of a building. In some jurisdictions, arson includes the deliberate burning of any structure.
➤ pyromania, setting a fire, torching.

art *n.* 1. In the law of **patents**, a mode or process of treating materials so as to produce a given result. 2. A creation of form and beauty. 3. Cunning or craft.
➤ skill, aptitude, craft, cunning, trade.

art. *n.* Abbreviation of **article**.

article [*ar* · tikl] *n.* 1. An individual thing or item. 2. A separate and distinct section of a legal document. USAGE: "Article I of the Constitution." 3. One of several clauses or provisions, for EXAMPLE, one of several **articles of impeachment**. 4. A written composition published in a newspaper or magazine.
➤ item, commodity, substance; column, editorial, essay; division, part, title.

articled clerk [*ar* · tikld] *n.* A lawyer's clerk or apprentice. Under a system inherited from England, lawyers used to be admitted to the **bar** after a period of instruction in law as a clerk in the offices of a practicing attorney. Now, graduation from law school and passing of a bar examination is required, although some states require a **clerkship** as well. *See* apprentice.

articles [*ar* · tiklz] *n. Plural* of **article**. Distinct divisions, parts, clauses, or provisions that, taken as a whole, make up a constitution, **charter**, statute, contract, or other written statement of principles or mutual understandings. *See* article.

articles of agreement [a · *gree* · ment] *n.* A **contract**.

articles of impeachment [im · *peech* · ment] *n.* The formal charges against the defendant in an **impeachment** proceeding.

articles of incorporation [in · kore · per · *ay* · shen] *n.* The **charter** or basic rules that create a corporation and by which it functions. Among other things, it states the purposes for which the corporation is being organized, the amount of **authorized capital stock**, and the names and addresses of the directors and incorporators. *See* certificate of incorporation; incorporation.

articles of partnership [*part* · ner · ship] *n.* Same as **partnership agreement**.

Articles of Confederation [*ar* · tiklz of kon · fed · er · *ay* · shen] *n.* The document that governed the **confederation** of the original 13 states before the Constitution was adopted. It formed a mere association of states, not the union of states into a nation, which the Constitution created.

Articles of War [*ar* · tiklz] *n. See* Code of Military Justice.

articulate [ar · *tik* · yoo · let] *adj.* Ability to express oneself clearly.
v. [ar · *tik* · yoo · late] 1. To prepare a written work composed of separate clauses or provisions. *See* articulated pleading. 2. To express one's thoughts clearly.
➤ *adj.* clear, coherent, eloquent, fluent, lucid ("the articulate argument").
v. enunciate, speak, state, vocalize, fit together ("The speaker articulated perfectly").

articulated pleading [*plee* · ding] *n.* A **pleading** in separate **counts**.

artifice [*ar* · ti · fis] *n.* Cunning; deception; a trick; a **fraud** USAGE: "His artifice was discovered."

artificial [ar · ti · *fi* · shel] *adj.* 1. Created by man, not nature. 2. Imitative; not original.
➤ manmade, synthetic, manufactured ("an artificial condition"); contrived, sham, spurious, specious ("an artificial argument").
artificial person [*per* · sen] *n.* A **person** or **entity** created by law and having an existence in law only, as distinguished from a **natural person**, that is, a human being. EXAMPLE: a corporation. *See* person.
artificial presumption [pre · *sump* · shen] *n.* A **presumption** created by the law and not based in logic or probability alone.

artisan's lien [*ar* · ti · zens leen] *n.* A craftsman's **lien** for his services in repairing an article of personal property. It includes the right to retain possession of the property until the craftsman has been paid for his work. An artisan's lien is a **possessory lien**. *See* mechanic's lien.

as *prep.* 1. To the same amount or degree; equally. 2. In the way that. 3. During; while. 4. For example. 5. Because; since.
as a matter of course [*mat* · er] *See* of course.
as agent [*ay* · jent] When written after the signature of a person who is signing a contract on behalf of a **principal**, these words relieve the person signing from **personal liability**. *See* representative capacity.
as interest may appear [*in* · trest may a · *peer*] *See* as their interests may appear.
as is A sale without **express warranty** or **implied warranty**. When an article is

sold "as is," the buyer takes a chance in making the purchase. USAGE: "I am selling you this car as is" implies "you look it over, and if you buy it you do so at your own risk." *See* all faults.

as of course *See* of course.

as per In accordance with. USAGE: "as per your instructions" means "in accordance with your instructions."

as their interests may appear [*in* · trests may a · *peer*] A provision in the **loss payable clause** of an insurance policy directing that, in the event of **loss**, the proceeds of the policy are to be allocated between the **named insured** and any holder of a **security interest** in the property, for EXAMPLE, a finance company or a bank.

ascendant [a · *send* · ent] *n.* A position of power or importance.
adj. Rising upward.
➤ *n.* ancestor, forefather, forebearer, sire.
adj. superior, dominant, eminent ("an ascendant position in the company").

ascendants [a · *send* · ents] *n.* Persons on one's genealogical line to the past. EXAMPLES: mother; grandmother; great-grandmother. *Compare* descendant. *See* lineal heir.

ascent [a · *sent*] *n.* 1. The transmission of property to one's **ascendants** under the **intestate laws**. *Compare* descent. 2. The act of going upward.

ascertain [as · *cer* · tane] *v.* To determine or find out, often in a conclusive way. USAGE: "We must ascertain the witness's whereabouts before trial."
➤ conclude, deduce, find out, prove, verify, determine, discover.

asked price [askd] *n.* *See* bid and asked.

asportation [as · por · *tay* · shen] *n.* The act of carrying away. With respect to **larceny**, the carrying away of the stolen goods after the taking.
➤ carrying away, moving, transfer, transmission.

assailant [a · *say* · lent] *n.* A person who assaults another person; the aggressor.
➤ attacker, aggressor, enemy, foe, hit man.

assassination [as · *sas* · sin · a · shun] *n.*
Murder by surprise attack, usually of a
political figure.
➤ murder, killing, destruction, slaying.

assault [a · *salt*] *n.* An act of force or
threat of force intended to inflict harm
upon a person or to put the person in fear
that such harm is imminent; an attempt to
commit a **battery**. The perpetrator must
have, or appear to have, the present ability
to carry out the act. *See* aggravated assault;
civil assault; criminal assault; simple assault.
v. To violate or harm; to attack.
➤ *n.* attack, advance, strike, violation
("The assault was aggressive").
v. abuse, advance, assail, jump, set
upon, bash, violate, storm ("The
pedestrian assaulted the child").

assault and battery [*bat* · er · ee] *n.*
An achieved assault; an assault carried
out by hitting or by other physical
contact. *See* battery.

assault with a deadly weapon [*ded* ·
lee *wep* · en] *n.* An assault aggravated
by the use of a lethal weapon. *See* deadly
weapon. *See also* aggravated assault.

assault with intent to commit murder
[in · *tent* to ko · *mit* mer · der] *n.* An
assault aggravated by a preconceived
intention to kill. *See* aggravated assault.

assault with intent to commit rape
[in · *tent* to ko · *mit*] *n.* An assault
aggravated by an intention to commit
rape. *See* aggravated assault.

assay [a · say] *n.* 1. An examination or test.
2. A test analysis of ore to determine its
quality, composition, weight, and the like.
v. To estimate the worth of.
➤ *n.* analysis, assessment, examination, test
("The doctor's assay wasn't promising").
v. appraise, evaluate, weigh ("He assayed
the property").

assembly [a · *sem* · blee] *n.* 1. The name
given to the **lower house** of the legislature in some states. *See* general assembly.
2. A constitutional right under the **First
Amendment**, particularly assembly for
the purpose of advancing political ideas
and airing grievances. *See* freedom of
association; unlawful assembly. 3. A
meeting of several persons.

➤ congregation, accumulation, band,
conference, gathering, group; attachment,
joining, manufacture, construction.

assent [a · *sent*] *v.* To affirm or agree to.
n. Consent; concurrence; demonstrated
approval. *See* mutual assent.
➤ *v.* accede, consent, defer, embrace,
conform to ("He assented to the offer").
n. acceptance, accession, approval,
concord, compliance, affirmation, accord
("The assent was welcome").

assert [a · *sert*] *v.* To state; to declare as
being true; to affirm; to allege.
➤ insist, advance, allege, attest, proclaim,
contend, state, profess.

assess [a · *sess*] *v.* 1. To estimate or make
an **appraisal**. 2. To determine the value
of property for the purpose of taxation.
3. To set or determine the amount of a
tax, fine, or contribution. *See* assessment;
jeopardy assessment. 4. To require contributions from the members of an association or other organization. 5. To analyze.
➤ evaluate, determine, size up, estimate.

assessable [a · *sess* · abl] *adj.* Liable to
assessment.

assessable insurance [in · *shoor* · ense]
n. Insurance whose premiums may be
increased if the **loss ratio** is high.

assessable stock *n.* **Stock** upon which
the corporation may levy an **assessment**
over and above the purchase price. *See*
stock assessment.

assessed value [*val* · yoo] *n.* The value of
property as estimated and fixed by the
government for purposes of taxation. *See*
value. *Also see* valuation.

assessment [a · *sess* · ment] *n.* 1. Imposing
of tax on the basis of a listing and valuation
of the property to be taxed. 2. Requiring
a payment above and beyond that which
is normal. EXAMPLE: the imposition of a 15
percent penalty on property taxes paid after
a certain date. 3. A call upon **subscribers**
to corporate stock to pay for their
subscriptions. 4. The act of assessing.
See assess. *See also* stock assessment.
➤ appraisal, determination, valuation,
estimation, judgment, investigation.

assessment district [*dis* · trikt] *n.* An
area benefited by a **public improvement**,

with the result that a **special assessment** is made against the property in that district to finance the improvement. *See* district.

assessment of damages [*dam · e · jez*] *n.* Setting the amount of **damages** owed by the losing **party** to the prevailing party in a legal action.

assessment ratio [*ray · shee · o*] *n.* The ratio of a property's **assessed value** to its **market value**. EXAMPLE: if real estate whose market value is $50,000 has an assessed value of $30,000, the assessment ratio is 3:5 or 60 percent.

assessment work *n.* A mining law term meaning work required to be performed on a mining claim each year to preserve one's right to the claim.

assessor [*a · sess · er*] *n.* 1. A public official who makes an **assessment** of property, usually for purposes of taxation. 2. An expert in a technical field who provides specialized advice to a judge during the trial of a case.
➤ charger, estimator, collector, evaluator.

asset [*ass · et*] *n.* Anything of value owned by a person or an organization. Assets include not only all real property and personal property, but **intangible property** such as **bills**, **notes**, stock, and **accounts receivable**. *See also* capital assets; liquid assets; marshaling assets; partnership assets; wasting assets.

asset seizure [*see · zher*] *n. See* civil forfeiture.

assets [*ass · ets*] *n. Plural* of **asset**. *See* asset.
➤ resource, capital, reserve, possessions, funds, money ("partnership assets").

asseveration [*a · sev · e · ray · shen*] *n.* The solemn affirmation of the truth of a statement.
➤ averment, deposition, assurance, protestation, testimony, profession.

assign [*a · sine*] *n. Singular* of **assigns**. *See* assigns.
v. 1. To transfer or grant property, or a **right** in property, to another. USAGE: "My uncle assigned all of his rights in this stock to me." 2. To designate or appoint. USAGE: "The court assigned an attorney to represent the defendant because he was

indigent." *See* assigned counsel; assigned risk. 3. To point out or specify. USAGE: "I will not assign blame for this misunderstanding."
➤ *v.* allot, allow, appoint, cast, delegate, empower.

assignable [*a · sine · abl*] *adj.* 1. Capable of being lawfully **assigned** or transferred; transferable. 2. Capable of being specifed or pointed out.
➤ conveyable, transmittable, transferable.

assignable error [*err · or*] *n.* An **error** occurring during trial which may be grounds for appeal. *See* assignment of errors; judicial error.

assignable lease *n.* A **lease** that can be transferred by the tenant without the permission of the landlord. *Compare* sublease.

assignable right *n.* A **right** that may be **assigned**, so as to transfer ownership. EXAMPLE: a department store's sale of its delinquent accounts to a collection agency.

assigned counsel [*a · sined koun · sel*] *n.* An attorney appointed by the court to defend a person accused of a crime who is without the means to employ legal assistance. Also known as appointed counsel. *See* right to counsel.

assigned risk [*a · sined*] *n.* In states where automobile liability insurance is compulsory, a system under which drivers who would ordinarily be denied coverage are assigned to insurance companies. *See* assign.

assignee [*a · sine · ee*] *n.* A person to whom a **right** is **assigned**. *See and compare* assignor.
➤ grantee, recipient, transferee, donee.

assignment [*a · sine · ment*] *n.* 1. A transfer of property, or a **right** in property, from one person to another. *See* equitable assignment. 2. A designation or appointment. *See* assign.
➤ responsibility, task, appointment, commission, authorization.

assignment for the benefit of creditors [*ben · e · fit of kred · i · terz*] *n.* An assignment and transfer by a debtor of all her property to a **trustee** to collect any amounts owed, to sell the property, and to distribute the proceeds among her **creditors**. *See* general assignment; preferential assignment; voluntary assignment; wage assignment.

assignment of contract [*kon* · trakt] *n.* The transfer by a **party** to a contract of his **interest** in the contract.

assignment of errors [*err* · orz] *n.* On appeal, a listing of **mistakes of law** or **mistakes of fact** alleged to have been committed by the **lower court**, which are designated by the **party** complaining of them as grounds for **reversal**.

assignor [a · sine · *or*] *n.* A person who **assigns** a **right**. *Compare* assignee.

assigns [a · *sines*] *n. Plural* of **assign**. Persons to whom a **right** or property is assigned; persons who have, will, or may receive something by **assignment**; **assignees** or potential assignees. The word "assigns" is customarily used in tandem with "**successors**" in the term **successors and assigns**. *See* successors and assigns.

assist [a · *sist*] *v.* To give support or aid.
➤ aid, promote, serve, foster, help, participate.

assistance [a · *sis* · tense] *n.* 1. **Public assistance**. 2. Aid; help.
➤ aid, help, succor, advocacy; support, welfare, subsidy, relief.

assistance of counsel [*koun* · sel] *n.* *See* right to counsel.

assistance writ [a · *sis* · tense] *n. See* writ of assistance.

assistant [a · *sis* · tant] *n.* One who helps or assists.
➤ clerk, helper, aide, associate, partner, collaborator, paralegal.

associate [a · *so* · see · et] *n.* 1. A person joined with one or more other persons in a common endeavor. 2. A person engaged in the practice of law with another attorney or attorneys, but not as a partner or member of the firm. 3. A member of an **association**.
v. 1. To combine with other parts; to connect together. 2. To befriend, accompany, or get together with others.
➤ *n.* partner, collaborator, assistant, helper, aide.

v. join, bring together, synthesize ("associate these seemingly unrelated ideas"); attend, combine, keep company with, mix, mingle, hang out ("He associated with criminals").

associate counsel [*koun* · sel] *n.* An attorney associated with the **attorney of record** in the handling of a civil action or in defending a criminal prosecution.

associate justice [*jus* · tiss] *n.* The title of any judge who is a member of an **appellate court**, except the chief justice.

association [a · so · see · *ay* · shen] *n.* Also called an **unincorporated association**, a collection of persons who have joined together for the pursuit of a common purpose or design. Unlike a corporation, an association has no legal existence independent of its members. On the other hand, an association that sometimes functions like a corporation may be treated as a corporation for some purposes by the law. An association may be organized for the purpose of making a profit, or it may be nonprofit in nature. *See* nonprofit association. *Also see* joint-stock company; limited partnership.
➤ organization, partnership, coalition, cartel, league, union ("National Association for Trial Advocacy"); relationship, connection, bond, dealings, fraternization ("her unlikely association with the complaining witness").

assume [a · *syoom*] *v.* 1. To undertake; to take upon oneself; to promise. EXAMPLE: to assume responsibility. 2. To presume; to expect; to suppose. EXAMPLE: to assume the truth of a statement. 3. To put on. EXAMPLE: to assume a disguise or a new identity.
➤ undertake, accept, adopt ("assume responsibility"); take over, put on ("assume a new identity"); presume, expect, suppose, accept ("to assume the truth of a statement").

assumed name [a · *syoomd*] *n.* A **fictitious name** or an alias.
➤ alias, pseudonym, nickname, moniker.

assumpsit [a · *sump* · sit] *(Latin) n.* A **common law action** that allows **damages** to be recovered for the failure to perform a contract.

A

assumption [a · *sump* · shen] *n.* The act of assuming. *See* assume.
➤ acceptance, taking on, adoption ("assumption of the risk"); belief, inference, theory, conjecture ("his assumption concerning delivery terms"); appropriation, seizure, usurpation ("assumption of power").

assumption clause *n.* 1. A clause in a deed, lease, or other conveyance, in which the person to whom property is transferred agrees to **assume** some obligation of the transferor. 2. A clause in a mortgage which provides that the mortgage may not be assumed without the consent of the **mortgagee**.

assumption of mortgage [*more* · gej] *n.* An agreement by which the **grantee** of mortgaged property assumes responsibility for the mortgage loan. *See* mortgage.

assumption of risk *n.* The legal principle that a person who knows and deliberately exposes herself to a danger assumes responsibility for the **risk**, rather than the person who actually created the danger. Assumption of risk is often referred to as **voluntary assumption of risk**. It is a defense to negligence.

assurance [a · *shoor* · ens] *n.* 1. A guaranty; a pledge; a promise. 2. Insurance. 3. A **conveyance** of real estate and the deed that conveys it. 4. Self-confidence.
➤ pledge, vow, commitment, guaranty, insurance; self-confidence, self-control.

assure [a · *shoor*] *v.* 1. To relieve doubt or give confidence to. 2. To make certain of.
➤ encourage, console, inspire, hearten; attest, vow, indemnify, pledge, endorse.

assured [a · *shoord*] *n.* A person who is insured.
adj. Guaranteed or confirmed. USAGE: "Ginsburg's confirmation was assured."
➤ *adj.* confirmed, ensured, guaranteed.

asylum [a · *sile* · em] *n.* 1. The right of a country or state to grant **immunity** from arrest to a person who has committed a crime in another jurisdiction. Most countries have mutually limited this right by signing **extradition treaties**. 2. A sanctuary; a refuge; a safe place.
➤ cover, den, haven, refuge, retreat, sanctuary.

at *prep.* A word whose meaning usually depends upon the context in which it is used. It signifies nearness when applied to a place; as a designation of time, it may denote a definite time or it may mean from or after a certain point in time.

at bar *adj.* "The case at bar" means "the case presently before the court." *See* bar.

at issue [*ish* · yoo] *adj.* A phrase referring to a case which is in a position to be decided by the court because the issues involved have been clearly stated by the parties. *See* joinder of issue.

at large *adj.* 1. Free; not restricted to a particular place. USAGE: "The prisoner escaped and is now at large." 2. Generally.
➤ loose, unrestrained, unconfined, free.

at large election [e · *lek* · shen] *n.* An election in which voters may cast their ballots for candidates for all positions, for EXAMPLE, an election in which one can vote for candidates for all of the seats on the city council, rather than being limited to candidates representing only the ward or district in which one lives.

at law *adj.* 1. Involving the rules of **law** rather than the rules of **equity**, or a **court of law** rather than a **court of equity**. *See and compare* equity; law. 2. By **operation of law**.

at maturity [ma · *choor* · e · tee] *adv.* A phrase sometimes used in a **promissory note** or similar instrument indicating the time when payment is due. *See* maturity; maturity date.

at sight Upon **presentment**. A **sight draft** is a **draft** payable at the time it is presented for payment, i.e., "at sight." *Compare* after sight.

at will *adj.* As one chooses, or as someone else chooses. *See* employment at will; estate at will; will.

ATLA Abbreviation of American Trial Lawyers Association.

atrocity [a · *tros* · ity] *n.* An event or situation which is appalling, catastrophic, or offensive.
➤ abomination, wickedness, savagery, infamy, iniquity.

attach [a · *tach*] *v.* 1. To seize property for the purpose of bringing it into the custody of the court. *See* attachment; writ of attachment. 2. To result from something else. EXAMPLE: the right of spouses to inherit from each other "attaches" upon their marriage. 3. To cause to adhere, bind, or fasten.
➤ staple, adhere, bind, accompany, combine, enlist; confiscate, seize, take ("to attach property"); attribute, ascribe, impute ("attach significance to the testimony").

attaché [a · ta · *shay*] *(French) n.* A member of the staff of an ambassador; a person attached to an embassy.

attached [a · *tachd*] *adj.* 1. Seized under a **writ of attachment**. 2. Connected; appended.
➤ confiscated, garnished, secured, sequestered, seized ("attached funds"); connected ("attached garage").

attachment [a · *tach* · ment] *n.* 1. The process by which a person's property is figuratively brought into court to ensure satisfaction of a **judgment** that may be rendered against him. In the event judgment is rendered, the property may be sold to satisfy the judgment. *See* writ of attachment. *Also see* foreign attachment; landlord's attachment. 2. Something connected to something else.
➤ seizure, confiscation, garnishment, dispossession; affixation, appending, securing ("the attachment of the seal on the document"); addendum, supplement, ancillary materials, supporting materials ("the attachments to the brief"); fondness, affection, loyalty, connection, affinity ("her attachment to the vice president").

attachment bond *n.* A **bond** posted by a person whose property has been **attached**. Because the bond provides **security**, the attached property can be freed until the matter is resolved.

attachment lien [*leen*] *n.* A **lien** that arises when property is **attached**; it is **perfected** when **judgment** is entered. *See* entry of judgment.

attack [a · *tak*] *v.* 1. To assault. 2. To challenge. USAGE: "My attorney intends to attack the statute on the ground that it is unconstitutional." *See and compare* collateral attack; direct attack.
n. 1. Any hostile or offensive action, especially those of a military nature. 2. The beginning or onset of something.
➤ *v.* assail, raid, molest, mug, hurt, overwhelm, hit.
n. physical assault, blitz, advance, assault, foray ("The attack was brutal"); start, onset, onslaught ("an attack of chicken pox").

attain [a · *tane*] *v.* To achieve or realize something. USAGE: "They attained their goal of discrediting the witness."
➤ achieve, accomplish, realize, earn, procure, reap

attainder [a · *tayn* · der] *n.* In England, in older times, attainder was the "non-person" status which the law gave to a person who was convicted of a **capital crime** and executed. Among other penalties, the property of an attained person was forfeited to the state. Attainder is prohibited in this country by the Constitution. *See* bill of attainder.

attempt [a · *temt*] *n.* An act done with the intent to commit a crime, which would have resulted in the crime being committed except that something happened to prevent it. The line between an attempt and mere preparations is often difficult to draw; it is a matter of degree.
v. To try or make an effort to do something.
➤ *n.* effort, exertion, fling, shot, undertaking, try ("The attempt was feeble").
v. try, make effort, endeavor ("The athlete attempted the jump").

attest [a · *test*] *v.* To swear to; to bear witness to; to affirm to be true or genuine. *See* attestation.
➤ adjure, announce, assert, aver, certify, swear, support, sustain.

attestation [a · tes · *tay* · shen] *n.* The act of witnessing the signing of a document, including signing one's name as a witness to that fact. *See* acknowledgment; authentication.
➤ endorsement, affirmation, certification, testimony, evidence ("an attestation clause").

attestation clause *n.* A clause, usually at the end of a document such as a deed

A

or a will, that provides evidence of attestation. EXAMPLES: "**signed, sealed, and delivered** in the presence of"; "**witness my hand and seal**." *See* testimonium clause.

attesting witness [a · *test* · ing *wit* · nes] *n.* A person who witnesses the signing of a document. *See* attestation.

attorn [a · *tern*] *v.* To transfer or turn over to another. *See* attornment.

➤ transfer, deliver, assign, convey, grant, relinquish.

attorney [a · *tern* · ee] *n.* An **attorney at law** or an **attorney in fact**. Unless otherwise indicated, generally means attorney at law.

➤ lawyer, counselor, advocate, legal advisor, barrister, counsel, legal eagle.

attorney at law *n.* Practice of law. A person who is licensed to practice law; a lawyer. *See* unauthorized practice of law.

attorney fees *n.* Compensation to which an attorney is entitled for her services. This is usually a matter of contract between the attorney and the client. *See* retainer. However, where authorized by statute, a court may enter an order in a lawsuit directing the payment of a **party's** attorney fees by the opposite party. In some types of cases, attorney fees are set by a statute that also requires that the fees be paid by the defendant if the plaintiff or claimant prevails in the **action**. EXAMPLE: under many **workers' compensation acts**, the claimant's attorney is entitled to a specified percentage of the claimant's award. *See also* contingent fee; lodestar rule.

attorney in fact *n.* An agent or representative authorized by his principal, by virtue of a **power of attorney**, to act for her in certain matters.

attorney of record [*rek* · erd] *n.* The attorney who has made an **appearance** on behalf of a **party** to a lawsuit and is in charge of that party's **interests** in the **action**. *See* entry of appearance.

attorney's lien [a · *tern* · ees leen] *n.* A **lien** that an attorney has upon money or property of her client (including papers and documents) for compensation due her from the client for professional services rendered. It is a **possessory lien**. *See also* charging lien.

attorney's work product [pro · dukt] *n.* *See* work product; work product rule.

attorney-client privilege [*klie* · ent *priv* · i · lej] *n.* Most information a client tells his attorney in connection with his case cannot be disclosed by the attorney, or anyone employed by the attorney or the attorney's firm, without the client's permission. *See* privilege; privileged communication; confidential relationship.

attorney general [a · *tern* · ee *jen* · e · rel] *n.* The chief law officer of the nation or of a state. The attorney general is responsible for representing the government in legal actions with which it is concerned, and for advising the chief executive and other administrative heads of the government on legal matters on which they desire an opinion. The **Attorney General of the United States** is appointed by the president and is the head of the Department of Justice. *Also see* Solicitor General of the United States.

attorney general's opinion [o · *pin* · yen] *n.* *See* opinion of the attorney general.

Attorney General of the United States [yoo · *nite* · ed] *n.* *See* attorney general.

attornment [a · *tern* · ment] *n.* The agreement of a tenant to accept one person in place of another as his landlord. *See* letter of attornment.

attractive nuisance [a · *trak* · tiv *nyoo* · sense] *n.* An unusual mechanism, apparatus, or condition that is dangerous to young children but is so interesting and alluring as to attract them to the premises on which it is kept. EXAMPLES: an abandoned mine shaft; an abandoned house; a junked car. *See* nuisance.

attractive nuisance doctrine [*dok* · trin] *n.* The principle in the law of **negligence** that a person who maintains an **attractive nuisance** on his property must exercise **reasonable care** to protect young children against its dangers, or be held responsible for any injury that occurs, even though the injured child trespassed upon his property or was otherwise at fault.

auction [*awk* · shen] *n.* A sale of property to the highest bidder. *See* bid.
➤ bargain, jam, sell-off, sale.

audit [*aw* · dit] *n.* 1. A formal or official examination and verification of accounts, vouchers, and other financial records as, for EXAMPLE, a **tax audit** or an **independent audit** of a company's books and records. *See also* field audit; internal audit; office audit. 2. Any verification of figures by an accountant.
v. To analyze and examine financial records and accounts.
➤ *n.* analysis, review, scrutiny, verification ("The audit is complete").
v. analyze, balance, investigate, examine, monitor, probe ("The accountant audited the books").

audit trail *n.* Financial records on which summary figures (as, for EXAMPLE, those set forth on a tax return or a **profit and loss statement**) are based, which prove the accuracy and integrity of the figures. An audit trail is sometimes referred to as a "paper trail."

auditor [*aw* · dit · er] *n.* 1. A person who conducts an audit. 2. A civil servant whose duty it is to examine the accounts of state officials to determine whether they have spent public funds in accordance with the law. 3. A person appointed by the court to examine accounts in dispute and to prepare a report to assist the court in reaching a decision.
➤ accountant, bookkeeper, cashier, inspector.

auspices [*au* · spi · sez] *n.* The approval, support, or patronage shown to another. USAGE: "He is here under my auspices."
➤ sponsorship, backing, encouragement, tutelage, management, guidance.

Australian ballot [*aw* · strale · yen *bal* · et] *n.* Term applied to the type of ballot used in the United States, i.e., a secret ballot containing the names of all candidates.

authentic [aw · *then* · tik] *adj.* Real; genuine; honest.
➤ genuine, real, accurate, actual, true, unadulterated, credible, reliable, valid, verifiable.
Ant. fake, faux.

authenticate [aw · *then* · ti · kate] *v.* To prove a thing to be genuine; to render authentic. *See* authentication.
➤ accredit, attest, certify, confirm, corroborate, legitimate.

authentication [aw · then · ti · *kay* · shen] *n.* 1. Such official **attestation** or certification as may be required for certain documents to be **admissible evidence**. EXAMPLES: the affixing of a **corporate seal** or a **notarial seal**; the issuing of a **certified copy** of a deed by the **clerk of court**. *See* acknowledgment; certificate of acknowledgment. 2. The process of proving that a document is genuine.
➤ verification, legitimation, documentation, evidence, acknowledgment, attestation.

author [aw · ther] *n.* 1. A person who produces a written work. 2. A person who originates something; a **maker**.
In **copyright** law, a person can be an author without producing any original material, provided she does something beyond copying, such as compiling or editing.
➤ producer, maker, originator, biographer, inventor, creator, planner.

authoritarianism [aw · tho · ri · *tare* · i · an · ism] *n.* The principle of unquestioning obedience to authority. *See* absolutism. *Compare* democracy.

authority [aw · *thaw* · ri · tee] *n.* 1. A decision on a **point of law**, made by a court or administrative agency, which must be taken into account in subsequent cases presenting similar facts and involving the same legal problem, although different parties are involved and many years have elapsed. *See* precedent. A **treatise** or a **law review** article may constitute **persuasive authority**, but never **binding authority**. *See* secondary authority. *Also see* citation. 2. The power of government. *See* governmental powers. 3. Certain agencies of government. EXAMPLES: a **port authority**; a **transit authority**; a **housing authority**. *See* civil authority. 4. Persons or agencies that exercise power or enforce the law. EXAMPLES: the police; the health department; administrative agencies. *See* color of authority. 5. The power of an **agent** to bind his **principal**. *See* actual authority;

A

apparent authority; express authority; implied authority; scope of authority.
➤ strength, prestige, charge, domination, esteem; power, right, ability ("She had actual authority").

authorization card [aw · ther · i · *zay* · shen] *n.* A form given to a worker by a union on which he may authorize the union to represent him in **collective bargaining** with his employer. A union which succeeds in soliciting signed authorization cards from a specified percentage of an employer's work force may be entitled to participate in a **representation election**. *See* certification of bargaining agent.

authorize [*aw* · ther · ize] *v.* To give permission to act; to give a right to act; to empower.
➤ assent, advocate, recommend, bless, vouch for, empower, confirm, legalize, sanction. ("to authorize an expenditure").

authorized capital stock [*aw* · ther · izd *kap* · i · tel] *n.* The maximum amount of **capital stock** that a corporation is authorized to issue under its **charter** or **articles of incorporation**.

auto theft [*aw* · toh] *n.* **Larceny** of an automobile. *Compare* car jacking; joyriding.

autocracy [aw · *tok* · re · see] *n.* A government ruled by one person, with no regard for the will of the people; a dictatorship. *See* dictator.
➤ absolutism, oppression, tyranny.

autograph [*aw* · to · graf] *n.* 1. A document written entirely in one's own handwriting. *Also see* holograph; holographic will. 2. A person's signature. *Compare* allograph. *v.* To write one's name; to inscribe.
➤ *n.* endorsement, signature, inscription, seal ("The autograph was authentic"). *v.* endorse, engross, inscribe ("The author autographed my copy of the book").

automobile guest [aw · toh · moh · *beel*] *n.* A person who is invited, either directly or indirectly, into a car by its owner or operator, and who accepts and rides for her own pleasure or business without conferring any benefit upon the owner or operator. If the guest is injured in an accident, the liability of the owner or operator is regulated by **guest statutes**. *See also* family purpose doctrine.

automobile insurance [aw · toh · moh · *beel* in · *shoor* · ense] *n.* An inclusive term which takes in the coverage of various **risks** involved in the ownership and operation of a motor vehicle; it includes **collision insurance**, **comprehensive insurance** (fire, flood, and theft and similar hazards), and insurance against liability for **personal injury** or damage to the property of others (**liability insurance**). *See also* no-fault insurance.

autonomy [aw · *tawn* · e · mee] *n.* Independence; self-government; the absence of political influence from outside or from foreign powers.
➤ independence, freedom, liberty, sovereignty, self-rule.

autopsy [*aw* · top · see] *n.* Opening, examination, and dissection of a dead body to determine the cause of death. An autopsy is also referred to as a **postmortem examination** or, simply, a **postmortem**.
➤ dissection, necrosis, pathological examination ("Dr. Lim Sang performed the autopsy.").

autoptic proference [aw · *top* · tik *prof* · er · ense] *n.* **Physical evidence** offered for viewing by the jury or judge. EXAMPLES: the murder weapon; the skull of the murder victim. *See* demonstrative evidence; real evidence.

autre vie [*oh* · tre vee] *(French) n.* "The life of another." *See* estate per autre vie.

autrefois [*oh* · tre · fwah] *(French) adv.* Formerly; previously.
  autrefois acquit [a · *kwit*] *n.* Previously acquitted. A **plea** by which a person accused of a crime interposes his previous acquittal of the same offense as a bar to further prosecution. *See* plea in bar. *See also* double jeopardy; prior jeopardy.
  autrefois convict [kon · *vikt*] *n.* Previously convicted. A **plea** putting forth a prior conviction for the same offense as a **defense**. *See* plea in bar. *See also* double jeopardy; prior jeopardy.

auxiliary [awg · *zil* · yer · ee] *adj.* Ancillary; subsidiary; supplementary.
n. An aide; a helper; a subordinate.

➤ *adj.* dependent, complementary, collateral, ancillary ("the auxiliary documents").
n. helper, accessory, accomplice, companion, partner, aide, subordinate.

avail [a · *vale*] *v.* 1. To be of use to. 2. To take advantage of.
➤ aid, assist, help, serve; accomplish, realize, produce, cause.

availability for work [a · vale · e · *bil* · i · tee] *n.* A reference to the requirement that a person be "ready and willing to accept available work" in order to qualify for unemployment insurance.

aver [a · *ver*] *v.* To allege; to **plead**; to assert; to state.
➤ allege, plead, assert, state.

average [*av* · er · ej] *n.* Mathematical term, meaning the sum of two or more numbers divided by the number of numbers composing the sum. In this use it does not imply a midpoint. In common usage, however, an average is the mean between extremes or between two or more quantities, measurements, distances, weights, or the like. For the application of "average" in **maritime law**, *see* general average loss; particular average; petty average.
v. To calculate the mean between extremes.
➤ *n.* normal, mean, middle, midpoint ("The average was two"); typical, normal, commonplace, unexceptional ("an average closing statement").
v. balance, even out, obtain the numerical mean, score, tally.

averment [a · *ver* · ment] *n.* An **allegation**; an assertion; a statement.
➤ positive statement, allegation, assertion.

avert [a · *vert*] *v.* To turn away from.
➤ divert, deflect, parry, prevent.

avoid [a · *voyd*] *v.* 1. To depart from. 2. To refrain from.
➤ cancel, vacate; elude, shun, avert, forbear.

avoidance [a · *voy* · dense] *n.* 1. The act of annulling or nullifying. *See* plea in confession and avoidance. 2. Evading; escaping. *See* tax avoidance.
➤ eluding, evasion, deviation, escape, bypass, resistance, eschewal.

avoidance of taxes [*tak* · sez] *n. See* tax avoidance.

avouch [a · *vouch*] *v.* To state as fact.
➤ acknowledge, affirm, proclaim, declare.

avow [a · *vow*] *v.* To profess openly.
➤ state, profess, confess, claim, declare, maintain, grant.

avowal [a · *vow* · el] *n.* 1. A direct statement or declaration. 2. A formal **offer of proof** during trial, after the judge has ruled that certain testimony is not **admissible evidence**, made to preserve a basis for appeal; that is, so that the **appellate court** will know what the witness's testimony would have been if the **trial court** had allowed him to testify.
➤ statement, admission, proclamation, protestation, confession.

avulsion [a · *vul* · shen] *n.* A sudden loss or addition to land as a result of the action of water or a sudden change in the course of a stream. *Compare* accretion.
➤ tearing away, separation by force, ripping, splitting.

award [a · *ward*] *n.* 1. The decision, decree, or **judgment** of an **arbitrator** or **administrative law judge**. 2. A jury's determination with respect to **damages**. 3. A court's order for the payment of **damages** or **costs**.
v. To confer, grant, or give.
➤ *n.* decision, decree, judgment, verdict ("The award is $500").
v. confer, grant, give, determine, donate, allot, settle, conclude ("The student was awarded a scholarship").

awry [uh · *rye*] *adj.* In an off-course direction.
➤ amiss, askance, astray, off course, wrong, bad.

ax *v.* To terminate or remove.
n. A cutting tool.
➤ *v.* fire, discharge, terminate, remove.
n. hatchet, cleaver.

axiom [*ak* · see · um] *n.* A principle so basic that its truth or accuracy is not disputed.
➤ principle, belief, maxim, truth, dogma.

babble [*bab* · bil] *n.* Talk or sounds that are incoherent, indistinct, or confused.
v. To speak foolishly or incoherantly: to blab.
➤ *n.* gibberish, gossip, jabber, muttering, drivel, ranting.
v. blab, chat, gibber, gossip, yak, run on, prate, rant, rave.

baby act [*bay* · bee] *n.* A term applied to a **plea** of **infancy** as a **defense** to a lawsuit.

BAC Abbreviation of **blood alcohol concentration**.

Bachelor of Laws [*bach* · e · ler] *See* LLB.

back *adj.* 1. Reverse. 2. From a time past.
v. 1. To support, usually with money. USAGE: "The bank has agreed to back my new business with a line of credit." 2. To **endorse**; to assume financial responsibility for. USAGE: "I am willing to be your cosigner if the bank requires someone to back your loan."
➤ *adj.* reverse, final, following, rear, former, overdue, past ("back pay").
v. abet, advocate, endorse, finance, sustain, uphold ("to back a rising musician").

back pay *n.* Unpaid wages to which an employee is entitled.

back pay order [*or* · der] *n.* The order of a court, **arbitrator**, or administrative agency that employees be given their back pay. Such orders are most common in cases involving the reinstatement of employees who were improperly discharged.

back taxes [*tak* · sez] *n.* 1. Taxes that are in arrears. 2. Taxes on which the

ordinary processes for collection have been exhausted.

backbond [*bak* · bond] *n.* An **indemnity bond**.

backdated [*bak* · day · ted] *adj.* Dated as of a date previous to the date on which a document or **negotiable instrument** is actually signed. USAGE: "A backdated check."

bad *adj.* 1. Worthless; invalid. 2. Not good. 3. Defective. 4. Of inferior quality. 5. Inadequate. 6. Wicked; evil.
➤ defective, inferior, inadequate, below standard, poor ("bad design"); evil, depraved, immoral ("bad intentions"); incorrect, faulty, questionable ("a bad move"); severe, harsh, cruel, tragic ("a bad winter").

bad check *n.* A check drawn on insufficient funds. *See* NSF check.

bad debt *n.* An uncollectible debt; a debt that is worthless because there is no likelihood of its recovery. The **Internal Revenue Code** provides that a bad debt is deductible from **gross income** in determining **taxable income**. The IRS maintains different standards for business and nonbusiness bad debts. A bad debt is deductible only if there was originally an expectation of repayment.

bad faith *n.* A devious or deceitful intent, motivated by self-interest, ill will, or a concealed purpose. The opposite of good faith. Bad faith is stronger than **negligence**, but may or may not involve **fraud**. EXAMPLE: an insurance company

B

engages in bad faith when it refuses, with no basis for its action, to pay a claim.

➤ abjection, deceit, conspiracy, treachery, deception, dishonesty, fraud, perfidy ("dealing in bad faith").

bad law *n.* A decision, ruling, or opinion that is not in accordance with law. *See* law.

bad title [*ty* · tel] *n.* **Title** which is so defective that a purchaser is under no obligation to accept it. *Compare* good title. *See* defective title.

badges of fraud [*bad* · jez] *n.* Suspicious circumstances that give the appearance or suggest the possibility of **fraud**. EXAMPLES: the sale of valuable property for a small fraction of its value; an attempt to conceal assets.

bail *n.* 1. The customary means of securing the release from custody of a person charged with a criminal offense, by assuring his appearance in court and compelling him to remain within the jurisdiction. 2. The **security** given for a defendant's appearance in court in the form of cash, real property, or a **bail bond**. 3. The person who is the **surety** on a bail bond. *v.* To secure the release from custody of a person charged with a crime, pending trial, by posting a bail bond.

➤ *n.* bond, guarantee, security, warrant, collateral.

v. sponsor, secure, release, post bond.

bail bond *n.* A **bond** given as **security** for the purpose of obtaining the release of a person in custody; it guarantees that the person released will return to court for trial. *See* bail.

bail bondsman [*bondz* · men] *n.* *See* bondsman.

bailable offense [*bale* · abl o · *fense*] *n.* An **offense** with which a defendant is charged from which she may be released on **bail**. Certain offenses, such as murder and armed robbery, are not bailable.

bailee [bay · *lee*] *n.* The person to whom property is entrusted in a **bailment**. *Compare* bailor.

➤ manager, overseer, supervisor, attendant, deputy.

bailee for hire *n.* A person or company that takes personal property into its care

and custody for compensation. EXAMPLES: an auto mechanic; a moving company; a storage company.

bailiff [*bay* · lif] *n.* A court attendant charged with maintaining order in the courtroom.

bailment [*bale* · ment] *n.* The entrusting of personal property by one person (the **bailor**) to another (the **bailee**) for a specific purpose, with the understanding that the property will be returned when the purpose is accomplished, the stated duration of the bailment is over, or the bailor reclaims it. EXAMPLES: placing one's furniture in storage; leaving one's coat in a restaurant checkroom. *See* gratuitous bailment; involuntary bailment; lucrative bailment; special bailment.

bailment for hire *n.* A bailment for compensation. *See* bailee for hire; lucrative bailment.

bailment for sale *n.* A **consignment**.

bailor [bay · *lore*] *n.* The person who entrusts property to another in a **bailment**. *Compare* bailee.

➤ grantor, assignor, transferor.

bailout [*bale* · out] *n.* 1. Any of a number of techniques available to owners of a business for minimizing tax impact upon the profits of the business. 2. Any circumstance in which a person is helped out of difficulty, usually financial, by another person.

bailout stock *n.* **Preferred stock** issued as nontaxable stock.

bait and switch *n.* A form of **fraud** in which a merchant advertises an item at a low price to entice customers into her store and then, claiming that the advertised article is no longer in stock, attempts to persuade the customer to purchase a higher priced item. Most states have made this practice a criminal offense.

Baker v. Carr [*bay* · ker ver · sus *kar*] *n.* A 1962 Supreme Court case, 369 U.S. 186, which established the constitutional requirement that representation in state legislatures be apportioned on the basis of population. This was the first in a series of cases in which the Supreme Court applied a **one person, one vote rule** to all elections for public office, whether federal, state, or local. *See* apportionment; apportionment of representatives.

balance [*bal* · ense] *n.* 1. That which remains after the deduction of a part, for EXAMPLE, the balance owed on an account. 2. Equilibrium.
v. 1. To equalize; to make equal. 2. To offset; to set off; to outweigh. 3. To harmonize.
➤ *n.* self-control, proportion, stability ("There was balance in the community").
v. make equal, neutralize, parallel ("The scales balanced").

balance due *n.* The amount owing on a debt after partial payment.

balance sheet *n.* A summarization of all the accounts of a business, showing debits and credits, but not showing the particular items used to make up the several accounts. *See* profit and loss statement.

balancing test [*bal* · en · sing] *n.* A principle of **constitutional law** which declares that the constitutional rights of each citizen must in each instance be balanced against the danger that their exercise presents to others or to the state. EXAMPLE: freedom of speech does not include the right "to cry fire in a crowded theater" if there is no fire.

ballistics [ba · *lis* · tiks] *n.* The science of motion and impact of projectiles, which can determine the direction, angle, and weapon from which a bullet was fired.

balloon mortgage [ba · *loon more* · gej] *n.* A **mortgage** whose final payment is considerably higher than any of the previous regular payments, the final payment representing much if not all of the entire principal. Balloon mortgages and **balloon notes** (*see* note) are illegal in some states.

balloon note [ba · *loon*] *n. See* balloon mortgage.

ballot [*bal* · et] *n.* 1. The means by which a voter indicates a preference when voting, for EXAMPLE, a paper ballot or a machine ballot. 2. A list of all candidates in an election, together with the offices for which they are competing.
➤ choice, lineup, tally, poll.

ban *n.* 1. A prohibition. 2. Excommunication. 3. An old word for a proclamation or notice. *See* bar.
v. 1. To prohibit. 2. To excommunicate. *See* bar.
➤ *n.* boycott, embargo, censorship, prohibition ("a ban on imports").
v. banish, bar, disallow, halt, eliminate, outlaw ("the movement to ban the manufacture of firearms").

banc [bonk] *(French) n.* Bench. *See en banc.*

banishment [*ban* · ish · ment] *n.* The expulsion or deportation of a person from a country by the government. *See* deportation.
➤ discharge, ostracism, segregation, dismissal, expulsion.

bank *n.* An institution that is in the business of receiving deposits of money, collecting and discounting **commercial paper** (*see* collection; discount), making loans, and similar functions involving the handling of funds or commercial transactions. *See and compare* collecting bank; commercial bank; intermediary bank; payor bank; savings bank.
➤ financial institution, credit union, repository, exchequer, coffer, safe, vault; hill, mound, dune, ridge.

bank account [a · *kount*] *n.* The deposits made by a customer, less his withdrawals, plus other charges the bank is entitled to make. *See and compare* checking account; savings account.

bank bills *n. See* bank note.

bank book *n.* A book in which a customer of a bank keeps account of her deposits, withdrawals, and balance. *See* passbook.

bank credit [*kre* · dit] *n.* The amount a bank is willing to lend a person based upon his credit. The amount may vary depending upon the **security** the borrower is able to provide.

bank draft *n.* A check, **draft**, or other **order instrument drawn** by a bank and payable upon **acceptance**.

bank examiner [eg · *zam* · in · er] *n.* A federal or state official authorized to

B

conduct an investigation of the accounts of a bank.

bank failure [*fale* · yoor] *n.* A state of **insolvency** in which a bank is unable to meet its obligations to depositors and other creditors.

bank note *n.* A **note** or **bill** issued by a bank promising to pay the **bearer** a stated sum **on demand**. Bank notes are a **medium of exchange**. *See* ordered.

banker's acceptance [*bank* · erz ak · *sep* · tense] *n.* An **acceptance** by a bank of a **draft** or a **bill of exchange**. A banker's acceptance is an instrument used for the purpose of extending credit.

banker's lien [*bank* · erz leen] *n.* The **lien** a bank has on all funds, **securities**, and other property of a depositor or customer who owes it money. *See and compare* mechanic's lien, attorney's lien.

bankrupt [*bank* · rupt] *adj./n.* 1. A person who is unable to pay her debts as they come due; an insolvent person. 2. A person who is entitled to the protection of the **Bankruptcy Code**.
➤ *adj.* insolvent, indigent, wiped out, penniless, destitute, broke, out of business.

bankruptcy [*bank* · rupt · see] *n.* 1. The circumstances of a person who is unable to pay his debts as they come due. 2. The system under which a debtor may come into court (**voluntary bankruptcy**) or be brought into court by his creditors (**involuntary bankruptcy**), either seeking to have his **assets** administered and sold for the benefit of his creditors and to be **discharged** from his debts (a *straight bankruptcy*), or to have his debts reorganized (a *business reorganization* or a *wage earner's plan*). A straight bankruptcy is called a **Chapter 7** proceeding because it is conducted under Chapter 7 of the **Bankruptcy Code**. Under a **Chapter 11** business reorganization, the debtor is permitted to continue business operations until a reorganization plan is approved by two-thirds of his creditors. Under a **Chapter 13** proceeding, an individual debtor who is a wage earner and who files a repayment plan acceptable to his creditors will be given additional time in which to meet his obligations.

➤ insolvency, failure, disaster, defaulting. *Ant.* solvency, success.

bankruptcy estate [es · *tate*] *n.* All of the property of the debtor at the time the **petition in bankruptcy** is filed.

bankruptcy judge *n.* A judge of a **bankruptcy court**.

bankruptcy proceedings [pro · *see* · dings] *n.* Any **proceedings** under the **Bankruptcy Code**; any proceedings relating to bankruptcy.

bankruptcy trustee [trus · *tee*] *n.* Same as **trustee in bankruptcy**.

Bankruptcy Code [*bank* · rupt · see] *n.* Federal bankruptcy legislation. There have been five major statutes, enacted respectively in 1800, 1841, 1867, 1898, and 1978. The last of these is the present Bankruptcy Code.

bankruptcy courts *n.* Federal courts that hear and determine only bankruptcy cases.

banning [*ban* · ing] *n.* The process of excluding or outlawing something. USAGE: "Literary critics were outraged at the banning of James Joyce's *Ulysses*."
➤ prohibiting, outlawing, excluding.

bar *n.* 1. The attorneys permitted to practice before a particular court, taken collectively. *See* bar association. *See and compare* integrated bar; voluntary bar. 2. The court itself, when one speaks of the "case at bar" or the "bar of justice." 3. A rail enclosing the judge and other **officers of the court**. 4. The place in some courtrooms occupied by a prisoner on trial. 5. A **defense** or **plea** that defeats an **action**. *See* plea in bar. 6. A prohibition; a ban.
v. To prevent; to prohibit; to exclude; to suspend; to block. *See* ban.
➤ *n.* barrier, snag, restraint, blockage ("a bar was placed in the doorway"); court, fend, tribunal, judiciary ("case at bar"); defense, plea ("a bar to his action").
v. prevent, block, exclude, hinder, secure ("to bar a cause of action").

bar association [a · so · see · *ay* · shen] *n.* A voluntary organization of members of the bar of a state or county, or of the bar of every state, whose primary function is promoting professionalism and enhancing the administration of justice; a **voluntary bar**. *See* state bar. *Compare* integrated bar.

bar examination [eg · zam · i · *nay* · shen] *n.* A written examination that every attorney must pass before being granted a license to practice law. Some states use their own tests, some use a standardized multistate examination, and some use both. *See* practice of law.

barbiturate [bar · *bit* · sher · ate] *n.* A class of prescription drugs that depress the central nervous system and are used as sedatives. Barbiturates are a **controlled substance** with a high potential for abuse leading to addiction; their possession, distribution, or sale is a criminal offense.

bare *adj.* Mere; limited; basic; scant; minimal.
   v. To reveal or expose information.
➤ *adj.* naked, open, bald ("the bare truth"). *v.* reveal, divulge, disclose, publish, unveil ("The witness bared all").
   bare contract [*kon* · trakt] *n.* A **contract** containing only the essential terms.
   bare licensee [lice · en · *see*] *n.* A **licensee**, i.e., a person whose presence on premises is neither invited nor resisted, but merely tolerated; a **mere licensee**.

bargain [*bar* · gen] *n.* An agreement between two or more persons; a **contract**.
   v. To negotiate; to talk about the terms of a contract.
➤ *n.* treaty, pact, settlement, deal, agreement, transaction, contract, covenant, stipulation. *v.* negotiate, deal, barter, haggle, dicker.

bargain and sale *adj.* A term for certain **sales agreements** (for both real property and personal property) containing provisions to be carried out at a future time. *See* executory contract.
   bargain and sale deed *n.* A **deed** conveying real property without **covenants**.
   bargain collectively [ke · *lek* · tiv · lee] *v. See* collective bargaining.

bargaining [*bar* · gen · ing] *adj.* Negotiating; discussing a contract.
   bargaining agent [*ay* · jent] *n. See* collective bargaining agent.
   bargaining agreement [a · *gree* · ment] *n. See* collective bargaining agreement.

bargaining unit [*yoo* · nit] *n. See* collective bargaining unit.

barratry [*bar* · a · tree] *n.* 1. The offense of stirring up quarrels or lawsuits. *Compare* champerty; maintenance. 2. A **maritime law** term for illegal or fraudulent acts by a ship's captain or crew which harm the ship's owner.
➤ troublemaking, champerty, litigiousness.

barren [*bahr* · en] *adj.* Empty; bare; incapable of reproduction.
➤ bare, empty, sparse, infertile, sterile, desolate, void.

barrister [*bar* · is · ter] *n.* 1. In England, a lawyer who is permitted to try cases in court. *Compare* solicitor. 2. An informal term for lawyer in the United States.

barter [*bahr* · ter] *n.* The trading of one thing for another, as opposed to paying with money.
   v. To negotiate for the acquisition of a thing or a service in exchange for another thing or service.
➤ *n.* trade, swap, exchange. *v.* exchange, swap, trade, haggle, negotiate ("It is customary to barter for goods in some countries").

base *adj.* 1. Basic. 2. Low; inferior; vile; impure; corrupt.
   n. A foundation; a starting point.
➤ *adj.* vulgar, corrupt, foul, vile, immoral ("base motives"); impure, adulterated, inferior ("base metal"). *n.* basis, foot, key, fundamental part, foundation.
   base animal [*an* · i · mel] *n.* Because of their "base nature," most animals (including, for EXAMPLE, bears, snakes, dogs, cats) cannot be the subject of **larceny**.
   base fee *n.* An **estate** in real property which has the possibility of lasting forever, but which may be put to an end by some event that blocks its continued existence. *See* fee. *Also see* determinable fee; qualified fee.
   base pay *n.* Wages, before the computation of overtime or the addition of bonuses. *Compare* gross pay.

baseless [*base* · less] *adj.* Without a foundation in fact; mistaken.

➤ unfounded, groundless, untenable, indefensible, unsubstantiated.

basis [*bay* · siss] *n.* 1. In tax law, the cost of property as of a certain date, upon which **depreciation** can be computed and gain or loss can be calculated when the property is sold or exchanged. *See* sale or exchange. *See also* accrual basis; adjusted basis; cash basis. 2. The foundation of anything. *See* laying a basis.

➤ foundation, authority, principle, premise ("basis for the argument"); cost ("the tax basis of the property").

basis patent [*pat* · ent] *n.* A **patent** in a virgin field; a **pioneer patent**.

bastard [*bas* · terd] *n.* A person born out of wedlock; also known as an illegitimate child.

➤ illegitimate child, adulterine, colt.

bastardy action [*bas* · terd · ee *ak* · shen] *n.* *See* paternity suit.

battered woman syndrome [*bat* · terd *wu* · men *sin* · drome] *n.* A psychological condition in which a woman commits physical violence against her husband or mate as a result of the continued physical or mental abuse to which he has subjected her. The courts are split with respect to the admissibility of **expert testimony** (in support of a plea of **self-defense**, for EXAMPLE) to prove the psychological effects of continued abuse. *See* abuse; spousal abuse. *See also* battery.

battery [*bat* · ter · ee] *n.* The unconsented-to touching or striking of one person by another, or by an object put in motion by him, with the intention of doing harm or giving offense. Battery is both a crime and a **tort**. *Compare* assault. *See* assault and battery. *Also see* simple battery; technical battery.

➤ beating, mugging, flogging, hitting, assault, thrashing, injury ("commit a battery"); batch, cluster, array ("a battery of elements").

bear *v.* 1. To yield; to produce; to generate; to bring in. USAGE: "I want to put my money in an account that bears interest." 2. To carry. USAGE: "Do Americans have a constitutional right to bear arms?"

➤ fund, provide, yield, produce, generate ("I want to put my money in an account that bears interest"); abide, stand, undergo, tolerate ("I cannot bear his presence"); bolster, uphold, prop, fortify, support ("bear weight").

bear arms *n.* *See* right to bear arms.

bear market [*mar* · ket] *n.* The stock market when the value of securities being traded is declining. *Compare* bull market.

bearer [*bare* · er] *n.* 1. The **holder** of a **negotiable instrument** payable to "bearer" or to "cash", i.e., a negotiable instrument not payable to a named person. The **Uniform Commercial Code** defines a bearer as the person in possession of an **instrument, document of title**, or **certificated security** payable to bearer or indorsed in blank. *See* indorsement in blank. 2. A person who is carrying something, particularly a message; a messenger.

➤ carrier, recipient, courier, possessor, holder, payee.

bearer bond *n.* A **bond** that by its terms, not by **indorsement**, is payable to the **holder**.

bearer instrument [*in* · stroo · ment] *n.* A **negotiable instrument** payable to bearer or to cash, or which is in any form that does not specify a **payee**.

bearer paper [*pay* · per] *n.* **Commercial paper** payable to bearer or to cash, or in any other form that does not designate a specific **payee**.

beat *v.* 1. To defeat, conquer, or subdue. 2. To assault physically.

➤ defeat, surmount, surpass, defeat; abuse, batter, hit, punch, pummel.

bed and board *n.* *See* divorce a mensa et thoro.

before [*be* · *for*] *adv./prep.* Prior to. "Before," like other inexact words, must be construed in the context in which it appears. Generally, when an act is required to be done a specified number of days before an event, the required number of days is computed by excluding the day on which the act is done and including the day on which the event is to occur.

➤ *adv.* ahead, afore, former, formerly, previous ("She filed for divorce before he did.").

prep. ahead of, in front of, preceding ("the case before the court").

before the court *prep.* In front of the court; **at bar.** USAGE: "the case presently before this court."

begging the question [*beg* · ing the *kwest* · shen] *n.* An argument that assumes the very thing in question has been proven. USAGE: "It begs the question to argue that one plus two equals three because three minus two equals one."

behalf [be · *haf*] *n.* In the name of; for the benefit, interest, or use of.
➤ defense, help, profit, service, benefit, benevolence.

belief [be · *leef*] *n.* Confidence of mind, based upon evidence that a fact exists, that an act was done, or that a statement is true. *Compare* faith; knowledge. *See* information and belief; reasonable belief.
➤ canon, creed, theory, persuasion, faith, doctrine; confidence, opinion, assurance, conviction.

belief-action principle [be · *leef ak* · shen *prin* · sipl] *n.* A principle of **constitutional law** which declares that a person can believe whatever she wants, but that if she acts upon her beliefs to the detriment of others, her constitutional right to do so must be weighed against the state's right to safeguard society as a whole. *See also* balancing test.

believable [be · *leev* · uh · bul] *adj.* That which is within the range of possibility.
➤ credible, plausible, trustworthy, tenable, convincing, reliable, conceivable.

belligerent [be · *lij* · e · rent] *adj.* Combative; hostile; quarrelsome; warlike. *n.* A nation carrying on war against another nation, or a group within a nation that has organized a provisional government and is carrying on war against the nation.
➤ *adj.* threatening, hostile, quarrelsome, combative, pugilistic.
n. combatant, aggressor.

below [be · *loh*] *adj.* 1. The **court below**; a **lower court.** USAGE: "The appeals court may not uphold the judgment of the court below." 2. In a position of lower rank; inferior. 3. Physically lower; under.

➤ beneath, down, underneath; inferior, under ("a rank below sergeant").

bench *n.* 1. A court. 2. The judges of a court. *See en banc.* 3. The seat upon which the judge sits when court is in session. 4. All judges and justices of a jurisdiction, collectively.
➤ bank, counter, board, worktable; judges, justices, chamber, tribunal, court.

bench trial [*try* · el] *n.* A trial before a judge without a jury; a **nonjury trial.**

bench warrant [*war* · ent] *n.* A **warrant** issued by a judge for a person's arrest.

beneficial [ben · e · *fish* · el] *adj.* Of benefit; profitable; advantageous.
➤ favoring, gainful, serviceable, useful, valuable.
Ant. harmful, deleterious.

beneficial association [a · so · see · *ay* · shen] *n. See* benevolent association.

beneficial enjoyment [en · *joy* · ment] *n.* Having the advantages of ownership of property. *See* enjoyment.

beneficial interest [*in* · trest] *n.* 1. An **interest** of value, worth, or use in property one does not own. EXAMPLE: the interest that the **beneficiary** of a **trust** has in the trust. 2. A property interest that inures solely to the benefit of the owner. 3. That which remains of the **estate** of a **decedent** after the payment of debts and the **expenses of administration.** 4. The right of a person having a **power of appointment** to appoint himself.
As is apparent, the meaning of the term is variable. Its appropriate definition is determined by the context in which it is used.

beneficial owner [*oh* · ner] *n.* A person who has **equitable title** to property, but not **legal title.**

beneficial power [*pow* · er] *n.* A **power** which has for its object the **grantee** of the power, and which is executed solely for her benefit. *See* power of appointment.

beneficial society [so · *sie* · e · tee] *n. See* benevolent association.

beneficial use *n. See* beneficial interest.

B

beneficial use and enjoyment
[en · *joy* · ment] *n.* *See* beneficial enjoyment; beneficial interest.

beneficiary [ben · e · *fish* · ee · air · ee] *n.* 1. A person who receives a benefit. 2. A person who has inherited or is entitled to inherit under a will. 3. A person for whom property is held **in trust**. 4. A person who is entitled to the proceeds of a life insurance policy when the insured dies. 5. A person designated by statute as entitled to the proceeds of a legal action such as a **wrongful death action**. *See* creditor beneficiary; donee beneficiary; third-party beneficiary.
➤ heir, recipient, successor, legatee, assignee.

benefit [*ben* · e · fit] *n.* 1. Anything that adds to the advantage or security of another. 2. A payment made under an insurance policy, pension, annuity, or the like. 3. **Statutory benefits**. *See* benefits.
v. To provide aid or assistance; to improve, enhance, or ameliorate.
➤ *n.* aid, asset, exhibition ("a benefit for the homeless"); advantage, profit, gain, utility, return ("the benefit of success").
v. help, build, aid, assist, serve, succor, avail ("The concert benefited the children's home").

benefit association [a · so · see · *ay* · shen] *n.* *See* benevolent association.

benefit of bargain rule [*bar* · gen] *n.* The rule that a person who is induced by **fraudulent misrepresentation** to make a purchase is entitled to recover as **damages** the difference between the real value and the represented value of the property.

benefit of clergy [*kler* · jee] *n.* The exemption of clergymen, under old English law, from criminal prosecution in **secular** courts. *See* without benefit of clergy.

benefit of counsel [*koun* · sel] *n.* *See* right to counsel.

benefit society [so · *sie* · e · tee] *n.* *See* benevolent association.

benefit theory [*thee* · e · ree] *n.* The principle that one who wishes to **rescind** a contract must restore the other party to the **status quo** by giving back any benefits received under the contract.

benefits [*ben* · e · fits] *n.* *Plural* of **benefit**. *See* benefit. Monetary or nonmonetary **consideration** paid or provided to an employee by an employer. EXAMPLES: sick pay; vacation pay; parental leave; health insurance. Such employee benefits are sometimes referred to as *nonstatutory benefits*, in contrast to *statutory benefits* such as workers' compensation coverage, unemployment insurance, and social security, which are provided because the law requires it.

benevolent [ben · *ev* · e · lent] *adj.* Charitable; philanthropic; prompted by good will or kind feelings.
➤ caring, considerate, humane, kind-hearted, charitable, philanthropic.

benevolent association
[a · so · see · *ay* · shen] *n.* An **association**, often a **fraternal benefit society**, formed for the purpose of providing financial aid or other assistance to its members.

benevolent corporation
[kore · per · *ay* · shen] *n.* A **corporation** created for **charitable** rather than business purposes; a **nonprofit corporation**; an **eleemosynary corporation**. *See* charitable organization.

bequeath [be · *kweeth*] *v.* To leave personal property or money by will; such a gift is called a **bequest** or a **legacy**. A gift of real property by will is properly called a **devise**, although the courts generally construe "bequeath" as synonymous with "devise" when it is used in connection with a **testamentary gift** of real estate. *See* testamentary disposition.
➤ grant, give, assign, remit, leave, provide.

bequest [be · *kwest*] *n.* Technically, a gift of personal property by will, i.e., a **legacy**, although the term is often loosely used in connection with a **testamentary gift** of real estate as well. *Compare* devise. *See* bequeath.
➤ gift, devise, endowment, heritage, legacy.

best *adj.* Of the highest quality. *Best* denotes superiority or preeminence.
v. To defeat; to beat.
➤ *adj.* choice, greatest, paramount, select, supreme, exemplary, superior, optimal, unrivaled.
v. surpass, conquer, defeat, outdo.

best evidence [*ev · i · dense*] *n.* The most superior proof of a fact; the most reliable proof, as contrasted with less reliable proof. USAGE: "An employee's timecard, not his supervisor's recollection, is the best evidence of his tardiness." *Compare* secondary evidence. *See* evidence.

best evidence rule *n.* The rule of evidence that a **party** must prove a disputed fact by the **best evidence** that is within his power to produce. *Compare* secondary evidence. *See* evidence.

best use *n. See* highest and best use.

bestiality [*bes · chee · al · i · tee*] *n.* Sexual intercourse with an animal, a crime in most states. *See also* buggery; crime against nature; sodomy.

bestow [*be · stoh*] *v.* To grant; to give; to confer. "Bestow" is a word frequently used in wills.
➤ grant, give, devote, favor, lavish.

bet *n.* A wager; an activity in which money or property is risked upon the occurrence of chance or upon the outcome of an uncertain event.
v. To risk money or property upon the occurrence of chance. *See* gambling; gaming.
➤ *n.* action, pledge, risk, lottery ("The bet was off").
v. gamble, speculate, venture ("to bet money").

betray [*be · tray*] *v.* 1. To reveal; to prove false. 2 To lead astray.
➤ divulge, declare, reveal, inform, disclose; cheat, defraud, dupe, violate, swindle.

better equity [*bet · er ek · wi · tee*] *n.* Of two **interests** that are just, the superior interest. *See* equity. *Also see* superior.

betterment [*bet · er · ment*] *n.* 1. An **improvement** to real estate which is more extensive than **ordinary repair** and which substantially increases the value of the property. 2. Gain; advancement; upgrading; furtherance.
➤ advancement, upgrading, progress.

betterment acts *n.* Statutes that obligate a landlord to compensate a former tenant for **improvements** the tenant made to real property, if the tenant acted in the belief that she had **title** to the property. Such

statutes are formally referred to as **occupying claimant acts**.

between [*be · tween*] *prep.* Intermediate. When used in designating time, "between" implies the exclusion of both the first and last day. "Between" is not "among"; thus, when designating persons, "between" applies only to two, "among" to three or more. USAGE: "I intend to divide my land between my two children and my personal effects among my three grandchildren."

beyond a reasonable doubt [*be · yond a ree · zen · ebl*] *n.* The degree of proof required to convict a person of a crime. A *reasonable doubt* is a fair doubt based upon reason and common sense, not an arbitrary or possible doubt. To convict a criminal defendant, a jury must be persuaded of his guilt to a level beyond "apparently" or "probably." Proof beyond a reasonable doubt is the highest level of proof the law requires. *Compare* preponderance of the evidence. *Also see* moral certainty.

beyond legal memory [*be · yond lee · gl mem · e · ree*] *See* legal memory.

BFOQ Abbreviation of **bona fide occupational qualification**.

BIA Abbreviation of **Bureau of Indian Affairs**.

biannual [*by · an · yoo · el*] *adj.* 1. Occurring once every two years; biennial. *Compare* semiannual. 2. Occurring twice a year.
➤ biennial, semiannual.

bias [*by · es*] *n.* Prejudice; preconception; partiality; favoritism; something that turns the mind and sways the judgment. *See also* discrimination.
v. To prejudice or taint.
➤ *n.* prejudice, preconception, partiality, leaning, inclination, proclivity, penchant, predilection.
v. skew, sway, prejudice ("that evidence could bias the jury").

bias of judge *n.* A judge's preconceived mental attitude, whether of hostility or favoritism, toward a litigant. *See* disqualified judge.

bias of juror [*joo · rer*] *n.* A juror's mental predisposition with respect to a litigant or to the litigation which renders the juror unable to form an objective opinion in the case. *See* disqualified juror.

bias of witness [*wit* · ness] *n.* *See* disqualified witness.

bicameral [by · *kam* · er · el] *adj.* Two-chambered, referring to the customary division of a legislature into two houses (a Senate and a House of Representatives).

bid *n.* An **offer**, especially one made at the letting of a contract (*see* letting a contract), an auction, or a **judicial sale**. *See* by-bidding; chilling bids; competitive bidding; lowest responsible bidder.
v. To invite; to make an **offer**, particularly at an auction or a **judicial sale**, or to secure a contract.
➤ *n.* try, proposal, suggestion, approach, price, offer, submission ("All bids were open").
v. demand, ask for, charge, greet, invite; submit, tender, propose, present; attempt, try, essay.
  bid and asked *adj.* In trading **securities** on the **over-the-counter market**, the *bid price* is the price a buyer is willing to pay, the *asked price* is the price at which a seller is willing to sell, and the difference between the two is the **market quotation**.
  bid bond *n.* A **bond** required of a person who bids on the letting of a contract for construction of a **public improvement**. The purpose of the bond is to **indemnify** the public against the consequences of a bidder's failure to follow through on the bid. *See* letting a contract; responsible bidder.
  bid in *n.* The act of the owner of property which has been put up at an auction in taking the property out of the auction by a protective bid, that is, a bid made to prevent a sacrifice of the property at less than its real value.
  bid off *v.* To purchase by bid at an auction or a **judicial sale**.
  bid price *n.* *See* bid and asked.
  bid shopping [*shop* · ing] *n.* Revealing the amount of a low bid in order to attract an even lower bid.

bidder [*bid* · er] *n.* A person who makes a bid.

biennial [by · *en* · i · al] *adj.* Same as **bi-annual**.

biennium [by · *en* · i · um] *n.* A period of two years.

bifurcate [*by* · fer · kayt] *v.* To separate into two parts.
➤ divide, partition, split, separate, dichotomize, halve, sunder.

bifurcated trial [*by* · fer · kay · ted *try* · el] *n.* A trial that is divided into two parts to provide separate hearings for different aspects of the same matter, for EXAMPLE, guilt and punishment, guilt and sanity, or **liability** and **damages**.

bigamous [*big* · a · muss] *adj.* Pertaining to or having the characteristics of **bigamy**.

bigamy [*big* · e · mee] *n.* The crime of knowingly marrying while married.

bigot [*big* · ut] *n.* One who is intolerant of others or prejudiced.
➤ dogmatist, fanatic, persecutor, zealot, redneck, segregationist, racist.

bilateral [by · *lat* · er · el] *adj.* 1. Involving two **interests**. 2. Having two sides. *Compare* unilateral.
➤ mutual, two-sided, reciprocal.
  bilateral contract [*kon* · trakt] *n.* A **contract** in which each **party** promises **performance** to the other, the promise by the one furnishing the **consideration** for the promise from the other. EXAMPLE: a contract for home heating oil (the dealer promises to deliver, the homeowner promises to pay). *Compare* unilateral contract.
  bilateral mistake [mis · *take*] *n.* Same as **mutual mistake**.

bilingual [by · *ling* · wel] *adj.* The ability to speak two languages. "Because she is bilingual, my secretary could translate the foreign opinion."

bill *n.* 1. A **complaint** in a suit in **equity**; i.e., a **bill in equity**. 2. A form of appeal to a higher court of rulings made by the court below during trial; i.e., a **bill of exceptions**. 3. A proposed law, presented to the legislature for enactment; i.e., a legislative bill. 4. Paper money. 5. A **bill of exchange** or **draft**; such a bill may be a **negotiable instrument** or a

nonnegotiable instrument. 6. In **commercial law**, an agreement reduced to writing. *See* bill of lading. 7. In criminal law, an **indictment** or the charge made against the accused in an indictment; i.e., a **bill of indictment**. 8. An action taken by a legislature when it sits as a court. *See* bill of attainder. 9. The charge for a purchase. The statement of an account presented to a debtor for payment.

v. To present an **account** for payment.

➤ *n.* proposed law, draft, resolution ("the bill before Congress"); invoice, account, fee, record, expenses, debit, cost ("the bill for legal services").

v. record, render, solicit, figure, charge money for goods ("to bill a customer").

bill in equity [*ek · wi · tee*] *n.* The **complaint** of a plaintiff in a **court of equity**.

bill of attainder [a · *tane* · der] *n.* A **legislative act** that inflicts capital punishment upon named persons without a judicial trial. Congress and the state legislatures are prohibited from issuing bills of attainder by the Constitution. *See* attainder.

bill of exceptions [ek · *sep* · shens] *n.* A means by which the **appellate court** is presented with **exceptions** taken or **objections** made during trial to rulings and decisions of the trial court.

bill of exchange [eks · *chaynj*] *n.* Same as **draft**.

bill of goods *n.* 1. A list of articles purchased. 2. A slang expression for a valueless item, by which a person indicates she has been misled into taking an action she regrets. USAGE: "He sold me a bill of goods."

bill of health *n.* 1. An official certification of the health of a ship, its cargo, and crew. 2. A physician's statement certifying to the good health of a person.

bill of indictment [in · *dite* · ment] *n.* A term for the formal document issued by a prosecutor, containing a criminal charge, before it is presented to the grand jury. If the grand jury determines the charge to be true, the bill is referred to as an **indictment**. *Also see* true bill.

bill of lading [*lay* · ding] *n.* A written acknowledgment by a **carrier** of the receipt of the goods described in the bill and an agreement to transport them to the place and the person specified in the bill. A bill of lading may be **negotiable** or **nonnegotiable**; in either event, it is a **document of title**.

bill of particulars [per · *tik* · yoo · lerz] *n.* 1. In criminal prosecutions, a more detailed statement of the offense charged than the **indictment** or **information** provides. A criminal defendant is entitled to a bill of particulars, as part of the **discovery** process, if the nature and extent of the offense are not alleged with sufficient particularity to allow the preparation of an adequate **defense**. 2. In civil actions, a more detailed statement of the **pleading**. An **adverse party** is entitled to be informed of the precise nature of the opposite party's **cause of action** or defense, in order to be able to prepare for trial and to protect himself against surprise at the trial.

bill of review [re · *vyoo*] *n.* A written request to a **court of equity**, asking it to review and reverse or revise its own decree.

bill of sale *n.* A document evidencing the transfer of **title** to personal property from a seller to a buyer.

bill of sight *n.* A bill issued by customs officers allowing an importer to inspect goods before paying duty on them.

bills and notes *n.* **Commercial paper**; **installments**, both **negotiable** and **nonnegotiable**. *See* note.

bills payable [*pay* · abl] *n.* An accounting term used in a **financial statement** to indicate the obligations a business owes. *See* account payable.

bills receivable [re · *seev* · abl] *n.* An accounting term used in a **financial statement** to indicate the obligations owed to a business. *See* account receivable.

Bill of Rights *n.* The first 10 amendments to the United States Constitution. The Bill of Rights is the portion of the Constitution that sets forth the rights which are the fundamental principles of the United States and the foundation of American citizenship.

bind *n.* A tight spot or predicament.

v. 1. To tie securely; to fasten; to restrain free movement. 2. To indenture; to obligate.

To create a legal obligation, either one's own or another person's. *See* binding.

➤ *n.* predicament, quandary, tight spot ("The commissioner was in a bind").

v. obligate, require, compel; restrict, hinder, restrain, yoke, detain.

bind-over hearing [*bined-oh* · ver *heer* · ing] *n.* A **preliminary hearing**; a **probable cause hearing**. *See* binding over.

binder [*bine* · der] *n.* 1. An interim **memorandum**, used when an insurance policy cannot be issued immediately, evidencing either that insurance coverage is effective at a specified time and continues until the policy is issued, or that the **risk** is declined and giving notice of that fact. 2. An **earnest money** deposit that preserves a buyer's right to purchase real estate.

➤ deposit, pledge, stake, collateral, escrow, security ("a binder on the deal").

binding [*bine* · ding] *adj.* That which one is obligated to follow, observe, or comply with; committed; obligatory. USAGE: "In my opinion, this is not a binding contract." *n.* A book's cover; a fastening.

➤ *adj.* compulsory, conclusive, obligatory, mandatory, necessary ("a binding agreement").

n. cover, adhesive, fastener.

binding authority [aw · *thaw* · ri · tee] *n.* Previous decisions of a higher court or statutes that a judge must follow in reaching a decision in a case. *See* authority. *Also see* precedent.

binding contract [*kon* · trakt] *n.* A **contract** that is enforceable. *Compare* voidable contract.

binding instructions [in · *struk* · shen] *n.* **Instructions** by the judge that the jury must follow. It is the jury's duty to apply the law which the judge advises them is applicable to the facts they find to be true. *See* jury instructions.

binding over [*oh* · ver] *v.* A court's action at a **preliminary hearing** or **probable cause hearing** setting a criminal defendant's bail and transferring her case to a trial court for trial. USAGE: "Based upon its **preliminary examination**, the Court finds the evidence sufficient to bind you over to the Superior Court for trial, and sets your bail at $10,000." *See* bind-over hearing.

bipartisan [by · *par* · ti · zen] *adj.* Referring to a governmental activity controlled or participated in equally by two political parties, generally Democratic and Republican. Statutes that create **boards** and **commissions** of national, state, and local government often provide that they be bipartisan in composition.

➤ dual, two-sided, duplicated, conciliatory.

bipartite [by · *par* · tite] *adj.* In two parts. USAGE: "A bipartite contract is a contract in two parts."

bkpt. An abbreviation of **bankrupt**.

Black Codes *n.* The name given the laws enacted in the states of the American South immediately after the Civil War, legalizing racial segregation.

black letter law [*let* · er] *n.* Fundamental and well-established rules of law.

black market [*mar* · ket] *n.* The sale or exchange of stolen goods or items that are banned (EXAMPLE: heroin) or restricted (EXAMPLE: prescription drugs), or that cannot legally be sold untaxed (EXAMPLES: cigarettes, liquor). *See* bootleg; contraband.

Blackacre [*blak* · ay · ker] *n.* The name of a hypothetical tract of land, often used in teaching the law of real property or **future interests**. *Also see* Whiteacre.

blacklist *n.* [*blak* · list] *n.* A list of persons who are to be avoided by those among whom the list is intended to circulate. Most commonly used to refer to lists of discharged employees, sent by the employer who fired them to other employers with the intention of preventing their employment. Such action is illegal in most states.

v. To put a person's name on a **blacklist**. *See* blacklist (*noun*).

➤ *v.* ban, bar, boycott, censure.

blackmail [*blak* · male] *n.* A form of the crime of **extortion**, usually by threat of exposure of some conduct of the victim which, if made public, would be harmful to him.

B

v. To demand unlawfully, backed by a demand for money or a threat of physical harm.
➤ *n.* ransom, extortion, exaction, payoff, hush money, bribery.
v. threaten, coerce, compel, demand, force, shake, squeeze.

blame *v.* To hold responsible; to find fault. *n.* 1. The responsibility for something of reproach; disgrace. 2. An expression of fault.
➤ *v.* accuse, fault, implicate, rebuke, reproach, condemn, execrate.
n. accusation, criticism, denunciation, reproof, reprobation, castigation ("I'll take the blame"); accountability, attribution, assignment ("allocation of blame").

blank *n.* 1. A space in a document that must be filled in to complete the meaning. 2. A form containing spaces that must be filled in to complete the transaction, for EXAMPLE, a blank contract or a blank check. *adj.* Plain; bearing no marks or writing.
➤ *n.* void, opening, gap, chasm, hollowness ("fill in the blank").
adj. bare, clean, empty, unfilled, unused ("a blank slate"); dull, expressionless, vacuous, impassive, noncommital ("a blank expression"); complete, absolute, utter, total, thorough ("the blank truth").

blank indorsement [en · *dorse* · ment] *n.* Also called a **general indorsement**, an indorsement of a **negotiable instrument** that specifies no **indorsee**. EXAMPLE: a check drawn payable to "John L. Jones" which he indorses, simply, "John L. Jones." *Compare* full indorsement. *See* indorsement.

blanket [*blank* · et] *adj.* Covering everything, for EXAMPLE, all members of a **class**, all **risks** to which the property of an insured is exposed, or all misconduct by a defendant. *v.* 1. To cover or spread over. 2. To hinder or obscure.
➤ *adj.* complete, total, all-encompassing ("a blanket power of attorney"); *v.* surround, envelop, overspread ("blanket the area"); cover, cloak, obscure, eclipse ("blanket the view").

blanket mortgage [*more* · gej] *n.* A **mortgage** in which more than one parcel of real estate is **security** for the debt.

blanket policy [*pol* · i · see] *n.* 1. An insurance policy that covers various **risks** and various types of property without specifying each item. EXAMPLE: a fire and theft policy that covers "all personal property located on the premises." 2. An insurance policy that covers property at more than one location. *See also* fleet coverage; floater policy.

blanket search warrant [*wahr* · ent] *n.* A single **search warrant** that describes separate areas or premises to be searched, or a search warrant that fails to specify the object of the search. Such a warrant violates the **Fourth Amendment**. *See* unreasonable search and seizure.

blasé [bla · *zay*] *adj.* Having the quality of indifference, frequently because the person is sated and bored.
➤ nonchalant, indifferent, unmoved, bored; knowing, worldly, sophisticated.

blasphemy [*blass* · fe · mee] *n.* Maliciously insulting the name of God or religion. Blasphemy was a crime at **common law** and still is in some states, although it is no longer enforced; the constitutionality of such laws is doubtful under the **First Amendment**.
➤ irreverence, swearing, indignity ("His blasphemy enraged the crowd.")

blatant [*blay* · tent] *adj.* Completely obvious.
➤ clear, manifest, noticeable, obvious, patent, plain.

blind *adj.* 1. Having only one opening or outlet. 2. Hidden; obscured. 3. Lacking sight.
➤ unexposed, inconspicuous, private, sheltered; heedless, indiscriminate, undiscerning, inattentive, indifferent; visionless, groping, visually impaired.

blind alley [*al* · ee] *n.* 1. An alley that can be exited only at the entrance; a dead-end street. 2. A dilemma.

blind intersection [*in* · ter · sek · shen] *n.* An intersection of streets at which a driver's view of vehicles approaching on the intersecting street is obscured.

blind trust *n.* An arrangement in which a person gives a **fiduciary** the power to manage her investments, surrendering the right even to know how they are being managed. An **investment trust** is a form of blind trust often used by persons elected or appointed to public office to avoid conflicts of interest. *See* trust.

blindness [*blind* · ness] *n.* Without sight, in whole or part. For purposes of eligibility for certain **statutory benefits** (EXAMPLES: veterans' benefits; social security; some disability insurance benefits), a person may be *legally blind* although partially sighted. *See* disability.
➤ sightlessness, defect, darkness, disability, handicap.

BLM Abbreviation of **Bureau of Land Management**.

bloc [blok] *n.* A group of persons, legislators, or organizations who support a common political or legislative goal even though they are of different political points of view. USAGE: "the farm bloc"; "the labor bloc."

blockage rule [*blok* · ej] *n.* The principle that a large block of corporate stock is not as easily marketable as a few shares and therefore, for tax purposes, may have less value than the sum of the individual shares making up the block.

blockbusting [*blok* · bus · ting] *n.* Circulating rumors that members of some minority group are moving into the neighborhood, as a scare tactic to induce people to sell their homes, usually at reduced prices. The **Fair Housing Act** and other anti-discrimination laws make such conduct illegal in most instances.

blood alcohol concentration (BAC) [*al* · ke · hol kon · sen · *tray* · shun] *n.* The amount of alcohol in the blood, commonly measured by blowing into a breath test device. A person's **BAC** is the standard for determining whether he was **driving while intoxicated**. *See* breathalyzer; evidential breath test.

blood relative [*rel* · e · tiv] *n. See* relation by blood.

blood test *n.* Blood drawn for the purpose of scientific, objective examination, for EXAMPLE, for determining a driver's **blood alcohol concentration** or to determine paternity. *See* HLA testing; paternity test.

bloodline [*blood* · line] *n.* The direct line of descent, especially in reference to animals.
➤ ancestry, parentage, family, descent, genealogy.

blotter [*blot* · er] *n.* A record of arrests made by the police and kept at the police station.
➤ booking, rough minutes, wastebook.

blue book *n.* 1. A publication listing the value of used automobiles by make, type, and year. 2. The name given the United States government's official directory of elected and appointed officeholders. 3. Similar directories in some state governments. 4. A particular reference volume used in legal research, *A Uniform System of Citation*, which gives the appropriate **citation** forms for all cases and statutes.

blue chip *adj.* A term describing first-class investments. USAGE: "This is a *blue chip stock*."
➤ high-priced, top quality, excellent.

blue chip stock *n. See* blue chip.

blue laws *n.* **Sunday closing laws**.

blue ribbon jury [*rib* · en *joo* · ree] *n.* A jury made up of persons specifically qualified to hear an especially complicated case.

blue sky laws *n.* State statutes intended to prevent **fraud** in the sale of **securities**. The term derives from investors who are "dumb enough to buy blue sky." *See* securities acts.

board *n.* 1. The board of directors of a corporation or the governing body of an **association**, i.e., shorthand for **board of directors**. USAGE: "the board" of General Motors; "the board" of the American Red Cross. 2. A group of individuals elected or appointed to supervise the carrying out of a governmental activity, for EXAMPLE, a **board of aldermen** or the **National Labor Relations Board**. A board that exercises **administrative** and **quasi-judicial** functions is often referred to as an *administrative board*. 3. Meals furnished to a person on a regular basis for pay. *See* boarder.

v. 1. To enter. 2. To supply meals for pay. 3. To cover up with planks.

➤ *n.* committee, trustees, directors, management, bureau, cabinet, commissionary ("the board of the Red Cross").

v. embark, enter, mount, climb ("board the bus"); secure, repair ("board up a broken window").

board of aldermen [*all* · der · men] *n.* The name given the city council in some cities. *See* alderman.

board of audit [*aw* · dit] *n.* A board created by the legislature in some states to approve the accounts of **public officers**.

board of directors [di · *rek* · terz] *n.* The **directors** of a corporation or **association** who act as a group in representing the organization and conducting its business.

board of education [ed · yoo · *kay* · shen] *n.* *See* school board.

board of equalization [ee · kwa · li · *zay* · shen] *n.* 1. A board of **local government** whose duty is to spread the tax burden evenly over all the taxable property within a **tax district**, so that some parts of the district are not unduly burdened and others unduly favored. 2. A board of state government whose duty is to equalize the burden of taxes between tax districts or between the counties or towns of a state. *See* equalization.

board of examiners [eg · *zam* · in · erz] *n.* A state board with the power to examine an applicant for a license to practice a profession or an occupation in which special learning is required.

board of health *n.* A local, county, or state board in charge of sanitary and hygienic matters, whose purpose is to protect the public health.

board of pardons [*par* · denz] *n.* *See* pardons board.

board of parole [pa · *role*] *n.* *See* parole board.

board of regents [*ree* · jents] *n.* A board that governs a state's public colleges and universities and, in some states, the entire public educational system.

board of review [re · *vyoo*] *n.* 1. A board established to review the decisions of an administrative agency. 2. A board

that hears appeals from property tax assessments. 3. In some cities, a board, sometimes called a **civilian review board**, that hears complaints of police brutality.

board of selectmen [sel · *ekt* · men] *n.* *See* selectmen.

board of supervisors [*soo* · per · vy · zerz] *n.* A **county board**; i.e., the governing body of a county.

board of tax appeals [a · *peelz*] *n.* *See* Tax Court.

board of trade *n.* 1. A group of people organized for the advancement of business interests. *See also* chamber of commerce. 2. An **association** of persons engaged in the business of buying and selling goods.

board of trustees [truss · *teez*] *n.* The **trustees** of an organization, commonly an institution, acting as a unit in directing the affairs of the institution.

boarder [*bore* · der] *n.* A person who pays to eat her meals regularly at one place, usually a house. If the arrangement also involves a room in which to sleep, it is referred to as room and board. *See* board; boarding house. *Compare* roomer.

➤ tenant, renter, guest.

boarding house [*bore* · ding] *n.* A place where a boarder lives. *See* board. *Compare* rooming house.

bodily [*bod* · e · lee] *adj.* Of or pertaining to the body.

bodily harm *n.* *See* bodily injury.

bodily heirs [airz] *n.* *See* heirs of the body.

bodily injury [*in* · je · ree] *n.* Physical harm or **injury** to the **person**; **personal injuries**.

body [*bod* · ee] *n.* 1. A human being's physical self. 2. A corporation. 3. The board of directors of a corporation; a **board**, **commission**, or other governmental body. 4. The main part of something. USAGE: "Paragraph 3 is the body of the contract." 5. A group of persons, things, or ideas regarded collectively. USAGE: "Your position is supported by a large body of law."

➤ bones, being, creature, crowd, text; board, commission ("the governing body");

B

main part, corpus, substance ("Paragraph 3 is the body of the contract").

body corporate [*kore* · per · et] *n.* A corporation, whether private or public. *See* private corporation; public corporation. *Also see* body politic and corporate.

body execution [eks · e · *kyoo* · shen] *n.* A **writ** enforcing a **judgment** against a person by causing him to be arrested and brought before the court. *See capias.*

body of the crime *n. See corpus delicti.*

body politic [*pol* · i · tik] *n.* All of the citizens who make up a governmental unit, such as a school district, village, township, town, borough, city, county, state, or country. *Also see* body politic and corporate; society.

body politic and corporate [*pol* · i · tik and *kore* · per · et] *n.* The government of certain **political subdivisions**, including towns, cities, and counties. *See* body corporate; body politic. *See also* municipal corporation.

bogus [*boh* · gus] *adj.* Phony; fake; false.
➤ counterfeit, phony, fake, false, sham, artificial, fraudulent, spurious ("a bogus check").

bogus check *n.* A check written on a bank in which the writer has no funds, or funds less than the amount of the check, which he offers knowing it will not be honored by the bank.

boiler room sales [*boy* · ler] *n.* High- powered and high pressure sales of **securities** of questionable value, over the telephone.

boilerplate language [*boy* · ler · plate lang · wej] *n.* Language common to all legal documents of the same type. Attorneys maintain files of such standarized language for use where appropriate. USAGE: "Make sure you read the boilerplate language on the sales contract."

bona fide [*bone* · ah *fide*] *(Latin) adj.* "Good faith"; real; honest. *Compare mala fide.*
➤ real, honest, true, sincere, legitimate, genuine, honorable, just.

bona fide occupational qualification [ok · yoo · *pay* · shen · el kwaw · li · fi · *kay* · shen] *n.* A permitted exception to the law forbidding discrimination in employment, for EXAMPLE, on the basis of gender. An employer may use a gender-based job description if sexual characteristics are essential to performance of the job. Such bona fide occupational qualifications are very few. EXAMPLES: some modeling assignments; some acting roles; a job as a wet nurse. The term bona fide occupational qualification is often shortened to **BFOQ**.

bona fide purchaser [*per* · che · ser] *n.* A person who purchases something in good faith for what it is worth, without knowing that anyone else has any legal interest in it. *See* buyer in the ordinary course of business; good faith purchaser; holder in due course; value.

bona fides [*bone* · ah *fiedz*] *adj. See* bona fide.

bond *n.* 1. A debt owed by a corporation or by the government to an investor. 2. The **written instrument** that evidences a debt. 3. An obligation to pay a sum of money upon the happening of a stated event. 4. A debt secured by a **mortgage**. *v.* To connect or join.

Bonds that represent debt and pay interest are called **investment bonds**. EXAMPLES of investment bonds issued by corporations include **convertible bonds, coupon bonds, guaranteed bonds, registered bonds, serial bonds**, and **term bonds**. (*Also see* junk bonds.) **Unsecured**, long-term corporate bonds are called **debentures**. EXAMPLES of investment bonds issued by government include **municipal bonds, savings bonds**, and **school bonds**. *See* government bonds.

Bonds that are obligations to pay money if a certain event takes place are generally classified either as **surety bonds** (which includes **bail bonds** and **performance bonds**), **fidelity bonds** (payable in the event of employee dishonesty, e.g., **embezzlement**), **indemnity bonds**, or **penal bonds**. Examples of indemnity and penal bonds include **appeal bonds, attachment bonds, bid bonds, completion bonds**, and **peace bonds**. Many bonds, depending on their precise terms, may properly be included in more than one of these classifications.

➤ *n.* bargain, contract, obligation, relationship, affiliation, affinity; binding, manacle, handcuff, chain.
v. fasten, fix, connect, fuse, bind ("to bond together").

bond issue [*ish* · yoo] *n.* 1. All of the bonds issued by a corporation or a **governmental entity** at a given point in time. 2. The process of creating bonds and delivering them to purchasers, owners, or holders.

bond premium [*pree* · mee · um] *n.* The amount above **face value** paid for a bond by the purchaser.

bonded [*bon* · ded] *adj.* 1. **Secured** by a bond. 2. Stored in a warehouse awaiting payment of customs duties. *See* bonded warehouse.
➤ secured, obligated, guaranteed.

bonded debt *n.* 1. An indebtedness of a corporation that is **secured** by a **bond issue**. 2. Monetary obligations undertaken by government for **governmental purposes**, to be paid out of taxes.

bonded warehouse [*ware* · house] *n.* A building designated by the customs authorities for the storage of imported merchandise until customs duties are paid on that merchandise.

bondholder [*bond* · hole · der] *n.* A person who is the **holder** or owner of a **government bond**, **mortgage bond**, **corporate bond**, or other **investment bond**. *See* bond.

bondsman [*bondz* · man] *n.* The person who guarantees a bond, particularly a **bail bond**. *See* surety.
➤ surety, guarantor, voucher.

bonification of tax [*bone* · i · fi · kay · shen] *n.* The suspension of taxes, particularly taxes on goods to be exported.

bonus [*bone* · us] *n.* 1. Something paid to an employee above agreed-upon wages. *Compare* base pay. 2. An extra payment to anyone for extra service or special performance. *See* incentive pay.
➤ fringe benefit, perquisite, additional compensation, tip, gratuity.

bonus stock *n.* Corporate stock issued free of cost or in exchange for property or services at an inflated value. *See* stock.

book *n.* 1. A bound volume; sheets held together by a ring or loop of wire. 2. Derived from or documented by books. *See* books.
v. 1. To charge someone formally for a crime. 2. To record something in a book. 3. To reserve or schedule an appearance.
➤ *n.* album, record, register, manuscript, manual, tract, publication.
v. accuse, arrest, indict ("book the assailant"); arrange for, order, organize ("book a band for the dance"); procure, slate, engage ("book the reservation").

book account [a · *kount*] *n.* Debit and credit entries regularly made in a book kept for that purpose.

book of account [a · *kount*] *n.* A book in which transactions with customers in a store are entered. It is admissible in evidence as a **book of original entry** under the **shopbook rule** exception to the **hearsay rule** if the entries were made in the **regular course of business** at or about the time of each transaction and if they were the first permanent record of the transaction. A book of account is also known as a **shopbook**. *See* exception to the hearsay rule. *See* journal.

book of original entry [o · *rij* · i · nel en · tree] *n.* The first permanent record by a storekeeper of a transaction with a customer, made in the **regular course of business** and within a reasonably short time after the transaction took place. *See* book of account.

book value [*val* · yoo] *n.* 1. **Assets** minus **liabilities**; cost less **depreciation**; **net worth**. A corporation's book value is the difference between its assets and liabilities divided by the total number of shares of its **outstanding stock**; in other words, the value shown on its balance sheets. 2. In the used-car market, a set value for every make, model, and year.

booking [*book* · ing] *n.* A police station term for the entry of an arrest and the charge for which the arrest was made. *See* blotter.

bookkeeper [*book* · keep · er] *n.* A person who maintains financial records.
➤ accountant, clerk, examiner, inspector.

B

bookkeeping [*book* · kee · ping] *n.*
Recording, in a systematic manner, the
financial transactions of an individual or
a business.
➤ accounting, recording.

bookmaker [*book* · maik · er] *n.* A person
who makes bets for others.
➤ gambler, bookie.

bookmaking [*book* · may · king] *n.*
Receiving bets on sports events, having
calculated the odds in advance, and paying
the winners after deducting a commission.
Bookmaking is a form of gambling and is
generally illegal.

books *n. Plural* of **book**. A shorthand
term for **book(s) of account, book(s) of
original entry, books and papers, books
and records**, and, sometimes, for records.
  books and papers [*pay* · perz] *n.* An
  informal term for records. *See* paper;
  records.
  books and records [*rek* · erdz] *n.*
  Informal term for records. *See* records.
  Also see corporate records.

boom *n.* 1. A time of growth and expansion.
USAGE: "A boom in business." 2. A loud
noise.
➤ gain, growth, expansion, upsurge, spread,
development, escalation; prosperity,
expansion, advancement

boot *n.* Something given in addition to
what was bargained for, or given to make
a bargain equal. USAGE: "He offered me
only $10,000, not the $20,000 the deal
was worth; but he threw in a weekend on
the Riviera to boot."
  v. To expel or oust.
➤ *v.* kick, oust, terminate ("to boot out of
the club").

bootleg [*boot* · leg] *adj./n.* Goods made,
transported, or sold illegally, especially
liquor. *See* black market; contraband.

bootstrap sale [*boot* · strap] *n.* A tax-saving
device by which the seller converts **ordinary income** from her business into **capital
gain** from the sale of corporate stock.

booty [*boo* · tee] *n.* Loot that is seized or
taken by force.
➤ spoils, plunder, loot.

born out of wedlock [*wed* · lok] *adj.* A
term referring to a child born to an
unmarried woman or a child born to a
married woman but fathered by a man
other than her husband. *See* bastard;
illegitimate child; wedlock.

borough [*bur* · oh] *n.* 1. A geographical
territory, usually of limited population,
which has been incorporated into a governmental unit possessing some of the
powers of a town. *See* town; township.
2. Any of the five administrative units
making up New York City. EXAMPLE: the
Borough of Brooklyn.
➤ geographical territory, area, division,
zone ("the borough of Manhattan").

borrow [*bahr* · oh] *v.* 1. To ask for and
receive a loan; that is, to request and accept
from another person the possession and
use of something of value with the stated
intention of returning it, a transaction
which may be for a definite or indefinite
period of time and with or without compensation. 2. To request and accept money
from another on a temporary basis, to be
repaid with interest. *Compare* lend. 3. To
use as one's own, expecially with ideas.
➤ use, receive, solicit ("borrow money");
copy, cite, paraphrase, imitate ("to borrow
another's theory").

borrowed employee rule [*bahr* · ohd
em · *ploy* · ee] *n.* See borrowed servant
rule.

borrowed servant rule [*bahr* · ohd *ser* · vent]
n. The rule of law that if the person to
whom an employee is lent is the **master**
of the employee at the moment the
employee's negligent act takes place, the
borrower is liable for the consequences
of the act; otherwise the lender is legally
responsible. *See* servant. *Also see*
master-servant rule.

borrower [*bahr* · oh · er] *n.* A person to
whom a loan is made. *Compare* lender.

bottom land [*bot* · om] *n.* Land that a
river overflows when it floods, unless it
is protected by flood control construction.

bottomry [*bot* · om · ree] *n.* A contract
for repayment of a loan made to equip
and supply a ship.

B

bought and sold notes *n.* Two notices from a broker that a transaction occurred, one going to the buyer (the **bought note**) and the other to the seller (the **sold note**).

bound *adj. See* bind; binding.

boundary [*boun* · dree] *n.* The limit or limits of a thing, particularly land.
➤ limit, perimeter, parameter, edge, margin, border, confines.

boundary action [*ak* · shen] *n.* A lawsuit to determine the boundary between adjoining landowners. Such an action is also called a *boundary suit*.

boycott [*boy* · kot] *n.* A joining together in a refusal to do business with a company, unless it changes practices felt to be injurious to those who are joining together, or to some of them, in an attempt to bring about modification of the practice. EXAMPLES of practices which might be the subject of a boycott of a company's service or product: a health club's refusal to grant membership to women; a manufacturer's policy of having most of its labor performed abroad. *See and compare* primary boycott; secondary boycott.
v. To refuse to participate, particularly as a response to a previous action.
➤ *n.* ban, embargo, exclusion, strike, rejection.
v. spurn, reject, ignore, exclude, picket, rebuff.

bracket [*brak* · et] *n.* A grouping. *See* tax bracket.

brain death *n.* Short reference term for the view that a person is dead even if some processes of the body continue when, for at least 24 hours, there is no response to pain or other stimuli, no significant reflexes, no respiration, no blood pressure, and no electrical activity in the brain. *Compare* chronic persistent vegetative state. *See* death.

branch *n.* 1. A part, division, or department of a larger body. EXAMPLE: a **branch of government**. 2. Any division, office, chapter, or similar unit of any organization. EXAMPLE: a **branch bank**. 3. A **line of descent** from a **common ancestor**. 4. An offshoot or extension.

v. To separate into different parts or directions.
➤ *n.* part, division, department, office, chapter, unit ("the Decatur branch"); offshoot, subordinate, subsidiary.
v. split, divide, elaborate ("to branch out into different markets").

branch bank *n.* 1. An office of a bank other than its main office. 2. A bank that functions as an extension of another bank, usually in a city or state other than the city or state in which the first bank is located and entitled to do business. Some states prohibit such an arrangement.

branch of government [*guv* · ern · ment] *n.* 1. One of the three divisions into which the Constitution separates the government of the United States, specifically, the **executive branch**, the **legislative branch**, and the **judicial branch**. These branches of government are sometimes referred to as **departments of government**. 2. A similar division in state government.

brand *n.* 1. A class of goods made by the same company. 2. A characteristic or unique kind.
v. 1. To mark. 2. To label a person, generally negatively.
➤ *n.* mark, sign, trademark, insignia, symbol ("A well-known brand"); type, style, kind, variety ("his brand of humor").
v. mark, engrave, identify, label ("to brand the cow"); stigmatize, defame, expose, defile, malign, deprecate ("to brand him as a traitor").

brandish [*bran* · dish] *v.* To wave or display in an agressive or threatening manner.
➤ show, display, dangle, wield, flaunt, swing, display ("to brandish the weapon").

bravado [*bra* · *va* · do] *n.* The assumption of bravery; foolhardiness.
➤ valor, pretense, arrogance, bluster, bombast, grandiosity, self-glorification.

brave *adj.* Having courage; showing no fear.
v. To withstand or endure.
➤ *adj.* courageous, dauntless, undismayed, resolute, valiant, fearless.
v. endure, bear, confront, suffer ("brave the cold weather").

brawl *n.* A fight.
v. To fight or quarrel, usually in public.

B

> *n.* fight, altercation, riot, uproar, disturbance, commotion, mêlée, row, fracas.
> *v.* fight, scrap, wrangle, bicker, clamor, quarrel, altercate.

breach *n.* A break; a breaking; a violation; the violation of an obligation, engagement, or duty. *See* anticipatory breach; continuing breach; material breach.
> evasion, neglect, dereliction, inobservance, default, nonadherence, repudiation ("breach of contract"); split, crack, crevice, schism, fissure, opening, gap ("a breach in the wall").

breach of contract [*kon* · trakt] *n.* Failure, without **legal excuse**, to perform any promise that forms a whole or a part of a **contract**, including the doing of something inconsistent with its terms.

breach of duty [*dyoo* · tee] *n.* The failure to do that which a person is bound by law to do, or the doing of it in an unlawful manner. *See* duty.

breach of promise [*prom* · iss] *n.* 1. The failure to keep a promise. 2. A breach of promise to marry. *See* promise of marriage. *Also see* heart balm statutes.

breach of promise to marry [*prom* · iss to *mahr* · ee] *n.* *See* promise of marriage. *Also see* heart balm statutes.

breach of the peace *n.* Conduct that violates the public order or disturbs the public tranquility. *See* disorderly conduct.

breach of trust *n.* A violation of duty in a variety of **fiduciary relationships**. The term is particularly applicable to a violation of duty by a **trustee**, whether **willful, fraudulent**, or merely **negligent**.

breach of warranty [*war* · en · tee] *n.* The violation of an **express warranty** or **implied warranty**.

break *v.* 1. To void or denounce a contract so it is no longer good. 2. To fracture or divide.
n. 1. A separation or rupture. 2. A recess; a pause. 3. An opportunity.
> *v.* breach, annul, violate, defy, disregard ("break an agreement"); fracture, sever, crack, snap, chip ("break the lamp").
n. breach, tear, separation, opening, rupture ("a break in the vertebra"); recess, respite, interval, breather, lull, hiatus, interlude ("a break in the conversation");

opportunity, chance, opening, occasion ("give him a break").

breakage [*brake* · ej] *n.* Loss of or damage to goods, particularly in transit.
> loss, damage.

breaking [*brake* · ing] *n.* 1. Any substantial act done to achieve **entry** within the meaning of the crime of **burglary**. *See* breaking and entering; housebreaking. 2. A **breakage**.
v. Separating; dividing; violating; breaching.

breaking a case *n.* 1. Law enforcement officers' coming to the point of solving a crime. 2. An informal taking of positions by the judges of an **appellate court** prior to their formal decision of the case before them.

breaking a close [*kloze*] *n.* A **trespass** upon **real property**. *See* close.

breaking and entering [*en* · ter · ing] *n.* Elements of the crime of **burglary**. *See* enter; entry.

breaking bulk *n.* The crime committed by a **bailee** who opens a package or container and takes a portion; a form of the crime of **larceny**. *See* bulk.

breathalyzer [*breth* · e · ly · zer] *n.* A trade name for an **evidential breath test**.

bribe *n.* A reward given or promised to induce a public official to perform an illegal act.
v. To influence official action by **bribery**.
> *n.* payoff, offering, illegal money, graft, kickback, lure, inducement, hush money, payola, blackmail.
v. buy, buy off, lure, influence, seduce, tamper, tempt.

bribery [*bry* · be · ree] *n.* The crime of giving something of value with the intention of influencing the action of a public official.
> corruption, perfidy, allurement, cajolery, inveiglement, connivance, venality, opportunism.

brief *n.* 1. A written statement submitted to a court for the purpose of persuading it of the correctness of one's position. A brief argues the facts of the case and the applicable law, supported by **citations** of **authority**. 2. A text that an attorney

prepares to guide her in the trial of a case. Called a *trial brief,* it can include lists of questions to be asked of various witnesses, points to be covered, and arguments to be made. 3. An outline of the published opinion in a case, made by an attorney or a paralegal for the purpose of understanding the case. 4. Short; concise; over quickly.
adj. 1. Short; succinct. 2. Fast, quick.
v. To inform a person about the facts of a situation.
➤ *n.* legal argument; summary, abstract, digest, outline, synopsis, review, abridgement, restatement.
adj. short, concise, succinct, pithy, curt, terse, hasty ("a brief review of the facts"); quick, fast, swift, hasty, temporary, momentary ("a brief visit").
v. advise, prepare, orient, inform, apprise, update ("Please brief me on this situation").

bringing action [*bring · ing ak · shen*] *n.* Same as **bringing suit**.

bringing suit [*bring · ing*] *n.* Beginning a lawsuit by filing papers that will result in the court's issuing **process** compelling the defendant to appear in court.

brink *n.* The edge or border of something.
➤ border, verge, boundary, edge, periphery, threshold ("on the brink of a major breakthrough in the case").

broad *adj.* Wide; expansive; tolerant; not narrow.
➤ wide, extensive, far-reaching, universal, large, unlimited, widespread ("broad appeal"); clear, apparent, evident, glaring, pronounced ("a broad hint").
  broad construction [*kon · struk · shen*] *n.* 1. The **construction** of a statute or other writing in a way that overlooks minor objections and trivial technicalities. 2. An interpretation of a constitutional provision, statute, ordinance, or other law that carries out its "true intent" or "spirit." USAGE: "It is legal to say and print most things, even if the majority of people disapproves, because the Supreme Court gives a broad construction to the **First Amendment**." *Compare* interpretation.

broadside objection [*brod · side ob · jek · shen*] *n.* An objection to

evidence on the general grounds of **incompetency, immateriality**, and **irrelevancy**, without specifying the grounds more particularly. Although used frequently in fiction, a broadside objection is generally not effective because it is too vague.

brocage [*broh · kej*] *n.* Same as **brokerage**.

broker [*broh · ker*] *n.* A person whose business is to bring buyer and seller together; an agent who, for a commission, negotiates on behalf of his principal in connection with entering into contracts or buying and selling any kind of property. As distinguished from a **factor**, a broker does not generally take possession of the property with respect to which he deals. *See* insurance broker; pawnbroker; real estate broker; securities broker.
➤ agent, middleman, proxy, representative, emissary, mediator, intermediary.

brokerage [*broh · ker · ej*] *n.* 1. The business of a **broker**. 2. A broker's commission.

brothel [*broth · el*] *n.* A house of prostitution.
➤ house of prostitution, whorehouse, bordello, parlor house, house of ill repute.

browbeat [*brow · beet*] *v.* To intimidate by using a domineering manner of speech.
➤ badger, bully, intimidate, harass, humiliate, tyrannize, domineer, oppress.

Brown v. Board of Education *n.* The Supreme Court's landmark 1954 decision, 347 U.S. 483, which declared that racial segregation in public schools violates the **equal protection clause** of the **Fourteenth Amendment**. *See* separate but equal. This case was argued by Thurgood Marshall, who later became the first black appointee to the Supreme Court.

browse *v.* To look over casually.
➤ scan, peruse, skim, survey, read, glance at.

brutal [*brew · tul*] *adj.* Ruthless or unfeeling.
➤ cruel, harsh, heartless, rough, uncivil, savage, vicious, severe, violent, ruthless.

brutality [*brew · tal · i · tee*] *n.* Severe treatment; cruelty.

B

➤ cruelty, inhumanity, violence, truculence, savagery, fierceness, ferocity, sadism, atrocity.

bubble [*bub* · l] *n.* A dishonest investment conceived by dishonest persons to defraud the investors.

bucket shop [*buk* · et] *n.* A sham brokerage where money is paid for the purchase of **commodities** or **securities** but orders to buy are never actually carried out.

budget [*bud* · jet] *n.* A projection of the revenues to be received and the expenses to be incurred in conducting a business or in the operations of a governmental body during a given period. *See and compare* capital budget; operating budget. *v.* To allocate expenditures in accordance with a plan.
➤ *n.* allotment, share, quota, account, statement, blueprint, allocation, allowance, reserve.
v. allocate, apportion, distribute, estimate.

bug *n.* 1. A disease-producing germ. 2. Insects or other pests. 3. Concealed surveillance.
v. 1. To survey unbeknownst to another person. 2. To disturb or annoy another.
➤ *n.* disease, germ, infection, virus; insect, pest, vermin; craze, obsession, mania, enthusiasm, rage; surveillance, monitor, device.
v. wiretap, monitor, spy, snoop, eavesdrop; bother, annoy, irk, irritate, disturb, pester.

buggery [*bug* · er · ee] *n.* Another term for the crime of **sodomy**. *See also* bestiality; crime against nature.
➤ sodomy, bestiality.

build *v.* 1. To expand upon or develop. 2. To construct or conceive.
➤ increase, accelerate, expand, enlarge, develop ("build a medical practice"); construct, engineer, produce, form, make, erect, create ("build a bridge").

builder [*bild* · er] *n.* A person who constructs or makes things.
➤ developer, owner, maker, manufacturer, architect, fabricator, crafter.

building [*bild* · ing] *n.* A permanent structure.

➤ structure, dwelling, construction, premises, edifice, home, house ("a beautiful building").

building and loan association [*bil* · ding and loan a · so · see · ay · shen] *n.* An organization of people cooperating by creating a common fund which may be loaned to any member for the purpose of building on property or purchasing property in order to build on it. A building and loan is not a **commercial bank**, and in most jurisdictions it is not classified as a **savings bank**, although in some states it constitutes a form of **savings and loan association** and is permitted to perform some banking functions.

building code [*bil* · ding] *n.* Standards, particularly relating to health and safety, prescribed by state statute or local ordinance, that must be followed in the construction of a building or other structure. Sometimes referred to as "code," as in "The wiring must be up to code."

building lines [*bil* · ding] *n.* Boundaries established by statute or ordinance, for reasons of public safety and health as well as tasteful effect, whose purpose is to provide open space between the buildings on a street and the street itself. Such lines are also known as **setback lines** or, simply, **setbacks**.

bulk *n.* 1. A quantity of unpackaged goods or cargo. 2. Unbroken packages. *See* in bulk. *Also see* breaking bulk. 3. The greater part; the largest or principal portion.
➤ size, mass, volume, substance ("a great amount of bulk"); majority, most, best, preponderance, lion's share ("I did the bulk of the work").

bulk mortgage [*more* · gej] *n.* A **mortgage** on goods **in bulk**.

bulk sale *n.* The transfer of a large portion of a business's inventory or supplies, not in the **ordinary course of business**. Bulk sales and other **bulk transfers** are regulated by the **Uniform Commercial Code** to protect creditors.

bulk sales acts *n.* State statutes intended to protect creditors against unregulated **bulk sales**. Such statutes have been replaced by the **Uniform Commercial Code**.

bulk transfer [*tranz* · fer] *n.* *See* bulk sale.

bull market [*mar* · ket] *n.* The stock market when the value of **securities** being traded is rising. *Compare* bear market.

bulletin [*bul* · et · in] *n.* 1. A published official report which contains material such as, for EXAMPLE, regulations issued by administrative agencies. 2. An announcement; a dispatch; a notification.
➤ announcement, dispatch, notification, statement, report, information, publication, release, news flash.

bullion [*bull* · yon] *n.* Gold or silver that has not yet been made into coins.

bumping [*bump* · ing] *n.* Occurs when an employee with greater seniority takes the job of an employee with less seniority during a layoff.

bunco [*bunk* · o] *n.* A swindle or fraud. *See* swindling.

bundle [*bun* · dil] *n.* 1. A grouping or collection. 2. A package to be mailed or shipped.
➤ collection, cluster, group, pile, assortment, array, package, box, parcel.

burden [*ber* · den] *n.* 1. Obligation; duty; responsibility. 2. Costs; expenditures; expenses.
v. To encumber; to strain.
➤ *n.* duty, obligation, responsibility, charge, requirement ("the burden of proof"); stress, hardship, strain, weight, grievance, difficulty, concern, worry ("a heavy burden").
v. encumber, strain, saddle with, afflict, oppress, impede, make responsible for ("I hate to burden you with this new assignment.").

burden of evidence [*ev* · i · denss] *n.* Same as **burden of going forward**.

burden of going forward [*goh* · ing *fore* · werd] *n.* The duty of a **party**, with respect to certain issues being tried, to produce evidence sufficient to justify a verdict before the other party is obligated to produce evidence to the contrary. This burden is also referred to as the **burden of evidence, the burden of proceeding,**

and the **burden of producing evidence**. The burden of going forward may shift back and forth between the parties during the course of a trial. *Compare* burden of proof. *See* prima facie case.

burden of persuasion [per · *sway* · zhen] *n.* The ultimate **burden of proof**; the responsibility of convincing the jury, or, in a **nonjury trial**, the judge, of the truth.

burden of proceeding [pro · *seed* · ing] *n.* Same as **burden of going forward**.

burden of producing evidence [pro · *dewss* · ing *ev* · i · denss] *n.* Same as **burden of going forward**.

burden of proof *n.* The duty of establishing the truth of a matter; the duty of proving a fact that is in dispute. In most instances the burden of proof, like the **burden of going forward**, shifts from one side to the other during the course of a trial as the case progresses and evidence is introduced by each side. *See* shifting the burden of proof. *See also* prima facie case; beyond a reasonable doubt; preponderance of the evidence.

bureau [*byoo* · roh] *n.* A subdivision of a **department of government**. EXAMPLES: the **Federal Bureau of Investigation** is within the Justice Department; the **Bureau of the Census** is within the Commerce Department; the **Bureau of Indian Affairs** is within the Interior Department.
➤ division, branch, office, department, ministry, board, authority ("the Bureau of Indian Affairs").

Bureau of Indian Affairs [*byoo* · roh of *in* · dee · en a · *fairz*] *n.* The agency of the federal government with responsibility for Indian affairs and for dealings between Native Americans and the government. The **BIA**, as it is referred to, is a **bureau** of the Interior Department. *See and compare* Indian; Native American. *Also see* Administration for Native Americans.

Bureau of Land Management (BLM) [*byoo* · roh of land *man* · ej · ment] *n.* The federal agency responsible for management of the more than 270 million acres of U.S. **public lands**, as well as the resources on and under the land, including timber, minerals, oil, gas, wildlife, and vegetation. *See* bureau.

Bureau of the Census [*byoo* · roh of the *sen* · sus] *n.* The official name of the **census bureau**.

bureaucracy [byoo · *rok* · re · see] *n.* The operation of government by **bureaus** and **departments** directed by levels of officials rigidly following rules and routines.
➤ administration, management, system; red tape, rules, regulations, forms.

Burford doctrine [*ber* · ferd *dok* · trin] *n.* A judicial doctrine under which federal courts generally decline to intervene in cases involving complicated state administrative regulations.

burglar [*ber* · gler] *n.* A person guilty of the crime of **burglary**.
➤ robber, thief, prowler, looter, felon, trespasser, marauder, criminal, pilferer.

burglary [*ber* · gler · ee] *n.* At **common law**, the offense of **breaking and entering** a dwelling at night with the **intent to commit a felony** (EXAMPLES: theft; murder). The crime of burglary has been broadened by statute to include entering buildings other than dwellings, with or without a breaking, and regardless of the time of day or night.
➤ robbery, larceny, breaking and entering, housebreaking, looting, crime, forcible entry, raiding, marauding.

burglary tools *n.* Tools or implements that can be adapted for use in cutting through or breaking open a building, room, safe, or the like. (EXAMPLES: a drill; a crowbar; a sledgehammer.) Possession of such tools is a criminal offense if they are possessed with the intention of using them for the purpose of **burglary**.

burial [*ber* · i · al] *n.* 1. A grave or tomb. 2. The act of burying.
➤ interment, funeral, sepulcher, entombment; hiding, shrouding, cover-up, concealment.

burn *v.* 1. To be on fire; to set on fire. 2. To be excited about; to be aroused or inflamed. 3. To cheat.
➤ incinerate, kindle, ignite, inflame, consume, glow, heat, flame, char; yearn, bristle, fume,

lust, be aroused, smoulder; deceive, defraud, bilk, chisel, take, swindle, gyp.

bursar [*bur* · ser] *n.* 1. The treasurer of a college. 2. A ship's **purser**.

bury *v.* 1. To conceal or cover. 2. To put to rest after death.
➤ conceal, cloak, hide, cover, shroud, stash; entomb, inter, inhume, lay to rest, embalm.

business [*biz* · ness] *n.* The work in which a person is regularly or usually engaged and from which she makes a living.
➤ trade, occupation, calling, activity, profession, field ("the cosmetology business"); concern, affair, responsibility, duty, interest, matter ("It's not your business"); commerce, manufacture, industry, intercourse, dealings ("doing business").

business agent [*ay* · jent] *n.* 1. A representative of a labor union engaged in dealing on behalf of the union. 2. An **agent** managing the business of his **principal**.

business corporation [kore · per · *ay* · shen] *n.* An ordinary corporation; a commercial corporation; a **for-profit corporation**. *Compare* nonprofit corporation. *See* corporation.

business day *n.* 1. Any day of the year except Sundays and holidays. 2. Any day of the year on which a given business regularly does business, usually Monday through Friday or Monday through Saturday. *Compare* calendar days.

business entry [*en* · tree] *n. See* book of account; book of original entry.

business entry rule [*en* · tree] *n. See* business records rule.

business expenses [eks · *pen* · sez] *n.* Expenses that are deductible from income for tax purposes, if ordinarily and necessarily incurred in operating a trade or business. *See* ordinary and necessary expense.

business guest *n. See* business invitee.

business insurance [in · *shoor* · ense] *n.* Same as **key man insurance**.

business interruption insurance [in · ter · *up* · shen in · *shoor* · ense] *n.* Insurance protecting against **loss** from the interruption of business, as distinguished from coverage upon merchandise or other property used in the business. *See* insurance.

business invitee [in · vy · *tee*] *n.* A person who comes upon premises at the invitation of the occupant, and who has business to transact. If a business invitee is injured as a result of some hazard on the premises, she is more likely to be able to hold the owner or occupant responsible at law than would a social guest or a **trespasser**. *Also compare* licensee. *See* invitee.

business judgment rule [*juj* · ment] *n.* The principle that courts should be reluctant to second-guess the decisions of corporate directors, even if those decisions are not in the best interests of the stockholders, as long as the decisions are within the power of the directors to make.

business license [*ly* · sense] *n.* A license granted by a city, town, or state, granting permission to a business to do business. *See* license.

business name *n.* The name under which a business is operated. In the case of an individual, it may be his real name or a fictitious name. *See* DBA; fictitious name.

business records [*rek* · erdz] *n.* A **book of original entry**; a **book of account**; all records kept in the **ordinary course of business**.

business records rule [*rek* · erdz] *n.* An **exception to the hearsay rule** which permits **business records** to be admitted into evidence even though they are **hearsay**.

business reorganization *n. See* bankruptcy.

business trust *n.* A corporation-like business organization in the form of a **trust**. It is also known as a **Massachusetts trust, Massachusetts business trust**, or **common law trust**. *See* corporation.

business visitor [*viz* · i · ter] *n. See* business invitee.

but-for rule *n.* A rule of **tort** law, now largely discarded, used to determine whether a defendant is legally responsible for a plaintiff's injuries. USAGE: "But for the driver's negligence, that pedestrian would not have been hurt." *See* proximate cause.

buttress [*but* · ress] *n.* To support or bolster.
➤ support, bolster, carry, uphold, strengthen, sustain, brace, shore up.

buy *n.* An item of value at a good price.
v. 1. To acquire possession; to purchase.
2. To bribe, induce, or influence.
➤ *n.* acquisition, deal, purchase, bargain ("a good buy").
v. purchase, obtain, procure, secure, acquire; bribe, corrupt, fix, palm, hire, pay off.

buy and sell agreement [a · *gree* · ment] *n.* A contract among partners or owners of a business which provides that if one wishes to leave the business, or dies, the others will buy her interest or merge it into their own interests in accordance with an agreed plan.

buyer [*by* · er] *n.* One who makes a purchase.
➤ purchaser, customer, client, consumer, user, vendee, patron, investor.
Ant. seller.

buyer in the ordinary course of business [*or* · din · e · ree corse of *biz* · nes] *n.* An important term in commercial transactions, defined by the **Uniform Commercial Code** as a person who buys goods in good faith and without knowledge that the sale violates the ownership rights or **security interest** of a third party. *See* bona fide purchaser; good faith purchaser.

by *prep.* 1. Through the act of. Signing a contract, **bill**, **note**, or other instrument with the name of the **principal**, followed by that of the **agent,** separated by the word "by," is a method of placing liability upon the principal and of avoiding **personal liability** for the agent. EXAMPLE: "John Jones, by Mary Smith." *Also see* for.
2. At or near a designated place or time.
3. In accordance with; under the authority of. 4. Because of; by reason of.

by law In accordance with law.

by operation of law [op · er · *ay* · shen] *See* operation of law.

by reason of [*ree* · zen] Because of.

by virtue of [*ver* · choo] By authority of; by reason of; by power of.

B

by-bidding [by-bid · ing] *n./v.* The making of sham bids at an auction for the purpose of inflating the final bid.

by-laws [by-lawz] *n.* 1. Rules and regulations created by corporations, **associations**, clubs, and societies for their governance. 2. In some municipalities, a synonym for ordinances. *Compare* charter.

bylaw [*bi* · law] *n.* A regulation adopted by a group or organization.

➤ rule, regulation, ordinance, order, canon, standard.

bystander [*bi* · stand · er] *n.* A person not directly involved in something; an observer.

➤ spectator, observer, witness, passer-by, eyewitness, nonparticipant, viewer, attestant, onlooker.

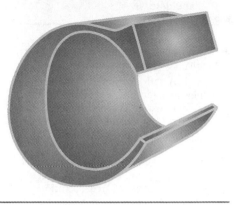

c A symbol for **copyright** when enclosed within a circle ©.

C corporation [see kore · per · *ay* · shen] *n.* Under the **Internal Revenue Code**, a **corporation** that has not elected **S corporation** status. Its income is taxed at the corporate level, its **dividends** at the shareholder level. *Compare* S corporation.

c.o. Abbreviation of **conscientious objector**; abbreviation of commanding officer.

c/o Abbreviation of care of.

CA Abbreviation of **Court of Appeals**. Also abbreviated C.A. or Ct. App.

ca Abbreviation of the Latin word *circa*, meaning "about." Often used with dates. USAGE: "ca. 1492."

cabinet [*kab* · i · net] *n.* A group of officials forming an advisory council to a head of government. The most notable is the Cabinet of the President of the United States, which consists of the heads of the most important departments of the federal government, including the Secretary of State, the Secretary of Defense, and the Attorney General.
➤ council, assembly, panel; closet, depository.
  cabinet officer [*off* · i · ser] *n.* A member of a cabinet.

cache [kash] *n.* 1. A hiding place. 2. A secure storage place.
➤ shelter, refuge, confinement; safe, repository, storehouse, warehouse.

cadaver [ka · *da* · ver] *n.* A corpse; a dead body.

caducary [ka · *doo* · ka · ree] *adj.* Relating to or subject to **escheat** or **forfeiture** of property.

CAF Abbreviation of **cost and freight**.

calamity [ka · *lam* · itee] *n.* A state of distress or misery; a disaster.
➤ disaster, cataclysm, misfortune, adversity.

calendar [*kal* · en · der] *n.* A list of cases ready for the court to dispose of, whether by trial or otherwise; a **court calendar**. A court calendar is also referred to as a **docket**. *See* trial calendar.
➤ diary, journal, register, schedule, lineup, program, chronology.

  calendar call *n.* The reading aloud of the calendar in court, to determine whether the cases listed are ready for trial or to set trial dates.

  calendar days *n.* Consecutive days, including Saturdays, Sundays, and holidays. *Compare* business day. *See* day.

  calendar month *n.* A month according to the calendar, i.e., a month computed not by counting 30 days, but by referring to the calendar for the month, regardless of the number of days it may contain. EXAMPLE: February, March, and April are calendar months although, of the three, only April has 30 days. *Compare* lunar month. *See* month.

  calendar year *n.* The period from January 1 through December 31. *Compare* civil year; fiscal year; tax year. *See* year.

caliber [*kal* · i · ber] *n.* Ability; status.

C

➤ quality, status, capability, eminence; ability, faculty, competence, acumen.

call *n.* 1. A notice of meeting or other gathering; a request to assemble or be present. EXAMPLE: a **calendar call**. 2. A demand for payment. EXAMPLES: a demand on a person who has **subscribed** to stock in a corporation (*see* subscribed stock) for an additional contribution to the **capital** of the corporation; an **assessment** made upon the members of an **association** or club. 3. An **option** to purchase **commodities** or stock or other securities at a given price within a specified period of time. *Compare* put. *See also* futures; futures contract. 4. A reference in a **legal description** of real estate (in a deed, for EXAMPLE) to natural objects, or other markers or **monuments**, which establish the boundaries of the property. *See* metes and bounds.
   v. 1. To address; to contact. 2. To summon.
➤ *n.* address, plea, bid, cry, entreaty ("the call for help was clear"); option, choice, alternative ("the right of put and call").
   v. command, order, invite, require, summon ("call to court for an appearance"); name, label, identify, designate, term ("call his speech defamation").

call option [*op* · shen] *n. See* call.

call premium [*pree* · mee · um] *n.* An extra sum, over and above **par value**, which a company must pay when it calls its **bonds** for **redemption** before **maturity**. *See* callable bonds.

call price *n.* The price at which a **callable bond** may be called or redeemed by its issuer. *See* redemption.

call-in pay [*kol*-in] *n.* Pay to which an employee is entitled when she is called in to work and no work is available.

callable [*kol* · abl] *adj.* That which is liable to **call**. EXAMPLES: a meeting; an **assessment**; a **bond**.
➤ redeemable, retrievable, reclaimable ("a callable bond").

callable bond *n.* A **bond**, also called a **redeemable bond**, that may be called for payment before its **maturity**. *See* call.

called meeting [*meet* · ing] *n.* A **special meeting** of an organization, held upon **notice**.

calumny [*kal* · um · nee] *n.* **Slander**; **defamation**; a false and malicious statement.
➤ slander, defamation, libel, vituperation, opprobrium, debasement.

cambist [*kam* · bist] *n.* A dealer in **negotiable paper**; a broker.
➤ dealer, broker.

camera [*kam* · e · ra] *n.* Room; chambers. *See* in camera.

camouflage [*kam* · uh · flazh] *v.* To disguise for the purposes of deception and avoiding identfication.
➤ conceal, cover up, embellish, obfuscate, disguise.

cancel [*kan* · sel] *v.* 1. To annul or set aside. 2. To strike out or strike through. 3. To terminate or revoke.
➤ call off, rub out, repeal, overthrow, annul, set aside, abrogate, rescind, quash, drop.

cancellation [kan · sel · *ay* · shen] *n.* 1. An erasure, blotting out, striking out, or crossing out of some portion of a written document or instrument. 2. The act of a **party** to a contract ending the contract after the other party has been guilty of **breach of contract**. Cancellation should be contrasted with **termination**, which provides the party ending the contract with fewer **remedies**.
➤ abandonment, reversal, recall, nullification, erasure, revocation, termination, withdrawal, rescission ("cancellation of the ethics committee meetings").

cancellation clause *n.* A provision in a contract that allows the parties to cancel the contract without obligation. *See* escape clause.

candid [*kan* · did] *adj.* Free from bias or malice; open; staightforward; honest.
➤ open, sincere, honest, straightforward, ingenuous, objective, genuine, frank, impartial ("to give a candid assessment").

candidate [*kan* · di · date] *n.* 1. A person who seeks office and who, in the case of a public office to be filled by election, has taken the steps required by the election law to have her name presented at the election so that the voters may vote for her. 2. A person who, after having been nominated, is presented to the voters at an election. *Compare* incumbent.

➤ bidder, suitor, seeker, job-hunter, nominee, contender.

cannabis [*kan* · e · bis] *n.* Short for **cannabis sativa**.

cannabis sativa [se · *tee* · va] *n.* Hemp; marijuana; hashish. These substances are illegal.

canon [*kan* · on] *n.* A law or rule.

➤ law, rule, statute, act, code, order; standard, criterion, measure, ethic, norm, test.

canon law *n.* Christian religious law, particularly that of the Roman Catholic church.

canonical disability [kan · *on* · ikl dis · a · *bil* · i · tee] *n.* **Defects** in personal relationships which, under **canon law**, allow the **annulment** of a marriage. EXAMPLES: impotence; a blood relationship between spouses (**consanguinity**). *Compare* civil disability.

canons of ethics [*kan* · onz of *eth* · iks] *n. See* Code of Judicial Conduct; Rules of Professional Conduct. *Also see* ethics.

canvass [*kan* · vess] *v.* 1. To solicit door-to-door or by telephone; to survey. EXAMPLES: taking orders for a product; making marketing surveys; appealing for votes for a political candidate. 2. To examine or review. EXAMPLE: recounting or validating the ballots cast in an election.

➤ solicit, survey, petition ("canvass the neighborhood"); examine, review, scrutinize, audit, probe, dissect ("canvass the ballots").

capable [*kape* · uh · bul] *adj.* Having a high level of ability or skill.

➤ effective, qualified, skilled, able, proficient, accomplished, efficient ("a capable soldier").

capacity [ke · *pass* · i · tee] *n.*
1. **Competency** in law. USAGE: "Generally, a minor does not have the capacity to enter into contracts." *See* legal capacity; mental capacity; testamentary capacity.
2. A person's ability to understand the nature and effect of the act in which he is engaged. USAGE: "Since he knows no English, he doesn't have the capacity to understand the contract." 3. The status in

which a person acts. USAGE: "When she agreed to buy the car, was she acting in her capacity as Bill's agent or was she acting for herself?" *See* criminal capacity; fiduciary capacity. 4. Ability or capability generally. USAGE: "Does Argentina have the capacity to respond to an attack by Brazil?" *See* earning capacity. 5. Available space. USAGE: "What is the cargo capacity of this ship?"

➤ competency, ability, capability, license, right ("capacity to contract"); skill, talent, ability, caliber, stature, capability ("a debater of great capacity"); position, duty, responsibility, job ("her capacity as warden").

capias [*kay* · pee · es] *(Latin) n.* Means "seize" or "take." A **writ** issued by a court directing the sheriff or marshal to take a defendant into custody and bring him before the court for a stated purpose.

capias ad respondendum [ad res · pon · *den* · dum] *adj./n.* "Seize for a response." A **writ** directing that a defendant in a civil action be produced in court on a specified day. *See* civil arrest.

capias ad satisfaciendum [ad sa · tis · fay · she · *en* · dum] *adj./n.* "Seize for satisfaction." A **writ** commanding that a **judgment debtor** be brought before the court to satisfy a debt. *See* civil arrest.

capias pro fine [pro *feen*] *adj./n.* "Seize for the fine." A **writ** to bring before the court a person who has not paid a fine imposed upon her.

capita [*ka* · pi · ta] *(Latin) n.* Means "heads"; "persons." *See* per capita.

➤ head, each.

capital [*ka* · pi · tel] *adj.* 1. Relating to wealth, **capital assets**, or capital. *See* capital. 2. Pertaining to loss of life. 3. Chief; most important; highest; major. *Note* that "capital" is not "**capitol**." *n.* 1. Wealth; **assets**. 2. Broadly, the total assets of a business. 3. Money or property used for the production of wealth. 4. That portion of the assets of a corporation used for conduct of the corporate business and for the purpose of creating profit. *See* authorized capital stock; floating capital; legal capital; stated capital. 5. An owner's **equity** in a business. 6. The city in which

C

a state's legislature meets. *Note* that "capital" is not "**capitol**." *See* seat; seat of government.

➤ *adj.* basic, outstanding, prime, vital, chief, primary, principal, cardinal, leading, controlling.

n. cash, stock, wealth, holdings, financial assets, funds, resources, principal.

capital assets [*ass* · ets] *n.* All **assets** except those excluded from that category by the **Internal Revenue Code**.

capital budget [*bud* · jet] *n.* 1. Portion of a budget devoted to a business's long-term assets (EXAMPLES: the physical plant; machinery; equipment). 2. A separate budget devoted to that purpose. *Compare* operating budget. *See* light.

capital case *n.* A case involving a **capital crime**.

capital crime *n.* A crime punishable by death.

capital equipment [ee · *kwip* · ment] *n.* Items used by a business to manufacture its product. EXAMPLE: machinery; equipment.

capital expenditures [eks · *pen* · di · choorz] *n.* Funds spent to purchase or improve **capital assets**.

capital gain *n.* Financial gain resulting from the **sale or exchange** of **capital assets**. *Compare* ordinary income. *See* gain.

capital gains tax *n.* Income tax upon financial gain resulting from the **sale or exchange** of **capital assets**. *See* gain.

capital goods *n. See* capital equipment.

capital loss *n.* For income tax purposes, a loss resulting from the **sale or exchange** of **capital assets**. *See* loss.

capital offense [o · *fense*] *n.* Same as **capital crime**.

capital punishment [*pun* · ish · ment] *n.* The death penalty as a punishment for crime.

capital stock *n.* 1. The shares of **stock** issued by a corporation. *See also* common stock. 2. The total wealth of a corporation, less its liabilities and obligations. 3. The maximum amount of stock that a corporation is authorized to issue. *See* authorized capital stock.

capital stock tax *n.* A tax on a corporation, for the privilege of doing business,

which is based upon the value of its **capital stock**.

capital structure [*struk* · cher] *n.* The relationship between the various types of indebtedness of a corporation. *See* capitalization; capitalization ratio.

capital surplus [*ser* · plus] *n.* Such **surplus** as a **corporation** may have over and above its **earned surplus**. *See also* accumulated surplus.

capitalism [*kap* · i · tel · izm] *n.* An economic system in which production (manufacturing, agriculture) and distribution (transportation) are privately owned and carried on for profit. *Compare* communism; fascism; socialism.

➤ free market economy, private enterprise, democracy, competition.

capitalization [kap · i · ta · li · *zay* · shen] *n.* The total value of the stocks, **bonds**, and other securities issued by a corporation. *See* capital structure.

capitalization ratio [*ray* · shee · o] *n.* The proportionate relationship of the value of each of the various types of **securities** issued by a corporation to the total value of its securities.

capitalize [*kap* · i · ta · lize] *v.* 1. To compute **periodic payments** on the basis of their value as money in hand; to convert future periodic payments into one present lump sum based upon their present value. *See* commuted value. 2. To provide **capital** for a business. 3. To take advantage of.

➤ exploit, gain, take advantage of, profit from, obtain; finance, subsidize, support.

capitation tax [kap · i · *tay* · shen] *n.* A direct tax imposed upon a person without regard to her income, **assets**, business, profession, or the like; a tax imposed at a **flat rate**.

capitol [*kap* · i · tel] *n.* The building in which a state legislature meets. *Note* that "capitol" is not "**capital**."

➤ statehouse, dome, center.

capitulary [ka · *pit* · yoo · lar · ee] *n.* A collection of laws. *See* code.

capricious [ka · *prish* · ess] *adj.* Changeable in purpose without reason; based upon whim or impulse rather than upon fact or law; arbitrary. *See* arbitrary and capricious.

➤ careless, impulsive, moody, arbitrary, whimsical, unreasonable, frivolous, flighty.

capriciously [ka · *prish* · ess · lee] *adv.* Impulsively; carelessly; in a **capricious** manner.

caption [*kap* · shen] *n.* 1. A taking or seizing. 2. A heading. As applied in legal practice, when "caption" is used to mean "heading," it generally refers to the heading of a court paper. EXAMPLE:

Miriam Brown	)	In the Court of Common
Plaintiff	)	Pleas of Bucks County,
	)	Pennsylvania
v.	)	Stanley Brown
	)	Civil Action No. 1234
Defendant	)	September Term, 1994

➤ heading, title, inscription ("the caption of the case").

captive [*kap* · tiv] *n.* A person who is being held against his or her will by force.

➤ hostage, pawn, prisoner, convict, subject ("held as a captive").

captivity [*kap* · tiv · i · tee] *n.* The state or condition of being a captive.

➤ bondage, custody, confinement, imprisonment, impoundment, internment.

car jacking [*kar* · jak · ing] *n.* **Larceny** of an automobile with the driver in it. *Compare* auto theft.

cardinal [*kar* · dih · nul] *adj.* 1. Essential; basic. 2. Important; key; main.

➤ basic, central, main, material, vital, rudimentary; dominant, outstanding, leading, prime, supreme, unparalleled, paramount, predominant.

care *n.* 1. Custody; safekeeping. 2. Attention; awareness; caution. Care is a word of variable and relative meaning that must always be interpreted in the context in which it appears. It is extremely important as a standard for determining **negligence**, in which context it always relates to the level of care that the law requires in the circumstances. *See and compare* due care; extraordinary care; great care; ordinary care; reasonable care; slight care.

v. 1. To give emotional weight to. 2. To nurture and support.

➤ *n.* custody, safekeeping, interest, regard, attention, awareness, caution.
v. beware, be cautious, guard; foster, nurture, watch, support, supervise.

careless [*kare* · less] *adj.* Heedless; negligent. Although in ordinary USAGE "careless" means "negligent," unlike "negligent," the word "careless" has no specific meaning for lawyers. Accordingly, "careless" should never be used in **pleadings** in place of "negligent." *See* negligent.

➤ unthinking, oblivious, unwary, heedless, unattentive, lax, casual, negligent.

caretaker [*kare* · tay · ker] *n.* A person who takes care of or maintains something.

➤ attendant, guardian, curator, warden; officeholder, administrator, superintendent.

carnal [*kahr* · nel] *adj.* Sensual; lustful.

➤ erotic, vulgar, worldly, sensual, lustful, fleshly, wanton.

carnal abuse [a · *byooss*] *n.* An unconsented-to sexual act that does not involve penetration. *Compare* carnal knowledge.

carnal knowledge [*naw* · ledj] *n.* Sexual intercourse; a sexual act involving penetration. *Compare* carnal abuse.

carriage [*kar* · ij] *n.* 1. Transportation of freight or passengers. 2. A person or animal's way of holding itself.

➤ posture, pace, demeanor, appearance, deportment ("her confident carriage"); transport, transportation, portage, shipment ("the carriage of goods").

carrier [*kar* · yer] *n.* 1. A transporter of passengers or freight. *See* common carrier; contract carrier; private carrier. 2. An insurance company. *See* insurance carrier. 3. A person or animal that carries or transmits a disease but is itself immune to the disease. *See* quarantine.

➤ runner, transporter, bearer, messenger ("a carrier for hire"); transmitter, possessor ("a carrier of tuberculosis").

carrier for hire *n.* A **private carrier** or a **common carrier** that charges for transportation.

C

carrier's lien [*kahr* · ee · erz leen] *n.* The **lien** of a carrier upon goods shipped, for the charges of transportation and storage.

carry [*kar* · ee] *v.* 1. To maintain on one's books as a debtor. USAGE: "The finance company said they would carry me for two months if I got laid off." 2. To transport. *See* carrier.
➤ achieve, attain, gain, prevail ("carry the day"); transport, move, haul, bring ("carry the packages").

carryback [*kar* · ee · bak] *n.* An income tax term for applying a **loss** occurring during one year in the recomputation of tax for an earlier year so as to reduce the earlier tax liability. *Compare* carryover.

carrying charge [*kar* · ee · ing *charj*] *n.* The charge included in an **installment sale contract** for the privilege of paying in installments. Such charges are in addition to interest and charges for the cost of **collection** and insurance. *See also* finance charge. USAGE: "How much are the carrying charges on this loan?"

carryover [*kar* · ee · oh · ver] *n.* An income tax term for applying a **loss** occurring during one year as a deduction in a later year. *Compare* carryback.

cartage [*kahr* · tej] *n.* 1. The act of transporting property. 2. The charges for transporting property.

carte blanche [kart *blonsh*] *n.* 1. The freedom to act in a situation as one thinks best, without restriction. 2. A blank card.
➤ freedom, unlimited authority, permit, sanction, free rein, power, discretion.

cartel [*kar* · tel] *n.* An association of industrial or financial interests that exists for the purpose of fixing prices, creating a **monopoly**, or cornering a market. A cartel is also referred to as a **trust**. *See* trust. *Also see* price-fixing.
➤ syndicate, coalition, association, consortium, block ("the oil cartel"); agreement, accord, bargain, deal ("the cartel with neighboring countries").

carter [*kar* · ter] *n.* A person or company that transports property; a **carrier**.

case *n.* 1. A contested question in a court of justice; a lawsuit; an **action**; a **legal action**;

a **cause of action**. 2. The written opinion of a judge or court deciding or commenting on a lawsuit. 3. An extinct form of legal action (more commonly known as an **action on the case** or **trespass on the case**), brought for **injury** resulting from a wrongful act other than the wrongful use of physical force.
➤ action, lawsuit, litigation, controversy, dispute, proceeding ("the case of *Roe v. Wade*"); example, instance, paradigm, illustration ("a case of mistaken identity"); thesis, reasoning, position, side, evidence, hypothesis ("We stated our case well").

case agreed [a · *greed*] *n.* Same as **agreed case**.

case and controversy [*kon* · tro · ver · see] *n. See* case or controversy.

case in chief *n.* Portion of a **party's** evidence that he produces at trial in support of his case, as opposed to evidence he may produce to counter his opponent's case. USAGE: "The opportunity to commit the crime is an element of our case in chief."

case in point *n.* 1. A **precedent**. USAGE: "I've been told there are a number of decisions supporting my client's position, but my research hasn't located a single case in point." *See also* on point. 2. An example. USAGE: "Of course some gases are lighter than air: helium and hydrogen are cases in point."

case law *n.* The law as laid down in the decisions of the courts in similar cases that have previously been decided. *See* common law. *Compare* statutory law.

case method [*meth* · ed] *n.* The method for the study of law most used in the United States; it is based upon analysis of the opinions written by judges and justices in actual cases. Also called the *case system.*

case of first impression [im · *presh* · en] *n. See* first impression.

case or controversy [*kon* · tro · ver · see] *n.* The Constitution gives the federal courts the power to decide various, specified types of "cases" and "controversies." Both words have essentially the same meaning. They give rise to the constitutional doctrine that courts will decide cases only when there is some actual disagreement, not merely a desire for a **hypothetical** declaration. *See* controversy.

case reports [re · *ports*] *n.* *See* reported cases.

case stated [*stay* · ted] *n.* Another term for **agreed case**.

casebook [*kase* · book] *n.* A book containing court decisions and other materials in a specific field of law, used for teaching law students. *Compare* hornbook.

cash *n.* Coin; money; money in hand, either in coin, currency, or other **legal tender**. A **cashier's check** or a **certified check** is the equivalent of cash, because payment is essentially guaranteed. *Compare* credit. *See* cash or its equivalent.
v. To exchange currency for commercial paper.
➤ *n.* coin, money, funds, currency, notes, legal tender.
v. make change, pay, draw, liquidate, redeem ("to cash a check").

cash basis [*bay* · siss] *n.* A method of accounting under which income is reported for tax purposes when it is actually received rather than when the right to receive it accrues. *Compare* accrual basis.

cash book *n.* A **book of account** of money received and paid out.

cash dividend [*div* · i · dend] *n.* An ordinary distribution to shareholders of corporate profit. A cash dividend, generally speaking, is not actually paid in cash; the term is used to distinguish the transaction from a **stock dividend**. *See* dividend.

cash flow *n.* The cash that remains after all the expenses of operating a business have been met; **net income** plus any amounts allowed for **depreciation**.

cash or its equivalent [ee · *kwiv* · a · lent] *n.* Money or that which is convertible into money when presented for payment. EXAMPLE: a **certified check**, but not a **promissory note**.

cash price *n.* A price that a seller sets for the cash sale of goods or services. In some instances, the cash price may be less than the price for the same goods or services sold on credit.

cash sale *n.* A sale in which payment of the purchase price and delivery of the goods take place at the same time.

cash surrender value [ser · *en* · der *val* · yoo] *n.* The **cash value** of a life insurance policy; the amount of money the owner of a life insurance policy would receive from the insurance company upon cashing the policy in.

cash value [*val* · yoo] *n.* 1. The amount of money an article or piece of property would bring if sold on the open market. Other terms for cash value include **market value** and **fair market value**. 2. The **cash surrender value** of a life insurance policy.

cashier's check [kash · *eerz*] *n.* A **bill of exchange**, drawn by a bank upon itself, and **accepted** by virtue of the act of issuance. *See* acceptance. The bank's issuance of the check is a guaranty that it will be **honored**. A cashier's check is the equivalent of cash. *Compare* certified check; money order; registered check.

castigate [*kas* · tih · gayt] *v.* To criticize severely.
➤ admonish, reprimand, chastise, criticize, thrash, excoriate, rebuke, upbraid.

castle doctrine [*kass* · l *dok* · trin] *n.* The doctrine that a person may use whatever force is required to defend his home and those in it. The principle derives its name from the maxim that "a man's home is his castle."

castration [kas · *tray* · shen] *n.* The severing of the testicles by surgery, drugs, or accident. Surgical or chemical castration is a controversial punishment for sex offenders used in some states. *Compare* sterilization.
➤ emasculation, asexualization, removal, sterilization, severing.

casual [*kazh* · wel] *adj.* Occasional; incidental; irregular, as opposed to regular; random.
➤ uncertain, unplanned, accidental, unexpected, spontaneous ("our casual encounter"); irregular, erratic, occasional, intermittent ("casual employment"); informal, relaxed ("casual dress").

casual employee [em · *ploy* · ee] *n.* A person employed temporarily, occasionally, intermittently, seasonally, not on a regular basis. The term has particular significance in labor law. *See also* casual employment.

casual employment [em · *ploy* · ment] *n.* Employment that is temporary or seasonal.

casualty [*kazh* · yoo · el · tee] *n.* A disastrous occurrence by chance or accident; a serious mishap or misfortune.
➤ disaster, accident, calamity, catastrophe, tragedy, misfortune.

casualty insurance [in · *shoor* · ense] *n.* Insurance covering damage done by the insured to the person or property of others, or damage done to the property of the insured. *See* insurance.

casualty loss *n.* An income tax deduction for a **loss** arising from fire, storm, flood, or other casualty to property owned by the taxpayer.

catalyst [*kat* · a · list] *n.* A force that motivates or impels something.
➤ inspiration, force, motivation, instigator, impetus.

catch time charter [*char* · ter] *n.* Boat rental based upon the time the boat is actually in use, as opposed to rental based upon a set amount per day.

catchall [*katch* · all] *n.* A clause or provision in a contract, will, or statute intended to broaden its application.
EXAMPLE (in a statute): "This provision shall apply to dogs, cats, caged birds, and such other animals as may be kept as domestic pets."

catching bargain [*kat* · shing *bahr* · gen] *n.* An agreement of an **expectant heir** for the sale of her **expectancy** at a grossly inadequate price and under circumstances that render the transaction unconscionable. *See* unconscionable contract.

categorical assistance [kat · e · *gore* · i · kel a · *siss* · tense] *n.* Publicly funded **entitlements** that are based upon the recipient's category or status, not upon need. EXAMPLES: most social security benefits; **VA mortgages**. *See* statutory benefits.

caucus [*kaw* · kus] *n.* A meeting of persons of the same political party or of the same views in general, held for the purpose of deciding upon a course of action that the participants should follow in a larger meeting to be held later.
➤ group, convention, gathering, conclave, session, assembly, meeting, council ("the Democratic caucus").

causa [*kow* · sah] *(Latin) n.* Cause; a cause; an action; a reason; a motive.

causa belli [*bel* · eye] *n.* A "cause of war."

causa mortis [*more* · tis] *n./adj.* "Because of death"; in expectation of death. *See* gift causa mortis.

causal relation [*kaw* · zel ree · *lay* · shen] *n.* *See* proximate cause.

causation [kaw · *zay* · shen] *n.* A causing; the producing of a result. *See* proximate cause. USAGE: "Causation is an essential element of a negligence action."
➤ production, origination, root, spawning, formation.

cause *n.* 1. An **action**; a lawsuit; a case; a **cause of action**. 2. A motive; a reason; an origin. *See* for cause; good cause; just cause; legal cause; reasonable cause. 3. That which brings about a result. *See* contributing cause; proximate cause. 4. An activity or goal supported by a number of people.
v. To bring about; to produce.
➤ *n.* stimulus, inducement, derivation, source, motive, agent ("the cause of the accident"); belief, conviction, faith, issue, purpose ("a charitable cause"); lawsuit, trial, case, legal proceeding ("cause of action").
v. bring into being, generate, create, sire, provoke, compel, launch, effectuate ("His bankruptcy caused his depression").

cause célèbre [kaws say · *leb* · re] *(French) n.* An incident or event that attracts great public attention; a famous case. USAGE: "The **Dred Scott case** was a *cause célèbre* in its day."

cause of action [*ak* · shen] *n.* Circumstances that give a person the right to bring a lawsuit and to receive **relief** from a court. *See* abatement of cause of action; accrual of cause of action; chose in action.

caution [*kaw* · shen] *n.* 1. Care; prudence; regard for danger. 2. A warning.

v. To warn or advise.

➤ *n.* warning, advice, vigilance, prudence, watchfulness, circumspection ("words of caution").

v. warn, tip off, alert, inform, forewarn, apprise, admonish. ("I cautioned you not to take that case.")

cautionary [*kaw* · shen · air · ee] *adj.* Reprimanding or warning.

cautionary instruction [in · *struk* · shen] *n.* A judge's **instruction** to a jury that they should avoid outside influences in their deliberations, refrain from talking with anyone about the case, and similar warnings. *See* jury instructions.

cautionary judgment [*juj* · ment] *n.* A **lien** placed by a plaintiff upon a defendant's property when it appears that the defendant is about to transfer or remove his property in order to defraud the plaintiff. Also known as a *cautionary lien.*

caveat [*ka* · vee · at] *(Latin) n.* Means "let him beware." 1. A notice to beware. 2. A formal objection, filed with a court, to a proposed action by the court.

➤ warning, caution, sign, alarm.

caveat emptor [*emp* · tor] "Let the buyer beware." This saying expresses the old **common law rule** that a buyer purchases at his peril. Today there are many exceptions to this rule (EXAMPLES: the **implied warranty of merchantability**; the **implied warranty of fitness for a particular purpose**).

caveator [*ka* · vee · a · tor] *n.* A person who files a *caveat.*

cc An abbreviation of **circuit court, civil case, criminal case, criminal court, county court, civil court**.

CCC Abbreviation of **Commodity Credit Corporation**.

CD *n.* 1. Abbreviation of and common short way of saying **certificate of deposit**. 2. Abbreviation of compact disc.

cease *v.* To stop an action.

➤ stop, desist, adjourn, quit, quell, suspend, terminate.

cease and desist order [dee · *zist or* · der] *n.* An order by an administrative agency or court that certain practices or activities must be stopped.

cede [seed] *v.* 1. To grant; to assign. A person transfers land to another person by **granting** or **conveying** it; a nation transfers territory by *ceding* it. 2. To give up; to yield; to surrender. *See* cession.

➤ abandon, yield, give up, forsake, release, relinquish ("A nation transfers territory by ceding it").

cedent [*see* · dent] *n.* A **grantor**; an **assignor**.

➤ grantor, assignor.

celebrate [*sel* · e · brate] *v.* 1. To observe; to perform. 2. To honor; to give publicity to an event.

➤ proclaim, rejoice, enjoy, eulogize, glorify, exalt, extol ("celebrate a victory"); observe, perform, conduct ("celebrate holiday rituals").

celebrity [see · *leb* · ri · tee] *n.* 1. A celebrated person. 2. Fame; status as a famous person.

➤ star, hero, famous person, luminary, big shot; fame, notoriety, prestige, repute, prominence.

cell *n.* A single room, as in "prison cell."

➤ cage, confinement, jail, prison, compartment, hole, nook, retreat, chamber.

censor [*sen* · ser] *n.* 1. A person who examines books, films, and other forms of expression to determine whether they are offensive to public morals. 2. A person who examines letters from persons in the military to ensure that they are not communicating information valuable to the enemy (a *military censor*). *See* censorship.

v. To examine, review, change, or delete.

➤ *n.* examiner, reviewer, critic, inspector.

v. forbid, restrict, suppress, withhold, examine, delete, expurgate, bowdlerize, abridge, amend, proscribe.

censorship [*sen* · ser · ship] *n.* The act of censoring. *See* censor. Censorship frequently involves a conflict with the First Amendment's right to free speech.

➤ forbiddance, banning, control, restriction, suppression, prohibition, stifling, purification, blockage, elimination.

C

censure [sen · shoor] *n.* Severe criticism; condemnation.
v. To find fault with; to criticise severly.
➤ *n.* disapproval, rebuke, reproach, reprimand, criticism, condemnation, denunciation, disapproval, castigation.
v. condemn, criticize, scold, reprimand, admonish, reprove, decry, assail, chastise, denigrate.

census [sen · sus] *n.* 1. An official counting of the inhabitants of a country, state, county, city, or other area or district. 2. An official count of the inhabitants of the United States taken by the government every 10 years as required by the Constitution. The census has come to include an enumeration of the resources of the country, as well as other statistics. *See* federal census.
➤ tally, tabulation, measurement, enumeration.

census bureau [sen · sus *byoo* · roh] *n.* Officially called the **Bureau of the Census**, the federal agency that takes the **federal census** and compiles and keeps the census records.

center [sen · ter] *n.* 1. Point of origin. 2. Most important or pivotal part.
➤ focus, midpoint, focal point, middle; essence, nucleus, heart, pith, gravamen, main point.

center of gravity doctrine [sen · ter of grav · i · tee *dok* · trin] *n.* A principle in the field of **conflict of laws** that a contract should be interpreted according to the laws of the state or country with which the matter in dispute has the most contacts.

central [sen · tral] *adj.* 1. Occupying a dominant or important position. 2. Midway.
➤ basic, essential, pivotal, primary, principal, dominant, elemental ("a central idea"); center, middle, medial, halfway ("central filing").
Ant. peripheral.

CEO Abbreviation of **chief executive officer**.
USAGE: "She is the CEO of our company."

ceremonial marriage [sehr · e · *mone* · ee · el *mehr* · ej] *n.* A marriage performed by an appropriate religious or civil official, after the parties have met all legal requirements (EXAMPLES: blood tests; securing a **marriage license**). *See* solemnization of marriage. *Compare* common law marriage; consensual marriage.

certain [ser · ten] *adj.* Unquestionable; free from doubt. *See* sum certain.
➤ definite, specific, ascertained, clear, explicit ("The price was certain"); confident, secure, assured ("Her demeanor was certain"); doubtless, conclusive, irrefutable, unquestionable, irrevocable ("certain defeat").

certainty [ser · ten · tee] *n.* Clarity; accuracy; precision; particularity.
➤ inevitability, sure thing, reality, verity, foregone conclusion ("It is a certainty that our client will be convicted"); confidence, assertiveness, assurance, credence, conviction ("The witness answered with certainty").

certificate [ser · *tif* · i · ket] *n.* A formal or official written declaration intended as an **authentication** of the fact or facts set forth therein. *See* license.
➤ pass, authorizing document, permit, ticket, affidavit, diploma, voucher, endorsement, assurance, credential.

certificate of acknowledgment [ak · *nol* · ej · ment] *n.* A written **acknowledgment** by a notary or other official that the person named in a document is who she claims to be and did, in fact, sign the document. *See also* attestation; authentication.

certificate of authentication [aw · then · ti · *kay* · shen] *n.* The written statement of a notary or other official taking an **acknowledgment** that he is the officer he claims to be and that the signature below the acknowledgment is, in fact, his. *See* authentication. *Also see* attestation.

certificate of convenience and necessity [kon · *vee* · nee · ense and ne · *sess* · i · tee] *n.* A certificate issued by an appropriate agency of government granting a private company permission to perform a **public service** for profit (EXAMPLES: the construction of a power plant for the extension of electric service; the operation of bus or air service as a **common carrier**).

certificate of deposit [de · *poz* · it] *n.* A **voucher** issued by a bank acknowledging the receipt of money on deposit which the bank promises to repay to the depositor. There are two kinds of certificates of deposit: **demand certificates** and **time certificates**. Demand certificates are ordinary savings accounts; the deposit can be withdrawn at any time, without penalty. Time certificates, which pay a higher rate of interest, are designed not to be cashed for a specified number of months or years. A certificate of deposit is often referred to simply as a **CD**. *See and compare* demand deposit; time deposit. A **Treasury certificate** is a form of certificate of deposit issued by the United States Treasury.

certificate of incorporation
[in · kore · per · *ay* · shen] *n.* 1. In some states, the same as **articles of incorporation**. 2. In some states, a certificate issued by the **Secretary of State** attesting that articles of incorporation have been filed and that the filing corporation is therefore a **legal entity** and capable of being sued. *See* incorporation.

certificate of need *n.* A certificate issued by an appropriate state agency giving an institutional provider of health care permission to expand its physical plant or to provide a new health service (EXAMPLE: permission to build a new wing or to provide emergency services).

certificate of occupancy
[ok · yoo · pen · see] *n.* A document issued by an appropriate agency of **local government** certifying that a newly con-structed or remodeled building is in com-pliance with all applicable building codes and may be occupied. *See* building codes.

certificate of participation
[par · tiss · i · *pay* · shen] *n.* 1. A certificate evidencing an **interest** in certain kinds of investments, for EXAMPLE, a **limited partnership**. 2. A **municipal bond** or other **government bond** which does not have or require voter approval and is therefore not an obligation of the governmental entity issuing it.

certificate of public convenience and necessity [*pub* · lik kon · *vee* · nee · ense and ne · *sess* · i · tee] *n.* Same as **certificate of convenience and necessity**.

certificate of stock *n.* *See* stock certificate.

certificate of title [*ty* · tel] *n.* 1. A document that shows who is the owner of the motor vehicle described in the document; often simply called "**title**." 2. In some jurisdictions, a document that shows the name of the owner of land identified in the document. *See* registration of land titles; Torrens title system.

certificated security [ser · *tif* · i · kay · ted se · *kyoo* · ri · tee] *n.* A **Uniform Commercial Code** term for a "share . . . or other interest in property of or an enterprise of the issuer," evidenced by "an instrument issued in bearer or regis-tered form." EXAMPLE: a share of stock in a corporation, evidenced by a **stock certificate**. *Compare* uncertificated security. *See* bearer bond; bearer instru-ment; registered security. *Also see* security.

certification [ser · ti · fi · *kay* · shen] *n.* 1. A formal **attestation** of a fact; an affirmation of the truth or accuracy of something. 2. The issuing of a certificate.
➤ assertion, substantiation, validation, endorsement, authentication, verification, license, declaration.

certification of bargaining agent
[*bar* · gen · ing *ay* · jent] *n.* A formal pronouncement by the **National Labor Relations Board**, or a similar state agency, that it has determined that a union seeking to represent an employer's employees represents a majority of those employees in an appropriate **collective bargaining unit** and is therefore their **collective bargaining agent**. *See* representation election.

certification of question [*kwes* · chen] *n.* A process through which a federal court refrains from deciding an issue involving a state law until that state's highest court has had the opportunity to do so, based upon the federal court's certification of the question involved.

certification of record on appeal
[*rek* · erd on a · *peel*] *n.* The trial judge's signed acknowledgment of the questions to be decided on appeal. *See* appeal.

certified [*ser* · ti · fide] *adj.* Confirmed; guaranteed; approved; authenticated.
➤ confirmed, guaranteed, approved, authenticated, validated, verified,

C

authorized, licensed, established ("a certified legal assistant").

certified case   *n.*   *See* certification of question.

certified check   *n.*   A **check** upon which the bank has stamped the words "certified" or "accepted," certifying that the check is drawn upon sufficient funds and will be **honored** when it is presented for payment. A certified check is the equivalent of cash. *See* acceptance. *Compare* cashier's check.

certified copy   [*kop* · ee]   *n.*   A copy of a document that is certified as a **true copy** by the official to whose custody the original is entrusted by law. EXAMPLE: a copy of a deed certified by the **recorder of deeds** as an exact copy of the recorded deed.

certified legal assistant (CLA)   [*lee* · gul uh · sis · tent]   *n.*   A legal assistant who has been certified by the **National Association of Legal Assistants**.

certified public accountant   [*pub* · lik a · *koun* · tent]   *n.*   Commonly referred to as a CPA; an accountant who has been certified by the state to practice as a **public accountant**.

certified question   [*kwes* · chen]   *n.*   *See* certification of question.

certified record   [*rek* · erd]   *n.*   *See* certification of record on appeal.

certify   [*ser* · ti · fy]   *v.*   1. To verify as true or accurate; to vouch for. 2. To guarantee. 3. To make or issue a certification.
➤ verify, validate, authenticate.

certiorari   [ser · sho · *rare* · ee]   *(Latin)*   *n.*   A **writ** issued by a **higher court** to a **lower court** requiring the **certification** of the **record** in a particular case so that the higher court can review the record and correct any actions taken in the case which are not in accordance with the law. The Supreme Court of the United States uses the **writ of certiorari** to select the state court cases it is willing to review. Commonly referred to as "cert." USAGE: "The court granted cert." *See* certification of record on appeal.

certitude   [*ser* · ti · tyood]   *n.*   The state of being certain or sure.

➤ certainty, irrefutability, undeniability, sureness.

cession   [*sesh* · en]   *n.*   A surrender; a yielding; a giving up. *See* cede.
➤ surrender, yielding, relinquishment, ceding, transfer, conveyance, release.

cestui   [*ses* · twee]   *(French)*   *n.*   Means "he who." A word that appears in French phrases used in the law, most notably, **cestui que trust** (he who benefits from a trust).

cestui que trust   [*ses* · twee keh]   *n.*   The **beneficiary** of a **trust**; the person for whose benefit property is held in trust.

cf.   Abbreviation meaning "compare" (from the Latin word for compare).

CFR   Abbreviation of **Code of Federal Regulations**. Also abbreviated as C.F.R.

ch.   Abbreviation of **chapter**.

chain   *n.*   A series of connected things; a series of things that follow from each other. *v.* To fasten or bind.
➤ *n.*   succession, series, order, progression, sequence ("chain of custody").
v.   bind, attach, hold, fasten, restrict ("chain the prisoner").

chain of causation   [kaw · *zay* · shen]   *n.*   A succession of events that link an act with a result; an element of **proximate cause**. *See* causation.

chain of custody   [*kuss* · te · dee]   *n.*   The succession of people who had possession or control of an object, or of the places an object was stored or located, from one point in time to another. In many instances, a chain of custody must be established for **physical evidence** to be admissible at trial. A chain of custody is sometimes called a *chain of possession*. *See* custody.

chain of title   [*ty* · tel]   *n.*   The succession of transactions through which **title** to a given piece of land was passed from person to person from its origins to the present day. *See also* abstract of title; title search.

chairman   [*chare* · man]   *n.*   The presiding officer of an organization's meeting.
➤ leader, head, director, presider, presiding officer.

challenge [*chal* · enj] *n.* An objection; a protest.
v. To object; to take exception to.
➤ *n.* objection, rejection, protest ("a challenge to juror 12"); test, contest, match, confrontation, adventure ("Winning this case will be a real challenge").
v. confront, dare, defy, contradict, impeach, dispute, question ("challenge the witness"); invite, summon, call, arouse ("challenge all comers").

challenge for cause *n.* An objection, for a stated reason, to a juror being allowed to hear a case. *Compare* peremptory challenge.

challenge to juror [*joo* · rer] *n.* *See* challenge for cause; peremptory challenge.

challenge to the jury array [*joo* · ree a · *ray*] *n.* *See* challenge to the panel.

challenge to the panel [*pan* · el] *n.* An objection to the entire **panel** from which a jury is to be selected, based upon partiality or upon misconduct of the court official who summoned the panel.

chamber [*chame* · ber] *n.* 1. A legislative or judicial body. 2. An enclosed space.
➤ panel, assembly, bench, committee, forum; compartment, box, cell, alcove, hall, parlor.

chamber of commerce [*chame* · ber of *kom* · erse] *n.* An association of business persons of a city or other area, organized to promote the commercial interests of the area.

chambers [*chame* · berz] *n.* The private office of a judge, where **parties** are heard and orders are entered in matters not required to be brought into **open court**.
USAGE: "The judge advised both attorneys that he would discuss the matter with them in chambers."

champerty [*cham* · per · tee] *n.* The crime of financing a lawsuit in exchange for a portion or all of the proceeds of the **action** if it is successful. *See and compare* barratry; maintenance.
➤ barratry, intermeddling, illegal bargain.

chance *n.* 1. That which occurs without reason or cause, by accident or because of luck. 2. A lottery or raffle ticket. *See* game of chance. 3. An opportunity.
v. To take place by accident; to risk.
➤ *n.* luck, good fortune, fortuitousness; possibility, contingency, likelihood, prospect.
v. attempt, risk, try, gamble.

chance verdict [*ver* · dikt] *n.* A **verdict** reached by tossing a coin or drawing lots. It is illegal. *See also* quotient verdict.

chancellor [*chan* · sel · or] *n.* 1. A judge of a **court of chancery** or **court of equity**. 2. In some states, the title of the **chief executive officer** of the state's system of public colleges and public universities. 3. The title of the chief officer of some universities.
➤ chief executive officer, secretary.

chancery [*chan* · ser · ee] *n.* *See* court of chancery; court of equity; equity.

change *n.* An alteration or modification.
v. To put one thing in the place of another; to exchange; to alter or make different; to vary.
➤ *n.* alteration, modification, conversion, transition, addition, deviation, innovation, variation, refinement, amendment.
v. make different, substitute, reverse, alter, redo, shift, modify, deviate, transform, reconstruct, reconfigure, amend, revise ("change the venue in the interest of fairness").

change of beneficiary [ben · e · *fish* · ee · ar · ee] *n.* Substitution of one person for another as the **beneficiary** of a life insurance policy.

change of venue *n.* Moving the trial of a case from one county or **judicial district** to another county or judicial district. The most common reason for a court to permit a change in the venue of a criminal trial is the defendant's inability to receive a fair trial, usually as the result of undue or unfair publicity. The issue is put before the court by means of a **motion for change of venue**.

changed circumstances [chaynjd *ser* · kum · stanse · ez] *n.* A term in **family law**, referring to grounds for modifying a support or custody order.

chapter [*chap* · ter] *n.* 1. A major section or division of a book or of a statute. *See*

C

also section; title. 2. A branch of a **fraternal benefit society** or similar organization, usually formed on the basis of the geographical location of its members.
➤ section, part, article, clause, portion ("Chapter 7 bankruptcy").

Chapter 11 [*chap* · ter ee · *lev* · en] *n.* *See* bankruptcy.

Chapter 13 [*chap* · ter ther · *teen*] *n.* *See* bankruptcy.

Chapter 7 [*chap* · ter *sev* · en] *n.* *See* bankruptcy.

character [*kar* · ak · ter] *n.* That which a person is, as demonstrated by what he says and does. In the law, "character" is generally used interchangeably with "reputation," although, strictly speaking, the two words have different meanings, as reputation relates not to who one is but to what people say about one. *See* character evidence. *Also see* reputation.
➤ individuality, integrity, attribute, disposition, personality, nature, kind; reputation, standing.

character evidence [*ev* · i · dense] *n.* Testimony relating to the regard in which a person is held in the community. *See* reputation.

chargé d'affaires [shar · *zhay* da · *fare*] *(French) n.* A **diplomatic representative** who takes the place of an ambassador when the ambassador is out of the country or when there is no ambassador.

charge *n.* 1. An obligation or indebtedness to be paid; a cost; an expense incurred. 2. Paying for something over a period of time, often in installments. EXAMPLE: a charge account. 3. A formal accusation of the commission of a crime. EXAMPLES: an **indictment**; an **information**. 4. A judge's instructions to a jury to aid them in their deliberations. *See* jury instructions. 5. A provision in a will under which real estate of the **testator** is subject to the payment of debts of the **estate**. 6. A **lien** or **encumbrance** upon land. 7. A person or thing given into the care or custody of another. USAGE: "When her parents died, she was put in the charge of her grandmother." *v.* 1. To impose an obligation, incur an expense, or create an indebtedness. 2. To

enter into a transaction in which payment will be made over a period of time. 3. To accuse; to blame.
➤ *n.* price, cost, fee, tariff, assessment, payment, debt, quotation ("The charge is 10 dollars"); indictment, accusation, complaint, arraignment, gravamen, citation, summons ("The charge against him was child molestation"); instruction, command, advice ("the charge to the jury"). *v.* encumber, entrust, delegate, assign ("charge the jury"); accuse, blame, indict, implicate, inculpate, incriminate ("charge the accused with theft").

charge account [a · *kount*] *n.* An **open-end credit** account.

charge back *n.* A setting off of one debt against another. *See* set off.

charge to the jury [*joor* · ee] *n.* *See* charge; jury instructions.

charge-off *n.* 1. Same as **write-off**. 2. A **bad debt** deduction for income tax purposes.

charge-sheet *n.* A police station **blotter** on which the names of those in custody, the charges against them, and the names of their accusers are entered.

charging lien [*leen*] *n.* One form of **attorney's lien**, specifically, the **lien** an attorney has for payment of his fee against a **judgment, account,** or **award** that the client owns or has an **interest** in, as a result of the attorney's professional efforts.

charisma [ka · *riz* · ma] *n.* Charm or appeal.
➤ allure, magnetism, charm, appeal ("The speaker had a great deal of charisma").

charitable [*char* · i · tebl] *adj.* Inclined to relieve others of the effects of circumstances such as poverty, illness, ignorance, and hunger.
➤ benevolent, eleemosynary, philanthropic, altruistic, giving, generous, magnanimous, humane ("charitable contribution"); forgiving, lenient, obliging, merciful, agreeable ("a charitable review").

charitable contribution [kon · tri · byoo · shen] *n.* 1. A gift for a **charitable purpose**. 2. A gift of money or other thing of value to a **charitable**

organization. Charitable contributions are deductible from income tax within the limitations imposed by the **Internal Revenue Code**. *See* charitable corporation; charitable deduction.

charitable corporation
[kore · per · *ay* · shen] *n.* A **corporation** organized and existing solely to engage in charitable activities. It issues no stock and earns no profit. *See* charitable organization; nonprofit corporation.

charitable deduction [dee · *duk* · shen] *n.* A tax deduction from federal income tax to which a taxpayer is entitled, within the limitations imposed by the **Internal Revenue Code**, for contributions or gifts made to a tax-exempt **charitable organization**. *See* charitable contribution.

charitable gift *n.* *See* charitable contribution.

charitable immunity doctrine
[im · *yoo* · ni · tee *dok* · trin] *n.* The principle that relieves a **charitable organization** from **tort** liability. Most states have eliminated or substantially curtailed the application of this time-honored doctrine.

charitable institution [in · sti · *tyoo* · shen] *n.* An **institution** organized for **charitable purposes**, with no element of private or corporate gain.

charitable organization
[or · ga · ni · *zay* · shen] *n.* Any entity created for a **charitable purpose** within the meaning of the **Internal Revenue Code**, contributions to which are deductible from federal income tax. (EXAMPLES: a **charitable corporation**; a **foundation**; a **charitable trust**; a **benevolent association**.) The advancement of religion, education, science, literature, and similar social interests beneficial to the community as a whole, are among the charitable purposes recognized by the Tax Code. *See* charitable deduction. A charitable organization is exempt from taxation under the Internal Revenue Code; in this connection, it is often referred to as an **exempt organization**.

charitable purpose [*per* · pes] *n.* The purpose for which an organization must be formed, and for which it must exist, if it

is to qualify as a **charitable corporation** under the **Internal Revenue Code**.

charitable trust *n.* A **trust** established for a **charitable purpose**. EXAMPLE: a trust whose purpose is to provide funds for the purchase of books for the public library.

charity [*char* · i · tee] *n.* Love of humanity; generosity.
➤ altruism, benevolence, donation, generosity, philanthropy.
Ant. greed, selfishness.

charter [*char* · ter] *n.* 1. A corporation's **articles of incorporation**, together with the laws that grant corporate powers. *See* corporation. 2. The basic law of an **association**; that is, the agreement or **compact** entered into by the founding members of the organization. 3. The basic law of a city or town. 4. The lease of a boat or ship.
v. [*char* · ter] 1. To grant a charter. 2. To hire a boat. 3. To hire any conveyance for exclusive use.
➤ *n.* treaty, document, privilege, decree, pact, conveyance, agreement, entitlement.
v. reserve, borrow, rent, hire, lease, let, engage ("to charter a bus").

charter of affreightment [a · *frate* · ment] *n.* A contract for the use or services of a ship for a period of time. *See* affreightment.

chattel [*chat* · el] *n.* Personal property that is visible, **tangible**, and movable. Animals are included within the definition of chattel. *See* movable property. *See and compare* personal chattels; real chattels.
➤ property, possessions, assets, belongings, tangibles, effects.

chattel mortgage [*more* · gej] *n.* A **mortgage** on personal property. Prior to the **Uniform Commercial Code**, a chattel mortgage was the preferred form of agreement for creating a **security interest** in goods. *See* secured transaction; security agreement.

chattel paper [*pay* · per] *n.* As defined by the **Uniform Commercial Code**, a document that reflects both a debt and a **security interest** in specific goods. *See* secured transaction.

C

check *n.* 1. A written order ("pay to the order of") directed to a bank to pay money to the person named. *See* cashier's check; certified check; NSF check; postdated check; third-party check; traveler's check. *See also* draft; negotiable instrument. 2. A restraint or limitation. USAGE: "That's a bad habit; you need to put a check on it." *v.* 1. To examine for accuracy. 2. To restrain or hold back.

➤ *n.* draft, note, negotiable instrument, banknote; inspection, examination, review, audit, analysis; obstruction, restraint, control, limitation, cessation.
v. inspect, examine, verify, assess, scrutinize, probe, question ("check the murder scene"); restrain, balance, curb, inhibit, constrain, harness ("check his power").

check-off *n.* The deduction of union dues by an employer from an employee's wages and the turning over of the amounts deducted to the union.

checking account [*chek* · ing a · *kount*] *n.* A bank account against which a depositor may draw an unlimited number of checks so long as he does not exceed the balance on deposit. *Compare* savings account.

chemical dependency [*kem* · i · kel dee · *pen* · den · see] *n.* A term that includes both alcoholism and drug addiction. *See* addict, drug dependency.

chicanery [chi · *kane* · e · ree] *n.* Trickery, which becomes **fraud** if the person who is the object of the deceit is deprived of something of value.

➤ deception, double dealing, dishonesty, trickery, subterfuge, treachery, machination.

chief *adj.* Highest in status, rank, or authority.

➤ dominant, leading, preeminent, foremost, ranking, paramount.

chief executive [eg · *zek* · yoo · tiv] *n.* Short for **chief executive officer**.

chief executive officer [*off* · i · ser] *n.* 1. The head of the **executive branch** or **executive department** of government. Such an individual is also referred to as the *chief magistrate.* EXAMPLES: the president of the United States; the governor of a state; the mayor of a city. 2. The officer of a corporation or other organization who has the most responsibility for managing its affairs, commonly referred to as the **CEO**.

chief judge *n.* The judge who assigns cases in a **district** or **circuit** where there is more than one judge. *See* president judge.

chief justice (CJ) [*juss* · tiss] *n.* The presiding justice of a court with three or more justices or judges who sit together. *See* presiding judge.

child *n.* 1. A very young person. *Compare* minor. 2. Offspring; progeny; descendant. *Compare* heir. "Child" is not a technical legal term with a definite meaning. Its meaning is always subject to construction in the context in which it is used. *See* after-born child; delinquent child; illegitimate child; neglected child; posthumous child; unborn child.

➤ kid, adolescent, minor, youth, juvenile, youngster.

child abuse [a · *byooss*] *n.* The physical, sexual, verbal, or emotional abuse of a young person. Child abuse includes the neglect of a child. It is a crime in every state. *See* child abuse reporting acts. *See also* protection order.

child abuse reporting acts [a · *byooss* re · *port* · ing] *n.* State statutes that make specified persons (EXAMPLES: physicians; teachers) responsible for reporting suspected child abuse. *See* designated reporter.

child labor [*lay* · ber] *n.* The employment of children. The age at which children are permitted to work, as well as their hours and some of the conditions of their employment, are regulated by state and federal laws. *See* Fair Labor Standards Act (FLSA).

child molestation [mo · les · *tay* · shen] *n.* Fondling or touching a child with sexual intent.

child neglect [ne · *glekt*] *n. See* child abuse.

child pornography [por · *nog* · re · fee] *n. See* obscene; pornography.

child stealing [*steel* · ing] *n.* The taking or removal of a child from a parent or from a person acting *in loco parentis*. This is also the crime committed when a child is abducted from the custody of one parent by the other, although it is commonly called **parental kidnapping**. *See* abduction. *Also see* kidnapping.

child support [se · *port*] *n.* 1. Money paid, pending divorce and after divorce, by one parent to the other for the support of their children. *Compare* alimony. *See* nonsupport; support. *See also* Reciprocal Enforcement of Support Act. 2. The obligation of parents to provide their children with the necessities of life.

chilling [*chil* · ing] *adj.* Tending to inhibit or restrain.
➤ inhibiting, dampening, restricting, curbing, restraining, impeding ("a chilling effect").

chilling bids [*chil* · ing] *n.* Conduct at an auction that is designed to inhibit bidding or dampen competition among bidders so that the highest amount bid is lower than it would otherwise have been.

chilling effect [*chil* · ing e · *fekt*] *n.* A reference to the **constitutional law** doctrine that action by the government that is not itself unconstitutional will nonetheless be disallowed if its effect is to inhibit ("chill") the free exercise of constitutional rights, particularly **First Amendment** rights.

chit *n.* 1. A voucher for a small sum of money owed for food or drink. 2. A promise to pay; a **promissory note**.

choate [*ko* · ate] *adj.* Complete; completely formed; perfect; whole. *Compare* inchoate.
➤ complete, completely formed, perfect, whole, ready, perfected ("a choate lien").

choice *n.* 1. An option or alternative. 2. Care in selection.
adj. Of high quality.
➤ *n.* option, selection, pick, alternative; decision, outcome, selection, judgment.
adj. select, top quality, prime.

choose *v.* To select freely after consideration.
➤ select, prefer, opt for, decide, embrace, resolve, settle.

chose [shohz] *(French) n.* A **thing**; a **chattel**; a **personal right**.

chose in action *n.* A right to bring a lawsuit; a **cause of** action. EXAMPLES: The right of a creditor to be paid; the right of an unpaid creditor to recover in a lawsuit.

chronic [*kron* · ik] *adj.* Recurring frequently; of long and continuous duration.
➤ habitual, unremitting, continuous, lingering, persistent, unyielding ("chronic knee problems").

chronic persistent vegetative state [*kron* · ik per · *sis* · tent veg · e · *tay* · tiv] *n.* A profound, prolonged, and irreversible coma in which a person nonetheless retains a degree of neurological function not present in the case of **brain death**. In some jurisdictions, in some circumstances, the use of life-support equipment may be discontinued and nutrition withdrawn from such persons.

churning [*chern* · ing] *n.* 1. A broker's violation of a customer's trust by engaging in superfluous transactions on the customer's account for the purpose of producing commissions for himself. This activity is a criminal offense. 2. Agitating; stirring up.

CIF Abbreviation of **cost, insurance, and freight**.

circuit [*ser* · kit] *n.* The area over which a **circuit court** has **jurisdiction**.
➤ district, area, section, jurisdiction, territory, division ("circuit court").

circuit court *n.* 1. A name given to certain courts, federal and state, by constitution and statute. 2. A court presided over by a judge or judges at different places in the same circuit.

Circuit Court of Appeals [a · *peelz*] *n.* The former name of the intermediate federal **appellate courts**, now called the **Court of Appeals of the United States**.

circular note [*ser* · kyoo · ler] *n.* Same as **letter of credit**.

circulating capital [*ser* · kyoo · layt · ing ka · pi · tel] *n. See* floating capital.

circumstantial [*ser* · kum · *stan* · shel] *adj.* Pertaining to circumstances, that is, to what appears to be the fact or the reality.
➤ indirect, inferential, deduced, conjectural, implicative ("circumstantial proof").

circumstantial evidence [*ev* · i · denss] *n.* Facts and circumstances from which a jury or a judge may reason and reach conclusions in a case. Many nonlawyers

C

erroneously believe that a criminal defendant cannot be convicted of a crime on the basis of circumstantial evidence. In fact, most convictions are based exclusively on circumstantial evidence, because, unless the defendant has confessed or there is an eyewitness, circumstantial evidence is the only kind of evidence available. *Compare* positive evidence. *See* evidence.

citation [sy · *tay* · shen] *n.* 1. A **writ** issued by a judge, ordering a person to appear in court for a specified purpose. 2. A written order issued by a police officer, usually for a relatively minor violation of the law, directing a person to appear in court on a stated day and time. EXAMPLE: a speeding ticket. *See* summons. 3. Reference to **authority** (a case, article, or other text) on a point of law, by name, volume, and page or section of the **court report** or other book in which it appears. EXAMPLE: *Roe v. Wade*, which is published in volume 410 of the **United States Reports**, at page 113, is properly **cited** as *Roe v. Wade*, 410 U.S. 113. *See also* parallel citation.
➤ writ, notice, order, bidding, notification, warrant, summons ("The driver received a citation"); reference, source, credit, attribution, documentation ("the citation for the case").

citator [sy · tay · ter] *n.* A system of books, the use of which allows a person doing legal research to locate every court opinion in which a particular case is cited, and to determine the context in which it is cited as well as whether it has been **affirmed, distinguished, followed, overruled**, or simply mentioned. The citator in common use is *Shepard's Citations;* "**sheparding**" has come to mean the same thing as "using a citator."

cite *n.* Short for **citation**.
v. 1. To summon or notify a person to appear in court. 2. To refer to as **authority** or **precedent**, or as a **case in point**. 3. To refer to in support of a position, point of view, or conclusion.
➤ *n.* citation, quotation.
v. summon, notify, name, inform, implicate, incriminate ("to cite for speeding"); refer to, adduce, indicate,

establish, specify, document ("cite adverse authority").

citizen [*sit* · i · zen] *n.* A person who has acquired citizenship by birth, naturalization, or other lawful means. *See* natural-born citizen; naturalized citizen. *See also* corporate citizenship.
 For the relationship of "citizen" and "citizenship" to the jurisdiction of the federal courts, *see* **diversity of citizenship**.
➤ denizen, resident, subject, inhabitant, taxpayer, voter.

citizen of a state *n.* A person who is a citizen of the United States is also a citizen of the state in which she lives.

citizen of the United States [yoo · *nite* · ed] *n.* A person born or naturalized in the United States.

citizen's arrest [*sit* · i · zenz a · *rest*] *n.* An arrest made by a person other than a police officer. A citizen's arrest is legal under certain circumstances.

citizenship [*sit* · i · zen · ship] *n.* The privilege of membership in a **body politic**; the status of a citizen.

city [*sit* · ee] *n.* A **municipal corporation** of the largest and highest class, usually under a government consisting of three branches: the **executive branch**, generally headed by a mayor; the **legislative branch**, usually called a city council or **board of aldermen**; and the **judicial branch**, commonly called a **municipal court** or **city court**. *Compare* town; township; village.
➤ large town, urban place, downtown, metropolis, village, municipality.

city charter [*char* · ter] *n. See* charter.

city council [*koun* · sel] *n. See* city. *Compare* city manager.

city court *n. See* municipal court.

city manager [*man* · e · jer] *n.* The chief administrative officer of a city under a form of municipal government known as the *city manager plan. Compare* commission form of government.

city manager form of government [*man* · e · jer form of guv · ern · ment] *n. See* city manager.

civic [*siv* · ik] *adj.* Relating to a community or civil affairs; of citizenship.

C

➤ common, community, governmental, official, public, municipal ("civic duty").

civil [*siv · el*] *adj.* 1. Pertaining to the enforcement of **private rights**, as distinguished from criminal prosecutions. *See* civil action. 2. Pertaining to the government or the relationship between the government and its citizens. *See* civil liberties; civil penalty; civil rights.

➤ community, civic, social, public, societal; noncriminal ("a civil case"); courteous, obliging, civilized, diplomatic, deferential, gracious, refined ("Civil behavior is required in the courtroom").

civil action [*ak · shen*] *n.* An **action** brought to enforce a **private right**, as contrasted with a criminal prosecution; a court **proceeding** brought by one **party** against another to correct a legal wrong. USAGE: "Medical malpractice is a civil action."

civil arrest [*a · rest*] *n.* A means by which a judge can secure the presence of a defendant in court until **final judgment** is rendered. *See capias ad respondendum; capias ad satisfaciendum.*

civil assault [*a · salt*] *n.* An **assault** for which the assailant is liable in a **civil action**. *Compare* criminal assault.

civil authority [*aw · thaw · ri · tee*] *n.* The **authority** vested in civil, as distinguished from military, officials.

civil case *n.* Same as **civil action**.

civil commitment [*ke · mit · ment*] *n.* 1. The jailing of a person for **nonsupport** or **civil contempt**. 2. The detention of the mentally ill, alcoholic, or drug addicted for treatment. *See commitment. See and compare* involuntary commitment; voluntary commitment. 3. The jailing of a person under **civil arrest**.

civil conspiracy [*ken · spir · e · see*] *n.* A combination of two or more persons acting together to accomplish an unlawful purpose, or to accomplish a lawful purpose by unlawful or criminal means, to the **injury** of another. To support a **cause of action** for civil conspiracy, **damage** must have resulted from the combination. *Compare* conspiracy.

civil contempt [*ken · temt*] *n. See* contempt of court. The dividing line between civil contempt and **criminal**

contempt is not always clear. Generally speaking, the contempt is civil when the court's purpose in conducting the contempt proceeding is to provide **relief** to a **private party** and to compel compliance with a court order. *Compare* criminal contempt.

civil court *n.* A court in which **civil actions**, as distinguished from **criminal prosecutions**, are tried. *Compare* criminal court.

civil death *n.* The termination of a person's **civil rights** because of his conviction of a felony. EXAMPLES: the right to vote; the right to bring a lawsuit; the right to hold public office. *See* civil disability.

civil disability [*dis · e · bil · i · tee*] *n.* A deprivation, by the law, of a person's **legal capacity**. EXAMPLES: a child of 11 years of age cannot enter into a valid contract (**infancy** is the **disability**); some mentally ill persons are considered by law not to have the capacity to make a valid will (**insanity** is the disability). *See* civil death.

civil disobedience [*dis · o · bee · di · ense*] *n.* The deliberate breaking of a law (and the willing acceptance of the resulting punishment) because the lawbreaker believes the law to be unjust and wishes, by her action, to call attention to the injustice.

civil fine *n. See* civil penalty.

civil forfeiture [*for · fit · sher*] *n.* A deprivation of money or property gained through criminal conduct. Also known as **asset seizure**, civil forfeiture is particularly common with respect to assets derived from violation of drug laws or property used or intended to be used in the commission of such violations. Civil forfeiture is a **civil action** (usually an **in rem action**), and does not depend upon a criminal conviction. *See* forfeiture.

civil fraud *n. See* tax fraud.

civil law *n.* 1. Law based upon a published **code** of statutes, as opposed to law found in the decisions of courts. EXAMPLE: the **common law** as opposed to the **Code Civil**. 2. Body of law that determines **private rights** and liabilities, as distinguished from criminal law.

See civil action. 3. The entire body of law adopted in a country or a state, as distinguished from **natural law** (sometimes called **moral law**) and from **international law** (the law governing relationships between countries). 4. The law of the Roman Empire, or modern law that has been handed down from Roman law. 5. The name of the body of law by which the State of Louisiana is governed. *See* Code Civil.

civil liability [ly · e · *bil* · i · tee] *n.* **Liability** to be sued in a **civil action**, as contrasted with **criminal liability**, which is liability to **criminal prosecution**.

civil liability insurance [ly · e · *bil* · i · tee in · *shoor* · ense] *n.* Insurance that indemnifies the policyholder against **civil liability**. *See* homeowners policy; liability insurance.

civil liberties [*lib* · er · teez] *n.* Political liberties guaranteed by the Constitution and, in particular, by the **Bill of Rights**, especially the **First Amendment**. EXAMPLES: freedom of speech; freedom of the press; freedom of association. *See also* civil rights.

civil penalty [*pen* · al · tee] *n.* Authorized by statutes governing specific **public wrongs**, civil penalties may be fines, **damages**, or both. EXAMPLE: a monetary penalty imposed by the **Federal Aviation Administration** on an airline that fails to maintain its planes in a manner assuring safety to the public. *See* penalty; statutory penalty.

civil procedure [pro · *see* · jer] *n.* The **rules of procedure** by which **private rights** are enforced; the rules by which **civil actions** are governed. There are both **Federal Rules of Civil Procedure**, followed in the federal courts, and **rules of civil procedure** of each of the states. *See also* rules of appellate procedure; rules of court; rules of evidence; rules of practice. *Compare* rules of criminal procedure.

civil rights *n.* 1. All the **rights** the law gives a person. 2. Constitutional or statutory guaranties against discrimination by reason of race, religion, national origin, gender, age, or disability.

civil rights amendments [a · *mend* · ments] *n.* The **Thirteenth Amendment,**

Fourteenth Amendment, and **Fifteenth Amendment** to the Constitution.

civil servant [*ser* · vent] *n.* 1. A **public employee**. 2. A public employee who is a member of the **civil service system**.

civil service [*ser* · viss] *n.* 1. All civilian employees of the federal government or state or local governments. 2. The **civil service system**, under which appointments to most state and federal government jobs, except those at the highest levels, are determined. It is a **merit system** that involves application of objective criteria, including the results of standardized examinations. *See* Civil Service Commission.

civil service system [*ser* · viss sis · tim] *n.* *See* civil service.

civil side *n.* The section of a **court calendar** that lists **civil cases**. *Compare* criminal side.

civil suit *n.* Same as **civil action**.

civil year *n.* A year consisting of $365\frac{1}{4}$ days, to account for leap year, as opposed to a calendar year of 365 or 366 days.

Civil Code [*sih* · vil] *n.* *See* civil law; Code Civil.

Civil Rights Acts [*sih* · vil] *n.* A term that may refer to any or all of the various statutes enacted by Congress relating to **civil rights**. The first of these were enacted in 1866, 1870, 1871, and 1875, in anticipation of the **Thirteenth Amendment**, and for the purpose of implementing that Amendment and the **Fourteenth Amendment**. These acts gave former slaves the right to sue and to testify in court, equal access to places of **public accommodation**, and the right to bring civil actions or to complain criminally for specified violations of their civil rights. The Civil Rights Act of 1957 created the **Commission on Civil Rights**. The Civil Rights Act of 1960 guaranteed to all citizens the right to register to vote. The **Civil Rights Act of 1964** assured access to places of public accommodation, public facilities, and education, without regard to religion, color, race, national origin, or sex; **Title VII** of that act prohibited discrimination in employment. **The Voting Rights Act of 1965** banned racial discrimination in local, state, or federal elections. The **Civil Rights Act of 1968**

(also called the **Fair Housing Act**) prohibited racial, religious, or ethnic discrimination in the sale or rental of housing. The **Civil Rights Act of 1991** provided for both **compensatory damages** and **punitive damages** for intentional discrimination or unlawful harassment in the workplace on the basis of sex, race, religion, or disability. Additionally, the **Age Discrimination in Employment Act** and the **Americans with Disabilities Act** are often classified as civil rights acts. States, as well as the federal government, have legislated extensively in the area of civil rights. *See also* Equal Employment Opportunity Commission.

Civil Rights Acts of 1964 [*sih · vil*] *n.* *See* Civil Rights Acts.

Civil Rights Acts of 1968 [*sih · vil*] *n.* *See* Civil Rights Acts.

Civil Rights Acts of 1991 [*sih · vil*] *n.* *See* Civil Rights Acts.

Civil Rights Commmission [*sih · vil rites ke · mish · en*] *n.* The popular name for the **Commission on Civil Rights**. *See* Commission on Civil Rights.

Civil Service Commission [*sih · vil ser · viss ke · mish · en*] *n.* The federal commission empowered to administer the federal **civil service system**. Each state has a civil service system as well. *See* civil service; commission.

civilian [*sih · vil · yen*] *n.* A person who is not a member of the military nor a police officer.
adj. Nonmilitary; secular.
➤ *n.* nonmilitary person, citizen, commoner, subject.
adj. nonmilitary, private, lay, secular, mundane.

civilian review board [*re · vyoo*] *n.* In some cities, a **review board** that hears complaints of police brutality.

CJ Abbreviation of **chief justice**. Also abbreviated C.J.

CLA Abbreviation of **certified legal assistant**. Also abbreviated C.L.A.

Claflin trust [*klaf · lin*] *n.* An **indestructible trust**.

claim *n.* 1. Something demanded as a matter of **right**. 2. A **civil case**. 3. With respect to **commercial paper**, a right to the **instrument** or its proceeds. 4. A **mining claim**. *See* claim jumping.
v. To assert; to ask for; to insist on; to challenge.
➤ *n.* assertion, contention, declaration, advocacy, insistence ("her claim of innocence"); accusation, plea, complaint, presentment, suit, cause of action ("a claim against the manufacturer").
v. assert, maintain, demand, lay claim to, solicit, require, defend, profess.

claim against decedent's estate [*a · genst de · see · dents e · state*] *n.* A debt that could have been enforced in a court against the **decedent** during his lifetime. *See* decedent's estate.

claim and delivery [*de · liv · e · ree*] *n.* In some states, the name of an **action** to recover personal property wrongfully taken or held and, in some circumstances, to recover **damages**.

claim for relief [*re · leef*] *n.* A **complaint** and, under the **Federal Rules of Civil Procedure**, any **pleading** "which sets forth . . . a claim, **counterclaim**, **cross-claim**, or **third-party claim**." *See* demand for relief; relief.

claim jumping [*jum · ping*] *n.* Taking advantage of the failure of a person who is mining **public land** to **perfect** her claim in the manner required by law, by perfecting a claim at the same location in order to obtain it for oneself. *See* mining claim.

claim of ownership [*oh · ner · ship*] *n.* Same as **claim of right**.

claim of right *n.* An entry upon land with the intent to claim and hold it for one's own, even though the claimant does not have **title** to the land and has no right to be on it.

claim of right doctrine [*dok · trin*] *n.* The tax law doctrine that a taxpayer who receives money that he may have to repay, because his right to retain it is in dispute, must nonetheless pay income tax on it for the tax year in which it was received.

claim of title [*ty · tel*] *n.* Same as **claim of right**.

claimant [*clay* · ment] *n.* One who claims or makes a claim; an applicant for justice; a plaintiff.
➤ petitioner, challenger, plaintiff, appellant, litigant, party, pleader.

claims adjuster [a · *just* · er] *n.* *See* adjuster.

Claims Court *n.* 1. A federal court whose **jurisdiction** is certain money claims against the United States. The full name of this court is the **United States Claims Court**; its former name was the Court of Claims. 2. In some states (New York, for EXAMPLE), a court for claims against the state.

clarify [*klar* · ih · fy] *v.* To make clear; to explain.
➤ explain, interpret, refine, illuminate, explicate, simplify, break down, analyze.

class *n.* 1. A number of persons who share something of significance in common other than their economic, educational, occupational, or social status. EXAMPLES: all males employed by the XYZ Company from 1989 to 1992; all females whose mothers used Fresh-N-Fancy deodorant between the years 1979 and 1986. *See* class action. 2. People grouped together according to economic, educational, occupational, or social status, or the like. USAGE: "working class"; "upper class." 3. Any division of persons or things by rank or on the basis of common characteristics. *v.* To classify.
➤ *n.* group, type, category, variety ("a constitutionally protected class"); style, standing, status.
v. group, classify, specify, separate ("The law classes this as a misdemeanor").

class action [*ak* · shen] *n.* An **action** brought by one or several plaintiffs on behalf of a class of persons. A class action may be appropriate when there has been **injury** to so many people that their voluntarily and unanimously joining in a lawsuit is improbable and impracticable. In such a situation, injured parties who wish to do so may, with the court's permission, sue on behalf of all. A class action is sometimes referred to as a **representative action**. *Also see* derivative action.

class directors [dih · *rek* · terz] *n.* **Corporate directors** whose terms of office are staggered. This is done to frustrate **takeovers**.

class gift *n.* A gift to a group of persons, the value of each of whose shares will depend on the number of people in the group when the gift becomes effective. EXAMPLE (in a will): "I bequeath the sum of $100,000 to my children, to be divided among them equally when the youngest of them shall reach the age of 18."

class legislation [lej · iss · *lay* · shen] *n.* All **legislation** involves some form of classification; the term "class legislation" really refers to "prohibited class legislation," i.e., legislation that makes **arbitrary** or **capricious** distinctions between members of the same class. Such legislation is unconstitutional under the **equal protection clause** of the **Fourteenth Amendment**. *See* suspect classification. *Also see* discrimination.

class of stock *n.* A type or classification of **stock** in a circumstance when a corporation issues more than one type. **Common stock** and **preferred stock** are EXAMPLES of different classes of stock.

class suit *n.* Same as **class action**.

classification [klas · i · fi · *kay* · shen] *n.* Arrangement by division into classes.
➤ allocation, allotment, analysis, arrangement, hierarchy, distribution, grouping, placement.

classification of cities [*sit* · eez] *n.* The grouping of cities within a state, usually on the basis of population, so as to make differences in their forms of government possible and legal.

classification of counties [*koun* · teez] *n.* In some states, the grouping of counties on the basis of population, so as to create differences in the powers possessed by their governments.

classification of offenses [oh · *fense* · ez] *n.* Crimes may be grouped on various bases. Most classications of offenses are related in some way to the seriousness or gravity of the criminal conduct. EXAMPLES: a **felony**, as opposed to a **misdemeanor**, as opposed to an **infraction**; a *malum in se* offense as distingushed from a *malum* *prohibitum* offense. *See also* degrees of crime; graded offenses.

clause *n.* 1. In the law, a sentence, a part of a sentence, or a paragraph in a will, contract, **pleading**, statute, constitution, or other legal document. EXAMPLES: the **equal protection clause** of the Constitution; a **cancellation clause**; an **attestation clause**. 2. A grammatical form.
➤ provision, section, part, passage, stipulation, condition.

Clayton Act [*klay* · ten] *n.* A federal statute that supplemented the **Sherman Act**, protecting the public against the effects of **monopolies** and **price-fixing**.

clean *adj.* Unsoiled; unblemished; honest; moral; healthy.
➤ blameless, chaste, faultless, precise, uncluttered.

clean bill of health *n.* *See* bill of health.

clean bill of lading [*lay* · ding] *n.* A **bill of lading** that contains no notations in the margin modifying the words in the bill itself.

clean hands doctrine [*dok* · trin] *n.* The principle that a complainant in a **court of equity** will be denied **relief** if he has conducted himself unjustly in the matter in dispute. Such a person is said in the law to have "unclean hands."

clean paper [*pay* · per] *n.* A **bill**, **draft**, **promissory note**, or similar instrument, with no attachments.

clear *adj.* 1. Free; free of; unrestricted. 2. Unmistakable; unequivocal. 3. Not clouded; not obscured. *See* clear title.
v. 1. To acquit; to exonerate. 2. To free; to liberate. 3. In banking, the payment by a bank of a check drawn on it. USAGE: "Because I haven't made a deposit for a month, I wasn't sure my check would clear the bank." *See* clearing.
➤ *adj.* understandable, open, apparent, sharp, unhindered, absolute, certain, decided, definite; absolved, discharged, innocent, dismissed.
v. clean, purify, refine, unclog, erase; exonerate, emancipate, acquit, liberate, discharge; make, net, realize, profit, acquire, earn.

clear and convincing evidence [kon · *vinss* · ing *ev* · i · dense] *n.* A degree of proof required in some civil cases, higher than the usual standard of **preponderance of the evidence**. *Also compare* beyond a reasonable doubt.

clear and present danger [*prez* · ent *dane* · jer] *n.* The test of whether speech is capable of creating such a substantial danger to the security of the country that it is not protected under the **First Amendment**. *See also* balancing test.

clear market value [*mar* · ket *val* · yoo] *n.* Same as **market value**.

clear title [*ty* · tel] *n.* **Good title**; **marketable title**; **title** to land or other property that is free from doubts or defects. *See* title. *Also see* good and valid.

clearance card [*kleer* · ens] *n.* A letter given to an employee by her employer, at the end of her employment, describing the nature and duration of the employment and the reasons for leaving. A clearance card is not necessarily a recommendation.

clearing [*kleer* · ing] *n.* 1. In banking, the exchanging of checks and balancing of accounts. *See* clear. 2. The act of a ship in leaving port. 3. An empty space; an open field.
➤ allowance, clearance, open space, empty space, margin.

clearinghouse [*kleer* · ing · house] *n.* 1. An association of banks whose purpose, daily, at one place and time, is to exchange checks and similar instruments held by one member and due from another. *See* clear; clearing. 2. Any association or place that exists for the exchange of information in a given area of human activity or interest.
➤ central location, exchange, distribution center.

clearly [*kleer* · lee] *adv.* Easily understood; unsmistakable; without doubt.
➤ distinctly, openly, overtly, surely, unmistakably, lucidly, undoubtedly.

clearly erroneous [*kleer* · lee err · *oh* · nee · us] *n.* A standard by which a trial court's **findings of fact** are reviewed. An **appellate court** will not set aside a trial court's findings of fact unless they are "clearly erroneous."

clemency [*klem* · en · see] *n.* 1. A willingness to forgive or to be lenient in punishment; the granting of a pardon or a **commutation of sentence**. *See* reprieve. 2. Leniency; mildness.
➤ forgiveness, compassion, fairness, lenience, charity, absolution, mercy, grace.

clerical [*kler* · i · kel] *adj.* 1. Pertaining to a clerk. 2. Pertaining to a clergyman.
➤ secretarial, routine, clerkly, office ("clerical work"); churchly, holy, pastoral, sacred ("clerical robes").
clerical error [*err* · er] *n.* A mistake in copying or writing; an error in form rather than in substance. *See* scrivener's error.

clerk *n.* 1. A person who keeps the records of a government office or a court. *See* clerk of court. 2. A person who keeps accounts, files, or records for another. 3. A person who sells goods in a store. 4. An attorney's clerk. *See* clerkship.
➤ assistant, salesperson, secretary, teller, recordkeeper, researcher, scribe, administrator ("clerk of the court").
clerk of court *n.* A public official who keeps the court's records.

clerkship [*klerk* · ship] *n.* 1. In some states, the service of a law student as an attorney's trainee, in order to qualify for admission to the bar. 2. Employment of a law student or a graduate attorney as a clerk by a licensed attorney or a judge.
➤ internship, employment.

client [*klie* · ent] *n.* 1. A person who employs an attorney. 2. A person who discusses with an attorney the possibility of hiring the attorney. 3. A person who employs almost any other person (EXAMPLES· an accountant; a stockbroker; a psychotherapist) for her professional expertise.
➤ customer, consumer, patron, purchaser, shopper, patronizer.
Ant. seller.
client privilege [*priv* · e · lej] *n. See* attorney-client privilege.
client security fund [se · *kyoo* · ri · tee] *n. See* IOLTA.

clinical [*klin* · i · kal] *adj.* 1. Relating to a clinic; direct observation. 2. Analytical or dispassionate.
➤ dispassionate, detached, impersonal, objective, scientific ("a clinical opinion").

close [klose] *adj.* 1. Near; nearby. 2. Intimate; tight.
n. [kloze] 1. A tract of land enclosed by a fence or an invisible boundary line. *See* breaking a close; closing. 2. An ending; a finish.
v. [kloze] 1. To finish; to conclude. 2. To seal; to wrap; to enclose.
➤ *adj.* near, tight, crowded, dense ("close quarters"); intimate, allied, devoted, confidential ("a close relationship").
n. premises; conclusion, ending, completion, termination ("to bring to a close").
v. complete, finish, agree to, seal, confirm ("close the deal"); terminate, conclude, suspend, cease ("close the account").
Ant. open; start.

close corporation [kore · per · *ay* · shen] *n.* 1. A **corporation** in which all the stock is owned by a few persons or by another corporation; sometimes also referred to as a **closely held corporation**. 2. Another term for a **family corporation**.

closed [klozed] *adj.* 1. Terminated; ended; concluded. 2. Sealed; wrapped; contained.
➤ finished, over, resolved, settled, shut, terminated, sealed.
Ant. unsettled; open.
closed corporation [kore · per · *ay* · shen] *n.* Same as **close corporation**.
closed shop *n.* A place of employment in that all employees are required by a **collective bargaining agreement** to be members of the union in order to be employed. *Compare* agency shop agreement; open shop; preferential shop.
closed-end mortgage [*klozed* · end more · gej] *n.* A **mortgage** that cannot be prepaid and under which the amount of the debt cannot be increased. *Compare* open-end mortgage.

closely held corporation [*klohs* · lee held kore · per · *ay* · shen] *n. See* close corporation.

closing [*kloze* · ing] *n.* 1. Making the **closing argument** (also referred to as a **final argument**) in a case; making a summation; summing up. 2. Completing a transaction, particularly a contract for the sale of real estate. USAGE: "We've practically bought the house; we'll sign the papers at the closing and the place will be ours." *See* closing costs.

adj. Following others (in importance).
➤ *n.* summation, ending, completion ("The closing was scheduled for 6:00 p.m.").
adj. final, summing-up, completing ("closing argument").
Ant. beginning.

closing argument [*ar* · gyoo · ment] *n.* *See* closing.

closing costs *n.* Payments required at a real estate closing to conclude the transaction. EXAMPLES: **escrow** funds; **appraisal** fees; attorney fees.

closing statement [*state* · ment] *n.* 1. The **final argument** in a case. 2. A document prepared in connection with a real estate closing that details the financial aspects of the transaction.

cloud on the title [*ty* · tel] *n.* An outstanding potential claim against real estate somewhere in the **chain of title**, which reduces the market value of the property. *See* defective title.

cluster zoning [*kluss* · ter *zone* · ing] *n.* In zoning law, a permitted use that departs from the requirements of the zoning regulations with respect to lot sizes on the condition that space be set aside for parks and similar public purposes. *See* zoning.

co- *prefix* Jointly; with; together; equally. A **comaker**, for EXAMPLE, is a person who signs a **note** or other **negotiable instrument** jointly with another person.

co-opt [*ko* · opt] *v.* To preempt; to take over.
➤ preempt, assume, usurp, absorb.

co. Abbreviation of company; abbreviation of county.

coaching [*koh* · ching] *v.* Instructing a witness before he takes the stand. Coaching is acceptable if it is confined to explaining to the witness how he should conduct himself and what he should expect; however, it is impermissible if it involves telling the witness what his testimony should be or whispering or signaling to him while on the stand.
➤ instructing, educating, training, teaching ("coaching the witness").

coalesce [ko · uh · *less*] *v.* To unite into a whole.
➤ combine, unite, fuse, solidify, consolidate, join, intermingle.

coalition [ko · a · *lish* · un] *n.* An alliance of parties for a joint action.
➤ alliance, league, society, partnership, union, party, mixture, association.

coassignee [ko · a · sine · ee] *n.* One of two or more persons to whom an **assignment** has been made. *See* assignee.

coastal [*kohs* · tel] *adj.* Pertaining to the land along the edge of the sea.
coastal waters [*waw* · terz] *n.* Waters along the shore of the sea, at any point before they meet the open ocean.

coax *v.* To manipulate or persuade.
➤ attract, bait, lure, prod, suggest, urge, cajole.

COBRA [*ko* · bra] *n.* Common acronym for the **Consolidated Omnibus Budget Reconciliation Act of 1985**.

cocaine [koh · *kane*] *n.* An illicit drug that induces an agitated emotional and physical state and can cause hallucinations. It creates psychological dependency in the user and often results in profound psychological addiction. A particularly powerful form of this drug is called crack cocaine or, simply, "crack." Inhaled by smoking, the onset of its effects is extremely rapid. Cocaine in any form is a **controlled substance**; its possession, distribution, or sale is a criminal offense.
➤ drug, controlled substance, crack, nose candy, snow, blow, white lady.

coconspirator [koh · kon · *spir* · e · ter] *n.* A person who participates with one or more other persons in a **conspiracy**. *See also* conspirator.
➤ abettor, collaborator, partner in crime, schemer, confederate, accomplice.
Ant. bystander.

coconspirator's rule [koh · kon · *spir* · e · ters] *n.* The rule of evidence that statements made by a person involved in a **conspiracy** may be used as evidence of the guilt of all the **conspirators**.

COD Acronym for of **collect on delivery**. Also abbreviated C.O.D.

C

code *n.* 1. The published statutes of a jurisdiction, arranged in systematic form. EXAMPLE: the **United States Code**. 2. A portion of the statutes of a jurisdiction, especially the statutes relating to a particular subject. EXAMPLES: a state's *criminal code* or *tax code*. 3. A secret language; encrypted material.
➤ rule, statute, ethics, canon, constitution, law, precedent ("code of professional responsibility"); secret, guidelines, cryptograph, cipher ("They wrote in code").

code pleading [*plee* · ding] *n.* The system of **pleading** in general use today, embodied in state codes or state **rules of civil procedure** and in the **Federal Rules of Civil Procedure**. Code pleading is much less rigid and technical than the system of **common law pleading**, which it replaced.

Code Civil [*siv* · il] *n.* A codification of French law made during the reign of Napoleon I, at his direction. The Code Civil is the basis of the laws of the State of Louisiana. The Code Civil is also referred to as the **Code Napoleon** or **Napoleonic Code**. *See also* civil law. *Compare* common law.

Code Napoleon [na · *pole* · ee · en] *n.* Same as **Code Civil**.

Code of Federal Regulations [*fed* · er · el reg · yoo · *lay* · shenz] *n.* An arrangement, by subject matter, of the rules and regulations issued by federal administrative agencies; commonly referred to as the **CFR** or abbreviated as C.F.R.

Code of Judicial Conduct [joo · *dish* · el kon · dukt] *n.* A set of principles and ethical standards promulgated by the **American Bar Association**, and subsequently adopted by a majority of states, which establish ethical standards, both personal and professional, for judges. *See* ethics. *Compare* Rules of Professional Conduct.

Code of Military Justice [*mil* · i · tar · ee juss · tiss] *n.* A code that encompasses the entire system of **military law** and military justice, substantive and procedural, civil and criminal, applicable to members of the military services of the United States.

codefendant [koh · de · *fen* · dent] *n.* One of two or more **defendants** in the same criminal prosecution or civil action.

codex [koh · deks] *(Latin) n.* A **code**.

codicil [kod · i · sil] *n.* An addition or supplement to a will, which adds to or modifies the will without replacing or revoking it. A codicil does not have to be physically attached to the will.
➤ addition, supplement, appendix, accessory, addendum, attachment, extension ("codicil to a will").

codification [kod · if · i · kay · shen] *n.* 1. The process of arranging laws in a systematic form covering the entire law of a jurisdiction or a particular area of the law; the process of creating a **code**. 2. The process of turning a **common law rule** into a statute.
➤ categorization, arrangement, classification, compilation, collection.

codify [kod · i · fy] *v.* To create a **code**. *See* codification.
➤ create, collect, arrange, systematize, assemble.

coemption [ko · *emp* · shen] *n.* Buying up all of a particular item.

coerce [ko · erse] *v.* To force or bring about by threats.
➤ force, dictate, intimidate, dominate, compel, press, bully, drive, terrorize.

coercion [ko · *er* · shen] *n.* Compulsion by the application of physical or mental force or persuasion. *See* duress; intimidation; undue influence.
➤ compulsion, pressure, duress, force, intimidation ("confession obtained by coercion"). *Ant.* volition.

coexecutors [koh · eg · *zek* · yoo · torz] *n.* Two or more persons appointed to act jointly as **executors** of the **estate** of a **testator**; **joint executors**.

cogent [ko · gent] *adj.* Having the power to convince; effective; compelling.
➤ forceful, logical, solid, sound, convincing, effective ("a cogent argument").

cognation [kog · *nay* · shen] *n.* Relationship by ties of blood or family. *See* relation by blood.

cognizable [*kog* · ni · zabl] *adj.* 1. Capable of being heard and determined by a court, i.e., within the **jurisdiction** of the court. 2. Knowable.
➤ accountable, justiciable, triable, proper, clear ("The offense was cognizable before the superior court").

cognizance [*kog* · ni · zense] *n.* 1. The assumption of **jurisdiction** by a court. 2. Awareness; acknowledgment; recognition.
➤ dominion, judicial notice ("The court has cognizance over maritime cases"); understanding, apprehension, attention, awareness ("The judge took cognizance of the objection").

cognovit note [kog · *noh* · vit] *n.* A **judgment note**.

cohabitation [ko · ha · bi · *tay* · shen] *n.* 1. Living together as man and wife, although not married to each other. *See* illicit cohabitation. 2. Living together. 3. Having sexual intercourse.
➤ living together, common-law marriage, alliance, union, residing together. *Ant.* separation.

coherent [ko · *here* · ent] *adj.* Logically ordered or integrated.
➤ logical, explanatory, cogent, unambiguous, understandable, concise, reasoned.

cohort [*ko* · hort] *n.* A partner in an activity.
➤ ally, associate, abettor, colleague, friend, partner, accomplice, sidekick, mate.

coif [koyf] *n.* A hat or cap worn by sergeants at law. *See* Order of the Coif.
➤ hat, cap.

coin *n.* Metal formed into a specific shape, size, and weight, stamped with a certain value, and declared by law to be money.

coincide [ko · in · side] *v.* 1. To agree or correspond. 2. To occur simultaneously.
➤ agree, approve, concur, endorse; correspond, coexist, match, confirm, synchronize, acquiesce.

coincidence [ko · *in* · si · dents] *n.* 1. Accord or agreement. 2. A surprising happening.
➤ agreement, accord, correlation, concurrence; accident, fortuity, fluke, happening.

coinsurance [ko · in · shoor · ense] *n.* With respect to insurance, a division of the **risk** between the insurer and the insured. EXAMPLE: a health insurance policy under which the insurance company is obligated to pay 80 percent of every claim and the insured pays 20 percent.

COLA [*koh* · la] *n.* Acronym for **cost-of-living adjustment**. In particular, the term "COLA" has become shorthand for the cost-of-living adjustments made annually in social security benefits.

cold *adj.* 1. Having a lower temperature than body temperature. 2. A lack of warmth.
➤ frozen, iced, chilly, nippy, glacial, shivery; aloof, passionless, reserved, unresponsive, distant, unemotional, frigid, phlegmatic.

cold-blooded *adj.* Performing a brutal act deliberately but without emotion.
➤ cruel, savage, merciless, ruthless, inhumane, callous, heartless, evil, emotionless.

collaborate [ko · *lab* · uh · rait] *v.* To work with others in an endeavor.
➤ collude, team up, cooperate, work together with, join with, coact.

collaborator [ko · *lab* · uh · ray · tor] *n.* One who works with or assists others.
➤ associate, partner, colleague, assistant, helper.

collapse [ke · *laps*] *v.* 1. To fall in or crumble. 2. To fail, especially in reference to a business enterprise. *n.* Failure; exhaustion.
➤ *v.* cave in, fold, give in, disintegrate ("The building collapsed"); fail, go under, falter ("The business collapsed"). *n.* downfall, failure, bankruptcy, destruction, disintegration.

collapsible corporation [ke · *lap* · sibl kore · per · *ay* · shen] *n.* A **corporation** organized under a prearranged plan for liquidation before any substantial amount of what would normally be taxable income can be realized. The **Internal Revenue Code**, however, provides for taxation of the proceeds of such a transaction.

collateral [ko · *lat* · er · el] *adj.* 1. Side-by-side, in the sense of a **collateral relative** such as an uncle or aunt. *Compare* lineal. 2. Accompanying. 3. Subordinate. 4. Indirect.

C

n. Stocks, **bonds**, or other property that serve as **security** for a loan or other obligation; property **pledged** to pay a debt.
➤ *adj.* indirect, secondary, accessory, related, additional, auxiliary, ancillary, subordinate, corresponding, side ("a collateral issue").
n. deposit, security, endorsement, pledge, promise ("He used my stock as collateral.")

collateral attack [a · *tak*] *n.* An attempt to challenge the validity of a **judgment**, decree, or order in an **action** or proceeding other than that in which it was obtained, which was brought for some other purpose. *Compare* direct attack.

collateral consanguinity [kon · sang · *gwin* · i · tee] *n.* A blood relationship based upon a **common ancestor**. EXAMPLES: aunts; uncles; cousins; nephews; nieces. *See* relation by blood.

collateral descendant [de · *send* · ent] *n. See* collateral descent.

collateral descent [de · *sent*] *n.* The determination of **hereditary succession** by counting the generations upward from the **intestate** to the nearest **common ancestor**, then downward, as, for EXAMPLE, from sister to sister or between cousins. *Compare* lineal descent. *See* descent.

collateral estoppel [es · *top* · el] *n.* Being barred from retrying in one court the same facts or issues that have already been the subject of a **judgment** in another court. Collateral estoppel is to be distinguished from *res judicata*, which prohibits the retrial of the same **cause of action**. *See* estoppel; estoppel by judgment.

collateral fraud *n.* Same as **extrinsic fraud**.

collateral heir [air] *n.* An **heir** by **collateral descent**. EXAMPLES: a brother; a cousin.

collateral inheritance tax [in · *her* · i · tense] *n.* A tax on property inherited by **collateral relatives** under a will or under the **intestate laws**.

collateral power [*pow* · er] *n.* A power to dispose of property given to a person who has no **interest** or **estate** in the property; also called a **naked power** or a **power without interest**. *See* power of appointment.

collateral relative [*rel* · e · tiv] *n. See* collateral consanguinity.

collateral source rule *n.* The rule that benefits received by the plaintiff from a source independent of the wrongdoer (for EXAMPLE, the plaintiff's insurance company) will not reduce the **damages** for which the wrongdoer is responsible.

collateral warranty [*war* · en · tee] *n.* A **warranty of title** to land made by a person other than the seller. A warranty from such a person is personal to the buyer and is not transferred when the buyer, in turn, sells the land.

collateral order rule [*or* · der] *n.* The principle that an **order of court** with respect to the form or manner in which a case is to be presented may be appealed even though it is not a **final order** in the case. *See* interlocutory appeal; interlocutory order.

collation [ko · *lay* · shen] *n.* 1. The blending and mixing of property belonging to different persons in order to divide it equally. *See* hotchpot. 2. Comparison of a copy with the original document. 3. Assembly of the pages of a document in sequence.
➤ comparison, blend, confirmation, matching, checking ("the collation of property"); assembling, organizing ("collation of pages").
Ant. separation, division.

collect [ko · *lekt*] *v.* 1. To receive or enforce payment. *See* collection. 2. To gather together; to gather in.
➤ amass, gather, incorporate, unite, accumulate, muster, congregate, flock, convene; acquire, secure, raise, dig up.
Ant. disburse, pay out.

collect on delivery [de · *liv* · e · ree] *n.* A provision (usually shortened to **COD**) in a shipping contract, whereby the carrier agrees to collect for the shipper, from the person to whom the goods are to be shipped, the sales price of the shipped item, in addition to the carrier's own charges. *See* consignee; consignor.

collecting bank [ko · *lek* · ting] *n.* Any bank that handles a **negotiable instrument** for **collection**, except the **payor bank**.

C

collection [ko · *lek* · shen] *n.* 1. The act of receiving payment of a debt, whether voluntarily paid or compelled by legal action. *See* costs of collection. 2. A term for the action required of a **payor bank** upon **presentment** of a **negotiable instrument**. 3. A group of things assembled.
➤ compilation, accumulation, digest, pile, gathering, contribution, group, clump. *Ant.* disbursement.

collection agency [*ay* · jen · see] *n.* A firm engaged in the business of collecting or receiving payment of claims or debts owed to others, as their agent.

collective [ko · *lek* · tiv] *adj.* In common; shared; participatory; cooperative. *n.* A group of persons working together on a common enterprise.
➤ *adj.* common, unified, consolidated, relating, assembled ("the law team's collective efforts"). *n.* organization, association, work team ("the farming collective").

collective bargaining [*bahr* · gen · ing] *n.* The negotiation of terms and conditions of employment between a union, acting on behalf of employees, and an employer or an association of employers. *See* collective bargaining agreement.

collective bargaining agent [*bahr* · gen · ing *ay* · jent] *n.* A union that engages in **collective bargaining** on behalf of an employer's employees.

collective bargaining agreement [*bahr* · gen · ing a · *gree* · ment] *n.* An agreement covering wages, hours, and working conditions, entered into between an employer and the union that is the **collective bargaining agent** for the employer's employees. *See* collective bargaining.

collective bargaining contract [*kon* · trakt] *n. See* collective bargaining agreement.

collective bargaining unit [*bahr* · gen · ing *yoo* · nit] *n.* An employee group permitted by law to be represented by a **collective bargaining agent**. EXAMPLES: all of an employer's maintenance employees, all of its drivers, or all employees in the finishing department.

collective mark *n.* A **trademark** or **service mark** used to identify a **trade association**, fraternal society, or union.

collector [ke · *lek* · ter] *n.* 1. A **special administrator** designated by the court to collect and preserve a **decedent's estate** until an **executor** or **administrator** is appointed. 2. A person appointed to collect taxes. *See* tax collector. 3. A person who works for a collection agency.

collide [*ko* · lide] *v.* 1. To disagree; to have opposite views. 2. To injure by bumping into.
➤ clash, conflict, dissent, disagree, oppose; crash, bump, smash, strike, converge.

collision insurance [ke · *lizh* · en in · *shoor* · ense] *n.* Automobile insurance that protects the owner or operator of a motor vehicle from **loss** due to damage done to his property by another. *Compare* liability insurance.

colloquium [ko · *loh* · kwee · um] *n.* 1. In an **action** for **defamation**, a section of the **complaint** that alleges that **libelous** or **slanderous** words were uttered concerning the plaintiff. 2. A conference or seminar on a particular subject.
➤ conference, group discussion, session, round table, seminar ("the colloquium on leadership").

collude [ke · *lood*] *v.* To act together or conspire, especially for a fraudulent or illegal purpose.
➤ conspire, plot, scheme, band together, unite, contrive. *Ant.* divide.

collusion [ke · *loo* · zhen] *n.* An agreement between two or more persons to defraud another person of her rights by use of the law or to achieve an object forbidden by the law. EXAMPLE: an agreement between a husband and wife to obtain a divorce by having one spouse commit an act that constitutes a ground for divorce.
➤ agreement for fraud, conspiracy, secret agreement, scheming, trickery, perfidy, plotting, contrivance.

collusive [ke · *loo* · siv] *adj.* Involving **collusion** or **fraud**.

collusive action [*ak* · shen] *n.* An **action** brought by **collusion** between the **parties** for the purpose of obtaining a

C

judicial opinion rather than deciding an actual controversy.

collusive divorce [di · vorss] n. A divorce obtained by **collusion** between the **parties**.

collusive joinder [join · der] n. A plaintiff's **joinder** of a defendant, in bad faith, for the purpose of conferring **jurisdiction** on a federal court. See joinder of parties.

color [kull · er] n. An apparent legal right; a seeming legal right; the mere semblance of a legal right. Although they may also refer to activity by private persons, terms such as **color of authority**, **color of law**, and **color of right** generally refer to actions taken by a representative of government (EXAMPLES: a police officer; a civil servant; any public official) which are beyond the authority granted by the law to his position or office, but which *appear* to be legal because of his official status. In many circumstances the government will be held responsible for such conduct even though it was unauthorized. If a deprivation of constitutional rights is involved, such conduct may also violate the **Civil Rights Acts**.
v. 1. To change the color of. 2. To influence or affect.
➤ n. deception, facade, falsification, misrepresentation, influence ("color of law"); pigment, color, dye, shade ("a lovely color"); complexion, description, features, likeness ("she has lost her color"). v. taint, prejudice, affect, influence ("His military background colored his perception of the case").

color of authority [aw · thaw · ri · tee] n. Authority derived from an election or appointment. See authority. USAGE: "He was acting under color of authority."

color of law n. An apparent **legal right**.

color of office [aw · fiss] n. An expression for acts performed by an official that are outside of the authority conferred by her office.

color of right n. A **right** based upon **color of authority**, **color of law**, **color of office**, or **color of title**.

color of title [ty · tel] n. That which gives the appearance of **title**, but is not

title in fact; that which, on its face, appears to pass title but fails to do so. EXAMPLE: a deed to land executed by a person who does not own the land.

colorable [kuhl · er · abl] adj. Apparently valid or legitimate, but actually false or questionable.
➤ deceptive, fraudulent, specious, bogus ("a colorable transaction"); plausible, credible, conceivable ("She possessed colorable authority").

colorable claim n. 1. A **claim** that superficially is legally well-founded, but that may actually be invalid. 2. In bankruptcy law, a groundless **claim of right** to property by a person in possession of the property against a **trustee in bankruptcy's** claim for possession.

colorable imitation [im · i · tay · shen] n. Something created for the purpose of having it appear to be the same as another product. See imitation.

coma [ko · ma] n. A state of unconsciousness brought about by a disease or injury.
➤ unconsciousness, sleep, stupor, torpor, trance.

comaker [koh · may · ker] n. A person who, with another or with others, signs a **note** or other **negotiable instrument** and thereby becomes fully liable for paying it. Compare cosigner. See maker.
➤ cosigner, originator ("Phil is the comaker on this promissory note").

combination [kom · bi · nay · shen] n. Two or more persons acting together to achieve a common objective. If the common objective is criminal in nature, the combination is a **conspiracy**.
➤ alliance, association, coalition, consortium, union ("an illegal combination in restraint of trade").
Ant. isolation, separation.

combination in restraint of trade [re · straint] n. An agreement between two or more persons that seeks to inhibit commerce by causing prices to increase beyond their natural level. Such combinations are illegal under the **antitrust acts**. See Clayton Act; monopoly; restraint of trade; Sherman Act.

combination patent [*pat* · ent] *n.* A **patent** granted to a **device** whose originality lies in the arrangement or composition of its components, none of which are new or original.

combine [*kom* · bine] *n.* A **combination in restraint of trade**.
v. To merge or mix items together.
➤ *n.* association, syndicate.
v. integrate, connect, merge, mix, link ("combine our resources").
Ant. sever, separate.

comity [*kom* · i · tee] *n.* 1. The recognition that one nation allows within its territory to the legislative, executive, or judicial acts of another nation; the extent to which the law of one nation is allowed to operate within the territory of another. This principle is sometimes referred to as the *comity of nations. See* conflict of laws. 2. Courtesy or consideration.
➤ recognition, willingness, accommodation, consideration, goodwill, reciprocity ("the comity of nations").
Ant. hostility.

comment [*kom* · ent] *n.* A statement that explains the author's opinion or ideas about a matter.
v. To make a comment.
➤ *n.* remark, note, notation, observation, assertion, explication, exposition.
v. remark, declare, explicate, expound, interject, discuss, opine.

commerce [*kom* · erss] *n.* 1. The purchase, sale, exchange, and distribution of goods and services among individuals, organizations, or nations. Although the term is generally synonymous with "trade," it sometimes has a broader significance, which may include social or sexual relations. 2. Short for **interstate commerce**. *See also* affecting commerce; foreign commerce. *See and compare* interstate commerce; intrastate commerce.
➤ exchange, marketing, commercialism, business, trade, interchange, industry.

commerce clause *n.* The clause in Article I, § 8, of the Constitution that gives Congress the power to regulate commerce between the states and between the United States and foreign countries. Federal statutes that regulate business and labor

(EXAMPLES: the **Fair Labor Standards Act**; the **Occupational Safety and Health Act**) are based upon this power. *See* interstate commerce.

commercial [ke · *mer* · shel] *adj.* Pertaining to the purchase and sale of goods, to buying and selling, or to commerce generally.
➤ monetary, wholesale, retail, bartering, for-profit ("a commercial transaction"); pecuniary, crass, exploitative ("his artwork is extremely commercial").

commercial bank *n.* An ordinary bank, as distinguished from a **savings bank**. *See* bank.

commercial domicile [*dom* · i · sile] *n.* A **domicile** acquired by residing in a country for the purpose of doing business there.

commercial frustration [frus · *tray* · shen] *n. See* frustration of contract doctrine; frustration of purpose.

commercial impracticability [im · prak · ti · ke · *bil* · i · tee] *n. See* impracticability.

commercial instrument [*in* · stroo · ment] *n. See* commercial paper.

commercial law *n.* The branch of the law that relates to shipping, insurance, the exchange of money, **brokerage, drafts, promissory notes**, and other matters of concern to merchants. *See* Uniform Commercial Code (UCC). *Also see* law merchant.

commercial loan *n.* A loan made by a lending institution to a business, as distinguished from a **personal loan** or a **consumer loan**.

commercial paper [*pay* · per] *n.* **Negotiable instruments**, including checks, **drafts, certificates of deposit**, and **promissory notes**. Commercial paper is regulated by Article 3 of the **Uniform Commercial Code**.

commercial speech *n.* Speech used for the purpose of commercial advertisement. Commercial speech does not benefit as fully from **First Amendment** guaranties as other speech. The government may, within limits, regulate commercial speech. EXAMPLE: a state is entitled to insist that advertising by a doctor or lawyer be "professional."

C

commercial use *n.* Use in a business in which one is engaged for profit. USAGE: "This property is zoned for commercial use."

commercial vehicle [*vee* · ikl] *n.* A motor vehicle used other than for pleasure or for the private convenience of the owner.

Commercial Code *n. See* Uniform Commercial Code (UCC).

commingle [ko · *ming* · gul] *v.* To merge; to mix. *See* marshal.

commingling [ko · *ming* · gling] *n.* Mingling; merging; mixing. *See also* marshaling assets, escrow account.

➤ combining, intermixing, merging, uniting, blending, marshaling.

commingling of funds *n.* The act of an agent, broker, attorney, or **trustee** in mingling his own funds with those of his client, customer, or **beneficiary**. Such conduct is unethical and often illegal as well.

commingling of goods *n.* A mixing of goods.

commission [ke · *mish* · en] *n.* 1. A governmental body, usually a board or similar agency, having **administrative** and **quasi-judicial** powers. EXAMPLES: the **Civil Service Commission**; the **Equal Employment Opportunity Commission**. 2. A group of persons charged with responsibility to perform some duty. EXAMPLE: the **Commission on Uniform State Laws**. 3. A **writ**; an authorization; a written authority from a competent source given to a **public officer** enabling her to exercise the powers or duties of her office. For EXAMPLE: a judge who is appointed, as opposed to an elected judge, serves by virtue of a commission from the governor. 4. A fee or payment calculated on a percentage basis, for EXAMPLE, a salesperson's remuneration. 5. The act of committing a crime. USAGE: "The witness testified that the defendant carried a gun during commission of the burglary."

➤ authority, duty, role, office, power ("her commission to enforce fair labor practices"); group, agency, board, council, panel, cabinet ("the tax commission").

commission agent [*ay* · jent] *n.* An **agent** who buys or sells on commission; a **factor**.

commission form of government [*guv* · ern · ment] *n.* A system of municipal government in which all executive and legislative power is held by a single elected or appointed board, usually consisting of the mayor and a few other public officials. *Compare* city manager form of government.

commission merchant [*mer* · chent] *n.* A **factor**.

Commission on Civil Rights [ke · *mish* · en on *siv* · el] *n.* A federal **commission** that collects and studies information on discrimination or denials of **equal protection of the laws** because of race, color, religion, sex, age, handicap, or national origin, or in the administration of justice in such areas as voting rights, enforcement of civil rights laws, and equality of opportunity in education, employment, and housing. The commission makes findings of fact but has no enforcement authority. *See* Civil Rights Acts.

Commission on Uniform State Laws [*yoo* · ni · form] *n.* A **commission**, composed of legal scholars, that proposes model legislation, called **model acts** or **model laws**, in various areas of the law. These are often adopted, in whole or in part, by individual states. EXAMPLES: the **Uniform Commercial Code**; the **Reciprocal Enforcement of Support Act**; the **Model Penal Code**. *See* uniform laws.

commissioner [ke · *mish* · e · ner] *n.* 1. A person having a **commission** to carry out a public office. In some cities, the chief of police is called the *police commissioner* or the *commissioner of public safety*. 2. A member of a **commission** or **board**. *See* county commissioners. 3. The former title of a **United States Magistrate**, i.e., United States Commissioner.

➤ administrator, manager, representative, delegate.

commissioner of court *n.* Same as **court commissioner**.

commit [ke · *mit*] *v.* 1. To effect or make a commitment. 2. To perpetrate, as to commit a burglary. *See* commission.

➤ enact, complete, perform, fulfill, achieve ("She committed the crime"); deliver, allocate, arrest, impound, incarcerate, imprison ("The person was committed to jail"); entrust, engage, invest, empower, convey ("commit funds").

commitment [ke · *mit* · ment] *n.* 1. The delivery of an arrested person for incarceration in jail in the absence of bail, pending trial. 2. The delivery of a convicted person to jail or prison to serve his sentence. 3. The detention of a mentally ill, alcoholic, or drug-addicted person or a person under **civil arrest**. *See* civil commitment; involuntary commitment; voluntary commitment. 4. The act of binding oneself, pledging, or contracting. *See* mortgage commitment.
➤ confinement, imprisonment, detention, restraint ("Because he was insane, his commitment was legal"); promise, assurance, obligation, vow, duty ("I had her commitment to pay the loan"); allegiance, duty, engagement, involvement ("commitment to the cause").

commitment fee *n.* A fee paid by a borrower to a lender, in addition to interest, for making a loan.

committee [ke · *mit* · ee] *n.* A group of persons selected by a larger body to perform some aspect of that body's responsibilities. EXAMPLE: the Judiciary Committee of the Senate reviews the qualifications of the president's judicial appointments and makes a recommendation to the full Senate with respect to **confirmation**. *See also* conference committee; executive committee.
➤ group, board, body, task force, council.

committee of the legislature [*leg* · iss · lay · cher] *n.* *See* legislative committee.

committee of the whole *n.* A legislature acting as a committee. A legislature may relax its normal rules of procedure and act as a committee to facilitate its work. Action taken by a committee of the whole is legal only if it is ratified by the legislature acting under its normal rules. *Compare* joint committee; select committee; standing committee.

committing magistrate [ke · *mit* · ing *maj* · is · trate] *n.* A judge, justice of the peace, or other judicial officer

authorized to commit a person arrested for the commission of a crime, pending **preliminary hearing** and trial. *See* commitment. *Also see* magistrate.

commodity [ke · *mod* · i · tee] *n.* 1. An article of commerce; a **movable** and **tangible** thing produced or used for sale or barter. 2. Certain farm products, such as grain or cotton, which are sold before they come into existence. *See* futures. 3. A useful thing.
➤ merchandise, possession, product, stock, material.

Commodity Credit Corporation [*kred* · it kore · per · *ay* · shen] *n.* A federal administrative agency that supports the price and availability of agricultural **commodities** through loans, purchases, and payments. The **CCC** also disposes of surplus farm commodities.

commodity exchange [eks · *chaynj*] *See* exchange.

common [*kom* · en] *adj.* 1. Customary; normal; accepted. USAGE: "The way I do it is common practice." 2. Shared; communal; collective. USAGE: "This is common property." 3. Vulgar; coarse; crude; low; inferior. USAGE: "He is a common thief." *n.* 1. That which is shared. *See* in common; tenancy in common. 2. An area in a community that is left undeveloped and is available for public use. In earlier days, a common was a pasture used by the inhabitants of the town for grazing their animals; today a common is a public park.
➤ *adj.* accepted, constant, mutual, prevailing, customary, established ("The way I do it is common practice"); shared, public, communal ("This is common property"); vulgar, low, second-rate, inferior, cheap ("Her manners were so common"). *Ant.* unusual; refined.
n. town center, park.

common ancestor [*an* · ses · ter] *n.* A person from whom two or more persons are descended. *See* ancestor; descendant.

common carrier [*kar* · yer] *n.* A person or company that represents itself as engaged in the business of transporting persons or property from place to place, for compensation, offering its services to the public generally. *See* carrier; carrier for hire.

C

common carrier's lien [*kar · yerz leen*] *n.* A **lien** on goods transported by a **common carrier**, which exists until the freight and storage charges are paid.

common council [*koun · sel*] *n.* More commonly called a city council; the legislative body of a city or other municipality, except for cities governed by a **city manager** or a **commission form of government**.

common disaster [*diz · ass · ter*] *n.* An occurrence that causes the death of two or more persons who have related **interests** in property; for EXAMPLE, a husband and wife, the heirs of a **common ancestor**, or beneficiaries under a will or an insurance policy. Different legal consequences may result depending upon whether it is possible to determine which of the persons survived the longest. *See* simultaneous death; simultaneous death acts. *See also* presumption of survivorship.

common drunk *n.* *See* habitual drunkard.

common enemy doctrine [*en · e · mee dok · trin*] *n.* The rule of law that a landowner is within her rights to repel **surface water** (EXAMPLE: water overflowing from a creek) from her land, even if it flows onto the property of an adjoining landowner.

common enterprise [*en · ter · prize*] *n.* *See* joint enterprise.

common law *n.* 1. Law found in the decisions of the courts rather than in statutes; **judge-made law**. *See* case law. *Compare* statutory law. 2. English law adopted by the early American colonists, which is part of the Untied States' judicial heritage and forms the basis of much of its law today. *Compare* civil law.
➤ case law, civil law, judge-made law. *Ant.* statutory law.

common law action [*ak · shen*] *n.* *See* action at common law.

common law crimes *n.* Conduct that was considered to be criminal by the **common law**. *Compare* statutory crimes.

common law lien [*leen*] *n.* A **lien** existing under the **common law**. *Compare* statutory lien.

common law marriage [*mar · ej*] *n.* A marriage entered into without ceremony, the parties agreeing between themselves to be husband and wife, followed by a period of **cohabitation**. Common law marriages are valid in some states and invalid in others. *See also* consensual marriage. *Compare* ceremonial marriage.

common law pleading [*pleed · ing*] *n.* A highly formal process of **pleading** a case, both **claim** and **defense**, the object of which was to put the matter in dispute **at issue** as precisely as possible. Common law pleading has been replaced in all jurisdictions by **code pleading**. *See* pleadings.

common law rule *n.* A **rule of law** created by and existing at **common law**.

common law trust [*kom · en law*] *n.* Same as **business trust**, **Massachusetts trust**, or **Massachusetts business trust**.

common nuisance [*nyoo · sense*] *n.* Same as **public nuisance**; that is, a **nuisance** that affects citizens at large. *Compare* private nuisance.

common pleas [*pleez*] *n.* A term for civil actions, as distinguished from criminal prosecutions.

common pleas court [*pleez*] *n.* *See* court of common pleas.

common purpose [*per · pes*] *n.* The intent of two or more persons acting together to commit a specific crime; also referred to as *common intent, common scheme,* or *common design.*

common situs picketing [*site · us pik · e · ting*] *n.* Picketing a contractor with whom a union has a labor dispute at a construction site at which many contractors are engaged. The object of such picketing is to exert the greatest possible economic pressure. As a rule, such picketing is illegal. *See* picketing.

common stock *n.* Ordinary **capital stock** in a corporation, the **market value** of which is based upon the worth of the corporation. Owners of common stock vote in proportion to their holdings, as opposed to owners of other classes of stock that are without **voting rights**. By contrast, however, common stock earns **dividends** only after other preferred classes of stock. *Compare* preferred stock. *See* stock.

common wall *n. See* party wall.

commonweal [*kom* · en · weel] *n.* The common welfare; the common good; the **public welfare**.

commonwealth [*kom* · en · welth] *n.*
1. The public; the entire body of people in a state or nation. *See* community.
2. A state or nation in which the people themselves govern through their elected representatives. 3. The official title of the states of Kentucky, Massachusetts, Pennsylvania, and Virginia. 4. A term for a self-governing territory of the United States. EXAMPLE: the Commonwealth of Puerto Rico.
➤ public citizens, society, democracy, federation, community.
Ant. individual.

Commonwealth Court [*kom* · en · welth] *n.* In Pennsylvania, a special court that has **jurisdiction** over most lawsuits brought against the state and many kinds of legal actions (not including criminal prosecutions) brought by the state.

communicate [ko · *mune* · i · kate] *v.* To share knowledge or information. Communication may be verbal or nonverbal.
➤ say, relate, give, notice, broadcast, narrate, utter, publicize, inform.

communication [kum · *yoo* · ni · kay · shen] *n.* A statement made in writing or orally by one person to another; the transfer of information, whether by speech, acts, signs, or appearances, and whether in person, in writing, or electronically. *See* marital communications privilege; privileged communication.
➤ discourse, dialogue, conversation, correspondence, interlocution; announcement, message, news, information, report.

communism [*kom* · yoo · niz · im] *n.* An economic system in which the state owns the means of production (manufacturing, agriculture, transportation) and in which, in theory, every citizen participates in production according to his ability and shares in what has been produced according to his need. A primary distinction between communism and **socialism** is that the

former is almost universally totalitarian and the latter generally democratic in greater or lesser degree. *Compare* capitalism; fascism.
➤ collectivism, socialism, state ownership, common property, Marxism.
Ant. capitalism.

community [ke · *myoo* · ni · tee] *n.*
1. People living in the same place (city, town, neighborhood) and subject to the same laws. 2. A place where people live together. 3. Society in general. 4. A group of people sharing common interests.
adj. Common ownership or possession.
➤ *n.* locality, society, neighborhood, town, colony, district, hamlet.
adj. shared, common, public.

community of interest [*in* · trest] *n.* A joint or common interest. *See* interest.

community property [*prop* · er · tee] *n.* A system of law under which the earnings of either spouse are the property of both the husband and the wife, and property acquired by either spouse during the marriage (other than by gift, under a will, or through inheritance) is the property of both. States that have adopted this system are called **community property states**. *Compare* equitable distribution.

community property state [*prop* · er · tee] *n. See* community property.

community trust *n.* A form of **charitable trust**.

commutation [kom · yoo · *tay* · shen] *n.*
1. Substituting one kind of payment for another. EXAMPLE: a lump-sum payment for installment payments. 2. Substituting one thing for another.
➤ change, alteration, abatement, modification, adjustment, lessening.

commutation of sentence [*sen* · tense] *n.* The substitution of a less severe punishment for a more severe punishment. *See* sentence. *Compare* amnesty; pardon; parole.

commutative [kem · *yoo* · te · tiv] *adj.* Pertaining to change or substitution ("commutative justice").

commutative contract [*kon* · trakt] *n.* A **contract** that involves mutual obligations, and in which the acts to be performed by

C

one **party** form the **consideration** for those to be performed by the other. *Compare* independent contract.

commutative justice [*jus* · tis] *n.* The concept that, for there to be justice in personal dealings, there must be fairness in equal measure on both sides. *Compare* distributive justice.

commuted value [kom · *myoo* · ted val · yoo] *n.* The **present value** of a **future interest**. Property or money that one can make use of today has less present value than property or money that one can only make use of at some future time (a future interest), because a person who has the present use of money or property can invest it or derive some other immediate benefit from it. *See* capitalize.

compact [*kom* · pakt] *n.* A contract, particularly a contract of an important and serious nature.
adj. Faking only a small space; short; condensed.
➤ *n.* contract, alliance, deal, pact, treaty ("We had a compact for peace").
adj. condensed, pressed, solid, hard, firm, thick, tight, small.

compact clause *n.* The clause in Article I of the Constitution which provides that, without the consent of Congress, no state can enter into an "agreement or compact" with another state or foreign country. *See* interstate compact.

company [*kum* · pe · nee] *n.* The joining of two or more persons for the carrying on of a business, usually, but not necessarily, a corporation. EXAMPLES: a finance company; an **investment company**. *See* joint-stock company; parent company; stock company.
➤ group, association, partnership, corporation, business group, enterprise, force ("John and Mary formed a company to sell shoes"); companionship, fellowship, friendship, camaraderie ("I like Jonathan's company").
Ant. individual; isolation.

company union [*yoo* · nyen] *n.* A labor union whose total membership consists of the employees of a single company and is controlled by the company.

comparable [*kom* · per · uh · bul] *adj.* That which can be compared; equivalent.

➤ similar, equivalent, corresponding, commensurate, equal.

comparable worth [*kom* · per · ebl] *n.* The concept that men and women are entitled to equal pay when their work requires equal skills or duties and is therefore of "comparable worth." Several states have adopted legislation putting this concept into practice in varying degrees. *See* Equal Pay Act.

comparative [kem · *par* · i · tiv] *adj.* Capable of being compared to others; similar.
➤ comparable, relative, proportionate, allocated, measured by comparison ("the doctrine of comparative negligence"). *Ant.* absolute.

comparative negligence [kem · *par* · i · tiv *neg* · li · jense] *n.* The doctrine adopted by most states that requires a comparison of the **negligence** of the defendant with the negligence of the plaintiff: the greater the negligence of the defendant, the lesser the level of **care** required of the plaintiff to permit her to **recover**. In other words, the plaintiff's negligence does not defeat her **cause of action**, but it does reduce the **damages** she is entitled to recover. Also called comparative fault. *Compare* contributory negligence.

comparative rectitude [kem · *par* · i · tiv *rek* · ti · tyood] *n.* The principle that, when both parties to a marriage are guilty of misconduct for which a divorce may be granted, the court will grant the divorce to the spouse who is less at fault.

compare [kom · *pare*] *v.* To note similarities and differences.
➤ measure, liken, juxtapose, analogize, differentiate, distinguish, contrast, weigh.

compel [kem · *pel*] *v.* To force; to force a response. A person who fails or refuses to answer **interrogatories** or to respond appropriately to an attempt to take his **deposition** may be forced to comply by means of a **motion to compel discovery**.
➤ coerce, impel, force, impose, oblige, require, threaten, decree.

compelling [kom · *pel* · ing] *adj.* Significant, powerful, or strong. Of a greater significance than legitimate or rational.

➤ powerful, strong, significant, emphatic, commanding, persuasive, overriding.

compelling state interest [kem · *pel* · ing state *in* · trest] *n.* A principle of **constitutional law** which holds that a state, whether by legislation or other action, may restrict personal rights only if it has an obligation to its citizenry as a whole to do so, for EXAMPLE, to ensure the public safety, maintain the public health, or to further its **police power**.

compensable [kem · *pens* · abl] *adj.* That which may, should, or must be compensated. **compensable injury** [*in* · je · ree] *n.* A job-related injury to an employee for which he is entitled to compensation under a **workers' compensation act**.

compensate [*kom* · pen · sate] *v.* 1. To **make whole**; to **indemnify**; to reimburse. 2. To pay.

➤ counterbalance, equilibrate, offset, stabilize; pay, reimburse, remunerate, satisfy.

compensating balance [*kom* · pen · say · ting *bal* · ense] *n.* The amount of money a person must keep on deposit with a bank as a requirement for a loan or a **line of credit**.

compensation [kom · pen · *say* · shen] *n.* 1. Remuneration for services, whether in the form of wages, salary, fees, or commissions. 2. Payment for **injury** or **loss**; **damages**. 3. Payment for injury or loss made under a **workers' compensation act** to an injured employee. *See* deferred compensation; just compensation; unemployment compensation acts.

➤ payment, reimbursement, payoff, consideration, settlement ("compensation for his work"); balancing, counterbalancing, redress, canceling out ("compensation for his handicap").

compensatory [kom · *pen* · se · to · ree] *adj.* Involving a reimbursement to make amends, to make equivalent, or to make reparations.

➤ remunerative, actual, repaying, atoning, redemptive, reimbursing, providing restitution ("compensatory damages").

compensatory damages [kem · *pen* · se · to · ree *dam* · e · jez] *n.* **Damages** recoverable in a lawsuit for **loss** or **injury** suffered by the plaintiff as a result of the defendant's conduct. Also called **actual damages**, they may include expenses, loss of time, reduced earning capacity, bodily injury, and mental anguish. *Compare* punitive damages.

competency [*kom* · pe · ten · see] *n.* 1. **Legal capacity.** USAGE: "Competency to stand trial." 2. Capability; qualification for performing a specific act.

➤ adequacy, capability, expertise, capacity.

competency hearing [*heer* · ing] *n.* A **proceeding** conducted to determine a person's soundness of mind, either for the purpose of standing trial in a criminal case or in the context of a **civil commitment**. *See* sound mind. *Also see* insanity; M'Naghten rule.

competent [*kom* · pe · tent] *adj.* 1. Having **legal capacity**. 2. Capable; qualified. 3. Sufficient; acceptable.

➤ eligible, qualified, capable, fit, polished, efficient, responsible, able. *Ant.* incapable, unable.

competent court *n.* A court having **jurisdiction**. *See* court of competent jurisdiction.

competent evidence [*ev* · i · dense] *n.* Evidence that tends to prove the matter in dispute; evidence that is legally admissible. *See* proof.

competent jurisdiction [joo · ris · *dik* · shen] *n.* *See* court of competent jurisdiction.

competent person [*per* · sen] *n.* 1. A person who has **legal capacity**. 2. A person legally qualified for a specific undertaking by age and mental capacity. *Compare* incompetent; incompetent person. *See* capacity.

competent witness [*wit* · ness] *n.* A person legally qualified to testify under oath; a person of appropriate age and mental capacity.

competition [kom · *pe* · tish · un] *n.* A contest between two rival parties.

➤ contest, rivalry, test, opposition, engagement, vying, encounter.

competitive [kom · *pet* · i · tiv] *n.* 1. Relating to or based on competition. 2. Open for competition.

C

C

➤ combative, opposing, rivaling, contending, contentious ("a competitive person"); public, unclosed, accessible, unrestricted ("competitive bidding").

competitive bidding [kem · pet · i · tiv bid · ing] *n.* Bidding for contracts for **public works** or goods or services required by the government, which contemplates the awarding of a contract to the **lowest responsible bidder**; that is, the lowest bidder most likely to complete the project in accordance with the **specifications**. Highway construction, the purchase of computers by a county, or the providing of lunches to a school district are EXAMPLES of undertakings normally requiring competitive bidding. *Compare* sole source contract.

compilation [kom · pih · lay · shen] *n.* A collection of statutes or data.
➤ gathering, arrangements, accumulation, selection.

compile [kom · pile] *v.* To collect and arrange.
➤ gather, group, accumulate, prepare, select, arrange, cumulate.

complain [kom · plane] *v.* 1. To criticize or find fault with. 2. To make formal charges initiating legal proceedings.
➤ disapprove, disparage, contravene, blame, protest, cavil, find fault with, deprecate, castigate ("complain about conditions"); charge, accuse, prosecute, arraign, sue, challenge, file a claim ("complain of a criminal act").

complainant [kom · play · nent] *n.* 1. The plaintiff in a lawsuit. 2. A person who files a formal accusation of a crime. 3. A person who makes any formal complaint. 4. The **prosecuting witness** in a criminal proceeding.
➤ plaintiff, claimant, petitioner, litigant.
Ant. defendant, respondent.

complaining witness [kom · play · ning wit · ness] *n. See* prosecuting witness, victim.

complaint [kom · playnt] *n.* 1. The initial **pleading** in a **civil action**, in which the plaintiff alleges a **cause of action** and asks that the wrong done him be **remedied** by the court. 2. A formal charge of a crime. 3. An objection, criticism, or protest.
➤ petition, charge, pleading, indictment, accusation ("Susan was served with a complaint"); objection, criticism, rebuke, protest, grievance ("Michael's complaint was justified").

complete [kom · pleet] *adj.* 1. Containing all necessary parts. 2. Made whole or brought to an end.
➤ full, absolute, inclusive, unimpaired, unrestricted, plenary, thorough, entire, blanket, unconditional ("complete liquidation"); closed, concluded, executed, done, terminated ("The deal is complete").

completion bond [kom · plee · shen] *n.* A **surety bond** guaranteeing payment of the cost of completing a construction contract if the contractor fails to complete it in accordance with the terms of the contract.

complex [kom · plecks] *adj.* Made from two or more parts; intricate; involved; difficult.
n. 1. A whole made up of interrelated parts. 2. An elaborate group of factors.
➤ *adj.* difficult, involved, abstruse, entangled, perplexing, complicated ("a complex case").
Ant. simple, easy.
n. development, compound, organization, structure, network; entanglement, maze, difficulty, complication.

compliance [kom · ply · ense] *n.*
1. Obedience; submission; conformance.
2. Assent; consent; acquiescence.
➤ assent, accommodation, concurrence, submission, yielding, agreement, cooperation.

comply [kom · ply] *v.* To conform one's behavior to another's request.
➤ concur, consent, obey, accommodate, defer to, satisfy.

component [kom · pone · ent] *n.* A part or ingredient; an element of a whole.
➤ part, section, segment, sector, unit, ingredient, aspect, factor.
Ant. whole.

compos mentis [kom · pes men · tis] *(Latin) adj.* Of sound mind; sane.

composite [kom · poz · it] *n.* An assembly of parts.
adj. Made of distinct parts.

➤ *n.* aggregate, medley, fusing, gathering, assembly, conjoining.
adj. fused, aggregated, assembled, joined, gathered.

composition [kom · po · *zish* · un] *n.* 1. An agreement or intellectual creation. 2. The general makeup or nature of something.
➤ agreement, compact, concession, release, settlement ("composition in bankruptcy"); makeup, organization, structure, constitution, nature ("the composition of the team").

composition with creditors
[kom · pe · *zish* · en with *kred* · i · terz] *n.* 1. An agreement between a debtor and her **creditors** under which, in exchange for prompt payment, the creditors agree to accept amounts less than those actually owed in satisfaction of their claims. *See* arrangement with creditors. 2. **Proceedings** under **Chapter 13** of the **Bankruptcy Code** for debt readjustment.

compound [kom · pound] *adj.* Composite; complex; mixed.
v. [kom · *pound*] 1. To compromise; to enter into a **composition with creditors**; to obtain **discharge** from a debt by the payment of a smaller sum. 2. To add to; to increase. 3. To create or form by mixing, combining, or uniting elements, ingredients, or parts.
n. 1. A mixture or blend. 2. A separated or segregated area.
➤ *adj.* composite, mixed, conglomerate.
v. blend, mix, combine, unite, merge ("To make a cake, you must compound the proper ingredients"); intensify, aggravate, widen, worsen, complicate ("compound the problem").
n. mixture, conglomeration, merger, blend; complex, site, campus ("held hostage at the compound").

compound interest [*in* · trest] *n.* Interest charged on interest by adding accrued interest to principal and computing interest for the next interest period upon the new principal. Compound interest is also called **interest on interest**. *Compare* simple interest. *See* interest.

compound larceny [*lar* · sen · ee] *n.* The offense of **larceny** compounded by the fact that the theft is from the victim's house or **person**. Unlike a burglar, a person who engages in a **larcenous** taking from a house has entered the house with the express or implied permission of the owner or occupant. Also referred to as **mixed larceny**. *Compare* burglary.

compounding a crime [kom · *poun* · ding] *n.* The agreement of a crime victim not to inform against or prosecute the perpetrator in return for money or something else of value. If the crime is a **felony**, the undertaking is often referred to as **compounding a felony**. Felony or **misdemeanor**, an agreement not to report or prosecute a crime is itself a crime. *See* misprision of felony.

compounding a felony [*fel* · a · nee] *n.* *See* compounding a crime.

comprehend [*com* · pree · hend] *v.* 1. To grasp the meaning of. 2. To recognize.
➤ understand, grasp, know, discern, fathom; cognize, apprehend.

comprehensive [kom · pre · *hen* · siv] *adj.* Inclusive; broad; complete; blanket.
➤ all-inclusive, all-embracing, consummate, total, unconditional, extensive.

comprehensive coverage [*kuv* · e · rej] *n.* A type of coverage provided by a policy of **comprehensive insurance**.

comprehensive insurance [in · *shoor* · ense] *n.* **Insurance** that provides coverage for various **risks** (EXAMPLES: fire; theft; flood; wind; hail), each of which could also be covered under separate policies.

compromise [*kom* · pre · mize] *n.* An agreement to end, by means of mutual concessions, a controversy over a claim that is disputed in good faith.
v. 1. To endanger; to put at risk. 2. To arbitrate or negotiate.
➤ *n.* agreement, bargain, concession, settlement, deal ("Our compromise brought peace").
v. expose, jeopardize, embarrass, imperil, weaken, discredit ("He compromised his values"); bargain, negotiate, trade off ("They compromised in order to settle their dispute.").

compromise and settlement [*set* · el · ment] *n.* An agreement to settle a dispute, followed by performance

C

of the promises contained in the agreement. *See* settlement.

compromise verdict [*ver* · dikt] *n.* A **verdict** reached as a result of the surrender by some members of the jury of their belief on one issue in the case in return for the abandonment by other members of their firm opinion on another issue. Because the result does not represent the approval of the jury as a whole, such a verdict may be set aside as improper.

comptroller [kon · *trole* · er] *n.* A corporate officer or public officer in charge of the financial affairs of a corporation or government agency or department.
➤ officer, accountant, registrar, inspector, examiner.

compulsion [kom · *pul* · shun] *n.* An irresistible impulse to do an act.
➤ coercion, force, oppression, urgency, obsession, craze, fetish, fixation, mania, infatuation, preoccupation.

compulsory [kem · *pul* · se · ree] *adj.* Brought about by **operation of law** or by moral considerations, or induced by the use of physical or mental force.
➤ obligatory, required, mandatory, involuntary, necessary ("compulsory counterclaim").
Ant. permissive.

compulsory arbitration [ar · bi · *tray* · shen] *n.* **Arbitration** required by statute. Compulsory arbitration is most common in connection with labor disputes.

compulsory counterclaim [*koun* · ter · klame] *n.* The **Federal Rules of Civil Procedure** require that any **demand** which the defendant has against the plaintiff, growing out of the same transaction or occurrence which is the subject matter of the plaintiff's **action**, must be **pleaded** in response to the plaintiff's suit, or be barred. *Compare* permissive counterclaim. *See* counterclaim.

compulsory examination [eg · zam · i · *nay* · shen] *n.* 1. A mental or physical examination ordered by a court. *See* motion for compulsory examination; motion. 2. Any required examination.
EXAMPLE: a medical examination required

for the purpose of providing **evidence of insurability**.

compulsory insurance [in · *shoor* · ense] *n.* Automobile liability insurance required as a condition of operating a motor vehicle.

compulsory joinder [*join* · der] *n.* The required **joining** of a **party**. The **joinder** of a person in a lawsuit is required if not to do so would deprive that person, or those already parties, of complete **relief** or cause substantial injustice. *See* joinder of parties. *Compare* permissive joinder.

compulsory nonsuit [*non* · syoot] *n.* *See* nonsuit.

compulsory payment [*pay* · ment] *n.* A payment compelled by force of law or by the threat of recourse to **legal process**. EXAMPLES: payment of income tax; payment of a debt because the creditor threatens **garnishment**.

compulsory process [*pross* · ess] *n.* A formal command compelling the attendance of a witness in court. Such a command is usually issued in the form of a **subpoena**, but may also be the subject of a **bench warrant**. *See* process.

computer crime [kem · *pyoo* · ter] *n.* A term that pertains both to using a computer or the data it contains to commit a crime, as well as to crimes against the computer or the material it holds. Most states and the federal government have enacted legislation making such tampering or theft a crime.

con *n.* In opposition to.
v. To trick or deceive.
➤ *n.* in opposition, against, dissenting ("We argued the point thoroughly, both pro and con").
v. deceive, cheat, scheme ("He conned us out of our money.").

conceal [kon · seal] *v.* To prevent the recognition of; to hide.
➤ hide, cloak, shield, obscure, shroud, protect, screen, seclude, veil, obfuscate ("to conceal the identity of the victim").

concealed weapon [ken · *seeld wep* · en] *n.* A weapon carried or placed so that it cannot easily be observed, even though it may not be totally invisible to everyone.

concealment [kon · seal · ment] *n.* A withholding of information; hiding of a person or information.
➤ hiding, disguise, evasion, obfuscation, furtiveness, camouflage, cover.

concealment of crime [ken · seel · ment] *n. See* misprision of felony. *Also see* compounding of crime.

concede [kon · seed] *v.* 1. To admit as true. 2. To admit defeat.
➤ assent, accept, settle, consent, endorse; submit, yield, surrender, succumb.

conceive [kon · seeve] *v.* 1. To comprehend by reason. 2. To originate.
➤ grasp, perceive, know, apprehend, realize; create, generate, originate, give birth to.

concentrate [kon · sin · trate] *v.* 1. To direct toward a common objective. 2. To focus or direct one's mental energy.
➤ accumulate, compress, congregate, focus, consolidate; contemplate, consider, scrutinize, think deeply, focus attention on, mediate, be engrossed in.

concept [kon · sept] *n.* An idea or theory.
➤ idea, thought, theory, opinion, postulate, assumption, presumption, tenet.

conception [ken · sep · shen] *n.*
1. Fertilization of the female ovum by the male sperm. 2. In **patent** law, the point at which an idea for an invention becomes patentable. To be patentable, an idea must include every essential characteristic of the complete and practical invention.
➤ fertilization, inception, formulation, beginning, invention.

concert of action rule [kon · sert of ak · shen] *n.* The rule that if one of the elements of a crime is such that it can only be committed by two persons acting together (EXAMPLES: **adultery**; **illicit cohabitation**), such mutual action cannot also be a **conspiracy**. This principle is also referred to as the **Wharton Rule**.

concerted [ken · ser · ted] *adj.* Planned or carried out together.
➤ coordinated, mutual, planned, premediated, united, consensual, conjoined, collaborative ("a concerted action").

concerted activity [ak · tiv · i · tee] *n.* In labor law, conduct engaged in by an employer's employees, a union, or others for the purpose of supporting **collective bargaining** demands. Concerted activity that constitutes an **unfair labor practice** (EXAMPLE: a **secondary boycott**) is prohibited by the **National Labor Relations Act**. However, *compare* concerted protected activity.

concerted protected activity [pro · tek · ted ak · tiv · i · tee] *n.* In labor law, conduct engaged in by two or more employees acting together for the purpose of influencing the terms and conditions of their employment, including but not limited to wages and hours. Such activity is protected by the **National Labor Relations Act** if it falls within the terms of that statute. EXAMPLES: joining a union; striking; picketing.

conciliation [kon · sil · ee · ay · shen] *n.* The voluntary resolution of a dispute in an amicable manner. One of the primary uses of **conciliators**, also called **mediators**, is in settling labor disputes. Professional conciliators are available for that purpose through the **Federal Mediation and Conciliation Service**. Conciliation differs from **arbitration** in that a conciliator, unlike an **arbitrator**, does not render a decision. *See* alternative dispute resolution; mediation.
➤ mediation, compromise, agreement, mitigation.

conciliator [kon · sil · ee · ay · tor] *n. See* conciliation.

conclude [kon · klude] *v.* 1. To finalize; to complete. 2. To determine.
➤ end, terminate ("to conclude the jury selection process"); rule, decide, declare, find, hold, deem, deduce.

conclusion [ken · kloo · zhen] *n.* 1. A deduction; i.e., the result of reasoning. 2. The end; the finish. 3. **Matter** in a **complaint** that comes after the plaintiff's statement of her **cause of action**.
➤ termination, end, completion, closure, payoff ("conclusion of the trial").
Ant. beginning.

conclusion of fact *n.* A **finding of fact**; a conclusion with respect to the

C

facts, reasoned or **inferred** from the evidence. EXAMPLE: a finding by a judge or jury that the defendant set fire to a barn, and that he intended to do so (*compare* conclusion of law).

conclusion of law *n.* A conclusion drawn by a court which, in conjunction with **findings of fact**, constitutes the basis of its decision in the case; the application of the appropriate legal principles to the case. EXAMPLE: whether the defendant who intentionally set fire to a barn (*see* conclusion of fact) is guilty of **arson**. *Note* that a conclusion of law is not the same as a **legal conclusion**. *Compare* legal conclusion.

conclusive [ken · *kloo* · siv] *adj.* Final; decisive of; the end of the matter; convincing.
➤ absolute, final, clear, compelling, indisputable ("conclusive evidence"); settled, completed, decided.
Ant. contestable, arguable.

conclusive evidence [*ev* · i · dense] *n.* Facts **in evidence** that are so convincing as to support **findings of fact** but that are not absolutely beyond contradiction.

conclusive presumption [pre · *zump* · shen] *n.* Same as **irrebuttable presumption**.

conclusively presumed [ken · *kloo* · siv · lee pree · zoomd] *adv.* *See* conclusive presumption; irrebuttable presumption.

concur [kon · *ker*] *v.* To agree with; to join with. *See* concurring opinion.
➤ agree, approve, come together, consent, support, condone, uphold; coincide, accompany, occur simultaneously.

concurrent [kon · *ker* · ent] *adj.* 1. Having the same **jurisdiction** or authority. *See* concurrent jurisdiction. 2. Occurring at the same time.
➤ coupled, accompanying, linked, merged, allied ("Concurrent powers may be exercised by both the federal and state governments").
Ant. incompatible, independent.

concurrent cause *n.* In the law of **negligence**, a **cause** that occurs at the same time as the **primary cause** to produce the injury, so that the injury

would not have happened in the absence of either. Contrast with **intervening cause**, i.e., a cause that succeeds or follows the primary cause.

concurrent conditions [kon · *dish* · ens] *n.* In a contract, conditions that must be performed simultaneously by each **party**; mutual **conditions precedent**.

concurrent covenants [*kov* · e · nent] *n.* **Covenants** in a contract that must be performed simultaneously.

concurrent jurisdiction [joo · ris · *dik* · shen] *n.* Two or more courts having the power to **adjudicate** the same class of cases or the same matter. *Compare* exclusive jurisdiction. *See* jurisdiction.

concurrent negligence [*neg* · li · jenss] *n.* Two or more independent acts of **negligence** which, together, cause or produce a single **injury** to a **third person** or to property.

concurrent powers [*pow* · erz] *n.* A **constitutional law** term which refers to powers that may be exercised concurrently by both the federal government and state governments.

concurrent resolution [re · zo · *loo* · shen] *n.* A **resolution** adopted by one house of a state legislature or of Congress and concurred in by the other. A concurrent resolution does not have the **force of law**. *Compare* joint resolution.

concurrent sentences [*sen* · ten · sez] *n.* Two or more sentences of imprisonment for crime in which the time of each is to run during the same period as the others, and not consecutively. *Compare* consecutive sentences.

concurring opinion [kon · *ker* · ing o · *pin* · yen] *n.* An **opinion** issued by one or more judges which agrees with the result reached by the **majority opinion** rendered by the court, but reaches that result for different reasons. *Compare* dissenting opinion; minority opinion. *See* concur.

condemn [ken · *dem*] *v.* 1. To declare a building unfit for use for reasons of public health or public safety and order its destruction. 2. To adjudge guilty; to pass sentence upon a person convicted of crime. 3. To **appropriate** property for **public use**. *See* condemnation. 4. To order the slaughter of diseased animals.

➤ convict, punish, damn, adjudicate, blame, appropriate.

condemnation [kon · dem · *nay* · shen] *n.* 1. An order adjudging a building unfit for use. 2. The passing of sentence upon a person convicted of crime. 3. The **legal process** by which government takes private property for **public use** through the exercise of the power of **eminent domain**. See taking. Also see expropriation. 4. Under **admiralty** law, the forfeiture of a ship or its cargo to the government for legal violations, including nonpayment of customs duties, or because the ship or cargo are unfit for use. 5. An order for the slaughter of diseased animals. *See* condemn.

➤ conviction, accusation, disproof, doom, damnation, taking.

condemnation proceeding [kon · dem · *nay* · shen pro · *see* · ding] *n.* Also called a *condemnation suit;* a judicial proceeding for determining **just compensation** for property taken by condemnation.

condition [ken · *dish* · en] *n.* 1. A provision in a contract, deed, will, or similar instrument that creates no right or duty in and of itself but merely limits or modifies rights and duties granted in the document. USAGE: "I don't have to pay her unless she finishes the work by the end of the year; it's a condition of the contract." *See and compare* express condition; implied condition. 2. Anything required to be done before something else is required to be done. USAGE: "I said I'd prepare dinner on the condition that she mows the lawn." 3. The shape or state something is in; its status. *v.* To prepare for use or activity.

➤ *n.* requirement, limitation, provision; contingency provision, prerequisite, specificiation; happening, position, posture, quality ("The condition of his hair was awful"). *v.* prepare, adapt, accustom, teach, warm up, inure, train, ready, modify.

condition of employment [em · *ploy* · ment] *n.* A matter with respect to which the **National Labor Relations Act** requires an employer to bargain collectively. EXAMPLES: wages; hours; vacation pay; seniority. *See* collective bargaining.

condition precedent [pree · *see* · dent] *n.* A condition that must first occur for a contractual obligation (or a provision of a will, deed, or the like) to attach. EXAMPLE: in a teacher's contract, a requirement that he submit the pupils' final grades before the school is obligated to compensate him for teaching the course. *Compare* condition subsequent.

condition subsequent [*sub* · se · kwent] *n.* In a contract, a condition that **divests** contractual liability that has already **attached** (or causes the **divestiture** of property rights granted by deed or will) upon the failure of the other **party** to the contract (or the **grantee** under the deed, or the **beneficiary** under the will) to comply with its terms. EXAMPLE: a provision in a **homeowners policy** that the insurance company's obligation to cover **loss** due to theft is **void** if the loss results from the doors being unlocked when the house is unoccupied. *Compare* condition precedent.

conditional [ken · *dish* · en · el] *adj.* Subject to **condition; contingent**; not absolute.

➤ contingent, incidental, dependent, qualified, provisional. *Ant.* absolute, unconditional.

conditional acceptance [ak · *sep* · tense] *n.* **Acceptance** of a **draft** containing some **qualification, limitation,** or **condition** different from that expressed on the face of the bill. *See* acceptance.

conditional bequest [be · *kwest*] *n.* *See* contingent bequest.

conditional contract [*kon* · trakt] *n.* Not simply a contract with conditions, but a contract whose very existence depends upon the occurrence of a condition.

conditional devise [de · *vize*] *n. See* contingent devise.

conditional estate [es · *tate*] *n. See* estate upon condition.

C

conditional fee *n.* An **estate** in land, also known as a **fee conditional** or **fee simple conditional**, which is limited to particular heirs. (EXAMPLES: **heirs of the body**; male heirs of the body.) If the **grantee** has no heirs of the type described in the condition, the estate reverts to the **grantor**. *See* fee. *Also see* limitation.

conditional indorsement [in · *dorse* · ment] *n. See* restrictive indorsement.

conditional legacy [leg · e · see] *n. See* contingent legacy.

conditional obligation [ob · li · *gay* · shen] *n.* An **obligation** that does not come into existence unless and until a specified uncertain event occurs. *Compare* simple obligation.

conditional pardon [*par* · den] *n.* A **pardon** that does not become effective until the person pardoned performs a specified act, or a pardon that is annulled upon the performance of a specified act.

conditional privilege [*priv* · e · lejd] *n. See* conditionally privileged communication.

conditional sale contract [*kon* · trakt] *n.* A **contract for the sale of goods** under which the buyer receives possession of the goods and the right to use them, but transfer of **title** to the buyer is conditioned upon payment of the full purchase price. *See also* chattel mortgage; installment sale.

conditional use permit [*per* · mit] *n.* A permit issued by a **zoning board** allowing an owner to use her property in a manner not common to other properties in the zone, but only with certain conditions. *Compare* variance. *See* zoning.

conditionally privileged communication [ken · *dish* · en · el · ee priv · e · lejd kum · yoo · ni · *kay* · shen] *n.* In the law of **defamation**, a **communication** made in good faith on a subject in which the person communicating has an **interest**, or with respect to which he has a **duty**, to a person having a corresponding interest or duty, even though the communication contains matter that, without privilege, would be grounds for a lawsuit for **libel** or **slander**. To be privileged, a communication must be made without **actual malice**. *See* privilege; privileged communication.

condominium [kon · de · *min* · ee · um] *n.* A multiunit dwelling, each of whose residents owns her individual apartment absolutely while owning a **tenancy in common** in the areas of the building and grounds used by all the residents. Commonly called a "condo." *Compare* cooperative apartment house.
➤ home, multiunit dwelling, separate ownership.

condonation [kon · do · *nay* · shen] *n.* 1. The forgiveness by one spouse of the other's conduct that constitutes grounds for divorce. Condonation is a **defense** to a divorce action based upon the conduct that has been condoned. 2. The act of overlooking or pardoning.
➤ forgiveness, pardon, overlooking, clemency, discharge, acquittal.

condone [kon · *dohn*] *v.* To allow, permit, or approve of a certain behavior or course of action.
➤ allow, tolerate, accept, bear with, permit, relent, yield.

conduct [*kon* · dukt] *n.* Personal behavior. *v.* [ken · *dukt*] to direct or manage.
➤ *n.* actions, behavior, performance, operation, style, way, code, method, comportment ("good conduct"). *v.* handle, operate, administer, direct, discharge, oversee, regulate ("to conduct a survey").

conduit [kon · *doo* · it] *n.* 1. A natural or artificial channel for movement. 2. An agent for distribution.
➤ channel, means, medium, method, path; agent, delegate, envoy, representative, middleman, intermediary.

confederacy [kon · *fed* · e · ra · see] *n.* 1. A joining together of people, groups of people, or nations, for a common purpose. *See also* confederation. 2. A joining together of people for an unlawful purpose, more commonly called a **conspiracy**.
➤ conspiracy, plot, scheme, collusion, alliance; affiliation, consolidation, combination, compact, combine, union. *Ant.* individual.

Confederacy [kon · *fed* · e · ra · see] *n.* The informal term for the 11 states of the American South that seceded from the

Union in 1860 and 1861 and formed the Confederate States of America.

confederation [kon · fed · e · *ray* · shen] *n.* An agreement or **compact** between two or more governments. *See* Articles of Confederation; federation.
➤ agreement, compact, league, group.

conference committee [*kon* · fer · ense kom · *it* · ee] *n.* A meeting of representatives of both houses of a legislature to resolve differences in the versions of the same **bill** passed by each, by working out a compromise acceptable to both bodies. *See* committee; legislative committee.

confess [kon · *fess*] *v.* To admit to an action; to acknowledge fault.
➤ admit, inculpate, reveal, declare, confirm, own up, acknowledge, concede.

confession [ken · *fesh* · en] *n.* 1. A voluntary admission by a person that he has committed a crime. *Compare* admission. *See and compare* voluntary confession; involuntary confession. 2. A declaration of one's sins to a priest. *See* priest-penitent privilege. 3. Any admission of wrongful behavior.
➤ admission, acknowledgement, declaration, disclosure, revelation. *Ant.* denial.

confession and avoidance [uh · *voy* · dense] *n. See* plea in confession and avoidance.

confession of judgment [*juj* · ment] *n.* The **entry** of a **judgment** upon the admission and at the direction of the debtor, without the formality, time, or effort involved in bringing a lawsuit. *See* judgment note.

confide [con · *fide*] *v.* 1. To trust with secrets. 2. To have faith in another.
➤ disclose, divulge, share, reveal; entrust, rely on, believe in, have faith in.

confidence [*kon* · fi · dense] *n.* 1. Reliance upon another. 2. An assurance of secrecy. 3. Trust in one's own abilities; self-assurance.
➤ belief, assurance, faith, self-possession, trust ("She has confidence in me"); secret, intimate information ("I will keep Mary's confidence about her child's father"). *Ant.* mistrust; public knowledge.

confidence game *n.* A swindling operation in which advantage is taken of the confidence or trust placed by the victim in the swindler. *Compare* false pretenses. *See* swindling.

confidence man *n.* A swindler; a trickster. *See* confidence game.
➤ swindler, trickster, bunco artist.

confidential [kon · fih · *den* · shel] *adj.* Pertaining to information that cannot be revealed, disclosed, or publicly disseminated.
➤ secret, classified, privileged, intimate, private, restricted, hidden, concealed, in camera.

confidential communication [kon · fi · *den* · shel kum · yoo · ni · *kay* · shen] *n.* Information of which unauthorized disclosure could be prejudicial to an important interest. Same as **privileged communication**.

confidential relationship [kon · fi · *den* · shel re · *lay* · shen · ship] *n.* A **fiduciary relationship**, and any informal relationship between parties in which one of them is duty-bound to act with the utmost good faith for the benefit of the other. Although the terms "confidential relationship" and "fiduciary relationship" are often used interchangeably, there is a distinction between them. "Fiduciary relationship" is a term correctly applicable to legal relationships (EXAMPLES: **guardian** and **ward**; **trustee** and **beneficiary**; attorney and client), while "confidential relationship" includes these as well as every other relationship in which one's ability to place confidence is important, such as, for EXAMPLE, business transactions in which one party relies upon the superior knowledge of the other.

confidentiality [kon · fi · den · shee · *al* · i · tee] *n.* The condition of being confidential or privileged. *See* privilege; privileged communication.

confine [ken · *fine*] *v.* 1. To place in a prison or similar institution. 2. Generally, to deprive a person or an animal of its liberty. *See* confinement.
➤ enclose, limit, bind, cage, detain, imprison, restrain, restrict. *Ant.* release, liberate.

confinement [ken · *fine* · ment] *n.* The state of being confined. *See* solitary confinement.
➤ detention, jail, imprisonment, restriction, constraint. ("Omar's period of confinement").
Ant. freedom.

confirm [kon · *ferm*] *v.* To remove doubt by an authoritative act; to verify or approve.
➤ corroborate, prove, attest, authenticate, ratify, verify, endorse, warrant, support.
Ant. question, doubt, challenge.

confirmation [kon · fer · *may* · shen] *n.*
1. Legislative approval of an appointment to high office made by the **chief executive**. EXAMPLE: the Senate's approval of the president's appointment of a Justice of the Supreme Court. 2. Approval necessary to make something valid or effective. 3. A contract that renders enforceable a previous agreement which, for one reason or another, might not have been valid. *See* ratification. 4. The act of making certain; verification.
➤ approval, authorization, endorsement, acknowledgment, verification ("confirmation of sale").

confirmation of estate [es · *tate*] *n.* A **conveyance** of real estate, or of a **right** or **interest** a person has in real estate, to another person who possesses the land, or has some other interest in it, which **cures** a **defect** existing in that person's interest.

confirmation of sale *n.* The formal approval by the court of an **executor's** or **administrator's** sale of property of a **decedent**. In some states, such approval is required to pass **title** to the property.

confiscate [kon · fis · kate] *v.* To seize private property by the authority of the government. Such a seizure or taking occurs as a penalty when property is **forfeit** because it was used in the commission of a crime (EXAMPLE: a car used to transport illicit drugs). Except for such a **forfeiture**, the government cannot take private property unless it pays **just compensation** as required by the **due process** provisions of the Constitution. *See also* eminent domain; taking.
➤ steal, seize, grab, impound, take.
Ant. restore.

confiscation [kon · fis · *kay* · shen] *n.* The act of confiscating. *See* confiscate.

confiscatory rate order
[ken · *fis* · ke · toh · ree rate *or* · der] *n.* An **order** by a **public service commission** or **public utility commission** setting the rates of a **common carrier** or **public utility** so low that the carrier or utility is deprived of a fair return on its investment.

conflict [*kon* · flikt] *n.* Opposition; disagreement; combat.
v. [kon · *flikt*] To run counter to; to oppose.
➤ *n.* clash, dispute, opposition, dissent, difference, controversy, hostility, resistence, rivalry.
v. contrast, contradict, vary, oppose, dissent, diverge, contend, refute.

conflict of interest [*kon* · flikt of *in* · trest] *n.* 1. The existence of a variance between the interests of the parties in a **fiduciary relationship**. EXAMPLE: the conduct of an attorney who acts both for her client and for another person whose interests conflict with those of her client. Ethical rules for attorneys specify various types of conflicts of interest and how they should be handled. 2. The condition of a public official or public employee whose personal or financial interests are at variance or appear to be at variance with his public responsibility. EXAMPLE: ownership, by the Secretary of Defense, of stock in a company that contracts with the Department of Defense for the manufacture of military equipment. *See* disclosure.

conflict of laws [*kon* · flikt] *n.* Area of the law that determines whether the law of some other state or country will be applied in a circumstance where the laws of more than one jurisdiction could apply and are in opposition to each other. An EXAMPLE of a situation in which liability laws might be in conflict: a manufacturing defect in a car made in Michigan, sold by a dealer in Texas to a Californian, who is driving the car in Oregon when a pedestrian is fatally injured due, in part, to the manufacturing defect. *See* center of gravity doctrine; *renvoi*.

conform [ken · *form*] *v.* 1. To be in harmony with. 2. To act in accordance with customs or standards of behavior.

➤ comply with, obey, observe, follow ("conform to the company's policy"); match, suit, follow, reconcile ("conform to the specifications").

conformed copy [ken · *formd*] *n.* A word-for-word copy of a document on which written entries are made to explain portions of the original that could not be reproduced, usually because a photocopy machine was not available or could not be used. EXAMPLE: a copy of a deed signed by Mary Jones might be conformed "s/Mary Jones."

conforming [ken · *form* · ing] *adj.* Complying with; in accordance with.

conforming goods *n.* Under the **Uniform Commercial Code**, goods are "conforming" when they comply with the seller's obligations under his contract with the buyer.

conforming use *n.* In zoning law, a **use** of a building that is permitted because it complies with the zoning ordinances and regulations. *Compare* nonconforming use.

confrontation [kon · fron · *tay* · shen] *n.* 1. A term that refers to the **Sixth Amendment** constitutional right of a defendant in a criminal case "to be confronted with the witnesses against him." 2. The clashing of ideas between opposing parties.

➤ conflict, argument, altercation, struggle, collision, strife, opposition, discord, hostility.
Ant. harmony, peace.

confuse [ken · *fyooz*] *v.* To puzzle; to perplex; to confound.

➤ puzzle, frustrate, mislead, fluster, bewilder, muddle, befuddle, mix up.
Ant. clarify, elucidate.

confusion [ken · *fyoo* · zhen] *n.* The state of being intermingled, mixed, merged, or blended together.

➤ disorder, unrest, disorientation, jumble, mess, tumult, commotion; ambiguity, incertitude, vagueness, enigma, dilemma.
Ant. clarity, comprehension.

confusion of debts *n.* Same as **confusion of rights**.

confusion of goods *n.* An intermingling of goods owned by different persons to such an extent that the property of each person can no longer be distinguished.

confusion of rights *n.* A merger of the rights of the creditor and the debtor in one person, thereby nullifying the debt. EXAMPLE: a tenant's inheritance, from his landlord, of the premises that she occupies under a lease.

conglomerate [kon · *glom* · e · rate] *n.* 1. A corporation that owns or controls many companies or other corporations which are involved in various and diverse businesses. 2. A cluster; a collection of things all together; a group.
v. To gather into a mass.
➤ *n.* corporation, monopoly, firm, giant, group.
Ant. individual.
v. mix, blend, mingle, join, associate.

congress [*kong* · gress] *n.* A formal gathering of delegates or representatives.
➤ delegation, assembly, association, conference, gathering, convetion.

Congress [*kong* · gress] *n.* The national legislature of the United States, consisting of the Senate and the House of Representatives. *See* congressman.

congressional [kon · *gresh* · en · el] *adj.* Pertaining to Congress or to an activity of Congress.

congressional districts [kon · *gresh* · en · el *dis* · trikts] *n.* The divisions of a state for the purpose of representation in the House of Representatives of the Congress of the United States, each district being separately represented by a member of the House. *See* apportionment of representatives; congressman; legislative districts.

congressional intent [in · *tent*] *n. See* legislative intent.

congressional investigations [kon · *gresh* · en · el in · ves · ti · *gay* · shenz] *n.* Investigations conducted by Congress, through its committees, to better understand what legislation is needed and to aid in drafting such legislation. *See* legislative committee.

Congressional Record [kon · *gresh* · en · el *rek* · erd] *n.* The official record of the **proceedings** of the Congress; printed daily.

congressman [*kong* · gress · man] *n.* 1. In strict usage, any member of the Congress, whether of the House of Representatives

or the Senate. 2. In common usage, a member of the House.
➤ representative, delegate, lawmaker, congresswoman.

conjecture [kon · *jek* · sure] *n.* A conclusion arrived at by guesswork.
➤ guess, presumption, supposition, surmise, speculation.

conjoint [kon · *joint*] *adj.* Related to or carried on by two or more in combination.
➤ combined, paired, associated, coupled ("a conjoint theft").

conjoint will *n.* Same as **joint will**.

conjoints [kon · *joints*] *n.* 1. Persons owning property together. 2. Husband and wife.

conjugal [kon · je · gul] *adj.* Pertaining to the marital relationship.
➤ matrimonial, spousal, paired, united, wedded. *Ant.* single.

conjugal rights *n.* The **rights** each spouse has in a marriage, arising out of the marriage. The legal term for such rights is **consortium**.

connect [ko · *nekt*] *v.* 1. To become joined. 2. To establish in relationship.
➤ blend, fuse, join, match, unite, intertwine; interrelate, associate, link, cohere.

connecting-up rule [ke · *nek* · ting-up] *n.* The rule that allows testimony or an exhibit to be introduced into evidence on the condition that its **relevancy** will later be shown by connecting it up with additional evidence. USAGE: "Your honor, if you permit just a few more questions, I'll connect that up."

connivance [ke · *nie* · vense] *n.* 1. A secret cooperation in an illegal act. 2. As a **defense** in an action for divorce, fraudulent consent by one spouse to the other spouse's engaging in conduct which constitutes grounds for divorce. *See* collusive divorce. *Compare* no-fault divorce.
➤ secret, conspiracy, concert, collusion, consent, overlooking, condoning, contrivance.

connubial [ke · *noo* · bee · el] *adj.* Pertaining to marriage.
➤ conjugal, married, nuptial, wedded, spousal ("connubial bliss").

consanguinity [kon · san · *gwin* · i · tee] *n.* Relationship by blood; having the blood of a **common ancestor**. *See* blood relation. *See and compare* collateral consanguinity; lineal consanguinity.
➤ affiliation, blood relationship, brotherhood, kindred, kinship. *Ant.* unrelated.

conscience [kon · shense] *n.* A person's natural judgment of right and wrong.
➤ principles, scruples, duty, inner voice, standards, ethics, moral sense.

conscientious [kon · shee · *en* · shes] *adj.* Conforming to moral goodness; hardworking.
➤ meticulous, fastidious, diligent, responsible ("The new paralegal was highly conscientious").

conscientious objector [kon · shee · *en* · shes ob · *jek* · ter] *n.* A person who seeks exemption from military service on religious grounds. Such objection may be based upon a person's conscience; membership in a particular religious denomination is not a requirement.

conscious [*kon* · shus] *adj.* 1. Having mental functions. 2. Perceiving or noticing with controlled thought or observation.
➤ awake, alert, alive, living; aware, attentive, heedful, mindful, understanding.

conscription [ken · *skrip* · shen] *n.* Requiring the performance of military service. *See* Selective Service System.

consecutive sentences [ken · *sek* · yoo · tiv sen · ten · sez] *n.* Sentences of imprisonment for crimes in which the time of each is to run one after the other without a break. *Compare* concurrent sentences.

consensual [ken · *sen* · shoo · el] *adj.* Created or brought about by consent.
➤ uncontested, approving, agreed upon, unopposed, unchallenged ("consensual sex").

consensual marriage [*mehr* · ej] *n.* A marriage in which vows are exchanged informally, without the involvement of either civil or religious authority. Generally, if such a marriage is to be valid, it must meet the criteria applicable to a **common law marriage**. A consensual marriage is also referred to as an **informal marriage**. *Compare* ceremonial marriage.

consent [ken · *sent*] *n.* Agreement; approval; acquiescence; being of one mind. Consent necessarily involves two or more persons because, without at least two persons, there cannot be a unity of opinion or the possibility of thinking alike. As a **defense** to a prosecution for rape, consent is an exercise of one's intelligence in making a choice between resistance and uncoerced assent, based upon knowledge of the significance of the act and of the moral issues involved.

v. To approve of or agree to.

➤ *n.* agreement, approval, acquiescence, concession, allowance, permission, accord, affirmation, concordance.

v. agree, accept, allow, approve, concede, yield, comply, sanction, ratify.

consent decree [de · *kree*] *n.* 1. A **judgment** in an **action** brought by an administrative agency (the **Environmental Protection Agency**, for EXAMPLE), in which the defendant declines to admit wrongdoing (polluting a river, for EXAMPLE) but agrees not to engage in the conduct alleged, in exchange for which the government's action is dropped. 2. A **decree** entered in an **equitable action** suit upon the consent of the **parties**. Such a decree is binding on the parties; they cannot subsequently appeal it or go to trial on the matter.

consent judgment [*juj* · ment] *n.* A **judgment** entered by consent of the parties for the purpose of executing a **compromise and settlement** of an **action**. A consent judgment is a contract between the parties, approved by the court, which is as conclusive as a judgment rendered by the court after a hearing. *See* final judgment.

consequence [*kon* · se · kwense] *n.* That which follows as the result or effect of a cause. *See* legal consequence; natural and probable consequence.

➤ result, outcome, effect, repercussion, reaction ("a consequence of drinking and driving"); significance, importance, influence, value, meaning ("A female president would be of great consequence").

consequential damages [kon · se · *kwen* · shel *dam* · e · jez] *n.* Indirect **losses; damages** that do not result from the wrongful act

itself, but from the result or the aftermath of the wrongful act. *See* incidental damages. *Compare* punitive damages.

conservation [*kon* · ser · vey · shun] *n.* Careful preservation or protection.

➤ preservation, protection, saving, fostering, maintenance.

conservator [ken · *ser* · ve · tore] *n.* 1. A person placed in charge of the property of an **incompetent person** by a court. *See also* guardian; custodian. 2. A preserver; a protector.

➤ guardian, protector, manager, preserver, overseer, caretaker.

conservatorship [ken · *ser* · ve · ter · ship] *n.* The legal arrangement under which a **conservator** holds the property of another.

consideration [ken · sid · e · *ray* · shen] *n.* 1. The reason a person enters into a contract; that which is given in exchange for performance or the promise to perform; the price bargained and paid; the inducement. Consideration is an essential element of a valid and enforceable contract. A promise to *refrain* from doing something one is entitled to do also constitutes consideration (*see* forbearance). 2. Motivation; incentive; inducement. 3. The act of giving thought to something; deliberation; contemplation. 4. Courtesy; respect; kindness.

See also adequate consideration; failure of consideration; fair consideration; good consideration; inadequate consideration; legal consideration; moral consideration; nominal consideration, past consideration; valuable consideration.

➤ value, incentive, recompense, inducement, reward, benefit ("Consideration is an essential element of a valid and enforceable contract"); kindness, respect, courtesy, thoughtfulness ("She had a lot of consideration for her mother"); thought, advisement, rumination ("Take it under consideration").

consign [ken · *sine*] *v.* To make a **consignment**.

➤ deliver, entrust, send, ship, transfer, authorize.

consignee [ken · sine · ee] *n.* The person to whom a carrier is to deliver a shipment of goods; the person named in a **bill of lading** to whom the bill promises delivery;

C

the person to whom goods are given on **consignment**, either for sale or safekeeping. *Compare* consignor. *See also* factor.
➤ receiver, salesperson, representative, seller.
Ant. consignor.

consignment [ken · sine · ment] *n.* The entrusting of goods either to a **carrier** for delivery to a **consignee** or to a consignee who is to sell the goods for the **consignor**. *See* bailment.
➤ entrusting, distribution, committal, transmittal.

consignment contract [kon · trakt] *n.* A consignment of goods to another (the **consignee**) with the understanding either that she will sell them for the **consignor** and forward the proceeds, or, if she does not, that she will return them to the consignor. A consignment is also known as a **bailment for sale**. *See* bailment.

consignor [ken · sine · or] *n.* A person who sends goods to another on **consignment**; the person named in a **bill of lading** as the person from whom goods have been received for shipment. *Compare* consignee.
➤ shipper, sender.
Ant. consignee.

consist [kon · sist] *v.* To be composed or made up of.
➤ be made up of, be composed of, contain, constitute, involve, entail, encompass.

consistent [kon · sis · tent] *adj.* Showing steady continuity; regular.
➤ uniform, consonant, regular, equal, equitable, logical, regular, dependable, unchanging, true, agreeing, compatible.

consolidate [ken · sol · ih · date] *v.* To unite into one mass or unit. USAGE: "The county is going to consolidate four high schools into a single school." *See* consolidation.
➤ unify, combine, connect, integrate, bind.
Ant. sever, disconnect, weaken.

Consolidated Omibus Budget Reconciliation Act of 1985
[ken · sol · ih · day · ted om · ni · bus buhd · jet reh · cun · cih · lee · ay · shen] *n.* A federal statute which provides that an employee who is covered by health insurance at her place of employment has the right to continued coverage for a specified

period of time after the termination of her employment, if she pays the premiums. This act is commonly referred to by its acronym, COBRA.

consolidated tax return
[ken · sol · ih · day · ted tax re · *tern*] *n.* A **tax return** filed by the **parent company** for all the members of an affiliated group of corporations in place of a separate corporate tax return filed by each corporation.

consolidation [ken · sol · ih · *day* · shen] *n.* A joining together of separate things to make one thing; an **amalgamation**.
➤ combination, alliance, fusion, incorporation, merger.
Ant. separation.

consolidation loan *n.* A loan taken for the purpose of repaying other loans, generally on more accommodating terms.

consolidation of actions [*ak* · shenz] *n.* The joining of separate suits into one suit for trial, by order of court, in the interest of justice or convenience. Generally, **actions** are consolidated only if they could originally have been brought as a single suit. *See* joinder.

consolidation of appeals [a · *peelz*] *n.* The joining of **appeals** from a single **judgment** or from different judgments that involve the same question and the same **parties**. **Appellate courts** may, without formally consolidating appeals, hear and determine two or more of them together for reasons of convenience or because of the similarity of the facts or questions involved.

consolidation of corporations
[kore · per · *ay* · shenz] *n.* A blending of two or more **corporations** in one, as a consequence of which their powers, privileges, and obligations pass to the new organization (the consolidated corporation) and the old companies cease to exist. For the distinction between consolidation and **merger**, *see* merger of corporations.

consortium [kon · *sore* · shum] *n.* 1. The **rights** and **duties** of both husband and wife, resulting from marriage. They include companionship, love, affection, assistance, comfort, cooperation, and sexual relations. *See* loss of consortium. 2. An alliance of business interests; a **cartel**; a **combine**; a **conglomerate**; a **syndicate**.

➤ conjugal fellowship, affection, intimacy, companionship ("She lost her husband's consortium because of his accident"); alliance, union, trust, pool, consolidation ("The cable company formed a consortium to keep prices high").

conspicuous [ken · *spik* · yoo · us] *adj.* Clearly visible; easily seen.

➤ clear, pronounced, well-marked, manifest, obvious, observable, visible, noticeable, distinct ("John Hancock's conspicuous signature").
Ant. concealed, hidden.

conspicuous clause *n. See* conspicuous term.

conspicuous place *n.* In the case of a posted notice, a place where the notice can be readily seen and where the notice itself will be readily discernible.

conspicuous term *n.* Word or words printed in such a manner that a **reasonable person** ought to have noted them. Various state and federal statutes require that certain provisions of certain kinds of contracts (particularly those involving credit) be "conspicuous."

conspiracy [ken · *spi* · re · see] *n.* An agreement between two or more persons to engage in a criminal act or to accomplish a legal objective by criminal or unlawful means. Conspiracy is a criminal offense (a **criminal conspiracy**); it is also a **wrong** which is grounds for a **civil action** if **damage** is suffered (a **civil conspiracy**). *See* withdrawal from conspiracy.

➤ connivance, counterplot, frame, plot, scheme, trickery.

conspire [ken · *spire*] *v.* To join in a secret agreement; to plot or scheme.

➤ agree, plan, plot, unite, abet, coact.

constable [*kon* · stebl] *n.* A **peace officer** whose duty is to maintain order and to serve **process** issued by justices of the peace and **magistrates**.

➤ peace officer, police officer, processor.

constant [*kon* · stent] *adj.* Marked by consistency; unchanging.
n. That which does not change; a regular occurrence.

➤ *adj.* continuous, invariable, dependable, incessant, sustained, stable, certain, unswerving.
n. standard, usual practice, regularity, pattern, form, certainty.

constitute [*kon* · sti · toot] *v.* 1. To set up, establish, make up, or form. 2. To appoint a person to an office or position.

➤ set up, establish, form, comprise, institute, create ("We constituted an apartment alliance").

constituted authorities [*con* · sti · too · ted aw · *thaw* · ri · teez] *n.* The lawfully appointed officers of the government.

constitution [kon · sti · *too* · shen] *n.* 1. The system of fundamental principles by which a nation, state, or corporation is governed. A nation's constitution may be written (EXAMPLE: the Constitution of the United States) or unwritten (EXAMPLE: the British Constitution). A nation's laws must conform to its constitution. A law that violates a nation's constitution is **unconstitutional** and therefore unenforceable. 2. The document setting forth the fundamental principles of governance. 3. The Constitution of the United States. 4. The structure or physical makeup of something.

➤ charter, code, formation, written law, supreme law; structure, frame, shape, arrangement.

Constitution [kon · sti · *too* · shen] *n.* The **Constitution of the United States**.

Constitution of the United States [kon · sti · *too* · shen of the yoo · *nie* · ted *states*] *n.* The fundamental document of American government, as adopted by the people of the United States through their representatives in the Constitutional Convention of 1787, as ratified by the states, together with the amendments to that Constitution.

constitutional [kon · sti · *too* · shen · el] *adj.* 1. In accordance with the Constitution of the United States; consistent with the Constitution; not in conflict with the Constitution. 2. In accordance with, consistent with, or not in conflict with a **constitution**, for EXAMPLE, a **state constitution** or the constitution of an

C

C

organization, such as a union or a **fraternal benefit society**. 3. In, grounded in, based upon, contained in, or relating to a constitution. *Compare* unconstitutional.

➤ approved, chartered, lawful, democratic, enforceable, permitted.

Ant. unconstitutional, impermissible, illegal.

constitutional amendment
[a · *mend* · ment] *n.* An amendment to a constitution. *See* amendment of constitution.

constitutional convention [ken · *ven* · shen] *n.* 1. A representative body that meets to form and adopt a constitution. EXAMPLE: the convention that met in Philadelphia in 1787 to draft and adopt the Constitution of the United States. 2. A representative body that meets to consider and adopt amendments to an existing constitution. Article V of the United States Constitution provides for the calling of a convention as a means of amending the Constitution.

constitutional courts *n.* Courts directly established by the Constitution, which are therefore beyond the power of Congress to abolish or alter. EXAMPLE: the **Supreme Court of the United States**.

constitutional law *n.* The body of principles that apply in the interpretation, construction, and application of the Constitution to statutes and to other governmental action. Constitutional law deals with **constitutional questions** and determines the **constitutionality** of state and federal laws and of the manner in which government exercises its authority.

constitutional limitations
[lim · i · *tay* · shenz] *n.* The provisions of a constitution that limit the legislature's power to enact laws.

constitutional office [*aw* · fiss] *n.* A public office created by a constitution, as distinguished from an office created by statute.

constitutional question [*kwes* · chen] *n.* *See* constitutional law.

constitutional right *n.* A **right** guaranteed by the Constitution of the United States or by a state constitution; a **fundamental right**. A constitutional right cannot be abrogated or infringed by Congress or by a state legislature.

constitutionality
[kon · sti · too · shen · *al* · i · tee] *n.* The quality of being **constitutional** or of being in accord with a constitution. USAGE: "Mr. Begner questioned the constitutionality of the ordinance which disallowed nude dancing in DeKalb County."

constrain [kon · *strane*] *v.* 1. To restrict the motion of. 2. To prevent the occurrence of.

➤ bind, confine, detain, restrict, restrain; prevent, prohibit.

construction [ken · *struk* · shen] *n.* 1. Determining the meaning of a constitution, statute, contract, will, or any other writing or document. USAGE: "Maria lost the lawsuit because of the court's construction of her contract with the defendant." *Compare* interpretation. *See* statutory construction. 2. The erection or creation of a building or other structure.

➤ definition, inference, translation, version, clarification ("strict construction of the Bill of Rights"); assembly, building, arrangement, origination, erection ("the construction of a house").

construction contract [*kon* · trakt] *n.* A **contract** for the construction of a building or other structure. The special characteristic of a construction contract is that the plans and specifications which control how the work is to be performed are incorporated into and made a part of the contract.

construction warranty [*war* · en · tee] *n.* A **warranty** furnished by the builder or seller of a new home, promising that it is free from basic defects. A construction warranty is sometimes referred to as a **homeowners warranty** or a **warranty of habitability**.

constructive [ken · *struk* · tiv] *adj.* 1. **Inferred, implied**, or **presumed** from the circumstances. 2. Productive; informative; helpful.

➤ effective, positive, practical, helpful, beneficial ("constructive criticism"); inferred, implied, presumed ("constructive eviction").

Ant. actual, direct.

constructive adverse possession
[*ad* · verse po · *zesh* · en] *n.* By statute in some states, payment of taxes on real

property one does not own, under **color of title** or **color of right**, is constructive **adverse possession** of that property. *See* constructive possession.

constructive contract [*kon* · trakt] *n.* Same as **quasi contract**.

constructive delivery [de · *liv* · e · ree] *n.* **Delivery** that does not involve an actual or immediate transfer of possession, but that is considered in law to be true delivery because the item to be delivered is made absolutely available to the recipient. EXAMPLE: delivery of **consigned** goods to a carrier is constructive delivery of the goods to the **consignee**. *Compare* actual delivery; symbolic delivery.

constructive desertion [de · *zer* · shen] *n.* Misconduct by a spouse so serious as to force the other spouse to leave and remain away. The spouse engaging in the misconduct, not the departing spouse, is guilty of **desertion**.

constructive discharge [*dis* · charj] *n.* In labor law, when an employer makes conditions on the job so difficult for an employee that she is compelled to resign her position. Such a resignation is considered, in law, not a **voluntary quit**, but a **discharge**. *See* wrongful termination.

constructive eviction [e · *vik* · shen] *n.* Interference by the landlord that renders the leased premises unfit for occupancy by the tenant or that deprives the tenant of the full use or enjoyment of the premises, causing him to abandon them.

constructive fraud *n.* A breach of duty, trust, or confidence that results in **damage** to another; it does not necessarily involve conscious wrongdoing. *Compare* actual fraud. *See* fraud.

constructive malice [*mal* · iss] *n.* Malice that can be **inferred** from the very fact that the wrongful act was committed; **malice in law**. *Compare* particular malice. *Also compare* actual malice; express malice. *See* malice. *See also* implied malice.

constructive notice [*noh* · tiss] *n.* Circumstances such that the law considers that **actual notice** took place, regardless of whether it did; a substitute for actual notice based upon a **presumption** of notice which is so strong that the law does not

permit it to be contradicted. EXAMPLE: a person who purchases real estate will not be permitted to prove he was unaware of a **defect** in the **title**, even if he was in fact unaware, if the defect was a **matter of record**. *See* record notice. Constructive notice is sometimes called *constructive knowledge. Compare* express notice; implied notice. *See* conclusive presumption. Also see legal notice; notice.

constructive possession [po · *zesh* · en] *n.* As opposed to **actual possession, possession** that the law **infers** from the circumstances; possession **in law** as opposed to possession **in fact**. EXAMPLE: a person claiming a tract of land under **color of right** or **color of title**, who is in actual possession of a portion of it, is in constructive possession of the entire tract. *See* constructive adverse possession; interruption of possession.

constructive receipt of income [re · *seet* of *in* · kum] *n.* For income tax purposes, income that is available to the taxpayer is taxed in the year it accrues (EXAMPLE: interest earned on a certificate of deposit) rather than in the year the taxpayer actually receives it.

constructive service [*ser* · viss] *n. See* constructive service of process.

constructive service of process [*ser* · viss of *pross* · ess] *n.* Another term for **substituted service of process**.

constructive trust *n.* A **trust**, created by **operation of law**, that is declared against a person who, by **fraud, duress**, or abuse of confidence, has obtained or holds **legal title** to property to which he has no moral or **equitable right**. In such a case, a court may declare that the person having legal title merely holds it **in trust** for the person from whom he obtained it. A constructive trust is also referred to as an **involuntary trust**. *Compare* resulting trust.

construe [kon · *strew*] *v.* To interpret; to determine the meaning of a word, sentence, document, or statute. *See* construction.
➤ interpret, restate, explain, clarify, convey, decode, decipher, infer, deduce.

consul [*kon* · sul] *n.* A person commissioned by a government to represent it in a foreign country for the

C

purpose of promoting and protecting its interests, particularly its commercial interests, and those of its citizens. A consul does not have diplomatic status. *Compare* ambassador.
➤ delegate, emissary, envoy, representative, ambassador.

consult [kon · *sult*] *v.* 1. To seek the advice of another. 2. To discuss with; to talk over.
➤ discuss, seek, advice, confer with, refer to; meet, discuss, exchange views, deliberate, confer.

consume [kon · *soom*] *v.* 1. To utilize; to use fully. 2. To do away with; to destroy.
➤ eat, employ, empty, exhaust, deplete, use, utilize, spend, waste ("consume energy"); destroy, annihilate, demolish, level, devastate ("consumed by fire").

consumer [kon · *soo* · mer] *n.* 1. A person who buys and uses products or services and who is affected by their cost, availability, and quality, as well as by laws regulating their manufacture, sale, and financing. *See* consumer credit; consumer credit protection acts; consumer goods. 2. Anyone who consumes.
➤ buyer, client, patron, purchaser, vendee, customer.

consumer credit [*kred* · it] *n.* Credit granted for the purpose of securing a **consumer loan**. *See* credit.

consumer credit protection acts
[kon · *soo* · mer *kred* · it pro · *tek* · shen acts] *n.* Also known as **truth in lending acts**; federal and state statutes which require, among other things, that contracts for the sale of **consumer goods** involving credit be written in plain language, that the **finance charges** be stated as a uniform **annual percentage rate**, and that goods purchased on credit or with credit cards be returnable within specified periods of time. *See* credit. *Also see* full disclosure.

consumer goods *n.* As defined by the **Uniform Commercial Code**, articles used primarily for personal, family, or household purposes.

consumer lease *n.* A lease of **consumer goods**, for EXAMPLE, a television set or a stereo.

consumer loan *n.* A loan made to a consumer for the purpose of purchasing

consumer goods, usually under a **conditional sale contract** involving **installment payments** and **finance charges**. *Compare* commercial loan. *See* consumer credit. *Also see* personal loan.

consumer price index [*in* · deks] *n.* Statistics compiled and published by the government on a regular basis, which reflect the current cost of living. *See* cost-of-living clause.

consummate [kon · sum · mate] *v.* To complete in all details; to fulfill.
➤ realize, achieve, accomplish, effectuate, fulfill, perfect ("to consummate the deal").

consummation [kon · sum · *ay* · shen] *n.* Completion; fulfillment.
➤ completion, perfection, realization, achievement, fulfillment.

consummation of marriage [*mar* · ej] *n.* Sexual intercourse after marriage. Non-consummation is grounds for **annulment of marriage** in many states.

consumption [kon · *sump* · shun] *n.* The utilization of goods to satisfy wants or desires.
➤ use, utilization, assimilation, depletion, waste, loss, destruction, exhaustion. *Ant.* conservation.

contact [kon · takt] *n.* A connection of two or more people or objects.
v. 1. To communicate with another. 2. To touch.
➤ *n.* touching, connection, meeting, impact, nexus, junction, joining ("offensive contact"); lead, referral, connection, tie, reference ("a business contact").
v. communicate with, reach, call, notify, correspond, inform, signal; touch, connect, join, overlap, abut, connect, attach, border.

contagious [kon · *tay* · jus] *adj.* Infectious; spreadable.
➤ communicable, infectious, spreadable, transmittable, transferrable, transmissible, infective ("a contagious disease").

contain [kon · tane] *v.* 1. To enclose; to keep inside. 2. To prevent from moving; to restrict.
➤ hold, include, embrace, be composed of, subsist of; restrain, bind, check, restrict, inhibit, jail, constrain, lock up, hold back.

contaminate [kon · *tam* · i · nate] *v.* To make impure or infect by combining with inferior or foreign substances.
➤ spoil, poison, pervert, corrupt, degrade, defile, ruin.

contemner [ken · *tem* · ner] *n.* Same as **contemnor**.

contemnor [ken · *tem* · nor] *n.* A person guilty of **contempt of court**.

contemplate [*kon* · tem · plate] *v.* 1. To consider in a careful or attentive way. 2. To foresee.
➤ ponder, deliberate, ruminate, cogitate, study, examine ("contemplate the risks"); anticipate, envision, foresee, expect, intend ("I do not contemplate calling any witnesses").

contemplation [kon · tem · *play* · shen] *n.* 1. Expectation; looking forward to. 2. Looking at or thinking about something intently.
➤ deliberation, rumination, pondering, consideration, thought, reverie; anticipation, intention, purpose, forethought, goal.

contemplation of death *n.* An expectation of death that motivates a person to act in a given way. More than the general fear of death which, it may be argued, everyone has, it is the fear of imminent death from some existing illness, accident, or immediate danger. **Gifts** made in expectation of death may be taxed differently than other gifts. *See and compare* gift causa mortis; inter vivos gift. *Also see* transfer in contemplation of death.

contemporaneous [kon · tem · per · *ay* · nee · us] *adj.* Occurring at the same time as another occurrence or event.
➤ concurrent, simultaneous, coexistent, contemporary, synchronous ("contemporaneous transaction").

contemporary [kon · *tem* · po · ra · ree] *n.* One who is the same or nearly the same as another in terms of age.
adj. 1. Occurring at the same time. 2. Modern; current; leading edge.
➤ *n.* peer, equal, colleague, friend.
adj. simultaneous, concurrent, related, coincident, attendant, linked; modern, recent, state-of-the-art, chic, avant-garde, fashionable, current, topical.

contempt [ken · *tempt*] *n.* 1. An act of disrespect toward a court or **legislative body**; deliberate disobedience of a court order. *See* contempt of court; contempt of Congress. 2. An act of disrespect generally.
➤ disregard, defiance, disrespect, violation, disobedience ("contempt of court"); disdain, scorn, hatred, abhorrence, opprobrium, loathing, condescension, scoffing, arrogance ("contempt for criminals").

contempt of Congress [*kong* · gress] *n.* Conduct disrespectful of Congress or its committees, which has the effect of obstructing them in their **proceedings**, including hearings and investigations. *See* legislative committee.

contempt of court *n.* Conduct that tends to bring the authority and administration of the law into disrespect or that embarrasses or obstructs the court's discharge of its duties. *See and compare* civil contempt; criminal contempt; direct contempt; indirect contempt.

contempt proceeding [pro · *see* · dingz] *n.* A hearing held by the court to determine if a person is guilty of contempt.

contemptible [kon · *temp* · ti · bul] *adj.* That which arouses scorn or disapproval.
➤ abhorrent, vile, evil, hateful, wicked, perfidious, despicable, depraved, base, deplorable.

contemptuous [kon · *temp* · choo · us] *adj.* Feeling or expressing contempt.
➤ scornful, derogatory, disparaging, disdainful, hateful, rude, haughty, pompous, arrogant, condescending.

contend [kon · *tend*] *v.* 1. To compete for something. 2. To present or advance a point of view; to assent.
➤ vie, disagree, compete, dispute, contradict, dissent; maintain, argue, advance, assert, hold, insist, state, attest.

content [*kon* · tent] *n.* 1. Meaning or significance. 2. The composition of information.
adj. [ken · *tent*] Satisfied; fulfilled.
➤ *n.* subject matter, thought, substance, meaning, nature, purpose, motif, thesis, essence, gist; form, structure, composition, framework.
adj. satisfied, pleased, happy, agreeable, appeased, willing, complacent.

C

contention [kon · *ten* · shun] *n.* 1. A position maintained during a debate or argument. 2. Disagreement; discord.

➤ position, claim, viewpoint, issue, ground, point, proposition; quarrel, opposition, friction, disaccord, antagonism, hostility, debate, dissent.

contents [*kon* · tents] *n.* The topics or materials covered.

➤ substance, essence, text, topics, scope, components, subject, sense.

conterminous [kon · *term* · in · us] *adj.* Adjoining; having a common boundary.

contest [*kon* · test] *n.* 1. An attempt to defeat the **probate** of a will, commonly referred to as an attempt to "set aside the will." 2. A competition; a struggle.
v. [ken · *test*] 1. To defend against a lawsuit; to litigate. 2. To dispute; to oppose.

➤ *n.* competition, struggle, battle, war, fight, engagement, disagreement, variance; game, sweepstakes, lottery.
v. oppose, dispute, challenge, question, counter, object to, fight, resist.

contested *adj.* 1. Litigated. USAGE: "contested divorce." 2. Disputed; opposed. USAGE: "contested claim." *Compare* uncontested.

context [*kon* · tekst] *n.* The words or language of a statute or other writing, in addition to the words or language being construed. USAGE: "You can't really understand the first paragraph of this agreement unless you read it in context, and that means reading the whole agreement."

➤ background, surroundings, environment, setting; meaning, tenor, purport, sense, scope.

contiguous [ken · *tig* · yoo · us] *adj.* In actual contact; touching; adjoining. USAGE: "Your land and mine are contiguous." *Compare* adjacent. *See also* abutting owners.

➤ abutting, adjacent, adjoining, against, beside, bordering, near, close, proximate, touching.

contingency [ken · *tin* · jen · see] *n.* An event that may occur.

➤ possibility, circumstance, likelihood, happening, chance, conditional event.

contingency fund *n.* A fund or account set up as a safeguard against anticipated but currently unspecifiable expenses. Also called a **contingency reserve**.

contingency reserve [re · *zerv*] *n.* Same as **contingency fund**.

contingent [ken · *tin* · jent] *adj.* Possible, but not certain to occur. *See* conditional.

➤ possible, dependent, conditioned, subordinate, provisional, subject to ("contingent claim").

contingent annuity [an · *yoo* · i · tee] *n.* An **annuity** payable upon the occurrence of a specified event the timing of which is beyond the control of the **annuitant**. EXAMPLE: the death of the annuitant's father.

contingent bequest [be · *kwest*] *n.* A **legacy** that is intended by the **testator** to **vest** only in the event of the occurrence of a specified **contingency**. EXAMPLE: $10,000 willed to Sam Smith "if and when he marries." *See* bequest.

contingent devise [de · *vize*] *n.* A **devise** that is intended by the **testator** to **vest** only in the event of the occurrence of a specified **contingency**. EXAMPLE: Land willed to Mary Jones "if and when she marries." *See* devise.

contingent estate [es · *tate*] *n.* An **estate in land** that is uncertain because it is dependent upon the happening of a future event. EXAMPLE: a **contingent remainder**.

contingent fee *n.* A fee for legal services, calculated on the basis of an agreed-upon percentage of the amount of money recovered for the client by his attorney. *See* attorney fees; fee.

contingent interest [in · *trest*] *n.* Same as **contingent estate**, except that one may have a contingent interest in personal property as well as in real property.

contingent legacy [*leg* · e · see] *n. See* contingent bequest.

contingent liability [ly · e · *bil* · i · tee] *n.* A **liability** that may or may not come into being, depending upon the occurrence or nonoccurrence of a future event. EXAMPLE: a **judgment** in a **pending action**.

contingent remainder [re · *mane* · der] *n.* A **remainder** in real property that is uncertain either because the person or persons who are to receive the property do not exist or are not identified at the time the will is written, or because their right to inherit is contingent upon the occurrence of some future event. EXAMPLE: "I leave my land to Bill Brown for as long as he lives and, should he have children, to his children after he dies." The **interest** or **estate** of Bill Brown's unborn children is a contingent remainder. *Compare* vested remainder.

continual [kon · *tin* · yoo · ul] *adj.* Occurring indefinitely in time; ongoing.
➤ perpetual, unending, everlasting, constant, persistent, endless, uninterrupted. *Ant.* intermittent.

continuance [ken · *tin* · yoo · ense] *n.* Adjournment of the hearing of a case from one date to another or to a later hour on the same day. USAGE: "Counsel's request for a continuance is granted." *Compare* recess.
➤ adjournment, stay, postponement, cessation; prolongation, protraction, extension, lengthening, repetition.

continuation [kon · tin · yoo · *ay* · shun] *n.* 1. A resumption after an interruption. 2. That which increases or lengthens something.
➤ resumption, reestablishment, reversion, reinstatement, recommencement, reopening ("continuation of a suit"); lengthening, protraction, addition, extension ("a continuation of the lien").

continue [ken · *tin* · yoo] *v.* 1. To grant a **continuance**. 2. To proceed. 3. To persevere.
➤ persist, persevere, pursue, prevail, forge ahead, progress ("continue to the end"); adjourn, delay, postpone, suspend, hold over, table, shelve ("continue the case"); remain, endure, stay, maintain ("continue as attorney of record").

continuing [ken · *tin* · yoo · ing] *adj.* Ongoing; constant; enduring.
➤ ongoing, constant, enduring, subsisting, present, incessant, repeated.

continuing breach *n.* A **breach of contract** that continues or is repeated over a period of time.

continuing contempt [ken · *temt*] *n.* A failure to free oneself from guilt of **contempt of court**. *Compare* purging contempt.

continuing contract [kon · trakt] *n.* A **contract** calling for **performance** over a period of time.

continuing easement [*eez* · ment] *n.* Same as **continuous easement**.

continuing jurisdiction [joo · ris · *dik* · shen] *n.* The power of a court to ensure that it has **jurisdiction** over a case until **final judgment**, once its jurisdiction has been activated by the commencement of an **action**.

continuing offense [o · *fense*] *n.* A continuous unlawful act or series of acts motivated by a single objective. Because of its nature, a continuing offense may be committed partly in one jurisdiction and partly in another, or in several others. EXAMPLE: a **conspiracy**.

continuing offer [*off* · er] *n. See* option.

continuing trespass [*tress* · pass] *n.* A permanent encroachment or intrusion upon the property of another. EXAMPLE: a sign that overhangs the adjoining property. *See* trespass. *See also* continuous easement; permanent trespass.

continuity [kon · ti · *new* · i · tee] *n.* Uninterrupted duration or coherence without significant change.
➤ coherence, consistency, connection, constancy, succession, flow.

continuous [kon · *tin* · yoo · us] *adj.* Uninterrupted; sustained.
➤ uninterrupted, unbroken, whole, sustained, ceaseless, constant, unceasing ("continuous adverse possession").

continuous easement [ken · *tin* · yoo · us *eez* · ment] *n.* An **easement** that exists without the necessity of human involvement. EXAMPLES: an overhanging roof; an overhanging sign. *Compare* discontinuous easement. *See also* continuing trespass.

contort [kon · tort] *v.* To disfigure a shape.
➤ distort, bend, deform, twist, convolute, pervert, disfigure.

contour [kon · toor] *n.* 1. The general form of something. 2. The line representing the outline of a form.
➤ outline, figure, form, profile, picture, silhouette; shape, frame, structure.

contra [kon · trah] *(Latin) adv.* Otherwise; the other way; disagreeing with; contrary to.

C

USAGE: "I doubt that we can sustain our legal position in this case; all of the **authority** is *contra*."
➤ against, opposite, adverse to, confronting, opposed to.

contraband [*kon · tra · band*] *n.* Anything possessed or transported in violation of law. EXAMPLES: marijuana; automatic weapons; untaxed alcoholic beverages or cigarettes. *See* black market; bootleg.
➤ illegal goods, bootlegged items, plunder, prohibited articles, smuggled goods.

contract [*kon · trakt*] *n.* An agreement entered into, for **adequate consideration**, to do, or refrain from doing, a particular thing. The **Uniform Commercial Code** defines a contract as the total legal obligation resulting from the parties' agreement. In addition to adequate consideration, the transaction must involve an undertaking that is legal to perform, and there must be **mutuality** of agreement and obligation between at least two **competent** parties.
   See adhesion contract; aleatory contract; bilateral contract; binding contract; breach of contract; conditional contract; conditional sale contract; constructive contract; exclusive contract; executed contract; executory contract; express contract; illusory contract; implied contract; installment sale contract; land contract; mutuality of contract; parol contract; quasi contract; subcontract; third-party beneficiary contract; unilateral contract; void contract; voidable contract; written contract.
   v. [*kon · trakt*] To enter into a **contract**. *See* contract
➤ *n.* agreement, understanding, bargain, compact, mutual promise, covenant, accord, arrangement, promise, assurance.
   v. agree, promise, engage, undertake, covenant, bargain, obligate, pledge; condense, shrink, recede, lessen.

contract against public policy [a · *genst* pub · lik *pol* · i · see] *n.* *See* public policy. *Compare* illegal contract.

contract carrier [*ka* · ri · er] *n.* A **carrier** that does not offer to transport goods for the public at large, but only for those with whom it decides to contract. *Compare* common carrier.

contract clause *n.* Clause of Article I of the Constitution which provides that states cannot pass any law that impairs the ability to contract. *See also* freedom of contract.

contract for deed *n.* *See* contract for sale of land; installment land contract.

contract for sale of goods *n.* A contract that, if **consideration** is paid, transfers **title** to **goods** from seller to buyer; also, a contract that obligates the seller to sell to the buyer at some future time. *See and compare* agreement of sale; agreement to sell. *See also* sales agreement.

contract for sale of land *n.* A contract in which one party agrees to sell and the other to purchase real estate. Contracts involving land must be in writing. *Note* that a contract for the sale of land is not a **deed**, but merely an agreement to transfer **title**. *See also* installment land contract.

contract implied in fact [im · *plide*] *n.* *See* implied contract.

contract implied in law [im · *plide*] *n.* *See* implied contract.

contract of adhesion [ad · *hee* · zhen] *n.* *See* adhesion contract.

contract of indemnity [in · *dem* · ni · tee] *n.* *See* indemnity.

contract of insurance [in · *shoor* · ense] *n.* *See* insurance contract.

contract of record [*rek* · erd] *n.*
1. A contract that has been **recorded**.
2. A phrase sometimes used with respect to a **judgment**.

contract of sale *n.* Same as **agreement of sale**. *See also* contract for sale of goods.

contractor [*kon* · trak · ter] *n.* 1. A person who contracts to render services for others, generally in building, excavating, and the like, who has control over the methods and means by which the work is accomplished. *See* independent contractor. *See also* general contractor; prime contractor; subcontractor. 2. A person who is a **party** to a contract.
➤ builder, architect, supplier, worker.

contractual [ken · *trak* · choo · el] *adj.* Pertaining to or based upon a **contract** or to a relationship between persons created by a contract.

➤ binding, obligatory, promised, settled, consensual, pledged, stipulated ("a contractual matter").

contractual obligation [ob · li · *gay* · shen] *n.* An **obligation** arising out of a **contract**.

contradict [kon · tra · *dikt*] *v.* To take issue with; to imply the opposite of.

➤ deny, refute, controvert, rebut, gainsay, contrast, argue, conflict, differ, dissent, counter.

contradiction [kon · tra · *dik* · shun] *n.* A situation in which inherent factors are inconsistent with each other.

➤ discrepancy, disagreement, incongruity, inconsistency, variance, controversion, rebuttal, negation.

contradictory [kon · tra · *dik* · tuh · ree] *adj.* Involving or causing a contradiction.

➤ inconsistent, clashing, irreconcilable, contrary, opposed, discrepant, negating, nullifying ("a contradictory statement").

contrary [*kon* · trair · ree] *adj.* In conflict or opposition to.

➤ counter, adverse, against, opposite, irreconcilable, at variance, contradictory, denying ("contrary to law").

contrast [*kon* · trast] *n.* The difference between two things.
v. [ken · *trast*] To compare the differences between things.
➤ *n.* difference, distinction, disparity, differentiation, antithesis, polarity.
v. differentiate, oppose, compare, distinguish.

contravene [kon · tra · *vene*] *v.* To go against; to violate. USAGE: "The court decided that the statute contravenes the Constitution."

➤ go against, violate, foil, thwart, disobey, frustrate, oppose, disregard, conflict with, nullify.

contribute [kon · *tri* · byoot] *v.* 1. To make a gift in conjunction with others. *See* contribution. 2. To participate. 3. To participate in causing a result. *See* contributing to delinquency.

➤ give, assist, donate, furnish, provide, aid ("contribute to charity"); help produce, participate, influence, help cause, advance ("contribute to his own injury"); indemnify, restore, return, reimburse, make restitution.

contributing cause [kon · *tri* · byoot · ing] *n.* A **cause** that is partially responsible for a result, i.e., a cause that contributes to a result. *See* contributory negligence.

contributing to delinquency [de · *link* · wen · see] *n.* The crime of causing or tending to cause the **delinquency** of a juvenile. *See* juvenile offender.

contribution [kon · tri · *byoo* · shen] *n.* 1. A payment of his share of a debt or **judgment** by a person who is jointly liable. *See* joint liability. 2. The right of a person who has satisfied a shared indebtedness to have those with whom she shared it contribute in defraying its cost. 3. A gift, commonly a **charitable gift**.

➤ donation, gift, charity, assistance, grant; collaboration, cooperation, help, interest, complicity, indemnification, restitution, reparation, repayment, satisfaction.

contribution between insurers [be · *tween* in · *shoor* · erz] *n.* The obligation of an insurance company that has issued a policy covering the same **loss** as that insured by another insurance company to contribute proportionally to the other insurer who has paid the entire loss.

contributory [kon · *trib* · yoo · tor · ee] *adj.* Added to; supplementary; joining with something else.

➤ assisting, auxiliary, aiding.

contributory negligence [*neg* · li · jense] *n.* In the law of **negligence**, a failure by the plaintiff to exercise **reasonable care** which, in part at least, is the cause of an injury. Contributory negligence defeats a plaintiff's **cause of action** for negligence in states that have not adopted the doctrine of **comparative negligence**. *Compare* comparative negligence.

contrite [kon · *trite*] *adj.* Penitent; apologetic for sins; humble.

➤ remorseful, penitent, apologetic, humble, sorrowful, regretful.

contrivance [kon · *trive* · ants] *n.* An artificial development or arrangement.

➤ plot, plan, mechanism, method, artifice, deception, fabrication, connivance.

contrive [kon · *trive*] *v.* 1. To devise or plan. 2. To create or develop artistically.

C

➤ scheme, conspire, collude, plot, organize; conceive, imagine, invent, create, fashion, improvise, develop.

control [ken · *trol*] *n.* The power or authority to direct or manage.
v. To exercise authority; to direct; to dominate; to command; to restrain.
➤ *n.* power, authority, jurisdiction, dominion, mastery, supervision, regulation, care, charge, dominance; restraint, moderation, deterrence, inhibition.
v. arrest, confine, constrain, restrain, prohibit; regulate, direct, govern, rule, oversee, command, supervise.

controlled substance [ken · *troled sub* · stense] *n.* A drug considered dangerous by the law because of its effects, which usually include intoxication, stupor, or addictive potential. Such drugs (EXAMPLES: heroin; cocaine; marijuana; **amphetamines; barbiturates**) are prohibited or their availability limited by federal and state **controlled substance acts**. The possession, distribution, or sale of a controlled substance is a criminal offense.

controlled substance acts *n.* *See* controlled substance.

controller [kon · *trole* · er] *n.* Same as **comptroller**.
➤ comptroller, accountant, inspector, auditor, bookkeeper, bursar.

controlling [ken · *trole* · ing] *adj.* Dominant; commanding; governing. A "controlling" decision is one to which other courts are legally obligated to conform.
➤ dominant, superior, precedential.

controlling interest [*in* · trest] *n.* 1. A majority of the shares of stock of a corporation. 2. Control of a corporation which is in the hands of less than a majority of the shareholders because many shareholders own only a limited number of shares. *See* majority interest; majority stockholders.

controversial [kon · tro · *ver* · shul] *adj.* Arousing debate; at issue; disputable; debatable.
➤ provocative, debatable, arguable, widely discussed, at issue, contestable, in dispute, contended, litigious.

controversy [*kon* · tro · ver · see] *n.* 1. An issue appropriate for a judicial ruling,

that is, a concrete dispute between **parties** with **adverse interests** that are substantial and capable of being remedied by a judicial order. 2. For the meaning of "controversy" as used in the Constitution, *see* case or controversy. 3. A dispute; an argument.
➤ lawsuit, case, legal action, legal proceeding; debate, altercation, dispute, squabble, disharmony, dissention, discord.

controvert [*kon* · tro · vert] *v.* To dispute or oppose.
➤ dispute, oppose, contest, counter, negate, rebut, refute, disprove, contravene, deny.

controverted [*kon* · tre · vert · ed] *adj.* Disputed; contested; challenged.

controverted facts *n.* Facts in issue; facts that are a matter of controversy before the court. When facts are in controversy, there is a basis for trial and, conversely, for the denial of **summary judgment**.

contumacious [kon · tyoo · *may* · shess] *adj.* Stubborn; disobedient; contemptuous. *See* contempt.

contumacy [*kon* · tyoo · ma · see] *n.* 1. Contemptuous disobedience of an order of the court. *See* contempt. 2. Refusal to submit to authority.

convene [ken · *veen*] *v.* 1. To call a meeting. 2. To assemble; to meet as a body.
➤ assemble, collect, mobilize, gather, summon, amass, round up, consolidate.

convenience [kon · *veen* · yence] *n.* 1. A useful or comfortable thing. 2. A suitable time or opportunity.
➤ accommodation, benefit, comfort, relief, support, avail, assistance ("the convenience of a second bathroom"); chance, freedom, opportunity, leisure, spare moment ("at your convenience").

convenience and necessity [ken · *vee* · ni · ense and ne · *sess* · i · tee] *n.* *See* certificate of convenience and necessity.

convenient [kon · *veen* · yent] *adj.* The quality of being easy to use or access.
➤ suitable, advantageous, accessible, easy, useful, carefree, nearby, available, commodious ("a convenient forum").

convention [ken · *ven* · shen] *n.* 1. An assembly of delegates for the purpose of

conducting particularly important affairs of a political party or another body. 2. An agreement between nations with respect to matters of relative lack of significance. *Compare* treaty. 3. Custom; protocol; form.
➤ meeting, gathering, forum, conclave, assembly; custom, protocol, tradition.

conventional [ken · *ven* · shen · el] *adj.* 1. Based or grounded upon a contract; expressly created by acts of the parties. 2. Customary; normal. 3. Correct; proper; suitable.
➤ standard, accepted, normal, regular, routine, approved, orthodox, established, familiar, usual, typical.

   conventional interest [*in* · trest] *n.* A rate of interest agreed upon by the parties, as distinguished from a rate of interest set by law. *See* legal interest.

   conventional lien [*leen*] *n.* A **lien** arising out of a contract between the parties rather than from a statute or a **judgment**.

   conventional mortgage [*more* · gej] *n.* A **mortgage** granted by a conventional lender, that is, a bank or a savings and loan institution rather than the **FHA** or **VA**.

converge [*kon* · verj] *v.* To move toward one point.
➤ unite, combine, approach, coalesce, merge, gather, congregate, convene.

conversation [kon · ver · *say* · shun] *n.* An exchange of ideas or thoughts between two or more persons.
➤ discourse, dialogue, discussion, colloquy, exchange, interchange, conference, rap.

conversion [ken · *ver* · zhen] *n.* 1. Control over another person's personal property which is wrongfully exercised; control applied in a manner that violates that person's **title** to or **rights** in the property. Conversion is both a **tort** and a crime. *See* fraudulent conversion. *Also see* involuntary conversion. 2. The act of exchanging a **convertible bond** or **convertible stock** for another **security**. 3. A transformation; a changeover; an alteration.
➤ change, transformation, shift, metamorphosis, transmutation ("his conversion to Judaism"); theft, larceny, misappropriation, deprivation, embezzlement ("the tort of conversion").

conversion by bailee [bay · *lee*] *n.* Appropriation by a **bailee** to his own use of property entrusted to him. *See* conversion. *Also see* appropriation; misappropriation.

conversion of insurance [in · *shoor* · ense] *n.* The exercise of the right that exists in some instances to exchange one type of insurance coverage for another with respect to the same **risk**. EXAMPLE: **term life insurance** for **whole life insurance**.

convert [ken · *vert*] *v.* 1. To **appropriate** the property of another person. *See* conversion. 2. To change or transform.
➤ steal, take, appropriate, embezzle, misuse; transform, change, alter, modify, refashion.

convertible [ken · *vert* · ibl] *adj.* Anything that can be changed to or for something else as a matter of **right**.
➤ exchangeable, transformable, interchangeable, permutable, adaptable, adjustable.

   convertible bonds *n.* **Bonds** issued with the privilege of converting them into other securities, usually the **common stock** of the issuing corporation.

   convertible debentures [deb · en · choorz] *n. See* convertible bonds; debenture.

   convertible stock *n.* Corporate stock that the stockholder is entitled to surrender for another **class of stock** or for other **obligations** of the corporation.

convey [kon · *vay*] *v.* 1. To transfer **title** to property from one person to another by deed, bill of sale, or other conveyance. *See* transfer. 2. To tranfer; to transmit. 3. To carry; to transport. 4. To indicate; to signify; to connote.
➤ transfer, give, deed, pass, assign, cede ("convey title"); communicate, tell, disclose, state ("convey an idea").

conveyance [kon · *vay* · ense] *n.* 1. The transferring of **title** to real property from one person to another. 2. Any document that creates a **lien** on real property or a debt or duty arising out of real estate. EXAMPLES: a lease; a **mortgage**; an **assignment**. 3. Any transfer of title to either real property or personal property. 4. A means of transportation. *See* absolute conveyance; fraudulent conveyance; involuntary conveyance; original conveyance; reconveyance; voluntary conveyance.

C

conveyancing [kon · *vay* · ense · ing] *n.*
The act of transfering **title** to or creating
a **lien** on real estate by deed, **mortgage**,
or other instrument. *See* transfer.

convict [*kon* · vikt] *n.* A person who is
under a sentence of imprisonment as the
result of having been convicted of a
crime. *See* conviction.
v. To find a person guilty of the crime
with which he is charged.
➤ *n.* criminal, felon, con, inmate, prisoner.
v. prove guilty, find guilty, punish, doom.

conviction [ken · *vik* · shen] *n.* 1. An
adjudication that a person is guilty of a
crime, either by a judge or jury or based
upon a plea of guilty. 2. The state of being
certain; a firm belief or opinion.
➤ certainty, opinion, belief.

convince [kon · *vince*] *v.* To persuade by
argument; to prove.
➤ persuade, sway, entice, convert, win
over, coax, influence, allure, enlist ("to
convince the jury of Omar's innocence").

convincing [kon · *vin* · sing] *adj.* Having
the power to show the truth of something.
➤ persuasive, compelling, credible, strong,
plausible, substantial, powerful
("a convincing argument").

convoy [*kon* · voy] *n.* An escort organized
for protection.
➤ escort, guard, fleet, contingent, group.

coobligor [koh · ob · *lie* · jer] *n.* A person
liable with one or more others on a
negotiable instrument or a contract; a
person liable on a **joint obligation** or a
joint and several obligation; a **joint
obligor**.

cooling-off period [kool · ing-off *peer* · i · ed]
n. 1. In labor law, a period often required
by statute or **collective bargaining
agreement** as a **condition precedent** to a
strike by the union or a **lockout** by the
employer, during which both parties
must attempt to resolve their differences
through **mediation** or negotiation. 2. A
period provided by law, otherwise known
as a *waiting period*, between the filing of
action for divorce and the hearing of the
case. 3. A period during which, in most
states, a buyer may cancel a purchase.

cooperate [ko · *op* · er · ate] *v.* To work in
union with others.
➤ collaborate, collude, participate, unite,
ally, act jointly, work together.

cooperation [ko · op · er · *ay* · shun] *n.* The
participation of a group to accomplish a
goal.
➤ participation, assistance, concert,
collaboration, complicity, reciprocity,
solidarity, agreement.
Ant. antagonism, uncooperativeness.

cooperation clause [koh · op · er · *ay* · shen]
n. A clause in an automobile liability
insurance policy that requires the insured
to cooperate with the insurance company
by attending all hearings and trials, giving
testimony, and agreeing to appropriate
settlements.

cooperative [koh · *op* · er · a · tiv] *adj.*
Willing; helpful; together.
n. A group enterprise for the mutual
benefit of its members. EXAMPLES: **a
cooperative store; a cooperative
marketing association**.
➤ *adj.* helpful, assisting, obliging, accommodating, harmonious, easy, synergistic.
n. alliance, collective, association,
federation, partnership, coalition.

cooperative apartment house
[a · *part* · ment] *n.* A multiunit dwelling
in which each tenant has an **interest** in
the corporation or other entity which owns
the building as well as a lease entitling
her to occupy a particular apartment within
the building. *Compare* condominium.

cooperative association
[a · soh · see · *ay* · shen] *n.* An **association**
that exists for the common advantage of
its members, financial or otherwise.

cooperative corporation
[kore · per · *ay* · shen] *n.* A **nonprofit
corporation** that issues no stock and
exists solely for the financial profit of its
members (as opposed to the financial
gain of the corporation) or to provide
them with goods or services.

cooperative marketing association
[*mar* · ket · ing a · soh · see · *ay* · shen] *n.*
A **cooperative association** of producers,
particularly farmers, organized to gain
the advantages of unified bargaining in
the sale of produce and the benefits of

C

shared costs; also referred to as a *farmer's cooperative*.

cooperative store *n.* A store operated by a **cooperative association** or a **cooperative corporation**.

coordinate [ko · *or* · din · ate] *v.* To bring together or organize for the purpose of achieving a goal. USAGE: "Eugenia will coordinate the search for a new associate."
➤ adjust, arrange, harmonize, combine, balance, synchronize, mesh, integrate, equalize.

coordination of benefits provision [ko · or · din · *ay* · shen of ben · e · fit pro · *vizh* · en] *n.* A clause in many insurance policies, especially health and accident policies, which provides that, notwithstanding the insured's ownership of other policies covering the same **risk**, she will receive benefits equal only to the total amount which she is out of pocket. *See* double insurance; insurance.

coowners [koh · *ohn* · erz] *n.* *See* coownership.

coownership [koh · *ohn* · er · ship] *n.* Ownership of property by more than one person. *See* cotenancy; joint tenancy; tenancy in common. **Also see** joint ownership.

coparcener [koh · *par* · se · ner] *n.* A **joint heir**.

copartner [*koh* · part · ner] *n.* A **partner**.

copartnership [koh · *part* · ner · ship] *n.* A **partnership**. *See* partnership.

copious [*kope* · ee · us] *adj.* Plentiful in number; abundant.
➤ ample, full, abundant, prolific, profuse, replete, generous, voluminous, bountiful.

copy [*kop* · ee] *n.* A reproduction of an original work. *Note*, however, that in the strict sense a copy is not necessarily a duplicate, that is, it is not necessarily a double or an exact reproduction of the original. *See* certified copy; examined copy.
v. To reproduce, imitate, or make a copy of.
➤ *n.* reproduction, transcript, duplicate, facsimile, likeness, image, impression; forgery, fake, imitation.
v. reproduce, duplicate, trace, print, transcribe; forge, cheat, plagarize, mimic, ape, falsify, infringe, impersonate.

copyright [*kop* · ee · rite] *n.* The right of an author, granted by federal statute, to exclusively control the reproduction, distribution, and sale of her literary, artistic, or intellectual productions for the period of the copyright's existence. Copyright protection extends to written work, music, films, sound recordings, photographs, paintings, sculpture, and some computer programs and chips. *See* right. *Also see* intellectual property; literary property.
v. To acquire a **copyright**. *See* copyright.
➤ *n.* authority, grant, license, permit, privilege, authorization.

coram nobis [*kor* · em *no* · bis] *(Latin) prep.* "In our presence"; before us. A **writ of coram nobis** is used to obtain review of a **judgment** by the court that rendered it. Its purpose is to correct **errors of fact** in criminal as well as civil cases. *Compare coram vobis.*

coram vobis [*kor* · em *vo* · bis] *(Latin) prep.* "In your presence"; before you. A **writ** which is essentially the same as a **writ of coram nobis**, except that it is addressed to an **appellate court** and requests it to review the **judgment** of the **trial court**.

corespondent [koh · res · *pon* · dent] *n.* The person who is accused by the plaintiff in an **action** for divorce of having committed **adultery** with the defendant. *Note* that "corespondent" is not "**correspondent**."

corner [*kore* · ner] *n.* 1. A point established by **survey** and located by references to distances and markers in a **legal description** of the boundaries of a tract of land. 2. The point at which converging lines meet. 3. A predicament.
v. 1. To acquire control of all or a preponderant quantity of a **commodity** in order to withhold it from the market for a time, thereby inflating the price, and then to sell it at the inflated price; to "corner the market." *See* monopoly. 2. To contract for future purchases of a commodity (**futures**) in an amount that exceeds the supply of the commodity, in order to inflate the price. *See* abbrochment; forestalling the market.

➤ *n.* crossing, junction, intersection; dilemma, jam, impasse, difficulty.
v. trap, seize, monopolize, control.

corollary [*kore* · o · lair · ee] *n.* Something that naturally follows.
➤ consequence, outcome, effect, conclusion, offshoot, outgrowth, addition, correlation.

coroner [*kor* · o · ner] *n.* A public official charged with responsibility for conducting inquiries, sometimes with the aid of a jury, into the death of persons who appear to have died from other than natural causes. Coroners have been replaced by **medical examiners** in most jurisdictions. *See* coroner's jury.

coroner's inquest [*in* · kwest] *n. See* inquest.

coroner's jury [*joo* · ree] *n.* A jury convened by a coroner to make an inquiry into the cause of a person's death.

corporal [*kore* · per · el] *adj.* Pertaining to the body; bodily.
➤ bodily, physical, fleshly ("corporal punishment").

corporal oath *n.* An oath in which the **affiant** raises her arm or touches the Bible with her hand; a **solemn oath**. *See* oath.

corporal punishment [*pun* · ish · ment] *n.* Punishment inflicted on the body. EXAMPLES: paddling; slapping; whipping.

corporate [*kore* · per · et] *adj.* Pertaining to a corporation.

corporate agents [*ay* · jents] *n.* The officers and employees of a corporation who have the authority to act for the corporation.

corporate bond *n.* A **bond** issued by a corporation that is the obligation of the corporation. *See* corporate securities.

corporate charter [*char* · ter] *n. See* charter. *Also see* corporate franchise.

corporate citizenship [*sit* · i · zen · ship] *n.* A corporation is a **citizen** of the state in which it is **incorporated**. It enjoys many of the constitutional rights guaranteed to a **natural person**.

corporate directors [de · *rek* · terz] *n.* **Directors** of a corporation; members of the board of directors of a corporation.

corporate distribution [dis · tre · *byoo* · shen] *n.* The distribution of money or other **assets** (EXAMPLE: a **dividend**) of a corporation to its shareholders.

corporate domicile [*dom* · i · sile] *n.* A corporation is **domiciled** in the state of its **incorporation**. *See* domicile.

corporate entity [*en* · ti · tee] *n.* The **corporation** itself, i.e., the corporation considered separate and apart from its stockholders. *See* entity.

corporate franchise [*fran* · chize] *n.* The powers granted a corporation by the state as specified in its **charter**. *See* franchise.

corporate liability [ly · e · *bil* · i · tee] *n.* The **liability** of a corporation for the acts of its directors, officers, shareholders, agents, and employees. *Compare* personal liability. *See* limited liability acts.

corporate officers [*off* · i · serz] *n.* The **officers** of a corporation. EXAMPLES: the president; the treasurer; the **comptroller**.

corporate purpose [*per* · pess] *n. See* articles of incorporation.

corporate records [*rek* · erdz] *n.* The **charter** and **bylaws** of a corporation, the minutes of the meetings of its board of directors and of stockholders' meetings, and the written evidence of its contracts and business transactions. *See* records. *Also see* books.

corporate reorganization [re · or · gen · i · *zay* · shen] *n.* 1. The process that takes place when a corporation is broken up or merges with or acquires another corporation. The process often, but not necessarily, involves corporations that are in financial distress; it generally involves a restructuring of corporate **capitalization**. A **reorganization** is always accompanied by significant tax considerations. *See* reorganized. 2. A corporate business reorganization under **Chapter 11** of the **Bankruptcy Code**. *See* bankruptcy.

corporate seal *n.* The **seal** of a corporation, used to validate corporate acts and documents as required by statute or by the **corporate charter**.

corporate securities [se · *kyoor* · it · eez] *n.* **Stock**, **bonds**, **notes**, and other documentation of indebtedness issued by a corporation to obtain funds to use in the corporation's business. *See* securities.

corporate stock *n.* **Stock** issued by a corporation. *See* corporate securities.

corporate veil *n.* *See* piercing the corporate veil.

corporation [kore · per · *ay* · shen] *n.* An **artificial person**, existing only in the eyes of the law, to whom a state or the federal government has granted a **charter** to become a **legal entity**, separate from its shareholders, with a name of its own, under which its shareholders can act and contract and sue and be sued. A corporation's shareholders, officers, and directors are not normally liable for the acts of the corporation. *See* corporate liability; limited liability acts.

　　See also benevolent corporation; business corporation; charitable corporation; close corporation; collapsible corporation; de facto corporation; de jure corporation; domestic corporation; eleemosynary corporation; family corporation; foreign corporation; municipal corporation; nonprofit corporation; nonstock corporation; private corporation; public corporation; quasi corporation.
➤ business, company, enterprise, organization, association, establishment, firm.

corporator [kore · per · *ay* · tor] *n.* Same as **incorporator**. *Compare* promoter.

corporeal [kore · *pore* · ee · el] *adj.* Possessing physical substance; pertaining to something that can be seen and touched; **tangible**. *Compare* incorporeal.
➤ tangible, bodily, actual, real, fleshly, physical, palpable ("corporeal existence").

corporeal hereditaments [herr · eh · *dit* · ah · ments] *n.* Physical or **tangible property**, whether real or personal, capable of being inherited. *Compare* incorporeal hereditaments. *See* hereditaments.

corporeal property [*prop* · er · tee] *n.* Property that has physical substance; **tangible property**. EXAMPLES: a tract of land; an automobile; an **heirloom**; a **chattel**. *Compare* incorporeal property.

corpse *n.* The dead body of a person.
➤ body, remains, victim, deceased, cadaver, dead body, stiff.

corpus [kore · pus] *(Latin) n.* Means "body." 1. The subject matter or **capital** of a **trust** or **estate**, or the principal of a fund, as distinguished from the income or interest. 2. The body or substance of anything.
➤ aggregate, bulk, quantity, sum, total, body, substance ("corpus of a trust").

corpus delicti [de · *lik* · tie] *n.* Means "the body of the crime"; the fact that a crime has actually been committed. EXAMPLES: in the case of murder, the corpse; in the case of **burglary**, the broken lock on the door; in the case of **assault**, the bruised face or the broken arm.

correct [ko · *rekt*] *v.* 1. To make right or amend. 2. To punish in order to reform or improve.
adj. Accurate, true.
➤ *v.* alter, modify, remedy, fix, adjust, amend; punish, reprimand, censure, chastise.
adj. proper, actual, true, exact, factual, careful, valid ("a correct statement of the law").

correction [ko · *rek* · shun] *n.* 1. A change to replace what was wrong. 2. The treatment and rehabilitation of criminals.
➤ alteration, modification, change, amendment, remedy, adjustment; improvement, reform, remediation, rehabilitation, penalty, discipline, reprimand, retribution, scolding.

correlate [*kor* · re · late] *v.* To establish a relationship between.
➤ connect, relate, coordinate, affiliate, match, parallel.

correlative [ke · *rel* · e · tiv] *adj.* Dependent, one thing upon another. EXAMPLES: right and wrong; **trustee** and **beneficiary**; husband and wife.

correlative rights *n.* Another term for the **reasonable use doctrine**, which governs the rights of a landowner along a river or stream to consume or divert water that would otherwise be available to his downstream neighbor. *See* reasonable use doctrine.

correspond [kor · ess · *pond*] *v.* 1. To communicate by writing letters back and forth. 2. To equal or parallel.
➤ communicate, notify, write, reply, contact; relate, fit, equal, approximate, correlate, harmonize, cohere, match.

correspondence [kore · ess · *pon* · dents] *n.* 1. Communication by sending letters. 2. The similarity between two or more items.
➤ communication, mail, letters, writing; similarity, equivalence, resemblance, agreement, congruity, uniformity, parity.

correspondent [kor · ess · *pon* · dent] *n.* 1. In banking or finance, a bank or other establishment that acts for or is involved in frequent commercial transactions with a similar organization located some distance away. 2. A person who communicates with another person in writing. *Note* that "correspondent" is not "**corespondent**."

corroborate [ke · *rob* · er · ate] *v.* To state facts that tend to support the truth of a statement made by another person.
➤ substantiate, confirm, affirm, verify, attest, validate, endorse, strengthen ("corroborate an alibi").

corroborating evidence [ke · *rob* · er · ay · ting *ev* · i · dense] *n.* Evidence from another source which tends to show the probability that the testimony of a prior witness is truthful. *Compare* cumulative evidence. *See* evidence.

corrupt [ko · *rupt*] *adj.* 1. Crooked; dishonest; malicious. 2. Debased; adulterated.
v. To pervert or pollute.
➤ *adj.* dishonorable, unprincipled, wicked, perfidious, insincere, venal; tainted, debased, degraded, profligate, rotten, foul, infected, polluted.
v. adulterate, spoil, pollute, subvert, pervert, defraud, degrade, infect, ravage, ruin, violate.

corrupt practices acts [ke · *rupt prak* · tiss · ez] *n.* Federal and state statutes that regulate expenditures by candidates for election as well as contributions to their election campaigns.

corruption [ko · *rup* · shun] *n.* 1. Dishonesty; crookedness. 2. Baseness. 3. Adulteration.

➤ deception, disloyalty, graft, perfidy, villainy, dishonesty, injustice, abuse of trust, knavery; evil, infamy, vice, depravity, turpitude; decay, infection, distortion, contamination.

cosign [ko · sine] *v.* To sign an instrument or document with another, creating a legal obligation on the part of the cosigner.
➤ endorse, certify, assure, insure, validate, underwrite, comake.

cosignee [ko · sy · nee] *n.* One who signs with another for a loan.
➤ comaker, guarantor, surety.

cosigner [ko · sine · er] *n.* A person who, with another or others, signs a **negotiable instrument** or other instrument or document and thereby becomes obligated to carry out its requirements. *Compare* **comaker**, a term used *only* in connection with negotiable instruments.

cost *n.* The amount of money, services, or property required to obtain something. *See* costs.
➤ price, rate, charge, worth, value, bill, fee ("the cost of a new car"); sacrifice, injury, consequence, loss, suffering ("the cost of war").

cost and freight *n.* A term, often shortened to **CAF**, which means that the price quoted to the purchaser includes the cost of the goods plus freight charges to the place of destination.

cost, insurance, and freight [in · *shoor* · ense] *n.* A term, often shortened to **CIF**, which means that the price quoted to the purchaser includes the cost of the goods plus freight and insurance charges to the place of destination.

cost-of-living adjustment [*liv* · ing a · *just* · ment] *n.* An adjustment in the amount of a benefit payment. (EXAMPLES: social security; federal civil service retirement benefits; some private pension and disability plans.) A cost-of-living adjustment is often referred to as a **COLA**. *See* statutory benefit.

cost-of-living clause [*liv* · ing] *n.* A provision in a **collective bargaining agreement** or other contract that ties wage or benefit increases to the cost of

C

living, generally as measured by the **consumer price index**.

cost-plus contract [kost-plus kon · trakt] *n.* A construction contract under which the contractor is entitled to recover her costs plus an agreed-upon percentage of those costs.

costs *n. Plural* of **cost**. The expense of pursuing a lawsuit. (EXAMPLES: a **filing fee**; an **appeal bond**.) The court may assess such costs against the losing **party**. Normally, however, costs do not include attorney fees. *See* court costs.

costs of collection [ke · lek · shen] *n.* A term found in a **promissory note**; the debtor's commitment to pay attorney fees for a plaintiff's attorney if the note is not paid and a successful lawsuit is commenced.

costs to abide the event [a · *bide* the e · *vent*] *n.* An order of an **appellate court** when it sends a case back for a new trial; means that the costs in the appellate court are to be paid by the **party** who is unsuccessful in the new trial.

cotenancy [ko · *ten* · en · see] *n.* The ownership of property by at least two persons (**cotenants**) in such a manner that they each have separate **interests**, but both have the **right of possession** of the property as a whole. The term includes **joint tenancy**, a **tenancy in common**, and a **tenancy by the entirety**. *See* tenancy.

cotenant [ko · *ten* · ent] *n.* One of two or more persons who are coowners under a **cotenancy**. *See* cotenant.

coterie [*ko* · te · ree] *n.* A close-knit group of persons with a strong common interest.
➤ circle, club, clique, group, clan, alliance, society.

coterminous [ko · *term* · in · us] *adj.* Same as **conterminous**.

cotrustees [koh · truss · *teez*] *n.* Two or more persons designated to act jointly as **trustees**.

council [*koun* · sil] *n.* The legislature of a city or other **municipality**. Also referred to as a **city council** or **common council**. *See* metropolitan council; town council. *Also see* city. *Note* that "council" is not "**counsel**."

➤ board, committee, advisors, cabinet, convention, caucus.

counsel [*koun* · sel] *n.* 1. An attorney; an attorney representing a **party** in a **legal action; legal counsel**. *See* assigned counsel; of counsel; right to counsel. 2. Advice; suggestions. *Note* that "counsel" is not "**council**."
v. To provide advice.
➤ *n.* attorney, lawyer, counselor, advocate, legal advisor; advice, guidance, opinion, warning, instruction.
v. advise, recommend, caution, urge, propose, instruct, direct.

counselor [*koun* · sel · er] *n.* An attorney.

count *n.* 1. A statement of a **cause of action** in a **complaint**. There may be several counts in one complaint. 2. A separate and distinct part of an **indictment** or **information** stating a separate and distinct offense. Division into counts is necessary when two or more offenses are charged in a single indictment or information. 3. The tally of votes cast in an election.
v. 1. To add up. 2. To have significance.
➤ *n.* claim, charge, allegation, declaration, cause of action, listing, enumeration.
v. measure, tally, calculate ("count the witnesses who might be called"); mean, matter, signify, weigh, rate ("his opinion doesn't count for much").

counter [*kown* · ter] *v.* To oppose or defend against an attack.
➤ oppose, offset, rebut, resist, contradict, defy.

counter-affidavit [*kown* · ter-af · i · *day* · vit] *n.* An **affidavit** responding to and contradicting the affidavit produced by an adversary.

counterclaim [*kown* · ter · klame] *n.* A **cause of action** on which a defendant in a lawsuit might have sued the plaintiff in a separate action. Such a cause of action, stated in a separate division of a defendant's **answer**, is a counterclaim. *See* compulsory counterclaim; setoff. *Also see* cross-action; cross-claim; cross-complaint.

counterfeit [*kown* · ter · fit] *adj.* False; imitation; sham.
n. Something made in imitation of something else for the purpose of deception.

C

v. To make a copy of something (EXAMPLES: currency; postage stamps; a painting) with the intention of deceiving or defrauding by passing the copy off as original or genuine.
➤ *adj.* false, imitation, sham, phony, fraudulent, bogus, forged.
n. fake, fraud, imitation, replica.
v. imitate, fake, mimic.
Ant. true, real, original.

countermand [kown · ter · *mand*] *v.* To revoke an order previously given.
➤ revoke, withdraw, change, cancel, annul, abolish.
Ant. offer.

counteroffer [koun · ter · off · er] *n.* A position taken in response to an **offer**, proposing a different deal. USAGE: "He responded with a counteroffer."

countersignature [kown · ter · sig · ne · choor] *n.* 1. A signature, often that of a subordinate, added to the signature of an officer or superior, in order to authenticate it. 2. Any subsequent or second signature on the same instrument, for EXAMPLE, as on a traveler's check.
➤ signature, cosignee, witness, underwriter.

country [kun · tree] *n.* A nation or land.
➤ nation, land, state, territory, citizenry.

county [kown · tee] *n.* A **political subdivision** of a state.
➤ subdivision, district, parish, region, municipal, corporation, province.

county board *n.* 1. Short for **board of supervisors** or *board of commissioners,* the governing body of a county. *See* commissioner. 2. Short for county *board of education* or county *school board,* the entity that coordinates local public school education policy in some states.

county commissioners [kum · *ish* · e · nerz] *n.* The members of the **county board**, often called **supervisors**. *See* commissioner.

county court *n.* Actually a **state court**, that is, a part of a state's judicial system. The **jurisdiction** of county courts varies from state to state with respect to the types of cases they are empowered to hear; however, the territorial jurisdiction of a county court is generally limited to the geographical boundaries of the county in which it is located. Many county courts are their state's **trial courts**. *See* original jurisdiction.

coupled with an interest [in · *trest*] *n. See* power coupled with an interest.

coupon [koo · pon] *n.* A certificate attached to a written **instrument**, which evidences the interest payable on the instrument to which it is attached. Such coupons, also known as **interest coupons**, are detachable from the instrument so that they can be presented for payment as they come due.
➤ certificate, share, interest, dividend, voucher, ticket, token, credit.

coupon bond *n.* A **bond** in which the interest, which is payable separately from the principal, is represented by detachable coupons.

coupon note *n.* A **promissory note** with coupons attached. The coupons are **notes** for **interest**, designed to be cut off and paid separately as they **mature**.

course *n.* The manner in which something normally occurs or develops. *See* due course; holder in due course.
➤ path, direction, route, passage, development, order, plan.

course of business [*biz* · ness] *n. See* ordinary course of business.

course of conduct [kon · dukt] *n.* A series of acts; a pattern of behavior.

course of employment [em · *ploy* · ment] *n.* For an employee to have a **compensable injury** under many **workers' compensation acts**, she must have received the injury "in the course of employment." Although court decisions construing this phrase vary in different jurisdictions, it is generally construed to mean within the period of employment and while the employee is engaged in the performance of her duties and furthering her employer's business. *Compare* **arising out of or in the course of employment**, a more generous standard present in the workers' compensation statutes of some states. *See also* scope of employment. The term likewise tends to receive a broader interpretation when the question is one of an employer's liability to third persons for injury resulting from the **negligence** of an employee.

C

court *n.* 1. A part of government, consisting of a judge or judges and, usually, administrative support personnel, whose duty it is to administer justice; the **judicial branch** of government. *See* county court; federal courts; state courts. 2. A place where justice is judicially administered. 3. All judges of the same jurisdiction. For EXAMPLE, all persons who sit as judges of the United States District Court for the Southern District of Texas, taken collectively, constitute "the court" for that judicial district. *Note* that in many instances the words "court" and "judge" are used interchangeably and, in context, have the same meaning. *v.* To invite or provoke into action.
➤ *n.* unit of government, forum, chamber, panel, bench, bar, justice, judge, session. *v.* invite, seek, attract, provoke ("to court danger").

court below *n.* A term used by an **appellate court**, or by attorneys appearing before an appellate court, to refer to the **trial court**.

court calendar [*kal* · en · der] *n. See* calendar. *Also see* docket.

court commissioner [ke · *mish* · e · ner] *n.* A person appointed by the court to perform specific duties in a case (EXAMPLES: taking testimony; conducting a **judicial sale**). *See also* master; master in chancery; referee.

court costs *n.* 1. **Court fees**. 2. The expenses involved in litigating an **action** (EXAMPLES: **witness fees**; the cost of a transcript), including **court fees** but excluding attorney fees. *Compare* expense of litigation. *See* costs; taxation of costs.

court en banc [on *bonk*] *n. See en banc.*

court fees *n.* The charges for the services of a **public officer**, particularly the **clerk of court**, rendered in connection with litigation. These are fixed by law. EXAMPLES: the fee for a certified copy of a document; **filing fees**. *Compare* attorney fees; costs.

court of admiralty [*ad* · mir · el · tee] *n. See* admiralty courts.

court of appeals [a · *peelz*] *n.* Often abbreviated as CA, C.A., or Ct. App. 1. A **Court of Appeals**. *See* Courts of Appeals of the United States. 2. The intermediate

appellate court in most states, although it is the highest appellate court in some, including New York. 3. A court in which appeals from a lower court are heard and decided.

court of bankruptcy [*bank* · rupt · see] *n. See* bankruptcy courts.

court of chancery [*chan* · se · ree] *n.* A **court of equity** in England and in some of the United States.

court of claims *n.* 1. The name formerly given to the United States Claims Court. *See* Claims Court. 2. The name given in some states to the court with **jurisdiction** over claims against the state.

court of common pleas [*kaw* · men pleez] *n.* The name given to **trial courts** in Pennsylvania and Ohio. *See* county court.

court of competent jurisdiction [*kom* · pe · tent joo · ris · *dik* · shen] *n.* A court that has the power and authority under the law to hear and decide the case before it. *See* jurisdiction.

court of equity [*ek* · wi · tee] *n.* A court having **jurisdiction** of **equitable actions**; a court that administers **remedies** which are **equitable** in nature. *Compare* court of law. *See* equity.

court of general jurisdiction [*jen* · e · rel joo · ris · *dik* · shen] *n.* Generally, another term for **trial court**; that is, a court having **jurisdiction** to try all classes of civil and criminal cases except those which can be heard only by a **court of limited jurisdiction**. *See also* original jurisdiction.

court of inferior jurisdiction [in · *feer* · ee · er joo · ris · *dik* · shen] *n. See* inferior court.

court of last resort [re · *zort*] *n. See* highest court.

court of law *n.* 1. A court having **jurisdiction** of **actions at law**, as distinguished from **equitable actions**. 2. Any court that administers the law of a state or of the United States. *Compare* court of equity.

court of limited jurisdiction [*lim* · i · ted joo · ris · *dik* · shen] *n.* A court whose **jurisdiction** is limited to civil cases of a certain type (EXAMPLE: **probate court**) or which involve a limited amount of money (EXAMPLE: **small claims court**), or whose jurisdiction in criminal cases is confined to **petty offenses** and **preliminary hearings** (EXAMPLE: **magistrate's court**). A court of limited jurisdiction is sometimes called a **court of special jurisdiction**. *Compare* court of general jurisdiction.

court of original jurisdiction [ah · *rij* · in · el joo · riss · *dik* · shen] *n.* *See* original jurisdiction.

court of oyer and terminer [*oi* · yer and *ter* · mi · ner] *n.* *See* oyer and terminer.

court of probate [*pro* · bate] *n.* *See* probate court.

court of record [*rek* · erd] *n.* Generally, another term for **trial court**. *See also* court of general jurisdiction.

court of special jurisdiction [*spesh* · el joo · ris · *dik* · shen] *n.* Same as **court of limited jurisdiction**.

court opinion [o · *pin* · yen] *n.* *See* opinion of court.

court order [*or* · der] *n.* 1. An **adjudication** by a court. 2. A ruling by a court with respect to a **motion** or any other question before it for determination during the course of a proceeding.

court record [*rek* · erd] *n.* *See* record.

court reporter [re · *port* · er] *n.* A person who stenographically (*see* stenographic notes) or by "voice writing" records court proceedings, from which, when necessary, he prepares a **transcript** that becomes a part of the **record** in the case.

court reports [re · *ports*] *n.* Official, published reports of cases decided by courts, giving the **opinions** rendered in the cases, with **headnotes** prepared by the publisher. *Also see* reporters.

court-martial [*kort*-mar · shel] *n.* A **military court** in which members of the armed services are tried for offenses under the **Code of Military Justice**. Courts-martial are of three types. A **summary court-martial**, which is limited to minor offenses, is held before a single officer who serves as judge and jury. An intermediate tribunal, a *special court-martial*, which deals with noncapital offenses, is conducted before a panel of officers, and provides many of the procedural safeguards associated with criminal trials in civilian courts. A *general*

court-martial is convened for the most serious violations of the Code, including capital cases, and is heard by a panel which includes an experienced judge.

Court of Appeals [kort of a · *peelz*] *n.* One of the 13 **Courts of Appeals of the United States**.

Court of Military Appeals [*mil* · i · te · ree a · *peelz*] *n.* A civilian court with **jurisdiction** to hear **appeals** from certain types of **court-martial** convictions. Its full name is the United States Court of Military Appeals.

Court of Military Review [*mil* · i · te · ree re · *vyoo*] *n.* Intermediate **appellate** military courts, one for each branch of the service (Army, Navy, Air Force, Marine Corps, and Coast Guard). The Court of Military Review hears appeals from the decisions of **courts-martial**; its decisions are reviewable by the **Court of Military Appeals**.

Courts of Appeals of the United States [a · *peelz* ... yoo · *ny* · ted] *n.* The intermediate **appellate court** in the federal court system, which is divided into 12 geographical **circuits** (each designated the United States Court of Appeals for that circuit) plus the United States Court of Appeals for the Federal Circuit, which hears appeals in **patent**, **copyright**, and **customs** cases, as well as appeals from the **Claims Court**.

covenant [*kov* · e · nent] *n.* 1. In a deed, a promise to do or not to do a particular thing, or an assurance that a particular fact or circumstance exists or does not exist. *See*, for EXAMPLE, covenant for further assurance; covenant for quiet enjoyment; covenant of seisin. *See also* concurrent covenants; dependent covenants; independent covenant; mutual covenants; restrictive covenant; title covenants. 2. A contract or agreement. *v.* To contract; to **pledge**; to make a binding promise.
➤ *n.* agreement, promise, pledge, vow, bond, compact, commitment ("covenant not to sue"). *v.* pledge, promise, agree.

C

covenant appurtenant [a · *per* · te · nent] *n.* Same as **covenant running with the land**.

covenant for further assurance [*fer* · ther e · *shoor* · ense] *n.* A covenant binding the **grantor** to perform any further acts as might be necessary to **perfect title**.

covenant for quiet enjoyment [*kwy* · et en · *joy* · ment] *n.* A covenant that **title** is good and that therefore the **grantee** will be undisturbed in her possession and use of the property. *See* good title.

covenant not to compete [kum · *peet*] *n.* A provision in an employment contract in which the employee promises that, upon leaving the employer, she will not engage in the same business, as an employee or otherwise, in competition with her former employer. Such a covenant, which is also found in **partnership agreements** and agreements for the sale of a business, must be reasonable with respect to its duration and geographical scope.

covenant not to sue *n.* In **tort** law, an agreement not to sue to enforce a **cause of action**. A covenant not to sue entered into with one **tortfeasor** does not release other **joint tortfeasors**.

covenant of seisin [*see* · zin] *n.* A covenant that the **grantor** has **title** to the property and the right to **convey** it. *See* seisin.

covenant of warranty [*war* · en · tee] *n.* *See* warranty deed.

covenant running with the land [*run* · ing] *n.* A covenant that passes with the land when the land is **conveyed**. Such a covenant imposes upon the next purchaser, and all subsequent purchasers, both the liability for performance and the right to demand performance. *See* running with the land.

covenantee [kov · e · nent · *ee*] *n.* The person to whom a **covenant** is made.

covenantor [kov · e · nent · er] *n.* The person making a **covenant**.

covenants for title [*ty* · tel] *n.* *See* title covenants.

cover [*kuv* · er] *n.* Under the **Uniform Commercial Code**, "cover" relates to the right of a buyer, if the seller has breached a **contract of sale**, to purchase the goods elsewhere (the "cover") and hold the seller liable for the difference between the cost of the cover and the original contract price.
v. As applied to insurance, "cover" means to protect oneself or one's property by purchasing insurance.
➤ *n.* replacement, exchange, alternate, buyer's right.
v. protect, wrap, hide, conceal, safeguard, camouflage.
Ant. reveal.

coverage [*kuv* · er · ej] *n.* The **risk of loss** covered by an insurance policy.
➤ reimbursement, premium, protection, warranty, guarantee.

covert [*ko* · vert] *adj.* 1. Hidden; concealed; secret. 2. Covered.
➤ undercover, hidden, clandestine, secret, mysterious, unseen.
Ant. manifest, open.

coverture [*kuv* · er · cher] *n.* The status and rights of a wife arising from the marriage relationship.
➤ marriage, nuptial bond, married state.
Ant. single.

CPA *n.* Abbreviation of and common short way of saying **certified public accountant**. Also abbreviated C.P.A.

crack *n.* Cocaine.
v. 1. To solve. 2. To lose control. 3. To break into.
➤ *n.* rock, coke, cocaine
v. break, solve ("crack the case"); collapse, break down, succumb, yield ("to crack up"); break, damage, sever, split ("to crack a dish").

crack cocaine [ko · *kane*] *n.* *See* cocaine.

craft union [*yoo* · nyen] *n.* A labor union whose membership is confined to persons who work in the same craft. EXAMPLES: painters; plumbers; electricians. *Compare* industrial union.

create [*cree* · ate] *v.* to bring into existence; to originate.
➤ develop, form, launch, originate, make, construct, cause.

credence [*cree* · dense] *n.* The state of being believable or credible.
➤ believability, certainty, trust, acceptance, faith.

C

credentials [kre · *den* · shelz] *n.* Documents that evidence a person's authority; something which shows that a person is who she says she is.
➤ authorization, recommendations, endorsement, qualifications, references.

credibility [kred · i · *bil* · e · tee] *n.* The capacity for being believed or credited; worthiness of belief.
➤ believability, integrity, trustworthiness, reliability, soundness.

credible [*kred* · ibl] *adj.* Believable. USAGE: "I think the witness is lying; his testimony isn't credible."
➤ believable, conceivable, creditable, honest, plausible, likely, worthy.
Ant. dubious, unlikely.

credit [*kred* · it] *n.* 1. Trust placed in a person's willingness and ability to pay when the obligation to pay is extended over a period of time without **security**. *See* consumer credit protection acts; letter of credit; line of credit. 2. The obligation owed by a debtor to a creditor. 3. An accounting term for what appears to be owing by one person to another. *Compare* debit. For use in the context of taxation, see **tax credit**.
v. 1. To acknowledge payment of or on account of a debt. 2. To post or enter a payment upon a ledger. *Compare* debit. 3. To give belief to a statement.
➤ *n.* rating, trust, standing, authority, loan, mortgage ("He has good credit").
v. accredit, accept, acknowledge, attribute to.

credit bureau [*byoo* · roh] *n.* A company that collects information concerning the financial standing, credit, and general reputation of others, which it furnishes to subscribers for a fee.

credit card *n.* A card issued for the purpose of enabling the owner to obtain goods, services, or money on credit.

credit insurance [in · *shoor* · ense] *n.* 1. An insurance policy purchased by a creditor insuring him against **loss** resulting from the inability of his debtors to pay their debts. 2. Insurance purchased by a debtor which pays her creditor in the event she is unable to pay because of her death or disability. *See* mortgage insurance.

credit life insurance [in · *shoor* · ense] *n.* *See* credit insurance.

credit line *n.* Same as **line of credit**.

credit rating [*ray* · ting] *n.* An assessment of a person's financial ability and promptness in the payment of his debts, generally rendered by a **credit bureau** in the form of a **credit report**.

credit report [re · *port*] *n.* A written report from a **credit bureau** giving a person's credit rating. It provides the details of the subject's credit and other significant financial transactions, usually for the previous seven to ten years.

credit union [*yoo* · nyen] *n.* A **cooperative association** organized to provide credit to its members at a rate of interest which is generally lower than the rate available from commercial **lending institutions**.

creditor [*kred* · it · er] *n.* A person to whom a debt is owed by a debtor.
➤ lender, assignee.
Ant. debtor.

creditor beneficiary [ben · e · *fish* · ee · ar · ee] *n.* A creditor who is the **beneficiary** of a contract made between the debtor and a third person. *See* third-party beneficiary.

creditors' meeting [*kred* · it · erz *meet* · ing] *n.* The **first meeting of creditors** of a **bankrupt**, required for the purpose of allowing the claims of creditors, questioning the bankrupt under oath, and electing a **trustee in bankruptcy**.

crime *n.* An offense against the authority of the state; a **public wrong**, as distinguished from a **private wrong**; an act in violation of the **penal code**; a **felony** or a **misdemeanor**. *See* criminal statute.
➤ felony, misdemeanor, criminal act, misconduct, delinquency, corruption, offense, lawlessness.

crime against nature [a · *genst nay* · cher] *n.* **Sodomy**, including **bestiality**. *Also see* buggery.

crime of moral turpitude [*more* · el *ter* · pi · tood] *n.* *See* moral turpitude.

crimen [*krim* · en] *(Latin) n.* A crime.

crimen falsi [*fall* · see] *n.* Any crime in which untruthfulness is an essential element or which involves untruthfulness that interferes with the administration of justice. EXAMPLES: **forgery; embezzlement; perjury**.

criminal [*krim* · i · nel] *adj.* 1. Pertaining to crime or punishment. 2. Involving crime; guilty of crime.

n. A person who has been convicted of committing a crime.

➤ *adj.* unlawful, felonious, illegal, notorious, blameworthy, noncivil ("criminal intent").

n. felon, culprit, violator, offender, delinquent, transgressor.

criminal act *n.* Any act punishable as a crime. *See* actus reus. *Compare* mens rea.

criminal action [*ak* · shen] *n.* A criminal prosecution.

criminal activity [*ak* · *tiv* · i · tee] *n.* Any activity that is a crime, including planning, fleeing from, or concealing the crime.

criminal anarchy [*an* · er · kee] *n.* The doctrine that government should be overthrown by force and violence. It is a **felony**. *See* anarchy.

criminal assault [a · *salt*] *n.* An **assault** for which the assailant may be criminally prosecuted, as opposed to **civil assault**. *See* criminal prosecution.

criminal attempt [a · *temt*] *n. See* attempt.

criminal capacity [ke · *pass* · i · tee] *n.* A person can be guilty of a crime only if he has the capacity to appreciate the criminal nature of his act. In the eyes of the law, certain persons are conclusively presumed to lack criminal capacity. EXAMPLES: insane persons; persons who have not reached the **age of reason**. *See* conclusive presumption; presumption.

criminal case *n.* The prosecution of a person for a criminal offense; a criminal prosecution. *Compare* civil case.

criminal charge *n.* An **indictment, information, complaint**, or other formal charge of the commission of a crime.

criminal conspiracy [ken · *speer* · e · see] *n. See* conspiracy.

criminal contempt [ken · *temt*] *n.* The dividing line between criminal contempt and **civil contempt** is not always clear. Generally, however, when the primary

purpose of a contempt proceeding is to preserve the court's authority, the contempt is criminal. EXAMPLES: personally insulting behavior directed by an attorney to the judge; a witness's unjustified refusal to answer a question. *See* contempt of court.

criminal conversation [kon · ver · *say* · shen] *n.* Seduction of a married person by a person other than one of the parties to the marriage. This is not a crime. *See* heart balm statutes. In some states it is a **tort** and grounds for a **civil action** against the seducer.

criminal court *n.* A court having **jurisdiction** of prosecutions for crimes. *Compare* civil court.

criminal information [in · fer · *may* · shen] *n. See* information.

criminal intent [in · *tent*] *n.* **Intent** to commit a crime as evidenced by the fact that the crime was committed. *Compare* specific intent. *See* mens rea; presumed intent.

criminal law *n.* Branch of the law that specifies what conduct constitutes crime and establishes appropriate punishments for such conduct. *Compare* civil law.

criminal liability [ly · e · *bil* · tee] *n.* **Liability** for arrest or prosecution. *Compare* civil liability.

criminal libel [*lie* · bel] *n.* A **durable** written or printed **defamation** which is **published** with **malice**.

criminal mischief [*miss* · chif] *n.* Same as **malicious mischief**.

criminal negligence [*neg* · li · jenss] *n.* A degree of **negligence** that exceeds **ordinary negligence** and that is punishable as a crime. The term **culpable negligence** is also applied to such conduct. *See* manslaughter; negligent homicide.

criminal offense [o · *fense*] *n.* A crime.

criminal pattern [*pat* · ern] *n. See* pattern.

criminal procedure [pro · *see* · jer] *n.* The **rules of procedure** by which criminal prosecutions are governed. *See* rules of criminal procedure. *Compare* civil procedure.

criminal proceeding [pro · *see* · ding] *n.* Any phase or aspect of a criminal prosecution, or the prosecution as a whole. *See* proceeding.

criminal prosecution
[pross · e · kyoo · shen] *n.* The process of arresting, charging, trying, and sentencing a person for the commission of a crime. A criminal sentence generally involves the imposition of a fine, imprisonment, or death. A criminal prosecution is brought by the **state**, as opposed to a civil action, which is brought by a **private party**.

criminal registration act
[rej · iss · *tray* · shen] *n.* A statute or local ordinance that requires a convicted **felon** to register with the authorities upon entering a community.

criminal side *n.* The section of a **court calendar** that lists criminal cases. *Compare* civil side.

criminal statute [*stat* · shoot] *n.* A statute that declares the conduct which it describes to be a crime, and establishes punishment for engaging in it.

criminal syndicalism [*sin* · dik · a · lzm] *n. See* syndicalism.

criminal trespass [*tress* · pess] *n.* The crime of entering on or into the property of another after having notice not to or refusing to leave after being told to do so. *See* trespass.

criminalize [*krim* · i · nel · ize] *v.* To make something a crime under the law. *Compare* decriminalization.

criminology [krim · in · *awl* · e · jee] *n.* The study of crime, criminals, and criminal punishment.

criterion [kry · *teer* · ee · on] *n.* The standard or basis against which something is judged.
➤ basis, standard, test, yardstick, guide, measure, model.

critical [*krit* · i · kul] *adj.* 1. Of great importance or signifance. 2. Judgmental; fault-finding.
➤ crucial, decisive, major, vital, grave ("the critical vote"); blaming, judgmental, carping, rebuking, disapproving ("critical mother").

critical stage [*krit* · i · kel] *n.* The point in a **criminal proceeding** at which a defendant's constitutional right to counsel is violated unless she has counsel or has been advised of her **right to counsel**.

criticize [*krit* · i · size] *v.* 1. To find fault with. 2. To evaluate or judge the facts or a situation.
➤ disparage, impugn, reprove, condemn, decry; adjudge, assess, appraise, rate, value.

crop insurance [in · *shoor* · ense] *n.* An insurance policy covering growing crops against **loss** from **risks** such as flood, hail, wind, hurricane, or plant disease.

cross *adv.* 1. Opposing; *contra*; against; conflicting. 2. Blocking; neutralizing. 3. Converging; intersecting; meeting.
v. 1. To mingle or blend. 2. To betray or hinder. 3. To intersect or meet.
adj. Annoyed, out-of-sorts; angry.
➤ *v.* blend, mingle, pollinate; betray, hinder, impede, interfere, obstruct, foil, frustrate; converge, intersect, meet, divide.
adj. angry, annoyed, crabby, grouchy, petulant, irritable, out-of-sorts.

cross-action [*kross*-ak · shen] *n.* 1. An **action** brought by a defendant in a lawsuit against the plaintiff based upon a **cause of action** arising out of the same transaction on which the plaintiff's suit is based. *See also* counterclaim. 2. An independent action brought by a defendant in a lawsuit against the plaintiff.

cross-appeal [a · *peel*] *n.* An **appeal** filed by the **appellee** from the same **judgment**, or some portion of the same judgment, as the **appellant** has appealed from. A cross-appeal is generally made a part of the review proceedings set in motion by the original appeal.

cross-claim [*kross*-klame] *n.* A **counterclaim** against a coplaintiff or a codefendant.

cross-complaint [kross-kem · *plaint*] *n.* A **complaint** a defendant in an **action** may file: (a) against the *plaintiff,* based upon *any* **cause of action** she has against him; or (b) against *anyone* (including persons not yet involved in the lawsuit) if she alleges a cause of action based upon the same transactions as those upon which the complaint against her is based, or if she claims an **interest** in property which is the subject of that complaint.

cross-demand [kross-de · *mand*] *n.* Any **demand** that a person makes against a person who is making a demand of him. In terms of **pleadings**, it comprises any claim that will reduce or overcome the claim of another, including a **counterclaim**, **cross-action**, **cross-claim**, or **cross-complaint**.

cross-examination
[kross-eg · zam · in · *ay* · shen] *n.* The interrogation of a witness for the opposing **party** by questions designed to test the accuracy and truthfulness of the testimony the witness gave on **direct examination**. The right to cross-examine witnesses in a criminal case is guaranteed by the Sixth Amendment. *See* examination.

cross-interrogatories
[kross-in · te · *rog* · e · tore · eez] *n.* **Interrogatories** propounded by a **party** who has himself been **served** with interrogatories.

cross-remainders [re · *mane* · derz] *n.* **Remainder** estates in property inherited under a will in which two or more persons are given **interests** that take effect only after the person or persons first named to participate in the **estate** have died or some other specified event has occurred.

crossing [*kross* · ing] *n.* 1. The trading-off by a broker of **securities** that one client wishes to sell for those that another client wishes to buy. 2. Passing over.
➤ passage, exchange, interchange, traverse, pathway.

crown cases [*kase* · ez] *n.* English criminal cases.

crucial [*kroosh* · al] *adj.* Important; essential; central.
➤ critical, determining, pivotal, vital, supreme, essential, decisive.

cruel [*kroo* · el] *adj.* Pitiless; brutal; heartless; without compassion.
➤ brutal, malevolent, savage, heartless, malicious, inhumane, oppressive.
Ant. kind, benevolent, loving.

cruel and inhuman treatment
[in · *hyoo* · men *treet* · ment] *n.* A ground for divorce. *See* cruelty.

cruel and unusual punishment
[un · *yoo* · zhoo · el *pun* · ish · ment] *n.* Forms of punishment for crime prohibited by the **Eighth Amendment**. The Supreme Court has determined that **corporal**

punishment inflicted by the state is cruel within the meaning of the Constitution, but that capital punishment is not.

cruelty [*kroo* · el · tee] *n.* The infliction of physical or mental pain or distress. As a ground for divorce, "cruelty" means physical violence or threats of physical violence, or mental distress willfully caused.
➤ brutality, harshness, spitefulness, viciousness, torture, violence ("cruelty to animals").
Ant. sympathy, kindness.

cruelty to animals [*an* · i · melz] *n.* Conduct, including **willful neglect**, that causes pain, suffering, and in some instances death to an animal. It is a crime, generally a **misdemeanor**. *See* animal rights.

cry *v.* 1. To notify, advertise, or sell by **outcry**. 2. To sound one's voice in pain or sorrow; to weep.
➤ notify, advertise, proclaim, pronounce, broadcast; weep, lament, whimper, moan, grieve.

ct. An abbreviation of **court**.

Ct. App. Abbreviation of **court of appeals**. Also abbreviated CA or C.A.

CTA Abbreviation of *cum testamento annexo*. *See* administrator CTA.

cudgel [*kud* · jell] *n.* A heavy club.
v. To beat with a club.
➤ *n.* bat, club, cane, stick, ferrule, weapon.
v. beat, pound, pummel.

culpable [*kulp* · abl] *adj.* Blameworthy; blamable; responsible; at fault.
➤ blameworthy, blamable, responsible, chargeable, punishable, answerable.
Ant. innocent.

culpable homicide [*hom* · i · side] *n.* 1. **Negligent homicide**. 2. Any type or degree of **homicide** for which a person is responsible other than murder.

culpable neglect [neg · *lekt*] *n.* The type of neglect that exists when **loss** or **damage** can reasonably be attributed to one's own carelessness.

culpable negligence [*neg* · li · jenss] *n.* Both in the law of **negligence** and as used in **criminal negligence** and **manslaughter** statutes, a conscious and wanton disregard of the probability that death or injury will result from the willful creation of an

C

unreasonable risk. *See also* culpable homicide; gross negligence; negligent homicide.

cum [kum] *(Latin) prep.* With; together with. *Cum* frequently appears in legal terminology using Latin words.

cum rights *n.* Stock sold with rights to purchase future stock of the corporation in a stated amount.

cum testamento annexo [tes · ta · *men* · to an · *eks* · o] *adj.* Means "with the will annexed." *See* administrator CTA.

cumulative [*kyoo* · myoo · le · tiv] *adj.* Adding to or added to something else; things added together. USAGE: "The cumulative effect of the 3 consecutive 10-year sentences he received is the same as if he had received a 30-year sentence."
➤ accruing, additive, advancing, amassed, increasing, totaling ("cumulative effect").

cumulative bequest [be · *kwest*] *n.* Same as **cumulative legacy**.

cumulative dividend [*div* · i · dend] *n.* An **accumulated dividend** on **preferred stock**, which must be paid before any **dividend** on **common stock** is paid. *Compare* noncumulative dividend. *See* dividend.

cumulative evidence [*ev* · i · dense] *n.* Additional evidence of the same kind, or from the same source, to the same point; evidence proving that which has already been proven. Evidence can be objected to on the ground that it is cumulative. Cumulative evidence is to be contrasted with **corroborating evidence**, which always comes from a different source and is often different in kind or character. *See* evidence.

cumulative legacy [*leg* · e · see] *n.* A **legacy** in addition to another legacy to the same person in the same will. EXAMPLE: a will bequeathing $8,000 to Mary Jones in the sixth paragraph and $5,000 to Mary Jones in the seventh paragraph. The **presumption** is that the **testator** intended the later **bequest** to be substitutional rather than cumulative, and Mary is therefore entitled only to the $5,000 bequest.

cumulative offense [o · *fense*] *n.* An **offense** that can be committed only by a repetition of acts of the same kind, which may occur on different days. EXAMPLE: the offense of being an **habitual drunkard**.

cumulative sentences [*sen* · ten · sez] *n.* Same as **consecutive sentences**.

cumulative stock *n.* *See* cumulative dividend.

cumulative voting [*voh* · ting] *n.* A method of voting for corporate directors under which each shareholder is entitled to cast a number of votes equal to the number of shares she owns times the number of directors to be elected, with the **option** of giving all her votes to a single candidate or of distributing them among two or more as she wishes. The effect of cumulative voting is to ensure minority representation on a Board of Directors. *See* minority representation.

curative [*kyoo* · re · tiv] *adj.* Tending to fix or remediate a situation.
➤ remedial, mending, correcting, healing ("curative legislation").

curative statute [*kyoo* · re · tiv *stat* · shoot] *n.* Legislation that corrects past errors or irregularities and validates acts that would otherwise be without legal effect, particularly irregularities in **conveyancing**.

curator [*kyoo* · ray · ter] *n.* A person appointed by the court to have charge of the property or the **person** of an **incompetent** or a minor. *See* conservator; guardian.
➤ guardian, conservator, manager, caretaker ("curator of the museum").

curator ad hoc [ahd hoke] *n.* A curator appointed to handle one matter only. *See ad hoc*.

curator ad litem [ahd *lie* · tem] *n.* A curator appointed for the purpose of bringing or defending a lawsuit. *See ad litem*.

cure *v.* To make healthy; to rectify. *n.* 1. Under the **Uniform Commercial Code**, a seller has the right to correct ("cure") his failure to deliver goods that conform to the contract if he does so within the period of the contract. 2. To remedy. *See* conforming goods. 3. To restore to health.
➤ *v.* heal, improve, better, rectify, relieve, restore, ameliorate.
n. recovery, improvement, remedy, restoration, correction, palliative, panacea, antidote, elixir, correction, remediation.

cure by verdict [*ver* · dikt] *v.* 1. When a **verdict** is favorable to the party against whom **error** was committed by the court, the error is deemed to be harmless. *See* harmless error; judicial error. 2. A verdict in a **party's** favor will cure **defects** in her **pleading** when **substantive rights** of the other party are not affected.

curfew [*ker* · few] *n.* A specific time in the evening after which persons must be off the streets. Curfews, which are generally established by city or town ordinance, most often apply to children.
➤ limitation, restriction, prohibition.

currency [*ker* · en · see] *n.* 1. A **medium of exchange**; money. 2. Paper money.
➤ money, legal tender, cash, bills, funds, dollars.

current [*ker* · ent] *adj.* Of this time.
➤ immediate, prevailing, contemporary, actual, customary.
Ant. past, uncommon.

current account [a · *kownt*] *n.* An account that involves ongoing dealings between the parties. *See* account.

current assets [*ass* · ets] *n.* Cash plus other **assets** that are short-term in nature and easily converted into cash. EXAMPLE: **accounts receivable**.

current earnings [*er* · ningz] *n.* Earnings of a corporation for the period during which a **dividend** is normally paid. *See* earnings.

current funds *n.* Money or **assets** easily converted to money; in the case of a corporation, its **working assets**.

current income [*in* · kum] *n.* **Income** due during the current **tax year**.

current liabilities [ly · e · *bil* · i · teez] *n.* **Liabilities** that, in the **ordinary course of business**, will be paid within one year.

cursory [*kurr* · suh · ree] *adj.* Hasty; brief; superficial.
➤ brief, hasty, indifferent, shallow, unmindful, harried, lax, perfunctory ("a cursory reading").
Ant. careful, thorough, meticulous.

curtail [kur · *tale*] *v.* To cut short or lessen.
➤ diminish, lessen, abate, reduce, cut short, abridge ("He promised to curtail his drinking").

curtesy [*ker* · te · see] *n.* The rights a husband had under the **common law** with respect to his wife's property. Today these rights have been modified in every state in various ways, but all states that retain curtesy in some form extend the same rights to both spouses. *Note* that "curtesy" is not "courtesy." *Compare* dower.

curtilage [*ker* · til · ayj] *n.* The open space around a house located within a common enclosure; a yard bordered by a fence or hedge.
➤ enclosure, yard, grounds.

custodial [kuss · *toh* · dee · el] *adj.* Referring to **custody** or to a **custodian**.
➤ confined, detained, supervised.

custodial account [a · *kount*] *n.* A bank account opened for the benefit of another person, usually a minor or **incompetent person**, but controlled by the person opening it.

custodial interrogation [in · terr · e · *gay* · shen] *n.* A term that arises from the **Miranda rule**, which provides that a person who has been taken into police custody cannot be questioned until he has been advised of his relevant constitutional rights, including the right to have an attorney present.

custodial search *n.* A police search of a person or property, which takes place after the person is in custody or the property has been seized. *See* search and seizure.

custodian [kuss · *toh* · dee · en] *n.* A person whose duty it is to safeguard and account for that which is given into his custody.
➤ caretaker, overseer, governor, curator, maintainer, protector, watchman, conservator, janitor.

custody [*kuss* · te · dee] *n.* 1. As applied to property, **control** and the obligation to safeguard. USAGE: "The bank has custody of my passport; it's in my safe deposit box." *Also see* chain of custody. 2. As applied to persons, physical control. (EXAMPLES: parents customarily "have custody" of their children; although, in the event of divorce, one parent may have **sole custody**, or both parents may have **joint custody** or **divided custody**; a

C

person arrested on a criminal charge is **in custody** from the moment of his arrest). Custody carries with it the obligation on the part of the **custodian** to maintain and care for the person in his **charge** for the duration of their relationship. *See* legal custody. *See also* custodial.
➤ care, control, protection, possession, management, preservation, restraint, impoundment, charge.

custom [*kuss* · tem] *n.* Often referred to as **custom and usage**; a practice that has acquired the **force of law** because it has been done that way for a very long time. *See* local custom; usage. *Compare* customs.
➤ habit, practice, convention, routine, established, precedent, procedure.

custom and usage [*yoo* · sej] *n. See* custom; usage.

customary [*kuss* · te · meh · ree] *adj.* Based on custom or accepted roles; regular; usual.
➤ accepted, expected, regular, frequent, popular, ordinary, established, habitual, commonplace.

customer [*kus* · te · mer] *n.* An individual who purchases products or services.
➤ buyer, client, user, purchaser, shopper, patron, consumer.

customhouse [*kuss* · tem · house] *n.* An office where customs duties are paid and where clearance is given to ships to enter or leave port.

customs [*kuss* · temz] *n.* 1. **Customs duties**. 2. The **Customs Service**. 3. A **customhouse**. *Compare* custom.
➤ duty, tax, tariff, toll, assessment ("The customs on my Dior dress was high").

Customs and Patent Appeals Court [*pat* · ent a · *peelz*] *n.* The former name for the court whose **jurisdiction** is now within the United States Court of Appeals for the Federal Circuit. *See* Courts of Appeals of the United States.

customs duties [*dyoo* · teez] *n.* The tax payable on the importation and exportation of merchandise or commodities and upon the goods themselves.

Customs Service [*ser* · viss] *n.* The United States Customs Service, a federal agency whose functions include assessing customs duties and preventing **contraband** from entering the country.

cut *n.* 1. A wound made by a sharp object. 2. A reduction. 3. A portion of.
v. 1. To divide or sever. 2. To break or interrupt. 3. To reduce the amount of.
➤ *n.* incision, gash, nick, cleavage, laceration; reduction, diminution, decrease; share, slice, part, portion, allotment, percentage.
v. sever, split, clip, nick, slash; shorten, lessen, lower, reduce, curtail; dilute, weaken, thin, adulterate.

cutback *n.* A reduction or diminution.
➤ reduction, decrease, lessening, curtailment ("a cutback in spending").

cutthroat pricing [*kut* · throte *pry* · sing] *n. See* predatory pricing.

cy pres [sie pray] *(French) n.* As nearly as practicable; as closely as possible. The doctrine that permits a **charitable gift** to be carried out as closely as possible to the intent of the donor if, for one reason or another, it cannot be carried out as directed by the donor. Under the doctrine of *cy pres*, the court can apply the gift to a charity with a similar purpose. *See also* deviation doctrine.

cycle [*sigh* · kul] *n.* 1. An interval of time. 2. A course of events.
➤ era, phase, period, age; chain, rhythm, succession, series.

cynical [*sin* · i · kul] *adj.* Expressing contemptuous distrust.
➤ sarcastic, sardonic, pessimistic, scornful, contemptuous, ironic, wry ("cynical view of human nature").

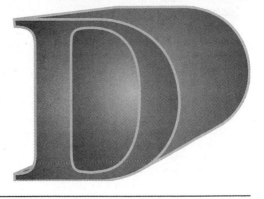

DA *n.* Abbreviation of **district attorney**. Also abbreviated D.A.

dab *n.* A gentle touch; a small quantity.
v. To touch lightly.
➤ *n.* bit, speck, spot, dollop, smidgen, drop.
v. daub, swab, pat.

dactylography [dak · ti · *log* · re · fee] *n.* The scientific study of fingerprints as a means of identification.
➤ fingerprint analysis, scientific analysis.

dally [*dah* · lee] *v.* To waste time; to delay or dawdle.
➤ dawdle, procrastinate, putter, linger, loiter, tarry.
Ant. hurry, expedite.

damage [*dam* · ej] *n.* The loss, hurt, or harm to person or property that results from **injury** which, in turn, is the negligent or deliberate invasion of a **legal right**. Although the words **damage**, **damages**, and injury are often treated as synonyms, there are important differences in their meanings. *Injury* is the illegal invasion of a legal right, i.e., a **wrong**; *damage* is the **loss**, hurt, or harm that results from the injury; and *damages* are the **reparation** awarded for the damage suffered. *See* compensatory damages. Additional damages may be awarded if the damage resulted from an injury that was inflicted recklessly or with **malice**. *See* punitive damages; treble damages.
v. To destroy or harm something or someone.
➤ *n.* loss, hurt, harm, destruction, impairment.
Ant. benefit.
v. harm, hurt, destroy, violate, blemish, abuse, mar, injure

damages [*dam* · e · jez] *n.* The sum of money that may be recovered in the courts as financial **reparation** for an **injury** or **wrong** suffered as a result of **breach of contract** or a **tortious** act. *Compare* damage. *See also* actual damages; compensatory damages; exemplary damages; irreparable damages; liquidated damages; mitigation of damages; nominal damages; punitive damages; special damages; speculative damages; treble damages.
➤ restoration, compensation, restitution, repayment, recovery, reparation, expenses, expiation ("There were significant damages in her case").

damnum [*dam* · num] *n.* (*Latin*) **Damage**; **loss**. *See* ad damnum clause; damages.
damnum absque injuria [*ahb* · skway in · *joo* · ri · ah] *n.* "Damage without a wrong." The sense of this legal maxim is that, without a wrong, there is no **cause of action**; it applies when an accident occurs and no one involved in the occurrence is at fault or **negligent**. (EXAMPLE: an accident caused by an **act of God**.) A **legal right** must be invaded for there to be a cause of action in **tort**. The mere fact that a person suffers **damage** of the kind recognized by law is not enough; there must also have been a **legal duty**, and someone must have violated that duty. When a duty is violated, a legal right is infringed. Damage ("*damnum*") without a wrong ("*injuria*") will not support a cause of action.

danger [*dane* · jer] *n.* A hazardous or troublesome situation.
➤ peril, risk, crisis, hazard, uncertainty, emergency.

dangerous [*dane* · jer · ess] *adj.* Able to cause injury; hazardous.
➤ hazardous, precarious, unsafe, harmful, destructive, injurious.

dangerous instrumentality [*dane* · jer · ess in · stroo · men · *tal* · i · tee] *n.* A thing so dangerous (EXAMPLES: explosives; hazardous waste; a gun) that if it causes injury the law may impose liability even though there was no **negligence**. A dangerous instrumentality is a basis for **absolute liability**. *See* instrumentality.

dangerous per se [*dane* · jer · ess per say] *adj.* A thing that may inflict injury without immediate human involvement. *See per se.*

dangle [*dang* · gul] *v.* To swing freely.
➤ hang, suspend, swing, entice, tempt.

dark *n.* 1. Low or no lightness. 2. In secrecy; in private.
adj. 1. Characterized by a lack of light. 2. Evil, wicked.
➤ *n.* night, shade, doom, dusk, twilight ("meet you at dark"); ignorance, secrecy, seclusion, mystery ("kept in the dark").
adj. dull, dim, indistinct, gloomy, faint, deep, mystical, mysterious, hidden, secret; evil, bad, satanic, corrupt, nefarious, wicked ("the dark side of his soul").

Dartmouth College case [*dart* · meth kol · ej] *n.* In *Trustees of Dartmouth College v. Woodward,* 17 U.S. 518 (1819), the Supreme Court decided that the **charter** of a **private corporation** is a contract under the **contract clause** of the Constitution and is therefore protected against impairment by the action of a state legislature. Decided in 1819, it is an extremely important case because the protection it provided to private contracts encouraged the growth of business very early in the history of the country.

dash *n.* 1. A light touch of something. 2. A short race. 3. Animated style.
v. 1. To move swiftly. 2. To ruin or foil.
➤ *n.* bit, drop, hint, sprinkling, touch, taste, smidgen, suggestion; sprint, run, race; style, flair, energy, esprit, vigor, vivacity, panache.
v. hasten, run, race, rush, bolt, scurry ("dash to the bank"); foil, dampen, discourage, frustrate, ruin, spoil ("dash his hopes").

dashing [*dash* · ing] *adj.* Gallant; sophisticated; attractive.
➤ gallant, dapper, debonair, stylish, flamboyant ("He certainly looked dashing in his new suit.").

data [*day* · tah] *n.* Collected information from which conclusions may be drawn; known facts.
➤ facts, information, documentation, evidence, compilations, statistics.

date *n.* 1. The time an occurrence is specified to have happened. Thus, for EXAMPLE, the date of a deed or other instrument is not the time when it was actually executed, but the time of its execution as stated in the deed itself. 2. In some uses, the time an occurrence actually happened. 3. A person of the opposite sex with whom one has a social engagement. 4. A social or other personal engagement.
v. To determine the day and time.
➤ *v.* determine, calendar, fix the time of.

date of issue [*ish* · yoo] *n.* An arbitrary date fixed as the beginning of the term for which **notes** and **bonds** of a **series** are to run, unrelated to the date on which they were put on the market.

date rape *n.* A form of **acquaintance rape** in which the victim is raped by her date. *See* rape.

day *n.* 1. A division of time consisting of 24 consecutive hours. 2. A division of time consisting of 24 consecutive hours computed from midnight to midnight. 3. A division of time consisting of 24 consecutive hours computed from the rising of the sun to the next rising of the sun.

day certain [*ser* · ten] *n.* A specified day; a particular day.

day in court *n.* A phrase meaning **due process of law**; i.e., the right to a hearing and the opportunity to have it.
➤ due process of law, hearing, opportunity, right to be heard.

daybook [*day* · book] *n.* An **account book** of **original entry** in which transactions are set down as they occur.

days of grace *n. See* grace period.

daze *n.* A shock; a state of confusion or dizziness.
v. To stupefy or confuse.

D

➤ *n.* shock, trance, coma, bewilderment, haze.
v. confuse, shock, astonish, mystify, perplex, stun.

DBA An abbreviation of, and commonly a short way of saying, "doing business as." A person's DBA is his or her **trade name**. EXAMPLES: a lawsuit involving a business owned by an individual named Gerri Jones who does business under the trade name Gerri's Jams might be captioned *Sam Smith v. Gerri Jones DBA Gerri's Jams*; a lawsuit involving a business owned by the ABC Corporation which does business under the trade name Merry Motels might be captioned *ABC Corporation DBA Merry Motels v. Sam Smith. See* doing business. *Also see* fictitious name.

DBE Abbreviation of *de bene esse.*

DBN Abbreviation of *de bonis non. See* administrator DBN.

DC Abbreviation of **district court**. Also abbreviated D.C. and dist. ct.

de [day] (*Latin*) *prep.* From; of; for; concerning; among; in. *De* is the first word of many Latin phrases and terms used in the law.

de bene esse [*bay* · nay *ess* · ee] For present use; of temporary validity; for what it is worth; conditionally. *See* deposition de bene esse.

de bonis non [*boh* · nis non] Short for *de bonis non administratis*, meaning "of goods not administered." *See* administrator DBN.

de facto [*fak* · toh] *adj.* **In fact**; in reality; existing even though it is illegal; existing without regard to legality or illegality. *Compare* de jure.
➤ in fact, in reality, existing.
Ant. de jure.

de facto corporation [*fak* · toh kore · per · *ay* · shen] *n.* A corporation **in fact**, but one that has failed to comply with the formal requirements for **incorporation**; an apparent corporation, asserted to be a corporation by its members and acting as a corporation with **color of law**. Such an organization is deemed a corporation with respect to everyone except the state. *Compare* de jure corporation.

de facto segregation [*fak* · toh seg · re · *gay* · shen] *n.* Racial imbalance in the public schools that is not a direct result of the law or any action of school officials, but rather is a result of economic, housing, or other social factors. *Compare* de jure segregation.

de jure [*zhoo* · reh] *adj.* **In law**; by lawful right; by virtue of law; rightfully. *Compare* de facto.
➤ rightful, authorized, lawful, sanctioned. *Ant.* de facto.

de jure corporation [*zhoo* · reh kore · per · *ay* · shen] *n.* A corporation created in compliance with all legal requirements, so that its right to exist and to exercise the powers described in its **charter** are protected against challenge by the state in **quo warranto** proceedings. *Compare* de facto corporation.

de jure segregation [*zhoo* · reh seg · re · *gay* · shen] *n.* Racial segregation imposed by law. *Compare* de facto segregation.

de minimis [*min* · i · mis] *adj.* "Of minimal concern" or "concerning insignificant matters."
➤ minimal, insignificant, trivial, unimportant.

de minimis non curat lex [*min* · i · mis non *kyoo* · rat leks] An expression in the law: "The law does not concern itself with insignificant matters." A court has the power to dismiss a case that it views as involving trifling matters and not affecting substantial rights.

de novo [*noh* · voh] *adj.* Anew; over again; a second time. USAGE: "de novo review."

de novo trial [*noh* · voh *try* · el] *n. See* trial de novo.

DEA Abbreviation of **Drug Enforcement Administration**.

dead *adj.* 1. No longer existing. 2. Lifeless; inactive; cold. 3. Defunct; of no value; inoperative; useless.
➤ lifeless, deceased, obsolete, useless, departed, expired, extinct.
Ant. living, alive, vital.

dead freight *n.* A shipping term that refers to the compensation owed a shipowner when the shipper fails to ship the full cargo agreed upon, resulting in a financial loss to the owner. *See* freight.

dead man's statute [*stat* · shoot] *n.* State statutes that bar testimony against the **estate** of a **decedent** by a person who is claiming some financial interest against the decedent. Such statutes often also apply to testimony against the estate of an **incompetent person**.

dead storage [*store* · ej] *n.* The safe-keeping of goods for a relatively long period of time. The battery is often removed from an automobile in dead storage so that the car cannot be moved under its own power. *Compare* live storage.

deadlock [*ded* · lok] *n.* A standstill; a lack of action.
➤ blockage, impasse, standstill, stoppage ("to face a deadlock").

deadly [*ded* · lee] *adj.* Capable of resulting in death.
➤ dangerous, destructive, lethal, fatal, hazardous, grave, murderous, perfidious ("assault with a deadly weapon").

deadly force [*ded* · lee] *n.* Force intended to cause death or likely to result in death; force intended to cause or likely to result in serious bodily injury.

deadly weapon [*ded* · lee *wep* · en] *n.* A weapon that is likely to cause death or serious bodily injury when used in the manner in which it was designed to be used.

dealer [*deel* · er] *n.* 1. A person who buys goods for resale. 2. In **securities** law, a person who buys and sells securities for himself, not as an agent or broker for a customer. 3. A person who buys and sells anything. 4. A person who sells drugs.
➤ wholesaler, merchant, broker, retailer, representative, vendor, middleman.
Ant. consumer.

death *n.* The end of life. The definition of death is different in different states, and may depend upon the legal issue involved. For EXAMPLE, for the purpose of **adjudicating** rights of inheritance, death occurs when all vital functions cease permanently; for the purpose of determining whether life-sustaining medical technology may be terminated, **brain death** may be the

appropriate standard. *Compare* life. *See* right to die. *See also* civil death; legal death.

There is a legal **presumption of death** after a person's disappearance and extended absence, usually for seven years. *See* Enoch Arden statutes; seven years' absence.
➤ end of life, expiration, annihilation, extinction, end, destruction.
Ant. life, resurrection.

death acts *n. See* wrongful death action.

death benefit [*ben* · e · fit] *n.* A sum of money paid to a beneficiary under a life insurance policy upon the death of the insured. Death benefits paid under the **Social Security Act** are a **statutory benefit**.

death certificate [ser · *tif* · i · ket] *n.* The official proof of death issued by an appropriate **public officer**. *See* certificate.

death duties [*dyoo* · teez] *n.* Another term for **inheritance taxes** or **estate taxes**. *See* duty.

death penalty [*pen* · el · tee] *n.* Another term for **capital punishment**. The death penalty is sought in particularly heinous criminal cases. Opponents of the death penalty view it as cruel and inhuman punishment in violation of the Eighth Amendment.

death taxes [*tak* · sez] *n.* Another term for **inheritance taxes** or **estate taxes**.

death warrant [*war* · ent] *n.* The order of a court commanding a sentence of death. *See* warrant.

deathbed declaration [*deth* · bed dek · le · *ray* · shen] *n. See* dying declaration.

debar [dee · *bar*] *v.* To exclude; to bar; to shut out. USAGE: "Because he is financially irresponsible, he was debarred from the bidding." *Note* that "debar" is not "**disbar**."
➤ exclude, bar, shut out.

debase [dee · *base*] *v.* 1. To adulterate. *See* adulteration. 2. To cheapen; to belittle.
➤ adulterate, cheapen, belittle, reduce, dishonor, pollute, contaminate.
Ant. upgrade, encourage.

debatable [dee · *bate* · uh · bul] *adj.* Inconclusive; ambiguous.

➤ arguable, in question, open to doubt, unresolved, disputable, suspect, dubious, conjectural ("a debatable point").

debate [de · *bate*] *v.* To discuss an issue with opposing arguments.

➤ discuss, altercate, controvert, wrangle, confute, consider, ponder.

debauchery [de · *baw* · che · ree] *n.* Excessive indulgence, including drunkenness and similar habits, seduction, and sexual immorality generally.

➤ self-indulgence, lust, excesses, seduction, vice, overindulgence.

debenture [de · *ben* · cher] *n.* An **unsecured**, long-term **corporate bond** or **note**. *See* long-term.

➤ unsecured bond, unsecured note.

debilitate [de · *bill* · ih · tayt] *v.* To impair; to weaken.

➤ cripple, enervate, weaken, eviscerate, exhaust, devitalize.

debit [*deb* · it] *n.* 1. An **obligation** charged or assessed against a debtor by a creditor. 2. An accounting term for what appears to be owing by one person to another. *Compare* credit.
v. 1. To charge. 2. To post or enter a charge upon a ledger. *Compare* credit.

➤ *n.* debt, indebtedness, obligation, arrears, liability.
Ant. credit.
v. charge, list, post.

debt *n.* 1. An unconditional and legally enforceable **obligation** for the payment of money. 2. That which is owing under any form of promise, including obligations arising under contract (EXAMPLES: a **mortgage**; an **installment sale contract**) and obligations imposed by law without contract (EXAMPLES: a **judgment**; **unliquidated damages**). A debt not presently due is nonetheless a debt. *See* antecedent debt; bad debt; judgment debt; legal debt; secured debt.

➤ obligation, liability, debit, dues, commitment, encumbrance.

debt limitation [lim · i · *tay* · shen] *n.* 1. A provision in a state constitution that places a limit on the total amount of indebtedness which the state, or cities and towns within the state, can legally incur. 2. A similar limit placed upon a corporation by its **articles of incorporation**.

debtee [*det* · ee] *n.* The person who is owed money by another; a creditor.

➤ creditor, lender.

debtor [*det* · er] *n.* 1. A person who owes another person money. 2. A person who owes another person anything. *See* debt.

➤ borrower, buyer, deadbeat.

debtor in possession [po · *zesh* · en] *n.* A debtor who continues to operate his business while undergoing a **business reorganization** under the **jurisdiction** of the **Bankruptcy Court**. *See* bankruptcy.

deceased [de · *seessd*] *n.* A dead person; a person who has died; a **decedent**.

➤ dead person, departed, decedent ("respect for the deceased").

decedent [de · *see* · dent] *n.* A legal term for a person who has died. *See* decedent's estate.

➤ deceased, testator, intestate, dead individual, departed.

decedent's estate [es · *tate*] *n.* The total property, real and personal, that a decedent owns at the time of her death.

deceit [de · *seet*] *n.* Any **false representation** by means of which a person misleads another and causes him harm. Deceit is a form of **fraud**.

➤ fraud, misrepresentation, cheating, dishonesty, trickery, duplication, falsification.

deceive [de · *seev*] *v.* To give a false impression; to mislead.

➤ delude, mislead, swindle, scam, defraud, dupe, hoodwink, screw, trick, victimize.

decent [*dee* · sent] *adj.* Conforming to standards of behavior; proper; honorable.

➤ proper, suitable, ethical, honorable, prudent, respectable, courteous, kind, thoughtful, obliging.

deception [de · *sep* · shen] *n.* The act of deceiving; deceit. *See* theft by deception.

➤ fraud, betrayal, trickery, pretense, duplicity, cunning, insincerity.

decide [de · *side*] *v.* To come to or make a **decision**.

➤ adjudge, conclude, hold, find, decree, determine, establish, resolve, rule.

D

decision [de · *sizh* · en] *n.* 1. The conclusion of a court in the **adjudication** of a case, or by others who function in an adjudicatory capacity, for EXAMPLE, an **arbitrator** or an administrative agency. Although "decision" and **opinion** are often used interchangeably, the words are not usually synonymous, as an opinion is an expression of the court's reasoning for its decision. More nearly synonymous are "decision" and **judgment**. *See* memorandum decision. 2. A conclusion or judgment.
➤ conclusion, resolution, agreement, judgment, adjudication, outcome, ruling.
decision on the merits [*merr* · its] *n. See* judgment on the merits.

declarant [de · *clar* · ent] *n.* A person who makes a **declaration**; a person who declares.
➤ speaker, affirmant, informer, deponent, witness.

declaration [dek · le · *ray* · shen] *n.* 1. An **unsworn statement**, whether written or oral, the significance of which lies in its **hearsay** character. EXAMPLES: a **declaration against interest**; a **dying declaration**. 2. A formal statement of fact made for an official purpose. EXAMPLE: a customs declaration, in which a person lists articles she has brought into the country. 3. In older legal practice, a plaintiff's initial **pleading**, known in modern practice as a **complaint** or **petition**. 4. A public pronouncement. 5. A pledge or promise. 6. Any statement or announcement. *See* declarant; declare.
➤ affirmation, statement, admission, profession, expression, proclamation, revelation.
declaration against interest [a · *genst in* · trest] *n.* A statement contrary to the financial or property interests of the declarant. Such a statement, made out of court, is admissible through a witness other than the declarant as an **exception to the hearsay rule**.
declaration of dividend [*div* · i · dend] *n.* The act of a corporation in creating a **dividend** to be paid to stockholders from **net income**. Such a declaration creates a debt owed by the corporation.
declaration of estimated tax [*ess* · ti · may · ted] *n.* A formal estimate of income anticipated during the forthcoming **tax year**, required under federal and state tax codes from corporations, **trusts**, and **estates**, and individuals who receive income that is not subject to withholding (generally, income other than wages). Such declarations must be accompanied by payment of the estimated tax.
declaration of intention [in · *ten* · shen] *n.* A formal declaration by an alien of his intention to become a citizen of the United States.
declaration of trust *n.* 1. A voluntary statement by which an owner of property acknowledges that she holds the property **in trust** for someone else. 2. The document creating a **trust**; a **trust instrument**. *See* deed of trust.

Declaration of Independence [in · de · *pen* · dense] *n.* The formal public announcement by the Continental Congress, on July 4, 1776, which recited the grievances of the American colonies against the British government and declared the colonies to be free and independent states. The Declaration of Independence does not have the **force of law**, but it is often important to read the Constitution with it in mind. *Compare* constitutional.

declaratory [de · *klar* · e · toh · ree] *adj.* Explanatory; clarifying; tending to remove doubt.
➤ elucidating, explanatory, clarifying, assertive ("declaratory judgment").
Ant. confusing.
declaratory judgment [*juj* · ment] *n.* A **judgment** that specifies the **rights** of the **parties** but orders no **relief**. Nonetheless, it is a **binding** judgment and the appropriate **remedy** for the **determination** of an **actionable** dispute when the plaintiff is in doubt as to his legal rights. *See also* summary judgment.
declaratory provision [pro · *vizh* · en] *n.* Part of a statute or ordinance that states the need which the legislation was enacted to fulfill; i.e., the statute's purpose. Declaratory provisions often begin with the word "whereas." *Compare* directory provision.
declaratory relief [re · *leef*] *n. See* declaratory judgment.

D

declaratory statute [*stat* · shoot] *n.* A statute enacted to clarify and resolve the law when the correct interpretation has been in doubt.

declare [de · *klare*] *v.* 1. To allege or set forth in a **pleading**. 2. To state; to assert; to utter; to announce.
➤ allege, admit, convey, attest, feel, disclose, assert, state.

declared dividend [de · *klared div* · i · dend] *n. See* declaration of dividend.

decline [de · *cline*] *v.* 1. To refuse to comply with. 2. To lower or fall.
n. A lessening or downward change.
➤ *v.* reject, renounce, repudiate, veto, spurn, repel ("decline representation"); fall, decay, drop, ebb, deteriorate, wane ("prices decline").
n. downfall, drop, descent, decay, deterioration, abatement, downturn, slide ("a decline in prices").

decrease [de · *kreese*] *v.* To reduce in size or number.
n. A reduction or lessening.
➤ *v.* diminish, subside, curtail, abate, deduct, recede, taper, quell.
n. fall, reduction, diminution, dwindling, loss, declination, attenuation.

decreasing term insurance [dee · *kree* · sing term in · *shoor* · ense] *n.* A type of **term insurance** under which the amount paid upon the death of the insured decreases over the life of the policy, although the premium payments remain the same. *See* life insurance; term life insurance.

decree [de · *kree*] *n.* 1. The **final order** of a **court of equity**, as opposed to a **judgment**, which is the final order of a **court of law**. For all practical purposes, the distinction between decrees and judgments no longer exists, and all **relief** in all **civil actions**, whether legal or equitable, is obtained by means of judgment. *See* decision. 2. An order, edict, or mandate.
v. To order; to dictate; to ordain; to enact.
➤ *n.* mandate, commandment, directive, ordinance, statute, decision, ruling.
v. order, dictate, ordain, enact, announce, command.
decree by consent [ken · *sent*] *n. See* consent decree.

decree nisi [*nie* · see] *n.* A conditional judgment that the court will make final unless a party **shows cause** why it should not be made final; an **interlocutory decree**. *See* nisi.

decree nunc pro tunc [nunk pro tunk] *n. See* nunc pro tunc order.

decree of divorce [di · *vorse*] *n.* A **final judgment** granting a **divorce**.

decriminalization [dee · krim · in · el · i · *zay* · shen] *n.* An action, usually by the legislature, rendering noncriminal some conduct that, before the action was taken, was a crime under the law. *Compare* criminalize. USAGE: "Some people advocate the decriminalization of marijuana."

decry [de · *kry*] *v.* To criticize or belittle.
➤ criticize, blame, vilify, disparage, traduce, condemn, defame, denounce.

dedicate [*ded* · i · kate] *v.* To make a **dedication**.
➤ pledge, commit, devote, endow, convey, apportion.

dedication [ded · i · *kay* · shen] *n.* 1. The setting aside of land for use by the public; a donation of land, or of an **easement** or other **interest** in land, by its owner for some public purpose. (EXAMPLE: a road through private property which the owner allows the public to use for the purpose of having access to a lake.) A public dedication of land may arise or be created by **adverse user**, deed, or **plat**. *See* dedication by deed; dedication by plat. 2. The setting aside or abandonment of property of any kind to public use. 3. Loyalty; faithfulness.
➤ setting aside, donation, endowment, conveyance, presentation, honor, celebration; commitment, devotion, allegiance, adherence.

dedication by adverse user [*ad* · verse] *n.* A dedication of land for public use that takes place by virtue of its having been used by the public over a period of time under a **claim of right** contrary to the interests of the true owner. *See* adverse possession; adverse user.

dedication by deed *n.* A dedication contained in a **deed**, setting forth the

D

exact public purpose for which the land is **conveyed** or for which an **interest** in it is set aside.

dedication by plat *n.* Also known as **statutory dedication**; dedication that takes place when a property owner, commonly a developer, subdivides a tract of land into lots to be built on, and by reference in the deed to a map or **plat**, sets aside property for streets, sidewalks, and public parks. *See* plat.

dedication of literary property [*lit · er · air · ee prop · er · tee*] *n.* Under **copyright** law, general publication of a work (as opposed, for EXAMPLE, to an author's limited circulation of her manuscript among a few friends) is considered a public dedication of the work and causes the author or owner to lose the right to copyright it. *See* public domain.

deductible [de · *duk* · tibl] *adj.* 1. In tax law, describes expenses that a taxpayer is permitted to subtract, in whole or in part, in computing her **taxable income**. EXAMPLES: interest on the mortgage on one's home; **casualty losses**; **charitable contributions**. *See* deduction. 2. Subtractible.
n. In insurance, the portion of a **loss** that the insured must pay from his own pocket before the insurance company will begin to make payment. USAGE: "Because my policy has a $500 deductible, my insurance company will pay only $2,000 of the $2,500 damage to my car."
➤ *adj.* removable, allowable, discountable.

deduction [de · *duk* · shen] *n.* 1. The amount allowed a taxpayer in reduction of **gross income** for the purpose of determining **adjusted gross income**. *See and compare* itemized deduction; standard deduction. 2. That which may be taken away or subtracted, particularly money. 3. That which is deduced or reasoned from something known or proven. *See* inference.
➤ subtraction, withdrawal, removal, exemption, allowance ("the home office deduction"); conclusion, assumption, understanding, inference, answer ("Holmes's deduction was accurate").

deed *n.* 1. A document by which real property, or an **interest** in real property, is **conveyed** from one person to another.

2. An act or action; something done or completed.
v. To transfer or **convey** by deed.
➤ *n.* instrument, release, assignment, conveyance, contract ("warranty deed"); achievement, action, accomplishment, performance ("good deed").
v. transfer, convey, grant ("to deed my interest to her").

deed absolute [*ab* · so · loot] *n.* Same as **absolute conveyance**.

deed of covenant [*kov* · e · nent] *n.* Same as **deed of warranty**.

deed of gift *n.* A deed **conveying** property without **consideration**.

deed of indenture [in · *den* · cher] *n.* *See* indenture.

deed of quitclaim [*kwit* · klame] *n.* Same as **quitclaim deed**.

deed of release [re · *leess*] *n.* Same as **quitclaim deed**.

deed of trust *n.* A deed that creates a **trust** in real estate and is given as **security** for a debt. A deed of trust is in the nature of a **mortgage**, but differs from a mortgage in that it is executed in favor of a disinterested third person as **trustee**, while a mortgage is executed directly to the creditor to be **secured**.

deed of warranty [*war* · en · tee] *n.* 1. A deed that contains **title covenants**. 2. A deed that contains **covenants** concerning the property conveyed and is a separate document from the deed that actually conveys the property.

deed poll [pole] *n.* A deed signed by the grantor only. *Compare* indenture.

deeded [*deed* · ed] *adj./adv.* **Conveyed** by **deed**.
➤ conveyed, granted, given, transferred.

deem *v.* 1. To presume, as used in statutes (for EXAMPLE, a statute providing that "persons of unsound mind shall be deemed **incompetent**"). Use of the term "deem" creates an **irrebuttable presumption**, unless the statute specifically provides otherwise. *See* presumption. 2. In ordinary conversation or writing, usually means judged or considered. USAGE: "I deem your conduct inappropriate."

➤ consider, believe, determine, perceive, regard, conceive.

deem advisable [ad · *vize* · ebl] *v.* Words that grant **discretionary power** to a **trustee** or **executor**. USAGE: "As my trustee shall deem advisable."

deep pocket [*pok* · et] *n.* A term applied to a defendant or potential defendant who is viewed as having **assets** sufficient to satisfy a **judgment** in a lawsuit or a potential lawsuit. USAGE: "Exxon is the defendant with the deep pocket."

deface [dee · *fayss*] *v.* 1. To mar or destroy an exterior or surface. EXAMPLES: painting graffiti on a wall; scratching symbols or words on gravestones. 2. To obliterate words or make them illegible. EXAMPLE: erasing or striking through names, dates, or numbers in a document. *See* obliteration.
➤ destroy, blemish, injure, damage, disfigure, tarnish, mar, mutilate, vandalize.

defalcation [dee · fal · *kay* · shen] *n.* 1. Referring to the act of a person entrusted with funds, the term includes, but is broader than, **embezzlement** and **misappropriation**, since it can involve either the failure to adequately account for funds or simply the failure to meet an obligation. 2. The reduction of one **demand** or debt by another opposing demand or debt; **setoff, counterclaim**, or **recoupment**.
➤ misappropriation, embezzlement, fraud, misuse; reduction, setoff, counterclaim, recoupment.

defamation [def · e · *may* · shen] *n.* **Libel** or **slander**; the written or oral **publication**, falsely and intentionally, of anything that is injurious to the good name or reputation of another person.
➤ libel, slander, defamatory statement, deprecation, belittlement, slur, vilification, traducement, opprobrium, calumny. *Ant.* praise.

defamatory [de · *fam* · e · tor · ee] *adj.* **Libelous** or **slanderous**; falsely injurious to reputation. *See* defamation; libel; slander.
➤ abusive, shameful, slanderous, injurious, detracting, derogatory, insulting ("defamatory statement"). *Ant.* laudatory.

defamatory per quod [per kwode] *adj. See* libelous per quod; slanderous per quod.

defamatory per se [per say] *adj. See* libelous per se; slanderous per se.

default [de · *fawlt*] *n.* 1. The failure of a person to pay money when due. 2. The failure to perform a duty or obligation. 3. The failure of a **party** to a lawsuit to appear in court when she is under a duty to appear or to **plead** when she is required to plead. 4. Fault; neglect; omission. *v.* 1. To fail to meet some legal obligation or duty. 2. To fail; to neglect; to omit.
➤ *n.* nonperformance, breach, neglect, negligence, evasion; fault, neglect, omission. *Ant.* compliance, performance. *v.* defraud, neglect, evade, dishonor, omit, shirk, fail ("He defaulted on his loan.").

default judgment [*juj* · ment] *n.* A **judgment** rendered in favor of a plaintiff based upon a defendant's failure to take a necessary step in a lawsuit within the required time.

defeasance [dee · *fee* · zens] *n.* The act of **annulling** or **voiding** a will, deed, or lease, or other contract upon the happening of a future event. *See* defeasible.
➤ cancellation, annulment ("a clause covering defeasance").

defeasance clause *n.* 1. The clause of a mortgage that specifies the conditions upon which the mortgage shall be **satisfied**. 2. A clause in a will, deed, lease, or other written instrument, the legal effect of which is to cancel or annul the instrument and release the parties from obligations under it upon the occurrence or nonoccurrence of a **condition subsequent**.

defeasible [dee · *feez* · ibl] *adj.* Subject to **defeasance**.
➤ voidable, revocable, dissoluble, removable. *Ant.* unalterable, irrevocable.

defeasible fee *n. See* determinable fee.

defect [dee · fekt] *n.* An absence of something necessary for completeness or **perfection**; an insufficiency; a deficiency; a flaw. *See* defective; design defect; hidden defect; latent defect; patent defect. *v.* [de · *fekt*] To flee; to depart; to quit; to renounce.

➤ *n.* imperfection, shortcoming, deformity, insufficiency, impairment, error, fault, flaw ("a latent defect").

v. abandon, depart, desert, reject, renounce, revolt ("defect to another country").

defect of form *n.* A defect in some nonessential aspect of a legal document, **instrument**, or **pleading** that does not affect the rights of the **parties**. EXAMPLE: an incorrect format. *Compare* defect of substance. *See* form.

defect of parties [*par* · teez] *n.* The failure to join as **parties plaintiff** or **parties defendant** persons whose presence in the **action** is necessary to determination of the action. *Also see* joinder; joinder of parties.

defect of substance [*sub* · stense] *n.* A defect in some essential aspect of a legal document, **instrument**, or **pleading**, i.e., a defect that affects the rights of the **parties**. EXAMPLES: the failure of a **complaint** to state a **cause of action**; a **defect of parties**; omission of the grantor's signature from a deed; the absence from a search warrant of a description of the place to be searched. *Compare* defect of form. *See* fatal defect.

defective [de · *fek* · tiv] *adj.* Imperfect; lacking completeness; having a defect or flaw of any kind.

➤ imperfect, impaired, flawed, abnormal, inadequate, unsound, nonmarketable, broken.

Ant. sound, sufficient, perfect.

defective pleading [*plee* · ding] *n.* A **pleading** that fails to conform with the **rules of civil procedure**.

defective record [*rek* · erd] *n.* 1. A defect in the recordation of a document such as a deed, will, or **lien**, for EXAMPLE, an imperfection in the copying process or an error in indexing the document. 2. A defect in the **record** of a trial. EXAMPLES: the loss of exhibits; the failure to fully transcribe a witness's testimony.

defective title [*ty* · tel] *n.* 1. The **Uniform Commercial Code** provides that **title** to a **negotiable instrument** is defective when the instrument, or any signature on it, is secured by **fraud, duress**, force, fear, or other unlawful means, or obtained for an **illegal consideration**.

2. Title to real estate is defective when it is not marketable. *See* marketable title.

defend [de · *fend*] *v.* 1. To contest an **action**, suit, or **proceeding**. 2. To oppose an attack.

➤ represent, advocate, vindicate, assert, protect, secure, watch, save, nourish, plead, prove a case, counter, argue for, propound.

Ant. attack.

defendant [de · *fen* · dent] *n.* The person against whom an **action** is brought. *Also see* respondent.

➤ accused, respondent, responding litigant, the party charged.

Ant. plaintiff.

defendant in error [*err* · er] *n.* The **party** against whom an appeal is taken to a higher court; an **appellee**.

defender [de · *fen* · der] *n.* One who defends another. *See* public defender.

➤ attorney, advocate, counsel, pleader.

defense [de · *fense*] *n.* 1. In both civil and criminal cases, the facts submitted and the legal arguments offered by a defendant in support of his claim that the plaintiff's case, or the prosecution's, should be rejected. The term "defense" may apply to a defendant's entire case or to separate grounds, called **affirmative defenses**, offered by a defendant for rejecting all or a portion of the case against him. 2. With respect to **commercial paper**, a legal basis for denying one's liability on an **instrument**. 3. Rebuttal; refutation. 4. Justification; excuse. 5. Protection against attack.

➤ explanation, rebuttal, vindication, justification, plea, rationalization ("a winning defense"); protection, preservation ("the defense of freedom of speech").

Ant. offense.

defense counsel [*kown* · sel] *n.* A trial lawyer who conducts the defense in a civil action or criminal prosecution. *Compare* prosecuting attorney.

defer [de · *fer*] *v.* 1. To put off to a future time; to postpone. 2. To yield.

➤ delay, detain, postpone, suspend, set aside; capitulate, submit, adapt, bow, assent, agree.

Ant. hasten; renounce, oppose.

deferred [de · *ferd*] *adj.* Put off to a future time; postponed.

deferred compensation
[kom · pen · *say* · shen] *n.* **Compensation** for services paid considerably after the services are rendered. (EXAMPLES: a pension; payments made under a **profit-sharing plan**.) As a rule, such compensation is taxed when it is actually received, not when it is earned. *See also* annuity; pension plan.

deferred income [*in* · kum] *n.* A tax law term for payments received before they are earned. (EXAMPLE: payment of $1,000 in 1994 to a tutor who is to provide 20 lessons in 1995.) **Accrual basis** taxpayers may defer paying taxes on such income until the services are rendered. *See* earned income.

deferred payments [*pay* · ments] *n.* Payments extended over a period of time; postponed payments. EXAMPLE: installment payments.

deferred prosecution
[pross · e · *kyoo* · shen] *n.* *See* diversion.

deficiency [de · *fish* · en · see] *n.* 1. A tax law term for an additional amount of tax owed by a taxpayer. 2. The amount by which the income tax owed by a taxpayer exceeds the amount shown to be owing on the return she filed. *See* deficiency assessment. 3. The amount still due the creditor after **foreclosure** of a mortgage or other **security**. *See* deficiency judgment. 4. Shortage; undersupply; lack.
➤ insufficiency, lack, shortage, inadequacy, absence, scantiness, want.
Ant. adequacy.

deficiency assessment [e · *sess* · ment] *n.* An **assessment** of additional tax made by the Internal Revenue Service or other taxing authority to cover a deficiency in income revealed upon an audit of the return filed by the taxpayer.

deficiency judgment [*juj* · ment] *n.* A **judgment** rendered against a **mortgagor** or other debtor for the amount of the deficiency when **foreclosure** fails to satisfy the **mortgage debt**.

deficit [*def* · i · sit] *n.* 1. The amount by which a sum of money is less than the amount required. 2. A deficiency.
➤ deficiency, arrears, lack, default ("Clinton's attempts to decrease the deficit").

deficit financing [*fine* · an · sing] *n.* Borrowing, particularly by government, to permit spending in excess of income.

define [de · *fine*] *v.* To determine the meaning of.
➤ describe, formulate, name, establish, label, explain, limit.

definite [*def* · ih · nit] *adj.* Authoritative; clear; precise.
➤ conclusive, sure, certain, fixed, ascertained, precise, positive, true, exact ("a motion for a more definite statement").
Ant. vague, fuzzy.

definite failure of issue [*def* · i · nit *fail* · yer of *ish* · ew] *n.* *See* die without issue.

definition [def · ih · *nish* · un] *n.* A statement of meaning.
➤ description, meaning, clarification, identification, denotation, signification.

definitive [de · *fin* · e · tiv] *adj.* 1. That which puts an end to litigation. USAGE: "Since no appeal has been taken, the court's final judgment is definitive." 2. Complete and accurate; final; conclusive.
➤ conclusive, complete, absolute, decisive, perfect, ultimate, final, clear.

defraud [de · *frawd*] *v.* To commit a **fraud**. *See* fraud.
➤ cheat, deceive, bamboozle, burn, delude.

defunct [de · *funkt*] *adj.* 1. No longer existing; dead; deceased. 2. Worthless.
➤ dead, expired, inoperative, invalid, obsolete, void, inactive, nonexistent.
Ant. functioning, working.

defy [de · *fie*] *v.* To refuse to obey; to challenge or resist.
➤ disregard, disobey, resist, oppose, flout, battle, repulse, challenge, frustrate ("to defy the judge's orders").

degradation [deg · ra · *day* · shun] *n.* The decline to a low, humiliated state.
➤ debasement, humiliation, ignominy, shame, odium, abjection.

degree [de · *gree*] *n.* 1. An abstract measure of importance or seriousness. USAGE: "**degree of care**"; "**degrees of crime**"; "**degrees of kinship**." 2. A unit of measurement for arcs and angles, often appearing in **legal descriptions** of real property, being 1/360th of a circle. 3. An award of rank

D

D

granted by a college or university upon completion of a course of study.
➤ magnitude, intensity, extent, range, caliber, level, rank.

degree of care *n.* A relative standard by which conduct is tested to determine whether it constitutes **negligence**. EXAMPLES: **due care**; **extraordinary care**; **ordinary care**; **reasonable care**. *See* care. *See also* highest degree of care; utmost care.

degree of consanguinity [kon · san · *gwin* · i · tee] *n.* The degree to which blood relatives are related to each other, i.e., the degree of closeness of the relationship. *See* consanguinity; prohibited degrees of consanguinity.

degree of proof *n.* The level of persuasiveness required in a lawsuit to prove the case. In civil actions, the measure is ordinarily **preponderance of the evidence**. In criminal prosecutions, proof **beyond a reasonable doubt** is required to convict.

degrees of crime *n.* The grades of a crime ranked according to seriousness. EXAMPLES: **first degree murder**; **second degree murder**. *See also* classification of offenses; graded offenses.

degrees of kinship [*kin* · ship] *n.* The relationship between a deceased person and her surviving kin for purposes of determining inheritance rights under the **intestate laws**. *See* kinship.

degrees of negligence [*neg* · li · jense] *n.* The classes or grades into which **negligence** is divided for the purpose of determining liability, ranging from **ordinary negligence** to **gross negligence**.

dehors [dee · *hohrz*] *(French) prep.* Beyond.
➤ beyond, unconnected, foreign to ("dehors the record").

dehors the record [de · *hohrz* the *rek* · erd] (from the *French*) *adv.* Outside the record; matters outside the transcript of the trial; outside of the courtroom.

del credere agent [*del kreh* · *de* · *reh ay* · *jent*] (from the *Italian*) *n.* An **agent** who guarantees his principal against the **default** of those with whom he contracts. *See* guarantee; warranty.

delay [de · *lay*] *n.* A stoppage; a pause.
v. To stop or postpone for a time.

➤ *n.* detainment, pause, stall, wait, interruption, suspension, postponement ("a delay in the proceedings").
v. arrest, block, retard, slacken, detain, hold up, postpone, prolong.

delegate [*del* · e · get] *n.* A person authorized to act for others, especially in political conventions and other state or national conventions; a representative.
v. [*del* · e · get] To appoint; to empower; to assign.
➤ *n.* agent, appointee, consul, representative, proxy, spokesperson ("Her delegate attended the conference").
v. authorize, appoint, commission, assign ("to delegate authority").

delegation [del · e · *gay* · shen] *n.* 1. The act of conferring authority upon, or transferring it to, another. USAGE: "By virtue of the **delegation of powers** contained in the Constitution, Congress is the branch of the federal government empowered to make laws." 2. The delegates from a particular state or other unit represented at a convention. USAGE: "She was an elected member of the Idaho delegation to the national convention of the Democratic Party."
➤ appointment, authorization, commissioning, assignment ("the delegation of authority from one person to another"); representatives, commission, organization, gathering ("She was appointed a member of the Georgia state delegation").

delegation of powers [*pow* · erz] *n.* 1. Provisions of the Constitution by which **executive powers** are delegated to the **executive branch** of the government, **legislative powers** to the **legislative branch**, and **judicial powers** to the **judicial branch**. 2. Delegation of constitutional power by one branch of government to another. Such delegation is permissible only if it is consistent with the principle of **separation of powers** set forth in the Constitution. 3. The transfer of power from the president to an administrative agency.

delete [de · *leet*] *v.* To eliminate, remove, or erase.
➤ cancel, erase, omit, remove, obliterate, excise, expel, efface ("delete paragraph 8 from the contract").
Ant. add, append.

deliberate [de · *lib* · e · ret] *adj.* By plan or preconceived design; carefully considered; not hasty. Use of the word "deliberate" in describing a crime conveys the idea that the perpetrator weighed the motives for his act and carefully considered the nature and the consequences of the crime, and that the act was not suddenly committed. *See* deliberation; premeditation.
v. [dee · *lib* · e · rate] 1. To formally meet, discuss, and consider. USAGE: "Now that the jury has been instructed by the judge, it will retire to deliberate its verdict." 2. To consider with care; to plan beforehand; to premeditate. *See* deliberation.
➤ *adj.* conscious, calculated, considered, willfully, intended, knowingly ("a deliberate mistake").
v. ponder, consider, think, contemplate, brood, ruminate, reflect, speculate ("The jury deliberated for three days before reaching a verdict").

deliberation [de · lib · e · *ray* · shen] *n.* A careful and thoughtful consideration; the process of reasoning the pros and cons of doing something; reflection; contemplation. *See* deliberate. *Also see* consideration; premeditation.
➤ examination, consideration, forethought, reflection, attention ("prolonged jury deliberations").

deliberative process privilege [de · *lib* · re · tiv *pross* · ess priv · i · lej] *n.* The **privilege** of the government to refuse to make available documents that reveal its policy-making processes.

delict [dee · *likt*] (*Latin*) *n.* Crime, offense, or **wrong**. A term used to describe both **torts** and crimes that are **public wrongs**. *See also corpus delicti*.

delinquency [de · *link* · wen · see] *n.* 1. Failure to pay a debt when due. *See* delinquent. 2. Failure to perform a duty. 3. A fault; a misdeed, a moral failing. USAGE: "He was found guilty of contributing to the delinquency of a minor." *See* contributing to delinquency.
➤ carelessness, failure, negligence, default, nonobservance, neglect ("delinquency in loan payments"); corruption, wrongdoing, misbehavior ("juvenile delinquency"). *Ant.* performance; good behavior.

delinquent [de · *link* · went] *adj.* 1. Behind in the payment of an **obligation**. USAGE: "This is a delinquent payment; it's 30 days late." 2. Guilty of improper conduct. *n.* 1. A person failing in duty. 2. A person of doubtful moral conduct. 3. A person who is behind in the payment of an obligation. 4. Short for juvenile delinquent. *See* juvenile offender.
➤ *adj.* outstanding, unpaid, tardy ("delinquent payments"); criminal, neglectful, immoral, scandalous ("a delinquent minor").
Ant. honest, innocent.
n. offender, wrongdoer, lawbreaker, undesirable, derelict, felon, hoodlum, miscreant, young offender.

delinquent child *n.* *See* juvenile offender.

deliver [de · *liv* · er] *v.* 1. To send; to hand over. 2. To set free. 3. To announce or proclaim. *See* delivery.
➤ convey, carry, remit, transfer, transport, turn over, send, forward; free, liberate, emancipate; announce, declare, express.

delivery [de · *liv* · e · ree] *n.* 1. A handing over; the surrender of **possession** to another. 2. Under the **Uniform Commercial Code**, with respect to **instruments, documents of title, chattel paper**, or **certificated securities**, the voluntary transfer of possession. Delivery is an important concept because some transactions are not legally complete in the absence of delivery; that is, delivery is an element of the transaction (EXAMPLES: **delivery of deed**; **delivery of gift**). Delivery need not be actual. It may be constructive or symbolic. *See and compare* actual delivery; constructive delivery; symbolic delivery.
➤ conveyance, passage, relinquishment, commitment, transferral, consignment; birth, childbirth, labor, bearing, birthing; speech, presentation, elocution.

delivery bond *n.* A **bond** given by a defendant to obtain the release of property that has been **attached**.

delivery of deed *n.* A **deed** will not transfer **title** unless it has been delivered, actually or constructively, by the grantor to the grantee or her agent. *See and compare* actual delivery; constructive delivery.

D

D

delivery of gift *n.* An actual, symbolic, or constructive transfer of possession of the subject matter of a gift to the person to whom the gift is made (the **donee**). No gift can be made, in law, unless the giver (the **donor**) demonstrates his intention to transfer **title** by surrendering control and possession. *See* gift. *See and compare* actual delivery; constructive delivery; symbolic delivery.

delude [de · *lood*] *v.* To mislead through misrepresentation.
➤ misstate, misrepresent, deceive, cheat, swindle, misguide, misinform.

delve *v.* To inquire into something; to investigate.
➤ inquire into, investigate, probe, peer, search, penetrate, unearth, ferret out.

demand [de · *mand*] *n.* 1. A claim of legal entitlement; a request to perform an obligation. 2. The assertion of a right to recover a sum of money.
v. To assert; to claim; to call for.
➤ *n.* requirement, order, ultimatum, claim, request ("make a demand for satisfaction of payment").
v. require, insist, assert, order, plead, summon, ask, request, necessitate.
demand certificate [ser · *tif* · i · ket] *n.* *See* certificate.
demand deposit [de · *pah* · zit] *n.* A bank deposit that may be withdrawn at any time. EXAMPLE: a savings account. *Compare* time deposit. *See* deposit. *Also see* certificate of deposit.
demand for relief [re · *leef*] *n.* The portion of a **complaint** or **claim for relief** that specifies the type of **relief** to which the plaintiff feels she is entitled and for which she requests **judgment**; also called a **prayer for relief**.
demand instrument [in · stroo · ment] *n.* *See* demand paper.
demand letter [*let* · ter] *n.* A letter requesting the performance of some obligation or making a claim for something to which the writer is entitled.
demand loan *n.* A loan that is **callable** at any time. *Compare* term loan.
demand note *n.* A **promissory note** payable when payment is demanded. *See* on demand.

demand paper [*pay* · per] *n.* **Commercial paper** payable when payment is demanded. *See* on demand.

demandant [de · *man* · dent] *n.* A person who makes a demand; a plaintiff.

demarcate [de · *mar* · kate] *v.* To set apart; to separate.
➤ mark, separate, border, demark, zone, delimit, limit.

demean [de · *meen*] *v.* To humiliate; to belittle.
➤ debase, belittle, humiliate, shame, deprecate, disparage, decry, derogate.

demeanor [de · *meen* · er] *n.* Conduct; deportment; bearing; attitude; the way a person carries himself. In evaluating a witness's truthfulness, a judge or jury is entitled to consider the witness's demeanor. USAGE: "The demeanor of that witness makes me question his credibility."
➤ presence, conduct, attitude, manner, style, bearing, conduct.

demesne [de · *meen*] *n.* Same as **domain**.

demise [de · *mize*] *n.* 1. A lease. 2. A deed. 3. The transfer of property by will. 4. Death.
v. To **convey**; to lease; to pass on by will or inheritance.
➤ *n.* lease, conveyance, transfer ("the demise of an estate"); decease, passing, fall, collapse, extermination ("High levels of crime led to the demise of the community").
v. lease, bequeath, transmit, confer, endow.

democracy [de · *mok* · re · see] *n.* A form of government in which all political power is possessed by the people and exercised by them either directly or through their elected representatives.
➤ commonwealth, equalitarianism, freedom, justice, representative government.

democratic [dem · o · *krat* · ik] *adj.* 1. Pertaining to democracy. 2. Not snobbish.
➤ representative, self-governing, egalitarian, constitutional; free, friendly, popular.

demonstrate [*dem* · un · strait] *v.* 1. To prove using evidence. 2. To illustrate using examples. 3. To publicly show feelings or support for a cause.
➤ show, establish, indicate, determine, prove; explain, illustrate, describe, express; march, strike, protest, rally.

demonstrative [de · *mahn* · stre · tiv] *adj.*
1. Provable by showing or demonstration.
2. Distinguishable from others of the
same class or kind. 3. Openly emotional.
➤ illustrative, clarifying, elucidating,
supportive ("demonstrative evidence");
expressive, passionate, effusive, emotional
("a demonstrative witness").

demonstrative evidence [*ev* · i · dense]
n. **Physical evidence** offered for viewing
by the judge or jury. EXAMPLES: the weapon
allegedly used in the crime; maps; clothing.
See autoptic proference.

demonstrative legacy [*leg* · e · see] *n.*
A **legacy** that specifies a particular fund
or particular property of the **testator** as
the primary source of payment of a sum
of money given in a will.

demur [de · *mer*] *n.* 1. To make a **demurrer**.
2. To object to; to take exception to; to
disagree. *Note* that "demur" is not "demure."
Compare demure; demurrer.
➤ challenge, protest, dissent, refute, balk,
disagree, object to, take exception to.

demure [de · *myoor*] *adj.* Shy; prudent;
cautious. USAGE: "Her demure demeanor
will improve her credibility as a witness."
➤ modest, retiring, bashful, coy, prudent, shy.
Ant. brash, outrageous.

demurrage [de · *mer* · ej] *n.* Money due as
compensation for the loss of earnings of a
ship or railroad car due to improper delay.

demurrer [de · *mer* · er] *n.* A method of
raising an objection to the legal sufficiency
of a **pleading**. A demurrer says, in effect,
that the opposing party's **complaint** alleges facts that, even if true, do not add
up to a **cause of action** and that, therefore,
the case should be **dismissed**. Demurrers
have been replaced in many, but not all,
jurisdictions by **motions** or **answers**,
which perform the same function. *See*
judgment on the pleadings; summary
judgment. *See also* general demurrer;
speaking demurrer; special demurrer.

demurrer to evidence [*ev* · i · dense] *n.*
An objection made by the defendant to
the plaintiff's **evidence** as a whole, which
concedes the truth of everything the plaintiff has attempted to prove by his evidence,
but argues that such facts do not, in law,

establish a right to **recover**. A demurrer to
evidence has largely been superseded in
modern practice by a **motion for directed
verdict** or its equivalent.

demurrer to interrogatory
[in · te · *rah* · ge · tore · ee] *n.* When a
witness refuses to answer a question,
giving a reason for her refusal, she
"demurs to the interrogatory."

denaturalize [dee · *nat* · shoor · e · lize] *v.* To
deprive a person of his citizenship, whether
acquired by naturalization or by birth.

denial [de · *ny* · el] *n.* 1. In a lawsuit,
contesting the **allegations** in the **pleading**
of an **adverse party**; a **traverse**. Denials
may be general or specific (*see* general
denial; specific denial), but they must be
unequivocal (*see* negative pregnant). 2. A
refusal; a rejection; a turndown.
➤ renunciation, rebuttal, contradiction,
challenge, dissent, disowning ("denial of
allegations"); rejection, refusal, turndown,
veto ("The trial proceeded after the
judge's denial of a directed verdict").
Ant. acknowledgment; granting.

denigrate [*den* · i · grayt] *v.* To belittle
the importance of.
➤ degrade, humiliate, belittle, smear, vilify,
denounce, defame, vituperate, divide,
dishonor.

denizen [*den* · i · zen] *n.* A citizen or
inhabitant.
➤ citizen, resident, occupant, inhabitant.

denote [de · *note*] *v.* To signify or stand
for. USAGE: "The star on the menu denotes
a low-fat item."
➤ mean, symbolize, signify, express,
designate.

denunciation [de · *nontz* · ee · ay · shun] *n.*
Public condemnation.
➤ tirade, calumny, aspersion, invective,
vilification, vituperation, incrimination,
deprecation, recrimination.

deny [dee · *ny*] *v.* 1. To refuse to grant. 2. To
reject; to contradict; to disown. *See* denial.
➤ disagree, controvert, disbelieve, negate,
oppose, refute ("to deny an allegation").
Ant. concede, grant.

department [de · *part* · ment] *n.* An
administrative unit within an organization.

D

➤ branch, section, office, agency, bureau, unit, division.

department of government [*guv* · ern · ment] *n.* 1. One of the three divisions into which the Constitution separates the government of the United States. Used in this sense, the term is synonymous with **branch of government**. *See also* executive branch; legislative branch; judicial branch. 2. A similar division in state government. 3. An administrative unit within a branch of government. EXAMPLES: the Department of Justice; the Department of Commerce.

departure [de · *par* · choor] *n.* 1. A retreat or exit. 2. A change from the norm. *See* variance.

➤ exit, retreat, removal, withdrawal ("His departure was scheduled for noon"); divergence, change, digression ("a departure from his usual approach").

dependency [dee · *pen* · den · see] *n.* 1. The state of being a **dependent person**. *See* dependent. 2. The condition of a person suffering from alcoholism or drug addiction. *See* chemical dependency. 3. A colony of a country.

➤ attachment, helplessness, contingency, connection, need.
Ant. self-sufficiency, independence.

dependent [dee · *pen* · dent] *adj* 1. **Contingent**; **conditional**. 2. Reliant; helpless; powerless.
n. 1. A person who is in need of aid or support because he entirely or partially lacks the means of supporting himself; i.e., a **dependent person**. 2. One entitled to support, as a spouse or child. *See* nonsupport. 3. In workers' compensation law, a person who relies for support upon the aid of another. 4. In tax law, a person whose relationship to the taxpayer is such that the taxpayer is entitled to claim her as an **exemption** when filing his income tax return. EXAMPLE: a child of the taxpayer who is less than 19 years of age.

➤ *adj.* clinging, reliant, helpless, under control of, parasitic ("A child is dependent on its parent"); contingent, ancillary, corollary ("dependent counterclaim").
Ant. autonomous; unconditional.
n. minor, charge, ward.

dependent conditions [kon · *dish* · ens] *n.* **Mutual promises**.

dependent covenants [*kov* · e · nents] *n.* **Covenants**, one of which is conditioned upon prior performance of the other, to be enforceable. *See* condition.

dependent person [*per* · sen] *n.* *See* dependent.

dependent promises [*prom* · iss · ez] *n.* *See* dependent covenants.

dependent relative revocation [*rel* · e · tiv rev · e · *kay* · shen] *n.* The doctrine that if a person revokes her will and has the intention to make a new will, but the new will is not made, it is **presumed** that she preferred to have her **estate** disposed of under the old will rather than under the **intestate laws**.

depict [de · *pikt*] *v.* To represent through pictures or ideas.

➤ characterize, exemplify, personify, render, sketch, typify, portray.

deplete [de · *pleet*] *v.* To lower the quantity of something; to reduce.

➤ dissipate, decrease, reduce, waste, exhaust, drain.

depletion [de · *plee* · shen] *n.* The act of consuming or wasting.

➤ emptying, exhausting, diminishment, draining, drying up, reduction, deduction.

depletion allowance [e · *louw* · ense] *n.* A deduction permitted under the **Internal Revenue Code** to the owner of growing timber, or oil, natural gas, or mineral deposits, as they are consumed by production or harvesting. *Compare* amortization; depreciation.

deplore [de · *plohr*] *v.* 1. To express grief. 2. To loathe; to condemn.

➤ regret, lament, mourn; hate, condemn, abhor, censure.

deponent [de · *pone* · ent] *n.* 1. A person who gives a **deposition**. 2. A person who gives sworn testimony in any form; an **affiant**; a witness.

➤ witness, attester, informant, testifier.

deport [de · *port*] *v.* 1. To banish from a place. 2. To behave and conform.

➤ banish, bar, exile, expel, oust, remove, evict, eject ("deport the alien"); carry,

D

behave, comport ("deport oneself professionally").

deportation [dee · por · *tay* · shen] *n.* The expulsion of an alien from a country in accordance with its immigration laws.
➤ banishment, exile, eviction, removal, extradition.

depose [dee · *poze*] *v.* 1. To give a **deposition** or state facts in an **affidavit**. USAGE: "I was deposed today in connection with my lawsuit against the hospital." 2. To take the deposition of someone else. USAGE: "My attorney will depose you tomorrow." 3. To remove a ruler, usually a king or dictator, from office.
➤ attest, state, testify, give sworn testimony ("depose the witness"); impeach, discharge, usurp, dismiss ("The monarchy was deposed").

deposit [de · *pah* · zit] *n.* 1. An article or money that has been **deposited**. *See* deposit *(verb). See also* certificate of deposit; demand deposit; depositary; depository; time deposit. 2. Anything left with a person for safekeeping or to preserve it. 3. An accumulation. USAGE: "The flood created a large deposit of soil."
v. 1. To put down money on account, as on layaway or as **earnest money**. *See* downpayment. 2. To put money or things in a place for storage or safekeeping, as in a **bailment**. 3. To put money in a bank account. 4. Anything left with a person for safekeeping or to preserve it. (EXAMPLE: a document filed with the **clerk of court**.) *See* filing.
➤ *n.* retainer, security, installment, pledge ("Miguel made a deposit on a new car"); accumulation, sediment, alluvium ("The flood created a large deposit of soil").
v. entrust, save, store, locate, amass, bank, hoard ("She deposits all her money into Swiss bank accounts").

deposit in court *n. See* payment into court.

deposit in trust *n. See* trust deposit.

deposit of earnest money [*er* · nest *mun* · ee] *n. See* earnest money.

deposit slip *n.* A receipt evidencing a deposit. *See* receipt.

depositary [de · *pah* · zit · air · ee] *n.* A person or an institution receiving a deposit for safekeeping. EXAMPLE: a **bailee**. *Note* that a "depositary" is not a "**depository**." *Compare* depository.

depositary bank *n.* Under the **Uniform Commercial Code**, the first bank to take a **negotiable instrument** for collection, even though it is also the **payor bank**.

deposition [dep · e · *zish* · en] *n.* 1. The transcript of a witness's testimony given under oath outside of the courtroom, usually in advance of the trial or hearing, upon oral examination or in response to written **interrogatories**. *See* discovery; examination of witness. 2. In a more general sense, an **affidavit**; a statement under oath.
➤ testimony, sworn testimony, testimony under oath, affidavit, declaration.
deposition de bene esse [day *bay* · nay es · ay] *n.* A deposition taken to be read into the **record** at trial because the witness cannot be present then. *See de bene esse.*

depositor [de · *pah* · zit · er] *n.* A person who makes a deposit, particularly a person who makes a deposit in a bank, including the **holder** of a **certificate of deposit**.
➤ customer, creditor, bailor.

depository [de · *pah* · zit · or · ee] *n.* A place where funds are **deposited** (EXAMPLE: a bank) or where valuable articles are put for safekeeping (EXAMPLE: a safe deposit box in a bank). *Note* that a "depository" is not a "**depositary**." *Compare* depositary.
➤ safe, vault, warehouse, treasury, archives.

depot [de · poe] *n.* A storage facility.
➤ station, terminal, repository, warehouse, storehouse.

depreciable [de · *pree* · shebl] *adj.* Capable of **depreciation**; that which may be depreciated. USAGE: "Is my computer a depreciable item?"

depreciated value [dee · *pree* · shee · ay · ted *val* · yoo] *n.* Original cost less **depreciation**.

depreciation [dee · pree · shee · *ay* · shen] *n.* 1. The lessening in worth of any property caused by wear, use, time, or obsolescence. *Compare* appreciation. 2. In computing income tax, a deduction allowed for the gradual loss of usefulness of a **capital asset** used in business or in the production of income. *See* useful life. *Compare* depletion.

D

➤ devaluation, reduction, deflation, depression, deterioration, erosion. *Ant.* appreciation.

depression [de · *pres* · shun] *n.* 1. A state of sorrow or despondency. 2. A decline in something.
➤ despondency, abjection, sorrow, melancholy, gloom, sadness; economic decline, recession, downturn, inflation, crisis, slump.

deprive [de · *prive*] *v.* To take something away; to deprive or dispossess.
➤ dispossess, divest, seize, wrest, expropriate.

deputy [*dep* · yoo · tee] *n.* 1. A person who is a subordinate of a **public officer**, performing the duties of office under the supervision of the public officer. EXAMPLES: a deputy sheriff; a deputy **clerk of court**. 2. A person appointed to act for another; a substitute, delegate, or agent.
➤ subordinate, assistant, delegate, substitute, appointee, surrogate, agent ("deputy clerk of court").

deraign [dee · *rane*] *v.* To prove; to vindicate; to prove by disproving the allegations of an adversary.
➤ prove, vindicate.

deranged [de · *raingd*] *adj.* Disturbed; crazy; insane.
➤ demented, confused, incompetent, mad, unbalanced, delusional, frenzied ("The deranged killer").

deregulate [dee · *reg* · yoo · late] *v.* To remove governmental controls, particularly from an industry, or from major aspects of an industry, as a whole. *Compare* regulate.
➤ decontrol, liberate, disencumber.

derelict [*der* · e · likt] *adj.* Abandoned; deserted; uninhabited.
n. 1. Personal property that the owner has abandoned. 2. A ship or ship's cargo abandoned with no hope of recovery and no intention of returning to it. 3. A vagrant.
➤ *adj.* forsaken, discarded, neglected, unwanted, abandoned, dilapidated.
n. outcast, tramp, wanderer, drifter.

dereliction [der · e · *lik* · shen] *n.* 1. Failure in the performance of duty; neglect of duty. 2. Abandonment of property; abandoned property. *See* renunciation. 3. An increase in land resulting from the withdrawal of

water that previously covered it; a **reliction**. *See also* accretion; avulsion.
➤ carelessness, evasion, delinquency, omission, neglect, default. *Ant.* accountability.

deride [de · *ride*] *v.* To laugh at in contempt; to make fun of or mock.
➤ disparage, scorn, taunt, mock, ridicule.

derivation [der · i · *vay* · shun] *n.* Source or origin.
➤ root, source, origin, ancestry, inception.

derivative [de · *riv* · e · tiv] *adj.* Something not original; something arising from another thing.
➤ secondary, subordinate, consequential, ensuing, resulting, caused, attributable ("a shareholder's derivative suit"). *Ant.* primary, direct.

derivative action [*ak* · shen] *n.* An **action** brought by one or more stockholders of a corporation to enforce a corporate right or to remedy a wrong to the corporation, when the corporation, because it is controlled by wrongdoers or for other reasons, fails to take action.

derivative evidence [*ev* · i · dense] *n.* **Evidence** uncovered as a result of leads obtained in an illegal search. Such evidence is inadmissible. *See* fruit of the poisonous tree doctrine; unreasonable search and seizure.

derivative liability [*ly* · e · *bil* · i · tee] *n. See* vicarious liability.

derivative suit *n.* Same as **derivative action**.

derive [de · *rive*] *v.* To deduce a conclusion; to draw out from.
➤ deduce, draw, infer, formulate, conclude, develop, determine, educe, glean.

derogation [der · e · *gay* · shen] *n.* 1. The partial or total **annulment** of a law by a subsequent statute. USAGE: "The modern statutory definition of **burglary** is in derogation of the **common law**." 2. The act of disparaging, detracting from, or undermining.
➤ repeal, annulment, abolishment.

derogatory clause [de · *rah* · ge · tor · ee] *n.* A clause that a **testator** secretly inserts in her will, which contains a provision that any will she makes later without that precise clause is **void**. This highly unusual provision is designed to protect the testator against subsequent attempts to exert **undue influence**.

descend [de · *send*] *v.* 1. To pass down to another. 2. To move down.
➤ endow, give, bequeath, bestow, pass down; fall, drop, dive, tumble, plunge, plummet.

descendant [dee · *sen* · dent] *n.* A person who is of the bloodline of an ancestor, no matter how remote. *Compare* ascendant. *See* descent.
➤ offspring, family, progeny, heir, lineage, kin. *Ant.* ascendant.

descent [de · *sent*] *n.* 1. **Hereditary succession**; the transmission of property upon the death of its owner **intestate** (without a will). The **line of descent** may be **collateral** or **lineal**. *See and compare* collateral descent; lineal descent. *Also see* consanguinity; heirs; immediate descent; intestate succession; succession. 2. The act of going downward.
➤ lineage, ancestry, bloodline, heritage, heirs, kin, pedigree, origin ("in the line of descent"); declination, sinking, descending, settlement ("The descent into the cave was hazardous.")
descent and distribution
[dis · tre · *byoo* · shen] *See* descent; distribution.

describe [de · *skribe*] *v.* To represent and explain in words.
➤ explain, express, narrate, recount, specify, relate, impart, state.

description [des · *krip* · shen] *n.* 1. A characterization of property contained in a mortgage, deed, or other instrument affecting **title** to real property, by means of which the property involved in the transaction may be identified. *See* legal description. 2. An oral or written narration.
➤ representation, identification, illustration, classification, portrayal, characterization ("a legal description"); narration, telling.

desecration [des · e · *kray* · shen] *n.* An act that violates the sacred. EXAMPLE: defacing a church, a synagogue, a mosque, or a public monument. Desecration can be a criminal act.

➤ defilement, debasement, blasphemy, profanation, sacrilege ("the desecration of the mosque").
Ant. adoration, righteousness.

desegregate [de · *seg* · ruh · gayt] *v.* To abolish the segregation or separation of races. *Brown v. Board of Education* mandated the desegregation of public schools.
➤ integrate, unify, mix, coalesce, intermingle, merge, assimilate.

desegregation [dee · seg · re · *gay* · shen] *n.* Doing away with laws and customs designed to separate the races. *Compare* segregation. *See also* integration.
➤ intermixing, integration.

desertion [de · *zer* · shen] *n.* 1. As a ground for divorce, a voluntary separation of one of the parties to a marriage from the other without the consent of or without having been wronged by the second party, with the intention to live apart and without any intention to return to cohabitation. *See* constructive desertion. *Also see* abandonment. 2. The criminal abandonment of a child in neglect of the parental duty of support. *See* nonsupport. 3. Under the **Code of Military Justice**, a member of the armed services is guilty of the criminal offense of desertion when: (a) without authority he is absent from his unit or place of duty with intent to remain away permanently; (b) he quits his unit or place of duty to avoid hazardous duty; or (c) without having been discharged from one of the armed forces, he enlists in the same or another of the armed forces or enters any foreign armed service. 4. In **maritime** law, the continued abandonment of a ship by a seaman during the term of his contract, without cause and with no intention to return. 5. The act of willful abandonment.
➤ abandonment, forsaking, renunciation, relinquishment, departure, abdication.

design [de · *zine*] *n.* 1. A purpose, usually combined with a plan of action. *See* formed design. 2. A sketch; a blueprint; a pattern; a plan; preparation.
v. To devise for a particular purpose.
➤ *n.* purpose, intention, objective, aspiration, hope, aim, goal; sketch, blueprint, pattern, plan, preparation.

D

D

v. craft, create, structure, devise, conceive, plan, invent, construct, arrange.

design defect [*dee* · fekt] *n.* A flaw or error in the design of an article that creates an unreasonable risk of injury for those who use the article. *See* defect. *Also see* product liability.

design patent [*pat* · ent] *n.* A **patent** of a design that gives an original and pleasing appearance to an article. *Compare* improvement patent; utility patent.

designated [*dez* · ig · nay · ted] *adj.* Appointed; chosen; selected.
➤ appointed, selected, chosen, assigned, denoted ("the designated driver").

designated reporter [*dez* · ig· · nay · ted re · *por* · ter] *n.* An individual who is obligated by **child abuse reporting acts** to report suspected child abuse to the authorities. EXAMPLES: a doctor; a nurse; a teacher.

designation [*dez* · ig · nay · shun] *n.* 1. An appointment to a post. 2. Name; mark; label.
➤ choosing, appointment, identification, denomination, indication; symbol, mark, token, sign, emblem, name.

desire [de · *zire*] *v.* To wish; to want; to request. When used in a will, "desire" may or may not accomplish a transfer of property, depending upon the context. *See* precatory words.
n. A want or longing for something.
➤ *v.* wish, want, request, hunger, need, covet, crave, solicit, pursue.
n. ambition, aspiration, wish, hunger, passion, yen, fondness, fancy, craving, lust, urge.

destination [des · te · *nay* · shen] *n.* The place at which a journey is to end.
➤ goal, object, plan, aim, ambition, design, intention.

destination contract [*kon* · trakt] *n.* A **contract** under which the **risk of loss** passes from the seller to the buyer at the point of destination.

destitute [*des* · te · toot] *adj.* Without means of support; poor; indigent.
➤ impoverished, needy, indigent, bereft, helpless, exhausted, poverty-stricken.
Ant. affluent.

destroy [dis · *troy*] *v. See* destruction.

destruction [dis · *truk* · shen] *n.* 1. For **tax deduction** and **insurance** purposes, a loss of value occurring without physical contact and invisible to the eye, instead of actual physical wreckage. (EXAMPLE: the destruction of an American business as a result of its **nationalization** by a foreign government.) In this sense, "destruction" means being rendered useless for the purpose for which a thing is intended or for which a person is trained, as opposed to total annihilation or demolition. 2. Actual physical ruin or devastation; annihilation; demolition; loss; ruin.
➤ defeat, rescission, elimination, liquidation, ruination, abolition; loss, ruin, annihilation, demolition.
Ant. creation.

desuetude [de · *sway* · tude] *n.* The discontinuation of.
➤ disuse, inaction, stoppage, suspension, nonuse, discontinuance.

detach [de · *tatch*] *v.* To sever or disconnect from another part.
➤ sever, remove, disentangle, disengage.

detail [de · *tale*] *v.* 1. To explain thoroughly. 2. To relegate authority.
n. A small part of a whole.
➤ *v.* explain, illuminate, particularize, elucidate, depict, delineate, narrate, tell ("detail your experience"); assign, allocate, order, impose, relegate.
n. aspect, part, item, component, ingredient, section, fragment.

detain [de · *tane*] *n.* To hold; to keep in custody; to arrest.
➤ restrain, stop, inhibit, obstruct, stall, constrain, hold, arrest, suppress ("to detain the suspect for questioning").

detainer [de · *tane* · er] *n.* 1. A **writ** for the continued detention of a prisoner. USAGE: "He finished his Ohio sentence last week, but he's still in custody on a Wisconsin detainer because that state wants him to stand trial on another charge." 2. The holding of a person without his consent. 3. The act of withholding property from its rightful owner. *See* forcible detainer; unlawful detainer.
➤ holding, detention, impoundment.

detention [de · *ten* · shen] *n.* 1. The holding of a person who has been arrested on a criminal charge. 2. Preventing a person from proceeding.

➤ confinement, detainment, custody, captivity, incarceration, imprisonment.

deter [de · *turr*] *v.* To discourage; to prevent from acting.

➤ dissuade, divert, deflect, block, thwart, ward off, repel, discourage.

deteriorate [de · *teer* · ee · oh · rayt] *v.* To decline in value.

➤ decline, depreciate, degrade, devalue, worsen, decay, retrogress.

determinable [de · *ter* · min · ebl] *adj.*
1. That which may be learned, found out, definitely decided upon, or settled.
2. That which is capable of ending or being brought to an end in the future, although its happening and the time of its happening are uncertain. EXAMPLE: a **determinable fee**.

➤ ascertainable, compatible, measurable, knowable, discoverable.

determinable fee *n.* An **estate in land** the existence of which is limited to (i.e. "determined by") the existence of a person and her heirs, and which will no longer exist if they no longer exist. In the case of a determinable fee, a **possibility of reverter** always remains in the grantor (that is, a **reversion** to the person who granted the estate, or to her heirs).

determinant [de · *ter* · mih · nent] *n.* An element that determines the nature of something.

➤ cause, factor, influence, essential element, driving force.

determinate [de · *ter* · min · et] *adj.* Having fixed limits; definite; made certain. *Compare* indeterminate.

➤ fixed, set, established, definite ("a determinate sentence").

determinate sentence [*sen* · tense] *n.*
1. A **sentence** whose duration is set by statute and cannot be reduced by a parole board based upon apparent rehabilitation, behavior in prison, or other considerations.
2. A sentence whose duration is set by statute and can be modified by the sentencing judge only in very special circumstances. *Compare* indeterminate sentence.

determination [de · ter · min · *ay* · shen] *n.*
1. A decision of a court or administrative agency. The term may connote either a final order in a case or merely a ruling made by the judge or **hearing officer** on a **procedural** question during the course of the trial or hearing. As "determination" applies to an administrative agency, it may also mean a purely **administrative**, as opposed to **quasi-judicial**, decision (for EXAMPLE, an **eligibility determination**). 2. The act of rendering a decision. 3. The discontinuance of an **estate** in real property. *See* determinable fee. 4. An ending; a termination; a conclusion. 5. Firm intention.

➤ judgment, conclusion, resolution, opinion, solution, declaration, recommendation ("The court's determination was in favor of the plaintiff"); resoluteness, strength, motive, purpose, tenacity ("As the attorney for the defendant, Bud was filled with determination").

determination letter [*let* · er] *n.* A letter issued by the **IRS** in response to a taxpayer's inquiry as to the tax implications of a given transaction. A determination letter that advises concerning the tax exemption status of a **charitable organization** is often referred to as a "501(c)(3) letter," after the section of the **Internal Revenue Code** that sets forth the criteria for such an exemption.

determinative [de · *ter* · min · a · tiv] *adj.* That which determines something. USAGE: "The judge's order is not determinative of the case; it is merely an **interlocutory order**."

determine [de · *ter* · min] *v.* Decide; **adjudicate**; settle finally.

➤ decide, define, settle, elect, establish, direct, impel, find, hold ("to determine the rights of the parties").

detinue [*det* · ih · noo] *n.* A **remedy** under the **common law** for the recovery of wrongfully held personal property. *See also* replevin.

detraction [de · *trak* · shen] *n.* 1. A removing of something. *See* duty of detraction. 2. Discrediting; disparagement; disrespect.

➤ removal, diversion, diminishment, abuse, defamation, aspersion, discrediting, disparagement, disrespect.

D

D

detriment [*det* · ri · ment] *n.*
1. **Consideration** for a contract, in the form not of something given, such as money or other thing of value, but rather in undertaking some responsibility one is not legally bound to undertake or in refraining from exercising some right one would otherwise have been entitled to exercise. EXAMPLE: a landlord's extension of a lease in exchange for the tenant's agreement not to bring suit for **damages** incurred by the tenant as a result of the landlord's **negligence**. 2. Harm; disadvantage. USAGE: "I relied upon his promise, to my detriment." *See* promissory estoppel.
➤ drawback, limitation, hindrance, impairment, affliction, liability, misfortune, harm, disadvantage.
Ant. benefit.

devastavit [dev · as · *tay* · vit] (*Latin*) *n.*
The act of an **executor** or **administrator** of a **decedent's estate** in mismanaging or wasting the **assets** of the estate, in violation of her duty as a **fiduciary**. *See* fiduciary.

develop [de · *vel* · ip] *v.* To cultivate the growth of.
➤ cultivate, grow, progress, unfold, improve, mature, proceed.

developer [de · *vel* · e · per] *n.* A person who enhances the commercial potential of real estate by subdividing land into building lots, constructing homes or commercial structures on them, and selling them. *See* subdivision.
➤ entrepreneur, promoter, planner, designer, organizer, contractor.

development [de · *vel* · ep · ment] *n.* 1. Land that has been **improved** by a developer. *See* improved land. 2. A happening or occurrence.
➤ advancement, progression, evolution, growth, improvement, expansion ("the development of modern technology"); circumstance, phenomenon, episode, happening, issue, situation, event, occurrence ("a new development in the case").

deviation [dee · vee · *ay* · shen] *n.* A departure from a route, plan, instruction, or agreement, or from a standard or norm.
➤ variance, variation, discrepancy, diversion, disparity, digression.

deviation doctrine [*dok* · trin] *n.* 1. In the law of **agency**, the rule providing that if the **agent** has digressed only slightly from the instructions of the **principal**, the principal is not excused from liability for the agent's **negligence**. *Compare* frolic of his own. *See also* dual purpose doctrine. 2. In the law of **trusts**, the doctrine that deviation from the **terms of the trust** is permitted to achieve the purpose intended by the creator of the trust. *See also* cy pres.

device [de · *vice*] *n.* 1. In **patent** law, an **invention**. 2. A scheme or strategy to work a trick or commit a **fraud**. 3. An emblem such as a business logo or a union label. 4. An apparatus; machine, appliance, or contrivance. *See* gambling device. 5. A means; a mechanism; an **instrumentality**.
➤ instrument, mechanism, contraption, invention, construction, apparatus ("an eating device"); scheme, plot, design, fraud, hoax ("a clever device to overthrow the government").

devious [*dee* · vee · us] *adj.* The quality of being deceitful or dishonest.
➤ crafty, cunning, sneaking, scheming, wily, insidious, deceitful, underhanded.
Ant. direct, honest, straightforward.

devise [de · *vize*] *n.* A gift of real property by will, although it is often loosely used to mean a **testamentary gift** of either real property or personal property. *Compare* bequest; legacy. *See also* conditional devise; contingent devise; general devise; lapsed devise; specific devise.
v. 1. To dispose of real property by will. By comparison, "**bequeath**" is a word used in wills to transfer personal property. However, the term "**devise and bequeath**" applies to both real property and personal property. *Compare* bequest; legacy. 2. To invent; to originate; to make; to plan.
➤ *n.* inheritance, legacy, transfer, conveyance ("the devise of the family jewels").
v. confer, bequeath, convey, endow ("She devised her business operation to her daughter"); plan, formulate, arrange, concoct, construct ("He devised a way to attract attention").

devise and bequeath [de · *vize* and be · *kweeth*] *v. See* devise.

devisee [de · vie · *zee*] *n.* The **beneficiary** of a **devise**.

devisor [de · *vie* · zor] *n.* A **testator** who makes a **devise**.

devoid [de · *voyd*] *adj.* Lacking or wanting. USAGE: "The criminal was devoid of a conscience."
➤ barren, wanting, lacking, desolate, uninhabited, deprived of, unsupplied.

devolution [de · vo · *loo* · shen] *n.* The transfer of property, or of a right or liability, from one person to another, usually by **operation of law**. *See* devolve.
➤ assignment, transference, delegation, transmission.

devolve [dee · *volv*] *v.* 1. To pass from one person to another, not as the result of some positive act or agreement between them, but by **operation of law**, as for EXAMPLE, by inheritance of an **estate**, **right**, or debt. *See* devolution. 2. To descend; to roll or tumble down.
➤ pass, transmit, grant, transfer, bequeath.

devote [de · *voht*] *v.* To commit or dedicate oneself to a person or cause.
➤ dedicate, assign, apply, heed, consecrate, pledge, consign.

diabolic [di · uh · *bol* · ik] *adj.* Having the quality of the devil; being mean, wicked, or cruel.
➤ demonic, evil, wicked, satanic, fiendish, horrible, monstrous, profane ("his diabolic scheme").

diagnose [*di* · ag · noce] *v.* To identify a disease or a problem.
➤ analyze, classify, estimate, specify, evaluate, interpret, recognize, pronounce.

diatribe [*di* · uh · tribe] *n.* An abusive speech or report.
➤ accusation, outburst, denunciation, upbraiding, attack, castigation, harangue.

dicker [*dik* · er] *v.* To barter or negotiate. *Compare* offer.
➤ barter, hassle, negotiate, trade, deal, haggle ("dicker about terms").

dicta [*dik* · ta] *n. Plural* of **dictum**, which is short for the *Latin* term ***obiter dictum***. Dicta are expressions or comments in a court opinion that are not necessary to support the decision made by the court; they are not **binding authority** and have no value as **precedent**. If nothing else can be found **on point**, an advocate may wish to attempt to persuade by **citing** cases that contain dicta. *Compare* authority. *See* persuasive authority.

dictate [*dik* · tayt] *v.* 1. To give instructions; to command. 2. To read out loud.
➤ command, compel, demand, prescribe, require ("dictate terms"); read, speak, say, record, transmit, utter ("dictate a report").

dictator [*dik* · tay · ter] *n.* An absolute ruler, answerable to no other power or authority.
➤ tyrant, ruler, authoritarian, autocrat.

dictum [*dik* · tum] *n. Singular* of **dicta**. *See* dicta.
➤ assertion, statement, comment, remark, observation, pronouncement ("judicial dictum").

die *v.* 1. To cease to exist. 2. To decline slowly toward death.
➤ expire, decease, perish, pass on; wither, recede, deteriorate, decay, decline.

die without issue [*ish* · ew] *v.* A phrase found in wills. It appears in the form of: "I leave Blackacre to William Bland, but if he dies without issue then to Marjorie Sharp." Such phrasing presents a question: Did the **testator** mean the death of Bland without surviving descendants (the *definite failure* construction), or did she mean the death of Bland's last descendant without surviving descendants (the *indefinite failure* construction), whenever that might be? The definite failure construction is mandatory in many states and is favored in a majority of others. *See* issue.

dies *[dee · ess]* (*Latin*) *n.* Days. *See sine die. See also* adjournment sine die.

diet [*die* · et] *n.* In some countries, the term for the legislature.

differ [*dif* · er] *v.* 1. To be of an opposite opinion. 2. To be different from another.
➤ disagree, oppose, take exception to, take issue, repudiate; vary, dissent, digress, disaccord.

D

D

different [*dif* · uh · rent] *adj.* Totally unlike another.
➤ diverse, unusual, dissimilar, atypical, varied, various, idiosyncratic, novel.

difficult [*dif* · ih · kult] *adj.* Hard to overcome or understand; complicated.
➤ complex, hard, problematic, perplexing, troublesome, obscure, arduous, complicated, profound, thorny.

diffident [*dif* · ih · dent] *adj.* Reserved and unattentive.
➤ cautious, demure, timid, unassuming, unsure, unpretentious, reserved, retiring, self-effacing.

diffuse [dih · *fyoos*] *adj.* 1. Unorganized and scattered. 2. Not concentrated or abridged. *v.* To spread wastefully or thinly.
➤ *adj.* dispersed, scattered, extended, prevalent; wordy, rambling, prolix, lengthy. *v.* extend, distribute, scatter, disperse.

digest [*die* · jest] *n.* A series of volumes containing summaries of cases organized by legal topics, subject areas, and so on. Digests are essential for legal research. *American Law Reports Annotated, Second Series* is an EXAMPLE of a digest. Searching ALR2d (*see* citation) for cases dealing with insurance claims for loss of sight, one would look first to the volume of that digest which deals with topic of "Insurance," then to the subject of "Risks and Losses Covered," and finally to the specific question, "Vision, loss of." Digests cover virtually all cases ever decided in the United States; some digests are limited to specific jurisdictions (EXAMPLES: federal cases; Michigan cases) or to specific fields in the law (EXAMPLES: labor law; tax law). Digests are updated continuously to ensure that they are current. *v.* To understand or synthesize. USAGE: "He was able to digest a tremendous amount of information."
➤ *n.* summary, abstract, synopsis, restatement, review. *v.* understand, consider, analyze, summarize.

digression [dih · *gres* · shun] *n.* A deviation; a straying.
➤ deviation, aside, straying, detour, variation, wandering; departure, divergence.

dilatory [*dil* · e · tor · ee] *adj.* 1. Intended to delay. 2. Inclined to delay; procrastinating; slow; not prompt.
➤ tardy, languid, neglectful, late, dawdling, forestalling, delaying, deferring ("a dilatory motion").
dilatory motion [*moh* · shen] *n.* A **motion** made for the purpose of delay.
dilatory plea [plee] *n.* A **plea** that tends to delay the trial of a case **on the merits**. (EXAMPLES: a **plea in abatement**; a **plea in bar**.) Under modern **rules of civil procedure**, dilatory pleas have been replaced by **motions** or **answers**.

dilemma [de · *lem* · uh] *n.* A choice between two unsatisfactory alternatives; a crisis; a quandary.
➤ predicament, quandary, confusion, puzzle, perplexity, problem, impasse.

diligence [*dil* · e · jens] *n.* Active attention to a matter; perseverance; the application of energy. "Diligence" is incapable of precise definition unrelated to the context in which it is used because its meaning depends upon the particular circumstances of the case. The concept of diligence is closely related to the concept of **care** and, like care, it is important as a standard for determining **negligence**. The law prescribes various degrees of diligence, ranging from **slight diligence** to **extraordinary diligence**. *See also* due diligence; reasonable diligence.
➤ perseverance, determination, assiduity, constancy, zeal, resolution, care, due care. *Ant.* laziness.

diligent [*dil* · ih · jent] *adj.* Hard-working; industrious.
➤ persistent, conscientious, hardworking, careful, industrious, assiduous, sedulous, tireless. *Ant.* lazy, careless.

diligent inquiry [*dil* · e · jent *in* · kwe · ree] *n.* Such **inquiry** as a motivated person, desiring to determine a fact, would usually and ordinarily make; inquiry made with diligence and in good faith, to learn the truth.

dilute [dih · loot] *v.* To weaken by mixing; to diminish the strength or flavor of something.
➤ weaken, adulterate, moderate, alter, attenuate.

diluvion [de · *loo* · vee · un] *n.* The gradual washing away of soil along the banks of a river. *Compare* alluvion.

diminish [de · *min* · ish] *v.* To reduce or lessen.
➤ shorten, lower, decline, abate, narrow, wither, lessen, assuage, temper, reduce, mitigate.

diminished [de · *min* · ishd] *adj.* Lessened; lowered; reduced.

diminished capacity [ke · *pass* · i · tee] *n.* The rule that a criminal defendant, although not sufficiently mentally impaired to be entitled to a **defense** of **insanity**, may have been so reduced in **mental capacity** (for EXAMPLE, by retardation, drugs, or alcohol) that he was incapable of forming the mental state necessary, in law, for the commission of certain crimes. *Compare* diminished responsibility. *See* insanity. *Also see* capacity.

diminished responsibility [re · spon · si · *bil* · i · tee] *n.* A concept very similar to **diminished capacity**, except that under the diminished responsibility rule a defendant's lowered mental capability is applied not to determine guilt, but rather, in **mitigation** of her sentence or to reduce the degree or severity of the crime. *See* degrees of crime.

diminution [dim · in · *yoo* · shen] *n.* A taking away or lessening.
➤ reduction, alleviation, abatement, minimizing, cutback ("diminution of damages").

diminution in value [*val* · yoo] *n.* A **measure of damages** for arriving at the amount of money a plaintiff is entitled to recover in a case where the value of his property has been reduced by the defendant's conduct.

diminution of damages [*dam* · e · jez] *n. See* mitigation of damages.

dingy [*din* · gee] *adj.* Soiled; drab; dreary.
➤ shabby, seedy, gloomy, drab, dull, rundown.

diplomatic [dip · le · *mat* · ik] *adj.*
1. Referring to a person trained in diplomacy; a **diplomatic representative**. 2. Tactful.
➤ cautious, prudent, discreet, tactful, civil.

diplomatic immunity [i · *myoo* · ni · tee] *n.* Exemption from both **civil liability** (EXAMPLES: liability for taxes or customs

duties; liability in **civil actions**) and **criminal liability** (EXAMPLES: liability to arrest or prosecution), which **diplomatic representatives** have when representing their country abroad.

diplomatic representative [rep · re · *zen* · te · tiv] *n.* Also referred to as a "diplomatic agent" or "diplomatic officer," an official who represents her government abroad. EXAMPLES: an ambassador; a **chargé d'affaires**.

dire *adj.* Terrible; drastic; dreadful.
➤ terrible, catastrophic, extreme, dismal, dreaded, grim, horrible, drastic, pressing, fearful ("dire circumstances").

direct [de · *rekt*] *adj.* Immediate or **proximate**.
v. To guide; to regulate; to control.
➤ *adj.* unbroken, continuous, immediate, uninterrupted, proximate; candid, blunt, forthright, plain, sincere, straightforward.
v. point, show indicate, steer ("I can direct you to the D.A.'s office."); govern, regulate, control ("to direct a play").

direct attack [e · *tak*] *n.* A challenge to the validity of a **judgment**, decree, or order asserted in the same **action** in which the judgment, decree, or order was rendered, to have it **vacated**, **suspended**, **annulled**, **enjoined**, **reversed**, or modified. *Compare* collateral attack.

direct cause *n.* Same as **proximate cause**.

direct contempt [ken · *temt*] *n.* Words spoken or acts done in the presence of the court that tend to undermine, embarrass, or prevent justice from being carried out. EXAMPLE: telling the judge that he is ignorant. *Compare* indirect contempt. *See* contempt; criminal contempt.

direct criminal contempt [*krim* · in · el ken · *temt*] *n.* Same as **direct contempt**.

direct damages [*dam* · e · jez] *n.* **Damages** that result immediately or **proximately** from a wrongful act, as distinguished from the remote or indirect consequences of a wrongful act. *Compare* remote damages. *See* direct loss.

direct evidence [*ev* · i · dense] *n.* Proof that speaks directly to the issue, requiring no support by other evidence; proof based solely upon the witness's own knowledge,

D

D

as distinguished from evidence from which **inferences** must be drawn if it is to have value as proof.

direct examination
[eg · zam · in · *ay* · shen] *n.* The first or initial questioning of a witness by the **party** who called her to the stand. *Compare* cross-examination; redirect examination. *See* examination.

direct injury [*in* · je · ree] *n.* An **injury** which is the direct result of the violation of a **legal right**. *See* direct damages. *Also see* proximate cause.

direct line *n. See* descent.

direct loss *n.* **Loss** or **damage** resulting from a **direct cause**, as distinguished from a **remote cause**. *See* direct damages.

direct payment [*pay* · ment] *n.* A payment that is absolute and unconditional as to time, amount, and the persons by whom and to whom it is to be made.

direct tax *n.* A tax (also called a **property tax** or an **ad valorem tax**) levied directly on real or personal property based upon value, or directly upon income (i.e., an **income tax**). Such a tax should be distinguished from an **indirect tax**, which is levied upon the importation, consumption, manufacture, or sale of articles and upon the privilege of doing business or engaging in a profession.

direct trust *n.* Same as **express trust**.

directed verdict [de · *rek* · ted *ver* · dikt] *n.* A **verdict** that a jury returns as directed by the judge. A judge directs a verdict when the **party** who has the **burden of proof** has failed to meet that burden. A **motion for directed verdict** is the **procedural** means by which a litigant requests the court to direct a verdict. *See* motion. *Compare* summary judgment.

direction [de · *rek* · shen] *n.* 1. A court's instruction to a jury. *See* jury instructions. 2. An instruction to an **agent**. 3. A command; an order. 4. Control; management.
➤ instruction, regulation, prescription, charge, rule, injunction, command, order ("follow the clerk's directions"); control, management, supervision ("Spielberg's creative direction").

director [de · *rek* · ter] *n.* 1. A person who, with other directors, oversees the business

of a corporation, sets corporate policy, and hires and supervises the employees who carry out that policy on a day-to-day basis. *See* board of directors. 2. The manager or chief administrative officer of an organization or enterprise, for EXAMPLE, the head of a Red Cross chapter. 3. A person who directs, controls, or manages.
➤ supervisor, boss, chief administrative officer, leader, chairperson, manager, president.

directory [de · *rek* · te · ree] *adj.* 1. That which is merely advisory, instructive, or which concerns form only, as opposed to that which is mandatory or which concerns matters of substance. 2. Sometimes, however, "directory" is used, in contrast to discretionary or **precatory**, to mean that which is required.
n. A listing of names, sometimes with other information such as addresses, telephone numbers, services offered, and so on.
➤ *adj.* advisory, instructive, nonbinding. *n.* catalogue, schedule, docket, register, index, record.

directory provision [pro · *vizh* · en] *n.* The part of a statute or ordinance that is permissive, as opposed to mandatory provisions of the same legislation. *Compare* declaratory provision; precatory words. *See* directory statute.

directory statute [*stat* · shoot] *n.* A statute whose provisions are a matter of form only and do not affect any **substantial right**, so that compliance is a matter of convenience rather than substance. *Compare* mandatory provision; mandatory statute.

directory trust *n.* A **trust** in which, by the **terms of the trust**, the trust funds are to be invested in a specified manner until the time when they are to be paid out. *Compare* discretionary trust.

disability [dis · e · *bil* · i · tee] *n.* 1. An absence of **legal capacity**. EXAMPLES: **infancy**; insanity; loss of rights because of conviction of a crime. *See* civil disability; legal disability. 2. Under **workers' compensation acts**, loss of earning power, loss of a limb or other body part, and, in some states, impairment of physical efficiency even though earning power has not been lost. 3. As used in most policies of disability insurance, inability to perform

D

the occupation that the insured was following at the time of the accident. 4. For purposes of disability benefits under the **Social Security Act**, inability by reason of a medically verifiable physical or mental impairment to engage in substantial and gainful activity appropriate to the claimant's age, education, training, experience, and mental and physical capacities. 5. Under the **Americans with Disabilities Act**, a physical or mental impairment that "substantially limits one or more of the major life activities." 6. A deprivation of ability; the state of being disabled; physical incapacity; physical disability. 7. Absence of competent power, whether physical, mental, legal, economic, or political. 8. A limitation; a restriction. *See also* general disability clause; partial disability; permanent disability; temporary disability; total disability.
➤ incapacity, unfitness, incompetence, inability ("His disability as a witness was detrimental to the case"); handicap, affliction, weakness, defect, disorder, impairment ("She suffered a permanent disability from the car accident").
Ant. advantage, strength.

disability clause *n.* A clause in an insurance policy providing for a waiver of premiums in the event of the insured's disability.

disability insurance [in · *shoor* · ense] *n.* Insurance that provides income in the event of disability.

disabled [dis · *ay* · buld] *adj.* 1. Experiencing a disability. 2. Crippled.
➤ broken, ill, weak, frail, infirm, made ineffective.

disadvantage [dis · ad · *van* · taj] *n.* A drawback; a flaw; a burden.
➤ drawback, hindrance, disability, restriction, handicap, difficulty, obstacle.

disaffirm [dis · e · *ferm*] *v.* To disclaim; to repudiate; to renounce; to disavow; to deny.
➤ disavow, recant, negate, veto, rescind, renege, renounce, deny, repudiate.
Ant. affirm.

disaffirmance [dis · e · *fer* · mens] *n.* 1. The refusal to fulfill a **voidable contract**. EXAMPLE: the refusal of a person, upon reaching her **majority**, to carry out a contract entered into when she was a minor.

2. Disclaimer; repudiation; disavowal; **renunciation**. *Compare* affirmance.

disagree [dis · uh · *gree*] *v.* To differ in opinion.
➤ differ, controvert, oppose, deny, diverge.

disagreement [dis · uh · *gree* · ment] *n.* 1. A dispute or argument. 2. Difference; dissimilarity.
➤ argument, contradiction, difference, feud, controversy, discrepancy, strife; variance, incongruity, clash, disparity.

disallow [dis · e · *louw*] *v.* To overrule; to reject; to deny.
➤ overrule, reject, deny, veto, forbid, repudiate, rebuff, spurn, abrogate.
Ant. grant.

disarm [dis · *arm*] *v.* 1. To take away the means of defense. 2. To win over to agreement.
➤ cripple, debilitate, weaken, disable, enervate; placate, mollify, pacify, assure, assuage.

disaster [diz · *ass* · ter] *n.* A catastrophe; a calamity; a misfortune. *See* common disaster.
➤ devastation, calamity, misery, ruin, fiasco, affliction, casualty.

disaster area [*air* · ee · uh] *n.* A locality that has experienced damage from a disaster, such as a major flood or hurricane, sufficiently extensive to qualify the affected population for emergency relief under state and federal statutes. **Casualty losses** occurring in disaster areas receive special tax consideration.

disaster loss *n.* *See* disaster area.

disbar [dis · *bahr*] *v.* To revoke an attorney's license to practice law. *See* disbarment; practice of law.
➤ disqualify, suspend, remove, rescind, expel ("to disbar an attorney for ethical violations").

disbarment [dis · *bahr* · ment] *n.* The revocation of an attorney's right to practice law. *See* practice of law. *See also* Rules of Professional Conduct.
➤ banishment, debarment, discharge, dismissal, ejection, eviction, removal.

disbursement [dis · *bers* · ment] *n.* Money paid out.
➤ payment, outlay, expense, remittance, fees.
Ant. receipt.

discharge [*dis* · charj] *n.* 1. A release from an obligation (such as a contract, a mortgage, or a **note**) because of performance or as a matter of grace. 2. The release of a debtor in a bankruptcy proceeding; a **discharge in bankruptcy**. 3. A release from custody. 4. Excusing a jury from further service. 5. To terminate an employee from employment. 6. The release of a member of the military from service. 7. **Release; satisfaction; rescission**. *v.* 1. To perform an obligation or duty; to satisfy a debt. USAGE: "All his debts were discharged by bankruptcy." *See* discharge in bankruptcy. 2. To free, liberate, or release, particularly from an obligation or duty. USAGE: "After **final settlement** of the estate, the court discharged the **administrator**." 3. To release a person from the military or from prison. USAGE: "The prisoner was discharged from custody." 4. To fire an employee. USAGE: "He was discharged from his job." 5. To unload or deliver cargo from a vessel or freight from a truck or railroad car.
➤ *n.* release, dismissal, termination, removal ("I received a discharge from the obligations of the contract"); accomplishment, fulfillment, execution, achievement ("discharge of duty").
v. perform, execute, effect, accomplish, comply, implement ("You must discharge your duty before taking on more work"); pay off ("discharge a debt"); extricate, absolve, acquit, liberate, emancipate ("She received an honorable discharge from the military"); fire, release, terminate, remove, sack, dismiss ("We discharged him for cause").

discharge in bankruptcy [*bank* · rupt · see] *n. See* discharge.

disciplinary rules [*dis* · i · plin · eh · ree] *n.* Rules and procedures for sanctioning attorneys guilty of professional misconduct. All jurisdictions have adopted such rules. Sanctions may include **disbarment**, suspension, probation, or reprimand. *See also* Rules of Professional Conduct.

discipline [*dis* · ih · plihn] *v.* 1. To bring (a group) under control. 2. To penalize in order to control. 3. To train through exercise. *n.* 1. An area of study. 2. Punishments or penalties.

➤ *v.* administer, command, supervise; castigate, penalize, reprove, punish; train, accustom, coach, condition, instruct. *n.* area, subject, course, curriculum; correction, punition, punishment.

disclaim [*dis* · *klame*] *v.* To renounce; to **waive**. *See* disclaimer.
➤ renounce, rescind, spurn, deny, cancel, disavow, annul.

disclaimer [*dis* · *klame* · er] *n.* 1. The refusal to accept, or the renunciation of, a right or of property. 2. The refusal to accept, or the renunciation of, an obligation. *See* limited warranty. 3. A denial; a rejection; a repudiation.
➤ relinquishment, renunciation, retraction, disowning, revocation, disavowal ("read the disclaimer carefully"). *Ant.* acceptance.

disclosure [*dis* · *kloh* · zher] *n.* 1. Under the **consumer credit protection acts**, the obligation to make the details of a credit transaction (EXAMPLE: the full amount of the finance charges) known to the purchaser. *See* disclosure statement. 2. The requirement that federal employees divulge any financial interests they have that might conflict with their government service. *See* conflict of interest. 3. The act of making known that which was unknown or not fully known. *Compare* nondisclosure.
➤ exposure, uncovering, acknowledgment, admission, publication, revelation. *Ant.* concealment.

disclosure statement [*state* · ment] *n.* The written statement required by **consumer credit protection acts** informing the consumer of the details of a credit transaction. Generally, the disclosure statement is incorporated into the consumer's contract.

discontinuance [*dis* · ken · *tin* · yoo · ense] *n.* 1. Same as **voluntary dismissal** or **nonsuit**. 2. The concluding, ending, or terminating of something.
➤ termination, cancellation, suspension, dismissal, cessation, abandonment.

discontinuing easement [*dis* · ken · *tin* · yoo · ing *eez* · ment] *n.* Same as **discontinous easement**.

discontinuous [dis · ken · *tin* · yoo · us] *adj.*
Lacking coherence; infrequent.
➤ infrequent, irregular, separated.

discontinuous easement
[dis · ken · *tin* · yoo · us *eez* · ment] *n.*
1. An **easement** whose use is infrequent
and therefore not apparent. *Compare*
apparent easement. 2. An easement that
exists only by human involvement.
EXAMPLE: a **right of way**. *Compare*
continous easement.

discount [*dis* · kount] *n.* 1. A reduction
from the regular sale price of an article.
2. In the banking business, the interest on
a loan charged in advance and deducted
from the loan when it is made; such a loan
is called a **discount loan**. 3. The purchase
of a **negotiable instrument** for an amount
less than its face value; i.e., purchase at
the **discount rate**. This practice is known
as **discounting**. *See also* rediscounting.
4. The lowered interest rate available under
some loans if repayment is made in a lump
sum rather than over a period of time.
5. The lowered rate of interest available
during the first years of an **adjustable
rate mortgage**.
v. 1. To give a **discount**; to purchase at a
discount. 2. To reduce the amount of;
belittle. *See* discount.
➤ *n.* reduction, markdown, rebate, break,
cutback, deduction.
Ant. increase.
v. reduce, belittle, ignore ("discount his
contribution to the project").

discount loan *n. See* discount.

discount rate *n.* 1. When **commercial
paper** is sold, the percentage of difference
between its face value and the amount for
which is is sold. 2. The rate established
by the **Federal Reserve Board** for loans
made by **federal reserve banks** to banks
in the **Federal Reserve System**.

discounting [*dis* · kount · ing] *n. See*
discount.

discourage [dis · *kur* · adj] *v.* To dishearten;
to deter; to dissuade.
➤ dissuade, dampen, caution, divert, daunt,
warn, demoralize, impede, inhibit, prevent.

discover [dis · *kuv* · er] *v.* To find or uncover.
➤ learn, uncover, unearth, deduce, determine,
ascertain, realize, conceive, detect.

discovered peril doctrine [dis · *kuv* · erd
peh · ril *dok* · trin] *n.* Same as **last clear
chance doctrine** or **humanitarian
doctrine**.

discovery [dis · *kuv* · e · ree] *n.* 1. A means
for providing a **party**, in advance of trial,
with access to facts that are within the
knowledge of the other side, to enable the
party to better try her case. A **motion to
compel discovery** is the **procedural** means
for compelling the **adverse party** to reveal
such facts or to produce documents, books,
and other things within his possession or
control. *See* deposition; interrogatories.
2. In **patent** law, the finding of something
new, such as a mechanical principle, that
may be adapted to produce a patentable
article. 3. In mining law, the finding of a
mineral deposit, the primary factor in
perfecting a mining claim. 4. A method
of acquiring territory on behalf of a nation.
5. Finding; disclosure; revelation.
➤ identification, exposure, uncovering,
disclosure, investigation, finding, breakthrough, pretrial device.

discredit [dis · *kred* · it] *v.* 1. To injure a
person's credit or reputation. 2. To impair
a person's believability. *See* credibility
➤ tarnish, downgrade, demean, disgrace,
puncture, impeach, malign, disparage.
Ant. support.

discreet [dis · *kreet*] *adj.* Careful or prudent,
especially concerning the maintenance of
confidentiality.
➤ guarded, judicious, sensitive, cautious,
careful, subtle, diplomatic.

discretion [dis · *kresh* · en] *n.* 1. The power
conferred upon an official to act according
to his own judgment and conscience, within
general rules of law only, uncontrolled by
the judgment or conscience of others. *See*
judicial discretion. 2. The freedom to act
without control other than one's own judgment. *See* legal capacity. 3. Tact; prudence;
consideration.
➤ will, choice, decision, selection, calculation,
consideration, precaution, tact, prudence
("I will leave that up to your discretion").

discretionary [dis · *kresh* · en · air · ee] *adj.*
That which is subject to a person's
discretion.

D

D

➤ optional, nonobligatory, elective, open, unrestricted ("discretionary power"). *Ant.* mandatory.

discretionary power [*pow* · er] *n.* A power conferred upon a person which she is free to exercise as she chooses. EXAMPLE: the power given an **executor** or **trustee** to sell or invest property "as she may deem advisable."

discretionary review [ree · *vyoo*] *n.* **Appellate court** review of a case that is not required by law; it takes place solely at the discretion of the court. *Certiorari* is an EXAMPLE of discretionary review. *See review.*

discretionary trust *n.* A **trust** in which broad discretion is **vested** in the **trustee** and is to be exercised by her in carrying out the purposes of the trust. *Compare* directory trust.

discriminate [dis · *krim* · ih · nayt] *v.* 1. To distinguish between different features. 2. To look at with disfavor or loathing; to show prejudice; to treat unequally.

➤ differentiate, separate, classify, compare, contrast, characterize ("discriminate between fine art and kitsch"); disfavor, reject, shun, hate, victimize, segregate, be bigoted ("discriminate against women").

discrimination [dis · krim · in · *ay* · shen] *n.* 1. The effect of **state action**, including statutes, official behavior, and officially sanctioned behavior, which distinguishes between **classes** of people in an arbitrary way in violation of the **equal protection clause** of the **Fourteenth Amendment**. Discrimination of this sort is often referred to as **invidious discrimination**. *See* suspect classification. *See and compare* de facto discrimination; de jure discrimination. 2. Conduct in violation of federal or state statutes which require that no distinction be made between people, in numerous areas of human activity (EXAMPLES: voting; education; employment), on account of race, religion, color, national origin, gender, age, or handicap. *See* Civil Rights Acts. *See also* Age Discrimination in Employment Act; Americans with Disabilities Act; Equal Pay Act. 3. Failure to treat everyone alike.

Note that discrimination (i.e., the failure to treat everyone alike) is not by itself illegal. (EXAMPLE: scheduling a makeup test so that all students whose last names begin with A through L take the examination on Monday, and all others on Tuesday.) What is illegal are the forms of unequal treatment prohibited by the Constitution or the law.

➤ bigotry, prejudice, partiality, injustice, unfairness, favoritism, hatred; acumen, keenness, taste, judgment, distinction, perspicacity.

discrimination by common carrier [*kom* · en ka · ree · er] *n.* An illegal arrangement by which a **common carrier** provides a lesser rate to one shipper of freight than it makes available to others in the same circumstances.

disease [de · zees] *n.* 1. An illness or ailment. 2. A harmful or destructive condition.

➤ illness, sickness, affliction, disorder, condition, infirmity.

disenfranchise [dis · en · *fran* · chize] *v.* To deprive a person of a right of citizenship (for EXAMPLE: the right to vote). *Compare* enfranchise.

➤ withhold, disinherit, disqualify, deprive, dispossess, disfranchise.

disfavor [dis · *faiv* · ur] *n.* The state of no longer being liked or respected. *v.* To look on with disapproval.

➤ *n.* unpopularity, shame, dislike, disregard, mistrust, disgrace. *v.* disapprove, offend, dislike.

disfranchise [dis · *fran* · chize] *n.* Same as **disenfranchise**.

disgrace [dis · *grase*] *n.* The loss of favor or dignity. *v.* To humiliate oneself; to lose standing.

➤ *n.* humiliation, abasement, indignity, blemish, dishonor. *v.* dishonor, humiliate, shame, abase, demean, ridicule, deride.

disguise [dis · *gise*] *n.* A covering used to alter the appearance of something. *v.* To change or conceal the appearance of.

➤ *n.* façade, front, mask, pretense, covering, masquerade, deception. *v.* conceal, deceive, mask, simulate, hide, alter, becloud.

dishonest [dis · on · est] *adj.* Not honest; deceitful. Characterized by a failure to tell the truth.

➤ lying, insincere, spurious, deceiving, deceptive, disreputable, nefarious, corrupt, unethical.
Ant. honest, ethical, upright, true.

dishonor [dis · *on* · er] *v.* 1. To refuse to accept or pay a **negotiable instrument** when it is duly presented for **acceptance** or payment, or when **presentment** is excused and the instrument is not accepted or paid. *Compare* honor. *See also* notice of dishonor. 2. To discredit; to disgrace; to shame.
n. Loss of respect or reputation.
➤ *v.* discredit, humiliate, disgrace, blemish, disrepute, abase, shame, degrade, defile; reject.
Ant. respect; accept.
n. shame, disgrace, scorn, indignity, aspersion, opprobrium.

disingenuous [dis · in · *gen* · yoo · us] *adj.* Insincere; dishonest.
➤ deceptive, artificial, misleading, dishonest, wily, unethical, insincere.

disinherit [dis · in · *herr* · it] *v.* To deny a person the right to inherit something.
➤ cut off, withhold, renounce, deprive, disclaim, forsake ("to disinherit the unrepentant son").

disinheritance [dis · in · *herr* · i · tense] *n.* The act of depriving an heir of his inheritance.
➤ abandonment, repudiation, renouncement, deprivation.
Ant. bestowal.

disinter [dis · in · *ter*] *v.* To remove a buried body from the grave. *See* exhumation.
➤ exhume, disentomb, resurrect, unearth.

disinterested [dis · in · ter · es · ted] *adj.* 1. Having no **interest** in a case or in its outcome. *Compare* interested; interested person; real party in interest. 2. In its common meaning, indifferent, unconcerned, uninterested.
➤ impartial, unbiased, uninvolved, fair, nonpartisan, neutral ("disinterested witness"); indifferent, detached, remote ("a disinterested demeanor").
Ant. biased; involved.

disinterested witness [*wit* · ness] *n.* A witness who is not biased by reason of any **interest** in the outcome of an **action**.

disjunctive allegations [dis · *junk* · tiv al · e · *gay* · shenz] *n.* *See* alternative pleading.

dismiss [dis · *miss*] *v.* 1. To order a case, **motion**, or prosecution to be terminated. A **party** requests such an order by means of a **motion to dismiss**. 2. To send away; to let out. 3. To fire an employee.
➤ suspend, eject, oust, remove, expel, fire, adjourn, disregard, ignore, refuse.
Ant. convene, embrace.

dismissal [dis · *miss* · el] *n.* 1. An order for the termination of a **civil action** without a trial of its issues, or without further trial. Whether a dismissal is a **final judgment** against the plaintiff depends upon whether it is a **dismissal with prejudice** or a **dismissal without prejudice**. *See also* discontinuance; involuntary dismissal; nonsuit; voluntary dismissal. 2. The termination of a criminal case at the request of the prosecutor, the result of which is to free the defendant. *See nolle prosequi.* 3. The discharge of an employee from his employment.
➤ termination, discharge, removal, elimination, discontinuance, disposal.

dismissal with prejudice [*prej* · e · diss] *n.* An order of **dismissal** which does not declare that the dismissal is "without prejudice"; a **final judgment** on the **merits** of the case. *Compare* dismissal without prejudice. *See res judicata.*

dismissal without prejudice [*prej* · e · diss] *n.* An order of **dismissal** which states that it is "without prejudice" means that the dismissal will not bar any new suit that the plaintiff might later bring on the same **cause of action**. *Compare* dismissal with prejudice.

disorderly [dis · *or* · der · lee] *adj.* 1. Against the peace, good order, morals, decency, or safety of the public. 2. Unruly; without order. 3. Untidy.
➤ unruly, riotous, boisterous, uncivil, undisciplined, rebellious, unmanageable.

disorderly conduct [*kon* · dukt] *n.* An act that breaches the peace, grossly offends public morality, or endangers public safety or public health. State statutes or local ordinances criminalizing such conduct are unconstitutional under the **due process clause** of the **Fourteenth Amendment**

D

unless they are sufficiently specific with respect to the conduct they prohibit. *See* breach of the peace; public nuisance.

disorderly house *n.* 1. A place where **disorderly conduct** habitually occurs. 2. A place frequented by criminals, intoxicated persons, drug addicts, prostitutes, or the like. *See* disorderly conduct; public nuisance.

disparage [dis · pa · rej] *v.* To discredit or defame a person or property.
➤ smear, belittle, ridicule, discredit, detract, dishonor, condemn, demean, downgrade, criticize.
Ant. acclaim.

disparagement [dis · pa · rej · ment] *n.* Discredit; detraction; dishonor; denunciation; disrespect.

disparagement of goods [prop · er · tee] *n.* Criticism that discredits the quality of merchandise or other property offered for sale. In certain cases, such criticism might constitute a business tort.

disparagement of title [ty · tel] *n.* Words or conduct that brings into question a person's **title** to particular property.

disparate [dis · pur · it] *adj.* Distinct in character or quality.
➤ different, unlike, divergent, distinct, separate, unequal.

disparity [dis · pur · ih · tee] *n.* A discrepancy between two things or two people.
➤ discrepancy, difference, incongruity, variation, imbalance, divergency ("disparity between his testimony today and his earlier statement").

dispatch [dis · patch] *n.* 1. A news item filed by a reporter. 2. Promptness and efficiency. *v.* 1. To send off. 2. To dispose of; to finish.
➤ *n.* communiqué, news flash; haste. *v.* send, rush, remit, expedite, transmit, hasten; complete, conclude, execute, fulfill, finalize.

dispel [dis · pell] *v.* To clear out or eliminate.
➤ dismiss, remove, release, diffuse ("dispel an inference").

dispensation [dis · pen · say · shen] *n.* Exemption from duties or penalties imposed by law. *See* exemption.
➤ permission, authorization, clearance, relinquishment, pardon, allowance.

dispense [dis · pents] *v.* 1. To give out in portions. 2. To prepare and disburse. 3. To do without.
➤ provide, apportion, dole out, do, assign, bestow, tender; operate, execute, manage, administer; absolve, discharge, release, exonerate.

displace [dis · plase] *v.* 1. To remove someone from a position. 2. To take the place of; to substitute.
➤ dislocate, dismiss, oust, evict ("The worker was displaced"); replace, substitute, supplant.

dispose [dis · poze] *v.* Always used with "of," as "dispose of." 1. To sell; to transfer; to **alienate**; to **grant**; to **convey**; to **bequeath**; to **devise**. *See* sound and disposing mind and memory. 2. To end; to settle; to resolve; to finalize. 3. To get rid of; to discard. *See* disposition.
➤ relinquish, sell, convey, bestow, discard, allocate; adapt, adjust, make willing, prepare, motivate.

dispose of *v.* *See* dispose.

disposing mind [dis · po · zing] *n.* *See* sound and disposing mind and memory; testamentary disposition.

disposition [dis · pe · zish · en] *n.* 1. The act of transferring or passing property. *See* fraudulent disposition; testamentary disposition. 2. A court's ruling, decision, or **judgment** in a case. USAGE: "The judge is ready to make a disposition." 3. The act of settling something, particularly a case; an arrangement. USAGE: "The insurance company made a satisfactory disposition of her claim." 4. The act of disposing of something. USAGE: "Disposition has been made of the body." 5. Frame of mind; nature or temperament.
➤ conveyance, transfer, relinquishment, disposal ("The will allowed for the proper disposition of property"); attitude, temperament, character, mood, humor, personality ("She has a lovely disposition").

dispositive [dis · pahz · e · tiv] *adj.* Controlling; conclusive; disposing.
➤ controlling, conclusive, disposing ("Those facts are damaging but not necessarily dispositive of this case").

D

dispositive facts *n.* Facts that will determine the outcome of a case.

dispossess [dis · po · *zess*] *v.* To oust; to put out of **possession** of real estate. *See* dispossession.
➤ expel, oust, eject, evict.
Ant. install, establish.

dispossess proceeding [pro · *see* · ding] *n.* An **action** brought against a tenant who is in default to oust him from the premises. *See* ejectment; eviction.

dispossess warrant [*war* · ent] *n.* A **warrant** issued by the court in a **dispossess proceeding** for the ouster of the tenant.

dispossession [dis · po · *zesh* · en] *n.* A forced or fraudulent changing of **possession** of land from one person to another; **ouster**. *See* ejectment.
➤ eviction, exile, foreclosure, usurpation, ejectment, displacement.

disprove [dis · *proov*] *v.* To prove something to be false; to refute.
➤ nullify, confute, prove false, negate, controvert ("He was able to disprove my theory of the case").

disputable presumption [dis · *pyoot* · ebl pre · *zump* · shen] *n.* Same as **irrebuttable presumption**.

dispute [dis · *pyoot*] *n.* A disagreement or controversy; in law, a disagreement or controversy that underlies a **legal action**.
USAGE: "This lawsuit grew out of a dispute between the parties."
v. 1. To argue against. 2. To disagree or challenge another's opinion.
➤ *n.* conflict, altercation, commotion, controversy, disturbance, feud, quarrel.
Ant. agreement.
v. contest, doubt, take exception, challenge, deny, contradict ("dispute the testimony"); debate, disagree, argue.

dispute resolution *n.* *See* alternative dispute resolution.

disqualification [dis · kwall · i · fi · *kay* · shen] *n.* That which makes a person ineligible for something; lack of qualification, especially for a public office or for jury duty. Disqualification for office may in some instances be for the want of a requirement such as a specific degree or professional license. A person would be disqualified

for jury duty if she had an **interest** in the matter to be heard.
➤ elimination, expulsion, exclusion, removal, denial, rejection; defect, disability, shortcoming.

disqualified [dis · *kwall* · e · fide] *adj./adv.* Made ineligible. *See* disqualification.
➤ ineligible, rejected, incompetent, subject to challenge.

disqualified judge *n.* A judge who is disqualifed to act in a particular case because of personal interest in the subject matter of the suit or because of his pre-conceived mental attitude. *See* bias of judge; recusation.

disqualified juror [*joo* · rer] *n.* A juror who is subject to **challenge** because of **mental disability**, bias, relationship to a **party**, **interest** in the suit, or similar reason. *See* bias of juror.

disqualified witness [*wit* · ness] *n.* A witness who is **incompetent** to testify because of her mental condition, inability to comprehend the oath, the **privileged** nature of her information, or **interest** in the result of the suit. *Compare* disinterested witness.

disqualify [dis · *kwall* · e · fy] *v.* To make ineligible. *See* disqualification.
➤ bar, expel, eliminate, exclude, disable.

dissect [dih · *sekt*] *v.* 1. To take apart in order to study. 2. To analyze the various parts of.
➤ cut up, dismember, section, take apart; analyze, inspect, scrutinize, investigate, examine.

disseisin [di · *see* · zin] *n.* Same as **dispossession**.

dissent [di · *sent*] *n.* 1. The point of view expressed by a judge who disagrees with the position taken the majority of judges in a case. *See* dissenting opinion. 2. Any disagreement with the views of another.
v. to disagree.
➤ *n.* nonagreement, objection, opposition, variance, noncompliance, protest, nonconcurrence.
v. disagree, dispute, challenge, contradict, argue, repudiate, refuse, decline.

D

dissenting opinion [di · *sen* · ting o · *pin* · yen] *n.* A written **opinion** filed by a judge of an **appellate court** who disagrees with the decision of the majority of judges in a case, giving the reasons for her differing view. Often a dissenting opinion is written by one judge on behalf of one or more other dissenting judges. *Compare* concurring opinion; majority opinion.

dissenting stockholders [di · *sen* · ting *stok* · hold · erz] *n.* A minority of **shareholders** who oppose the action taken by the majority. *See* appraisal remedy.

dissolution [dis · e · *loo* · shen] *n.* A breaking up; the separation of a thing into its component parts.
➤ termination, cessation, finish, nullification, discontinuance, liquidation, disintegration, dissipation.
Ant. establishment, creation.

dissolution of corporation [kore · per · *ay* · shen] *n.* The termination of a **corporation's** existence and its abolishment as an **entity.** *See* liquidation; liquidation of corporation.

dissolution of marriage [*ma* · rej] *n.* 1. The termination of a marriage, whether by **annulment**, **divorce a vinculo**, or **no-fault divorce**. 2. A term for divorce in some no-fault divorce states.

dissolution of partnership [*part* · ner · ship] *n.* The change in the relation of **partners** caused by any partner's ceasing to be associated in the carrying on of the business. Any such change brings about the dissolution of the **partnership**. *See* partnership. *Also see* liquidation; liquidation of partnership.

dist. ct. *n.* Abbreviation of **district court**. Also abbreviated DC and D.C.

distinct [dis · *tinkt*] *adj.* 1. Presenting a clear impression. 2. Apart from others; unique.
➤ clear, evident, pronounced, well-defined, explicit; different, special, discrete, unique.

distinctive [dis · *tink* · tiv] *adj.* Characteristic; able to be distinguished from others.
➤ characteristic, distinguishing, particular, uncommon, idiosyncratic, salient ("her distinctive accent").

distinguish [dis · *ting* · wish] *v.* 1. To explain why a particular case is not

precedent or **authority** with respect to the **matter in controversy**. 2. To point out significant differences; to differentiate.
➤ separate, differentiate, classify, divide, categorize, characterize.

distinguishable [dis · *ting* · wish · ebl] *adj.* That which may be **distinguished**. If a case is distinguishable from another case, the precedent in the former case may not be applicable.

distort [dis · *tort*] *v.* To bend or alter.
➤ bend, color, slant, change, falsify, misconstrue ("distort the truth").

distrain [dis · *train*] *v.* To seize a tenant's goods for nonpayment of rent. *See* distress. *See also* landlord's lien.
➤ seize, impound, attach, sequester, appropriate.

distraint [dis · *traint*] *n.* The act of **distraining.** *See* distrain.

distress [dis · *tress*] *n.* 1. At **common law**, a landlord's act **distraining** a tenant's goods in **satisfaction** of unpaid rent. 2. Taking goods or **chattels** out of the possession of a wrongdoer into the **injured party's** possession to secure satisfaction for the wrong. 3. Misfortune; hardship; anxiety; stress.
➤ confiscation, impoundment, dispossession, attachment ("distress for payment"); suffering, agony, torment, pain, despair ("Jennifer suffered much distress after the accident").

distressed sale [dis · *trest*] *n.* 1. A sale at which merchandise is sold at a discount because of some difficulty experienced by the seller. EXAMPLES: a "lost our lease" sale; a fire sale. 2. A **foreclosure sale** or **tax sale**.

distribute [dis · *trib* · yoot] *v.* 1. To make distribution of the property of an **intestate estate** to the persons entitled to it. 2. To apportion; to allocate; to prorate. 3. To expend. 4. To disseminate. 5. To dole out; to give.
➤ apportion, allot, classify, allocate, deliver, disseminate, divide, organize.
Ant. collect.

distributee [dis · *trib* · yoo · tee] *n.* 1. A person entitled to share in the **estate** of a **decedent** who died without a will. *See* heirs. 2. In its nontechnical sense, a person

who receives any portion of a **decedent's estate** under a will. *See* distribution.
➤ recipient, beneficiary, heir, donee.

distribution [dis · tre · *byoo* · shen] *n.* 1. The act of the **administrator** of an **intestate estate** in allocating the **decedent's** property among her heirs. 2. The disposal by the **executor** of the **estate** of a decedent who died **testate**; i.e., leaving a will. 3. A **corporate distribution**. 4. Allocation; appropriation; a doling out.
➤ allocation, assignment, organization, grouping, allotment, transference, arrangement. *Ant.* accumulation.

distributive [dis · *trib* · yoo · tiv] *adj.* Relating to distribution; that which apportions, allots, or allocates.

distributive finding [*fine* · ding] *n.* A **finding of fact** in favor of both **parties** by a judge or jury, that is, partly for the plaintiff and partly for the defendant.

distributive justice [*juss* · tiss] *n.* The concept that justice requires the benefits and burdens of a society to be fairly allocated among its members. *Compare* commutative justice.

distributive share *n.* The share of an **intestate estate** to which a **distributee** or heir is entitled after payment of the debts of the estate and the **estate tax**. *See* distribution.

district [dis · trikt] *n.* A geographical unit within a state, county, or other **political subdivision** within which some aspect of government is administered. EXAMPLES: a **school district**; a **judicial district**; a **congressional district**; a **tax district**.
➤ region, unit, zone, section, province, domain, community.

district attorney (DA) [a · *tern* · ee] *n.* A public officer, usually elected, who conducts **actions**, generally criminal prosecutions, on behalf of his state in his district, usually a county. *Compare* United States Attorney.
➤ prosecutor, prosecution, state's attorney, accuser.

district court (DC) *n.* 1. A **District Court of the United States**. 2. In many states, the name for the major **court of original jurisdiction**, that is, the court in which most civil lawsuits and criminal

prosecutions are initially brought. *See also* inferior court; trial court.

District Courts of the United States [yoo · *nite* · ed] *n.* Officially termed United States District Courts, the **courts of original jurisdiction** for both criminal prosecutions and civil cases arising under federal statutes, cases involving federal **constitutional questions**, and suits by and against citizens of different states. Each state and territory, and the District of Columbia, has at least one federal **judicial district**.

districting [*dis* · trik · ting] *v.* *See* apportionment of representatives; reapportionment.

disturbance [dis · *terb* · ants] *n.* Disorder; confusion; interruption.
➤ unrest, confusion, disorder, revolt, tumult, affray, clamor, turmoil ("a disturbance in the courtroom").

disturbing the peace [dis · *ter* · bing] *n.* Same as **breach of the peace**.

diverse [die · *verse*] *adj.* Different or dissimilar. USAGE: "They come from diverse backgrounds."
➤ different, mixed, varied, heterogeneous, sundry, various, unlike.

diversion [di · *ver* · zhen] *n.* 1. Short for **pretrial diversion** or **diversion program**. 2. Alteration of the normal or natural course of something; detour; deviation. 3. Distraction. 4. Tactic. 5. Amusement; recreation; pleasure.
➤ detour, digression, distraction, deflection ("The defendant's trick created a menacing diversion for the jury"); hobby, pastime, recreation, entertainment ("Sailing can be a wonderful diversion").

diversion program [*pro* · gram] *n.* Any one of a number of processes designed to bring about disposition of criminal charges before trial, often with no criminal conviction, provided the defendant successfully completes a treatment program or in some other specified way demonstrates his rehabilitation. This process is also sometimes referred to as **pretrial diversion, deferred prosecution**, or **intervention**. Diversion or intervention that is designed to take place after conviction is called **posttrial diversion** or **posttrial intervention**.

D

D

diversity [die · *ver* · sih · tee] *n.* 1. Variety or difference among a group of people on things. 2. A shortened form of "diversity of citizenship." USAGE: "Is there diversity in this case so that we can remove the federal court?"
➤ variety, multiplicity, assortment, variation ("cultural diversity").

diversity jurisdiction [di · *ver* · se · tee joo · ris · *dik* · shen] *n.* The **jurisdiction** of a federal court arising from **diversity of citizenship**, when the **jurisdictional amount** has been met. *See also* amount in controversy.

diversity of citizenship [di · *ver* · se · tee of *sit* · i · zen · ship] *n.* A ground for invoking the **original jurisdiction** of a federal **district court**, the basis of **jurisdiction** being the existence of a controversy between citizens of different states. *See* District Courts of the United States; diversity jurisdiction. *Compare* federal question.

divest [di · *vest*] *v.* 1. To deprive or cause the loss of a **right** or **title**. 2. To deprive; to strip. *See* divestiture.
➤ forfeit, displace, strip, discharge, remove, deprive.
Ant. confer, give.

divestiture [di · *vest* · i · cher] *n.* 1. An order of court requiring a corporation to sell off some of its **assets**, particularly another company or companies it owns. Divestiture is a **remedy** available under the **antitrust acts**. 2. The act of divesting or the condition of being divested. *See* divest. 3. The surrender of a **right** or **title**.
➤ giving up, surrendering, deprivation, removal.

divided custody [di · *vy* · ded *kuss* · te · dee] *n.* An arrangement under which the child of divorced parents lives a portion of the time with one parent and a portion of the time with the other. **Legal custody**, however, remains at all times with only one of the parents. *Compare* joint custody; sole custody. *See* custody.

dividend [*div* · e · dend] *n.* 1. A payment made by a corporation to its stockholders, either in cash (a **cash dividend**), in stock (a **stock dividend**), or out of **surplus earnings**. *See* accumulated dividend; cumulative dividend; liquidation dividend;

noncumulative dividend; scrip dividend. 2. In the case of a **mutual insurance company**, a portion of the premium paid to the insured that is not required to pay claims or to operate the business. 3. A gain or profit.
➤ profit, benefit, reward, share, allowance, bonus.

divisible [di · *viz* · ebl] *adj.* Able to be divided or separated into component parts. *See* severable.
➤ severable, detachable, breakable, separable.

divisible contract [*kon* · trakt] *n.* A **contract** whose parts are capable of separate or independent treatment; a contract that is enforceable as to a part which is valid, even though another part is invalid and unenforceable. *Compare* indivisible contract. *See* severability of contract.

divisible divorce [di · *vorss*] *n.* A concept under which a divorce decree that is unenforceable for one reason or another with respect to alimony or child support may nonetheless be completely effective to dissolve the marriage. *See* Estin doctrine.

divisible offense [o · *fense*] *n.* A crime that cannot be committed without at the same time committing one or more other crimes. EXAMPLE: it is impossible to commit **murder** without committing **battery**. *See* lesser included offense.

divorce [di · *vorss*] *n.* A dissolution of the marital relationship between husband and wife. *Compare* alimony. *See* collusive divorce; foreign divorce; no-fault divorce. *v.* To end an existing relationship or situation.
➤ *n.* separation, division, break, breakup, parting, rupture, disunion.
v. rescind, dismiss, annul, cease, dissolve.

divorce a mensa et thoro [ah *men* · sa et *thoh* · roh] *n.* A decree that terminates the right of **cohabitation**, and **adjudicates** matters such as custody and support, but does not dissolve the marriage itself. A divorce a mensa et thoro is often referred to as **legal separation**, **judicial separation**, or **limited divorce**. *Compare* absolute divorce; divorce a vinculo matrimonii; no-fault divorce. *See mensa et thoro. See also* separate maintenance.

divorce a vinculo matrimonii
[ah *vin* · kyoo · loh mat · ri · *moh* · ni · eye]
n. A decree that dissolves the marriage because of **matrimonial misconduct**. Also called absolute divorce. *Compare* divorce a mensa et thoro; no-fault divorce. *See a vinculo matrimonii.*
divorce from bed and board *n.* Same as **divorce a mensa et thoro.**

divulge [di · *vulge*] *v.* To make known.
➤ reveal, confess, communicate, admit, proclaim, expose, impart.
Ant. conceal.

DNA fingerprinting [*fing* · er · prin · ting] *n.* A method for for identifying the perpetrator of a crime by comparing tissue (EXAMPLES: blood; skin; semen) found at the scene of the crime with similar tissue from the defendant. It is also a method for extablishing paternity. DNA (short for deoxyribonucleic acid) is a basic material in all living cells, which transmits the hereditary pattern. DNA evidence is admissible in some jurisdictions in criminal prosecutions and, in most jurisdictions, in **paternity suits**. Other terms for DNA fingerprinting are **HLA testing** and **genetic marker testing**.

DNR Abbreviation of "do not resuscitate." *See* do not resuscitate order.

do not resuscitate order [ree · *suss* · i · tate or · der] *n.* A physician's order on the chart of a hospitalized patient, which directs that if the patient's heart should stop beating, or if he stops breathing, no effort should be made to revive him. Usually shortened to **DNR**, such an order is given only with respect to a terminally ill patient whose death is imminent. A multitude of legal issues are associated with DNRs. *See also* durable power of attorney, healthcare proxy; living will.

dock *n.* 1. The place reserved in the courtroom for a prisoner on trial for commission of a crime. 2. A wharf or pier.
v. 1. To reduce or decrease. 2. To land a boat.
➤ *n.* pier, harbor, wharf, landing.
v. deduct, abridge, decrease, reduce, subtract ("dock his pay").

docket [*dok* · et] *n.* 1. A list of cases for trial or other disposition; a **court calendar**.

2. A list of cases and a summary of what occurred in those cases, although not a **record** in the sense of a **transcript**.
v. To make an **entry** in a **docket**. *See* docket (*noun*).
➤ *n.* register, agenda, program, diary, plan, calendar, record ("entered in the docket").
v. record, enter ("to docket a case").

Doctor of Jurisprudence [*dok* · ter of joor · is · *proo* · dense] *n.* Same as **Juris Doctor**.

doctor-patient privilege [*dok* · ter-*pay* · shent *priv* · i · lej] *n.* *See* physician-patient privilege.

doctrine [*dok* · trin] *n.* A **rule of law** or a legal principle. EXAMPLES: the **last clear chance doctrine**; *cy pres*; the **Miranda rule**.
➤ dogma, theory, philosophy, belief, rule, principle, tradition.

document [*dok* · yoo · ment] *n.* Anything with letters, figures, or marks (EXAMPLES: printed words; photographs; pictures; maps) recorded on it. *See* ancient document.
v. to make a record of; to support with evidence.
➤ *n.* report, publication, paper, instrument, certificate, form, record.
v. authenticate, substantiate, prove, demonstrate.
document of title [*ty* · tel] *n.* Any document which in the **regular course of business** is treated as evidencing that the person in possession of it is entitled to receive, hold, and dispose of the document and the goods to which it pertains. EXAMPLES: a **bill of lading**; a **warehouse receipt**. *See* title.

documentary [dok · yoo · *men* · ta · ree] *adj.* Pertaining to or arising out of a document.
documentary draft *n.* A **draft** with a number of attached documents.
documentary evidence [*ev* · i · dense] *n.* A document or other writing that tends to establish the truth or falsity of a matter at issue. (EXAMPLES: a deed; a **negotiable instrument**; **books and records**; photographs.) When oral evidence is given, it is the person (i.e., the witness) who speaks; when documentary evidence is involved, it is the document that "speaks." *Compare* testimony.

D

documentary stamp tax *n. See* revenue stamps.

doing business [*doo* · ing *biz* · ness] *n.* Carrying on business; engaging in business. In the case of a corporation, the exercise of some of the functions for which the corporation was organized.

doing business in a state *n.* For purposes of bringing suit against a corporation in a given state, the corporation may generally be said to be "doing business" in any state in which it transacts some portion (customarily expressed as "minimum contacts") of its ordinary or customary business. *See* minimum contacts test. *Also see* localization doctrine.

domain [doh · *mayn*] *n.* 1. Absolute ownership and control of land. USAGE: "This farm is my domain." 2. Real property of which one has absolute ownership and control. USAGE: "I have domain over this farm." Land owned by the government is **public domain**. (USAGE: "All national parks are in the public domain.") So are literary and artistic works on which the **copyright** has expired or which are not subject to copyright. *See* dominion. *Also see* eminent domain.
➤ kingdom, holding, territory, estate, province ("your personal domain"); jurisdiction, authority, command ("The government has domain over this piece of land").

Dombrowski doctrine [dom · *brow* · skee dok · trin] *n.* A rule of **constitutional law** under which federal courts can **enjoin** a state prosecution for violation of a statute which is so vague that it violates the defendant's rights under the **First Amendment**, particularly if the prosecution is in bad faith. *See* vagueness doctrine. *Also see* equitable restraint doctrine.

domestic [de · *mes* · tik] *adj.* 1. Pertaining to the home. *See* domestic relations. 2. Pertaining to one's own state, as distinguished from **foreign states**, i.e., other states of the United States. *See and compare* domestic corporation; foreign corporation. 3. National, as distinguished from international. USAGE: "Domestic travel is less expensive than travel outside the country."
➤ local, native, household, indigenous, national. *Ant.* foreign.

domestic corporation [kore · per · *ay* · shen] *n.* A **corporation** organized under the laws of the state. *Compare* foreign corporation.

domestic judgment [*juj* · ment] *n.* As opposed to a **foreign judgment**, a **judgment** rendered by a court in the jurisdiction in which the rights or liabilities that are the subject of the judgment are involved.

domestic relations [re · *lay* · shenz] *n.* The field of law relating to domestic matters, such as marriage, divorce, support, custody, and adoption; **family law**.

domicile [*dom* · i · sile] *n.* The relationship that the law creates between a person and a particular locality or country. Domicile is a person's permanent home or **permanent abode**. Although in a particular context "domicile" may have the same meaning as "**residence**," the terms are not synonymous because, while a person may have only one domicile, she may have many residences. *See* abode; permanent residence; place of abode. *See also* corporate domicile; matrimonial domicile; national domicile. USAGE: "Although he has residences in a number of different countries, he is domiciled in Chicago."
v. To create or maintain a **domicile**. *See* domicile.
➤ *n.* residence, abode, establishment, home ("She claimed Tampa, Florida, as her permanent domicile.").
v. locate, occupy, dwell, abide ("Because the defendant was domiciled there, the complaint was filed in Clayton County").

domicile of choice *n.* The place a person voluntarily chooses for himself, as opposed to his **domicile of origin** or domicile conferred upon him by **operation of law**.

domicile of origin [*orr* · e · jin] *n.* The place where a person is domiciled at the moment of her birth.

domiciliary [dom · i · *sil* · ee · er · ee] *adj.* Referring to the place where a person makes his home. *See* domicile.
n. A person who has a **domicile** or is domiciled. USAGE: "She is a domiciliary of the State of Alabama."
➤ *n.* citizen, native, dweller, inhabitant, resident.

domiciliary administration
[ad · min · is · *tray* · shen] *n.* As contrasted with **ancillary administration**, the **administration** of a **decedent's estate** in the state in which she was **domiciled**; **principal administration**.

dominant [*dom* · i · nent] *adj.* Principal; paramount; predominant; ruling. *Compare* servient.
➤ commanding, primary, supreme, chief, superior, principal.

dominant estate [es · *tate*] *n.* Same as **dominant tenement**. *Compare* servient estate.

dominant tenement [*ten* · e · ment] *n.* Real property that benefits from an **easement** which burdens another piece of property, known as the **servient tenement**. *Compare* servient tenement. *See also* appurtenant easement.

dominion [de · *min* · yen] *n.* Ownership and control. *See* domain.
➤ jurisdiction, power, domination, supremacy ("dominion over property").

donate [*doh* · nate] *v.* To give; to contribute; to bestow.
➤ award, bequeath, bestow, grant, pledge. *Ant.* receive.

donation [doh · *nay* · shen] *n.* 1. A gift. 2. The act of giving; the act of making a gift.
➤ offering, grant, gift, contribution, handout.

donative intent [*doh* · ne · tiv in · *tent*] *n.* The intent to make a gift. It is necessary to show donative intent to prove that a sum of money is a gift rather than income under tax laws.

donee [doh · *nee*] *n.* 1. A person to whom a gift is made. *See* grantee. 2. A person who is the recipient of a **power of appointment**; a **donee of a power**.
➤ transferee, heir, recipient, beneficiary, grantee. *Ant.* donor.

donee beneficiary
[ben · e · *fish* · ee · er · ee] *n.* Same as **third-party beneficiary**. The benefit a donee beneficiary receives from the contract between two other persons is a **gift**.

donee of a power [*pow* · er] *n.* *See* donee.

donor [*doh* · nor] *n.* A person who makes a gift.

➤ giver, contributor, donator, grantor. *Ant.* recipient.

doomed *adj.* Condemned; lost; hopeless.
➤ condemned, predestined, ruined, undone, destroyed, sentenced, sunk.

dope *n.* 1. A person of low intelligence. 2. Slang for information. USAGE: "Give me the dope on the *Brown University* case." 3. A term for illegal drugs. Dope can refer to a number of different drugs, including marijuana, crack, or heroin.
➤ idiot, dunce, fool, dolt; news, information, lowdown, scoop; drug, narcotic.

dormant [*dor* · ment] *adj.* Inactive; in abeyance; sleeping.
➤ inactive, inert, passive, latent, quiescent, abeyant, inoperative, suspended, static, silent. *Ant.* active, manifest.

dormant judgment [*juj* · ment] *n.* A **judgment** that, because of the lapse of time and the failure to take any steps to continue to enforce it, can no longer be executed without being **revived**. *See* execution; revival of judgment.

dormant partner [*part* · ner] *n.* Same as **silent partner**.

dormant title [*ty* · tel] *n.* An unclaimed **title** to real estate.

double [dubl] *adj.* Multiplied by two; duplicate; matching.
➤ twofold, dual, paired, duplicate, twin. *Ant.* single, solo.

double hearsay [*hear* · say] *n.* The testimony of a witness as to a statement made to a second person outside of court by a third person. **Hearsay** is the testimony of a witness as to a statement made outside of court by a second person. Hearsay testimony is not admissible unless it falls within an **exception to the hearsay rule**. Double hearsay, which is also called **multiple hearsay**, is never admissible. *See* hearsay; hearsay rule.

double indemnity [in · *dem* · ni · tee] *n.* A benefit payable under an insurance policy at twice **face value** if **loss** occurs under certain conditions. EXAMPLE: under a life insurance policy, the death of the insured by accidental, as opposed to natural, causes.

D

D

double insurance [in · *shoor* · ense] *n.* Coverage of the same **risk** and the same **interest** by different insurance companies. *See* contribution between insurers; excess insurance.

double jeopardy [*jep* · er · dee] *n.* A rule originating in the **Fifth Amendment** that prohibits a second punishment or a second trial for the same offense. It is sometimes referred to as **former jeopardy** or **prior jeopardy**. *See* jeopardy.

double patenting [*pat* · en · ting] *n.* The obtaining of a second **patent** by the same applicant on the same invention; a practice prohibited under patent law.

double pleading [*plee* · ding] *n.* The **pleading** of more than one **cause of action** in the same paragraph of a **complaint**. Although this practice was not permitted under **common law pleading**, it is now universally acceptable under **code pleading**.

double taxation [tak · *say* · shen] *n.* 1. Taxing the same individual or property twice, for the same purpose, by the same governmental body and by a tax of the same kind, in the same year. Such taxation is **unconstitutional**. 2. Taxing the income of a corporation, and then taxing it again when it is distributed to shareholders in the form of **dividends**. The second taxation occurs in the form of the **personal income tax** which each shareholder must pay; this form of double taxation is legal.

double wills *n.* Another term for **reciprocal wills**. *See also* mutual wills.

doubt *n.* 1. The state of mind that exists when evidence fails to cause one to believe the existence of a fact. *See* beyond a reasonable doubt. The opposite of doubt is certainty. 2. Uncertainty.
v. To question or mistrust.
➤ *n.* uncertainty, suspicion, concern, hesitation, indecision, ambivalence, insecurity. *v.* suspect, dispute, question, distrust, challenge.

doubtful [*dowt* · ful] *adj.* 1. Lacking a definite opinion. 2. Uncertain; questionable.
➤ dubious, hesitant, uncertain, ambivalent ("the juror's doubtful veracity"); questionable, unconvincing, speculative ("The report was of doubtful accuracy").

doubtful title [*dout* · ful *ty* · tel] *n.* **Title** that is open to reasonable doubt; title that will probably cause a purchaser to be involved in litigation.

dower [*dow* · er] *n.* The **legal right** or **interest** that a wife acquires by marriage in the property of her husband. Dower, which was very important under the **common law**, ensured that a widow was able to live upon and make use of a portion of her husband's land, usually a third, as long as she lived. Dower, as such, no longer exists or has been substantially modified in most states, but every state retains aspects of the concept for the protection of both spouses (EXAMPLES: **elective share**; **election** by spouse; **election under the will**). *Note* that "dower" is not "**dowry**." *Compare* curtesy.

downpayment [*down* · pay · ment] *n.* 1. A portion of the purchase price paid at the time of sale or delivery, with the balance to be paid later. 2. An initial sum of money paid when something is purchased on an **installment sale contract**.

dowry [*dow* · ree] *n.* Under the **Code Civil**, the property a woman brings to her husband when she marries.
➤ portion, allotment, settlement.

draconian [dra · *kone* · ee · en] *adj.* Harsh or severe. This term derives from the seventh-century B.C. Athenian statesman Draco, who developed an extremely harsh code of laws.
➤ ruthless, rigid, austere, stringent, uncompromising, strict, brutal ("This calls for draconian measures"). *Ant.* mild.

draconian laws [dra · *kone* · ee · en] *n.* Laws that are unreasonably harsh or severe.

draft *n.* 1. An **order** in writing by one person on another (commonly a bank) to pay a specified sum of money to a third person **on demand** or at a stated future time. EXAMPLES: a check; a **bill of lading**; a **warehouse receipt**. *See* bank draft; documentary draft; overdraft; sight draft; time draft. 2. Compulsory military service. 3. A preliminary version of a document or plan. USAGE: "rough draft"; "first draft."

v. 1. To make a preliminary version of a document. 2. In the case of the **Selective Service System**, to require a person to perform military service.

➤ *n.* money order, check, banknote, negotiable paper ("a bank draft"); version, attempt ("first draft of my brief").

v. frame, draw, prepare, compose ("You must draft your will.").

draftsman [*drafts* · men] *n.* Also called *draftsperson* or *drafter.* 1. A person who prepares a deed, will, or other legal instrument. USAGE: "He is an excellent legal draftsman." 2. A person who draws designs or plans for buildings, other construction, or machines.

➤ creator, designer, inventor, maker, planner.

dragnet clause [*drag* · net] *n.* A mortgage provision that makes the mortgaged property **security** for all of the **mortgagor's** debts to the **mortgagee**, past, existing, and future.

drainage district [*drain* · ej *dis* · trikt] *n.* A territorial division created by government for the purpose of establishing and maintaining a project for the drainage of lands within the district. *See* public corporation; quasi corporation.

dram shop acts *n.* State statutes that make bars and liquor stores liable for **injury** or **damage** caused by persons who become intoxicated from consuming alcoholic beverages they purchased there. *Compare* vicarious liability.

drastic [*dras* · tik] *adj.* Radical in action or effect; severe; extreme.

➤ extreme, radical, desperate, severe, strong, dire, forceful ("drastic measures").

draw *n.* An advance of money to a person (for EXAMPLE, a commission sales person or a partner in a law firm) who has incurred out-of-pocket expenses or who, by virtue of her contract or her work, is expected to produce the money.

v. 1. To prepare a **draft** of a legal document; to draft. 2. To create, make, or sign a **negotiable instrument**. 3. To take or accept an advance. 4. To withdraw money from a bank account.

➤ *n.* extraction, withdrawal, depletion, advance ("I made a draw on my checking account").

v. draft, prepare, make, compose ("draw up the papers"); extract, deplete, exhaust, withdraw ("Do you wish to draw on your savings account?").

Ant. deposit.

draw on *v.* To prepare, sign, and deliver a **draft** for **acceptance**; to **make** a draft. *See* draw; drawee; drawer.

drawback [*draw* · bak] *n.* A disadvantage or shortcoming.

➤ disadvantage, shortcoming, weakness, flaw, hitch, lack, obstacle.

drawee [draw · *ee*] *n.* The person upon whom a **draft** is **drawn**; the person to whom a draft is presented for **acceptance** and payment. The drawee of a check is always a bank. *Compare* drawer.

drawer [draw · *er*] *n.* The **maker** of a **draft**. *Compare* drawee.

drawn *n. See* draw.

Dred Scott case *n.* The famous case of *Scott v. Sanford*, 60 U.S. 393, decided by the Supreme Court in 1857, which ruled that neither slaves nor former slaves were citizens of the United States even if they lived in states where slavery was illegal. This decision was nullified by the **Thirteenth** and **Fourteenth Amendments**.

dress *v.* 1. To put clothes on. 2. To arrange the alignment of. 3. To treat wounds; to sterilize.

n. Clothing; attire.

➤ *v.* clothe, adorn, bedeck, wear, don; adjust, align, straighten, trim; bandage, treat, sterilize, cover, cleanse.

n. clothing, attire, uniform, costume, apparel, appearance, garb.

drivel [*drihv* · ul] *n.* Childish, foolish, or uniportant talk.

➤ nonsense, babble, foolishness, gibberish, rubbish.

driving under the influence (DUI) [*dry* · ving under the *in* · flew · ense] *n.* Same as **driving while intoxicated**.

driving while ability impaired [*dry* · ving while a · *bil* · i · tee im · *pared*] *n.* In some states, the same as **driving while**

D

intoxicated; in others, a lesser offense involving a lower **blood alcohol concentration** than that required for **DWI**.

driving while intoxicated [*dry* · ving while in · *tok* · si · kay · ted] *n.* Often shortened to **DWI**, the crime of operating a motor vehicle while under the influence of alcoholic beverages or drugs. In some jurisdictions, driving while intoxicated may be called either **drunk driving**, **driving under the influence (DUI)**, or **driving while ability impaired (DWAI)**. *See* blood alcohol concentration; breathalyzer; drunk-o-meter; evidential breath test.

drop *v.* 1. To stop worrying about. 2. To trickle out.
n. 1. A small quantity. 2. A descent from higher to lower.
➤ *v.* abandon, desert, quit, relinquish, reject, forsake, cancel; drip, dribble, ooze, trickle.
n. particle; descent, decline, depth.

drug *n.* 1. Any substance used or manufactured for use as a medicine for humans or animals, including over-the-counter and prescriptive preparations. *See* over-the-counter medication; prescription. 2. Any substance, whether manufactured or found in nature, that is used to induce intoxication. As applied in this sense, the word "drug" refers to a substance that (although it may be medicine) has not been prescribed, has either **psychoactive** or addictive qualities, generally causes drug dependency or chemical dependency, and is a **controlled substance**. EXAMPLES: alcohol; marijuana; **amphetamines**; **barbiturates**; cocaine; heroin. *See also* addict; addiction; alcoholism.
➤ medication, compound, remedy, prescription, medicine, dope, pill, pharmaceutical.
drug addict [*ad* · ikt] *n.* *See* addict.
drug addiction [e · *dik* · shen] *n.* *See* drug dependency; chemical dependency.
drug dependency [de · *pen* · den · see] *n.* Habituation or addiction to a drug. *See* chemical dependency.

Drug Enforcement Administration (DEA) [en · *forss* · ment ad · min · is · *tray* · shen] *n.* The law enforcement agency that enforces federal criminal statutes relating to drugs.

drug paraphernalia [pehr · e · fer · *nayl* · ya] *n.* *See* paraphernalia.
drug program [*proh* · gram] *n.* *See* treatment program.

drunk *n.* One who is drunk or impaired by alcohol.
adj. Intoxicated by alcohol.
➤ *n.* alcoholic, inebriate, dipsomaniac, lush, boozer, drunkard.
adj. intoxicated, inebriated, under the influence, saturated, sotted.

drunk driving [*drunk dry* · ving] *n.* *See* driving while intoxicated.

drunk-o-meter [drunk · *omm* · e · ter] *n.* A trade name for an **evidential breath test**.

drunkard [*drunk* · erd] *n.* *See* habitual drunkard.

drunkenness [*drunk* · en · ness] *n.* The condition of a person who is intoxicated. *See* intoxication. *See also* public drunkenness.
➤ inebriation, intoxication, being under the influence.

dry *adj.* 1. Jurisdictions in which it is illegal to sell alcoholic beverages; in some by the bottle or can, in some by the glass, and in some totally. USAGE: "This is a dry county." 2. Nonproductive. 3. Without moisture.
➤ bare, barren, depleted, dull, boring, monotonous, plain, simple, tedious; sober.
dry mortgage [*more* · gej] *n.* A **mortgage** that provides that the **mortgagor** shall have no **personal liability**; i.e., liability for payment of the **mortgage debt** above and beyond the value of the mortgaged property.
dry trust *n.* Same as passive trust.

dual citizenship [*dew* · el sit · i · zen · ship] *n.* The status of a person who is a citizen of two countries, for EXAMPLE, the country of his birth and, if different, the country of which his parents are citizens. *See* citizenship.

dual purpose doctrine [*dew* · el per · pes dok · trin] *n.* If an employee performs a personal errand while traveling on his employer's business, he nonetheless remains in the **course of employment** within the meaning of the law of **agency** if the employer's business was the primary purpose of the travel. The employer is not relieved of liability for any injury to a third person occurring as a result of the employee's **negligence**. *See* deviation doctrine. *Compare* frolic of his own.

duces tecum *[dew · ses tee · kem]* *(Latin) adj.* Means "bring with you." *See* subpoena duces tecum.

due *adj.* 1. Owing; payable. 2. Fitting; suitable.
➤ outstanding, unpaid, collectable ("The loan payment is due"); proper, reasonable, lawful, appropriate, rightful, ready ("due care").

due bill *n.* An acknowledgment of a debt in writing; an IOU.

due care *n.* That degree of care which a person of **ordinary prudence** would exercise in similar circumstances. Same as **ordinary care** or **reasonable care**. *See* care. *See and compare* high degree of care; extraordinary care; slight care.

due course *n.* The ordinary course of events. *See* holder in due course; payment in due course. *See also* ordinary course of business.

due date *n.* The date on which a **promissory note** or other obligation, by its terms, is to be paid or met ("falls due"); **maturity date**.

due diligence *[dil · i · jense]* *n.* Amount of diligence that a reasonable and **prudent person** would exercise under the same circumstances. Same as **ordinary diligence** or **reasonable diligence**. A finding of negligence requires a showing that the defendant did not act with due diligence. *See* diligence; due care.

due notice *[noh · tiss]* *n.* Sufficient notice. In a case where the amount of **notice** to be given is prescribed by law, that amount "due notice," and only such notice is sufficient notice in law.

due process *[pross · ess]* *n. See* due process of law.

due process clause *[pross · ess]* *n.* Actually a reference to two due process clauses, one in the **Fifth Amendment** and one in the **Fourteenth Amendment**. The Fifth Amendment requires the federal government to accord "due process of

law" to citizens of the United States; the Fourteenth Amendment imposes a similar requirement upon state governments. *See* due process of law.

due process hearing *[pross · ess heer · ing]* *n.* An **administrative hearing** held to comply with the **due process clause**. EXAMPLE: a **parole revocation hearing**.

due process of law *[pross · ess]* *n.* Law administered through courts of justice, equally applicable to all under established rules that do not violate fundamental principles of fairness. Whether a person has received due process of law can only be determined on a case-by-case basis. In all criminal cases, however, it involves, at the very least, the right to be heard by a fair and impartial tribunal, the defendant's right to be represented by counsel, the right to cross-examine witnesses against him, the right to offer testimony on his own behalf, and the right to have advance notice of trial and of the charge sufficient in detail and in point of time to permit adequate preparation for trial. Due process requirements for criminal prosecutions are considerably more rigorous than those for civil cases. "Due process of law" is guaranteed by both the **Fifth Amendment** and the **Fourteenth Amendment**. *See* due process clause. *See and compare* procedural due process; substantive due process.

dues *n.* Annual or other regular payments made by a member of a club, union, or association to retain membership. *Compare* initiation fee.
➤ payments, assessments, charges, fees.

DUI Abbreviation of **driving under the influence**.

duly *[dew · lee]* *adv.* When used before any word implying action, "duly" means that the act was done properly, regularly, and according to law. EXAMPLES: "duly authorized"; "duly witnessed"; "duly sworn."
➤ fittingly, properly, rightly, correctly, regularly.

dumb *adj.* 1. Without the power to speak. 2. Lacking in intelligence.
➤ mum, mute, impaired, voiceless; stupid, dense, moronic, idiotic, foolish.

D

D

dummy [*dum* · ee] *n.* A person who poses as acting for himself, but who is, in reality, acting for another who is the **interested person**; a **straw man**. *See also* real party in interest.
➤ stand in, double, duplicate, counterfeit, copy ("a dummy corporation").
Ant. principal.

dummy corporation [kore · per · *ay* · shen] *n.* A **corporation** organized and appearing to act as a corporation, but in reality organized with the motive of avoiding **personal liability** and having no legitimate corporate purpose.

dumping [*dum* · ping] *n.* 1. The sale in the United States of foreign merchandise at less than its fair value, a practice prohibited by federal statutes known as **dumping acts**. 2. Cutting the price of merchandise for a quick sale. 3. Disposing of trash, garbage, or other solid waste by putting it in a land-fill or dump. The management of solid waste is regulated by the **Environmental Protection Agency** in conjunction with state and local authorities.

dumping acts *n. See* dumping.

dun *v.* To demand payment of a debt, particularly an overdue debt.
➤ urge, press, insist, importune, besiege.

dupe *v.* To trick or deceive.
➤ deceive, defraud, overreach, outwit, fool, hoodwink, con, rip off.

duplicate [*dew* · pli · ket] *n.* 1. An exact reproduction of anything, whether achieved by making an impression (EXAMPLE: carbon paper), by photography (EXAMPLE: photo-stating), or by any other means. *Compare* copy. 2. A double or twin of anything.
v. [*dew* · pli · kate] To make an exact copy of something.
➤ *n.* replica, twin, copy, facsimile, reproduction.
Ant. original.
v. reproduce, replicate, copy, clone.

duplicity in pleading [dew · *pliss* · e · tee in *plee* · ding] *n. See* double pleading.

durable [*dew* · rebl] *adj.* Lasting; enduring; ongoing; permanent; continuing.
➤ lasting, enduring, ongoing, permanent, sturdy, strong, hardy, sound, tough.

durable power of attorney [*pow* · er of a · *tern* · ee] *n.* A **power of attorney** that remains effective even though the **grantor** becomes mentally incapacitated. Some durable powers of attorney become effective *only* when a person is no longer able to make decisions for herself.
EXAMPLES: A **healthcare proxy**; a **living will**. *See* advance directive. *See also* mental disability; mental incapacity.

duration [dew · *ray* · shen] *n.* The period of time during which a thing exists.
➤ extent, tenure, span, term, course, while, phase.

duress [dew · *ress*] *n.* Coercion applied for the purpose of compelling a person to do, or to refrain from doing, some act. (EXAMPLE: threatening to burn down a person's house in order to make her sign a contract.) Duress may be a **defense** in a civil action. (EXAMPLE: a contract entered into under duress is **voidable**.) Duress may also be a defense to a criminal prosecution if the defendant committed the crime out of a well-grounded fear of death or serious bodily harm. *See* coercion; intimidation; undue influence.
➤ oppression, force, subjection, constraint, coercion, pressure, compulsion.
Ant. free will, volition.

Durham rule [*doo* · rem] *n.* A test for establishing **insanity** for the purpose of a **defense** to criminal prosecution, in some jurisdictions. Under this test, a defendant's criminal responsibility is determined on the basis of whether his unlawful act was the result or "product" of "**mental disease** or **mental defect**." The *Durham defense* is similar to the **irresistible impulse** defense. *Compare* M'Naghten rule.

duty [*dew* · tee] *n.* 1. A **legal obligation**, whether imposed by the **common law**, statute, court order, or contract. USAGE: "When a **right** is invaded, a **duty** is vio-lated." A **tort** is committed only when there has been a **breach of duty** resulting in **injury**. 2. Any obligation or responsibility. 3. A tax upon the importation of goods into a country or upon the goods imported.
➤ responsibility, requirement, role, assignment, charge, mandatory act, pledge, obligation; tax, import tax.

duty of detraction [dee · *trak* · shen] *n.* A duty or tax imposed on **legacies** received by aliens and residents of other states.

duty of tonnage *n.* *See* tonnage duty.

DWAI *n.* Abbreviation of and short for **driving while ability impaired**.

dwell *v.* 1. To live in; to reside; to occupy. 2. To linger over or be engrossed in.

➤ reside, remain, inhabit, live, stay, occupy; prolong, linger, continue, brood over.

dwelling [*dwel* · ing] *n.* A house or other shelter in which people live.

➤ residence, home, habitation, shelter, quarters, abode.

DWI Abbreviation of and short for **driving while intoxicated**.

dying [*die* · ing] *adj.* Approaching death or an end.

➤ expiring, passing, deteriorating, declining, waning, receding, obsolete ("a dying doctrine").

dying declaration [*dy* · ing dek · le · *ray* · shen] *n.* A statement made by the victim of a homicide when he is about to die, and has no hope of recovery, concerning the circumstances under which his injury was inflicted. A dying declaration is admissible as an **exception to the hearsay rule**. *See* hearsay; hearsay rule.

dying without issue [*dy* · ing without *ish* · ew] *n.* *See* die without issue.

D

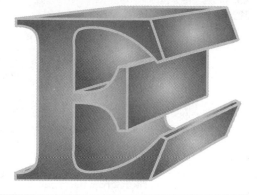

e.g. (*Latin*) Abbreviation of *exempli gratia*, meaning "for the sake of an example"; for example. USAGE: "There are many kinds of negotiable instruments, e.g., checks, promissory notes, drafts and certificates of deposit."

eager [*eeg* · ur] *adj.* Marked by enthusiasm.
➤ willing, interested, aspiring, excited, ready, passionate, pushy, desirous, voracious, enthusiastic.
Ant. reluctant, inhibited.

EAP Abbreviation of **employee assistance program**.

earmark [*eer* · mark] *n.* A distinctive characteristic.
➤ feature, label, mark, symbol, sign, trademark, identification, stamp, attribute.

earmarked [*ear* · markt] *adv.* Set aside for a specific purpose; money, goods, or other property that has been identified in some manner so that it can be distinguished from other things of the same sort. USAGE: "Don't sell those; they have been earmarked for charity."

earn *v.* 1. To make money. 2. To deserve.
➤ gain, draw, win, acquire ("earn wages"); deserve, merit, rate ("earn the promotion").

earned [urnd] *adj.* 1. Received as a result of labor or service. 2. Merited; deserved. 3. Gained; acquired.

earned income [*in* · kum] *n.* Income received for work or for the performance of some service. *Compare* unearned income.

earned income credit [*in* · kum *kred* · it] *n.* A tax credit on **earned income** for low income workers with dependent children,

as defined by the **Internal Revenue Code**.

earned premium [*pree* · mee · um] *n.* Portion of a premium payment that relates to coverage for a period for which the **carrier** is presently responsible, as opposed to coverage for a period which has not yet occurred. EXAMPLE: With respect to a $500 premium paid for a year's fire insurance, after six months the earned premium is approximately $250; at that point, the **unearned premium** is also approximately $250, because insurance premiums are paid in advance.

earned surplus [*ser* · plus] *n.* Portion of a corporation's **surplus** derived from **undivided profits**. *See also* accumulated surplus; capital surplus.

earnest [*ur* · nest] *adj.* Intense; enthusiastic; serious.
➤ sincere, diligent, serious, resolute, conscientious, intent, purposeful, impassioned, heartfelt.
Ant. insincere, dishonest.

earnest money [*er* · nest *mun* · ee] *n.* A downpayment of part of the **purchase price** made to bind the bargain; a deposit.
➤ deposit, installment, downpayment, retainer, pledge.

earning capacity [*er* · ning ke · *pass* · i · tee] *n.* A person's ability to earn money. Earning capacity is an element considered in measuring **damages** recoverable for **personal injury**.

earnings [*er* · ningz] *n.* 1. A person's gains from her services or labor; that which

E

gainful employment yields; wages. 2. Profits from the investment of **capital**. *See* future earnings; net earnings.

➤ salary, profits, wages, revenue, proceeds. *Ant.* losses.

earnings per share *n.* The amount of the annual dividend on a share of **common stock**.

easement [*eez* · ment] *n.* 1. A right to use the land of another for a specific purpose. EXAMPLE: a **right of way** given by a land-owner to a utility company to erect and maintain power lines. 2. A right to use water, light, or air. *See* easement of light and air. *Also see* affirmative easement; apparent easement; continuous easement; discontinuous easement; express easement; implied easement; negative easement; prescriptive easement; public easement; secondary easement.

➤ privilege, liberty, servitude, advantage, right of way.

easement appendant [a · *pen* · dent] *n.* Same as **appurtenant easement**.

easement appurtenant [a · *per* · te · nent] *n.* *See* appurtenant easement.

easement by implication [im · pli · *kay* · shen] *n.* *See* implied easement.

easement by prescription [pre · *skrip* · shen] *n.* *See* prescriptive easement.

easement in gross *n.* As contrasted with an **appurtenant easement**, an easement in gross does not exist so that the owner of adjoining property may better enjoy his property; rather, it is a personal interest in the use of another's land, unrelated to his own. (EXAMPLE: a right to take water from the property of another.) An easement in gross may be a right in either real property or personal property, depending upon its intended duration. *See and compare* dominant tenement; servient tenement.

easement of access [*ak* · sess] *n.* The right of an owner of real property bordering a public road to come from and go to the highway without being obstructed. *See* way of necessity.

easement of light and air *n.* An easement for the enjoyment of light and air unobstructed by structures on the adjoining premises. *See* ancient lights.

easement of necessity [ne · *sess* · i · tee] *n.* *See* way of necessity.

eavesdropping [*eevs* · drah · ping] *n.* 1. The crime of hanging about or entering a person's home for the purpose of covertly listening to conversation. 2. Wiretapping; i.e., electronic eavesdropping.

➤ listening, snooping, prying, spying, wiretapping, bugging.

EBT *n.* Abbreviation of **evidential breath test**.

economic [ek · e · *nom* · ik] *adj.* Relating to the production, distribution, or consumption of wealth.

➤ financial, monetary, pecuniary, fiscal.

economic strike [ek · e · *nom* · ik] *n.* A strike for the purpose of bringing about changes in wages, hours, or other conditions of employment. Economic strikers have fewer legal protections than **unfair labor practice** strikers.

edge *n.* 1. A favorable margin. 2. A section adjacent to a border.

➤ benefit, lead, advantage, odds ("He has an edge over his opponent."); border, fringe, rim, boundary, limit, bounds ("the edge of his property").

edict [*ee* · dikt] *n.* A command or prohibition proclaimed by a **sovereign** and having the effect of law.

➤ order, regulation, ordinance, mandate, injunction, pronouncement, dictate, judgment, law. *Ant.* suggestion.

educate [*ed* · joo · kate] *v.* To train by formal instruction.

➤ instruct, prepare, teach, guide, direct, inform, train, tutor.

education [ed · joo · *kay* · shun] *n.* The process of developing knowledge.

➤ knowledge, learning, preparation, schooling, training, erudition, guidance, scholarship, instruction.

EEOC Abbreviation of **Equal Employment Opportunity Commission**.

effect [e · *fekt*] *n.* 1. Outcome; result; consequence. 2. Power to bring about a result. 3. Impression. *Note* that "effect" is not "**affect**" or "**effects**." *See also* in effect; legal effect.

v. To cause; to bring about; to accomplish; to produce. *Note* that to "effect" is not to "**affect**."
➤ *n.* outcome, result, consequence, aftermath, impression.
v. cause, enforce, execute, produce, create, initiate.

effective [e · *fekt* · iv] *adj.* 1. In force; in effect; in operation. 2. Proficient or skillful.
➤ useful, practical, accomplished, productive, adequate, proficient, functional, pragmatic.

effective assistance of counsel [e · *sis* · tense of *koun* · sel] *n.* *See* right to counsel.

effective date *n.* The date when a statute becomes law or a contract or other legal obligation becomes binding.

effects [e · *fekts*] *n.* 1. One's belongings, especially things of a personal nature; personal effects. 2. Personal property, although the term is sometimes loosely used to mean both real property and personal property. The word "effects," when used in a will, has generally been construed to mean personal effects, but, depending upon context, it has also been construed to mean all of the personal property owned by the **testator**.
➤ belongings, possessions, holdings, personalty, goods, assets, resources.

effectuate [e · *fek* · tyoo · ate] *v.* To carry out; to put into effect.
➤ enforce, cause, enact, execute.

efficient [e · *fish* · ent] *adj.* 1. Able to produce a result. 2. Capable; competent.
➤ competent, productive, capable, effective, timesaving.
Ant. ineffective, unproductive.

efficient cause *n.* In the law of negligence, the act or omission that directly brought about the occurrence which inflicted **injury** and resulted in liability. *See* procuring cause. *See also* proximate cause.

efficient intervening cause [in · ter · *vee* · ning] *n.* Same as **intervening cause**.

effort [*ef* · urt] *n.* An exertion of power to accomplish a goal.
➤ energy, exertion, vigor, work, assiduity, arduousness, undertaking.

egress [*ee* · gress] *n.* A passage out; an exit.
➤ exit, escape, way out, outlet.

eight-hour laws [*ate*-our] *n.* Federal and state statutes that limit the number of hours most types of employees may work during a 24-hour period. The federal act known as the **Fair Labor Standards Act** requires overtime pay after eight hours, as do some state acts. *See* wage and hour laws.

Eighteenth Amendment [*ay* · teenth e · *mend* · ment] *n.* The Eighteenth Amendment to the Constitution, adopted in 1919, prohibited the manufacture, sale, or importation of alcoholic beverages. It is known as the Prohibition Amendment. It was repealed in 1933 by the **Twenty-first Amendment**.

Eighth Amendment [e · *mend* · ment] *n.* Part of the **Bill of Rights**, the Eighth Amendment forbids excessive bail, excessive fines, and **cruel and unusual punishment**.

eject [ee · *jekt*] *v.* 1. To throw out from within. 2. To drive out with force.
➤ remove, throw out, dislodge, displace; oust, expel, jettison, discard.

ejectment [ee · *jekt* · ment] *n.* An **action at common law** for the right to possession of land. *See also* forcible detainer; forcible entry and detainer.

ejusdem generis [ee · *jus* · dem *jen* · e · ris] (*Latin*) *adj.* Of the same kind or class.

ejusdem generis rule *n.* The rule of construction that when things are enumerated in a document (such as a contract, will, or statute), followed by a more general description, the general description will be understood to relate only to things similar in kind to those enumerated.

elder [*el* · dur] *n.* 1. A person who is older. 2. A leader.
adj. Older.
➤ *n.* senior, veteran, chief, superior, leader.
adj. older, superior, preceding ("my elder brother").

elder abuse [*el* · der a · *byooss*] *n.* The physical, sexual, verbal, or emotional abuse or neglect of an elderly person.

elect [e · *lekt*] *v.* 1. To make a choice. 2. To select a person for office by a majority vote or a **plurality vote**.
➤ choose, accept, decide, conclude, determine, opt for.
Ant. reject, appoint.

election [e · *lek* · shen] *n.* 1. The expression of a choice by eligible voters of persons to fill public, corporate, or other office. *See* at large election; general election; representation election; special election. 2. Choosing between two or more rights which are so inconsistent that the choice of one eliminates the possibility of choosing the other or others. EXAMPLE: when the law gives a taxpayer a choice of two methods of computing a tax, and she chooses one, she cannot also choose the other. 3. Any exercise of choice.
➤ selection, designation, choice, nomination.
Ant. rejection.

election between dower and will [be · *tween dow* · er] *n. See* election by spouse.

election by spouse *n.* The doctrine that forces a surviving spouse to an election between his or her **statutory share** of the property of the deceased spouse and the benefits provided by the will. *See* election under the will; elective share. *See also* curtesy; dower.

election contest [*kon* · test] *n.* Also referred to as a *contested election*; occurs when objection is made to the manner in which an election was conducted, which objection, if proven, would cause the election to be invalidated.

election district [*dis* · trikt] *n.* A territorial unit of a state, county, or city established with respect to various offices, national or local, to be filled by election.

election of defenses [de · *fense* · ez] *n.* The doctrine, applicable to both civil actions and criminal prosecutions, that a defendant is required to elect a specific **defense** upon which he will rely.

election of remedies [*rem* · e · deez] *n.* 1. A requirement often present in the law that a **party** to a lawsuit must choose between two or more different types of **relief** allowed by law on the same set of facts. The adoption of one has the effect of barring use of the others. *See* remedy. *Also see* waiver by election. 2. The act of choosing between two or more different types of relief allowed by law on the same set of facts.

election precinct [*pree* · sinkt] *n. See* election district.

election under the will [*un* · der] *n.* The doctrine that a person who is given a benefit (a **legacy** or **devise**) under a will must choose between that benefit and any interest in the **testator's** property granted to him by statute. *See* election by spouse; elective share; statutory share.

electioneering [e · *lek* · shen · *eer* · ing] *n.* The solicitation of votes. It is a criminal offense when conducted at certain times and places on election day.

elective [e · *lek* · tiv] *adj.* 1. Pertaining to election to office, or to offices that must be filled by election. 2. Optional; **discretionary**.
➤ optional, discretionary, nonobligatory, voluntary, facilitative.
Ant. mandatory, obligatory.

elective franchise [*fran* · chize] *n.* The right to vote.

elective share *n.* In some states, the **share** a surviving spouse may elect to take in the **estate** of the deceased spouse. In such jurisdictions, it replaces **dower**. An elective share is also referred to as a **statutory share**. *See* election by spouse; election under the will.

elector [e · *lek* · ter] *n.* 1. An eligible voter. *See* registered voter. 2. A **presidential elector**, that is, a member of the **electoral college**.
➤ voter, representative, proxy, stand-in, delegate.

electoral college [e · *lek* · te · rel *koll* · ej] *n.* The body empowered by the Constitution to elect the president and vice president of United States, composed of **presidential electors** chosen by the voters at each presidential election. In practice, however, the electoral college votes in accordance with the popular vote.

electronic eavesdropping [ih · lek · *tron* · ik eevs · drah · ping] *n. See* eavesdropping; wiretapping.

electronic surveillance [ih · lek · *tron* · ik ser · *vale* · enss] *n.* *See* eavesdropping; wiretapping.

eleemosynary [el · ee · e · *moss* · en · er · ee] *adj.* Charitable.

➤ nonprofit, generous, charitable, altruistic, humanitarian ("an eleemosynary institution"). *Ant.* commercial.

eleemosynary corporation [kore · per · *ay* · shen] *n.* Same as **charitable corporation**.

eleemosynary purpose [*per* · pes] *n.* Same as **charitable purpose**.

elegant [el · e · *gant*] *adj.* Of high quality or value.

➤ formal, beautiful, cultivated, classy, dignified.

element [*el* · e · ment] *n.* A component or essential part of something. EXAMPLE: **fraudulent conversion** is an essential element of the crime of embezzlement.

➤ part, portion, section, substance, segment, member, feature, ingredient ("an element needed to prove negligence").

elementary [el · e · *men* · tree] *adj.* Dealing with the simplest principles of.

➤ basic, simple, primary, easy, foundational, obvious, rudimentary ("Elementary, my dear Watson!").

elevation [el · e · *vay* · shun] *n.* 1. The height above a given level. 2. A rise in stature or class.

➤ rise, altitude, steepness; advancement, stature, coronation, sanctification, eminence.

Eleventh Amendment [e · *lev* · enth a · *mend* · ment] *n.* An amendment to the Constitution that prohibits the federal courts from hearing lawsuits brought against a state by a person who is not a citizen of that state.

eligibility [el · e · je · *bil* · e · tee] *n.* The status of a person or thing that is eligible for something.

➤ suitability, acceptability, worthiness, preference ("eligibility for the NFL draft"). *Ant.* unacceptability.

eligibility determination [de · ter · min · *ay* · shen] *n.* A decision by an administrative agency with respect to a person's entitlement to a benefit administered by the agency (EXAMPLE: unemployment

compensation benefits). *See* determination; initial determination.

eligible [*el* · e · jibl] *adj.* Qualified; fit; suitable. EXAMPLE: Legally qualified to be appointed or elected to public office. *See* eligibility.

➤ fit, proper, qualified, acceptable, suitable, worthy, satisfactory.

eligible voter [*voh* · ter] *n.* A person who is entitled to vote, having met all legal requirements such as minimum age and residency; a **qualified voter**. *See* registered voter.

eliminate [e · *lim* · i · nayt] *v.* 1. To disqualify or eject. 2. To do away with or end.

➤ disallow, prohibit, exempt, expel, disregard, disqualify, oust; eradicate, demolish, stamp out, exterminate, expurgate, obliterate.

elisor [e · *lie* · zer] *n.* A person appointed to perform duties of a sheriff or coroner when such an official is disqualified or unable to act.

elite [e · *leet*] *adj.* Best; choice; selected. *n.* A small, select, and powerful group; high-class people.

➤ *adj.* select, noble, privileged, choice, top flight, first class, aristocratic ("an elite group").
n. select group, upper class, aristocracy, gentry, nobility, high society, privileged class ("to be a member of the elite").

elude [e · *lood*] *v.* To avoid, flee, or escape.

➤ evade, escape, flee, outwit, avoid ("elude the police").

emancipated minor [e · *man* · si · pay · ted *mine* · er] *n.* A person who has not yet attained the **age of majority** who is totally self-supporting or married. A parent emancipates his minor child when he surrenders control and authority over the child and gives her the right to her earnings. Emancipation also terminates the parent's legal duty to support the minor child. *See* emancipation.

emancipation [e · man · si · *pay* · shen] *n.* 1. Release of a minor from parental control. *See* emancipated minor. 2. Liberation from slavery. 3. The act of freeing or liberating.

➤ liberation, discharge, release, unletting, unbridling. *Ant.* subjugation, servitude.

E

E

embargo [em · *bar* · goh] *n.* 1. An order of government forbidding the entry or departure of a particular country's ships or planes, sometimes imposed in carrying on war, at other times imposed in control of trade. 2. An order of government forbidding the importation of a specified commodity from a particular foreign country.
➤ restriction, prohibition, stoppage, detention, blockade.

embarrass [em · *barr* · as] *v.* To cause a state of self-conscious distress.
➤ fluster, upset, disquiet, mortify, humiliate, shame, abash, annoy, disconcert.

embassy [*em* · be · see] *n.* 1. An ambassador and his staff; those persons representing their government in a foreign country. 2. The residence and headquarters of an ambassador.
➤ delegation, consulate, legation, commission, committee.

embezzlement [em · *bezl* · ment] *n.* The **fraudulent conversion** of property, including but not limited to money, with which a person (EXAMPLES: an employee; a **bailee**; a **trustee**) has been entrusted.
➤ abstraction, misappropriation, misuse, theft, larceny, defalcation, peculation, pilferage.

emblements [*em* · bul · ments] *n.* Corn, wheat, rye, potatoes, garden vegetables, and other crops produced annually through labor. A tenant whose labor has produced emblements has the right to carry them away after the **tenancy** ends.
➤ crop, output, production, produce, yield.

embody [em · *bod* · ee] *v.* 1. To include in a document, **instrument**, statute, or other writing. USAGE: "Our contract fully embodies our deal." 2. To include or incorporate as a part of something.
➤ include, incorporate, blend, assimilate, contain; represent, personify, epitomize, show, symbolize, typify.

embrace [em · *brays*] *v.* 1. To take in and include as part of a whole. 2. To enclose in one's arms ("to embrace a point of view").
➤ adopt, endorse, sanction, comprehend; caress, hold, hug ("to embrace a person").

embracery [em · *bray* · se · ree] *n.* The crime of attempting to corrupt, influence, instruct, or induce a jury in any way, except by the evidence and the arguments of counsel in open court, to be more favorable to one side of a case than the other. *See* obstructing justice.

embryo transplantation [*em* · bree · oh tranz · plan · *tay* · shen] *n.* A medical technique that involves the implantation of a fertilized embryo in a woman's womb with the goal of having her carry it to term and giving birth. *See also* in vitro fertilization; surrogate motherhood.

emend [i · *mend*] *v.* 1. To edit errors from a document. 2. To correct.
➤ correct, improve, edit, amend.

emergency [e · *mer* · jen · see] *n.* A sudden, extremely important, and unexpected occurrence.
➤ urgency, extremity, jam, predicament, distress, plight, squeeze, exigency.

emergency doctrine [*dok* · trin] *n. See* sudden emergency doctrine.

emergency treatment [*treat* · ment] *n.* Medical treatment, including surgery, may be undertaken in an emergency, without consent, for an unconscious adult or for a child, if no one is available who is legally capable of giving consent.

eminent domain [*em* · i · nent doh · *main*] *n.* The power of the government to take private property for a public use or public purpose without the owner's consent, if it pays just compensation. The process by which this is done is called **condemnation**. *Also see* expropriation; taking.
➤ condemnation, expropriation, compulsory acquisition.

emission [ee · *mish* · en] *n.* 1. Something that is discharged. (EXAMPLE: fumes discharged from the exhaust system of an automobile.) Many emissions, including those from vehicles, factories, and backdoor barbecues, are air pollutants and are regulated by the **Environmental Protection Agency** in conjunction with state and local authorities. *See* pollution. 2. The act of issuing or sending forth.
➤ discharge, exhalation, issue, transmission, venting, leakage, expulsion.
Ant. reception.

emoluments [e · *moll* · yoo · ments] *n.*
1. Gain received from holding office, including salary, fees, and **perquisites**.
2. Gain, including wages or salary, received from any employment.
➤ wages, benefits, gain, reward, earnings, allowance.

empanel [em · *pan* · el] *v.* Same as **impanel**.

empirical [em · *pihr* · ih · kul] *adj.* 1. Relying on observation alone. 2. Able to be proven or disproven through observation.
➤ experimental, sensed, verified, concrete, scientific.
Ant. speculative, theoretical.

empiricism [em · *peer* · e · sizm] *n.* Searching for knowledge by experiment rather than by attempting to apply theoretical principles.

employ [em · *ploy*] *v.* 1. To enter into a contract of employment; to hire. 2. To use.
➤ hire, retain, recruit, engage, appoint ("to employ workers"); use, utilize, practice, consume, handle, exercise ("to employ a technique").

employee [em · *ploy* · ee] *n.* A person who works for another for pay in a relationship that allows the other person to control the work and direct the manner in which it is done. The earlier legal term for employee was **servant**. *Compare* independent contractor. *Also compare* agent.
Note that statutory definitions of "employee" may differ, depending upon the purpose of the statute. For EXAMPLE, although the distinctions between the definitions of employee in the **Social Security Act**, the **Fair Labor Standards Act**, and the **National Labor Relations Act** may seem insignificant, they may, in any given instance, be critical.
➤ servant, worker, agent, laborer, helper, personnel, jobholder.

employee assistance program
[e · *sis* · tense *proh* · gram] *n.* An employer-sponsored program, often in conjunction with an insurance company or a **health maintenance organization**, which provides treatment referrals for employees impaired or disabled by chemical dependency or other problems requiring counseling services. It is often referred to by its abbreviation, **EAP**.

Employee Retirement Income Security Act
[em · *ploy* · ee re · *tire* · ment *in* · kum se · *kyoo* · re · tee] *n.* Better known by its acronym, **ERISA**; a federal statute that protects employee pensions by regulating pension plans maintained by private employers, the way in which such plans are funded, and their **vesting** requirements. ERISA has important tax implications for both employers and employees. *See* vested pension.

employer [em · *ploy* · er] *n.* A person who hires another to work for her for pay in a relationship that allows her to control the work and direct the manner in which it is done. The earlier legal term for employer was **master**.
➤ master, contractor, director, boss, chief.
Ant. employee, servant, agent.

employers' liability acts [em · *ploy* · erz ly · e · *bil* · i · tee] *n.* Now called **workers' compensation acts**. Employers' liability acts abolished or substantially restricted the **defenses** previously available to an employer (EXAMPLES: **contributory negligence; assumption of risk**) when an employee brought suit for an injury incurred on the job. *See also* Federal Employees' Liability Act (FELA).

employment [em · *ploy* · ment] *n.* 1. The relationship between an employee and an employer. *See* course of employment; full-time employment; part-time employment; scope of employment. 2. That which occupies a person's time. *Compare* gainful employment.
➤ livelihood, service, business, trade, vocation, occupation, job, profession, work.

employment at will *n.* A hiring for an indefinite period of time. In the absence of an agreement to the contrary, all employment is **at will** and either the employer or the employee may terminate it at any time.

en [on] (*French*) *prep.* In; into; on. The word *en* introduces various French phrases used in the law.

en banc [*bonk*] *prep.* Means "on the bench." A court, particularly an **appellate court**, with all the judges sitting together (*sitting en banc*) in a case. *See also* full bench.

enable [en · *ay* · bul] *v.* To make possible.
➤ empower, facilitate, endow, legalize, capacitate.

enabling [en · *ay* · bling] *adj.* That which empowers one to do something he would otherwise not have the power to do.

enabling act *n.* 1. A statute that grants new powers or authority to persons or corporations. 2. A statute that gives the government the power to enforce other legislation or that carries out a provision of a constitution. The term also applies to a clause in a statute granting the government the power to enforce or carry out that statute. Such a provision is called an **enabling clause**.

enabling clause *n. See* enabling act.

enabling legislation [lej · is · *lay* · shen] *n. See* enabling act.

enact [en · *akt*] *v.* 1. To pass a statute; to create **statutory law**. 2. To establish by law; to decree. 3. To perform; to effect. *See* enactment.
➤ codify, decree, command, establish, dictate, proclaim, execute.
Ant. repeal.

enacting clause [en · *akt* · ing] *n.* Portion of a statute that proclaims the authority by which it is enacted. EXAMPLE: "Be it enacted by the legislature of the State of New York, as follows."

enactment [en · *akt* · ment] *n.* 1. A statute. 2. The process by which a legislative **bill** becomes law.
➤ legislation, law, act, rule, ordinance, measure, statute.

encourage [en · *kerr* · ej] *v.* 1. To abet; to incite; to induce. 2. To support; to give hope; to hearten.
➤ advocate, approve, assist, boost, enliven, excite.
Ant. deter.

encroachment [en · *kroach* · ment] *n.* 1. An intrusion upon the land of another, or upon a highway or sidewalk, by occupying it, fencing or walling in a portion of it, or erecting a structure that protrudes into it. USAGE: "The sign over your store is much too large; it is an encroachment upon the sidewalk." *See* continuing trespass; trespass. 2. Infringement; intrusion.

➤ invasion, wrong, violation, infringement, trespass.

encumber [en · *kum* · ber] *v.* To obligate; to burden; to create an **encumbrance**.
➤ burden, hinder, block, cramp, hamper, retard.
Ant. unburden.

encumbrance [en · *kum* · brenss] *n.* 1. An interest in land that exists in someone other than the owner of the land. It reduces the value of the land, but does not prevent the owner from transferring **marketable title**. EXAMPLES: a **lien**; a mortgage; an **easement**. 2. Any hindrance or impediment.
➤ lien, charge, liability, impediment, claim, easement.

end *n.* 1. The goal which one undertakes. 2. The point that marks the close of something.
v. To reach a conclusion.
➤ *n.* aim, idea, target, goal, intent ("the ends of justice"); close, termination, fulfillment, conclusion, consummation, finish ("the end of my questions for this witness").
v. close, terminate, destroy; result, conclude.

endangered [en · *dane* · jerd] *adj.* Threatened with extinction or harm.
➤ imperiled, jeopardized, threatened, unprotected.

endangered species [en · *dane* · jerd *spee* · seez] *n.* Wildlife that is in danger of becoming extinct through all or a significant portion of its range. A succession of federal statutes provide for the conservation and restoration of endangered wildlife and prohibit various kinds of acts that are harmful to endangered species.

endorse [en · *dorse*] *v.* To inscribe with a title; to sign one's name to in order to obtain money. *See and compare* endorsement; indorse; indorsement.
➤ advocate, affirm, approve, certify, confirm, guarantee.

endorsement [en · *dorse* · ment] *n.* Same as **indorsement**, with the same meaning. When the word is used in the law (that is, in court opinions and statutes), particularly with respect to **negotiable instruments**, it is generally spelled with an *i*, whereas when it occurs in literature and other

E

nonlegal contexts it usually begins with an *e*. *Carefully read* indorsement.

➤ affirmation, approval, favor, qualification, recommendation, advocacy.

endowment [en · *dow* · ment] *n.* A gift of real or personal property to an institution, such as a college or a library, for its permanent support.

➤ award, benefit, bequest, donation, grant, property, funding.

endowment insurance [in · *shoor* · ense] *n.* A life insurance policy that provides for payment to the insured of the **face value** of the policy after a specified number of years, but to another named person if the insured dies before payment is due to be made.

enfeoffment [en · *feff* · ment] *n.* The act of giving a person ownership and possession of a **fee**, that is, ownership and possession of an **estate in land**.

enforce [en · *forss*] *v.* To put into effect; to carry out.

➤ administer, apply, dictate, execute, fortify. *Ant.* disregard.

enforceable [en · *forss* · ebl] *adj.* That which can be put into effect or carried out, referring to legal rights. EXAMPLES: a contract; a judgment. *Compare* unenforceable.

➤ binding, lawful, effective. *Ant.* unenforceable, void.

enforcement [en · *forss* · ment] *n.* 1. The act of putting the law into effect or of making sure that the law is carried out. 2. Short for law enforcement authorities. 3. Putting anything into effect.

➤ execution, administration, fulfillment, management, obligation. *Ant.* waiver.

Enforcement of Foreign Judgments Act [en · *forss* · ment of *for* · en juj · ments] *n.* A **Uniform Law**, the purpose of which is to give to the **holder** of a **foreign judgment** the same **rights** and **remedies** as the holder of a **domestic judgment**. *See* full faith and credit; judgment.

enfranchise [en · *fran* · chize] *v.* 1. To give a person a right or a privilege. *See* franchise. 2. To permit a person to vote. *Compare* disenfranchise.

➤ liberate, entitle, authorize. *Ant.* encumber.

engage [en · *gayj*] *v.* 1. To actively take part in something. 2. To hire someone. 3. To compete in an athletic event or to do battle with an enemy.

➤ undertake, involve, participate, entertain ("to engage in a particular activity"); hire, appoint, obtain, secure ("They engaged the services of a maid to help with the party"); fight, combat, compete, contest ("The combatants engaged one another fiercely during the competition").

engaged in commerce [en · *gayjd* in *kom* · erss] *adv.* A reference to the power of Congress, under Article I of the Constitution, to regulate businesses engaged in **interstate commerce**.

engrossment [en · *grose* · ment] *n.* 1. Drafting, in final form, a legislative **bill** that is ready to be enacted into a statute. 2. The act of copying any document in final form. *See* ingrossing. 3. Buying up large quantities of a **commodity** in order to control the market. *Also see* abbrochment; monopoly.

enhanced [en · *hanst*] *adj.* Increased, especially in value.

➤ strengthened, intensified, augmented, enlarged. *Ant.* depreciated.

enigma [un · *nig* · muh] *n.* Something that is difficult to understand; a mystery.

➤ puzzle, mystery, paradox, confusion, problem, perplexity, riddle, conundrum.

enjoin [en · *joyn*] *v.* 1. To restrain by **injunction**. 2. To forbid. 3. To command; to order.

➤ command, direct, charge, decree, ordain, exact, forestall, frustrate.

enjoy [en · *joy*] *v.* 1. To own or possess. USAGE: "He enjoyed a high standard of living." 2. To derive pleasure from.

➤ own, hold, keep, maintain, partake; like, love, appreciate, savor, relish.

enjoyment [en · *joy* · ment] *n.* 1. The ability to exercise a right, for EXAMPLE, use, possession, or ownership. *See* covenant for quiet enjoyment. 2. Receiving substantial economic benefit from property without necessarily having **title**. *See* beneficial enjoyment. 3. Pleasure; fun; satisfaction.

E

➤ satisfaction, amusement, gratification, fun, diversion, use, tenancy, usage. *Ant.* loathing.

enlargement [en · *larj* · ment] *n.* 1. An extension of time granted to a **party** to comply with a requirement of law or an order of court. Thus, for EXAMPLE, a **motion for enlargement of time** is a formal request that the court grant additional time for an appeal. See motion. 2. An increase in size; an expansion.

➤ appreciation, growth, increase, augmentation, amplification, extension, exaggeration.

enlargement of time *n.* See enlargement.

Enoch Arden statutes [*ee* · nok *ar* · den *stat* · shoot] *n.* Legislation that creates a presumption of death when a person, particularly a spouse, has been absent for an extended period of time. *See* seven years' absence.

enroll [en · *role*] *v.* 1. To enter upon the record; to register. *See* roll. 2. To sign up.

➤ impanel, engage, inscribe, catalogue, chronicle, list, register, matriculate.

enrolled bill [en · *rold*] *n.* A **bill** that has been enacted by both houses of the legislature.

enrolled bill rule *n.* The rule that there is a **conclusive presumption** that an enrolled bill was properly enacted, and therefore the courts will not adjudicate that question or concern themselves with technical errors that may exist with respect to the statute.

ensue [en · *soo*] *v.* To follow or come after, usually in some predictable order.

➤ follow, develop, happen, transpire, proceed.

ensure [en · *shoor*] *v.* Same as **insure**.

entail [en · *tail*] *v.* 1. To create an **estate** with a limitation upon succession, i.e., a **fee tail**. 2. To involve. USAGE: "The trial of a lawsuit entails a great deal of preparation."

➤ demand, obligate, necessitate, impose, involve, require, encompass.

entanglement [en · *tang* · gul · ment] *n.* 1. A predicament. 2. Something which is complicated and confusing.

➤ dilemma, predicament, problem, strait; confusion, disorder, chaos, tumult, disarray.

enter [en · ter] *v.* 1. To go into. EXAMPLES: to enter a house in order to take possession; to enter a building in order to commit a **felony**. *See* breaking and entering. 2. To make a note of something; to make an entry of any kind. *See* book of original entry. 3. To make a record; to put something **on the record**. EXAMPLE: a guilty plea. 4. To register for a competition. *See* entry.

➤ go into, board, insert, set foot, arrive, penetrate, infiltrate ("She entered into a binding agreement"); post, list, enroll, docket, document, calendar ("The clerk entered the defendant's appearance on the docket").

enterprise [en · ter · prize] *n.* An undertaking or venture, especially one involving business. *See* joint enterprise.

➤ activity, plan, campaign, scheme, engagement, undertaking; business, corporation, industry.

entertain [en · ter · *tain*] *v.* 1. To consider. USAGE: "The court said it would not entertain my lawsuit because there is no **controversy**." 2. To amuse.

➤ hear, adjudicate, resolve; amuse, perform for, host, treat, welcome.

entertainment expense [en · ter · *tain* · ment eks · *pense*] *n.* A deduction from income for tax purposes, if it is a necessary business expense.

entice [en · *tice*] *v.* To lure or tempt by trickery.

➤ lure, tempt, seduce, invite.

enticement of a child [en · *tice* · ment] *n.* Inviting, inducing, or luring a child into a place for the purpose of committing a sexual act upon the child. *See* child abuse; child molestation.

entire [en · *tire*] *adj.* Whole; undivided; indivisible.

➤ complete, full, comprehensive, undivided ("entire interest"). *Ant.* partial.

entire contract [kon · trakt] *n.* 1. A **contract** in which the **consideration** given is for the performance of every part of the contract, i.e., for the performance of the contract as a whole. *Compare* severable contract. 2. The contract as a whole. In construing any provision of a contract, the entire contract should be considered. *Compare* severable contract.

entire day *n.* A day of 24 hours, usually beginning and ending at midnight.

entire interest [*in* · trest] *n.* Absolute **title**; an unshared **interest**. EXAMPLE: a **fee simple**; an **entire tenancy**.

entire output contract [*out* · put *kon* · trakt] *n.* A contract in which the seller binds herself to the buyer to sell to the buyer the entire output of a product she manufactures, and the buyer binds himself to buy all of the product. *See* requirement contract.

entire tenancy [*ten* · en · see] *n.* Sole ownership; ownership that is neither joint nor in common. *See* tenancy by the entirety. *See and compare* joint tenancy; tenancy in common.

entirety [en · *tire* · tee] *n.* A whole of anything, as distinguished from a part of it; an undivided whole. USAGE: "The joint estate of a husband and wife is called a **tenancy by the entirety**." *See* joint tenancy; *compare* tenancy in common.
➤ whole, aggregate, completeness, totality, gross.
Ant. part.

entitle [en · *ty* · tel] *v.* To give a person a **right** in or **title** to anything.
➤ authorize, warrant, permit, empower, charter, qualify ("this clause entitles me to rescind the contract").
Ant. disqualify.

entitlement [en · *ty* · tel · ment] *n.* 1. A benefit that an eligible person has a right to receive from the government, which the government cannot refuse or take away without **due process of law**. EXAMPLES: **public assistance**; social security benefits. 2. That to which a person has a legitimate claim.
➤ right, claim, birthright, interest.

entity [en · ti · tee] *n.* An existence; something that exists; a being, actual or artificial. EXAMPLES: a corporation; a partnership; a **trust**; an administrative agency; an **artificial person**; a **natural person**. *See* legal entity.
➤ body, unit, existence, individual, object, being, item.
Ant. illusion.

entrapment [en · *trap* · ment] *n.* Inducing a person to commit a crime he is otherwise not inclined to commit, in order to bring a criminal prosecution against him. Such conduct by law enforcement authorities is an **affirmative defense** to a prosecution for the crime into which the defendant was entrapped. *See* predisposition.
➤ temptation, deception, beguilement, ensnarement.

entry [en · tree] *n.* 1. In **burglary**, the act of going into a place for the purpose of committing a **felony**. It may consist of either total physical intrusion or the insertion of some part of the body or an instrument connected to the body (EXAMPLES: a hand; a hook; a gun). *See* breaking and entering. 2. The act of going upon real property. A **writ of entry**, for EXAMPLE, is a **writ** used for the purpose of recovering possession of real property by an owner or **tenant** who has been wrongfully deprived of possession. *See* right of entry; right of reentry; unlawful entry. 3. The act of making a record of something by noting it in a book or upon a paper. *See* book of original entry. *Also see* enter.
➤ penetration, intrusion, infiltration, insertion, arrival ("The burglar's entry onto the estate immediately set off the alarm"); report, account, chronicle, document ("entry of judgment").

entry of appearance [e · *peer* · enss] *n.* The document filed by an attorney asserting that the attorney is representing a particular client. It is necessary to file an entry of appearance with the court before representing a client in court. *See* appearance.

entry of court order [*or* · der] *n.* *See* entry of judgment.

entry of decree [de · *kree*] *n.* *See* entry of judgment.

entry of judgment [*juj* · ment] *n.* Recording a **judgment** in a **judgment book** or filing it with the clerk. Entry of judgment is a **ministerial act** rather than a **judicial act**. *Compare* render judgment.

enumerate [e · *nyoo* · mer · ate] *v.* To count; to specify; to itemize; to name; to list. USAGE: "The rights spelled out in the Bill of Rights are sometimes referred to as enumerated rights."

E

➤ list, record, itemize, specify, detail, count ("The powers that the Constitution expressly gives to the president are enumerated in Article I.").

enumerated powers [e · *nyoo* · me · ray · ted *pow* · erz] *n.* Powers specifically granted by the Constitution to one of the three **branches of government**. Another term for enumerated powers is **express powers**. *Compare* implied power. *See also* executive powers; judicial powers; legislative powers.

environment [en · *vy* · ren · ment] *n.* The objects one is surrounded by; all of the elements which act upon an organism or an ecological community.

➤ surroundings, environs, habitat, atmosphere, conditions, milieu, ecosystem.

environmental impact statement [en · vy · ren · *men* · tel *im* · pakt *state* · ment] *n.* Under state and federal statutes, detailed declarations required with respect to proposed projects or legislation that might have an influence upon the environment. *See* Environmental Protection Agency.

Environmental Protection Agency [en · vy · ren · *men* · tel pro · *tek* · shen ay · jen · see] *n.* The duties of this agency of the federal government, often referred to by its abbreviation, **EPA**, are numerous and broad in scope. Its basic mission is to reduce and control pollution of every kind, in some instances by direct intervention and in others by working with or overseeing agencies of state and local government.

envoy [*en* · voy] *n.* A high-ranking representative sent by one government to another, usually for some special purpose or specific undertaking.

➤ consul, legate, agent, delegate, emissary.

eo [*ee* · oh] (*Latin*) *prep.* That.

eo nomine [*nom* · i · nee] *n.* Means "by that name"; in that name; by that title.

EPA Abbreviation of **Environmental Protection Agency**.

ephemeral [e · *fem* · e · ral] *adj.* Lasting for a very short time.

➤ fleeting, brief, evanescent, passing, transient, transitory, momentary, elusive. *Ant.* permanent.

epitome [e · *pit* · e · mee] *n.* An ideal example or model.

➤ embodiment, essence, model, representative ("the epitome of sleaze").

equal [*ee* · kwel] *adj.* 1. Alike; the same as. 2. Impartial; not discriminating; unbiased.

➤ alike, uniform, just, unbiased, impartial, balanced, even ("equal opportunity"); identical, same, coequal ("equal partners").

equal protection [pro · *tek* · shen] *n. See* equal protection of the laws.

equal protection clause [pro · *tek* · shen] *n.* The clause in the **Fourteenth Amendment** which dictates that no state may "deny to any person within its jurisdiction the **equal protection of the laws**." *See* equal protection of the laws.

equal protection of the laws [pro · *tek* · shen] *n.* Constitutional guaranty which specifies that the rights of all persons must rest upon the same rules under the same circumstances. Put another way, every state must give equal treatment to every person who is similarly situated or to persons who are members of the same **class**. "Equal protection of the laws" is a requirement of the **Fourteenth Amendment**. *See* equal protection clause.

equal time doctrine [*dok* · trin] *n. See* fairness doctrine.

equal time rule *n. See* Equal Time Act.

Equal Employment Opportunity Commission [*ee* · kwel em · *ploy* · ment op · er · *tew* · ni · tee kuh · *mish* · en] *n.* A federal agency whose purpose is to prevent and remedy discrimination based on race, color, religion, national origin, age, or sex with respect to most aspects of employment including hiring, firing, promotion, and wages. The commission, which is known as the **EEOC**, enforces many federal **Civil Rights Acts** and antidiscrimination statutes. *See* discrimination.

Equal Pay Act [*ee* · kwel] *n.* A federal statute that requires men and women to be paid equally for the same work. *See* comparable worth.

Equal Rights Amendment [*ee* · kwel rights a · *mend* · ment] *n.* A proposed constitutional amendment, passed by Congress in 1972, which failed for lack of ratification

E

by three-fourths of the states. The proposed amendment, generally referred to as the **ERA**, provided that "equality of rights under the law shall not be abridged by the United States or any state on account of sex."

Equal Time Act [*ee* · kwel] *n.* A federal statute which requires that if a radio or television station makes time available to one candidate for public office, it must make time available on the same basis to all candidates for that office. *Compare* fairness doctrine.

equalization [ee · kwe · li · *zay* · shen] *n.* The process or act of making things equal or creating uniformity.
➤ standardization, regulation, leveling, accommodation, balancing.

equalization board *n. See* board of equalization.

equalization of taxes [*tak* · sez] *n.* Carried out by **boards of equalization**; the process of adjusting the total **assessments** on all real estate in a **tax district** to equalize them with the total assessments in other tax districts in the state, the goal being equality and uniformity in taxation.

equitable [*ek* · wi · tebl] *adj.* 1. Adjective describing a claim that the law may recognize as a matter of fairness or justice, even though it is not based upon a **legal right**. *See* equitable right; equity. 2. Fair; just.
➤ just, fair, impartial, proper, honest, objective, rightful.
Ant. biased, unfair.

equitable action [*ak* · shen] *n.* Although the distinction between a **suit in equity** and an **action at law** has been abolished in most states, all actions now being simply **civil actions**, the concept of an equitable action still exists with respect to the **remedy** sought, as historically certain types of **relief** were available only in a **court of equity**. (EXAMPLES: an **injunction**; **specific performance**.) Equitable actions are designed to remedy **injuries** that cannot adequately be redressed by an action at law. *See* equitable relief.

equitable adoption [e · *dop* · shen] *n.* The principle that a child may enforce **in equity** a promise to adopt him, at least to the extent that he will be given rights of inheritance with respect to the property of the person who made the promise.

equitable assignment [e · *sine* · ment] *n.* A writing or act which does not in law amount to an **assignment**, and which a **court of law** will not enforce as an assignment, but which a **court of equity** will. EXAMPLES: an **executory contract**; a **deed of trust**.

equitable defense [de · *fense*] *n.* A **defense** formerly recognized only by a **court of equity**. Now, under most state **rules of civil procedure**, both equitable as well as **legal** defenses may be raised in all civil actions.

equitable distribution [dis · tri · *byoo* · shen] *n.* Some jurisdictions permit their courts, in a divorce case, to distribute all property obtained during the marriage on an "equitable" basis, that is, without regard to whose name the property is in. In deciding what is equitable, the court takes into consideration factors such as the length of the marriage and the contributions of each party, including homemaking. *Compare* community property.

equitable easements [*eez* · ments] *n.* A term sometimes used to describe **covenants running with the land**. They may be the subject of **equitable relief**, enforced **in equity** by **injunction**. *See* easement. *Also see* restrictive covenant.

equitable election [e · *lek* · shen] *n.* 1. **Election under the will**. 2. **Election of remedies**. *See* election.

equitable estate [es · *tate*] *n.* An interest in property recognized only **in equity**. EXAMPLE: the interest of a beneficiary of a **trust**.

equitable estoppel [es · *top* · el] *n.* Same as **estoppel in pais**.

equitable interest [*in* · trest] *n. See* equitable right; equitable title.

equitable lien [leen] *n.* A right recognized **in equity** but not **at law**, to have specific property, or its proceeds, applied to the payment of a particular debt or class of debts. *See* lien.

equitable mortgage [*more* · gej] *n.* An **instrument** not enforceable **at law** as a **mortgage**, but given the effect of a mortgage **in equity**. EXAMPLES: an agreement

E

to execute a mortgage; an agreement that attempts to create a mortgage but is imperfect in form.

equitable ownership [*oh* · ner · ship] *n.* *See* equitable title.

equitable recoupment [ree · *koop* · ment] *n.* A reduction in the amount of money or property owed to the plaintiff by the defendant because of money or property owed by the plaintiff to the defendant. *See* recoupment.

equitable relief [re · *leef*] *n.* A **remedy** available **in equity** rather than **at law**; generally **relief** other than money **damages.** EXAMPLES: an **injunction**; **specific performance**.

equitable remedy [*rem* · e · dee] *n.* *See* equitable relief.

equitable restraint doctrine [re · *straint* dok · trin] *n.* The rule that deters federal courts from **enjoining** a criminal prosecution in state court from taking place unless the prosecution is in bad faith. *See* Dombrowski doctrine.

equitable right *n.* A **right** that a court will protect as a matter of **equity**, even though it is not a **legal right**.

equitable servitudes [*ser* · vi · tyoodz] *n.* Same as **equitable easements**.

equitable title [*ty* · tel] *n.* **Title** recognized as ownership **in equity**, even though it is not **legal title** or **marketable title**; title sufficient to give the party to whom it belongs the right to have the legal title transferred to him. EXAMPLE: the title held by a purchaser under a **contract for sale of land**.

equity [*ek* · wi · tee] *n.* 1. A system for insuring justice in circumstances where the **remedies** customarily available under conventional law are inadequate; a system of **jurisprudence** less formal and more flexible than the **common law**, available in particular types of cases to better ensure a fair result. Although **courts of equity** and **courts of law** have been merged, their equity powers are still distinct. *See* equitable action; equitable relief. 2. Short for **court of equity**. 3. Fairness; justice; right. 4. A person's interest in property after subtracting the amount he owes on the property from its **fair market value**. USAGE: "I have

paid off all but $10,000 of the $100,000 mortgage on my home, which is worth $120,000, so my equity is now $110,000."

➤ fairness, justice, rightness, ethics, uprightness, propriety ("the equity of the situation"); interest, security, stake, claim ("my equity in my house").

equity capital [*kap* · i · tel] *n.* The portion of the assets of a corporation provided by the sale of stock. *See* capital; capital assets; capital stock.

equity court *n.* *See* court of equity.

equity financing [*fine* · an · sing] *n.* Selling corporate stock to generate **capital**. *See* capital; equity capital.

equity jurisdiction [joo · ris · *dik* · shen] *n.* A court's power to grant **relief** not available **at law** when justice so demands.

equity loan *n.* Also known as a **home equity loan**; a bank loan secured by the homeowner's equity in her home.

equity of partners [*part* · nerz] *n.* The right a **partner** has to have partnership assets pay the debts of the partnership before any of the partners can claim any right to any of the assets. *See* partnership.

equity of redemption [ree · *demp* · shen] *n.* The right of a mortgagor who has defaulted upon his mortgage payments to prevent foreclosure by paying the debt in full. *See* redemption.

equivalent [ee · *kwiv* · e · lent] *adj.* Of equal value, weight, or force.
n. 1. In patent law, an invention that accomplishes the same result as that achieved by a patent alleged to have been infringed. *See* infringement of patent. 2. A thing of equal value, weight, or force.
➤ *adj.* commensurate, corresponding, comparable, parallel, like, exact.
Ant. dissimilar.
n. correspondent, match, parallel, peer, substitute, twin.
Ant. opposite.

equivocal [e · *kwiv* · uh · kul] *adj.* Uncertain; doubtful.
➤ ambiguous, nebulous, vague, imprecise, recondite, puzzling, unresolved, uncertain.

equivocate [e · *kwiv* · uh · kayt] *v.* To avoid committing oneself; to avoid an issue.

E

➤ dodge, elude, evade, avoid, hedge, prevaricate, misstate, deceive.

ERA Abbreviation of **Equal Rights Amendment**.

eradicate [e · *rad* · ih · kayt] *v.* To destroy; to erase or expunge.

➤ demolish, obliterate, purge, eliminate, expurgate, destroy, remove, delete.

erasure [e · *ray* · sher] *n.* A rubbing, scraping, or wiping out; a method of altering a document.

➤ elimination, cancellation, removal, effacement, annulment, expungement. *Ant.* insertion.

erasure of record [*rek* · erd] *n. See* expungement of record.

ergo [*ehr* · go] (*Latin*) *adv.* Therefore; accordingly; consequently.

➤ therefore, accordingly, consequently.

Erie v. Tompkins [*ee* · ree *ver* · ses *tomp* · kinz] *n.* The case in which the Supreme Court (304 U.S. 64), in 1938, established the doctrine that, except for cases involving federal statutes or the Constitution, the law to be applied in any case in federal court is the law of the state in which the federal court is located.

ERISA [e · *riss* · ah] Acronym for **Employee Retirement Income Security Act**.

erode [ee · *rode*] *v.* To wear away; to decay.
➤ decay, recede, wear away, deteriorate, abrade, weaken.

error [*err* · er] *n.* 1. A mistake of the court during the trial of a lawsuit that forms a basis for filing an appeal requesting an **appellate court** to review the **proceedings**. *See* fundamental error; harmless error; judicial error; prejudicial error; reversible error. 2. A mistake by anyone. *See* clerical error.

➤ mistake, misinterpretation, fault, defect, flaw, miscalculation, misapprehension, aberration, deviation.

error coram nobis [*koh* · rem *noh* · bis] *n. See coram nobis.*

error coram vobis [*koh* · rem *voh* · bis] *n. See coram vobis.*

error in fact *n. See* error of fact.

error in law *n. See* error of law.

error of fact *n.* A **mistake of fact** committed by the court.

error of law *n.* A **mistake of law** committed by the court.

escalator clause [*es* · ke · lay · ter] *n.* 1. A clause in a **contract of sale** or a lease made during a period when prices and rentals are controlled by the government, allowing the seller or landlord to increase the price the buyer or tenant must pay if such increases are permitted by the government during the life of the agreement. 2. A provision in a contract that permits the contract price to increase as costs increase. *See* cost-of-living adjustment; cost-of-living clause.

escape [es · *kape*] *v.* To flee from or avoid. *n.* 1. The crime committed by a prisoner who unlawfully leaves custody without the use of force. *Compare* prison breaking; rescue. 2. The crime committed by a warden or guard who permits a prisoner to leave custody unlawfully. 3. The flight of a person seeking to avoid arrest. 4. Any effort by a person to avoid danger.

➤ *v.* flee, dodge, vanish, disappear, evade, break out, bolt, flee; avert, shun. *Ant.* capture.
n. break, release, evasion, departure, liberation, retreat.

escape clause *n.* A clause in a contract relieving one or more of the parties of liability for nonperformance under certain specified circumstances. *See* cancellation clause.

escheat [es · *cheet*] *n.* The right of the state to take **title** to property after the death of a person who has not disposed of the property by will and has left no heirs to inherit it.
➤ reversion, forfeiture, seizure, appropriation.

Escobedo rule [es · ko · *bee* · doh] *n.* In *Escobedo v. Illinois*, 378 U.S. 478, decided by the Supreme Court in 1964, a murder suspect held by the police for questioning was denied the right to consult his attorney, who was in a nearby room. The Court held that whenever a police investigation is no longer general, but focuses on a specific person, that person is entitled to the assistance of counsel; if he is denied access to counsel at the investigative stage of the proceeding, a subsequent conviction will be set aside. *See* right to counsel.

E

escrow [es · kroh] *n.* A written instrument (EXAMPLES: stock, bonds, a deed), money, or other property deposited by the **grantor** with a third party (the **escrow holder**) until the performance of a condition or the happening of a certain event, upon the occurrence of which the property is to be delivered to the **grantee**. USAGE: "The down payment is being held in escrow." *adj.* Being held separate.
➤ *adj.* separate, designated, specified ("Keep the money in an escrow account.").

escrow account [e · kount] *n.* A bank account in the name of the depositor and a second person, the deposited funds being returnable to the depositor or paid to a third person upon the happening of a specified event. (EXAMPLE: money for the payment of property taxes which a **mortgagor** pays into the escrow account of the **mortgage company** or bank.)

escrow contract [kon · trakt] *n.* A contract that describes the rights of the parties to an escrow.

escrow holder [hole · der] *n.* The third party to an escrow.

espionage [es · pee · en · ahzh] *n.* The crime of obtaining national defense information and communicating it to a foreign nation; spying.
➤ spying, treason, betrayal, mutiny, eavesdropping.

Esq. Abbreviation of **esquire**.

esquire [es · kwire] *n.* A term applied to attorneys; it is customary to add it to an attorney's name as a title when addressing the attorney by letter. USAGE: "Mary Brown, Esquire" or "Mary Brown, Esq."

essence [ess · enss] *n.* 1. The essential element. USAGE: "Time is of the essence in this deal; if the goods are not delivered by midnight, our contract is off." 2. The gist or substance of anything.
➤ core, heart, nature, lifeblood, marrow, soul, backbone.
Ant. periphery.

essence of the contract [kon · trakt] *n.* The vital aspect of the contract.

essential [e · sen · shul] *adj.* 1. Of the utmost importance. 2. Belonging to the very nature of a thing.
➤ important, required, needed, primary, requisite, mandatory; inherent, intrinsic, fundamental.

establish [es · tab · lish] *v.* 1. To prove a fact by evidence. USAGE: "The jury believes that the defendant's guilt has been established." 2. To originate, to create; to found and set up.
➤ prove, convince, demonstrate, show, validate, confirm, substantiate ("It has been established that the couple will no longer reside together."); form, build, start, initiate, launch, commission ("She established the business 10 years ago.")

establishment clause [es · tab · lish · ment] *n.* The provision of the **First Amendment** which states that "Congress shall make no law respecting an establishment of religion, or prohibiting the free exercise thereof." It means that neither a state nor the federal government can set up a state religion; neither can pass laws that aid one religion, aid all religions, or prefer one religion over another; neither can force or influence a person to go to or remain away from a church, synagogue, mosque, or other place of worship, or force him to proclaim a belief or disbelief in any religion.

estate [es · tate] *n.* 1. The **right, title, and interest** a person has in real or personal property, either **tangible** or **intangible**. Estates in real property (**estates in land** or **landed estates**) include both **freehold estates** (EXAMPLES: a **fee simple**; a **fee tail**; a **life estate**) and **estates less than freehold** (EXAMPLES: **estates for years; estates at will**). 2. The property itself. 3. The property left by a **decedent**; i.e., a **decedent's estate**. *See* gross estate; net estate. 4. The property of a **bankrupt**; i.e., a **bankruptcy estate**. 5. The property of a **ward** or mentally incompetent person. 6. A person's social standing or standing in the community. *See* absolute estate; conditional estate; dominant estate; equitable estate; expectant estate; future estate; landed estate; particular estate; qualified estate; residuary estate; servient estate; separate estate; trust estate; vested estate.
    Note that to fully understand the definitions of the many kinds of estates in land that the law recognizes, it is necessary to

know that a **tenant** is not only a person who leases an apartment, a house, or commercial premises, but is anyone who, although not owning land, has certain rights with respect to occupying or using it. *See* tenant. *See also* tenancy.

➤ assets, wealth, property, fortune, personalty, effects, land, property.

estate at sufferance [*suf* · ranss] *n. See* tenancy at sufferance.

estate at will *n. See* tenancy at will.

estate by purchase [*per* · ches] *n.* An estate acquired by any method except **descent**.

estate by the curtesy [*ker* · te · see] *n.* An estate acquired through the right of **curtesy**.

estate by the entirety [en · *tire* · teez] *n.* The estate of husband and wife owning land together as **tenants by the entirety**. *See also* tenancy by the entirety.

estate duty [*dew* · tee] *n. See* estate tax.

estate for years *n.* An estate that terminates after a specific number of years. EXAMPLE: real property occupied under a 10-year lease.

estate from year to year *n. See* tenancy from year to year.

estate in bankruptcy [*bank* · rupt · see] *n. See* bankruptcy estate.

estate in common [*kom* · en] *n.* The common estate of persons holding property as **tenants in common**. *See also* tenancy in common.

estate in expectancy [eks · *pek* · ten · see] *n. See* expectant estate.

estate in fee *n. See* fee simple; fee conditional; fee tail.

estate in joint tenancy [*ten* · en · see] *n.* The joint estate of persons holding property as **joint tenants**. *See also* joint tenancy.

estate in land *n.* An estate in real property. *See also* landed estate.

estate in possession [po · *zesh* · en] *n. See* vested estate.

estate in remainder [ree · *mane* · der] *n. See* remainder.

estate in reversion [ree · *ver* · zhen] *n. See* reversion.

estate in severalty [*sev* · rel · tee] *n.* An estate held by a person as the sole **tenant** without any other person having an

interest. This is the most common and usual way of holding an estate, and all estates are deemed to be of this sort unless expressly declared to be otherwise. *Compare* joint tenancy; tenancy in common. *See* severalty.

estate less than freehold [*free* · hold] *n.* Any estate whose duration is less than that of a **life estate**. EXAMPLES: an **estate for years**; an **estate at will**; an **estate at sufferance**. *See* freehold.

estate of freehold not of inheritance [*free* · hold not of in · *herr* · i · tense] *n.* A **life estate**. A life estate does not pass to the heirs of the **tenant**. *Compare* estate of inheritance. *See* freehold.

estate of inheritance [in · *herr* · i · tense] *n.* Also known as a **fee**, a **freehold** interest in land that is inheritable; i.e., an interest which the **tenant** is not only entitled to enjoy for his own lifetime, but which, after his death, if he leaves no will, his heirs will inherit under the **intestate laws**.

estate per autre vie [per *oh* · tre vee] *n.* An estate that is to last for the life of a person other than the **tenant**. EXAMPLE: "I give Blackacre to my son-in-law, Samuel Jones, for as long as my daughter, Mary Brown Jones, shall live." *See* autre vie.

estate tail *n. See* fee tail.

estate tax *n.* A tax imposed by the federal government and most states upon the transmission of property by a deceased person. The tax is imposed upon the net estate of the **decedent** without reference to the recipients' relationship to the decedent or to the amount a recipient receives. An estate tax is a **transfer tax**. *Compare* inheritance tax.

estate upon condition [up · *on* ken · *dish* · en] *n.* An estate whose existence, enlargement, or termination is conditioned upon the happening of a particular event. Such conditions are either expressed in the deed, will, or other instrument that creates the estate, or they are implied by law. An estate upon condition is also referred to as a **conditional estate**. *Also see* limitation of estate.

estate upon condition expressed [up · *on* ken · *dish* · en eks · *prest*] *n. See* estate upon condition.

E

estate upon condition implied [up · *on* ken · *dish* · en im · *plide*] *n. See* estate upon condition.

estate upon limitation [up · *on* lim · it · *ay* · shen] *n.* An estate created by using **words of limitation**.

estimate *n.* The act of appraising; an opinion or judgment.
v. To judge the appropriate worth of something.
➤ *n.* guess, judgment, valuation, appraisal, rating, assessment.
v. guess, determine, figure, predict, reckon, surmise, suspect.

estimated [*est* · ih · may · ted] *adj.* Arrived at through an educated guess or rough calculation.
➤ approximated, calculated, speculated, surmised ("estimated worth of the property").

estimated tax [*est* · i · may · ted] *n. See* declaration of estimated tax.

Estin doctrine [*est* · in *dok* · trin] *n.* The rule of law that even though the **full faith and credit** clause of the Constitution requires that a court in one state enforce a divorce decreed by a court in another state, that requirement does not extend to a support order that is part of the decree, unless the original court had **personal jurisdiction** over the spouse whom it ordered to pay support. *See* divisible divorce; foreign judgment.

estop [es · *top*] *v.* To bar; to stop; to prevent. *See* estoppel.
➤ impede, restrict, hinder, thwart, block, restrain, preclude.
Ant. authorize.

estopped [es · *topd*] *adv.* Barred; prevented; stopped from. *See* estoppel.

estoppel [es · *top* · el] *n.* A prohibition imposed by law against uttering what may actually be the truth.
There are two classes of estoppel. A person may be estopped by his own *acts or representations* (that is, not be permitted to deny the truth or significance of what he said or did) if another person who was entitled to rely upon those statements or acts did so to her detriment. This type of estoppel is also known as **equitable estoppel** or **estoppel in pais**. The second type of

estoppel is *legal estoppel*. It includes **matters of record** such as marriage, divorce, judgments, and deeds, as well as the findings of a court. Estoppel must be distinguished from **waiver**, which is the voluntary surrendering of a known right. *See* collateral estoppel; judicial estoppel; promissory estoppel.
➤ impediment, prohibition, restraint, ban, bar, obstruction.
Ant. allowance.

estoppel by contract [*kon* · trakt] *n.* 1. A restriction against denying the truth of facts agreed upon by virtue of entering into a contract. 2. A prohibition against denying the validity or significance of acts done in performance of a contract.

estoppel by deed *n.* A bar that prevents a **party** to a deed from asserting any **right** or **title** in **derogation** of the deed or from denying the truth of any facts asserted in it.

estoppel by judgment [*juj* · ment] *n.* The bar that a **judgment** creates against relitigating facts or issues.

estoppel by laches [*lach* · ez] *n. See* laches.

estoppel by record [*rek* · erd] *n.* 1. A prohibition against denying the truth of facts contained in a legislative or judicial record. *See* legislative record; record. 2. A bar against denying facts adjudicated by a court.

estoppel by silence [*sy* · lenss] *n.* An estoppel that arises when a person who is under a duty to speak fails to do so and thereby leads another person to do or not to do something that is prejudicial to him. *See* estoppel in pais.

estoppel certificate [ser · *tif* · i · ket] *n.* A certification from a bank to a prospective purchaser of real estate with respect to the status of the mortgage.

estoppel in pais [pay] *n.* Also known as **equitable estoppel**; a term applied to a situation in which a **party** is denied the right to plead or prove a fact because of something she has done or has failed to do. *See pais*.

estovers [es · *toh* · verz] *n.* 1. The right of a tenant of farm land to take from the premises timber needed for fuel, for the repair of buildings and fences, or for

E

other agricultural needs. 2. Support to which a person is entitled from an **estate**. 3. Alimony.

➤ support, alimony.

et [et] *(Latin) conj.* And; also.

et al. [*ahl*] Short for *et alia*, meaning "and others." (EXAMPLE: "Mary Brown et al." means "Mary Brown and others.") This abbreviation is commonly used in court papers, the *et al.* often referring to a list of unlisted plaintiffs or defendants.

et cetera [*set* · e · ra] "And so forth"; and so on; and others; and the rest. Commonly written in its abbreviated form, **etc**.

➤ and others, and so on, and so forth.

et seq. [*sek*] Short for *et sequitur*, meaning "and what follows." For EXAMPLE, a reference to "page 110 et seq." means "page 110 and the following pages."

et ux. [*uks*] Short for *et uxor*, meaning "and wife." For EXAMPLE, until recently it was common, in deeds and other formal documents, to refer to a man and his wife as "Samuel Johnson et ux."

etc. [et · *set* · e · ra] Short for **et cetera**. Etc. is the common way of writing *et cetera*.

ethical [*eth* · ih · kul] *adj.* 1. Having the quality of being honest and moral. 2. Permissible behavior by attorneys according to the Rules of Professional Conduct.

➤ good, honest, principled, professional, moral, uncorrupted, honorable, virtuous, upright.

ethics [*eth* · iks] *n.* 1. A **code** of moral principles and standards of behavior for people in professions such as law or medicine (EXAMPLES: the **Code of Judicial Conduct**; the **Rules of Professional Conduct**). *See* legal ethics; judicial ethics. 2. A body of moral principles generally.

➤ principles, values, morals, mores, criteria, canon, rules.

euthanasia [yooth · e · *nay*˙ · zha] *n.* The act of causing death to end pain and distress. Also referred to as **mercy killing**. *See* do not resuscitate order.

evasion [ee · *vay* · zhen] *n.* Avoiding something by flight or deception, especially a penalty or obligation.

➤ avoidance, dodging, fabrication, escape, shunning.
Ant. confrontation.

evasion of tax *n. See* tax evasion.

evasive [ee · *vay* · siv] *adj.* Elusive; nonresponsive; slippery. USAGE: "The witness's answer is evasive."

➤ misleading, vague, ambivalent, covert.
Ant. forthright, open, direct.

event [e · *vent*] *n.* 1. A happening or ocurrence. 2. The effect or result.

➤ happening, transaction, affair, incident, episode, development; end, conclusion, outcome, consequence.

evergreen contract [*ev* · er · green *kon* · trakt] *n.* A contract that automatically renews itself from term to term unless one **party** gives the other notice in advance of his intention to terminate the agreement.

evict [ee · *vikt*] *v.* To oust or dispossess.

➤ displace, oust, expel, dispossess, turn out, eject, kick out, uproot ("to evict a tenant for nonpayment of rent").

eviction [ee · *vik* · shen] *n.* The act of putting a tenant out of possession of premises that she has leased. *See* constructive eviction; partial eviction. *See also* ejectment.

➤ expulsion, ouster, ejection, dislodgement, removal, dispossession.

evidence [*ev* · i · denss] *n.* The means by which any matter of fact may be established or disproved. Such means include testimony, documents, and physical objects. The law of evidence is made up of rules that determine what evidence is to be admitted or rejected in the trial of a civil action or a criminal prosecution and what weight is to be given to admitted evidence. *Compare* proof. *See* admissible evidence. *See also* best evidence; character evidence; circumstantial evidence; competent evidence; corroborating evidence; cumulative evidence; demonstrative evidence; documentary evidence; extrinsic evidence; legal evidence; material evidence; newly discovered evidence; opinion evidence; parol evidence; prima facie evidence; rebuttal evidence; relevant evidence; rules of evidence; secondary evidence; state's evidence.
v. To demonstrate; to establish; to reveal; to show; to indicate; to prove.

➤ *n.* verification, substantiation, authentication, certification, corroboration, testimony, confirmation, proof ("based on the evidence").

v. certify, attest, reveal, display, demonstrate, prove, establish, suggest ("proof evidencing a crime").

evidence aliunde [ah · *lyun* · day] *n.* Evidence from another source or another place; **parol evidence**; **extrinsic evidence**. *See* aliunde.

evidence in mitigation [mit · i · *gay* · shen] *n. In a civil action,* proof of facts tending to show that the plaintiff is not entitled to the amount of **damages** that might otherwise be recoverable. *See* mitigation; mitigation of damages. *In a criminal prosecution,* proof of facts tending to show that a convicted defendant's punishment should not be as severe as it might otherwise be or that the degree of the crime should be reduced. *See* mitigating circumstances.

evidence of debt *n.* Any written instrument revealing a monetary obligation. EXAMPLES: a bond; a mortgage; a **note**.

evidence of insurability [in · shoor · e · *bil* · i · tee] *n.* Evidence an insurance company requires before it will issue a life insurance policy. EXAMPLE: a medical examination and report.

evidence of title [*ty* · tel] *n.* A deed or other instrument establishing **title** to property, particularly real estate.

evidencing [*ev* · i · den · sing] *adv.* Proving; establishing; demonstrating; showing.

evident [*ev* · i · dent] *adj.* That which is obvious or noticeable.

➤ plain, clear, obvious, apparent, discernible, noticeable, visible, unhidden, ostensible.

evidential breath test [ev · i · *den* · shel] *n.* A scientific device that gives blood alcohol readings. It operates on the principle that blood alcohol in the body is concentrated in a constant ratio to the concentration of blood in the lung. An **EBT** is the only type of breath test that is admissible evidence. *See* blood alcohol concentration; breathalyzer; drunk-o-meter.

evidentiary facts [ev · i · *den* · sher · ee] *n.* Facts admissible in evidence. *See* probative facts; ultimate facts.

evoke [ee · *voke*] *v.* To bring to mind; to cite with support.

➤ elicit, produce, arouse, generate, summon, stimulate ("evoke a response").

ex [eks] *(Latin) prep.* From; out of; in; of; in accord with; by reason of.

ex contractu [kon · *trak* · too] Means "from contract" or arising out of a contract. The term refers to legal actions based upon **breach of contract**. *Compare ex delicto.*

ex curia [*koo* · ree · ah] Out of court; elsewhere than in court.

ex delicto [de · *lik* · toh] Means "from a wrongful act" or arising out of a wrongful act. The term refers to **civil actions** based upon **torts** or crimes. *Compare ex contractu.*

ex dividend [*div* · i · dend] Stock sold "ex dividend" is stock sold without its **dividend**. The term refers to an agreement between the buyer and seller that, although the buyer has bought the stock, the seller owns the **stock dividend** that has been declared by the corporation but not yet paid.

ex officio [oh · *fish* · ee · oh] Means "from office," i.e., by virtue of office. A term for a person's right to hold a particular office by virtue of the fact that she holds another office. EXAMPLE: the right of a mayor, in some cities, to sit on the police commission.

ex parte [*par* · tay] Means "of a side," i.e., from one side or by one **party**. The term refers to an **application** made to the court by one party without notice to the other party.

ex parte divorce [*par* · tay di · *vorss*] *n.* A divorce **proceeding** in which only one spouse participates. If the failure to participate is due to inadequate notice, any divorce decree granted is invalid.

ex parte injunction [*par* · tay in · *junk* · shen] *n.* An **injunction** issued without prior notice to the **adverse party**.

ex parte order [*par* · tay *or* · der] *n.* An **order** made by the court upon the **application** of one of the parties to an **action** without notice to the other party.

ex post facto [*fak* · toh] *adj.* Means "after the thing is done" or after the act is committed. *See* ex post facto law.

ex post facto law [*fak* · toh] *n.* A law making a person criminally liable for an act that was not criminal at the time it was committed. The Constitution prohibits both Congress and the states from enacting such laws.

ex rel. [rell] *prep.* Short for *ex relatione*, a Latin term that means "on the relation of" or on the information of. It indicates an **ex rel. action**, that is, a legal action brought by the state upon the instigation of a private party, known as a **relator**, who has a **beneficial interest** in the action.

ex rel. action *n. See ex rel.*

ex relatione [rel · ah · she · *oh* · nee] *See ex rel.*

ex- A *prefix* indicating a former title or previous status. EXAMPLES: ex-congresswoman; ex-spouse.

ex. Sometimes used as an abbreviation of **exhibit**.

exact [eg · *zact*] *adj.* Marked by thorough examination or precision.
➤ precise, literal, accurate, particular, strict, express ("the exact wording").

examination [eg · zam · i · *nay* · shen] *n.* 1. In connection with legal **proceedings**, a word commonly understood to mean questioning a person under oath or **affirmation**. 2. Inspection; close observation; investigation; search. 3. A test.
➤ investigation, inquiry, research, analysis, observation, questioning, search, inspection.

examination before trial [be · *fore* try · el] *n. See* deposition; discovery.

examination in chief *n.* Same as **direct examination**.

examination of bankrupt [*bank* · rupt] *n.* A questioning of the **bankrupt** under oath by his creditors, as provided by the **Bankruptcy Code**, concerning the conduct of his business, his dealings with his creditors, the amount, kind, and whereabouts of his property, and all other matters that may affect administration and settlement of the **bankruptcy estate** or granting of his **discharge in bankruptcy**.

examination of invention [in · *ven* · shen] *n.* Same as **examination of patent**.

examination of patent [*pa* · tent] *n.* An examination made by the **Office of Patents and Trademarks** with respect to every **patent** applied for to determine if the alleged invention is patentable.

examination of title [*ty* · tel] *n. See* title search.

examination of witness [*wit* · ness] *n.* Obtaining the testimony of a witness by oral questions and answers made under oath in open court. *See and compare* cross-examination; direct examination.

examine [eg · *zam* · in] *v.* 1. To inspect or observe. 2. To ask questions of a witness at trial.
➤ inspect, analyze, scrutinize, study, monitor, observe; question, interview, interrogate.

examined copy [eg · *zam* · ind *kop* · ee] *n.* A copy of a document that has been compared with the original and accords with it.

examiner [eg · *zam* · in · er] *n.* An officer or other person who is authorized to conduct an examination or investigation and, in some circumstances, a full hearing. *See* bank examiner; hearing examiner; medical examiner; trial examiner.
➤ investigator, researcher, inspector, reviewer, questioner.

examining court [eg · *zam* · in · ing] *n.* A court that conducts a **preliminary hearing** in a criminal case.

examining trial [eg · *zam* · in · ing] *n.* Same as **preliminary hearing**.

except [ek · *sept*] *prep.* Other than; excluding. *v.* To take or reserve an **exception** to a ruling or order of a court; to object in a judicial or administrative proceeding. *Note* that "except" is not "accept."
➤ *prep.* other than, exluding, saving, apart from ("Except for his inability to type, he was an excellent secretary."). *v.* pass, reject, delete, excuse, remove, disallow, ignore ("As a student she was excepted from jury duty."). *Ant.* incorporate.

exception [ek · *sep* · shen] *n.* 1. A protest against a ruling of the **trial court** with respect to an **objection**, entered by the objecting party so that she may include the ruling in her **bill of exceptions** if she appeals. In most jurisdictions today, however, an objection carries with it an automatic exception. 2. In a deed or other conveyance, the withholding of a right that would otherwise pass to the grantee. *Compare* reservation. 3. Exclusion;

E

noninclusion; exemption. 4. Any objection or protest.

➤ protest, complaint ("The exception will be taken into consideration"); separation, departure, segregation, omission ("an exception to the rule").

exception in deed *n.* A withdrawal of some portion of the real estate granted by a deed that otherwise would pass to the grantee. *Compare* reservation.

exception in insurance policy [in · *shoor* · ense *pol* · i · see] *n.* A provision in an insurance policy that withdraws a named **risk**, or named risks, from coverage under the policy. EXAMPLE: An automobile liability policy that excludes from coverage **loss** occurring while the vehicle is being driven by a person under the age of 18.

exception in statute [*stat* · shoot] *n.* A clause in a statute that removes from application of the statute some persons, places, or things which, without the proviso, would be included. *See* proviso in statute.

exception to the hearsay rule [*hear* · say] *n.* **Hearsay evidence** that is exempted from the general rule against the admissibility of hearsay and is therefore admissible notwithstanding the rule. EXAMPLES: a **dying declaration**; a **declaration against interest**; **business records**. *See* hearsay; hearsay rule.

excess [ek · *sess*] *adj.* Surplus; beyond normal limits.
n. A surplus or overage.
➤ *adj.* extra, surplus, overflow, spare, excessive ("excess baggage").
Ant. scarce, lacking.
n. surplus, overage, extra.

excess insurance [in · *shoor* · ense] *n.* An insurance policy under which the insurance company is liable only for the amount of **loss** or damage in excess of the coverage provided by other policies owned by the insured.

excess of jurisdiction [joo · ris · *dik* · shen] *n.* An act of a judge that is not authorized by law and is therefore unlawful. EXAMPLE: an order entered in a case that the court has no right to hear. *See* jurisdiction.

excessive [ek · *sess* · iv] *adj.* Beyond usual limits; exceeding appropriate boundaries.

➤ disproportionate, extreme, exorbitant, superfluous, exaggerated ("excessive damages").
Ant. modest, insufficient.

excessive bail *n.* Prohibited by the **Eighth Amendment**; bail set at an amount higher than is reasonably related to ensuring that the accused will appear to stand trial. *See* bail.

excessive damages [*dam* · e · jez] *n.* An award of **damages** by a verdict that appears to have been rendered under the influence of passion or prejudice, or one that is inordinately unwarranted by the facts.

excessive fine *n.* A criminal penalty forbidden by the **Eighth Amendment**; a fine that is highly disproportionate to the offense.

excessive force *n.* Force beyond that which is necessary or reasonable in the circumstances. EXAMPLE: force greater than is required for self-defense.

excessive interest *n.* *See* usury.

exchange [eks · *chaynj*] *n.* 1. A mutual transfer of property for property, generally other than money for money; a trade, barter, or swap. *Compare* sale. *See* sale or exchange. 2. A place of business where the marketing of securities is conducted; a stock exchange; a **securities exchange**. 3. A place where grain, cotton, wool, and the like are bought and sold; a **commodity exchange**. 4. An exchange of the money of one country for the money of another at a rate which depends upon the respective values of the two currencies in the money markets of the world. 5. A transfer of money from one person to another at a distant place at an agreed rate of exchange. 6. A word indicating negotiability, when it appears on the face of an instrument calling for the payment of money to a named payee. EXAMPLE: a **bill of exchange**.
v. To trade or transfer.
➤ *n.* trade, deal, transfer, replacement, substitution ("He asked for 50 dollars in exchange for his cleaning services.")
v. transfer, swap, trade, transpose, substitute ("to exchange an item of clothing for a different size").

exchange broker [*broh* · ker] *n.* 1. A broker who makes and concludes deals for others in matters of money or merchandise. 2. A broker who negotiates **bills of exchange** drawn in foreign countries or on other places in the same country. 3. A broker who transacts business on a stock exchange or a **commodity exchange**.

exchange rate   Same as **rate of exchange**.

excise   [ek · *size*]   *v.*   1. To remove, as by an incision. 2. To tax, expecially privileges or luxuries.

➤ cut, remove, extract, take out; tax, charge, collect, demand, exact.

excise tax   [*ek* · size]   *n.*   Any tax except an income tax or a property tax; a tax on the manufacture, sale, or use of goods (EXAMPLES: cigarette tax; gasoline tax) or on certain transactions or occupations (EXAMPLES: a **documentary stamp tax**; a business tax).

excited   [ek · *site* · ed]   *adj.*   In the state of being happy or aroused.

➤ active, emotional, ardent, strong, aroused, stirred, eager, inflamed.

excited utterance   [ek · *site* · ed *utt* · er · enss]   *n.*   A declaration made under the stress of excitement; it is an exception to the **hearsay rule** and is therefore admissible evidence.

exclusion   [eks · *kloo* · zhen]   *n.*   1. The action of a judge in ruling evidence to be inadmissible. 2. The amount of money a person can give away without paying a gift tax. 3. A provision in an insurance policy that removes a specified **risk**, person, or circumstance from coverage. *See* exception in insurance policy. 4. The act of keeping out or apart.

➤ rejection, omission, dismissal, elimination, disallowance, nonacceptance, repudiation.

exclusionary rule   [eks · *kloo* · zhen · air · ree]   *n.*   The rule of **constitutional law** that evidence secured by the police by means of an **unreasonable search and seizure**, in violation of the **Fourth Amendment**, cannot be used as evidence in a criminal prosecution. *See* fruit of the poisonous tree doctrine; *Mapp v. Ohio. See also* derivative evidence.

exclusive   [eks · *kloo* · siv]   *adj.*   Shutting out other occurrences or possibilities; not shared.

➤ restricted, private, limited, unique, not shared.

exclusive agency   [*ay* · jen · see]   *n.*   A contract of **agency** under which the principal gives the agent the sole right to sell. *Compare* exclusive right to sell.

exclusive bargaining agent [*bar* · gen · ing *ay* · jent]   *n.*   The union certified as the employees' **collective bargaining agent** under the **National Labor Relations Act**.

exclusive contract   [*kon* · trakt]   *n. See* entire output contract.

exclusive control   [ken · *trol*]   *n.*   A degree of control that excludes the possibility that any other person or thing had any degree of control whatsoever. Exclusive control is a requirement of the doctrine of *res ipsa loquitur*.

exclusive jurisdiction   [joo · ris · *dik* · shen]   *n.*   **Jurisdiction** when only one court has the power to adjudicate the same class of cases or the same matter. *Compare* concurrent jurisdiction. *See* jurisdiction.

exclusive license   [*ly* · sens]   *n.*   1. A **license** to do something that is not given to anyone else. 2. A grant by the owner of a patent to another person of the sole right to make, use, or sell the patented article. 3. A license granted by the owner of a **trade name** or **trademark** giving the licensee the sole right to sell the licensor's products or services. *Also see* franchise.

exclusive listing   [*list* · ing]   *n. See* exclusive right to sell.

exclusive possession   [po · *zesh* · en]   *n.*   Same as **sole possession**.

exclusive power of appointment [*pow* · er of a · *point* · ment]   *n.*   A **power of appointment** that permits the **donee** to exclude from the distribution any member of the class which the appointment was intended to benefit. *See* donee of a power. *Compare* nonexclusive power of appointment.

exclusive representation [rep · ree · zen · *tay* · shen]   *n. See* exclusive agency; exclusive bargaining agent.

exclusive right   *n.*   A sole right; a right granted to no one else.

exclusive right to sell   *n.*   The right of a sales agent to be the sole sales agent, free from all competition including competition from the principal. Exclusive right to sell agreements are particularly common in connection with sales of real estate. Called *exclusive listings*, their effect is to prevent the homeowner from selling his home without paying a commission to the agent. *See* listing agreement. *See and compare* multiple listing; nonexclusive listing; open listing.

exculpate [*eks · kul · pate*] *v.* 1. Absolve; exonerate; acquit. 2. Condone; excuse; forgive; pardon. *Compare* inculpate.
➤ vindicate, justify, dissolve, clear, pardon. *Ant.* convict.

E

exculpatory [*eks · kul · pe · toh · ree*] *adj.* Tending to free from blame or to acquit of a criminal charge. USAGE: "I think the defendant will be acquitted; virtually all of the evidence was exculpatory." *Compare* inculpatory.

exculpatory clause *n.* A clause in a contract or other legal document excusing a **party** from liability for his wrongful act. EXAMPLE: a provision in a lease relieving a landlord of liability for trespass.

excusable [*eks · kyoo · zebl*] *adj.* That which may be forgiven or overlooked.
➤ pardonable, forgivable, permissible ("excusable negligence").

excusable homicide [*hom · i · side*] *n.* A homicide committed in the course of performing a lawful act, without any intention to hurt (for EXAMPLE, by accident) or committed in self-defense. *Compare* justifiable homicide.

excusable neglect [*neg · lekt*] *n.* Dilatory neglect that may be forgiven or overlooked by a court, upon a showing of good reason therefor. For EXAMPLE, a court may authorize the opening of a **default judgment** after expiration of the time normally allowed. The court may authorize belated action in some circumstances if the failure to act was due to excusable neglect. *See* open a judgment. *Also see* dilatory.

excusable negligence [*neg · li · jenss*] *n.* *See* excusable neglect.

excuse [*eks · kyooss*] *n.* A reason for being relieved from a duty or obligation. *v.* 1. To relieve from liability. 2. To relieve from a duty or obligation.

➤ *n.* explanation, vindication, defense, rationalization ("a lame excuse").
v. pardon, vindicate, exculpate, forbear; absolve, liberate ("excuse from duty").

execute [*ek · se · kyoot*] *v.* 1. To sign a document. USAGE: "I will not deliver the goodsuntil you execute the contract." *See* execution. 2. To complete, perform, or carry out a mission, command, transaction, duty, or obligation. EXAMPLE: a **capias** is a writ by which a judge directs an officer to carry out ("execute") the court's order for the defendant's arrest. 3. To put a person to death in accordance with a sentence of death. *See* capital punishment.
➤ accomplish, perform, achieve, administer, complete ("She was quick to execute her obligations under the contract"); eliminate, finish, liquidate, condemn, assassinate ("The prisoner was scheduled to be executed at 9 a.m.").

executed [*ek · se · kyoot · ed*] *adj.* 1. Completed, performed, or carried out. 2. Signed. 3. Put to death.
➤ cut, signed, completed; killed, terminated, destroyed.

executed agreement [*a · gree · ment*] *n.* *See* executed contract.

executed consideration [*kon · sid · e · ray · shen*] *n.* **Consideration** that has been fulfilled; something given and received before the making of the contract. *See* past consideration.

executed contract [*kon · trakt*] *n.* A **contract** whose terms have been fully performed. *Compare* executory contract.

executed estate [*es · tate*] *n.* Same as **vested estate**.

executed gift *n.* A **gift** that has been delivered by the donor with the intent to transfer **title**, and that has been accepted by the donee.

executed remainder [*re · mane · der*] *n.* Same as **vested remainder**.

executed trust *n.* A **trust** in which every aspect of **disposition** is spelled out in the **trust instrument**.

executed writ *n.* A **writ** whose command has been fully carried out by the officer to whom it was directed.

execution [ek · se · *kyoo* · shen] *n.* 1. A
writ or **process** for the enforcement of a
judgment. *See* body execution; general
execution; junior execution; levy of execution; special execution. 2. The act of an
officer in serving a writ or process. 3. The
performance or carrying out of a mission,
command, duty, or obligation. 4. The
signing of a document or instrument. 5. The
carrying out of a sentence of death. 6. The
completion of any transaction.
➤ fulfillment, achievement, performance,
conclusion, accomplishment ("the execution of a contract"); capital punishment,
death, elimination, condemnation, hanging,
electrocution ("The execution was
administered by electric chair.").

execution creditor [*kred* · i · ter] *n.* A
creditor who has recovered a **judgment**
against a person obligated to him and has
caused an execution to be issued on the
judgment.

execution lien [leen] *n.* A **lien** created
by or in connection with a **levy of
execution**.

execution sale *n.* A **public sale** by a
sheriff or similar officer of property seized
under a writ of execution following a
levy of execution. *See also* judicial sale.

executioner [ek · se · *kyoo* · shen · er] *n.*
A person who carries out or executes a
death sentence.

executive [eg · *zek* · yoo · tiv] *adj.*
Pertaining to the administration or
enforcement of the law.
n. 1. A person who enforces the law, as
distinguished from a person who makes
the law or a person who interprets the law.
2. A person who manages or administers.
➤ *adj.* managerial, presidential, official,
administrative ("executive decree").
n. chief, supervisor, boss, director, chairperson, president ("a corporate executive").

executive agency [*ay* · jen · see] *n.*
Another term for administrative agency.

executive agreement [a · *gree* · ment] *n.*
An agreement with a foreign government,
made by the president acting within her
executive powers.

executive branch *n.* 1. With the
legislative branch and the **judicial
branch**, one of the three divisions into
which the Constitution separates the
government of the United States. These
branches of government are also referred
to as **departments of government**. The
executive branch is primarily responsible
for enforcing the laws. 2. A similar division
in state government.

executive committee [ke · *mit* · ee] *n.*
1. A committee of the directors of a
corporation authorized to act for the board
of directors between meetings of the board
with respect to ordinary business of the
corporation. 2. A committee of administrative personnel of any organization able to
act for the orgainization with respect to the
management of its daily business.

executive department [dee · *part* · ment]
n. 1. Another term for the **executive branch**
of the federal government or of a state
government. 2. A unit within the executive
branch of government. EXAMPLES: the
Department of Justice; the Department of
Commerce.

executive employee [em · *ploy* · ee] *n.*
An employee who may have administrative
duties but who has at least some managerial authority, i.e., the power to direct
others and to participate in the management
of the enterprise.

executive officer [*off* · i · ser] *n.*
1. Any **officer** upon whom **executive
powers** of federal or state government
are conferred. EXAMPLES: the president of
the United States; the attorney general of
the United States or of a state; the governor
of a state. 2. An officer of a corporation
who has or shares responsibility for determining and overseeing the affairs of the
corporation.

executive order [*or* · der] *n.* An order
issued by the **chief executive officer**
(EXAMPLES: the president of the United
States; the governor of a state; the mayor
of a city) of government, whether national,
state, or local.

executive powers [*pow* · erz] *n.* The
powers vested in the **executive branch** of
the United States government by Article
II of the Constitution or in the executive
branch of the government of a state, city, or
town by its constitution or **charter**. *Compare* judicial powers; legislative powers.

E

E

executive privilege [*priv* · i · lej] *n.* The privilege of the president of the United States to refuse to make certain confidential commuications available to public scrutiny or to review by any **branch of government** other than the **executive branch**.

executive session [*sesh* · en] *n.* A meeting of a governmental body, usually a legislative body (EXAMPLE: a city council), that is closed to the public. In many jurisdictions, the enactment of legislation in executive session is prohibited by **sunshine laws**.

executor [eg · *zek* · yoo · tor] *n.* A person designated by a **testator** to carry out the directions and requests in the testator's will and to dispose of his property according to the provisions of his will. *Compare* administrator. *See also* personal representative.
➤ administrator, fiduciary, custodian, personal representative.

executory [eg · *zek* · yoo · tor · ee] *adj.* Not yet fully performed, completed, fulfilled, or carried out; to be performed, either wholly or in part; not yet executed. *See* execute.
➤ incomplete, unfulfilled, contingent, deficient, partial, unexecuted.
Ant. executed, completed.

executory contract [kon · trakt] *n.* A **contract** yet to be performed, each **party** having bound herself to do or not to do a particular thing. *Compare* executed contract.

executory estate [es · *tate*] *n.* All **future estates** except **remainders** and **reversions**; a **contingent estate**. *See* future interest; vested estate.

executory interest [*in* · trest] *n.* Same as **executory estate**.

exemplar [*eg* · zem · plar] *n.* An example; a sample; a specimen. EXAMPLE: mug shots; fingerprints; **DNA fingerprinting**.
➤ example, sample, specimen.

exemplary damages [eg · *zemp* · le · ree *dam* · e · jez] *n.* Same as **punitive damages**.

exempli gratia [eg · *zemp* · lee *grah* · tee · ah] (*Latin*) "For the sake of an example," for example, or by way of example. Commonly abbreviated **e.g.**

exemplification [eg · zemp · li · fi · *kay* · shen] *n.* The **authentication** of a copy of a document by **attestation** or certification. *See* certified copy.
➤ authentication, certification, verification.

exemplified copy [eg · *zemp* · li · fide *kop* · ee] *n.* An **authenticated** copy; a copy of a public document or record verified by official seal. *See* certified copy.

exempt [eg · *zemt*] *adj.* Excused; free of an obligation that is binding on others.
v. To release from an obligation or duty; to excuse.
➤ *adj.* immune, privileged, freed, favored, excused ("The company was exempt from investigation.").
Ant. accountable, responsible.
v. waive, excuse, absolve, clear, discharge ("I was exempted from the written examination.").
Ant. obligate, encumber.

exempt income [*in* · kum] *n.* 1. Income on which one need not pay income tax. 2. Income not subject to **garnishment**.

exempt organization [or · ga · ni · *zay* · shen] *n.* *See* charitable organization.

exemption [eg · *zemp* · shen] *n.* 1. Freedom or release from some legal duty or obligation (EXAMPLES: military service; jury duty). 2. The privilege granted a debtor to retain a portion of his property or earnings free from the claims of his creditors and from bankruptcy. 3. An allowance granted by way of a deduction when computing one's taxable income. EXAMPLES: a tax exemption for a dependent; a **personal exemption**. 4. The person for whom an exemption may be claimed in an income tax return.
➤ immunity, liberty, absolution, dispensation.
Ant. obligation.

exemption statutes [stat · shoots] *n.* State statutes that exempt certain types of property owned by a **judgment debtor**, or property of a specified value, from **levy of execution** and **public sale**. *See* homestead exemption.

exercise [*eks* · er · size] *n.* The act of using or making use of.
v. To use; to make use of. USAGE: "Under my contract, I will lose my option to

purchase the truck unless I exercise it by the end of the month."
➤ *n.* use, utilization; drill, practice; physical labor.
v. utilize, employ, apply, practice, administer.
Ant. disregard.

exhaustion [eg · *zaws* · chen] *n.* The state of having spent all available energy.
➤ fatigue, weariness, debility, enervation, draining.

exhaustion of remedy [eg · *zaws* · chen of *rem* · e · dee] *n.* 1. The doctrine that when the law provides an **administrative remedy**, a party seeking **relief** must fully exercise that remedy before the courts will intervene. 2. The doctrine, applicable in many types of cases, that the federal courts will not respond to a party seeking relief until she has exhausted her remedies in state court.

exhibit [eg · *zib* · it] *n.* 1. Any paper or thing offered in evidence and marked for identification. 2. A document attached to and made a part of a **pleading**, transcript, contract, or other legal paper.
v. To show or display something.
➤ *n.* attachment, document, display, illustration, transcript ("Please refer to exhibit A.").
v. show, display, reveal, uncover, illustrate.

exhumation [eg · zoo · *may* · shen] *n.* The removal of a body from the grave.
➤ removal, unearthing, disentombment, resurrection.
Ant. burial.

exigence [*eg* · zi · jenss] *n.* Same as **exigency**.
➤ urgency, necessity, exigency.

exigency [*eg* · zi · jen · see] *n.* An urgency; something requiring immediate attention.
➤ imperativeness, flight, crisis.

exigent [*eggs* · ih · jent] *adj.* Requiring urgent aid or assistance.
➤ pressing, urgent, vital, crucial, grave, essential ("exigent circumstances").

exist [eg · *zist*] *v.* 1. To continue to survive despite adverse situations. 2. To be living.
➤ endure, survive, subsist, live; live, breathe, continue, remain, last.

exoneration [eg · zon · e · *ray* · shen] *n.* 1. The act of clearing a person of a charge or accusation of guilt. 2. A release or discharge from liability.
➤ dismissal, clearance, release, acquittal, exculpation.

expatriation [eks · pay · tree · *ay* · shen] *n.* A voluntary change of citizenship from one country to another. EXAMPLE: the act of choosing the citizenship of the second country, by a child born in the United States who possesses **dual citizenship** and who has attained her **majority**.
➤ migration, withdrawal, renouncement, relegation.
Ant. immigration.

expect [eks · *pekt*] *v.* 1. To look forward to. 2. To consider something as certain; to predict.
➤ await, anticipate, look forward to; assume, predict, suppose, infer, surmise.

expectancy [eks · *pek* · ten · see] *n.* 1. An **estate** which one anticipates receiving (EXAMPLES: a **reversion**; a **remainder**), as opposed to an estate which one presently possesses or enjoys. 2. Something that is anticipated.
➤ contingency, likelihood, probability, presumption.

expectancy tables [*tay* · blz] *n. See* mortality tables.

expectant *adj.* Having hope; anticipating.
➤ hopeful, anticipating, readying, prospective ("an expectant mother").

expectant estates [es · *tates*] *n.* **Future interests**.

expectant heir *n.* A person who expects to inherit property. *Compare* heir apparent; heir presumptive.

expectant right *n. See* expectancy; expectant estates.

expectation [eks · pek · *tay* · shun] *n.* The prospect of an event occurring.
➤ anticipation, contemplation, prospect, expectancy, hope, preconception, promise.

expedite [*eks* · pe · dite] *v.* To speed along or hasten.
➤ speed, facilitate, accelerate, quicken, encourage, dispatch, push forward.

E

E

expense [eks · *pense*] *n.* The cost of a thing or of a service; the charge made for something; a paying out. *See* business expenses; operating expenses; ordinary and necessary expense; out-of-pocket expense.
➤ cost, charge, rate, payment, price, value, debit, sacrifice, surrender, loss, forfeit.
expense of litigation [lit · i · *gay* · shen] *n.* Court costs and attorney fees.
expenses of administration [ad · min · is · *tray* · shen] *n. See* administration expenses.

experience [eks · *peer* · ee · ense] *n.* 1. Practical knowledge gained by training and practicing. 2. Something personally lived through; the events that combine to make up a life.
➤ skill, training, proficiency, exposure, competence, expertise ("experience in litigation"); event, occasion, adventure, occurrence, situation ("a scary experience").

experience rating [eks · *peer* · ee · ense *ray* · ting] *n.* An insurance company's record with respect to **losses** in connection with a particular type of **risk** against which it insures its policyholders, for EXAMPLE, automobile collision or residential burglary.

experience tables [eks · *peer* · ee · ense *tay* · blz] *n. See* mortality tables.

expert [*eks* · pert] *n.* A person who has special skill or knowledge in a given field. *See* expertise.
adj. Highly proficient, or professional.
➤ *n.* authority, professional, specialist, virtuoso, scholar, veteran, master ("an expert in the field of forensic medicine"). *Ant.* layperson.
adj. skilled, qualified, competent, accomplished, proficient ("an expert witness").
expert opinion [uh · *pin* · yen] *n. See* expert testimony; expert witness.
expert testimony [*tes* · ti · moh · nee] *n.* The **opinion evidence** of an **expert witness**; the testimony of a person particularly skilled, learned, or experienced in a particular art, science, trade, business, profession, or vocation who has a thorough knowledge concerning such matters that is not possessed by people in general.
expert witness [*wit* · nes] *n.* A person who is so qualified, either by actual experience or by careful study, as to enable him to form a definite opinion of his own respecting a subject about which persons having no particular training, experience, or special study are incapable of forming accurate opinions. *See* expert testimony.

expertise [eks · per · *teez*] *n.* The knowledge possessed by an expert.
➤ knowledge, skill, wisdom, experience, facility.

expiration [eks · per · *ay* · shun] *n.* Coming to an end; termination due to lapse of time.
➤ conclusion, termination, ending, discontinuation.

explain [eks · *plane*] *v.* To make known or understandable.
➤ clarify, elucidate, unravel, define, illuminate, solve, untangle.

explicit [eks · *pliss* · iht] *adj.* Clear and definite.
➤ clear, definite, exact, obvious, manifest, unambiguous, lucid, stated, expressed, understandable ("explicit directions"). *Ant.* implicit, obscure.

exploit [eks · *ployt*] *v.* 1. To take advantage of for one's own purposes. 2. To put to productive use.
➤ abuse, victimize, oppress, persecute, take advantage of; use, operate, apply, avail, utilize.

export [*eks* · port] *adj.* Relating to goods shipped out of the country.
n. Singular of **exports**. *See* exports.
v. [eks · *port*] To ship goods out of the country.
➤ *n.* trade goods, wares, articles ("musical export").
v. convey, transport, converge, send out ("to export goods").
export tax *n.* A tax on goods shipped out of the country or on the act of shipping goods out of the country.

exportation [eks · por · *tay* · shen] *n.* The sending of goods from one country to another country. *Compare* importation.
➤ sending, transporting.
Ant. importation.

exports [*eks* · ports] *n.* Goods shipped from one country to another country.
➤ goods, trade goods, shipments, shipped wares.

expository statute [eks · *pos* · i · tor · ee *stat* · shoot] *n.* A statute enacted for the purpose of construing or interpreting an existing statute.

exposure [eks · *poh* · zher] *n.* The state of being visible or public. *See* indecent exposure.
➤ uncovering, acknowledgment, display, openness, publicity, disclosure, divulgence.

express [eks · *press*] *adj.* Stated; declared; clear; explicit; not left to implication. *Compare* implied.
v. To put into words; to verbalize; to state; to declare.
➤ *adj.* stated, declared, clear, explicit, precise, unmistakable ("an express duty").
v. put into words, verbalize, indicate, communicate, state, declare, articulate ("He expressed his concerns.").

express agency [*ay* · jen · see] *n.* Same as **actual agency**.

express assumpsit [a · *sump* · sit] *n.* An undertaking to do something that is supported by an express promise. *See assumpsit.*

express authority [aw · *thaw* · ri · tee] *n.* Authority expressly granted to or conferred upon an agent or employee by a principal or employer. *Compare* apparent authority.

express condition [ken · *dish* · en] *n.* A **condition** that is stated rather than implied.

express contract [*kon* · trakt] *n.* A **contract** whose terms are stated by the parties.

express easement [*eez* · ment] *n.* An **easement** created by agrement, **grant**, **reservation**, **exception**, or **covenant**. *See* exception in deed.

express invitation [in · va · *tay* · shen] *n.* A written or spoken **invitation** given to a person by the owner or occupant of realty, permitting the person to enter the property. *Compare* implied invitation. *See* invitee.

express malice [*mal* · iss] *n.* 1. For the purpose of **first degree murder**, a deliberate or premeditated design to inflict injury or take life. 2. For the purposes of the law of **defamation**, **malice in fact** as distinguished from **implied malice**. *See* malice.

express notice [*no* · tiss] *n.* **Actual notice** communicated by direct information. *Compare* constructive notice; implied notice. *See* notice.

express permission [per · *mish* · en] *n.* As used in statutes imposing liability upon an automobile owner for injury caused to her car when operated by another person, means the owner's prior knowledge of the intended use and her consent to it.

express powers [*pow* · erz] *n.* Same as **enumerated powers**.

express repeal [re · *peel*] *n. See* repeal of statute.

express trust *n.* A **trust** created by a direct or positive **declaration of trust**.

express waiver [*way* · ver] *n.* **Waiver** by express or positive act or words. *Compare* implied waiver.

express warranty [*war* · en · tee] *n.* A **warranty** created by the seller in a **contract for sale of goods**, in which the seller, orally or in writing, makes representations regarding the quality or condition of the goods. *Compare* implied warranty.

expression [ex · *press* · shun] *n.* 1. A verbalization; a formulation; an assertion. 2. Facial appearance.
➤ manifestation, exhibition, indication, sign ("an expression of his intent"); assertion, communication, remark, declaration ("the expression of his idea"); look, countenance, grimace, air, aspect ("a surprised expression").

expropriate [eks · *pro* · pree · ate] *v.* To **condemn** property for public use. *See* condemnation; eminent domain.
➤ seize, assume, impound, confiscate, foreclose ("The land was expropriated for state use.").

expropriation [eks · pro · pree · *ay* · shen] *n.* 1. The taking of private property by the government for public use through the exercise of the power of **eminent domain**. *See* condemnation; taking. 2. The act of taking something from someone.
➤ appropriation, taking, assumption, seizure, condemnation.

expulsion [eks · *pul* · shen] *n.* 1. The forcing of a person out of a school or an

E

association, society, corporation, legislative body, or the like. 2. A driving out.
➤ banishment, discharge, dismissal, ban, rejection, ousting ("expulsion from school").

expunge *v.* To erase, delete, or strike.
➤ erase, eradicate, delete, omit, extirpate, exclude, abolish.

expungement [eks · *punj* · ment] *n.* The act of erasing, deleting, removing, destroying, obliterating, or wiping out.
➤ abolition, obliteration, extermination, annihilation ("the expungement of the monarchy").
　expungement of record [*rek* · erd] *n.* With some variance from state to state, every jurisdiction provides for the removal of criminal convictions of certain offenses from a person's record, particularly first offenses. *See* first offender.

extant [eks · *tent*] *adj.* Alive or existing.
➤ alive, existing, surviving, living. *Ant.* extinct.

extend [eks · *tend*] *v.* 1. To spread or stretch out to a fuller length. 2. To hold out; to offer.
➤ broaden, widen, add, augment, enlarge, lengthen, continue ("extend the porch"); offer, proffer, put forth, present, hold out, give ("extend my thanks").

extended benefits program [eks · *ten* · ded *ben* · e · fits *pro* · gram] *n.* A program created by and funded under federal statutes that provide for the payment of additional unemployment compensation benefits after the weeks of eligibility under state statute have been used up.

extension [eks · *ten* · shen] *n.* A stretching; a lengthening; a prolongation; a continuance.
➤ enlargement, continuation, prolongation, addition, elongation, stretching ("I was given an extension of time for my paper.").
　extension of debt *n.* *See* extension of time.
　extension of lease *n.* The lengthening of the term of a lease by mutual agreement between the lessee and lessor. *Note:* an extension is not a renewal. *Compare* renewal of lease.
　extension of note *n.* *See* extension of time.

extension of time *n.* 1. Prolonging the time for payment of a note to a date beyond the due date stated in the note. 2. Modification of an obligation by giving additional time for performance. 3. Relief granted to a debtor by a **bankruptcy court**. 4. An enlargement of time. 5. Any lengthening of a previously set period of time.

extenuating [eks · *ten* · yoo · ay · ting] *adj.* Tending to moderate or mitigate.
➤ mitigating, alleviating, diminishing, explanatory, exculpating ("extenuating circumstances").

extenuating circumstances [eks · *ten* · yoo · ay · ting *ser* · kum · stan · sez] *n.* Facts that reduce the damages in a civil case or the penalty in a criminal case. *See* mitigating circumstances; mitigation of damages.

extenuation [eks · *ten* · yoo · *ay* · shen] *n.* The reduction of damages in a civil case or punishment in a criminal case.
➤ mitigation, moderation, reduction, justification ("an extenuation of the sentence").

exterritorial [eks · terr · i · *tor* · ee · el] *adj.* The status of persons (EXAMPLES: visiting diplomats; an ambassador) who live in a country but are not subject to its laws. *Compare* extraterritoriality.

extinguishment [eks · *ting* · wish · ment] *n.* Discharge; destruction; termination; cancellation. *See* release.
➤ elimination, discharge, destruction, termination, cancellation, suffocation ("extinguishment of the debt").
　extinguishment of debt *n.* The termination or cancellation of a debt, whether by payment, **merger in judgment**, **novation**, or otherwise.
　extinguishment of easement [*eez* · ment] *n.* The termination of an **easement**, whether by **abandonment of use**, merger of the **dominant tenement** and the **servient tenement, release,** or otherwise.
　extinguishment of rent *n.* The termination of a tenant's liability for rent, whether by acquisition of **title** to the land or by a **release** granted by the landlord.

extort [eks · *tort*] *v.* 1. To coerce; to intimidate. 2. To commit the crime of **extortion.**

➤ extract, cheat, blackmail, demand, wrest, coerce ("They extorted money from the government.").

extortion [eks · *tor* · shen] *n.* The criminal offense of obtaining money or other thing of value by duress, force, threat of force, fear, or **color of office**. *See also* coercion; duress; intimidation.

➤ coercion, intimidation, fraud, stealing, oppression ("the criminal extortion of funds").

extra [*eks* · tra] *adj.* Outside of; out of; beyond; better than expected.

➤ *adj.* excess, additional, spare, ancillary ("an extra pair of glasses").
adv. particularly, extremely, especially ("be extra careful").
n. addition, complement, bonus, supplement ("The free air conditioning was an added extra for buying the car.").

extra dividend [*div* · i · dend] *n.* Sometimes called an extraordinary dividend; a **dividend** paid by a corporation beyond **ordinary dividends**.

extra session [*sesh* · en] *n. See* special session.

extra vires [*esk* · tra *vy* · reez] (*Latin*) *adj.* Same as *ultra vires*.

extra work *n.* Services undertaken by a contractor in addition to the work covered by the contract, for which extra compensation is sought.

extradition [eks · tra · *dish* · en] *n.* The surrender by one nation or state to another of a person accused or convicted of an offense within the territory of the second.

➤ surrendering, deportation, transfer.

extradition treaty [*tree* · tee] *n.* A **treaty** between two nations that provides for the extradition from one to the other of persons charged with or convicted of offenses listed in the treaty.

extradotal property [eks · tra · *doh* · tal *prop* · er · tee] *n.* In Louisiana, the portion of the property of a married woman that is not part of her **dowry**.

extrajudicial [eks · tra · joo · *dish* · el] *adj.* That which occurs aside from or independent of the court or of judicial action; outside of the court's jurisdiction; outside of the courtroom.

➤ private, separate, independent, out-of-court ("an extrajudicial statement").

extrajudicial statement [*state* · ment] *n.* Any statement made outside of court.

extralateral rights [eks · tra · *lat* · er · el] *n. See* apex rule.

extralegal [eks · tra · *leeg* · el] *adj.* Beyond the control or authority of the law. *Note* that extralegal does not mean illegal.

➤ out of reach, unattainable, beyond, out-of-court, nonlegal.

extraneous [eks · *tray* · nee · us] *adj.* 1. Something coming from outside. 2. Not pertinent; irrelevant. *See* aliunde.

➤ irrelevant, unneeded, impertinent, inadmissible, inessential, foreign ("extraneous information").

extraneous evidence [*ev* · i · dense] *n. See* parol evidence.

extraordinary [eks · *trore* · di · nar · ee] *adj.* Not of a usual, regular, or customary kind; remarkable; uncommon; rare.

➤ bizarre, inconceivable, outstanding, rare, individual, unusual, remarkable, uncommon ("extraordinary diligence").

extraordinary care *n.* A very high degree of care; the highest degree of care; the greatest care. *Compare* slight care. *See* care.

extraordinary diligence [*dil* · i · genss] *n.* A very high degree of diligence; the highest degree of diligence; the greatest diligence. *See* diligence.

extraordinary remedies [*rem* · e · deez] *n.* **Remedies** that provide types of **relief** not obtainable in an ordinary **action at law** or **equitable action**. EXAMPLES: *certiorari*; *mandamus*; *quo warranto*. *See* extraordinary writs.

extraordinary session [*sesh* · en] *n. See* special session.

extraordinary writs [ritz] *n.* **Writs** that provide **extraordinary remedies**. (EXAMPLES: a **writ of certiorari**; a **writ of mandamus**; a **writ of quo warranto**.) Extraordinary writ is the modern term for **prerogative writ**.

extraterritoriality [eks · tra · terr · i · tor · ee · *al* · i · tee] *n.* The operation of the laws of a state or country beyond its geographical boundaries. An act that is a wrong according to the law of the jurisdiction where it occurred, rather than the law of the jurisdiction where suit is brought, is an EXAMPLE of an extraterritorial wrong. *Compare* exterritorial.

extreme [esk · *treem*] *adj.* 1. Exceeding the norm; beyond reason or convention. 2. Existing at a very high degree; far away.
➤ intense, extensive, excessive, drastic, harsh, egregious, outrageous; last, furthest, final, outermost, ultimate, terminal, utmost. *Ant.* moderate, mild.

extreme cruelty [eks · *treem krew* · el · tee] *n.* A ground for divorce. It is not confined to physical violence, but also includes conduct that wounds the feelings and sensibilities so severely as to impair physical or mental health.

extremis [eks · *treem* · iss] *See in extremis.*

extrinsic [eks · *trin* · sik] *adj.* Outside; from outside; derived from outside; foreign. *Compare* intrinsic.

➤ foreign, extraneous, imported, outside, irrelevant, unrelated, peripheral, contingent.

extrinsic evidence [*ev* · i · dense] *n.* Evidence from another source or another place; **parol evidence**; **evidence aliunde**.

extrinsic fraud *n.* **Fraud** that is collateral to the issues tried in the case in which the **judgment** was rendered and that constitutes grounds for setting aside the judgment; fraud that prevents a party from having a trial or from presenting his side of the case fully and fairly. EXAMPLE: A party misrepresenting to the court that he had given his adversary notice of the action. *Compare* intrinsic fraud.

eyewitness [*eye* · wit · ness] *n.* A person who testifies to what she has seen.
➤ bystander, observer, onlooker, corroborator, identifier, spectator.

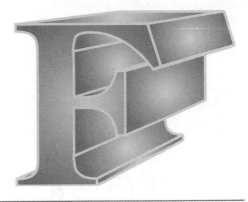

FAA Abbreviation of **Federal Aviation Agency**.

fabricate [*fab* · ri · kate] *v.* 1. To falsify; to forge; to deceive. 2. To construct; to manufacture.
➤ falsify, defraud, concoct, produce ("She gave fabricated testimony"); construct, manufacture, compose, create ("fabricate the product").

fabricated evidence [*fab* · ri · kay · ted *ev* · i · dense] *n.* Evidence that has been manufactured and is false in whole or in part.

face *n.* 1. The surface or front of any object or other thing. 2. The printed and written matter appearing on the front of an **instrument**, document, **judgment, pleading**, or statute. USAGE: "The court will decide whether this is your signature, but the check seems valid on its face." *See* face of instrument.
v. To confront. USAGE: "She was ready to face her accusers."
➤ *n.* appearance, disguise, display, visage, surface, front.
v. confront, encounter, challenge, meet, defy.

face amount [a · *mount*] *n.* Same as **face value**.

face of instrument [*in* · stroo · ment] *n.* 1. The words and numbers that appear on an **instrument**, and the legal consequences produced by those words and numbers and by those words and numbers only; that is, without regard to any **extrinsic evidence** relating to their meaning. 2. **Face amount** or **face value**. 3. The side of an instrument upon which the terms and conditions appear.

face of judgment [*juj* · ment] *n.* The amount for which the **judgment** was rendered, without interest.

face of policy [*pol* · e · see] *n.* All of the provisions of an insurance policy, as opposed to merely the front page. *Compare* face value.

face of the record [*rek* · erd] *n.* The entire **record** in a case, not merely some part of it; the record as a whole.

face value [*val* · yoo] *n.* The value printed or otherwise appearing on the face of stock, **bonds**, insurance policies, and similar instruments; that is, without regard to any dividends, interest, or, in the case of life insurance, any additional **indemnity** that is or might be payable. *See also* par value.

facilitate [fe · *sil* · e · tayt] *v.* To aid or assist; to bring about.
➤ aid, assist, advance, enable, speed up, foster, expedite, simplify, make possible ("to facilitate his release from prison").

facilitation [fe · sil · e · *tay* · shen] *n.* 1. The act of helping to make a crime easier to accomplish. 2. Any act of assistance.
➤ furtherance, promotion, expedition.

facilities [fe · *sil* · e · teez] *n. Plural* of **facility**.

facility [fe · *sil* · e · tee] *n.* 1. Proficiency or skill. 2. Something created, constructed, or used to make something else easier to do. USAGE: "A bank is a facility that facilitates the saving of money." *See* facilitation.
➤ ease, efficiency, aptitude; accommodation, network, resource, training place.

facility of payment clause [*pay* · ment] *n.* A clause in an insurance policy that permits the insured and the beneficiary to appoint persons who may receive benefit payments for the beneficiary. In certain circumstances, such a clause may make it easier for an insurance company to discharge its liability.

facsimile [fak · *sim* · i · lee] *n.* An exact and precise copy or reproduction of anything. A signature reproduced by rubber stamp is a "facsimile signature."
➤ reproduction, copy, replica, simulation, likeness.

fact *n.* An actual occurrence, as distinguished from the legal consequences of the occurrence; something that took place, not something that might or might not have occurred; an act or deed; that which exists; that which is real; that which is true. For the critically important distinction between a question of *fact* and a question of *law*, *see and compare* question of fact; question of law. *See also* accessory after the fact; accessory before the fact; evidentiary facts; matter of fact; probative facts; ultimate facts.
➤ verifiable truth, experience, actuality, reality, occurrence, certainty, matter.

fact findings [*fine* · dingz] *n.* *See* finding of fact. *Compare* conclusion of law.

fact questions [*kwes* · chenz] *n.* *See* question of fact.

fact-finding body [*fakt*-fine · ding *bod* · ee] *n.* A board or body, usually of an administrative agency, that is empowered to make **findings of fact**.

facto [fak · toh] (*Latin*) Fact; in fact; in deed. *See de facto; ex post facto; ipso facto.*

factor [fak · ter] *n.* 1. A part or element. 2. A person employed to receive goods from a **principal** and to sell them for compensation, usually in the form of a commission referred to as **factorage**. A factor is a **bailee** who is sometimes called a **consignee** or **commission merchant**. *Compare* broker.
➤ ingredient, determinant, consideration, instrumentality, point; bailee, consignee, commission, merchant.

factor's lien [*leen*] *n.* The **lien** that a factor has on his principal's goods for his commissions and expenses.

factorage [*fak* · ter · ej] *n.* Commissions or other compensation paid to a **factor** for his services.

factorizing process [*fak* · ter · ize · ing *pross* · ess] *n.* Another term for **garnishment**.

factors' acts Statutes in many states that enable a factor to do anything with respect to the owner's goods that the owner could, and making the owner responsible for the factor's conduct and protecting **bona fide purchasers** in any transaction with the factor.

facts *n.* *See* fact.

facts in issue [*ish* · ew] *n.* The facts upon which the plaintiff bases her **cause of action**, and which the defendant disputes in his **pleadings**.

factual [*fak* · tyoo · ul] *adj.* Relating to the facts; objective; true.
➤ accurate, undistorted, faithful, unbiased, undisputed, authentic, realistic, verifiable, objective, true ("a factual account").

faculty [*fak* · ul · tee] *n.* 1. the mental capacity or ability to perform an act. 2. An organization of educators.
➤ ability, proficiency, talent, aptitude, capacity, competency ("his faculty at math"); instructors, professors, lecturers ("a fine faculty").

fail *v.* 1. To fall short; to not succeed. 2. To refuse. *But compare* refusal; refuse. 3. To neglect or to not perform. *But compare* neglect. 4. To become worthless. 5. To become insolvent. 6. To lapse. 7. To decline in health. 8. To collapse. *See* failure.
➤ refuse, abort, abandon, desert, forsake; decline, deteriorate, fall, miscarry.

failed bank *n.* *See* bank failure.

failing [*fayl* · ing] *n.* 1. The state of not succeeding. 2. Weakness or defect.
➤ defect, deficiency, fault, flaw, Achilles heel.

failing circumstances [*fail* · ing *ser* · kem · stan · sez] *n.* The situation in which a person finds himself, or a business finds itself, when debts become increasingly difficult to pay as they come due; the approach of insolvency.

failure [*fail* · yer] *n.* 1. A lack of success; inability; the fact of having fallen short.

F

EXAMPLE: **failure of proof**. 2. Refusal. EXAMPLE: **failure to bargain collectively**. *But compare* refusal; refuse. 3. Neglect or nonperformance. EXAMPLE: **failure to prosecute**. *But compare* neglect. 4. Worthlessness. EXAMPLE: **failure of consideration**. 5. Insolvency. EXAMPLE: **bank failure**. 6. A lapse. EXAMPLE: **failure of issue**. 7. A decline in health. EXAMPLE: heart failure. 8. Collapse. EXAMPLE: **bank failure**. *See* fail.
➤ inability, inadequacy, nonperformance, nonsuccess, defeat ("failure to reach your quota"); defaulter, deadbeat, loafer, nonperformer, underachiever ("He was considered a failure by his peers").

failure of bank *n.* *See* bank failure.

failure of consideration [ken · sid · e · *ray* · shen] *n.* The circumstance that exists when the **consideration** for a contract, which was sufficient at the time the contract was entered into, has become worthless, has ceased to exist, or has been invalidated, usually by failure of one of the parties to keep his promise or as a result of a defect in the consideration. *Compare* want of consideration.

failure of evidence [ev · i · dense] *n.* *See* failure of proof.

failure of issue [ish · ew] *n.* The death of a person without children. The term refers to the circumstance in which an **estate** cannot be acquired as provided by will because there has been a death **without issue**. *See* die without issue.

failure of proof *n.* In the trial of a lawsuit, an absence or failure of proof with respect to facts alleged, with the result that the **cause of action** or **defense** fails.

failure of record [rek · erd] *n.* The failure of a party to produce a record (EXAMPLE: a certified copy of a recorded deed) after alleging its importance to her case.

failure to bargain collectively [barg · en ke · lek · tiv · lee] *n.* An employer's refusal to negotiate in good faith, as required by the **National Labor Relations Act**, with a union that is the **collective bargaining agent** for its employees. *See* collective bargaining.

failure to make delivery [de · *liv* · e · ree] *n.* Failure to make a delivery as required by the law or by contract; misdelivery.

failure to prosecute [pross · e · kyoot] *n.* A plaintiff's failure to appear in court and proceed with his case, or his failure to pursue it diligently. *Note* that "prosecute," as used in the context of "failure to prosecute," relates to a civil action, not a criminal prosecution. Failure to prosecute a lawsuit is a ground for its dismissal. *See* want of prosecution.

failure to state a cause of action [ak · shen] *n.* *See* demurrer; demurrer to evidence.

faint *adj.* 1. Slight; not easily discernible. 2. Light-headed or weak.
➤ weak, light-headed ("to feel faint"); ambiguous, obscure, dark ("a faint light in the distance").

faint pleading [plee · ding] *n.* A false or deceptive **pleading**, intended to deceive persons who are not involved in the lawsuit.

fair *adj.* Equitable; honest; just; neutral; objective; openminded; unbiased.
➤ impartial, unprejudiced, nonpartisan, unbiased, detached ("a fair trial"); mediocre, intermediate, medium, moderate, reasonable ("a fair ball player").

fair and impartial trial [im · *par* · shel try · el] *n.* A trial conducted in accordance with the requirements of **due process of law**.

fair cash value [val · yoo] *n.* The reasonable cash price for which something can be sold in the market after reasonable efforts have been made to find the purchaser who will give the highest price. Fair cash value is almost synonymous with **actual cash value** or **fair market value**.

fair comment [kom · ent] *n.* Doctrine applicable to the news media, concerning press comment on matters of public interest; as long as the report is based on honest belief of truthfulness, fair comment is a defense to a **libel** action if the report or comment proves to be inaccurate. *See* conditionally privileged communication; journalists' privilege; privileged communication. *Compare* defamation.

F

fair competition [kom · pe · *tish* · en] *n.* Open, equitable, and just competition, fair between competitors and to their customers. *Compare* unfair competition.

fair consideration [ken · sid · e · *ray* · shen] *n.* A fair and reasonable price for the subject matter of a contract; **adequate consideration**; something more than **nominal consideration**.

fair hearing [*hear* · ing] *n.* A term that refers to the **due process** requirements for administrative hearings. The requirements are not as strict as the **fair and impartial trial** criteria applicable to court cases. *See* due process of law.

fair market price [*mar* · ket] *n.* **Market value**. *See* fair market value.

fair market value (FMV) [*mar* · ket *val* · yoo] *n.* Actual value; value in money. The amount a buyer will pay and a seller will accept when neither is under pressure to buy or sell and both have a reasonable degree of knowledge of the relevant facts. Fair market value is virtually synonymous with **actual cash value**, **fair cash value**, and **fair value**. When there is no market, it is sometimes necessary for a court to construct a fair market value, relying upon **expert testimony** with respect to a hypothetical buyer and seller in the same circumstances. *See* market.

fair preponderance of evidence [pre · *pon* · de · rense of ev · i · dense] *n.* Same as **preponderance of evidence**.

fair return [re · *tern*] *n.* Also referred to as fair rate of return and fair return on investment; an important factor in the setting of public utility rates by public utility commissions. A public utility's rates may be no higher than those required to give its investors a "fair return" on their investment.

fair sale *n.* A **judicial sale** conducted according to law at an auction at which all persons have the right to appear and bid.

fair trade acts *n.* Statutes, now repealed, that allowed producers and distributors of brand name goods to set the minimum and maximum retail prices of their goods.

fair trial [*try* · el] *n.* Same as **fair and impartial trial**.

fair use doctrine [*dok* · trin] *n.* The principle that entitles a person to use copyrighted material in a reasonable manner, including a work's theme or idea, without the consent of the copyright owner.

fair value [*val* · yoo] *n.* *See* fair market value.

Fair Credit Billing Act [*kred* · it *bil* · ing] *n.* One of the federal **consumer credit protection acts**, which provides a procedure for the correction of disputed bills in transactions involving credit.

Fair Credit Reporting Act [*kred* · it re · *port* · ing] *n.* A federal statute that regulates credit bureaus with respect to their release and use of credit reports. The Act prohibits the reporting of outdated information and the reporting of information for employment purposes. It requires accuracy and relevancy in reporting, as well as due regard for confidentiality, and provides consumers the opportunity to correct inaccurate information in their files.

Fair Debt Collection Practices Act [ke · *lek* · shen *prak* · tiss · ez] *n.* One of the federal **consumer credit protection acts**, whose purpose is to eliminate improper collection practices by debt collection agencies (EXAMPLES: contacting a debtor at work; telephoning a debtor at home at unreasonable hours).

Fair Housing Act [*how* · zing] *n.* Another name for the **Civil Rights Act of 1968**, which prohibits practices that deny housing to anyone because of race, color, religion, or national origin.

Fair Labor Standards Act [*lay* · ber *stan* · derdz] *n.* A federal statute that establishes a maximum work week for certain employees, sets a minimum hourly wage, and imposes restrictions on child labor. The Act covers employers in **interstate commerce** and other employers, including state and local government. Additionally, all states have statutes governing hours; most also have minimum wage requirements. *See* wage and hour acts. *Also see* hours of labor; overtime; overtime pay.

fairness [*fayr* · nus] *n.* The state of being just and equitable.
➤ justice, equity, honesty, rectitude, equality, uprightness, integrity, open-mindedness. *Ant.* bias, prejudice.

fairness doctrine [*fair* · nes *dok* · trin] *n.* A regulation of the **Federal Communications Commission** that required television and radio stations to provide fair coverage of differing points of view on controversial public issues. The fairness doctrine was abolished by the commission in 1987. *Compare* Equal Time Act.

faith *n.* Confidence; trust; credit; credence. *Compare* belief; knowledge. *See and compare* bad faith; good faith.
➤ trust, assurance, dependence, loyalty, allegiance, certitude, belief, hope, conviction.

fake *n.* An imitation of an object; an imposter.
v. To deceive, alter, or manipulate.
➤ *n.* forgery, copy, imitation, reproduction, hoax, replica, fabrication.
v. deceive, pretend, simulate, dupe, feign, counterfeit.

fallacy [*fal* · uh · see] *n.* A mistake, defect, or falsehood.
➤ mistake, misinterpretation, deception, distortion, illusion, delusion.

false *adj.* 1. Accidentally untrue or inaccurate. 2. Intentionally or knowingly untrue.
➤ untrue, concocted, deceiving, fallacious, distorted; dishonest, hypocritical, perjured, malicious; adulterated, counterfeit, fake, simulated.

false advertising [*ad* · ver · tie · zing] *n.* Making untrue and fraudulent statements in order to encourage the buying of products or services. It is a crime. It may also expose the advertiser to **civil liability** for fraud. False, misleading, or deceptive advertising is an **unfair trade practice** which is subject to legal action by the **Federal Trade Commission**.

false and fraudulent [*fraw* · dyoo · lent] *adj.* A term referring to a representation which the person making it knows to be untrue.

false answer [*an* · ser] *n.* A sham **answer** filed in response to a **complaint**; a **pleading** that is pure pretext. *See* false pleading; frivolous pleading.

false arrest [a · *rest*] *n.* An arrest made by a person with no legal authority to do so. False arrest is both a **tort** and a crime,

and is a form of **false imprisonment**. *See* arrest. *Also see* malicious arrest.

false check *n.* A check drawn upon a bank in which the maker has no funds and no credit, and which he has no reason to believe will be honored. *See* check.

false entry [*en* · tree] *n.* 1. An untrue entry in an **book of account** or similar record of account. 2. A criminal offense by a bank officer or employee who makes inaccurate entries in reports or statements of the bank with the intent to injure or defraud.

false impersonation [im · per · sen · *ay* · shen] *n.* 1. The criminal offense of assuming the name and identity of another person as a means of committing a **fraud**. 2. The crime of pretending to be a police officer or a public official.

false imprisonment [im · *priz* · en · ment] *n.* The unlawful restraint by one person of the physical liberty of another. Like **false arrest**, to which it is closely related, it is both a **tort** and a crime.

false instrument [*in* · stre · ment] *n.* A counterfeit **instrument**. *Compare* false making.

false making [*may* · king] *n.* A forgery that does not involve a material alteration, that is, does not alter an existing genuine **instrument** or attempt to masquerade as the act of a genuine and existing person. EXAMPLE: Sam Blue tells Mr. Brown his name is George Green, borrows $50 from Brown, and gives him an IOU signed "George Green." *Compare* false instrument; counterfeit.

false oath *n.* An intentional untruth stated under oath with respect to a material matter in a **bankruptcy proceeding**. *See* false swearing; perjury.

false personation [per · sen · *ay* · shen] *n.* Same as **false impersonation**.

false pleading [*plee* · ding] *n.* A **pleading** that is good in form, but that the pleading party knows is false in fact. *See* false answer; frivolous pleading.

false pretenses [pre · *ten* · sez] *n.* The crime of obtaining the money or property of another by **fraudulent misrepresentation**. The essential elements of the offense are an intentional false statement concerning a **material fact,** in reliance on which **title** or possession is surrendered. *See* fraud. *Compare* larceny.

false representation [rep · ree · zen · *tay* · shen] *n.* A misrepresentation; a **fraudulent misrepresentation**. *See* representation. *Also see* false pretenses.

false statement [*state* · ment] *n.* For purposes of criminal law, a statement that is willfully false.

false swearing [*sware* · ing] *n.* Knowingly and intentionally stating under oath, but not necessarily in court, that which is not true. EXAMPLE: lying in an affidavit. *Compare* perjury.

false verdict [*ver* · dikt] *n.* A verdict not reached by due deliberation and consideration of the evidence. EXAMPLES: a verdict arrived at by drawing lots; a **quotient verdict**.

falsi crimen [*fall* · see *krim* · en] *n.* *See* crimen falsi.

falsify [*fal* · sih · fie] *v.* To misrepresent or tamper with; to make false.
➤ alter, lie, misrepresent, misreport, doctor, misstate, tamper with, twist ("falsify the records").

family [*fam* · i · lee] *n.* A word of great flexibility, the meaning of which varies according to the context in which it appears. In its most common usage, it means the persons who live under one roof and under one head or management. A family is not necessarily limited to a father and mother (or a father or mother) and children.

In another of its common uses, "family" refers to persons who are of the same bloodline, or are descended from a common ancestor. As used in **public assistance** statutes, "family" generally means persons whose support the law requires the person seeking assistance to provide. In **exemption statutes**, it means those who live with or are a part of the debtor's household. Other EXAMPLES of areas of the law in which "family" may have various meanings include **homestead exemptions, decedents' estates,** wills, insurance, workers' compensation, and zoning.

➤ classification, progeny, descendants, paternity, genealogy; brood, household, family unit, issue.

family agreement [a · *gree* · ment] *n.* Same as **family settlement**.

family allowance [a · *louw* · ense] *n.* An amount paid out of the assets of a **decedent's estate** for the necessary expenses of the widow and children until final settlement of the estate.

family arrangement [a · *raynj* · ment] *n.* Same as **family settlement**.

family car doctrine [*dok* · trin] *n.* Same as **family purpose doctrine**.

family corporation [kore · per · *ay* · shen] *n.* A corporation most of whose stock is held by the members of one family. *See* close corporation.

family court *n.* A court whose **jurisdiction** varies from state to state. It may hear domestic relations cases; it may hear juvenile court matters; it may also try child abuse cases and oversee **paternity suits**.

family law *n.* Area of the law concerned with domestic relations.

family purpose doctrine [*per* · pes *dok* · trin] *n.* Also called the **family car doctrine**; the rule that the owner of an automobile purchased or used for the pleasure or convenience of his family is liable for injuries inflicted by the negligent operation of the vehicle by any member of the family. *See also* automobile guest.

family settlement [*setl* · ment] *n.* An agreement by the members of a family settling the distribution of family property among them, including an agreement among heirs as to the distribution of a **decedent's estate** without **administration**.

Fannie Mae [*fan* · ee may] *See* Federal National Mortgage Association.

Farm Credit Administration [*kred* · it ad · min · is · *tray* · shen] *n.* A federal agency with facilities for refinancing farm indebtedness. The Farm Credit Administration oversees the **federal farm credit system**.

farm credit institutions [*kred* · it in · sti · *too* · shenz] *n.* The institutions that make up the **federal farm credit system**, including **Federal Land Banks**,

F

federal intermediate credit banks, and banks for cooperatives. *See* cooperative marketing association.

farm labor [*lay* · ber] *n.* *See* agricultural labor.

farm laborer [*lay* · ber · er] *n.* *See* agricultural labor.

FAS Abbreviation of **free alongside ship**; abbreviation of **fetal alcohol syndrome**.

fascism [*fash* · izm] *n.* An economic and political system characterized by one-party dictatorship, extreme nationalism, and private ownership of the means of production under a highly centralized government. *Compare* capitalism; communism; socialism.
➤ regimentation, bureaucracy, racism, absolutism.

fatal [*fay* · tel] *adj.* 1. Causing death; deadly or mortal. 2. Ruinous. 3. Crucial; critical.
➤ deadly, lethal, destructive, calamitous ("fatal injury"); critical, crucial, decisive, determining ("fatal error").

fatal defect [*dee* · fekt] *n.* *See* fatal variance.

fatal error [*err* · er] *n.* Same as **prejudicial error**.

fatal injury [*in* · je · ree] *n.* A **personal injury** resulting in death.

fatal variance [*vair* · ee · ense] *n.* In pleading, a significant difference between the **pleadings** and the **proof** in a **civil action**, or the **indictment** (or **information**) and the **evidence** in a **criminal prosecution**. In a civil case, a variance becomes a "fatal variance" or a "fatal defect" if it so misleads the adverse party that she cannot properly prepare her **action** or defense. In a criminal case, a variance is fatal, and will result in a reversal of the conviction, if it deprives the defendant of the opportunity to prepare a defense or exposes him to **double jeopardy**. *Compare* immaterial variance.

fault *n.* A wrongful act or omission. Neglect or violation of a legal duty; lack of prudence; failure to exercise care. In the language of the law, "fault" indicates negligence. In ordinary language, however, fault is not committed to negligence; it includes simple blame and moral failure as well.
v. To blame or criticize.

➤ *n.* negligence, blame, frailty, malfeasance, oversight, inadequacy, flaw, imperfection, weakness.
v. criticize, chastise, condemn, censure ("She faulted the board of directors for making the wrong decision").

faulty [*fall* · tee] *adj.* Marked with a defect; blemished.
➤ flawed, inferior, inadequate, improper, defective, blemished, imperfect, substandard, aberrant ("faulty wiring").

favor [*fayv* · er] *n.* 1. Support or encouragement for another. 2. A friendly feeling toward another. 3. An act of kindness or graciousness.
v. To show support for a cause or person.
➤ *n.* encouragement, endorsement, support ("win his favor"); partiality, disposition, liking, inclination, favoritism, fondness ("the candidate of favor"); kindness, good deed, courtesy ("Do me a favor.")
v. prefer, support, promote, champion, advance, endorse, back, boost.

favoritism [*fav* · ur · ih · tizm] *n.* The show of affection or fondness for one and not another; bias.
➤ partiality, bias, prejudice, fondness, discrimination, proneness, one-sidedness. *Ant.* impartiality.

FBI Abbreviation of **Federal Bureau of Investigation**.

FCC Abbreviation of **Federal Communications Commission**.

FDA Abbreviation of **Food and Drug Administration**.

FDIC Abbreviation of **Federal Deposit Insurance Corporation**.

fear *n.* A strong feeling caused by an awareness of danger.
v. To feel terror toward or because of someone or something.
➤ *n.* fright, trepidation, worry, anxiety, apprehension, concern, dread, terror.
v. apprehend, dread, fret, be afraid of, be concerned about, be terrified of.

feasance [*fee* · zenss] *n.* The doing or performing of an act. *Compare* malfeasance; misfeasance; nonfeasance.

feasible [*fee* · zih · bul] *adj.* Capable of being accomplished.

F

> doable, workable, viable, conceivable, manageable.

feasor [*fee · zor*] *n.* One who does something or commits a wrong. *See* tortfeasor.

featherbedding [*fedh · er · bed · ing*] *n.* The practice, on the part of employees, of inducing their employer to hire and use more workers than the job requires.

feature [*feet · chur*] *n.* 1. A prominent quality or characteristic. 2. Something offered as being particularly attractive.
> characteristic, mark, trait, point, quality; specialty, lead, item, main attraction.

federal [*fed · er · el*] *adj.* 1. Pertaining to the government of the United States of America. 2. Pertaining to the Constitution of the United States and to laws enacted under its authority. 3. Pertaining generally to a community of **sovereign states**.
> United States, national, central, constitutional, associated, merged.

federal act *n. See* federal statutes.

federal agency [*ay · jen · see*] *n.* Any administrative agency, board, bureau, commission, corporation, or institution of the federal government, usually in the **executive branch** of government. EXAMPLES: the **Federal Communications Commission**; the **Occupational Safety and Health Administration**; the **National Labor Relations Board**.

federal census [*sen · ses*] *n.* The census taken every 10 years by the federal government, as required by the Constitution.

federal common law [*kom · en*] *n.* The body of decisions by the federal courts in those limited fields where the Constitution does not require the federal courts to apply state law, namely, in the interpretation and application of the Constitution and federal statutes, and in international law and admiralty. *See Erie v. Tompkins.*

federal corporation [*kore · per · ay · shen*] *n.* A corporation chartered by Congress or organized under federal law.

federal courts *n.* Any of the **United States Courts**.

federal crimes *n.* Acts that have been made criminal by federal statute.

federal enclave [*en · klave*] *n.* A federal facility or institution located on land owned or leased by the federal government within a state. EXAMPLE: a military base.

federal farm credit system [*kred · it sis · tem*] *n. See* Farm Credit Administration; farm credit institutions.

federal government [*guv · ern · ment*] *n.* 1. The government of the United States of America. 2. The government of a community of independent and **sovereign states** united by **compact**. *Compare* state government.

federal instrumentality [*in · stroo · men · tal · e · tee*] *n.* A means used by the federal government to carry out a federal statute or governmental purpose, generally through a federal administrative agency. USAGE: "The **Federal Aviation Administration** is the instrumentality through which the federal government carries out its commercial aviation policy." *See* instrumentality.

federal jurisdiction [*joo · ris · dik · shen*] *n.* The **jurisdiction** of the federal courts. Such jurisdiction is based upon the **judicial powers** granted by Article III of the Constitution and by federal statutes. EXAMPLE: **diversity jurisdiction**. *Also see* federal question.

federal laws *n. See* federal statutes.

federal legislation [*lej · is · lay · shen*] *n. See* federal statutes.

federal magistrate [*maj · is · trate*] *n. See* magistrate.

federal offenses [*o · fen · sez*] *n. See* federal crimes.

federal preemption [*pree · emp · shen*] *n. See* preemption.

federal question [*kwes · chen*] *n.* A question created by any case arising under the Constitution or any treaty or statute of the United States; it also exists in any case based upon **diversity of citizenship**. The federal courts have **jurisdiction** over a case if it involves a federal question. *See* federal jurisdiction.

Federal Aviation Administration [*fed · er · el ay · vee · ay · shen ad · min · is · tray · shen*] *n.* The federal agency that regulates commercial air traffic and enforces safety regulations. It is a branch of the Department of Transportation.

Federal Bureau of Investigation [*fed · er · el byoo · roh of in · ves · ti · gay · shen*] *n.* Popularly known as the **FBI**, an agency organized for the purpose of investigating violations of the law, particularly federal crimes. The FBI maintains a clearinghouse for fingerprints and other identification data, as well as a national crime laboratory, and collaborates with state and local law enforcement agencies. Among the duties assigned to it is the protection of the internal security of the United States. The FBI is a division of the Department of Justice.

Federal Code [*fed · er · el*] *n.* *See* United States Code.

Federal Communications Commission [*fed · er · el kum · yoo · ni · kay · shenz kum · ish · en*] *n.* The federal regulatory agency for radio and television, telegraph, telephone, cable television, and satellite communication. It is commonly referred to as the **FCC**.

Federal Deposit Insurance Corporation (FDIC) [*fed · er · el de · paw · zit in · shoor · ense kore · per · ay · shen*] *n.* An agency of the United States government that insures depositors against loss due to the insolvency of any bank it insures. *Compare* Federal Savings and Loan Insurance Corporation.

Federal Employees' Compensation Act [*fed · er · el em · ploy · eez kom · pen · say · shen*] *n.* A federal statute that provides workers' compensation benefits for employees of the United States government who are injured or killed as a consequence of their employment. *See* workers' compensation acts.

Federal Employers' Act [*fed · er · el em · ploy · erz*] *n.* A federal statute that provides workers' compensation benefits to employees of railroads. *See* workers' compensation acts.

Federal Housing Administration [*fed · er · el how · zing ad · min · is · tray · shen*] *n.* Commonly referred to as the **FHA**; an agency of the United States that supports the availability of housing and of a sound mortgage market by insuring bank mortgages granted to borrowers who meet its standards.

Federal Insurance Contributions Act [*fed · er · el in · shoor · ense kon · tri · byoo · shenz*] *n.* The federal statute that funds social security and Medicare by taxing employers, the wages of employees, and the earnings of the self-employed. Most people are aware of this law because of the **FICA** deduction that appears on their pay stubs.

Federal Land Banks [*fed · er · el*] *n.* Banks that provide farm loans. They are established by federal statute and supervised by the **Farm Credit Administration**.

Federal Mediation and Conciliation Service [*fed · er · el mee · dee · ay · shen* and *ken · sil · ee · ay · shen ser · viss*] *n.* A federal agency whose duties are to assist parties to labor disputes to settle their differences through **conciliation** and **mediation**. Additionally, the Service provides arbitrators for the **arbitration** of labor disputes. *Compare* American Arbitration Association.

Federal National Mortgage Association [*fed · er · el nash · e · nel more · gej a · soh · see · ay · shen*] *n.* A federal agency created to supply a market for mortgages insured by the **Federal Housing Administration** or guaranteed by the **Veterans Administration**. The agency is commonly referred to as **Fannie Mae** (from its initials, FNMA). *Compare* Government National Mortgage Association.

Federal Register [*fed · er · el rej · is · ter*] *n.* An official publication, printed daily, containing regulations and proposed regulations issued by administrative agencies, as well as other **rulemaking** and other official business of the **executive branch** of government. All regulations are ultimately published in the **Code of Federal Regulations**.
federal regulations [*reg · yoo · lay · shenz*] *n.* *See* Code of Federal Regulations; *Federal Register.*

Federal Reserve Banks [*fed · er · el ree · zerv*] *n.* Banks incorporated under the Federal Reserve Act, which are members of the **Federal Reserve System** and operate under the supervision of the **Federal Reserve Board**. Federal Reserve Banks

F

act as government **depositories** and **fiscal agents** of the government and receive and maintain the **legal reserves** of banks in the Federal Reserve System.

Federal Reserve Board [*fed* · er · el ree · *zerv*] *n.* An independent board, appointed by the president, that oversees banks in the **Federal Reserve System**. It establishes **legal reserve** requirements, **discount rates** for bank loans, and maximum limits on the interest that banks may pay on deposits. *See* Federal Reserve Banks.

Federal Reserve System [*fed* · er · el ree · *zerv sis* · tem] *n.* A system of banks operating under the supervision of regulatory agencies established by federal legislation. It promotes sound banking practices and facilitates the flow of credit and money essential to the country's economy. *See* Federal Reserve Banks; Federal Reserve Board.

Federal Rules of Appellate Procedure [*fed* · er · el rules of a · *pel* · et pro · *see* · jer] *n.* A body of rules that govern appeals to the **United States Courts of Appeals**. *See* rules of appellate procedure.

Federal Rules of Civil Procedure [*fed* · er · el rules of *siv* · il pro · *see* · jer] *n.* A comprehensive set of rules governing procedure in civil cases in **United States District Courts**. *See* rules of civil procedure.

Federal Rules of Criminal Procedure [*fed* · er · el rules of *krim* · i · nel pro · *see* · jer] *n.* A comprehensive set of rules governing procedure in criminal cases in **United States District Courts**. *See* rules of criminal procedure.

Federal Rules of Evidence [*fed* · er · el rules of *ev* · i · dense] *n.* A body of rules governing procedure with respect to evidence in both civil and criminal cases in **United States District Courts**. *See* rules of evidence.

Federal Savings and Loan Insurance Corporation (FSLIC) [*fed* · er · el say · vingz and loan in · *shoor* · ense kore · per · *ay* · shen] *n.* An agency of the United States government that insures depositors against loss due to the insolvency

of any savings and loan association it insures. *See* Resolution Trust Corporation. *Compare* Federal Deposit Insurance Corporation.

federal statutes [*stat* · shoot] *n.* Statutes enacted by Congress.

Federal Tort Claims Act [*fed* · er · el] *n.* An Act of Congress that allows the federal government to be sued for most **torts** committed by its employees and agents. The Act largely nullifies the doctrine of **sovereign immunity** as it applies to the federal government, with some exceptions, including discretionary acts of public officials. *See* official immunity.

Federal Trade Commission [*fed* · er · el trade ke · *mish* · en] *n.* A federal agency empowered to prevent **unfair trade practices, unfair methods of competition**, and acts or practices in **restraint of trade** that have been declared unlawful by federal statutes. The **FTC** administers and enforces the federal **antitrust acts** and promotes competition.

federalism [*fed* · er · el · izm] *n.* 1. Pertaining to a system of government that is federal in nature. 2. The system by which the states of the United States relate to each other and to the federal government.

Federalist Papers [*fed* · er · e · list *pay* · perz] *n.* A series of political essays written by Alexander Hamilton, James Madison, and John Jay advocating the adoption of the United States Constitution. The Federalist Papers are often referred to by the courts in interpreting the Constitution.

federation [fe · de · *ray* · shen] *n.* A combination of nations, states, or other bodies existing for a common purpose. *See also* confederation.
➤ coalition, alliance, syndicate, union, association.

fee *n.* 1. A charge made for the services of a professional person, such as a lawyer or physician. *See* attorney fees; contingent fee. 2. A statutory charge for the services of a public officer. EXAMPLE: court fees. 3. An amount charged for a privilege. EXAMPLE: a tuition fee. 4. An **estate** in real property that may be inherited (USAGE: "Robin holds her land in fee; Lee has a fee interest in his farm.") When "fee" is used without **words of limitation** (for EXAMPLE, **base fee**, **conditional fee**, **determinable fee**, or **qualified fee**), it always means **fee simple**. *See* estate of inheritance. *Compare* estate less than freehold; estate of freehold not of inheritance.

➤ compensation, wage, payment, commission, charge ("fixed fee"); estate, property, inheritance, holding ("absolute fee").

fee conditional [ken · *dish* · en · el] *n.* Same as **conditional fee**.

fee estate [es · *tate*] *n.* A fee in land; an **estate in fee**.

fee expectant [eks · *pek* · tent] *n.* A fee that is limited to a man and his wife and their **lineal descendants**.

fee simple [*sim* · pl] *n.* Also known as a **fee simple absolute**; the most complete **estate in land** known to the law. It signifies total ownership and control. It may be inherited free of any condition, limitation, or restriction by particular heirs. *Compare* fee tail. *See* estate of inheritance.

fee simple absolute [*sim* · pl *ab* · so · loot] *n.* Same as **fee simple**.

fee simple conditional [*sim* · pl ken · *dish* · en · el] *n.* Same as **conditional fee**.

fee simple defeasible [*sim* · pl de · *feez* · ibl] *n.* *See* base fee; determinable fee; qualified fee.

fee simple determinable [*sim* · pl de · *ter* · min · ebl] *n.* Same as **determinable fee**.

fee simple estate [*sim* · pl es · *tate*] *n.* *See* fee simple.

fee tail *n.* An **estate in land** that is given to a person and her **lineal descendants** only, the heirs in general being deprived of any interest in the estate. In the absence of lineal descendants, the estate reverts to the donor. A fee tail estate given only to the donor's female lineal descendents is called a *fee tail female*; a fee tail estate limited to the donor's male lineal descendents is called a *fee tail male*. *See* entail. *See also* estate of inheritance; heirs of the body; reversion. *Compare* fee simple.

fee tail female [*fee* · male] *n.* *See* fee tail.

fee tail male *n.* *See* fee tail.

feign [fayn] *v.* To make a false impression; to pretend.

➤ pretend, imagine, disguise, conceal.

feigned [faynd] *adj.* Pretended; affected; artificial.

➤ pretended, specious, spurious, fraudulent, fake, bogus ("a feigned smile").

feigned action [faynd *ak* · shen] *n.* *See* fictitious action.

FELA Abbreviation of **Federal Employers' Liability Act.**

fellow servant [*fel* · oh *ser* · vent] *n.* 1. An employee who, with his coworkers, is an employee of the same employer and, with them, is engaged in common work under common supervision. 2. Short for **fellow servant doctrine**.

fellow servant doctrine [*dok* · trin] *n.* The **common law rule** that exempts an employer from liability to her employees for injuries they suffer as a result of the negligence or misconduct of their coworkers ("fellow servants"). Because of the enactment of **workers' compensation acts**, this rule has relatively little modern application.

felon [*fel* · en] *n.* A person who has been convicted of a **felony**.

➤ criminal, wrongdoer, offender, convict, miscreant.

felonious [fe · *lone* · ee · es] *adj.* 1. A legal term meaning done with the intent to commit a crime, that is, with **criminal intent**. *See* felonious intent. 2. Having the quality of a felony. EXAMPLE: **felonious assault**. 3. Unlawful; wrongful. 4. Malicious; evil; treacherous.

➤ villainous, criminal, illegal, heinous, malignant, unlawful, wrongful.

felonious assault [a · *salt*] *n.* An **assault** that is a **felony** (EXAMPLE: **aggravated assault**), as opposed to an assault that is a **misdemeanor** (EXAMPLE: **simple assault**).

felonious homicide [*hom* · i · side] *n.* The killing of a human being without justification or excuse, that is, **murder** or **manslaughter**.

felonious intent [in · *tent*] *n.* 1. The intent to commit a **felony**. *See* criminal intent. 2. As an element of the crime of **larceny**, the taking and carrying away of

F

another person's property without his consent, or without right or excuse, combined with an intent to deprive him of that property permanently.

feloniously [fe · *lone* · ee · us · lee] *adv.* 1. Doing a felonious act. 2. Acting with intent to commit a **felony**.

felony [*fel* · a · nee] *n.* A general term for more serious crimes (EXAMPLES: **murder; robbery; larceny**), as distinguished from lesser offenses, which are known as **misdemeanors**. In many jurisdictions, felonies are crimes for which the punishment is death or more than one year of imprisonment. Persons convicted of felonies are generally incarcerated in prisons or penitentiaries, as opposed to local jails.
➤ gross offense, serious offense, transgression, wrongdoing, crime.

felony murder [*mer* · der] *n. See* felony murder rule.

felony murder rule [*mer* · der] *n.* The rule that a death which occurs by accident or chance during the course of the commission of a **felony** is **first degree murder**. (EXAMPLE: If, during the course of an **armed robbery** by Robbers A and B, Robber A accidentally shoots and kills the storeowner, Robber B as well as Robber A is guilty of murder.) The felony murder rule, which is a **common law** doctrine, has been modified by statute in most states. *See* murder. *Compare* misdemeanor manslaughter rule.

feme [fem] (*French*) *n.* A woman.

feme covert [*ko* · vert] *n.* A married woman. At **common law** the status of married women was impaired by **legal disabilities** (EXAMPLE: lack of legal capacity to enter into contracts). *Compare feme sole;* feme sole trader. *See also* civil disability.

feme sole [soul] *n.* An unmarried woman. *Compare feme covert.*

feme sole trader [soul *tray* · der] *n.* A married woman who engages in business on her own account, separate from her husband. *See and compare feme sole;* feme covert.

femme [fem] (*French*) *n.* Same as **feme**.

fence *n.* 1. A railing or enclosure which frequently marks the boundary line for a piece of property. 2. A person who receives and deals in stolen goods.
➤ railing, barrier, hedge, enclosure; thief, burglar, receiver.

feoffment [*feff* · ment] *n.* At **common law**, a transfer of a **freehold estate** in land.

ferae naturae [*fare* · ee nah · *tyoo* · ree] (*Latin*) *n.* Wild animals.

fertile octogenarian rule [fertl awk · toh · jen · *air* · i · en] *n.* In the law of **future interests**, a name sometimes given to the rule that the law does not recognize the possibility that a man or a woman cannot beget or bear a child after a certain age. *See also* possibility of issue extinct.

fetal alcohol syndrome [*fee* · tel *al* · ke · hol *sin* · drome] *n.* The name given to the group of symptoms that may appear in the newborn infants of women who drink heavily during pregnancy, including severe mental retardation, cardiac defects, and physical deformity. Fetal alcohol syndrome is often referred to by its abbreviation, **FAS**.

fetal rights [*fee* · tel] *n.* The rights accorded to a fetus. *See* life.

fetus [*fee* · tes] *n.* In the human female, the offspring in the womb, after approximately the third month of pregnancy.

FHA Abbreviation of **Federal Housing Administration**.
FHA mortgage [*more* · gej] *n. See* Federal Housing Administration.

fi. fa. [*fy* · fah] (*Latin*) Short for *fieri facias*. Lawyers often say "*fi. fa.*" when referring to a **writ of fieri facias**.

fiat [*fee* · at] *n.* An authoritative order issued by a person who has the power to enforce it.
➤ proclamation, decree, ordinance, pronouncement, mandate ("issued by fiat").

FICA [*fy* · kah] *n.* Acronym for **Federal Insurance Contributions Act**.

fiction of law [*fik* · shen] *n. See* legal fiction.

fictitious [*fik* · tish · es] *adj.* Imaginary; not real; counterfeit; false; not genuine.
➤ imaginary, counterfeit, false, pretend, untrue, deceptive, misrepresented, simulated.

fictitious action [*ak* · shen] *n.* A lawsuit brought for the purpose of obtaining a judicial opinion, without an actual or existing controversy between the parties. *Compare* case or controversy.

fictitious name *n.* 1. An artificial name that a person or a corporation adopts for business or professional purposes. *See* DBA; trade name. 2. A false name used by a person intending to deceive or to perpetrate a **fraud**. *See* alias.

fictitious party [*par* · tee] *n.* A **party** in whose name an action has been brought without any authority to do so. A person who files such a suit is guilty of contempt of court.

fictitious payee [pay · *ee*] *n.* The rule is that when an **instrument** is made payable to an existing person, with no intention that she shall have any interest in it, it is considered to be payable to a "fictitious payee." In other words, a real person may be a fictitious person within the meaning of **negotiable instruments** law.

fidelity [fi · *del* · i · tee] *n.* 1. Loyalty; good faith; the keeping of promises; 2. Accuracy.
➤ loyalty, good faith, devotion, fealty, allegiance, honor, dedication; accuracy, adherence, precision ("fidelity to the original version").

fidelity and guaranty insurance [gar · en · *tee* in · *shoor* · ense] *n.* Insurance against **loss** due to dishonesty, default, or inaccuracy. EXAMPLES: **title insurance**; **credit insurance**. Some fidelity and guaranty insurance, similar in form and purpose to a **fidelity bond**, insures against employee dishonesty.

fidelity bond *n.* A **bond** in the form of an insurance contract which indemnifies against **loss** resulting from embezzlement or other misuse of funds by an officer or an employee. *See* indemnification. *Also see* fidelity and guaranty insurance.

fidelity insurance [in · *shoor* · ense] *n.* Same as **fidelity and guaranty insurance**.

fides [*fie* · deez] (*Latin*) *n.* Faith; trust; honesty. *See* bona fide.

fiduciary [fi · *doo* · she · air · ee] *adj.* That which is based upon trust or confidence; the relationship between a fiduciary and his principal.

n. A person who is entrusted with handling money or property for another person. EXAMPLES: attorney and client; **guardian and ward; trustee and beneficiary**.
➤ *adj.* trustworthy, reliable, confidential ("fiduciary duty").
n. trustee, guardian, executor, custodian, caretaker ("She is a fiduciary for her clients.")

fiduciary bond *n.* A **bond** required of a fiduciary (EXAMPLES: an **executor**; an **administrator**; a **guardian**) as a condition of managing an **estate**.

fiduciary capacity [ke · *pass* · i · tee] *n.* The position of a person who acts on behalf of another in matters involving property or money. The term implies a position of trust and power in which confidence is placed and responsibility and good faith are required. *See* fiduciary relationship.

fiduciary contract [kon · trakt] *n.* A contract that relies upon the integrity of the party trusted rather than upon her credit or ability. EXAMPLE: a **bailment**.

fiduciary duty [*dew* · tee] *n.* The duty to act loyally and honestly with respect to the interests of another; the duty the law imposes upon a fiduciary.

fiduciary relationship [re · *lay* · shen · ship] *n.* A relationship between two persons in which one is obligated to act with the utmost good faith, honesty, and loyalty on behalf of the other. EXAMPLES: attorney and client; **trustee and beneficiary; conservator and ward**. A fiduciary relationship is often loosely but inaccurately considered to be the equivalent of a **confidential relationship**. *Compare* confidential relationship.

field audit [*aw* · dit] *n.* An examination by the Internal Revenue Service of a taxpayer's books and records, conducted at the taxpayer's home or business establishment, to determine the accuracy of his income tax return. *See* audit. *Compare* office audit.

field sobriety test [so · *bry* · e · tee] *n.* A test used by police to establish whether probable cause exists to charge a motorist with driving while intoxicated. It may take a number of forms. EXAMPLES: walking a line; counting backwards from 10. *See* sobriety checkpoint.

F

field warehousing [*ware · how · zing*] *n.* An arrangement whereby manufacturers and merchants of wholesale goods borrow money on the security of goods stored in warehouses. Under this method of business financing, the debtor has access to the security for the purpose of selling it.

fieri facias [*fie · e · rye fay · shee · ass*] *(Latin)* *n.* Means "cause it to be done"; short for **writ of fieri facias**. A *fieri facias* is a **writ of execution**, the ordinary **writ** for the seizure and sale of the property of a **judgment debtor**.

FIFO [*fie · foe*] *n./adj.* Acronym for **first in, first out**, an accounting method for establishing the value of business inventory when goods are so intermingled that they cannot be identified without specific invoices. The FIFO method hypothesizes that inventory consists of the goods most recently purchased or produced. *Compare* LIFO.

Fifteenth Amendment [*fif · teenth a · mend · ment*] *n.* An amendment to the Constitution which provides that "the right of citizens of the United States to vote shall not be denied or abridged by the United States or by any state on account of race, color, or previous condition of servitude."

Fifth Amendment [*a · mend · ment*] *n.* An amendment to the Constitution that guarantees the right to grand jury indictment if one is accused of having committed a serious crime, the right not to be placed in **double jeopardy**, the right not to be compelled to incriminate oneself, the right to **due process of law**, and the right not to have one's private property taken by the government without just compensation. The Fifth Amendment applies only to the federal government. Its requirements are made applicable to state and local government through the **Fourteenth Amendment**.

fighting words [*fite · ing*] *n.* Words which tend to incite a breach of the peace; a category of speech that the Supreme Court has declared is not protected by the **First Amendment** guaranty of freedom of speech.

file *n.* 1. The **record** in a case, kept by the clerk of court. 2. A place where documents are deposited and kept, usually in covers marked and tabbed so that they can be easily located.
v. 1. To deposit a document (EXAMPLE: a **pleading**) with a public officer (EXAMPLE: the clerk of court) to have it preserved as one of the records of her office. 2. To place a document, or even a small object, in a place of deposit, usually indexed or marked in a manner making it easy to locate in the future. *See* record; recorded.

➤ *n.* archives, portfolio, census, information, record ("The file was under lock and key"). *v.* deliver, register, enter, submit ("We filed the documents with the proper authorities"); categorize, organize, collate, arrange, index ("They filed our names in alphabetical order").

filiation proceeding [*fil · ee · ay · shen pro · see · ding*] *n.* Same as **affiliation proceeding**.

filing [*file · ing*] *n.* The act of depositing a document with a **public officer** to preserve it as one of the records of his office. *See* file.

filing fee *n.* The fee charged by a public officer for the filing of a **pleading** or other document in that office.

filing laws *n.* Statutes that require the filing of an **instrument** as a condition of its complete effectiveness.

final [*fine · el*] *adj.* 1. Terminating all dispute, controversy, or doubt. 2. Conclusive; the end, ultimate, or last.
➤ concluding, ultimate, terminal, ending ("final adjudication"); absolute, decisive, irrefutable, unappealable ("final offer").

final adjudication [*a · joo · di · kay · shen*] *n.* *See* final judgment.

final and appealable order [*a · peel · ebl or · der*] *n.* *See* final order.

final appealable order [*a · peel · ebl or · der*] *n.* *See* final order.

final argument [*ar · gyoo · ment*] *n.* At the end of a trial, each party's summation of his case to the jury immediately before the jury is instructed by the judge and retires to deliberate its verdict. Final argument may also be made to the judge in a case without a jury. Also called closing argument.

final decision [de · *sizh* · en] *n.* Same as **final judgment**.

final decree [de · *kree*] *n.* *See* final judgment.

final determination [de · ter · me · *nay* · shen] *n.* *See* final judgment.

final disposition [dis · po · *zish* · en] *n.* *See* final judgment.

final hearing [*heer* · ing] *n.* The hearing that results in a final decision. *See* hearing.

final judgment [*juj* · ment] *n.* A **judgment** that determines the merits of the case by declaring that the plaintiff is or is not entitled to recovery. For purposes of the doctrine of *res judicata*, any judicial decision that is not conditional or subject to change in the future by the same court. For purposes of appeal, a judgment that terminates the litigation between the parties on the merits and leaves nothing to be done but to enforce what has been decided.

final order [*or* · der] *n.* *See* final judgment.

final passage [*pass* · ej] *n.* The completion of legislative action in the adoption of a bill so that it becomes law (i.e., a statute).

final settlement [*setl* · ment] *n.* 1. The winding up of a **decedent's estate** and the discharge of the **administrator**. 2. A determination by the government of the amount it must pay (for EXAMPLE, to a contractor). The term does not necessarily imply the existence of a dispute.

final submission [sub · *mish* · en] *n.* In a trial before a judge without a jury, final submission occurs when the court takes the case under advisement, after the evidence has been presented, the arguments made, and the briefs filed. In a jury case, it takes place when the court directs the jury to retire for consideration of the case.

finance [*fine* · ans] *n.* The management of money and credit.
v. To obtain money or credit for a person or purpose; to furnish funds.
➤ *n.* commerce, investment, economics, revenue, fiscal matters ("The bank was involved in high finance").

v. capitalize, promote, subsidize, underwrite, invest ("The investor financed the endeavor").

finance charge *n.* The charge under an installment sale contract for the privilege of paying in installments. *Compare* interest. *See also* carrying charge.

finance company [*kum* · pe · nee] *n.* A company engaged in making loans to individual consumers and businesses.

financial [fin · *an* · shel] *adj.* Pertaining to finances; fiscal; monetary.
➤ pecuniary, monetary, budgetary, economic, banking ("the financial situation").

financial institution [in · sti · *too* · shen] *n.* Any organization, business, or person authorized under state or federal law to engage in financial transactions with the public. EXAMPLES: a bank; a savings and loan association; a credit union; a finance company.

financial reports [re · *ports*] *n.* *See* annual report; financial statement; income statement; profit and loss statement.

financial responsibility laws [res · pon · se · *bil* · e · tee] *n.* State statutes requiring proof of financial reliability (in the form of, for EXAMPLE, insurance or a bond) as a condition of operating a motor vehicle.

financial statement [*state* · ment] *n.* A summary of the assets and liabilities of a person or a business, usually including an **income statement** or a **profit and loss statement**. *Note* that "financial statement" is not "**financing statement**."

financial worth *n.* The value of a person's property less what he owes; assets less liabilities.

financing statement [*fine* · an · sing *state* · ment] *n.* A notice of the existence of a **security interest** in goods, which a creditor is entitled to file with the appropriate public officer, usually the **Secretary of State**. The designated public office varies from state to state. *Note* that "financing statement" is not "**financial statement**." *See* perfecting a security interest.

find *v.* 1. In the trial of a lawsuit, to arrive at a conclusion or decision with respect to facts that are in contention. USAGE: "This

F

court (or jury) finds the defendant not guilty." *See and compare* finding of fact; conclusion of law. 2. To locate; to discover; to come upon; to learn of.

➤ achieve, acquire, attain, procure, gain; discover, locate, detect, ascertain, decipher, uncover, expose ("Scientists will find a cure"); determine, establish, decree, decide, conclude, adjudge ("the jury finds").

finder [*fine* · der] *n.* A person who undertakes for a fee to locate and connect people who wish to collaborate in business ventures. *See* finder's fee.

➤ locater, agent, broker, investigator.

finder's fee [*fine* · derz] *n.* A fee charged by a finder for finding and connecting business collaborators.

finding [*fine* · ding] *n.* A conclusion with respect to a **question of fact**. Findings are made by juries, judges, arbitrators, and administrative agencies, among others. *See and compare* general finding; special finding.

➤ decision, recommendation, verdict, ascertainment, pronouncement, deduction ("The court's finding is for the plaintiff").

finding of fact *n.* A conclusion with respect to disputed facts in a legal action, reasoned or inferred from the evidence. *Compare* conclusion of law. *See also* conclusion of fact.

finding of law *n* Same as **conclusion of law**.

fine *n.* A monetary penalty imposed as punishment upon a person convicted of a crime. *Compare* civil penalty. *See* forfeiture. *See also* excessive fine. *v.* To sentence a person convicted of a crime to pay a monetary penalty as punishment. *adj.* 1. Having a delicate, exquisite quality. 2. Superior in quality.

➤ *n.* assessment, damages, punishment, reparation, penalty. *v.* charge, impose, confiscate, levy, penalize, tax. *adj.* splendid, excellent, masterly, exquisite ("a fine painting"); clear, dry, sunny ("a fine day").

fingerprints [*fing* · er · prints] *n.* The marks left by the lines on a person's fingers. No two people have identical fingerprints. Therefore, fingerprints have significant value as evidence for purposes of identification. *See* DNA fingerprinting.

➤ prints, marks, identification, impression, trademark, characteristic.

fire insurance [in · *shoor* · ense] *n.* Insurance that indemnifies the insured against **loss** to property (EXAMPLES: a house; the contents of a house; a commercial building) due to fire.

fire sale *n.* A sale of goods marked down in price because of fire, smoke, or water damage. Fire sales are regulated by law in many jurisdictions to protect consumers from fraudulent practices.

firearm [*fire* · arm] *n.* Any weapon from which shot or shell is discharged by the explosion of gunpowder. (EXAMPLES: a rifle; a shotgun; a revolver.) Even if such a weapon has been rendered harmless, it is a firearm in the eyes of the law if it can easily be restored.

➤ weapon, gun, pistol, shotgun, revolver, munitions.

firearms acts *n.* *See* gun control laws.

firm *adj.* Fixed; certain; solid; irrevocable. *n.* 1. A business establishment; an unincorporated business, particularly a partnership. 2. The members of a partnership, as a group.

➤ *adj.* definite, secured, abiding, unalterable ("a firm offer"). *n.* enterprise, establishment, partnership, organization, office, conglomerate, institution ("a reputable firm").

firm name *n.* The name under which a firm transacts its business. *See* trade name.

firm offer [*off* · er] *n.* Under the **Uniform Commercial Code**, an offer to buy or sell goods made in a signed writing which, by its terms, gives assurance that it will be held open. A firm offer is not revocable for **want of consideration** during the time it states it will be held open, or if no time is stated, for up to three months.

first *adj./adv.* Before all others in order of time, progression, rank, or importance.

➤ *adj.* initial, paramount, premiere, introductory, prime, champion, dominant, ruling. *adv.* beforehand, initially, originally, to start with.

first degree murder [de · *gree mer* · der] *n.* Murder committed deliberately with **malice aforethought**, that is, with premeditation. *Compare* second degree murder. *See* murder.

first impression [im · *presh* · en] *n.* Phrase referring to a case that has not arisen before and that is without precedent to govern it. USAGE: "Surrogate motherhood has not been the subject of litigation in our state; this is a case of first impression."

first in, first out *adj. See* FIFO.

first lien [*leen*] *n.* A **lien** having priority over any other lien on the same property. If the property is sold, the first lien must be satisfied from the proceeds of the sale before any **junior encumbrance** can be satisfied. *See also* first mortgage.

first meeting of creditors [*meet* · ing of *kred* · i · terz] *n. See* creditors' meeting.

first mortgage [*more* · gej] *n.* A **mortgage** having priority over any other **lien** on the same property. *See also* first lien.

first of exchange [eks · *chaynj*] *n.* The first of a set of **bills of exchange** drawn in duplicate or triplicate. When any one of the bills is honored, the others are void.

first offender acts [o · *fen* · der] *n.* State and federal statutes that authorize judges to give relatively lenient sentences to persons convicted of a crime for the first time. Additionally, although the provisions of such statutes vary, they typically permit first offenders to enter a **diversion program** in lieu of prosecution, and provide for expungement of conviction for the first offenders who are convicted but not rearrested within a specified period of time. *See* expungement of record.

first option [*op* · shen] *n.* Same as **first refusal**. *See* right of first refusal.

first refusal [re · *few* · zel] *n. See* right of first refusal.

first-class title [*first*-klas] *n.* Title that is good and valid; **clear title; marketable title**.

First Amendment [a · *mend* · ment] *n.* An amendment to the Constitution that guarantees freedom of religion, freedom of speech, and freedom of the press, as well as freedom of association (the right "peaceably to assemble") and the right to petition the government for redress of grievances.

fiscal [*fis* · kel] *adj.* Bearing upon matters of finance generally.

➤ monetary, treasury, capital, commercial.

fiscal agent [*ay* · jent] *n.* An agent acting for a governmental body or a private institution with respect to its financial affairs, paying and receiving on its behalf and serving as a **depository** of its funds. *See* agent.

fiscal year *n.* An accounting period of 12 consecutive months. Both businesses and individuals may choose any such 12-month period as their tax year. A fiscal year is often referred to by its abbreviation, **FY**.

fish and game laws *n.* State and federal statutes that establish seasons when specified fish and game may be caught or hunted, limit the number that may be taken, specify size limits, and prohibit the taking of some species altogether. *See* open season.

fishing expedition [*fish* · ing eks · pe · *dish* · en] *n.* The use of **discovery** not in order to better try a **cause of action**, but to determine whether there is in fact a cause of action. EXAMPLE: using a **subpoena duces tecum** for the purpose of searching for evidence and witnesses.

fitness [*fit* · ness] *n.* Suitability; appropriateness.

➤ suitability, aptness, value, usefulness, utility ("fitness to practice law").

fitness for a particular purpose [*fit* · ness for a per · *tik* · yoo · ler per · pes] *n.* The **Uniform Commercial Code** provides that if a buyer of goods relies upon a seller's judgment in selecting goods to be used for a particular purpose, there is an **implied warranty** that the goods are suitable for that purpose. *See* implied warranty.

fix *v.* 1. To set in order; to arrange. 2. To hold steady. 3. To repair or mend something damaged. 4. To determine or establish.

➤ adjust, arrange, regulate, coordinate, establish ("fix prices"); affirm, set, secure, confirm ("fix your salary"); repair, heal, improve, rectify, refurbish, recondition, service ("fix the stove"); settle, determine, establish, resolve ("fix the meeting time").

F

F

fixed *n.* 1. Established or set. USAGE: "fixed by law." 2. Permanent; definite; stable; not varying. USAGE: "fixed charges." 3. Agreed upon dishonestly. USAGE: "fixed fight"; "price-fixing." 4. Firmly attached.
➤ permanent, established, situated, steady, entrenched; undeviating, unfaltering, enduring, persistent.

fixed amount [a · *mount*] *n.* A specific or specified amount; a **sum certain**. To be **negotiable**, an **instrument** must be payable in a "fixed amount." *See* negotiable instrument.

fixed assets [*ass* · ets] *n.* The **assets** of a business that will not readily be consumed; permanent assets. EXAMPLES: land; buildings; **capital equipment**. *Compare* liquid assets.

fixed by law *n.* Established, set, or prescribed by statute or regulation. USAGE: "The amount Medicare will pay the doctor varies with the procedure and is fixed by law."

fixed charges [*char* · jez] *n.* Expenses a business will incur whether or not it operates or produces. EXAMPLES: property taxes; mortgage interest; rent; depreciation.

fixed costs *n.* *See* fixed charges.

fixed income [*in* · kum] *n.* Income that tends not to vary with respect to when it is received and that is relatively uniform in amount. EXAMPLES: social security payments; annuity payments; interest on bonds.

fixed liability [ly · a · *bil* · i · tee] *n.* Debts that are certain, unvarying in amount, ongoing, and, generally, long-term.

fixed prices [*pry* · sez] *n.* 1. Mutually agreed-upon prices. 2. An agreement between producers and distributors of a product to sell the product at a set price. Such agreements are usually illegal under both state and federal statutes. *See* price-fixing.

fixed rate mortgage [*more* · gej] *n.* A **mortgage** in which the **rate of interest** is absolute, that is, is not adjusted from time to time. *Compare* adjustable rate mortgage.

fixing bail [*fik* · sing] *n.* The determination by a judge of the amount of bail a defendant must put up to be released from custody. *See* bail; bail bond.

fixture [*fiks* · cher] *n.* An article, previously personal property, that, by being physically affixed to real estate, has become part of the real property; something so connected to a structure for use in connection with it that it cannot be removed without doing injury to the structure. EXAMPLES: a chandelier; an outdoor television antenna; a furnace. *See* trade fixtures.
➤ attachment, permanent addition, immovable object.

flagrante delicto [flay · *gran* · tee dee · *lik* · tow] (*Latin*) *adj.* Means "while the wrong is occurring." *See in flagrante delicto.*

flat rate *n.* A set amount paid for goods or services regardless of the number of items purchased or the amount of time or the degree of skill required in rendering the service. USAGE: "The magazine charges a flat rate of $500 for a quarter-page ad, regardless of the number of words." A **per capita tax** is an EXAMPLE of a tax imposed on a flat rate basis.

flaw *n.* A defect, deficiency, or weakness.
➤ defect, weakness, blemish, shortcoming, imperfection, deficiency ("The flaw in his reasoning became evident.").

flee *v.* To run away or escape. *See* flight; flight to avoid prosecution.
➤ abscond, evade, abandon, depart ("to flee the jurisdiction").

flee to the wall *n.* *See* retreat to the wall.

fleeing from justice [*flee* · ing from *jus* · tiss] *n.* *See* flight; flight to avoid prosecution.

fleet coverage [*kuv* · e · rej] *n.* Inclusion of all the vehicles operated by the insured (usually a business) under an automobile liability policy. Coverage is extended automatically as newly acquired vehicles are added to those already insured. *See* blanket policy.

flight *n.* 1. The **common law** offense of running away after being accused of a crime. 2. Escape; retreat; hasty departure. 3. The act of flying.
➤ fleeing, exfiltration, retreat, departure, escape.

flight to avoid killing [a · *void kil* · ing] *n.* *See* retreat to the wall.

flight to avoid prosecution [a · *void* pros · e · *kyoo* · shen] *n.* Departing a place (or concealing oneself) with the intention of avoiding arrest, prosecution, or punishment for a crime, whether or not prosecution has begun or is pending. *See* flight; fugitive from justice.

flim-flam [*flim*-flam] *n.* A confidence game; **bunco**.
v. To engage in a confidence game; to cheat, swindle, or bilk.
➤ *n.* confidence game, fraud, sham, deception, bunco.
v. cheat, dupe, trick, swindle.

float *n.* 1. Checks that are in the banking system in the process of collection. 2. **Floating capital**. 3. **Floating debt**.
v. 1. To launch, activate, or initiate something; to start something up. USAGE: "The company is considering whether to float stock to pay for the land it is purchasing." 2. To allow the value of a nation's currency, relative to other currencies, to fluctuate solely in accordance with the laws of supply and demand. 3. To drift; to glide; to fly.
➤ *v.* launch, activate, initiate, start up ("to float stock"); drift, glide, fly ("float through the air").

floater policy [*flote* · er *pol* · e · see] *n.* An insurance policy covering property that is frequently moved between locations. *Also see* blanket policy.

floating [*flote* · ing] *adj.* 1. Ongoing; fluctuating, not fixed; uncommitted. 2. Drifting; gliding; flying.
➤ ongoing, fluctuating, uncommitted; drifting, gliding, flying, hovering, wafting.
floating capital [*kap* · i · tel] *n.* Uninvested funds that have been set aside for the payment of current or general expenses. Also referred to as **circulating capital**.
floating charge *n. See* floating lien.
floating debt *n.* 1. Short-term debt, payable at an early date, which arises from current operations and with respect to which no provision for payment has been made. 2. The indebtedness of a governmental unit, the payment of which has not been provided for budgetarily through taxation or otherwise.

floating indebtedness [in · *det* · ed · ness] *n. See* floating debt.
floating interest rate [*in* · trest] *n.* An interest rate that is not constant; an interest rate that fluctuates based upon the current cost of borrowing money. *See* adjustable rate mortgage.
floating lien [leen] *n.* A security arrangement in which the inventory that stands as **security** is left with the debtor, to be handled and even sold in the course of business. It is a continuing **charge** on the assets of the company creating it, but it permits the company to deal freely with the property. Inventory acquired after the **lien** is created is security for the lien as well. *See* after-acquired property; lien.
floating policy [*pol* · i · see] *n. See* floater policy.

flood *n.* An overwhelming quantity of something; an excess of.
v. To overflow with a large quantity.
➤ *n.* torrent, deluge, downpour, inundation.
v. inundate, overwhelm, immerse, overflow, engulf.

flood insurance [in · *shoor* · ense] *n.* An insurance policy that protects the insured against **loss** of or damage to property caused by flood. It is required by banks as a condition of obtaining a mortgage on property located in a place that is liable to flooding.

floor *n.* 1. A person's right to address a meeting. USAGE: "The delegate from Missouri has the floor." 2. The portion of a legislative chamber reserved for members. USAGE: "We were admitted to the Senate visitors' gallery, but not to the floor." 3. A minimum price or wage level. USAGE: "The **Fair Labor Standards Act** establishes a floor for the wage an employer may legally pay an employee." 4. The bottom level or lowest surface of anything.
➤ base, bottom, minimum, minimum level.
floor plan *n.* A drawing that shows the layout and dimensions of all the rooms on a single floor or story of a building.
floor plan financing [*fine* · an · sing] *n.* A security arrangement most common among automobile dealerships. Automobile dealers purchase new cars by borrowing against the cars in their possession

(whether or not they are actually on the "floor" of the showroom). The vehicles are released from their status as collateral as they are sold and the proceeds of the sale are applied to the debt. *See* security.

flotsam [*flot* · sem] *n.* 1. Goods that are floating in the sea as a result of shipwreck. *Compare* jetsam. 2. Odds and ends of little value.

flow *n.* An uninterrupted, continuous movement.
v. To move smoothly; to derive from a source.
➤ *n.* movement, discharge, circulation.
v. move, drain, discharge, emit.

flowage [*floh* · ej] *n.* A right to overflow the land of another in maintaining an artificial body of water, for EXAMPLE, a fish pond. A right of flowage is obtained by **grant** or **easement**, or reserved in a **conveyance** (*see* reservation).

FLSA Abbreviation of **Fair Labor Standards Act**.

FMCS Abbreviation of **Federal Mediation and Conciliation Service**.

FNMA Abbreviation of **Federal National Mortgage Association**.

FOB Abbreviation of **free on board**.

foetus [*fee* · tes] *n.* Same as **fetus**.

FOIA Abbreviation of **Freedom of Information Act**.

follow [*foll* · oh] *v.* 1. To remain consistent with a previous decision. USAGE: "The court's decision in this case followed its decision in *Smith v Jones*." *See* authority; precedent. 2. To pursue. 3. To come after; to result from.
➤ displace, ensue, supervene, succeed; trail, pursue, persecute, escort; accord, emulate, harmonize, reflect; appreciate, apprehend, realize.

Food and Drug Administration
[ad · min · is · *tray* · shen] *n.* Commonly referred to by its abbreviation, **FDA**; a federal agency within the Department of Health and Human Services. It is responsible for safeguarding public health and safety by protecting the consumer from adulterated, misbranded, or fraudulent food products, cosmetics, and drugs. No drug may be legally marketed unless it is first approved by the FDA.

for *prep.* 1. On behalf of. Signing a contract, bill, note, or other instrument with the name of the agent, followed by that of the principal, separated by the word "for," is a method of placing liability on the principal and avoiding personal liability for the agent. EXAMPLE: "John Jones for Mary Smith." *Also see* by. 2. Because of; on account of; by reason of. EXAMPLE: "for value" means "because of **consideration**" (or "because of **valuable consideration**") given by one party to the other. 3. Throughout or during a given period of time. USAGE: "It rained for three days."
➤ concerning, notwithstanding, supposing, pro, toward.

for account of [a · *kount*] A form of indorsement of checks and other commercial paper that identifies the person entitled to the proceeds of the instrument. *See also* payable to order.

for cause 1. For legal cause, that is, upon grounds provided by constitution or statute. EXAMPLES: a **challenge for cause** to a juror; the removal for cause of a public official. *See* cause; good cause; legal cause. 2. The termination of a person's employment for just cause.

for collection [ke · *lek* · shen] *See* restrictive indorsement.

for deposit [de · *paw* · zit] *See* restrictive indorsement.

for deposit only [de · *paw* · zit] *See* for deposit.

for hire Describes a vehicle operated to carry passengers or freight for a charge. *See* common carrier.

for profit [*prof* · it] A business or other enterprise whose purpose is to make money. Thus, a corporation that is not a **charitable corporation** is referred to as a **for-profit corporation**. *Compare* nonprofit corporation.

for purpose of argument [*per* · pes of ar · gyoo · ment] *See* arguendo.

for the record [rek · erd] *See* of record.

for use *See* use.

for use and benefit [*ben* · e · fit] *See* use.

F

F

for value [*val* · yoo] For **consideration**. *See* holder for value; purchaser for value.

for value received [*val* · yoo re · *seevd*] *See* value received.

for whom it may concern [ken · *sern*] In an insurance policy, a phrase that extends the protection of the policy to anyone who has an **insurable interest** in the property.

for-profit corporation [kore · per · *ay* · shen] *n. See* for profit.

forbearance [for · *bare* · ense] *n.* 1. The act of holding back from doing something one has a right to do. (EXAMPLE: refraining from commencing a lawsuit.) Withholding of action one has a legal right to undertake is sufficient **consideration** for a contract. 2. Giving a debtor additional time for payment. 3. Submitting or yielding without complaint.
➤ holding back, refraining, inaction; patience, delay, mercy.

force *n.* 1. Physical power or strength exerted against a person (EXAMPLE: **robbery**) or thing (EXAMPLE: **forcible entry**). 2. Power exerted through deceit. EXAMPLE: fraud. *See* coercion. *Compare* duress. 3. Any effective exercise of power. USAGE: "force of law" means the law itself or that which has the effect or power of law. *See also* excessive force; forcible detainer; forcible entry and detainer; in force; irresistible force.
v. To press on against resistance; to compel someone to do an act.
➤ *n.* coercion, duress, stimulus, potential; gumption, determination, obligation, persuasiveness.
v. compel, obtrude, demand, impose, coerce, oblige, constrain.

force majeure [forss ma · *zhoor*] (*French*) *n.* A force that humans can neither resist, foresee, nor prevent; an **act of God**. Some contracts contain a force majeure clause, which excuses nonperformance if the contract cannot be performed because of the occurrence of an unforeseeable and irresistible event.

force of law *n. See* force.

forced heir *n.* A person who cannot be disinherited by a **testator** (EXAMPLE: a surviving spouse who is entitled to an elective share), except when there is a legal cause for disinheritance.

forced sale *n. See* execution sale; judicial sale.

forcible [*for* · sibl] *adj.* 1. With force; resulting in force; having the quality of force. 2. Effective; convincing.
➤ aggressive, potent, vehement, vigorous ("a forcible attack"); effective, convincing ("a forcible argument").

forcible detainer [de · *tane* · er] *n.* 1. A **summary remedy** for regaining possession of real property from one who continues to hold the property after his right to possession has expired or has been lawfully terminated. *See also* ejectment; eviction. *Compare* forcible entry and detainer. 2. The act of a person who remains in possession of land after her right to do so has ended. *See* detainer.

forcible entry [*en* · tree] *n.* 1. An entry into a house or other structure with at least some degree of actual force. *See* breaking; breaking and entering; burglary. 2. An entry on real property which is in the possession of another person, without her consent and by actual force or threats of force, causing her to surrender possession of the property. *Compare* trespass.

forcible entry and detainer [*en* · tree and de · *tane* · er] *n.* 1. A **summary remedy** for obtaining possession of real property by a person who has been wrongfully put out or kept out of possession. *See also* ejectment; eviction. *Compare* forcible detainer. 2. The act of a person who wrongfully deprives another of possession of land.

forcible trespass [*tress* · pass] *n.* Occurs when conduct amounting to a breach of the peace is used to intimidate a person into surrendering personal property. *See* trespass.

forebearance [for · *bare* · ense] *n.* Refraining from doing that which a person can do.
➤ resisting, refraining, endurance, patience, temperance, holding back.

foreclose [for · *kloze*] *v.* 1. To cut off the right to recover **security** that has been mortgaged; to obtain a **foreclosure**

decree. *See* foreclosure. 2. To block; to close off; to terminate.

➤ block, confiscate, forfeit, bar.

foreclosure [for · *kloh* · zher] *n.* 1. A legal action by which a **mortgagee** terminates a **mortgagor's** interest in mortgaged premises. *See* mortgage. *Compare* equity of redemption. 2. The enforcement of a **lien, deed of trust**, or mortgage on real estate, or a **security interest** in personal property, by any method provided by law. *See* statutory foreclosure; strict foreclosure. *See also* execution sale; judicial sale.

➤ blockage, obstruction, confiscation, prohibition, removal, dispossession, removal, eviction.

foreclosure decree [de · *kree*] *n.* A decree that orders the sale of mortgaged real estate, the proceeds to be applied in satisfaction of the debt. *See* decree.

foreclosure sale *n.* A sale of mortgaged premises in accordance with a **foreclosure decree**; a **judicial sale**. *See also* equity of redemption; redemption.

forego [for · *goe*] *v.* To precede. *Compare* forgo.

➤ go before, precede.

foregoing [for · *goh* · ing] *adj.* Preceding; previously mentioned.

➤ antecedent, precedent, prior, above ("to serve the foregoing matter").

foreign [*forr* · en] *adj.* 1. Belonging to, of, or from another nation, country, state, or jurisdiction. 2. Alien; strange; imported; unfamiliar; extrinsic.

➤ alienated, borrowed, extraneous, inaccessible; irrelevant, impertinent, inconsistent.

foreign administrator [ad · *min* · is · tray · ter] *n.* *See* foreign personal representative.

foreign attachment [a · *tach* · ment] *n.* The **attachment** of property owned within the jurisdiction by a nonresident defendant.

foreign bill of exchange *n.* A **bill of exchange** that is not payable in the state or country in which it was **drawn**.

foreign charity [*cha* · ri · tee] *n.* A charity that is to be administered in a state or country outside the jurisdiction in which the donor is or was domiciled.

foreign commerce [*kom* · erss] *n.* *See* foreign trade.

foreign consul [*kon* · sul] *n.* *See* consul.

foreign corporation [kore · per · *ay* · shen] *n.* 1. A corporation incorporated under the laws of one state, doing business in another. *See* doing business in a state. 2. Under federal statutes, including the Internal Revenue Code, a corporation organized outside the United States. Under the Code, special tax considerations apply to U.S.-owned foreign corporations, i.e., foreign corporations in which citizens or residents of the United States hold a controlling interest. *Compare* domestic corporation.

foreign court *n.* The court of a foreign state or nation. *See* foreign judgment.

foreign currency [*ker* · en · see] *n.* The money of a foreign country.

foreign divorce [di · *vorss*] *n.* A divorce granted in a state or country other than the couple's state of residence.

foreign exchange [eks · *chaynj*] *n.* 1. The act of converting the money of one country to the money of another. 2. The procedure by which money issued by one country pays debts owed in another.

foreign executor [eg · *zek* · yoo · tor] *n.* *See* foreign personal representative.

foreign judgment [*juj* · ment] *n.* A **judgment** rendered by a court of a foreign country or a court of a sister state. *Compare* domestic judgment.

foreign jurisdiction [joo · ris · *dik* · shen] *n.* A **jurisdiction** other than the jurisdiction where the **forum** is located.

foreign law *n.* The law of a jurisdiction other than the jurisdiction that is asked to apply it.

foreign personal holding company [*per* · sen · el *hole* · ding kum · pe · nee] *n.* A **foreign corporation** whose income is primarily **personal holding company** income and at least 50 percent of whose stock is owned by less than six individuals (as opposed to less than six corporations or partnerships) who are U.S. citizens or residents. *See* holding company.

foreign personal representative [*per* · sen · el rep · re · *zen* · te · tiv] *n.* An **executor** or **administrator** who administers a **decedent's estate** in a state other than the state in which she was appointed; an ancillary executor or administrator. *See* personal representative. *Also see* ancillary administration.

foreign representative [rep · re · *zen* · te · tiv] *n.* An ambassador or other diplomatic representative.

foreign service of process [*ser* · viss of *pross* · ess] *n.* **Service of process** in a state or country foreign to the state or country from which the process (EXAMPLES: an arrest warrant; a **complaint**) issued. *See also* long arm statutes.

foreign state *n.* 1. Another state of the United States. 2. Another country.

foreign tax credit [*kred* · it] *n.* A credit against United States income tax which, in some circumstances, is available to U.S. citizens or residents who pay income tax to a foreign country. The credit is designed to ease the burden of double taxation.

foreign trade *n.* Commerce between countries; the importation and exportation of goods.

foreign will *n.* A will executed in a state other than the state in which it is offered for probate.

foreman [*for* · men] *n.* 1. A member of a jury or grand jury who acts as its spokesperson. 2. A person in charge of a group of employees; a supervisor.
➤ spokesperson, supervisor, leader.

forensic [fo · *ren* · sik] *adj.* Pertaining to or belonging to the courts.
➤ judicial, legal, argumentative, controversial, disputable, contestable, litigious, juristic ("forensic medicine").

forensic medicine [*med* · e · sin] *n.* The science of medicine as it relates to the law and legal proceedings. *See* medical jurisprudence.

forensic pathology [path · *all* · e · jee] *n.* Branch of medicine that pertains to the causes of disease and death as they relate to the law and legal proceedings.

forensic psychiatry [sy · *ky* · e · tree] *n.* The science of psychiatry as it relates to the law and legal proceedings.

foreseeable [for · *see* · ebl] *adj.* That which may be anticipated or known in advance; that which a person should have known.

In the law of negligence, a person is responsible for the consequences of his acts only if they are foreseeable. *See* proximate cause.
➤ imminent, prospective, forthcoming.

foreseeable injury [*in* · jer · ee] *n.* An **injury** that a **reasonably prudent person** should reasonably have anticipated was a likely result of a given act or failure to act.

forestalling the market [for · *stall* · ing the *mar* · ket] *n.* Same as **abbrochment**.

forfeit [*for* · fit] *n.* That which is forfeited or subject to forfeiture.
v. To lose, particularly as a result of a default or neglect, or the commission of a crime or offense. One may forfeit, among other things, money, property, or rights. *See* forfeiture. *See also* fine; penalty. *Compare* confiscate.
➤ *n.* loss, non-contest.
v. abandon, relinquish, renounce, sacrifice, surrender, escheat, repudiate, shun, eschew, forsake, spurn, waive.

forfeiture [*for* · fit · sher] *n.* A deprivation of money, property, or rights, without compensation, as a consequence of a default or the commission of a crime; **civil forfeiture**. USAGE: "His car is subject to forfeiture because he used it to transport marijuana." *See* civil forfeiture. *See also* confiscation; fine; penalty.
➤ dispossession, confiscation, seizure, punishment.

forfeiture of bond *n.* The loss of something pledged as **security** because of a breach of a condition of the bond. EXAMPLE: the **surety's** obligation to pay to the court the amount of the **bail bond** if the defendant fails to appear in court.

forge *v.* 1. To commit a **forgery**. 2. To shape by hammering. 3. To move ahead.
➤ counterfeit, design, duplicate, imitate, reproduce; construct, invent, build, manufacture.

forgery [*for* · jer · ee] *n.* The **false making**, **material alteration**, or **uttering**, with intent to defraud or **injure**, of any writing that, if genuine, might appear to be legally effective or the basis for legal liability. Forgery is a crime. *See* uttering a forged instrument. *See also* counterfeit.

F

F

➤ falsification, fraudulence, misrepresentation, manipulation.

forgo [for · *goe*] *v.* To deny oneself of something; to do without.
➤ do without, pass up, abjure, relinquish, renounce, waive, abstain, desist.

form *n.* 1. A printed instrument (EXAMPLE: a **complaint**; a court order; a contract) with blank spaces for the insertion of such details as may be required to make it a complete document. 2. **Procedure** rather than **substance**. *See and compare* procedural; substantive. 3. Appearance rather than substance; the opposite of substance. *See and compare* matter of form; matter of substance.
➤ datasheet, paper, application, chart; ceremony, behavior, fashion, method, style; arrangement, appearance, conformation, formation.

forma pauperis [*for* · ma *paw* · per · iss] *See in forma pauperis.*

formal [*for* · mel] *adj.* 1. Certain; fixed; firm; set; explicit. 2. Pertaining to matters of form rather than of substance. *See and compare* matter of form; matter of substance.
➤ certain, fixed, firm, set, explicit, traditional. *Ant.* informal, casual.
formal contract [*kon* · trakt] *n.* 1. A signed, written contract, as opposed to an oral contract. 2. A contract that must be in a certain form to be valid. EXAMPLE: a **negotiable instrument**. *Compare* informal contract; parol contract. *See also* specialty.
formal party [*par* · tee] *n.* Same as **nominal party**.

formalize [*for* · mel · ize] *v.* to give official status to.
➤ legalize, legitimate, validate, make official, legitimize ("to formalize an agreement").

formed design [de · *zine*] *n.* A plan or course of conduct conceived deliberately and with premeditation. *See* deliberate; deliberation.

former [*for* · mer] *adj.* Prior in point of time. *See autrefois;* autrefois acquit; autrefois convict. *Also see* entries beginning "*prior*," such as **prior adjudication**; **prior jeopardy**; **prior testimony**.
➤ prior, previous.
former jeopardy [*jep* · er · dee] *n.* Same as **double jeopardy**.

forms of action [*ak* · shen] *n.* Many forms of action existed at **common law**. (EXAMPLES: **trespass**; ***assumpsit; ex contractu; ex delicto*.**) These technical forms of action have been abolished, leaving today only one form of action in civil lawsuits: the **civil action**.

fornication [for · ni · *kay* · shen] *n.* Sexual intercourse between unmarried persons. If one of the partners to the act is married, that partner is guilty of adultery; the unmarried partner is guilty of either fornication or adultery, depending upon the jurisdiction. The crime of fornication is rarely punished. *See also* cohabitation; illicit relations.
➤ copulation, seduction, coition, intercourse.

forswear [for · *sware*] *v.* To swear falsely. *See* false swearing. *Compare* perjury.
➤ perjure, deceive, lie, equivocate.

forthwith [forth · *with*] *adv.* 1. With reasonable diligence; within a reasonable time. 2. Immediately.
➤ immediately, directly, instantly, promptly, abruptly.

fortiori [for · she · *or* · ee] *See a fortiori.*

fortuitous [for · *too* · i · tes] *adj.* Accidental; occurring by chance. *See* accident.
➤ unexpected, accidental, surprise, unintended, unexpected, chance, haphazard ("a fortuitous event").
fortuitous event *n.* An accident; something happening by chance. *See* accidental death; accidental injury.

forum [*for* · em] *n.* 1. A place where **jurisdiction** is. 2. A court; a tribunal; a jurisdiction. 3. A place for discussing ideas; an opportunity for public debate.
➤ tribunal, bench, judiciary, court, assembly, platform, panel, arena, space.
forum non conveniens [non kon · *veen* · yenz] (*Latin*) *n.* Means "inconvenient jurisdiction." The legal principle that a court is empowered to decline **jurisdiction** when it serves justice and the convenience of the parties to try the case in another forum.
forum shopping [*shop* · ing] *n.* Attempting to have one's case heard by the court one believes most likely to sustain one's claim.

forward [*for* · ward] *adj.* Pertaining to the future; advanced.
v. To transmit; to put something on its way to an ultimate destination; to ship. *See* forwarder.
➤ *adj.* advanced, accelerated; rude, offensive, harsh, aggressive.
v. aid, expedite, cultivate, foster; consign, send, remit, transport.
forward contract [*kon* · trakt] *n.* Same as **futures contract**.

forwarder [*for* · war · der] *n.* A person who arranges with carriers for goods to be transported over a distance, from one party to another. A forwarder also assumes responsibility for packing, storage, and such other handling as may be required.

foster [*foss* · ter] *v.* Encourage; protect; cherish; nourish.
adj. Substitute.
➤ *v.* promote, support, encourage, protect, cherish, nourish, accommodate, stimulate; harbor, help, oblige, sustain.
adj. substitute, replacement ("foster parents").
foster child *n.* A child brought up by a person who is not her biological parent. *Compare* adoption.
foster home *n.* The household or home in which a foster child is raised.
foster parent [*pair* · ent] *n.* A person who rears a foster child.

found *v.* 1. Determined as a fact. USAGE: "The judge found that the defendant was telling the truth." *See also* find; finding; finding of fact. 2. Located or discovered for **jurisdictional** purposes. EXAMPLE: a corporation is "found," and therefore may be served with **process**, in a jurisdiction in which it is **doing business**. *See* service of process. 3. Established a foundation or basis. EXAMPLE: a grand jury indorses the words "not found" on a **bill of indictment** when it determines there is insufficient basis for criminal prosecution.
➤ begin, initiate, create, introduce, commence, ("to found a company"); erect, base, support, raise ("to found an argument on fact").

foundation [foun · *day* · shen] *n.* 1. One form of **charitable organization**, especially one involving a large and permanent fund. 2. Preliminary evidence necessary to establish a basis for admitting other evidence. EXAMPLE: testimony as to who killed the butler is inadmissible unless the "foundation has been laid" by testimony that the butler is dead. *See* admissible evidence. 3. Base; basis. 4. Support; underpinning.
➤ endowment, charity, institute, society; authority, rationale, purpose, justification; base, basis, support, underpinning ("the building's foundation").

founded [*found* · ed] *adv.* Grounded; arises from. USAGE: "her motion is well founded" means there is a strong basis (in law, in fact) for the **motion**.
➤ grounded, supported, established ("a well-founded idea").
founded on [*found* · ed] *adv.* Based upon. USAGE: "Her **cause of action** is founded on his conduct."

four corners [*kor* · nerz] *n.* The face of a document or instrument. The expression generally relates to the act of construing a document based upon the document alone, without recourse to **extrinsic evidence**. *See* plain language rule. *Compare* parol evidence.

Fourteenth Amendment [*four* · teenth a · *mend* · ment] *n.* An amendment to the Constitution that requires the states (as opposed to the federal government—*compare* Fifth Amendment) to provide **due process of law**, and to ensure **equal protection of the laws**, "to any person within [their] jurisdiction." The Fourteenth Amendment also prohibits states from abridging "the **privileges and immunities** of citizens." *See* due process clause; equal protection clause; privileges and immunities clause.

Fourth Amendment [a · *mend* · ment] *n.* An amendment to the Constitution prohibiting searches without search warrants and requiring that search warrants be issued only upon **probable cause**. *See* search and seizure.

fracas [*fray* · cus] *n.* A noisy fight or disturbance.
➤ battle, brawl, scuffle, fight, fuss, fray, disturbance.

F

F

fractional [*frak* · shen · el] *adj.* Small, being no more than a portion or fraction of the whole.

➤ partial, divided, incomplete, segmented ("a fractional share of corporate stock").

fractional share *n.* 1. A fractional part of a share of corporate stock. 2. The proportion or fraction of a corporation that a given shareholder owns.

frame *v.* 1. To draft a document. USAGE: "The Founding Fathers framed our Constitution." 2. To cause the arrest or conviction of a person based upon false evidence.
n. The basic structure of an object.

➤ *v.* conceive, contrive, invent, formulate, prepare ("frame an argument"); draft, write ("frame a statute"); set up, entrap ("frame the suspect").
n. structure, edifice, skeleton, support, body, form, anatomy.

franchise [*fran* · chize] *n.* 1. A right or privilege conferred by law. EXAMPLE: the right to vote. *See* elective franchise; enfranchise. 2. A privilege of doing something, conferred by law, that does not belong to all citizens. EXAMPLE: a grant to a public utility of the right to provide a public service. *See also* corporate franchise. 3. A license granted by the owner of a **trade name** or **trademark** permitting the licensee to sell the licensor's products or services and retain the profits. Most "chain" fast food restaurants, for EXAMPLE, are franchises; so is the Atlanta Falcons football team (the National Football League is the licensor or franchisor). *See* franchisee; franchisor.

➤ license, authorization, privilege, exemption.

franchise tax *n.* A tax imposed on the privilege of carrying on a business.

franchisee [*fran* · chize · *ee*] *n.* A person or company that is granted the right to operate a **franchise**. *See* licensee.

franchisor [*fran* · chize · *or*] *n.* A person or company that owns and grants a **franchise**. *See* licensor.

frank *adj.* 1. Direct and to the point. 2. Abusive-sounding or rude.
v. To mark for mailing without postage. *See* franking privilege.

➤ *adj.* direct, unembellished, forthright, honest; abrasive, rude.
v. mail, send.

franking privilege [*priv* · i · lej] *n.* The privilege of mailing material without postage; it is possessed by senators and congresspersons, among other federal officials.

FRAP Abbreviation of **Federal Rules of Appellate Procedure**.

fraternal [fre · *ter* · nel] *adj.* 1. Related; shared; common; mutual. 2. Brotherly.

➤ related, shared, common, mutual, brotherly, friendly, intimate, kind.

fraternal benefit association [*ben* · e · fit a · so · see · *ay* · shen] *n.* Same as **fraternal benefit society**.

fraternal benefit society [*ben* · e · fit so · sy · e · tee] *n.* An unincorporated group of persons organized solely for mutual benefit and to advance a common, usually charitable, cause. Customarily, the principal form of assistance that such a society provides to its members is the payment of death benefits, usually through "fraternal insurance." *See* mutual benefit society.

fraud *n.* Deceit, deception, or trickery that is intended to induce, and does induce, another to part with anything of value or surrender some legal right. *See* actual fraud; badges of fraud; constructive fraud; extrinsic fraud; false representation; intrinsic fraud; mail fraud; misrepresentation; tax fraud; wire fraud.

➤ misrepresentation, dishonesty, collusion, beguilement, deception, guile, deceit, chicanery, trickery.

fraud in fact *n.* Actual fraud. *Compare* constructive fraud; fraud in law.

fraud in law *n.* Constructive fraud. *Compare* actual fraud; fraud in fact.

fraud in the essence [*ess* · ense] *n.* Deception with respect to a document a person signs. EXAMPLE: a sale based upon a **fraudulent misrepresentation**. *See* essence.

fraud in the factum [*fak* · tum] *n.* Same as **fraud in the essence**.

fraud in the inducement [in · *dewss* · ment] *n.* Fraud exercised in inducing a person to sign an instrument or to enter into an agreement or transaction. *See* intrinsic fraud.

frauds, statute of [*stat* · shoot] *n. See* statute of frauds.

fraudulent [*fraw* · je · lent] *adj.* 1. That which is done with intent to defraud. 2. Deceitful; dishonest. *See* fraud.
➤ deceptive, devious, phony, bogus, dishonorable, deceitful, dishonest, spurious, crooked.

fraudulent assignment [a · *sine* · ment] *n. See* fraudulent conveyance.

fraudulent concealment [ken · *seal* · ment] *n.* Suppressing or hiding a material fact that one has a duty to communicate. EXAMPLE: the failure of a bankrupt to fully disclose her property to her **trustee in bankruptcy**.

fraudulent conversion [ken · *ver* · zhen] *n.* An essential element of the crime of **embezzlement**, consisting either of an appropriation of money or other property to one's personal use after obtaining lawful possession of it, or of using it for the benefit of anyone other than its owner. *See* conversion.

fraudulent conveyance [ken · *vay* · ense] *n.* A **conveyance** in fraud of creditors; a transaction by means of which the owner of real or personal property attempts to put the property beyond the reach of his creditors.

fraudulent disposition [dis · pe · *zish* · en] *n. See* fraudulent conveyance.

fraudulent misrepresentation [mis · rep · re · zen · *tay* · shen] *n.* Words spoken or written with the knowledge or belief that they are false, and with the purpose of deceiving and inducing action in reliance. *See* essence; intrinsic fraud.

fraudulent practice [*prak* · tiss] *n.* Fraudulent conduct.

fraudulent preference [*pref* · rense] *n.* 1. The act of a debtor in making payment to one of her creditors by paying him with the intention of defrauding other creditors. 2. Under the **Bankruptcy Code**, a transfer of property to a creditor which gives him an advantage over other creditors. Although such a transfer may be disallowed by the **trustee in bankruptcy**, it is not necessarily a criminal act. *See* preference.

fraudulent representation [rep · re · zen · *tay* · shen] *n.* Same as **fraudulent misrepresentation**.

fraudulent sale *n. See* fraudulent conveyance.

fraudulent transfer [*trans* · fer] *n. See* fraudulent conveyance.

FRCP Abbreviation of **Federal Rules of Civil Procedure**.

free *adj.* 1. Without cost; without charge. 2. Without restraint or coercion; unrestricted; not obstructed; to be enjoyed without limitations. 3. Not bound. 4. Not enslaved.
v. 1. To liberate; to release. 2. To acquit; to exonerate.
➤ *adj.* unconstrained, unimpeded, emancipated, unencumbered ("a free man"); cleared, exonerated, spared, disencumbered, excused ("free and clear").
v. discharge, liberate, release; acquit, pardon, exonerate.

free alongside ship [a · *long* · side] *adv.* In a commercial contract, a term signifying that the seller is responsible for the cost of transporting the goods to dockside. Commonly expressed by its abbreviation, **FAS**.

free and clear *adv.* Not encumbered by a mortgage or other **lien**, unencumbered. USAGE: "We own our property free and clear." *See* encumbrance.

free election [e · *lek* · shen] *n.* An election in which every voter is allowed to cast his ballot, or to refrain from voting, as his own judgment and conscience dictate.

free exercise clause [*ek* · ser · size] *n.* The clause in the **First Amendment** that prevents Congress from prohibiting the "free exercise" of religion. *See* freedom of religion.

free on board *adv.* A commercial term meaning that the charges for transporting goods to the **FOB** point, that is, to the destination, are to be paid by the seller.

free port *n.* A port, or a section of a port, where goods may be unloaded, warehoused, or reshipped without going through customs or paying duty.

freedom [*free* · dum] *n.* 1. A social and political characteristic of a nation that guarantees the civil liberties of its inhabitants. 2. Liberty; absence of restraint; independence.

F

F

➤ liberty, autonomy, deregulation, authorization, independence, abolition, emancipation, salvation, immunity.

freedom of assembly [a · *sem* · blee] *n. See* freedom of association.

freedom of association [a · so · see · *ay* · shen] *n.* The **First Amendment** right of the people "peaceably to assemble."

freedom of contract [*kon* · trakt] *n.* A phrase relating to the **contract clause** of the Constitution, which provides that "no state shall ... pass any ... law impairing the obligation of contracts." This provision is a constitutional guaranty of the right to acquire and possess property and to dispose of it as one wishes.

freedom of expression [eks · *presh* · en] *n.* A term that covers religious freedom, freedom of speech, and freedom of the press, all of which are protected by the **First Amendment**.

freedom of religion [re · *lij* · en] *n.* The **First Amendment** stipulates that "Congress shall make no law respecting an establishment of religion, or prohibiting the free exercise thereof." This provision guarantees the freedom to believe or not to believe and, subject to law, the right to act upon one's religious belief or lack of belief. It also prohibits financial assistance to religion from public funds.

freedom of speech *n. See* freedom of speech and of the press.

freedom of speech and of the press *n.* The **First Amendment** provides that "Congress shall make no law ... abridging the freedom of speech or of the press." It embraces the concept that the expression or publication of thought and belief, free from government interference, is essential to the well-being of a free society, and should be limited only to prevent abuse of that right.

freedom of the press *n. See* freedom of speech and of the press.

Freedom of Information Act (FOIA) [*free* · dum of in · fer · *may* · shen] *n.* A federal statute that requires federal agencies to make available to the public, upon request, material contained in their files, as well as information on how they function. The Act contains various significant exemptions from disclosure, including information compiled for law enforcement purposes.

freehold [*free* · hold] *n.* An **estate in fee** or a **life estate** in real property. *See and compare* estate less than freehold; estate of freehold not of inheritance.

freehold estate [es · *tate*] *n.* A freehold.

freeze *v.* To preserve the status quo; to maintain things as they presently are. EXAMPLES: an employer's decision to maintain present pay levels or suspend salary increases; a court order prohibiting withdrawals from a bank account.

➤ stop, suspend, inhibit, dishearten, preserve.

freight *n.* 1. The charge for a carrier's services in transporting and delivering property. 2. The cargo carried by a carrier. *See* dead freight.

➤ conveyance, encumbrance, burden, fare, tonnage.

freight booking [*book* · ing] *n.* Making specific arrangements, in advance, for the transportation of goods.

freight forwarder *n. See* forwarder.

fresh *adj.* Prompt; immediate; current; timely.

➤ prompt, immediate, current, timely ("fresh pursuit"); young, dewy, new.

fresh complaint rule [kum · *playnt*] *n.* The doctrine, no longer universally endorsed by the courts, that the credibility of the complainant in a sexual assault case is strengthened if she reported the crime promptly.

fresh pursuit [per · *sute*] *n.* 1. The pursuit of a person by a police officer from the time of commission of an offense, or from discovery of the offense, for the purpose of arresting him. An officer giving immediate chase may pursue a suspect into a neighboring state, and, if permitted by that state, make the arrest there. Fresh pursuit is also referred to as **hot pursuit**. 2. A person may use reasonable force to recover property from a thief if she pursues and apprehends him immediately.

friend *n.* A companion or acquaintance. *See* next friend.

➤ confidant, companion, cohort, compatriot, ally, partner, comrade.

friend of the court *n.* Same as *amicus curiae*.

friendly [*frend* · lee] *adj.* Receptive; sympathetic; amicable.

➤ receptive, sympathetic, amicable, amiable, courteous, civil, accessible, auspicious. *Ant.* hostile.

friendly suit *n.* Same as **amicable action**.

friendly takeover [*take* · over] *n.* The voluntary merger of one corporation into another. *Compare* hostile takeover. *See* merger of corporations; takeover. *Compare* hostile takeover.

fringe benefits [*ben* · e · fits] *n.* Benefits received by an employee in addition to wages or salary. EXAMPLES: vacation pay; health insurance; a pension.

frisk *v.* To search a person, particularly for a weapon, by running one's hands over his clothing. A frisk conducted by a police officer is subject to the **search and seizure** requirements of the **Fourth Amendment**. *Compare* stop and frisk.

➤ inspect, scan, explore, investigate, search, probe, scrutinize.

frivolous [*friv* · e · les] *adj.* Obviously insufficient; trivial; trifling; unimportant.

➤ trivial, impractical, superficial, senseless, volatile, insufficient, trifling ("a frivolous appeal").

frivolous appeal [a · *peal*] *n.* An **appeal** taken on grounds that are trivial and obviously insufficient.

frivolous pleading [*plee* · ding] *n.* A **pleading** that is good in form but false in fact and not pleaded in good faith. *See* false pleading. *Also see* false answer.

frivolous suit *n.* A lawsuit brought with no intention of determining an actual controversy. EXAMPLE: an action initiated for purposes of harassment.

frolic [*froll* · ik] *n.* Something that is fun or amusing.

v. To run around merrily.

➤ *n.* antic, spree, fun, amusement; mischief, caprice.

v. play, romp, revel, prance, carouse, cavort.

frolic of his own [*froll* · ik] *n.* The conduct of an employee or agent who has departed from the **scope of employment** (that is, from doing his employer's or principal's

business) to do something for himself. (EXAMPLE: a delivery driver who deviates from his route and spends an hour at the zoo.) The principal or employer is not liable for injury to a third party caused by the negligence of an agent or employee who is on a "frolic of his own."

from *prep.* A word which expresses the concept of a starting point in matters of time or distance. It can cause confusion in determining whether the day or point from which a calculation is to be made should be included in or excluded from the computation. It should be construed according to the intention of the parties and the equities of the case.

➤ separating, against, taken away.

front *n.* 1. That which faces forward. 2. That which comes before or ahead of something else. 3. That which serves as a cover or disguise for some other undertaking. 4. Appearance; outward impression; façade.

adj. Lead; first; beginning.

v. To face; to look at or onto something.

➤ *n.* forward, beginning, façade, foreground; aspect, demeanor, disguise, manner.

adj. advanced, first, frontal, headfirst, preliminary ("front money").

v. confront, border, overlay, meet.

front money [*mun* · ee] *n.* Money that must be invested or that is otherwise required before a venture or enterprise can be undertaken.

frontage [*frun* · tej] *n.* The length of property, in feet or other linear measurement, along a street, highway, body of water, or abutting property.

fronting [*frun* · ting] *n.* *See* front.

fronting and abutting [a · *but* · ing] *adj.* Bordering; adjacent; adjoining. *See* abut. *Also see* abutting owners; adjoining landowners.

frozen [*froh* · zen] *adj.* Unable to be changed or moved.

➤ immobilized, restricted, unavailable, inaccessible ("His assets were frozen").

frozen asset [*froh* · zen *ass* · et] *n.* An **asset** that cannot be converted to cash easily or quickly. *Also see* freeze.

F

fruit *n.* That which accrues; the accrual; the yield; the result; the product; the return. USAGE: "Profit is the fruit of **capital**."
➤ benefit, consequence, return, ware, accrual, product, return.

fruit and tree doctrine [*dok* · trin] *n.* The tax law doctrine that income is the fruit of the labor of the person who earned it and, as such, is his tax liability, which he cannot avoid by making a gift of the income to someone else.

fruit of the poisonous tree doctrine [*poy* · zen · es tree dok · trin] *n.* The **constitutional law** doctrine that evidence, including **derivative evidence**, obtained as the result of an illegal search is inadmissible. *See* exclusionary rule; Fourth Amendment; unreasonable search and seizure.

fruits of crime *n.* Anything acquired as the result of committing a crime.

frustrate [*frus* · trait] *v.* To feel or make someone discouraged.
➤ foil, hinder, obstruct, prevent, cancel, check, confound.

frustration [*frus* · *tray* · shen] *n.* The prevention of accomplishment of purpose.
➤ dissatisfaction, annoyance, nuisance, circumvention.
Ant. satisfaction.

frustration of contract doctrine [*kon* · trakt *dok* · trin] *n.* A doctrine that frees the parties to a contract from the obligation of performance in circumstances where the purpose of the contract has been substantially frustrated. *See* frustration of purpose.

frustration of purpose [*per* · pes] *n.* An event that may excuse nonperformance of a contract because it defeats or nullifies the objective in the minds of the parties when they entered into the contract. An EXAMPLE of such an event is the death of an animal that one party has agreed to sell to the other. *See* frustration of contract doctrine.

FSLIC Abbreviation of **Federal Savings and Loan Insurance Corporation**.

FTC Abbreviation of **Federal Trade Commission**.

fugitive [*few* · je · tiv] *n.* A person who flees, especially from justice; an escapee; a runaway. *See* fugitive from justice.
➤ deserter, runaway, outlaw, outcast, refugee, escapee.

fugitive from justice [*jus* · tiss] *n.* A person who departs a jurisdiction (or conceals herself within the jurisdiction) to avoid arrest, prosecution, or punishment for a crime, even if she believes herself innocent. *See also* flight to avoid prosecution.

full *adj.* Complete; wholly sufficient; not lacking in any significant respect; ample.
➤ complete, adequate, plenteous, plentiful, ample, sated.

full age *n.* The status of a person who has become an adult in the eyes of the law; the **age of majority**; **legal age**.

full answer [*an* · ser] *n.* An answer that is factually complete and legally sufficient. *See* answer.

full bench *n.* The court with all the judges sitting in a case, particularly an **appellate court**. *See* bench; *en banc*.

full blood *n.* The relationship between children of the same father and mother.

full cash value [*val* · yoo] *n.* Same as **market value**.

full court *n.* Same as **full bench**.

full cousin [*kuz* · in] *n.* A first cousin.

full coverage [*kuv* · er · ej] *n.* Insurance coverage that indemnifies the insured for the full amount of the **loss**.

full disclosure [dis · *kloh* · zher] *n.* Revealing all of the details of something. The term refers to a duty the law imposes on persons in specific circumstances. EXAMPLE: the **consumer credit protection acts** require disclosure of the complete terms upon which credit is extended. *See also* disclosure statement.

full faith and credit [*kred* · it] *n.* A reference to the requirement of Article IV of the Constitution that each state give "full faith and credit" to the "public acts, records, and judicial proceedings" of every other state. This means that a state's judicial acts must be given the same effect by the courts of all other states as they receive at home.

full hearing [*hear* · ing] *n.* A **proceeding** in which one not only has the right to present evidence, but is also afforded a reasonable opportunity to know the claims of the opposing **party** and to respond to them.

full indorsement [in · *dorse* · ment] *n.* An **indorsement** which is not a mere signature, but which also orders payment to a named indorsee. EXAMPLE: a check drawn to John Jones and indorsed "pay to the order of Bill Smith, [signed] John Jones."

full name *n.* First name, middle name, if any, and surname; first name, middle initial, and surname.

full settlement [*setl* · ment] *n.* The resolution of all claims, demands, and disputes.

full value [*val* · yoo] *n.* Same as **market value**.

full warranty [*war* · en · tee] *n.* A **warranty** that is not confined to specified defects and that covers labor as well as materials. *Compare* limited warranty.

full-time employment [em · *ploy* · ment] *n.* The circumstance of an employee who is fully employed (customarily, 40 hours per week) on a regular basis, as distinguished from part-time, casual, seasonal, or temporary employment. *See* regular employment.

function [*funk* · shen] *n.* A performance or act required of a person in the course of her employment or in carrying out a duty. *See* judicial function; ministerial function.
➤ task, role, responsibility, duty, purpose, utility.

fund *n.* 1. Usually stated in the *plural*, a sum of money, either in hand or deposited in a bank. 2. Usually stated in the *plural*, an accumulation of pecuniary resources (EXAMPLES: stock; bonds), not limited to money. *See* current funds; mutual fund; sinking fund. 3. Money or other assets set aside for a particular purpose. 4. One of the accounts of a state or public body to be applied for a particular purpose. EXAMPLES: a highway fund; a school fund. *See* funded debt; public funds. *Compare* general fund.
v. 1. To finance; to subsidize; to underwrite; to **capitalize**. *See* funded. 2. To convert an

obligation (for EXAMPLE, a **draft**) into a more permanent form with an extended time of payment (for EXAMPLE, a bond).
➤ *n.* endowment, reserve, stock, treasury, accumulation, reservoir, pool.
v. capitalize, endow, finance, subsidize, underwrite, contribute, donate.

fundamental [fun · da · *men* · tel] *adj.* At the foundation; basic; essential; underlying; primary.
➤ integral, requisite, substantive, elemental, basic, essential, underlying, primary.

fundamental error [*err* · er] *n.* An error of the court that goes to the foundation of a case or deprives a litigant of **due process**; judicial error of such severity that it will be reviewed on appeal even if it is not specifically cited as a ground for appeal. *See* error.

fundamental law *n.* The principles of law upon which a nation is founded; a nation's constitution. *See* fundamental rights.

fundamental rights *n.* The rights expressly guaranteed by a nation's constitution. *See* fundamental law.

funded [*fun* · ded] *adj.* Refers to money that has been set aside or for which financial provision has been made.

funded debt *n.* An obligation of national, state, or local government for which revenues have been provided in order to pay the interest and to make future payments upon the principal so that the debt will gradually be reduced.

funds *n.* Plural of **fund**. *See* fund.

fungible [*fun* · jibl] *adj.* Of such a nature as to be consumable by use and totally replaceable **in kind**.
n. Commonly stated in the *plural* (**fungibles**). 1. **Commodities** of a nature such that one is identical with another and each is a replacement for the other. EXAMPLES: wheat; oats; corn. 2. Goods or **securities** of which any unit is the equivalent of any other like unit. EXAMPLE: 100 shares of the same class of a corporation's stock.
➤ *adj.* replaceable, interchangeable ("Wheat is a fungible commodity").

fungible goods *n.* *See* fungible.

F

F

fungible stock *n.* *See* fungible.

fungibles [*fun* · jiblz] *n.* *Plural* of **fungible**. *See* fungible.

furnish [*fer* · nish] *v.* Within the meaning of the **controlled substance acts** and liquor laws, to supply, provide, give, sell, deliver, or distribute.
➤ give, accommodate, invest, prepare, bestow, transfer, distribute.

further [*fer* · thur] *adj.* Additional; more; supplemental; added; future.
adv. [*fer* · thur] Additionally; moreover; furthermore.
v. To advance; to encourage; to promote; to foster; to abet.
➤ *adj.* added, extra, more, farther.
adv. additionally, distant, again.
v. advance, encourage, promote, assist, facilitate, help, aid.

further advance [ad · *vanse*] *n.* An additional loan made to a mortgagor by a mortgagee, often secured by the original mortgage. *See* advance. *See also* future advance.

further assurance [a · *shoor* · ense] *n.* *See* covenant for further assurance.

further hearing [*hear* · ing] *n.* *See* further proceedings.

further instructions [in · *struk* · shenz] *n.* Same as **additional instructions**.

further proceedings [pro · *see* · dingz] *n.* Additional proceedings, usually in the same case. *See* proceeding.

furtherance [*fer* · thur · ense] *n.* The act of helping something advance, progress, or move forward.
➤ advancement, advocacy, progression, elevation, backing.

future [*few* · cher] *adj.* Pertaining to a time which is to come; prospective.
n. What will happen in a time to come; an advancement or development.
➤ *adj.* approaching, destined, imminent, yet to come, succeeding ("future damages").
n. eternity, outlook, prospect, afterward.

future advance [ad · *vanse*] *n.* A loan made to a mortgagor or other debtor by a mortgagee or other secured **party** after the initial loan for which the mortgage or security agreement was given. Future advances are usually secured under an express provision of the mortgage or security agreement. *See also* further advance.

future damages [*dam* · e · jez] *n.* A sum of money awarded a plaintiff as compensation for the consequences of a defendant's wrongful act that will occur in the future; **prospective damages**. EXAMPLE: damages for loss of future earnings. *See* damages.

future earnings [*ern* · ingz] *n.* Income to be earned later from an occupation, profession, or business.

future estate [es · *tate*] *n.* An **estate in land**, whether **vested** or **contingent**, that is to come into existence at a future time; a **future interest**. *Compare* present estate; present interest. *See* future interest.

future goods *n.* Goods that do not yet exist. Future goods may be the subject of a present contract to sell. *See* futures.

future interest [*in* · trest] *n.* 1. An **estate** or **interest** in land or personal property, including money, whether **vested** or **contingent**, that is to come into existence at a future time. EXAMPLES: a **remainder**; a **reversion**; payments or income to be received in the future. *Compare* future estate. *Also compare* present estate; present interest. 2. A name sometimes given to the area of the law governing property interests which are to come into existence in the future.

future-acquired property [-a · *kwired* prop · er · tee] *n.* *See* after-acquired property.

futures [*few* · cherz] *n.* **Commodities** that are the subject of a **futures contract**.

futures contract [*kon* · trakt] *n.* A **contract** for the sale of a **commodity** (EXAMPLES: grain; cotton) to be delivered at a future time. Although the price is fixed when the contract is entered into, the value of the contract fluctuates with changes in the market value of the commodity.

fuzzy *adj.* Lacking in definition or clarity.
➤ ambiguous, unclear, indefinite, unfocused, dim, blurred.
Ant. clear, lucid.

FY Abbreviation of **fiscal year**. USAGE: "FY 1994" (or "FY '94") means "fiscal year 1994."

gag order [*or* · der] *n.* 1. An order of court prohibiting the parties, attorneys, or witnesses in a case from discussing the case with the press. 2. An order of court prohibiting the press from reporting on the trial of a case. Such an order is generally unconstitutional under the **First Amendment**. 3. An order by a judge that a defendant who is disrupting a trial be gagged and bound.

gain *n.* 1. Earnings; profits; proceeds; return; yield; interest; increase; addition. 2. In tax law, excess of revenue over expense. *Compare* loss.
   v. To win a competition; to increase; to acquire possession.
➤ *n.* acquisition, profit, appreciation, enhancement.
   v. accomplish, attain, procure, consummate, get, profit, secure, achieve.

gain derived from capital [de · *rived* from *kap* · i · tel] *n.* A profit or yield produced by property, as distinguished from an increase in the value of the property itself. *See* capital. *Compare* capital gain.

gainful [*gain* · ful] *adj.* Profitable; rewarding; lucrative.
➤ beneficial, lucrative, profitable, advantageous, rewarding ("gainful employment").

gainful employment [em · *ploy* · ment] *n.* Paid employment.

gamble [*gam* · bul] *v.* To wager on an uncertain outcome.
➤ bet, jeopardize, risk, imperil, challenge.

gambling [*gam* · bling] *n.* The act of taking a monetary risk on the chance of receiving a monetary gain; staking money or property on luck. Gambling is illegal in some jurisdictions and regulated in others. *See* bet.

gambling contract [*kon* · trakt] *n.* A **contract** in which the parties agree that one of them will gain, and one will lose, money or property upon the happening of an event whose occurrence is uncertain and in which neither has an interest other than the possibility of gain or loss. (EXAMPLE: Sarah agrees to pay Joe $100 if the Los Angeles Dodgers win the pennant, and Joe promises to pay Sarah $100 if they don't.) A gambling contract is unenforceable unless it arises from a specific form of gambling in a jurisdiction where that form is legal. *See* lottery. *Also see* gambling policy. *Compare* insurance contract.

gambling device [de · *vise*] *n.* Any instrument, means, mechanism, contrivance, or thing used for gambling, although capable of being used for other purposes. EXAMPLES: playing cards; dice; a slot machine.

gambling policy [*pol* · e · see] *n.* Also called a **wager policy**, a life insurance policy in which the beneficiary has no pecuniary interest in the life of the insured, or any policy of insurance in which the insured has no **insurable interest** in the subject of the policy. In other words, an insurance policy which is a **gambling contract** rather than an **insurance contract**.

game *n.* 1. A recreation, sport, amusement, or pastime. 2. Wild animals, birds, and fish. *adj.* Having an inflexible, undaunting spirit.
➤ *n.* entertainment, festivity, amusement, recreation.
   adj. courageous, gallant, spirited, unafraid ("a game performer").

game laws *n.* *See* fish and game laws.

game of chance *n.* A game in which victory is largely or entirely determined by luck rather than skill. *See* chance.

gaming [*gay* · ming] *n.* Same as **gambling**. *See* gambling.

gaming contract [*kon* · trakt] *n.* Same as **gambling contract**.

gaming device [de · *vise*] *n.* Same as **gambling device**.

gang *n.* 1. A group of persons who associate with each other for criminal purposes. 2. A group of persons who associate with each other for social purposes.
➤ crew, crowd, posse, troop, ring, team, bunch, clan, club.

GAO Abbreviation of **General Accounting Office**.

garageman's lien [ga · *rahzh* · menz lee · en] *n.* The **lien** of a person in the business of operating a garage for storage of a motor vehicle.

garnish [*gar* · nish] *v.* 1. To warn; to notify. 2. To cause a **garnishment** to be levied on a **garnishee**; to garnishee a debtor. 3. To decorate or ornament, particularly food.
➤ attach, impound, seize, levy, sequester ("to garnish wages"); decorate, adorn, beautify, grace ("to garnish the rack of lamb").

garnishee [gar · nish · *ee*] *n.* The person upon whom a **garnishment** is served, usually a person indebted to the defendant or in possession of money or property of the defendant. *Compare* garnishor.
v. To commence a **garnishment** proceeding; to serve a notice of garnishment; to cause the garnishment of a debtor of the defendant.

garnishment [gar · nish · ment] *n.* A **proceeding** by a creditor to obtain satisfaction of a debt from money or property of the debtor which is in the possession of a third person or is owed by such a person to the debtor. EXAMPLE: because Ron owes back taxes, the IRS (the creditor, also called the **garnishor** or plaintiff) initiates a garnishment against Ron (the debtor, also called the defendant) by serving a notice of garnishment of Ron's wages upon his employer, the ABC Company (the **garnishee**). *Note* that a garnishment is distinguished from an **attachment** by the fact that the money or property reached by the garnishment

remains in the hands of the third party until there is a **judgment** in the action involving the basic debt.
➤ attachment, levy, appropriation, collection.

garnishor [gar · nish · *or*] *n.* The person who initiates a **garnishment**, generally a creditor of the defendant. *Compare* garnishee.

gas lease *n.* *See* oil and gas lease.

Gault decision [gawlt de · *sizh* · en] *n.* *Application of Gault*, 387 U.S. 1, a 1967 decision of the Supreme Court, ruled that, in juvenile court proceedings, a juvenile has many of the rights guaranteed to adults in the **Bill of Rights** and the **due process clause** of the **Fourteenth Amendment**, including the right to confront and cross-examine adverse witnesses, the right to assistance of counsel, and protection against self-incrimination.

gay rights *n.* A term whose origins are in the movement for legal equality for homosexuals (gay men and lesbian women). Many jurisdictions have enacted ordinances prohibiting discrimination based upon sexual orientation in housing, employment, or public accommodation. USAGE: "He was an advocate for gay rights."

gender discrimination [*jen* · der dis · krim · i · *nay* · shen] *n.* *See* sex discrimination.

general [*jen* · e · rel] *adj.* Common to many, or to the greatest number; widely spread; prevalent; extensive though not universal; having a relation to all; common to the whole. EXAMPLES: attorney general; **general assembly**; **general creditor**.
➤ common, ordinary, generic, prevalent, routine, extensive, average, popular.

general act *n.* Same as **general law**.

general administrator [ad · *min* · is · tray · ter] *n.* An **administrator** who administers the whole of the **estate** of a **decedent**, without limitation. *Compare* special administrator. *See* administration of estate. *Also compare* ancillary administration.

general agent [*ay* · jent] *n.* An agent authorized to perform all acts connected with the business of his principal. *Compare* special agent. *See* agent. *Also see* managing agent.

G

general appearance [a · *peer* · ense] *n.*
An **appearance** whereby the party appearing submits herself to the **jurisdiction** of the court, thereby waiving all jurisdictional defects. *Compare* special appearance.

general assembly [a · *sem* · blee] *n.* The official title of the legislature in 19 states.

general assignment [a · *sine* · ment] *n.* An **assignment** by a debtor of all his property to pay all of his creditors, share and share alike. *See* assignment for the benefit of creditors.

general assignment for the benefit of creditors [a · *sine* · ment for the *ben* · e · fit of *kred* · it · erz] *n. See* assignment for the benefit of creditors.

general assistance [a · *sis* · tense] *n. See* general relief.

general average contribution [*av* · rej kon · tri · *byoo* · shen] *n.* A contribution by all of the parties in a maritime venture to make good the loss suffered by one of them in saving the cargo or ships of the others or in sustaining any other extraordinary expense for the general benefit of all. *Compare* particular average. *See* Jason clause.

general average loss [*av* · rej] *n. See* general average contribution.

general bequest [be · *kwest*] *n. See* general legacy.

general charge *n.* Same as **general instruction**.

general circulation [ser · kyoo · *lay* · shen] *n. See* newspaper of general circulation.

general contractor [*kon* · trak · ter] *n.* A contractor, also called a prime contractor, who contracts to manage a construction project as a whole. The prime contractor employs and oversees any subcontractors.

general court *n.* The official title of the legislature in Massachusetts and New Hampshire.

general court-martial [-mar · shel] *n. See* court-martial.

general creditor [*kred* · it · or] *n.* A creditor whose claim is unsecured by a mortgage, **judgment lien**, or other **lien**, and is not entitled to priority. *Compare* secured creditor.

general custom [*kus* · tem] *n. See* custom.

general damages [*dam* · e · jez] *n.* **Damages** that are the natural and probable result of the wrongful acts complained of. *Compare* special damages.

general demurrer [de · *mer* · er] *n.* A **demurrer** attacking a **pleading** on the ground that the allegations are insufficient to state a **cause of action** or **defense**; i.e., a demurrer directed to matters of **substance** rather than of form or **procedure**. *Compare* special demurrer.

general denial [de · *ny* · el] *n.* A **pleading** that denies every allegation of the opposing party's previous pleading (for EXAMPLE, the **complaint**) without denying them specifically or separately. *Compare* specific denial. *See* denial.

general deposit [de · *pah* · zit] *n.* A deposit in which the thing to be returned to the depositor is not the identical item, but its equivalent. EXAMPLE: money deposited in a savings account in a bank. *Compare* special deposit. *See* deposit.

general devise [de · *vize*] *n.* A **devise** that does not refer to specific real estate. EXAMPLE: "I give and devise all of my real property to State University." *Compare* specific devise.

general disability clause [dis · e · *bil* · i · tee] *n.* A clause in a disability insurance policy which provides that total disability under the policy is not limited to the insured's inability to perform the duties of his regular occupation or profession, but includes the inability to perform gainful employment generally.

general election [e · *lek* · shen] *n.* An election held for the purpose of selecting officers to succeed to office upon the expiration of the terms of the officers currently occupying those offices. *Compare* special election. *See* election.

general exception [ek · *sep* · shen] *n.* An **exception** directed to matters of substance rather than of form. *Compare* special exception. *See* general demurrer.

general execution [ek · se · *kyoo* · shen] *n.* A **writ** of execution that directs the sheriff to levy upon any property of the defendant, as distinguished from a **special execution**, which specifies the property to be sold. *See* execution.

G

general executor [eg · *zek* · yoo · tor] *n.* An **executor** who administers the whole of the **estate** of a **decedent**, without limitation. *Compare* special executor.

general finding [*fine* · ding] *n.* A finding by a court on the basis of which it determines the existence or nonexistence of liability. EXAMPLE: "This court determines all the issues of fact in this case in favor of the plaintiff." *Compare* special finding. *See* finding.

general fund *n.* The basic fiscal account from which a governmental unit operates; a fund not set aside for a particular purpose. *See* fund.

general guaranty [*gair* · en · tee] *n.* A guaranty available to anyone who accepts the offer. *Compare* special guaranty. *See* guaranty.

general guardian [*gar* · dee · en] *n.* A guardian of both the **person** and the **estate** of a **ward**. *Compare* guardian ad litem. *See* guardian.

general indorsement [in · *dorse* · ment] *n.* Same as **blank indorsement**. *Compare* special indorsement.

general instruction [in · *struk* · shen] *n.* An instruction by the court to the jury relative to the case as a whole. EXAMPLE (in a jury charge): "If you find that the plaintiff has proven the things I have referred to by a preponderance of the believable evidence, your verdict will be for the plaintiff; if you find that the plaintiff has not proven all of the things I have specified, then your verdict will be for the defendant." *See* jury instructions; preponderance of the evidence. *Compare* special instruction.

general intangibles [in · *tan* · jiblz] *n.* Under the **Uniform Commercial Code**, "any personal property … other than goods, accounts, **chattel paper**, documents, **instruments**, and money." *See* intangible; intangible property.

general jurisdiction [joo · ris · *dik* · shen] *n. See* court of general jurisdiction.

general law *n.* A statute that applies to all persons, or to all persons in the circumstances described in the statute. *Compare* special legislation.

general ledger [*lej* · er] *n. See* ledger.

general legacy [*leg* · e · see] *n.* A **legacy** of personal property or money that may be satisfied out of the general **estate** of the **testator**, as opposed to a legacy of a particular item of personal property or of money from a specific fund. *Compare* specific legacy.

general legislation [lej · is · *lay* · shen] *n. See* general law.

general lien [leen] *n.* The right of a creditor to repossess an article, not merely as **security** for a sum due on the purchase of that article, but for any amount owed by the debtor to the creditor in the regular course of business. *Compare* special lien. *See* lien.

general malice [*mal* · iss] *n.* **Malice** toward a group of persons or toward people or society in general; a disposition to kill or maim regardless of the consequences.

general orders [*or* derz] *n.* Same as **rules of court**.

general partner [*part* · ner] *n.* A **partner** in an ordinary partnership, as distinguished from a **limited partnership**. "General partner" is synonymous with "partner." *Compare* special partner. *See* general partnership.

general partnership [*part* · ner · ship] *n.* An ordinary **partnership**, as distinguished from a **limited partnership**. "General partnership" is synonymous with "partnership." *See* general partner.

general plea *n. See* general denial.

general power of appointment [*pow* · er of a · *point* · ment] *n.* A **power of appointment** that may be exercised in favor of anyone whom the **donee** of the power chooses. *See* donee of a power. *Compare* limited power of appointment.

general power of attorney [*pow* · er of a · *ter* · nee] *n. See* power of attorney.

general relief [re · *leef*] *n.* A form of **public assistance** available only to the very poor, usually on an emergency basis and for a short period of time, to provide food, clothing, and temporary housing. It is often referred to simply as **GR**. *See* welfare.

general reputation [rep · yoo · *tay* · shen] *n. See* reputation.

general retainer [re · *tain* er] *n.* The act of employing the services of an attorney

G

for a specified period of time, often a year, for such services as the client may request. *Compare* special retainer. *See* retainer.

general session [*sesh* · en] *n.* 1. A regular session of the legislature. *Compare* special session. *See* session. 2. A regular term of court.

general statute [*stat* · shoot] *n.* *See* general law.

general tenancy [*ten* · en · see] *n.* *See* tenancy at will.

general term *n.* A regular term of court. *Compare* special term. *See* term of court.

general verdict [*ver* · dikt] *n.* The final determination by the jury as to the truth of the matter before them and as to liability. *Compare* special verdict.

general warranty [*war* · en · tee] *n.* A **warranty** contained in a deed, by which the grantor promises to protect the grantee and her heirs against all claims from whatever source. *Compare* special warranty.

General Accounting Office [*jen* · e · rel a · *koun* · ting *off* · iss] *n.* An independent federal agency that oversees the accounting and auditing of much of the federal government's fiscal operations. It is commonly referred to as the **GAO**.

General Services Administration [*jen* · e · rel *ser* · viss · ez ad · min · is · *tray* · shen] *n.* The federal government's purchasing and supply agency. The **GSA** contracts for the construction of federal buildings and other facilities and manages government property.

generation [jen · e · *ray* · shen] *n.* 1. Creation; production. 2. A stage in the sequence of natural **descent**. USAGE: "My grandfather, my father, and I represent three generations."
➤ production, evolution, causation, origination; era, age, epoch, span.

generation-skipping transfer tax [-skip · ing *trans* · fer] *n.* A federal tax on **testamentary** or *inter vivos* transfers of property between persons separated by two or more generations. This tax allows the government to collect **transfer taxes** (*see* estate tax; gift tax) that would otherwise be unassessed because the transfer of the property skipped a generation.

generic [jen · *err* · ik] *adj.* 1. Pertaining to a kind, class, or group. 2. General; inclusive.
➤ common, all-inclusive, universal, collective, broad, nonspecific, nonexclusive.

generic drug *n.* The common or chemical name of a prescription drug approved by the **Food and Drug Administration**, as opposed to its brand name.

generic drug laws *n.* State statutes that permit pharmacists to substitute a **generic drug** when a brand-name drug has been prescribed.

genetic marker testing [jen · *et* · ik *mar* · ker] *n.* *See* DNA fingerprinting; HLA testing.

gentleman's agreement [*jentl* · menz a · *gree* · ment] *n.* An agreement based solely upon trust; it is unenforceable in law as a contract. *Note* that a gentleman's agreement is not the same as an informal agreement; an informal agreement or informal contract *is* a contract.

gentrification [jen · tri · fi · *kay* · shen] *n.* The process of redeveloping an aging urban area into a more well-to-do district.
➤ redevelopment, restoration, repair, upgrading.

genuine [*jen* · yoo · in] *n.* Real or original, as opposed to false, fictitious, or counterfeit.
➤ authentic, accurate, legitimate, unquestionable, original, veritable, authenticated ("a genuine document").

genuine instrument [*in* · stroo · ment] *n.* An instrument (EXAMPLES: a check; a note; a bond) that is what it purports to be; an instrument that is free of forgery or counterfeiting.

germane [jer · *main*] *adj.* Relevant; applicable; pertinent; appropriate; apropos.
➤ appropriate, connected, suitable, relative, pertinent, relevant, apropos.

gerrymandering [*jerr* · ee · man · der · ing] *n.* Manipulating the boundary lines of a political district (EXAMPLE: a **congressional district**) to give an unfair advantage to one political party or to dilute the political strength of voters of a particular race, color, or national origin. *See* apportionment of representatives.

gestation [jes · *tay* · shen] *n.* The process of fetal development in the womb during the period from conception to birth.
➤ evolution, growth, incubation, ripening.

G

G

Gibbons v. Ogden [*gib* · enz *ver* · sus *og* · den] *n.* A Supreme Court decision of 1824 (22 U.S. 1) which first established the concept that Congress's power under the **commerce clause** of the Constitution is restricted to **interstate commerce**, and does not apply to **intrastate commerce**.

Gideon v. Wainright [*gid* · ee · en *ver* · sus *wain* · rite] *n.* A 1963 Supreme Court decision (372 U.S. 335) which held that the right to counsel, as guaranteed by the **Sixth Amendment**, applies to state court criminal trials as well as to the federal courts, and that criminal defendants in state courts who cannot afford to hire an attorney must have one provided to them.

gift *n.* A voluntary transfer of property by one person to another without any **consideration** or compensation. For there to be a gift, the **donor** must intend to make a gift, and it must be delivered to and accepted by the **donee**. *See* delivery of gift; donative intent.

➤ endowment, benefaction, allowance, donation ("a gift to the hospital"); talent, attribute, flair, capacity ("the gift of gab").

gift causa mortis [*kow* · sa *mor* · tis] *n.* A gift of personal property made by the donor in expectation of his death, i.e., in **contemplation of death**. To complete a gift causa mortis, there must be delivery of the gift, the donor must die as anticipated, the donee must survive him, and the gift must not have been revoked in the meantime. *Compare* testamentary gift. *See causa mortis.*

gift in contemplation of death [kon · tem · *play* · shen] *n.* *See* gift causa mortis.

gift in trust *n.* A gift in which the donee receives only **equitable title** to the subject matter of the gift. *See* declaration of trust.

gift inter vivos [*in* · ter *vy* · vose] *n.* *See* inter vivos gift.

gift over [*oh* · ver] *n.* A gift "over" to another donee after the term of the previous donee's gift has ended. EXAMPLE: "I devise and bequeath my farm to Mary for life, and after her death to Joe **in fee**." The devise to Joe is a gift over.

gift tax *n.* A tax on the transfer by gift, by a living person, of money or other property. The federal government and most states impose gift taxes. By comparison, there are distinctly different tax consequences if the transfer of the gift occurs upon the death of the donor (*see* estate tax; inheritance tax). Additionally, special tax considerations apply to gifts made by living persons in **contemplation of death** (*see* gift causa mortis). A gift tax is a **transfer tax**.

gift to a class *n.* *See* class gift.

Gifts to Minors Act [*mine* · erz] *n.* *See* Transfers to Minors Act.

gilt-edged securities [*gilt*-edjd se · *kyoo* · ri · teez] *n.* Stocks, bonds, and other securities that are the safest for investment. *Compare* blue chip stock.

Ginnie Mae [*jin* · ee may] *See* Government National Mortgage Association.

gist *n.* The essence of something; the essential point.

➤ essence, basis, substance, main point, reason, gravamen, keystone ("the gist of an argument").

gist of an action [*ak* · shen] *n.* The ground or foundation of a lawsuit; the **gravamen** of a **complaint**.

give *v.* 1. To make a gift. *See* gift. 2. To convey; to transfer; to grant. USAGE (in a deed): "give, grant, sell, and convey." USAGE (in a will): "give and bequeath."

➤ contribute, bequeath, convey, donate, provide, grant, bestow, confer, commit, transmit.

GNMA Abbreviation of **Government National Mortgage Association**.

GNP Abbreviation of **gross national product**.

go *v.* 1. To move along symbolically, as in the passing of **title** from one person to another. USAGE: "I want everything to go to my wife." 2. To move along physically. USAGE: "I want to make sure both of these exhibits go into evidence."

➤ advance, proceed, depart, progress, move, pass.

goal *n.* An objective or purpose.

➤ target, aim, ambition, purpose, object, objective, mission, intention ("to achieve a goal").

going [*goh* · ing] *adj.* 1. Forward or onward. 2. Ongoing; functioning.

➤ forward, onward, ongoing, existing, functioning ("a going concern").

going and coming rule [*kum* · ing] *n.* Under most **workers' compensation acts**, the rule that an employee cannot recover benefits for injuries she sustains while going to or returning from work.

going business [*biz* · ness] *n. See* going concern.

going concern [ken · *sern*] *n.* A business in operation. A firm is a going concern, even though it is not fully solvent, as long as it continues to undertake its line of business in **good faith** with the hope of succeeding.

going forward with the evidence [*for* · ward with the ev · i · dense] *n. See* burden of going forward.

going private [*pry* · vet] *n.* The method by which a **publicly held** corporation becomes a **privately held** corporation.

going public [*pub* · lik] *n.* The method by which a corporation becomes a **publicly held** corporation, that is, offers its stock for sale to the public at large.

going value [*val* · yoo] *n.* Same as **going-concern value**.

going-concern value [-ken · *sern* val · yoo] *n.* 1. The value of a business as a functioning unit, as opposed to the value of its assets considered piecemeal. 2. The value of a business as a **going concern**, as distinguished from a business that is not yet established.

golden parachute [*gole* · den pehr · e · shoot] *n.* A phrase used to describe contracts between corporations and their directors and executives, which provide such officials with certain financial advantanges if they leave the corporation because of a takeover. An EXAMPLE of a golden parachute provision might be severance pay equal to a year's salary.

golden rule contention [ken · *ten* · shen] *n.* An argument made by attorneys to jurors that, in assessing liability (in a civil case) or guilt (in a criminal case), they should put themselves in the place of the injured party or victim and render a verdict such as they would wish to receive were they in such a position.

good *adj.* 1. Valid; clear; absolute; marketable. **Good title,** for EXAMPLE, means **clear title** or **marketable title**. *See* free and clear. 2. Genuine, as opposed to forged or counterfeit. USAGE: "This dollar bill is good." 3. As applied to a **negotiable instrument**, certain of payment. USAGE: "How do you know this note is good?" 4. As applied to articles offered for sale, of **merchantable quality**. USAGE: "Even though it's used, this car is good." 5. Beneficial. 6. Effective.

➤ admirable, commendable, exceptional, reputable, stupendous; honorable, innocent, irreproachable, respectable; legitimate, reliable, worthy, valid.

good and valid [*val* · id] *adj.* Description of **title** that is clear and marketable. *See* marketable title. *See also* free and clear; good title.

good and valuable consideration [*val* · yoo · ebl ken · sid · e · *ray* · shen] *n. See* good consideration; valuable consideration.

good behavior [bee · *hay* · vyer] *n.* 1. Law-abiding conduct. 2. The conduct required of a prisoner to justify reducing the time to be served.

good cause *n.* A substantial reason, in law, for taking action or a legal excuse for nonperformance or inaction. EXAMPLE: A court has "good cause" for granting a **continuance** if to do otherwise would deprive a litigant of a fair trial. *See* cause; for cause; legal cause; just cause.

good character [*kehr* · ek · ter] *n. See* character; reputation. *See also* good moral character.

good consideration [ken · sid · e · *ray* · shen] *n.* Merely **moral consideration**, and therefore not **consideration** adequate to support a contract except in circumstances in which it is reinforced by **love and affection**. *See* adequate consideration; legal consideration.

good faith *n.* Fairness and equity; the absence of improper motive or of a negligent disregard of the rights of others; the honest and reasonable belief that one's conduct is proper; the opposite of fraud and deceit. USAGE: "He acted in good faith."

G

good faith bargaining [*bar* · ge · ning] *n.* 1. The sincere intention on the part of each **party** to a labor dispute to explore all possibilities for settling the matter. 2. An open-minded and honest desire to enter into a **collective bargaining agreement**.

good faith purchaser [*per* · ches · er] *n.* *See bona fide* purchaser; buyer in the ordinary course of business.

good moral character [*more* · el kehr · ek · ter] *n.* Character as demonstrated by conduct that conforms to generally accepted community moral standards.

good order [*or* · der] *n.* When applied to goods, means they are in satisfactory condition.

good repair [re · *pair*] *n.* Reasonable or proper repair.

good repute [re · *pyoot*] *n.* Good reputation. *Also see* character.

good Samaritan doctrine [se · *mehr* · i · ten dok · trin] *n.* The doctrine that a person who intervenes to aid someone in impending danger has a duty to exercise care so as not to leave the object of the rescue in worse condition than if he had not intervened. If failure to exercise **due care** results in injury, the rescuer will be held liable. In some jurisdictions, the good Samaritan doctrine is referred to as the **rescue doctrine**. *Note* that the law does not require one to be a good Samaritan—only to exercise due care if she chooses to be a good Samaritan.

good time *n.* A length of time by which a convict's prison term is shortened because of his good behavior while in prison. USAGE: "Good time may not exceed one-half of the prisoner's total sentence."

good title [*ty* · tel] *n.* Valid and **marketable title**. *Compare* bad title.

goods *n.* A term of variable meaning, sometimes signifying all personal property or **movables**, sometimes limited to merchandise held for sale or in storage, sometimes meaning **tangible property** only, and sometimes including **intangible property** such as **securities**. Securities, money, and **things in action**, however, are not "goods" within the definition of the **Uniform Commercial Code**; **commodities**, including **futures** and **fungibles**, are. *See* contract

for sale of goods. Also see confusion of goods; future goods.

➤ belongings, chattels, encumbrances, property; merchandise, vendibles, wares, materials.

goods and chattels [*chat* · elz] *n.* Personal property; sometimes means personal property other than **intangible property**.

goodwill [good · will] *n.* The benefit a business acquires, beyond the mere value of its **capital stock** and **tangible assets**, as a result of having a good reputation and the respect of the public. Goodwill is **intangible property**. However, goodwill is a function only of a **going concern**, and therefore can be assigned a value for accounting purposes only in connection with the sale of a business that is a going concern. *See* going-concern value.

➤ kindliness, benevolence, rapport, favor, amity, friendship.

govern [*guv* · ern] *v.* 1. To direct; to control; to rule. 2. To regulate; to manage. 3. To be **authority** for something; to be a **precedent**. USAGE: "Judicial opinions are governed by precedent."

➤ control, administer, conduct, dictate, regulate, manage, oversee ("govern a state"); influence, incline, guide, regulate ("Judicial opinions are governed by precedent").

governance [*guv* · er · nenss] *n.* 1. Exercising governmental power. 2. Any exercise of power or control over the conduct of others.

governing body [*guv* · er · ning *bod* · ee] *n.* A group of persons who, usually by virtue of the offices they hold, establish the policies under which an organization or governmental unit operates. EXAMPLES: the board of directors of a corporation; a county's board of supervisors.

government [*guv* · ern · ment] *n.* 1. A system of administration by which a nation or state, or any political subdivision of a state (EXAMPLES: a county; a city; a town; a township), is governed. *See* local government. 2. Any system by which any group of people is governed. *See* govern.

➤ management, supervision, guidance, leadership, administration, bureaucracy.

G

government bond *n.* A **bond** issued by government.

government contract [*kon* · trakt] *n. See* public contract.

government corporation [kore · per · *ay* · shen] *n.* A corporation created by statute through which governmental functions are exercised; a governmental agency. EXAMPLE: The **Government National Mortgage Association**. *Compare* public corporation.

Government National Mortgage Association [*guv* · ern · ment *nash* · e · nel *more* · gej a · soh · see · *ay* · shen] *n.* A **government corporation** created by federal statute that guarantees **securities** backed by bank mortgages insured by the **FHA** or guaranteed by the **VA**. This process increases the overall supply of credit available for the purchase of housing by the public. The agency is commonly referred to as **Ginnie Mae**, from its initials, **GNMA**. *Compare* Federal National Mortgage Association.

government survey [*ser* · vay] *n.* The survey of lands in the **public domain**, conducted by the federal government, under which land is laid out in **townships**, **sections**, and **quarter sections**. *See* survey.

governmental [guv · ern · *men* · tel] *adj.* Pertaining to government or to a government; of the government; by the government.

➤ administrative, bureaucratic, regulatory, municipal, public.

governmental act *n.* An act done in the course of carrying out the administration of government; any exercise of the **police power**.

governmental agency [*ay* · jen · see] *n. See* administrative agency.

governmental body [*bod* · ee] *n.* 1. A unit of a **branch of government** or of a **department of government**. EXAMPLES: a court; a legislature; an administrative agency. 2. A **political subdivision**. *See* governmental entity; governmental unit.

governmental duties [*dew* · teez] *n.* 1. The duties imposed upon a city, town, or village by the state, to be exercised for the benefit of the public. EXAMPLES: police and fire protection; public health and safety. 2. The responsibilities imposed upon a government by its constitution.

governmental entity [*en* · ti · tee] *n.* 1. A government. 2. A **political subdivision**. 3. A governmental agency. *See* entity. *Also see* governmental unit.

governmental functions [*funk* · shenz] *n.* The activities engaged in by a government in carrying out its governmental duties.

governmental immunity [im · *yoo* · ni · tee] *n. See* sovereign immunity.

governmental instrumentality [in · stroo · men · *tal* · i · tee] *n.* A means or agency used by government to carry out a governmental purpose. *See* instrumentality. *Also see* administrative agency; agency; federal instrumentality.

governmental powers [*pow* · erz] *n.* The power exercised by the government, as a **sovereign**, which enables it to fulfill its governmental functions.

governmental purpose [*per* · pes] *n.* As described in the preamble to the Constitution, any activity of government designed to: "establish justice, insure domestic tranquility, provide for the common defense, promote the general welfare, and secure the blessings of liberty." *See also* public purpose.

governmental subdivision [sub · di · *vizh* · en] *n. See* governmental unit.

governmental unit [*yoo* · nit] *n.* 1. A **political subdivision**. 2. A governmental agency. *Also see* governmental entity.

governor [*guv* · er · ner] *n.* The chief executive of a state.

➤ chief executive, head, leader, director, administrator, manager, official.

GPM Abbreviation of **graduated payment mortgage**.

GR Abbreviation of **general relief.**

grace *n.* An indulgence; a favor; mercy; clemency. *See* of grace.

➤ indulgence, favor, mercy, clemency, forgiveness, leniency, pardon.

grace period [*peer* · ee · ed] *n.* An additional amount of time in which to satisfy an obligation or pay a debt. In commercial law, the promisor is generally permitted to make payment within three days after the date specified in a **negotiable instrument**

as the due date; this rule of grace does not, however, apply to checks. In most states, life and health insurance premiums may be paid 30 days after the date on which they are due. Many types of contracts (EXAMPLES: installment contracts; **security agreements**) typically provide for grace periods. *Compare* moratorium.

grade *n.* 1. An incline, as in a highway. 2. The rank or degree of a thing in order of its importance or seriousness.
v. 1. To evaluate or rank. 2. To make flush with the rest of the surface.
➤ *n.* incline, rank, degree, step, stage.
v. evaluate, mark, rank, brand, class, value, rate ("grade his presentation"); flatten, level, even ("grade the road").

grade crossing [*kross* · ing] *n.* The intersection of a road and a railroad at a grade.

graded offenses [*gray* · ded o · *fen* · sez] *n.* Crimes that the law separates into degrees or classes, usually based upon severity. EXAMPLE: **first degree murder** as distinguished from **second degree murder**. *See also* classification of offenses; degrees of crime.

graduated [*grad* · joo · ay · ted] *adj.* Measured; progressive; increasing; incremental.
➤ measured, progressive, increasing, continuous, regular, perceptible ("a graduated tax").

graduated lease *n.* A lease that provides for periodic increases in rent over its term.

graduated payment mortgage [*pay* · ment *more* · gej] *n.* A **mortgage** in which the amount of the monthly payments increases over the life of the mortgage in accordance with a preestablished schedule. It is often referred to by its abbreviation, **GPM**. *Compare* adjustable rate mortgage; fixed rate mortgage.

graduated tax *n.* A tax that increases as the amount or value of the thing taxed increases. EXAMPLE: the federal income tax. *See also* progressive tax.

graft *n.* An illegal or otherwise unfair payoff; bribery.
➤ corruption, kickback, bribery, blackmail, profiteering, illegal profit.

grand *adj.* 1. Impressive in size or importance. 2. Marked with a great display.
➤ elevated, great, outstanding; formal, pompous, ceremonial.

grand jury [*joo* · ree] *n.* A body whose number varies with the jurisdiction, never less than 6 nor more than 23, whose duty it is to determine whether **probable cause** exists to return **indictments** against persons accused of committing crimes. The right to indictment by grand jury is guaranteed by the **Fifth Amendment**. *See* special grand jury.

grand larceny [*lar* · sen · ee] *n.* **Larceny** of property above a specified value. The minimum differs from state to state. *Compare* petty larceny.

grand theft *n.* Another term for **grand larceny**.

grandfather clause [*grand* · fah · thur] *n.* In a statute regulating a business, occupation, or other activity, a provision exempting persons already engaged in such activity from the requirements of the statute. If a grandfather clause applies, the protected parties are said to be "grandfathered."

grant *n.* 1. A word used in conveying real property; a term of **conveyance**. *See* granting clause. 2. The conveyance or transfer itself. 3. Also called a **grant-in-aid**, funds awarded by the government or by a foundation for a specific purpose such as, for EXAMPLE, scientific research. 4. That which is conveyed, conferred, or given. EXAMPLES: land; money; a patent; a corporate charter.
v. 1. To **convey**; to **bequeath**; to **devise**. USAGE (in a deed): "grant, bargain and sell." 2. To bestow; to confer; to give; to give away. 3. To concede; to acknowledge; to admit.
➤ *n.* allocation, gift, contribution, privilege, endowment, donation.
v. authorize, allow, relinquish; award, donate, assign, allot; consent, yield, agree, acknowledge.

grant-in-aid *n.* *See* grant.

grantee [gran · *tee*] *n.* The person to whom a **grant** is made; the party in a deed to whom the **conveyance** is made. *Compare* grantor.

G

grantee-grantor indexes [-gran · *tor* in · dek · sez] *n. See* grantor-grantee indexes.

granting clause [*gran* · ting] *n.* Words in a deed or will that indicate the grantor's intention to make a **conveyance** of land.

grantor [gran · *tor*] *n.* The person who makes a **grant**; the party in a deed who makes the **conveyance**. *Compare* grantee.

grantor-grantee indexes [-gran · *tee* in · dek · sez] *n.* Volumes maintained in most county courthouses that list every deed, mortgage, **secured transaction**, and **lien** of every type ever recorded in the county. All transactions are alphabetically indexed, both by grantor (the grantor-grantee index) and by grantee (the grantee-grantor index). *Compare* tract index.

gratis [*gra* · tiss] *adj.* Without compensation; free of charge.
➤ free, without charge, pro bono, complimentary, unrecompensed, expenseless ("I will perform these services gratis.").

gratuitous [gre · *too* · it · ess] *adj.*
1. Something that is given, done, or promised, with nothing given, done, or promised in return, that is, without **consideration**. EXAMPLE: a **gratuitous bailment**. 2. Done for free, without charge, or voluntarily. USAGE: "***Pro bono*** legal representation is gratuitous." 3. Done without cause; unsolicited; unsought. USAGE: "He gives a lot of gratuitous advice."
➤ indefensible, unessential, unjustified, unprovoked; complimentary, charitable, voluntary, free, donated; unsolicited, unsought.

gratuitous bailee [bay · *lee*] *n. See* gratuitous bailment.

gratuitous bailment [*bail* · ment] *n.* A **bailment** for the sole benefit of the **bailee**; that is, one in which no compensation is involved. EXAMPLE: borrowing a book from a friend.

gratuity [gre · *too* · i · tee] *n.* 1. A tip. 2. A present; a gift; a reward; an **honorarium**.
➤ gift, contribution, bonus, dividend, tip, honorarium; graft, kickback, hush money.

gravamen [*grah* · va · men] *n.* 1. The basis of a **complaint**; the **gist of an action**. USAGE: "Bill's alleged use of excessive force is the gravamen of Sam's lawsuit against him." 2. Essence; substance; gist; material part; basis.
➤ substance, core, foundation, nucleus, focal point, thrust, essence, gist, cornerstone.

gravity [*grav* · i · tee] *n.* 1. Seriousness; severity; importance. 2. Weight; heaviness. 3. The force that pulls all bodies (all mass) toward the earth.
➤ acuteness, severity, urgency, momentousness, consequence; pressure, weight, heaviness, force.

great *adj.* 1. Marked by a relative largeness or large number. 2. Characterized by importance or magnificence.
➤ extraordinary, large, prodigious, extreme, outrageous ("great bodily harm"); outstanding, influential, significant, noteworthy, superior ("a great oration").

great bodily harm [*bod* · i · lee] *n. See* great bodily injury.

great bodily injury [*bod* · i · lee in · je · ree] *n.* A phrase that appears in **tort** law but has no single definition. It can, on the one hand, mean merely a significant, as opposed to a trivial, injury; on the other, it can connote very specific serious injuries, including, for EXAMPLE, loss of limbs or loss of their use, bodily disfigurement, or injuries that result in long-term disability. *See* personal injury. *Also see* bodily injury; serious bodily injury.

great care *n.* The degree of care a **prudent person** usually exercises concerning her own affairs of great importance.

green card *n.* A document that evidences an alien's status as a **resident alien**.

Green River ordinance [*riv* · er or · di · nenss] *n.* A type of **ordinance** that forbids salespersons and peddlers from soliciting people at their homes and business establishments.

grievance [*gree* · venss] *n.* 1. A formal complaint filed by an employee or by an employee's union claiming that the employer has violated the **collective bargaining agreement**. 2. A similar complaint filed against a union by an employer. 3. Any complaint about a wrong or an injustice.
➤ affliction, hardship, injustice, injury, complaint, protest, allegation, accusation, objection.

grievous [*gree* · vus] *adj.* Oppressive; burdensome; causing suffering. USAGE: "grievous bodily injury" (see great bodily injury).
➤ severe, painful, disturbing, offensive, unbearable.

gross *adj.* 1. Without deduction; as a whole; entire; total. EXAMPLES: gross earnings; gross income; gross pay. *Compare* net. 2. Blatant; extreme; flagrant. 3. Coarse; crude; unrefined. 4. Large; obese. *n.* Twelve dozen (144). *See* in gross.
➤ *adj.* obvious, apparent, flagrant, exorbitant, unmitigated; large, obese, portly, corpulent; callous, lewd, obscene, coarse; whole, entire, all, aggregate, total, sum.

gross alimony [*al* · i · mone · ee] *n. See* lump-sum alimony.

gross earnings [*ern* · ingz] *n.* Total income, before expenses. *See* gross income. *Compare* net earnings.

gross estate [es · *tate*] *n.* 1. The value of all property left by a **decedent**, before payment of taxes and expenses. 2. The value of all taxable property in a **decedent's estate**. *Compare* net estate.

gross expenses [eks · *pen* · sez] *n.* Total expenses.

gross income [*in* · kum] *n.* 1. Total income. 2. The whole or entire profit from a business. 3. Under the Internal Revenue Code, "all income from whatever source derived," before allowance for deductions or exemptions. *Compare* net income. *See* adjusted gross income.

gross income tax [*in* · kum] *n. See* gross receipts tax.

gross lease *n.* A **lease** that binds the landlord to pay all expenses (EXAMPLES: taxes; utilities). *Compare* net lease.

gross misdemeanor [mis · de · *mean* · er] *n.* A **misdemeanor** of a more serious nature than the ordinary misdemeanor; generally a misdemeanor for which the punishment prescribed by law is imprisonment *and* a fine, as opposed to imprisonment *or* a fine, or both. Sometimes referred to as a "high and aggravated misdemeanor."

gross national product [*nash* · en · el *prod* · ukt] *n.* Commonly called the **GNP**, the market value of all the goods and services a nation produces in a given period.

gross neglect of duty [neg · *lekt* of *dew* · tee] *n.* As a ground for removal of a public official from office, a breach of duty so serious as to endanger the public welfare. *See* neglect of duty; removal for cause.

gross negligence [*neg* · li · jenss] *n.* Willfully and intentionally acting, or failing to act, with a deliberate indifference to how others may be affected. *Compare* ordinary negligence. *See* negligence. *Compare* constructive fraud.

gross pay *n.* Total salary, wages, or commissions, before payroll deductions for taxes, social security, and the like. *Compare* net pay. *See* gross earnings; gross income.

gross proceeds [pro · seedz] *n. See* gross receipts.

gross profit [*prof* · it] *n.* The difference between what something sells for and what it cost, before expenses. *Compare* net profit.

gross receipts [re · *seets*] *n.* The total income of a business before deductions of any kind.

gross receipts tax [re · *seets*] *n.* A tax on the **gross receipts** of a business.

gross revenue [*rev* · e · new] *n.* Same as **gross income**. *Compare* net revenue.

gross sales *n.* The entire amount of all the sales of a business. As used in statutes imposing a tax on "gross sales," the term means the gross prices paid by a business for goods, not the prices at which it resells the goods to consumers.

gross weight *n.* The weight of a shipment of goods, including the weight of containers, boxes, crates, and the like; the weight of any packaged article, including the weight of its packaging. *Compare* net weight.

ground *n.* 1. Often expressed in the *plural* (**grounds**), the basis for a **cause of action**; a reason. USAGE: "My attorney says I have insufficient grounds for a lawsuit against the dealer who sold me the car." 2. The earth or soil.
➤ basis, premise, pretext, rationale, foundation ("ground for a lawsuit"); earth, soil, land ("on hallowed ground").

ground of action [*ak* · shen] *n.* The basis of or cause for an **action**. *See* cause of action.

G

ground rent *n.* Rent paid under a **ground rent lease**.

ground rent lease *n.* A long-term **lease** of land, commonly for 99 years, typically entered into by the tenant so that it can construct income-producing buildings (EXAMPLES: office buildings; shopping malls).

ground water [*waw* · ter] *n.* The water on or below the surface of the ground. Ground water, which is a source for wells and springs, may be either a **natural watercourse**, **percolating waters**, or **surface waters**.

grounds *n.* *Plural* of **ground**. *See* ground.

group *n.* 1. For insurance purposes, any defined body of people who exist in some relationship to each other. (EXAMPLES: all employees of the XYZ Company; all members of the State Medical Society.) 2. A number of persons or things assembled together, with or without relationship to each other.
v. To gather together; to arrange or assemble.
➤ *n.* accumulation, congregation, conglomerate, formation, body.
v. assemble, arrange, classify, associate, collect, congregate, meet, organize, marshal.

group annuity [e · *new* · i · tee] *n.* A contract providing for pensions in the form of **retirement annuities** for a group of employees. The terms of the contract are stated in a **master policy**; the individual employee's participation is evidenced by a certificate issued to him. *See* annuity. *Also see* pension plan.

group health insurance [in · *shoor* · ense] *n.* *See* group insurance.

group home *n.* A residential facility that provides services for persons who do not need the structure of an institution but who require a protective environment (EXAMPLE: battered women) or a sheltered transitional environment to assist their re-entry from an institution into the community as independent and productive persons (EXAMPLE: certain long-term psychiatric patients). A **halfway house** is one EXAMPLE of a group home.

group insurance [in · *shoor* · ense] *n.* 1. A contract providing life, accident, or health insurance for a group of employees.

The terms of the contract are contained in a **master policy**; the individual employee's participation is demonstrated by a certificate of insurance which she holds. 2. A contract providing life, accident, or health insurance for any defined group of people. The contract is a master policy and is entered into between the group policyholder (for EXAMPLE, the American Automobile Association; the American Bar Association) and the insurance company for the benefit of the policyholder's members.

group libel [*ly* · bel] *n.* A statement that **libels** a group, such as, for EXAMPLE, a town's police department. Plaintiffs who are members of the group must show that the statement was made "of and concerning" them to succeed in a libel action.

group policy [*pol* · i · see] *n.* *See* group insurance.

grouping of contracts [*groop* · ing of *kon* · trakts] *n.* Same as **center of gravity doctrine**.

growing crop [*groh* · ing] *n.* A crop in the process of growth. Some cases hold that a "growing crop" may be either above or below the surface of the soil, although other cases hold that a crop is not a "growing crop" unless it shows above the ground.

growth *n.* 1. The evolution or metamorphosis of an object or person. 2. A progresive advance from a lower to a higher form.
➤ development, ripening, unfolding, maturation; increase, expansion, accumulation, aggrandizement, inflation.

GSA Abbreviation of **General Services Administration**.

guarantee [gair · en · *tee*] *n.* 1. Same as **guaranty**. 2. A person to whom a guaranty is given. 3. A **warranty**.
v. 1. To make or give a **guaranty**. 2. To assure; to vouch; to endorse; to **warrant**.
➤ *n.* attestation, certification, commitment, oath, warranty.
v. pledge, promise, assure, endorse.

guaranteed [gair · en · *teed*] *adj.* Secure; definite; **vested**.
➤ approved, affirmed, vested, confirmed, definite, attested, secure.
Ant. contingent, at risk.

G

G

guaranteed bond *n.* A **bond** guaranteed by a corporation other than the corporation that issued it.

guaranteed stock *n.* **Preferred stock** whose dividends are guaranteed by a corporation other than the issuing corporation. *See* issue.

guarantor [*gair* · en · tor] *n.* A person who makes or gives a **guaranty**.

guaranty [*gair* · en · tee] *n.* A promise to pay the debt or satisfy the obligation of another person in the event that person does not make payment or fails to perform. The person making the guaranty is called the **guarantor**, the person whose debt is guaranteed is the **debtor**, and the person to whom the guaranty is made is the **creditor** or **guarantee**. *Compare* surety. *Also compare* suretyship; warranty. *See* absolute guaranty; special guaranty.
➤ engagement, pledge, promise, covenant, indemnity, security.

guaranty insurance [in · *shoor* · ense] *n.* A guaranty in the form of insurance against **loss** as a result of default or insolvency (EXAMPLE: nonpayment of credit card debt), misconduct (EXAMPLE: embezzlement), or breach of contract (EXAMPLE: **defective title** to real estate). *See* credit insurance; fidelity and guaranty insurance; title insurance.

guardian [*gar* · dee · en] *n.* A person empowered by the law to care for another who, by virtue of age (EXAMPLE: a minor) or lack of mental capacity (EXAMPLE: a psychotic person), is legally unable to care for himself. Guardianship may also involve the duty to manage the estate (i.e., the property) of the incompetent person. A person supervised by a guardian is called a **ward**. *See* guardianship. *Also see* conservator; next friend; testamentary guardian.
➤ protector, custodian, sponsor, curator, champion.

guardian ad litem [*ly* · tem] *n.* A person appointed by the court to represent and protect the interests of a minor or an incompetent person during litigation. *See* ad litem.

guardian by nature *n.* See natural guardian.

guardianship [*gar* · dee · en · ship] *n.* 1. The office or the functions and duties of a **guardian**. 2. The relationship between a guardian and the person for whom she acts, called the **ward**, whom the law regards as incapable of managing his own affairs.

guest *n.* 1. A person stopping at a hotel, motel, restaurant, or other place of public accommodation for food or lodging. *See* business invitee. 2. An **automobile guest**. *See* guest statutes. 3. A person who receives the hospitality of another; a social guest; an **invitee**.
➤ patron, invitee, confidante, recipient, caller.

guest statutes [*stat* · shoots] *n.* State statutes that govern the liability of the owner or operator of a motor vehicle for injury to an **automobile guest**. Under such statutes, the owner or driver is liable to a guest only for injury resulting from **gross negligence**. *See also* family purpose doctrine.

guilt *n.* 1. Criminality; responsibility for violating the law. 2. Shame; blame; fault. *Compare* innocence.
➤ misconduct, turpitude, dishonesty, delinquency; dishonor, blame, liability, remorse, regret.

guilty [*gill* · tee] *adj.* 1. The plea of a defendant in a criminal prosecution admitting having committed the crime with which she is charged. 2. The finding by a judge, or the verdict of a jury, that a defendant in a criminal case has committed the offense with which he is charged. 3. Blameworthy; responsible; culpable; remiss.
➤ culpable, accountable, condemned, incriminated, blameworthy, responsible, culpable.

guilty knowledge [*naw* · ledj] *n.* See scienter.

guilty mind *n.* General criminal intent. *See also mens rea*.

guilty plea [plee] *n.* See guilty.

guilty verdict [*ver* · dikt] *n.* See guilty.

gun *n.* A firearm.
➤ firearm, rifle, pistol, weapon, shotgun, arms.

gun control laws [ken · *trol*] *n.* Federal and state statutes regulating the manufacture, sale, use, and possession of firearms. Such statutes typically impose waiting periods for the purchase of a firearm, require a license, and prohibit concealment. *See* concealed weapon.

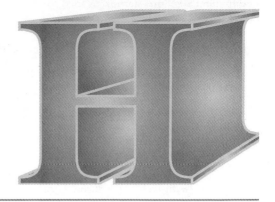

habeas corpus [*hay* · bee · ess *kore* · pus] (*Latin*) *n.* Means "you have the body." A **writ** whose purpose is to obtain immediate relief from illegal imprisonment by having the "body" (that is, the prisoner) delivered from custody and brought before the court. A **writ of habeas corpus** is a means for attacking the **constitutionality** of the statute under which, or the proceedings in which, the original conviction was obtained. There are numerous writs of habeas corpus, each applicable in different procedural circumstances. The full name of the ordinary writ of habcas corpus is *habeas corpus ad subjiciendum.*

habendum clause [ha · *ben* · dum] *n.* Part of a deed that specifies the nature of the **estate** being conveyed to the grantee. *Habendum* is a form of the Latin word "have." "To have and to hold in **fee simple**" is an EXAMPLE of the language of a habendum clause.

habit [*hab* · it] *n.* A pattern of repeated behavior.
➤ custom, inclination, course of conduct, practice, pattern, procedure, routine, repetition.

habitability [hab · i · te · *bil* · i · tee] *n.* The condition of premises that are habitable. *See* warranty of habitability.

habitable [*hab* · i · tebl] *adj.* Fit for habitation; reasonably fit to be lived in. *See* habitability.
➤ livable, fit, acceptable, occupiable, tenantable.
Ant. uninhabitable.

habitable repair [re · *pair*] *n.* Good repair; such state of repair as makes a building fit for occupancy. USAGE (in a lease): "The landlord shall maintain the premises in a state of habitable repair."

habitancy [*hab* · i · ten · see] *n.* A place at which a person resides with the intent to make and regard it as a home. *See* domicile; residence.
➤ home, residence, dwelling.

habitation [hab · i · *tay* · shen] *n.* A place of abode, either permanent or temporary; a residence. *Compare* domicile.
➤ domicile, abode, residence, dwelling, home; occupation, possession, residence, tenancy.

habitual [hab · *it* · shoo · el] *adj.* By habit; constant; customary; accustomed; usual; common; ordinary; regular.
➤ constant, customary, hardened, accustomed, usual, common, ordinary, regular, routine, recurrent ("habitual intoxication").

habitual criminal [*krim* · in · el] *n.* A repeat offender; a convicted person who has a prior criminal record; a **recidivist**. *See* habitual offender statutes.

habitual drunkard [*drunk* · erd] *n.* 1. Also termed a **common drunk**, a person who has been convicted of habitual drunkenness. 2. A person who drinks alcoholic beverages to excess and with habitual frequency. *See* alcoholic.

habitual drunkenness [*drunk* · en · ness] *n.* 1. The offense of having more than one conviction for public drunkenness. 2. A condition of frequent intoxication.

habitual intoxication
[in · tok · si · *kay* · shen] *n.* Same as **habitual drunkenness**.

habitual offender statutes [o · *fen* · der *stat* · shoots] *n.* State statutes that impose a greater punishment for a second or subsequent conviction than for the first. *See* habitual criminal.

habitually [hab · *it* · shoo · e · lee] *adv.* By habit; customarily. *Note* that habitually does not mean "exclusively" or "entirely." *See* habitual.
➤ customarily, regularly, traditionally.

had *v.* As used in legal language, brought, commenced, or maintained. USAGE: "Can an **action** be had in this situation?" *See* have.
➤ brought, commenced, maintained.

haggle [*hag* · gull] *v.* To argue over the terms of a deal; to barter.
➤ argue, bargain, negotiate, quibble, wrangle, deal, dicker ("to haggle about terms").

half blood *n.* A person who shares one parent in common with another person. EXAMPLES: a half brother; a half sister.

half brother [*bruth* · er] *n.* A man or boy who shares one parent in common with another person.

half sister [*sis* · ter] *n.* A woman or girl who shares one parent in common with another person.

halfway house [*haf* · way] *n.* A facility in which persons recently discharged from a rehabilition facility (EXAMPLES: a drug and alcohol treatment program; a psychiatric hospital) or prison live for a time and are given support and assistance in readjusting to society at large. *See also* group home; rehab program; treatment program.

hallucinogen [ha · *loo* · sin · o · jen] *n.* Any drug that induces hallucinations. (EXAMPLES: LSD; psilocybin; PCP; mescalin; peyote.) Hallucinogenic drugs are regulated by **controlled substance acts**.

halt *v.* To disrupt the progress of; to suspend action.
n. A stop or pause.
➤ *v.* stop, block, curb, deter, restrict, restrain, discontinue, interrupt, arrest.
n. stop, pause, respite, cessation, delay, stoppage, truce, lapse, lull.

hand down *v.* To issue a **judgment**, decision, or opinion in a case. USAGE: "The court handed down its decision yesterday."
➤ decide, judge, opine, reveal, publish.

handcuff *n.* Chains used to secure the wrists.
v. To make powerless; to restrict or restrain.
➤ *n.* shackle, chain, harness, collar, pinion.
v. shackle, tie, fasten, manacle, lash, leash.

handicap [*han* · dee · kap] *v.* To put others at a disadvantage; to hinder.
n. An encumbrance that impairs one's abilities.
➤ *v.* hinder, interfere, obstruct, frustrate, burden, cripple, impede, hamper.
n. obstruction, blockade, disadvantage, liability, deficiency, impairment.

handicapped [*han* · di · kapt] *adj.* Having a disability. *See* Americans with Disabilities Act; disability.
➤ disabled, physically challenged, impaired.

handle [*han* · dul] *v.* To manage; to deal with; to take care of.
➤ regulate, supervise, guide, administer, oversee, direct, have charge of.

handwriting [*hand* · rite · ing] *n.* The form of writing done by an individual, without the aid of a machine.
➤ script, penmanship, writing, hand, longhand, autography.

happening [*hap* · pen · ing] *n.* Something that occurs; an event.
➤ event, occurrence, action, incident, matter, phenomenon.

harass [huh · *rass*] *v.* To disturb persistently; to badger.
➤ annoy, hound, molest, intimidate, persecute, badger, plague, pester, torment, hassle.

harassment [ha · *rass* · ment] *n.* Words or conduct intended to pester, upset, disturb, or cause emotional distress. In certain circumstances, harassment can be **actionable**. EXAMPLES: sexual harassment in the workplace; abuse of a debtor under the **Fair Debt Collection Practices Act**. *See* sexual harassment.
➤ annoyance, badgering, irritation, disturbance, aggravation, intimidation, abuse.

harbor [*harr* · ber] *v.* 1. To hide or conceal a person. 2. To keep, shelter, or protect. *See* harboring a criminal.
➤ keep, hide, conceal, shelter, protect ("to harbor a refugee").

H

harboring a criminal [*harr* · ber · ing a *krim* · in · el] *n.* Concealing, sheltering, or protecting a criminal. Harboring a criminal is itself a criminal act and almost indistinguishable from acting as an **accessory after the fact**.

hard labor [*lay* · ber] *n.* A special condition sometimes imposed as part of a prison sentence for a criminal conviction. It does not mean rigorous labor; it only means that labor is compulsory while in prison.
➤ compulsory labor, bondage, servitude.

harm *v.* to injure or impair.
n. Injury or damage.
➤ *v.* hurt, cripple, abuse, inflict, damage, injure, impair ("to harm his chances for advancement").
n. injury, misfortune, damage, detriment, aggravation, evil, disservice ("I mean you no harm").

harmful [*harm* · ful] *adj.* Capable of causing harm or injury.
➤ destructive, dangerous, injurious, detrimental, deleterious, harmful, evil. *Ant.* safe, benevolent.

harmless error [*harm* · less *err* · er] *n.* Trivial or merely formal error; a ruling or other action by a judge in the trial of a case which, although erroneous, is not prejudicial to substantial rights, does not affect the final outcome of the case, and does not form a basis for appeal. *Compare* prejudicial error; reversible error. See error.

harmonize [*harr* · mun · ize] *v.* 1. To construe apparent inconsistencies in a legal document; to reconcile seeming conflict between two statutes or between two judicial decisions in a manner that gives effect to both. 2. To accommodate; to reconcile; to integrate.
➤ bring into accord, adapt, accommodate, reconcile, integrate.

harry [*har* · ree] *v.* To torment incessantly.
➤ harass, badger, heckle, tease, pester, bully, bother, hound, offend, provoke.

hashish [*hash* · eesh] *n.* A drug made from the resin of the cannabis sativa plant. Hashish is a **controlled substance**; its possession, sale, or distribution is a criminal offense. *Compare* marijuana.

haste *n.* Extreme speed; hurry.

➤ hurry, eagerness, rush, frenzy, flurry, dash, dispatch, scurry, urgency ("In his haste, he forgot the chart.").

Hatch Act *n.* An Act of Congress prohibiting public employees from participating in political activity that involves taking "an active part in political management or political campaigns." Every state has also enacted a "little Hatch Act."

have *v.* 1. To possess, either temporarily or permanently. 2. To possess a legal right. USAGE: "Do I have a **cause of action** in this situation?" *See* had.
➤ possess, hold.

have and hold *See* habendum clause.

havoc [*hav* · uk] *n.* Chaos; destruction.
➤ chaos, disorder, shambles, ruin, devastation.

hazard [*haz* · erd] *n.* 1. In insurance law, the **risk**, likelihood, or probability of **loss**. *See* moral hazard. 2. Danger; peril.
v. To expose oneself to a loss.
➤ *n.* peril, threat, crisis, danger, menace, uncertainty.
v. venture, endanger, jeopardize, speculate, dare, risk, gamble ("to hazard a guess").

hazardous [*haz* · er · dess] *adj.* 1. In insurance law, susceptible to **loss**. 2. Dangerous; unsafe; perilous; risky.
➤ dangerous, harmful, unsafe, risky, perilous, insecure, difficult.

hazardous contract [*kon* · trakt] *n.* A contract whose performance depends on an uncertain event.

hazardous employment [em · *ploy* · ment] *n.* Employment involving a high degree of risk of injury or death.

hazardous occupation [awk · yoo · *pay* · shen] *n.* *See* hazardous employment.

hazardous substance [*sub* · stense] *n.* *See* hazardous waste.

hazardous waste *n.* Industrial, commercial, medical, and other waste—solid, liquid, or otherwise—that poses a threat to human life or health, or to the environment. The storage, transportation, and disposal of hazardous substances are regulated by federal and state statutes. *See* solid waste; toxic waste; waste. *Also see* pollution.

HB Abbreviation of **House Bill**.

head *n.* 1. Leader; chief; the person in charge, whether of an administrative agency or a business. 2. Top; front. 3. Ability; intelligence.

➤ leader, chief, person in charge, authority, principal person ("head of household"); brain, aptness, faculty, gift, aptitude, intellect, instinct, sense, intuition ("a good head for business").

head of family [*fam · i · lee*] *n.* The person who is under a legal or moral obligation for the support of a family. A **homestead** occupied by a head of family is exempt from **execution** to the extent provided by the **homestead exemption statutes**.

head of household [*house · hold*] *n.* 1. In tax law, a single person, other than a surviving spouse, who provides a home for certain persons, generally dependents. Also, married persons who live apart are each a head of household. A head of household is entitled to pay federal income tax at a lower rate than other single persons. 2. A **head of family**. *See* homestead; homestead exemption.

head tax *n.* A **capitation tax**.

headnote [*hed · note*] *n.* A summary statement that appears at the beginning of a **reported case** to indicate the points decided by the case.

➤ summary, annotation, summation.

health *n.* A state of well-being; freedom from sickness. *See* bill of health; public health; sound health.

➤ well-being, fitness, soundness, strength, vitality.

health insurance [in · *shoor* · ense] *n.* Insurance that indemnifies the insured for medical expenses incurred as a result of sickness or accident.

health laws *n.* Statutes, ordinances, and regulations designed to promote and protect the health of the public. EXAMPLES: food inspection laws administered by the **Food and Drug Administration**; statutes regulating hazardous substances; quarantine regulations. *See* public health.

health maintenance organization [*main · ten · enss* or · *ge · ni · zay* · shen] *n.* A network of healthcare providers (EXAMPLES: doctors; hospitals) who provide medical services under a group insurance plan which requires that an insured be treated only by providers within the **HMO** or by providers to whom the insured is referred by the HMO. *Compare* preferred provider organization.

health officer [*off · i · ser*] *n.* A public employee who is empowered to enforce health laws.

healthcare proxy [*helth · kare prok · see*] *n.* A written document allowing a person's agent or **attorney in fact** to make healthcare decisions for her in the event she is no longer able to make such decisions for herself. *See* advance directive; durable power of attorney; right to die. *Compare* living will.

hear *v.* 1. To consider a **motion**; to try a case. USAGE: "Judge Smith has been assigned to hear this case." *See* hearing. 2. To listen; to understand. 3. To become aware of information.

➤ try, hold court, adjudicate ("hear a case"); understand, heed, submit, listen, note, notice ("hear his point"); discover, gather, glean, learn, ascertain, determine ("Did you hear the jury's verdict?").

hear and determine [de · *ter* · min] *v.* To consider and decide all the questions involved in a case.

hearing [*heer · ing*] *n.* A **proceeding** in which evidence is introduced and witnesses are examined so that **findings of fact** can be made and a determination rendered. Although, in a general sense, all trials can be said to be hearings, not all hearings are trials. The difference is in the degree of formality each requires, with the rules of procedure being more relaxed in hearings.

A hearing may be conducted by a court, an administrative agency, an **arbitrator**, or a committee of the legislature, as well as by many other public bodies. *See* administrative hearing; fair hearing; final hearing; public hearing; rehearing.

➤ trial, inquiry, litigation, adjudication, review, legal proceedings, case.

hearing examiner [eg · *zam* · in · er] *n.* The title of the person who functions as a judge with respect to an administrative hearing. In some states, and in the federal system, the title **administrative law judge** is used instead. *See* hearing officer.

hearing officer [*off* · i · ser] *n.* Same as **hearing examiner**, although, in some circumstances, a hearing officer, unlike a hearing examiner, does not have the power to **adjudicate**, her authority being limited to making recommendations to the appropriate administrative agency. *See also* administrative law judge.

hearsay [*heer* · say] *n./adj.* The testimony of a witness as to a statement made to him outside of court, or made to someone else who told him what was said, that is offered in court to prove the truth of the matter contained in the statement. *See* hearsay rule. *See also* double hearsay.
➤ *n.* secondhand information, gossip, report, indirect evidence, grapevine, rumor ("hearsay testimony").

hearsay evidence [*ev* · i · dense] *n.* Same as **hearsay**.

hearsay rule *n.* The rule that hearsay testimony is not admissible unless it falls within an exception to the hearsay rule. *See* exception to hearsay rule.

heart balm statutes [*stat* · shoots] *n.* Legislation in many states abolishing the **right of action** for seduction, **breach of promise to marry, alienation of affections**, and **criminal conversation**.

heat *n.* 1. An intensity of feelings. 2. The feeling of or degree of thermal elevation or hotness.
➤ passion, insanity, emotion; warmth, swelter, torridity.
Ant. premeditation; chill.

heat of passion [*pash* · en] *n.* The expression for a mental state on the part of a criminal defendant adequate in law to reduce the crime of **murder** to **manslaughter**. In this context, "heat" means an emotional state which created reasonable provocation (EXAMPLES: anger; fury; panic), and before a sufficient time had elapsed for reason to return. *Compare* premeditation.

hedge *v.* to protect oneself by being cautious.
➤ evade, avoid, dodge, equivocate, prevaricate, sidestep.

hedging [*hed* · jing] *n.* 1. A transaction by which a person who has made a contract for sale or purchase of a **commodity** protects herself against loss resulting from market fluctuation, by making a countercontract for the purchase or sale of an equal quantity of the commodity. 2. Avoiding the consequences of losing a bet by setting up a strategy to minimize the loss.

hedonic damages [hee · *don* · ik *dam* · e · jez] *n.* **Damages** awarded by some courts for loss of enjoyment of life or of life's pleasures. *Compare* loss of consortium.

heed *v.* To give attention to.
➤ follow, obey, comply with, be guided by, hear, notice.

heighten [*hite* · en] *v.* 1. To make more intense or increase. 2. To become greater.
➤ augment, intensify, enhance, enlarge, magnify; raise, uplift, build up.

heinous [*hay* · nuss] *adj.* Cruel, repulsive, or malicious.
➤ hateful, dreadful, diabolic, mean, despicable, shameful, villainous ("a heinous crime"). *Ant.* good, loving, caring.

heir [air] *n. Singular* of **heirs**. *See* heirs.
➤ successor, descendant, inheritor, recipient, beneficiary, donee ("my heirs and assigns").

heir apparent [a · *pehr* · ent] *n.* A person who is related to another in such a way that she is certain to inherit the **estate** of that person if she outlives him and he dies **intestate**. *Compare* expectant heir; heir presumptive.

heir by devise [de · *vize*] *n.* A contradictory expression, meaning a person to whom land is **devised** by will, not a person who inherits it.

heir collateral [ke · *lat* · e · rel] *n. See* collateral descendant.

heir expectant [eks · *pek* · tent] *n.* Same as **expectant heir**.

heir male *n.* A **testator's** nearest male blood relative.

heir presumptive [pre · *zum* · tiv] *n.* A person who would be an heir if the ancestor were to die right now, but whose possibility of inheritance may be destroyed by the birth of someone more nearly related or by the person's death before that of the ancestor. *Compare* heir apparent; expectant heir.

heirloom [*air* · loom] *n.* An object owned by a family for generations. *See* mixed property.
➤ antique, gift, bequest, heritage, legacy.

H

heirs [airz] *n.* 1. *Plural* of **heir**. 2. Persons who are entitled to inherit real or personal property of a **decedent** who dies **intestate**; persons receiving property by **descent**. 3. Although not technically correct, the word is often used to indicate persons who receive property through a decedent's will. *Note* that "heirs" and "children" do not have the same meaning (*see* child); nor do "heirs" and "**next of kin**." *Also see* forced heir; joint heirs; lawful heirs; legal heirs; lineal heirs; natural heirs; right heirs.

heirs and assigns [a · *synz*] *n.* Words in a deed or will that pass a **fee simple absolute** to the grantee. The word "heirs," or the words "heirs and assigns," do not convey any interest in the property to the grantee's heirs; they are **words of limitation** whose function is to indicate the *nature* of the estate conveyed to the *grantee. Compare* words of purchase.

heirs at law *n.* Essentially the same as **heirs**.

heirs by blood *n.* **Words of limitation** that refer to descendants or ascendants. *Compare* heirs of the body. *See* heirs and assigns.

heirs of the body [*bod* · ee] *n.* **Words of limitation** that refer to **descendants** only. *Compare* heirs by blood. *See* heirs and assigns.

held *v.* 1. In reference to property, may mean actual possession, the right to possession, or having **title**. USAGE: "She held that property **in trust** for her brother." 2. In reference to the decision of a court, means decided. USAGE: "The court held that the plaintiff had no **cause of action**." 3. To have or to keep, permanently or temporarily, in a particular manner or without limitation. *See* hold; holding.
➤ decided, asserted, adjudicated ("The court held that privity was not required"); conducted, administered ("held court"); possessed, owned ("held title").

help *v.* To give support to; to promote. *n.* 1. Assistance; relief. 2. Employee; assistant.
➤ *v.* aid, assist, avail, accommodate, benefit, improve, remedy, facilitate. *n.* aid, assistance, favor, succor, support, backing, guidance; aide, assistant, worker, servant, auxiliary, representative.

helpless [*help* · less] *adj.* 1. Vulnerable. 2. Powerless; imcapable.
➤ unarmed, unprotected, exposed, vulnerable; impotent, powerless, weak, feeble, dependent, debilitated, infirm, paralyzed, incapable.

henceforth [*henss* · forth] *adv.* From this point forward; from now on. *Note,* however, that "henceforth" may or may not mean "forever," depending upon the context in which it is used. *See also* hereafter.
➤ from now on, following, succeeding.

hereafter [heer · *aff* · ter] *adv./n.* After now; at some future time. *Note* that "hereafter" sometimes, but not necessarily, conveys the idea of "forever." *See* perpetuity. *See also* henceforth.
➤ *adv.* after now, at some future time, later, afterwards.

hereby [*heer* · by] *adv.* By this (action, document, or **instrument**).

hereditaments [herr · eh · *dit* · a · ments] *n.* Property, rights, or any other thing capable of being inherited, whether **corporeal** or **incorporeal**, and whether **real** or **personal**. *See and compare* corporeal hereditaments; incorporeal hereditaments; incorporeal right. *See and compare* personal property; real property.
➤ land, real property, personal property, inheritance.

hereditary [herr · *ed* · i · terr · ee] *adj.* Passed along by inheritance; inherited. *See* inherit.
➤ biological, genetic, inherited, innate, instinctive, inborn, native, lineal, constitutional, congenital. *Ant.* learned, acquired.

hereditary succession [sek · *sesh* · en] *n.* The passing of **title** under the laws of **descent**. *Also see* inheritance.

herein [*heer* · in] *adv.* A word used to locate a reference in a document. It may refer to a specific part, page, or paragraph of the document, or to the entire document. USAGE: "as set forth herein at page 97"; "as set forth herein."

hereinabove [heer · in · e · *buv*] *adv.* Same as **hereinbefore**.

hereinafter [heer · in · *af* · ter] *adv.* A word used to locate a reference to something mentioned later in the same document. USAGE: "as set forth hereinafter at page 201."

H

hereinbefore [heer · in · be · *for*] *adv.* A word used to locate a reference to something mentioned previously in the same document. USAGE: "as set forth hereinbefore at page 3."

hereinbelow [heer · in · be · *loh*] *adv.* Same as **hereinafter**.

hereto [*heer* · too] *adv.* To this. EXAMPLE: to this document, to this time. EXAMPLE (in a contract): "the diagram which is marked Appendix A and attached hereto."

heretofore [*heer* · to · for] *adv.* At a time previous to this time; before the present; formerly. EXAMPLE (in a court opinion): "The fact that the gun was not loaded was heretofore unknown to this court."
➤ previously, until now, before the present, formerly.

hereunder [heer · un · der] *adv.* Same as **herein**.

herewith [heer · *with*] *adv.* With this. EXAMPLE (in a letter): "I am forwarding my check for $25 herewith."

heroic [he · *row* · ik] *adj.* Marked by courage or daring.
➤ brave, bold, noble, valiant, courageous, dauntless, stalwart, resolute ("a heroic escape").

heroin [*herr* · o · in] *n.* A highly addictive narcotic drug, derived from morphine, which blunts the senses and induces euphoria and sleep. It can be injected or inhaled by smoking. Heroin is a **controlled substance**; its possession, distribution, or sale is a criminal offense.

hesitant [*hez* · i · tant] *adj.* Reluctant or undecided.
➤ reluctant, timid, undecided, tentative, wavering, cautious, doubting.

hesitate [*hez* · ih · tayt] *v.* Wait or hold off.
➤ dally, delay, wait, waver, pause, falter, demur.

heterogeneous [het · er · oh · *geen* · ee · us] *adj.* Different; diverse; mixed.
➤ mixed, different, varied, dissimilar, diverse, assorted ("a heterogeneous group"). *Ant.* homogeneous.

hidden [*hid* · en] *adj.* That which is out of sight.
➤ latent, concealed, masked, veiled, submerged, undisclosed ("a hidden defect").

hidden defect [*hid* · en *dee* · fekt] *n. See* latent defect.

hide *v.* To keep out of sight.
➤ conceal, shroud, suppress, veil, obscure, harbor, envelop, deceive.

high *adj.* 1. Elevated in rank, order, degree, importance, or status. 2. Tall; lofty.
➤ elevated, important, significant ("The high court of this state"); tall, lofty ("a high structure").

high court *n.* An informal way of referring to the Supreme Court of the United States or the highest court in a state judicial system. *See also* highest court.

high degree of care [de · *gree*] *n.* **Great care**; more than **ordinary care**. *Compare* reasonable care. *See* care.

high seas *n.* Areas of the ocean beyond the territorial jurisdiction of any nation.

high tide *n.* The highest point to which tidal waters rise. *See* high water line.

high water line [*waw* · ter] *n.* 1. As applied to tidal waters, the point reached by the water at high tide. 2. As applied to fresh water lakes, the customary line or level of the water.

high water mark [*waw* · ter] *n.* Same as **high water line**.

higher court [*hy* · er] *n.* Any court that is above a **lower court**, usually an **appellate court**. USAGE: "This case should be decided by a higher court." *Compare* high court; highest court.

highest [*hy* · est] *adj.* Supreme; paramount; foremost; top.
➤ supreme, major, paramount, foremost, top, best ("the highest and best use for this piece of property").

highest and best use *n.* Refers to a method for determining the value of real property, which assumes hypothetically that the property will be put to the most profitable use possible.

highest court *n.* The highest court of a state; the Supreme Court of the United States; a court whose decisions are not subject to review by a higher court.

highest degree of care [de · *gree*] *n.* **Extraordinary care**; **utmost care**. *See also* care.

H

highway [*hy · way*] *n.* A road used by the public at large. *Compare* private road.
> road, roadway, street, freeway, expressway, avenue, interstate.

highway robbery [*rob · e · ree*] *n. See* hijacking. In slang parlance, an exorbitant price: "That bill is outrageous; it's highway robbery."

hijack [*hy · jak*] *v.* To steal goods or vehicles while they are in use.
> abduct, seize, take, intercept, capture, snatch, take captive ("to hijack an airplane").

hijacking [*hy · jak · ing*] *n.* 1. **Robbery** of a vehicle (EXAMPLES: a truck; a train; a plane), or its cargo, or both, while in transit. 2. **Air piracy**. *Compare* car jacking.
> robbery, kidnapping, abduction, capturing, commandeering, air piracy.

hinder [*hin · der*] *v.* To obstruct; to block; to impede.
> obstruct, block, impede, frustrate, restrain, bar, interfere, curb, crimp.

hint *v.* To allude to; to indicate or suggest. *n.* A suggestion or obscure reference.
> *v.* suggest, intimate, imply, indicate, refer, connote ("to hint at the answer"). *n.* clue, suggestion, indication, allusion, insinuation ("a subtle hint").

hire *n.* 1. The amount paid for a person's services. 2. The amount paid for use of an article.
v. 1. To employ a person. 2. To contract for services (EXAMPLE: a band) or for the use of something (EXAMPLE: a taxicab).
> *n.* payment, charge, fee ("We could not afford her hire").
v. employ, enlist, retain, contract ("Their company won't hire ex-convicts").

hiring hall [*hy · ring*] *n.* In certain industries, a facility operated by a union, or by a union and employers jointly, where employers find and hire employees.

historic [*hiss · tor · ik*] *adj.* Of great importance or significance.
> of major importance, famous, well-known, significant, crucial ("a historic appointment to the Court").

historic site [*hiss · tor · ik*] *n.* A place or building significant in American history, which may be protected against alteration

or destruction if the federal government accepts an appropriately made request to register it in the National Register of Historic Places.

hit and run *n.* The crime of not stopping and remaining at the scene of an accident. *See* leaving the scene of an accident.

hitherto [*hith · er · too*] *adv.* Previously; before this time.
> previously, once, until now, formerly.

HIV Abbreviation of human immunodeficiency virus, the virus that causes AIDS.

HLA testing [*test · ing*] *n.* Abbreviation of human leukocyte antigen testing. An HLA blood test is a paternity test. *See* DNA fingerprinting.

HMO Abbreviation of **health maintenance organization**.

hoard *v.* To possess and keep more than is reasonably necessary.
> accrue, accumulate, store, store away, keep in reserve, collect, gather.

hoax *n.* A trick; a prank; a scam.
v. To fool into believing; to trick.
> *n.* ruse, scheme, deceit, sham, trick, fraud, chicanery, pretense, joke, dupery. *v.* trick, fool, delude, deceive, dupe, swindle.

Hobbs Act *n.* One of the federal **antiracketeering acts**, which criminalizes interference with **interstate commerce** by robbery, physical violence, or **extortion**. *See also* Racketeer Influenced and Corrupt Organizations Act (RICO).

hold *v.* 1. To own or to have **title** to something. EXAMPLE: to be a holder of a **negotiable instrument**. 2. To possess, occupy, and maintain authority over real property. USAGE: "He holds a **life estate** in that property." 3. To retain in one's keeping. USAGE: "She holds that money **in trust** for her son." 4. To make a decision interpreting the law. USAGE: "What did the court hold in this situation last year?" 5. To conduct; to administer; to manage; to oversee. USAGE: to "hold a hearing." 6. To have official power or authority. USAGE: to "hold office"; to "hold an election." 7. To place in custody; to restrain. USAGE: to "hold for questioning." 8. To have or to keep, permanently or temporarily. 9. To grasp; to grip. *See* held; holding.

n. A control or influence over another.

➤ *v.* own, have title to ("To hold a negotiable instrument"); possess, occupy ("He holds a life estate in that property"); retain, control ("He holds that money in trust for his sister"); decide, rule, announce, decree, settle ("What did the court hold in this situation last year?"); conduct, administer, manage, oversee ("The agency will decide whether to hold a hearing ") occupy, maintain, direct, be in charge of ("to hold office"); grasp, grip ("hold my hand").

n. domination, power, control, sway, domination, influence, authority, grasp, possession ("She's really got a hold on me").

hold harmless [*harm* · less] *adj./v.* To enter into a **hold harmless agreement**; to **save harmless**.

hold harmless agreement [*harm* · less a · *gree* · ment] *n.* An agreement by which one party promises to protect the other against future liability, loss, or damage. A hold harmless agreement is also called a **save harmless agreement**. *See* hold harmless. *See also* indemnify; indemnity.

hold harmless clause [*harm* · less] *n.* *See* hold harmless.

hold out *v.* 1. To present oneself or another as possessing a certain status or position; to present someone as one's representative; to represent oneself as the agent of another. USAGE: "Why did John hold himself out as Mary's broker when he negotiated the sales agreement?" *See* agency by estoppel; apparent authority. 2. To stand firm; to refuse to yield.

n. A person such as an athlete or employee who has not come to terms with the employer. USAGE: "Our pitchers are signed but Sanders is still a hold out."

hold up *v.* 1. To delay or interrupt. 2. To rob. *n.* 1. A robbery. 2. A problem or postponement.

➤ *v.* postpone, delay, impede, interrupt, halt, restrain ("hold up the proceedings"); rob, plunder, sack, take by theft ("hold up the bank").

n. robbery, crime, burglary, stickup; problem, trouble, wait, snag, delay.

holder [*hole* · der] *n.* 1. A person who has the legal right to enforce a **negotiable instrument** or who is entitled to receive, hold, and dispose of a **document of title** and the goods to which it pertains. With respect to an **instrument** payable to or in the name of "bearer," the person in possession is the "holder"; with respect to an instrument payable to or in the name of an identified person, that person is the "holder" *if* she is in possession of the instrument. 2. A person who has the ownership, possession, or use of any property.

➤ owner, possessor, bearer, keeper, recipient.

holder for value [*val* · yoo] *n.* A person who has given **consideration** for a **negotiable instrument** that he **holds**. *See* hold.

holder in due course *n.* A holder of a **negotiable instrument** who gave value for it and took it in good faith and without notice of any **claim** or **defense** against it. *Compare* bona fide purchaser; holder in good faith.

holder in good faith *n.* A person who **takes** or **holds** property, including a **negotiable instrument**, without knowledge of any **defect** in **title**. *See* good faith; good title. *See* take; hold.

holding [*hole* · ding] *n.* 1. The proposition of law for which a case stands (*see* precedent); the "bottom line" of a judicial decision. *Compare* opinion. *Also compare* dicta. *Also see* held; hold. 2. Most often used in the *plural* to mean property. *See* holdings. *v.* *See* hold.

➤ *n.* decision, conclusion, order, adjudication, bottom line ("the court's holding").

holding company [*kum* · pe · nee] *n.* A corporation that owns a dominant interest in one or more other corporations through ownership of their **securities**. To qualify for certain advantages under federal tax law, a holding company must hold at least 80 percent of the stock of any corporation it controls. *See* foreign personal holding company. *Compare* investment company.

holding over [*oh* · ver] *n.* *See* holdover tenant.

holding period [*peer* · ee · ed] *n.* In tax law, the period of time a taxpayer holds property before disposing of it.

holdings [*hole* · dingz] *n.* *Plural* of **holding**. Property, real or personal; assets. EXAMPLES: land; corporate stock.

➤ property, belongings, assets, goods.

H

holdover tenant [*hold* · oh · ver *ten* · ent] *n.* A tenant who continues in possession without the consent of the landlord after expiration of the lease.

holiday [*hol* · i · day] *n.* 1. A day set aside for commemoration of some great national or historical event and on which work is not ordinarily performed. 2. A day declared a **legal holiday** by statute.
➤ observance, celebration, day off, occasion, vacation.

holograph [*hol* · o · graf] *n.* A document written entirely in one's own handwriting.

holographic [hol · uh · *graf* · ik] *adj.* Written in one's own handwriting.
➤ written, handwritten, penned, printed, scripted, inscribed ("holographic will").

holographic will [hol · o · *graf* · ik] *n.* A will that is entirely written and signed by the **testator** in his own handwriting. In many states, the requirement that the signing of a will be witnessed is not imposed in the case of a holographic will, because a successful counterfeit of another person's handwriting is very difficult; the requirement that the will be entirely in handwriting is therefore thought to be sufficient protection against **forgery**.

homage [*hom* · aj] *n.* A show of respect.
➤ honor, regard, reverence, allegiance, exaltation, veneration ("to pay homage to Attorney Gould").

home *n.* 1. A word whose legal significance may be either "house," "**residence**," or "**domicile**," depending upon the context in which it appears. 2. One's native land.
➤ residence, domicile, house, abode, domain; native land, birthplace, motherland, fatherland.

home equity loan [*ek* · wi · tee] *n. See* equity loan.

home port *n.* The port where a vessel is registered or where one or more of the owners resides.

home rule *n.* The right of a city, town, or county to self-government with respect to purely local matters. A state's constitution may or may not confer such a right upon its cities and towns. *Also see* local option.

homeowners insurance [in · *shoor* · emse] *n. See* homeowners policy.

homeowners policy [*home* · ohn · erz *pol* · i · see] *n.* An insurance policy that insures homeowners against most common **risks**, including fire, burglary, and **civil liability**. *See* liability; liability insurance.

homeowners warranty [*war* · en · tee] *n.* Same as construction warranty.

homestead [*home* · sted] *n.* 1. In a legal sense, the right to own real property free and clear of the claims of creditors, provided the owner occupies the property as her home. *See* head of family; head of household. 2. In a more general sense, the place of residence of the family.
➤ dwelling, domicile, home, residence.

homestead exemption [eg · *zemp* · shen] *n.* Under **homestead exemption statutes**, the **immunity** of real property from **execution** for debt, provided the property is occupied by the debtor as the head of the family. *See* head of family.

homestead exemption statutes [eg · *zemp* · shen *stat* · shoots] *n.* State statutes that provide for a **homestead exemption**.

homework [*home* · werk] *n.* Also called **industrial homework**, work, usually **piecework**, performed for an employer at one's own home (EXAMPLE: making dresses), rather than at the employer's place of business, ordinarily a factory. Homework is regulated by federal and state law.

homicide [*hom* · i · side] *n.* The killing of a human being. Homicide may be non-criminal (**excusable homicide** or **justifiable homicide**) or criminal (**felonious homicide**). Excusable or justifiable homicide includes killing by accident (*see* homicide by misadventure) or in **self-defense**. A felonious homicide is either **murder** or **manslaughter**. Manslaughter homicide includes **negligent homicide** and **vehicular homicide**. *See also* reckless homicide.
➤ murder, manslaughter, slaying, assassination, killing, slaughter, felony, elimination, termination of life, extermination.

homicide by misadventure [mis · ad · *ven* · cher] *n.* A killing by pure accident, without any intention to harm, while doing a lawful act. EXAMPLE: while Thomas is chopping wood, the head flies off his axe and fatally injures a bystander.

Hon. An abbreviation of **honorable**.

honest [*on* · est] *adj.* Trustworthy; truthful.
➤ genuine, sincere, frank, ethical, moral, true, just, decent, trustworthy.

honesty [*on* · es · tee] *n.* Uprightness; trustworthiness.
➤ candor, openness, truthfulness, fairness, candor, integrity, sincerity.

honor [*on* · er] *n.* Honesty; integrity; principle; trustworthiness; virtue.
v. 1. To pay or **accept** a **negotiable instrument** when it is duly **presented**. *Compare* dishonor. *See* acceptance. 2. To praise; to acclaim; to value.
➤ *n.* honesty, integrity, principle, trustworthiness, virtue, veracity, credibility, dignity. *v.* credit, redeem, make good ("The store honors personal checks"); praise, acclaim, value, venerate, extol, revere, recognize, commemorate ("to honor the dead").

honorable [*on* · er · ebl] *adj.* Reputable; trustworthy; conscientious.
n. A title of courtesy for judges, members of Congress, and other high-ranking government officials. Often shortened to **Hon.** USAGE: "Honorable" (or "The Honorable" or "Hon.") Shirley Jones, Judge, Court of Common Pleas.
➤ *adj.* honest, good, moral, right, meritorious.

honorable discharge [*dis* · charj] *n.* A formal declaration given by the government to a member of the armed services upon the completion of service, certifying that he or she served conscientiously and faithfully.

honorarium [on · e · *rare* · ee · um] *n.* 1. A fee paid for services rendered gratuitously or in circumstances where there is no legal obligation for payment. *See* gratuity. 2. A reward for an act or service where the law or custom prohibit an agreed-upon payment.
➤ emolument, commission, payment, consideration, recompense, salary, compensation, stipend.

honorary trust [*on* · e · *rare* · ee] *n.* A **trust** based purely upon moral or ethical obligations and not enforceable in a court.

hoodlum [*hude* · lum] *n.* A person, generally a youth, who commits acts of violence or who breaks laws.
➤ scoundrel, ruffian, juvenile delinquent, thief, villain, mobster, miscreant, rogue, peculator.

hoodwink [*hud* · wenk] *v.* To cheat or deceive.
➤ fool, trick, deceive, outwit, beguile, dupe, cheat.

horizontal [horr · i · *zawn* · tel] *adj.* Parallel to the ground; lengthwise.
➤ even, level, straight, parallel to the ground, lengthwise.

horizontal agreement [a · *gree* · ment] *n.* An agreement by which competing producers or dealers on the same level seek to prevent competition by controlling the market price of a **commodity**, customers, products, or sales territories. *Compare* vertical agreement. *See* price-fixing; restraint of trade.

horizontal integration [in · te · *gray* · shen] *n.* *See* horizontal merger.

horizontal merger [*mer* · jer] *n.* A merger of two companies that are in competition with each other. Depending upon the circumstances, a horizontal merger may also be a **horizontal restraint of trade**. *Compare* vertical merger. *See* merger.

horizontal price-fixing [*price*-fik · sing] *n.* **Price-fixing** in **restraint of trade** under a **horizontal agreement**. *Compare* vertical price-fixing.

horizontal property acts [*prop* · er · tee] *n.* State statutes relating to cooperative apartment houses, condominiums, and similar structures.

horizontal restraint of trade [re · *straint*] *n.* **Restraint of trade** carried out under a **horizontal agreement**. *Compare* vertical restraint of trade.

hornbook [*horn* · book] *n.* 1. A book that explains the fundamental aspects of an area or field of the law (EXAMPLES: contract law; insurance law) in basic terms. A hornbook is usually concise. 2. An elementary work in any field. *Compare* casebook; treatise.
➤ digest, manual, abstract, study guide, treatise, commentary, exposition, outline, dissertation, capsule, elementary work, primer, elementary law ("The hornbook on torts").

hornbook law *n.* A fundamental legal principle, free of ambiguity and universally accepted. USAGE: "It is hornbook law that without **consideration** there is no contract."

H

hostage [*hoss* · tej] *n.* A person held captive by another and threatened with bodily harm or death if his captor's demands are not met.
➤ prisoner, captive, pawn, victim.

hostile [*hoss* · tel] *adj.* 1. Antagonistic; adverse; argumentative. 2. Warlike; bellicose; belligerent.
➤ antagonistic, adverse, argumentative, warlike, bellicose, belligerent, combative ("a hostile demeanor"); uncooperative, opposed ("a hostile witness").

hostile environment [en · *vi* · ron · ment] *n.* As frequently used in judicial opinions concerning sexual harassment, a situation in which sexually offensive conduct is permitted to infect the workplace, making it unpleasant or difficult for an employee to do her job. *See* sex discrimination.

hostile fire *n.* In insurance law, an unintended fire or a fire that has spread from the place where it was contained.

hostile possession [po · *zesh* · en] *n.* *See* adverse possession.

hostile takeover [*take* · over] *n.* The involuntary merger of one corporation into another. *Compare* friendly takeover. *See* takeover. *See also* merger of corporations.

hostile witness [*wit* · ness] *n.* A witness who may be **cross-examined** or **impeached** by the party who called him, because of malice or prejudice he displayed toward that party in his **direct examination**. *Compare* adverse witness. *See* impeachment of witness.

hot *adj.* 1. Stolen. 2. Hazardous or dangerous to possess. 3. Furious; enraged; provoked. 4. Warm; burning; scalding.
➤ stolen, pilfered; furious, enraged, provoked, angry, excited, frenzied; warm, burning, scalding.

hot blood *n.* Same as **heat of passion**.

hot cargo clause [*kar* · go] *n.* A provision in a **collective bargaining agreement** under which union members have the right to refuse to handle the goods of any other employer with whom the union is involved in a labor dispute.

hot goods *n.* Stolen property.

hot pursuit [per · *soot*] *n.* Same as **fresh pursuit**.

hotchpot [*hotch* · pot] *n.* The blending and mixing of property belonging to different persons in order to divide it equally. With respect to a **decedent's estate**, making allowance for the value of property given by the **decedent** as **advancements** to her **heirs** or **distributees** during her lifetime, so that the whole may be divided in accordance with the **intestate laws**, each share being charged with what has already been received. *See* distribution.

hours of labor [*lay* · ber] *n.* The time, in hours per day or per week, spent by an employee working for his employer. Hours of labor are regulated by the federal **Fair Labor Standards Act** and by similar state statutes. *See* overtime; overtime pay.

house *n.* 1. A building where people live. 2. Some buildings where people assemble for a particular purpose. EXAMPLES: a house of worship (a church, synagogue, or mosque). 3. The **lower house** of the two halves of a bicameral legislature, e.g., the House of Representatives.
➤ abode, dwelling, domicile, residence; business, establishment, company.

house counsel [*koun* · sel] *n.* An attorney who represents a single client (EXAMPLE: a corporation; a union), usually on a full-time basis. Also called in-house counsel.

House Bill *n.* A legislative **bill** that originates in the House of Representatives of the United States Congress or of a state legislature. Every such bill is assigned a number, preceded by the designation "**HB.**" *Compare* Senate Bill.

House of Representatives [rep · re · *zen* · te · tivz] *n.* 1. The **lower house** of Congress. Its 435 members are elected every 2 years. 2. One of the two houses of a bicameral state legislature. *See* house.

housebreaking [*house* · brake · ing] *n.* Another term for **burglary**.
➤ burglary, stealing, thievery, looting, raiding, plundering, filching.

household [*house* · hold] *n.* Persons who live together as a family in the same place. *See also* family; head of family; head of household.
adj. Relating to the family home or day-to-day activities.

➤ *n.* family, residence, homestead, lodging. *adj.* domestic, residential; everyday, common, routine.

housing authority [*how* · zing aw · *thaw* · ri · tee] *n. See* public housing.

HR Abbreviation of **House of Representatives**.

humanitarian [hyoo · man · ih · *tare* · ee · en] *adj.* Showing interest in the welfare of others.
➤ philanthropic, compassionate, benevolent, charitable, human, kind, humane ("a humanitarian gesture").
Ant. selfish, greedy.

humanitarian doctrine [hyoo · man · i · *tare* · ee · en *dok* · trin] *n.* Another term for the **last clear chance doctrine**. *See* discovered peril doctrine.

humanity [hue · *man* · ih · tee] *n.* 1. Humankind; people. 2. The quality of being caring or compassionate. USAGE: "The light sentence showed the judge's humanity."
➤ people, mankind, humankind, human beings; caring, compassion, charity, benevolence.

humiliate [hue · *mill* · ee · ate] *v.* To shame or embarrass.
➤ disgrace, shame, abase, embarrass, malign, put down, mock, ridicule.

hung jury [*joo* · ree] *n.* A jury that cannot reach a unanimous verdict.

husband-wife privilege [*huz* · bend-wife *priv* · i · lej] *n.* Same as **marital communications privilege**.

hybrid class action [*hy* · brid class *ak* · shen] *n.* An **action** brought by one or several plaintiffs on behalf of others to determine rights with respect to specific property. This is not a typical **class action**, as the interests of the members of the class are separate and distinct. However, each has an interest of some sort in the property and therefore in the outcome of the lawsuit.

hypothecate [hy · *poth* · e · kate] *v.* To **pledge** property as **security** for the performance of an act (EXAMPLE: repaying a debt), without transferring possession of the property. *See* hypothecation.
➤ pledge, mortgage.

hypothecation [hy · poth · e · *kay* · shen] *n.* A **pledge** in which the pledged property remains in the possession of the debtor. *See* hypothecate.

hypothesis [hy · *poth* · e · sis] *n.* Something not proven, but assumed for the purpose of argument. *See* arguendo.
➤ assumption, theory, supposition, postulate, presumption.

hypothesize [hy · *poth* · e · size] *v.* To assume; to suppose; to presume; to theorize.
➤ assume, suppose, presume, theorize.

hypothetical [hype · e · *thet* · i · kel] *adj.* Something that is a hypothesis; that which is merely assumed to be true; theoretical.
➤ theoretical, assumed, imaginary, supposed ("a hypothetical question").

H

i.e. *(Latin)* Abbreviation of *id est*, meaning "that is," "it is," or "that is to say." USAGE: "The seller insisted that payment be made in cash or its equivalent, i.e., in cash or with a certified check or a cashier's check."

ibid. [*ib* · id] *(Latin)* Short for *ibidem,* meaning "in the same place"; in the same volume.

ICC Abbreviation of **Interstate Commerce Commission**.

id *(Latin)* *n.* 1. That; it. 2. The part of the human personality which wants and desires.
id est *See* i.e.

id. *(Latin)* Short for *idem;* means "previously referred to" or "the same." *Id.* is used in legal writing when the author is citing the immediately preceding authority. EXAMPLE: If the author of a brief has cited the case of *Trimble v. Gordon,* 430 U.S. 762, immediately following which she refers to page 765 of the *Trimble* decision, the correct citation is "*Id.* at 765." *Compare infra; supra.*

idea [eye · *dee* · uh] *n.* A concept; a belief.
➤ concept, thought, belief, proposal, notion, meaning, essence, conviction, view.

identical [eye · *dent* · ih · kul] *adj.* Exactly the same.
➤ alike, matching, twin, uniform, indistinguishable, duplicate.

identification [eye · den · ti · fi · *kay* · shen] *n.* The act of demonstrating or proving that a person or thing is the person or thing it is alleged, supposed, or represented to be. *See* authentication; DNA fingerprinting; fingerprints; lineup; voiceprinting.
➤ verification, authentication, ascertainment, recognition.

identify [eye · *dent* · ih · fie] *v.* To recognize or notice; to assert the identity of.
➤ specify, name, designate, determine, recognize ("identify the perpetrator").

identity [eye · *den* · ti · tee] *n.* Sameness; the state of being the same as someone or something is alleged, supposed, or represented to be. *See* identification.
➤ sameness, resemblance, similarity; individuality, uniqueness.
Ant. universality, dissimilarity.
  identity of interests [*in* · trests] *n.* A circumstance that exists when parties who are separate in name only (EXAMPLE: a corporation and its **wholly owned subsidiary**) are, in legal effect, the same.
  identity of parties [*parr* · teez] *n.* Refers to persons or parties whose interests are so bound together that a **judgment** in a lawsuit against one is automatically *res judicata* in a lawsuit brought against the other on the same facts. *See* party.

idiocy [*id* · ee · e · see] *n.* A form of mental incapacity.
➤ mental retardation, lunacy, insanity, imbecility.
Ant. genius, sanity.

idle [*eye* · dul] *adj.* 1. Inactive. 2. Without employment.
➤ inactive, disengaged, inert, still; jobless, unoccupied, lazy, slothful, unemployed.

ignorance [*ig* · ner · ense] *n.* A lack or absence of knowledge, not a matter of being mistaken.
➤ lack of knowledge, unenlightenment, unawareness, incomprehension, unfamiliarity, absence of knowledge.
Ant. comprehension, brilliance, knowledge.

ignorance of fact *n.* A circumstance that occurs either when a fact that really exists is unknown, or when a fact that supposedly exists really does not.

ignorance of the law *n.* A lack of knowledge of the applicable law.

ignorance of the law is no excuse [eks · *kyooss*] A legal saying referring to the **presumption** that everyone knows the law and that therefore ignorance of the law is no **defense**.

illegal [il · *lee* · gul] *adj.* Unlawful; contrary to law; illicit.
➤ unlawful, contrary to law, illicit, felonious, forbidden, improper, unauthorized, proscribed.

illegal consideration [ken · sid · e · *ray* · shen] *n.* An act or promise to act that is contrary to law or **public policy**. A contract cannot be based upon illegal consideration. *See* consideration.

illegal contract [*kon* · trakt] *n.* An agreement prohibited by law or that violates the law. *Note* that a contract is not illegal simply because it is invalid, **void, voidable**, or unenforceable.

illegal entry [*en* · tree] *n.* A federal offense committed by an alien who enters the country at an unauthorized time or place, or by fraudulent means, or to avoid examination by the **INS**.

illegal interest [*in* · trest] *n.* **Usury**; interest in excess of the rate allowed by law.

illegal search *n. See* unreasonable search and seizure.

illegality [il · lee · *gal* · i · tee] *n.* Unlawfulness. Illegality is not synonymous with irregularity, which is merely a failure to conform to a rule of procedure.
➤ unlawfulness, wrongdoing, criminality, malfeasance, transgression.

illegally obtained evidence [il · lee · gul · ee ub · *taned* ev · i · dense] *n.* Evidence obtained in a manner that would cause it to be inadmissible under the **exclusionary rule**. EXAMPLE: evidence obtained based upon a search warrant issued without **probable cause**, or a coerced confession.

illegitimate [il · le · *jit* · i · met] *adj.*
1. Contrary to law. 2. Wrong; erroneous;

improper; invalid. 3. As commonly used, an illegitimate child. *Compare* legitimate.
➤ unlawful, impermissible; wrong, erroneous, improper, invalid; bastard.

illegitimate child *n.* A child born to parents who are not married to each other. *Compare* legitimate child. *See* born out of wedlock.

illicit [il · *liss* · it] *adj.* Unlawful; illegal; forbidden by law. *Compare* licit.
➤ unlawful, illegal, forbidden by law, not permitted, improper, banned, proscribed, unauthorized.
Ant. authorized.

illicit cohabitation [ko · hab · i · *tay* · shen] *n.* Living together as man and wife, although not married to each other. This was a crime at **common law**. *See* cohabitation. *Compare* illicit relations.

illicit intercourse [*in* · ter · corse] *n. See* illicit relations.

illicit relations [re · *lay* · shenz] *n.* **Adultery** or **fornication**. *Compare* illicit cohabitation.

Illinois land trust [il · i · *noy*] *n. See* land trust.

illiterate [il · *lit* · er · it] *adj./n.* A term describing a person who is unable to read or write; unlearned; untaught.

illusory [il · *loose* · e · ree] *adj.* Based upon illusion; imaginary; fictitious; unreal; false.
➤ imaginary, fictitious, unreal, false, misleading, delusive, spurious, sham, seeming.

illusory contract [*kon* · trakt] *n.* An "agreement" that is not a contract in law because it is based upon an **illusory promise**. *See* contract.

illusory promise [*prom* · iss] *n.* A promise whose performance is completely up to the promisor. EXAMPLE: a promise by Jones to work for Brown for one year "unless I resign earlier." Because the carrying out of such a promise is optional, there is no mutuality, and therefore the promise cannot form the basis of a valid contract.

illustrate [*il* · luss · trayt] *v.* To demonstrate or exemplify.
➤ explain, demonstrate, clarify, illuminate, show, expound ("let me illustrate my point").

I

illustration [il · luss · tray · shun] n. 1. A representative example. 2. A drawing to accompany text.
➤ showing, example, depiction, explanation, demonstration, representation, case in point.

imbecility [im · be · sil · i · tee] n. A form of mental incapacity.
➤ mental incapacity, mental deficiency, feeble-mindedness.

imbracery [em · braiss · e · ree] n. Same as **embracery**.

imbue [im · bew] v. To infuse or saturate.
➤ instill, indoctrinate, permeate, drench, inculcate, pervade.

imitation [im · i · tay · shen] n. False likeness. See colorable imitation; infringement of trademark.
➤ forgery, fraud, reproduction, duplication, infringement.

immaterial [im · e · teer · ee · el] adj. Not material; irrelevant; not pertinent; of no consequence. See also impertinent.
➤ not material, irrelevant, not pertinent, not important, of no consequence, insignificant, unessential, minor, beside the point. Ant. material, relevant, significant.

immaterial allegation [al · e · gay · shen] n. An unessential, unnecessary, or superfluous **allegation** in a **pleading**. See also impertinent matter. Compare material allegation.

immaterial averment [a · ver · ment] n. Same as **immaterial allegation**.

immaterial evidence [ev · i · dense] n. Evidence that has little or no bearing upon the issues in a case or that does not tend to prove a **material fact**. Compare material evidence. See also irrelevant evidence.

immaterial issue [ish · oo] n. An issue or question with respect to a point that will not determine the outcome of the case.

immaterial variance [vair · ee · ense] n. An inconsistency between what a party **pleads** and what she **proves**, which is not so substantial as to mislead or prejudice the other party in maintaining his **cause of action** or **defense**. Compare fatal variance. See variance.

immediate [i · mee · dee · et] adj. 1. Close; near. 2. Prompt; instant. Immediate is an indefinite and elastic word as it applies to time, distance, and place. Its meaning is always relative to the event and dependent on the circumstances. EXAMPLE: "immediate vicinity" may mean either nearby or adjoining.
➤ close, near, direct, proximate; prompt, instant, speedy, timely; impending, upcoming.

immediate cause n. A phrase often used erroneously as a synonym for **proximate cause**. However, unlike proximate cause, it is not necessarily the primary cause of an occurrence, but rather the last in a string of events causing the occurrence.

immediate danger [dane · jer] n. Same as **imminent peril**.

immediate descent [de · sent] n. Under the **intestate laws**, inheritance directly by the heir without an intervening **degree of kinship** or **consanguinity**. EXAMPLES: from father to son; from grandfather to grandson when the father is dead. Compare mediate descent.

immediate family [fam · i · lee] n. Generally, a person's spouse, children, parents, and brothers and sisters.

immediate notice [noh · tiss] n. As used in insurance policies, notice given within a reasonable time after discovery of the **loss**.

immediately [i · mee · dee · et · lee] adv. 1. Promptly; with reasonable speed and without unnecessary delay. 2. Without engaging in intervening activity.
➤ promptly, instantly, at once, directly. Ant. later.

immemorial [im · e · more · ee · el] adj. Before human memory; in very ancient times. See legal memory. USAGE: "Milton has been telling stories since time immemorial."
➤ dateless, archaic, ancestral.

immigrant [im · i · grent] n. 1. A person who enters a country with the intention of living there permanently. 2. In the United States, every alien except those classes of aliens specified in the Immigration and Nationality Act. See immigration; permanent resident.
➤ foreigner, nonnative, alien, emigrant.

immigration [im · i · gray · shen] n. The coming of foreigners into a country for purposes of remaining there permanently. See immigrant; permanent resident.

➤ migration, admission, expatriation, alien entry, ingress, transmigration.

Immigration and Naturalization Service [im · i · *gray* · shen and nat · sher · e · li · *zay* · shen *ser* · viss] *n.* The federal agency with responsibility for administering the immigration laws. The duties of the **INS**, as it is more commonly known, include ascertaining the eligibility of persons who apply for entry into the country, determining the legal status of aliens, conducting naturalization **proceedings**, and carrying out deportations.

Immigration Service [im · i · *gray* · shen *ser* · viss] *n. See* Immigration and Naturalization Service.

imminent [*im* · i · nent] *adj.* About to happen. *Note* that "imminent" is not "eminent," which means distinguished or prominent.

➤ probable, impending, unavoidable, inevitable, close ("imminent danger").

imminent danger [*dane* · jer] *n.* Immediate danger of death or great bodily harm sufficient to justify a person who kills in self-defense.

imminent peril [*perr* · il] *n.* Danger so suddenly and immediately at hand that a person may be excused for not exercising reasonable judgment.

imminently dangerous article [*im* · i · nent · lee *dane* · jer · ess *ar* · tikl] *n.* Same as **dangerous instrumentality**.

immoral [im · *more* · el] *adj.* 1. Contrary to the welfare of the general public as measured by the standards of behavior of the community. 2. Although commonly used to refer solely to sexual misconduct, correct use may also include the following meanings, among others: unethical; unscrupulous; corrupt; dishonest; depraved; deviant; wicked; evil. *Compare* moral.

➤ unethical, unscrupulous, corrupt, dishonest, depraved, deviant, wicked, evil. *Ant.* moral, honest.

immoral consideration [ken · sid · e · *ray* · shen] *n.* **Consideration** contrary to good morals. *Compare* moral consideration. *See* immoral contract.

immoral contract [kon · trakt] *n.* An agreement based upon **immoral**

consideration. (EXAMPLE: a contract to commit a crime.) Such a contract is unenforceable.

immorality [im · more · *al* · i · tee] *n.* Conduct, behavior, or practices that are immoral.

➤ corruption, wrong, delinquency, debauchery.

immovables [im · *move* · eblz] *n.* Property that cannot be moved from place to place; real property. *Compare* movables.

immune [ih · *myoon*] *adj.* A high degree of resistance.

➤ sheltered, screened, exempt, excused, unexposed, safe, protected ("immune from prosecution").

immunity [im · *yoo* · ni · tee] *n.* 1. An exemption granted by law, contrary to the general rule; a **privilege**. Immunity may be granted to a class of persons (EXAMPLE: the immunity of conscientious objectors from military service) or to an individual (EXAMPLES: **immunity from prosecution**; the **privilege against self-incrimination**). *See also* interspousal immunity; judicial immunity; legislative immunity; sovereign immunity; waiver of immunity. 2. A state of invulnerability to disease.

➤ exemption, privilege, indemnity, release, insusceptibility, guarantee, absolution, safety ("absolute immunity").

immunity from prosecution [pross · e · *kyoo* · shen] *n.* A guaranty to a person that if he testifies against others he will not be prosecuted for his own criminal conduct. Immunity from prosecution is of two types, **transactional immunity** and **use immunity**.

impact [*im* · pakt] *n.* 1. The effect or significance of something. 2. Collision; force. *v.* To hit or strike with force.

➤ *n.* effect, meaning, consequence ("What was the impact of his speech?"); crash, collision, brunt, contact, striking ("The impact of the cars"). *v.* crash, smash, collide, touch, jolt.

impact rule [*im* · pakt] *n.* The rule, existing in only a few states, that for a plaintiff to recover **damages** for mental anguish in a **negligence** action, impact must have occurred, or at a minimum, there must have been physical contact.

impair [im · *pare*] *v.* To weaken or hinder. USAGE: "Alcohol usage impaired the attorney's ability to provide competent representation."
➤ hurt, hinder, stifle, taint, waste, weaken, deplete, devalue.
Ant. strengthen.

impairment [im · *pair* · ment] *n.*
1. Limitation; a lessening or reduction in quality, value, or strength. 2. Disability.
➤ limitation, defect, error, flaw, obstruction, disability, handicap.
impairment of capital [*kap* · i · tel] *n.* An undersupply in the **capital** of a corporation, but not necessarily insolvency.
impairment of obligation of contracts [ob · li · *gay* · shen of *kon* · trakts] *n.* A reference to the **contract clause** of the Constitution, which provides that the states cannot pass laws "impairing the obligation of contracts." *See* freedom of contract.

impanel [im · *pan* · el] *v.* To enroll; to list. The act of the clerk of court in listing the names of persons who have been selected for jury duty. *See* jury list; jury panel.
➤ list, enroll, enter, schedule, docket.

imparl [im · *parl*] *v.* To delay a lawsuit for the purpose of discussing a settlement.

impartial [im · *par* · shel] *adj.*
1. Indifferent as between the parties to a lawsuit. 2. Neutral; unbiased.
➤ fair, unbiased, neutral, unprejudiced, objective ("an impartial observer").
impartial juror [*joo* · rer] *n.* A juror who will render a verdict solely on the basis of the evidence.
impartial jury [*joo* · ree] *n.* A jury made up of **impartial jurors**. The **Sixth Amendment** guarantees every criminal defendant the right to be tried by an "impartial jury."
impartial trial [*try* · el] *n.* *See* fair and impartial trial.

impass [*im* · pass] *n.* A deadlock or dilemma. USAGE: "Negotiations had broken down; they were at an impass."
➤ cessation, stop, standstill, stalemate, dilemma, discontinuance, block.

impeach [im · *peech*] *v.* 1. To charge a public officer with defective performance in office. *See* malfeasance in office;

misfeasance in office. 2. To question the truthfulness of a witness or the authenticity of a document. 3. To accuse; to blame; to censure. 4. To question; to challenge. *See* impeachment.
➤ accuse, blame, censure, contradict, dispute, denounce, decry, castigate.

impeachment [im · *peech* · ment] *n.* 1. The constitutional process by which high elected officers of the United States, including the president, may be removed from office. The accusation (**articles of impeachment**) is made by the House of Representatives and tried by the Senate, which sits as an impeachment court. Under the Constitution, the grounds for impeachment are "treason, bribery, or other high crimes and misdemeanors." 2. The act of questioning a witness's credibility or the authenticity of a document. 3. The act of accusing, blaming, or censuring. 4. The act of questioning or challenging. *See* impeach.
➤ indictment, complaint, charge, castigation, vilification, censure, disapproval, reproof, discrediting, removal.
impeachment of verdict [*ver* · dikt] *n.* An attack against a verdict based upon the inappropriateness of the jury's deliberations or the manner in which it arrived at the verdict.
impeachment of witness [*wit* · nes] *n.* An attack on the credibility of a witness by proof that the facts about which he has testified are false, that his general reputation is bad, that he has previously made contradictory or inconsistent statements, or that he is biased or hostile. *See* impeach. *Also see* prior inconsistent statements; Jencks rule.

impediment [im · *ped* · i · ment] *n.* 1. A bar; a disqualification; a **civil disability**. EXAMPLE: failure to have reached one's majority is an **impediment to marriage**. 2. Any obstruction or obstacle.
➤ bar, disqualification, obstruction, obstacle, blockade, deterrent, barrier, hindrance.
impediment to marriage [*mehr* · ej] *n.* A **civil disability** that prevents marriage.

impel [im · *pell*] *v.* To drive forward.
➤ start, urge, motivate, mobilize, incite, launch, instigate, prompt, propel.

I

imperative [im · *perr* · e · tiv] *adj.*
Mandatory; compulsory; commanding.
➤ mandatory, urgent, compulsory, obligatory,
crucial, commanding.
Ant. unimportant, voluntary.

imperfect [im · *per* · fekt] *adj.* 1. As used
in the law, lacking in some essential legal
requirement. 2. Incomplete; flawed;
defective.
➤ incomplete, flawed, defective, deficient,
faulty, lacking, tainted, impaired,
unsatisfactory.

impermissible [im · per · *miss* · ih · bul]
adj. Illegal, inadmissible.
➤ illegal, wrongful, actionable, unsanctioned,
proscribed, punishable.

impersonation [im · per · se · *nay* · shen] *n.*
The act of pretending to be another. *See*
false impersonation.
➤ imitation, copy, fraud, representation.

impertinent [im · *per* · tin · ent] *adj.*
1. Having no bearing upon the issues raised
by the pleadings; irrelevant; immaterial;
inapplicable. 2. Impudent; irreverent;
disrespectful. *Compare* pertinent.
➤ irrelevant, inapplicable, unimportant,
unrelated; rude, disrespectful, surly,
abusive, discourteous.
  impertinent matter [*mat* · er] *n.* Matter
  in a **complaint** or other **pleading** which
  does not belong there. The court may order
  it to be stricken. *See* strike. *Also see*
  immaterial allegation; scandalous matter.

impetus [*im* · pe · tus] *n.* The motivation
or cause for something.
➤ stimulus, incentive, boast, pressure, push,
propellant, motive.

implausible [im · *plaus* · ih · bul] *adj.*
Doubtful; unbelievable; outrageous.
➤ unbelievable, incredible, unlikely,
questionable, inconceivable ("an
implausible alibi").

implead [im · *pleed*] *v.* 1. To institute an
impleader. 2. To sue.
➤ join, bring in, sue.

impleader [im · *pleed* · er] *n.* A defendant's
action in bringing into a lawsuit, as an
additional defendant, a party whom the
defendant asserts is responsible to the
plaintiff for the **damages** or other **remedy**
the plaintiff seeks. *Compare* interpleader;

joinder; joinder of parties. *See* implead.
See also third-party practice.

implicate [im · plih · kayt] *v.* To accuse;
to connect a person with criminal activity.
➤ involve, accuse, associate, inculpate,
incriminate, link, expose, entangle.
Ant. dissociate.

implicated [*im* · pli · kay · ted] *adj.* Involved.
➤ involved, accused, incriminated, linked,
connected.

implication [im · pli · *kay* · shen] *n.*
Something implied.
➤ suggestion, innuendo, insinuation, hint;
connection, involvement, complicity.

implicit [im · *pliss* · it] *adj.* Not directly
stated; implied.
➤ unstated, tacit, implied, suggested,
understood, unspoken, latent, virtual.
Ant. explicit, manifest.

implied [im · *plide*] *adj.* Something
intended although not expressed, or not
expressed in words. *Compare* express.
Also compare infer; inferred.
➤ implicit, suggested, inferred, assumed,
insinuated, tacit, undeclared ("an implied
contract").
Ant. express, explicit.

implied abrogation [ab · re · *gay* · shen]
n. *See* implied repeal.

implied acceptance [ak · *sep* · tense] *n.*
The acceptance of an offer understood from
the circumstances and from the acts of the
parties rather than specific words of acceptance. *See* acceptance; offer and acceptance.

implied agency [*ay* · jen · see] *n.* An
actual agency, the existence of which is
proven by deductions or inferences from
the facts and circumstances of the situation,
including the words and conduct of the
parties. *See* implied power. *Compare*
agency by estoppel; apparent authority.
Also compare actual authority.

implied agreement [a · *gree* · ment] *n.*
Same as **implied contract**.

implied authority [aw · *thaw* · ri · tee]
n. The authority of an agent to do whatever acts are necessary to carry out her
express authority. EXAMPLE: an attorney
retained to commence a legal action has
the implied authority to file such pleadings
as she feels are appropriate.

implied by law *n.* Arising by **operation of law**.

implied condition [ken · *dish* · en] *n.* A **condition** that is not expressed but that is **inferred** by the law from the acts of the parties.

implied confession [ken · *fesh* · en] *n.* An accused's admission of guilt inferred from the fact that he submits himself to the mercy of the court. *See* confession. *Also see* admission.

implied consent [ken · *sent*] *n.* Acquiescence or assent inferred from conduct that demonstrates concurrence. *Compare* informed consent. *See* implied consent statutes.

implied consent statutes [ken · *sent stat* · shoots] *n.* State statutes which provide that every person who operates a motor vehicle on the state's highways impliedly consents to permit the state to test the alcohol concentration in her blood to determine if she is guilty of driving while intoxicated. *See* blood alcohol concentration.

implied consideration [ken · sid · e · *ray* · shen] *n.* **Consideration** deduced from the conduct of the parties, rather than expressly stipulated.

implied contract [*kon* · trakt] *n.* Implied contracts are of two types: contracts *implied in fact,* which the law infers from the circumstances, conduct, acts, or the relationship of the parties rather than from their spoken words; and contracts *implied in law,* which are **quasi contracts** or **constructive contracts** imposed by the law, usually to prevent **unjust enrichment**.

implied covenant [*kov* · e · nent] *n.* An unexpressed **covenant** that the law will infer from language used in a deed or lease.

implied dedication [ded · i · *kay* · shen] *n.* 1. Passive acquiescence by an owner of land to its use by the public. 2. Affirmative acts by the owner of land that demonstrate an intent to devote the property to public use. *See* dedication.

implied easement [*eez* · ment] *n.* An **easement** created by **operation of law** on the theory that whenever a person **conveys** land adjacent to land he retains, he intends to include in the **conveyance** whatever rights are necessary for beneficial use

and enjoyment of the property he has conveyed. *Compare* implied reservation.

implied in fact *n.* *See* implied contract.

implied in law *n.* *See* implied by law.

implied intent [in · *tent*] *n.* 1. Intention to commit a crime, inferred from the fact that the crime was committed. *See* intent. *See also* criminal intent; *mens rea*; specific intent. 2. Intention deduced from conduct.

implied invitation [in · va · *tay* · shen] *n.* An act, other than an **express invitation**, by an owner or occupant of premises which reasonably causes or allows a person to believe that it is intended that she enter the premises. *See* business invitee; invitation; invitee.

implied malice [*mal* · iss] *n.* **Malice** inferred from a vicious or spiteful act intentionally committed. *Compare* actual malice; express malice. *See* constructive malice.

implied notice [*noh* · tiss] *n.* A kind of **actual notice** rather than **constructive notice**; notice which the law presumes a person had because he was aware of the facts generally and was easily able to **perfect** his knowledge. *Compare* express notice. *See* presumption.

implied power [*pow* · er] *n.* 1. The power necessary to carry out a **power** expressly granted. EXAMPLE: the power of a corporation to do those things necessary to accomplish the purposes for which it was organized. 2. The power of a department or an agency of government to perform such acts as are necessary to achieve the objectives of the statute or constitution under which the agency was established. *See also* inherent power. *Compare* enumerated powers.

implied promise [*prom* · iss] *n.* A nonexistent promise created by the law as the basis for a contract **implied in law**. *See* implied contract.

implied repeal [re · *peel*] *n.* *See* repeal of statute.

implied reservation [re · zer · *vay* · shen] *n.* The inferred **reservation** of a **right** or an **easement** from a **conveyance** of land, when such right or easement is essential to enjoyment of the land retained by the grantor. *See* reservation. *Compare* exception; implied easement.

I

implied trust *n.* A **trust** created by the law on the basis of legal **presumptions** as to the intention of the parties, usually to prevent fraud. EXAMPLES: a **constructive trust**; a **resulting trust**.

implied waiver [*way* · ver] *n.* A **waiver** inferred from the conduct of the parties. *Compare* express waiver.

implied warranty [*war* · en · tee] *n.* In the sale of personal property, a **warranty** by the seller, inferred by law (whether or not the seller intended to create the warranty), as to the quality or condition of the goods sold.

Under the **Uniform Commercial Code**, the most important implied warranties are the *implied warranty of merchantability* and the *implied warranty of fitness for a particular purpose*. In any sale of goods, a warranty of merchantability (fitness for general or customary purposes) is implied if the seller normally sells such goods. An implied **warranty of fitness for a particular purpose** exists when the seller has reason to know the purpose for which the buyer wants the goods and the buyer is relying on the seller to furnish goods suited to that purpose.

implied warranty of fitness for a particular purpose [war · en · tee of *fit* · ness for a per · tik · yoo · ler *per* · pess] *n.* *See* implied warranty.

implied warranty of merchantability [*war* · en · tee of mer · chen · te · *bil* · i · tee] *n.* *See* implied warranty.

imply [im · *plie*] *v.* To suggest without stating directly; to intimate.
➤ insinuate, indicate, hint, connote, denote, allude, suggest.

import [im · port] *n.* *Singular* of **imports**. *See* imports.
v. [im · *port*] To bring or ship goods into the country.
➤ *n.* importance, significance, meaning, seriousness.
v. introduce, carry, transport, convey, ship.

important [im · *por* · tent] *adj.* Of significant worth or value.
➤ momentous, noteworthy, powerful, outstanding, illustrious, major, grand; urgent, crucial, critical, vital, necessary.

importation *n.* The sending of goods from one country to another. *Compare* exportation.

imports [*im* · ports] *n.* Goods brought into one country from another.

impose [im · *poze*] *v.* 1. To place a burden or duty upon a person. USAGE: "impose a tax"; "impose sentence"; "impose on (one's) hospitality." 2. To take unwanted advantage of someone.
➤ burden, inflict, levy, order, enact ("Do you think the government will impose a new tax?"); intrude, interpose, interfere, transgress, force, infringe ("he always imposes himself").

imposition [im · po · *zish* · en] *n.* 1. A tax. 2. A burden. *See* impose.
➤ tax, impost, charge, duty, toll, levy; burden, constraint, encroachment, encumbrance, hindrance.

impossibility [im · poss · i · *bil* · i · tee] *n.* That which cannot be done. *Compare* impracticability.
➤ futility, insurmountability, infeasibility, unattainability, failure, unfeasibility, difficulty, failure.

impossibility of performance [per · *form* · enss] *n.* A rule of contract law that excuses a party from performing under a contract when, through no fault of her own, performance is not possible. EXAMPLES: when the subject matter of the contract ceases to exist (a house under a contract of sale burns to the ground); when the transaction is made illegal (after a contract for their sale is entered into, the possession of handguns is prohibited by statute). *See also* frustration of contract doctrine; frustration of purpose. *Compare* impracticability; legal impossibility.

impossible [im · *poss* · ih · bul] *adj.* That which seems unable to be done or achieved.
➤ unachievable, unworkable, absurd, unobtainable, inconceivable, preposterous, hopeless.

impost [*im* · post] *n.* A tax; a duty. *See* customs duties.
➤ tax, duty, levy.

impotence [*im* · pe · tenss] *n.* Inability, on the part of a male, to have sexual intercourse. Impotence is a ground for annulment of marriage in some jurisdictions, and for divorce in others. *Note* that impotence is not sterility.

➤ inability, incapacity, weakness, ineffectiveness, powerlessness, ineptitude, incapacity, sterility, barrenness.

impotent [im · pe · tent] *adj.* Incapable of achieving a result; without power.
➤ powerless, helpless, ineffective, sterile, effete, barren, prostrate.

impound [im · *pound*] *v.* To hold animals, goods, documents, or funds in legal custody.
➤ take possession of, secure, seize, confiscate, sequester, appropriate.

impounding the record [im · *pound* · ing the rek · erd] *n. See* sealing of the record.

impracticability [im · prak · ti · ke · *bil* · i · tee] *n.* 1. A legal term unique to the **Uniform Commercial Code**, from the provision of the **UCC** that excuses a seller from the obligation to deliver goods when delivery has become unrealistic because of unforeseen circumstances. *Compare* impossibility of performance; legal impossibility. 2. The state of being unworkable, unrealistic, or not capable of successful or worthwhile accomplishment.

impracticable [im · *prak* · tih · ke · bul] *adj.* Incapable of being accomplished.
➤ unattainable, unfeasible, impossible, unrealizable, unmanageable, unwieldy, unviable.
Ant. feasible.

impress [im · *press*] *v.* 1. To affect or influence. 2. To seize.
➤ reach, touch, affect, influence, inspire, stir; seize, impound, acquire, levy, take, sequester.

imprisonment [im · *priz* · en · ment] *n.* 1. The detention of a person following a sentence for a crime or while awaiting trial on a criminal charge. 2. Any restraint upon a person, contrary to his wishes, which deprives him of his freedom of movement. *See* false imprisonment.
➤ detention, restraint, confinement, detainment, incarceration.

improper [im · *prop* · er] *adj.* Not in accordance with truth or proper behavior.
➤ incorrect, indecent, unallowable, unsuitable, forbidden, erroneous, unsound, immoral ("improper advances").

impropriety [im · pro · *pry* · eh · tee] *n.* 1. An act of misconduct. 2. That which is socially unacceptable.
➤ imprudence, indiscretion, misbehavior, incorrectness; tactlessness, bad taste, indecorum, indecency, indelicacy.

improve [im · *proov*] *v.* 1. To increase the value of something by alteration or addition. 2. To make better.
➤ make better, upgrade, enhance, enrich, fix, renovate ("to improve one's position").

improved land [im · *proovd*] *n.* Land whose value has been increased by grading, landscaping, introduction of utilities, the construction of buildings, and the like.

improvement [im · *proov* · ment] *n.* 1. Anything that enhances the value of real property permanently. EXAMPLES: buildings; fences; landscaping; a swimming pool. *Compare* repair. 2. A change for the better.
➤ bettering, enhancement, advancement, enrichment, renovation.

improvement bond *n.* A **bond** issued by a municipality or other **public authority** to finance public improvements (EXAMPLES: school construction; sewer installation).

improvement patent [*pat* · ent] *n.* A **patent** to modify an existing invention so as to increase its usefulness or effectiveness. *Compare* design patent; utility patent.

improvidently granted [im · *prov* · i · dent · lee gran · ted] *adv.* A term sometimes used by a court to describe an order or **judgment** that it feels it granted unwisely.

impugn [im · *pyoon*] *v.* To condemn; to make adverse comments.
➤ assail, criticize, discredit, denounce, contest, disbelieve, raise questions about, oppose.

impulse [im · puls] *n.* An uncontrollable action or thought.
➤ desire, inclination, drive, force, stimulant ("an uncontrollable impulse").

impulsive [im · *pul* · siv] *adj.* Acting without thought; emotional; spontaneous.
➤ bold, rash, unthinking, spontaneous, hasty, risky, sudden, unadvised, unconsidered.
Ant. planned.

impunity [im · *pyoon* · ih · tee] *n.* Freedom from punishment or harm.

I

➤ exemption, absolution, freedom, immunity, protection, privilege ("act with impunity").

impute [im · *pewt*] *v.* To attribute, ascribe, or charge. *See* imputed.

➤ ascribe, attribute, credit, assign, attach.

imputed [im · *pew* · ted] *adj.* 1. That which is attributed to a person, not because she personally performed the act (or personally had knowledge or notice), but because of her relationship to another person for whose acts, omissions, knowledge, or notice she is legally responsible. USAGE: "The neglect by his paralegal in this matter will be imputed to attorney Jones." *See* agency. 2. Blamed; implicated; ascribed; charged.

➤ attributed, blamed, implicated, ascribed, charged ("The paralegal's neglect is the attorney's imputed neglect").

imputed knowledge [*nawl* · edj] *n.* 1. An agent's knowledge that is binding upon his principal because of their **agency relationship**. 2. Knowledge of facts charged to a person because anyone of ordinary common sense would know them. 3. That which a person has a duty to know and the means of knowing. *Compare* actual knowledge; personal knowledge. *See* knowledge.

imputed negligence [*neg* · li · jenss] *n.* The **negligence** of one person which, by reason of her relationship to another person, is chargeable to the other person. EXAMPLE: an employer is liable for the negligence of his employee which occurs within the **scope of employment**.

in *prep.* Within. "In" generally indicates location. The word *in* also precedes many Latin and French phrases in the law and can have various meanings, including in, on, to, into, within, while, according to, in the course of, at, and among.

in absentia [ab · *sen* · sha] (*Latin*) Means "in absence"; although absent. USAGE: "I received my degree *in absentia* because I was in the Army by graduation day."

in action [*ak* · shen] *See* chose in action.

in aid of In support of.

in autre droit [*oh* · tre drwah] (*French*) Means "in the right of another"; on another's behalf; as a representative of another. EXAMPLE: an action brought by a **guardian** on behalf of his **ward**. *Compare* in his (or her) own right. *See* representative capacity.

in banc [bonk] (*French*) Same as *en banc*.

in bank Same as *en banc*.

in bar *See* plea in bar.

in being [*bee* · ing] In existence; alive. A fetus is sometimes considered a **life in being** in the law of **future interests**.

in blank A term of reference to any instrument drafted and executed with blank spaces left to be filled in later. EXAMPLE: a check signed by the maker, with the name of the payee, or the amount, or both, not filled in. *See* blank indorsement.

in bulk As a lot; all together; not broken down into individual items or articles. *See* bulk; bulk sale; in gross.

in camera [*kam* · e · ra] **In chambers**; in private. A term referring to a hearing or any other judicial business conducted in the judge's office or in a courtroom that has been cleared of spectators. USAGE: "an in camera inspection of the evidence."

in chambers [*chame* · berz] Refers to any judicial business, including a hearing, conducted in the judge's office. *See* in camera.

in chief *See* case in chief.

in commerce [*kawm* · erss] A reference to **interstate commerce**. *See* commerce. *See also* affecting commerce; commerce clause; engaged in commerce.

in common [*kawm* · en] That which is shared, used, done, or owned by more than one person. EXAMPLES: a public park; a condominium; a **tenancy in common**. *Compare* joint. *See* common. *Compare* several; severalty.

in contemplation of death [kon · tem · *play* · shen] *See* contemplation of death.

in corpore [*kore* · po · re] (*Latin*) In body; in substance. *See* corporeal.

in custody [*kus* · te · dee] Under the direct or indirect restraint of the police. *See* custody. *Also see* custodial interrogation; Miranda rule.

in due course In its proper time; in the usual order of things. *See* holder in due course; payment in due course.

in effect [e · *fekt*] 1. Of legal consequence; in force; in operation. *See* effective. 2. In fact. 3. Being the same thing as; essentially; effectively.

I

in equity [*ek* · wi · tee] 1. In a **court of equity**. 2. In fairness; in accordance with the rules of equity. *See* equity.

in esse [*ess* · ee] (*Latin*) In being. *See* in being; life in being.

in evidence [*ev* · i · dense] Before the court, having been offered and received into evidence. USAGE: "That fact is not in evidence."

in extremis [eks · *trem* · iss] (*Latin*) Literally, "the outer edges," meaning the last stage before death; at the point of death.

in fact Real; in reality; referring to something that actually occurred as opposed to a **legal fiction** or something that the law presumes to have occurred. *Compare* in law.

in fee Having or owning a **fee estate** or a fee interest in land. *See* fee.

in flagrante delicto [flay · *gran* · tee dee · *lik* · tow] (*Latin*) Means, literally, "while the wrong is blazing," i.e., in the act of committing an offense; red-handed.

in force Legally effective; in effect. USAGE: "This contract will be in force until the last day of the month." *See* enforceable.

in forma pauperis [*for* · mah *paw* · per · iss] (*Latin*) Means "in the form (or manner) of a poor person." A term pertaining to the exemption from court costs that may be granted to indigent persons to enable them to file a lawsuit or an appeal.

in full 1. Relating to complete performance, especially of a monetary obligation. USAGE: "payment in full." 2. All the facts.

in full settlement [*setl* · ment] *See* full settlement.

in futuro [fyoo · *tyoo* · roh] (*Latin*) In the future; at a future time.

in good order [*or* · der] *See* good order.

in gross 1. Taken as a whole; without deduction. *See* gross. *See also* in bulk. 2. A term referring to certain kinds of rights that attach to the person rather than to land. EXAMPLE: **easement in gross**.

in his (or her) own right 1. Refers to a lawsuit brought by a person on his or her own behalf, as opposed to a suit a person brings in a **representative capacity**. *Compare* in autre droit. 2. Referring to owning property, as distinguished from holding **title** as the representative of another person (for EXAMPLE, a **trustee** for a **beneficiary** or a **guardian** for a **ward**).

in issue [*ish* · ew] *See* at issue.

in kind 1. Payment in goods or services instead of money. 2. Repayment of loaned goods (EXAMPLE: clothing) or commodities (EXAMPLE: coffee) with goods or commodities of the same kind rather than the identical things borrowed. *See* in specie; kind.

in law 1. Under the law. 2. That which is presumed or implied by the law to have occurred, as distinguished from that which occurred in fact. 3. In **law** as opposed to in **equity**. *Also compare* in equity.

in lieu of [loo] In place of; instead of; in substitution for. USAGE: "Will you allow me to pay in Canadian funds in lieu of U.S. currency?"

➤ in place of, for, instead of, in substitution for.

in limine [*lim* · e · nee] (*Latin*) Means "at the outset." Appears in the context of **motion in limine**, a motion made before the commencement of a trial which requests the court to prohibit the adverse party from introducing prejudicial evidence at trial. *See* motion.

in litem [*ly* · tem] (*Latin*) *See* ad litem.

in loco parentis [*loh* · koh pa · *ren* · tis] (*Latin*) Means "in the place of parents." Describes a person who, in the absence of a child's parent or guardian, and without formal legal approval, temporarily assumes a parent's obligations with respect to the child. EXAMPLE: a foster parent.

in open court [*o* · pen] Proceedings in court in public session rather than **in chambers** or **in camera**.

in pais [pay] (*French*) *See* pais. *Also see* estoppel in pais.

in pari delicto [*pah* · ree de · *lik* · toh] (*Latin*) Equally at fault.

in pari materia [*pah* · ree ma · *teer* · ee · ah] (*Latin*) Meaning "in connection with the matter"; in connection with the same subject. USAGE: "These two statutes are *in pari materia* because they both regulate the same activity."

in perpetuity [per · pet · *yoo* · i · tee] Forever.

in person [*per* · sen] Refers to appearing without counsel and personally conducting a lawsuit in which one is a party. *See* appearance. *See also* in propria persona; *pro se*.

I

in personam [per · *soh* · nam] (*Latin*) Means "in person." *See* in personam action. *Compare* in rem.

in personam action [per · *soh* · nam ak · shen] A legal action whose purpose is to obtain a **judgment** against a person, as opposed to a judgment against property. Most lawsuits are in personam actions. *See* in personam; judgment in personam; jurisdiction in personam. *Compare* in rem action; quasi in rem action.

in personam judgment [per · *soh* · nam juj · ment] *See* judgment in personam.

in personam jurisdiction [per · *soh* · nam joo · ris · *dik* · shen] *See* jurisdiction in personam.

in possession [po · *zesh* · en] Holding possession; having possession.

in propria persona [*pro* · pree · ah per · *soh* · nah] (*Latin*) Literally, "in one's proper person"; same meaning as in person and *pro se*.

in re [ray] (*Latin*) "In the matter of." Certain types of lawsuits, particularly *ex parte* proceedings and **in rem actions**, are captioned "In re." An EXAMPLE of a caption or heading in such a proceeding might be: *In re William Smith and Mary Smith, Father and Mother of Ronald Smith, a Minor.*

in rem [rem] (*Latin*) Means "in the thing." *See* in rem action. *Compare in personam.*

in rem action [ak · shen] A **legal action** brought against property (EXAMPLES: an **action to quiet title**; a **civil forfeiture**), as opposed to an action brought against the person. An EXAMPLE of the caption or heading of an action *in rem* brought by the government might be: *United States v. A Parcel of Land Known as 123 Main Street, Middleboro, Ohio. Compare* in personam action. *Also compare* quasi in rem action. *See* judgment in rem; jurisdiction in rem.

in session [*sesh* · en] *See* session.

in situ [*sy* · too] (*Latin*) "At the site"; in position. *See* situs.

in specie [*spee* · shee] (*Latin*) 1. **In kind**. 2. Payment in gold or silver coins rather than paper money. USAGE: "payment *in specie*."

in stirpes [*ster* · peez] (*Latin*) *See* per stirpes.

in terrorem clause [ter · *raw* · rem] A clause in a will which provides that a beneficiary who contests the will shall be deprived of his **bequest** or **devise**.

in the course of employment [em · *ploy* · ment] *See* course of employment.

in the matter of [*mat* · er] A form of captioning a case, sometimes used instead of *in re* and meaning the same thing.

in the ordinary course of business [*or* · din · e · ree course of *biz* · ness] *See* ordinary course of business.

in the presence of the court [*prez* · ense] *See* presence of the court.

in the scope of employment [em · *ploy* · ment] *See* scope of employment.

in toto [*toh* · toh] (*Latin*) Completely; in the whole; altogether.

in transit [*tran* · zit] In passing; while passing through; while in or on a conveyance or carrier. *See* transit.

in trust 1. The status of property held by a **trustee**. 2. A phrase used in a document when a person intends to create a **trust**.

in vitro fertilization [*vee* · tro fer · ti · li · *zay* · shen] Medical procedure by which the ovum of a woman who is unable to conceive normally is fertilized with a male sperm, in a test tube or similar artificial environment, and then implanted in her uterus so that she may carry the embryo to term and give birth. *See also* embryo transplantation; surrogate motherhood.

inability [in · uh · *bil* · ih · tee] *n.* The lack of sufficient power or skill.
➤ inadequacy, helplessness, failure, ineptness, incompetency, incapability, powerlessness.

inactive [in · act · iv] *adj.* 1. Not engaged in activity. 2. A feeling of weakness.
➤ idle, inert, inoperative; deficient, lacking, incapable, unsatisfactory; feeble, helpless, disabled.

inadequate [in · *ad* · e · kwet] *adj.* 1. Insufficient; deficient. 2. Ineffective.
➤ incomplete, wanting, lacking, defective, substandard, faulty, inapt, scanty, weak.

inadequate consideration [ken · sid · e · *ray* · shen] *n.* A price given for the subject matter of a contract that is worth less than its value. *Compare* adequate consideration. *See* consideration.

inadequate damages [*dam* · e · jez] *n.* An **award** so small that it bears no reasonable relation to the loss suffered by the plaintiff. *See also* inadequate remedy at law. *See* damages.

inadequate remedy at law [*rem* · e · dee] *n.* A term meaning the plaintiff's rights are more effectively remedied by granting an **injunction, specific performance**, or some other form of **equitable relief** than by awarding **damages**. *Compare* adequate remedy at law. *See* remedy.

inadmissible [in · ad · *mis* · ibl] *adj.* That which should not be admitted, allowed, or considered.
➤ objectionable, not allowed, banned, disallowed, unacceptable, excludable, barred, improper.

inadmissible evidence [ev · *i* · dense] *n.* Evidence that a court may not admit and consider in a case before it. EXAMPLE: **hearsay evidence**.

inalienable [in · *ale* · yen · able] *adj.* 1. Incapable of being **conveyed** or transferred; nontransferable. 2. Incapable of being withdrawn or taken away. *Compare* alienable. *See* alien; alienate.
➤ nontransferable, absolute, permanent, inherent, unforfeitable ("inalienable rights").

inalienable rights *n.* Fundamental **constitutional rights**; inherent rights. EXAMPLES: freedom of speech; **due process of law**; **equal protection of the laws**.

inapplicable [in · ap · *lik* · ebl] *adj.* Inappropriate; irrelevant; that which cannot be applied. *Compare* applicable.
➤ inappropriate, improper, irrelevant, extraneous, immaterial ("The statute is inapplicable to this activity").

inauguration [in · awg · yer · *ay* · shen] *n.* 1. The ceremony by which a person elected to high office is installed into office. 2. A beginning; the act of putting into effect.
➤ beginning, putting into effect, induction, consecration, swearing in.

Inc. Abbreviation of **Incorporated**, which often forms a part of a company's complete corporate name. EXAMPLE: "Jack & Jill, Inc."

incapacity [in · ke · *pass* · i · tee] *n.* 1. Lack of legal competency. 2. Lack of ability to understand. *Compare* capacity. 3. Under **workers' compensation acts**, disability.
➤ feebleness, dotage, incompetence, inability, infirmity, weakness, helplessness, lack of fitness.

incarcerate [in · *kar* · ser · ate] *v.* To imprison; to confine in a prison or jail.
➤ jail, confine, imprison, hold captive, restrain ("to incarcerate the convicted criminal").

incendiary [in · *sen* · dee · e · ree] *adj.* Describes any substance that tends to start a fire or that is used to start a fire. *n.* A person guilty of **arson** or an attempt to commit arson.
➤ *n.* arsonist, houseburner, pyromaniac.

incentive [in · *sen* · tiv] *n.* Lure; inducement; motivation.
➤ motivation, inducement, impulse, cause, catalyst, motive, allure, attraction ("an incentive to succeed").

incentive pay [in · *sen* · tiv] *n.* Employee compensation over and above regular salary or wages as an inducement for additional production. *See* bonus.

inception [in · *sep* · shen] *n.* 1. The initial stage. 2. The beginning.
➤ initial stage, starting point, birth, genesis, initiation; beginning, commencement, start. *Ant.* end; death, extermination.

incest [*in* · sest] *n.* Sexual intercourse between persons so closely related that the law prohibits their marriage to each other.

inchoate [in · *koh* · ate] *adj.* Imperfect; not completely formed; just beginning.
➤ imperfect, inadequate, not completely formed, partial, developing, undeveloped, beginning, rudimentary ("inchoate interest"). *Ant.* perfected, completed.

inchoate dower [*dow* · er] *n.* A wife's right to receive an interest in real estate owned by her husband if she survives him and has not previously released her interest. *See* dower.

inchoate interest [*in* · trest] *n.* An interest that has not yet developed. EXAMPLE: **inchoate dower**. *See* interest.

inchoate lien [*leen*] *n.* A **lien** that is ineffective with respect to everyone but

I

the creditor and the debtor because it has not been recorded.

inchoate right *n.* *See* inchoate interest.

incident [*in* · si · dent] *adj.* Likely to happen; normally occurring.
n. 1. An event or occurrence of significance because of its connection with a main or principal event or occurrence. 2. Any event or occurrence.
➤ *adj.* following, related to, relative to, associated, implicated.
n. event, occasion, happening, occurrence, experience.

incident of ownership [*oh* · ner · ship] *n.* That which tends to indicate ownership. EXAMPLE: having the right to change the beneficiary of a life insurance policy indicates that one owns the policy. *See also* indicia of ownership.

incident to employment [em · *ploy* · ment] *n.* A term defining compensable injuries under **workers' compensation acts**. The phrase has the same meaning as "in the line of duty." *See also* course of employment; scope of employment.

incidental [in · si · *den* · tel] *adj.* Secondary to the main reason or purpose; dependent; linked.
➤ secondary, subordinate, minor, additional, dependent, linked, contingent.
Ant. primary.

incidental beneficiary [ben · e · *fish* · ee · e · ree] *n.* A person to whom the benefits of a contract between two other people accrue merely as a matter of happenstance. An incidental beneficiary may not sue to enforce such a contract. *Compare* third-party beneficiary. *See* beneficiary.

incidental damages [*dam* · e · jez] *n.* The term used in the **Uniform Commercial Code** for **consequential damages**. They include charges incurred in connection with stopping delivery or returning goods when there has been a **breach of contract**. *See* damages.

incidental use *n.* In zoning law, a use of premises that is collateral to the main use.

incite [in · *site*] *v.* 1. To arouse to action, sometimes to violence or riot. 2. To instigate.
➤ arouse, stir up, encourage, goad, inflame, instigate, set in motion, awaken, energize.

included offense [o · *fenss*] *n.* *See* lesser included offense.

inclusive [in · *cloos* · iv] *adj.* All-encompassing; all-inclusive.
➤ all-embracing, comprehensive, extensive, exhaustive, full, sweeping, broad.
Ant. exlusive, selective.

income [*in* · kum] *n.* The gain derived from **capital** or from labor, including profit gained through a sale or conversion of **capital assets**. *See also* adjusted gross income; earned income; fixed income; gross income; net income; ordinary income; taxable income; unearned income.
➤ wages, salary, earning, profit, livelihood.

income-bearing [*bare* · ing] *adj.* Producing income. EXAMPLE: a bond that yields interest.

income-producing property [pro · *doos* · ing *prop* · er · tee] *n.* Same as **income property**.

income property [*prop* · er · tee] *n.* Property owned for the purpose of producing income. EXAMPLE: an apartment building.

income statement [*state* · ment] *n.* An itemization of a person's income and expenses during a specific period. *See also* financial statement; profit and loss statement.

income tax *n.* A tax based on income, personal or corporate. The **Internal Revenue Code**, which is the federal tax law, taxes income from "whatever source derived." Many states and municipalities tax income as well.

income tax return [re · *tern*] *n.* *See* tax return.

incommunicado [in · kum · yoo · ni · *kah* · doh] *adj./adv.* Cut off from being able to communicate with anyone. USAGE: "The police held her incommunicado for eight hours after her arrest."
➤ isolated, cutoff, sequestered, separate.

incompatibility [in · kum · pat · e · *bil* · e · tee] *n.* A conflict in personality and temperament. As a requirement for **no-fault divorce**, a conflict so deep it cannot be altered or adjusted, rendering it impossible for the parties to continue to live together in a normal marital relationship.

incompatible [in · kum · *pat* · ih · bul] *adj.*
1. In a state of disagreement or conflict.
2. Mutually exclusive; contradictory.
➤ antagonistic, discordant, disagreeing, uncongenial, hostile; contradictory, conflicting, antithetical ("incompatible arguments").

incompetence [in · *kawm* · pe · tense] *n.*
Incapacity or inadequacy. *See* incompetency; incompetent person.
➤ incompetency, neglect, inability, inadequacy, ineptness.

incompetency [in · *kawm* · pe · ten · see] *n.*
1. The condition, state, or status of an **incompetent person**. 2. Lack of ability. *Compare* competency.

incompetent [in · *kawm* · pe · tent] *adj.*
Invalid; unqualified; inept; inadequate. *n.* A term commonly used for **incompetent person**. *See* incompetency.
➤ *adj.* invalid, unqualified, incapable, inept, inefficient, bungling, inadequate, deficient, insufficient.
Ant. competent, skilled, able.

incompetent evidence [*ev* · i · dense] *n.*
Invalid evidence. (EXAMPLE: testimony that violates the **parol evidence rule**.) Incompetent evidence is inadmissible. *Compare* competent evidence. *See* inadmissible evidence.

incompetent person [*per* · sen] *n.* A person (EXAMPLES: a minor; an insane person) who is not legally qualified for a specific activity (EXAMPLES: giving testimony; entering into a contract) by reason of **nonage** or **mental incapacity**. *Compare* competent; competent person.

incomprehensible
[in · kom · pre · *hen* · sih · bul] *adj.*
Incapable of being understood.
➤ unfathomable, puzzling, inconceivable, inexplicable, unimaginable, amazing.

inconclusive [in · kon · *kloo* · siv] *adj.*
Subject to disproof; subject to rebuttal; not conclusive. USAGE: "The plaintiff's case was dismissed because the evidence in support of his claim was inconclusive." *Compare* conclusive presumption.
➤ unproven, unpersuasive, weak, unconvincing, indefinite, unsubstantiated, uncorroborated.

inconsequential [in · kon · sih · *kwen* · shul] *adj.* Of no significance; trifling, trivial.
➤ unimportant, trifling, minor, trivial, immaterial, irrelevant ("an inconsequential detail").
Ant. important, significant, material.

inconsistency [in · kun · *sis* · ten · see] *n.*
A contradiction or irregularity.
➤ contradiction, variance, difference, disparity, divergence, inconsonance ("an inconsistency in his testimony").

inconsistent [in · kun · *sis* · tent] *adj.* Not in harmony or accord; contradictory of one another.
➤ incompatible, contradictory, conflicting, discordant, opposing.
inconsistent statements [*state* · ments] *n. See* prior inconsistent statements. *See also* quasi admission.

inconspicuous [in · kon · *spik* · yoo · us] *adj.* Not easily noticed.
➤ unnoticed, unobtrusive, unseen, unperceivable, indistinct, hidden, blurred.

incontestability provision
[in · kon · test · a · *bil* · i · tee pro · *vizh* · en] *n.* A provision in a life or health insurance policy that, after a specified period of time, the insurer shall be unable to challenge the validity of the policy on the basis of the untruthfulness of the application. *See also* preexisting condition clause.

incontestable [in · kon · *test* · ih · bul] *adj.* Irrefutable; incapable of being disputed.
➤ clear, conclusive, irrefutable, unassailable, undeniable, unambiguous.

incontrovertible [in · kon · tre · *ver* · tibl] *adj.* So clear as to be beyond dispute.
➤ incontestable, definitive, conclusive, certain, noncontestable.

inconvenience [in · kun · *vee* · nee · enss] *n.* Annoyance; bother; hardship. *See* forum non conveniens.
➤ annoyance, nuisance, bother, burden, hardship, hindrance, hassle.

incorporate [in · *kore* · per · ate] *v.* 1. To form a corporation. 2. To combine in one unit; to include.
➤ combine, include, merge, weave, fuse, mix ("incorporate graphs into the presentation").

incorporated [in · *kore* · per · ay · ted] *adj.* Formed as a corporation.

incorporation [in · kore · per · *ay* · shen] *n.* 1. The act of forming a corporation. 2. The act of combining one thing with another.

incorporation by reference [*ref* · e · renss] *n.* Making a document a part of another document by referring to it in the second document with the stated intention of including it. USAGE: "Our written agreement of August 11, 1992, is hereby incorporated into this contract by reference."

incorporator [in · *kore* · per · ay · ter] *n.* A person who, alone or with others, forms a corporation.

incorporeal [in · kore · *pore* · ee · el] *adj.* Having no body or substance; without physical existence. *Compare* corporeal. *See also* intangible.
➤ intangible, bodiless, nonphysical, nonmaterial, spiritual.
Ant. tangible, material.

incorporeal hereditaments [herr · eh · *dit* · ah · ment] *n.* An inheritable right arising out of physical property, usually land, but not a right in the property itself. EXAMPLE: the right to receive rent from real property. *Compare* corporeal hereditaments; corporeal property. *See* intangible property.

incorporeal property [*prop* · er · tee] *n.* A property interest in a **legal right**. *Compare* corporeal property. *See* incorporeal right.

incorporeal right *n.* A **right** that has no tangible substance. EXAMPLE: the right to sue (i.e., a **cause of action**). *See* intangible property. *Also see* chose in action.

incorrect [in · ko · *rekt*] *adj.* Wrong; improper; faulty.
➤ mistaken, wrong, unfactual, inaccurate, false, amiss, erroneous.

incorrigible [in · *korr* · i · jibl] *adj.* 1. Unmanageable; used to refer to an unmanageable child. *See* juvenile offender. 2. Incapable of being corrected or reformed.
➤ unmanageable, disobedient, uncontrollable, unruly, unreformable, unsalvageable, wicked, unrepentant.

increase [*in* · kreese] *n.* An enlargement or growth.

v. [in · *kreese*] To become greater in size or worth.
➤ *n.* addition, gain, hike, boost, enlargement, growth, rise, accrual. *v.* enlarge, proliferate, expand, extend, supplement, raise, surge.

incredible [in · kred · ih · bul] *adj.* 1. Extraordinary; wonderful. 2. Improbable; unbelievable.
➤ fabulous, wonderful, awesome, amazing; absurd, impossible, ridiculous, preposterous, unthinkable, suspect, suspicious.

increment [*in* · kre · ment] *n.* Increase; an addition; that which is gained; the amount of increase.
➤ increase, addition, advancement, raise.

incriminate [in · *krim* · i · nate] *v.* 1. To charge with a crime. 2. To reveal a person's involvement in a crime. 3. To reveal one's own involvement in a crime. *See* incrimination; self-incrimination.
➤ implicate, involve, impeach, connect, indict, charge ("Jeff's statement incriminated Tonya").

incriminating [in · *krim* · i · nay · ting] *adj.* Accusing; blaming; that which incriminates.

incriminating circumstance [*ser* · kum · stanse] *n.* A circumstance tending to show that a crime has been committed, or that some particular person committed it.

incriminating evidence [*ev* · i · dense] *n.* Evidence tending to show that a person has committed a crime.

incriminating statement [*state* · ment] *n.* A statement that connects, or tends to connect, the accused with a crime.

incrimination [in · krim · i · *nay* · shen] *n.* The act of accusing a person of a crime, furnishing evidence against a person, or revealing one's own criminal involvement. *See* incriminate; self-incrimination.
➤ accusation, indictment, blame, decrial, impeachment.

incroachment [in · *kroach* · ment] *n.* Same as **encroachment**.

inculcate [*in* · kul · kayt] *v.* To instruct or impart.
➤ instill, inspire, indoctrinate, educate, propagandize, impress, imbue, preach.

inculpate [*in* · kul · pate] *v.* 1. To incriminate; to accuse a person of a crime. 2. To blame. *Compare* exculpate.
➤ incriminate, accuse, charge, impute, blame, denounce.

inculpatory [in · *kul* · pe · tore · ee] *adj.* That which tends to incriminate. USAGE: "I think the defendant will be convicted because his own testimony was inculpatory." *Compare* exculpatory.
➤ incriminating, damning, damaging, blaming, accusatory, impugning. *Ant.* exculpatory.

incumbent [in · *kum* · bent] *n.* A person who holds an office. *Compare* candidate.
➤ officeholder, occupant, official, bureaucrat. *Ant.* candidate.

incumber [in · *kum* · ber] *v.* Same as **encumber**.

incumbrance [in · *kum* · brenss] *n.* Same as **encumbrance**.

incur [in · *kerr*] *v.* To bring upon oneself; to become liable or responsible, either by operation of law or by one's conduct. EXAMPLES: to incur a penalty by late payment of taxes; to incur someone's anger by behaving wrongfully.
➤ undertake, assume, acquire, become responsible, bring on ("incur a penalty for noncompliance with the regulations").

indebted [in · *det* · ed] *adj.* Obligated on a debt, whether or not the debt is due; obligated to make a payment.
➤ accountable, bound, liable, obligated, answerable for, beholden, encumbered.

indebtedness [in · *det* · ed · ness] *n.* Being in debt. "Indebtedness" may refer to a person's total debt (that is, everything she owes to everyone) or to a single debt.
➤ liability, debts, responsibility; appreciation, gratitude.

indecent [in · *dee* · sent] *adj.* Unfit to be seen or heard; grossly vulgar; lewd; lascivious; obscene.
➤ vulgar, lewd, lascivious, obscene, immoral, unseemly ("indecent exposure").

indecent assault [a · *salt*] *n.* The act of a man in taking indecent liberties (EXAMPLE: fondling, without consent) with a woman; **sexual assault**. In some jurisdictions,

indecent assault is a gender-neutral offense and applies equally to perpetrators of either sex. *See* lewd and lascivious cohabitation.

indecent exposure [ex · *poh* · zher] *n.* Exposing one's private parts in a manner, and at a time and place, which is offensive to public decency. *See* public indecency.

indecent language [*lang* · wej] *n.* Language that is obscene, profane, or shocking to the moral sense. *See* profanity.

indecent liberties [*lib* · er · teez] *n. See* indecent assault.

indefeasible [in · de · *fee* · zibl] *adj.* That which cannot be taken away. *See* vested; vested right.
➤ inalienable, incontrovertible, immutable, incontestable, irreversible, confirmed, binding, settled.

indefinite [in · *def* · i · nit] *adj.* Temporary; uncertain; open; open-ended; indeterminate.
➤ temporary, uncertain, vague, ill-defined, boundless, open, open-ended, indeterminate, unclear. *Ant.* certain, permanent.

indefinite failure of issue [*fail* · yer of *ish* · ew] *n. See* die without issue.

indemnification [in · dem · ni · fi · *kay* · shen] *n.* 1. The act of indemnifying or being indemnified. *See* indemnify. 2. Payment made by way of compensation for a **loss**. *See* indemnity.
➤ restitution, amends, compensation, insurance, payment, reparation.

indemnify [in · *dem* · ni · fy] *v.* 1. To compensate or reimburse a person for **loss** or damage. 2. To promise to compensate or reimburse in the event of future loss or damage. *See* indemnity. *See also* hold harmless; save harmless.
➤ compensate, reimburse, secure, make amends, guarantee, restore, repay, redeem.

indemnitee [in · dem · ni · *tee*] *n.* A person who is to be indemnified. *Compare* indemnitor.

indemnitor [in · dem · ni · *tor*] *n.* A person who indemnifies another. *Compare* indemnitee.

indemnity [in · *dem* · ni · tee] *n.* 1. A contract to compensate another in money or property for a **loss** she might suffer as

I

the result of conduct which might occur; a **contract of indemnity**. EXAMPLE: a **performance bond**. 2. Compensation paid under a contract of indemnity. *See* indemnification. 3. A benefit payable under an insurance policy. *See* indemnity insurance. *Also see* double indemnity.

➤ repayment, security, restitution, assurance, restoration.

indemnity bond *n.* A **bond** to **indemnify** the **indemnitee** against **loss** from the conduct of the **indemnitor** or from the conduct of a third person.

indemnity insurance [in · *shoor* · ense] *n.* Insurance providing **indemnification** for actual **loss** or damage, as distinguished from **liability insurance**, which provides for payment of a specified sum upon the occurrence of a specific event regardless of what the actual loss or damage may be.

indemnity policy [*paw* · li · see] *n.* *See* indemnity insurance.

indenture [in · *den* · cher] *n.* 1. A deed executed by both parties. *Compare* deed poll. 2. Sometimes loosely used to refer to any deed, written contract, mortgage, or other instrument embodying a **security interest** in real property. 3. A contract between bondholders and the corporation or governmental body issuing the bond as to the terms of the debt. 4. A contract binding one person to work for another as an apprentice.

indenture of trust *n.* *See* trust indenture.

independent [in · de · *pen* · dent] *adj.* Free from the control of another; unconnected. *See* autonomy.

➤ unrestricted, separate, autonomous, sovereign, nonpartisan, free, unbound, unassociated, self-reliant.

independent adjuster [a · *just* · er] *n.* An adjuster of claims against insurance companies who works for various companies as an independent contractor and not as a regular employee of any.

independent audit *n.* An audit conducted by an accountant or other auditor who is not an employee or agent of the person or firm being audited. *Compare* internal audit. *See* audit.

independent contract [*kon* · trakt] *n.* A contract whose enforceability does not depend upon the performance of any other contract or promise. *Compare* commutative contract. *See* contract.

independent contractor [*kon* · trak · ter] *n.* As distinguished from an employee, a person who contracts to do work for another person in her own way, controlling the means and method by which the work is done but not the end product. An independent contractor is the agent of the person with whom she contracts. *Compare* employee. *See* contractor.

independent counsel [*koun* · sel] *n.* Under federal statute, counsel who may be specially appointed to investigate and prosecute high government officials for crimes committed in office. *See* counsel. *See also* special counsel; special prosecutor.

independent covenant [*kov* · e · nent] *n.* A **covenant** in a contract or deed, the breach of which may entitle the **injured party** to recover **damages**.

independent intervening cause [in · ter · *vee* · ning] *n.* Same as **intervening cause**.

independent paralegal [*pehr* · e · leeg · el] *n.* A paralegal who works at a "paralegal firm" (as opposed to a law firm) or freelance and who is retained by an attorney or a law firm on a temporary basis. There is an increasing tendency for courts to hold that an independent paralegal is not engaged in the unauthorized practice of law if she works under the direct supervision of an attorney. *Compare* unauthorized practice of law.

independent source rule *n.* Although evidence gained as the result of government misconduct cannot be used in a criminal prosecution, the facts obtained by such conduct are admissible if the government gained knowledge of these facts from an independent source. *See* fruit of the poisonous tree doctrine. *See also* inevitable discovery rule.

indestructible [in · de · *struk* · tih · bul] *adj.* Incapable of being destroyed or terminated.

➤ endless, indefeasible, perpetual, permanent, enduring, unbreakable.

indestructible trust [in · de · *struk* · tibl] *n.* A **trust** that may not be terminated by the **beneficiary**. *See* termination.

indeterminate [in · de · *ter* · min · et] *adj.*
Uncertain; not determined; not fixed; not made certain.

➤ open, vague, imprecise, unclear, amorphous, nebulous, unspecified, unresolved.

indeterminate sentence [*sen* · tense] *n.*
A prison sentence that is for no less than a minimum period and no more than a maximum period, its exact duration to be determined by the prison or parole authorities based upon behavior in prison or similar considerations. *Compare* determinate sentence.

index [*in* · deks] *n.* 1. A list of subjects treated in a printed work, usually arranged alphabetically, together with the page number at which the subject is found or discussed. An index customarily appears at the end of the book or other work to which it pertains, although it may sometimes be contained in a separate volume or series of volumes. *See* grantor-grantee indexes; tract index. 2. An indicator.
v. To connect the cost or value of things (EXAMPLES: wages; pension payments; interest; rent) to an economic indicator, such as the **consumer price index**. *See also* cost-of-living adjustment (COLA); cost-of-living clause.

➤ *n.* list, inventory; indication, basis, rule, formula, symbol.
v. list, classify, codify, inventory, docket, file.

Indian [*in* · dee · en] *n.* 1. A Native American; a member of the race of people native to North America and South America. 2. A native of India.
Note that many indigenous Americans do not look upon "Indian" as an accurate or appropriately descriptive term. Accordingly, the term "Native American," which is preferred, has come into common usage. However, "Indian" was used in statutes enacted before the mid-1970s, as well as in the judicial opinions interpreting those statutes. In this regard, *compare* the title of the **Bureau of Indian Affairs** (established in 1824) with the title of the **Administration for Native Americans** (created in 1974). The terms listed here are of pre-1970 origin.

Indian Affairs Bureau [a · *fairz byoo* · roh]
n. See Bureau of Indian Affairs.

Indian Claims Commission [ke · *mish* · en]
n. A commission established by Congress to hear and determine claims by Indian tribes against the government.

Indian lands *n.* Lands held in trust for a tribe or nation of Native Americans by the United States; that is, lands held or administered for the use and benefit of Native Americans.

Indian reservation [rez · er · *vay* · shen]
n. Land set aside by the United States for occupancy by Native Americans.

Indian title [*ty* · tel] *n.* The right of Native Americans to occupy land, originating by virtue of their prior occupancy of the continent. This **title** cannot be **conveyed**. Indian title is also called **aboriginal title**.

Indian tribe *n.* A body of Native Americans united in a community under one leadership or government and inhabiting a particular territory.

indicate [*in* · dih · kayt] *v.* To signify or suggest.

➤ imply, signify, suggest, allude to, evidence, intimate, hint, mean, attest.

indication [in · dih · *kay* · shun] *n.* A suggestion; a clue; evidence.

➤ hint, suggestion, forewarning, evidence, mention, sign, warning, symptom, omen, indicator ("an indication of foul play").

indicia [in · *dish* · a] *n.* Indicators; indications; signs; evidence; things furnishing information or suggesting a conclusion. USAGE: "The sale of his business for almost nothing, and the fact that he concealed his assets, are indicia of fraud." *See* badges of fraud.

➤ indicators, indications, signs, evidence, expressions, tokens.

indicia of ownership [*oh* · ner · ship] *n.* Evidence, usually **documentary evidence**, of **title** to real or personal property. EXAMPLES: a deed to land; a **bill of sale** of **personalty**; a **stock certificate**; a **certificate of title**. *See also* incident of ownership.

indict [in · *dite*] *v.* 1. To formally charge with the commission of a crime. *See* indictment. *Also see* grand jury. 2. To blame; to accuse.

➤ charge, arraign, implicate, prosecute, blame, accuse.

indictable [in · *dite* · ebl] *adj.* Subject or liable to **indictment**. USAGE: "Rape is an **indictable offense**."
➤ prohibited, illegal, impermissible, punishable.

   indictable offense [o · *fense*] *n.* A crime prosecuted by **indictment** rather than by **information**. Generally, this means a **felony** rather than a **misdemeanor**.

indicted [in · *dite* · ed] *adj.* 1. Formally charged with the commission of a crime. *See* indictment. 2. Blamed; accused.
➤ formally charged, blamed, accused.

indictee [in · dite · *ee*] *n.* A person against whom a grand jury has returned an **indictment**.

indictment [in · *dite* · ment] *n.* 1. A charge made in writing by a grand jury, based upon evidence presented to it, accusing a person of having committed a criminal act, generally a **felony**. It is the function of the prosecution to bring a case before the grand jury. If the grand jury indicts the defendant, a trial follows. 2. The formal, written accusation itself brought before the grand jury by the prosecutor. *Compare* information. *See and compare* no bill; true bill. *See also* bill of indictment. 3. Any serious criticism or attempt to blame.
➤ complaint, denunciation, allegation, charge, incrimination, accusation.

indifferent [in · *dif* · rent] *adj.* 1. Neutral as to the parties or the subject matter involved in litigation; disinterested; impartial. 2. Aloof; reserved; passive; detached.
➤ neutral, disinterested, impartial, aloof, reserved, passive, detached, unemotional ("an indifferent attitude").

indigent [*in* · di · jent] *adj.* Poor; a person who has no money, or almost none, and no property, and is unable to support himself. Legal counsel must be appointed to represent a criminal defendant who cannot afford to hire an attorney. An **indigent defendant's** right to counsel is guaranteed by the **Sixth Amendment**. *See* assigned counsel; *in forma pauperis;* right to counsel.
➤ poor, needy, deprived, poverty-stricken, penniless.

   indigent defendant [de · *fen* · dent] *n.* *See* indigent.

indignities [in · *dig* · ne · teez] *n. Plural* of **indignity**. As a ground for divorce, means degrading conduct demonstrating hatred or contempt. EXAMPLES: recurring ridicule; habitually unwarranted criticism; persistently abusive language. *See* intolerable indignity; mental cruelty.

indignity [in · *dig* · ne · tee] *n.* Insult; humiliation; an affront to self-respect. *See* indignities.
➤ insult, humiliation, cruelty, disrespect, degrading conduct.

indirect [in · di · *rekt*] *adj.* Not direct; roundabout; circuitous; not resulting directly from an act or cause, but more or less remotely connected with it.
➤ not direct, roundabout, circuitous, deviating, ancillary, oblique, inferential, collateral. *Ant.* direct.

   indirect contempt [ken · *temt*] *n.* An act committed elsewhere than in the courtroom or before the judge which tends to obstruct the administration of justice or to bring the court into disrespect. EXAMPLE: intimidating a witness out of the presence of the court. *Compare* direct contempt. *See* contempt. *See and compare* civil contempt; criminal contempt.

   indirect evidence [*ev* · i · dense] *n.* Evidence whose value as proof rests solely upon the **presumptions** and **inferences** arising from it. *See* circumstantial evidence.

   indirect tax *n.* A tax other than one imposed directly upon income; a tax other than one imposed upon property on the basis of its value. An indirect tax is most often levied upon an activity (EXAMPLE: importing goods) or a privilege (EXAMPLE: engaging in business). *Compare* direct tax.

indiscretion [in · dis · *kress* · shun] *n.* An act that goes against society's morals; a mistake.
➤ mistake, poor judgment, imprudence, injudiciousness, thoughtlessness, misdeed, misconduct.

indispensable [in · dis · *pen* · sebl] *adj.* Essential; vital; that which cannot be dispensed with.
➤ essential, vital, mandatory, crucial, required, necessary, cardinal, imperative.

I

indispensable evidence [*ev · i · dense*] *n.* Evidence without which proof of a specific fact is impossible.

indispensable party [*par · tee*] *n.* A person who must be a **party** to an **action** for the action to exist and be maintained and for an appropriate **judgment** to be rendered; a person who has a stake in the outcome of litigation of such a nature that a determination cannot be made without affecting her interests. Although the **Federal Rules of Civil Procedure** have replaced "indispensable party" (and "**necessary party**") with "**persons needed for just adjudication**," the original terms retain their importance under many states' **rules of civil procedure**. *See* joinder of parties.

individual [*in · de · vid · joo · el*] *adj.* Personal; separate; single; particular. *n.* 1. A **natural person**, as distinguished from a corporation or other **artificial person**. 2. One person, as distinguished from a group of people.
➤ *adj.* personal, separate, single, particular, unique, specific.
n. person, autonomous entity, distinct person, body, party, character, human being.

individual retirement account [*re · tire · ment a · kount*] *n.* Under the **Internal Revenue Code**, individuals who are not included in an employer-maintained retirement plan may deposit money (up to an annual maximum amount set by the Code) in an account for the purchase of **retirement annuities**. No tax is paid on income deposited to an **IRA**, and the proceeds are taxable only when they are withdrawn. *See* Keogh plan.

indivisible [*in · di · viz · ibl*] *adj.* Incapable of division; inseparable.
➤ entire, inseverable, united, inseparable, unsunderable ("One nation, indivisible").

indivisible contract [*kon · trakt*] *n.* A contract whose parts are incapable of separate or independent treatment, so that if a portion is invalid the entire contract is unenforceable. *Compare* divisible contract. *See* severable contract.

indorse [*in · dorse*] *v.* To sign one's name on the back of a document, especially a check. *See* indorsement.

➤ support, back, finance, recommend, authorize, authenticate, sign, ratify, validate.

indorsee [*in · dor · see*] *n.* The person to whom a **negotiable instrument** is indorsed by name. *Compare* bearer. *See* indorse.

indorsee in due course *n.* A person who in good faith, **in the ordinary course of business**, for value, acquires a **negotiable instrument** duly indorsed to her, indorsed generally, or payable to **bearer**. *See* general indorsement.

indorsement [*in · dorse · ment*] *n.* 1. The writing of one's name on the back of a **negotiable instrument**, by which a person transfers **title** to the paper to another person. 2. Loosely speaking, signing one's name on the back of any document. 3. Approval; backing; support. Used in this sense, the word is generally spelled *endorsement*. *See* endorsement.
   See further accommodation paper; blank indorsement; conditional indorsement; full indorsement; general indorsement; restrictive indorsement; special indorsement.
➤ sanction, consent, permission, support, backing, encouragement, confirmation.

indorsement for account of [*a · kount*] *n. See* for account of.

indorsement for collection [*ke · lek · shen*] *n. See* for collection; restrictive indorsement.

indorsement for deposit [*de · paw · zit*] *n. See* for deposit; restrictive indorsement.

indorsement in blank *n. See* blank indorsement.

indorsement without recourse [*with · out ree · korse*] *n. See* without recourse.

indorser [*in · dor · ser*] *n.* The person who indorses a **negotiable instrument**. *Compare* indorsee.

induce [*in · doose*] *v.* To lead on; to influence; to cause; to persuade.
➤ lead on, influence, cause, persuade, pressure, motivate, precipitate, actuate.

inducement [*in · doose · ment*] *n.* 1. In contract law, that which motivates a person to enter into a contract. *See* consideration. 2. That which motivates, influences, or persuades a person to do anything.

➤ motivation, motive, impulse, catalyst, cause, attraction, stimulant ("an inducement to make the deal").

induction [in · *duk* · shen] *n.* 1. The act of being made a member of one of the armed forces. *See* Selective Service System. 2. The act of bringing about or causing.
➤ inauguration, installation, ordination, selection.
Ant. expulsion.

industrial [in · *dust* · ree · el] *adj.* Pertaining to industry or trade.
➤ commercial, mass-produced, mechanized, manufactured, technological, standardized.

industrial development [de · *vel* · ep · ment] *n.* The process of obtaining industries for a region (e.g., a state, a city), constructing manufacturing plants, and the like.

industrial disease [de · *zeez*] *n. See* occupational disease.

industrial homework [*home* · werk] *n. See* homework.

industrial relations [re · *lay* · shenz] *n.* A term embracing all aspects of the relationship between employers and employees or unions that represent them. EXAMPLES: **collective bargaining**; **arbitration** or **mediation** of disputes; implementation of **OSHA** requirements or the provisions of the **Fair Labor Standards Act**.

industrial union [*yoon* · yen] *n.* A labor union organized without regard to the particular skills of its members, taking in instead all employees of an entire industry. *Compare* craft union.

industry [in · dust · ree] *n.* 1. A distinct branch of trade or business. EXAMPLES: the automobile industry; the garment industry. 2. A business or plant engaged in the production of goods, particularly a manufacturing plant employing a large number of people. 3. Diligence or enterprise.
➤ field, business, enterprise, profession, production, work; diligence, drive, zeal, persistence, activity, determination.

inebriation [in · *ee* · bree · ay · shun] *n.* The state of drunkenness or intoxication.
➤ drunkenness, insobriety, intemperance, intoxication.

ineffective [in · e · *fek* · tiv] *adj.* Not producing a desired effect.
➤ unproductive, fruitless, useless, invalid, futile, ineffectual, powerless, nugatory.

ineligibility [in · el · i · je · *bil* · e · tee] *n.* The state of being **ineligible**.

ineligible [in · *el* · i · jibl] *adj.* Lacking eligibility. USAGE: "She is ineligible for unemployment compensation benefits because she is no longer trying to find work."
➤ disqualified, unsuitable, disallowed, unentitled, inapplicable.
Ant. eligible.

inept [in · *ept*] *adj.* Incompetent, unskilled; clumsy.
➤ unqualified, unfit, inefficient, clumsy, unable, awkward, incompetent, bungling, inappropriate.

inequality [in · e · *kwal* · ih · tee] *n.* Prejudice; a lack of balance.
➤ prejudice, partiality, imbalance, discrepancy, injustice, inconsistency, bias, disproportion.

inescapable peril [in · es · *kayp* · ebl *pehr* · il] *n.* Same as **inevitable accident**.

inevitable [in · *ev* · i · tebl] *adj.* Unable to be avoided; unavoidable.
➤ unalterable, ineluctable, certain, sure, destined, definite, imminent.
Ant. uncertain.

inevitable accident [*ak* · se · dent] *n.* An occurrence that is purely happenstance and that could not have been avoided even if everyone involved had used **due care** to prevent it. (EXAMPLE: an **act of God**.) Inevitable accident is also referred to as **inescapable peril**. *See* accident; accidental injury; unavoidable accident. *Compare* negligence.

inevitable discovery rule [dis · *kuv* · e · ree] *n.* The **fruit of the poisonous tree doctrine** does not bar the introduction into evidence of facts obtained by a search that violates the **Fourth Amendment**, or a confession secured in violation of the **Sixth Amendment**, if the facts would have been discovered whether or not the illegal conduct occurred. *See also* independent source rule.

inexact [in · eggs · *act*] *adj.* Not exactly correct; indefinite.
➤ estimated, unclear, rough, unspecified, imperfect, imprecise, hazy ("an inexact science").

inexcusable [in · eks · *kyooz* · ih · bul] *adj.* Without justification.
➤ unforgivable, indefensible, reprehensible, unpardonable, heinous, cruel, unjustifiable.

inexplicable [in · eks · *plik* · uh · bul] *adj.* Beyond explanation or comprehension.
➤ mysterious, puzzling, undecipherable, incomprehensible, baffling, enigmatic.

infamous [*in* · fem · ess] *adj.* Notorious; ill-famed; despicable; villainous.
➤ notorious, ill-famed, despicable, villainous, disreputable, profligate, perfidious, heinous.
infamous crime *n.* A phrase with more than one connotation, which can mean: (1) **treason**; (2) any crime of dishonesty included within the term *crimen falsi*; (3) any crime that would affect the future credibility of the person convicted of it; (4) any **felony**; (5) any crime punishable by **infamous punishment**.
infamous punishment [*pun* · ish · ment] *n.* In modern times, punishment for a **felony** rather than punishment for a **misdemeanor**; that is, any crime for which the punishment is more than one year of imprisonment.

infamy [*in* · fa · mee] *n.* 1. The state of disgrace resulting from conviction of an **infamous crime**. *See* civil death. 2. Shame; dishonor; disgrace.
➤ disgrace, discredit, disrespect, shame, notoriety, aspersion, opprobrium ("a day that will live in infamy").

infancy [*in* · fen · see] *n.* 1. The status of a person who has not reached the **age of majority** and who therefore is under a **civil disability**; **nonage**; **minority**. 2. A civil disability resulting from the fact that one has not yet attained one's **majority**. *See* legal disability. 3. The period of life during which one is a very young child. *See* child. 4. The beginning period of anything.
➤ childhood; inception, start, conception, genesis.

infant [*in* · fent] *n.* A very young person. *See* infancy.
➤ child, minor, juvenile, toddler, tot, youngster, kid.

infanticide [in · *fan* · ti · side] *n.* The deliberate killing of a child shortly after its birth.

infect [in · *fekt*] *v.* To make unfit by damaging; to pollute or contaminate.
➤ contaminate, impair, taint, sully, stain, pollute, debase.

infer [in · *fer*] *v.* To reason and conclude from a known fact. *See also* inferred. *Compare* implied.
➤ reason, conclude, deduce, construe, assume, glean, intuit, surmise, ascertain.

inference [*in* · fe · rense] *n.* 1. That which may be reasoned from the evidence as being true or proven; a **conclusion of fact**. *Compare* presumption. *Also compare* conclusion of law. *See* finding of fact. *See also* conclusive evidence. 2. That which is inferred. *See* infer.
➤ belief, assumption, deduction, conclusion, conjecture ("a likely inference").

inferential [in · fe · *ren* · shel] *adj.* Pertaining to or based upon **inference**.

inferior [in · *feer* · ee · er] *adj.* Less or lower in power, authority, or rank; subordinate.
➤ of lower rank, secondary, lesser, under, junior, subordinate, subsidiary, minor ("an inferior court"); faulty, poor, shoddy, imperfect, second-rate, unacceptable, defective ("an inferior product").
inferior court *n.* 1. A **court of original jurisdiction**, as distinguished from an **appellate court**; a **trial court**. *See* original jurisdiction. *See also* lower court. 2. A **court of limited jurisdiction**.

inferred [in · *ferd*] *adj.* Concluded from a known fact or a fact believed to be true. *See* infer; inference. *Compare* implied.
➤ concluded, deduced, reasoned, presumed, constructed.

infidelity [in · fi · *del* · i · tee] *n.* 1. Unfaithfulness in marriage. As a ground for divorce in some states, infidelity is the same as **adultery**. 2. Disloyalty generally.
➤ unfaithfulness, betrayal, cheating, adultery, disloyalty, deceit.
Ant. loyalty, fealty.

infirm [in · *ferm*] *adj.* 1. Defective; weak; lacking purpose. USAGE: "Your legal argument is infirm." 2. Sickly; feeble in mind or body.
➤ defective, weak, purposeless ("Your legal argument is infirm"); sickly, feeble, powerless ("I am feeling infirm").

I

infirmative [in · *ferm* · e · tiv] *adj.* Tending to weaken or to lessen. Testimony that weakens the effectiveness of other evidence is "infirmative testimony." *See* exculpatory.
➤ exculpatory, invalidating ("infirmative testimony").

infirmity [in · *ferm* · i · tee] *n.* 1. A defect in some aspect of a legal document, **pleading**, argument, or the like. EXAMPLE: a **defect of parties**. 2. A disability; a disease; physical or mental weakness.
➤ defect, disability, disease, weakness, frailty, debility, incapacity.

inflated [in · *flay* · ted] *adj.* Blown up or increased; exaggerated.
➤ enlarged, swollen, dilated, air-filled, distended ("an inflated balloon"); amplified, embellished, overpriced, overvalued, excessive ("inflated worth"); vain, boastful, immodest, overdone, pompous, conceited ("inflated sense of self").

inflation [in · *flay* · shun] *n.*
1. Augmentation; increase. 2. the increase in the amount of money needed to purchase items.
➤ extension, enlargement, upsurge, distension, aggrandizement; currency devaluation, price increase.

inflict [in · *flikt*] *v.* To impose or administer.
➤ impose, mete out, apply, wound, punish, force, hurt, harm ("to inflict punishment").

influence [*in* · flew · ense] *n.* Pressure applied to undermine or override a person's judgment or willpower. *See* undue influence.
v. To alter, move, sway, or affect. *See* undue influence.
➤ *n.* power, authority, pressure, manipulation, force, leadership, leverage.
v. alter, move, sway, affect, direct, guide.

inform [in · *form*] *v.* 1. To communicate to another. 2. To make known what had been secret; to disclose.
➤ notify, advise, explain, relate, proclaim, publish ("inform the attorney"); divulge, betray, inculpate, reveal, disclose ("inform on a friend").

informal [in · *form* · el] *adj.* Lacking in form; not in accordance with formal rules or requirements. *Compare* formal.

➤ unofficial, common, unauthorized, casual, ordinary, relaxed, perfunctory, spontaneous, unconventional.

informal agreement [a · *gree* · ment] *n.* Same as **informal contract**.

informal contract [*kon* · trakt] *n.* A contract not in the customary form, often an **oral contract**. *See* parol contract. *Compare* formal contract; written contract. *Also compare* gentleman's agreement.

informal marriage [*mehr* · ej] *n.* Same as **consensual marriage**.

informant [in · *form* · ent] *n.* One who supplies information. *See* informer.
➤ source, spy, stool pigeon, tipster; adviser, envoy, communicator.

information [in · fer · *may* · shen] *n.* 1. An accusation of the commission of a crime, sworn to by a district attorney or other prosecutor, on the basis of which a criminal defendant is brought to trial for a **misdemeanor** and, in some states, for a **felony**. 2. In some jurisdictions, which prosecute felonies only on the basis of **indictment** by a grand jury, an **affidavit** alleging **probable cause** to bind the defendant over to await action by the grand jury. *See* binding over.
3. Knowledge of acquired facts.
➤ knowledge, facts, material, news; wisdom, enlightenment ("I need more information"); charge, accusation, complaint, allegation ("felony information").

information and belief [be · *leef*] *n.* A phrase used in the law to limit a declaration (EXAMPLES: a **complaint**; an **allegation**) so that it is understood to be made upon information *believed* to be true as opposed to information *known* to be true. A district attorney swears to an **information** "upon information and belief." *See* upon information and belief.

informed [in · *formd*] *adj.* Based upon thought and information. USAGE: "His choice was an informed decision."
➤ knowledgeable, conscious, aware, forewarned, prepared, notified, apprised. *Ant.* unaware.

informed consent [in · *formd* ken · *sent*] *n.* Agreement to permit something to occur (usually surgery or some other medical procedure), after having been given as

I

much information as necessary to make an intelligent and rational ("informed") decision. A physician, hospital, or other healthcare provider may be held responsible for injury caused by a risk that was not disclosed.

informed intermediary [in · *formd* in · ter · *mee* · dee · e · ree] *n.* Trained professionals who are interposed in the chain of commerce between manufacturer and consumer. In the law of **product liability**, a pharmaceutical company may in certain circumstances successfully defend against an **action** brought by a person injured by a prescription drug which the company manufactured, if the company shows that it informed prescribing physicians ("informed intermediaries") of the risks involved. *See* intermediary.

informer [in · *form* · er] *n.* A person who supplies information to the authorities concerning a violation of the law, whether as a volunteer or after being questioned. *See also* qui tam action.
➤ informant, divulger, spy, source, tipster, tattler, reporter, notifier, messenger.
informer's privilege [in · *form* · erz *priv* · i · lej] *n.* The **privilege** of the prosecution, in certain instances, to maintain the confidentiality of an informer. *See* privileged communication.

infra [in · fra] (*Latin*) *adv.* Below; beneath; under; within. *Infra* is used in legal writing when the author refers to an **authority** which she also cites at a later point in the work. EXAMPLE: If at footnote 40 of her brief the author has cited "Children and Young Persons Act, 1969," she might, at footnote 26, refer to that reference as follows: "See *infra* note 40." *Compare ibid.; id.; supra.*

infraction [in · *frak* · shen] *n.* 1. A minor violation of law. EXAMPLE: a traffic citation. 2. A breach; an infringement. *See also* petty offense.
➤ violation, breach, infringement, transgression, lawbreaking, noncompliance, contravention. *Ant.* compliance.

infringe [in · *frinj*] *v.* To violate or interfere with a right, law, privilege, or duty. *See* infringement.

infringement [in · *frinj* · ment] *n.* A violation of a right or privilege; an encroachment.

➤ violation, misfeasance, invasion, encroachment, interference, breach ("infringement of patent").
infringement of copyright [*kop* · ee · rite] *n.* Using any portion of copyrighted material without the consent of the copyright owner. *Compare* fair use doctrine. *See* copyright.
infringement of patent [*pat* · ent] *n.* The manufacture, use, or sale of a **patent** or **process patent** without the authorization of the patent owner.
infringement of trademark [*trade* · mark] *n.* A use or imitation of a **trademark** in such manner that a purchaser of goods is likely to be deceived into believing that they are the goods of the owner of the trademark.

infuse [in · *fyooz*] *v.* To combine or introduce one thing to another; to soak or saturate.
➤ instill, implant, ingrain, imbue, inculcate, introduce.

ingredient [in · *greed* · ee · ent] *n.* Something that is a portion of the whole.
➤ component, part, element, section, unit, aspect, factor.

ingrossing [in · *groh* · sing] *n.* The act of copying any document in final form. *See* engrossment.

inhabitant [in · *hab* · i · tent] *n.* A person who has a **domicile** or a fixed residence in a particular place. Sometimes "inhabitant" is used synonymously with "resident"; sometimes it is used more narrowly, with a meaning comparable to "**domiciliary.**"
➤ resident, citizen, native, dweller, tenant, occupant.

inherent [in · *hehr* · ent] *adj.* Pertaining to an inseparable quality or integral part of a thing or a person.
➤ intrinsic, innate, ingrained, integral, inseparable, natural, essential. *Ant.* incidental, extrinsic.

inherent danger [*dane* · jer] *n.* Danger characteristic of certain work or of a certain product, which does not arise solely from the method of performing the work or from a defect in the product. Such a product (EXAMPLE: explosives), or such work (highway construction involving the use of explosives), is said to be "inherently dangerous."

I

inherent defect [*dee* · fekt] *n.* *See* latent defect.

inherent power [*pow* · er] *n.* Power basic to a situation or position, although not backed by an express grant of authority. The federal government has inherent powers not expressly or impliedly given it in the Constitution. EXAMPLE: the power to regulate navigation. *See also* implied power.

inherent power of court [*pow* · er] *n.* Power essential to a court's ability to function in dispensing justice. EXAMPLE: the power to punish **contempt**.

inherent right *n.* A fundamental right that a person has by virtue of having been born a human being. *See* inalienable rights.

inherently dangerous [in · *hehr* · ent · lee *dane* · jer · ess] *adj.* *See* inherent danger.

inherit [in · *hehr* · it] *v.* 1. To take or receive property, including money, as an heir by **descent**. The word is sometimes loosely used also to mean taking under a will. *See* inheritance. 2. To have certain characteristics through heredity.
➤ take by succession, be left, be the heir of, acquire, receive, obtain, succeed, take over.

inheritance [in · *hehr* · i · tense] *n.* Strictly speaking, the taking or receiving of property as an heir by **descent**. In everyday language, taking under a will *or* by descent. *See* inherit; intestate succession; succession.
➤ legacy, devise, bequest, endowment, birthright, share, dispensation.

inheritance tax *n.* A tax on the privilege of taking the property of a **decedent** by **descent** or under a will, but not a tax on the decedent's right to dispose of his property or a tax on the property itself. *Compare* estate tax.

inhibit [in · *hib* · it] *v.* To discourage from an act; to restrict or prevent.
➤ restrain, restrict, arrest, prohibit, hinder, suppress, prevent, cramp, forbid, repress.

inhuman treatment [in · *hyoo* · men *treet* · ment] *n.* *See* cruel and inhuman treatment.

initial [in · *ish* · el] *adj.* Relating to the beginning; the first.
v. To place or write one's initials, usually on a document. USAGE: "Please initial each copy of the contract."

➤ *adj.* beginning, first, introductory, maiden, incipient, original, early ("initial meeting"). *Ant.* terminal.
v. sign, authorize, mark, approve.

initial carrier [*kehr* · ee · er] *n.* 1. The first **carrier** in a pair or series of connecting carriers; the carrier who received the goods from the shipper. 2. The carrier contracting with the shipper (not necessarily the carrier who is the first link in transportation).

initial determination [de · ter · mi · *nay* · shen] *n.* The eligibility determination made by the **Social Security Administration** when a claimant applies for social security benefits. Subsequent administrative determinations on appeal may reverse an initial denial of benefits.

initials [i · *nish* · elz] *n.* The first letters of a person's first and last (or first, middle, and last) names, often used in place of a signature.

initiation [ih · nish · ee · *ay* · shen] *n.* A rite or introduction.
➤ introduction, admission, indoctrination, induction, baptism ("his initiation into the fraternity").

initiation fee [i · nish · ee · *ay* · shen] *n.* A sum paid to a club, union, or other association in order to join.

initiative [i · *nish* · ye · tiv] *n.* 1. A process in many states by which the voters directly enact or reject legislation or constitutional amendments at the polls, independent of the legislature. *Compare* recall; referendum. 2. An initial step leading to action; ambition.
➤ first step, first move, beginning; determination, drive, aggressiveness, enthusiasm, leadership.

inject [in · jekt] *v.* To introduce or put in.
➤ infuse, saturate, drive in, instill, introduce, imbue ("to inject some humor into the conversation").

injudicious [in · joo · *dish* · us] *adj.* Unwise; careless.
➤ unsound, unreasoned, hasty, inexpedient, reckless, incautious, unwise.

injunction [in · *junk* · shen] *n.* 1. A court order that commands or prohibits some act or course of conduct. It is preventive in nature and designed to protect a plaintiff from **irreparable injury** to his property or property rights by prohibiting or

commanding the doing of certain acts. (EXAMPLE: a court order prohibiting unlawful picketing.) An injunction is a form of **equitable relief**. *See* affirmative relief; restraining order; specific performance. *See also* ex parte injunction; mandatory injunction; permanent injunction; preliminary injunction; preventive injunction; temporary injunction. 2. A command; a mandate; an order.
➤ ban, stay, order, enjoinder, interdiction, restraint, mandate, prohibition.

injunctive relief [in · *junk* · tiv re · *leef*] *n.* **Relief** resulting from an **injunction**.

injure [*in* · jer] *v.* 1. To interfere with a person's legal rights. *See* actionable wrong; injury. 2. To harm, damage, or reduce the value of property. *See* damage. 3. To physically hurt or wound a person.
➤ harm, damage, misuse, mistreat, abuse, violate, tarnish, hurt, wound.

injured [*in* · jerd] *adj.* 1. Wronged; damaged. 2. Hurt; wounded.
➤ damaged, aggrieved, offended, hurt, violated ("The injured party filed in federal court").

injured party [*par* · tee] *n.* A person wronged by the action of another; a person having a **right of action**. *See* innocent and injured.

injurious falsehood [in · *joo* · ree · es *false* · hood] *n.* A **defamation** that causes **damage**.

injury [*in* · jer · ee] *n.* 1. The invasion of a **legal right**; an **actionable wrong** done to a person, her property, or her reputation. (*Compare* "**damage**," which is the loss, hurt, or harm resulting from "injury.") *Note* that an injury, as the law uses that term, is not limited to physical harm done to the body; *note too* that, in the language of the law, an injury to the body (that is, a **personal injury**) may mean death as well as mere physical harm. *See* irreparable injury; permanent injury; private injury; public injury; reparable injury. 2. In everyday language, damage or harm to the physical structure of the body. *See* accidental injury; bodily injury.
➤ wrong, damage, loss, detriment, harm, offense.
Ant. benefit.

injustice [in · *juss* · tiss] *n.* An act that deprives a person of a **legal right**; an **injury**; that which is unjust.
➤ injury, wrong, unfairness, inequality, inequity, prejudice, transgression, bias, abuse, partiality.
Ant. fairness.

inland [*in* · land] *adj.* Within a country; carried on within a country; domestic as opposed to foreign.
➤ internal, domestic, heartland.
inland bill *n.* A **bill of exchange** that is both drawn and payable within the state.
inland bill of exchange [eks · *chaynj*] *n.* Same as **inland bill**.
inland marine insurance [me · *reen* in · *shoor* · ense] *n.* A term originally related to insurance covering ships or cargoes on nonoceanic U.S. waters, but which now relates to broad categories of insurance, including **floater policies** on jewelry and clothing. *Compare* marine insurance.
inland navigation [nav · i · *gay* · shen] *n.* Navigation upon **inland waters**.
inland rules of navigation [nav · i · *gay* · shen] *n.* Navigation rules made by local authorities with respect to rivers and lakes or other **inland waters**.
inland waters [*waw* · terz] *n.* Rivers, lakes, bays, gulfs, and all other bodies of water within, or partly within, the boundaries of the United States. Inland waters do not include **tidal waters** or the ocean. *See* navigable waters.

inmate [*in* · mate] *n.* 1. A person confined with others in a prison, penitentiary, or jail, or involuntarily in a hospital or similar place. 2. A person who lives in a common residence, usually a rooming house or the like, with others.
➤ prisoner, convict, captive; roomer, dweller, occupier.

innate [*in* · ayt] *adj.* Biological; inherited; native.
➤ inborn, hereditary, fundamental, basic, natural, essential, congenital, native.

innocence [*in* · e · sense] *n.* Absence of guilt. *See also* presumption of innocence.
➤ blamelessness, sinlessness, naiveté, purity, inexperience.
Ant. guilt, cunning; sophistication.

I

innocent [*in* · e · sent] *adj.* 1. In a technical legal sense, not guilty, that is, a finding by a judge or jury that the prosecution has failed to meet its **burden of proof**. 2. In the general sense, free from wrongdoing or not knowingly involved in wrongdoing. 3. Pure; trustful; naive.
➤ faultless, blameless, not guilty; pure, trustful, naive.
Ant. guilty, culpable; sophisticated, worldly.

innocent agent [*ay* · jent] *n.* A person who, at the direction of his principal, engages in an act in violation of the law but who incurs no legal guilt, either because he lacks the **capacity** to commit a crime or because he was entirely unaware of the circumstances that made his act a crime. *See* agent.

innocent and injured [*in* · jerd] *n.* A person wronged by another, particularly an *innocent and injured spouse*, i.e., a spouse who is the plaintiff in a divorce action and who has given his or her partner no grounds for divorce.

innocent party [*par* · tee] *n.* A person who unintentionally participates in some wrongful activity.

innocent purchaser [*per* · che · ser] *n.* Same as **bona fide purchaser**. *See also* buyer in the ordinary course of business; good faith purchaser.

innocent trespasser [*tress* · pass · er] *n.* A person who trespasses under **color of right** or in good faith by mistake. *See* trespasser.

innovation [in · uh · *vay* · shun] *n.* A change; an invention.
➤ change, departure, modification, revision, modernization, alteration.

inoperative [in · *op* · e · re · tiv] *adj.* Not in effect; ineffective; worthless.
➤ not in effect, ineffective, worthless, deficient, broken, inadequate, imperfect.

inoperative will *n.* A will that is ineffective because the **dispositions** attempted by the **testator** are contrary to law.

inquest [*in* · kewst] *n.* 1. An investigation conducted by a coroner or medical examiner, sometimes with the aid of a jury, to determine the cause of a person's death when death is due, or apparently due, to unlawful, violent, or suspicious means. 2. Any official inquiry before a jury.

➤ inquiry, search, investigation.

inquest jury [*joo* · ree] *n.* A jury summoned by a coroner or medical examiner to determine the cause of death.

inquire [in · *kwire*] *v.* To look for information; to ask.
➤ ask, probe, investigate, examine, explore, look into, quiz.

inquiry [*in* · kwe · ree] *n.* 1. A judicial or other legal examination or investigation. 2. Any seeking after information. *See* diligent inquiry.
➤ inquest, investigation, examination, hearing; question, query, interrogatory.

inquisitorial system [in · kwiz · e · *toh* · ree · el sis · tem] *n.* The system of criminal justice in continental Europe and in countries whose legal procedures derive from those of continental Europe, for EXAMPLE, South American countries. Under the inquisitorial system, a court does not base its determination of guilt or innocence solely upon the evidence presented by the prosecutor, but investigates the facts on its own as well. *Compare* accusatory system. *Compare also* adversary system.

INS Abbreviation of **Immigration and Naturalization Service**.

insane [in · *sane*] *adj.* Of unsound mind. *See* insanity.
➤ unsound, deranged, demented, absurd, bizarre, mad.

insane delusion [de · *loo* · zhen] *n.* The product of an unsound mind, a belief in the existence of things that do not exist, contrary to all evidence and reason.

insanity [in · *san* · i · tee] *n.* A term for a condition of the mind, which has no medical or scientific meaning (*compare* psychosis) and whose legal meaning depends upon the context in which it is used. Specifically, the law's definition of insanity varies with the type of matter involved: insanity as a defense to a criminal charge, insanity as a reason for denying a person his physical liberty, or insanity as a **civil disability** that deprives a person of the **legal capacity** to conduct such ordinary affairs of life as entering into contracts, making a will, or the like.

I

Insanity as a criminal defense. Different states use different tests or standards for determining whether a criminal defendant was insane (that is, whether he had the capacity to form **criminal intent**) at the time he committed the crime. The most important of these tests are the **M'Naghten rule, irresistible impulse**, and, most frequently used, the **Model Penal Code's** standard, lack of capacity "as a result of mental disease or defect" to appreciate the criminality of one's conduct or to conform one's conduct to the requirements of law. The law also requires that a criminal defendant be sane at the time of trial, and permits imposition of the death penalty only if the person convicted is sane at the time of execution. *See* mental defect; mental disease. *See also* Durham rule.

Insanity as a basis for deprivation of personal liberty. State laws vary with respect to the circumstances under which a person may be committed to an institution against her will by reason of insanity. Generally, however, the mental condition of the person involved must be such as to cause her to be harmful to herself or to others, or it must render her unable to provide herself with shelter, food, or clothing or to know how to use such necessities of life if they are provided for her. In all events (except in limited situations of brief duration), involuntary commitment may not occur without a judicial hearing and, with respect to persons who are simply unable to provide for themselves, may be undertaken only for the purpose of treatment. *See* civil commitment; commitment. *Also see* mental incapacity.

Insanity as a legal disability. Insanity is also a **legal disability** which, among other things, may void a contract or a will or constitute grounds to annul a marriage. For such purposes, insanity is generally defined as an impairment of the mind of a character such that it is impossible for the person so afflicted to understand the nature and consequences of her acts or the character of the transaction in question. In such circumstances, it is necessary to appoint a **guardian** or **conservator** to make disposition of the incompetent person's property. See capacity; competency; testamentary capacity. See also civil disability.

➤ madness, lunacy, derangement, mental illness, disorientation, dementia.

inscription [in · *skrip* · shen] *n.* 1. Another term for the registration or recording of a deed, mortgage, or other instrument. 2. Words, letters, or signs engraved upon stone, metal, or the like so that they will be as permanent as possible.

➤ registration, recording, engraving, dedication, notation, caption, autograph, legend.

insecure [in · se · *kyoor*] *adj.* 1. Uncertain; unconfident. 2. Unsafe or unprotected.

➤ uncertain, vulnerable, frail, unconfident; risky, unreliable, unprotected, unassured, precarious.

Ant. secure, confident; protected.

insecurity clause [in · se · *kyoo* · ri · tee] *n.* A provision in an **installment sale contract** or other agreement that permits the seller to demand the entire balance due if she believes the buyer is unable or unwilling to pay. *Compare* acceleration clause.

inseparable [in · *sep* · er · uh · bul] *adj.* Indivisible; incapable of being separated.

➤ indivisible, joined, consolidated, fused, intertwined, intimate, devoted ("The twins were inseparable").

insertion [in · *ser* · shun] *n.* An addition or attachment; something that is put in or interjected.

➤ addition, interjection, addendum, supplement, penetration.

insider [in · *sy* · der] *n.* 1. An officer or director of a corporation or any other person who is in a position to acquire knowledge of the business and condition of the corporation through his official position. 2. A person on the inside of any group, especially a person who has special knowledge or unique opportunities as a result. *adj.* Nonpublic; undisclosed.

➤ *n.* officer, director, member, intimate, associate.

adj. private, protected, nonpublic, undisclosed ("insider information").

insider information [in · fer · *may* · shen] *n.* The information acquired by a director or officer of a corporation or other insider.

It is information unavailable to the public and upon which **insider trading** is based.

insider trading [*tray* · ding] *n.* A transaction in the stock of a corporation by a director, officer, or other insider, buying and selling on the basis of information obtained by her through her position in the company. Insider trading is regulated by the **Securities Exchange Act**.

insight [*in* · site] *n.* Awareness; perception.
➤ intuition, cognizance, perception, realization, keenness, acuteness, acumen, understanding.

insignificance [in · sig · *nif* · ih · kants] *n.* Lack of importance.
➤ unimportance, immateriality, irrelevance, triviality, insubstantiality.

insist [in · *sist*] *v.* To be emphatic about; to demand or require.
➤ stress, urge, demand, dictate, command, require, emphasize, impose.

insolvency [in · *sol* · ven · see] *n.* 1. The status of a person when his total assets are of insufficient value to pay his debts. 2. The inability of a person to pay her debts as they become due or in the **ordinary course of business**. *Compare* solvency. *See* bankruptcy.
➤ bankruptcy, destitution, indebtedness, default, ruin, failure.
Ant. financial stability, solvency.

insolvency proceeding [pro · *see* · ding] *n. See* assignment for the benefit of creditors; bankruptcy proceedings; receivership.

insolvent [in · *sol* · vent] *adj.* The state or condition of a person who is in a state of **insolvency**. *Compare* solvent.
n. A person who is in a state of insolvency.
➤ *adj.* bankrupt, indigent, destitute, broke, impecunious, ruined.

inspection [in · *spek* · shen] *n.* The act of looking something over closely, sometimes formally, usually for the purpose of verifying its accuracy or authenticity. Under the **Uniform Commercial Code**, the buyer of goods is entitled to inspect the article tendered by the seller to see if it conforms to the contract and, if it does not, to reject it. *See* conforming goods.

➤ examination, investigation, evaluation, observation, checking.

inspection laws *n.* Federal, state, and local laws designed to promote health and safety by protecting the public from hazards such as the unsanitary processing of food, the improper packaging of articles for sale, or unsafe working conditions. EXAMPLES: food inspection laws administered by the **FDA**; inspections conducted by **OSHA** to insure workplace safety. *See* sanitary codes.

inspection of documents [*dok* · yoo · ments] *n.* In either a civil or a criminal case, the inspection of documents material to the case which are in the possession of an **adverse party** or of the prosecution, as authorized by the **rules of civil procedure** or the **rules of criminal procedure**. *See also* Jencks rule.

inspection of records [*rek* · erdz] *n.* A reference to the right to freely examine and copy public records.

inspire [in · *spire*] *v.* To stimulate or encourage.
➤ stimulate, influence, prompt, urge, encourage, stir, induce, incite, influence, imbue.

install [in · *stall*] *v.* 1. To induct or place in office. *See* inauguration; induction. 2. To make anything ready for use.
➤ induct, place, set up, position, affix, connect, hook up.
Ant. remove, dismantle.

installation [in · ste · *lay* · shen] *n.* 1. Establishment; setting up. 2. Equipment. *See* install.
➤ furnishing, launching, induction, coronation; machinery, furnishings, station, system.

installment [in · *stall* · ment] *n.* 1. A payment of money due, the balance of which is to be paid at other agreed-upon times. 2. One of a number of parts of something furnished or performed over a period of time.
➤ partial payment, allotment, segment, portion, parcel, section.

installment contract [*kon* · trakt] *n.* A contract that requires or authorizes the delivery of goods in separate lots. *Compare* installment land contract.

installment land contract [*kon* · trakt] *n.* A contract for the purchase of real estate that provides for payment of the purchase price in installments and for **title** to be conveyed upon the completion of payment. *Compare* installment contract. *See also* contract for sale of land.

installment loan *n.* A loan to be repaid in fixed amounts over a period of time. *See* installment note.

installment note *n.* A promissory note payable in two or more specified amounts at different stated times. It is the instrument on which an installment loan is based.

installment payments [*pay* · ments] *n.* Payments at fixed intervals until the entire principal and interest on an obligation are satisfied. Installment payments are made under **installment contracts, installment notes,** or **installment sale contracts,** as well as other types of agreements. Articles sold under an installment sale contract are said to be purchased on the *installment plan.* Commercial installment sales and installment loans are regulated by **consumer credit protection acts.**

installment sale *n.* A sale of goods or services in which the purchase price is payable in installments. *See also* conditional sale contract.

installment sale contract [*kon* · trakt] *n.* A contract the subject of which is an **installment sale**. *See* contract.

instance [*in* · stenss] *n.* 1. A request. USAGE: "The judge dismissed the complaint at the instance of the defendant." 2. An example. USAGE: "Can you cite an instance in which intent is not a required element of a crime?"
➤ urging, request ("At the instance of the judge, he concluded his argument quickly"); example, case in point, situation ("in this instance").

instant [*in* · stent] *adj.* 1. Present; current; at hand. USAGE: "the instant case" means "the present case." *See* at bar. 2. Quick; fast; sudden.
n. A moment; duration of the blink of an eye.
➤ *adj.* present, current, at hand ("the instant case"); quick, immediate, fast, sudden ("the instant appearance of the witness").
n. moment, blink of an eye, flash, jiffy, second.

instantaneous [in · sten · *tay* · nee · es] *adj.* Occurring in an instant; occurring without delay.
➤ immediate, direct, spontaneous, simultaneous, speedy, prompt, quick.
instantaneous death *n.* A death that occurs in an instant or before the passage of any significant amount of time after the injury that caused it. If death is truly instantaneous, there can be no recovery for pain and suffering.

instanter [in · *stan* · ter] *adv.* Instantly; this instant; at once; immediately.
➤ instantly, at once, immediately.

instigate [*in* · sti · gate] *v.* 1. To incite, especially the commission of a crime. 2. To rouse to action, especially to a bad act.
➤ incite, stir up, induce, generate, provoke, rouse.
Ant. hamper, suppress.

instigation [in · sti · *gay* · shen] *n.* The act of instigating. *See* instigate.
➤ prodding, encouragement, initiation, prompting, suggestion.

institute [*in* · ste · toot] *n.* 1. An organization whose purpose is the carrying out of scholarly work. EXAMPLES: the **American Law Institute**; the **Practising Law Institute**. 2. An educational institution, especially a school providing advanced training for particular work.
v. To start; to establish. USAGE: "I'm going to institute an action" means "I'm going to file a lawsuit."
➤ *n.* organization, foundation, academy, college, university, association, institution, school ("the American Law Institute").
v. start, establish, commence, begin, launch ("I'm going to institute a new policy.").

institution [in · ste · *too* · shen] *n.* 1. Something that has been established, particularly an organization or place that is educational or charitable in nature and has a public or community purpose. EXAMPLES: a county juvenile detention facility; a state psychiatric hospital; a private university. 2. A place of business; a business establishment. EXAMPLES: a bank; a stock exchange. 3. The act of instituting or establishing something.
➤ establishment, organization, alliance, center, association, academy, school ("a

I

fine institution"); custom, norm, code, law, tradition ("the institution of slavery").

institutional [in · sti · *too* · shen · el] *adj.* Pertaining to an institution.

institutional decision [de · *sizh* · en] *n.* A decision made by an organization rather than an individual.

institutional lender [*len* · der] *n.* An institution in the business of making loans for profit. EXAMPLES: a bank; a mortgage company.

instruct [in · *strukt*] *v.* To direct; to order; to give instructions. *See* jury instructions.
➤ direct, order, give instructions, guide, teach, advise, tutor.

instructions [in · *struk* · shenz] *n.*
1. Directions; information; guidelines.
2. Short for **jury instructions**.
➤ directions, orders, guidelines, information, advice, charges.

instructions to the jury [in · *struk* · shenz to the *joo* · ree] *n. See* jury instructions.

instrument [*in* · stroo · ment] *n.* 1. A **negotiable instrument**. 2. A **stock certificate**, bond, or similar security. 3. Any writing that evidences a right to the payment of money and is not itself a **security agreement** or lease. 4. Any formal legal document evidencing an agreement or the granting of a right. EXAMPLES: a contract; a deed; a mortgage; a will. 5. A tool; a device for performing work or accomplishing a purpose. 6. A factor; a force; a catalyst; an agent; a means. *See* instrumentality.
➤ record, legal document, writing, contract; tool, device, apparatus, equipment, machinery.

instrumental trust [in · stroo · *men* · tal] *n.* A **ministerial trust**.

instrumentality [in · stroo · men · *tal* · i · tee] *n.* A means of accomplishing something; an **agency**. *See* dangerous instrumentality; federal instrumentality.
➤ means, method, agency; operation, device, tool, vehicle, resource.

instrumentality rule *n.* Same as **alter ego rule**.

insubordination [in · sub · or · di · *nay* · shen] *n.* Willful refusal to obey orders, particularly the instructions of an employer.

➤ disobedience, noncompliance, impudence, unruliness, defiance.
Ant. submissiveness, obedience.

insufficient [in · suh · *fish* · ent] *adj.* Inadequate; not enough.
➤ lacking, deficient, meager, sparse, depleted, wanting, paltry, slight.

insufficient evidence [*ev* · i · denss] *n.* Not enough evidence **in law** to support a verdict, a requirement for the granting of a **motion for directed verdict**, a **motion for judgment notwithstanding the verdict**, or a **motion for new trial**.

insufficient funds *n.* The absence of sufficient funds in a bank account for payment of a check drawn by the depositor. *See* NSF check; overdraft.

insurability [in · shoor · e · *bil* · i · tee] *n.* Having the qualities needed to be insurable; the capability of being insured.

insurable [in · *shoor* · ebl] *adv.* Capable of being insured. EXAMPLE: as a condition of purchasing life insurance, being in sound health at the time the policy is issued.

insurable interest [*in* · trest] *n.* An **interest** from whose existence the owner derives a benefit and whose nonexistence will cause her to suffer a **loss**. The presence of an insurable interest is essential to the validity and enforceability of an insurance policy because it removes it from the category of a **gambling contract**. An insurable interest in life insurance, for EXAMPLE, is: (a) one's interest in his own life; (b) one's natural interest in the continued life of a blood relative; or (c) any reasonable expectation of financial benefit from the continued life of another (one's debtor, business partner, etc.). See key man insurance.

insurance [in · *shoor* · ense] *n.* A contract (the policy) by which one party (the insurer), in return for a specified **consideration** (the premium) agrees to **compensate** or **indemnify** another (the insured) on account of **loss, damage**, or **liability** arising from an unknown or **contingent** event (the **risk**). There are almost as many kinds of coverage as there are risks. EXAMPLES of some of the most common types of insurance are **accident insurance, automobile insurance, credit life insurance, disability insurance, fire insurance, flood**

I

insurance, health insurance, homeowners insurance, liability insurance, life insurance, major medical insurance, malpractice insurance, mortgage insurance, and **title insurance**.

The law does not permit a person to insure against the consequences of acts or transactions that violate **public policy**, for EXAMPLE, gambling losses. Most importantly, the law requires a person to have an **insurable interest** in whatever she wishes to insure. *See* gambling contract; gambling policy.

See also all-risk insurance; business insurance; business interruption insurance; casualty insurance; coinsurance; collision insurance; comprehensive insurance; credit insurance; crop insurance; decreasing term insurance; endowment insurance; excess insurance; fidelity insurance; fidelity and guaranty insurance; group health insurance; group insurance; guaranty insurance; indemnity insurance; inland marine insurance; key man insurance; last survivor insurance; marine insurance; national service life insurance; no-fault insurance; ordinary life insurance; public liability insurance; self-insurance; straight life insurance; term life insurance; unemployment insurance; whole life insurance; workers' compensation insurance.
➤ indemnification, assurance, coverage, policy, warranty, covenant, security, guarantee, indemnity against contingencies, precaution, safeguard.

insurance adjuster [a · *just* · er] *n. See* adjuster; independent adjuster.

insurance agent [*ay* · jent] *n.* A person authorized by an insurance company to represent it when dealing with third persons in matters relating to insurance. *Compare* insurance broker. *See* agent.

insurance binder [*bine* · der] *n. See* binder.

insurance broker [*broh* · ker] *n.* A person who acts as an **intermediary** between the insured and the insurer, who is not employed by any insurance company. The broker solicits insurance business from the public, and having obtained an order, either places the insurance with a company selected by the insured or, if the insured does not select a **carrier**, then with a company

of the broker's choice. Depending upon the circumstances, an insurance broker may represent either the insured, or the insurer, or both. *See* broker. *Compare* insurance agent.

insurance carrier [*kehr* · ee · er] *n.* A company engaged in the business of issuing insurance policies; an insurance company.

insurance commissioner [kum · *ish* · e · ner] *n.* The head of a department of state government which regulates insurance companies in that state. *See* insurance department.

insurance company [*kum* · pe · nee] *n.* A company engaged in the business of issuing insurance policies. *See* mutual insurance company. *Compare* stock insurance company.

insurance contract [*kon* · trakt] *n.* The formal name for an insurance policy.

insurance department [de · *part* · ment] *n.* A state administrative agency established for the purpose of supervising and regulating insurance companies. *See* insurance commissioner.

insurance policy [*pol* · i · see] *n.* A contract to compensate or **indemnify** a person for **loss** arising from a contingent occurrence.

insurance premium [*pree* · mee · um] *n.* Money paid to an insurer for an insurance policy. *See* premium.

insurance trust *n. See* life insurance trust.

insure [in · *shoor*] *v.* 1. To enter into a contract of insurance as an insurer; to issue an insurance policy. 2. To guarantee. 3. To make sure.
➤ obtain insurance, secure against loss, underwrite, guard, safeguard, shield, back, check, warrant, arrange, provide, assure, reassure.

insured [in · *shoord*] *adj.* Covered by an insurance policy.
n. A person protected by an insurance policy; a person whose property is protected by an insurance policy. One need not be the **named insured** (i.e., named in the policy) to be covered. A standard automobile insurance policy, for EXAMPLE, usually covers any person operating the insured vehicle with the permission of the named insured.

insurer [in · *shoor* · er] *n.* 1. Generally, an insurance company, that is, the party who assumes the **risk** under an insurance policy and agrees to compensate or **indemnify** the insured. 2. One who guarantees something.
➤ indemnitor, indemnifier, guarantor, assurer, surety, underwriter.

insurer's liability [in · *shoor* · erz ly · e · *bil* · i · tee] *n.* **Absolute liability.**

insurgent [in · *ser* · jent] *n.* A person who participates in an insurrection; a rebel.
➤ rebel, rioter, revolutionary, agitater, mutineer, traitor, insurrectionist, reformer, dissident, guerrilla, resister.
Ant. loyalist, obedient, jingoist.

insurrection [in · ser · *rek* · shen] *n.* An uprising against the government; a rebellion. *Compare* revolution.
➤ uprising, riot, coup d'état, insurgence, revolution, subversion, coup, anarchy, sedition, outbreak, disturbance, revolt.

intangible [in · *tan* · jibl] *adj.* Without physical substance; nonmaterial; **incorporeal.** *Compare* tangible.
n. A thing which may or may not have value, but has no physical substance; an **intangible asset** or **intangible property.** EXAMPLES: a **cause of action**; a **copyright**; an **account receivable**; **goodwill.** *Compare* tangible property.
➤ *adj.* nonphysical, abstract, imperceptible, impalpable, transcendental, nonmaterial, metaphysical, disembodied, soulful, intellectual, philosophical, theoretical, psychic.
intangible asset [*ass* · et] *n.* **Intangible property** that has value. *Compare* tangible asset.
intangible property [*prop* · er · tee] *n.* 1. An **incorporeal right** unrelated to a physical thing. EXAMPLES: a right to sue (i.e., a **cause of action**); a right to inherit property. 2. Property that has no intrinsic value, but evidences something of value. EXAMPLE: a stock certificate (which evidences a share in the ownership of the corporation that issued it). *Compare* tangible property.
intangible value [*val* · yoo] *n.* The worth of **intangible property.**

intangibles [in · *tan* · jiblz] *n. Plural* of **intangible.** 1. **Intangible property,** collectively, is often referred to simply as "intangibles." 2. **General intangibles.**

intangibles tax *n.* A tax levied upon the value of **intangible property** or upon transactions involving intangibles.

integrated [in · te · *gray* · ted] *adj.* 1. Desegregated. See integration. *Also see* desegregation. 2. Coordinated; consolidated; commingled.
➤ desegregated, mixed, assimilated, coordinated, organized, cohesive, complete.
integrated agreement [a · *gree* · ment] *n.* See integrated contract.
integrated bar *n.* A type of involuntary bar association that exists in some states, to which all attorneys practicing in the state must belong. Created by statute or rule of court, it is, in effect, a governmental body. *Compare* voluntary bar.
integrated contract [kon · trakt] *n.* A written contract that contains all the terms and conditions of the parties' agreement. It must expressly say so. (EXAMPLE: "This contract represents the entire agreement between the parties.") An integrated contract cannot be modified by **parol evidence.** *See* contract.

integration [in · te · *gray* · shen] *n.* 1. The bringing together of people of all races. *Compare* segregation. 2. Making something part of a larger thing; combining; commingling; consolidating; merging. *See* consolidation; merger. *See and compare* horizontal integration; vertical integration.
➤ desegregation, assimilation, union, harmonization, coexistence.
Ant. separation.

intellectual property [in · te · *lek* · choo · el *prop* · er · tee] *n.* Property (EXAMPLES: **copyrights; patents; trade secrets**) that is the physical or tangible result of original thought. Modern technology has brought about widespread infringement of intellectual property rights. EXAMPLE: the unauthorized reproduction and sale of videotapes, audiotapes, and computer software. *See* infringement of copyright; infringement of patent; literary property; piracy.

intemperance [in · *tem* · per · ense] *n.* 1. The habitual and excessive use of intoxicating liquor. *See* habitual drunkard; habitual drunkenness. 2. Lack of restraint in one's habits and conduct.

➤ excess, self-indulgence, abandon, extravagance, exaggeration, insatiability, unreasonableness, self-gratification, gluttony, debauchery, insobriety, drunkenness, alcoholism.
Ant. restraint.

intend [in · *tend*] *v.* To have in mind; to act with purpose or design.

➤ mean, plan, aim, calculate, premeditate, propose, scheme, resolve, plot, design.

intended use doctrine [in · *ten* · ded use *dok* · trin] *n.* The rule of **product liability** law that a manufacturer or seller of a product is liable for injury resulting from its use only if the product was used for the purpose for which it was intended.

intent [in · *tent*] *n.* Purpose; the plan, course, or means a person conceives to achieve a certain result. Intent is an essential element of any crime except a **strict liability crime** or a **regulatory offense**, and some **petty offenses** and **infractions**. Intent is not, however, limited to conscious wrongdoing, and may be inferred or presumed. *Compare* motive. *See* criminal intent; felonious intent; legislative intent; specific intent; testamentary intent; transferred intent. *See also* malice; malice aforethought; *mens rea;* premeditation; *scienter.*

➤ determination, scheme, plan, resolve, view, goal, contemplation, will, leaning, premeditation, end, mark, resolution, target, aim, ambition, destination, object, objective, idea ("intent of Congress"); drift, implication, connotation, essence, indication, signification, message, significance ("Your intent is clear").

intent to commit a felony [kum · *it* a *fel* · e · nee] *n.* An essential element of the crime of **burglary**.

intent to kill *n.* In some jurisdictions, an essential element of the crime of **aggravated assault**.

intention [in · *ten* · shen] *n.* Purpose; plan; object; aim; goal. The **intention of the parties** is the most important factor in interpreting a contract. *Also see* declaration of intention; testamentary intent.

➤ course, proclivity, purpose, route, propensity, purpose, plan, object, aim,

goal ("the intention of the parties"); penchant, bias, leaning, impetus, current.

intention of the parties [*par* · teez] *n.* *See* intention.

intentional [in · *ten* · shen · el] *adj.* Done with **intent** or with an intention; knowingly.

➤ preplanned, calculated, plotted, intended, considered; contemplated, resolved, purposeful, schemed, designed, contrived, willed, prearranged, voluntary.
Ant. fortuitous, unintended, accidental.

intentional injury [*in* · je · ree] *n.* An injury inflicted by positive, willful, and aggressive conduct, or by design, as opposed to an injury caused by negligence or resulting from an accident. *See* injury.

intentional tort *n.* *See* intentional injury; tort.

intentionally [in · *ten* · shen · el · ee] *adv.* *See* intentional.

inter [in · tur] (*Latin*) *adv.* Between; among; during. *Compare intra.*

inter alia [*ay* · lee · ah] "Among others"; among other things; among other matters.

inter se [say] "Among themselves"; between themselves. USAGE: "What are the rights and liabilities of the company's stockholders inter se, as opposed to their obligations to the creditors of the corporation?"

inter vivos [*vy* · vose] *adj.* Between living persons.

inter vivos gift [*vy* · vose] *n.* A gift between living persons that becomes absolute and irrevocable during the lifetime of the parties. *Compare* testamentary gift. *See* gift; gift causa mortis.

inter vivos transfer [*vy* · vose *trans* · fer] *n.* A transfer of property made during the lifetime of the owner. EXAMPLE: an **inter vivos gift**. *Compare* testamentary disposition.

inter vivos trust [*vy* · vose] *n.* A **trust** that is effective during the lifetime of the creator of the trust; a **living trust**. *Compare* testamentary trust.

interception [in · ter · *sep* · shen] *n.* 1. Listening to or recording telephone conversations or other forms of electronic communication. It is prohibited by federal and state statutes. See eavesdropping; wiretapping. 2. The act of hindering, obstructing, or otherwise interfering with something.

➤ wiretapping, eavesdropping, bugging, electronic surveillance; blockage, hindrance, obstruction, impedance, frustration.

intercourse [*in · ter · korse*] *n.* 1. Dealings between persons or nations. EXAMPLES: trade; correspondence. 2. Interchange of thought and feeling. 3. Sexual intercourse.

➤ commerce, business, trade, exchange, communication, dealings; intimacy, copulation, fornication, sexual relations, carnal knowledge.

interdict [*in · ter · dikt*] *v.* To forbid; to prohibit.

interest [*in · trest*] *n.* 1. A **right**; a **claim**; a **share**; a **title**. EXAMPLES: a **leasehold interest**; a **security interest**; a **vested interest**. *See* right, title, and interest. *See also* absolute interest; admission against interest; adverse interest; beneficial interest; conflict of interest; declaration against interest; equitable interest; executory interest; future interest; insurable interest; legal interest; party in interest; pecuniary interest; possessory interest; terminable interest. 2. The compensation allowed by law, or fixed by the parties, for the use or **forbearance** of borrowed money. *Compare* carrying charge; finance charge; penalty. *See* accrued interest; compound interest; conventional interest; excessive interest; floating interest; illegal interest; interest on interest; legal interest; rate of interest; simple interest. 3. Concern. *See* compelling state interest. 4. Curiosity.

➤ stake, holding, portion, property, part, ownership, possession, investment, stock, percentage ("an interest in the company"); premium, profit, gain, return, increase; accrual, dividend; benefit, enrichment, boon, advantage; solicitude, attention, concern, heed, notice, regard, anxiety, conscientiousness, wariness; thoughtfulness, preoccupation, enthusiasm, mindfulness ("an interest in the child's welfare"); pursuit, avocation, engrossment, pastime ("diverse interests").

interest coupon [*koo · pon*] *n. See* coupon.

interest on interest *n.* **Compound interest**.

interest rate *n.* The charge made by a lender for the privilege of borrowing money; the rate of interest.

interest upon interest *n.* Same as **interest on interest**.

interest-bearing [*behr · ing*] *adj.* A term applied to any transaction that generates interest. *See* investment. USAGE: "An interest-bearing bond."

interested [*in · tres · ted*] *adj.* Having an **interest**. *Compare* disinterested.

➤ influenced, biased, concerned, prejudiced, undetached, jaundiced, affected, connected, engaged, involved ("an interested party"). *Ant.* detached, uninvolved.

interested party [*par · tee*] *n. See* interested person; real party in interest.

interested person [*per · sen*] *n.* 1. A person who has an **interest** in a lawsuit; a person who will be directly affected by the outcome of litigation. EXAMPLES: a plaintiff or a defendant. 2. A person having an interest in something. EXAMPLE: an heir to an **intestate estate**. *See* real party in interest. *Compare* dummy; stranger.

interference [*in · ter · feer · ense*] *n.* 1. Violation of a person's right to be secure in her business relationships (*interference with business*) or in her contractual relationships (*interference with contract*). Such interference, if it is intentional and unreasonable, is a **tort**. *See* malicious interference with contract; tortious interference with contract. 2. An obstruction, hindrance, or interruption.

➤ obstruction, interruption, interloping, intrusion, prying, resistance, interference, interposition ("interference with contract").

interference proceeding [*pro · see · ding*] *n.* A **proceeding** before the **Patent and Trademark Office** to determine the **priority** between two inventions that conflict with each other.

interim [*in · ter · im*] *adj.* That which is temporary, between, or in the meantime. *See* interlocutory; *pro tempore*. *n.* Intermission; break in the proceedings.

➤ *adj.* temporary, makeshift ("an interim appointment"). *n.* intermission, recess, pause, interlude, meantime, interregnum, break. *Ant.* future, permanent.

interim officer [*off · i · ser*] *n.* A person appointed to temporarily perform the duties of an office.

interim order [*or* · der] *n.* An order by a court or administrative agency that provides **temporary relief**; an **interlocutory order**. EXAMPLE: a **temporary injunction**.

interlineation [in · ter · lin · ee · *ay* · shen] *n.* 1. The act of writing between lines that have already been written or printed, for the purpose of making additions or corrections. 2. That which is written between lines already written. *Compare* interpolation.
➤ insertion, interjection, placement, sliding in, infusion, interpolation, supplement, inset.

interlocking directorate [in · ter · *lok* · ing di · *rek* · ter · ate] *n.* The relationship between two or more corporations that have directors or officers in common.

interlocutory [in · ter · *lok* · you · tore · ee] *adj.* 1. Not determinative of the case, but relating to a decision or order by a judge on a point or matter, such as a procedural question, arising during the course of the proceeding. 2. Temporary; interim; not final. *Compare* final order.
➤ provisional, tentative, intermediary, interim ("an interlocutory appeal"); transient, intervening.
Ant. permanent.

interlocutory appeal [a · *peel*] *n.* An appeal of a ruling or order with respect to a question that, although not determinative of the case, must be decided for the case to be decided. *See* appeal; appealable order.

interlocutory decision [de · *sizh* · en] *n.* *See* interlocutory order.

interlocutory decree [de · *kree*] *n.* *See* decree nisi.

interlocutory order [*or* · der] *n.* An order that is not final; an order that is only intermediate and does not determine or complete the **action**. *Compare* final judgment.

interloper [*in* · ter · loh · per] *n.* 1. A person who does business without a required license. 2. An intruder; a trespasser.
➤ intermeddler, trespasser, busybody, infiltrater, encroacher, raider, crasher.

intermarriage [in · ter · *mehr* · ej] *n.* Marriage between persons of different races, religions, or groups. *See* miscegenation.

intermeddle [in · ter · *med* · ul] *v.* To intrude upon; to interfere wrongfully.

➤ invade, trespass, intrude, infringe, interrupt, intercept, hinder, inhibit, thwart.

intermeddler [in · ter · *med* · ler] *n.* A person who intrudes into or interferes with a business or with property without the legal right to do so. *See* interference; interloper; trespasser. *Compare* volunteer.
➤ invader, trespasser, interloper, intruder.

intermediary [in · ter · *mee* · dee · e · ree] *n.* A person through whom a transaction is performed for another; a go-between. EXAMPLE: a broker.
➤ mediator, arbitrator, broker, middleman, go-between, moderator, medium, emissary.

intermediary bank *n.* Any bank to which an item is transferred in the course of **collection** except the **depositary bank** or **payor bank**.

intermediate [in · ter · *mee* · dee · et] *adj.* Occurring between two events; **interlocutory**; intervening.
➤ halfway, in-between, median, intermediary, central, mid, equidistant, intervening, transitional, interposed.
Ant. terminal.

intermediate account [a · *kount*] *n.* An **account** filed by an **executor, administrator**, or **guardian** between the filing of the **inventory** of an **estate** and the **final settlement**.

intermediate appellate court [a · *pel* · et] *n.* The lower court of a two-level appellate system; an **appellate court** whose decisions are subject to review by a higher appellate court. *See* appellate.

intermediate court *n.* *See* intermediate appellate court.

intermediate order [*or* · der] *n.* Same as **interlocutory order**.

intermediate units [*yoo* · nits] *n.* The entities that coordinate local public school education policy in many states, replacing county or district boards of education. They administer programs mandated by state and federal law. *See* county board; school board.

intermingle [in · ter · *ming* · gling] *v.* To mix different elements; to commingle; to associate with.
➤ mix, commingle, confuse, pool, join, merge, interblend, interlace, mesh.

I

intermingling of goods [in · ter · *ming* · gling] *n.* A mixing of the goods of one person with the goods of another so that they cannot be separated according to the rights of each owner with respect to each item. *See* commingling; commingling of goods. *See also* confusion of goods.

intermittent easement [in · ter · *mit* · ent *eez* · ment] *n.* 1. An **easement** that is only used occasionally. 2. An easement that is usable only at times.

intermixture of goods [in · ter · *miks* · cher] *n.* Same as **intermingling of goods**.

intern [*in* · tern] *n.* A recently graduated student in a professional field who functions as an assistant while she completes her studies. EXAMPLE: a medical intern in a hospital.

v. [in · *tern*] To confine; to restrict freedom of movement to a limited geographical area. Such confinement (an EXAMPLE of which is the detention of enemy aliens during wartime) is called **internment**.

➤ *n.* journeyman, novice, apprentice, trainee, neophyte, graduate, assistant.
v. confine, restrict, detain.

internal [in · *tern* · el] *adj.* 1. Pertaining to the inside; within. 2. Domestic as opposed to foreign.

➤ inner, innermost, inmost, home, in-house, civil, municipal, state, national ("internal audit"); inborn, congenital, intrinsic, basic, fundamental ("internal quality").

internal audit [*aw* · dit] *n.* An **audit** performed by auditors who are employees of the company or other entity being audited, as distinguished from an **independent audit** conducted by outside auditors; a self-audit.

internal commerce [*kawm* · erss] *n.* Same as **intrastate commerce**.

internal improvement [im · *proov* · ment] *n.* **Public improvements**.

internal revenue [*rev* · e · new] *n.* The revenues of the federal government raised from domestic sources (EXAMPLES: income tax; **estate tax**; **excise taxes**), as opposed to revenues raised from customs duties.

internal security [se · *kyoo* · ri · tee] *n.* A term describing activities of government (particularly law enforcement) designed to protect the government and the people against subversive activities.

Internal Revenue Bulletin [in · *tern* · el *rev* · e · new *bull* · et · in] *n.* The ***IRB*** is the official publication of the Internal Revenue Service for announcing official rulings (EXAMPLE: **revenue rulings**) and for publishing **executive orders**, legislation, judicial decisions, and similar items of significance relating to the administration of the tax laws.

Internal Revenue Code [in · *tern* · el *rev* · e · new] *n.* A compilation of all federal statutes that impose taxes (EXAMPLES: income tax; **estate tax**; **gift tax**; **excise tax**) or provide for the administration of such laws.

Internal Revenue Service [in · *tern* · el *rev* · e · new *ser* · viss] *n.* Popularly known as the **IRS**, the organization that administers and enforces the **Internal Revenue Code**. The Internal Revenue Service is an agency within the Department of the Treasury.

international [in · ter · *nash* · e · nel] *adj.* Between two or more nations or between persons of different nations.

➤ foreign, worldwide, global, universal, cosmopolitan.
Ant. domestic, national.

international agreement [a · *gree* · ment] *n.* A treaty or other formal agreement between nations.

international commerce [*kawm* · erss] *n.* *See* foreign trade.

international courts *n.* *See* International Court of Justice.

international law *n.* The rules and principles that govern relations and dealings between nations. *Compare* comity. *See and compare* private international law; public international law. *Also see* conflict of laws.

International Court of Justice [in · ter · *nash* · e · nel court of *juss* · tiss] *n.* The principal judicial body of the United Nations.

International Monetary Fund [in · ter · *nash* · e · nel *mon* · e · teh · ree] *n.* A fund established and administered by the United Nations as the largest source of international credit readily available to member nations.

internment [in · *tern* · ment] *n.* 1. The act of interning someone. *See* intern. 2. The situation of a person who is interned.
➤ detention, confinement.

interplea [*in* · ter · plee] *n.* 1. A **proceeding** in which a claimant to property that has been **attached** may have her rights to the property determined. 2. A **plea** that allows a defendant in a lawsuit involving property rights to assert that he has no interest in the property and to demand that he be relieved of any legal obligations arising out of the property. *Also see* interplead; interpleader.

interplead [in · ter · *pleed*] *n.* To file an **interpleader** in a lawsuit. *Compare* implead.

interpleader [in · ter · *pleed* · er] *n.* A **remedy** that requires rival claimants to property held by a distinterested third party (EXAMPLES: a **stakeholder**; a person who is in debt to the claimants) to litigate their demands without entangling him in their lawsuits. *See* interplea; interplead. *See also* third-party practice. *Compare* impleader; joinder; joinder of parties.

Interpol [*in* · ter · pawl] *n.* An international agency that coordinates the law enforcement activities of the countries that belong to it. "Interpol" is short for "International Criminal Police Organization."

interpolation [in · ter · pe · *lay* · shen] *n.* Adding words to an **instrument** or document in order to alter it. *Compare* interlineation.
➤ injection, introduction, change, rewriting.

interpose [in · ter · *poze*] *v.* 1. To introduce; to insert; to interject. USAGE: to "interpose a defense" means to "present a defense" in a lawsuit. 2. To intervene.
➤ add, introduce, insert, interject, enter.

interpret [in · *ter* · pret] *v.* 1. To construe; to explain; to draw out meaning. 2. To translate from a foreign language. *See* interpretation.
➤ explain, decipher, understand, untangle, translate ("to interpret a statute").

interpretation [in · ter · pre · *tay* · shen] *n.* The process of finding the true meaning of words. "Interpretation" is not synonymous with "**construction**," which has to do with determining the significance not simply of words, but the legal meaning of an entire writing, such as a contract, will, or statute. *Compare* construction.
➤ construction, clarification, definition, analysis, understanding.

interpretation clause *n.* A clause contained in many statutes in which terms used in the statute are defined. It usually appears in the beginning of the statute.

interpreter [in · *ter* · pre · ter] *n.* A person who interprets testimony in court or at a **deposition** for a witness who does not speak English or is hearing-impaired.
➤ translator, assistant, explicator.

interrogation [in · terr · e · *gay* · shen] *n.* 1. The questioning of a criminal suspect by the police. *See* custodial interrogation; Escobedo rule; Miranda rule. 2. The questioning of any person.
➤ grilling, inquisition, catechizing, cross-examination, scrutiny, testing, questioning ("He waived his *Miranda* rights prior to the interrogation").

interrogatories [in · te · *raw* · ge · toh · reez] *n.* 1. Written questions put by one party to another, or, in limited situations, to a witness in advance of trial. Interrogatories are a form of **discovery** and are governed by the **rules of civil procedure**. *Compare* deposition. 2. Questions.
➤ questions, inquiries.

interrupt [*in* · ter · rupt] *v.* To hinder; to stop; to bother or interfere with.
➤ meddle, intrude, disturb, stop, suspend, break in, delay, prevent, disconnect.

interruption [in · te · *rup* · shen] *n.* A break in continuity; the suspension of something.
➤ interference, severance, suspension, stoppage, intermission, disturbance, pause, hiatus, standstill, cessation, recess, interlude. *Ant.* continuation.

interruption of possession [po · *zesh* · en] *n.* An interruption in the continuity of the possession of an adverse claimant (*see* adverse possession). The effect is to restore **constructive possession** to the owner.

intersection [in · ter · *sek* · shun] *n.* A place where two or more things cross.
➤ crossing, juncture, junction, connection, meeting point, crossroads.

I

interspousal [in · ter · *spouw* · zel] *adj.* Between husband and wife.

➤ marital, conjugal, matrimonial, connubial, nuptial, paired, hymeneal, wedded, uxorial ("the doctrine of interspousal immunity").

interspousal immunity [im · *yoo* · ni · tee] *n.* The doctrine in some states that one spouse may not sue the other for a **tort** committed by one against the other. This rule is not to be confused with the **marital communications privilege**, which relates to spouses not testifying against each other.

interspousal transfers [*trans* · ferz] *n.* Transfers of property between husband and wife.

interstate [*in* · ter · state] *adj.* Between states. *Compare* intrastate.

interstate commerce [*kawm* · erss] *n.* **Commerce** between states; that is, from a given point in one state to a given point in another. Most federal statutes dealing with business or labor (EXAMPLES: **consumer credit protection acts**; the **Fair Labor Standards Act**), as well as many other federal statutes, are based upon the **commerce clause** of the Constitution, which gives Congress the power "to regulate commerce… among the several states." The term "commerce" is often used as a short reference for "interstate commerce." For EXAMPLE, "**affecting commerce**" means "affecting interstate commerce" and "**engaged in commerce**" means "engaged in interstate commerce." *See* commerce clause. *Compare* intrastate commerce.

interstate compact [*kawm* · pakt] *n.* A formal agreement between states. *See* compact; compact clause.

interstate extradition [eks · tre · *dish* · en] *n. See* extradition; extradition treaty.

Interstate Commerce Commission (ICC) [*in* · ter · state *kawm* · erss ke · *mish* · en] *n.* A federal agency whose duty is to regulate interstate carriers other than airlines (EXAMPLES: trucking companies; bus lines; trains) and, in particular, to ensure that their rates are fair and their service appropriate.

intervene [in · ter · *veen*] *v.* 1. To become a **party** to a lawsuit by means of **intervention**; to interpose oneself as a party. 2. To occur between; to interrupt. 3. To step in; to come between; to mediate.

➤ interfere, involve, meddle, intercede, settle, negotiate, reconcile.

intervening [in · ter · *veen* · ing] *adj.* 1. Acquiring the status of a **party** to an **action** by means of **intervention**. 2. That which occurs between two events; intermediate (EXAMPLE: in counting the number of days intervening between Thanksgiving and Christmas, one excludes those two days). 3. The act of stepping in or coming between. USAGE: "The **mediator** has agreed to assist by intervening in the labor dispute."

➤ intruding, interfering, obtrusive, parenthetical, infringing, interrupting, breaking in, intercepting.

intervening agency [*ay* · jen · see] *n.* An act or omission that interrupts the connection between cause and effect. *See* intervening cause.

intervening cause *n.* A **cause** that intrudes between the **negligence** of the defendant and the **injury** suffered by the plaintiff, breaking the connection between the original wrongful act or omission and the injury, and itself becoming the **proximate cause** of the injury. *Compare* concurrent cause.

intervening efficient cause [e · *fish* · ent] *n.* Same as **efficient intervening cause**.

intervening force *n. See* intervening cause.

intervening lien [*leen*] *n.* A **lien** that, in point of time or **of record**, comes between other liens or other **conveyances** or transfers of the same property. *See* priority of liens.

intervenor [in · ter · *vee* · nor] *n.* A person who becomes a **party** to a lawsuit by means of a **proceeding** known as **intervention**.

intervention [in · ter · *ven* · shen] *n.* 1. The **proceeding** by which a person not originally a **party** to an **action**, in order to protect her rights, may join one of the original parties in maintaining the action or in asserting a **defense** against some or all of the parties. Intervention is controlled by the **rules of civil procedure**. *See* intervene. 2. Short for **pretrial intervention** or **posttrial intervention**. *See* diversion program.

➤ intrusion, interference, intermeddling, encroachment, interruption, obstruction, overstepping, incursion, insertion, interjection ("intervention in the case");

arbitration, ministry, intercession, negotiation ("intervention by the referee").

interview [in · ter · vyoo] *n.* A conversation comprised of questions and answers for the purpose of gaining information or evaluation.
v. To ask questions of; to evaluate.
➤ *n.* meeting, audition, consultation, examination, evaluation, conference.
v. examine, question, interrogate, quiz, sound out, consult.

intestacy [in · *tess* · ste · see] *n.* The status of the **estate** or property of a person who dies without leaving a valid will. *See* intestate. *Compare* testacy.

intestate [in · *tess* · tate] *adj.* Pertaining to a person, or to the property of a person, who dies without leaving a valid will. USAGE: "John left an **intestate estate**." *See* intestacy; partial intestacy. *Compare* testate.
n. 1. A person who dies without leaving a valid will. USAGE: "John is an intestate." 2. The status of a person who dies without leaving a valid will. USAGE: "John died intestate." *See* intestate. *Compare* testate.

intestate estate [es · *tate*] *n.* The **estate** of a person who dies without leaving a valid will.

intestate laws *n.* State statutes that set forth the rules by which property passes when a person dies intestate. *See* descent; devolution; devolve. *Also see* intestate succession; partial intestacy.

intestate property [*prop* · er · tee] *n.* Same as **intestate estate**.

intestate succession [suk · *sesh* · en] *n.* Inheritance from a person who dies **intestate**. *Compare* testate succession. *See* succession.

intimate [*in* · tih · mit] *adj.* Very close; personal; private.
➤ friendly, guarded, confidential, personal, private, secret, sexual ("an intimate conversation").

intimidation [in · tim · i · *day* · shen] *n.* The act of putting a person in fear by threatening to commit an unlawful act. Intimidation does not necessarily involve an act of violence or even a threat of violence. *Compare* threat. *See also* coercion; duress; extortion; undue influence.
➤ coercion, duress, extortion, undue influence.

into [in · too] *adv.* Within; inside of. Courts have held "into" to be comparable to "to," but not to "through."
➤ within, inside of.

intolerable indignity [in · *taw* · le · rebl in · *dig* · ni · tee] *n.* An **indignity** amounting to **mental cruelty**, and therefore a ground for divorce in some states.

intolerance [in · *tol* · er · ants] *n.* Attitudes or behavior characterized by bias or bigotry.
➤ partiality, narrow-mindedness, bias, prejudice, racism, aversion, dislike, hatred, bigotry, repulsion.

intoxicant [in · *tok* · si · kent] *n.* Any substance that causes intoxication. EXAMPLES: alcoholic beverages; heroin; barbiturates; airplane glue. *See* controlled substance; drug.
➤ controlled substance, drug.

intoxicated [in · *tok* · si · kay · ted] *adj.* Being in a state of intoxication; inebriated; drunk. *See* driving while intoxicated.
➤ drunk, drunken, inebriated, plastered, loaded, high, dazed, befuddled, alcoholic.
Ant. sober.

intoxicating liquor [in · *tok* · si · kay · ting *lik* · er] *n.* Any beverage that produces intoxication when consumed in sufficient quantities. *See* alcoholic beverage; intoxicant.

intoxication [in · tok · si · *kay* · shen] *n.* 1. A disturbance of mental or physical capacities resulting from the use of alcohol, drugs, or other substances; a substance-induced impairment of a person's judgment or sense of responsibility. *See* habitual drunkenness; public intoxication. *See also* driving while intoxicated. 2. Inebriation; drunkenness.
For the relationship between intoxication and responsibility for criminal conduct, *see and compare* involuntary intoxication; voluntary intoxication.
➤ inebriation, drunkenness, dipsomania, incompetence, intemperance, insobriety, alcoholism.
Ant. sobriety.

intra [*in* · tra] (*Latin*) *adv.* Within; within the bounds of. *Compare* inter.

intrastate [*in* · tra · state] *adj.* Wholly within the boundaries of a state. *Compare* interstate.

I

intrastate commerce [*kawm* · erss] *n.* **Commerce** that takes place within the boundaries of one state. *Compare* interstate commerce.

intrinsic [in · *trin* · zik] *adj.* Describes that which is a part of the fundamental nature of something; inherent. *Compare* extrinsic.
➤ internal, fundamental, natural, indwelling, permanent, authentic, real, inner, basic, indigenous, innate, constitutional, substantial, congenital, underlying. *Ant.* incidental.

intrinsic fraud *n.* 1. **Fraud** committed in the trial of a case or with respect to an issue involved in the case. EXAMPLES: **perjury**; bribing a witness; forging an exhibit. 2. **Fraud in the inducement**. *Compare* extrinsic fraud.

intrinsic value [*val* · yoo] *n.* The true or inherent value of a thing; the value of the thing itself. The intrinsic value of an article may be very different from the amount of money required to purchase it or the cost of manufacturing it. EXAMPLE: measured by the paper and ink of which it is made, a thousand-dollar bill has almost no intrinsic value. *Compare* market value.

introduce [*in* · tro · dooss] *v.* 1. To present or put forward. USAGE: "Rubin introduced the knife into evidence." 2. To recommend or sponsor. USAGE: "The president introduced new tax savings."
➤ enter, offer, submit, present, put forward, tender, proffer; institute, announce, inaugurate, start, launch, pioneer.

introduced evidence [in · tre · *doosd ev* · i · dense] *n.* Evidence offered by a party in the trial of a case and admitted or received by the court. *See* offer of proof. *See also* admissible evidence.

introduction of evidence [in · tre · *duk* · shen of *ev* · i · dense] *n.* See introduced evidence.

intruder [in · *troo* · der] *n.* 1. A person who enters a place without invitation, particularly after having been told not to. *See* trespasser. 2. A person who involves himself in anything in circumstances where his involvement is unwelcome. *See* intermeddler.
➤ trespasser, aggressor, invader, infiltrator, raider, encroacher, unlawful entrant. *Ant.* guest, invitee.

invalid [in · *val* · id] *adj.* Illegal; of no force or effect. *Compare* valid.
n. [*in* · ve · lid] A sick person.
➤ *adj.* unfounded, faulty, inoperative, untrue, ineffective, illegal.
n. shut-in, convalescent, cripple, amputee, victim, patient, stricken person, paraplegic.

invalidate [in · *val* · i · date] *v.* To render something illegal or to deprive it of legal effect. USAGE: "I'm certain the court will invalidate this contract."
➤ overrule, cancel, reverse, abolish, void.

invasion [in · *vay* · zhen] *n.* An intrusion upon the property or rights of another.
➤ intrusion, incursion, interference, trespass, overstepping, intermeddling, inroad, breach, penetration, assault.

invasion of corpus [*kore* · pus] *n.* Also called **invasion of principal**; making payments from the principal or *corpus* of a **trust** when the trust income is insufficient to support the payments required by the **terms of the trust**.

invasion of principal [*prin* · sipl] *n. See* invasion of corpus.

invasion of privacy [*pry* · ve · see] *n.* A violation of the **right of privacy**. *See* privacy.

invent [in · *vent*] *v.* 1. To think of something new, particularly a new device, and of a method of creating it, and to follow through with its creation. 2. To create. 3. To make up or falsify. *See* invention.
➤ formulate, develop, author, fashion, originate, devise, conceive, hatch, imagine, produce, patent, envisage, dream up ("invent a new design"); pretend, distort, fabricate, concoct, fake, make up ("invent an alibi").

invention [in · *ven* · shen] *n.* 1. The act of creating something patentable. *See* patent. *See also* device. *Compare* discovery. 2. The thing that has been invented. 3. The act of creating something new. 4. The act of making something up or falsifying. *See* invent.
➤ finding, discovery, creation, improvisation, concoction, composition, innovation, fabrication.

inventor [in · *ven* · ter] *n.* A person who creates an invention.
➤ author, maker, creator, deviser, pioneer, improviser.

inventory [in · ven · tor · ee] *n.* 1. An itemized list or schedule of **assets**, property, or other articles, sometimes with notations of their value. EXAMPLES: a list of a merchant's stock in trade (that is, the items she has in stock or on hand); the list of an auctioneer at a **foreclosure sale**; a list possessed by a sheriff serving a **writ of execution**, a **trustee in bankruptcy**, or the **administrator** of an **estate**. 2. Goods held for sale or lease (stock in trade) or raw materials consumed in a business.
➤ itemized list, menu, checklist, stocklist, catalog, index, accounting, roster, register, account, enumeration, statement, tally.
inventory search *n.* See custodial search.

inverse [in · *verse*] *adj.* Reversed; opposite; contradictory.
➤ opposite, backward, contrary, transposed, inverted, converse.

inverse condemnation [kon · dem · *nay* · shen] *n.* A suit brought against the government by a property owner who has been adversely affected by a taking of his property for public use without the payment of just compensation and without a **condemnation proceeding**. See condemnation. See also eminent domain.

invest [in · *vest*] *v.* 1. To use money to generate income. See investment. 2. To install in office. 3. To **vest**. 4. To devote (time or energy).
➤ speculate, lay out, put out capital, sink money into, support, venture ("invest in a fund"); endow, vest, license, confer, appoint, commission, entrust, mandate, delegate, ordain, authorize, sanction, grant, enable ("invest with authority").

investigate [in · *ves* · ti · gate] *v.* To inquire; to look into; to make an investigation.
➤ inspect, look into, seek evidence, track, inquire into, probe, observe, examine, analyze, scrutinize, dissect, explore.

investigation [in · ves · ti · *gay* · shen] *n.* 1. An inquiry, either judicial, legislative, or administrative, for the discovery and collection of facts concerning a particular matter or matters. See discovery; examination; inspection. 2. Inquiry; looking into something; research.
➤ inquiry, examination, inspection, research, exploration, scrutiny, search, study.

investigatory [in · *ves* · ti · ga · tor · ee] *adj.* Having the quality or character of an investigation.

investigatory interrogation [in · terr · o · *gay* · shen] *n.* The routine questioning of a person by a police officer in circumstances where the person being questioned has not been accused of criminal conduct and has not been deprived of his freedom of action in any significant way. The constitutional protections of the **Miranda rule** do not apply in the case of an investigatory interrogation. See interrogation.

investigatory powers [*pouw* · erz] *n.* Authority conferred upon administrative agencies or legislative committees to inspect, to require the disclosure of information, and, usually, to call witnesses and to compel them to testify under oath.

investigatory stop *n.* See stop and frisk.

investment [in · *vest* · ment] *n.* 1. The act of placing money or **capital** where it will yield an income or revenue. EXAMPLES: making an interest-bearing loan; purchasing stock, bonds, or other securities; buying **income property**. See investment property; investment security; legal investment. 2. A property or a deal into which money is put for the purpose of producing income or revenue.
➤ financing, venture, capital, speculation, stock, portfolio, holding, securities.

investment adviser [ad · *vy* · zer] *n.* A person who engages in the business of counseling others as to the advisability of purchasing or selling **securities** or who, as a regular business, issues analyses of or reports concerning securities.

investment bank *n.* A financial institution engaged in the business of **underwriting** new **securities**.

investment bonds *n.* One form of **investment security**. EXAMPLES: coupon bonds; **municipal bonds**; **serial bonds**.

investment company [*kum* · pe · nee] *n.* An issuer of **securities** that is primarily engaged in the business of investing, reinvesting, or trading in securities. *Compare* holding company.

investment contract [kon · trakt] *n.* 1. Under federal statute, a transaction in

I

which money is invested in a common enterprise involving the efforts of others from which a profit is anticipated. 2. Any contract providing for the investment of **capital** in a way intended to produce profit.

investment credit [*kred* · it] *n.* A direct credit against federal income tax, as opposed to a tax deduction, for money invested by a business in **capital** items such as **capital equipment**.

investment fund *n.* *See* investment trust; mutual fund.

investment income [*in* · kum] *n.* *See* unearned income.

investment property [*prop* · er · tee] *n.* Same as **income property**.

investment security [se · *kyoo* · ri · tee] *n.* As distinguished from ordinary **commercial paper**, a **security** normally traded on a **securities exchanges**.

investment tax credit [*kred* · it] *n.* *See* tax credit.

investment trust *n.* A corporation that puts its **assets** into stocks, bonds, or other investments and distributes the profits to shareholders of the trust. *See* mutual fund.

investor [in · *vest* · er] *n.* A person who makes investments; a person who invests.

invidious [in · *vid* · ee · us] *adj.* Hostile or malicious.
➤ hostile, offensive, malicious, overt ("invidious discrimination").

invidious discrimination [in · *vid* · ee · us dis · krim · i · *nay* · shen] *n.* Discrimination of the type forbidden by the **equal protection clause** of the **Fourteenth Amendment**; discrimination that is arbitrary, irrational, and not related to any legitimate purpose. *See* discrimination.

invitation [in · vi · *tay* · shen] *n.* An express or implied offer or request by a person who owns or occupies real estate, made to another person, to enter or pass through the property. An invitation is to be distinguished from mere permission. *See and compare* express invitation; implied invitation. *Also see* invitee. *Compare* trespass.
➤ enticement, attraction, allurement, petition, offer, solicitation, overture, inducement, provocation, stimulus.

Ant. rejection, expulsion.

invitation to bid *n.* Notice given by one who wishes a job done, to those viewed as likely candidates for doing it, describing the job (i.e., providing specifications) and requesting bids. *See* letting a contract.

invited error [in · *vy* · ted *ehr* · er] *n.* A party who causes a court to commit **error** cannot use that error as a basis for appeal. *See* judicial error.

invitee [in · vy · *tee*] *n.* A person who enters the premises of another at the latter's invitation, or for business purposes, or for their mutual advantage. EXAMPLES: a restaurant patron; a customer of a store; a plumber called to repair a leaky faucet; a social guest. *Compare* licensee, but *note* that the distinction between invitee and licensee has been abandoned in some jurisdictions. *See* business invitee; mutual advantage rule. *See and compare* express invitation; implied invitation. *Also compare* trespasser.
➤ guest, patron, customer.

invoice [in · voiss] *n.* A list of the items included in a sale, although not itself the bill of sale; a list of items included in a shipment to a purchaser or **consignee**. An invoice usually itemizes the value of the listed items.
➤ written account, statement, bill, account; inventory, reckoning, enumeration.

involuntary [in · *vol* · en · te · ree] *adj.* Not voluntary; unwilling; independent of choice; that which is coerced or done under duress.
➤ forced, unwilling, coercive, obligatory, mandatory, imperative, unintentional, automatic.
Ant. voluntary, willful.

involuntary alienation [ayl · yen · *ay* · shen] *n.* A loss of **title** to property due to **attachment**, **levy**, sale for taxes, bankruptcy, or similar proceedings. *Compare* voluntary alienation. *See* alienation.

involuntary bailment [*bail* · ment] *n.* A **bailment** created by accident as a result of the owner of personal property accidentally, but without negligence, leaving it in the possession of another. EXAMPLE: belongings left behind by a hotel guest.

involuntary bankruptcy [*bank* · rupt · see] *n.* A bankruptcy initiated by one's creditors. *See* bankruptcy; bankruptcy proceedings. *Compare* voluntary bankruptcy.

involuntary commitment [ke · *mit* · ment] *n.* The process by which a person suffering from a mental illness is admitted to a mental institution, against his will, for diagnosis and is detained for treatment. The law imposes significant restrictions on the circumstances under which such a commitment may occur, its purpose, and its duration; the law also imposes strict **procedural due process** requirements with respect to involuntary commitments. *Compare* voluntary commitment. *See* insanity. *Also see* civil commitment; commitment.

involuntary confession [ken · *fesh* · en] *n.* A **confession** obtained by means of fear or threats of violence, or by promises of reward or **immunity**. An involuntary confession is inadmissible as evidence against a criminal defendant. *Compare* voluntary confession.

involuntary conversion [ken · *ver* · zhen] *n.* The loss or destruction of property as a result of theft, **casualty**, or **condemnation**. *See* conversion.

involuntary conveyance [ken · *vey* · ense] *n.* A transfer of real estate without the consent of the owner, usually as the result of a **judgment** or an order of court. *Compare* voluntary deed. *See* conveyance.

involuntary deposit [de · *pawz* · it] *n.* Same as **involuntary bailment**.

involuntary discontinuance [dis · ken · *tin* · yoo · ense] *n.* The forcing of a case out of court for some error in **pleading** or technical omission. It is a form of **involuntary dismissal**. *Compare* voluntary discontinuance. *See* discontinuance.

involuntary dismissal [dis · *miss* · el] *n.* The **dismissal** of a lawsuit by the court, either prior to **judgment** or by virtue of a judgment against the plaintiff based upon the verdict of the jury or the decision of the court after trial. *Compare* voluntary dismissal.

involuntary intoxication [in · tok · si · *kay* · shen] *n.* Intoxication that is not self-induced. (EXAMPLE: the condition of a person who is given a drug without realizing it.) Involuntary intoxication

is an **affirmative defense** to a criminal charge. *Compare* voluntary intoxication.

involuntary manslaughter [*man* · slaw · ter] *n.* The unintentional killing of a human being by a person engaged in doing some unlawful act not amounting to a **felony**, or in doing some lawful act in a manner tending to cause death or great bodily injury. *See* manslaughter. *See and compare* murder; voluntary manslaughter.

involuntary nonsuit [*non* · soot] *n.* See nonsuit.

involuntary servitude [*ser* · vi · tood] *n.* The status of a person who is forced to work for another, with or without pay; **peonage**. *Compare* slavery. Both involuntary servitude and slavery were abolished by the **Thirteenth Amendment**. *See* servitude.

involuntary transfer [*trans* · fer] *n.* Same as **involuntary conveyance**.

involuntary trust *n.* Same as **constructive trust**. *Compare* voluntary trust.

involve [in · *volv*] *v.* 1. To bring into a circumstance. 2. To engage in an activity.
➤ implicate, accuse, incriminate, inculpate, draw in, charge ("involve a codefendant"); relate, support, participate, enter into, collude, collaborate, connect, act in concert.

IOLTA [eye · *ol* · ta] Acronym for Interest on Lawyers' Trust Accounts. In states with IOLTA programs, lawyers who hold funds belonging to clients deposit such money into a common fund, the interest on which is used for charitable, law-related purposes such as legal services to the poor. Some states' IOLTA programs are voluntary; some are mandatory.

iota [eye · oh · tuh] *n.* A minute amount; the smallest amount possible.
➤ fragment, morsel, scintilla, bit, drop, dab, shred, trace, grain.

IOU [eye · oh · *yoo*] *n.* A **memorandum** of debt, consisting of the three letters *I*, *O*, and *U* (standing for "I owe you"), a statement of amount, and the debtor's signature.

ipso facto [ip · soh fak · toh] (*Latin*) "By the fact itself"; by the very fact; by the act itself.

IRA [*eye* · rah] Acronym for **individual retirement account**.

IRB Abbreviation of *Internal Revenue Bulletin*.

IRC Abbreviation of **Internal Revenue Code**.

iron safe clause [*eye* · ern] *n.* A provision in a fire insurance policy requiring the insured to keep her books, inventories, and other records in a fireproof safe or other place safe from fire. Under an iron safe clause, such data are the only acceptable proof of the value of the items covered by the policy, and their destruction by fire releases the insurance company from its obligations under the policy.

ironclad [*eye* · urn · klad] *adj.* Firm; definite.
➤ definite, firm, final, certain, strict ("an ironclad agreement").

irrational [ir · *rash* · uh · nul] *adj.* Illogical; lacking reason or sense.
➤ unsensible, unreasonable, ridiculous, illogical, injudicious, ludicrous.

irrebuttable [ir · re · *but* · ebl] *adj.* That which cannot be rebutted, denied, or contradicted.
➤ conclusive, incontestable, definite.
irrebuttable presumption
[pre · *zump* · shen] *n.* Also called a **conclusive presumption**; an inference of fact so strong that it amounts to a rule of law, which the court will not permit to be contradicted by a showing of fact to the contrary. EXAMPLE: A statute which declares that a person in a state of intoxication is conclusively presumed to be unable to operate and control a motor vehicle on the highway. *See* presumption. *Compare* rebuttable presumption.

irreconcilable [ir · rek · en · *sy* · luh · bul] *adj.* Not capable of being solved or harmonized.
➤ irretrievable, irremedial, unsolvable, conflicting.

irreconcilable differences
[ir · rek · en · *sy* · lebl *dif* · ren · sez] *n.* A requirement for divorce or dissolution of marriage in some states with **no-fault divorce** laws. The term itself means that, because of dissension and personality conflicts, the marriage relationship has been destroyed and there is no reasonable expectation of reconciliation. *See also* irremedial breakdown of marriage; irretrievable breakdown of marriage.

irrecusable [ir · re · *kyoo* · zih · bul] *adj.* Relating to an imposed obligation which is incapable of being refused or rejected.
➤ imposed, mandated, required.

irrecusable obligation [ir · re · *kyoo* · zebl ob · li · *gay* · shen] *n.* An obligation to which one has not consented, but which cannot be avoided. EXAMPLE: an obligation imposed by law, such as a **constructive trust**.

irrefutable [ir · ree · *fyoot* · ih · bul] *adj.* Definitive; conclusive; incapable of being challenged.
➤ firm, positive, proven, indisputable, certain, sure, evident ("irrefutable proof").

irregular [ir · *reg* · yoo · ler] *adj.* Different; departing from the normal or regular.
➤ abnormal, out of order, nonconforming, erratic, inconsistent, variable, improper, flawed, aberrant, intermittent.

irregular judgment [ir · *reg* · yoo · ler *juj* · ment] *n.* A **judgment** that fails to conform to some necessary **rule of practice** or **rule of procedure** and is therefore subject to reversal.

irregularity [ir · reg · yoo · *lehr* · i · tee] *n.* 1. A failure to follow appropriate and necessary **rules of practice** or **rules of procedure** by omitting some act essential to the orderly conduct of a lawsuit or conducting it in an improper manner. 2. A failure to comply with rules or requirements imposed by law. (EXAMPLE: a competitive bid that does not conform to specifications.) Irregularity will render a transaction unenforceable only if it is substantial. *Compare* illegality.
➤ deviation, nonconformity, divergence, aberration, abnormality.

irrelevancy [ir · *rel* · e · ven · see] *n.* Lack of relevancy, whether in a **pleading** or in evidence; that which is not related to any pertinent or material issue in the case; that which is redundant. *Compare* relevancy.

irrelevant [ir · *rel* · e · vent] *adj.* Not material; having the quality of irrelevancy. *Compare* relevant. *See* immaterial; impertinent; impertinent matter.
➤ not relevant, impertinent, unconnected, extraneous, immaterial, unrelated, inapplicable, beside the point, foreign,

not germane, inappropriate ("irrevelant evidence").
Ant. pertinent, material, germane.

irrelevant allegation [al · le · *gay* · shen] *n.* Same as **immaterial allegation**.

irrelevant evidence [*ev* · i · dense] *n.* Evidence that is not material or pertinent; evidence that does not tend to prove a **material fact** or a fact at issue in the case. Irrelevent evidence is inadmissible. *Compare* relevant evidence. *See* evidence.

irremedial breakdown of marriage [ir · re · *mee* · dee · el *brake* · down of mehr · ej] *n.* A requirement for **no-fault divorce** in some states. *See also* irreconcilable differences; irretrievable breakdown of marriage.

irreparable [ir · *rep* · er · rebl] *adj.* Unrepairable; that which cannot be repaired, corrected, or adequately compensated. *See* compensation.
➤ irreversible, beyond repair, irremediable, irrevocable, beyond correction, hopeless, lost, remediless, incurable, unfixable, unsalvageable.
Ant. salvageable.

irreparable damage [*dam* · ej] *n.* In the law of **injunctions**, an **injury** of such a nature that there is no adequate **remedy** in a **court of law** and for which, therefore, recourse must be sought in a **court of equity**; an injury that cannot be satifactorily or completely compensated with money. The term does not refer to the *amount* of **damage** caused, or the *amount* of the **damages**, but to the *difficulty of measuring* the amount of the damages. *Compare* reparable injury.

irreparable harm *n.* *See* irreparable damage.

irreparable injury [*in* · je · ree] *n.* *See* irreparable damage. *Compare* reparable injury.

irresistible [ir · re · *zis* · tibl] *adj.* That which cannot be resisted; that which is compelling or overpowering.
➤ overwhelming, unavoidable, compelling, overpowering, inexorable, formidable, omnipotent, vigorous, invincible.
Ant. resistible.

irresistible force *n.* An overwhelming force; a force that cannot be resisted. EXAMPLE: a mob. *See* act of God; *force majeure.*

irresistible impulse [*im* · pulse] *n.* An impulse to commit an act that one is powerless to control. "Irresistible impulse" is the test used in some jurisdictions to determine insanity for purposes of a criminal **defense**. This test asks: Although the defendant is able to understand the nature and consequences of her act, and to understand that it is wrong, is she unable because of mental disease to resist the impulse to do it? *Compare* M'Naghten rule. *See* insanity.

irretrievable breakdown of marriage [ir · re · *treev* · ebl *brake* · down of mehr · ej] *n.* A requirement for **no-fault divorce** in some states. *See* irreconcilable differences; irremedial breakdown of marriage.

irreversible [ir · re · *ver* · sih · bul] *adj.* Permanent; irrevocable.
➤ persistent, irrevocable, lost, final, perpetual ("an irreversible condition").
Ant. temporary.

irreversible coma [ir · re · *ver* · sibl *koh* · ma] *n.* Same as **chronic persistent vegetative state**.

irrevocable [ir · *rev* · e · kebl] *adj.* That which cannot be abrogated, annulled, or withdrawn; not revocable.
➤ irreversible, final, unmodifiable, inextinguishable, unalterable, immovable, indissoluble, immutable, fixed ("an irrevocable offer").
Ant. revocable.

irrevocable offer [*off* · er] *n.* Same as **firm offer**.

irrevocable trust *n.* A **trust** in which the **settlor** permanently gives up control of the trust property. *Compare* revocable trust.

IRS Abbreviation of **Internal Revenue Service**.

issuance [*ish* · yoo · ense] *n.* The act of issuing. *See* issue.

issue [*ish* · yoo] *n.* 1. **Securities** offered for sale at a particular time, either to the public or privately, by a corporation or by government; an **offering**. EXAMPLES: corporate stock (a **stock issue**); **municipal bonds** (a **bond issue**). *See and compare* private offering; public offering. 2. Under the **Uniform Commercial Code**, the first delivery of a **negotiable instrument** to anyone by its **maker** or **drawer** for the purpose of giving rights in the instrument. 3. A material point or question arising out of the **pleadings** in a case, which is disputed by the parties and which they wish the court to decide. *See and compare* issue of fact; issue of law. *See also* at issue; joinder of issue. 4. All persons who are descendants of one ancestor, including all future descendants. However, when used in a will, "issue" will be taken to mean children or grandchildren, or all *living* descendants, if that is the **testator's** clear intention. "Issue" may or may not include adopted children, depending upon state law. *v.* To come from; to come out; to come out of; to put out; to bring out; to distribute; to give out. USAGE: "the corporation will issue stock tomorrow"; "he requested that the court issue its decision."

➤ *n.* issuance, dissemination, publication, presentation, exhibition, emergence, disclosure, dispensation, granting ("a stock issue"); question, cause, problem, dispute, contention, topic, subject, affair, theme, disputed, matter ("an issue in this case"); heirs, progeny, children, grandchildren, decendants, posterity, family, lineage, seed, line, young ("die without issue"). *v.* print, disseminate, publish, announce, distribute, reveal, enunciate, circulate, release.

issue of fact *n.* Issue that arises when a fact is alleged or asserted by one party and is disputed by the other. In a jury trial, the jury decides issues of fact; in a bench trial, issues of fact are decided by the judge. *Compare* issue of law.

issue of law *n.* Issue that arises when the facts are not in dispute and the question before the court is the conclusion of law to be drawn from the facts. *Compare* issue of fact.

issuer [*ish · oo · er*] *n.* 1. An entity that issues securities. EXAMPLES: a corporation; a city; the government of the United States. 2. Anyone who issues something.

item [*eye · tem*] *n.* 1. Under the **Uniform Commercial Code**, "an **instrument** or a promise or order to pay money handled by a bank for **collection** or payment." 2. A specific subject or matter contained in an **appropriation act**. 3. An entry in an account. 4. An article or thing. 5. A distinct or separate part.

➤ entry, piece, particular, object, feature, aspect, circumstance, thing, subject, point, detail, sample, ingredient, member.

itemize [*eye · tem · ize*] *v.* To state or list items individually or in detail. USAGE: "Did you itemize your tax deductions this year?" *See* itemized deductions.

➤ individualize, catalog, particularize, rank, inventory, tabulate, designate, register one-by-one, enumerate ("itemize the losses").

itemized deductions [*eye · tem · ized de · duk · shenz*] *n.* Deductions from **adjusted gross income** that are available in certain circumstances to taxpayers who do not choose to use the **standard deduction**. EXAMPLES: state and local taxes; interest on the mortgage on one's home. *See* deduction.

ivory tower [*eye · vuh · rcc tow · ur*] *n.* Literally, a scholar's retreat. In common USAGE, "living in an ivory tower" means that a person and his ideas are too theoretical, impractical, or unrealistic to work in the "real world."

J Abbreviation of **judge** and **justice**. USAGE: "Marshall, J., dissenting."

jactitation [jak · ti · *tay* · shen] *n.* A false claim or boast. At **common law**, if such a claim caused **injury** it was **actionable**.
➤ false claims, boast, brag, vanity, pretension, swagger, puffery.
jactitation of title [*ty* · tel] *n.* Same as **slander of title**.

JAG [jag] Acronym for **Judge Advocate General**. *See* Judge Advocate General.

jail *n.* A place of confinement, usually maintained by a county or municipality, for persons convicted of **misdemeanors** or for persons accused of crime and awaiting trial who are not able to furnish bail or are not entitled to bail. *Compare* penitentiary; prison.
v. To confine or imprison.
➤ *n.* house of detention, gaol, correctional institution, lockup, brig, prison, pen, penitentiary, penal institution, reformatory, cell.
v. lock up, restrain, restrict, imprison, isolate, take into custody, incarcerate.

Jane Doe *n.* The feminine version of **John Doe**; a fictitious name often used in court papers when the unidentified party is known to be a woman.

Jason clause [*jay* · sun] *n.* A clause in a ship's **bill of lading** that imposes upon each of the owners of the ship's cargo the obligation to make a **general average contribution** in the event of **loss** to the property of any one or more of them.

jaywalking [*jay* · waw · king] *n.* Crossing a street diagonally or, under some ordinances, at a place other than a designated crossing.

JD Abbreviation of **Juris Doctor** or **Doctor of Jurisprudence**, the primary degree awarded by most law schools, replacing the LLB. *Compare* LLD; LLM.

jealous [*jel* · us] *adj.* Suspecting unfaithfulness in another; distrustful; insecure.
➤ envious, covetous, possessive, suspicious, insecure, doubting, distrustful.

Jencks rule *n.* The rule that a defendant in a federal criminal prosecution has the right to examine government papers to be better able to cross-examine or **impeach** government witnesses. *Also see* cross-examination; impeachment.

jeopardize [*jep* · er · dize] *v.* To risk; to endanger.
➤ imperil, threaten, endanger, risk, stake, gamble.

jeopardy [*jep* · er · dee] *n.* 1. In a criminal case, the danger of conviction and punishment to which a defendant is exposed when he is brought to trial. The **Fifth Amendment** guarantees that a person cannot "for the same offense ... twice be put in jeopardy"; that is, the government cannot expose a person to **double jeopardy** by trying him twice for the same crime. 2. Danger; peril; exposure.
➤ exposure, threat, peril, insecurity, danger, precariousness, venture, uncertainty, endangerment, instability.
jeopardy assessment [a · *sess* · ment] *n.* An accelerated procedure by which the IRS assesses and collects taxes if it is concerned that a taxpayer may conceal **assets** to evade payment.

jetsam [*jet* · sem] *n.* Goods thrown overboard to save a ship during a storm or similar occurrence, which float in the water or are cast onto the beach by the wind and tide. *Compare* flotsam. *See* jettison.

jettison [*jet* · i · sen] *v.* The voluntary throwing overboard of part of the cargo to save a ship in distress. *See* jetsam.

➤ throw away, cast, cast aside, discharge, expel, dismiss, eject, eliminate, drop, reject.

Jim Crow *adj./n.* A term for **de jure segregation**.

JNOV Abbreviation of **judgment notwithstanding the verdict** or **judgment non obstante veredicto**.

job lot *n.* A commercial term for goods of various kinds, or of various brands, brought together for sale in one lot, usually to a retailer. *See* lot.

jobber [*job* · ber] *n.* 1. An intermediary who buys from a manufacturer or whole-saler and sells to retailers. *See also* broker; factor. 2. A person or business engaged in piecework.

➤ middleman, supplier, representative, salesperson, broker, wholesaler, cosigner, operator.

John Doe *n.* A **fictitious name** often substituted for a party's real name in the title of an **action** or proceeding until the real name can be learned. Thus, there are John Doe actions, John Doe summonses, and John Doe warrants. The term "John Doe" is also used in court papers to protect privacy.

join *v.* 1. To merge or combine. 2. To contest legally.

➤ merge, connect, link, attach, unify, collaborate; take on, contest, engage ("The issue was joined.").

joinder [*join* · der] *n.* 1. Uniting, in a single **complaint**, two or more elements of a lawsuit (EXAMPLES: **joinder of claims**; **joinder of parties**), each of which could be the basis of a separate suit. 2. Uniting two or more **indictments** or **informations** in a single criminal prosecution. 3. A person's acceptance of an agreement or other trans-action to which she is not otherwise bound. 4. Acting jointly with one or more other persons; joining.

Joinder in **civil actions** is governed in considerable detail by the **rules of civil procedure**; in **criminal cases** by the **rules of criminal procedure**. *See* collusive joinder; compulsory joinder; misjoinder; nonjoinder; permissive joinder; proper parties. *See also* consolidation of actions; impleader; interpleader; third-party practice.

➤ uniting, joining, merger, consolidation.

joinder of actions [*ak* · shenz] *n.* *See* consolidation of actions.

joinder of claims *n.* The joining of claims in a lawsuit. A party asserting a claim against the opposing party, whether as an original claim, **counterclaim**, **cross-claim**, or **third-party claim**, may join as many claims as she has. *See* claim.

joinder of counts *n.* The joining of separate offenses in an **indictment** or **information**. *See* joinder of offenses. *See also* count.

joinder of defendants [*de* · *fen* · dents] *n.* Jointly charging two or more criminal defendants in the same **indictment** or **information**, a permissible procedure if they are alleged to have participated in the same criminal act or acts.

joinder of indictments [*in* · *dite* · ments] *n.* Two or more **indictments** or **informations** tried together, a joinder which may be ordered by the court if the offenses could have been joined in a single indictment or information. *See* joinder of offenses.

joinder of informations [*in* · for · *may* · shenz] *n.* *See* joinder of indictments.

joinder of issue [*ish* · ew] *n.* An issue of fact appropriate to be decided by the court because it has been clearly stated by the parties, each with opposite contentions. *See* at issue; issue.

joinder of offenses [*o* · *fen* · sez] *n.* The charging of two or more offenses in separate counts of a single **indictment** or **information**. Such joinder is permissible if the offenses charged are of the same or similar character or are based upon an act or acts that make up a common scheme or plan. *See* joinder of indictments.

joinder of parties [*par* · teez] *n.* The uniting of two or more **parties** as plaintiffs or as defendants in a lawsuit. Under the

J

Federal Rules of Civil Procedure, the court must decide whether a "just adjudication" *requires* the joinder of a party who has not been brought into the lawsuit. The Federal Rules refer to such parties as **persons needed for just adjudication**. By comparison, in many states the **rules of civil procedure** make a distinction between **indispensable parties** (who must be joined if the lawsuit is to go forward) and **necessary parties** (who must be joined if possible). *Also see* proper parties.

joint *adj.* In the language of the law, means united or bound together with respect to rights or obligations. It is important to distinguish between "joint," which refers to common interests, and "**joint and several**," which refers to interests which are, at one and the same time, *both* common *and* separate. *Also compare* several.

    EXAMPLE (**joint liability**): If X and Y both sign a **promissory note** in favor of Z, the note is a **joint obligation** and both X and Y have **joint liability**. (A note executed by two people is a **joint and several obligation** only if it expressly says so.) Therefore, in the event of default on the note, if Z brings suit *only* against X, X has the right to demand that Y be joined in the action (*see* joinder).

    EXAMPLE (**joint and several liability**): If Drs. A and B, performing surgery together, engage in medical malpractice that injures patient C, C has a **cause of action** against both surgeons, *or* either one, and if she sues both, and secures a **judgment** against both, she may enforce the judgment against either A or B, *or* against both (apportioning the total as she chooses). This is because, as **joint tortfeasors**, Drs. A and B have **joint and several liability**.

n. 1. Slang terminology for jail. 2. A marijuana cigarette.

➤ *adj.* mutual, collaborative, combined, concerted, common, allied, united, merged, collective, unified, consolidated, communal, undivided, inseparable.

    n. jail, pen, house, rack, slammer; marijuana cigarette, doobie, hooter, spliff, blunt.

joint account [a · *kount*] *n.* An account in the name of two or more persons (EXAMPLE: a bank account), either of whom may make withdrawals. A joint account

may be held as a **joint tenancy with the right of survivorship** or as a **tenancy in common**. *See* multiparty account.

joint action [*ak* · shen] *n.* A lawsuit brought by two or more persons acting for their common interest. *See* joinder.

joint adventure [ad · *ven* · cher] *n. See* joint venture.

joint and mutual wills [*myoo* · chew · el] *n.* Two wills, generally but not necessarily **reciprocal wills**, contained in the same document and executed by both **testators**. *Also see* mutual wills. *Compare* joint will.

joint and several [*sev* · rel] *adj.* Together and individually; a term indicating both unity and individuality. USAGE: "There is **joint and several liability** in this case because the plaintiff has the right to hold either or both defendants responsible for his injuries." *Compare* several.

joint and several liability [*sev* · rel ly · e · *bil* · i · tee] *n.* 1. The **liability** of two or more persons who enter into an agreement promising, individually and together, to perform some act (EXAMPLES: pay money; serve as **surety**; furnish goods). Thus, there are joint and several **notes**, **bonds**, mortgages, and other contracts. The legal effect is that if default or breach occurs, the **promisee** can sue either or both **promissors**. However, such liability is always based upon express language in the agreement (EXAMPLE: "jointly and severally") or upon language from which **severalty** can be implied (EXAMPLE: "I" rather than "we"). *Compare* joint liability; several liability. 2. The liability of two or more persons who jointly commit a **tort** (**joint tortfeasors**).

joint and several obligation [*sev* · rel ob · li · gay · shen] *n.* An **obligation** (EXAMPLES: a **note**; a **bond**; a mortgage) which two or more persons have **jointly and severally** made themselves responsible to satisfy. *Compare* joint obligation. *See* joint and several; joint and several liability.

joint and survivorship annuity [ser · *vy* · ver · ship a · *new* · i · tee] *n.* An **annuity** payable jointly to two persons during the period they are both alive, and upon the death of one, to the other. *Compare* joint annuity.

J

joint annuity [a · *new* · i · tee] *n.* An **annuity** payable jointly to two persons during the period they are both alive, terminating upon the death of either one. *Compare* joint and survivorship annuity.

joint bank account [a · *kount*] *n. See* joint account.

joint cause of action [*ak* · shen] *n. See* joinder.

joint committee [ke · *mit* · tee] *n.* A committee composed of representatives of both houses of Congress or of a state legislature, appointed for the purpose of negotiating a compromise with respect to pending legislation. *See* conference committee; legislative committee.

joint contract [*kon* · trakt] *n.* A contract under which an obligation is incurred by two or more persons. *Compare* joint and several; several liability. *See* contrast.

joint creditors [*kred* · it · erz] *n.* Persons who are creditors under a contract giving them joint rights.

joint custody [*kuss* · te · dee] *n.* An arrangement whereby both parties to a divorce retain legal custody of their child and jointly participate in reaching major decisions concerning the child's welfare. *Compare* divided custody; sole custody.

joint debtors [*det* · erz] *n.* Persons who are jointly indebted on the same obligation.

joint debtors' acts [*det* · erz] *n.* Statutes existing in many states which permit a court to enter **judgment** against one or more defendants in a lawsuit, while allowing the suit to continue against the others.

joint enterprise [*en* · ter · prize] *n.* 1. A term applicable in the law of **negligence** which indicates an undertaking for the mutual benefit or pleasure (*compare* joint venture) of two or more persons, as a result of which the negligence of one of the participants may be imputed to the others. A "joint enterprise" is also referred to as a **common enterprise**. *See* imputed negligence. 2. A **joint venture**.

joint estate [es · *tate*] *n.* A **joint tenancy**.

joint executors [eg · *zek* · yoo · terz] *n.* Two or more persons acting jointly as **executors** in the **administration** of **decedent's estate**; **coexecutors**; joint **personal representatives**.

joint heir [air] *n.* A person who inherits jointly with another heir or other heirs. *See* heir.

joint indictment [in · *dite* · ment] *n.* An **indictment** charging two or more persons as criminal defendants. A joint indictment is appropriate when the offenses alleged arise out of acts carried out in common.

joint liability [lie · e · *bil* · i · tee] *n.* The **liability** of two or more persons as if they were one person so that, in the absence of statute providing otherwise (*see* joint debtors' acts), if one of them is sued the other or others liable with her must be joined as defendants. *See* joinder; jointly. *Compare* joint and several; joint and several liability; several liability; severalty.

joint lives *n.* A period of time that terminates upon the death of either one of two named persons. USAGE: "The public library will receive title to the building when either Sam or Mary dies because they hold a **life interest** in it for their joint lives."

joint negligence [*neg* · li · jense] *n. See* joint tort; joint tortfeasors.

joint obligation [ob · ly · *gay* · shen] *n.* An **obligation** (EXAMPLES: a **note**; a **bond**; a mortgage) which two or more persons have jointly made themselves responsible to satisfy. *Compare* joint and several obligation; several obligation.

joint obligor [ob · *ly* · jore] *n.* Same as **coobligor**.

joint offense [o · *fense*] *n.* A crime committed by two or more persons acting jointly. *See* conspiracy.

joint ownership [*oh* · ner · ship] *n.* 1. In one sense, a **joint tenancy** or a **tenancy by the entirety**. 2. In another sense, any property owned together with another, including a **tenancy in common** and **community property**.

joint policy [*pol* · li · see] *n.* An insurance policy on the lives of two or more persons, but usually a married couple, the beneficiary being the survivor.

joint possession [po · *zesh* · en] *n.* Possession of property shared by two or more persons.

joint resolution [rez · e · *loo* · shen] *n.* A **resolution** adopted by both houses of a state legislature or of Congress. In most

J

jurisdictions, a joint resolution is not a law, although a congressional resolution has the effect of law if it is signed by the president. *Compare* concurrent resolution.

joint return [re · *tern*] *n.* A single income tax return filed by a husband and wife reporting their combined incomes. Although married persons are entitled to file separately, their total tax liability is usually greater if they do.

joint tax return [re · *tern*] *n. See* joint return.

joint tenancy [*ten* · en · see] *n.* An **estate in land** (EXAMPLES: a **fee simple estate**; a **life estate**; an **estate for years**) or in **personal property** (EXAMPLE: a savings account) held by two or more persons jointly, with equal rights to share in its enjoyment. The most important feature of a joint tenancy is the **right of survivorship**, which means that upon the death of a joint tenant the entire estate goes to the survivor (or, in the case of more than two joint tenants, to the survivors, and so on to the last survivor). *See* tenancy by the entirety. *Compare* tenancy in common.

joint tenancy with the right of survivorship [*ten* · en · see with the right of ser · *vy* · ver · ship] *n.* Same as **joint tenancy**.

joint tenant [*ten* · ent] *n.* One of two or more tenants under a **joint tenancy**.

joint tort *n.* A **tort** perpetrated by **joint tortfeasors**.

joint tortfeasors [*tort* · fee · zerz] *n.* Two or more persons whose acts, together, contribute to producing a single injury to a third person or to property. Joint tortfeasors are **jointly and severally** liable. *See* joint and several liability; joint tort. *See also* concurrent negligence. *Compare* several liability.

joint trespass [*tress* · pass] *n.* A **trespass** committed by two or more persons, or by one or more of them at the bidding or with the encouragement of the others.

joint trial [*try* · el] *n.* A single trial of two or more persons for the same offense. *See* joinder of indictments; joinder of informations; joinder of offenses.

joint trustees [trus · *teez*] *n.* Same as **cotrustees**.

joint venture [*ven* · cher] *n.* Sometimes referred to as a **joint adventure**; the relationship created when two or more persons combine jointly in a business enterprise (*compare* joint enterprise) with the understanding that they will share in the profits or losses and that each will have a voice in its management. Although a joint venture is a form of partnership, it customarily involves a single business project rather than an ongoing business relationship.

joint will *n.* A single instrument that contains the wills of two or more persons and is **jointly** executed by them. Customarily, a joint will disposes of property that the **testators** own either jointly or in common. *Compare* joint and mutual wills; reciprocal wills.

joint-stock association [a · so · see · *ay* · shen] *n.* Same as **joint-stock company**.

joint-stock company [*kum* · pe · nee] *n.* An **unincorporated association** for the purpose of carrying on business. Like a corporation, it issues **capital stock**; unlike a corporation, but like a partnership, the members are normally liable for the acts of the organization. *See* personal liability.

jointly [*joint* · lee] *adv.* Unitedly; sharing together; in **unity of interest**, **right**, or **liability**; not separate. In **community property states,** virtually all property owned by married persons is the jointly owned property of both parties to the marriage. In the remaining states, property is jointly owned only if **title** is in both spouses (EXAMPLES: both names on a deed, bank account, or **certificate of title**). *See and compare* joint tenancy; tenancy by the entirety; tenancy in common.

➤ unitedly, in concert, in conjunction, in combination, collectively, in common, mutually, conjointly.
Ant. individually, separately.

jointly and severally [*sev* · re · lee] *adv. See* joint and several; several.

journal [*jer* · nel] *n.* 1. In bookkeeping, the record to which **original entries** are transferred. *See* book of account; book of original entry. 2. The log in which the daily **proceedings** of a legislature are recorded. EXAMPLE: the **Congressional Record**.

J

3. A magazine or periodical, particularly one of a professional or academic nature. EXAMPLE: a law review. 4. Any daily record of events, thoughts, or observations.
➤ chronicle, register, log, registry, ledger, notebook, diary, periodical, calendar, magazine.

journal entry [*en* · tree] *n.* 1. An entry in a **book of account**. 2. An entry in a journal.

journal entry rule [*en* · tree] *n.* The rule that courts may look into the journals of the legislature to determine whether a statute was passed in accordance with constitutional requirements.

journalist [*jer* · nel · ist] *n.* One who communicates the news to the public.
➤ writer, commentator, correspondent, newsperson, reporter.

journalists' privilege [*jer* · nel · ists *priv* · i · lej] *n.* The press's **privilege** of commenting on **public figures**, with respect to matters of public interest, so long as such comment is based upon honest belief of its truthfulness and is without **malice**. *See* conditionally privileged communication; fair comment. *See also* shield laws.

journeyman [*jer* · nee · man] *n.* A worker who has learned her trade, having progressed beyond the status of an apprentice. **Collective bargaining agreements** between **craft unions** and employers provide for a higher rate of pay for journeymen than for apprentices.
➤ worker, artisan, employee.

joyriding [*joy* · ry · ding] *n.* The temporary taking of a motor vehicle without the owner's consent but with no intent to deprive the owner of it permanently. Joyriding, which is referred to in some states as **unauthorized use of a motor vehicle**, is a crime. *Compare* auto theft, car jacking.

JP Abbreviation of **justice of the peace**.

judge *n.* A public officer who conducts or presides over a court of justice. The words "judge," "court," and "justice" are often used interchangeably and, in context, have the same meaning. *See also* justice of the peace; magistrate.
v. To form an opinion after weighing the evidence and arguments.

➤ *n.* justice, adjudicator, surrogate, magistrate, arbitrator, chancellor, jurist, decider, arbiter.
v. consider, conclude, reckon, settle, referee, try, pronounce, decree, find, opine, hold.

judge advocate [*ad* · vo · ket] *n.* A military officer who is appointed to serve as a judge or a lawyer in a military court. *See* court-martial. The title of the chief legal officer of each branch of the military is **Judge Advocate General**.

judge pro tempore [*tem* · po · ray] *n.* Same as **pro tempore judge**.

judge trial [*try* · el] *n.* A **bench trial**. *Compare* jury trial.

judge-made law *n.* 1. Law created by the decisions of judges, as opposed to statutory law; **precedent**. 2. **Judicial legislation**. 3. **Common law**.

Judge Advocate General [juj *ad* · vo · ket *jen* · e · rel] *n.* The title of the chief legal officer of each branch of the military service. In each branch of the military, the corps responsible for administering **military law** is referred to as JAG, the acromym for Judge Advocate General.

judgment [*juj* · ment] *n.* 1. In a civil action, the final determination by a court of the rights of the parties, based upon the **pleadings** and the evidence; a decision. 2. In a criminal prosecution, a determination of guilt; a conviction. 3. In everyday usage, the formation of an opinion. 4. In everyday usage, good sense or discretion. *See also* arrest of judgment; confession of judgment; declaratory judgment; default judgment; deficiency judgment; dormant judgment; entry of judgment; estoppel by judgment; final judgment; foreign judgment; money judgment; render judgment; revival of judgment; summary judgment; vacation of judgment; void judgment.
➤ decree, holding, ruling, conclusion, opinion, award, sentence, finding, adjudication, verdict, arbitration ("the judgement of the court"); understanding, perception, acumen, insight, reasoning, discrimination, discernment ("a woman of judgment").

judgment book *n.* Same as **judgment docket**.

judgment by default [de · *fawlt*] *n. See* default judgment.

judgment creditor [*kred* · i · ter] *n.* A creditor who has secured a judgment against his debtor which has not been satisfied.

judgment debt *n.* A debt for which judgment has been entered. *See* entry of judgment.

judgment debtor [*det* · er] *n.* A person against whom a judgment, which has not been satisfied, has been entered. *See* entry of judgment.

judgment docket [*dok* · et] *n.* A book or **docket** maintained by the **clerk of court** in which are recorded all **judgments** that have been entered, and, among other things, the date of entry, the parties, and whether the judgment was satisfied. *See* entry of judgment.

judgment execution [ek · se · *kyoo* · shen] *n.* *See* execution; execution creditor; execution lien.

judgment in personam [per · *soh* · nam] *n.* A **judgment** against a person, as distinguished from a judgment against a specific piece of property or against a specific account. A judgment *in personam* may be satisfied out of any property owned by the **judgment debtor**. *Compare* judgment in rem. *See* in personam action; jurisdiction in personam.

judgment in rem *n.* A judgment in an **action** brought against property, or brought to enforce a **right** in property, as distinguished from a judgment against a person. *Compare* judgment in personam. *See in rem*; in rem action; jurisdiction in rem. *See also* judgment quasi in rem.

judgment lien [leen] *n.* A **lien** created by **entry of judgment**. It gives the **judgment creditor** the right to **attach** the property of the **judgment debtor** to satisfy the judgment.

judgment non obstante veredicto [*juj* · ment non ob · *stan* · teh veh · reh · *dik* · toh] (*Latin*) *n.* Means "judgment notwithstanding the verdict." *See* judgment notwithstanding the verdict.

judgment note *n.* A **promissory note** that contains a provision authorizing the creditor to obtain a **judgment** against the debtor on the **note** without the formalities involved in bringing suit. Judgment notes are not valid in all states. *See* confession of judgment; warrant of attorney.

judgment notwithstanding the verdict [not · with · *stan* · ding the *ver* · dikt] *n.* Also referred to as a **judgment NOV**, a **judgment** rendered by the court in favor of a **party**, notwithstanding the fact that the jury has returned a verdict against that party.

judgment NOV *n.* Short for **judgment notwithstanding the verdict** and **judgment non obstante veredicto**.

judgment nunc pro tunc [nunk pro tunk] *n.* *See nunc pro tunc*.

judgment on the merits [*mehr* · its] *n.* A judgment based on the **substantive rights** of the parties, as distinguished from a judgment based upon procedural points. *See* merits.

judgment on the pleadings [*plee* · dingz] *n.* A judgment rendered in favor of the defendant when the plaintiff's **complaint** fails to state a **cause of action**, or in favor of the plaintiff when the defendant's **answer** fails to state a legally sufficient **defense**. *See* pleadings. *See also* demurrer; summary judgment.

judgment proof *n.* Refers to persons (for EXAMPLE, indigent persons or insolvent persons) against whom, because of their circumstances, a **judgment** has no value because it cannot be enforced.

judgment quasi in rem [*kway* · sye] *n.* A judgment affecting property that determines only the rights of the **parties** with respect to the property, not the rights of all persons who might have an interest in it. EXAMPLE: a judgment in an action involving the administration of a **trust** (beneficiaries other than the plaintiff may have an interest in the **trust estate**); a judgment in a **receivership** (other creditors); a judgment in a case involving **marshaling assets** (other **mortgagees**). *See* quasi in rem action. *Compare* judgment in personam; judgment in rem.

judgment rendered [*ren* · derd] *See* render judgment.

judgment roll *n.* A collection of papers that, in some states, the clerk must file when she **dockets** the **judgment** in a case. The contents of a judgment roll differ according to state statute, but usually include the **summons**, the **affidavits of service**, the **pleadings**, the **jury instructions**, and the decision or the judgment.

J

judicature [*joo* · di · ka · cher] *n.* 1. The administration of justice. 2. The profession of those who are involved in the administration of justice. EXAMPLES: judges; lawyers; court clerks. 3. Judicial **jurisdiction** or power.
➤ administration, judiciary; jurisdiction, power.

judicial [joo · *dish* · el] *adj.* 1. Pertaining to courts or judges and their functions. 2. Relating to that which is issued by a court or judge. EXAMPLE: a judicial order; a judicial opinion. 3. Decided on the basis of the facts and the law. *Note* that "judicial" is not "**judicious.**"
➤ juristic, legal, judiciary ("a judicial act"); discriminating, wise, sagacious, prudent, just, fair, magisterial, perspicacious ("a judicial demeanor").

judicial act *n.* 1. The act of a judge in applying the law to the facts in the case before her. 2. The act of a judge in adjudicating the rights of parties who appear before the court. *See also* judicial function; judicial powers. *Compare* administrative act; legislative act; ministerial act.

judicial branch *n.* 1. With the **legislative branch** and the **executive branch**, one of the three divisions into which the Constitution separates the government of the United States. These **branches of government** are also referred to as **departments of government**. The judicial branch is primarily responsible for interpreting the laws. 2. A similar division in state government.

judicial circuit [*ser* · kit] *n.* *See* circuit; circuit court.

judicial cy pres [sye pray] *n.* *See cy pres.*

judicial decision [de · *sizh* · en] *n.* A decision by a court. *See* decision.

judicial department [de · *part* · ment] *n.* Same as **judicial branch**.

judicial determination [de · term · min · *ay* · shen] *n.* A **judicial decision**; a **ruling** by a court.

judicial dicta [*dik* · ta] *n.* *See dicta.*

judicial discretion [dis · *kresh* · en] *n.* Refers to a judge's right to use her own judgment so long as she follows the law and does not act arbitrarily. *See* discretion. *Compare* judicial restraint.

judicial districts [*dis* · trikts] *n.* 1. Areas into which a state is divided for purposes of judicial administration and jurisdiction. 2. The territorial units of the **District Courts of the United States**. *See* district court. *See also* circuit; circuit court.

judicial error [*ehr* · er] *n.* An error committed by the court itself. EXAMPLE: allowing **hearsay** testimony as evidence in violation of the **hearsay rule**. *See* error.

judicial estoppel [es · *top* · el] *n.* A prohibition against denying the truth of declarations one has made during the course of judicial proceedings, for EXAMPLE, in testimony or in **pleadings**. *See* estoppel.

judicial ethics [*eth* · iks] *n.* *See* Code of Judicial Conduct; ethics.

judicial foreclosure [for · *kloh* · zher] *n.* *See* judicial sale. *Also see* foreclosure; foreclosure sale.

judicial function [*funk* · shen] *n.* An act that is within the power of the judiciary to perform. *Compare* legislative function. *See* judicial act; judicial powers.

judicial immunity [im · *yoo* · ni · tee] *n.* The protection from **personal liability** which the law grants a judge for his actions, so long as they are judicial acts; that is, legitimate judicial functions or lawful exercises of judicial power. *Compare* legislative immunity. *See* immunity.

judicial legislation [lej · is · *lay* · shen] *n.* A judicial decision that encroaches upon the function of the legislature by making law rather than interpreting the law. *See* judge-made law; make law.

judicial lien [leen] *n.* A **lien** obtained by means of **judicial process**. EXAMPLES: an **attachment lien**; a **judgment lien**.

judicial notice [*noh* · tiss] *n.* Refers to a judge's action in finding a fact to be true without requiring either party to prove it to be true. Judicial notice substitutes for proof. A judge may appropriately take judicial notice with respect to, among other things, historical, geographical, or scientific facts or principles which are commonly accepted and believed to be beyond contradiction as, for EXAMPLE, the fact that John Kennedy was elected president of the United States in 1960, the fact that France is located in Europe, and the fact that water boils at 212 degrees Fahrenheit at sea level and standard pressure. *Compare* official notice. *See* finding of fact.

J

judicial officer [*off* · i · ser] *n.*
1. A judge or other person (EXAMPLES: a justice of the peace; a **magistrate**) who is appointed or elected to perform duties that are principally judicial. *See* judicial function. 2. Any employee of the **judicial branch** of government.

judicial opinion [o · *pin* · yen] *n.* An **opinion** issued by a court.

judicial order [*or* · der] *n.* A **court order**.

judicial powers [*pow* · erz] *n.* 1. The powers granted to a court or to the **judicial branch** of government by its constitution and statutes. 2. The power of a court to perform a judicial act or to carry out a judicial function. *Compare* executive powers; legislative powers.

judicial proceeding [pro · *see* · ding] *n.* A **proceeding** before a judge or similar judicial officer, as distinguished from a proceeding before an administrative agency. *Compare* administrative proceeding.

judicial process [*pross* · ess] *n.* 1. All the acts of a court from the beginning of an **action** to the end. 2. The means by which a defendant is compelled to appear in court and by which he is notified that an action has been commenced against him. EXAMPLES: a **writ**; an **arrest warrant**. *See* process.

judicial question [*kwes* · chen] *n.* A question appropriate for a court to decide; a question involving interpretation of law. *See* question of law.

judicial remedy [*rem* · e · dee] *n.* A **remedy** that a court, as opposed to an administrative agency, is empowered to grant. *Compare* administrative remedy.

judicial restraint [re · *straint*] *n.* Refers to a judge's duty not to allow his personal views to influence his **decision** in a case. *Compare* judicial discretion.

judicial review [re · *vyoo*] *n.* 1. Review by a court of a decision or ruling of an administrative agency. 2. Review by an **appellate court** of a determination by a lower court. *See* review.

judicial sale *n.* A sale carried out under the order or **judgment** of a court. EXAMPLES: a **foreclosure sale**; a **tax sale**. *See* execution sale; sheriff's sale.

judicial separation [sep · e · *ray* · shen] *n.* Same as **divorce a mensa et thoro**,

divorce from bed and board, and **limited divorce**.

judicial system [*sis* · tem] *n.* Same as **judiciary**.

judicial writ *n.* A **writ** issued by a court, as opposed to a writ issued by some other authority.

judiciary [joo · *dish* · ee · ehr · ee] *n.* 1. The system of courts within a nation, state, or other governmental unit. 2. The **judicial branch** of government.
➤ courts, bench, system of justice.

judicious [joo · *dish* · ess] *adj.* Wise; well-considered; with the use of good judgment. *Note* that "judicious" is not "**judicial**."
➤ wise, well-considered, prudent, astute, rational, logical ("a judicious prosecutor").

jump *v.* 1. To move suddenly off the ground. 2. To run away from a situation. 3. To assault another.
➤ leap, vault, spring; escape, avoid, neglect, evade; attack, mug.

jump bail *n.* To flee a jurisdiction, or conceal oneself within a jurisdiction, while released on bail. *See also* bail bond; forfeiture of bond.

junior [*joo* · nyer] *adj.* 1. Of secondary importance, rank, or right. USAGE: "A second mortgage is junior to a first mortgage." *Compare* senior. 2. Younger.
➤ younger, subordinate, second, secondary, lesser ("A junior mortgage is one filed after the first mortgage").
Ant. senior.

junior encumbrance [en · *kum* · brense] *n.* A mortgage or other **lien** that is of lesser **priority** in law than another mortgage or lien. *Compare* senior encumbrance.

junior execution [ek · se · *kyoo* · shen] *n.* An **execution** issued after the issuance of another execution on the same property or against the same defendant.

junior interest [*in* · trest] *n.* An **interest** or **right** in property subordinate to another person's interest or right in the same property. EXAMPLES: a **junior mortgage**; a **junior lien**; a **junior execution**. *Compare* senior interest.

junior lien [leen] *n.* A **lien** that is inferior in **priority** to another lien. *Compare* senior lien.

J

junior mortgage [*more* · gej] *n.* A **mortgage** that is inferior in **priority** to another mortgage. *See* second mortgage. *Compare* senior mortgage.

junk bonds *n.* Corporate **bonds** that are below investment quality; that is, a high-risk investment. As with high-risk investments generally, junk bonds yield a high rate of interest.

junket [*jung* · kit] *n.* A trip, usually taken at the expense of the public or at the expense of a gambling casino.

➤ trip, excursion, frolic, tour.

jurat [*joor* · at] *n.* The certification that an **affidavit** has been duly sworn by the **affiant** before a duly authorized person (EXAMPLE: a notary public). The jurat usually appears at the end of the affidavit. Its customary form is: "Subscribed and sworn to before me," followed by the date, signature, and title of the official.

jure [*zhoo* · reh] (*Latin*) *n.* Law; in law. *See de jure.*

juridical [joo · *rid* · i · kel] *adj.* Pertaining to the law; pertaining to the administration of justice.

➤ legal, judicious, judicial.

Juris Doctor [*joor* · is *dok* · ter] *n.* The primary degree given by most law schools. It is commonly expressed in its abbreviated form, **JD** or J.D.

jurisdiction [joo · ris · *dik* · shen] *n.* A term used in several senses: 1. In a general sense, the right of a court to **adjudicate** lawsuits of a certain kind. EXAMPLES: the right of juvenile courts to hear cases involving juvenile offenders; the power of federal courts to adjudicate **federal questions**. 2. In a specific sense, the right of a court to determine a particular case; in other words, the power of the court over the subject matter of, or the property involved in, the case **at bar**. 3. In a geographical sense, the power of a court to hear cases only within a specific territorial area (EXAMPLES: a state; a county; a federal **judicial district**). *See* venue. 4. Authority; control; power. 5. District; area; locality. *See* circuit; circuit court; county court; district; district court; judicial districts.

The term also applies to the authority of an administrative agency to hear and determine a case brought before it.

See also admiralty jurisdiction; ancillary jurisdiction; appellate jurisdiction; concurrent jurisdiction; continuing jurisdiction; court of competent jurisdiction; court of general jurisdiction; diversity jurisdiction; equity jurisdiction; excess of jurisdiction; exclusive jurisdiction; federal jurisdiction; foreign jurisdiction; general jurisdiction; limited jurisdiction; military jurisdiction; original jurisdiction; pendent jurisdiction; personal jurisdiction; plenary jurisdiction; primary jurisdiction; probate jurisdiction; special jurisdiction; subject matter jurisdiction; territorial jurisdiction; want of jurisdiction ("to have jurisdiction on a matter or a person").

➤ capacity, authority, authorization, right, charter, judicature, license, sovereignty ("to have jurisdiction over a matter or a person"); territory, region, domain, district, circuit, state, quarter, field, province ("The matter has not been decided in this jurisdiction").

jurisdiction clause *n.* An essential clause in any **pleading** that contains a **claim for relief**, which states the grounds upon which the court's jurisdiction is based.

jurisdiction in personam [per · *soh* · nam] *n.* The jurisdiction a court has over the person of a defendant. It is acquired by **service of process** upon the defendant or by her voluntary submission to jurisdiction. Voluntary submission may be implied from a defendant's conduct within the jurisdiction, for EXAMPLE, by **doing business in a state** or by operating a motor vehicle within a state (*see* implied consent statutes). Jurisdiction in personam is also referred to as **personal jurisdiction**. *See and compare* jurisdiction in rem; jurisdiction quasi in rem. *See in personam*; in personam action; judgment in personam.

jurisdiction in rem *n.* The jurisdiction a court has over property situated in the state. *See and compare* jurisdiction in personam; jurisdiction quasi in rem. *See in rem*; in rem action; judgment in rem.

jurisdiction of the person [*per* · sen] *n.* Same as **jurisdiction in personam**.

jurisdiction of the subject matter [sub · jekt *mat* · er] *n. See* subject matter jurisdiction.

jurisdiction quasi in rem [*kway* · sye] *n.* The jurisdiction a court has over the defendant's **interest** in property located

J

within the jurisdiction. *See and compare* jurisdiction in personam; jurisdiction in rem. *See also* judgment quasi in rem; quasi in rem action.

jurisdictional [joo · ris · *dik* · shen · el] *adj.* Pertaining to **jurisdiction**.

jurisdictional amount [a · *mount*] *n.* The amount of money in dispute may determine whether a court has **jurisdiction** of the case. **Small claims courts**, for EXAMPLE, are empowered only to hear cases involving limited amounts of money as set by state statutes. The **diversity jurisdiction** of federal courts is based upon a jurisdictional amount set by federal statute. *See* amount in controversy.

jurisdictional dispute [dis · *pyoot*] *n.* A conflict between two or more unions over whose members are entitled to perform work of various kinds.

jurisdictional facts *n.* Facts that must be present for a court to be able to assume **jurisdiction** in a case. The **amount in controversy** and **diversity of citizenship** are EXAMPLES of jurisdictional facts.

jurisdictional plea *n.* A **plea** or **answer** that contests the court's **jurisdiction**.

jurisprudence [joor · is · *proo* · dense] *n.* The science of law; legal philosophy.
➤ philosophy, theory, legal foundation, philosophy of law, system of laws.

jurist [*joor* · ist] *n.* A person who is learned in the law; a judge; a professor of law.
➤ learned counsel, law professor, legal authority, legal expert.

juror [*joor* · er] *n.* A person on a jury.
➤ factfinder, trier of fact, appraiser, arbiter.

jury [*joor* · ee] *n.* A group of women and men selected according to law to determine the truth. Juries are used in various types of legal proceedings, both civil and criminal. *See* advisory jury; blue ribbon jury; coroner's jury; grand jury; hung jury; impartial jury; petit jury; polling the jury; sequestration of jury; special jury; striking a jury; struck jury; traverse jury; trial jury.
➤ factfinder, trier of fact, reviewers, panel, veniremen, array, arbiters.

jury box *n.* Portion of the courtroom where the jury is seated during the trial of a case.

jury challenge [*chal* · enj] *n. See* challenge for cause; challenge to the panel; peremptory challenge.

jury charge *n. See* jury instructions.

jury commissioner [kum · *ish* · en · er] *n.* An official who is responsible for compiling **jury lists**, drawing jurors for a panel, and summoning jurors on the panel for duty. *See* jury panel.

jury instructions [in · *struk* · shenz] *n.* Directions given to the jury by the judge just before she sends the jurors out to deliberate and return a verdict, explaining the law that applies in the case and spelling out what must be proven and by whom. *See* charge. *Also see* additional instructions; cautionary instruction; mandatory instruction; model jury instructions; peremptory instruction; request for instructions.

jury list *n.* A list of names of all persons in a jurisdiction who are subject to call for jury duty or who have been placed on the **jury panel**.

jury of peers *n. See* peer.

jury panel [*pan* · el] *n.* 1. The **jury list**. 2. The jury impaneled for the trial of a particular case. *See* impanel.

jury question [*kwes* · chen] *n.* A **question of fact**, as opposed to a **question of law**; that is, a question that is for the jury, rather than the judge, to decide.

jury room *n.* The room in a courthouse where the jury conducts its deliberations.

jury tampering [*tam* · per · ing] *n. See* tampering.

jury trial [*try* · el] *n.* A trial in which the jurors are the judges of the facts and the court is the judge of the law. Trial by jury is guaranteed in all criminal cases by the **Sixth Amendment**, and in most civil cases by the **Seventh Amendment**. *Compare* bench trial. *See* summary jury trial.

jury wheel *n.* A device for selecting, on a random basis, the names of persons to form a **jury panel**.

just *adj.* Right or fair according to law; legally right; lawful.
➤ rightful, equitable, principled, honest, merited, due, fair, reasonable, rational, unbiased, fitting, appropriate, authentic, justifiable, constitutional, judicious, bona fide, factual.
Ant. inequitable, unfair.

J

just cause *n.* A fair cause relied upon in good faith. USAGE: "She is receiving unemployment compensation benefits even though she was fired, because she was not discharged for just cause." *See* for cause.

just cause of provocation [prov · uh · *kay* · shen] *n.* *See* provocation.

just compensation [kom · pen · *say* · shen] *n.* A term originating in the **Fifth Amendment** prohibition against the government taking private property for public use without "just compensation," meaning that the government can exercise the power of **eminent domain** only if it provides payment that is fair both to the person whose property is taken and to the public, which must pay for it. Such payment includes the monetary value of the property taken and the **damages** caused by the taking. *See* condemnation; condemnation proceeding; inverse condemnation.

just debts *n.* In the law of wills, all claims that could have been enforced by an **action** against the **decedent** in his lifetime.

justice [*juss* · tis] *n.* 1. The goal of a society which demands that its courts diligently apply its laws to the facts of each case, in every case. *See* commutative justice; distributive justice. *See also* miscarriage of justice; obstructing justice. 2. The title of a judge, especially the judge of an **appellate court**.
➤ fairness, equity, even-handedness, fair play, legality, impartiality, uprightness, integrity, probity, rectitude.

justice of the peace *n.* A **judicial officer** who presides over a **court of limited jurisdiction**, his authority usually being restricted in civil actions to cases in which the amount in dispute is very small and, in criminal cases, to prosecutions for minor offenses and to **preliminary hearings**. *See* justice's court.

justice's court *n.* A court presided over by a justice of the peace. *See* magistrate's court.

justiciable [jus · *tish* · ebl] *adj.* Appropriate for determination by a court.
➤ litigable, prepared for court action, actionable, ready, suitable ("a justiciable controversy").
Ant. premature, moot.

justiciable controversy [*kon* · tro · ver · see] *n.* A case in which there is an actual disagreement with respect to a right that is actually claimed, as opposed to a hypothetical or theoretical dispute. *See* case or controversy; controversy. *Compare* academic question.

justifiable [jus · ti · *fy* · ebl] *adj.* Sanctioned by law; defensible. *See* sanction.
➤ rightful, merited, defensible, acceptable, reasonable, allowable, vindicable, valid, proper.
Ant. unwarranted, unexcused.

justifiable cause *n.* Same as **probable cause**.

justifiable homicide [*hom* · i · side] *n.* A **homicide** committed in self-defense or intentionally in carrying out a legal duty as, for EXAMPLE, a police officer who kills an armed robber during the course of a robbery. *Compare* excusable homicide.

justification [jus · ti · fi · *kay* · shen] *n.* 1. A legal excuse for committing an act that otherwise would be a **tort** or a crime. EXAMPLES: a newspaper does not commit **libel** if it honestly believes its false statement concerning the mayor is true (*see* fair comment; journalists' privilege); killing in self-defense is not a crime. 2. An explanation; a reason; an excuse.
➤ explanation, rationalization, vindication, apology, basis, foundation, alibi.

juvenile [*joo* · ve · nile] *adj.* Young; youthful; immature.
n. A young person; an adolescent.
➤ *adj.* childish, inexperienced, puerile, sophomore, irresponsible, infantile, unwise, adolescent.
Ant. adult; mature.
n. infant, youth, youngster, minor, teenager, stripling, kid, ward, teen.

juvenile court *n.* A court having **special jurisdiction** over delinquent and neglected children. *See* child neglect; delinquent child; juvenile offender. *Also see* Gault decision; status crime.

juvenile delinquent [de · *link* · went] *n.* Same as **juvenile offender**.

juvenile offender [o · *fen* · der] *n.* A minor who breaks the law. A juvenile offender is sometimes referred to as a **delinquent child** or a **youthful offender**. *See also* status crime.

juxtapose [*jux* · ta · pose] *v.* To place next to each other.
➤ border, abut, adjoin, connect, neighbor.

J

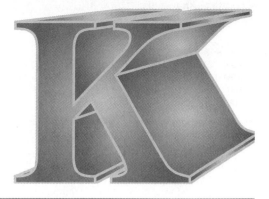

kangaroo court [kang · ge · *roo*] *n.* An unauthorized, self-appointed "court" set up to justify an action that its members intended to take in the first place. *See also* lynching.
➤ lynching, lynch mob, mob justice.

KB Abbreviation of **King's Bench**.

keen *adj.* 1. Enthusiastic. 2. Sharp or piercing. 3. Very intelligent; astute.
➤ enthusiastic, interested, fervent, spirited, avid, impassioned ("a keen interest"); sharp, incisive, acute, cutting ("a keen edge"); astute, shrewd, wise, perceptive, intelligent, clever, brilliant ("a keen mind").

keep *v.* 1. To maintain; to carry on; to conduct; to manage. USAGE: "keep books"; "keep the peace"; "keep in repair." 2. To hold in custody or in one's possession; to protect. USAGE: "keep valuables"; "keep on deposit."
➤ maintain, carry on, conduct, manage, hold; tend, nurture, feed, subsidize, support; prevent, detain, deter, inhibit, stop, restrain.
keep books *n. See* bookkeeping.
keep in repair [re · *pair*] *n.* Term in a lease provision that binds the tenant to maintain the premises in as good repair as they were when the lease was made.
keep the peace *n.* To maintain public order; to prevent a **breach of the peace**.

keeper [*keep* · er] *n.* 1. A person who has the care, custody, or management of anything. EXAMPLE: the warden of a jail. 2. A person who is in possession of a thing, place, or business, whether or not he is the owner. EXAMPLES: a **bailee**; a **depositary**.
➤ custodian, caretaker, warden, guard, protector.

keeping [*keep* · ing] *n.* Maintaining; conducting; managing.
➤ maintaining, conducting, managing, caring for ("keeping a gaming house"); accordance, agreement ("in keeping with the contract").
keeping a disorderly house [dis · *or* · der · lee] *n. See* disorderly house.
keeping a gaming house [*gay* · ming] Maintaining a place where people are allowed to assemble for the purpose of betting or gambling.

Keogh Plan [*kee* · oh] *n.* The type of retirement plan that self-employed professionals (EXAMPLES: attorneys; physicians) and individuals or partners in an **unincorporated** business activity (EXAMPLES: realtors; plumbers) may set up under the **Internal Revenue Code** to obtain the tax advantages available to employees under a **qualified pension plan**. *Compare* individual retirement account (IRA).

key man insurance [in · *shoor* · ense] *n.* Life or disability insurance purchased by a business on a vital member or employee of the company, with the company as beneficiary. Its purpose is to lessen the adverse economic impact to the business of the death or disability of a person whose contribution is considered highly important to the organization.

kickback [*kik* · bak] *n.* The payment of money back to a customer or purchaser as an inducement to use or buy services, material, or goods from the person making the payment. The taking of such a payment is a criminal offense. It is a federal offense for a public official to solicit a kickback from a

contractor involved in the construction or repair of any public work, or any other work financed by loans or grants from the government. *See also* bribery.
➤ graft, bribe, payoff, payola, cut.

kiddie tax [*kidd · ee*] *n.* A slang term for the federal income tax on the **unearned income** of children under the age of 14.

kidnap [*kid · nap*] *v.* To take a person, against her will, without legal justification, through force, fraud, or intimidation.
➤ abduct, seize, snatch, steal, remove, grab, entice, shanghai.

kidnapping [*kid · nap · ing*] *n.* The crime of taking and detaining a person against his will by force, intimidation, or fraud. *See also* abduction; child stealing; hostage; parental kidnapping.
➤ abduction, child stealing, seizure, hijacking.
kidnapping for ransom [*ran · sem*] *n.* Kidnapping for the purpose of holding the victim for ransom; that is, demanding money or some other **consideration** for the person's release. It is an aggravated form of kidnapping and, accordingly, the penalty is greater than for kidnapping when no ransom is involved. (For kidnapping across state lines, *see* Lindbergh Law.)

kill *v.* 1. To end or terminate. 2. To take the life of.
➤ defeat, destroy, crush, nullify, invalidate ("kill the bill"); murder, injure, slay, liquidate, slaughter, assassinate ("to kill an innocent bystander").

kin *n.* Relatives; persons related by blood or **consanguinity**. *See* relation by blood. *See also* next of kin.
➤ relatives, relations, family.

kind *n.* Type; category; class. *See* in kind.
adj. Gentle; amiable; tender.
➤ *n.* type, category, class, sort, variety, grouping, classification.
adj. gentle, considerate, giving, altruistic, loving, good, generous, benevolent.

King's (Queen's) Bench *n.* Short for Court of King's Bench, an English court with both **general jurisdiction** and **appellate jurisdiction**. King's Bench is important to Americans because it was the court that created much of the English **common law**, which forms the foundation of our law.

When a queen is on the throne, this court is called **Queen's Bench**.

kinship [*kin · ship*] *n.* The circumstance of being related by blood; the fact of being kin.
➤ ancestry, family, friendship, brotherhood, sisterhood.

kiting [*kite · ing*] *n.* Using bad checks to get money, specifically: 1. drawing checks against deposits that have not been credited because the deposits are made up of other checks which are still in the banking system for **collection** (*see* float); or 2. drawing checks against deposits that have not been made, taking the chance that money will be deposited before the checks are presented.

kleptomania [klep · te · *may* · nee · a] *n.* An irresistible and pathological impulse to steal.

knock and announce rule [a · *nounss*] *n.* The rule that a law enforcement officer may forcibly enter a house, whether to make an arrest or conduct a search, only if she has first identified herself as an officer and stated her purpose, and has been refused admittance.

knocked down *adj.* An expression used in auctions, meaning "sold." Property is said to be "knocked down" (or **struck off**) when the auctioneer, by the fall of her hammer or otherwise, signifies to the bidder that he is entitled to the property upon paying the amount of his bid.

know all men *n.* Formal words used in various kinds of legal **instruments** as a way of giving notice to **all the world**. USAGE: "Know all men by these presents." *See* presents; these presents.

knowingly [*noh · ing · lee*] *adv.* With knowledge; deliberately; consciously; intentionally. *See* deliberate; intent; intention; intentional; *mens rea.* As used in the criminal law and applied to a criminal defendant, "knowingly" means that the accused possessed **intent**, a necessary element of most crimes; in other words, that he knew what he was doing and understood the probable results.
➤ with knowledge, deliberately, consciously, intentionally, purposely, willfully.

knowingly and willfully [*wil* · ful · ee] *adv.* A term used in some criminal statutes, meaning a deliberate failure to obey the law.

knowledge [*naw* · ledj] *n.* A clear awareness of the truth; an accurate perception of the facts; the state of knowing. *See scienter. Also see* notice. *See and compare* actual knowledge; imputed knowledge; personal knowledge.
➤ cognizance, awareness, perception, recognition, information; wisdom, erudition, learning, intelligence.

known *adj.* Understood; acknowledged; recognized.

➤ famous, familiar, popular, noted, celebrated; recognized, perceived, understood.

kook *n.* An idiotic or bizarre person. USAGE: "Don't listen to that kook."
➤ nut, crackpot, crank, lunatic, flake, fruitcake.

kowtow [*kow* · tow] *v.* To show submissive respect; to grovel.
➤ grovel, stoop, fawn, cower, pander, flatter.

kudos [*koo* · doze] *n.* Honor, praise, or acclamation.
➤ praise, acclaim, glory, honor, distinction, esteem.

K

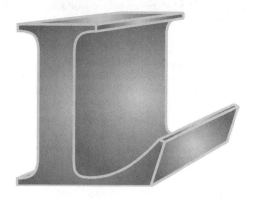

label [*lay* · bul] *v.* To describe or distinguish.
n. A marking or description.
➤ *v.* classify, denominate, brand, identify,
designate, stamp, call.
n. tag, identification, brand, mark,
description, characterization, logo, design.

labor [*ley* · ber] *n.* 1. In common usage,
physical work, although the word refers
with equal accuracy to work involving the
application of professional or intellectual
skills. 2. Work performed for a wage or
salary, as opposed to work performed in
order to realize a profit. 3. The body or group
of persons who work for wages, as a class
and as distinguished from management.
See child labor; labor dispute; unfair labor
practice.
v. To work; to exert oneself.
➤ *n.* work, occupation, undertaking, toil,
enterprise, task, responsibility; energy,
exertion, effort.
v. work, agonize, struggle, toil, slave,
travail, strain.
labor agreement [a · *gree* · ment] *n.*
See collective bargaining agreement.
labor contract [*kon* · trakt] *n. See*
collective bargaining agreement.
labor dispute [dis · *pyoot*] *n.* A
controversy between an employer and its
employees or their **collective bargaining
agent** concerning wages, hours, or other
working conditions, or concerning union
representation.
labor laws *n.* Federal and state statutes
and administrative regulations that govern
such matters as hours of work, minimum
wages, unemployment insurance, safety

and **collective bargaining**. EXAMPLES: the
National Labor Relations Act; the **Fair
Labor Standards Act**; the **Occupational
Safety and Health Act**.
labor organization [or · gan · i · *zay* · shen]
n. Same as labor union.
labor relations acts [re · *lay* · shenz] *n.*
Federal and state statutes that regulate
relations between management and
labor. EXAMPLE: the **National Labor
Relations Act**.
labor union [*yoo* · nyen] *n.* An
association of workers formed for the purpose of engaging in **collective bargaining**
with employers on behalf of workers
concerning wages, hours, and other terms
and conditions of their employment. *See*
collective bargaining agent. *See also*
craft union; industrial union.

Labor Relations Act [re · *lay* · shenz] *n.*
See National Labor Relations Act.

Labor Relations Board [re · *lay* · shenz] *n.*
See National Labor Relations Board.

Labor Standards Act [*stan* · derdz] *n. See*
Fair Labor Standards Act (FLSA).

laborer [*lay* · ber · er] *n.* A person who
performs labor for compensation.
➤ worker, employee, help, toiler.

laborer's lien [*lay* · ber · erz leen] *n.* The
statutory right given a worker or employee
to have her wages satisfied out of the
property of her employer if her employer
fails to pay her. *See* lien.

laches [*lach* · ez] *n.* The **equitable** doctrine
that a plaintiff's neglect or failure to assert
a right may cause the court to deny him

361

relief if, as a result, the defendant has changed position so that the defendant's rights are at risk.

➤ delay, nonfeasance, laxity, procrastination, laggardliness, inattention, remissness.

lack of *See* phrases beginning "**want of**."

laden in bulk [*lay* · den] *adj.* A shipping term referring to a ship loaded with a loose, unboxed, or unkegged cargo.

lading [*lay* · ding] *n.* *See* bill of lading.

lame duck *n.* 1. An elected official who is completing his term in office after having been defeated for reelection. 2. An elected official who, by law, cannot succeed herself in office. Both are "lame ducks" because they have lost their political strength.

Lame Duck Amendment [a · *mend* · ment] *n.* *See* Twentieth Amendment.

land *n.* 1. As used in the law, the soil and everything attached to it, whether naturally (EXAMPLES: trees; water; rocks) or by man (EXAMPLES: buildings; **fixtures**; fences), extending from the surface downward to the center of the earth and upward endlessly to the skies. *See* air rights. *See also* improved land; mineral land; posted land; tidelands; unimproved land; wetlands. "Land" is properly used interchangeably with "real estate," "real property," and "**realty**." "Property" is often used by itself to mean "land." *See* contract for sale of land; covenant running with the land; installment land contract. 2. An **interest** in land or an **estate in land**. *See* landed estate; landed interest. EXAMPLES: a **fee simple**; a **life estate**. *See* estate. 3. A country, especially one's country of birth or citizenship. *See* law of the land.
  v. To accomplish or attain.
➤ *n.* real estate, property, earth, terrain, soil, ground, nation, realty, territory, acreage.
  v. earn, win, achieve, acquire ("to land a contract").

land bank *n.* A bank created by federal statute for the purpose of making loans on agricultural land at low interest rates. Often used interchangeably with **soil bank**.

land contract [*kon* · trakt] *n.* *See* contract for sale of land; installment land contract.

land development [de · *vel* · ep · ment] *n.* *See* developer; development.

land grant *n.* A **grant** of **public lands** by the government. EXAMPLES: a grant of public land to a state by Congress to create and maintain a state-supported college or university (i.e., a **land grant institution**); a grant of land by a state to a railroad to support the construction of a railroad line. *See* land patent.

land grant institution [in · sti · *too* · shen] *n.* A college or university that has received a **land grant** from Congress.

land patent [*pat* · ent] *n.* 1. A **conveyance** or grant of land to an individual by the government. 2. A deed or other document conveying government land to an individual. *See* land grant; patent.

land sale contract [*kon* · trakt] *n.* *See* contract for sale of land; installment land contract.

land tax *n.* Same as **property tax**.

land trust *n.* 1. A property ownership arrangement in which a **trustee** holds both **legal title** and **equitable title** to the trust property, and the **beneficiary** retains the power to direct the trustee as well as the power to manage and receive the income from the trust property. Such an arrangement is also referred to as an **Illinois land trust**. *See* trust. 2. A nonprofit, tax-exempt organization whose function is to protect conservation resources by acquiring and holding land under agreements that prohibit use of the land for development or other commercial purposes.

land use planning [*plan* · ing] *n.* *See* land use regulation.

land use regulation [reg · yoo · *lay* · shen] *n.* Government regulation of the way in which land is used. Zoning statutes and ordinances are EXAMPLES of land use regulation.

Land Court *n.* A Massachusetts court that has **jurisdiction** over most **actions** affecting real estate or involving **title** to land.

Land Department [de · *part* · ment] *n.* *See* Bureau of Land Management.

Land Management Bureau [*man* · ej · ment byoo · roh] *n.* *See* Bureau of Land Management.

L

Land Office [*off* · iss] *n.* A common way of referring to the General Land Office, the federal agency that was the predecessor of the **Bureau of Land Management**.

landed [*lan* · ded] *adj.* Owning land; having real estate.

landed estate [es · *tate*] *n.* 1. Real property. 2. The **interest** or **estate** that a person has in land. *See* estate in land.

landed interest [*in* · trest] *n.* The **interest** or **estate** that a person has in land.

landed property [*prop* · er · tee] *n.* Real property.

landlord [*land* · lord] *n.* An owner of real property who leases all or a portion of the premises to a tenant. A landlord is also called a **lessor**; a tenant is called a **lessee**.
➤ lessor, landowner, possessor, proprietor. *Ant.* lessee.

landlord's attachment [a · *tach* · ment] *n.* A **remedy** provided a landlord by statute for enforcement of his **landlord's lien**. *See* attachment.

landlord's lien [*land* · lordz leen] *n.* A **lien** for rent which is in arrears, which a landlord has on a tenant's personal property located on the leased premises. *See* distrain; distraint.

landmark [*land* · mark] *n.* 1. A natural or manmade object (EXAMPLES: an embedded rock; an iron stake) that serves as a **monument** or a marker of a land boundary. *Also see* natural monuments. 2. A building or other structure of historical significance. *See* historic site. 3. Adjective for a court decision of great significance in establishing an important legal **precedent**. (EXAMPLE: *Roe v. Wade.*) Such a decision is often referred to as a **landmark decision** or a **landmark case**. *Also see* leading case.
➤ *n.* monument, marker, stake, feature. *adj.* significant, precedential, decisive, key ("a landmark decision").

landmark case *n. See* landmark.

landmark decision [de · *sizh* · en] *n. See* landmark.

landowner [*land* · oh · ner] *n.* A person who owns real property.
➤ landlord, owner, proprietor, possessor, title holder.

lands, tenements, and hereditaments *n.* A term found in deeds and other documents relating to land, which expresses the most inclusive **interest** a person can own in real property, i.e., an inheritable interest in the land and everything on it or under it (EXAMPLES: structures, minerals), and all rights arising out of it (EXAMPLES: the right to collect rent; the right to harvest timber).

lapse *n.* A termination or extinguishment, particularly of a **right** or **privilege**; a **forfeiture** caused by a person's failure to perform some necessary act or by the nonoccurrence of some **contingency**.
v. To cease; to expire; to terminate.
➤ *n.* termination, extinguishment, forfeiture; break, pause, recess.
v. cease, expire, terminate, discontinue, abate, pass, revert, terminate.

lapse statute [*stat* · shoot] *n. See* antilapse statutes.

lapsed *adj.* Terminated; extinguished; expired; no longer in force.
➤ terminated, extinguished, expired, elapsed, outdated ("a lapsed devise").

lapsed devise [de · *vize*] *n.* A **devise** that was good when the will was made but that has failed since then because of the death of the **devisee** before the death of the **testator**. *Compare* lapsed legacy. *See* antilapse statutes.

lapsed legacy [*leg* · e · see] *n.* A **legacy** that was good when the will was made but that has failed since then because of the death of the **legatee** before the death of the **testator**. *Compare* lapsed devise. *See* antilapse statutes.

lapsed policy [*pol* · i · see] *n.* An insurance policy that is no longer in force because of failure to pay the premium.

larcenous [*lar* · sen · ess] *adj.* Thieving or stealing; describes the type of intent that is an essential element of the crime of **larceny**. USAGE: "She did not take the ring with the intention of borrowing it; she took it with larcenous intent."
➤ thieving, criminal, predatory, felonious, rapacious.

larceny [*lar* · sen · ee] *n.* The crime of taking personal property, without consent, with the intent to **convert** it to the use of someone other than the owner or to deprive the owner of it permanently. Larceny does not involve the use of force or the threat of force. *See lucri causa. Also see* compound larceny; grand larceny; mixed larceny; petty larceny; simple larceny. *Compare* robbery. *Also compare* burglary; false pretenses; theft.

➤ theft, embezzlement, burglary, pilferage, misappropriation, stealing.

larceny by bailee [bay · *lee*] *n.* The taking or **conversion** to his own use by a **bailee** of property entrusted to him. *See* bailment.

larceny by fraud or deception [de · *sep* · shen] *n.* The taking of personal property, accomplished by fraud, stealth, or trick, with the intent to deprive the owner of his property permanently.

larceny by trick *n. See* larceny by fraud or deception.

larceny from the person [*per* · sen] *n.* Stealing any article from the **person** of the owner, or from her immediate custody, but without force. EXAMPLE: pickpocketing.

larceny of automobile [*aw* · te · mu · beel] *n. See* auto theft.

larceny of lost, mislaid, or misdelivered property [mis · *laid* or mis · de · *liv* · erd] *n.* The taking or **conversion** to one's own use of property one knows is lost, mislaid, or misdelivered, without making a reasonable effort to locate the owner. *See* lost property; misdelivery; mislaid property.

lascivious [le · *siv* · ee · ess] *adj.* Lewd; lustful; tending to produce carnal or lewd emotions. *See* lewd and lascivious cohabitation.

➤ lewd, lustful, erotic, licentious, indecent, bawdy, improper, promiscuous.

last *adj.* 1. Final; ultimate; concluding; definitive. 2. Least; lowest; worst.
v. To continue or endure.

➤ *adj.* final, ultimate, concluding, definitive, newest, latest, lowest, worst, above, foregoing, former.
v. endure, survive, continue, persevere, remain, withstand ("built to last a lifetime").

last antecedent rule [an · te · *see* · dent] *n.* A rule of **statutory construction** which requires that modifying words be construed as applying to those words immediately

preceding or following them, and not to words more remotely placed in the sentence.

last clear chance doctrine [*dok* · trin] *n.* A rule of **negligence** law by which a negligent defendant is held liable to a plaintiff who has negligently placed himself in peril, if the defendant had a later opportunity than the plaintiff to avoid the occurrence that resulted in injury. In some jurisdictions, the doctrine is referred to as the **discovered peril doctrine** and in others as the **humanitarian doctrine**.

last illness [*il* · nes] *n.* The illness that was the cause of a person's death.

last in, first out *See* **LIFO**.

last known address [a · *dress*] *n.* The place to which **process** (EXAMPLE: a **notice of action**) is to be sent when a statute authorizes **substituted service** by mail.

last resort [re · *zort*] *n.* Describes a court from whose **judgments** or decisions no appeal can be taken; the highest court to which a case can be taken. *See* highest court.

last will *n.* Same as **will**. The word "last" may connote "final wishes," or it may signify that the will is the most recent in a series of wills made by the **testator**.

last will and testament [*tes* · te · ment] *n.* Same as **last will**.

late *adj.* 1. No longer alive; dead. 2. Not on time; tardy; overdue.

➤ dead, departed, deceased; tardy, dilatory, lagging, delayed, unpunctual.

latent [*lay* · tent] *adj.* Hidden from view; concealed; not discoverable by ordinary inspection. *Compare* patent.

➤ hidden, concealed, not discoverable, submerged, veiled, passive, inactive, lurking ("latent defect").
Ant. obvious, manifest.

latent ambiguity [am · big · *yoo* · i · tee] *n.* An uncertainty in an **instrument** or document that does not appear in the words themselves, but only from the application of the writing to extrinsic circumstances which are obscure, ambiguous, or apparently illogical. EXAMPLE: a bequest to "my cousin John" by a **testator** who has two cousins named John. *See* ambiguity.

L

latent deed *n.* A deed kept hidden for 20 years or more. *See* deed.

latent defect [*dee* · fekt] *n.* 1. A defect not observable by casual inspection; a hidden defect in a structure or manufactured article, not discoverable by a reasonable examination. *Compare* patent defect. *See* defect; design defect. 2. **Defective title** to real estate that is not easily discoverable even though it is a matter of **public record**.

lateral [*lat* · e · rel] *adj.* From or toward the side.
➤ sideways, from the side, flanked.

lateral hire *n.* A person hired by a new firm or organization at the same level that the person previously held.

lateral support [sup · *ort*] *n.* The right of a landowner to support for her land in its natural state from the land adjoining it. A landowner has a duty not to alter his land in a way (for EXAMPLE: by excavation) that deprives the adjoining landowners of lateral support for their soil. *Compare* subjacent support.

laundering [*lawn* · der · ing] *n.* The federal crime of passing illegally acquired money through a legitimate business in order to obscure its source and give it the appearance of having been obtained legally.
➤ fraud, deception, illegal passing.

law *n.* 1. The entire body of rules of conduct created by government and enforced by the authority of government. EXAMPLES: a constitution; statutes; ordinances; regulations; judicial decisions. *See* law of the land. 2. A specific rule of conduct, such as a particular statute. USAGE: "The **Clayton Act** is a very important law." 3. The rule or rules of conduct that govern a specific activity occurring among or between persons or between a person and the state, or which govern the result in a particular case. USAGE: "The **Miranda rule** and the **Sixth Amendment** are the law in this situation" (or "in this case"). *See and compare* private law; public law. 4. The rules of conduct governing behavior in specific areas or fields of human activity. EXAMPLES: family law; contract law; constitutional law; criminal law.

The distinction between a **question of law** and a **question of fact** is extremely

important. *See and compare* question of law; question of fact. *Also see* matter of law.

It is also important to distinguish law from morals and morality. Human beings decide for themselves what is moral and what is immoral; morality does not involve formal sanctions. Law, on the other hand, is created by the state and is enforced by its authority.

See adjective law; administrative law; canon law; case law; civil law; commercial law; common law; conclusion of law; conflict of laws; constitutional law; criminal law; foreign law; general law; international law; local law; maritime law; martial law; mercantile law; military law; moral law; municipal law; natural law; organic law; parliamentary law; penal law; positive law; practice of law; private law; procedural law; prospective law; public law; remedial laws; retrospective legislation; revenue law; substantive law; unwritten law; written law.
➤ rules of conduct, mandate, code, constitution, statute, ordinance, regulation, judicial decision, command, act, precedent, authority, canon, holding.

law clerk *n. See* clerkship.

law court *n. See* court of law.

Law Day *n.* 1. By Act of Congress, May 1, a day set aside each year for publicly honoring the American system of law and justice. 2. The **maturity date** of a **bond** or mortgage.

law enforcement agency [en · *forss* · ment ay · jen · see] *n.* An agency of government with responsibility to enforce laws, particularly the criminal laws. EXAMPLES: the FBI; state or local police; a sheriff's department.

law enforcement authority [en · *forss* · ment aw · *thaw* · ri · tee] *n.* Same as **law enforcement agency**.

law enforcement officer [en · *forss* · ment *off* · i · ser] *n.* A person employed by a law enforcement agency for the purpose of seeing that the law, particularly the criminal law, is obeyed; a police officer; a peace officer.

law journal [*jern* · el] *n.* A publication containing articles pertaining to the law or of interest to lawyers. A **law review** is one type of law journal. Law journals are also published by bar associations and other organizations.

L

law judge *n.* A judge of a **court of law**, as opposed to a **court of equity**. *See also* administrative law judge.

law list *n.* A directory of persons who practice law, often together with other information such as the schools from which they obtained their degrees, the fields of the law in which they specialize, and the like. A law list may encompass attorneys nationwide or be as limited as a single city or county, or a particular field of specialization.

law merchant [*mer* · chent] *n.* A term referring to the law governing transactions between merchants, which evolved over many years as a part of the English **common law**. In its contemporary form in the United States, it is an element of **commercial law** and is largely governed by the **Uniform Commercial Code**.

law of marque [mark] *n.* *See* letters of marque and reprisal.

law of nations [*nay* · shenz] *n.* Same as **public international law**. *See also* international law.

law of nature [*nay* · cher] *n.* *See* natural law.

law of the case *n.* 1. A term referring to the principle that a decision of an **appellate court** is controlling at all subsequent stages of the litigation, and that upon **remand** the **trial court** must strictly follow the appellate court's rulings. This principle is related to the doctrine of *res judicata*. 2. A term referring to the rule that **instructions** given by the court to the jury are binding upon the jury, and, on appeal, are binding upon any party who has failed to take **exceptions**.

law of the flag *n.* A term referring to the law of the nation whose flag is flown by a particular seagoing vessel. Certain maritime matters are determined according to the law of the country whose flag the vessel flies.

law of the forum [*fore* · em] *n.* The law of the jurisdiction in which the case is litigated.

law of the land *n.* 1. A country's total law, including its constitution and all of its statutes and judicial decisions.

2. A reference to the mandate of the **supremacy clause** of the Constitution.

law of the road *n.* *See* rules of the road.

law officer [*off* · i · ser] *n.* 1. An attorney employed by government, or by an agency of government, to provide it with legal representation and legal counsel. EXAMPLES: a deputy attorney general; an assistant district attorney. 2. A law enforcement officer.

law reporters [re · *port* · erz] *n.* *See* law reports.

law reports [re · *ports*] *n.* Also called **law reporters** or, simply, **reporters**; volumes containing the opinions of courts in actual cases, sometimes with **annotations** showing additional cases on the same point as the reported cases. Law reports first appear in the form of **advance sheets** and are later republished in bound volumes. *See also* court reports.

law review [re · *vyoo*] *n.* A publication containing articles by law professors and other authorities, with respect to legal issues of current interest, and summaries of significant recent cases, written by law students. Being on the law review is a high honor for law students. Another name for a law review is **law journal** or legal periodical.

Law School Admissions Test [ad · *mish* · enz] *n.* Usually referred to by its acronym **LSAT**; the standardized examination that virtually all law schools require of applicants for admission. An applicant's LSAT results are evaluated in conjunction with his or her undergraduate performance and other factors.

lawful [*law* · ful] *adj.* According to law; not prohibited by law. Although "lawful" and "legal" are often used interchangeably, "lawful" more nearly suggests the concept of being in accord with the spirit or substance of the law, whereas "legal" conveys the idea of compliance with the form of the law.

► legal, legitimate, permitted, permissible, sanctioned, warranted, proper, legalized, licit ("lawful activity").

lawful arrest [a · *rest*] *n.* 1. An **arrest** based upon a legal **warrant** or otherwise based upon **probable cause**. 2. A proper **civil arrest**.

lawful damages [*dam* · e · jez] *n.* Such **loss** resulting from **injury** as the law compensates. *See* damages.

lawful force *n.* The amount of force permitted to be used in self-defense or by a police officer in making an arrest.

lawful goods *n.* Items or substances that may be sold or imported or exported without violating the law; articles that are not **contraband**.

lawful heirs [airz] *n.* Same as **heirs**, i.e., those persons who are entitled to inherit the property of a **decedent** who dies **intestate**. *Compare* lawful issue; legal heirs.

lawful interest [*in* · trest] *n.* *See* legal interest.

lawful issue [*ish* · yoo] *n.* Descendants; **heirs of the body**. *Compare* lawful heirs. *See* issue.

lawful money [*mun* · ee] *n.* Same as **legal tender**.

lawful representative [rep · re · *zen* · te · tiv] *n.* A person who succeeds to the rights of another person. EXAMPLES: an heir; a **legatee**; a **receiver**. *Compare* legal representative. *See* succession.

lawless [*law* · less] *adj.* Describes a person who does not observe the law or refuses to be governed by it.
➤ illegal, wrongful, criminal, disobedient, chaotic, violent, disorganized, anarchistic, uncontrolled.

laws *n.* *Plural* of **law**. *See* law.

lawsuit [*law* · sewt] *n.* An informal term for an **action** or **proceeding** in a civil court, but not for a criminal prosecution.
➤ action, proceeding, suit, case, cause of action, cause.

lawyer [*law* · yer] *n.* An attorney. *See also* attorney at law; barrister; counselor; solicitor.
➤ attorney, barrister, counselor, solicitor, legal advocate, counsel, practitioner, mouthpiece, jurist.

lax *adj.* The state of being careless, casual, or permissive.
➤ slack, careless, casual, remiss, negligent, indifferent, sloppy.

lay *adj.* Pertaining to laypersons, as opposed to professionals, experts, or members of the clergy. *See* layperson.
v. 1. To create or build. 2. To hand over. 3. To put down.
➤ *adj.* nonexpert, nonprofessional, amateur ("a lay witness"); nonclerical ("a lay deacon").
v. create, build, undergird ("to lay a foundation"); present, hand over ("to lay the case before the judge"); put down, bury, end ("to lay to rest").

lay advocate [*ad* · ve · ket] *n.* A nonlawyer who represents persons before an administrative agency or other nonjudicial bodies. Many government agencies permit nonlawyers, including paralegals, to engage in such representation.

lay judge *n.* 1. In some jurisdictions, a person who is not **learned in the law** who sits as an assistant to the trial judge. 2. A layperson who, in some states, presides over a **court of limited jurisdiction**. (EXAMPLE: a justice of the peace.)

lay witness [*wit* · ness] *n.* A witness, other than an **expert witness**, who possesses no expertise in the field about which she testifies. Except in limited circumstances in some jurisdictions, a lay witness is not permitted to testify as to her opinion, but only as to things she actually observed. *See* opinion evidence. *Compare* expert opinion; expert testimony.

layaway [*lay* · a · way] *n.* An arrangement for purchasing goods in which the buyer reserves an item with a downpayment or deposit and claims it only upon paying the balance in full. USAGE: "The item was purchased on layaway."

laying [*lay* · ing] *v.* The act of establishing, creating, or constructing.
➤ establishing, creating, making, constructing ("laying a foundation").

laying a basis [*bay* · sis] *n.* *See* laying a foundation.

laying a foundation [foun · *day* · shen] Introducing evidence for the purpose of making other evidence, not yet introduced, relevant and material. This phrase is often uttered by an attorney during the trial of a case. EXAMPLE: To lay a foundation sufficent to enable a tape recording of a conversation

L

to be admissible evidence, a witness must first authenticate it; that is, establish that it is genuine.

laying the venue [*ven* · yoo] Stating in a **complaint** or **petition** the county or **judicial district** in which the plaintiff seeks to bring the **action**.

layman [*lay* · man] *n. See* layperson.

layoff [*lay* · off] *n.* A temporary or permanent termination of a person's employment by his employer. The term is most often used when the termination is brought about by a lack of available work.
➤ discharge, suspension, firing, unemployment, removal, termination.

layperson [*lay* · per · sen] *n.* 1. A nonprofessional person, as opposed to a person in one of the professions. USAGE: "He is not a physician, he is a layperson." *Compare* professional. 2. A nonexpert, as opposed to an expert. *See* lay witness. 3. A person who is not a member of the clergy, as opposed to a person who is.
➤ nonprofessional, amateur, nonexpert.

LBO Abbreviation of **leveraged buyout**.

lead counsel [*kouwn* · sel] *n.* The attorney who is in charge of her side of a case (i.e., the plaintiff's side or the defendant's side), with other counsel assisting her.

leading [*lee* · ding] *adj.* 1. Primary; most important; chief. 2. Guiding; directing.
➤ primary, most important, predominant, foremost, chief ("a leading case"); guiding, directing, suggestive ("a leading question").

leading case *n.* A case that derives its importance from the fact that it settled or finally determined a significant point of law. *Brown v. Board of Education* is an EXAMPLE of a leading case; it is also a **landmark case**. However, not every leading case is a **landmark case**.

leading object rule [*ob* · jekt] *n.* The rule that a contract to guarantee the debt of another must be in writing (*see* statute of frauds) does not apply if the **promissor's** "leading object" or "main purpose" in giving the guaranty was to benefit himself. (EXAMPLE: A is injured as a result of the negligence of B's minor son. B promises to pay A's medical bills in return for A's agreement not to sue.) This rule is also

referred to as the **main purpose rule**. *See also* original promise.

leading question [*kwes* · chen] *n.* A question put to a witness that suggests the answer the questioner desires. (EXAMPLE: "You did as you were told, didn't you?") Leading questions are generally not allowed on **direct examination**, but are permitted on **cross-examination**.

learned [*ler* · ned] *adj.* Knowledgeable; educated; wise.
➤ knowledgeable, educated, accomplished, wise, judicious, well-informed.

learned in the law [*ler* · ned] 1. A person who has studied the law academically (i.e., graduated from law school), as distinguished from a person who has acquired legal knowledge through her experience in the legal system, for EXAMPLE, a **lay judge**. 2. A phrase properly applicable to any attorney.

lease *n.* 1. A contract for the possession of real estate in consideration of payment of rent, ordinarily for a term of years or months, but sometimes **at will**. The person making the **conveyance** is the landlord or **lessor**; the person receiving the right of possession is the tenant or **lessee**. *See* tenancy at will. 2. Under the **Uniform Commercial Code**, a contract transferring the right to possession and use of personal property ("**goods**") for a term in return for **consideration**. The person granting possession of the goods is the lessor; the person receiving possession is the lessee.
    See assignable lease; consumer lease; graduated lease; gross lease; ground rent lease; leasehold; mineral lease; mining lease; month to month lease; net lease; percentage lease; perpetual lease; proprietary lease; sublease; underlease.
    v. 1. To create a **tenancy** in real property. *See* leasehold. 2. To transfer possession of personal property for a specified period of time.
➤ *n.* contract, agreement, grant, instrument. *v.* let, rent, convey, grant, charter, hire.

lease with option to purchase [*op* · shen to *per* · chess] *n.* A lease that provides the **lessee** with the **option**, at the end of the term (or, under some leases, at any time during the term), to purchase the property for a specified sum.

leaseback [*leess* · bak] *n. See* sale and leaseback.

leasehold [*leess* · hold] *adj.* The **interest** or **estate** of a **lessee** under a **lease**. The lessee's interest or estate is also referred to as a **leasehold interest** or **leasehold estate**.

leasehold estate [es · *tate*] *n. See* leasehold.

leasehold interest [*in* · trest] *n. See* leasehold.

leasehold value [*val* · yoo] *n.* The monetary value of a leasehold.

leave *n.* Permission, authorization.
  v. 1. To make a **disposition** of something, particularly by will. 2. To deposit; to abandon; to discard. 3. To depart; to go out from.
  ➤ *n.* permission, authorization, license, sanction; absence, parting, break, removal, pause ("take leave").
  v. dispose of, give, grant, deposit, abandon, discard; depart, retreat, embark.

leave and license [*ly* · sense] *n.* A **defense** to an **action** in **trespass**, which states that the conduct complained of was engaged in with the permission of the plaintiff. *See* license.

leave of absence [*ab* · sense] *n.* Absence from work with the employer's permission. (EXAMPLE: sick leave.) A leave of absence may be with or without pay.

leave of court *n.* Permission of the court. Leave of court is required when permission to take a certain step in an **action** is discretionary with the court. EXAMPLE: leave of court is required for a person to appear as *amicus curiae. See* judicial discretion.

leaving the scene of an accident [*lee* · ving … *ak* · si · dent] *n.* The crime committed by the operator of an automobile who departs from the site of an accident in which he is knowingly involved without identifying himself or providing other information required by law. This offense is also commonly referred to as **hit and run**.

ledger [*lej* · er] *n.* A **book of account** to which the daily transactions of a business are posted, having been taken from the business's **books of original entry** or

journals. A book of account that reflects all of the assets and liabilities of a company is a **general ledger**.
  ➤ book of account, register, diary, journal, accounts, logbook, passbook, record.

legacy [*leg* · uh · see] *n.* Accurately, a gift of personal property by will, although the term is often loosely used to mean any **testamentary gift**; a **bequest**. *Compare* devise. *See* conditional legacy; contingent legacy; cumulative legacy; demonstrative legacy; general legacy; lapsed legacy; pecuniary legacy; residuary legacy; specific legacy; vested legacy.
  ➤ grant, bequest, endowment, present ("to receive a legacy"); tradition, history, meaning ("the legacy of Thurgood Marshall").

legacy tax *n.* Same as **inheritance tax**.

legal [*lee* · gl] *adj.* 1. According to law; not prohibited by law. 2. In accordance with statute. 3. By means of judicial proceedings. 4. That which is inferred or presumed by the law. *See* inference; legal presumption. 5. Created by law. EXAMPLE: a **legal entity**. 6. According to law rather than **equity**. 7. Pertaining to the law. *Compare* moral.
  Although "legal" and "lawful" are often used interchangeably, "legal" more nearly connotes the idea of compliance with the form of the law, while "lawful" suggests the concept of being in accord with the spirit or substance of the law.
  ➤ authorized, permitted, sanctioned, proper, constitutional, legitimate, formal, statutory, allowable, rightful, decreed, enforcible.

legal action [*ak* · shen] *n.* 1. Any lawsuit. 2. An **action at law**, as opposed to an **action in equity**. 3. An action before an administrative agency to enforce a **right**.

legal age *n.* The age at which a person acquires the **capacity** to enter into contracts, make **conveyances** and transfers of property, and otherwise conduct business as an adult; the **age of majority**. Legal age varies from state to state. It may also differ in the same state depending upon the activity involved. EXAMPLE: many states set different ages for entering into marriage, making a will, and purchasing alcoholic beverages. *See* majority; minority. *Compare* age of consent; legal capacity.

L

legal aid *n.* The customary term for *pro bono* legal assistance provided to indigent persons by attorneys and paralegals, and often coordinated by state or local bar associations. *Compare* Legal Services Corporation.

legal assistant [e · *sis* · tent] *n.* Same as **paralegal**.

legal authority [aw · *thaw* · ri · tee] *n.* 1. The power of the law to require obedience. 2. **Precedent**. USAGE: "What is your legal authority for that contention?"

legal capacity [ke · *pass* · i · tee] *n.* 1. The ability to execute binding contracts, deeds, wills, etc.; **capacity**. *Compare* incapacity; legal incapacity. 2. The right to sue and be sued.

legal capital [*ka* · pi · tel] *n.* The minimum amount of **capital** a corporation must have to commence business or remain in business.

legal cause *n.* 1. The **proximate cause** of an **injury**. 2. **Probable cause**. 3. Cause that the law deems sufficient.

legal conclusion [kun · *kloo* · zhen] *n.* A statement of the result in a situation which involves application of the law to a set of facts without having set forth the **material facts** supporting it. EXAMPLE: A person expresses a legal conclusion when she says "the defendant committed **arson** *because* he intentionally started the fire" *if* the **legal issue** is *whether* the defendant intentionally started the fire. *Note* that a legal conclusion is not the same as a **conclusion of law**. *Compare* conclusion of law.

legal consequence [*kon* · se · kwenss] *n.* *See* legal effect.

legal consideration [ken · sid · e · *ray* · shen] *n.* **Consideration** sufficient to support a contract; **adequate consideration**; actual consideration as distinguished from **moral consideration**.

legal counsel [*koun* · sel] *n.* *See* counsel.

legal custody [*kuss* · te · dee] *n.* 1. Custody in accordance with law. EXAMPLES: custody of a minor by a court-appointed guardian; restraint of a person pursuant to lawful **detainer**; custody of a child after divorce. 2. With respect to the custody of a child after divorce, a right awarded to one parent to make the major decisions concerning the welfare of the child of both, even though the other parent may have physical custody of the child from time to time. However, *see* joint custody. *Also see* custody; divided custody; sole custody.

legal death *n.* 1. **Brain death**. 2. **Civil death**.

legal debt *n.* An **obligation** enforceable in an **action at law**. *See* debt.

legal demand [de · *mand*] *n.* A **demand** made in proper form. Thus, for EXAMPLE, if a contract states that suit may be not be brought for its enforcement unless performance has first been demanded in writing, then only a written demand is a legal demand.

legal dependent [de · *pen* · dent] *n.* A person whom one is legally bound to **support**; a person who has the right to appeal to the law to require another to support him. EXAMPLE: a person's minor child. *See* dependent.

legal description [des · *krip* · shen] *n.* In deeds and mortgages, a description of the real estate that is the subject of the **conveyance**, by boundaries, distances, and size, or by reference to maps, surveys, or **plats**. *See* metes and bounds.

legal disability [dis · e · *bil* · i · tee] *n.* Same as **civil disability**. *Compare* physical disability.

legal discretion [dis · *kresh* · en] *n.* Same as **judicial discretion**.

legal duty [*dew* · tee] *n.* An obligation imposed by the law. *See* duty.

legal effect [ef · *ekt*] *n.* 1. In force; valid; effective. USAGE: "This mortgage is of no legal effect because it isn't signed." 2. The consequence or result of some action or circumstance as a **matter of law**. USAGE: "The legal effect of an illegal search is that the evidence obtained is inadmissible."

legal entity [*en* · ti · tee] *n.* An **entity** created by the law; an **artificial person**. EXAMPLE: a corporation.

legal ethics [*eth* · iks] *n.* The code of conduct among lawyers which governs their moral and professional duties toward one another, toward their clients, and

L

toward the courts. *See* ethics; Rules of Professional Conduct.

legal evidence [*ev* · i · dense] *n.* Evidence that is admissible. *See* admissible evidence.

legal excuse [eks · *kyooss*] *n.* An excuse sufficient in law to permit a person to avoid a legal duty. EXAMPLES: **excusable homicide**; **excusable neglect**. *See* excuse.

legal fiction [*fik* · shen] *n.* A nonexistent status or circumstance that the law pretends is real in order to achieve justice. A **lost grant** is an EXAMPLE of a legal fiction.

legal fraud *n.* Same as **constructive fraud**.

legal heirs [airz] *n.* A term that may mean either **heirs** or **next of kin**. *See* lawful heirs.

legal holiday [*hol* · i · day] *n.* A day declared a holiday by statute. Generally, the courts, public offices, and banks are closed, as are other businesses, and **legal process** may not be served, although state statutes vary with respect to the kind of business that can be legally transacted.

legal impediment [im · *ped* · i · ment] *n.* The lack of a quality or qualification required by law. USAGE: "failure to register is a legal impediment to voting"; "failure to have achieved **legal age** is a legal impediment to marriage."

legal impossibility [im · poss · i · *bil* · i · tee] *n.* A person who is unable to commit a crime because of *legal impossibility* cannot be convicted of a crime he intends or attempts. (EXAMPLE: A child who has not attained the **age of reason**, and who is therefore **conclusively presumed** to be unable to commit murder, cannot be convicted of murder under any circumstances.) By contrast, a person who is unable to complete a criminal act because of *factual impossibility* may nonetheless be criminally responsible. (EXAMPLE: An adult who, at close range, points a pistol at the head of a person he intends to kill and pulls the trigger, mistakenly believing the gun to be loaded, is guilty of attempted murder.) *See and compare* impossibility of performance; impracticability.

legal incapacity [in · ke · *pass* · i · tee] *n.* The inability to execute binding contracts, to marry, etc., due to lack of **capacity** or some other **legal impediment**. *Compare* legal capacity. *See* incapacity. *Also see* civil disability.

legal injury [*in* · je · ree] *n.* An invasion or violation of a legal right.

legal insanity [in · *san* · i · tee] *n.* A term that refers to the way in which the law defines **insanity**. *Note* that the term "insanity" has no scientific or medical meaning.

legal interest [*in* · trest] *n.* 1. The rate of interest fixed by statute (usually the maximum allowable rate) that will be in effect between the parties in the absence of an agreement between them fixing the rate. *Compare* usury. *See* interest. 2. A **right**, **claim**, or **share**. *See* legal right; legal title.

legal investments [in · *vest* · ments] *n.* In certain states, high-quality investments designated by the state's banking authorities as allowable investments for banks and **investment companies**, particularly with respect to **trust funds**. Legal investments are also called **legal lists**.

legal issue [*ish* · ew] *n.* 1. A question arising in a case with respect to the law to be applied or the meaning of the law. *See* question of law. 2. **Lawful issue**.

legal jeopardy [*jep* · er · dee] *n.* Another term for the **jeopardy** to which a criminal defendant is vulnerable when she is brought to trial. *See* double jeopardy.

legal liability [ly · e · *bil* · i · tee] *n.* The **liability** to which a defendant in a **civil action** is exposed.

legal lists *n.* Same as **legal investments**.

legal malice [*mal* · iss] *n.* **Constructive malice** or **express malice**. *See* malice in law.

legal malpractice [mal · *prak* · tiss] *n.* An attorney's failure to exercise on behalf of his client the knowledge, skill, and ability ordinarily possessed and exercised by members of the legal profession. Like medical malpractice, legal malpractice is a **tort** if it results in **injury**. *See* malpractice.

legal memory [*mem* · e · ree] *n.* That which is "**beyond legal memory**" is that which occurred a long time ago, in law usually at least 20 or 30 years before. The term is synonymous with **ancient** and is a **legal fiction**. *See* ancient document;

L

ancient judgment; ancient lights. *See also* lost grant.

legal name *n.* A person's given or Christian name in combination with the surname or family name.

legal negligence *n.* Same as **negligence in law** or **actionable negligence**.

legal notice [*noh · tiss*] *n.* 1. Such **notice** as complies with the requirements of the law. In some circumstances, legal notice is notice that the law implies either because a person had knowledge of the actual facts (**actual notice**) or because he failed to make inquiry when he reasonably should have (**implied notice**); in other contexts, it is notice that the law considers to have taken place whether or not it did (**constructive notice** or **public notice**); in still others, it is notice actually communicated by direct information. 2. Notice given by publication in a **newspaper of general circulation**. *See* publication. *See also* record notice.

legal obligation [ob · li · *gay* · shen] *n.* 1. A debt; a **legal debt**. 2. An obligation to do what the law requires one to do. *Compare* moral obligation.

legal opinion [o · *pin* · yen] *n.* An assessment by an attorney for the benefit of her client, usually in writing, of the requirements of the law as it applies to a situation with which the client is concerned.

legal presumption [pre · *sump* · shen] *n.* A **presumption of law** rather than a **presumption of fact**.

legal proceeding [pro · *see* · ding] *n.* Any **action** brought in a court or before an administrative agency. *See* proceeding. *See and compare* administrative proceeding; judicial proceeding. *Also see* adversarial proceeding.

legal process [*pross* · ess] *n.* 1. **Process**. 2. More broadly, process that is in proper form and issued for a lawful purpose. 3. In another sense, the system by which laws are applied or administered, i.e., the legal system or the judicial system.

legal question [*kwes* · chen] *n.* *See* legal issue.

legal rate of interest [*in* · trest] *n.* *See* legal interest.

legal remedy [*rem* · e · dee] *n.* A **remedy** available through legal action.

legal representative [rep · re · *zen* · te · tiv] *n.* A person who handles another person's legal affairs, but not in the capacity of an attorney; a **personal representative**. EXAMPLES: an **executor**; an **administrator**. *Compare* lawful representative.

legal research [*ree* · serch] *n.* A study of **precedents** and other **authority** for the purpose of developing or supporting a legal theory or position. Most legal writing (briefs, memoranda, etc.) is based upon legal research and involves application of that research to the facts of the case.

legal reserve [re · *zerv*] *n.* 1. The amount of money or **assets** the law requires a bank to have set aside to insure depositors' opportunities to withdraw cash as they wish. 2. The amount of money or assets necessary for a life insurance company to have available at any given time to enable it to pay all claims. *See* reserve.

legal residence [*rez* · i · dense] *n.* A person's **permanent residence**; the equivalent of **domicile**.

legal right *n.* A claim recognizable in an **action** brought in a court or before an administrative agency; a **right** recognized by the law.

legal separation [sep · e · *ray* · shen] *n.* *See* divorce a mensa et thoro.

legal services [*lee* · gl *ser* · viss · ez] *n.* *See* Legal Services Corporation.

legal tender [*ten* · der] *n.* Coin and currency of the country issuing it; lawful money.

legal title [*ty* · tel] *n.* **Title** that evidences apparent ownership, as distinguished from **equitable title**, which indicates a **beneficial interest**. EXAMPLE: Smith owns the Lay-Z Ranch and has **record title**; Smith conveys the Lay-Z to Jones under a **contract for sale of land**, but has not yet executed a deed to Jones. In these circumstances, Smith has legal title to the Lay-Z and Jones has equitable title.

Legal Services Corporation [*lee* · gl *ser* · viss · ez kore · per · *ay* · shen] *n.* Known as "Legal Services," a program providing representation and other legal services in connection with certain types

L

of civil matters (EXAMPLES: disputes with landlords; claims by creditors) to persons unable to afford an attorney. The program is created by federal statute and is publicly funded. *Compare* legal aid.

legalese [leeg · el · *eez*] *n.* The use by lawyers of specialized words or phrases, rather than plain talk, when it serves no purpose; legal jargon. Contemporary commentators eschew legalese in favor of direct, effective use of language.

legality [le · *gal* · i · tee] *n.* The condition of conformity with the law; lawfulness.
➤ lawfulness, permissibility, constitutionality, rightfulness, sanction.

legalization [lee · ge · li · *zay* · shen] *n.* The act of making legal or lawful that which is illegal or unlawful; legalizing. *See* legalize. *See also* decriminalization; legitimation.
➤ legitimation, validation, legalizing, authorization, sanction, ratification, approval.

legalize [*lee* · ge · lize] *v.* To make legal or lawful that which is illegal or unlawful; to confirm something already done. *See* legalization.
➤ make legal, legitimate, approve, authorize, sanction, validate, legislate, decriminalize, permit.

legally [*lee* · ge · lee] *adv.* According to law; properly.
➤ legitimately, properly, appropriately, formally, justifiably.

legally adopted [e · *dop* · ted] *adj.* Adopted according to law. *See* adoption.

legally blind *adj. See* blindness.

legally constituted court [kon · sti · tew · ted] *n.* A court existing under the authority of the law. *Compare* kangaroo court.

legally sufficient title [se · *fish* · ent ty · tel] *n.* **Marketable title**.

legally sworn *n.* Put under oath. *See* sworn.

legatee [leg · e · *tee*] *n.* A person who receives personal property as a beneficiary under a will, although the word is often loosely used to mean a person who receives a **testamentary gift** of either personal property or real property. *Compare* devisee.
➤ recipient, devisee, beneficiary, donee, legal heir.

legation [le · *gay* · shen] *n.* 1. A country's diplomatic representative, and her staff, in the foreign country to which they have been assigned. *See* ambassador. 2. The residence or headquarters of a foreign diplomatic representative. *See* embassy.
➤ diplomatic representative, ambassador, consulate, delegation, envoy; embassy, headquarters.

legislate [*lej* · is · late] *v.* To make or enact a law by legislation.
➤ codify, prescribe, ordain, enact, establish, formulate, rule.

legislation [lej · is · *lay* · shen] *n.* Laws (EXAMPLES: statutes; ordinances) enacted by a legislative body (EXAMPLES: Congress; a state legislature; a city council). *Compare* judge-made law; judicial legislation. *Also compare* regulation. *See* class legislation; remedial legislation; retrospective legislation; special legislation.
➤ law, regulation, statute, ordinance, ruling, measure, act.

legislative [*lej* · is · lay · tiv] *adj.* 1. Pertaining to the enactment of laws. 2. Pertaining to legislation. 3. Pertaining to the legislature.
➤ congressional, statutory, parliamentary, codified, statutory.

legislative act *n.* 1. The act of a legislator in voting on legislation. 2. A statute or ordinance. 3. Any act by a legislature that carries out a **legislative function**. *Compare* administrative act; judicial act.

legislative apportionment [a · *por* · shen · ment] *n. See* apportionment of representatives.

legislative body [*bod* · ee] *n.* A legislature or a **legislative committee**.

legislative branch *n.* 1. With the **judicial branch** and the **executive branch**, one of the three divisions into which the Constitution separates the government of the United States. These **branches of government** are also referred to as **departments of government**. The legislative branch is primarily responsible for enacting the laws. 2. A similar division in state government.

legislative committee [ke · *mit* · ee] *n.* A committee of a house of the legislature or of any legislative body. A legislative committee reviews proposed legislation in the area of activity over which it has

L

jurisdiction and recommends passage, amendment, or rejection of the legislation to the full legislature. *See* conference committee; joint committee; standing committee.

legislative court *n.* A court created by a legislative act rather than by a constitutional provision.

legislative department [de · *part* · ment] *n.* Same as **legislative branch**.

legislative districts [dis · trikts] *n.* The divisions of a state for the purpose of representation in each of the houses of its legislature. *See* district. *See also* congressional districts.

legislative function [*funk* · shen] *n.* An act that is within the power of the legislature to perform. *Compare* judicial function. *See also* legislative act; legislative powers.

legislative history [*hist* · e · ree] *n.* Recorded events that provide a basis for determining the **legislative intent** underlying a statute enacted by a legislature. The records of **legislative committee** hearings and of debates on the floor of the legislature are among the sources for legislative history. *Compare* plain meaning rule.

legislative immunity [im · *yoo* · ni · tee] *n.* The protection from **personal liability** which the law grants a legislator for her actions so long as they are legislative acts; i.e., legitimate legislative functions or lawful exercises of legislative power. *Compare* judicial immunity. *See* immunity.

legislative intent [in · *tent*] *n.* That which the legislature wanted or intended to achieve when it enacted a statute. Legislative intent is considered when construing the meaning of words in a statute. *See* legislative history; plain meaning rule.

legislative investigation [in · ves · ti · *gay* · shen] *n.* See investigation.

legislative powers [*pow* · erz] *n.* 1. The powers granted to a legislature or to the **legislative branch** of government by its constitution and statutes. 2. The power of a legislature to perform a legislative act or to carry out a legislative function. *Compare* executive powers; judicial powers.

legislative rule *n.* In **administrative law**, a regulation having the force of law, promulgated by an administrative

agency carrying out a statutory mandate empowering or requiring it to regulate.

legislator [*lej* · is · lay · ter] *n.* A member of a legislature.

➤ council member, senator, lawmaker, delegate, representative, congressperson.

legislature [*lej* · is · lay · cher] *n.* 1. The **branch of government** that enacts **statutory law**, usually consisting of two houses, a Senate and a House of Representatives, made up of members representing districts and elected by the voters of those districts. Congress is the national legislature. *See* state legislature. 2. Any body having legislative powers. EXAMPLES: a city council; a **board of aldermen**; a **board of supervisors**.

➤ house, chamber, assembly, parliament, senate, council.

legitimacy [le · *jit* · i · mes · ee] *n.* 1. Lawfulness; genuineness; validity; correctness. 2. The state of having been born in wedlock.

➤ lawfulness, genuineness, validity, correctness, authenticity.

legitimate [le · *jit* · i · met] *adj.* 1. Lawful. 2. Genuine; valid; correct; right. 3. As commonly used, a legitimate child. *Compare* illegitimate.
v. [le · jit · i · *mate*] To make lawful; to make legitimate. EXAMPLE: making an illegitimate child legitimate (**legitimation**).

➤ *adj.* lawful, genuine, valid, correct, right, proper, rightful, verifiable ("the legitimate heir").
v. make lawful, certify, validate, legalize, license ("to legitimate a child").

legitimate child *n.* A child born to parents who are married to each other. *Compare* illegitimate child.

legitimation [le · jit · i · *may* · shen] *n.* 1. The legal proceeding by which an illegitimate child is given the status of a legitimate child. 2. Making lawful that which was unlawful.

lemon laws [*lem* · en] *n.* State statutes providing that a purchaser of a new car may return it within a specified period of time, and is entitled to receive a refund or a comparable replacement if the car is substantially defective and if reasonable efforts to repair it have failed. In some states, lemon

L

laws also apply to other vehicles, such as boats and motorcycles.

lend *v.* 1. To make a loan; that is, to allow another person to have the use and possession of something, for a definite or indefinite period of time, and with or without compensation. *Compare* borrow. 2. To give another person the temporary use of money, to be repaid with interest, i.e., the act of lending money or lending credit. 3. When used in a will, to give, **devise**, or **bequeath**.
➤ supply, furnish, lease, let, loan, provide, advance.
Ant. take, withhold, borrow.

lender [*len* · der] *n.* 1. A person who makes a loan; a person who lends. *Compare* borrower. 2. A **lending institution**.
➤ creditor, seller, bank, supplier, loaner.

lending [*len* · ding] *n.* The act of making a loan. *See* lend.

lending agency [*ay* · jen · see] *n. See* lending institution.

lending credit [*kred* · it] *n. See* lend.

lending institution [in · sti · *tew* · shen] *n.* A company engaged in the business of making loans. EXAMPLES: a bank; a savings and loan association.

lending money [*mun* · ee] *n. See* lend.

lese majesty [lees *maj* · es · tee] *(French) n.* A crime against the **sovereignty** of the state; **treason**.

lessee [less · ee] *n.* The person receiving the right of possession of real property, or possession and use of personal property, under a lease. A lessee of real estate is also known as a tenant. *Compare* lessor.
➤ renter, possessor, leaseholder, boarder, tenant.

lesser included offense [*less* · er in · *kloo* · ded o · *fense*] *n.* A criminal offense included within the crime for which a defendant has been **indicted**, and for which he may be convicted under the **indictment** so long as he is not convicted of the more serious offense; a crime that cannot be committed without at the same time committing one or more other crimes. EXAMPLE: It is impossible to commit **first degree murder** without also committing both **second degree murder, voluntary manslaughter**, and

battery. *See* divisible offense. *See also* merger of offenses.

lesser offense [*less* · er o · *fense*] *n. See* lesser included offense.

lessor [less · or] *n.* The person conferring the right of possession of real property, or possession and use of personal property, under a lease. A lessor of real estate is also known as a landlord. *Compare* lessee.
➤ lender, creditor, owner, landlord.

let *n.* In old deeds and other **conveyances**, an obstruction, hindrance, or impediment. USAGE (in a deed): "The grantee shall have the right to use this **easement** without let or hindrance."
v. 1. To award a contract to a contractor selected from among two or more bidders for a job. *See* letting a contract. *Also see* bid. 2. To lease property. USAGE: "Did she let her apartment?" 3. To allow.
➤ *n.* obstruction, hindrance, impediment ("without let or hindrance").
v. allow, authorize, permit, endorse ("let the decision stand"); lease, sublet, convey, lend ("Did she let her apartment?").

lethal [*lee* · thel] *adj.* Capable of producing death; deadly.
➤ deadly, mortal, fatal, murderous, devastating ("a lethal weapon").

lethal weapon [*wep* · en] *n.* A **deadly weapon**.

letter [*let* · er] *n.* 1. A document granting or delegating some specific power or authority. EXAMPLES: a **letter of credit**; a **letter of intent**. *Also see* letters. 2. A written communication, usually through the mail, from one person to another. 3. The precise or literal meaning. EXAMPLE: the **letter of the law**.
➤ document, written communication, missive, message, note, memo.

letter of advice [ad · *vyss*] *n.* Under the **Uniform Commercial Code**, a communication from the **drawer** of a **draft** to the **drawee** advising that a described draft has been drawn.

letter of attornment [a · *tern* · ment] *n.* A letter from a landlord to a tenant advising her that the premises have been sold and instructing her to pay rent to the new owner. *See* attornment.

letter of credit [*kred* · it] *n.* A written promise, generally by a bank, that it will honor **drafts** made upon it by a specified customer so long as the conditions described in the letter are complied with; a document which states in legal form that the bank has extended credit to the owner of the letter and will pay his bills. Transactions involving letters of credit are governed by the **Uniform Commercial Code**.

letter of intent [in · *tent*] *n.* A letter **memorializing** a preliminary understanding between two or more persons, written by one of them to the other (or others) to serve as a basis for the formal agreement they intend to execute.

letter of the law *n.* A literal or exact reading of a statute or other law. *Compare* spirit of the law.

letter ruling [*roo* · ling] *n.* A written statement issued to a taxpayer by the Internal Revenue Service, in which interpretations of tax laws are made and applied to a specific set of facts.

letters *n.* *Plural* of **letter**. Documents granting or delegating some specific power or authority. EXAMPLES: **letters of administration**; letters testamentary; **letters patent**. *Also see* letter.

letters of administration [ad · min · is · *tray* · shen] *n.* A document issued by the **probate court** appointing the **administrator** of the **estate** of a person who has died without leaving a will. *Compare* letters testamentary. *See* administration.

letters of administration CTA [ad · min · is · *tray* · shen] *n.* **Letters of administration** issued to an **administrator CTA**.

letters of administration DBN [ad · min · is · *tray* · shen] *n.* **Letters of administration** issued to an **administrator DBN**.

letters of marque *n.* *See* letters of marque and reprisal.

letters of marque and reprisal [mark and re · *prize* · el] *n.* A term relating to the power given Congress by the Constitution to authorize privately owned ships, during time of war, to attack the ships of hostile nations and seize their cargoes. In modern times, international treaties and the existence of the United Nations have rendered this practice obsolete. *See marque.*

letters patent [*pat* · ent] *n.* The document issued by the government granting a **patent**.

letters rogatory [*roh* · ge · toh · ree] *n.* A request by a court in one country, made to a foreign court, to obtain information desired in a case pending before it by having a witness who is located within the jurisdiction of the foreign court answer written **interogatories**.

letters testamentary [tes · te · *men* · te · ree] *n.* A document issued by the **probate court** appointing the **executor** of the **estate** of a **decedent** who died leaving a will. *Compare* letters of administration. *See* testamentary.

letting [*let* · ing] *v.* 1. Awarding a contract. *See* letting a contract. 2. Leasing. *See* lease; let. 3. Allowing.
➤ awarding, granting ("letting a contract"); leasing, renting, chartering ("letting a studio").

letting a contract [*kon* · trakt] The steps in awarding a contract, particularly for construction or repair of a public building or other public improvement, including the invitation to bid, receipt of bids, and award of the contract to the **lowest responsible bidder**. *See* public contract.

leveraged buyout [*lev* · er · ejd *by* · out] *n.* A transaction in which management or an outside entity purchases all of the outstanding stock of a **publicly held** corporation, largely with borrowed funds. The debt created by the transaction becomes a liability of the acquired corporation. A leveraged buyout is often referred to as an **LBO**.

levy [*lev* · ee] *n.* 1. The action of government in imposing and collecting a tax under authority of law. *See* assessment. 2. The seizure of property by the sheriff or other officer under a **writ** to ensure payment of a **judgment debt** or to pay it. Such a levy is called a **levy of execution**. *See* writ of attachment; writ of execution. 3. Any imposition of a burden.
v. 1. To **assess**; to impose; to require; to demand. 2. To **attach** property by judicial order.

L

➤ *n.* tax, toll, duty, fine, charge; seizure, attachment, arrogation, appropriation ("a levy of execution").
v. assess, impose, require, demand, exact, inflict ("to levy taxes"); seize, attach, confiscate, declare, instigate, originate ("to levy property").
levy of execution *n. See* levy.

levying war [*lev* · ee · ing] *n.* One of the acts of **treason** against the United States enumerated in the Constitution. *See* insurrection.

lewd *adj.* Lascivious; lustful; wanton; tending to produce carnal emotions. *See* lewdness.
➤ lascivious, lustful, wanton, indecent, obscene, gross, prurient.
lewd and lascivious cohabitation [le · *siv* · ee · ess ko · ha · bi · *tay* · shen] *n.* 1. A man and a woman openly engaging in **adultery** or **fornication**. 2. Under some state statutes, rarely enforced today, a man and woman living together outside of marriage. *See* illicit cohabitation; illicit relations. *See also* open and notorious.

lewdness [*lewd* · nes] *n.* Gross sexual indecency. Lewdness is a crime under some state statutes. Public commission of the indecent act is a necessary element of the crime. *See* indecent exposure.
➤ indecency, obscenity, wantonness, debauchery.
Ant. purity, chastity.

lex [leks] *(Latin) n.* Law; the law; a law.
lex fori [*fore* · eye] *n.* Means "law of the forum," a term relating to a decision by a court that the **substantive law** to be applied in the case is the law of the **jurisdiction** or **forum** where the lawsuit has been brought, as opposed to the law of the jurisdiction or forum in which the events giving rise to the lawsuit occurred. *Compare lex loci.*
lex loci [*loh* · sie] *n.* Means "law of the place," a term relating to a decision by a court that the **substantive law** to be applied in the case is the law of the **jurisdiction** or **forum** where the events giving rise to the lawsuit occurred, as opposed to the law of the jurisdiction or forum in which the lawsuit has been brought. *Compare lex fori.*

LEXIS [*lex* · iss] *n.* A computerized system for legal research. Its database includes almost all reported cases from state and federal courts, all federal statutes, the statutes of many states, federal regulations, and law review articles.

leze majesty [lees *maj* · es · tee] *(French) n.* Same as *lese majesty*.

liability [ly · e · *bil* · i · tee] *n.* 1. Although broadly speaking "liability," as used in the law, means legal responsibility, it is a general term whose precise meaning depends upon the context in which it appears. Among its usages are: a debt one is required to pay; an obligation one must discharge; the circumstance one is in when he has breached a contract; a person's responsibility after she has committed a **tort** that causes **injury**. It is also accurate to speak of the "criminal liability" of a person who has violated a criminal statute. 2. In everyday speech, a burden or an unfavorable situation or circumstance.
See absolute liability; derivative liability; employers' liability acts; fixed liability; joint and several liability; joint liability; legal liability; limitation of liability; limited liability acts; parental liability; personal liability; primary liability; product liability; secondary liability; several liability; strict liability; stockholders' liability; vicarious liability.
➤ responsibility, debt, obligation, indebtedness, encumbrance; handicap, disadvantage, shortcoming.
liability created by statute [*stat* · shoot] *n.* A liability created by statute, as opposed to one created by contract; a liability that would not exist except for the statute creating it.
liability insurance [in · *shoor* · ense] *n.* An insurance policy under which the insurance company agrees to protect the insured against liability arising from an act or omission of the insured that causes **injury** to a third person or to the third person's property. EXAMPLES: **malpractice insurance**; **civil liability insurance**. *Also see* automobile insurance.

liable [*lie* · ebl] *adj.* 1. Having legal responsibility; responsible; accountable; answerable; obligated. USAGE: "The law

L

holds people liable for breach of contract."
See liability. 2. Likely to; subject to;
susceptible to. USAGE: "The hurricane is
liable to hit at any moment." *Note* that
"liable" is not "**libel**."
➤ responsible, accountable, answerable,
obligated ("The law holds people liable
for breach of contract"); likely to happen,
subject, susceptible, prone ("The hurricane
is liable to hit any moment").

libel [*lie* · bul] *n.* A false and **malicious**
publication, expressed either in printing,
writing, or by signs and pictures, tending
to harm a person's reputation and expose
him to public hatred, contempt, or ridicule.
Note that "libel" is not "**liable.**" *Compare*
slander. *See* malice; publication. *Also see*
criminal libel; defamation; group libel;
trade libel.
➤ defamation, slander, malice, denunciation,
accusation, aspersion, calumny, vilification.

libel per quod [kwode] *n. See* libelous
per quod.

libel per se [say] *n. See* libelous per se.

libelant [*lie* · bel · unt] *n.* The plaintiff in
a suit in **admiralty**. *Compare* libelee.
➤ plaintiff, complainant.

libelee [*lie* · bel · ee] *n.* The defendant in
a suit in **admiralty**. *Compare* libelant.
➤ defendant, answerable party.

libelous [*lie* · bel · ess] *adj.* Containing or
constituting **libel; defamatory**.
➤ defamatory, damaging, maligning,
injurious, slanderous, vilifying, scandalous,
disparaging ("libelous remark").

libelous per quod [kwode] *n.* A term
referring to written or printed words that are
not **defamatory** in and of themselves and
with respect to which, therefore, **injury**
and **damages** must be proven. *See per quod.*
See also actionable per quod; slanderous
per quod. *Compare* libelous per se.

libelous per se [say] *n.* A term referring
to written or printed words that are presumed
to be **defamatory** because they necessarily
cause **injury** to the reputation of the person
about whom they are spoken. (EXAMPLES:
words that imply criminal conduct; words
that could subject a person to professional
disgrace; words implying infection with
a loathsome and communicable disease.)

When words are libelous per se, **actual
damages** need not be proven. *See per se.*
See also actionable per se; slanderous per
se. *Compare* libelous per quod.

liberal [*lib* · e · rul] *adj.* 1. Giving;
generous; expansive. 2. Great; abundant;
profuse. 3. Open-minded; progressive.
➤ broad, generous, flexible, extended,
loose, casual ("liberal interpretation");
generous, bountiful, unsparing, magnanimous, lavish; tolerant, unbiased, neutral,
impartial, flexible, enlightened, receptive,
progressive ("liberal in his thinking").

liberty [*lib* · er · tee] *n.* A basic right granted
by the Constitution of the United States,
which contemplates not only an absence
of physical restraint but personal freedom
encompassing every form of individual
prerogative that is not taken away by a
valid law enacted for the common good.
See civil liberties; personal liberty.
➤ freedom, independence, privilege, right,
emancipation, choice, autonomy.

liberty of contract [*kon* · trakt] *n. See*
freedom of contract.

liberty of port *n.* A phrase in a **marine
insurance** policy that permits the insured
ship to call at and use only the ports specified in the policy other than the port of
destination. *Compare* liberty of the globe.

liberty of the globe *n.* A phrase in a
marine insurance policy that permits
the insured ship to go to any part of the
world. *Compare* liberty of port.

license [*ly* · sense] *n.* 1. A special privilege,
not a right common to everyone. *See*
privilege. 2. Permission (EXAMPLES: a
marriage license; a fishing license) to do
something that, if it were not regulated
would be a right. 3. A privilege conferred
on a person by the government to do
something she otherwise would not have
the right to do. EXAMPLES: the privilege of
incorporation; the privilege of operating
as a **public utility** or a **common carrier**.
See corporate franchise; franchise. 4. A
requirement imposed as a means of regulating a business. EXAMPLE: a liquor license.
5. Permission to practice a profession,
engage in an occupation, or conduct a
business. EXAMPLES: a license to practice
law; a business license; a real estate license.

L

6. The privilege of entering upon real property for a specific or limited purpose. *See* licensee. *Compare* trespasser. *Also compare* adverse user; easement.
7. Authorization by the owner of a **patent** to make, use, or sell the patented article; permission by the owner of a **trademark** or **copyright** to use the trademark or to make use of the copyrighted material. *See* exclusive license. 8. An **affirmative defense** to an **action** in **trespass**. *See* leave and license. 9. A certificate evidencing an official grant of permission or authorization. EXAMPLES: a driver's license; a hunting license. 10. Permission to do or not to do something. 11. Unrestrained freedom.
v. To authorize to do something. EXAMPLES: to license attorneys; to license gun owners.
➤ *n.* privilege, authorization, sanction, permission, entitlement.
v. authorize, legitimize, sanction, approve, validate, regulate.

license fee *n.* A charge made by a governmental body for the issuance of a license. It may be imposed for the purpose of raising revenue, for the privilege of engaging in the activity authorized by the license, or to defray the expense of issuing the license.

license tax *n.* Same as **license fee**.

licensee [ly · sen · *see*] *n.* 1. A person who enters upon the property of another for his own convenience, pleasure, or benefit, uninvited but tolerated by the owner. EXAMPLE: a pupil visiting a factory as part of a school group (but not at the suggestion of the company). *Compare* invitee, but *note* that the distinction between a licensee and an invitee has been abandoned in some jurisdictions. *Also compare* trespasser. *See* bare licensee; mere licensee. 2. A person possessing a license as, for EXAMPLE, a licensed driver, plumber, or physician. 3. A person to whom the owner of a **patent**, **copyright**, or **trademark** grants a right of use. *Compare* licensor. *Also see* franchisee.

licensing [*ly* · sen · sing] *n.* The act or process of granting or issuing a license.

licensor [ly · sen · *sore*] *n.* The grantor of a license. EXAMPLES: a state; a city; the owner of a **patent**. *Compare* licensee. *Also see* franchisor.

licentiousness [ly · *sen* · shes · ness] *n.* 1. Lack of moral restraint. 2. Ruthless disregard of the rights of others.
➤ obscenity, immorality, lasciviousness; lawlessness, recklessness, wantonness.

licit [*liss* · it] *adj.* Legal; lawful; permitted by law; allowed. *Compare* illicit.
➤ legal, lawful, legitimate, admissible, allowed.
Ant. unlawful, illegitimate.

lie *n.* An untruth told intentionally.
v. 1. To be appropriate or available as a **remedy**. USAGE: "An **action** for **damages** will not lie unless there has been **injury**."
2. To tell a falsehood intentionally. *See* perjury. 3. To be positioned or located.
➤ *n.* perjury, deception, deceit, forgery, slander, tale, fraud.
v. be maintainable, subsist, be available, be warranted, stand ("An action for damages will not lie unless there has been injury"); beguile, con, deceive, falsify, pervert, fabricate ("The suspect lied"); be, sit, exist, occupy, reach, remain ("to lie in bed").

lie detector *n.* *See* polygraph.

lie in wait *v.* *See* lying in wait.

lien [*leen*] *n.* A **claim** or **charge** on, or **right** against, personal property, or an **encumbrance** on real property, for the payment of a debt. A lien may be created by statute (EXAMPLES: a **tax lien**; an **attachment lien**) or by agreement between the parties (EXAMPLES: a **mortgage** on **real estate**; a **security agreement** covering **personal property**). In some instances, a lien permits the creditor to retain the debtor's property in his possession until the debt is satisfied. Such a lien is called a **possessory lien**. (EXAMPLES: a **landlord's lien**; an **attorney's lien**.) There is a great variety of liens. Among others, *see* banker's lien; charging lien; equitable lien; execution lien; factor's lien; first lien; floating lien; general lien; inchoate lien; judicial lien; laborer's lien; maritime lien; materialman's lien; mechanic's lien; retaining lien; secret lien; special lien; statutory lien; vendor's lien; warehouseman's lien.
➤ debt, obligation, mortgage, interest ("The mortgage is a lien on the house").

lien creditor [*kred* · i · tor] *n.* A **creditor** whose debt is secured by a **lien**. EXAMPLES: an **execution creditor**; a **judgment creditor**.

L

lien of attachment [a · *tach* · ment] *n.* *See* attachment lien.

lien of judgment [*juj* · ment] *n.* *See* judgment lien.

lien state *n.* *See* mortgage.

lien theory state [*theer* · ee] *n.* *See* mortgage.

lienee [lee · *nee*] *n.* The owner of property subject to a **lien**.

lienholder [*leen* · hole · der] *n.* Same as **lienor**.

lienor [lee · *nor*] *n.* The owner or holder of a lien.

life *n.* The state of being alive or existing as a person. The law does not prescribe a single point in time when human life begins. What legal exactness there is changes with the matter in question and ranges from the point of conception, through the end of the first trimester of pregnancy or the point at which the fetus becomes **viable**, to the moment of birth and, in certain instances, beyond birth. Matters which may, in law, yield different points of commencement for human life include inheritance rights, the right of government to regulate abortions, claims for **damages** arising from negligent injury to the fetus, maternal fetal neglect resulting from alcoholism or drug addiction, and the treatment of **anencephalic** newborns. *See* person; personhood; unborn child; viability; viable child; wrongful birth; wrongful pregnancy.

Similar legal issues are associated with the question of when life ends. *See* death; right to die.

➤ endurance, survival, subsistence, animation, cycle, span, duration, course, endurance, period ("for the life of the car"); vitality, animation, vivacity, esprit, soul, vigor ("the life of the party").

life annuity [a · *new* · i · tee] *n.* 1. A contract to pay to a person a specific sum of money each year for the remainder of her life. 2. The annual sum paid. *See* annuity.

life care contract [*kon* · trakt] *n.* An agreement commonly entered into between nursing homes for the elderly and their clients, under which the facility promises to provide care for the remainder of the client's life in exchange for the client's property or financial resources.

life estate [es · *tate*] *n.* An **estate** that exists as long as the person who owns or holds it is alive. Its duration may also be for the lifetime of another person (EXAMPLE: "to Sarah so long as Sam shall live").

life expectancy [eks · *pek* · ten · see] *n.* From a statistical point of view, how long a person of a particular age and sex may be expected to live. *See* mortality tables.

life imprisonment [im · *priz* · en · ment] *n.* *See* imprisonment.

life in being [*bee* · ing] *n.* In the law of **future interest**, the balance of the lifetime of a person who is alive at the time the will takes effect.

life insurance [in · *shoor* · ense] *n.* A contract (the policy) in which the insurer, in exchange for the payment of a premium, agrees to pay a specified sum to a named beneficiary upon the death of the insured. *See* decreasing term insurance; ordinary life insurance; straight life insurance; term life insurance; whole life insurance.

life insurance trust [in · *shoor* · ense] *n.* A **trust** in which the **trust estate** consists of life insurance policies payable to the trust upon the death of the insured.

life interest [*in* · trest] *n.* An **interest** in real property or personal property that is to terminate upon the death of the owner or holder of the interest, or upon the death of some other designated person. EXAMPLES: a **life estate**; a **personal right** to use or profit from another's land (*see* easement in gross; *profit à prendre*).

life policy [*pol* · i · see] *n.* A life insurance policy. *See* policy.

life sentence [*sen* · tense] *n.* *See* sentence.

life tables [*tay* · blz] *n.* *See* mortality tables.

life tenancy [*ten* · en · see] *n.* A **life estate**.

life tenant [*ten* · ent] *n.* A person who holds a **life estate**.

LIFO [*lie* · foe] *adj.* The acronym for **last in, first out**, an accounting method for establishing the value of business inventory when goods are so intermingled

L

they cannot be identified without specific invoices. The LIFO method hypothesizes that inventory consists of those goods that have been on hand the greatest length of time, that is, the goods that were purchased first. *Compare* FIFO.

light *n.* 1. Illumination. 2. Context; point of view.
adj. 1. Illuminated. 2. Cheery; being in high spirits. 3. Not heavy.
v. To brighten or ignite. *See* easement of light and air.
➤ *n.* illumination, shining, glow, aurora, beacon, lamp ("light up ahead"); angle, approach, insight, slant, view, interpretation ("to see in a new light").
adj. radiant, lucent, clear, bright, well-lit; carefree, chipper, merry, perky, sunny, up, weightless ("She was in a light mood"); easy, casual, flimsy ("light work").
v. animate, brighten, illuminate, ignite, shine, highlight, turn on ("to light the lamp").
light and air *n.* *See* easement of light and air.

lighterage [*lite* · e · rej] *n.* 1. The transportation of goods by barge; the loading of a ship from a barge; the unloading of a ship onto a barge. 2. The charges for such services.

lights *n.* *See* ancient lights.

limine [*lim* · e · nee] (*Latin*) *n.* Beginning; outset; threshold. *See* in limine.

limit [*lim* · it] *n.* 1. A boundary; a border; the outer line of a thing. 2. A restriction; a restraint.
v. To restrain; to restrict; to impose a limitation.
➤ *n.* extreme, edge, border, perimeter, bounds, compass, confines, edge, end ("the city limits"); bar, cap, check, obstacle, limitation, blockade ("the limit of our involvement").
v. restrict, suppress, hinder, bar, block, obstruct, control ("to limit access").
Ant. facilitate, expand.

limitation [*lim* · i · *tay* · shen] *n.* That which limits; a restriction. EXAMPLES of various kinds of limitations that the law imposes include: the period of time during which a lawsuit may be initiated (**limitation of action**); the duration of an **estate in land** (**limitation of estate**); the amount of **damages** for which a person will be held responsible (**limitation of liability**). These and other limitations are listed and defined *below*.
➤ impediment, drawback, constraint, hindrance, cramp, condition, restraint, qualification, reservation, disadvantage ("The system has limitations").
Ant. expansion, benefit.

limitation of action [*ak* · shen] *n.* The period of time during which a civil action may be brought after the **injury** occurs or becomes known; the period of time during which a criminal prosecution may be initiated after the crime is committed. **Limitation periods** (also referred to as **statutory periods**) vary in length from jurisdiction to jurisdiction with the type of action being litigated or crime being prosecuted. *See* statutes of limitations. *Also see* tolling the statute.

limitation of estate [*es* · *tate*] *n.* A provision in a deed, will, or other grant stating a point in time at which, or an event upon the occurrence of which, the **estate** will terminate and pass to the next taker; words that determine the nature or duration of an estate. *See* limitation over. *See also* estate upon condition; words of limitation.

limitation of indebtedness [*in* · *det* · ed · ness] *n.* *See* debt limitation.

limitation of liability [*ly* · e · *bil* · i · tee] *n.* 1. A provision in a contract that places a ceiling on liability for **loss** or **injury**. Such provisions are most commonly found in certain kinds of **bailments** (EXAMPLES: damage to personal property left with a storage company; the loss of baggage by an airline) and in insurance policies. 2. A statute that puts a cap on liability with respect to certain types of **damages** or that otherwise restricts liability. *See* limited liability acts.

limitation over [*oh* · ver] *n.* The **estate** that becomes available by the terms of a deed, will, or other grant, following the termination of a prior estate. EXAMPLE: a **remainder** after a **life estate**. *See* limitation of estate.

limitation period [*peer* · ee · ed] *n.* *See* statutes of limitations.

limitations, statute of [*stat* · shoot] *n.* *See* statute of limitations.

L

limited [*lim · i · ted*] *adj.* 1. A word that follows a company's name and indicates that the business is a corporation, especially in England and Canada, although some American corporations also use the term (or its abbreviation, **Ltd.**) in place of "Inc." EXAMPLE: "Jack & Jill Limited." *See* limited company. 2. A word used to signify a partnership other than a **general partnership**. *See* limited partnership. 3. In the law of property, restricted by a **limitation**. 4. Narrow; restricted; enclosed within a certain limit.
➤ confined, bounded, prescribed, checked, curbed, fixed ("Our options are limited"); dull, narrow, simple, slow, unimaginative ("He is of limited mind").

limited admissibility
[ad · miss · i · *bil* · i · tee] *n.* A term referring to evidence that is admissible for one purpose but not for other purposes. EXAMPLE: **hearsay evidence** may be admitted for the purpose of proving what A said to B, but not to prove the truth of what A said to B. *See* admissibility.

limited company [*kum* · pe · nee] *n.* A company in that the liability of a shareholder is limited to the amount he has invested in shares, i.e., a corporation. *See* limited liability acts. *See also* limited partnership.

limited divorce [di · *vorss*] *n.* 1. A **divorce a mensa et thoro**. 2. A decree of divorce that dissolves the marriage but does not provide for custody or support.

limited fee *n.* A **conditional fee**, **determinable fee**, or **qualified fee**. EXAMPLE: a **fee tail**. *See also* base fee.

limited guaranty [gehr · en · *tee*] *n.* A contract of **guaranty** that applies to only one transaction.

limited jurisdiction [joo · ris · *dik* · shen] *n. See* court of limited jurisdiction.

limited liability [ly · e · *bil* · i · tee] *n. See* limited liability acts; limitation of liability.

limited liability acts [ly · e · *bil* · i · tee] *n.* 1. Statutes that restrict **liability** to an amount less than the law would otherwise allow or that confine liability to **damages** for certain types of wrongs. EXAMPLE: the **Federal Tort Claims Act**. 2. Statutes that restrict the liability of corporate shareholders to the amount they have invested in or preclude the **personal liability** of corporate

directors unless they have acted beyond their legal authority. *See* limitation of liability; limited company.

limited owner [*oh* · ner] *n.* The owner of an **interest** in property which is not an **absolute interest**. EXAMPLE: the owner of a **life estate**, as opposed to the owner of a **fee simple**.

limited partner [*part* · ner] *n.* A partner in a **limited partnership** whose liability is limited to the sum she contributed to the partnership as **capital**; a **special partner**. *See* partner. A limited partner is not involved in managing or carrying out the business of the partnership. *Compare* general partner.

limited partnership [*part* · ner · ship] *n.* A **partnership** in which the liability of one or more of the partners is limited to the amount of money they have invested in the partnership. *Compare* general partnership.

limited power of appointment [*pow* · er of a · *point* · ment] *n.* A **power of appointment** exercisable only in favor of those persons, or that class of persons, designated in the instrument creating the power. (EXAMPLE: the power granted the **executor**, in the will, to divide the **estate** among the **testator's** grandchildren as the executor believes appropriate.) A limited power of appointment is also referred to as a **special power of appointment**. *Compare* general power of appointment.

limited publication [pub · li · *kay* · shen] *n.* Prior to securing a **copyright**, an author, composer, or artist may publish his work on a restricted basis ("limited publication") without forfeiting his right to have the material copyrighted. EXAMPLE: the private circulation of a manuscript.

limited warranty [*war* · en · tee] *n.* 1. A **warranty** that is limited in duration or confined to specified **defects**. 2. A warranty providing less than a **full warranty** provides.

Lindbergh Law [*lind* · berg] *n.* A federal statute that makes **kidnapping** a federal crime if the victim is transported from one state to another or to a foreign country. This statute was a reaction to the 1932 kidnapping of the infant son of aviator Charles A. Lindbergh.

L

line *n.* 1. A course of **descent** or **succession**. USAGE: "**maternal line**"; "**paternal line**"; "**direct line**." 2. A boundary; a demarcation; a limit. 3. A **carrier's** route. *See also* building lines; high water line.
➤ rim, edge, border, perimeter, limit, boundary, cutoff ("property line").

line item veto [*eye* · tem *vee* · toh] *n.* The right of a governor under most state constitutions to veto individual appropriations in an **appropriation act** rather than being compelled either to veto the act as a whole or to sign it into law. The president of the United States does not have a line item veto.

line of credit [*kred* · it] *n.* The maximum amount of credit a credit card holder, bank customer, or store patron is authorized to use. *See* credit.

line of descent [de · *sent*] *n.* *See* descent. *See also* collateral descent; lineal descent.

line of duty [*dew* · tee] *n.* A term relating to those acts performed by military personnel or law enforcement officers in fulfilling their duty. The equivalent term in civilian employment is **scope of employment**.

line of high water [*waw* · ter] *n.* *See* ordinary high tide.

lineage [*lin* · ee · ej] *n.* Race; family, **descendants** from or **ascendants** to a **common ancestor**.
➤ race, family, descendants, ancestry, heritage, kin, progeny, girth, blood, stirpes, stock, succession.

lineal [*lin* · ee · el] *adj.* In a direct line. *Compare* collateral. *Also see* lineals.
➤ hereditary, ancestral, uninterrupted, continuous, undeviating ("lineal progression").

lineal ascendants [a · *sen* · dents] *n.* A person's grandparents, great-grandparents, etc. *See* ascendant.

lineal consanguinity [kon · sang · *gwin* · i · tee] *n.* The blood relationship between individuals from whom a person is descended in a direct line of **ascent** (EXAMPLE: father; grandfather; great-grandfather) or between individuals descended from a person in a direct line of **descent** (EXAMPLE: daughter; granddaughter; great-granddaughter). *See and compare* ascendant; descendant. *See* consanguinity.

lineal descendant [de · *sen* · dent] *n.* A person in the direct line of **descent**. EXAMPLES: one's child, grandchild, or great-grandchild. *Compare* collateral descendant. *See* descendant.

lineal descent [de · *sent*] *n.* Inheritance in the direct line of the **intestate**; that is, from a parent or grandparent to a child or grandchild (or from a child or grandchild to a parent or grandparent). *See* descent. *Compare* collateral descent.

lineal heir [air] *n.* A person entitled to inherit by lineal ascent or lineal descent. *See* lineal descent. *Also see* lineal ascendant; lineal descendant; lineals.

lineals [*lin* · ee · elz] *n.* Persons who share a **common ancestor** with the **decedent**. *See* lineal heir.

lineup [*line* · up] *n.* A police practice in which a number of individuals, including the criminal suspect, are displayed to the victim of the crime or other witnesses to determine if one of the individuals can be identified as the perpetrator of the offense. *Compare* show-up.
➤ group, array, arrangement, formation, showing, inspection, row ("the police lineup").

link-in-chain *adj.* The **privilege against self-incrimination** protects an individual not only against having to answer questions that are directly incriminating, but also against having to answer questions that may link him to criminal conduct in the chain of evidence.

liquid [*lik* · wid] *adj.* As used in the law and in commerce, easily convertible into cash.
➤ convertible, interchangeable, fluid, free, negotiable, quick ("The bonds are very liquid and may be cashed in at any time"). *Ant.* frozen, nontransferable.

liquid assets [*ass* · ets] *n.* **Assets** that are easily convertible into cash. *See* asset.

liquidate [*lik* · wi · date] *v.* 1. To pay, discharge, or satisfy a debt. 2. To determine or make certain the amount of a debt either by agreement or by legal action. 3. To cash; to convert **assets** to cash. 4. To break up, do away with, wind up, or dissolve. USAGE: "After Jim died his partner liquidated the business." 5. To kill; to murder.

L

See liquidated; liquidating; liquidation. *See also* dissolution; winding up.

➤ discharge, clear, cancel, honor, pay off, quit ("liquidate my debts"); cash, convert, exchange, realize ("liquidate the bonds"); abolish, annihilate, eliminate, kill, remove, wipe out ("liquidate the company"). *Ant.* incur; create.

liquidated [*lik* · wi · day · ted] *adj.* 1. In reference to a debt, paid, discharged, or satisfied. 2. In reference to a debt, determined or made certain as to amount, matured, settled, or agreed upon. 3. Cashed; converted into cash. 4. In reference to the affairs of a business, dissolved or wound up. 5. Killed; murdered. See liquidate; liquidating; liquidation. *See also* dissolution; winding up.

➤ ascertained, determined, declared ("liquidated damages").

liquidated account [a · *kount*] *n.* An **account** the amount of which is agreed upon by the parties or fixed by **operation of law**.

liquidated claim *n.* A **claim** the amount of which is agreed upon by the parties or which can be determined by applying rules of law or by mathematical calculation. *Compare* unliquidated claim.

liquidated damages [*dam* · e · jez] *n.* A sum agreed upon by the parties at the time of entering into a contract as being payable by way of compensation for **loss** suffered in the event of a **breach of contract**; a sum similarly determined by a court in a lawsuit resulting from breach of contract. *Compare* unliquidated damages. For the distinction between a penalty and liquidated damages, *see* penal bond; penalty.

liquidated debt *n.* A debt that has been paid or for which it is certain as to how much is due. *Compare* unliquidated debt. *See* debt.

liquidated demand [de · *mand*] *n.* A **demand** that is undisputed as to amount. *Compare* unliquidated claim.

liquidating [*lik* · wi · day · ting] *adj.* The act of paying, cashing, making certain, settling, winding up, or dissolving. *See* liquidate; liquidated; liquidation. *See also* dissolution.

liquidating partner [*part* · ner] *n.* A **partner** who, upon dissolution of the partnership, is responsible for its **liquidation**. *See* dissolution of partnership.

liquidating trust *n.* A **trust** whose purpose is its own **liquidation** as soon as circumstances permit.

liquidation [lik · wi · *day* · shen] *n.* 1. The extinguishment of a debt by payment. 2. The ascertainment of the amount of a debt or **demand** by agreement or by legal proceedings. 3. The winding up of a corporation, partnership, or other business enterprise upon dissolution by converting the **assets** to money, collecting the **accounts receivable**, paying the debts, and distributing the surplus if any exists. *See* liquidate; liquidated. *See also* bankruptcy; corporate distribution; dissolution; receivership.

➤ elimination, abolition, rescission.

liquidation dividend [*div* · i · dend] *n.* A distribution to shareholders of a corporation, or members of any firm or business enterprise, of the surplus remaining after liquidation of the business and payment of creditors. *See* dividend.

liquidation of corporation [kore · per · *ay* · shen] *n. See* liquidation.

liquidation of partnership [*part* · ner · ship] *n. See* liquidation.

liquidator [*lik* · wi · day · ter] *n.* A person who is appointed to **liquidate** a business; a **receiver**.

liquidity [li · *kwid* · i · tee] *n.* A word referring to the degree of ease with which one's **assets** can be converted to cash. *See* liquid.

liquor [*lik* · er] *n.* Same as alcoholic beverage. *See also* intoxicating liquor.

➤ spirits, inebriant, drink, alcohol, intoxicant, extract, elixir ("They drank liquor on New Year's Eve").

liquor laws *n.* State and federal statutes, both civil and criminal, regulating the production, sale, and use of alcoholic beverages. *See* dram shop acts.

lis [liss] *(Latin) n.* A suit, **action**, controversy, or dispute.

lis pendens [*pen* · denz] *(Latin) n.* A pending suit or pending **action**. Refers to the **jurisdiction**, power, or control a court has over the property involved in a suit during litigation. The *doctrine of lis pendens* states that a pending suit is notice to **all the world**, and therefore a person who purchases

L

real property involved in the pending litigation will be bound by the **judgment** in the case. *See* notice of lis pendens.

list *n.* 1. A **docket**; a **court calendar**. 2. A written series of items or persons' names. EXAMPLES: an inventory; a **jury list**. *See also* blacklist.
v. 1. To register or enroll something. EXAMPLES: to list property for sale with a real estate agent (*see* listing agrement); to register a **security** with a stock exchange (*see* listed security). 2. To offer for sale. *See* list price. 3. To write down a series of items, persons, or the like, in some order and for some purpose. *See* listing.
➤ *n.* account, agenda, inventory, manifest, poll, record, contents, schedule, roster, outline ("the jury list").
v. itemize, docket, enroll, calendar, log, chart ("list the home for sale").

list of creditors [*kred* · i · terz] *n.* A list of the people to whom a **bankrupt** owes money, with the amounts owed, which he must furnish to the **Bankruptcy Court**.

list price *n.* The publicized price of goods, from which a discount may be given. *Compare* wholesale price.

listed [*list* · ed] *adj.* Contained on a list. *See* list; listing.

listed security [se · *kyoo* · ri · tee] *n.* Stock or other securities traded on a stock exchange. *Compare* unlisted security.

lister [*list* · er] *n.* A public employee who lists property for purposes of taxation; a **tax assessor**. *See* tax rolls.

listing [*list* · ing] *n.* The act of putting a thing on a list, registering it, or offering it for sale. *See* list; listed.

listing agreement [a · *gree* · ment] *n.* A contract between an owner of real property and a real estate agent under which the agent is retained to secure a purchaser for the property at a specified price, for a commission. For various types of real estate listing contracts, *see and compare* exclusive right to sell; multiple listing; nonexclusive listing; open listing.

listing of taxable property [*taks* · ebl *prop* · er · tee] *n.* *See* tax rolls.

litem [*ly* · tem] *(Latin) adj.* Means "of litigation"; pertaining to litigation. *See ad litem;* guardian ad litem.

literacy [*lit* · e · re · see] *n.* The ability to read and write.
➤ ability to read, intelligence, learning, education, background, cultivation ("The state has a low literacy rate").

literacy test *n.* A test formerly administered by election authorities in some states as a device for disenfranchising African-American voters. Such tests are now rarely given because their earlier discriminatory application has been prohibited by the **Voting Rights Act** of 1965. *See* Civil Rights Acts.

literal [*lit* · e · rel] *adj.* Word-for-word; strict.
➤ strict, verbatim, correct, actual, true, plain ("a literal interpretation of the Constitution").
Ant. loose, creative, virtual.

literal construction [ken · *struk* · shen] *n.* *See* strict construction.

literary [*lit* · e · re · ree] *adj.* Pertaining to or knowledgeable about literature, books, or authors.
➤ published, poetic, artistic, educated, bookish, classical, formal, well-spoken ("The professor seemed very literary").

literary profits laws [*prof* · its] *n.* *See* Son of Sam laws.

literary property [*prop* · er · tee] *n.* The **interest** of an author, or anyone to whom she has transferred her interest, in her own work; the exclusive right of an author to use and profit from her own written or printed intellectual production. *See* intellectual property; literary work. *Also see* infringement of copyright.

literary work *n.* In **copyright** law, "works, other than audiovisual works, expressed in words, numbers, or other verbal or numerical symbols or indicia, regardless of the nature of the material objects, such as books, periodicals, manuscripts, phonorecords, film, tapes, disks, or cards, in which they are embodied."

litigant [*lit* · i · gant] *n.* A **party** to a lawsuit; a person engaged in litigation.
➤ litigator, disputant, contender, challenger, adversary, opponent, party ("The litigants

L

in the case were both injured in the accident").

litigate [*lit* · i · gate] *v.* To maintain or defend a **legal action**; to be a **party** to a lawsuit. *See* litigation.

➤ dispute, contest at law, file, sue, prosecute, appeal ("She will not litigate that cause of action").

litigated [*lit* · i · gay · ted] *adj.* Subjected to litigation; having been the subject matter of litigation. USAGE: "That matter (or issue, or fact) has been fully litigated; the judge has admitted a considerable amount of evidence on the point."

litigation [lit · i · *gay* · shen] *n.* 1. A **legal action**; a lawsuit. 2. The area of the law concerning trial work.

➤ judicial contest, prosecution, action, lawsuit, case, cause ("Massive amounts of litigation have backlogged the courts").

litigious [li · *tij* · ess] *adj.* 1. Pertaining to litigation. 2. Eager or excessively willing to litigate.

➤ argumentative, combative, pugnacious, militant, belligerent, bellicose.

littering [*lit* · er · ing] *n.* The offense of throwing or depositing trash, garbage, waste, or other material on or near a public highway or public land, on or near coastal waters or inland waters, or on the property of another person.

littoral [*lit* · e · rel] *adj.* Pertaining to the shore of a lake or ocean, as opposed to the shore or bank of a stream or river. *Compare* riparian.
n. Sometimes referred to as "littoral land"; the shore of a lake or ocean.

➤ *adj.* coastal, waterfront, beach.

littoral owner [*own* · er] *n.* The owner of land on the shore of a lake or ocean. *Compare* riparian owner.

littoral rights *n.* The rights of a **littoral owner**. *Compare* riparian rights.

live [lyve] *adj.* 1. Having life; the state of being alive. *See* viable. 2. Active.
v. [liv] 1. To reside or dwell in a place. *See* living. 2. To exist; to be; to have life. *See* viable.

➤ *adj.* living, breathing, animate, aware, conscious ("a live cat"); active, alert, brisk, current, dynamic, hot, vital ("The crowd is live tonight").

v. dwell, room, being, abide, bide, bunk, nest ("I live upstairs"); breathe, persist, prevail, persevere, continue ("He will live only for a few more days").

live storage [*store* · ej] *n.* The safekeeping of something for a relatively brief period of time. EXAMPLE: the overnight garaging of an automobile. *Compare* dead storage. *See* bailment.

livery [*liv* · e · ree] *n.* 1. The keeping of horses and vehicles for hire. 2. The stabling of horses. USAGE: "livery stable." 3. The leasing of vehicles, with or without a driver. *See* hire; lease. 4. Under old English law, a ceremonial transfer of title to land (*livery of seisin*).

livery conveyance [ken · *vay* · ense] *n.* A vehicle used to transport passengers for hire as a **private carrier**, but not as a **common carrier**.

livery of seisin [*see* · zin] *n. See* livery.

lives in being [lyves in *bee* · ing] *n. See* life in being.

living [*liv* · ing] *adj./adv.* 1. Residing or dwelling in a place. *See* reside. 2. Existing; being. *See* life; viable.

➤ surviving, being, existing, ongoing, continuing ("The tree is still living").

living apart [a · *part*] *n.* A term referring to a separation of husband and wife, with no intention of resuming the marital relationship; permanent separation.

living in adultery [a · *dull* · te · ree] *n.* The act of a man and woman who are known to be unmarried living together openly as if they were married. *Compare* adultery. *See* cohabitation; illicit cohabitation. *Also see* illicit relations; lewd and lascivious cohabitation.

living issue [*ish* · ew] *n.* One's living descendants. *See* issue.

living together [to · *geh* · ther] *n. See* cohabitation.

living trust *n.* 1. An **inter vivos trust**. 2. An **active trust**.

living will *n.* A document in which a person sets forth directions regarding medical treatment to be given if she becomes unable to participate in decisions regarding her medical care. *Compare* advance directive; durable power of attorney; healthcare proxy. *See* right to die.

L

LJ Abbreviation of **law journal**; abbreviation of **law judge**.

LLB Short for **Bachelor of Laws**, formerly the primary degree awarded by most law schools, now replaced by the **JD**.

LLD Short for Doctor of Laws, an advanced law degree.

LLM Short for Master of Laws, an advanced law degree.

loading [*loh* · ding] *v.* 1. In calculating a charge for any service, the inclusion of items that have no real bearing upon what is a reasonable charge. 2. In calculating a premium, the addition by an insurance company of administrative or operating expenses. 3. The placing of goods on a plane, ship, railroad car, or truck.
➤ stacking, putting, inserting, packing, heaping, burdening, lading.

loan *n.* The act of lending; the act of loaning. *See* loan Also see commercial loan; consolidation loan; consumer loan; demand loan; equity loan; installment loan; personal loan; short-term loan; small loan acts; term loan.
   v. To deliver or transfer money or other personal property to a borrower who promises to return it or its equivalent, often, particularly in the case of money, with interest.
➤ *n.* financing, advance, credit, allowance, mortgage, floater ("a loan on the house").
   v. allow, credit, lend, provide, stake, touch.

loan association [a · so · see · *ay* · shen] *n.* *See* building and loan association; savings and loan association.

loan commitment [ke · *mit* · ment] *n.* *See* mortgage commitment.

loan company [*kum* · pe · nee] *n.* Same as **finance company**.

loan for consumption [ken · *sump* · shen] *n.* A lending of personal property that is to be consumed and returned **in kind**. EXAMPLE: the loan of a cup of salt. *Compare* loan for use.

loan for use *n.* A lending of personal property which is to be used and returned. EXAMPLE: the loan of a salt shaker. *Compare* loan for consumption.

loan participation [par · tiss · i · *pay* · shen] *n.* A term describing the involvement of a number of lenders in a single loan, sharing both the risk and the potential profit. *See* participation.

loan ratio [*ray* · shee · oh] *n.* Percentage of a property's value that a **secured loan** represents relative to the value of the property that secures it. EXAMPLE: the loan ratio of a $160,000 mortgage on real estate with a market value of $200,000 is 80 percent. *Compare* loan-to-value ratio.

loan value [*val* · yoo] *n.* The maximum amount of money that can be borrowed on a life insurance policy. The loan value of life insurance depends upon the policy's **cash surrender value**.

loan-to-value ratio [-val · yoo *ray* · shee · oh] *n.* Percentage of a property's purchase price that a loan secured by the property represents. *Compare* loan ratio.

loaned employee rule [loned em · *ploy* · ee] *n.* *See* borrowed servant rule.

loaned servant rule [loned *ser* · vent] *n.* *See* borrowed servant rule.

loanshark [*lone* · shark] *n.* A person who lends money at excessive or illegal interest rates and engages in **extortion** to motivate repayment. *See* usury.
➤ usurer, extortionist.

lobbying [*lob* · ee · ing] *n.* Attempting to persuade legislators to vote for or against a bill pending in a state legislature or in Congress.

lobbying acts *n.* Federal and state statutes requiring the registration of lobbyists and otherwise regulating their activities.

lobbyist [*lob* · ee · ist] *n.* A person who engages in lobbying, whether for a fee or as a concerned citizen.
➤ advocate, espouser, representative, ally, supporter.

local [*loh* · kel] *adj.* Pertaining to a particular, confined, or limited place. EXAMPLE: "**local government**" means county, city, or town government, as distinguished from national or state government.
➤ localized, native, home, regional, narrow, restricted ("local government").
   Ant. national, general.

L

local action [*ak* · shen] *n.* An **action** that can be brought only where the **cause of action** arose, because that is the only place it could arise. EXAMPLE: an **action to quiet title** to real estate. *Compare* transitory action. *See and compare* in personam action; in rem action.

local agent [*ay* · jent] *n.* An **agent** who represents her principal in a particular place such as a county, town, or city. Her geographical limitations do not necessarily limit her authority, and she may, indeed, be a **general agent**. Generally, **service of process** may be made on a **foreign corporation** by serving its local agent.

local assessment [a · *sess* · ment] *n.* *See* special assessment.

local chattel [*chat* · el] *n.* A thing attached to realty; a **fixture**. *See* chattel.

local court *n.* A court whose **jurisdiction** is confined to a specific locality. EXAMPLES: a **county court**; a **municipal court**.

local custom [*kus* · tem] *n.* A custom that exists in a particular county, city, or town. It may have the force of law locally. *See* custom; custom and usage.

local government [*guv* · ern · ment] *n.* *See* local.

local improvement [im · *proov* · ment] *n.* A **public improvement** that confers a special benefit on the property in a particular locality.

local improvement assessment [im · *proov* · ment a · *sess* · ment] *n.* *See* special assessment.

local law *n.* 1. The law of the jurisdiction in which the **action** is pending. 2. State, as distinguished from federal, law. 3. The law of one state, as distinguished from the law of another state. 4. A law enacted by a municipality or other **political subdivision**; an ordinance. 5. A statute directed only to a specific part of a state, or that applies only within a single city, county, or town. *Compare* general law.

local legislation [lej · is · *lay* · shen] *n.* *See* local law.

local option [*op* · shen] *n.* The right given by a state's constitution or statutes to a town, city, or county to decide for itself whether a certain state law shall take effect within its area. EXAMPLE: whether to permit or prohibit the sale of alcoholic beverages is often left to local option. *See also* home rule.

local ordinance [*or* · di · nense] *n.* *See* local law; ordinance.

local rules *n.* **Rules of court** that are applicable in a single **judicial district**.

local statute [*stat* · shoot] *n.* *See* local law.

local tax *n.* A tax imposed by and for the benefit of a municipality, county, town, or other **political subdivision**, as distinguished from a state tax or federal tax of general application.

local union [*yoon* · yen] *n.* A union of employees employed at plants in a specific geographical area, or at one plant, but chartered by a national union or international union. *See* labor union.

local usage [*yoo* · sej] *n.* *See* local custom.

localization doctrine [lo · ke · li · *zay* · shen dok · trin] *n.* The doctrine that a **foreign corporation** subjects itself to the laws of the state in which it operates if it does sufficient business there for a sufficient period of time. *See* doing business in a state; long arm statutes; minimum contacts test.

locate [*loh* · kate] *v.* 1. To select, survey, and settle the boundaries of a tract of land; to designate a particular portion of land by geographical boundaries. 2. To become settled in a place. 3. To designate a place for something.
➤ establish, move to, reside, camp, stay, take, root, dig in ("The company chose to locate in Delaware").

location [*loh* · kay · shen] *n.* 1. With respect to land, a description of its boundaries; a **legal description** of real estate. *See also* locative calls. 2. The act of locating or describing something, especially land. 3. In mining law, a series of acts by which the **locator** of a claim preempts a portion of public mineral lands and establishes his right to exploit it. *See* public land. 4. The place where a thing or person can be found.
➤ spot, area, residence, locale, neck of the woods, region ("pinpoint the ship's location").

locative calls [*lok* · e · tiv] *n.* Landmarks, **monuments**, and other physical objects on land, or referred to in a **legal description**

of land, which establish boundaries. *Also see* location.

locator [*loh* · kay · ter] *n.* A person who locates and establishes the boundaries to land, particularly mining claims.

lockout [*lok* · out] *n.* The closing of the workplace by the employer, or the withholding of work, to enhance the employer's bargaining position in labor negotiations. *See* collective bargaining; collective bargaining agreement.
➤ work stoppage, labor dispute, close-out.

lockup [*lok* · up] *n.* In a police station, a place for the temporary confinement of persons under arrest.
➤ place of detention, jail, facility, prison.

loco parentis [*loh* · koh pa · *ren* · tis] *(Latin) adj. See in loco parentis.*

locum tenens [*loh* · kum *ten* · enz] *(Latin) n.* Means "holding the place." An assistant or deputy who holds the office of a person whose term has expired is *locum tenens* until he is superseded by a person legally authorized to actually hold the office.

locus [*loh* · kus] *(Latin) n.* A place; a locality.
➤ place, point, locality ("the locus of the burglary").

  locus in quo *n.* Means "the place in which." USAGE: "the *locus in quo* of the burglary" means "the place where the burglary occurred."

lodestar [*lode* · star] *n.* Something that guides or points the way.

  lodestar rule *n.* A standard applied by courts in fixing the amount of attorney fees allowed by statute. The number of hours spent on the case, and a reasonable rate per hour (i.e., the **prevailing rate**), are the "lodestar," to be adjusted by other relevant factors such as the quality of the work performed and the nature of the result obtained by the attorney.

lodger [*lod* · jer] *n.* A person who lives in the home of another person (i.e., a lodging house). Because a lodger lives in another person's home, he does not have all of the rights the law gives a tenant. *See* boarder.
➤ roomer, guest, boarder, tenant, dweller, lessee.

lodging house [*lod* · jing] *n.* A house where rooms are rented to guests, with or without board, by the week or month. *See* lodger.
➤ abode, domicile, hotel, inn, quarters, boarding house, bed and breakfast.

log rolling [*roh* · ling] *n.* 1. The technique of submitting a constitutional amendment or **proposition** to the voters in a form that requires them, in order to approve one portion of the measure, also to approve portions they might otherwise not have voted for. 2. A similar practice in submitting a **bill** to the legislature for adoption. 3. The practice whereby a member of the legislature votes for the bill of another member with the understanding that she will receive his support for a measure in which she is interested.
➤ trading favors, playing politics.

logical [*loj* · ih · kul] *adj.* Characterized by reason and consistency.
➤ consistent, reasonable, sound, coherent, lucid, analytical ("logical deduction").
Ant. emotional, unreasonable.

logical relevancy [*loj* · i · kel *rel* · e · ven · see] *n. See* relevancy.

logrolling *See* log rolling.

loiter [*loy* · ter] *v.* To stand around idly. *See* loitering.
➤ linger, wander, dally, loaf, tarry, lag, halt, pause, get not place fast, put off, idle ("Don't loiter in the hall").

loitering [*loy* · ter · ing] *n.* 1. The offense of idling or lounging about, either in a public place or on private property. Many loitering statutes and ordinances have been held to be **unconstitutionally vague**. *See* vagrancy; vagueness doctrine. 2. Standing around or spending one's time idly; being dilatory.
➤ idling, dallying, hanging around, lingering.

long *adj.* 1. In the language of the stock market, a trader in **securities** is "long" or **long on the market** when he takes the full price risk, i.e., he gains if the market price goes up and loses if it declines. 2. Extended; drawn-out; stretched; lengthy; not short.
➤ deep, expanded, far-reaching, extended, widespread, considerable ("Alaska is a long way away").
Ant. confined, short.

L

long arm statutes [*stat* · shoots] *n.*
State statutes providing for **substituted
service of process** on a **nonresident** corporation or individual. Long arm statutes
permit a state's courts to take **jurisdiction**
over a nonresident if she has done business in the state (provided the **minimum
contacts test** is met), or has committed a
tort or owns property within the state. *See*
doing business in a state; foreign service
of process; localization doctrine;
nonresident motorist statutes.

long on the market [*mar* · ket] *adv. See*
long.

long-term *adj.* Relating to a relatively lengthy
period of time. *Compare* short-term.

long-term debt *n.* A debt that is not due
for at least one year. *Compare* short-term
debt.

long-term financing [*fine* · an · sing] *n.*
A loan with a term of at least one year.
Compare short-term financing.

longevity pay [lon · *jev* · i · tee] *n.*
Additional pay allowed members of the
military for lengthy service.

look out [look owt] *v.* To watch for; to
notice.
➤ beware, watch for, be alert, be wary, have
a care, heads up, notice, pay attention.

looking and listening [*look* · ing and
liss · en · ing] *n.* The duty of a person,
before crossing a railroad track, to use her
senses in a way a **reasonably prudent
person** would in similar circumstances
to determine whether it is safe to cross.

lookout [*look* · out] *n.* 1. A reference to the
requirement that a motorist must use **due
diligence** in anticipating and discovering
the presence of others on the road to avoid
injury to them or to himself. 2. A person
who participates in a crime by watching
at a distance to prevent discovery of the
criminal activity.
➤ guard, sentinel, scout, watcher, sentry, patrol ("The lookout watched for the police").

loophole [*loop* · hole] *n.* A means of
avoidance or evasion, particularly a means
for evading the law.
➤ ambiguity, vagueness, omission, windfall,
opening, opportunity ("The new tax law
has several loopholes").

lose *v.* 1. To be deprived of. 2. To suffer
defeat. *See* lost.
➤ misplace, miss, mislay, vanish, be
deprived of ("to lose a book"); forfeit,
fail, abort, fall short, suffer defeat,
succumb ("to lose the Superbowl").

loss *n.* A deprivation. The word "loss"
connotes both the act of losing and the
thing lost. It is not a word of hard and
fast meaning. It does not necessarily
mean actual monetary loss; it may refer
to an event such as a death, or the end of
a friendship, or to anything that is gone
and cannot be recovered.
  In the law, the word "loss" chiefly
appears in the context of **liability, injury,**
or **damage** and **damages,** and therefore,
not surprisingly, insurance. *In the context
of insurance,* loss is the consequence of
the occurrence of the **risk** against which
the insurance company has agreed to
indemnify the insured. The term is also
applied extensively *in tax law,* where it is
used in contradistinction to gain, and refers
to transactions involving an excess of
expense over revenue. *See* risk of loss.
Also see actual loss; capital loss; casualty
loss; direct loss; disaster loss; general
average loss; net operating loss; pecuniary
loss; profit and loss statement; proof of
loss; salvage loss; total loss.
➤ damage, deprivation, depletion, casualty,
mishap, grief, detriment, ruin ("Her loss
wasn't as great as she thought").

loss of bargain [*bar* · gen] *n. See*
benefit of bargain rule.

loss of consortium [ken · *sore* · shem] *n.*
The loss of a spouse's assistance or companionship, or the loss of a spouse's ability or willingness to have sexual relations.
If such loss results from a **tort,** it gives rise to
a **cause of action** in favor of the partner
of the spouse **injured** by the tort. *See*
consortium.

loss of earning capacity [*ern* · ing
ke · *pass* · i · tee] *n.* Harm done to a
person's ability to earn money in the
future. *Compare* loss of earnings. *See*
earning capacity.

loss of earnings [*ern* · ingz] *n.* Earnings
or wages of which a person has actually
been deprived. It is an element of **damages**

L

in a **tort** action. *Compare* loss of earning capacity. *See* earning capacity.

loss of eye *n.* In a disability insurance policy, a term referring either to the actual loss of an eye or to the loss of its use.

loss of limb *n.* *See* loss of member.

loss of member [*mem* · ber] *n.* In a disability insurance policy, a term referring either to the actual severance of a part of the body, especially a limb, or to the loss of its use. *See* member. *Also see* loss of use; member.

loss of use *n.* 1. The loss of the ability to use a **member**, equivalent to the actual loss of the member. 2. A deprivation of the opportunity to make use of property, for EXAMPLE, the inability to use an automobile that has been put out of commission by a collision.

loss payable clause [*pay* · ebl] *n.* A clause in an insurance policy purchased by the owner of real property or personalty which provides that, in the event of loss, the proceeds of the policy are to be paid to the holder of the **security interest** in the property (EXAMPLES: in the case of fire insurance on real estate, the bank or other mortgagee; in the case of collision insurance on an automobile, usually the finance company). A loss payable clause generally provides that if the loss is shared by the **named insured** and one or more mortgagees or **lienors**, the proceeds are to be allocated among them "**as their interests may appear**."

loss payee [pay · *ee*] *n.* The person or persons designated in a **loss payable clause**.

loss ratio [*ray* · shee · oh] *n.* An insurance term meaning the relation which total losses paid during a given period bear to the total premiums earned during the same period.

loss reserve [re · *zerv*] *n.* An insurance term meaning the amount set aside by the insurance company for losses not yet incurred and losses incurred but not yet made the subject of claims.

lost *adj.* 1. No longer possessed. *See* lost property. 2. Gone; vanished. 3. Destroyed.
➤ misplaced, missing, mislaid, gone, disappeared ("the lost treasure map"); destroyed, vanquished, defeated, demolished ("lost in battle"); confused, unclear, bewildered, mystified ("The new clerk was lost").

lost corner [*kore* · ner] *n.* A point in a survey of land whose position cannot be determined beyond a reasonable doubt either from traces of the original marks or from other evidence, and whose location can be established only by reference to one or more independent corners.

lost grant *n.* The **legal fiction** that a person who has been in possession of real property for a long time, and has acted as if she owned it, has done so under an **ancient** or "lost" grant or **title**.

lost property [*prop* · er · tee] *n.* Personal property with which the owner has involuntarily and unintentionally parted through neglect or carelessness. *See* larceny of lost, mislaid, or misdelivered property. *Compare* abandoned property; mislaid property.

lost will *n.* A will that is known to have existed but that cannot be found after careful and thorough search. In some states, the contents of a lost will can be proven through **parol evidence**; in others it cannot.

lot *n.* 1. A **tract** or **parcel** into which land has been divided. 2. A group; a number of things or persons, often assorted, taken as a group. EXAMPLE: a **job lot**. 3. A unit of shares of stock traded on a stock exchange. *See* odd lot; round lot. 4. Tossing or drawing an object as a means of making a decision or a choice. USAGE: "chosen by lot." *See* lottery. 5. That which fate or fortune bestows. USAGE: "her lot in life."
➤ plot, plat, block, subdivision, tract; group, pack, batch, crew.

lot book *n.* A **plat book**.

lottery [*lot* · e · ree] *n.* Any scheme, plan, or procedure under which, for a price, a prize or prizes are distributed by lot or by chance, but most commonly the distribution of monetary prizes by selling numbered tickets and later, at a previously announced time, choosing the winning numbers by lot or chance. A lottery is a gambling scheme and is therefore illegal except in some jurisdictions where it is regulated. Many states conduct lotteries as a state activity for the purpose of generating public funds.

L

➤ game of chance, bet, gamble, scheme, sweepstake, draw, raffle, wager ("the Florida lottery").

Louisiana law [loo · wee · zee · *an* · a] *n.* The law of the State of Louisiana, which has its background in the **civil law**, as opposed to the other states of the United States, whose law is rooted in the **common law**. *See* Code Civil.

love and affection [a · *fek* · shen] *n.* **Consideration** adequate to support a contract with a near relative, but not a contract with a **stranger**; i.e, **good consideration** but not **valuable consideration**. *See* adequate consideration; legal consideration; moral consideration.

low tide *n.* The lowest point to which tidal waters ebb. *See* low water line.

low water line [*waw* · ter] *n.* The point tidal waters reach at low tide.

low water mark [*waw* · ter] *n.* Same as **low water line**.

lower [*low* · er] *adj.* 1. Relatively low or below in status, rank, or order. 2. Physically situated underneath or below.
v. To diminish or demote.
➤ *adj.* inferior, inadequate, incompetent.
v. demote, defame, mitigate, decline.

lower court *n.* 1. An **inferior court**, usually a **trial court**. 2. A **court of limited jurisdiction**.

lower house *n.* The House of Representatives of the Congress of the United States or of any bicameral legislature. *Compare* upper house. *See* state legislature. *Also see* legislature.

lower riparian owner [ry · *pair* · ee · en oh · ner] *n.* A **riparian owner** who owns land downstream from an **upper riparian owner**.

lowest responsible bidder [*lo* · est res · *pon* · sibl bid · er] *n.* A **responsible bidder** with the lowest bid.

loyalty [*loy* · el · tee] *n.* Adherence to law or to the government; faithfulness to a person or to a principle.
➤ allegiance, fealty, devotion, bond, faith, support ("He has shown great loyalty to his country").

loyalty oath *n.* An **oath** pledging support for the government and disclaiming allegiance to foreign doctrines or affiliations. It is required of certain public employees whose duties bear upon national security. Such an oath is of dubious **constitutionality** unless it is narrowly worded and limited in its application. *See also* oath of allegiance.

LR Abbreviation of **law review**; abbreviation of **law reports**.

LS Abbreviation of *locus sigilli*, meaning "the place of the seal." The letters "LS" are often printed on a document required to be **under seal** to indicate the place at which the seal should be affixed; sometimes they appear instead of a seal, but serve the same purpose. *See* scroll.

LSAT [*ell* · sat *or* el · ess · ay · *tee*] *n.* Acronym for **Law School Admissions Test**; "LSAT" is the customary way of referring to that examination. It is also referred to as the "L-SAT."

LSD Abbreviation of lysergic acid diethylamide, a hallucinogenic drug that often produces temporary psychosis as a side effect. LSD is a **controlled substance**; its possession, distribution, or sale is a criminal offense. *See* hallucinogen.
➤ acid, sunshine, hallucinogen.

Ltd. Abbreviation of **Limited**, which often forms a part of a company's complete corporate name. USAGE: "Jack & Jill Ltd."

lucid [*loo* · sid] *adj.* Clear; coherent; understandable; rational; sane.
➤ clear, coherent, understandable, rational, sane.
Ant. incomprehensible.

lucid interval [*in* · ter · vel] *n.* A period of sanity experienced by some insane persons, during which they are **competent** to transact their affairs (EXAMPLES: marry; make a will; enter into contracts). *See* insanity. *See also* competent person; legal capacity.

lucrative [*loo* · kre · tiv] *adj.* Profitable.
➤ profitable, worthwhile, money-making, fruitful, productive, advantageous ("to sign a lucrative contract").

lucrative bailment [*bail* · ment] *n.* A **bailment for hire**.

L

lucri causa [*loo* · kree *kaw* · zah] *(Latin)* *n.* Means "for the sake of gain." *Lucri causa* is an element of the crime of **larceny**.

lump sale *n.* 1. A sale of several things in one lot for a lump sum. 2. A **judicial sale** of several distinct **parcels** of real estate together, or several articles of personal property, for a single gross sum.

lump sum *n.* One sum covering all amounts to be paid.

lump-sum alimony [*al* · i · moh · nee] *n.* An award of **alimony in gross**, that is, an award of one lump sum to be paid either in installments or as a lump sum. *See* alimony. *Also see* periodic alimony.

lump-sum payment [*pay* · ment] *n.* A payment in one sum, as distinguished from payment in installments.

lump-sum settlement [*setl* · ment] *n.* The **commutation** of periodic payments into one lump sum to be accepted as full payment and **satisfaction**.

lumping sale [*lump* · ing] *n.* Same as **lump sale**.

lunacy [*loon* · e · see] *n.* **Insanity**.
➤ insanity, mania, foolishness, abnormality, madness, dementia.

luxury tax [*lug* · zhe · ree] *n.* An **excise tax** imposed on luxury items. EXAMPLES: fur coats; liquor.

lying in wait [*ly* · ing] *n.* Concealing oneself in order to ambush a person with the intention of doing him bodily harm or of killing him.

lynch law *n.* A term referring to doing something without legal authority which can be done only with legal authority, particularly administering punishment. *See* lynching. *Compare* kangaroo court.
➤ lawlessness, mob rule, terrorism, anarchy, mobocracy.

lynching [*lin* · ching] *n.* Summarily punishing a person for an alleged offense without legal authority, generally by putting him to death.

L

M'Naghten rule [me · *naw* · ten] *n.* A test employed in a number of jurisdictions for determining whether a criminal defendant had the **capacity** to form **criminal intent** at the time he committed the crime of which he is accused. Specifically, the M'Naghten rule is that an accused is not criminally responsible if he was laboring under such a defect of reason from disease of the mind that he either did not know the nature of his act or, if he did, that he did not know it was wrong. The M'Naghten rule is also referred to as the **right and wrong test**. *Compare* Durham rule; irresistible impulse. *See* insanity.

mad *adj.* 1. Crazy; insane. 2. Showing displeasure or anger. 3. Eager; showing intense feeling.
➤ crazy, insane, demented, unstable, unbalanced, psychotic; angry, infuriated, incensed, livid, furious ("mad at the world"); impassioned, keen, wild, ardent, enthusiastic ("to be mad about music").

made *adj.* 1. Signed; executed. USAGE (at the signature line of an instrument such as a contract or deed): "**made and executed**." *See* make. 2. Proven. USAGE: "The judge said the plaintiff made her case." 3. Created; produced; constructed; manufactured.
➤ constructed, formed, designed, assembled, fabricated, created, built ("a man-made object").

made and executed [ek · se · kyoo · ted] *adj.* Signed. *See* signed, sealed, and delivered.

made known *adj.* A term used by a **declarant** to indicate that he is without personal knowledge of the facts and that his knowledge is limited to what he has been told. *Compare* personally known to me.

magisterial [maj · i · *steer* · ee · el] *adj.* Pertaining to a **magistrate** or her functions.
➤ important, formal, elevated, pompous, arrogant, prodigal.

magisterial district [*dis* · trikt] *n.* The geographical **jurisdiction** of a **magistrate** or justice of the peace.

magisterial precinct [*pree* · sinkt] *n.* Same as **magisterial district**.

magistrate [*maj* · is · trate] *n.* 1. A judge of a **court of limited jurisdiction**; that is, a judge of a court whose **jurisdiction** is restricted to **misdemeanors** and to **preliminary hearings** on **felony** charges, or to civil claims involving small amounts of money. EXAMPLE: a justice of the peace. 2. A **United States Magistrate**; that is, a federal judicial officer who has some of the powers of a judge of a federal district court, including the power to conduct preliminary hearings in criminal cases and hearings on **pretrial motions** in civil cases. *See* committing magistrate. *See also* District Courts of the United States.
➤ judge, judicial officer, official, arbiter.

magistrate's court *n.* A court presided over by a **magistrate**; a **court of limited jurisdiction**. EXAMPLES: a **justice's court**; a **police court**.

Magna Carta [*mag* · na *car* · ta] (*Latin*) *n.* Same as **Magna Charta**.

Magna Charta [*mag* · na *car* · ta] (*Latin*) *n.* "Great charter," a document that was issued by King John of England in 1215 and is the basis of English and American constitutional protections. Its guaranties relating to life, liberty, and property are embedded in the Constitution of the United States and in every state constitution in the United States.

mail fraud *n.* The use of the mails to perpetrate a **fraud**. It is a federal crime. The essence of the offense is using the mails to make a **fraudulent misrepresentation** for the purpose of obtaining money or anything else of value. The crime is also known as **using the mails to defraud**. *See also* wire fraud.

mail order divorce [*or · der di · vorss*] *n.* A divorce granted by a foreign country, upon the application of one or both parties to the marriage, without either party being a **domiciliary** or a resident of that country. (EXAMPLE: a **Mexican divorce**.) Such a divorce is **void** in every state in the United States.

mailable matter [*male · ebl mat · er*] *n.* Matter that, under applicable statutes and regulations, may be transmitted by mail.

mailbox rule [*mayl · bahks rool*] *n.* Rule in contract law that acceptance of an offer is effective upon dispatch (i.e., mailing) by the offeree and not upon receipt by the offeror. Sometimes called the implied agency rule because the Post Office is deemed to be the agent of the offeror. This rule applies to the acceptance of an offer, but not to the making, rejection, or revocation of an offer.

mailed *adj./adv.* Describes an item when it is appropriately enveloped or packaged, addressed, and stamped, and deposited in a proper place for the receipt of mail. *See* mailable matter.

In contract law, acceptance of an offer takes place when the acceptance is mailed, unless the parties have made another arrangement or a statute provides otherwise.

maim *v.* To mutilate a limb, member, or any essential part of the body of another person; to commit the crime of **mayhem**.
➤ cripple, maul, incapacitate, break, disable, mar.

main *adj.* Principal; leading; chief in importance, strength, or extent.

➤ principal, leading, chief, cardinal, major, fundamental ("the main thrust of his argument").
Ant. subordinate.
main purpose rule [*per · pes*] *n.* Same as **leading object rule**.

maintain [*main · tain*] *v.* 1. To commence or carry on an **action**. USAGE: "She is determined to maintain her lawsuit." 2. To keep in condition or repair. USAGE: "The lease requires him to maintain the apartment in good repair." 3. To operate, support, or carry something on indefinitely. EXAMPLE: **maintaining a nuisance**. 4. To support; to provide care for; to subsidize; to preserve; to nourish. USAGE: "He maintains both of his parents as well as his wife and children." 5. To assert; to declare. USAGE: "Even though she was convicted, she continues to maintain that she is innocent." *Also see* maintenance.
➤ prosecute, pursue, persevere, keep on, continue, preserve, conserve, uphold ("She is determined to maintain her lawsuit"); service, save, preserve, protect, overhaul ("maintain the car"); sustain, care for, finance, nourish, shelter, nurture ("He maintains both of his parents as well as his children"); advocate, affirm, fight for, insist, profess, state ("Even though she was convicted, she continues to maintain that she is innocent").
Ant. damage, abandon, deny, discontinue.
maintain a nuisance [*main · tain a nyoo · sense*] *v.* To carry on or operate a **nuisance** on an ongoing or continuing basis, as distinguished from merely being aware of its existence.

maintenance [*main · ten · ense*] *n.* 1. Making repairs and otherwise keeping premises or machinery in good condition. *See* maintain. 2. The **support** of a person. *Also see* separate maintenance. 3. Stirring up litigation; **officious intermeddling** in a lawsuit in which one has no **interest** or **standing**, by assisting a party, with money or in some other way, to **maintain** the **action**. *See* champerty. *Compare* barratry.
➤ upkeep, conservation, preservation, care, repair, protection ("Bring the car in for scheduled maintenance"); help, aid, finances, alimony, subsistence, livelihood ("maintenance for her health").

M

major [*may* · jer] *adj.* Greater; larger; more powerful; more important.

n. 1. A person who has attained his **majority**; a person who is no longer a minor. *See* adult; age of majority; full age; legal age. 2. In college, the academic area in which one concentrates or specializes. USAGE: "Her major was English."

➤ *adj.* greater, larger, more powerful, main, leading, principal, preeminent, outstanding, notable, significant.

major dispute [dis · *pyoot*] *n.* As opposed to a **minor dispute**, a railroad labor dispute that the **Railway Labor Act** requires be submitted to **mediation** before a strike can be called. *Compare* minor dispute.

major medical insurance [*med* · i · kel in · *shoor* · ense] *n.* Insurance that covers especially costly medical, surgical, or hospital expenses; insurance that **indemnifies** the insured for medical expenses exceeding a stipulated minimum amount. *See* medical insurance.

majority [ma · *jaw* · ri · tee] *n.* 1. **Legal age**; **full age**; the age at which a person acquires the **capacity** to contract; the age at which a person is no longer a minor. The **age of majority** varies from state to state and differs depending upon the purpose. (EXAMPLES: eligibility for a driver's license; eligibility to vote; the right to purchase alcoholic beverages). *See* legal capacity. 2. More than half of anything. *Compare* minority.

➤ legal age, full age, age of responsibility, drinking age, estate, manhood ("He has now reached the age of majority"); plurality, bulk, mass, lion's share, most, preponderance ("She has a majority of the shares of stock").

majority interest [*in* · trest] *n. See* majority stockholders; controlling interest.

majority of electors [e · *lek* · terz] *n. See* majority vote.

majority of qualified electors [*kwaw* · li · fide e · *lek* · terz] *n. See* majority vote.

majority opinion [o · *pin* · yen] *n.* 1. An **opinion** issued by an **appellate court** that represents the view of a majority of the members of the court. *Compare* concurring opinion; dissenting opinion; minority opinion; plurality opinion. 2. The opinion of the majority of the members of any group.

majority rule *n.* A majority of those who actually vote in an election, as opposed to a majority of those eligible to vote. *See* eligible voter; majority vote.

majority stockholders [*stok* · hole · derz] *n.* Stockholders who, as a group, own more than 50 percent of the stock of a corporation. *See* stockholder. *See also* controlling interest.

majority view *n.* An interpretation of a principle of law concurred in by the courts in a majority of states. *Compare* minority view.

majority vote *n.* A vote of more than half of the voters who actually vote, as distinguished from eligible voters. *Compare* plurality vote.

make *v.* 1. To **draw** or execute an **instrument**; to sign. USAGE: "I'll make a check to your **order**." See made; made and executed; maker. 2. To cause to be or to happen. USAGE: "**make a law**"; "make money"; "make a promise." 3. To form; to create; to manufacture; to construct; to accomplish.

➤ fabricate, create, originate, manufacture, cast, erect ("to make a law"); execute, draft, prepare ("I'll make a check to your order"); induce, compel, coerce, cause, require ("make me do it").

make a contract [*kon* · trakt] *v.* To arrive at an agreement and put it into effect. In the case of a written contract, it includes reducing the agreement to writing and signing it.

make a law *v.* To enact a statute or ordinance. *Compare* make law.

make a record [*rek* · erd] *v.* 1. To physically prepare a **record**; i.e., to assemble the transcript, **pleadings**, exhibits, etc. 2. To offer or present evidence "for the record" during a trial, usually to ensure a basis for appeal. *See* record. *Also see* offer of proof.

make law *v.* A term that refers to the action of a court in deciding a case in a manner never before decided or interpreting a statute in a manner in which it was never previously interpreted. *Compare* make a law. *See* judge-made law.

M

make whole *v.* To return a person who has suffered a **loss** to the position she was in prior to the loss. The purpose of **compensatory damages** is to make a plaintiff whole for loss or **injury** she suffered as a result of the defendant's conduct.

maker [*may* · ker] *n.* 1. A person who obligates himself by executing a check, **promissory note**, **draft**, or other **negotiable instrument**. *See* drawer. *Also see* accommodation maker. 2. A manufacturer; a creator; an originator.
➤ author, producer, fabricator, creator.

mala [*may* · lah] *(Latin) adj.* Bad; wrong; evil.
  mala fide [*fie* · dee] Means "in bad faith." *Compare bona fide.*
  mala in se [*in saye*] *See malum in se.*
  mala prohibita [pro · *hib* · i · tah] *See malum prohibitum.*

maladministration
[mal · ad · min · is · *tray* · shen] *n.* Inefficient administration; poor, but not necessarily corrupt, administration.
➤ inefficiency, ineffectiveness, blundering, bungling, misfeasance.

malefactor [*mal* · e · fak · ter] *n.* 1. A person convicted of a crime; a criminal. 2. A person who is guilty of anything.
➤ criminal, offender, felon, villain, outlaw, perpetrator ("The malefactor was sentenced to 10 years").

malfeasance [mal · *feez* · ense] *n.* The doing of a wrongful act or an unlawful act. *Compare* misfeasance; nonfeasance.
➤ dereliction, wrongful conduct, mismanagement, misdeed, negligence, carelessness, transgression.
  malfeasance in office [*aw* · fiss] *n.* The performance by a public official of an official act that is illegal or wrongful. *Compare* misfeasance in office. *See* official misconduct.

malice [*mal* · iss] *n.* State of mind that causes the intentional doing of a wrongful act without **legal excuse** or **justification**; a condition of mind prompting a person to the commission of a dangerous or deadly act in deliberate disregard of the lives or safety of others. The term does not necessarily connote personal ill will. It can and frequently does mean **general malice**.

See actual malice; constructive malice; express malice; implied malice; particular malice; premeditated malice. *See also* malicious; malicious act. *Compare* intent.
  *As an element of **murder***, all those states of mind that prompt a person to kill another person without legal excuse or justification; an intent to do the deceased **great bodily harm**.
  *As an element of **malicious prosecution***, a prosecution motived either by personal malice (EXAMPLE: anger) or by an unjustifiable purpose (EXAMPLE: **extortion**). *Also see* malicious use of process.
  *In the law of **defamation***, to be **actionable** malice must be **actual malice** or **express malice**, as distinct from **implied malice** or **constructive malice**. *Also see* criminal libel. A **privileged communication** is conditioned upon an absence of malice. *See* conditionally privileged communication; journalists' privilege. *Also see* libel; slander.
  *In the law of **damages***, additional damages may be awarded if the **damage** to the plaintiff resulted from an **injury** inflicted recklessly or with malice. *See* punitive damages.
➤ willfulness, animosity, callousness, hate, bad blood, evil, grudge, intent, deliberation.
malice aforethought [a · *fore* · thawt] *n.* An **intent to kill** or injure, or the deliberate commission of a dangerous or deadly act in disregard of the lives or safety of others. The word "**aforethought**" does not refer to the intent to take life, but to the malice.
malice in fact *n.* **Actual malice**; **express malice**; a positive intention to injure another person. Malice in fact deprives a defendant in a **defamation** action of the ability to defend on the ground that his statement is **privileged**. *See* conditionally privileged communication. *Compare* constructive malice; implied malice; malice in law.
malice in law *n.* Malice that is inferred from the fact that a vicious or spiteful act is intentionally committed; **implied malice**; **constructive malice**. EXAMPLE: **libel per se** (**injury** is **presumed**).
malice prepense [*pree* · pense] *n.* Same as **malice aforethought**.

malicious [mel · *ish* · ess] *adj.* 1. Motivated by **malice**; with **intent** and without **legal**

M

excuse or **justification**. 2. Malevolent; wicked; evil; vicious; callous. *See* willful.

➤ malevolent, wicked, evil, nasty, spiteful, vicious, callous ("a malicious act").

malicious abuse of process [a · *byooss* of *pross* · ess] *n.* The **willful** and **intentional** misuse of **process** for a purpose other than the purpose for which it was designed. EXAMPLE: subjecting an **adverse party** to excessive litigation expenses by the unrestrained use of process, such as **depositions**, **interrogatories**, **motions to compel discovery**, and the like. *See* abuse of process. *Compare* malicious use of process.

malicious act *n.* A wrongful act intentionally done without **legal excuse** or **justification**; an injurious or lethal act committed without regard to its consequences.

malicious arrest [a · *rest*] *n.* A form of **malicious prosecution**.

malicious injury [*in* · je · ree] *n.* A wrongful **injury** intentionally inflicted by one person upon another without **legal excuse** or **justification**, or without regard to its consequences. *See* legal injury.

malicious interference with contract [in · ter · *feer* · ense with *kon* · trakt] *n.* Intentional and unreasonable interference with a person's right to be secure in her contractual and business relationships. It is a **tort**, sometimes referred to as **tortious interference with contract**. EXAMPLE: a physician, for arbitrary reasons, causing a nurse to be removed from a hospital's "on call" list by threatening not to admit patients to the hospital.

malicious mischief [*miss* · chif] *n.* The **willful** destruction of the property of another. It is a **tort** and, in most jurisdictions, a crime as well. Malicious mischief is also called **criminal mischief**. *See* mischief.

malicious prosecution [pross · e · *kyoo* · shen] *n.* A **criminal prosecution** or **civil suit** commenced **maliciously** and without **probable cause**. After the termination of such a prosecution or suit in the defendant's favor, the defendant has the right to bring an **action** against the original plaintiff for the **tort** of "malicious prosecution." *See* malicious arrest; malicious use of process.

malicious use of process [*pross* · ess] *n.* The use of **process** for a purpose for which

it was intended, but out of personal **malice** or some other unjustifiable motive (EXAMPLE: to **extort** money) and without **probable cause**. It is, in effect, a form of **malicious prosecution**. *Compare* malicious abuse of process.

maliciously [mel · *ish* · es · lee] *adv.* 1. With harmful motive and in **willful** or **reckless disregard** of the rights of others. 2. In a malevolent, nasty, or spiteful manner.

malinger [mel · *ing* · ger] *v.* To pretend illness or disability in order to avoid work or to evade one's duty.

malingerer [mel · *ing* · ger · er] *n.* One who malingers (feigns illness, injury, or incapacity).

➤ loafer, dodger, evader, shirker.

malpractice [mal · *prak* · tiss] *n.* The failure of a professional person to act with **reasonable care**; misconduct by a professional person in the course of engaging in his profession. *See* legal malpractice; medical malpractice.

➤ misconduct, incompetence, negligence, carelessness, dereliction, misdeed, violation, transgression ("legal malpractice").

malpractice insurance [in · *shoor* · ense] *n.* A type of **liability insurance** that protects professional persons (EXAMPLES: attorneys; physicians; psychotherapists) from liability for **negligence** and other forms of malpractice. It is also called **professional liability insurance**.

malum [*may* · lum] *(Latin) n.* Bad; evil; wrong.

malum in se [in say] *n.* Naturally evil or wicked; immoral; illegal from the very nature of the act on the basis of principles of natural, moral, or public law, independent of the fact that it is punished by the state. EXAMPLES: **murder**; **robbery**; **incest**. *Compare malum prohibitum. See* natural law; moral law; public law.

malum prohibitum [pro · *hib* · i · tum] *n.* A wrong which is a wrong only because it is prohibited by law. EXAMPLE: driving on the lefthand side of the road. *Compare malum in se.*

management [*man* · ej · ment] *n.* 1. The persons who oversee, control, or direct a

M

business or other enterprise. *Compare* labor. 2. The act of controlling or directing.

➤ leaders, directors, administrators, authority, board, front office ("The management laid the employee off"); government, control, handling, administration, direction, rule ("poor management of the company").

manager [*man · e · jer*] *n.* 1. A person in charge of another's business or operations or the general business of a corporation; in some corporations, the head of one of several departments or one or more branches. 2. One who has responsibility for conducting or directing anything. *See* managing agent. *Also see* city manager form of government.

➤ administrator, director, supervisor, boss, conductor, overseer.

managing agent [*man · e · jing ay · jent*] *n.* A person to whom a corporation has given general powers involving the exercise of judgment and discretion in conducting the corporation's business. *See* agent; manager. *Also see* general agent.

mandamus [man · *day* · mus] (*Latin*) *n.* Means "we command." A **writ** issuing from a **court of competent jurisdiction**, directed to an **inferior court**, board, or corporation, or to an officer of a **branch of government** (judicial, executive, or legislative), requiring the performance of some **ministerial act**. A **writ of mandamus** is an **extraordinary remedy**. *See* writ of mandamus.

mandate [*man · date*] *n.* 1. An order or command issued by a court. 2. A requirement; an ultimatum; a directive. *v.* To require; to order; to command.

➤ *n.* direction, edict, decree, charge, command, fiat ("the mandate of the people"). *v.* require, order, command ("The court mandated desegregation").

mandatory [*man · de · tore · ee*] *adj.* Compulsory, not a matter of discretion; required to be done or performed. *Compare* directory; permissive.

➤ obligatory, imperative, required, binding, forced, imperious ("a mandatory provision"). *Ant.* voluntary, elective.

mandatory injunction [*in · junk · shen*] *n.* An **injunction** that compels a defendant to do a particular positive act involving a change of existing conditions. EXAMPLE: an injunction to stop a **secondary boycott**.

mandatory instruction [*in · struk · shen*] *n.* A **jury instruction** which directs that if the jury finds that a specified set of facts have been proven, then it must decide the case in favor of a specific party.

mandatory provision [*pro · vizh · en*] *n.* A provision in a statute or ordinance that, if not followed, renders the **proceedings** to which it relates illegal and **void**. *See* mandatory statute. *Compare* directory provision.

mandatory sentencing [*sen · ten · sing*] *n.* The statutory requirements in some jurisdictions that persons convicted of certain crimes be sentenced to prison for a period of time prescribed by statute. Mandatory sentencing displaces a judge's discretionary power to sentence a defendant to a different term or to impose probation or a suspended sentence. *See* sentencing. *Also see* mandatory statute.

mandatory statute [*stat · shoot*] *n.* 1. A statute that leaves nothing to discretion in carrying out its terms. 2. A statute that relates to **substantive rights** and not to matters of form. A mandatory statute often uses the word "shall." *Compare* directory statute. *See* mandatory provision.

manifest [*man · i · fest*] *adj.* Evident or obvious to the senses, particularly to the eyes or to the mind; plain; clear. *n.* 1. A document that lists items being warehoused or shipped. 2. A document that lists the cargo or passengers of a ship or plane. *v.* To reveal; to exhibit; to express.

➤ *adj.* open, obvious, not hidden, apparent, bold, clear-cut ("The reasoning was manifest"). *v.* show, reveal, demonstrate, display, declare, expose, express, exhibit, evidence, evince. *Ant.* latent, hidden; conceal, cloak.

manifesto [*man · i · fes · toh*] *n.* A statement issued to the public by a government, an organization, or a group of people stating its policy with respect to social, economic, or political matters and describing the reasons for its positions or its acts.

➤ announcement, proclamation, broadcast, credo, affirmation, edict.

M

manipulation of stock
[man · ip · yew · *lay* · shen] *n.* *See* stock manipulation.

Mann Act *n.* A federal statute that makes it a **felony** to transport a woman or girl in **interstate commerce** or **foreign commerce** for immoral purposes. *See* interstate commerce.

manner [*man* · ur] *n.* 1. Behavior or conduct. 2. A characteristic style; a method or approach.
➤ behavior, conduct, bearing, look, tone; method, approach, style, habit, custom, routine.

manslaughter [*man* · slaw · ter] *n.* The killing of a human being, without **premeditation** or **malice** and without **legal excuse** or **justification**. **Voluntary manslaughter** occurs when a **homicide** is intentional but the result of **sudden passion** or great **provocation**. **Involuntary manslaughter** is an unintentional killing in the course of doing an unlawful act not amounting to a **felony** or while doing a lawful act in a reckless manner. There are various degrees of manslaughter, which are not consistent from jurisdiction to jurisdiction. *Compare* excusable homicide; justifiable homicide. *Also compare* murder. *See* criminal negligence; culpable negligence. *Also see* negligent homicide; negligent manslaughter.

manual [*man* · yoo · el] *adj.* Pertaining to the hands or to work done by hand.
n. Written directions for performing a certain task or certain work.
➤ *adj.* hand-operated, physical, menial, arduous, standard ("Peter grew tired from the manual labor").
n. primer, guidebook, handbook, bible, compendium ("The manual contained the assembly instructions").
Ant. automatic, mechanized; scholarly treatise.

manual delivery [de · *liv* · e · ree] *n.* Physical delivery of an article by one person to another; hand delivery.

manual labor [*lay* · ber] *n.* Physical labor; work done by hand, which relies largely on physical strength rather than to skill.

manufacture [man · yoo · *fak* · cher] *n.* The process of converting raw or unfinished material into a form suitable for use.
v. To make, build, or produce from raw or processed materials, by hand or by machine, into a form suitable for use.
➤ *n.* construction, production, assembling, creation, casting, completion.
v. build, assemble, fashion, form, cast, frame ("The company manufactured cars").

manufacturer [man · yoo · *fak* · cher · er] *n.* A person or company engaged in manufacturing. *See* manufacture.
➤ maker, builder, capitalist, industrialist, company.

manufacturer's liability
[man · yoo · *fak* · cher · erz ly · e · *bil* · i · tee] *n.* *See* product liability.

manufacturing corporation
[man · yoo · *fak* · cher · ing kore · per · *ay* · shen] *n.* A corporation engaged in the business of converting raw or processed material into a form suitable for use. *See* manufacture.

manufacturing establishment
[man · yoo · *fak* · cher · ing es · *tab* · lish · ment] *n.* A place, normally a factory, where machinery is used to produce a finished product from raw materials. *See* manufacture.

manumission [man · yoo · *mish* · en] *n.* Liberation from a condition of servitude by the voluntary act of the master.
➤ liberation, enfranchisement.
Ant. slavery.

Mapp v. Ohio [map *ver* · sus o · *hy* · oh] *n.* A 1961 decision of the Supreme Court (367 U.S. 643) holding that evidence seized by the police in violation of the **Fourth Amendment** ban on **unreasonable searches and seizures** is inadmissible in a criminal prosecution in state court, under the **exclusionary rule**, which applies to the states by virtue of the **Fourteenth Amendment**.

Marbury v. Madison [*mar* · bur · ee *ver* · sus *mad* · i · sen] *n.* An 1803 decision of the Supreme Court (5 U.S. 137) of great significance in American **constitutional law**, which established the constitutional doctrine that the Constitution grants to the **judicial branch** of government the

M

power of **judicial review**, that is, the power to decide whether the actions of the **legislative branch** (for EXAMPLE, statutes enacted; investigations conducted) and the **executive branch** (for EXAMPLE, **executive orders** and **appointments**) are constitutional.

margin [*mar* · jin] *n.* 1. A sum of money, or its value in **securities**, deposited with a broker by a customer to protect the broker against loss in buying or selling for the customer due to the rise and fall of the market. *See* margin account. 2. An edge; leeway; slack. 3. A border; a boundary.
➤ rim, fringe, confine, skirt, bound, edge, brim ("the margin of the page").

margin account [a · *kount*] *n.* A system used by **securities brokers** to finance the purchase of **securities**, under which the customer makes purchases by paying the broker only a percentage of the cost of the securities to be bought, the broker pledges her own credit to finance the balance of cost, and the securities themselves serve as collateral. **Commodities** are purchased in this manner as well. *Also see* short sale.

margin call *n.* A demand made upon a customer by a **securities broker** to increase the money or **securities** on deposit in the customer's **margin account**, generally because of a deterioration in the value of the collateral securities.

margin transaction [tran · *zak* · shen] *n.* A transaction in **securities** or **commodities** made through a broker on a **margin account**. Such a transaction is often referred to as "buying on margin." *See* on margin.

marihuana [mehr · i · *wan* · ah] *n.* Same as **marijuana**.

marijuana [mehr · i · *wan* · ah] *n.* The cannabis sativa plant, a drug. Marijuana is a **controlled substance**; its possession, sale, or distribution is a crime. **Hashish** is produced from the resin of marijuana. The presence of marijuana in the blood or urine may be detected by **radioimmunoassay**. *See* THC. The police nickname for marijuana is "GLM" (for "green leafy material"). Hemp is also produced from the cannabis sativa plant.
➤ pot, weed, reefer, grass, smoke, doobie.

marine [ma · *reen*] *adj.* Pertaining to the sea, or to transportation, commerce, or other activity relating to the sea or to navigation. Marine actions and transactions are generally governed by the law of **admiralty**.
➤ aquatic, oceanic, naval, pelagic, coastal, maritime ("marine life").
Ant. terrestrial.

marine contract [kon · trakt] *n.* Same as **maritime contract**.

marine insurance [in · *shoor* · ense] *n.* An insurance policy covering the **risk of loss** to a ship or its cargo from the perils of the sea. *Compare* inland marine insurance.

marital [*mehr* · i · tel] *adj.* Pertaining or relating to marriage, the marriage relationship, or the married state.
➤ spousal, matrimonial, conjugal, nuptial, wedded ("marital status").

marital agreement [a · *gree* · ment] *n.* An agreement between two people who are married to each other (a **postnuptial agreement**), or two people who are about to marry (a **prenuptial agreement**), with respect to the disposition of the marital property or property owned by either spouse before the marriage, with respect to the rights of either in the property of the other, or with respect to support. *See also* property settlement.

marital communications privilege [kum · yoo · ni · *kay* · shenz priv · i · lej] *n.* Neither spouse may testify with respect to private communications between them, and either may prevent the other from doing so, except with respect to proceedings, civil or criminal, specifically exempted by statute (EXAMPLE: a prosecution of one spouse for a crime against the other). Whether the nontestifying spouse may waive the privilege by consenting to the testimony depends upon the law of the jurisdiction. The marital communications privilege is sometimes referred to as the **husband-wife privilege**. *See* privileged communication. *Compare* interspousal immunity.

marital deduction [de · *duk* · shen] *n.* In computing the **taxable estate**, a deduction allowed under both the federal **estate tax** and **gift tax** with respect to property passing from one spouse to the other.

M

marital duties [*dew* · teez] *n.* The obligations of spouses to each other as a result of marriage. EXAMPLE: **consortium**. *Compare* marital rights.

marital portion [*pore* · shun] *n.* A term that may refer to either **dower** or **dowry**.

marital property [*prop* · er · tee] *n.* Property acquired by the parties during the marriage, which a court will divide between the former spouses upon dissolution of the marriage if the parties have not themselves made disposition by **marital agreement**. *See and compare* community property; equitable distribution; separate property.

marital rights *n.* The rights of both spouses created by marriage. EXAMPLES: **consortium**; rights relating to **marital property**. *Compare* marital duties.

marital settlement [*setl* · ment] *n. See* marital agreement.

marital share *n.* Same as **marital portion**.

maritime [*mehr* · i · time] *adj.* Pertaining to the sea; pertaining to **navigable waters**.
➤ naval, oceanic, aquatic, seafaring, riparian, pelagic.
Ant. terrestrial.

maritime belt *n. See* territorial waters.

maritime contract [*kon* · trakt] *n.* A contract relating to a transaction involving transportation on **navigable waters**.

maritime law *n.* The law dealing with rights and obligations with respect to the use of **navigable waters** for the transportation of persons or property by ships, either commercially or noncommercially. The United States system of maritime law is a federal system, which is governed by federal statute as interpreted and applied by **admiralty courts**. *Also see* admiralty; admiralty jurisdiction.

maritime lien [leen] *n.* A **lien** on a vessel in favor of a person furnishing it with supplies, repairs, or other necessaries for use on **navigable waters**. Such a lien may also arise from a **maritime tort**.

maritime tort *n.* An **injury** to person or property of which **admiralty courts** will take **jurisdiction** because it occurred on **navigable waters**.

mark *n.* 1. A sign or symbol (EXAMPLES: an "X"; a thumbprint) made by an illiterate or disabled person as a substitute for a complete signature. A mark is a valid signature when witnessed as required by state statute. 2. A **trademark**; a **service mark**; a **collective mark**. 3. An indication of something; an indicator; indicia; evidence. USAGE: "Possession is only one mark of ownership." *See also* badges of fraud. 4. Another spelling of **marque**. 5. A line; a dividing line. EXAMPLES: high water mark; low water mark. 6. A sucker; a dupe.
➤ indicator, signal, trademark, identification, symbol, initials, indicator ("A bill of sale is a mark of ownership"); line, border ("low water mark"); criterion, standard, norm, indication, sign, measure ("a mark of excellence").

marker [*mar* · ker] *n. See* monument.

market [*mar* · ket] *n.* 1. A place designated for selling things—items such as **securities** and **commodities**, for EXAMPLE, as well as merchandise or food. *See* over-the-counter market; stock market. 2. A region where things are sold or can be sold. USAGE: "Our company is trying to break into the Asian market." 3. The state of business and prices on a stock exchange or **commodity exchange**. For EXAMPLE, "the stock market is falling" means the price of the average share on the stock exchange is falling. 4. A short term for stock market. 5. The degree of demand for something. For EXAMPLE, "there is an active market for gold" means that a lot of gold is being bought and sold. *See* forestalling the market; money market; open market.
➤ trade center, exchange, marketplace, bazaar, mart, shop ("Get me some bread from the market"); region, section ("Our company is trying to break into the Asian market"); consumer demand, want, vogue, call, need, interest ("There is an active market for gold").

market price *n.* 1. The price of something as determined by the demand for it in relation to the supply. *See* market value. 2. The quoted price. *See* market quotations.

market quotations [kwo · *tay* · shenz] *n.* The current prices for **commodities** or **securities** bought and sold on a stock exchange or **commodity exchange**.

M

market rate *n. See* market price.

market value [*val* · yoo] *n.* The price a buyer will pay for something, and a seller will accept for it, when both have a reasonable knowledge of the appropriate facts and neither is under undue pressure to buy or to sell; the amount being paid in the **open market**. *See* fair market value; market price. *See also* actual cash value; fair cash value.

marketable [*mar* · ket · ebl] *adj.* Salable; that which can be sold.
➤ saleable, merchantable, commercial, in vogue, vendable, tradable ("marketable title").

marketable title [*ty* · tel] *n.* A **title** free from **encumbrances** for which a person of **reasonable prudence** and intelligence, who is well informed as to the facts and their legal significance, would be willing to pay **fair market value**. Property to which the owner has marketable title is salable property. *See* clear title; good title; legal title; record title. *Compare* bad title; unmarketable title.

marketing contract [*mar* · ket · ing *kon* · trakt] *n.* A contract between a **cooperative marketing association** and its members, under which the members commit themselves to market their products exclusively through the association and the association agrees to obtain the best possible price for the products.

marking up [*mark* · ing up] *n.* The detailed revision of a **bill** by a **legislative committee**.

markup [*mark* · up] *n.* In arriving at the selling price of an item, the amount the seller adds to cost to cover overhead and permit a profit.
➤ increase, profit, margin.

marque [mark] (*French*) *n.* A seizure of goods.

marque and reprisal [re · *prize* · el] *n. See* letters of marque and reprisal.

marriage [*mehr* · ej] *n.* 1. The relationship of a man and a woman legally united as husband and wife. Marriage is a contract binding the parties until one dies or until a divorce or annulment occurs. *See* marital duties; marital rights. 2. The act of

becoming married; the marriage ceremony. *See* common law marriage; consensual marriage; informal marriage; plural marriage; proxy marriage; putative marriage; restraint of marriage; void marriage; voidable marriage.
➤ matrimony, wedlock, nuptial state, nuptials, sacrament, espousal ("to be joined in marriage").
Ant. divorce.

marriage certificate [ser · *tif* · i · ket] *n.* A **certificate** that evidences a marriage, prepared by the person officiating at the ceremony and usually required by state law. *Compare* marriage license.

marriage license [*ly* · sense] *n.* Authorization to marry issued by the state in which the ceremony is to occur. It is a **condition precedent** to a **ceremonial marriage**. *Compare* marriage certificate.

marriage portion [*pore* · shen] *n.* Same as **marital portion**.

marriage settlement [*setl* · ment] *n.* Same as **marital agreement**.

married woman [*woom* · en] *See feme covert*; feme sole trader.

marshal [*mar* · shel] *n.* 1. A **United States Marshal**; i.e., an officer of the **executive branch** of the federal government, whose duties are to execute the orders of the federal courts, for EXAMPLE, **summonses, writs**, or **warrants**. 2. Generally, a court officer with the authority to carry out **legal process**. 3. A town or village police officer, in some jurisdictions.
v. To assemble; to arrange and dispose of in proper order; to collect; to round up. *Also see* commingle; commingling.
➤ *n.* officer, deputy, chief, bailiff.
v. gather, shepherd, allocate, regiment, array, direct, lead, order ("marshal the payroll").

marshaling [*mar* · shel · ing] *n.* Assembling; arranging and disposing of things in proper order; collecting; rounding up. *See* marshal.
➤ collecting, commingling, arranging, prioritizing.

marshaling assets [*ass* · ets] *n.* 1. The collecting of **assets**, often by a **trustee in bankruptcy** or a **receiver**, for the purpose of paying debts in accordance with their **priority**. *See* commingle; commingling. 2. The principle that when two or more creditors seek satisfaction out of the assets of their common debtor, and one of them is entitled to resort to two funds but the other has recourse to only one of the funds, the first creditor may be required to seek satisfaction from the fund the second creditor cannot touch, so that the second creditor may, if possible, have her claim satisfied out of the fund that is subject to the claims of both creditors. The situation arises when, for EXAMPLE, a senior mortgagee has a **lien** on two parcels of land, and a junior mortgagee has a lien on only one of the parcels (*see* junior mortgage; senior mortgage).

marshaling liens [leenz] *n.* An expression sometimes used in place of **marshaling assets**.

martial law [*mar* · shel] *n.* Law created and administered by military authorities, by means of which a civilian population is governed or controlled, usually in time of war or when the civil authority is otherwise unable to function. *Note* that martial law is not **military law**. *Compare* military law.

marvelous [*mar* · ve · lus] *adj.* 1. Causing wonder or amazement. 2. Extraordinarily impressive; wonderful.
➤ amazing, astounding, incredible, extraordinary, fantastic, unbelievable ("Otis's marvelous catch"); great, fantastic, splendid, spectacular, divine, magnificent ("Darling, you look marvelous").

Mary Carter agreement [*mare* · ee *kar* · ter a · *gree*ment] *n.* An agreement in which a codefendant secretly settles a lawsuit with the plaintiff and continues as an **illusory** codefendant; i.e., an agreement that creates a sham defendant who may have an interest in seeing a verdict rendered against his codefendant. Mary Carter agreements are illegal in some states; in others, they are legal under some circumstances.

mask *n.* 1. A cover for the face. 2. A guise; false appearance.
v. To disguise an object or person.
➤ *n.* cover, façade, veil, visor; pretense, pretext, simulation, semblance, veneer, posture.
v. hide, cover, dissemble, pretend.

mass *n.* An aggregate of people or things.
➤ carload, bundle, block, accumulation, mob, gob, bunch ("a mass of people").

mass picketing [*pik* · e · ting] *n.* The use of pickets in large numbers in a labor dispute. Mass picketing is a form of intimidation and is subject to **injunction** as well as to an **action** for **damages** if it results in **injury** to the employer's business. It may also be an **unfair labor practice**. *See* picket.

Massachusetts business trust [mass · e · *chew* · sets *biz* · ness] *n.* Same as **Massachusetts trust**, **business trust**, or **common law trust**.

Massachusetts trust [mass · e · *chew* · sets] *n.* Same as **Massachusetts business trust**, **business trust**, or **common law trust**.

master [*mas* · ter] *adj.* Dominant; principal, main; controlling.
n. 1. A somewhat outdated, but sometimes still used, term for employer. *See* employer. *Also see* master and servant. 2. A person appointed by the court to assist with certain judicial functions (EXAMPLE: taking testimony) in a specific case. *See* master's report. *Also see* special master. 3. A person who possesses the highest degree of skill in her trade. USAGE: "master plumber"; "master electrician." *Compare* apprentice; journeyman. 4. The person in command of a ship, usually called "captain." 5. A person who has control or authority over others.
v. To become proficient at; to learn thoroughly.
➤ *adj.* first, paramount, dominant, principal, main, controlling ("the master agreement").
n. officer, official, employer, boss, director, leader, commandant, head ("office master"); artisan, expert, professional ("a master at karate").
v. learn, study, excel, grasp, acquire, understand, comprehend ("to master a foreign language").

master agreement [a · *gree* · ment] *n.* In labor law, a **collective bargaining agreement** between a union and a trade association or the major employers in an industry. Such an agreement controls the terms of the employment which the association's members provide to their employees.

master and servant [*ser* · vent] *n.* The equivalent of the more modern terms "employer" and "employee." *See* servant.

M

master in chancery [*chan* · se · ree] *n.* In a **court of chancery**, an officer of the court who assists the judge and performs such judicial duties (EXAMPLE: taking testimony) and **ministerial duties** (EXAMPLE: administering oaths) as the judge assigns. Many of the duties of a master in chancery are similar to those of a **court commissioner** or **referee**. *See* master's report.

master policy [*pol* · i · see] *n.* An insurance policy, usually life or health insurance, providing coverage to the members of a group (EXAMPLE: a bar association). The contract is between the carrier and the group. *See* group annuity; group insurance.

master's report [*mas* · terz re · *port*] *n.* A written report that a **master** or a **master in chancery** is required to file with the judge upon performing judicial duties.

master-servant rule [*mas* · ter-ser · vent] *n.* *See respondeat superior.*

material [ma · *teer* · i · el] *adj.* 1. Important; relating to substance rather than form; going to the merits; relevant. *Compare* immaterial. 2. Pertaining to the physical, **tangible**, or **corporeal**, as distinguished from the **intangible, incorporeal**, or spiritual.
n. 1. Any substance used in manufacturing or construction. *See* materialman; materialman's lien. 2. Facts or ideas incorporated by a writer into his work.
➤ *adj.* important, relevant, significant, influential, consequential, applicable, primary, substantial ("material witness"). *Ant.* insignificant, unimportant, irrelevant. *n.* supplies, goods, fabric, bolt, cloth, stock ("We didn't have enough material for the dress"); data, evidence, facts, information, notes ("material to support the thesis").

material allegation [al · e · *gay* · shen] *n.* A statement in a **pleading** essential to the **claim** or **defense**, which cannot be stricken from the pleading without leaving the pleading insufficient. *See* striking a pleading. *Compare* immaterial allegation.

material alteration [all · te · *ray* · shen] *n.* An **alteration** of a written **instrument** that gives the instrument a legal effect or significance different from that which it originally had.

material breach *n.* A **breach of contract** sufficiently substantial to give the **injured party** the right to **rescind** the contract or to maintain an **action** for **damages**, or both.

material error [*err* · er] *n.* *See* prejudicial error.

material evidence [*ev* · i · dense] *n.* Evidence that goes to the **substantive** matters in dispute or has a legitimate bearing and effective influence on the decision of the case; evidence which is pertinent. *See* evidence, relevant evidence. *Compare* immaterial evidence. *Also see* competent evidence.

material fact *n.* 1. A **fact** that has the capacity to induce a person to take an action, for EXAMPLE, make a contract, buy something, or enter into a marriage. 2. For purposes of **pleading**, a fact that constitutes a necessary part of the plaintiff's **cause of action** or the defendant's **defense**. 3. For purposes of **summary judgment**, a fact upon which the outcome of the litigation depends. 4. For the purpose of **voiding** an insurance policy, a fact which if known to the agent would have caused her either to decline coverage or to quote a higher premium.

material misrepresentation [mis · rep · re · zen · *tay* · shen] *n.* *See* material representation.

material mistake [*mis* · take] *n.* A mistake so substantial that it is apparent the parties did not act with knowledge of the true facts. (EXAMPLE: a recital of 3,000 acres in a land lease, when the **lessor**, in fact, owns only 1,000 acres.) A material mistake usually justifies **reformation** or **rescission** of an agreement. *See* mistake. *Compare* mutual mistake.

material representation [rep · re · zen · *tay* · shen] *n.* A statement or **representation** of fact that influences a person to do something (EXAMPLE: make a purchase) she would not have done if the statement or representation had not been made. A fraudulent or deliberately inaccurate statement that is intended to cause, or causes, a person to act in **reliance** is called a **material misrepresentation** or a **fraudulent misrepresentation**.

material variance [*vehr* · i · ense] *n.* *See* fatal variance.

M

material witness [*wit* · ness] *n.* A witness who is vital because she is the only person, or one of only a few people, who witnessed an event of great importance to a decision in a case or to the successful conclusion of an investigation.

materialman [ma · *teer* · i · el · man] *n.* A person who supplies materials for the construction of a building or other structure. *See* materialman's lien.

materialman's lien [ma · *teer* · i · el · manz leen] *n.* A **lien** provided by law, often under a **mechanic's lien** statute, for the protection of a person who supplies materials for use in the construction of a building or other improvement. *See* materialman.

maternal [muh · *ter* · nul] *adj.* Relating to the mother; caring; nurturing.
➤ motherly, protective, nourishing, sensitive, caring, warm, tender.

maternal line [ma · *ter* · nel] *n.* A line of inheritance or ancestry from or through the mother. *Compare* paternal line.

mathematical [math · e · *mat* · ih · kul] *adj.* Concerning mathematics; statistical; accurate.
➤ accurate, scientific, exact, statistical, computed, meticulous.
Ant. unproven, speculative.

mathematical evidence
[math · e · *mat* · i · kel ev · i · dense] *n.* Evidence based upon mathematical computation or demonstration; evidence that is certain and reliable. *See* demonstrative evidence. *Compare* moral evidence.

matrimonial [mat · ri · *moh* · ni · el] *adj.* Pertaining to marriage or to the married state.
➤ betrothed, conjugal, engaged, marital, nuptial, wedded.

matrimonial action [*ak* · shen] *n.* A legal action based upon or arising out of the marital relationship. EXAMPLES: an action for divorce; an action for **separate maintenance**.

matrimonial cohabitation
[koh · hab · i · *tay* · shen] *n.* A term meaning two people living together as husband and wife or living together by all appearances as husband and wife. *See* common law marriage.

matrimonial domicile [*dom* · i · sile] *n.* The place where two people live together as husband and wife. *See* domicile.

matrimonial misconduct [mis · *kon* · dukt] *n.* An offense against the vows of marriage.

matter [*mat* · er] *n.* 1. Facts that make up a **ground of action** or defense. USAGE: "His amended complaint contains **new matter**." Matter should not be confused with evidence; evidence is that which tends to prove the existence of a fact or facts. *See* proof. 2. A case; a controversy. 3. A subject or subject matter; a question; an issue; a transaction. *See* in the matter of; subject matter jurisdiction. 4. Printed material. 5. That which has substance; that which is composed of material.
➤ issue, topic, question, problem, case, proposition ("the matter in question"); amount, body, material, object, stuff, thing ("gray matter").

matter in controversy [*kon* · tre · ver · see] *n.* The subject of the litigation; the matter concerning which suit is brought and upon which the trial proceeds. *See* amount in controversy; case or controversy. *See also* matter in issue.

matter in dispute [dis · *pyoot*] *n.* Same as **matter in controversy**.

matter in issue [*ish* · ew] *n.* The question presented by the **pleadings**; the matter upon which the plaintiff's **action** is based and which the defendant **controverts** by her **answer**. *See* matter in controversy.

matter of course *n.* *See* of course.

matter of fact *n.* Whether something is true or real; whether an event took place; in a case involving a jury, that which is for the jury to decide based upon the evidence. *Compare* matter of law. *See* fact; question of fact.

matter of form *n.* That which relates to the *manner* in which a **cause of action** is **pled**, or the *form* in which it is pled, as distinguished from a **matter of substance**, which goes to the existence of a cause of action. *See* form. *See and compare* matter of fact; matter of law.

matter of law *n.* The application, meaning, or interpretation of the law by which a case is to be decided. Matters of law are always decided by the judge, as

M

opposed to the jury. *Compare* matter of fact. *See* law; question of law.

matter of record [*rek* · erd] *n.* A matter or **proceeding** entered on the court records; a matter recorded in the place and manner required by law. EXAMPLES: a **judgment** entered on the **judgment docket**; the official transcript of a trial; a deed or mortgage recorded with the **recorder of deeds**. *See* entry of judgment.

matter of substance [*sub* · stense] *n.* A matter going to the existence or merits of a case. *Compare* matter of form.

mature [ma · *choor*] *adj.* 1. Due and payable. 2. Full-grown; ripe; fully developed. *v.* 1. To become due and payable. USAGE: "When does this **note** mature?" *See* due date. 2. To ripen; to develop fully; to reach maturity.
➤ *adj.* experienced, ripe, dependable, adult, grown up, wise, seasoned, of age ("The boy seemed mature for his age").
v. ripen, come of age, perfect, age, maturate, evolve ("When does this promissory note mature?").

matured [ma · *choord*] *adj.* To be completed and ripe for payment. *See* mature; maturity. *See also* liquidated; liquidated claim.
➤ ripened, come due, due, finished ("The bond has matured").

maturity [ma · *choor* · i · tee] *n.* The state of full development, readiness, or completion.
➤ development, readiness, perfection, prime, reliability, dependability, advancement, cultivation, completion.

maturity date *n.* The date specified in a **negotiable instrument** for payment; the due date.

maxim [*mak* · sim] *n.* A time-tried rule of thumb based upon reason, but not a law in itself, which courts may apply when appropriate, particularly in **equitable actions**. EXAMPLES: "let the buyer beware!" (*see caveat emptor*) or "he who seeks equity must do so with clean hands" (*see* **clean hands doctrine**).
➤ precept, canon, teaching, adage, dictum, rule.

may *v.* 1. A word used to express permission; a term that the courts generally construe as advisory or optional rather than mandatory. *Compare* shall. *See and compare*

directory provision; directory statute; mandatory provision; mandatory statute. 2. A word used to express possibility or contingency. USAGE: "The trier of fact may assess punitive damages if warranted."

mayhem [*may* · hem] *n.* A form of **aggravated assault**, the crime of maliciously disabling or disfiguring a person. *See* maim.
➤ anarchy, commotion, disorder, pandemonium, trouble, violence.

mayor [*may* · er] *n.* The chief municipal officer of a city or town, charged with responsibility for overseeing the administration of the municipality where she has been elected or appointed.
➤ executive, chief executive, officer, administrator, politician.

mayor's court [*may* · erz] *n.* A **municipal court** or **city court** presided over by the mayor. *See* court of limited jurisdiction.

McCulloch v. Maryland [mih · *kull* · a *ver* · sus *mehr* · i · land] *n.* A landmark Supreme Court case, decided in 1819 (17 U.S. 316), which established the doctrine that Congress has the **implied power** to enact legislation necessary to carry out those powers expressly granted to it by the Constitution.

McNabb-Mallory rule [mik · *nab*-mal · e · ree] *n.* A rule of **constitutional law**, applicable to federal prosecutions, that if a person is not promptly **arraigned** after his arrest, any confession he gives may be inadmissible. Some delay is permitted, however, as delineated in the **Federal Rules of Criminal Procedure** and other federal statutes. *See* arraignment.

mean *n.* A midpoint between extremes or between two or more quantities, measurements, distances, weights, or the like. *Compare* average. *v.* To intend. USAGE: "He did not mean to cause problems, but he did."
➤ *n.* average, midpoint, medium, balance, center, par.
v. suggest, propose, imply, design, wish, try.

mean high tide *n.* The average height of all high tides at a given location over a period of years. Mean high tide is also referred to as ordinary high tide.

mean low tide *n.* Also referred to as ordinary low tide, the line of the average

M

low tide taken at a specific point over a period of years.

meander [me · *an* · der] *v.* To follow a winding course.

➤ twist, snake, wander, change, drift, roam.

meander line *n.* A line established in surveying land adjacent to a river or stream, running from one point to another along the bank. It provides a means of determining the quantity of land to be paid for by a purchaser of a tract bounded by a stream or river. *See* survey.

meaning [*meen* · ing] *n.* The thing that is conveyed, signified, or intended.

➤ message, significance, content, interpretation, purpose, essence, message, gist, purport ("the meaning of the statute").

means *n.* 1. Financial resources. *See* visible means of support. 2. An instrumentality or method for accomplishing a purpose. 3. Wherewithal; capability. *See* ways and means committee.

➤ assets, backing, bankroll, budget, income, stake ("the means to support the family"); aid, equipment, instrumentality, medium, organ, mode ("the means to an end").

means test *n.* The requirement for certain kinds of publicly funded aid (EXAMPLE: **AFDC**) that the recipient be indigent or of limited financial resources. *See* pauper's oath.

measure [*mezh* · er] *n.* 1. The standard by which the size, weight, quantity, or quality of anything is determined. EXAMPLES: inches; bushels; acres. 2. A term for a statute or **resolution** enacted by a legislative body.

➤ criterion, standard, gauge, scale, yardstick, test ("What is the measure for ocean depth?"); act, enactment, statute, regulation, bill, rule ("the price-supports measure").

measure of care *n.* *See* standard of care.

measure of damages [*dam* · e · jez] *n.* The rules for arriving at the amount of **damages** a person is entitled to recover in a given lawsuit.

mechanic's lien [me · *kan* · iks *lee* · en] *n.* A **lien** created by law for the purpose of securing payment for work performed or materials furnished in constructing or repairing a building or other structure. *Also see* materialman's lien.

mechanical equivalent [me · *kan* · i · kel e · *kwiv* · e · lent] *n.* In **patent** law, a term for a **device** that accomplishes the same result as that achieved by the patent alleged to be infringed. *See* infringement of patent.

mediate [*mee* · dee · it] *adj.* In the middle; secondary; subordinate; indirect.
v. [*mee* · dee · ayt] To intercede; to step in; to arbitrate. *See and compare* arbitration; mediation.

➤ *adj.* secondary, subordinate, indirect ("mediate descent").
v. negotiate, settle, judge, intercede, moderate, referee, arbitrate ("to mediate a dispute").

mediate descent [de · *sent*] *n.* In the most common use of the term, **descent** to an heir through an intermediate link of **consanguinity**. EXAMPLE: from grandfather to grandson (the father having died). *Compare* immediate descent.

mediation [mee · dee · *ay* · shen] *n.* The voluntary resolution of a dispute in an amicable manner. One of the primary uses of **mediators**, also called **conciliators**, is in settling labor disputes. Professional mediators are available for that purpose through the **Federal Mediation and Conciliation Service**. Mediation differs from **arbitration** in that a mediator, unlike an **arbitrator**, does not render a decision. *See* alternative dispute resolution; conciliation.

➤ intervention, conciliation, negotiation, interposition, arbitration, intercession.

Mediation and Conciliation Service [mee · dee · *ay* · shen and ken · sil · ee · *ay* · shen *ser* · viss] *n.* *See* Federal Mediation and Conciliation Service.

mediator [*mee* · dee · ay · tor] *n.* An impartial person trained to assist parties in resolving their disputes amicably. The terms "mediator" and "conciliator" are used interchangeably. *Compare* arbitrator. *See* mediation.

➤ go-between, intermediary, referee, liaison, advocate, medium, umpire, conciliator.

Medicaid [*med* · i · kade] *n.* A program of publicly funded medical and hospital care for persons with limited income or no income. It is a form of **public assistance** jointly subsidized by the federal government

M

and the states; a **means test** is imposed to determine eligibility. *Compare* Medicare. *See* public funds.

medical examiner [*med · i · kel eg · zam · i · ner*] *n.* 1. In some jurisdictions, a public official who has the same authority as a coroner. 2. A physician retained by an insurance company to examine applicants for insurance, particularly life insurance.

medical insurance [*med · i · kel in · shoor · ense*] *n.* Insurance providing for the payment of medical expenses in the event of sickness or accident. *See* insurance.

medical jurisprudence [*med · i · kel joo · ris · proo · dense*] *n.* A branch of the science of medicine having to do with legal questions. *See* jurisprudence. *Also see* forensic medicine.

medical malpractice [*med · i · kel mal · prak · tiss*] *n.* A physician's negligent failure to observe the appropriate **standard of care** in providing services to a patient; also, misconduct while engaging in the practice of medicine. Like **legal malpractice**, medical malpractice is a **tort** if it causes **injury**. *See* malpractice.

medical record [*med · i · kel rek · erd*] *n.* A record kept by physicians and by hospitals reflecting a patient's progress in treatment, medications administered or prescribed, and the like. The form and content of medical records are governed by state statute.

Medicare [*med · i · kare*] *n.* A program of medical and hospital insurance for older Americans provided by the federal government and financed by **social security** funds. Age, not financial need, determines eligibility. *Compare* Medicaid.

medium of exchange [*me · di · um of eks · chaynj*] *n.* Anything used as money, or anything that can be exchanged for goods, services, or other things of value. *See* legal tender.

meet *v.* 1. To come together; to contact. 2. To convene for a common purpose.
➤ connect, join, abut, link; face, greet, come across, assemble, rally, convene, gather.

meeting [*meet · ing*] *n.* 1. An assembly or gathering of people, usually for a specific purpose. EXAMPLES: a stockholders' meeting;

a union meeting; a prayer meeting. *See* annual meeting; called meeting; creditors' meeting; regular meeting; special meeting; stated meeting; town meeting. 2. A coming together from opposite directions. EXAMPLE: a **meeting of the minds**.
➤ assembly, convocation, caucus, gathering, congregation, session, rally ("Stockholder's meeting").

meeting of creditors [*kred · i · terz*] *n.* *See* creditors' meeting.

meeting of the minds *n.* The mutual assent of the parties to a contract with respect to all of the principal terms of the contract. A meeting of the minds is essential to the creation of a legally enforceable contract, but in the event of a dispute, the courts will look to the objective evidence rather than the subjective intention of a party.

member [*mem · ber*] *n.* 1. A person who belongs to an organization, or a person who is part of a family. 2. A part of the body, for EXAMPLE, a leg, hand, or toe.
➤ associate, fellow, teammate, enrollee, initiate ("fraternity member"); arm, component, element, limb, organ, piece ("to maim or lose a member").

member bank *n.* A bank that is a member of the **Federal Reserve System**.

member of Congress [*kong · gress*] *n.* A member of the Congress of the United States, either the House of Representatives (a congressperson) or the Senate (a senator), although the term is often used to mean only members of the House.

membership corporation [*mem · ber · ship kore · per · ay · shen*] *n.* A **nonprofit corporation** existing for charitable, fraternal, religious, or educational purposes. The participants are members rather than shareholders.

memoranda [*mem · o · ran · da*] *n.* *Plural* of **memorandum**. *See* memorandum.

memorandum [*mem · o · ran · dum*] *n.* 1. A writing made for the purpose of preserving events or ideas in one's memory or communicating them to someone else; a means of reminding oneself or others of something to be done or remembered. 2. A writing made for the purpose of recording and evidencing the terms of an agreement prior

M

to drafting it, i.e., a **memorandum of understanding**. 3. A writing made for the purpose of recording or evidencing any transaction. 4. For the purpose of meeting the requirements of the **statute of frauds** or (as to contracts for the sale of goods over $500) of the **Uniform Commercial Code**, a signed writing containing the terms of the contract.

➤ memo, notation, recapitulation, dispatch, letter, summary, precis, message ("The memorandum concerned safety precautions").

memorandum check *n.* A **check** with "Memorandum" or "Mem." written across it, not intended for **presentation** to the bank, but simply as evidence of a debt owed by the **maker** to the **payee** to be satisfied by the maker.

memorandum decision [de · *sizh* · en] *n.* A court decision, usually consisting of a brief paragraph announcing the court's **judgment**, without an in-depth opinion.

memorandum of law *n.* A written statement submitted to a court for the purpose of persuading it of the correctness of one's position. It is similar to a brief, although usually not as extensive.

memorandum of understanding [un · der · *stan* · ding] *n. See* memorandum.

memorandum sale *n.* Same as **sale on approval**.

memorial [mem · *or* · i · el] *n.* 1. A **memorandum**. 2. A petition or protest presented in writing to the legislature or to the **chief executive officer** of the government (EXAMPLES: the president; the governor; the mayor). 3. A short note, **abstract**, **memorandum**, or rough draft of the **orders of court** from which full records may be made later. 4. Something erected in remembrance of a person or event; a monument.
adj. Commemorative.

➤ *n.* memorandum, petition, protest, note. *adj.* commemorative, monumental, ceremonial, dedicatory, celebrative ("memorial statue").

memorialize [mem · *or* · i · el · ize] *v.* 1. To write down or otherwise informally make a record of an event or a transaction, to preserve it in memory or to communicate

it to someone else. *See* memorandum. 2. To petition by **memorial** those who govern. 3. To commemorate.

➤ honor, dedicate, observe, conserve ("memorialized in solid gold").

memory [*mem* · e · ree] *n.* 1. Historically in the law, the words "memory" and "mind" had the same meaning, i.e., **mental capacity**. EXAMPLE: The phrase "sound and disposing mind and memory," commonly found in wills, is a declaration by a **testator** that she possesses **testamentary capacity**, that is, the mental capacity to make a will. *See* mind and memory. *Also see* legal memory; refreshing memory. 2. In more common, and more modern, usage, the power to retain knowledge and to recognize and recall past knowledge. *See* recollection. *Also see* past recollection recorded; present recollection recorded; present recollection revived.

➤ remembrance, recall, recreation, recollection, subconsciousness, thought ("The witness's memory isn't as good as it used to be").

mens [menz] *(Latin) n.* Mind; intention; reason; understanding; will.

mens rea [*ray* · ah] *n.* An "answerable intent," i.e., an intent for which one is answerable; an evil intent; a guilty mind; a **criminal intent**. In combination with *actus reus* (a guilty or criminal act), *mens rea* is an essential element of any crime except **regulatory crimes** or **strict liability crimes** and some **petty offenses** and **infractions**. *Mens rea* may be inferred or presumed. *See* intent; presumed intent; *scienter. Compare* specific intent.

mensa et thoro [*men* · sa et *thoh* · roh] *(Latin) adj.* Means "bed and board." *See* divorce a mensa et thoro.

mental [*men* · tel] *adj.* Pertaining to the mind and the emotions.

➤ psychic, rational, thinking, brainy, cerebral, thoughtful, psychological.

mental anguish [*ang* · wish] *n.* 1. Mental suffering, as distinguished from physical pain, but including the mental reaction to physical pain; **pain and suffering**. **Damages** are recoverable for mental anguish caused by a **tort**. 2. A ground for divorce, more commonly referred to as **mental cruelty**. 3. Grief; distress; fright; anxiety; depression.

M

mental capacity [ke · *pass* · i · tee] *n.*
The ability to understand the nature and
character of the transaction in which one is
involved (EXAMPLES: making a contract; committing a crime). *See* capacity; competency.
Compare mental incapacity.

mental condition [kon · *dish* · en] *n.* 1. A
term referring to **mental capacity** or **mental
incapacity**. *See also* insanity. 2. A term
meaning state of mind or mental state.

mental cruelty [*crew* · el · tee] *n.* As a
ground for divorce, conduct by one spouse
that is damaging to, or that can damage,
the mental or physical health of the other
spouse. *See* indignities; mental anguish.

mental defect [*dee* · fekt] *n.* A defect in
the mind of a person. For purposes of the
Durham rule of criminal responsibility,
a condition that caused the criminal act
for which the defendant is being tried.
See insanity. *Compare* mental disease.

mental disability [dis · e · *bil* · i · tee] *n.*
A **disability** of the mind that substantially
affects mental or emotional processes.
See insanity.

mental disease [di · *zeez*] *n.* A disease
affecting the mind. For purposes of the
Durham rule of criminal responsibility,
a condition that caused the criminal act
for which the defendant is being tried.
See insanity. *Compare* mental defect.

mental illness [*ill* · ness] *n.* *See* insanity.

mental incapacity [in · ke · *pass* · i · tee]
n. The inability to understand the nature
and character of the transaction in which
one is involved (EXAMPLES: making a contract; committing a crime). *See* capacity;
competency. *Compare* mental capacity.

mental incompetent [in · *kawm* · pe · tent]
n. *See* incompetent person; mental
incapacity.

mental reservation [rez · er · *vay* · shen]
n. Doubts or misgivings a person has about
a promise she has made or an act she has
performed or is about to undertake.

mention [*men* · shun] *v.* To state, express,
or refer to something.
n. Notice; acclaim; praise.
➤ *v.* inform, state, tell, notify, remark, assert,
declare.
n. acclaim, honor, accolade, respect,
tribute, laudation, praise.

mercantile [*mer* · ken · tile] *adj.*
Commercial; pertaining to trade and
commerce in merchandise; pertaining to
the business or activities of merchants.

mercantile agency [ay · jen · see] *n.*
Another term for a credit bureau.

mercantile law *n.* Same as **commercial
law**. *See also* law merchant.

mercantile paper [*pay* · per] *n.* Same
as **commercial paper**.

merchandise [*mer* · chen · dize] *n.* Goods,
wares, and **commodities** commonly
bought and sold by merchants.
v. To engage in commercial activity; to
trade; to market.
➤ *n.* commodity, effects, material, wares,
stock, moveables ("The store's
merchandise").
v. advertise, buy and sell, promote, trade,
traffic, handle ("They merchandise the
event of Christmas").

merchant [*mer* · chent] *n.* 1. A person who
regularly trades in a particular type of
goods. 2. Under the **Uniform Commercial
Code**, "a person who deals in goods of the
kind or otherwise by his occupation holds
himself out as having knowledge or skill
peculiar to … the … goods involved in the
transaction." The law holds a merchant
to a higher standard than it imposes upon
a casual seller; his transactions may carry
with them an **implied warranty of
merchantability**. *See* implied warranty.
3. A retailer of merchandise. *See also*
commission merchant; law merchant.
➤ dealer, seller, buyer, broker, trader, vendor
("The merchant sold us the lamp").

merchantability [mer · chen · te · *bil* · i · tee]
adj. 1. The **Uniform Commercial Code**
provides that there is an **implied warranty**
that goods are **merchantable** if the seller
is a merchant with respect to goods of that
kind. *See* implied warranty of merchantability. *Compare* implied warranty of
fitness for a particular purpose. 2. In
common usage, salability.

merchantable [*mer* · chen · tebl] *adj.* 1. Under
the **Uniform Commercial Code**, as the
term relates to goods, fit for general or customary purposes. *See* merchantability. *Also
see* implied warranty of merchantability.

M

Compare implied warranty of fitness for a particular purpose. 2. In common usage, of good quality and salable, but not necessarily the best.

➤ fit, saleable, marketable ("merchantable quality").

merchantable quality [*kwaw* · li · tee] *n.* *See* merchantable.

merchantable title [*ty* · tel] *n.* A **marketable title**.

mercy killing [*mer* · see *kil* · ing] *n.* Another term for **euthanasia**.

mere [meer] *adj.* Nothing more than; a minimum; bare.

➤ pure, simple, bald, plain, utter, unmixed, minimum, bare.

mere licensee [ly · sen · *see*] *n.* Only a **licensee** (as distinct from, for EXAMPLE, an **invitee**); a **bare licensee**.

mere volunteer [vol · un · *teer*] *n.* Only a volunteer, i.e., a person to whom a **legal obligation** is not generally owed. *See* officious intermeddler.

meretricious [mehr · re · *trish* · us] *adj.* 1. False. 2. Based upon deception; fraudulent. 3. Sexually immoral or lewd. 4. Flashy; tawdry; cheap.

➤ immoral, obscene, lewd, cheap; blatant, showy, trashy, superficial, sham, hollow, plastic, bogus, deceptive, lying, misleading.

meretricious marriage [*mehr* · ej] *n.* A marriage in which either one or both of the parties lacks **capacity**. If, for EXAMPLE, Sam marries Janet who already has a husband, the marriage is meretricious because Janet lacked the capacity to marry.

merger [*mer* · jer] *n.* The combining of one of anything with another or others; the absorption of one thing by another; a disappearing into something else. EXAMPLES: a **merger of corporations**; a **merger of contracts**; a **merger of offenses**.

➤ federation, union, consolidation, alliance, fusion, tie-in, combination.

merger in contract [*kon* · trakt] *n.* The process by which negotiations lose their **legal effect** when the **contract** is signed. *Compare* merger of contracts.

merger in judgment [*juj* · ment] *n.* The **extinguishment** of a **cause of action** in a **judgment**. EXAMPLE: The obligation to pay

money under a separation agreement is superseded by a judgment for alimony.

merger of contracts [*kon* · trakt] *n.* The **extinguishment** of an agreement when the parties substitute another agreement for it. *Compare* merger in contract.

merger of corporations [kore · per · *ay* · shenz] *n.* A joining of two (or more) corporations in which one goes out of existence, leaving a single survivor which possesses the powers and owns the stock and other property of both (or all). *See* horizontal merger; vertical merger.

Although the terms "merger" and "**consolidation**" are often used interchangeably, they are actually quite different. In a merger, one of the combining corporations continues in existence and absorbs the others; in a consolidation, the combining corporations are dissolved and lose their identity in a new **corporate entity** that takes over the property and powers, as well as the rights and liabilities, of the constituent corporations. *See* consolidation of corporations.

merger of crimes *n.* *See* merger of offenses.

merger of estates [es · *tates*] *n.* *See* merger of property interests.

merger of offenses [o · *fen* · sez] *n.* The doctrine that when a **lesser offense** is a component of a more serious offense, prosecution can be only for the greater offense. EXAMPLE: a person cannot be prosecuted for both **robbery** and **larceny** arising from a single act. *See* lesser included offense. *See also* merger of sentences.

merger of property interests [*prop* · er · tee in · trests] *n.* 1. The absorption of one **estate** into another, when a greater estate and a lesser estate coincide and meet in one and the same person without any intermediate estate. EXAMPLE: when the owner of a **life estate** purchases the **remainder**. 2. The uniting of **legal title** and **equitable title** in one person.

merger of rights of action [*ak* · shen] *n.* *See* merger in judgment.

merger of sentences [*sen* · ten · sez] *n.* A defendant who, on the basis of two separate **indictments**, is convicted of two separate crimes arising from a single act (EXAMPLE: **murder** and **battery**) may be

M

sentenced on the more serious conviction, but not on both. *See* merger of offenses. *See also* lesser included offense.

merit [*mehr* · it] *n.* Worth; quality; value. *v.* To earn or deserve.
➤ *n.* value, worth, quality, stature, goodness, superiority ("The case was decided on its merits").
v. rate, invite, qualify for, be worthy of, prompt, deserve, earn ("It did not merit my attention").

merit increase [*in* · kreess] *n.* In labor law, an increase in pay given in recognition of the quality of an employee's work, as opposed to a pay raise granted on the basis of length of service or seniority.

merit system [*sis* · tem] *n.* In government service, a system of hiring and promotion in employment which is carried out on the basis of ability. *See also* Civil Service Commission.

meritorious [mehr · i · *toh* · ree · us] *adj.* Worthy; deserving praise; having merit.
➤ sound, praiseworthy, commendable, choice, excellent, noble ("a meritorious undertaking").
Ant. worthless.

meritorious consideration [ken · sid · e · *ray* · shen] *n.* Same as **good consideration**.

meritorious defense [de · *fense*] *n.* A **defense** that goes to the **merits of the case**; a defense warranting a hearing, although it may not be a perfect defense or a defense assured of succeeding.

merits [*mehr* · its] *n.* Also referred to as the **merits of the case**; the essential or **substantive** issues of a case, as opposed to questions of **practice** or **procedure**. USAGE: "Since the defendant's **answer** raises **questions of fact**, the case will be decided **on the merits** and not on the plaintiff's **motion for summary judgment**." *See* judgment on the merits.

merits of the case *See* merits.

mescalin [*mes* · ke · lin] *n.* A hallucinogenic drug, also called **peyote**, that can produce temporary psychosis as a side effect. Mescalin is a **controlled substance**; its possession, distribution, or sale is a criminal offense. *See* hallucinogen.

mesne [meen] (*French*) *adj.* Intermediate; intervening; occupying a middle or mean position.

mesne encumbrance [en · *kum* · brense] *n.* An **encumbrance** that is prior in right to one encumbrance and subsequent in right to another.

mesne process [*pross* · ess] *n.* **Process** issued between the commencement of a suit and final judgment.

mesne profits [*prof* · its] *n.* Intermediate **profits**; profits accruing between two points in time. *See profit à prendre.*

messuage [*mess* · wayzh] *n.* A dwelling house with its adjacent buildings and **curtilage**.

metes and bounds [meets] *n.* A property description, commonly in a deed or mortgage, that is based upon the property's boundaries and the natural objects and other markers on the land. *See* legal description.

methadone [*meth* · e · dohn] *n.* Short for methadone hydrochloride, a synthetic narcotic used in the treatment of severe pain. It is also employed in the treatment of narcotic addiction for purposes both of detoxification and of temporary maintenance. Methadone is a **controlled substance**.

methamphetamine [meth · am · *fet* · e · meen] *n.* A form of **amphetamine**.

methedrine [*meth* · e · dreen] *n.* A trade name under which **amphetamine** is marketed.

metropolitan [met · re · *pol* · i · ten] *adj.* Pertaining to a large city or metropolis.
➤ municipal, urban, populated, sophisticated, city, modern, urbane ("metropolitan area").

metropolitan area [*air* · ee · eh] *n.* A city and its suburbs. *Compare* metropolitan district.

metropolitan council [*kouwn* · sil] *n.* A public body with policymaking responsibility for a **metropolitan district**.

metropolitan district [*dis* · trikt] *n.* A district comprising a number of neighboring cities and towns, established by statute for the purpose of providing coordinated public services. (EXAMPLES: a **water district**; a **sewer district**).

Mexican divorce [*mek* · si · ken di · *vorss*] *n.* A term referring to a divorce granted in Mexico, either by mail or by the mere **appearance** of a plaintiff spouse who is neither a resident nor a **domiciliary** of Mexico. Such divorces have no validity in any state of the United States. *See* mail order divorce.

mid-channel [mid-chan · el] *n.* The middle of a navigable river.

middle thread [thred] *n.* The hypothetical middle or center line of a river or stream, generally equally distant from either bank.

middleman [*midl* · man] *n.* 1. A person who buys from a manufacturer or wholesaler and sells to a consumer; a retailer. 2. A broker. 3. A person who brings parties together.

➤ go-between, broker, liaison, intermediary, factor, attorney, envoy ("The attorney was the middleman in the adoption").

midnight deadline [*mid* · nite *ded* · line] *n.* A time limit imposed by the **Uniform Commercial Code** upon **collecting banks**, under certain circumstances, in the process of **collection**.

migratory divorce [*my* · gre · toh · ree di · *vorss*] *n.* A divorce obtained by a person who changed his residence or **domicile** to another state for the length of time required to secure a divorce in that state, but with no intention of remaining there. *See* divorce.

mileage [*my* · lej] *n.* 1. Compensation for the cost of travel in the course of performing one's duties. Mileage is paid, for EXAMPLE, to public officials, jurors, witnesses, and to some employees by their employers. *Compare* per diem. 2. The distance between two points, in miles.

➤ reimbursement, payment, allotment, compensation, levy, rate ("We were given mileage for the trip to and from the courthouse"); distance traveled, distance.

military [*mil* · i · teh · ree] *n./adj.* 1. Pertaining to the Army, Navy, Air Force, Marine Corps, or Coast Guard. 2. Pertaining to war or to warfare.

➤ *n.* army, navy, air force, marine corps, troops, legions, divisions, militia ("the military advanced on the enemy").

adj. spartan, warlike, combative, armed, aggressive, gladiatorial ("The vehicle had a military design").

military appeals [a · *peelz*] *n. See* Court of Military Appeals; Court of Military Review.

military commission [ke · *mish* · en] *n.* A tribunal established by the military for the trial and punishment of offenses against **martial law.** *See* military offense.

military court *n.* A court whose members are members of the military, with **jurisdiction** to hear and determine cases involving **military law** or offenses against **martial law.** EXAMPLES: a **court-martial**; a **military commission**; a **Court of Military Review**.

military draft *n. See* Selective Service System.

military government [*guv* · ern · ment] *n.* Government established by the military authorities occupying the territory of a hostile nation during wartime or as a result of war, or established within the military's own country during time of insurrection (as was the case during the Civil War). *See* martial law.

military jurisdiction [joo · ris · *dik* · shen] *n.* There are three kinds of military jurisdiction: jurisdiction exercised under **military law**; jurisdiction exercised under **military government**; and jurisdiction exercised under **martial law.** *See* jurisdiction.

military justice code [*juss* · tiss] *n. See* Code of Military Justice.

military law *n.* The **Code of Military Justice** and other statutory provisions for the governance of men and women in the armed forces. *Note* that military law is not **martial law.** *Compare* martial law.

military offense [o · *fense*] *n.* A violation of **military law.** EXAMPLES: sleeping on guard duty; desertion.

military testament [*tes* · ta · ment] *n. See* military will.

military tribunal [try · *byoo* · nel] *n. See* military court. *Also see* military commission.

military will *n.* Most states relax their formal requirements for wills for members of the armed services, particularly during wartime. Thus, for EXAMPLE, it is possible in

M

some jurisdictions for a serviceman or servicewoman who is a minor to make a valid oral will or an unwitnessed written will. *See* nuncupative will.

militia [mi · *lish* · eh] *n.* An organization of citizens in each state, trained in military discipline and skills, who may be called to duty in emergencies but are not kept in military service, as is the regular army. A state's **National Guard** units are its militia.
➤ volunteers, minutemen, reserves, standbys.

mill *n.* A monetary unit of the United States, used solely for accounting purposes, particularly for computing property taxes; it is the equivalent of one thousandth of one dollar or one tenth of one cent. *See* millage.

mill rate *n.* Same as **millage**.

millage [*mil* · ej] *n.* Tax on real property calculated at a rate of $1 per $1,000 of **assessed value**. The terms "millage" and "**mill rate**" are used interchangeably. *See* mill.

mind *n.* The ability to will, decide, direct, permit, or assent; **mental capacity**. *See* state of mind.
➤ intelligence, faculties, judgment, reasoning, psyche, intellect.

mind and memory [*mem* · e · ree] *n.* A term commonly found in wills (USAGE: "sound and disposing mind and memory"); a declaration by a **testator** that he has the **mental capacity** to make a will. *See* memory. *Also see* capacity; testamentary capacity.

miner's inch [*my* · nerz] *n.* A unit of measurement of the rate at which water is discharged. It is a commonly applied in western states and is a factor in the context of water rights. EXAMPLE: in California, by statute, the official miner's inch of water equals .025 cubic feet per second (through a standard opening under standard pressure). \

mineral [*min* · e · rel] *n.* Any naturally occurring substance that can be extracted from the earth, including oil and gas. The word is a comprehensive one; if its ordinary meaning is to be restricted, the language used, whether in a **conveyance**, statute, or any other context, must clearly show that intent.

mineral deed *n.* 1. A **conveyance** of a landowner's **interest** in minerals lying beneath the surface of the land. Such a grant has the effect of separating **title** to the minerals from the title to the land. 2. A conveyance of previously deeded title to minerals contained in the land. *See* deed. *Also see* mineral right.

mineral land *n.* Land made valuable by the deposits of useful or precious minerals it contains.

mineral lease *n.* A contract that grants the right to explore for minerals and, if they are located, to extract them from the land and remove them from the premises. *Compare* mineral deed. *See* mineral royalty. *Also see* mining lease; oil and gas lease.

mineral right *n.* A right to explore for and extract minerals from land, whether by virtue of a **mineral deed**, or under a **mineral lease** or **mining lease**, or otherwise.

mineral royalty [*roy* · el · tee] *n.* Money paid under a **mineral lease** or **mining lease** requiring the lessee to pay the owner of the land an amount computed on the basis of the quantity extracted. Such contracts customarily provide that a specified quantity be taken within a stated period of time, and, failing that, that a stipulated sum of money be paid. *Note* that a **royalty** is to be distinguished from a **rental**.

mini-trial [*min* · ee-try · el] *n.* A voluntary, nonbinding form of **alternative dispute resolution** sometimes used in complex commercial cases (EXAMPLE: **patent infringement**) that would otherwise result in a lengthy trial. A summary presentation is made to a panel composed of executives of both litigants, presided over by a jointly selected neutral moderator who advises the parties of the strengths and weakness of their respective claims, after which the parties meet to discuss the possibility of settlement. *Compare* summary jury trial.

minimum [*min* · i · mum] *n.* The least amount; the smallest quantity.
➤ margin, bottom line, smallest amount, dab, least, slightest ("minimum standards for admission").

minimum contacts test [*kon* · takts] *n.* A doctrine under which a state court is permitted to acquire **personal jurisdiction**

over a nonresident, although he is not personally served with **process** within the state, if he has had such a substantial connection with that state that **due process** is not offended by the court's exercise of jurisdiction over him. *See* personal service of process. *See also* doing business in a state; localization doctrine; long arm statutes.

minimum fee schedule [*sked · jool*] *n.* A schedule of the minimum fees a bar association permits its members to charge for legal services. The courts have held that minimum fees are in **restraint of trade**; accordingly, where such schedules still exist, they are merely advisory.

minimum royalty [*roy · el · tee*] *n.* Under some **royalty** agreements, the amount which a **licensee** of a **patent** is obligated to pay its owner or holder, whether or not she uses the patent.

minimum sentence [*sen · tense*] *n.* The lightest sentence permitted for a particular crime.

minimum wage *n. See* minimum wage laws.

minimum wage laws *n.* State and federal statutes establishing a minimum rate of wages to be paid employees. The **Fair Labor Standards Act** is the federal minimum wage statute. *See* wage and hour acts.

mining [*my · ning*] *n.* The act of extracting minerals, including coal, ore, and metal, from the earth.

mining claim *n.* A **parcel** of public mineral land that has been appropriated according to law by a prospector who has discovered a precious metal or other valuable mineral on it or under it. It is **property** and can be, bought, sold, and **conveyed**, and will pass by **descent**. *See* public land.

mining lease *n.* A **lease** of land that grants to the **lessee** the right to mine and remove minerals. Some mining leases involve the payment of **rent** (*see* mining rent); under others, the lessee pays a **royalty** (*see* mineral royalty). *See also* mineral lease. *Compare* mineral deed.

mining location [*lo · kay · shen*] *n.* The act of **perfecting** a mining claim. *See* locator.

mining rent *n.* The **consideration** for a **mining lease**. *Compare* mineral royalty; royalty. *Also compare* mineral deed.

minister [*min · i · ster*] *n.* 1. A person who performs services for another; an **agent**. 2. In some countries, the title of the head of a department of the government or the head of the entire government. *See* prime minister. 3. A representative of one government to another government, i.e.; a diplomatic representative. EXAMPLE: an ambassador. 4. A clergyperson; a minister of the gospel. *v.* To attend to or assist.

➤ *n.* secretary, commissioner, chief, consul, delegate, prime minister ("the minister of defense"); pastor, clergyman, father, parson, preacher, lecturer ("married by a minister"). *v.* cater to, wait on, accommodate, pander, nurse, tend ("I will minister to his cuts").

ministerial [*min · i · steer · i · el*] *adj.* 1. Pertaining to delegated authority. *See* delegate. 2. Pertaining to a **minister** or other agent. *See* minister.

➤ implemental, administrative, subsidiary, ancillary, clear, fixed ("He has ministerial authority").

ministerial act *n.* An act that a person performs under the authority of a superior, in a prescribed manner, in accordance with the requirements of the law and without exercising his own judgment or discretion. EXAMPLE: the **entry** of an order of court by a **clerk of court**. *See* entry of judgment. *Also see* administrative act.

ministerial duty [*dew · tee*] *n.* An official duty whose performance is commanded by law and required to be carried out in a specific manner, no aspect of which is left to the discretion of the official. *See* ministerial act.

ministerial function [*funk · shen*] *n.* A function of a public official that does not involve the exercise of discretion or judgment. *See* ministerial act.

ministerial officer [*off · i · ser*] *n.* A public official whose duties involve little or no discretion. *See* ministerial duty.

ministerial trust *n.* A **trust** in which the **trustee** is called upon to exercise almost no discretion in carrying out her responsibilities. *See also* passive trust. *Compare* discretionary trust.

M

minor [*my · ner*] *adj.* Insignificant; slight; small; trivial; petty.
n. A person who has not yet attained her **majority**; a person who has not reached **legal age**; a person who has not acquired the **capacity** to contract. *See* infancy; infant. *See also* legal capacity. *Compare* age of majority; full age.
➤ *adj.* inferior, trivial, secondary, slight, insignificant, small ("only minor damage").
n. adolescent, baby, youngster, infant, juvenile, child ("She was still a minor under the law.")

minor dispute [*dis · pyoot*] *n.* As opposed to a **major dispute**, a labor dispute involving the railroads that the **Railway Labor Act** requires the parties to submit to **compulsory arbitration**.

minor offense [*o · fense*] *n. See* petty offense.

minority [*my · naw · ri · tee*] *n.* 1. The status of a minor. 2. The period during which one is a minor. 3. An ethnic, racial, or religious group different from the majority. 4. A group to whom the protection of the **equal protection clause** of the **Fourteenth Amendment** applies; a **suspect class**. 5. Less than half of anything. *Compare* majority.
➤ nonage, childhood, infancy, juvenility, youth ("The children still are in their minority"); outvoted number, less than half, secondary group, lesser proportion, handful ("a minority position").

minority opinion [*o · pin · yen*] *n.* 1. A **dissenting opinion** in a case issued by one or more members of the court. *Compare* majority opinion. *See* opinion. 2. The opinion of a minority of the members of any group.

minority representation [*rep · re · zen · tay · shen*] *n.* Representation achieved by a minority of voters, usually under a system of voting that provides for protection of their interests. **Cumulative voting** is an EXAMPLE of such a system.

minority stockholders [*stok · hole · derz*] *n.* **Stockholders** of a corporation who, taken as a group, hold an insufficient number of shares to elect directors or otherwise control the management of the corporation. *See* stockholders.

minority view *n.* An interpretation of a principle of law favored by the courts of some states, but not concurred in by the courts in a majority of states. USAGE: "Applying strict liability to landlord-tenant relations is still a minority view." *Compare* majority view.

minutes [*min · ets*] *n.* 1. A **memorandum** of what occurred in court. 2. The record of the business transacted at a meeting of the stockholders or directors of a corporation. 3. A record of the **proceedings** of any group. *See* minutes book.
➤ notes, summary, outline, transcript, memorandum ("the minutes of the meeting").

minutes book *n.* 1. A book in which the **proceedings** of a court are entered by the clerk. 2. A book in which the proceedings at meetings of a corporation's stockholders or directors are recorded.

Miranda rule [*mi · ran · da*] *n.* The **Fifth Amendment** and the **Fourteenth Amendment** to the Constitution require that, before a suspect who is in custody may be questioned, she must be informed that she has the right to remain silent and that anything she says may be used against her in court, be given the right to have an attorney present during questioning, and be advised that if she cannot afford an attorney one will be provided for her. If an interrogation occurs in the absence of these warnings, or in the absence of the suspect's attorney, any confession obtained is inadmissible unless the defendant has intelligently and knowingly waived her "Miranda rights." *See Miranda v. Arizona.*

Miranda v. Arizona [*mi · ran · da ver · sus ehr · i · zoh · na*] *n.* A landmark decision of the Supreme Court (384 U.S. 436) in 1966, dealing with **custodial interrogation**, confessions, self-incrimination, and the right to counsel. The constitutional requirements announced by the Court in this case have come to be known as the **Miranda rule**.

misadventure [*mis · ad · ven · cher*] *n.* An accident; bad luck. *See* homicide by misadventure.
➤ setback, mishap, casualty, debacle, failure, lapse.

M

misapplication [mis · ap · li · *kay* · shen] *n.*
The act of making a wrongful use of
something. *See* misappropriation.
➤ misuse, abuse, misappropriation,
squandering, illegal handling, corrupt use.

misappropriate [mis · uh · *pro* · pree · ayt]
v. To take or use wrongfully or illegally;
to steal.
➤ take, swindle, rob, defalcate, defraud,
embezzle, usurp ("misappropriate funds").

misappropriation
[mis · a · pro · pree · *ay* · shen] *n.* The
act of dishonestly taking or removing
property or of putting it to a dishonest
use; a **conversion** of property.
misappropriation of funds *n.* The act
of a person in wrongfully taking or using
another's money that has been entrusted to
her for a specific purpose. *See* wrongful
abstraction. *Also see* embezzlement.

misbranding [mis · *bran* · ding] *n.*
Offering an article for sale with a false
or misleading label.

miscarriage [mis · *kehr* · ej] *n.* 1. The
expulsion of a fetus from the womb before
it is **viable**. An abortion is a miscarriage
that is brought about intentionally. 2. A
failure to attain an intended, desired, or just
result. EXAMPLE. a miscarriage of justice.
➤ stillbirth, spontaneous abortion ("to have
a miscarriage"); defeat, error, misadventure,
miss, nonsuccess, perversion ("miscarriage
of justice").
miscarriage of justice [*juss* · tiss] *n.*
A decision in a lawsuit inconsistent with
substantial justice; a result in a case that
disregards or denies a party's essential rights.

miscegenation [mis · sej · e · *nay* · shen] *n.*
The intermarrying, cohabiting, or inter-
breeding of persons of different races. State
statutes criminalizing such acts have been
held unconstitutional under the **equal
protection clause** of the **Fourteenth
Amendment**.

miscellaneous [mis · sel · *ane* · ee · us] *adj.*
Diverse; varied.
➤ varied, mixed, collected, unclassified, jum-
bled, diversified, ("miscellaneous items").

mischarge [*mis* · charj] *n.* An error on the
part of a court in its charge or instructions
to the jury. Whether a mischarge is

reversible error depends upon the degree
to which it affected the **substantive rights**
of the **appellant**. *See* jury instructions.

mischief [*mis* · chif] *n.* Conduct resulting
in annoyance or **injury**. *See* malicious
mischief.
➤ wrongfulness, wrongdoing, annoyance,
misconduct, prank.

misconduct [mis · *kon* · dukt] *n.*
1. Disobedience of some established and
definite rule or law; intentional wrongdoing,
as opposed to **negligence** or failure to
exercise **due care**. Misconduct by counsel
(EXAMPLE: willfully and repeatedly offering
prejudicial evidence), by the judge
(EXAMPLE: highly improper remarks), or by
a member of the jury (EXAMPLE: deciding
the case on the basis of information other
than the evidence) may be grounds for a
new trial if it prevents either of the parties
from receiving a fair trial. 2. Improper
conduct generally. *See* malfeasance;
misfeasance.
➤ dereliction, misdeed, offense, impropriety,
naughtiness, transgression.
misconduct in office [*off* · iss] *n. See*
official misconduct.

misconstrue [mis · kon · *strew*] *v.* To
misunderstand; to get an incorrect
impression.
➤ misinterpret, confuse, mistake,
misunderstand, misconceive, misread.

miscue [*mis* · kew] *n.* A mistake or error.
➤ mistake, error, blunder, slip, fumble.

misdelivery [mis · de · *liv* · e · ree] *n.*
1. The delivery of mail, freight, or other
items to a person other than the person to
whom they were sent. 2. The surrender of
goods by a **carrier** or other **bailee** to
someone other than the one to whom they
were **consigned**. *See* larceny of lost,
mislaid, or misdelivered property.

misdemeanant [mis · de · *meen* · ent] *n.* A
person who has committed a **misdemeanor**.

misdemeanor [mis · de · *meen* · er] *n.* A
crime not amounting to a **felony**. In many
jurisdictions, misdemeanors are offenses
for which the punishment is incarceration
for less than a year (generally in a jail,
rather than in a prison or the penitentiary)
or the payment of a fine. *Compare* infraction;
petty offense.

M

➤ offense, transgression, wrong, misdeed, violation, trespass, impropriety.

misdemeanor manslaughter rule [*man* · slaw · ter] *n.* Paralleling the **felony murder rule**, a doctrine in some jurisdictions which declares that any death that takes place during the commission of a misdemeanor is **involuntary manslaughter**.

misdirection [mis · di · *rek* · shen] *n.* 1. Same as **mischarge**. 2. The wrong course.

➤ mischarge, misinformation, misguidance; mistaken course, error, aberrance, failure.

misfeasance [mis · *fee* · zense] *n.* The improper performance of a lawful act. *Compare* malfeasance; nonfeasance.

➤ dereliction, negligence, transgression, wrongfulness, peccadillo, breach.

misfeasance in office [*off* · iss] *n.* The performance by a public official, in an official capacity, of a legal act in an illegal or improper manner. *Compare* malfeasance in office. *See* official misconduct.

mishandle [*mis* · han · dul] *v.* To maltreat, damage, or abuse.

➤ misuse, squander, waste, misdirect ("mishandle funds").

misjoinder [mis · *join* · der] *n.* The **joinder of actions**, **claims**, **indictments**, or **parties** that, under the **rules of civil procedure** or the **rules of criminal procedure**, should not be joined. *See* joinder of actions; joinder of claims; joinder of indictments; joinder of parties.

mislaid [mis · *lade*] *adj.* Put in the wrong place and forgotten. *Compare* abandoned; lost.

mislaid property [*prop* · er · tee] *n.* Property that the owner has voluntarily and intentionally placed in a location which he has since forgotten. *Compare* abandoned property; lost property. *See* larceny of lost, mislaid, or misdelivered property.

mislead [mis · *leed*] *v.* To lead astray; to give false information.

➤ deceive, betray, misrepresent, misdirect, dupe, scam, delude, defraud, inveigle.

mismanage [mis · *man* · aj] *v.* To administer or handle in an incompetent manner.

➤ misuse, maladminister, mishandle, administer inefficiently, bungle, neglect.

misnomer [mis · *no* · mer] *n.* A mistake in a name, for EXAMPLE, in an **accusation**, **indictment**, or **pleading**, or in an instrument such as a deed or mortgage.

➤ slip, misusage, misnaming, malapropism.

mispleading [mis · *plee* · ding] *n.* Committing an error in a **pleading**.

misprision [mis · *prizh* · en] *n.* Contempt of authority or of the government as exhibited, for EXAMPLE, by **obstruction of justice**, the concealment of a crime, or **contempt of court**, or, in the case of a public official, by neglect of duty. *See* compounding a crime.

misprision of felony [*fell* · e · nee] *n.* The offense of failing to inform the authorities of a **felony** of which one has knowledge, coupled with a positive act of concealment. EXAMPLE: covering up evidence.

misprision of treason [*tree* · zen] *n.* The concealment or failure to promptly disclose to the authorities knowledge of the commission of an act of **treason**.

misrepresent [mis · rep · re · *zent*] *v.* To portray something falsely; to mislead or deceive.

➤ fabricate, distort, lie, deceive, falsify, prevaricate, delude, warp, exaggerate.

misrepresentation [mis · rep · re · zen · *tay* · shen] *n.* The statement of an untruth; a misstatement of fact designed to lead one to believe that something is other than it is; a false statement of fact designed to deceive. *See* fraud; fraudulent misrepresentation; material representation; misrepresentation.

➤ fraud, deception, deceit, distortion, fabrication, exaggeration ("the misrepresentation of a material fact").

mistake [mis · *take*] *n.* 1. An erroneous mental conception that influences a person to act or to decline to act; an unintentional act, omission, or error arising from ignorance, surprise, imposition, or misplaced confidence. "Mistake" is a legal concept especially significant in contract law because, depending upon the circumstances, it may warrant **reformation** or **rescission** of a contract. 2. An error; a misunderstanding; an inaccuracy. *See* mutual mistake; unilateral mistake.

M

➤ misconception, inaccuracy, lapse, slip, confusion, erratum ("a mistake of identity").

mistake of fact   *n.*   A belief in the existence of a nonexistent fact **material** to a transaction; or ignorance, unconsciousness, or forgetfulness of a fact material to a transaction. *See* fact.

mistake of law   *n.*   An erroneous conclusion as to the **legal effect** of a set of facts by one having full knowledge of the facts.

mistrial   [*mis* · try · el]   *n.*   A trial that has been terminated by the judge prior to its conclusion because the jury is unable to reach a verdict (*see* hung jury), because of **prejudicial error** that cannot be corrected or eliminated by any action the court might take (EXAMPLE: the prosecutor's use of racial slurs), or because of the occurrence of some event that would make it pointless to continue (EXAMPLE: the death of a juror). A mistrial is the equivalent of no trial having been held. *Compare* new trial.

➤ abrogation, termination, cancellation.

mitigating   [*mit* · ih · gay · ting]   *adj.*   That which tends to qualify, modify, or lighten something.

➤ exonerative, modifying, cushioning, softening, alleviating, relieving ("mitigating circumstances").

mitigating circumstances   [*mit* · i · gay · ting *ser* · kem · stan · sez]   *n.*   Circumstances that lessen blame or reduce the degree of civil or criminal responsibility, for EXAMPLE, the reduction of **murder** to **manslaughter** because the defendant acted with **provocation**. Compare aggravating circumstances. *See* mitigation of damages; mitigation of punishment. *See also* extenuating circumstances.

mitigation   [mit · i · *gay* · shen]   *n.*   That which lessens severity or reduces harshness. *Compare* aggravation.

➤ reduction, abatement, moderation, softening, extenuation, lessening ("mitigation of damages").
Ant. aggravation.

mitigation of damages   [*dam* · e · jez]   *n.*   Facts that tend to show that the plaintiff is not entitled to as large an amount of **damages** as would otherwise be recoverable. The law obligates an **injured party**

to mitigate his **injury**, i.e., to do all he reasonably can to avoid or lessen the consequences of the other party's wrongful act. EXAMPLE: a landlord whose tenant abandons a one-year lease after two months and refuses to make further rental payments, is entitled to recover the lost rental only if and to the extent that she has made reasonable efforts to find a substitute tenant. *See* mitigating circumstances.

mitigation of punishment   [*pun* · ish · ment] *n.*   Reduction of a criminal sentence by the judge on the basis of "mitigating factors," for EXAMPLE, the fact that the defendant has no prior convictions or has made restitution to the victim. *See* mitigating circumstances.

mixed   [mixd]   *adj.*   Combined; mingled; commingled; blended; fused.

➤ blended, merged, composite, brewed, kneaded, united.

mixed action   [*ak* · shen]   *n.*   An **action** relating to both real property and personal property; i.e., an action at one and the same time both *in rem* and *in personam.* EXAMPLE: an action for recovery of possession of real property and for **damages** for **injury** to the property. *See* in personam action; in rem action.

mixed insurance company [in · *shoor* · ense *kum* · pe · nee]   *n.*   An insurance company with the characteristics of both a **mutual company** and a **stock company**. *See* mutual insurance company.

mixed larceny   [*lar* · sen · ee]   *n.*   Same as **compound larceny**.

mixed nuisance   [*new* · sense]   *n.*   A **nuisance** that is both public and private in its effects. *See and compare* private nuisance; public nuisance.

mixed presumption   [pre · *zump* · shen] *n.*   A **presumption of law and fact**.

mixed property   [*prop* · er · tee]   *n.* Property that, for certain purposes, the law considers to be, at one and the same time, both real property and personal property. EXAMPLES: **fixtures; heirlooms;** tombstones.

mixed question of law and fact [*kwes* · chen]   *n.*   A question that is composed of two questions: a **question of law** to be decided by the judge and a **question of fact** to be decided by the jury.

M

MO *n.* Abbreviation of *modus operandi* or "method of operation," referring to a pattern of criminal conduct.

mob *n.* A number of people assembled for the purpose of doing violence to persons or property. *See* riot; unlawful assembly.
➤ throng, horde, mass, assemblage, gang, pack.

model [*mod · l*] *n.* A plan, design, sample, or standard to be reproduced, imitated, or copied.
➤ plan, archetype, mold, prototype, image, facsimile ("model jury instructions").
model acts *n. See* Uniform Laws.
model jury instructions [*joo · ree in · struk · shenz*] *n.* In many jurisdictions, sample **jury instructions** that trial judges are required to follow when charging a jury. *See* charge.
model laws *n. See* Uniform Laws.

Model Penal Code [*mod · l pee · nel*] *n.* A proposed criminal code prepared jointly by the **Commission on Uniform State Laws** and the **American Law Institute**.

Model Rules of Professional Conduct [*mod · l rules of pro · fesh · en · el kon · dukt*] *n. See* Rules of Professional Conduct.

modification [*mod · i · fi · kay · shen*] *n.* A change, alteration, or amendment.
➤ qualification, deviation, limitation, inflection, variation, amendment, refinement, change, alteration.
modification of judgment [*juj · ment*] *n.* Under the **Federal Rules of Civil Procedure**, and most states' **rules of civil procedure**, a **judgment** may be modified in circumstances in which it is equitable to do so, in order that it will accurately reflect what was decided. Grounds for modification generally include clerical error, inadvertence, excusable neglect, fraud, misrepresentation, and newly discovered evidence.

modify [*mod · ih · fie*] *v.* To change, adjust, or moderate. EXAMPLE: "modify a sentence."
➤ adjust, alter, revamp, revise, amend, refine, change, improve.

modus [*moh · dus*] (*Latin*) *n.* Mode; manner; method.
modus operandi [*op · e · ran · dee*] *n.* Often shortened to **MO**, it means "method

of operating." USAGE: "The police believed they were looking for a serial killer because each homicide appeared to involve the same *modus operandi.*"

moiety [*moy · e · tee*] *n.* 1. A part; a fraction of a thing; 2. A half.

molestation [*mo · les · tay · shen*] *n.* Physical abuse; improper sexual contact. *See* child molestation.
➤ abuse, mischief, annoyance, malice, affliction, persecution, interference.

mollify [*mol · ih · fie*] *v.* To pacify or appease; to reduce the severity of.
➤ assuage, pacify, quiet, subdue, calm.

monarchy [*mon · er · kee*] *n.* A government in which all power is in the hands of a single person.

monetary [*mon · e · ter · ee*] *adj.* Pertaining to money.
➤ budgetary, capital, financial, fiscal, pecuniary.
monetary loss *n.* A loss measured in money. *See* loss.
monetary value [*val · yoo*] *n.* Value measured in money. *See* value.

money [*mun · ee*] *n.* 1. In a specific sense, currency, both coin and paper; cash; the **medium of exchange** recognized by the country issuing it. 2. In a general sense, wealth; everything that represents property and passes from hand to hand without regard to **title**. *See* legal tender; scrip.
➤ capital, cash, revenue, greenback, coin, specie, legal tender; assets, wealth, affluence, fortune, wherewithal, treasure.
money claim *n.* A **claim** or **demand** for money based upon a contract, express or implied, as opposed to a claim for **damages** or a claim for **equitable relief**; a **liquidated claim**. *See* express contract; implied contract.
money counts *n.* In **common law pleading**, the "money counts" in **actions** in *assumpsit* were **money had and received**, **money lent**, and **money paid**.
money demand [*de · mand*] *n. See* money claim.
money had and received [*re · seevd*] *n. See* money counts.

M

money judgment [*juj* · ment] *n.* A **judgment** ordering the payment of a sum of money by one party to the other; a judgment that can be fully satisfied by the payment of money.

money laundering [*lawn* · de · ring] *n.* *See* laundering.

money lent *n.* *See* money counts.

money made *n.* Money collected by a sheriff under a **writ of execution**.

money market [*mar* · ket] *n.* The **market** for trading in short-term securities (EXAMPLES: **certificates of deposit**; **Treasury notes**).

money order [*or* · der] *n.* A **negotiable instrument** purchased from a bank, a telegraph company, the post office, or other authorized **drawee** for the purpose of paying a debt or transmitting money to a third person. Liability for payment rests solely on the drawee. *See also* registered check. *See* postal money order.

money paid *n.* *See* money counts.

moneyed corporation [*mun* · eed kore · per · *ay* · shen] *n.* 1. A corporation organized for profit; a **business corporation** rather than a **charitable corporation**. 2. A corporation having the powers of a bank or finance company.

monition [moh · *nish* · en] *n.* A court order, particularly one ordering a person to appear and specifying the consequences of failure to do so.
➤ summons, warning, admonition.

monopoly [muh · *nop* · e · lee] *n.* A means by which a company, or several companies, suppress competition by illegally acquiring the power to control the manufacture or sale of an article or **commodity** and, by so doing, acquire the power to fix prices. Monopolization is prohibited by a series of federal **antitrust acts**, including the **Sherman Act** and the **Clayton Act**. *See also* price-fixing; restraint of trade.
➤ domination, corner, oligopoly ("The company has a monopoly on the business"); cartel, trust, amalgamation, consortium, holding ("The company is a monopoly").

month *n.* Unless another meaning is specifically noted, means a calendar month, as distinguished from a lunar month, which is a period of 30 days.

month to month lease *n.* A **lease** in which no definite term is agreed upon and the rent is a certain amount per month. Such a lease is generally terminable upon 30 days' notice. *See* month to month tenancy.

month to month tenancy [*ten* · en · see] *n.* 1. **Tenancy** under a **month to month lease**. 2. A **tenancy at will**. 3. The tenancy of a tenant who is a **holdover**.

monument [*mon* · yoo · ment] *n.* 1. A tombstone. 2. A marker of stone or metal placed at a point of historical interest. 3. With respect to real estate, a physical object, whether natural or artificial (EXAMPLES: a tree; a stone; a fence), on the ground that establishes a boundary line. *See* landmark; marker; natural monument.
➤ footstone, memorial, headstone, tombstone, pillar, gravestone ("The monument marked his resting place"); reminder, shrine, landmark, marker, tribute ("The monument commemorated the battle").

moonlighting [*moon* · lite · ing] *v.* Working a second job in addition to one's regular job.

moonshine [*moon* · shine] *n.* Alcoholic liquor that is illegally manufactured.

moot *adj.* Of no actual significance. USAGE: "It's now a moot point."
➤ academic, theoretical, abstract, speculative, of no practical importance, hypothetical, debatable, unsettled.

moot case *n.* A case involving only abstract questions; a case without any actual controversy between the parties. (EXAMPLE: after filing an action under the **lemon law** seeking a refund of the purchase price of his new car, but before a hearing is held, the plaintiff is given a full refund by the dealer.) Generally, the courts will not hear a case that has become moot. *Compare* test case. *See* case or controversy. *Also see* moot question.

moot court *n.* An imitation court in which law students try imaginary cases or argue fictitious appeals in order to learn how to conduct real ones.

M

moot question [*kwes* · chen] *n.* A question that has already been settled, resolved, or decided. *Compare* academic question; hypothetical question.

moral [*mor* · el] *adj.* 1. Pertaining to virtue or right conduct; relating to the distinction between right and wrong. It is important to distinguish "moral," "morals," and "morality" from "law" and "legal." Human beings decide for themselves what is moral and immoral; morality does not involve formal sanctions. Law, on the other hand, is created by the state and is enforced by its authority. 2. Pertaining to that which is logical or probable, based upon what regularly occurs in the natural world and in human experience. *See* moral certainty; moral evidence. *Also see* ethics.
n. A lesson or principle extracted from a situation or story.
➤ *adj.* ethical, honest, above-board, principled, honorable, worthy ("a moral person").
n. lesson, principle, canon, truism, point, teaching, proverb ("the moral of the story").

moral certainty [*ser* · ten · tee] *n.* The equivalent of proof **beyond a reasonable doubt**, that is, proof sufficient to satisfy a jury of reasonable persons (*see* reasonable man test) that the defendant is guilty of the crime charged. *Compare* preponderance of the evidence.

moral coercion [koh · *er* · zhen] *n.* A form of duress; **undue influence** or taking undue advantage of another person's financial distress or extreme need. *See* coercion.

moral consideration
[ken · sid · e · *ray* · shen] *n.* **Consideration** that is good only in conscience, not in law, except in circumstances where **good consideration** is **adequate consideration**. EXAMPLE: **love and affection** may be moral consideration sufficient to support a contract with a near relative. *Compare* valuable consideration. *See* legal consideration.

moral duress [dew · *ress*] *n. See* moral coercion.

moral evidence [*ev* · i · dense] *n.* Evidence that has **probative value**, even though it is not **demonstrative evidence** or **mathematical evidence**, because, based upon human experience, it is logical or probable. *See* evidence.

moral fraud *n.* Same as **actual fraud**.

moral hazard [*haz* · erd] *n.* In the law of fire insurance, the chance or **risk** of the insured himself destroying the property by fire, or permitting it to be destroyed, for the purpose of collecting the insurance. *See* arson.

moral law *n.* The "law of conscience"; ethics; morality. *Compare* positive law.

moral obligation [ob · li · *gay* · shen] *n.* A commitment arising from ethical motives, as distinguished from a **legal obligation**. A moral obligation is not enforceable; a legal obligation is. *See* ethics.

moral turpitude [*ter* · pi · tewd] *n.* Depraved conduct; immoral conduct. A crime of moral turpitude is a vile, depraved, or highly immoral crime (EXAMPLE: child molestation).

morality [more · *al* · i · tee] *n.* Pertaining to morals.
➤ virtue, integrity, honor, ethics, honesty.

morals [*more* · elz] *n.* Principles of right and wrong conduct. *See* moral.
➤ personal principles, standards, behavior, conduct, scruples, ideas, ethics.

moratorium [more · e · *toh* · ree · um] *n.* A period during which a person, usually a debtor, has a legal right to postpone meeting an obligation. An individual creditor may declare a moratorium with respect to her debtor, or a moratorium may be imposed by legislation and apply to debtors as a class. *Compare* grace period.
➤ postponement, pause, freeze, discontinuance, stoppage, abeyance, stay, respite.

more definite statement
[*def* · i · nit *state* · ment] *n.* A **motion for more definite statement** is made by a defendant in response to a vague or ambiguous **complaint**. *Also see* motion.

more or less *adv.* Approximately, about, almost; a phrase used to cover some slight or unimportant inaccuracy, or possible inaccuracy, when describing size, quantity, or distance, particularly in a **legal description** of land.

morgue [morg] *n.* A place where the bodies of unidentified dead persons are kept to be viewed for the purpose of identification or, when death occurred under suspicious circumstances, so that an **inquest** may be performed.

M

mortal [*more* · tel] *adj.* Death-producing; deadly; fatal; lethal.
n. A being, especially a person, who is not immortal and will, therefore, eventually die.
➤ *adj.* deadly, fatal, lethal, dire, extreme ("a mortal wound").
n. animal, being, body, human, soul, person.

mortality [*more* · *tal* · i · tee] *n.* 1. The death rate in a country, state, or other region, or among a class of persons, a race, an age group, or the like. 2. Death. 3. The vulnerability to death that all humans share.
➤ human race, humanity, mankind, vulnerability, frailty, evanescence, mortals ("limited by one's mortality").
mortality tables [*tay* · blz] *n.* Also referred to as **actuarial tables**, statistical tables showing the probable life expectancy of a person of a given sex and age.

mortgage [*more* · gej] *n.* 1. A **pledge** of real property to **secure** a debt. Which one of at least three possible legal principles defines the rights of the parties to a given mortgage depends upon the state in which the mortgaged property is located. In states that have adopted the *lien theory*, the mortgagee (creditor) has a **lien** on the property; the mortgagor (debtor) retains **legal title** and is entitled to possession unless his interest is terminated by a **foreclosure decree**. In *title theory* states, a mortgage transfers **title** and a theoretical right of possession to the mortgagee; title reverts to the mortgagor upon full payment of the mortgage debt. A *third group of states* employs hybrid versions of the lien and title theories, with characteristics of both. 2. A written agreement pledging real property as security.
See adjustable rate mortgage; assumption of mortgage; balloon mortgage; blanket mortgage; bulk mortgage; chattel mortgage; closed-end mortgage; conventional mortgage; deed of trust; equitable mortgage; FHA mortgage; first mortgage; fixed rate mortgage; future advance; graduated payment mortgage; junior mortgage; open-end mortgage; purchase money mortgage; reverse equity mortgage; second mortgage; senior mortgage; trust deed; VA mortgage.
v. 1. To place real property under a **mortgage**. *See* mortgage 2. To obligate; to **pledge**.

➤ *n.* encumbrance, indebtedness, debt, obligation, security, pledge ("a mortgage on the property").
v. hypothecate, obligate, encumber, stake, post, hock ("They mortgaged the farm").
mortgage bond *n.* A **bond secured** by a mortgage.
mortgage certificate [ser · *tif* · i · ket] *n.* A **certificate of participation** evidencing a person's status as a **mortgagee**, with others, of a **parcel** of real estate.
mortgage clause *n. See* mortgagee clause.
mortgage commitment [ke · *mit* · ment] *n.* A legally binding letter given by a lending institution to a borrower stating the terms on which it will grant the borrower a mortgage on a specific piece of real estate.
mortgage company [*kum* · pe · nee] *n.* A company in the business of making mortgage loans, which it then sells to other businesses or individuals who invest in mortgages.
mortgage debt *n.* The debt or obligation **secured** by a **mortgage**.
mortgage foreclosure [fore · *kloh* · zher] *n. See* foreclosure.
mortgage insurance [in · *shoor* · ense] *n.* 1. Insurance purchased by a **mortgagor** that pays the mortgage if the mortgagor is unable to because of death or disability. 2. Insurance purchased by a **mortgagee** insuring him against **loss** resulting from the mortgagor's inability to make payment. Mortgage insurance is a form of credit insurance.
mortgage loan *n.* A loan secured by a mortgage. *See* loan.
mortgage note *n.* A **note** that evidences a loan for which real estate has been mortgaged.
mortgage of goods *n. See* chattel mortgage; secured transaction; security agreement; security interest.
mortgage point *n. See* points.

mortgagee [more · ge · *jee*] *n.* The person to whom a **mortgage** is made; the lender. *Compare* mortgagor.
mortgagee clause *n.* A clause in an insurance policy covering mortgaged property which provides that, in the

event of a **loss**, payment will be made to the mortgagee to the extent of her loss. *See* as interest may appear.

mortgagee in possession [poh · *zesh* · en] *n.* A phrase describing the right of a mortgagee who is lawfully in possession of mortgaged property to remain in possession unless and until the mortgage is satisfied. *See* possession.

mortgagor [more · ge · *jor*] *n.* A person who **mortgages** his property; the borrower. *Compare* mortgagee.

mortis causa [*more* · tis *kow* · sa] *(Latin) n. See causa mortis*.

mortmain statutes [*mort* · mane] *n.* Statutes formerly existing in England which restricted the amount of land that could be controlled by those whose control would prevent the land from being inherited, particularly the Church.

most favored nation clause [*fay* · verd *nay* · shen] *n.* A clause in a **treaty** providing that the citizens of both countries signing the treaty are entitled to all the rights and privileges granted under any treaty by either of them to the citizens of "the most favored nation" with whom they have relations.

motion [*moh* · shen] *n.* 1. An application made to a court for the purpose of obtaining an order or **rule** directing something to be done in favor of the applicant. (EXAMPLE: a defendant's **motion to dismiss** is a formal request to the court that the plaintiff's lawsuit be terminated without further consideration.) The types of motions available to litigants, as well as their form and the matters they appropriately address, are set forth in detail in the **Federal Rules of Civil Procedure** and the **rules of civil procedure** of the various states, as well as in the **Federal Rules of Criminal Procedure** and the various states' **rules of criminal procedure**. Motions may be written or oral, depending on the type of **relief** sought and on the court in which they are made. Some common motions are listed below, defined by reference. 2. Under **parliamentary rules**, the method of presenting a **resolution** or other measure for debate and decision by the assembled group.

➤ request, petition, proposition, plan, demand, offering ("a motion to dismiss").

motion for change of venue [*ven* · yoo] *n. See* change of venue; venue.

motion for compulsory examination [kem · *pul* · se · ree eg · zam · i · *nay* · shen] *n. See* compulsory examination.

motion for directed verdict [di · *rek* · ted *ver* · dikt] *n. See* directed verdict.

motion for enlargement of time [en · *larj* · ment] *n. See* enlargement.

motion for judgment on the pleadings [*juj* · ment on the plee · dings] *n. See* judgment on the pleadings.

motion for more definite statement [*def* · i · nit *state* · ment] *n. See* more definite statement.

motion for new trial [*try* · el] *n. See* new trial.

motion for protective order [pro · *tek* · tiv *or* · der] *n. See* protective order.

motion for summary judgment [*sum* · e · ree *juj* · ment] *n. See* summary judgment.

motion in arrest of judgment [a · *rest* of *juj* · ment] *n. See* arrest of judgment.

motion in bar *n. See* plea in bar. *Also see* bar.

motion in limine [*lim* · e · nee] *n. See in limine*.

motion to amend [a · *mend*] *n. See* amend.

motion to compel discovery [kum · *pel* dis · *kuv* · e · ree] *n. See* compel.

motion to dismiss [dis · *miss*] *n. See* dismiss; dismissal.

motion to quash indictment [in · *dite* · ment] *n. See* quash.

motion to strike *n. See* strike.

motion to suppress [sup · *press*] *n. See* suppress; suppression; suppression of evidence.

motion to vacate judgment [*vay* · kate *juj* · ment] *n. See* vacation of judgment.

motive [*moh* · tiv] *n.* The reason that leads the mind to desire a result; that which leads the mind to engage in a criminal act; that which causes the mind to form **intent**; the reason for an **intention**. *See* criminal intent; *mens rea*; specific intent.

➤ inducement, rationale, stimulus, drive, spur, passion, provocation, purpose, causation. *Ant.* result.

movable [*move* · ebl] *adj.* Referring to that which may be moved from one place to another. *See* movables.

➤ transportable, adaptable, not fastened, removable, mobile, conveyable.

movable freehold [*free* · hold] *n.* Real property that is prone to being diminished or increased in size by the encroaching or receding ocean or a change in the course of a stream. *See* freehold.

movable property [*prop* · er · tee] *n.* **Personal property**; **movables**.

movables [*move* · eblz] *n.* **Personal property**; **movable property**. *Compare* immovables.

➤ chattels, personal property, personalty, goods, possessions.

movant [*move* · ent] *n.* A party who makes a **motion**; a **moving party**.

➤ petitioner, complainant, applicant.

move *v.* 1. To make a **motion** to a court. 2. To present a **resolution** or other measure at a meeting to be debated and voted upon. *See* motion. 3. To change one's point of view or that of another person.

➤ petition, demand, request, propose, propound, urge ("He moved for a new trial").

movent [*move* · ent] *n.* *Same* as **movant**.

moving papers [*move* · ing *pay* · perz] *n.* **Affidavits** or other **documents** (EXAMPLE: a **memorandum of law**) submitted in support of a **motion**. *See also* supporting affidavit; supporting papers.

moving party [*move* · ing *par* · tee] *n.* *See* movant.

mug *n.* 1. A face; a mouth. 2. A thug; a ruffian. *v.* 1. To **assault** a person, especially from behind, with the **intent** to **rob**. 2. To photograph a person who is being booked. *See* booking. *Also see* mug book. 3. To deliberately make a funny face.

➤ *v.* accost, assault, attack, rob ("to be mugged in the park").

mug book *n.* A volume containing photographs ("mug shots") of convicted criminals, maintained by law enforcement authorities for the purpose of identifying suspects.

mugging [*mug* · ing] *n.* *See* mug.

mulct [mulkt] *n.* A fine; a penalty. *v.* 1. To impose a fine or penalty. 2. To take something by fraud or deceit.

➤ *n.* fine, penalty, punishment. *v.* fine, penalize, punish, cheat, defraud, deceive, swindle.

multi- [*mul* · ti-] *(Latin) adj.* 1. Many; many times. 2. More than two.

multidistrict litigation [mul · ti · *dis* · trikt lit · i · *gay* · shen] *n.* Under the **Federal Rules of Civil Procedure**, "when **civil actions** involving one or more common questions of fact are pending in different districts [EXAMPLE: an **infringement of trademark**] occurring on a nationwide basis, such actions may be transferred to any district for coordinated or consolidated pretrial proceedings." EXAMPLES: **depositions**; **interrogatories**. *See* District Courts of the United States.

multifariousness [mul · ti · *fare* · ee · ess · ness] *n.* 1. The **joinder** of two or more **actions** or **claims**, contrary to the **Federal Rules of Civil Procedure** or state **rules of civil procedure**. *See also* misjoinder. 2. Complexity; intricacy.

➤ misjoinder; diversity, variety, intricacy.

multilateral agreement [mul · ti · *lat* · e · rel a · *gree* · ment] *n.* An agreement participated in by more than two parties.

multinational corporation [mul · ti · *nash* · e · nel kore · pe · *ray* · shen] *n.* A corporation with branches in a number of countries.

multiparty account [mul · ti · *par* · tee a · *kount*] *n.* A **joint account**, **POD account**, or **trust account**.

multiple [*mul* · tipl] *adj.* Many; a number of; more than one.

➤ several, plural, divergent, assorted, many, mixed.

multiple access [*ak* · sess] *n.* A **defense** in a **paternity suit**; the fact that the mother of the child had sexual relations with men other than the defendant. *Compare* nonaccess.

M

multiple counts *n.* More than one **count** in a **complaint** or **indictment**. *See* joinder of claims; joinder of counts; joinder of indictments.

multiple hearsay [*hear* · say] *n.* **Double hearsay**, triple hearsay, etc. *See* hearsay.

multiple listing [*list* · ing] *n.* A **listing agreement** under which the seller's real estate agent may permit other brokers to attempt to sell the property and, if successful, to share the sales commission. *See and compare* exclusive right to sell; nonexclusive listing; open listing.

multiple offenses [o · *fen* · sez] *n.* Conduct that violates more than one criminal statute. (However, *see* lesser included offense; merger of sentences.)

multiple sentence [*sen* · tense] *n.* **Consecutive sentences** or **concurrent sentences**.

multistate corporation [*mul* · ti · state kore · pe · *ray* · shen] *n.* A corporation that does business in more than one state or that has branches in several states. *See* doing business; doing business in a state.

municipal [myoo · *niss* · i · pel] *adj.* 1. Belonging or pertaining to a city, town, or other local government. 2. Public or governmental, as distinguished from private.
➤ urban, community, neighborhood, city, civic, town, metropolitan ("municipal ordinance").

municipal bond *n.* A **bond** issued by a state or a municipality to raise money for municipal expenses from a source other than taxation. *See* municipal securities. *Compare* municipal warrant.

municipal by-law [*by*-law] *n. See* by-law.

municipal charter [*char* · ter] *n. See* charter.

municipal corporation [kore · per · *ay* · shen] *n.* A **political subdivision** (EXAMPLES: a county; a city; a town; a village) created by the state legislature, with the power to administer the affairs of the community (by, for EXAMPLE, enacting ordinances) as well as the responsibility for enforcing the authority of the state within its territorial limits with respect to the functions delegated to it by the state (by, for EXAMPLE, arresting persons who violate state criminal statutes). Municipal

corporations are **legal entities** which can sue and be sued. *See* body politic and corporate; public corporation. *See also* quasi-municipal corporation.

municipal court *n.* A local court whose **territorial jurisdiction** is limited to the geographical boundaries of the municipality in which it is located and whose **subject matter jurisdiction** is generally confined to enforcing municipal ordinances and trying petty offenses, and to civil cases involving claims for small amounts of money. *See also* police court; small claims court.

municipal law *n.* 1. In the narrow and most usual sense of the term, the law pertaining to **local government**. 2. In a broad sense, the law of a state or nation, as distinguished from **international law**.

municipal officer [*off* · i · ser] *n.* An officer of a **municipality**. EXAMPLE: a mayor. *See* officer.

municipal ordinance [*or* · din · ense] *n. See* ordinance.

municipal securities [se · *kyoo* · ri · teez] *n.* **Municipal bonds** and **municipal warrants**.

municipal warrant [*war* · ent] *n.* An **order** drawn by a **municipal officer** disbursing municipal funds in payment of a debt of the municipality. *See* disbursement; order. *Also see* municipal securities. *Compare* municipal bond.

municipality [myoo · niss · i · *pal* · i · tee] *n.* A **municipal corporation**, for EXAMPLE, a county, city, or town. *See* body politic and corporate.
➤ metropolis, town, country, village, township, parish.

muniment of title [*myoo* · ni · ment of *ty* · tel] *n.* A document evidencing **title** to real estate, especially a **title deed** which, with other records, establishes a **chain of title**. *See also* title search.

murder [*mer* · der] *n.* The **intentional** and **premeditated** killing of a human being (**first degree murder**); the intentional killing of a human being, without premeditation, but with **malice aforethought**, express or implied (**second degree murder**). Under most state statutes, a **homicide**

M

that occurs during the commission of a **felony** is first degree murder, as are homicides perpetrated by lying in wait, torture, poison, and other criminal acts from which premeditation or deliberation can be inferred. Similarly, a homicide that results from deliberately doing a dangerous or deadly act with disregard for the safety of others is second degree murder, **malice** being inferred from the act itself. *Compare* manslaughter. *See* felony murder rule. *See also* degrees of crime.

➤ liquidation, slaughter, killing, slaying, homicide, execution, unlawful killing.

must *v.* A word used to express obligation or necessity; a term that the courts generally construe as mandatory rather than directory. *See and compare* may; shall. *n.* Something mandatory.

➤ *n.* charge, imperative, requirement, mandate, obligation.

mute *adj.* Silent; speechless; incapable of speaking.

➤ soundless, dumb, taciturn, wordless, reserved, silent, quiescent.

mutilation [myoo · ti · *lay* · shen] *n.* 1. As it relates to an instrument or document, any act, short of destruction, that makes the instrument imperfect. EXAMPLE: tearing or obliterating parts of a will. 2. Committing the crime of **mayhem**. *See* maim.

➤ confusion, injury, maiming, hurt, destruction, disfiguration, defacing.

mutiny [*myoo* · ti · nee] *n.* In **military law**, a revolt against authority by two or more subordinates acting together.
v. To revolt against commanding officers.

➤ *n.* disobedience, insurrection, revolt, riot, strike ("a shipwide mutiny").
v. disobey, insurrect, rebel, resist, rise up ("The crew was ready to mutiny at the slightest excuse").
Ant. submission, obedience.

mutual [*myoo* · choo · el] *adj.* Reciprocal, or the same on both sides of a transaction or relationship, as, for EXAMPLE, **mutual promises**, **mutual mistake**, or mutual affection.

➤ bilateral, interchanged, related, leagued, collaborative, connected.

mutual account [a · *kount*] *n.* An **account** with debits and credits, i.e., an account involving two persons that is maintained as an **open account** with the understanding that there will ultimately be an adjustment of the balance.

mutual advantage rule [ad · *van* · tej] *n.* A test for determining whether a person who enters upon premises with the owner's permission is an **invitee** or a **licensee**. If the owner receives a benefit or advantage from the visit (EXAMPLE: a pizza delivered as ordered), the visitor is an invitee; if not, he is a licensee. In some jurisdictions this distinction is critical in determining the **standard of care** required of the owner. *See also* business invitee.

mutual agreement [a · *gree* · ment] *n.* *See* mutual assent.

mutual assent [a · *sent*] *n.* A **meeting of the minds**; consent; agreement. Required for contract formation. *See* assent.

mutual benefit association [*ben* · uh · fit a · so · see · *ay* · shen] *n.* *See* benevolent association.

mutual benefit society [ben · uh · fit so · *sy* · e · tee] *n.* *See* benevolent association.

mutual company [*kum* · pe · nee] *n.* A **cooperative corporation** whose members are at one and the same time the customers and owners of the company, sharing the profits according to the volume of business they do with the company. *See* mutual insurance company.

mutual covenants [*kuv* · e · nents] *n.* **Covenants** that are concurrent, that is, the performance of one is a **condition precedent** to the obligation to perform the other. *See* mutual promises.

mutual fund *n.* An **investment company** that issues shares in itself and uses the proceeds from the sale of its stock to invest in the **securities** of other corporations.

mutual insurance [in · *shoor* · ense] *n.* An insurance policy issued by a **mutual insurance company**.

mutual insurance company [in · *shoor* · ense kum · pe · nee] *n.* An insurance company established and operated as a **mutual company**, issuing no **capital stock**, whose members are at

M

one and the same time the owners of the company, the insurers, and the insured. *See* insurance company. *Compare* stock company; stock insurance company.

mutual mistake [mis · *take*] *n.* A **mistake of fact** that is reciprocal and common to both parties to an agreement, each laboring under the same misconception with respect to a **material fact**. Such a mistake will justify **reformation** of the contract, and may warrant its **rescission**. EXAMPLES: an incorrect **legal description** in a deed, resulting in the grantee receiving more land than either of the parties intended; two ships named the "Peerless." *Compare* unilateral mistake.

mutual promises [*prom* · iss · ez] *n.* Promises exchanged by contracting parties, one being the **consideration** for the other. *See* contract. *Also see* mutual covenants.

mutual wills *n.* 1. Wills in which the **testators** name each other as beneficiaries. 2. Wills executed in accordance with an agreement between two persons to dispose of their property in a particular manner. *See* reciprocal wills.

mutuality [myoo · choo · *al* · i · tee] *n.* Two persons having the same relationship toward each other with respect to a particular right, obligation, burden, or benefit; the condition of being mutual. Mutuality is essential to the existence of a binding contract.

➤ reciprocity, interchange, correspondence, interdependence, correlation, exchange.

mutuality of contract [*kon* · trakt] *n.* A **meeting of the minds** of the parties; i.e., mutual assent. *See* mutuality of obligation.

mutuality of obligation [ob · li · *gay* · shen] *n.* A term referring to the rule of law that there must be "mutuality" in a contract; that is, it must be binding upon both parties if it is to be valid and enforceable. *See* mutuality of contract.

mystery [*mis* · te · ree] *n.* That which is difficult to understand or solve.

➤ puzzle, riddle, enigma, obscurity, quandary, perplexity ("The identity of the real killer remained a mystery").

mystify [*miss* · tih · fie] *v.* To confuse or bewilder.

➤ baffle, perplex, elude, stump, deceive, hoodwink.

M

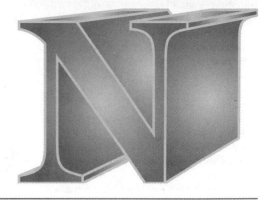

n.a. 1. Not applicable. 2. In banking, no account.

N.B. (*Latin*) Abbreviation of *nota bene*, meaning "note well." "N.B." is used in writing to emphasize the importance of a statement or fact in the way that *Note* is used throughout this dictionary.

nab *v.* To seize or take; to apprehend or arrest.
➤ capture, arrest, pick up, catch, apprehend ("the police nabbed the elusive suspect").

naive [*ni* · eev] *adj.* Innocent; simple; childlike.
➤ innocent, credulous, simple, trusting, unschooled, unworldly, plain, unaffected, gullible.
Ant. sophisticated, worldly.

naked [*nay* · ked] *adj.* 1. Plain; bare. 2. Nude; unclothed.
➤ plain, bare, nude, defenseless, conspicuous, noticeable, observable, overt, evident, perceptible.
   naked possession [po · *zesh* · en] *n.* Possession without **title** or **color of title**. *See* possession.
   naked possibility [poss · e · *bil* · e · tee] *n.* A mere possibility. *See* possibility.
   naked power [*pow* · er] *n.* Same as **collateral power**.
   naked promise [*prom* · iss] *n.* A promise for which there is no **consideration** and which, therefore, is not binding. *See* contract. *See also nudum pactum*.

NALA [*nah* · lah] *n.* Acronym for **National Association of Legal Assistants**.

NALS [nalz or en · ay · el · *ess*] *n.* Acronym for **National Association of Legal Secretaries**.

named *adj.* Specifically mentioned or designated.
➤ articulated, designated, appointed.
Ant. anonymous, unknown.

named insured [in · *shoord*] *n.* The person specified in an insurance policy as the insured person (EXAMPLE: under an automobile insurance policy, usually the owner of the car), as distinguished from others who may also be protected by the policy (EXAMPLE: an **automobile guest**). *Compare* additional insured.

Napoleonic Code [ne · poh · lee · *awn* · ik] *n.* Same as **Code Civil**.

narcotic [nar · *kot* · ik] *adj.* Relating to drugs that blunt the senses and induce sleep. *See* narcotics.

narcotics [nar · *kot* · iks] *n.* Highly addictive drugs, usually opiates, that blunt the senses, including pain, and induce sleep. Narcotics are **controlled substances**; their possession, distribution, or sale is a criminal offense.
➤ dope, anesthetic, analgesic, painkiller, drug, contraband, opiate, sedative, controlled substance.

narrative [*nehr* · e · tiv] *n.* A story; an account; at tale.
➤ story, telling, tale, description, communication, rendition, depiction.

narrative testimony [*nehr* · e · tiv *tes* · ti · moh · nee] *n.* A method of receiving **testimony** in which the witness is asked to state the facts and is allowed to do so uninterrupted by questions from counsel.

narrow [*nehr* · oh] *adj.* 1. Restricted; tight. USAGE: "a narrow passageway." 2. Intolerant; closed-minded. USAGE: "a narrow person."
➤ restricted, tight, constricted, strict; intolerant, closed-minded, partisan, bigoted, provincial.

narrow interpretation [*nehr* · oh in · ter · pre · *tay* · shen] *n.* An interpretation of a constitutional provision, statute, or ordinance that gives a restricted meaning to the words. *See* interpretation.

narrowly tailored [*nah* · row · lee *tay* · luhrd] *adj.* The quality of a statute that remedies the existing problem without affecting more activities than necessary. *Compare* overbreadth doctrine.

NASD Abbreviation of National Association of Securities Dealers, a **trade association** that oversees the ethical and professional standards of its members and maintains **NASDAQ**.

NASDAQ [*naz* · dak] *n.* Acronym for National Association of Securities Dealers Automated Quotations system. NASDAQ controls the **over-the-counter market** in **securities**. OTC securities are listed and traded through the NASDAQ system.

nation [*nay* · shen] *n.* A **body politic** of people occupying a specific geographical territory and politically organized under one government; a state or country independent of any other sovereign power, with an organized government, a system of laws, and the power to enter into agreements with other nations.
➤ republic, sovereignty, union, community, democracy, commonwealth.

national [*nash* · en · el] *adj.* 1. Pertaining to the United States. 2. Pertaining to a nation.
➤ civil, domestic, federal, governmental, political, widespread, nationwide ("the national government").

national bank *n.* A bank **incorporated** under federal statutes, as opposed to a **state bank**.

national debt *n.* The total sum of money owed by the government of the United States.

national domicile [*dom* · i · sile] *n.* The nation in which a person has her **domicile**,

as distinguished from her state or local domicile.

national emergency [e · *mer* · jen · see] *n.* Any event, including but not limited to war, that threatens the stability or safety of a nation. EXAMPLE: an economic crisis on a national scale. *Compare* national security.

national government [*guv* · ern · ment] *n.* 1. The government of the United States; the federal government. 2. The government of a nation.

national origin [*or* · i · jin] *n.* A term referring to the country in which a person or his ancestors were born.

national security [se · *kyoo* · ri · tee] *n.* Any matter relating to the safety of a nation. *Compare* national emergency.

National Association of Legal Assistants [*nash* · en · el a · so · see · *ay* · shen of *leeg* · el a · *sis* · tents] *n.* A national organization of legal assistants and paralegals whose purpose is to enhance professionalism and the interests of those in the profession, as well as to advance the administration of justice generally. Among its other undertakings, **NALA** has established a "Code of Professional Responsibility" for paralegals and legal assistants and provides professional certifications, continuing education, and assistance in job placement. A person who receives certification through NALA is entitled to so indicate by the use of "**CLA**" (**Certified Legal Assistant**) after his or her name.

National Association of Legal Secretaries [*nash* · en · el a · so · see · *ay* · shen of *leeg* · el sek · re · tare · eez] *n.* A national organization of legal secretaries whose purpose is continuing legal education and professionalism. Membership in **NALS** provides publications, seminars and workshops, and other educational tools. NALS also grants professional legal secretary certification to qualified applicants.

National Crime Information Center [in · fer · *may* · shen sen · ter] *n. See* NCIC.

National Federation of Paralegal Associations [*nash* · en · el fed · e · *ray* · shen of pehr · e · *leeg* · el a · so · see · *ay* · shenz] *n.* An association of paralegal and legal assistant organizations nationwide whose

N

purpose is to enhance professionalism and the interests of those in the profession, as well as to advance the administration of justice. Among its other undertakings, **NFPA** has established the "Affirmation of Responsibility," a code of professional conduct for paralegals and legal assistants, and provides continuing education and assistance in job placement.

National Guard [*nash* · en · el gard] *n.* An organization of men and women maintained as a reserve for the Army and the Air Force, serving their states during disasters and civil disturbances and subject to being called to regular service in time of war. The National Guard is a **militia**.

National Labor Relations Act [*nash* · en · el *lay* · ber re · *lay* · shenz] *n.* Actually several Acts of Congress, including the **Wagner Act** and the **Taft-Hartley Act**, which, collectively, regulate relations between management and labor by, among other things, prohibiting certain activities (**unfair labor practices**) that unreasonably hamper employers in the conduct of their business or that interfere with the right of employees to be effectively represented by unions of their choice.

National Labor Relations Board [*nash* · en · el lay · ber re · *lay* · shenz] *n.* A federal administrative agency created by the **National Labor Relations Act** for the purpose of enforcing the Act. Commonly referred to as the **NLRB**.

National Service Life Insurance [*nash* · en · el *ser* · viss life in · *shoor* · ense] *n.* A special type of life insurance provided to military personnel at low rates by federal statute.

nationality [nash · en · *al* · i · tee] *n.* Belonging and owing allegiance to a nation as a result of having been born there or through **naturalization**. Nationality is not a characteristic that applies only to human beings; corporations, ships, and flags, for EXAMPLE, also possess nationality. *See* foreign corporation; register of ships. *See also* citizenship.
➤ native land, origin, citizenship, allegiance, community, country.

nationalization [nash · en · e · li · *zay* · shen] *n.* The taking over of a business or an industry by the government.
➤ seizing, taking over, socialization, appropriation.

Native American [*nay* · tiv a · *mehr* · i · ken] *n.* An indigenous American. Although many indigenous Americans prefer the term "Native American" to "Indian," for historical reasons statutes relating to Native Americans generally refer to "Indians" and are so indexed in most code books and reference volumes. *See* Bureau of Indian Affairs; Indian Claims Commission; Indian lands; Indian reservation; Indian title; Indian tribe; *and see especially* Indian. *Compare* Administration for Native Americans.

natural [*nat* · sher · el] *adj.* 1. Occurring in accordance with the course of nature or the operation of **natural laws**; existing in nature; native. 2. Normal; ordinary. 3. Foreseeable. 4. Spontaneous.
➤ normal, everyday, accustomed, customary, typical; spontaneous; foreseeable; innate, inherent, untaught, fundamental, genetic ("his natural talent for oratory").

natural affection [a · *fek* · shen] *n.* The affection that a person's near relative is presumed to have for her. *See* love and affection.

natural and probable consequence [*prob* · ebl *kon* · se · kwense] *n.* A result that might naturally be expected to follow from a given act; a result that a **reasonable person** would have foreseen. USAGE: "His conduct amounted to negligence because the explosion was a natural and probable consequence of what he did." *See* probable consequence.

natural boundary [*boun* · de · ree] *n.* 1. A line formed by nature (EXAMPLE: a stream) that creates a boundary of a **parcel** of land. 2. A line drawn between two **natural monuments** that establishes a boundary. *See* boundary.

natural child *n.* A child born to its parents, as opposed to an adopted child. *Compare* adoption.

natural consequence [*kon* · se · kwense] *n.* *See* natural and probable consequence.

N

natural day *n.* The 24-hour period from midnight to midnight, as opposed to any 24-hour period.

natural death *n.* 1. Death resulting from natural causes rather than from, for EXAMPLE, **negligence**, accident, or violence. 2. Death from natural causes rather than **civil death**.

natural death acts *n.* State statutes granting people the right to make **living wills** and to establish **healthcare proxies**.

natural guardian [*gar* · dee · en] *n.* A child's mother or father, as distinguished from a **guardian** appointed by the court.

natural heirs [airz] *n.* **Heirs of the body**.

natural law *n.* 1. A term referring to the concept that there exists, independent of manmade law, a law laid down (depending upon one's beliefs) by God or by nature, which human society must observe in order to be happy and at peace. *See* natural right. *Compare* positive law. 2. A sequence of events in nature that always occur in the same manner if the circumstances are the same. EXAMPLE: the law of gravity.

natural laws *n.* *See* natural law.

natural monuments [*mon* · yoo · ments] *n.* Natural objects used in describing land boundaries. EXAMPLES: trees; rocks. *See* natural boundaries. *See also* legal description.

natural objects of bounty [*ob* · jekts of *boun* · tee] *n.* The members of a deceased person's family whom one would normally think of as his beneficiaries. USAGE: "I would have thought Sam's kids would have been the natural objects of his bounty, but he left everything to the Humane Society."

natural person [*per* · sen] *n.* A human being, as distinguished from an **artificial person** created by law, such as a **corporation**.

natural right *n.* A **right** existing under **natural law**, independent of manmade law. EXAMPLE: the right of a human being to exist. *Compare* positive law.

natural succession *n.* The passing of property from one person to another by **descent**. *See* succession.

natural watercourse [*waw* · ter · kohrss] *n.* A river or other natural stream, or natural channel for water, as distinguished from a manmade stream or artificial channel for water.

natural-born citizen [*sit* · i · zen] *n.* A citizen by birth, as distinguished from a citizen who has been naturalized. *Compare* naturalized citizen. *See* citizen.

naturalization [nat · sher · e · li · *zay* · shen] *n.* The process and the act of conferring nationality and citizenship upon a person who is not a natural-born citizen. *See* naturalized citizen.

➤ acceptance, admission, enfranchisement.

naturalization court *n.* A court with the power to administer the oath of allegiance (i.e., grant citizenship) to an alien whose eligibility for citizenship has been determined; specifically, a state **court of record** or any **District Court of the United States**. *See* naturalized citizen.

naturalization proceeding [pro · *see* · ding] *n.* A hearing before the **Immigration and Naturalization Service** or a federal district court to determine an applicant's eligibility for naturalization. *See* District Courts of the United States.

naturalized citizen [*nat* · sher · e · lized *sit* · i · zen] *n.* A person who has become a citizen through **naturalization**. *Compare* natural-born citizen. *See* citizen.

navigable [*nav* · i · gebl] *adj.* Sufficiently wide and deep for a ship to travel on.

➤ transversable, passable, unobstructed, negotiable ("navigable waters").

navigable river [*riv* · er] *n.* *See* navigable waters.

navigable waters [*waw* · terz] *n.* Any body of water, whether **inland waters, territorial waters,** or open sea, that is used, or capable of being used, as a route for trade and travel. United States **admiralty courts** have **jurisdiction** over "navigable waters of the United States." *Compare* nonnavigable waters.

navigate [*nav* · ih · gayt] *v.* To control the course of travel; to sail.

➤ travel, steer, guide, maneuver, traverse, journey.

navigation [nav · i · *gay* · shen] *n.* The science of guiding a ship, plane, etc. from place to place. *See* inland rules of navigation; rules of navigation.

NCIC *n.* The customary way of referring to the **National Crime Information**

Center, a computerized network used by police departments across the country to determine if there are outstanding warrants on a suspect or an arrestee, to locate missing persons, and to trace stolen vehicles, guns, and the like. *Compare* rap sheet.

ne exeat [nee *eks* · ee · at] *(Latin) v.* Means "do not leave"; refers to a **writ** forbidding a person from going beyond the geographical jurisdiction of the court or the state until she has secured a **bond** assuring satisfaction of the plaintiff's claim against her.

nearest male heir [*neer* · est male air] *n.* Same as **heir male**.

necessaries [*ness* · e · sair · eez] *n.* Things reasonably necessary for maintaining a person in accordance with his position in life. Thus, depending upon the person's economic circumstances, "necessaries" may not be limited simply to those things required to maintain existence, i.e., shelter, food, clothing, and medical care. *See* nonsupport; support.
➤ essentials, needs, requirements, prerequisites, necessities, fundamentals. *Ant.* luxuries.

necessary [*ness* · e · sair · ee] *adj.* 1. Essential; indispensable. 2. Appropriate; convenient; useful. *See also* necessaries; necessitous.
➤ essential, indispensable, required, imperative ("a necessary party"); appropriate, convenient, useful; unalterable, irrevocable, settled, certain ("necessary damages"). *Ant.* optional.

necessary and proper clause [*prop* · er] *n.* Article I of the Constitution grants to Congress the power to make all laws "necessary and proper" for carrying out its constitutional responsibilities. The Supreme Court has long interpreted this provision to mean that Congress has the right not only to enact laws that are absolutely indispensable, but any laws that are reasonably related to effectuating the powers expressly granted to it by the Constitution. *See and compare* enumerated powers; implied powers.

necessary damages [*dam* · e · jez] *n.* Same as **general damages**.

necessary easement [*eez* · ment] *n. See* way of necessity.

necessary expense [eks · *pense*] *n. See* ordinary and necessary expense.

necessary party [*par* · tee] *n.* A person who must be a **party** to an **action** for the court to grant complete relief; a party who must be **joined** if at all possible. Although the **Federal Rules of Civil Procedure** have replaced "necessary party" (and **indispensable party**) with the concept of **persons needed for just adjudication**, the original terms retain their importance under many states' **rules of civil procedure**. *See* joinder of parties.

necessary repairs [re · *pairz*] *n.* Repairs that are necessary if premises are to be usable for the purpose for which they are being leased *Compare* good repair; ordinary repair.

necessities [ne · *sess* · i · teez] *n. See* necessaries; necessity.

necessitous [ne · *sess* · i · tuss] *adj.* 1. Destitute; impoverished; needy; indigent. 2. Referring to that which must be done.
➤ destitute, impoverished, needy, indigent, disadvantaged ("necessitous circumstances"). *Ant.* wealthy.

necessitous circumstances [*ser* · kem · stan · sez] *n.* The condition of a person who lacks the **necessaries** of life.

necessity [ne · *sess* · i · tee] *n.* 1. That which is necessary; that which must be done. *See* certificate of convenience and necessity; certificate of need; way of necessity; work of necessity. 2. That which is compelled by natural forces and cannot be resisted. Necessity is a **defense** in a criminal prosecution if the defendant committed the crime to prevent a more serious harm from occurring. EXAMPLE: reckless driving by a driver, to avoid the gunshots of officers who are attempting to make an unlawful arrest, may not be a crime.
➤ essential, imperative, need, fundamental requirement, prerequisite ("a necessity for survival"); power, impulse, coercion, motivation ("public necessity").

need *n.* 1. The use or want of something. 2. Being without a necessity. *v.* To want or require something.

N

➤ *n.* demand, precondition, obligation, requirement, necessity ("the need for complete honesty"); absence, scarcity, deprivation, paucity, shortage ("to be in need").
v. require, demand, want, yearn, crave, desire, lack, long for, covet.

negate [*neg* · ate] *v.* To nullify or override.
➤ contradict, nullify, repeal, undo, void, gainsay, annul.

negative [*neg* · e · tiv] *adj.* Expressing denial, refusal, or opposition. *Compare* affirmative.
n. 1. A denial; a reason given in opposition to something. 2. An answer "no." *Compare* affirmative.
v. To deny, veto, reject, or refuse to consent.
➤ *adj.* disapproving, dissenting, opposing, objecting, adverse, cynical, rejecting, contravening.
n. denial, refusal, refutation, disavowal.
v. deny, veto, reject, refuse, consent.

negative averment [a · *ver* · ment] *n.* In a **pleading**, a **denial** coupled with an **allegation**.

negative condition [ken · *dish* · en] *n.* A **condition** grounded upon the nonoccurrence of some event.

negative covenant [*kov* · e · nent] *n.* A **covenant** that requires the **covenantor** to refrain from doing something. EXAMPLES: a **covenant not to compete**; a **restrictive covenant**.

negative easement [*eez* · ment] *n.* An **easement** whose effect is to prevent the owner of land subject to the easement from doing something he would be entitled to do if no easement existed. EXAMPLE: If the owner of Whiteacre and Blackacre, adjoining tracts of land, conveys Whiteacre to the Church of the Eternal and **covenants** that no building shall be erected on adjoining land within 150 feet of Whiteacre, that covenant is a negative easement with respect to Blackacre. *Compare* affirmative easement.

negative evidence [*ev* · i · dense] *n.* Testimony that an alleged fact is not so; testimony that denies rather than affirms. *Compare* positive evidence.

negative pregnant [*preg* · nent] *n.* In a **pleading**, a denial that carries within it an implied admission. (EXAMPLE: If a **complaint** alleges the defendant to be a corporation organized under the laws of California, an **answer** which denies that the defendant is organized under the laws of California is "pregnant" with the admission that the defendant is a corporation.) Pleading in this form is frowned upon by the courts.

negative testimony [*tess* · ti · moh · nee] *n.* See negative evidence.

neglect [*neg* · lekt] *n.* 1. The failure to do or perform some work, act, or duty, required by one's status or by law, or as required in one's business or occupation (EXAMPLES: a person's duty as a parent; as a **fiduciary**; as an attorney; as a contractor; as a landlord). Depending upon the context in which it appears, the word "neglect" may imply a deliberate failure to act, or it may mean either carelessness or simple oversight. *See* abuse; child abuse. *Compare* - willful neglect. 2. Carelessness; disregard; oversight.
v. 1. To fail to do something or to omit doing it. 2. To refuse to do something. *But compare* refusal; refuse.
➤ *n.* delinquency, disdain, disregard, inconsideration, indifference.
v. overlook, abandon, procrastinate, discount, omit, ignore.

neglect of duty [*dew* · tee] *n.* The failure of a public official to perform a duty required of her by virtue of her office or by law. *Compare* gross neglect of duty.

neglected child [*neg* · lekt · ed] *n.* A child who is abandoned, neglected, or cared for in an inadequate or unreasonable manner. *See* child abuse.

negligence [*neg* · li · jense] *n.* The failure to do something that a **reasonable person** would do in the same circumstances, or the doing of something a reasonable person would not do. Negligence is a **wrong** generally characterized by carelessness, inattentiveness, and neglectfulness rather than by a positive intent to cause **injury**. *See* negligence in law. *Compare* reckless; willful and wanton negligence.
   See also actionable negligence; active negligence; comparative negligence; concurrent negligence; contributory negligence; criminal negligence; culpable negligence; degrees of negligence; gross negligence;

N

imputed negligence; joint negligence; legal negligence; ordinary negligence; passive negligence; simple negligence; slight negligence; subsequent negligence; supervening negligence; wanton negligence; willful negligence.

➤ thoughtlessness, default, breach of duty, oversight, delinquency, irresponsibility, carelessness, dereliction, recklessness, inattentiveness ("The doctor's negligence caused the tumor to go undetected").

negligence in law   *n.*   1. A breach of the duty to use **care**; the failure to observe a duty established by law which **proximately** causes **injury** to the plaintiff. *See* proximate cause. 2. **Negligence per se**.

negligence per se   [per say]   *n.* Negligence that is beyond debate because the law, usually a statute or ordinance, has established a **duty** or **standard of care** that the defendant has violated, as a result of which he has caused **injury** to the plaintiff. EXAMPLE: failure to stop at a stop sign, as required by law, which is the **proximate cause** of injury to another driver or a pedestrian. *See per se. See also* absolute liability; negligence in law; strict liability.

negligent   [*neg* · li · jent]   *adj.*   1. Being responsible for an act of **negligence**.
2. Careless; heedless; inattentive; lax.
3. Reckless.

➤ careless, heedless, inattentive, lax, reckless, irresponsible, delinquent.

negligent homicide   [*hom* · i · side]   *n.* The crime of causing the death of a person by negligent or reckless conduct. *See and compare* manslaughter; second degree murder. *See* culpable negligence. *Also see* reckless endangerment; reckless homicide; vehicular homicide.

negligent manslaughter   [*man* · slaw · ter] *n.*   In some states, a form of **negligent homicide**.

negligently   [*neg* · li · jent · lee]   *adv.*   *See* negligent.

negotiability   [ne · go · sha · *bil* · i · tee]   *n.* The quality of being **negotiable**. *See* words of negotiability.

negotiable   [ne · *go* · shebl]   *adj.*
1. Transferable by **indorsement** or **delivery**. EXAMPLE: a **negotiable instrument**.

2. Subject to negotiation; bargainable. USAGE: "My usual fee is $100 an hour, but it's negotiable." *Compare* nonnegotiable.

➤ transferable, assignable, alienable ("a negotiable instrument"); open, undetermined, malleable, bargainable ("Her fee was negotiable").
Ant. nonnegotiable; fixed.

negotiable instrument   [*in* · stroo · ment] *n.*   Under the **Uniform Commercial Code**, a signed writing that orders or promises payment of money if: it is unconditional, it is in a fixed amount, it is payable **on demand** to **bearer** or to **order** or at a definite time, and it "does not state any undertaking or instruction by the person promising or ordering payment to do any act in addition to the payment of money." (EXAMPLES: a check; a money order; a **certificate of deposit**; a **bond**; a **note**, a **bill of lading**; a **warehouse receipt**.) Negotiable instruments are also referred to as **commercial paper** or **negotiable paper**.

➤ draft, check, bond, note, money order, instrument.

negotiable order of withdrawal account [*or* · der of with · *draw* · el a · *kount*]   *n.* More commonly called a **NOW account**; a savings account on which checks can be drawn.

negotiable paper   [*pay* · per]   *n.   See* negotiable instrument.

negotiable words   *n.   See* words of negotiability.

negotiate   [ne · *go* · shee · ate]   *v.*   1. To transfer a **negotiable instrument** to a third person by **indorsement** or **delivery**. 2. To bargain; to discuss the terms of a contract. *See* negotiable; negotiation. *See also* negotiated plea.

➤ deal, mediate, bargain, arrange, discuss.

negotiated plea   [ne · *go* · shee · ay · ted plee] *n.*   A **plea** entered by a defendant in a criminal case after **plea bargaining** with the prosecution.

negotiation   [ne · go · shee · *ay* · shen]   *n.*
1. The act of transferring a **negotiable instrument** to a third person by **indorsement** or **delivery**. 2. Communication, whether in the form of discussions, or in writing, or otherwise, in attempting to arrive at an agreement; the act or process

N

of bargaining. *See* negotiable; negotiation. *See also* negotiated plea.
➤ agreement, compromise, mediation, discussion, arbitration.

negotiations [ne · go · shee · *ay* · shenz] *n.* *See* negotiation.

nemo [*nee* · moh] (*Latin*) *n.* Meaning "No one"; nobody; no man; no person. The word "*nemo*" appears as the first word of many legal maxims. EXAMPLE: *Nemo dare potest quod non habet* ("No one is able to give what he does not have").

neonatal [nee · o · *nay* · tel] *adj.* Pertaining to a newborn child or children.

neonatal tissue [*tish* · yew] *n.* The live tissue or cells of a newborn child.

nepotism [nep · e · tizm] *n.* The act of appointing a person to public office because she is related by blood or marriage to the person making the appointment. (EXAMPLE: the mayor appointing his sister-in-law to the position of chief of police.) It has also come to mean favoring relatives in business transactions or promotions.
➤ partiality, injustice, unfairness, partisanship, cronyism, preferential treatment.

net *adj.* Pertaining to that which is left after deductions.
n. 1. A loosely woven fabric. 2. That which remains after deducting for charges such as cost, interest, taxes, and the like; short for **net income**, **net profit**, **net worth**, etc. USAGE: "Although the gross receipts of the business exceeded $100,000 this year, after we pay all of our operating expenses our net [i.e., net profit] will be less than $10,000." *Compare* gross.
➤ *adj.* remaining, residual, surplus, unspent ("net profits").
n. cloth, netting, fabric; gain, profit, return, accumulation, taxes.

net assets [*ass* · ets] *n.* Total **assets** minus total **liabilities**.

net balance [*bal* · ense] *n.* As applied to the proceeds of a sale, the balance of the proceeds after deducting the expenses related to the sale. *See* balance.

net before taxes [be · *for tak* · sez] *n.* **Gross profit** less all costs and expenses except taxes. *See* net profit.

net contract [*kon* · trakt] *n.* *See* net listing.

net earnings [*ern* · ingz] *n.* **Gross receipts** or **gross revenue**, less **operating expenses**; **gross income** less **gross expenses**, including taxes; **net profit**. *See* net income; net pay. *Compare* gross expenses.

net estate [es · *tate*] *n.* The **estate** of a **decedent** after deduction of debts, funeral expenses, and **expenses of administration**. *Compare* gross estate. *See* taxable estate.

net income [*in* · kum] *n.* **Gross income** less **ordinary and necessary expenses**; **taxable income**. *Compare* gross income. *See* net earnings.

net lease *n.* A **lease** that binds the tenant to pay all expenses (EXAMPLES: utilities; taxes). *Compare* gross lease. *See* net rent.

net listing [*list* · ing] *n.* A contract in which the owner of property agrees to pay the broker, as her commission, everything she obtains over a specified amount for the sale of the owner's property.

net operating loss [*op* · e · ray · ting] *n.* The excess of **operating expenses** over **gross income** or **gross revenue**.

net pay *n.* Salary, wages, or commissions, after payroll deductions for taxes, social security, etc.; take-home pay. *Compare* gross pay. *See* net earnings; net income.

net premium [*pree* · mee · yum] *n.* The amount of a life insurance premium less any **dividend** to which the insured is entitled.

net price *n.* The price of goods or real estate, after subtracting commissions, discounts, and any other deductions.

net proceeds [*pro* · seedz] *n.* The **proceeds** of a sale, less commissions or other charges that an agent making the sale may rightfully deduct. *Compare* gross proceeds.

net profit [*prof* · it] *n.* **Gross profit** less all costs and expenses including taxes; **net earnings**. *See* net before taxes.

net rent *n.* Rent paid under a **net lease**.

net return [re · *tern*] *n.* **Net income**; **net profit**.

net revenue [*rev* · e · new] *n.* For most purposes, the same as **net income**. *Compare* gross revenue.

N

net weight *n.* The weight of a shipment of goods, less the weight of containers, boxes, crates, and the like; the weight of any packaged article less the weight of its packaging. *Compare* gross weight.

net worth *n.* The value of an entity's **assets** minus its **liabilities**. A statement of net worth is generally exchanged by the parties in a **matrimonial action**.

net worth method [*meth* · ed] *n.* For purposes of federal income tax, a method of calculating the income of a taxpayer whose records are inadequate: her **net worth** as of the beginning of the **tax year** is subtracted from her net worth as of the end of the tax year.

net yield *n.* The return on an investment, after deducting its costs (EXAMPLES: **brokerage**; commissions).

neurosis [new · *roh* · sis] *n.* A mental disorder characterized by anxiety, as opposed to severe derangement. It is also referred to as **psychoneurosis**. *Compare* psychosis.

➤ disorder, insanity, abnormality, affliction, derangement, inhibition, instability.

neutrality acts *n.* Federal statutes that prohibit the government or any citizen of the United States from engaging in certain acts in support of countries that are at war with each other if the United States is not at war with any of the belligerents. EXAMPLES of prohibited acts: soliciting funds in support of a belligerent government; traveling on the ship of a belligerent country.

new *adj.* A word whose meaning always depends upon the context in which it appears. Those meanings include: original; novel; fresh; mint; recent; recently manufactured; newly made; newly discovered; not previously used; unexplored; different; better.

➤ original, novel, fresh, mint, recent, unexplored, different.

new and useful [*yooss* · ful] *adj.* The two characteristics an invention must possess for it to be **patentable**.

new cause of action [*ak* · shen] *n.* In connection with an amended **pleading**, a phrase applied to a **cause of action** that is based upon facts different from those in the original pleading, or to a cause of action that involves **parties** not named in the original pleading. *See* amendment of pleading.

new evidence [*ev* · i · dense] *n.* *See* newly discovered evidence.

new issue [*ish* · yew] *n.* **Securities** issued to the public for the first time. *See* issue.

new matter [*mat* · er] *n.* **Allegations** that may properly be the subject of amended pleadings (*see* amendment of pleadings) or **supplemental pleadings**; material not originally pled or events occurring after the original pleading was filed.

new promise [*prom* · iss] *n.* A promise that is substituted for an earlier promise, which either the **promisor** cannot keep or the **promisee** cannot enforce. *See* promise. *Also see* contract.

new trial [*try* · el] *n.* A trial that may be ordered by the **trial court** itself, or by an **appellate court** on appeal, when **prejudicial error** has occurred or when, for any other reason, a fair trial was prevented. **Newly discovered evidence**, faulty **jury instructions**, and juror misconduct are common EXAMPLES of grounds for a new trial, which may be granted by the court on its **own motion** or upon a party's **motion for a new trial**. *See* trial de novo.

newly discovered evidence [*nyoo* · lee dis · *kuv* · erd *ev* · i · dense] *n.* Evidence discovered after the verdict or **judgment** in a case. Newly discovered evidence is a ground for a new trial if it involves **material facts** *discovered after* trial which *occurred prior* to the trial, if those facts could not have been discovered in time for the trial, even by the exercise of **due diligence**. EXAMPLE: a confession by Bill, after Jane's conviction, that he, not she, committed the murder.

newsman's privilege [*nyooz* · manz *priv* · i · lej] *n.* *See* shield laws.

newspaper of general circulation [*nyooz* · pay · per of *jen* · e · rel ser · kyoo · *lay* · shen] *n.* A newspaper subscribed to by the general public, published at regular intervals, which contains material of general interest. Statutes commonly provide that **legal notice** take the form of notice published in a newspaper

N

of general circulation. *Compare* official newspaper.

next *adj.* 1. Immediately following. USAGE: "Yours is the next motion to be heard." 2. Nearest; adjacent. USAGE: "Go to the courtroom next to the elevator."
➤ following; consequent, ensuing; closest, proximate, nearby, neighboring, adjacent.

next friend *n.* A person appointed by the court to concern herself with the interests of a minor or other **incompetent**, and to act on his behalf. Such an appointment is less formal than a **guardianship**, but is often similar in its responsibilities. *Compare* friend of the court.
➤ guardian, appointee.

next of kin *n.* A person's next of kin may be either her **blood relatives**, or those persons who would inherit from her under the laws of **intestate succession**.

NFPA [*nif · pa*] Acronym for **National Federation of Paralegal Associations**.

nighttime [*nite · time*] *n.* At **common law**, the period between sunset and sunrise. (*See* burglary.) In many states, "nighttime" has been redefined by statute.
➤ twilight, dusk, dark, nightfall.

nihil [*nee · hil*] (*Latin*) *n.* Nothing; not. The word "*nihil*" appears as the initial word of many legal maxims and phrases. For EXAMPLE, *nihil habit* ("he has nothing") is a **return** that a sheriff makes on a **writ** which she has been unable to serve on a defendant.

nil *n.* Nothing; zero.
➤ nothing, zero, naught.

Nineteenth Amendment [*nine · teenth a · mend · ment*] *n.* The amendment to the Constitution that prohibits the government, federal or state, from denying or restricting a citizen's right to vote on the basis of gender. Its effect was to give women the right to vote.

Ninth Amendment [*a · mend · ment*] *n.* An amendment to the Constitution which provides that the fact that certain rights are enumerated in the Constitution "shall not be construed to deny or disparage others retained by the people." The Supreme Court has held that **privacy** is an EXAMPLE of such a retained right. *See* right of privacy.

nisi [*nie · sie*] (*Latin*) *adj.* The word "*nisi*" conveys the idea of condition. Thus, for EXAMPLE, a **decree nisi** is a conditional judgment which the court will make final unless the **party** affected by it **shows cause** why it should not be made final. *See* order to show cause.

nisi decree [*de · kree*] *n.* *See* decree nisi.

nisi prius [*pree · us*] *adj.* Meaning "unless before." A term designating a **trial court**, as opposed to an **appellate court**.

NLRB Abbreviation of **National Labor Relations Board**.

no 1. None; none at all; zero. 2. A negative answer; a denial.
➤ none, zero; denial, rejection.

no action clause *n.* A clause in a **liability insurance** policy which provides that the insurance company is not obligated to **indemnify** its policyholder unless a lawsuit (an action) has been brought against the policyholder by an **injured** third party and has resulted in a **judgment** for **damages** or in an out-of-court settlement.

no arrival, no sale [*a · ry · vel*] *n.* A term in a **contract for sale of goods**, which means that if the goods do not arrive at their destination, **title** does not pass to the buyer and she is not liable for the purchase price.

no bill *n.* An **indorsement** meaning **not found** or **not a true bill**, which a **grand jury** enters on an **indictment** when it declines to **indict**. *Compare* true bill.

no caused [*kawzd*] *v./adj.* Same as **nonsuited**.

no contest [*kon · test*] *n.* *See nolo contendere*.

no evidence [*ev · i · dense*] *n.* A phrase that may mean either inadequate evidence or, literally, no evidence at all. *See and compare* insufficient evidence; scintilla rule.

no eyewitness rule [*eye · wit · ness*] *n.* The rule that when there is no eyewitness to an event involving a fatality, the **presumption** is that the **decedent** exercised **ordinary care** for his own safety, unless there is evidence clearly indicating the contrary. *See* contributory negligence.

no funds *n.* *See* insufficient funds; NSF check.

N

no goods *n. See nulla bona.*

no recourse [*ree* · korss] *n. See* without recourse. *Also see* nonrecourse.

no-contest clause [*kon* · test] *n. See* incontestability provision.

no-fault divorce [di · *vorss*] *n.* A term for the requirements for divorce in jurisdictions in which the party seeking the divorce need not demonstrate that the other party is at fault. The requirements differ from state to state. EXAMPLES include **irreconcilable differences**, **irremedial breakdown of marriage**, and **irretrievable breakdown of marriage**.

no-fault insurance [in · *shoor* · ense] *n.* A type of automobile insurance required by law in many states, under which the insured is entitled to **indemnification** regardless of who was responsible for the injury or damage. Proof of **negligence** is not a condition of liability under such a policy. *See* insurance.

no-par stock *n.* Stock with no **par value**. *See* stock.

no-strike clause *n.* A provision in a **collective bargaining agreement** that prohibits the union from striking, usually in specified circumstances or unless it has first taken certain steps, for EXAMPLE, submitting the dispute to **mediation**. *See* strike.

nol pros'd [nawl prosst] *v.* A use of the term *nol. pros.* as a verb to indicate the **discontinuance** of either a civil action or a criminal prosecution. USAGE: "Because there wasn't enough evidence, the district attorney nol pros'd the case against Lee." *See nolle prosequi. See also* voluntary dismissal.

nol. pros. [nawl pross] (*Latin*) *v.* Abbreviation and short form of *nolle prosequi.*

nolle prosequi [*no* · le *pross* · e · kwee] (*Latin*) *n.* Means "unwilling to pursue." 1. In a criminal case, an entry **of record** by the prosecutor by which she declares her intention not to prosecute the case further. 2. In a civil action, an entry on the record by the plaintiff by which he declares that he will proceed no further with the case.

nolo contendere [*no* · lo kon · *ten* · de · ray] (*Latin*) *n.* Means "I do not wish to contend."

A **plea** in a criminal case, also referred to as **no contest**, which, although it is essentially the same as a guilty plea, and carries the same consequences with respect to punishment, can be entered only with **leave of court**, because it is not an admission of responsibility and cannot be used against the defendant in a civil action based upon the same facts.

nolo contendere plea [plee] *n. See nolo contendere.*

nominal [*nom* · i · nel] *adj.* 1. In name only. 2. Minimal; very small; inconsequential; insubstantial; insignificant.
➤ minimal, inconsequential, insubstantial, insignificant, simple.

nominal capital [*kap* · i · tel] *n.* In the context of a business, **capital** that either exists only in name or is insignificant in amount.

nominal consideration [ken · sid · e · *ray* · shen] *n.* **Consideration** in a nominal amount. (EXAMPLE: "**one dollar**.") Nominal consideration is commonly the stated consideration, or the consideration **of record**, when the parties want the actual amount of the consideration to be kept between themselves.

nominal damages [*dam* · e · jez] *n.* **Damages** awarded to a plaintiff in a very small or merely symbolic amount. Such damages are appropriate in a situation where: (1) although a legal right has been violated, no **actual damages** have been incurred, but the law recognizes the need to vindicate the plaintiff (*see* vindictive damages); or (2) some **compensable injury** has been shown, but the amount of that injury has not been proven.

nominal defendant [de · *fen* · dent] *n. See* nominal party.

nominal partner [*part* · ner] *n.* A person who appears to be a **partner**, or a person whom the partnership **holds out** as a partner, but who has no real or substantial interest in the firm or the business.

nominal party [*par* · tee] *n.* 1. A person suing or defending an **action** for the benefit of another. 2. A person who is a **party** in an action, but who is not a **real party in interest**. EXAMPLE: a person joined as a party to comply with a technical **rule of**

N

practice, not because he has an **interest** in the subject matter of the action.

nominal plaintiff [*plane* · tif] *n. See* nominal party.

nominal right *n.* A technical but likely inconsequential right, as opposed to a **substantive right**.

nominal trust *n.* A **passive trust**; a **dry trust**.

nominate [*nom* · i · nayt] *v.* 1. To name or to designate. 2. To select or choose a person to be a candidate for office.
➤ designate, select, choose, draft, recommend.

nomination [nom · i · *nay* · shen] *n.* The act of nominating. *See* nominate.
➤ choice, designation, recommendation, appointment.

nominee [nom · i · *nee*] *n.* 1. A person who has been nominated as a candidate. 2. An agent, delegate, deputy, or other representative of another person; a person who has been named or designated to act on behalf of another. USAGE: "the winner of the contest will be chosen by the mayor or her nominee" means "the winner will be chosen by the mayor or by someone the mayor selects to make the decision." *See* nominate.
➤ aspirant, candidate, entrant, bidder.

nominee trust *n.* A **trust** in which, by the **terms of the trust**, the **trustee** is authorized to hold trust property in the name of a third person or a group of persons nominated by the trustee. *See* nominate.

non (*Latin*) Not; no. A word used in combination with another word, or as a prefix, to indicate the negative or the absence of something.

non compos mentis [*kom* · pess men · tiss] *adj.* Mentally incompetent; of unsound mind. *See* mental incapacity. *See also* insanity.

non obstante [ob · *stan* · tay] *adv.* Notwithstanding.

non obstante veredicto [ob · *stan* · tay ver · e · *dik* · toh] *adj.* Means "notwithstanding the verdict." See judgment notwithstanding the verdict. See also judgment non obstante veredicto; judgment NOV.

non pros'd [prosst] *v.* A use of the term ***non pros***. as a verb to indicate a **dismissal** because of a **failure to prosecute; nonsuited**. USAGE: "His suit was non pros'd because he failed to appear at trial." *See non prosequitur*; nonsuit.

non pros. [pross] *n.* Abbreviation and short form of ***non prosequitur***.

non prosequitur [pross · *ek* · wi · ter] *n.* Means "he does not pursue." The name of a **judgment** that was available to a party at **common law** if the **adverse party** failed to take some action in a lawsuit as required by the **rules of procedure**, for EXAMPLE, filing an **answer** within the prescribed time. Today, such a failure would result in a **dismissal**. *See* failure to prosecute. *See also* default judgment; nonsuit.

non sequitur [*sek* · wi · ter] *n.* Means "it does not [logically] follow." USAGE: "It's a *non sequitur* to conclude that because Bill wasn't sentenced to prison the last time, he won't be this time."

non-par-value stock [*val* · yoo] *n.* Same as **no-par stock**.

nonabatable nuisance [non a · *bay* · tebl *new* · sense] *n.* A **permanent nuisance**. *Compare* abatable nuisance.

nonacceptance [non · ek · *sep* · tense] *n.* 1. Under the **Uniform Commercial Code**, the right of a buyer to reject goods that fail to conform to the contract. 2. The refusal of a **drawee** to pay a **draft** as **presented**. *See* acceptance; dishonor. 3. A refusal or rejection.

nonaccess [non · *ak* · sess] *n.* A **defense** in a **paternity suit**; i.e., the fact that the alleged father of the child had no opportunity to have sexual relations with the plaintiff.

nonage [*noh* · nij] *n.* The status of a person under the **age of majority; minority**.
➤ infancy, minor, minority.

nonapparent easement [non · a · *pehr* · ent *eez* · ment] *n.* An **easement** that is not obvious to the eye. *Compare* apparent easement. *See* discontinuous easement.

nonappearance [non · e · *peer* · ense] *n.* 1. The failure of a defendant to enter an **appearance** in an **action**. 2. The failure of a **party** or witness to appear in court in

response to notice, a subpoena, or other **process**.
➤ default, truancy, nonattendance, absenteeism, nonpresence.

nonbailable [non · *bale* · ebl] *adj.* A crime for which, by statute, no bail may be set. Murder and armed robbery are examples of nonbailable offenses. *See* bail; bailable offense.

noncancelable policy [non · *kan* · se · lebl *paw* · li · see] *n.* An insurance policy that, by its terms, cannot be canceled by the insurance company.

nonconforming [non · ken · *for* · ming] *adj.* Noncompliant; different; deviating.
➤ contrary, noncompliant, dissenting, differing, defiant, deviant, unique, unconventional.

nonconforming use [non · ken · *for* · ming] *n.* In zoning law, a use of a building or land that is permitted, even though it does not comply with current regulations, because the use conforms to the law in effect at the time the use began. *Compare* conforming use. *See* grandfather clause.

noncontestability clause [non · ken · tes · te · *bil* · i · tee] *n.* Same as **incontestability provision**.

noncontestable [non · ken · *tes* · te · bul] *adj.* Incapable of being disputed or challenged.
➤ incontrovertible, undeniable, nonchallengeable, nondebatable ("this provision is noncontestable").

noncumulative dividend [non · *kyoo* · myoo · le · tiv *div* · i · dend] *n.* A **dividend** on **preferred stock** that does not accumulate (*see* accumulated dividend) if the corporation does not distribute it to its shareholders; a dividend that the corporation has no duty to pay once the year in which it **accrues** has passed.

noncumulative stock *n. See* noncumulative dividend.

nondisclosure [non · dis · *kloh* · zher] *n.* The failure to reveal a fact, regardless of whether there was an intent to conceal the fact. *Compare* disclosure.
➤ concealment, silence, withholding.

nonexclusive listing [non · eks · *kloo* · siv *lis* · ting] *n.* With respect to real estate, a **listing agreement** with the features of an exclusive listing, except that the owner retains the right to sell her property without using the agent and without becoming liable to the agent for a commission. *See and compare* exclusive right to sell; multiple listing; open listing.

nonexclusive power of appointment [non · eks · *kloo* · siv *pow* · er of a · *point* · ment] *n.* A **power of appointment** under which the **donee** is not permitted to exclude from the **distribution** any member of the class designated by the **donor**. *Compare* exclusive power of appointment. *See* objects of a power.

nonfeasance [non · *fee* · zense] *n.* The failure of a person to act. *See and compare* malfeasance; misfeasance.
➤ disregard, omission, dereliction, failure, avoidance.
Ant. misfeasance, action.

nonintervention will [non · in · ter · *ven* · shen] *n.* A will that directs the **executor** to administer the **decedent's estate** without court supervision.

nonjoinder [non · *join* · der] *n.* The failure to join a **party** necessary for a just **adjudication** of an **action**. *See* joinder. *See and compare* indispensable party; necessary party; persons needed for just adjudication.

nonjury trial [non · *joor* · ee *try* · el] *n.* A trial before a judge without a jury; a **bench trial**.

nonleviable [non · *lev* · ee · ebl] *adj.* Property that, by virtue of an **exemption statute** (EXAMPLE: a **homestead exemption**), cannot be levied upon. *See* levy; writ of attachment.

nonmailable matter [non · *male* · ebl *mat* · er] *n.* Material that cannot lawfully be deposited in the United States mails. EXAMPLES: material of irregular size; **contraband** (i.e., **controlled substances**, obscene matter, etc.).

nonnavigable waters [non · *nav* · i · gebl] *n.* Any body or bodies of water that are not **navigable**.

N

nonnegotiability [non · ne · go · sha · *bil* · i · tee]
n. The quality of being **nonnegotiable**.
Compare negotiability.

nonnegotiable [non · ne · *goh* · shebl] *adj.*
1. A document or instrument not
transferable by **indorsement** or **delivery**.
EXAMPLES: a lease; a deed; a mortgage. 2. Not
subject to negotiation; not bargainable.
USAGE: "My fee is $100 an hour, and it is
nonnegotiable." *Compare* negotiable.
➤ nontransferable, non-assignable ("a
nonnegotiable lease"); closed, set,
established, not bargainable.

nonnegotiable instrument
[*in* · stroo · ment] *n.* An **instrument** that
is not **negotiable**.

nonpar stock *n.* Same as **no-par stock**.

nonpayment [non · *pay* · ment] *n.* The failure of a debtor to pay a debt when it is due.
➤ delinquency, evasion, arrearage, remissness, repudiation.

nonperformance [non · per · *form* · ense] *n.*
1. Failure to do or perform an act in
accordance with the terms of a contract;
breach of contract. 2. The failure or
inability to do that which one is obligated
to do or wishes to do.
➤ dereliction, omission, evasion,
infringement, noncompliance.
Ant. compliance.

nonprofit [non · *prof* · it] *adj.* Not done
for profit. *See* profit.
➤ altruistic, philanthropic, unselfish,
magnanimous, benevolent, eleemosynary.

nonprofit association
[a · so · see · *ay* · shen] *n.* An **association**
organized for purposes other than making
a profit, usually purposes that are educational, fraternal, or charitable in nature.
EXAMPLES: a sorority; a labor union; many
religious congregations. *See* charitable
organization; charitable purpose.

nonprofit corporation
[kore · per · *ay* · shen] *n.* A **nonstock
corporation** organized for purposes other
than making a profit, generally for charitable or educational purposes. EXAMPLE: a
private college or a **private university**.
Compare profit corporation. *See* charitable
corporation.

nonprofit institution [in · sti · *too* · shen]
n. See charitable institution.

nonprofit organization
[or · ga · ni · *zay* · shen] *n.* A **nonprofit
association, nonprofit corporation**, or
any **charitable organization**.

nonrecourse [non · *ree* · korss] *adj.* A
term referring to the legal inability of a
person to look to another, or to other
property, for the satisfaction of a debt or
demand. Thus, a "nonrecourse loan" is a
loan in which the only **asset** available to
the creditor in the event of default is the
property that **secures** the loan, the debtor
having no **personal liability**. *Compare*
recourse. *Also see and compare* with
recourse; without recourse.

nonresident [non · *rez* · i · dent] *n.* 1. A
person who does not reside within the
jurisdiction. 2. A person who is in a place
other than his residence. 3. A **foreign
corporation**. *See* foreign service of process; long arm statutes. *Compare* resident.
➤ nonoccupant, nondomiciliary, noncitizen,
alien, foreigner, visitor, interloper.

nonresident alien [*ayl* · yen] *n.* A
person who is neither a citizen nor a
resident of the United States. *Compare*
resident alien. *See* alien.

nonresident motorist statutes
[*moh* · ter · ist *stat* · shoots] *n.* State
statutes that give the courts of a state
jurisdiction over nonresidents who operate
their motor vehicles on the highways of
the state. *See* long arm statutes. *See also*
foreign service of process.

nonsane [non · *sane*] *adj.* Unsound mind.
See insanity.

nonstock corporation [non · *stok*
kore · per · *ay* · shen] *n.* A corporation,
usually a **nonprofit corporation**, that
issues no stock and whose members have
no ownership or **proprietary interest**.
See corporations.

nonsuit [*non* · soot] *n.* 1. A **judgment**
given by a court against a plaintiff who
fails to appear for trial or who, upon trial,
is unable to prove her case; a **dismissal**.
A nonsuit in these circumstances is called
an **involuntary nonsuit**. 2. A judgment by
a court against a plaintiff who consents

to the judgment is called a **voluntary nonsuit**. *See and compare* involuntary dismissal; voluntary dismissal. *See* peremptory nonsuit. *See also* default judgment; directed verdict; *non prosequitur.*
➤ default, dismissal, directed verdict.

nonsuited [non · *soot* · ed] *adv.* The status of a plaintiff against whom a **nonsuit** has been entered; in some jurisdictions, to be nonsuited is to be "**no caused.**"

nonsupport [non · sup · *port*] *n.* 1. The crime committed by a parent who willfully fails to provide his or her minor child with the **necessaries** of life. 2. The crime committed by a husband or wife who willfully fails to provide a dependent spouse with necessaries. 3. A ground for divorce in some states. *See also* Reciprocal Enforcement of Support Act.
➤ default, neglect, noncontribution, failure to provide, irresponsibility.

nonuse [non · *yooss*] *n.* The state of not being used.
➤ forbearance, abstinence, disuse.

nonuser [non · *yoo* · zer] *n.* Failure to use, particularly relative to **rights** in land. The absence of a **user** (EXAMPLE: failure to use an **easement**) may result in loss of the right. *Note* that "nonuser" does not refer to a person; it is a legal concept. *See* adverse possession; adverse user.

nonvoting stock [*non* · voh · ting] *n.* Corporate stock that does not carry with it the right to vote on the conduct of corporate affairs. *Compare* voting stock.

norm *n.* That which is regularly done; the standard; the custom.
➤ standard, custom, average, rule, generality, habit.

not A word expressing the negative or communicating refusal or denial.
not a true bill *n.* An **indorsement** that a grand jury enters on a **bill of indictment** when it declines to **indict**. *See and compare* no bill; true bill. *See also* not found.
not found *v.* An **indorsement** that a grand jury enters on a **bill of indictment** when it declines to **indict**. *Compare* found. *See and compare* no bill; true bill. *See also* not a true bill.

not guilty [*gill* · tee] *n.* 1. A plea entered in a criminal case by a defendant who denies having committed the crime with which she is charged. 2. The verdict of a jury that acquits a criminal defendant. 3. The **judgment** of a court, sitting without a jury, that the prosecution has failed to prove its case against a criminal defendant. *Compare* innocent.
not guilty plea [*gill* · tee plee] *n. See* not guilty.
not guilty verdict [*ver* · dikt] *n. See* not guilty.
not negotiable [ne · *goh* · shebl] *n.* Same as **nonnegotiable**.
not satisfied [*sat* · is · fide] *n.* Same as **no goods** or *nulla bona*.
not-for-profit corporation [*prof* · it kore · per · *ay* · shen] *n.* Same as **nonprofit corporation**.

nota bene [*no* · ta ben · ay] *(Latin) v.* Means "note well." *See N.B.*

notarial [noh · *tare* · ee · el] *adj.* Pertaining to a notary public or to the functions of a notary public.
notarial act *n.* The act of a notary public, for EXAMPLE, an **acknowledgement** or a **jurat**.
notarial seal *n.* The official seal of a notary public. A notarial seal affixed to a document creates a **rebuttable presumption** that the document is authentic. *See* authenticate; authentication.

notary [*noh* · te · ree] *n.* Same as **notary public**.

notary public [*noh* · te · ree *pub* · lik] *n.* A **public officer** whose function is to attest to the genuineness of documents (for EXAMPLE, deeds and **affidavits**) and to administer oaths. *See* attestation; authentication.

note *n.* 1. A written promise by one person to pay another person a specified sum of money on a specified date; a term used interchangeably with **promissory note**. A note may or may not be **negotiable**, depending upon its form. *See* negotiable instrument. *See also* balloon note; circular note; demand note; installment note; judgment note; mortgage note; time note; Treasury note. 2. A notation or **memorandum**.

N

v. 1. To observe or notice. 2. To make an official entry.

➤ *n.* commentary, observation; voucher, draft ("bank note"); significance, importance, distinction ("person of note"). *v.* observe, regard, realize, witness, notice; record, register, docket, document, enter, mark down.

note of protest [*pro* · test] *n.* A **memorandum** of the **protest** of a **negotiable instrument, indorsed** by a notary at the time of protest. *Compare* notice of protest.

notice [*noh* · tiss] *n.* 1. As defined by judicial decision, "information concerning a fact, actually communicated to a person by an authorized person, or actually derived by him from a proper source." **Due process** requires notice and the opportunity to be heard. 2. A formal declaration of intention. USAGE: "Robin will be leaving the company at the end of the month; she gave notice yesterday." 3. Information; intelligence; knowledge. *See* actual notice; constructive notice; due notice; express notice; immediate notice; implied notice; judicial notice; legal notice; official notice; personal notice; public notice; without notice. *Also see* knowledge. *v.* 1. To acknowledge by thought or action. 2. To observe or perceive.

➤ *n.* communication, information, announcement, release, statement; awareness, intelligence, knowledge; heed, consideration, watchfulness, care, caution; warning, admonition, caveat. *v.* apprise, inform, impart, publish, reveal, proclaim ("notice a hearing"); observe, mark, spot, detect, perceive, witness, note, see, view ("to notice what the perpetrator was wearing").

notice acts *n.* *See* recording acts.

notice of action [*ak* · shen] *n.* 1. The formal notice which informs a person that a civil action has been instituted against him; a **summons**. 2. *Lis pendens*. *See* notice of lis pendens.

notice of appeal [a · *peel*] *n.* The process by which **appellate review** is initiated; specifically, written notice to the **appellee** advising her of the **appellant's** intention to appeal.

notice of appearance [a · *peer* · ense] *n.* A written notice filed in an **action**, or given orally in open court, by a **party's** attorney that she is **appearing** in the proceeding. A party who chooses to represent himself is also required to file a notice of appearance. *Compare* notice to appear. *See* appearance.

notice of deposition [dep · e · *zish* · en] *n.* Written notice that a **party** to a lawsuit must give to all other parties before taking a **deposition**.

notice of dishonor [dis · on · er] *n.* A notice that a **negotiable instrument** has been **dishonored** by **nonacceptance** or **nonpayment**. *See* dishonor. *See also* acceptance; payment.

notice of dismissal [dis · *mis* · sel] *n.* A notice filed by the plaintiff advising the defendant of the **voluntary dismissal** of the **action**.

notice of judgment [*juj* · ment] *n.* Notice to a **party** against whom a **judgment** has been rendered advising her of its **entry**. In some jurisdictions, such notice is required by statute; in others, it is a matter of **constructive notice**.

notice of lis pendens [liss *pen* · denz] *n.* A formal notice filed with the **recorder** or the **clerk of court** or other public officer, for the purpose of giving notice to **all the world** that the property listed in the notice is the subject of litigation. For EXAMPLE: a bank files a *lis pendens* with the clerk of court when foreclosing on property. *See lis pendens*.

notice of loss *n.* Notice of the occurrence of a **loss** under an insurance policy, which the policy requires the insured to give to the insurance company within a specified period of time. *See* proof of loss.

notice of motion [*moh* · shen] *n.* A formal notice by a **party** to an **action** that a **motion**, the purpose of which is stated in the notice, will be made to the court on a stated date.

notice of order [*or* · der] *n.* *See* notice of judgment.

notice of pendency [*pen* · den · see] *n.* *See* notice of lis pendens.

notice of protest [*pro* · test] *n.* A certificate issued by a notary public advising that the **instrument** described in the certificate (EXAMPLES: a **draft**; a **bill of lading**) has been **dishonored**. *See* protest. *Compare* note of protest.

notice of suit *n.* *See* notice of action.

notice of trial [*try* · el] *n.* Notice given by a **party** to the **adverse party** of his intention to have the case placed on the **trial calendar**.

notice to appear [a · *peer*] *n.* A court order in the form of a **summons** directing a person to appear or suffer the consequences stated in the notice. *See* show cause order. *Compare* notice of appearance.

notice to creditors [*kred* · i · terz] *n.* Formal notice required by the **Bankruptcy Code** to be given with respect to certain aspects of the bankruptcy proceedings (EXAMPLES: **creditors' meetings**; the date for filing **proofs of claims**).

notice to plead *n.* A notice filed by the plaintiff advising the defendant that if he does not file a **pleading** in response to the **complaint** within the time specified in the **rules of procedure**, the plaintiff will take a **default judgment**.

notice to produce [pro · *dooss*] *n.* Formal notice given by a **party** to the **adverse party** to produce books, papers, or other evidence for use at trial or to prepare for trial. This procedure is one method of **discovery**.

notice to quit *n.* Formal notice given by a landlord to a tenant terminating a tenancy or in anticipation of the end of the term of the lease. Such notice is often a precondition to a landlord's legal right to evict a tenant. *See* eviction. *See also* ejectment.

notify [*noh* · tih · fie] *v.* To inform; to give notice to.
➤ contact, communicate, inform, proclaim, state, tell, divulge, announce.

notorious [no · *tore* · ee · es] *adj.* 1. Well known; a matter of public knowledge. 2. Unfavorably known. 3. Scandalous; infamous; shady.
➤ disreputable, scandalous, infamous, well-known, prominent, preeminent.

notorious adultery [a · *dul* · te · ree] *n.* *See* lewd and lascivious cohabitation. *See also* adultery; cohabitation; open and notorious.

notorious possession [po · *zesh* · en] *n.* *See* adverse possession; open and notorious.

notwithstanding [not · with · *stan* · ding] *adv.* In spite of; nonetheless; despite; nevertheless. *See* judgment notwithstanding the verdict.
➤ nonetheless, although, despite.

NOV Abbreviation of *non obstante veredicto*.

novation [no · *vay* · shen] *n.* The extinguishment of one obligation by another; a substituted contract that dissolves a previous contractual duty and creates a new one. Novation, which requires the mutual agreement of everyone concerned, replaces a contracting party with a new party who had no rights or obligations under the previous contract. *Compare* accord and satisfaction; substitution.
➤ replacement, extinguishment, substitution.

novel [*nov* · el] *adj.* New; original; fresh. *n.* A book that may be **copyrighted** and for which various kinds of rights may be sold; a work of fiction.
➤ *adj.* new, original, unique, atypical, creative, unorthodox, singular, unusual, uncommon.
n. story, narrative, fiction, tale.

novel case *n.* A case for which there is no **precedent**; a **case of first impression**.

novelty [*nov* · el · tee] *n.* 1. In patent law, a requirement for the **patentability** of an invention; namely, that it be a thing of distinct individuality not previously known or used. 2. That which has novel characteristics; that which is novel.
➤ innovation, rarity, mutation, specialty.

NOW account [a · *kount*] *n.* Acronym and common name for **negotiable order of withdrawal account**.

now for then *adj./adv.* *See* nunc pro tunc.

NSF check *n.* A check drawn on insufficient funds; a bad check. *See* overdraft.

nude *adj.* 1. Bare; mere. 2. Naked; unclothed.
➤ bare, mere; naked, unclothed, exposed, garmentless, unclad, stripped.

nude contract *n.* Same as *nudum pactum*.

N

nudum pactum [*noo* · dum *pak* · tum] (*Latin*) *n.* Means "bare agreement." A mere promise unsupported by **consideration**. *See* contract. *See also* naked promise.

nugatory [*noo* · ge · tore · ee] *adj.*
1. Without effect; invalid; futile.
2. Worthless; without value. USAGE: "His will was nugatory because he never executed it."
➤ invalid, futile, worthless, unenforceable, ineffective, meaningless, null, inadequate, inoperative.

nuisance [*noo* · sense] *n.* 1. Anything a person does that annoys or disturbs another person in her use, possession, or enjoyment of her property, or which renders the ordinary use or possession of the property uncomfortable. (EXAMPLES: noise; smoke; a display of **public indecency**; an **encroachment**.) What constitutes a nuisance in a particular case depends upon numerous factors, including the type of neighborhood in which the property is located, the nature of the act or acts complained of, their proximity to the persons alleging **injury** or **damage**, their frequency or continuity, and the nature and extent of the resulting injury, damage, or annoyance. 2. An annoyance; an inconvenience; a bother. *See* abatable nuisance; abatement of nuisance; absolute nuisance; common nuisance; maintaining a nuisance; mixed nuisance; permanent nuisance; private nuisance; public nuisance; qualified nuisance; temporary nuisance.
➤ annoyance, inconvenience, bother, intrusion, aggravation, devilment, hindrance, problem.
Ant. benefit.

nuisance at law *n.* Same as **nuisance per se**.

nuisance in fact *n.* Conduct that is not a nuisance under all circumstances, but that is legally objectionable because of the manner in which it is conducted or the location at which it occurs. *Compare* nuisance per se.

nuisance per se [per say] *n.* An act, occupation, or structure that is considered a nuisance at all times and under any circumstances, regardless of location or surroundings. *Compare* nuisance in fact. *See per se.*

nul [*null*] (*Latin*) *adj./n.* No; no one; none.
nul tiel record [teel *rek* · erd] *n.* From the *Latin,* meaning "no such record." A **plea** at **common law** when a defendant disputes the **record** upon which an **action** on a **judgment** is based.
nul waste In an **action** of **waste**, a **plea** denying that the defendant committed waste.

null *adj.* 1. Of no legal effect.
2. Nonexistent.
➤ nonexistent, valueless, absent, ineffective, invalid ("their agreement was null and void").
null and void *adj./adv.* That which binds no one; that which is of no effect; that which is incapable of creating legal rights or obligations. (USAGE: "If you deface that check it will be null and void.") Although the usual meaning of "null and void" is **voidable**, it is sometimes construed to mean **void**. *See and compare* void; voidable.
nulla bona [*null* · a *bone* · a] (*Latin*) *n.* Meaning "no goods." A **return** that a sheriff makes on a **writ of execution** when he is unable to find any property of the defendant on which to make a **levy**.

nullification [null · i · fi · *kay* · shen] *n.*
1. The act of creating a **nullity** or of making something **null**. *See* nullify.
2. The state of being a nullity.
➤ cancellation, voiding, revocation, suspension, discontinuance.

nullify [*null* · i · fy] *v.* To **annul**; to **void**, to **vacate**.
➤ cancel, annul, rescind, void, vacate, revoke, abate, undo, vitiate.

nullity [*null* · i · tee] *n.* That which is without legal effect; that which is **null**. EXAMPLE: a marriage that is subject to **annulment**.
➤ erasure, naught, nihilism, nonreality, futility, invalidity.
nullity suit *n.* An **action** for **annulment**.

number [*num* · ber] *n.* 1. A numeral; an integer. 2. An aggregate. USAGE: "A number of Senators supported the unusual bill.").
➤ numeral, digit, figure; aggregate, amount, portion.

numbers [*num* · berz] *n.* *See* numbers game.

numbers game [*num* · berz] *n.* An illegal lottery in which the participants bet on numbers chosen at random. The winning numbers correspond to a set of numbers, published on a daily basis, that change every day, for EXAMPLE, the last three numbers of the balance in the United States Treasury. *See* gambling.

nunc pro tunc [nunk pro tunk] (*Latin*) *adj.* Means "now for then." A term applied to the power of the court to allow acts to be done retroactively; that is, the power to give an act the same force and effect it would have had if it had been performed on time. Thus, for EXAMPLE, there are *nunc pro tunc* **amendments,** *nunc pro tunc* **filings** and *nunc pro tunc* **judgments**.

nunc pro tunc order [*or* · der] *n.* An **order of court** permitting an act to be performed retroactively.

nuncupative [nun · *kyoo* · pah · tiv] *adj.* Oral; not written.
➤ oral, spoken, unwritten, declared, voiced, parole.

nuncupative will [*nung* · kyoo · pay · tiv] *n.* A will declared orally by a **testator** during his **last illness**, before witnesses, and later reduced to writing by a person who was present during the declaration. *See also* military will; oral will.

nuptial [*nup* · chew · al] *adj.* Relating to marriage or a wedding.
➤ marital, matrimonial, spousal, conjugal, connubial.

N

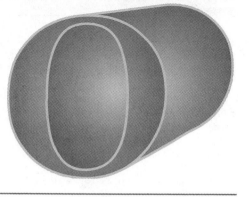

OASDI Abbreviation of **Old Age, Survivors' and Disability Insurance**.

oath *n.* 1. A calling on God to witness what one avers as truth. 2. Any form of **attestation** incorporating an appeal to a sacred or revered being by which a person signifies that he is bound in conscience to perform an act or to speak faithfully and truthfully. In most jurisdictions, the question "do you swear to tell the truth" has been replaced by "do you **swear** or **affirm**." In other jurisdictions, the term "oath" has been construed to include "**affirmation**." *See* corporal oath; false oath; loyalty oath; pauper's oath; solemn oath. *Also see* jurat; perjury. *Compare* affirmation.
➤ promise, affidavit, affirmation, avowal, pledge, attestation ("oath of allegiance").

oath of allegiance [a · *lee* · jense] *n.* An oath by which a person swears loyalty to the United States and to the Constitution; a form of **loyalty oath**. An oath of allegiance is required of, among others, aliens who are applying for **naturalization** and persons being sworn into a **constitutional office**.

oath of office [*off* · iss] *n.* An oath taken by a person being sworn into **office** in which she declares she will faithfully perform the duties of the office. *See* oath of allegiance.

obedient [o · *beed* · ee · ent] *adj.* Compliant with the demands of a superior.
➤ compliant, dedicated, dutiful, faithful, pliant, behaved, submissive, tractable.

obey [oh · *bay*] *v.* To follow; to comply with.
➤ submit, succumb, comply, conform, follow, serve, perform.

obfuscate [*ob* · fuss · skayt] *v.* 1. To make something unclear. 2. To make insensible or senseless.
➤ confuse, muddle; stupefy, befuddle. *Ant.* clarify.

obiter [*oh* · bih · ter] (*Latin*) *prep.* Means "in passing"; incidentally; by the way.
obiter dicta [*dik* · ta] Means "comments in passing." *See* dicta.
obiter dictum [*dik* · tum] Means "A comment in passing." *See* dicta.

object [*ob* · jekt] *n.* 1. The goal toward which effort is directed; the purpose of an undertaking or course of action. 2. A material thing; any tangible thing that can be seen or perceived by the senses. *v.* [ob · *jekt*] 1. To make an **objection** during the course of a trial or hearing. 2. To **except**; to protest. 3. To disapprove.
➤ *n.* aim, article, idea, motive, point, purpose, goal ("the object of a statute"). *v.* oppose, attack, controvert, protest, dispute, except, disapprove ("to object to a question").
object of a statute [*stat* · shoot] *n.* The aim or purpose of a statute; the reason a statute was enacted. The object or intent of a statute is considered when interpreting the statute. *See* statutory construction.

objection [ob · *jek* · shen] *n.* 1. The customary method, during a trial or hearing, of calling the attention of the judge or **hearing officer** to some aspect of the **proceeding** which one believes to be illegal or improper (EXAMPLE: an attempt by the **adverse party** to introduce **hearsay evidence**), and of seeking a ruling on the matter. 2. An **exception**; a protest; disapproval.

➤ censure, challenge, disapproval, grievance, opposition, protest.

objectionable [ob · *jek* · shun · uh · bul] *adj.* 1. Bad; repulsive; repugnant. 2. Improper; inadmissible.

➤ unappealing, obnoxious, displeasing, disgraceful, unsavory, repulsive, vile ("his objectionable manner"); improper, unsuitable, inadmissible ("objectionable evidence").

objects of a power [*pow* · er] *n.* Persons belonging to a **class** who are eligible as **appointees** or **beneficiaries** of a **power of appointment**. *See and compare* exclusive power of appointment; nonexclusive power of appointment.

objects of bounty [*boun* · tee] *n. See* natural objects of bounty.

obligation [ob · li · *gay* · shen] *n.* 1. That which binds a person, either legally, morally, or socially. (EXAMPLES: a promise; a contract; a debt; an oath; a duty; a moral responsibility.) *See* moral obligation; social duty. 2. That which a person is bound to do. 3. In the very narrowest sense, a **bond** or deed **under seal**. *See* contractual obligation; joint and several obligation; joint obligation; legal obligation; simple obligation.

➤ commitment, contract, assignment, promise, accountability, duty, responsibility.

obligation under seal *n. See* specialty.

obligee [ob · li · *zhee*] *n.* The person to whom an obligation is owed; a **promisee**. *Compare* obligor.

obligor [ob · li · *zhor*] *n.* The person who owes an obligation to another; a **promisor**. *Compare* obligee.

obliteration [ob · li · te · *ray* · shen] *n.* The wiping out or removal of written letters, words, or figures by erasing, tearing, cutting, or striking through them with a pen, pencil, or typewriter; any form of total destruction. Obliteration makes a will unenforceable in some jurisdictions. *Compare* rasure.

➤ repeal, removal, murder, abolition, abatement, elimination, erasure.

obscene [ob · *seen*] *n.* Offensive to generally accepted ideas of what is appropriate. *Note* that, although they are often used interchangeably, "obscene"

and "pornographic" are not synonymous. Strictly speaking, conduct of all sorts may be an obscenity; **pornography**, however, is limited to **lewd** and **licentious** portrayals of erotic behavior.

The Supreme Court has determined that pornographic material is obscene, and therefore not entitled to the **First Amendment** guaranty of **freedom of expression**, *only if :* (1) the average person, applying contemporary community standards, would find that the work, taken as a whole, appeals to the **prurient interest**; and (2) the work depicts or describes, in a patently offensive way, sexual conduct specifically defined by the applicable state law; and (3) the work, taken as a whole, lacks serious literary, artistic, political, or scientific value. Thus, government cannot take action against material alleged to be obscene, or against its distributors, unless the material violates all three of these criteria. However, because government does have a "compelling interest" in preventing the exploitive use of children, it may absolutely prohibit the viewing, possession, or distribution of child pornography. *See* compelling state interest.

➤ offensive, atrocious, improper, loathsome, lustful, suggestive, pornographic, wanton, vulgar.

obscenity [ob · *sen* · i · tee] *n.* Printed matter, visual material, or language that is **obscene**.

➤ indecency, immorality, abomination, impropriety, vulgarity, smut, pornography.

obscure [ob · *skyoor*] *adj.* 1. Not clearly understood or known. 2. Remote; concealed.
v. To hide from view; to make indistinct.

➤ *adj.* complex, profound, deep, hidden, egoteric, abstruse; remote, isolated, private, foreign.
v. mislead, veil, becloud, obfuscate, suppress, blur.

obsess [ob · *sess*] *v.* To think about or dwell upon something or someone excessively.

➤ dominate, compel, craze, dement, possess, torment, bedevil.

obsession [ob · *sess* · shun] *n.* An irresistible compulsion; a consuming desire.

➤ compulsion, fanaticism, mania, passion, preoccupation.

O

obsolescence [ob · se · *less* · ense] *n.* The state or condition of being outmoded or no longer of use. "Obsolescence" reduces the **market value** of property and, for that reason, may have significant tax consequences, particularly with respect to **capital equipment** and other **capital assets**.
➤ uselessness, supercession, disuse.

obsolete [ob · se · *lete*] *adj.* No longer used; out of date.
➤ ancient, antiquated, disused, outmoded, unfashionable.

obstruct [ob · *strukt*] *v.* To introduce obstacles or impediments; to hinder, to impede; to prevent.
➤ prevent, impede, hinder, barricade, curb, suppress.

obstructing [ob · *struk* · ting] *v.* Introducing obstacles or impediments; hindering, impeding; preventing.

obstructing justice [*juss* · tiss] *n.* The crime of impeding or hindering the administration of justice in any way. EXAMPLES: intimidating a witness; bribing a juror. *See also* obstructing process.

obstructing process [*pross* · ess] *n.* The crime of impeding or interfering with **service of process**. EXAMPLE: deliberately misleading a process server with the respect to the whereabouts of a person she is attempting to **serve** or the location of property upon which she is attempting to **levy**.

obstructing the mails *n.* The crime of impeding or interfering with the passage or delivery of mail.

obstruction [ob · *struk* · shun] *n.* A barrier; a hindrance; an obstacle.
➤ barrier, hindrance, limitation, restriction, constraint, prevention, preclusion.

obstruction of justice [ob · *struk* · shen of *juss* · tiss] *n. See* obstructing justice.

obtaining money or property by false pretenses [pre · *ten* · sez] *n. See* false pretenses.

obvious [*ob* · vee · yus] *adj.* Apparent; conspicuous; evident; patent.
➤ apparent, conspicuous, evident, noticeable, distinct, unmistakable, overt, explicit.
Ant. subtle, latent.

obvious danger [*dane* · jer] *n.* In the law of **negligence**, a danger readily observable by a person of ordinary intelligence. *See* obvious risk.

obvious defect [*dee* · fekt] *n. See* patent defect. *Compare* latent defect.

obvious risk *n.* A risk that is, or should be, readily apparent to a person of ordinary intelligence. Taking an obvious risk may be, but is not necessarily, an act of **negligence**. *See* risk. *Also see* obvious danger.

occupancy [*ok* · yoo · pen · see] *n.*
1. Possession **in fact** (*see* possession); the use and enjoyment of premises by a tenant, whether she holds the property under a lease, as a **life tenant**, or otherwise.
2. The taking possession of those things which previously belonged to no one, with the intention of acquiring a right of ownership. *See* adverse possession.
   Physical occupancy of property and *legal possession* are not necessarily identical. In the eyes of the law, a person may be in actual possession of property although he is not on the property physically.
➤ control, possession, tenancy, tenure, residency.
Ant. relinquishment.

occupancy of the field *n.* A doctrine of **constitutional law** which declares that when Congress has enacted legislation (the **Smith Act**, for EXAMPLE) in an area where national oversight and control is needed, it must be presumed that Congress intended that the federal government should "occupy the field," and therefore the states may not enact legislation governing the same matter. *See* preemption.

occupant [*ok* · yoo · pent] *n.* A person in possession of premises, enjoying and using the property. *See* use; enjoyment.
➤ dweller, inhabitant, inmate, tenant, resident.

occupation [*ok* · yoo · *pay* · shen] *n.* 1. The use and enjoyment of real property. *See* occupancy; occupant. 2. A profession, vocation, calling, employment, or trade. 3. The principal activity or business of one's life. 4. Any activity in which a person is engaged.
➤ livelihood, trade, avocation ("a noble occupation"); use, possession,

O

domination, influence ("occupation of the premises").

occupation tax *n.* A tax imposed on persons engaged in particular occupations or certain businesses or professions. *Compare* license tax; property tax; sales tax.

occupational [ok · yoo · *pay* · shen · el] *adj.* Pertaining to an occupation.

occupational disease [di · *zeez*] *n.* As opposed to a work-related physical injury, a disease resulting from a particular kind of employment or a disease known to be an occupational hazard. (EXAMPLE: bysinosis, or "brown lung disease," is an occupational disease of workers in textile mills.) Occupational diseases are **compensable injuries** under state **workers' compensation acts**.

occupational hazard [*haz* · erd] *n.* A danger or risk of injury or disease that is inherent in a particular occupation. *See* occupational disease.

Occupational Safety and Health Act [ok · yoo · *pay* · shen · el *safe* · tee] *n.* An Act of Congress, commonly referred to as **OSHA**, the purpose of which is to eliminate dangerous conditions in the workplace. *See* Occupational Safety and Health Administration (OSHA).

Occupational Safety and Health Administration [ok · yoo · *pay* · shen · el *safe* · tee and health ad · min · i · *stray* · shen] *n.* Created by the **Occupational Safety and Health Act, OSHA** is a federal administrative agency that promulgates occupational safety and health standards, issues regulations, conducts inspections, issues citations, and imposes penalties for noncompliance with its regulations.

occupy [ok · yoo · pie] *v.* 1. To engage one's mental energy. 2. To hold or take possession of.
➤ absorb, engage, fascinate, engross, excite ("occupy the mind"); own, possess, inhabit, reside in ("occupy a house").

occupying claimant [ok · yoo · py · ing *klame* · ent] *n.* The term for a person who, while occupying premises either as a tenant or in the belief that he had good title, made **improvements** for which he is seeking reimbursement after vacating the premises. An **action** upon such a claim is

maintained under statutes known as **betterment acts** or **occupying claimant acts**.

occupying claimant acts *See* occupying claimant; betterment acts.

occur [oh · *kur*] *v.* To take place; to happen.
➤ happen, transpire, materialize, proceed, arise.

odd *adj.* 1. Peculiar; weird. 2. Irregular; out of the ordinary. 3. Extra; miscellaneous.
➤ peculiar, strange, unconventional, weird, eccentric; uneven, irregular; varied, various, sundry, miscellaneous.

odd lot *n.* 1. A transaction in stock involving less than 100 shares. *Compare* round lot. 2. Not the usual number in which an item is sold. EXAMPLE: five cans of beer rather than a six-pack.

of *prep.* A word indicating possession, direction, distance, source, derivation, cause, motive, reason, inclusion, kind, category, or other connection.

of age The status of a person who has obtained his **majority**. A person who is of age for one purpose may not be of age for another. *See* minor. *Also see* age of majority.

of counsel [*koun* · sel] 1. Describes an attorney assisting another attorney in the handling or trial of a case. 2. Signifies an attorney who is not a member or an employee of a law firm, but who is associated with the firm for limited purposes, such as handling particular kinds of matters.

of course 1. As a matter **of right**. The term refers to an action to be taken during the course of litigation that can be taken without the permission of the court. 2. A term indicating concurrence, agreement, or assent. *See* of grace.

of grace As a favor, kindness, or indulgence. The term is applied to permission that is granted, or approval that is given, when there is no duty to do so. *Compare* of course; of right. *See* grace; grace period.

of record [*rek* · erd] A term meaning **recordation** or **entry** on or in the **records**. It is applied not only to the recording of instruments or documents (EXAMPLES: deeds; mortgages) deposited with the appropriate

O

public officer (EXAMPLE: a **recorder of deeds**) for that purpose, but also to statements and testimony recorded in the official transcript of a case. USAGE: "Inasmuch as the district attorney stated in open court that she intends to *nol. pros.* the **indictment**, her statement is a matter of record."

of right *See* of course; right.

of the essence [*ess · ense*] *See* essence.

offend [*uh · fend*] *v.* 1. To outrage or provoke someone. 2. To disobey or break the law.
➤ insult, affront, provoke, snub; disobey, transgress, infringe.

offender [*o · fen · der*] *n.* A person who commits an offense.
➤ violator, lawbreaker, transgressor, felon, wrongdoer.

offense [*o · fense*] *n.* 1. A crime. Although "offense," as the term is generally used, means a **felony** or a **misdemeanor**, it may also include **infractions** and **petty offenses** as well as **regulatory crimes**. 2. A hurt; a wrong; a misdeed; wrongdoing. *See* continuing offense; divisible offense; joinder of offenses; joint offense; lesser included offense; merger of offenses; multiple offenses; same offense.
➤ infraction, malfeasance, transgression, wrongdoing; hurt, wrong, misdeed.

offensive [*o · fen · siv*] *adj.* 1. In the context of the law of **nuisances**, noxious, unsanitary, unsightly, or noisy. 2. Pertaining to aggression or attack. 3. Causing hurt, anger, displeasure, or disgust.
➤ noxious, abhorrent, detestable, objectionable, reprehensible; noxious, unsanitary, unsightly; aggressive, forward.

offensive touching [*tuch · ing*] *n.* An element of the crime or **tort** of **battery**.

offensive weapon [*wep · en*] *n.* Generally speaking, a **deadly weapon**.

offer [*off · er*] *n.* 1. A proposal made with the purpose of obtaining an **acceptance**, thereby creating a **contract**. *See* offer and acceptance. 2. A **tender of performance**. 3. A statement of intention or willingness to do something. 4. An **offer of proof**. 5. With respect to the **over-the-counter marketing** of **securities**, the asked price of an **offering**. *See* bid and asked. 6. A proposal; a proposition; a bid. *See* counteroffer; firm offer; irrevocable offer.

v. 1. To propose for acceptance or rejection. USAGE: "I offered him the choice of going with me or staying home." 2. To propose for consideration. USAGE: "I offered him my advice." 3. To propose to do something. USAGE: "I offered to marry him."
➤ *n.* proposal, suggestion, endeavor, proposition, submission, bid.
v. present, advance, propose, provide, award, suggest. extend.

offer a bribe *n. See* bribe.

offer and acceptance [*ak · sep · tense*] *n.* Essential elements in the creation of a legally enforceable contract, reflecting mutual assent or a **meeting of the minds**. In the case of a **bilateral contract**, acceptance is the **offeree's** communication that she intends to be bound by the **offer**; in the case of a **unilateral contract**, the offeree accepts by **performing** in accordance with the terms of the offer.

offer for the record [*rek · erd*] *n. See* offer of proof.

offer of compromise [*kom · pre · mize*] *n.* An offer to adjust or compromise a claim or dispute for the purpose of settling the matter without litigation and without admitting liability.

offer of evidence [*ev · i · dense*] *n.* Same as **offer of proof**.

offer of judgment [*juj · ment*] *n.* Under the **Federal Rules of Civil Procedure**, a defendant may serve an **adverse party** with an offer to allow a **judgment** to be taken against her for the amount of money or property specified in the offer. Similar procedures are available under the **rules of civil procedure** of many states.

offer of proof *n.* An "offer of proof" is made during the trial of a case after the court has ruled that a particular question cannot be asked of a witness, or that the witness may not answer a particular question, or that some other evidence (EXAMPLES: a document; a weapon) is inadmissible. In making an offer of proof, the **party** who offered the rejected evidence or testimony states **for the record**, usually out of the hearing of the jury, the fact that would have been proven had the court ruled the evidence admissible. This procedure allows an **appellate court** to determine whether the court's ruling was in error.

O

offeree [off · er · *ree*] *n.* A person to whom an offer is made. *Compare* offeror.

offering [off · er · *ring*] *n.* **Securities** offered for sale to the public or privately at a particular time by a corporation or by government. *See and compare* private offering; public offering.

➤ donation, contribution, gift, benefaction, bequest, subsidy, alms ("an offering at church"); sale, issue, distribution ("a stock offering").

offering circular [*ser* · kyoo · ler] *n.* *See* prospectus.

offering price *n.* The price per share of an **offering**.

offeror [off · er · *ror*] *n.* A person who makes an **offer**.

office [*off* · iss] *n.* 1. A function in which a person is employed carrying out the business of government. "Office" in this sense is synonymous with **public office**. Although the office may be either appointive or elective, the word implies a position with at least some degree of authority in carrying out the constitutional and statutory responsibilities of government (as opposed, for instance, to purely nondiscretionary or clerical duties). *See* constitutional office; political office; public office; public officer; public official; public trust. 2. A position of trust in nongovernmental, private employment. EXAMPLES: the president of a corporation; the **trust officer** of a bank. 3. A department, division, or branch of a corporation or of government. USAGE: "the West Coast office"; "the home office"; the **Patent and Trademark Office**. *See* principal office. *Also see* Land Office. 4. A place where business is transacted.

➤ business, appointment; occupation, employment, charge, responsibility; department, division, branch ("the home office").

office audit [*aw* · dit] *n.* An examination by the IRS of a taxpayer's books and records, conducted at an IRS office; the taxpayer brings his supporting documents to the office. *Compare* field audit.

office copy [*kop* · ee] *n.* 1. A **certified copy** of a **public record**. 2. A working copy.

Office of Thrift Supervision [soo · per · *vizh* · en] *n.* An **office** of the United States Treasury Department that charters federal **savings and loan associations** and regulates federal and state-chartered **thrift institutions**, taking such action as is necessary to enforce compliance with federal law. *See* Resolution Trust Corporation.

officeholder [*off* · iss · *hole* · der] *n.* A person elected or appointed to **office**, generally **public office**.

➤ official, appointee, incumbent.

officer [*off* · i · ser] *n.* 1. A person who holds a position of trust or authority in the government, in a corporation or other private organization, or in the armed services; a person who holds an **office**. *See* corporate officers; executive officer; judicial officer; ministerial officer; municipal officer; public officer; trust officer. 2. A police officer, usually a uniformed officer. *See* law enforcement officer; peace officer.

➤ commander, administrator, agent, official, representative; policeman, cop, inspector.

officer of the court *n.* Anyone who is an employee of the court (EXAMPLES: a judge; a **bailiff**; a **marshal**; a clerk) or a person who, although not an employee of the court, is obligated to conduct himself in a manner that furthers the administration of justice (EXAMPLE: any attorney admitted to practice before the court).

official [o · *fish* · el] *adj.* Pertaining to an **office** or to an **officer**; pertaining to that which is ordered, authorized, or certified by an officer or authorized or required by law. *n.* An **officer**; a **public officer**; a **public official**.

➤ *adj.* accredited, approved, valid, licensed, recognized, formal, legitimate, sanctioned. *n.* administrator, manager, executive, bureaucrat, dignitary, leader.

official act *n.* An act done by an **officer** in performing the duties of her **office**; that is, an act done in her official capacity.

official immunity [im · *myoo* · ni · tee] *n.* A legal doctrine which declares that a government official is exempt from **civil liability** for **injury** resulting from his conduct if his action that caused the injury was within the scope of his authority and required the exercise of discretion. *See* scope of authority. *See also* Federal Tort Claims Act; sovereign immunity.

official misconduct [mis · *kon* · dukt] *n.* **Malfeasance in office, misfeasance in office**, or **nonfeasance**.

official newspaper [*nyooz* · pay · per] *n.* A newspaper in which the **legal notices** of government are published. It may or may not be a **newspaper of general circulation**.

official notice [*no* · tiss] *n.* The equivalent of **judicial notice** by an administrative agency; also referred to as **administrative notice**.

official oath *n. See* oath of office.

official records [*rek* · erdz] *n.* **Records** made by an official of the government in the course of performing her official duties. (EXAMPLES: correspondence; memoranda; data; minutes.) Official records are admissible in the federal courts and in federal **administrative proceedings**, as well as in most state courts, as an **exception to the hearsay rule**, to prove the transactions they **memorialize**. *See* public record.

official reports [re · *ports*] *n. See* court reports; reporters.

official seal *n.* The seal affixed to a document by a **public officer**. Various offices and departments of government, state and federal, have and use their particular seal. *See* seals. *See also* corporate seal.

official transcript [*tran* · skript] *n. See* transcript.

Official Gazette [o · *fish* · el ge · *zet*] *n.* A weekly publication of the **Patent and Trademark Office**, listing **patents** issued and **trademarks** registered.

officiate [o · *fish* · ee · ate] *v.* To perform an official duty or function. EXAMPLE: to perform the office of a priest, minister, rabbi, or imam at a religious service.
➤ oversee, manage, administer, conduct, direct.

officious [o · *fish* · us] *adj.* Meddlesome; offering unrequested and unwanted advice or services.

➤ meddlesome, dictatorial, obtrusive, interfering, domineering ("an officious intermeddler").

officious intermeddler [in · ter · *med* · ler] *n.* A person who involves himself in someone else's business. *See* mere volunteer.

officious will *n.* A **will** in which the **testator** leaves her property to her family. *See* natural objects of bounty.

offset [*off* · set] *n.* 1. A claim made for the purpose of reducing or nullifying another claim; a **counterclaim**; a **recoupment**; a **setoff**. 2. A balancing or compensating factor; a deduction. 3. The practice of investing in a foreign nation's industry to "repay" that nation for business transacted in the investor's nation.
v. To balance against; to equalize.
➤ *n.* counterclaim, recoupment, setoff, deduction.
v. counterbalance, compensate, equalize, countervail, neutralize.

oil and gas lease *n.* A grant of the right to remove oil and gas from land; a form of **mineral lease**.

oil lease *n. See* oil and gas lease.

old *adj.* 1. Advanced in years. 2. Traditional; established.
➤ used, elderly, worn, matured, declining, decayed, rundown; established, vintage, familiar, veteran, age-old, standing. *Ant.* contemporary, modern.

Old Age, Survivors' and Disability Insurance [ser · *vie* · verz and dis · e · *bil* · i · tee in · *shoor* · ense] *n.* The system administered under the **Social Security Act** by which retirement, disability, dependent, and related benefits are provided to older and disabled Americans. It is popularly known as social security. *See* Social Security Act.

oligarchy [*aw* · li · gar · kee] *n.* A government that is administered by only a few persons. *Compare* democracy.

olograph [*aw* · lo · graf] *n.* Same as **holograph**.

ombudsman [*om* · budz · man] *n.* A public official to whom citizens can address complaints concerning the government. The ombudsman's function is to investigate

O

such complaints, particularly those relating to infringements of individual rights, and attempt to mediate an amicable resolution. *See* alternative dispute resolution.
➤ referee, agent, moderator, representative.

omission [o · *mish* · en] *n.* 1. Not doing something required by the law. 2. A failure to act; a failure to do something that ought to be done.
➤ breach, neglect, cancellation, disregard, exclusion, oversight, repudiation.

omit [oh · *mit*] *v.* To leave out; to exclude.
➤ bypass, pass over, leave out, exclude, delete, neglect ("he omitted an important detail").

omnibus [*om* · ni · bus] *adj.* (from the *Latin*, meaning "for all") Pertaining to a number of items at one time.

omnibus bill *n.* A legislative **bill** covering various separate and unrelated matters.

omnibus clause *n.* A clause in an automobile liability insurance policy that extends coverage under the policy to persons using the insured automobile with the permission of the **named insured**.

on *prep.* Upon; at; by; adjacent; around; adjacent to; beside; atop; near; nearby; in contact with the surface of a thing and supported by it.
➤ about, above, forward, adjacent, near.

on account [a · *kount*] 1. A sale on credit. 2. A partial payment to be applied to the balance due on an account.

on all fours Refers to a judicial opinion in a case that is very similar to another case, both with respect to the facts they involve and the applicable law. *See* precedent. *Compare* on point.

on approval [a · *proov* · el] *See* sale on approval.

on call Same as **on demand**.

on demand [de · *mand*] A **note** that must be paid when payment is requested. *See* demand. Under the **Uniform Commercial Code**, a **negotiable instrument** is **payable on demand** if it states that it is payable on demand or **at sight**, or otherwise indicates that it is payable at the will of the holder, or does not state any time of payment.

on information and belief [in · for · *may* · shen and be · *leef*] *See* upon information and belief. *Also see* information and belief.

on margin [*mar* · jin] 1. A purchase of **securities** from a **margin account**. 2. Any purchase on credit.

on or about [a · *bout*] A phrase used to cover some slight or unimportant inaccuracy, or possible inaccuracy, when stating the date on which an event occurred. Thus, for EXAMPLE, an **indictment** might charge that the injury that caused death was inflicted "on or about May 13, 1993," or a **contract of sale** might call for delivery "on or about November 9, 1994."

on or about the person [*per* · sen] A phrase common to statutes relating to concealed weapons, making it a crime for a person to conceal a weapon on, attached to, or near his body. *See* person. *Also see* on the person.

on or before [be · *fore*] This phrase in a contract gives the **promisor** the assurance that her obligation will be fully satisfied (for EXAMPLE, to pay money or to render a service) even though she performs it in advance of the performance date specified in the agreement. In other words, "on or before" a specified date means "by" that date.

on point Refers to a judicial opinion that, with respect to the facts involved and the applicable law, is similar to but not **on all fours** with another case. *Compare* on all fours. *See* precedent.

on sight Same as **at sight**.

on the merits [*mehr* · its] A case that was decided on the basis of its true issues rather than on **procedural** questions. *See* merits; merits of the case.

on the person [*per* · sen] Refers to wearing or carrying something either on one's body or in or on one's clothing. *See* person. *Also see* on or about the person.

on the record [*rek* · erd] Same as **of record**.

on the relation of [re · *lay* · shen] *See* ex rel.

one *adj./pron.* 1. A single unit. 2. A person, usually either unnamed or named but unknown. USAGE: "one is free to do as one wishes"; "the victim was one Mary Jones."

➤ *adj.* alone, individual, lone, odd, only, single ("Just one vote shy").
pron. person, individual.

one dollar [*doll* · er] *n.* A **recital** of **nominal consideration**. It is not uncommon for deeds, particularly older deeds, to recite a consideration of "one dollar" rather than the amount actually paid for the property. Other forms of this recital are "one dollar in hand paid" and "one dollar and other valuable consideration."

one person, one vote rule [*per* · sen] *n.* **Equal protection of the laws** requires the rule of "one person, one vote" in state legislatures; that is, **legislative districts** that are roughly equal in population must be the geographical basis on which representatives are elected to both houses of a state's legislature. *See Baker v. Carr.*

one-sided *adj.* Biased; partial; unequal.
➤ unfair, unjust, slanted, prejudiced, interested, uneven ("a one-sided deal").

onerous [*ohn* · e · ress] *adj.* 1. Burdensome; oppressive; demanding. 2. Not without **consideration**.
➤ burdensome, oppressive, demanding, cumbersome, fatiguing, overwhelming.

onerous contract [*kon* · trakt] *n.* A contract supported by a valid **consideration**. *See* valid.

onerous deed *n.* A deed executed by the grantor for a **valuable consideration**.

onerous gift *n.* A gift that imposes some obligation upon the **donee**.

onset [*on* · set] *n.* 1. The beginning of something. 2. An attack.
➤ beginning, inception, outbreak, coming, dawn; advance, assault, charge.

onus [*own* · us] *n.* 1. Something one is bound to do through an obligation; a burden or duty. 2. Blame; accusation.
➤ burden, duty, responsibility, affliction, load, task, encumbrance; accusation, charge, fault, blemish, dishonor, infamy, degradation.

open [*oh* · pen] *adj.* 1. Not settled. 2. Available. 3. Candid; honest. 4. Exposed. 5. Not secret; not concealed. 6. Uncensored. 7. Obvious. 8. Unrestricted; unobstructed; free. 9. Public.

v. 1. To bring up; to broach. 2. To begin; to commence; to introduce. 3. To unseal; to unbind.

➤ *adj.* receptive, unprejudiced ("open to suggestion"); apparent, manifest ("open defiance"); equivocal, available, undecided ("an open question"); candid, honest, exposed; uncensored, obvious; unrestricted, unobstructed, free, public ("open admission").
v. begin, expose, breach, display, initiate, originate ("open a file").

open a bid *v.* To unseal the bids received following advertisement for bids in the **letting** of a contract, for the purpose of determining the most favorable bid. *See* bid. *Also see* letting a contract.

open a case *v.* To make an opening statement at the start of a trial. *See* opening statement.

open a file *v.* To begin representation of a client.

open a judgment [*juj* · ment] *v.* To bring a previously entered **judgment** before the court for the purpose of considering whether it should be modified or vacated. *See* entry of judgment, modification of judgment; vacation of judgment.

open a rule *v.* To change a **rule absolute** to a **rule nisi** or **decree nisi**.

open account [a · *kount*] *n.* 1. An account whose balance has not been determined. 2. An account that has not been closed, settled, or stated in circumstances where further dealings between the parties are anticipated. *See* account stated. 3. An **open-end credit** arrangement. 4. A transaction whose terms have not been completely agreed upon or are expressly understood to be subject to change.

open and notorious [no · *tore* · ee · us] *adj.* A phrase applied to a number of concepts and terms in the law, which refers to acts that are deliberately not concealed and that are conspicuous and a matter of public knowledge. Thus, for EXAMPLE: *open and notorious possession* means conduct sufficient to put a person of **ordinary prudence** on notice that his land is the subject of **adverse user** or **adverse possession**; and *open and notorious adultery* refers to a man and woman openly engaging in

O

adultery or **fornication**, or openly living together outside of marriage. *See* lewd and lascivious cohabitation; notorious adultery.

open and notorious adultery
[no · *tore* · ee · us a · *dull* · te · ree] *n. See* open and notorious. *Also see* adultery.

open and notorious possession
[no · *tore* · ee · us po · *zesh* · en] *n. See* open and notorious. *Also see* adverse possession.

open bulk *n.* Goods in the mass or goods that are unsealed and exposed to view.

open court *n.* 1. A court that is in session. 2. A court session that is open to the public, as distinguished from a session conducted by a judge in her **chambers**. *See* in chambers. *Also see* public trial.

open listing [*liss* · ting] *n.* A **listing agreement** in which the owner does not give the agent the **exclusive right to sell** the property; that is, the owner is free to concurrently employ additional agents for that purpose. *See and compare* exclusive right to sell; multiple listing; nonexclusive listing.

open market [*mar* · ket] *n.* A market that is not restrained by private agreements between buyers and sellers or regulated by the government; a free market. *See* market.

open meeting laws [*meet* · ing] *n. See* sunshine law.

open policy [*pol* · i · see] *n.* Same as **unvalued policy**.

open possession [po · *zesh* · en] *n. See* adverse possession; open and notorious.

open season [*see* · zen] *n.* The period or periods in a year when fish or game may be caught or hunted. The fish and game laws specify different periods for different species.

open shop *n.* A place of employment governed by a **collective bargaining agreement** which stipulates that membership in the union is not a condition of being hired or of keeping one's job. *Compare* agency shop agreement; closed shop.

open the door An expression for the situation in which a **party** becomes entitled to introduce otherwise inadmissible evidence because the **adverse party** introduced similar or related evidence.

USAGE: "I'm going to allow the question, counselor; after all, you opened the door on direct examination."

open trial *n. See* public trial.

open-end *adj.* A transaction that has no set limits as to duration and amount and can be modified by either party at any time. EXAMPLE: an **open-end mortgage**.

open-end credit [*kred* · it] *n.* The extension of credit under any form of **open account**, usually with the express agreement that the balance may not exceed a certain amount and that a specified percent of the balance must be paid on a regular basis. Credit cards and charge accounts are common forms of open-end credit accounts.

open-end lease *n.* A lease with no fixed termination date. *See* lease.

open-end mortgage [*more* · gej] *n.* A **mortgage** under which the mortgagor is permitted to borrow additional money.

opening statement [*state* · ment] *n.* A statement made by the attorney for each party at the beginning of a trial, outlining to the judge and jury the issues in the case and the facts that each side intends to prove.

operate [*op* · e · rate] *v.* 1. To carry out; to effectuate; to produce an effect. 2. To perform surgery.
➤ perform, run, execute, accomplish, function, engage.

operating [*op* · e · rate · ing] *v.* 1. Carrying out, effectuating, or executing. 2. Performing surgery.

operating budget [*bud* · jet] *n.* 1. Portion of a budget concerned with **operating income** and **operating expenses**. 2. A separate budget devoted to those matters. *Compare* capital budget.

operating expenses [eks · *pen* · sez] *n.* The cost of running a business; the expenses incurred in operating a business.

operating income [*in* · kum] *n.* Income that a business derives from operation of the business itself, as opposed to income derived from investments. *See* income.

operating loss *n. See* net operating loss.

operation of law [*op* · e · *ray* · shen] *n.* Through law, as opposed to by contract or through the action of a person or other entity. For EXAMPLE, a person who receives property by inheritance (i.e., under the **intestate laws**), rather than under a will, receives the property by "operation of law."

operative [*op* · e · re · tiv] *adj.* Effective; functioning; central; key.
n. 1. An **agent**. 2. A detective. 3. A spy. 4. An employee or laborer.
➤ *adj.* accessible, functional, efficacious, practicable, serviceable, capable, efficient. *n.* investigator, detective, spy, secret agent; employee, worker, working person.

operative part *n.* *See* operative words.

operative words *n.* 1. The words in an instrument that give it its particular legal character. For EXAMPLE, the words "grant, bargain and sell" in an instrument make that instrument a **deed**. *See* grant. 2. Words (or any part or portion of a document) that determine legal rights, obligations, or liabilities. EXAMPLE: the words "I killed Joe" (in a statement given by a criminal defendant to the police) tend to establish the defendant's guilt. *See* confession.

opiate [*oh* · pee · et] *n.* Any narcotic, or any drug with a narcotic effect. *See* opium.

opinion [o · *pin* · yen] *n.* 1. A written statement by a court that accompanies its **decision** in a case and gives the court's reasons for its decision. Although "decision" and "opinion" are often used interchangeably, the terms are not synonymous: a decision is the **judgment** in the case; an opinion gives the reasoning on which the judgment is based. *See* advisory opinion; concurring opinion; dissenting opinion; majority opinion; minority opinion; per curiam opinion; plurality opinion; slip opinion. 2. A **legal opinion** given to a client by his attorney. 3. A conclusion a person has drawn from facts she has observed; a statement of belief rather than a statement of fact. *See* expert opinion; title opinion.
➤ judgment, conclusion, decree, ruling, position, order ("opinion of the court"); persuasion, conviction, viewpoint, belief, outlook ("her opinion of the new associate").

opinion evidence [*ev* · i · dense] *n.* The testimony of a witness with respect to what she believes to be the truth or what she has concluded to be a fact based upon her observations. Generally, opinion

evidence is admissible only if given by an **expert witness** (*compare* lay witness). *See* expert testimony.

opinion of court *n.* *See* opinion.

opinion of the attorney general [a · *tern* · ee *jen* · rel] *n.* 1. A **legal opinion** prepared by the **attorney general** of a state for the purpose of advising the governor or other state **executive officers** with respect to the meaning or requirements of the laws they administer. 2. An opinion of the Attorney General of the United States with respect to a question of law, requested by the president or the head of any **executive department** of the federal government.

opium [*oh* · pee · yum] *n.* A narcotic drug manufactured from a species of poppy. Opium is a **controlled substance**; its possession, distribution, or sale is a criminal offense.

opportunity [op · ur · *tune* · ih · tee] *n.* Option; chance.
➤ chance, luck, occasion, propitiousness, time, turn ("opportunity to be heard").

oppose [uh · *poze*] *v.* To object to; to contest.
➤ counter, contend, rebut, protest, fight, debate, disagree ("oppose a motion").

opposite party [*ah* · po · sit *par* · tee] *n.* Same as **adverse party**.

oppression [o · *presh* · en] *n.* 1. The exercise of authority by a public official in a manner that violates a person's rights. 2. Cruel, severe, and unduly dominating acts that subject a person to **injury**. Oppressive acts may constitute both a crime and a **tort**.
➤ abuse, hardship, persecution, injustice, domination, torment, cruelty.

option [*op* · shen] *n.* 1. An **offer**, combined with an agreement supported by **consideration** not to revoke the offer for a specified period of time; a future contract in which one of the parties has the right to insist on compliance with the contract, or to cancel it, at his election. In other words, "option" is short for **option contract. Commodities** and **securities** are commonly bought and sold on the basis of *future* options. *See* futures; futures contract. *See also* call option; first option; put option; qualified stock

O

option; stock option. *See and compare* call; put. 2. Something that can be chosen. *See* settlement option. 3. The right or power to choose. *See* local option. 4. A choice.

➤ advantage, offer, choice, preference, prerogative, selection ("option to purchase").

option contract [kon · trakt] *n. See* option.

option to purchase [per · chess] *n.* A contract in which the owner of property agrees with another person that that person shall have the right to buy the property at a specified price within a specified period of time. An option to purchase is a common provision in a lease; it confers upon the tenant the option to purchase the leased premises.

option to renew [re · nyoo] *n.* A right to choose to renew a lease, granted to the tenant by the lease.

optionee [op · shen · ee] *n.* A person who receives an **option**.

OR Abbreviation for **own recognizance**, it means "own bond" and relates to the circumstance in which a judge releases a criminal defendant on his promise to return to court for trial, rather than compelling him to post a **bail bond**. OR release is also referred to as **release on own recognizance** or **ROR, personal recognizance**, or **OR bond**. *See* recognizance.

OR bond *n. See* OR.

oral [ohr · el] *adj.* By word of mouth; spoken, as opposed to written. *See* parol; verbal.

➤ spoken, articulate, narrated, voiced, uttered, unwritten.

oral argument [ar · gyoo · ment] *n.* A **party**, through her attorney, usually presents her case to an **appellate court** on appeal by arguing the case verbally to the court, in addition to submitting a brief. Oral argument may also be made in support of a **motion**. *See* argument.

oral confession [ken · fesh · en] *n.* A voluntary admission by a person, made orally, that he has committed a crime. *See* confession.

oral contract [kon · trakt] *n.* A contract that is not in writing, or part of which is not in writing; a **parol contract**. Unless the subject of an oral contract is covered

by the **statute of frauds**, it is just as valid as a written contract; often, however, its enforceability is limited because its terms cannot be proven. *See* contract. *Also see* informal contract.

oral trust *n.* A **trust** created by verbal declaration. Only personal property, as opposed to real property, may be the subject of an oral trust.

oral will *n.* Same as **nuncupative will**.

ordain [or · dane] *v.* 1. To enact an ordinance or to make a law of any kind. 2. To decree; to order; to mandate; to command; to legislate. 3. To bestow the office of priest, minister, or rabbi upon a person.

➤ establish, anoint, designate, install, nominate; decree, order, mandate, command.

ordeal [or · deal] *n.* 1. An ancient method of criminal trial based upon the belief that if a person was innocent God would save him from death or injury when he was subjected to a severe physical test. Thus, among other tests, ancient courts conducted ordeals by fire, by boiling water, and by hot iron. *See* trial by ordeal. 2. A severe test; a tribulation; a trying experience.

➤ tribulation, affliction, torment, adversity, calamity.

order [or · der] *n.* 1. A determination made by a court; an **order of court**. 2. A determination made by an administrative agency. 3. A written direction (EXAMPLES: a check; a **bill of lading**) from one person to another to pay money or to deliver goods to a third person; **order paper**; an **order instrument**. *See* negotiable instrument. 4. A list of goods or merchandise that a person wants a dealer to sell to her. 5. A command or direction.

See decision; decree; judgment. *See also* appealable order; court order; executive order; interlocutory order; intermediate order; payable to order; protection order; protective order; restraining order; stop-loss order; stop order; stop-payment order. *v.* To command or compel.

➤ *n.* decree command, mandate, demand, judgment ("order of the court"); arrangement, grouping, layout, pattern, placement, rotation ("order of creditors").
v. dictate, require, rule, demand, ordain, prescribe ("to order that the lawyer be disbarred").

O

order instrument [*in* · stroo · ment] *n.*
See negotiable instrument.

order nisi [*nee* · sie] *n. See* decree nisi.

order nunc pro tunc [nunk pro tunk] *n.*
See nunc pro tunc; nunc pro tunc order.

order of court *n.* 1. An **adjudication** by
a court. 2. A ruling by a court with respect
to a **motion** or any other matter before it
for determination during the course of a
proceeding.

order of filiation [fil · ee · *ay* · shen] *n.*
An order of court determining the paternity
of an illegitimate child. *See* affiliation
proceeding; paternity suit.

order paper [*pay* · per] *n.* A **negotiable
instrument**; i.e., an instrument that recites
an unconditional promise to pay a fixed
amount of money, and which is payable to
order and meets all the other requirements
of negotiability.

order to show cause *n.* An order of court
directing a **party** to appear before the court
and to present facts and legal arguments
showing cause why the court should not
take a certain action adversely affecting
that party's interests. Orders to show cause
are often granted *ex parte*. A party's failure
to appear or, having appeared, his failure
to show cause, will result in a **final
judgment** unfavorable to him. *See* show
cause. *Also see* decree nisi.

Order of the Coif [*or* · der of the koif] *n.*
An honorary society of lawyers, whose
membership is based on high achievement
in law school.

ordinance [*or* · di · nense] *n.* 1. A law of a
municipal corporation; a **local law**
enacted by a city council, town council,
board of supervisors, or the like. 2. A rule
established by authority. *See* ordinance.
➤ command, mandate, law, regulation, order,
statute, rule.

ordinary [*or* · di · ner · ee] *adj.* Usual;
normal; common.
n. In some states, a judicial officer with
limited powers, similar to a **master** or
referee.
➤ *adj.* usual, normal, common, reoccurring,
routine, traditional, conventional,
reasonable.

ordinary and necessary expense
[*ness* · e · ser · ree eks · *pense*] *n.* Under
tax law, to be deductible as a **business
expense**, an expenditure must be both
"ordinary" and "necessary." An **ordinary
expense** is one that is customary or usual
in the particular business, trade, or industry. A **necessary expense** is an expense
that is appropriate and helpful, although
not necessarily essential, to the taxpayer's
business.

ordinary care *n.* Same as **due care** or
reasonable care.

ordinary course of business [*biz* · ness]
n. That which is customarily done in
business, as distinguished from that which
is rarely done, unusual, or fraudulent.
See also regular course of business.

ordinary diligence [*dil* · i · jense] *n.*
Same as **due diligence** or **reasonable
diligence**.

ordinary dividend [*div* · i · dend] *n.* A
regular dividend paid by a corporation, as
distinguished from an **extra dividend** or
a **stock dividend**.

ordinary expense [eks · *pense*] *n. See*
ordinary and necessary expense.

ordinary high tide *n.* Same as **mean
high tide**.

ordinary income [*in* · kum] *n.* Income
from regularly recurring sources (EXAMPLES:
income from one's business; interest on
one's savings account; **stock dividends**), as
distinguished from, for EXAMPLE, **capital
gains**. "Ordinary income" is a tax law term.
See income.

ordinary interest [*in* · trest] *n.* **Simple
interest** calculated on the basis of a 360-
day year rather than a 365-day year.
Compare compound interest.

ordinary life insurance [in · *shoor* · ense]
n. **Straight life insurance** or **whole life
insurance**, as opposed to **term life
insurance** or **group insurance**.

ordinary low tide *n.* Same as **mean low
tide**.

ordinary negligence [*neg* · li · jense] *n.*
The failure to exercise the **degree of care**
that a **reasonably prudent person** would
have exercised in similar circumstances; the
failure to use **ordinary care** or **due care**.
Compare gross negligence. *See* negligence.

O

ordinary person [*per* · sen] *n.* *See* reasonable man test.

ordinary prudence [*proo* · dense] *n.* *See* reasonable man test.

ordinary prudent man [*proo* · dent] *n.* *See* reasonable man test.

ordinary prudent person [*proo* · dent *per* · sen] *n.* *See* reasonable man test.

ordinary repairs [re · *pairz*] *n.* In the law of landlord and tenant, repairs necessary to keep the premises in good condition. EXAMPLES: plumbing repair; painting; wallpapering.

ordinary risks of employment [em · *ploy* · ment] *n.* Dangers that are normal aspects of a person's employment.

ordinary skill *n.* Degree of skill that persons engaged in a particular occupation usually employ, as opposed to that degree of skill possessed by a few persons of extraordinary talent or ability. "Ordinary skill" is the standard for determining the **negligence** of a professional person.

ordinary wear and tear *n.* *See* wear and tear.

organic [or · *gan* · ik] *adj.* 1. Fundamental; basic; structural. 2. Derived from plants or animals as opposed to minerals.
➤ fundamental, basic, structural, inherent, biological, innate, primary.

organic law *n.* A constitution; the basic or fundamental law of a state or nation. *See* constitution.

organization [or · ge · ni · *zay* · shen] *n.* 1. A group of persons joined together to engage in a common activity or to pursue a common purpose. EXAMPLES: a corporation; an **unincorporated association**; a labor union; a sorority. 2. The act of organizing.
➤ group, alliance, league, coalition, affiliation, consortium, federation.

organized crime [or · ge · nized] *n.* A criminal enterprise involving a pattern of racketeering activity. *See* Racketeer Influenced and Corrupt Organizations Act (RICO).

origin [or · ih · jin] *n.* 1. The birth or beginning of something. 2. Ancestry; heritage.
➤ beginning, cause, birth, genesis, foundation; descent, heritage, lineage, bloodline. *Ant.* death, termination.

original [o · *rij* · i · nel] *adj.* 1. Pertaining to that which is done for the first time. EXAMPLES: an **original conveyance**; a **book of original entry**. 2. Pertaining to that from which a copy is made. 3. Fundamental; founding; earliest. 4. First; primary. *n.* The first copy; the master. USAGE: "File the original with the clerk.")
➤ *adj.* innovative, introductory, unique, clever, basic, formative, fundamental, earliest, first, primary.
n. standard, archetype, paradigm, precursor, model, first, source, pattern.

original contractor [*kon* · trak · ter] *n.* A **prime contractor** or **general contractor**. *Compare* subcontractor.

original conveyance [ken · *vey* · ense] *n.* A **conveyance** by which an **estate** or **use** is created; a **primary conveyance**.

original deed *n.* *See* original conveyance.

original document [*dok* · yoo · ment] *n.* *See* original evidence.

original document rule [*dok* · yoo · ment] *n.* *See* best evidence rule; original evidence.

original entry [*en* · tree] *n.* *See* book of original entry. *See also* book of account.

original evidence [*ev* · i · dense] *n.* An original document, as opposed to a copy or duplicate, that is introduced into evidence. The **original document rule** states that the original of a document is the **best evidence** of the truth or accuracy of the matter **memorialized** in the document. *See* best evidence rule.

original evidence rule [*ev* · i · dense] *n.* *See* original evidence.

original intent [in · *tent*] *n.* A term applied to the view of some scholars and jurists that judicial interpretation of the Constitution should be based on the words of the Constitution itself and the framers' "original intent," not on a contemporary understanding of the Constitution in the context of current realities. Adherents of this doctrine are sometimes referred to as **strict constructionists**.

original jurisdiction [joo · ris · *dik* · shen] *n.* The **jurisdiction** of a **trial court**, as distinguished from the jurisdiction of an **appellate court**. *See also* court of general jurisdiction.

original package [*pak* · ej] *n.* A shipped package that is delivered by the seller to the carrier for transportation, and then delivered unopened to the **consignee**. Under a rule of **constitutional law** known as the **original package doctrine**, no state may impose a tax upon goods imported from a foreign country so long as the goods remain in their original package.

original package doctrine [*pak* · ej *dok* · trin] *n. See* original package.

original process [*pross* · ess] *n.* A **summons**; the **process** by which an **action** is commenced.

original promise [*prom* · iss] *n.* A promise to **guarantee** the debt of another which, contrary to the basic rule (*see* statute of frauds), need not be in writing because it is made for the purpose of promoting the interests of the **promisor**. *See* leading object rule.

origination fee [o · rij · i · *nay* · shen] *n.* A fee charged a borrower by a lender (EXAMPLE: a mortgage company) for arranging a loan. It covers the cost of a credit check and other expenses of obtaining financing.

orphans' court [*or* · fenz] *n.* The name given **probate court** in some states.

OSHA [*oh* · sha] *n.* Acronym for both the **Occupational Safety and Health Administration** and the **Occupational Safety and Health Act.**

ostensible [os · *ten* · sibl] *adj.* Apparent; seeming.
➤ alleged, presumable, assumed, purported, plausible, apparent, seeming ("his ostensible purpose").

ostensible agency [*ay* · jen · see] *n.* An **agency** created by a course of conduct. EXAMPLE: the agency of a husband to make purchases on his wife's credit, established as a result of her consent to his doing so on numerous occasions in the past.

ostensible authority [aw · *thaw* · ri · tee] *n.* Same as **apparent authority**.

ostensible ownership [*ohn* · er · ship] *n.* The appearance of ownership by someone other than the owner, stemming from the conduct of the owner.

ostensible partner [*part* · ner] *n.* A person who, although not a **partner**, incurs

the liability of a partner because he is held out, or holds himself out, as a member of the partnership. *See* hold out.

OTC Abbreviation of **over-the-counter**. *See* over-the-counter market. *Also see* over-the-counter medication.

other insurance provision [*uth* · er in · *shoor* · ense pro · *vizh* · en] *n. See* coordination of benefits provision; excess insurance.

oust *v.* To carry out an **ouster**; to expel.
➤ banish, repudiate, discharge, expulse, remove, eject.

ouster [*oust* · er] *n.* 1. The **dispossession** from real property of a person entitled to possession. *Compare* ejectment; eviction. 2. A removal.
➤ deportation, banishment, deprivation, ejection, expulsion.

ouster of jurisdiction [joo · ris · *dik* · shen] *n.* A court's loss of **jurisdiction**, usually because of events occurring after the **action** is brought.

out *adv.* Away from; not in.
➤ absent, expired, finished, extinguished.

out of court *adj.* Not in or before the court.

out of pocket [*pok* · et] *adj.* Spent; disbursed. *See* disbursement.

out of term *adj.* Between **terms of court**; a time when no session of the court is held.

out-of-court settlement [*setl* · ment] *n.* 1. The ending of a controversy by agreement, before it gets to court. 2. The settlement of a lawsuit after the **complaint** has been **served**, and without obtaining or seeking judicial approval.

out-of-pocket expense [eks · *pense*] *n.* An expense usually paid for with cash. *See* expense.

outbuilding [*out* · bil · ding] *n.* A building used in connection with a main building located on the same piece of property. EXAMPLE: a garage; a barn. *See* outhouse.

outcome [*owt* · kum] *n.* The result; the conclusion.
➤ result, decision, resolution, finding, ruling, culmination, consequence, aftermath ("the outcome of the case").

O

outcome test [*out* · kum] *n.* The rule that, in a **diversity of citizenship** case, the federal court should apply state law to ensure the same result as would have been attained in state court.

outcry [*out* · kry] *n.* 1. To notify or sell by crying out. EXAMPLE: an auctioneer offering an item for sale and asking for bids. *See* auction. 2. The crying out of a person who is assaulted. 3. A strong protest. USAGE: "There was a great deal of public outcry for a change in that law."
➤ clamor, outburst, protest, uproar, complaint, accusation, disapproval, castigation.

outdated [owt · *day* · ted] *adj.* Out of use; old; obsolete.
➤ archaic, obsolete, primitive, old-fashioned, passé.
Ant. contemporary.

outer door [*out* · er] *n.* A door for entering or exiting premises, whether the premises are a house or an apartment located in a building with other apartments. The term is of significance with respect to the rule that prohibits an officer from forcing an "outer door" for the purpose of serving **process**.

outhouse [*out* · house] *n.* 1. An **outbuilding**. 2. An outdoor privy.

outlaw [*out* · law] *n.* 1. A person who has violated the law. 2. A fugitive; a **fugitive from justice**.
v. To make something illegal.
➤ *n.* criminal, fugitive, crook, desperado, hoodlum, recidivist, bandit, robber, felon.
v. ban, condemn, exclude, forbid, illegalize.

outlawed [*out* · lawd] *adj.* Barred by the **statute of limitations**.

outlay [*out* · lay] *n.* An expense; money advanced on a transaction.
➤ expense, cost, disbursement, charge, expenditure.

outlet [*owt* · let] *n.* An exit or egress.
➤ opening, gate, vent, egress, access.

outmoded [owt · *moad* · ed] *adj.* Old; dated.
➤ outdated, obsolete, out-of-fashion, anachronistic, passé, dated ("an outmoded style of dress").

output [*owt* · put] *n.* That which is produced.
➤ proceeds, product, return, result, yield, harvest, crop.

output contract [*out* · put *kon* · trakt] *n.* *See* entire output contract.

outrage [*out* · rayj] *n.* 1. An aggravated **wrong** that inflicts grave **injury** to a person's body or mind. EXAMPLE: a rape. 2. An offensive act; an affront.
v. To shock or enrage.
➤ *n.* injustice, violation, abomination, transgression, violence.
v. exasperate, provoke, infuriate, discombobulate, affront, anger, arouse, disgust, gall.
Ant. benefit, pacify.

outrageous [owt · *ray* · jus] *adj.* Extreme; shocking.
➤ shocking, wild, unwarranted, atrocious, excessive, despicable, intolerable ("outrageous behavior").

outright [*out* · rite] *adj.* Completely; totally; without strings attached.
➤ complete, absolute, direct, thorough, unequivocal ("an outright lie").
outright gift *n.* An absolute gift. *See* gift.

outside salesperson [*out* · side *saylz* · per · sen] *n.* A person who sells her employer's product by calling upon potential buyers at their places of business, rather than soliciting business by telephone. The expenses incurred by an outside salesperson may be taken by her as tax deductions.

outstanding [out · *stan* · ding] *adj.* 1. Unpaid; unsettled. USAGE: "**outstanding stock**"; "**outstanding balance**." 2. Prominent; distinguished.
➤ uncollected, unresolved, in arrears, existing, remaining ("an outstanding charge"); distinctive, excellent, memorable, extraordinary, distinguished ("an outstanding performance").
outstanding accounts [a · *kounts*] *n.* Unpaid accounts, both good and bad. *See* account.
outstanding and open account [o · pen a · *kount*] *n.* An unpaid or unsettled account. *See* account.
outstanding balance [*bal* · ense] *n.* The amount owed on a debt. *See* balance.
outstanding debts *n.* Debts that are due and owing. *See* debt.

O

outstanding stock *n.* Shares of **stock** issued by a corporation. Outstanding stock is an **obligation** of the corporation. *Compare* treasury stock.

over [*oh* · ver] *adj./adv.* 1. A word used to indicate the transferring of a case from one court to another. *See* binding over. 2. A word used to indicate the **continuance** of a case from one **session** or **term of court** to another. USAGE: "The judge said he would put the case over until next term." 3. A word applied to a **contingent estate**, sometimes called an "estate over." *See* contingent devise; contingent remainder. 4. Above. 5. Higher in position. 6. Excessive.
➤ *adj.* closed, completed, concluded, ended, finished, settled.
adv. beyond, exceeding, transcending, surpassing; on top of, above.

over insurance [in · *shoor* · ense] *n.* Same as **excess insurance**.

over-the-counter market [-*count* · er *mar* · ket] *n.* A market in **securities** other than the stock exchange; securities transactions directly between brokers. The over-the-counter securities market (the **OTC**) trades through the **NASDAQ** system. *See* market.

over-the-counter medication [*count* · er med · ı · *kay* · shen] *n.* Medication that can legally be purchased at a retail store without a prescription. *Compare* controlled substance.

overbreadth doctrine [*oh* · ver · bredth *dok* · trin] *n.* The doctrine that a statute is unconstitutional if its language is so broad that it unnecessarily interferes with the exercise of constitutional rights, particularly **First Amendment** rights, even though the purpose of the statute is to prohibit activities that the government may constitutionally prohibit. EXAMPLE: a statute that seeks to outlaw child pornography by criminalizing all obscene books, magazines, and films. *Compare* vagueness doctrine; narrowly tailored.

overcharge [*oh* · ver · charj] *n.* 1. A charge greater in amount than is permitted by law. EXAMPLE: **usury**. 2. A charge by a **common carrier** or **public utility** in excess of the **tariffs** approved by the **public service commission** or the **Interstate Commerce Commission**. 3. Any excessive charge.

v. To charge more than is appropriate or allowed.
➤ *n.* excess, additional charge.
v. deceive, cheat, fleece, rip off.

overcome [oh · ver · *kum*] *v.* 1. To exceed, outweigh, or defeat. 2. To stun or overwhelm.
➤ surmount, transcend, rise above, prevail, triumph; overwhelm, stun, bowl over, daze, crush.

overdraft [*oh* · ver · draft] *n.* The condition that arises when a customer of a bank draws a check in an amount greater than the amount of money he has on deposit in the bank. *See* insufficient funds; kiting; NSF check.

overdue [o · ver · *dew*] *adj.* Past due; having run beyond **maturity**.
➤ late, delinquent, outstanding, unsettled, belated ("an overdue payment").
overdue paper [*pay* · per] *n.* A **negotiable instrument** or other written evidence of **obligation** that was not paid **at maturity**. *See* evidence of debt.

overestimate [oh · ver · *ess* · tih · mate] *v.* To overrate the worth or value of a person or thing.
➤ exceed, enlarge, magnify, overstate, misjudge, maximize.

overhang [*oh* · ver · hang] *n.* That which extends or projects over. (EXAMPLES: a roof that extends over adjoining property; a sign that extends over the sidewalk.) An overhang may constitute a **continuous easement**. *See also* encroachment; easement.
v. To extrude or extend.
➤ *n.* projection, eave, awning, protuberance.
v. bulge, jut, loom, portend, protrude, extend, project.

overhead [*oh* · ver · hed] *n.* The continuing or regular costs of operating a business. EXAMPLES: wages and salaries; rent; telephone; office supplies.
➤ budget, cost, expenses, outlay, upkeep.

overissue [o · ver · *ish* · ew] *n.* An **issue** of **stock** by a corporation in excess of the amount of stock authorized by its **charter**.

overlook [*oh* · ver · *look*] *v.* 1. To forgive or disregard. 2. To oversee or administer.
➤ excuse, forgive, pardon, disregard ("overlook this transgression"); guide,

O

oversee, govern, administer, steer, command ("overlook the project").

overreach [oh · ver · *reech*] *v.* 1. To bring an end to. 2. To go beyond a set limit. 3. To lead astray knowingly; to take advantage of.
➤ abolish, obliterate, overturn, disrupt, remove, topple, surmount; exceed, go beyond; deceive, intimidate, take advantage of.

overreaching [o · ver · *ree* · ching] *n.* Taking unfair advantage in bargaining. Overreaching by one party might cause a contract to be voided. *See* adhesion contract; unconscionability.
➤ misconduct, trickery, circumvention, misleading, undermining.

override [o · ver · *ride*] *v.* To exercise one's authority or will so as to nullify the action of another or others. EXAMPLES: in many states it is possible for the voters to override a **legislative act** by **referendum**; Congress, by a two-thirds vote of both houses, can override a presidential veto.
➤ nullify, counteract, void, supersede, defeat, dominate.

overrule [o · ver · *rool*] *v.* To disallow; to override; to reverse; to veto; to annul; to nullify. The *overruling of precedent* is the **nullification** of a prior decision as **precedent**; it occurs when the same court, or a higher court in a later case, establishes a different rule on the same point of law involved in the earlier case. When a decision is overruled, it is said to be "reversed." *See* reversal; reverse. A judge *overrules an objection* when she refuses to sustain the **objection**.
➤ void, abrogate, invalidate, disallow, override, reverse, quash, veto, annul, nullify. *Ant.* allow, sustain.

overt [o · *vert*] *adj.* 1. In the language of the law, relates to an act as opposed to the mere intention to engage in an act. 2. Open; observable.
➤ open, exposed, conspicuous, noticeable, perceptible, observable.

overt act *n.* An act that carries an **intent** into effect; an act from which intent may be **presumed**. Although intent may make an otherwise innocent act criminal, mere guilty intention, without an "overt act," is never criminal. *See* act.

overthrow [oh · ver · *throh*] *v.* To defect; to oust.
n. A revolt or revolution whereby one group takes power from another.
➤ *v.* abolish, obliterate, overturn, disrupt, remove, topple, surmount.
n. revolt, insurrection, revolution, ouster, coup d'état.

overtime [*oh* · ver · time] *n.* Work performed over and above the period of one's regular work hours. *See* Fair Labor Standards Act (FLSA); wage and hour acts.

overtime pay *n.* Extra pay for working overtime. *See* Fair Labor Standards Act (FLSA); wage and hour acts.

overture [*oh* · ver · tchyoor] *n.* A proposal; an introduction; an opening.
➤ beginning, advance, approach, proposal, invitation, proposition.

owe *v.* 1. To be legally indebted. 2. To be under a political, moral, or social obligation.
➤ be behind, be in arrears, be bound, be obligated, be indebted.

owing [*oh* · wing] *adj.* Due; unpaid.
➤ due, unpaid, attributable, outstanding, payable.

own *adj.* Pertaining to that which belongs to oneself.
v. To be the owner of anything.
➤ *adj.* inherent, intrinsic, personal, private, particular.
v. control, dominate, hold occupy, retain.

own motion [*moh* · shen] *n.* A term referring to a **disposition** made by a court or other tribunal during the course of a **proceeding**, without a **party** having requested it. USAGE: "Neither the plaintiff nor the defendant requested a continuance; the judge put the case over until January on his own motion." *See sua sponte.*

own recognizance [re · *kog* · ni · sense] *n.* Often referred to as **OR** [oh · *arr*]; the circumstance in which a judge releases a criminal defendant on his promise to return to court for trial, rather than compelling him to post a **bail bond**. "Own recognizance" is the same as **personal recognizance**. (USAGE: "The judge released him on his own recognizance.") OR release is also referred to as **release on own recognizance** or **ROR**. *See* recognizance.

O

owner [*oh* · ner] *n.* A person who has **title** to property and **dominion** over it. *See* ownership. *See also* coownership; part owner; record owner; reputed owner; riparian owner.
➤ buyer, landlord, possessor, proprietor.
owner in fee *n.* *See* fee simple; fee simple absolute.
owner of record [*rek* · erd] *n.* *See* record owner.

ownership [*oh* · ner · ship] *n.* The rights of an owner, including the right to possess and control property. *See* coownership; incident of ownership; indicia of ownership; joint ownership; ostensible ownership; owner; sole and unconditional ownership; sole ownership; unconditional ownership.
➤ claim, occupancy, possessorship, tenancy, dominion, control, seisin, title, tenure.

oyer and terminer [*oi* · yer and *ter* · mi · ner] *v.* A phrase derived from old English and *French*, meaning "hear and determine." Its modern application is **court of oyer and terminer**, a term for criminal courts in some states.

oyez [*oi* · yez] *v.* A word derived from the *French*, meaning "hear ye"; a cry uttered by the **tipstaff** or **bailiff** in some courts when the judge enters the courtroom at the beginning of a session of court.

O

PA Abbreviation of **professional association**.

PAC [pak] *n.* Acronym for **political action committee**. A PAC is a committee or other body organized to receive funds in support of candidates for elective office. The activities of PACs are regulated by federal statute.

pacify [*pass* · ih · fy] *v.* To calm or appease.
➤ appease, settle, soothe, please, placate, relieve, harmonize, mollify, calm.
Ant. antagonize.

pack *v.* 1. To use illegal means to select a jury sympathetic to one's client. An attorney who does so is said to be **packing a jury**. 2. To put together for transportation or storage. 3. To crowd or cram together.
n. An accumulation of things or people.
➤ *v.* arrange, load, collect, charge.
n. assemblage, bundle, collection, lot, mass, troop, gang.

package [*pak* · ej] *n.* 1. A bundle or parcel made up of several smaller parcels combined in one box or other receptacle for transportation. *See* original package. 2. Something envisioned as a whole. EXAMPLE: a "package deal."
➤ bundle, batch, container, amalgamation, baggage, parcel.

packing a jury [*pak* · ing a *joo* · ree] *n.* Using illegal means to insure that a jury is made up of persons favorably disposed to one of the parties to the case. *See* jury.

pact *n.* A **compact**; a contract; an agreement. *See* nudum pactum.
➤ alliance, arrangement, treaty, transaction, concord.

pactum [*pak* · tum] (*Latin*) *n.* Means "contract." *See* nudum pactum.

paid *adj.* **Satisfied**; remunerated.
➤ satisfied, remunerated, resolved, compensated.

paid in *adj.* Money or property given to an organization in exchange for an interest in the organization. Thus, for EXAMPLE, a member of a bar association who has paid his dues is "paid in" or "paid up," and receives membership in the organization; a person who has contributed to the **paid-in capital** of a corporation receives stock in the corporation.

paid-in capital [*kap* · i · tel] *n. See* paid in.

paid-up stock *n.* Corporate stock issued to a stockholder, the cost of which he has paid in full. *See* stock. *See also* corporate securities; corporate stock.

pain *n.* Hurt; suffering; distress.
➤ discomfort, anguish, suffering, torment, affliction, misery, ordeal.

pain and suffering [*suf* · e · ring] *n.* Mental anguish or physical pain. **Damages** may be recoverable if the pain and suffering is caused by a **tort**.

pais [pay] (*French*) *n.* 1. The country. 2. Outside of court. *See* estoppel in pais.

palatable [*pal* · uh · tih · bul] *adj.* 1. Of an endurable or average quality. 2. Pleasant to the sense of taste.
➤ acceptable, agreeable, satisfactory, unobjectionable; tasty, savory, appetizing, delicious.

palimony [*pal* · i · moh · nee] *n.* **Alimony** paid upon the breakup of a live-in relationship between two people who were not married to each other. In some states, such payment may be ordered by a court if the parties entered into an **express contract** or if the court finds the existence of an **implied contract**. In others, court-ordered palimony is based upon *quantum meruit*. In still others, palimony is considered to be contrary to **public policy** and is not recognized by the law.

palliate [*pal · ee · ayt*] *v.* 1. To reduce the intensity of. 2. To grant relief; to clear charges.
➤ ease, abate, curb, curtail, pacify, reduce; excuse, absolve, release, exonerate, clear, forgive.

palming off [*pawm · ing*] *n.* A form of **fraudulent misrepresentation** in which a seller of goods misrepresents himself as someone else, or represents the goods as belonging to someone else, with the purpose of inducing a buyer to purchase something she would not otherwise buy. *See* misrepresentation.

Palsgraf rule [*pallz · graf*] *n.* In the law of **torts**, the rule that a person is liable only for **foreseeable injury** resulting from her **negligence**, and not for harm that could not have been foreseen or predicted.

paltry [*pol · tree*] *adj.* Small or insignificant.
➤ insignificant, small, minute, scanty, negligible, piddling, trivial ("a paltry amount").

pamphlet law [*pam · flet*] *n.* In most states, the **Secretary of State** or the legislature publishes a limited number of copies of all statutes enacted by the legislature as they are enacted and before they are **codified**. These "pamphlet laws" are then distributed to public officials, public offices, and libraries throughout the state, and are available upon request to the general public as well.

panacea [*pan · uh · see · uh*] *n.* A cure-all; a solution.
➤ cure-all, remedy, solution, answer, balm, cure.

pander [*pan · der*] *n.* A pimp; a **panderer**. *v.* 1. To pimp. 2. To gratify the desires of others; to cater to others; to accommodate.

panderer [*pan · der · er*] *n.* Same as **pander**.

pandering [*pan · der · ing*] *n.* Soliciting customers for a prostitute; pimping. *See* solicit.
➤ soliciting, pimping, hustling.

panel [*pan · el*] *n.* 1. The jury **impaneled** for the trial of a case. *See* jury list; jury panel. 2. A group of **appellate court** judges, customarily three, who hear and decide a case in the place of the entire membership of the court. 3. A number of **commissioners** who have the authority of the entire **commission**. 4. An **arbitration panel**; i.e., a number of **arbitrators** who hear and decide a case. 5. Any group of persons who hear and determine a matter together.
➤ forum, body, committee, board, assembly, jurors, triers of fact, jury.

panhandling [*pan · hand · ling*] *n.* Public begging.

paper [*pay · per*] *n.* 1. A document or documents, including **books and records**. 2. An instrument or instruments, **negotiable** or **nonnegotiable**. EXAMPLES: **commercial paper; documents of title**. *See and compare* negotiable instrument; nonnegotiable instrument. 3. Legal papers; i.e., documents utilized or involved in a lawsuit. (EXAMPLES: **documentary evidence**; a **complaint**; an **answer**; a **brief**.) *Note* that the **Fourth Amendment** guaranty against **unreasonable searches and seizures** applies to "papers and effects" as well as to "persons [and] houses." *See* accommodation paper; bearer paper; chattel paper; clean paper; ship's papers; valuable papers.
➤ certificate, instrument, record, document; composition, essay, report.

paper money [*mun · ee*] *n.* Paper currency issued by the government; the equivalent of a government **bank note**. *See* money. *Also see* legal tender; medium of exchange.

paper title [*ty · tel*] *n.* Apparent title to real estate, supported by a chain of **conveyances** rather than by a **chain of title**. In other words, the appearance of title based upon a series of deeds or other conveyances which seem to pass **title**, but do not.

papers [*pay · perz*] *n. Plural* of **paper**. *See* paper.

P

par *n.* 1. The status of stock when it may be purchased for its **face value**. USAGE: "My stock is at par." *See* par value. 2. Equality in standing, status, or rank. USAGE: "A general in the army is on a par with an admiral in the navy." 3. The average or norm; a standard. USAGE: "His recent work has been below par."
➤ equivalence, correspondence, unity, equilibrium, balance; average, norm, expectations.

par value *n.* The value of a **share of stock** or of a **bond**, according to its **face**; the named or nominal value of an **instrument**. The par value and the **market value** of stock are not synonymous; there is often a wide difference between them. The issuer of a bond is obligated to redeem it at par value upon **maturity**. *See* stated value. *See also* no-par stock.

paradigm [*par* · uh · dime] *n.* An archetype; a model.
➤ model, archetype, guide, standard, pattern.

paralegal [*pehr* · e · leeg · el] *n.* A person who, although not an attorney, performs many of the functions of an attorney under an attorney's supervision. The **American Bar Association** defines a paralegal as a "person, qualified through education, training, or work experience, who is employed or retained by a lawyer, law office, governmental agency, or other entity in a capacity or function which involves the performance, under the ultimate direction and supervision of an attorney, of specifically designated substantive legal work, which work, for the most part, requires a sufficient knowledge of legal concepts that, absent such assistant, the attorney would perform the task." Another term for paralegal is **legal assistant**.
➤ legal assistant, paraprofessional, aide, lay advocate, legal technician.

parallel citation [*pehr* · e · lel sy · *tay* · shen] *n.* A **citation** to a court opinion or decision that is printed in two or more **reporters**. EXAMPLE: *Roe v. Wade* is officially cited as 410 U.S. 113, with parallel citations to 93 S. Ct. 705 and 35 L. Ed. 2d 147, which means that the written opinion in the *Roe* case is published in volume 410 of the United States Reports at page 113, *and* in

volume 93 of the *Supreme Court Reporter* at page 705, *and* in volume 35 of *United States Supreme Court Reports, Lawyers' Edition, Second Series* at page 147. *See* court reports. *Also see* United States Reports.

paramount [*pehr* · e · mount] *adj.* Above everyone or everything; dominant; prevailing; first.
➤ superior, unsurpassed, dominant, prevailing, supreme.
paramount right *n.* A superior right. EXAMPLE: a **senior mortgage** is paramount to a **junior mortgage**. *See* right.
paramount title [*ty* · tel] *n.* A superior title. EXAMPLE: **legal title** is paramount to **paper title**. *See* title.

paraphernal property [pehr · e · *fer* · nel *prop* · er · tee] *n.* Same as **extradotal property**.

paraphernalia [pehr · e · fer · *nayl* · ya] *n.* 1. At **common law**, the property of a wife which she had a right to possess separately from her husband. EXAMPLES: clothing; jewelry. 2. *Drug paraphernalia* are articles used in connection with the taking of illicit drugs. (EXAMPLE: hypodermic syringes; opium pipes.) Possession of drug paraphernalia is illegal in most states. 3. Equipment; accessories; miscellaneous articles.
➤ gear, property, furnishings, accessories, supplies, equipment, accessories, articles.

parasite [*par* · ih · site] *n.* One who depends on and lives off another.
➤ scavenger, leech, borrower, sycophant, sponge, barnacle, scrounger.

parcel [*par* · sel] *n.* 1. A lot or tract of real estate. 2. A bundle; a small package; a portion of a package.
v. 1. To divide real estate into separate lots or parcels. *See* parcel (*noun*). 2. To allocate into portions and distribute. USAGE: "I think my mother parceled out my father's effects fairly."
➤ *n.* package, lot, tract, plot, enclosure. *v.* apportion, partition, distribute, allow, prorate.

parcener [*par* · sen · er] *n.* Same as **coparcener**. *See* joint heir.

pardon [*par* · den] *n.* 1. An act of grace by the chief executive of the government, for EXAMPLE, a governor or the president, relieving a person of the legal consequences of a crime of which she has been convicted. A pardon erases the conviction. *Compare* commutation of sentence. *Also compare* amnesty; parole; reprieve. *See* clemency; conditional pardon; pardons board. 2. Forgiveness; absolution.

v. To forgive or excuse.

➤ *n.* release, forgiveness, exoneration, clemency, vindication.

v. excuse, exonerate, vindicate, acquit, release.

pardons board *n.* A **board** of state government authorized to grant pardons and **commutations** to persons convicted of crimes. *Compare* parole board.

parens patriae [pahr · enz pat · ree · ay] (*Latin*) *adj.* Meaning "the parent of the country."

***parens patriae* doctrine** [dok · trin] *n.* The doctrine that **dependent** and **incompetent persons** are under the protection and control of the state. This concept empowers the state, within the limits imposed by the Constitution, to institutionalize orphans, individuals with serious mental defects, and others who are unable to care for themselves. *See* institution.

parent [pair · ent] *n.* Depending upon the circumstances, and the statute being applied to those circumstances, "parents" may mean either biological parents or adoptive parents, or both, and may refer to the parents of either a legitimate child, an illegitimate child, or both. The term may also apply to one who stands *in loco parentis*, including a foster parent, a **guardian**, or an agency of the state concerned with child welfare.

➤ procreater, antecedent, ancestor, mother, father, predecessor, progenitor, begetter.

parent company [kum · pe · nee] *n.* A corporation that owns all or the majority of the stock of another corporation. The corporation owned by the parent company is called a **subsidiary** or a **wholly owned subsidiary**.

parent corporation [kore · per · ay · shen] *n.* *See* parent company.

parental [pa · ren · tel] *adj.* Pertaining to parents or to being a parent.

➤ maternal, paternal, motherly, fatherly ("parental rights").

parental kidnapping [kid · nap · ing] *n.* A form of **kidnapping** in which a child is abducted from the custody of one parent by the other parent. *See* abduction. *Also see* child stealing.

parental liability [ly · e · bil · i · tee] *n.* In some states, by statute, parents are liable for damage caused by their children resulting from the parents' failure to supervise them.

parental rights *n.* The rights of a parent with respect to his or her child. EXAMPLES: the right to impose discipline; the right to manage the child's affairs; the right to prevent adoption.

pari delicto [pah · ree de · lik · toh] (*Latin*) *See* in pari delicto.

pari materia [pah · ree ma · teer · ee · ah] (*Latin*) Means "in connection with the matter." *See* in pari materia.

pari-mutuel betting [peh · ree-myoo · chew · el bet · ing] *n.* A form of wagering at race tracks in which those who bet on the winning animal share the total stakes, less a percentage to the management and the state. Pari-mutuel betting is legal in most states if done at state-regulated tracks or at state-approved betting establishments.

parish [pehr · ish] *n.* 1. A **political subdivision** in Louisiana, corresponding to a county in other states. 2. An administrative unit of a church or religious organization, headed by a minister or priest.

➤ territory, archdiocese, community, church, subdivision.

parity [pehr · i · tee] *n.* 1. A term applied to the system by which the federal government subsidizes farmers by insuring that the prices they receive for their products are maintained at a level equal to the prices they received during a specified base period. These **subsidies** are also referred to as **price supports**. *See* subsidy. 2. Equality; par; evenness.

➤ uniformity, equilibrium, semblance, balance, subsidy ("parity in the NFL").

parlance [par · lens] *n.* The language used to describe people, places, or things.

➤ speech, vocabulary, manner, terminology ("in contemporary parlance").

Parliament [par · le · ment] *n.* The legislature of the English government, consisting of the House of Lords and the House of Commons.

parliamentary [par · le · *men* · te · ree] *adj.* 1. Relating or pertaining to the English Parliament. *See* Parliament. 2. Relating or pertaining to legislation or to a legislature.
➤ legislative, deliberative, orderly.

parliamentary law *n.* The body of law that governs the way in which the meetings of a legislature are conducted. *See* parliamentary rules.

parliamentary rules *n.* The rules adopted by an organization (EXAMPLES: a union; a corporation) to govern the conduct of its meetings. *See* Roberts Rules of Order.

parochial [pe · *roh* · kee · el] *adj.* 1. Pertaining to a **parish**. 2. Provincial; unsophisticated; limited.
➤ narrow, provincial, regional, sectional, confined, insular, bigoted ("a parochial view").

parochial school *n.* A school operated by a church or religious organization, providing both religious instruction and general academic education. *See and compare* private school; public school.

parol [pa · rull] *adj.* Oral; by word of mouth; spoken, as opposed to written. Note that "parol" is not "parole."
➤ oral, unwritten, nuncupative, voiced, uttered ("parol evidence").

parol contract [*kon* · trakt] *n.* 1. An **oral contract**. 2. At **common law**, a contract not **under seal**.

parol evidence [*ev* · i · dense] *n.* The oral or verbal testimony of a witness; specifically, testimony relating to the terms of a written agreement. *See* parol evidence rule. *Also see aliunde*; evidence aliunde.

parol evidence rule [*ev* · i · dense] *n.* Under the parol evidence rule, evidence of prior or **contemporaneous** oral agreements that would change the terms of a written contract are inadmissible. In other words, the intention of the parties, as evidenced by the language of a written contract, cannot be varied by parol proof of a different intention. The **presumption** is that the written contract incorporated all of the terms of the contract. *See* parol evidence.

parole [pa · *role*] *n.* 1. The release of a person from imprisonment after serving a portion of her sentence, provided she complies with certain conditions. Such conditions vary, depending upon the case, but they generally include stipulations such as not associating with known criminals, not possessing firearms, and not leaving the jurisdiction without the permission of the parole officer. Parole is not an act of **clemency**; it does not set aside the sentence. The **parolee** remains in the **legal custody** of the state and under the control of her parole officer. She may be returned to prison if she breaches the specified conditions. However, **due process** requires that parole cannot be revoked without a hearing. *See* revocation hearing. *Also see* due process hearing. *See and compare* amnesty; commutation of sentence; pardon; reprieve. 2. Word of honor.
v. To release from confinement.
➤ *n.* release, freedom, emancipation, conditional release.
v. discharge, release, liberate, let out, disimprison, unchain, unfetter.

parole board *n.* A **board** of state government authorized to grant paroles to persons imprisoned for crimes. *Compare* pardons board.

parole officer [*off* · i · ser] *n.* A **public officer** assigned by the **parole board** to supervise a **parolee** and to monitor his compliance with the conditions of his parole.

parole revocation hearing [rev · e · *kay* · shen *heer* · ing] *n.* *See* revocation hearing.

parolee [pa · *role* · ee] *n.* A person who has been released from prison on parole.

part *n.* Less than the whole; a component; a piece; a portion; a segment; a share.
v. 1. To move away from. 2. To separate or divide.
➤ *n.* portion, section, allocation, measure, chunk, division, piece ("the major part of the estate"); role, performance, representation, character, portrayal ("playing the part").
v. leave, depart, escape, withdraw, remove; separate, disentangle, divide, sunder, subdivide.

P

part owner [*oh* · ner] *n.* One of two or more persons who own property as coowners. *See* coownership. *See also* cotenancy; joint tenancy; tenancy in common.

part performance [per · *for* · mense] *n.* **Performance** by a party to a contract that is less than full performance. Part performance of an **oral contract** for the sale of real estate removes the contract from the application of the **statute of frauds**; that is, it allows the court to order the enforcement of the contract even though it was not reduced to writing, if not to do so would cause the partially performing party injustice or hardship or would result in fraud. *Compare* substantial performance.

part-time employment [em · *ploy* · ment] *n.* The circumstance of an employee who is less than fully employed. Part-time employment may nonetheless be **regular employment**. *Compare* full-time employment. *Also compare* casual employment; seasonal employment; temporary employment.

partial [*par* · shel] *adj.* 1. Relating or pertaining to a part. *See pro tanto.* 2. Biased; prejudiced.
➤ fragmentary, fractional, limited ("partial payment"); biased, prejudiced, unobjective, interested ("The judge recused himself as being partial to the defendant").

partial average [*av* · e · rej] *n.* *See* particular average.

partial disability [dis · e · *bil* · i · tee] *n.* A disability resulting in only a partial loss of earning capacity, the plaintiff or claimant still being capable of performing some gainful employment; a disability that is less than total. *Compare* total disability. *See* disability. *Also see* loss of member; loss of use; partial loss.

partial eviction [e · *vik* · shen] *n.* An **eviction** of a tenant from a part of the leased premises. However, a partial eviction may constitute a **constructive eviction** from the entire premises.

partial incapacity [in · ke · *pass* · i · tee] *n.* *See* partial disability.

partial intestacy [in · *tess* · te · see] *n.* An **intestacy** with respect to only a portion of a **decedent's estate**, the balance of the estate having been disposed of by will.

partial loss *n.* 1. The **destruction** of only a portion of insured property. *See* loss. 2. The loss at sea of a part of a ship's cargo. *See* general average contribution; particular average. 3. Loss of use of part of a bodily member; loss, in part, of the use of a portion of the body. *See* loss of member.

partial payment [*pay* · ment] *n.* 1. A payment of a part of a debt. 2. An **installment payment**.

partial performance [per · *form* · ense] *n.* *See* part performance.

partial release [re · *leess*] *n.* A release of one or more **parcels** of real estate from a **blanket mortgage** upon payment of a portion of the mortgage debt. *See* release.

partial verdict [*ver* · dikt] *n.* A verdict in a criminal case in which the defendant is found guilty on some **counts** of the **indictment** and acquitted on others. *See* verdict.

participate [par · *tiss* · i · pate] *n.* To have a part or share of something in common with others; to experience in common with others; to take part in. USAGE: "participate in the discussion"; "participate in the loan" (*see* loan participation); "participate in the crime." *See* participation.
➤ share, join, partake, contribute, encourage, experience.

participation [par · tiss · i · *pay* · shen] *n.* The act of participating. **Loan participation** and **coinsurance** are EXAMPLES of legal arrangements involving participation; **aiding and abetting** is "participation in a crime"; "participation in a **work stoppage**" disqualifies an employee from receiving unemployment compensation benefits. *See* participate.
➤ involvement, engagement, cooperation, partaking.

participation loan *n.* *See* loan participation.

particular [par · *tik* · yoo · ler] *adj.* 1. Pertaining to a single or individual person or thing; separate; distinct. 2. Pertaining to a special person or thing. 3. Discriminating or fussy.
➤ definite, distinguished, individual, specific, distinct; discriminating, choosy, fussy ("She is very particular about her food").

P

particular average [*av* · e · rej] *n.* 1. A term used in contrast to "general average," indicating a **loss** to a ship's cargo that is absorbed solely by the owner or owners of the particular cargo that has been destroyed. 2. A term synonymous with **partial loss** when used in a **marine insurance** policy. *Compare* general average contribution.

particular estate [es · *tate*] *n.* A limited **estate** (EXAMPLES: a **life estate**; an **estate for years**) that precedes a **future estate**, especially where the future estate is a **remainder**.

particular lien [*leen*] *n.* A **lien** upon a particular piece of property for labor performed on it or material supplied to it. EXAMPLE: a **mechanic's lien** on an automobile for the cost of repairs or parts that were installed.

particular malice [*mal* · iss] *n.* Ill will or a grudge against a particular person; a desire to have revenge on a particular person. *Compare* constructive malice. *See* malice.

particular tenant [*ten* · ent] *n.* The **tenant** of a **particular estate**. *See* tenant.

particularity [par · tik · you · *lehr* · i · tee] *n.* In detail; specificity. **Pleadings** must allege **matter** with "particularity." The **remedy** for failure to plead with sufficient particularity is a **more definite statement**.
➤ precision, fastidiousness, meticulousness, detail, care, carefulness.

particulars [par · *tik* · yoo · lerz] *n.* Details; specifics. *See* bill of particulars. *Also see* particularity.
➤ specifications, details, features, niceties, articles, specifics.

parties [*par* · teez] *n. Plural* of **party**. The several meanings of "parties" are fully defined under **party**. *See* party.

partisan [*part* · ih · zan] *adj.* One-sided.
➤ partial, predisposed, clannish, factional, party, slanted, subjective ("a partisan view").
Ant. open, balanced, bipartisan.

partition [par · *tish* · en] *n.* 1. A division made between two or more persons of land or other property belonging to them as coowners. *See* coownership. 2. A **legal action** by which land or other property belonging to two or more persons is divided between them by court order. 3. A wall; a fence; a divider.
v. To separate or divide.
➤ *n.* division, splitting, apportionment, allotment, segmentation; wall, fence, divider.
v. separate, section, parcel out, divide.

partition deed *n.* A deed that achieves a partition of real estate.

partner [*part* · ner] *n.* A member of a **partnership**. *See* dormant partner; general partner; limited partner; liquidating partner; nominal partner; ostensible partner; silent partner; special partner.
➤ participant, associate, confrere, collaborator, confederate, member, teammate, aid, ally.

partnership [*part* · ner · ship] *n.* An undertaking of two or more persons to carry on, as coowners, a business or other enterprise for profit; an agreement between or among two or more persons to put their money, labor, and skill into commerce or business, and to divide the profit in agreed-upon proportions. Partnerships may be formed by **entities** as well as individuals; a corporation, for EXAMPLE, may be a **partner**. *See* coownership.

For federal income tax purposes, a partnership is a **for profit** enterprise (including a **syndicate, group, pool**, or **joint venture**) that is not a corporation. *See* articles of partnership; dissolution of partnership; equity of partners; general partnership; limited partnership; liquidation of partnership; secret partnership; special partnership; universal partnership.
➤ federation, alliance, league, association, collaboration, business, enterprise, undertaking.

partnership agreement [a · *gree* · ment] *n.* The agreement signed by the members of a partnership that governs their relationship as partners. It is sometimes referred to as **articles of partnership**.

partnership assets [*ass* · ets] *n.* All **assets** belonging to the partnership, as opposed to the personal assets of the partners.

partnership association [a · so · see · *ay* · shen] *n.* A business organization that is a type of **artificial person** standing halfway between a **limited partnership** and a **corporation**. Unlike a

P

general partnership, its members have **limited liability** for the obligations of the partnership. *Also see* professional corporation.

partnership debts *n.* Debts owed by the partnership, as opposed to the personal debts of the partners.

party [*par* · tee] *n.* 1. A person who has engaged in a transaction or made an agreement (i.e., a party to a contract). EXAMPLES of the use of the word "party" in this context include: **secured party; multiparty account; third-party beneficiary**. In this sense of the word, a person who has had dealings of any sort with another is a "party" to those interactions. Thus, a person who participates in the commission of a crime is a party to the crime and a person who is the victim of a **tort** is an **injured party**. *See also* innocent party. 2. One of the opposing litigants in a lawsuit; e.g., a defendant or a plaintiff; a **petitioner**; an **appellant**; an **appellee**. EXAMPLES of this use of the word "party" include: **indispensable party; joinder of parties; necessary party**. *See also* adverse party; nominal party; proper parties; substitution of parties; third-party complaint. 3. As the term is used in connection with an appeal, the appellant (also called **plaintiff in error**) and the appellee (also called **respondent or defendant in error**). *See also* aggrieved party. 4. For some purposes, a person interested in the outcome of litigation, who may or may not be a **party of record**, for EXAMPLE, a **party in interest** or a **real party in interest**. 5. A person.

➤ adversary, participant, litigant, disputant, claimant, conspirator, collaborator, partner, partaker; political organization, coalition, league, group, caucus.

party aggrieved [a · *greevd*] *n.* Same as **aggrieved party**.

party defendant [de · *fen* · dent] *n.* Same as **defendant**.

party in interest [*in* · trest] *n.* *See* real party in interest.

party litigant [*lit* · i · gant] *n.* A person named as a party to an **action** or suit. *See also* party of record.

party of record [*rek* · erd] *n.* A person formally named as a party to an **action** or

an appeal, as distinguished from a person who has an **interest** in the subject matter of the litigation. *Compare* real party in interest.

party plaintiff [*plain* · tif] *n.* Same as **plaintiff**.

party to a crime *n.* The status of each person concerned in the commission of a crime, whether their involvement is direct or indirect. Any party to a crime may be guilty of commission of the crime.

party to be charged *n.* As used in connection with the **statute of frauds**, the party against whom the contract is sought to be enforced.

party wall *n.* A common wall dividing and supporting two buildings which it separates. Customarily, the adjoining landowners own the wall as **tenants in common**. However, the wall may rest entirely on the land of one owner and still have the legal characteristics of a party wall.

pass *n.* 1. A short leave of absence for a person in the military service. 2. Permission to enter or leave a place where such permission is required, for EXAMPLE, a military base or a manufacturing plant. 3. Permission to ride as a passenger on a common carrier (for EXAMPLE, a train or plane) without paying a fare, or to attend an event (for EXAMPLE, a movie or concert) without paying the price of admission.
v. 1. To **vest** title, or to **convey** or transfer title or some other **legal interest** from one person to another by will, **conveyance, intestacy,** or otherwise. USAGE: "After Leslie died, the house passed to her daughters, Robin and Lee." *See* title. 2. To enact a statute. USAGE: "House Bill 3221 passed the legislature yesterday and the governor signed it today." *See* passage. 3. To pronounce, render, or impose a sentence. USAGE: "When will the judge pass sentence?" 4. To **render judgment** in a case (USAGE: "the court will not pass judgment until tomorrow"), to make a ruling in a case (USAGE: "the court will not pass upon the motion until it reconvenes"), or to form and express an opinion about someone or something (USAGE: "passing judgment on the basis of appearances is often a mistake"). 5. To **utter** a **forgery** or to circulate counterfeit currency. USAGE: "They arrested her when

P

she attempted to pass the counterfeit bills." *See* uttering a forged instrument. 6. To approve; to be approved. USAGE: "The car passed inspection."

➤ *n.* license, authorization, sanction, legalization, validation; route, way, opening, pathway.

v. ratify, approve, adopt ("pass a bill"); succeed, accomplish, achieve ("pass the course"); declare, render, decide, announce ("pass sentence"); transfer, give, grant, deed ("pass title").

passage [*pass* · ej] *n.* 1. Enactment of legislation. 2. A passageway. 3. The act of moving from one place to another.

➤ authorization, endorsement, confirmation, validation, acceptance ("passage of the bill"); route, channel, conduct, path ("Northwest Passage"); segment, piece, selection, excerpt, segment ("a passage from the text").

passbook [*pass* · book] *n.* A booklet carried by a depositor in which the bank enters the amount and dates of deposits and withdrawals to or from a savings account.

passenger [*pass* · en · jer] *n.* 1. A person who rides in an automobile or other conveyance, as distinguished from the driver or operator of the vehicle. A passenger may or may not be an **automobile guest** within the meaning of a state's **guest statute**. *Compare* automobile guest. 2. A person who has paid a fare or is given a pass and travels in a conveyance (EXAMPLE: a bus; a plane) operated by a common carrier.

➤ guest, traveler, commuter, client, patron.

passim [*pass* · im] (*Latin*) *adv.* Means "here and there." A term used to indicate that a certain idea or reference appears throughout a book or an article.

passion [*pash* · en] *n.* 1. Strong emotion. 2. Love; desire. *See* heat of passion.

➤ anger, excitement, emotion, fervor, rapture, ire, fire, zeal; lust, adoration, craving, excitement, affection, eroticism.

passive [*pass* · iv] *adj.* 1. Inactive. 2. Dormant. 3. Submissive.

➤ inactive, dormant, submissive, docile, obliging.
Ant. active, involved.

passive negligence [*neg* · li · jense] *n.* **Negligence** that lies in the failure to do an act, as opposed to the negligent doing of an act. *Compare* active negligence.

passive trust *n.* A **trust** in which the **trustee** has no duties to perform, and in which the **beneficiary** of the trust has the entire management of the **estate**; a **dry trust**; a **nominal trust**. *Compare* active trust.

passport [*pass* · port] *n.* A document issued by a nation to a citizen, requesting foreign countries to permit the bearer to pass freely and safely.

➤ authorization, license, visa, travel permit.

past *adj.* Former; previous; prior.
n. A bygone time.

➤ *adj.* former, previous, prior, obsolete, old ("past consideration").
n. old days, history, yesteryear, antiquity, yesterday ("nostalgia for the past").

past consideration [ken · sid · e · *ray* · shen] *n.* **Consideration** given *prior* to entering into a contract. Past consideration is not sufficient consideration to support a contract.

past due *n.* Overdue; having run beyond **maturity**.

past recollection recorded
[rek · e · *lek* · shen re · *kor* · ded] *n.* When a witness once had knowledge about a matter, but presently has insufficient recollection to enable her to testify accurately from memory, she may read into evidence the contents of a **memorandum** or other writing that she made or **adopted** concerning the matter, if the matter was fresh in her memory when she made or adopted the writing. Past recollection recorded is not inadmissible under the **hearsay rule**. *See and compare* present recollection recorded; present recollection revived; recorded past recollection.

patent [*pat* · ent] *adj.* Obvious; self-evident; apparent.
n. 1. The exclusive right of manufacture, sale, or use granted by the federal government to a person who invents or discovers a device or process that is **new and useful**. *See* process patent. *Also see* device; discovery; invention. 2. The grant of a right, privilege, or authority by the government. EXAMPLE: a **land patent**. *See* animal patent;

P

basis patent; combination patent; design patent; double patenting; examination of patent; improvement patent; infringement of patent; letters patent; pioneer patent; plant patent; utility patent.

v. [*pat* · ent] To obtain a **patent** upon an invention. *See* patent (*noun*).

➤ *adj.* obvious, visible, noticeable, apparent, evident, unmistakable, tangible, definite, indubitable.

n. permit, license, certificate, trademark, right, legal right.

patent ambiguity [am · big · *yoo* · i · tee] *n.* An uncertainty that appears on the **face** of a document and is of such a nature that it is impossible to determine the intention of the party or parties to the document. EXAMPLE: "I **devise and bequeath** all of my property to most of my children." *See* ambiguity.

Patent and Trademark Office [*pat* · ent and *trade* · mark *off* · iss] *n.* Authorized by the Constitution and established by Congress, this **office** of the federal government registers all **trademarks** and grants all **patents** issued in the United States. Its duties also include examining patents (*see* examination of patent), hearing and deciding appeals from inventors and trademark applicants, and publishing the *Official Gazette*.

patent appeals [a · *peelz*] *n. See* Customs and Patent Appeals Court.

patent defect [*dee* · fekt] *n.* A **defect** observable by casual inspection; an obvious defect in a structure or manufactured article, readily discoverable by a reasonable examination. *Compare* latent defect.

patent infringement [in · *frinj* · ment] *n. See* infringement of patent.

patent medicine [*med* · i · sin] *n.* An over-the-counter medication; a medication concocted by a manufacturer, often according to a secret formula. *Note* that a patent medicine is generally *not* patented; however, it is often protected by **trademark**. *See* proprietary drug.

patent rights *n.* The rights a **patentee** receives with respect to her invention as a result of having been granted a patent for it.

patentability [*pat* · ent] *n.* The quality of being **patentable**.

patentable [*pat* · ent · ebl] *adj.* Entitled to receive a **patent**. To be patentable, an idea must include every essential characteristic of the complete and practical invention.

patentee [pat · en · *tee*] *n.* A person who receives a **patent**.

paternal line [pa · *ter* · nel] *n.* A line of **inheritance** from or through the father. *Compare* maternal line.

paternity [pa · *ter* · ni · tee] *n.* The status of being a father.

adj. Related to fatherhood.

➤ *n.* fatherhood, derivation, ancestry, lineage, descent.

paternity proceeding [pro · *see* · ding] *n. See* paternity suit.

paternity suit *n.* A **proceeding** to establish the paternity of a child born out of wedlock, usually for the purpose of compelling the father to support the child. *See also* affiliation proceeding.

paternity test *n. See* DNA fingerprinting; genetic marker testing; HLA testing.

pathological [path · e · *loj* · ikl] *adj.* 1. Caused by disease. 2. Relating to disease. *See* pathology.

➤ demented, deranged, unbalanced, abject.

pathology [path · *aw* · le · jee] *n.* The branch of medicine concerned with the nature and symptoms of disease.

patient [*pay* · shent] *adj.* Restrained; unhurried; tolerant; accepting; forbearing. *See* forbearance.

n. A sick or injured person under the care of a physician, dentist, nurse, or other health professional.

➤ *adj.* diligent, sympathetic, unperturbed, balanced, determined, indefatigable, relentless, steadfast, persistent, unflappable.

n. victim, convalescent, sufferer, invalid, sick person, client.

patient forbearance rule [for · *bair* · ense] *n.* The rule that **cohabitation** with one's spouse is not **condonation** of cruelty or **indignities** when the **injured** spouse hopes that the marriage can be saved by "patient forbearance." *See* injured party; innocent and injured. *Also see* forbearance.

P

Patient Self-Determination Act [*pay* · shent self-de · ter · mi · *nay* · shen] *n.* A federal statute that requires every hospital which participates in **Medicaid** or **Medicare** to ask all admitted patients whether they have an **advance directive** (EXAMPLES: a **healthcare proxy**; a **living will**), and, if so, to document that fact in the patient's medical chart. Additionally, the hospital must advise all such patients of their right to refuse or select treatment under state law. *See* right to die.

patient-physician privilege [-fi · *zish* · en *priv* · i · lej] *n. See* physician-patient privilege.

patrimony [*pat* · ri · mo · nee] *n.* 1. An **estate** inherited from one's father or through the **paternal line**. 2. Any inherited estate.

patronage [*pay* · tren · ej] *n.* 1. The power to appoint persons to public office. 2. Offices or favors obtained by an office-holder as a result of the power to make such appointments or to grant such favors. 3. Sponsorship; backing; support. 4. Customers or patrons of a store or business, collectively.
➤ sponsorship, advocacy, guardianship, auspices, sustenance.

pattern [*pat* · ern] *n.* 1. A repetition of acts. In some instances, liability, both criminal and civil, is based on "patterns of conduct." EXAMPLES: **RICO** convictions require proof of "a pattern of racketeering activity"; a finding of **civil contempt** often requires proof of repeated disobedience of a court order. 2. A model; an example; a prototype.
➤ standard, classification, repetition, method, outline; model, example, prototype.

paucity [*paws* · ih · tee] *n.* A shortage.
➤ lack, dearth, shortage, scarcity, inadequacy. *Ant.* plethora, abundance.

pauper [*paw* · per] *n.* An indigent person; a person who is unable to support himself and must receive public aid. Paupers may sue without paying court costs (*see in forma pauperis*) and have a constitutional right to have counsel appointed to represent them in criminal cases (*see* assigned counsel; *Gideon v. Wainright*; right to counsel).

➤ indigent, beggar, insolvent, mendicant, debtor.

pauper's oath *n.* An **affidavit** or **oath** required of a pauper seeking publicly funded assistance (EXAMPLES: **AFDC**; court-appointed counsel), verifying that she is indigent. *See* means test. *See also* assigned counsel; right to counsel.

pause *n.* A temporary stop in activity. *v.* To hesitate or discontinue a movement or action.
➤ *n.* break, delay, stoppage, respite, stay, interval, intermission, hesitation. *v.* stop, suspend, deliberate, wait, hold back, consider, dwell, discontinue.

pawn *n.* A **bailment** of personal property as **security** for a debt or other obligation. *See* pawnbroker. *v.* To **pledge** personal property as **security** for payment of a debt. *See* pawnbroker.
➤ *n.* collateral, instrument, medium, vehicle. *v.* mortgage, stake, obligate, post, deposit, encumber, pledge.

pawnbroker [*pawn* · bro · ker] *n.* A person whose business is the lending of money with interest, **secured** by items of personal property that are deposited with her. If the borrower defaults on the loan, the pawnbroker has the right to sell the pawned items. *See* pawn.

pay *n.* Compensation, particularly for work or services, whether in the form of wages, salary, or commissions. *See* payment. *v.* To **discharge** a debt; to compensate another for goods or property received or services rendered.
➤ *n.* compensation, consideration, income, wage ("to receive high pay"). *v.* expend, remit, honor, settle, disburse ("to pay your bills").

pay any bank *n.* A form of **restrictive indorsement**. Under the **Uniform Commercial Code**, after an item has been indorsed with the words "pay any bank" or similar indorsement, only a bank may acquire the rights of a **holder** until either the item has been returned to the customer initiating collection, or the item has been specially indorsed by a bank to a person who is not a bank.

P

payable [pay · ebl] adj. 1. In the usual sense of the term, "due" or "to be paid," rather than "may be paid." 2. In the occasional sense of the term, "capable of being paid." n. An **account payable**.

➤ adj. mature, owed, in arrears, due, redeemable, collectable.

payable after sight Words indicating that a **draft** is payable after **acceptance**.

payable on death See POD account.

payable on demand [de · mand] Words that make an **instrument** a **demand instrument**. See demand paper.

payable to bearer [bear · er] Words that make an **instrument** a **bearer instrument; words of negotiability**. See bearer paper.

payable to order [or · der] **Words of negotiability**.

payables [pay · eblz] n. **Accounts payable**.

payee [pay · ee] n. 1. A person to whom a payment is made or is to be made. 2. A person designated in a check, **bill**, or **note** as the person to whom payment is to be made. Compare payor.

payer [pay · er] n. Same as **payor**.

payment [pay · ment] n. The **discharge** of an obligation by the **delivery** and **acceptance** of money, or of something equivalent to money, which is accepted by the person to whom payment is due. See compulsory payment; downpayment; lump-sum payment; voluntary payment.

➤ satisfaction, defrayal, subsidy, reimbursement, remittance, amortization, outlay.

payment in due course n. 1. With respect to **negotiable instruments**, payment to the **holder** at or after the **maturity** of the instrument, in **good faith** and **without notice** that his title is defective. See defective title. 2. Payment of any obligation in the ordinary course of events. See due course.

payment into court n. A deposit with the **clerk of court**, of money or other property, to be disbursed later in accordance with the rights of the **parties** as ordered by the court.

payor [pay · or] n. 1. A person who makes a payment or is obligated to make a payment. 2. The person who **makes** a check, **bill**, or **note**. Compare payee.

payor bank n. A bank that is the **drawee** of a **draft**. Compare collecting bank.

payroll [pay · rol] n. 1. A list of employees to be paid, with the amounts due each of them. 2. The amount needed by an employer to pay all of its employees the money due them for a particular pay period.

payroll tax n. Taxes owed by an employer on its payroll (EXAMPLES: social security tax; unemployment compensation tax) and by the employees on their pay (EXAMPLES: social security tax; income tax).

PBGC Abbreviation of **Pension Benefit Guaranty Corporation**.

PC 1. Abbreviation of **professional corporation**. It often forms a part of the name under which a professional corporation does business. The law firm of Smith and Smith, if it is a professional corporation, might, for EXAMPLE, hold itself out to the public as "Smith & Smith, Esqs., PC." See professional corporation. 2. Abbreviation of **penal code**. 3. Abbreviation of "personal computer." 4. Abbreviation of "politically correct."

PCP n. Abbreviation of phenylcyclohexyl piperidine or phencyclidine, a drug formerly manufactured as a veterinary anesthetic. In low doses, it produces a feeling of euphoria in humans; it also produces severe anxiety and psychosis. PCP is a **controlled substance**; its possession, distribution, or sale is a criminal offense.

peace n. As used in the language of the law, the tranquility enjoyed by members of a community where good order rules; the sense of security that is necessary for everyone's comfort and for which all governments are created. See breach of the peace; justice of the peace.

➤ quiet, order, tranquility, harmony, concord, security, goodwill, serenity, unanimity, cooperation.

peace bond n. A **bond** that a court requires be posted by a person who has threatened to commit a **breach of the peace**.

peace officer [off · i · ser] n. A law enforcement officer; a police officer.

peaceable [peess · ebl] adj. Peaceful; without force.

➤ peaceful, gentle, calm, amicable, unbellicose.

peaceable entry [*en* · tree] *n.* An entry upon real estate achieved without the use of force.

peaceable possession [po · *zesh* · en] *n.* Possession of real estate that is not contested by litigation or resisted by force. *See* possession.

peaceful [*peess* · ful] *adj.* Nonaggressive; nonviolent; passive.

➤ nonaggressive, nonviolent, passive, patient, lawful.

peaceful assembly [a · *sem* · blee] *n. See* First Amendment; freedom of association.

peaceful picketing [*pik* · e · ting] *n.* **Picketing** without violence, intimidation, or physical obstruction.

peculation [pek · yoo · *lay* · shen] *n.* **Embezzlement** of **public funds** by a **public official**.

➤ embezzlement, deception, cheating, misappropriation.

pecuniary [pe · *kyoo* · nee · e · ree] *adj.* 1. Involving money; pertaining or relating to money; financial. 2. That which has monetary value.

➤ monetary, financial, fiscal, budgetary ("contrary to his pecuniary interest").

pecuniary benefit [*ben* · e · fit] *n.* A benefit that has a value in money. *See* benefit.

pecuniary bequest [be · *kwest*] *n.* Same as **pecuniary legacy**.

pecuniary condition [ken · *dish* · en] *n.* A person's **net worth**.

pecuniary damages [*dam* · e · jez] *n.* **Damages** capable of being calculated in terms of their monetary value. *See* pecuniary injury; pecuniary loss.

pecuniary injury [*in* · je · ree] *n.* An **injury**, the **damages** from which are measurable in money. *See* pecuniary damages; pecuniary loss.

pecuniary interest [*in* · trest] *n.* A direct monetary interest in the outcome of a case, the **letting** of a contract, or the like. A juror or a judge is disqualified from sitting in judgment in a case involving a matter or **party** in which he has a pecuniary interest, such as, for EXAMPLE, ownership of stock in a corporation that is a defendant in a **stockholders' derivative action** before his court.

pecuniary legacy [*leg* · e · see] *n.* A **legacy** consisting of a sum of money.

pecuniary loss *n.* A loss of money; a loss by which money, or that which has a monetary value, may be acquired. As used in connection with a **wrongful death action**, the **beneficiaries'** economic loss due to the premature death of the **decedent**.

pederasty [*ped* · e · ras · tee] *n.* Intercourse *per os* or *per anus* between males, particularly between a man and a boy. Pederasty involving consenting adults, commonly called **sodomy**, is a criminal act in some states. Pederasty involving an adult and a minor is a crime in every jurisdiction.

pedestrian [ped · *ess* · tree · en] *n.* A person walking on a sidewalk, street, or highway. *adj.* Common; unimaginative.

➤ *n.* stroller, walker, bystander. *adj.* unimaginative, mediocre, commonplace, uninteresting, dreary, trite, prosaic, uninspired, everyday ("a pedestrian performance").

peeping tom [*peep* · ing] *n.* A person who secretly observes others, usually through open windows, generally to achieve sexual gratification; a **voyeur**.

➤ voyeur, eavesdropper, invader.

peer *n.* 1. An equal. USAGE: "The **Sixth Amendment** guaranty of trial by an impartial jury means, among other things, the right to be tried by a jury of one's peers." 2. A member of the British nobility.

➤ associate, colleague, equal, equivalent, match, mate.

penal [*peen* · el] *adj.* Relating to punishment.

➤ punitive, disciplinary, castigatory, retributive, corrective ("the penal system").

penal action [*ak* · shen] *n.* 1. In the broad sense of the term, a **criminal prosecution**. 2. A **civil action** in which the wrongdoer is subject to a **fine** or **penalty** payable to the wronged party, or is liable for **punitive damages**, i.e., damages over and above **actual damages**. *See also* civil penalty.

penal bond *n.* A **bond** requiring the **obligor** to pay a specified sum of money as a penalty if she fails to perform the obligation that is the subject of the bond. In the event of default, the **collateral** that **secures** the bond is **forfeit**. A penal bond

P

is distinguishable from a bond providing for **liquidated damages**. *Compare* simple bond. *See* penalty. *Also see* penal sum.

penal code *n.* The published criminal statutes of a jurisdiction. *See* code. *Also see* Model Penal Code.

penal institution [in · sti · *too* · shen] *n.* A correctional institution; a jail, prison, or penitentiary.

penal law *n.* *See* penal code; penal statute.

penal statute [*stat* · shoot] *n.* 1. A statute that defines and prescribes the punishment for a criminal offense, i.e., imprisonment, **fine**, or **forfeiture**. 2. A statute that provides a **penalty** enforceable in a **civil action**. *Also see* civil penalty. 3. A statute (for EXAMPLE, a **wrongful death statute**) that provides for **punitive damages**. *See* penal action. *Also see* statute.

penal sum *n.* The amount of the penalty specified in a **penal bond**. *Compare* liquidated damages.

penalize [*pen* · uhl · eyz] *v.* To punish or discipline.
➤ punish, cost, fine, mulct, confiscate, forfeit, condemn, castigate.
Ant. reward.

penalty [*pen* · el · tee] *n.* 1. In the broad sense of the term, the consequences imposed by the law upon those who violate the law, particularly the criminal law. *See* fine; forfeiture; imprisonment. 2. A punishment for the nonperformance of an act, or for the performance of an unlawful act, whether by **civil action** or by **criminal prosecution**. *See* civil penalty; penal action; penal bond; penal statute. 3. Liability to which the law subjects a wrongdoer in favor of the **aggrieved party**. Such liability may involve a fine or **punitive damages**. *See* civil penalty; penal action; penal statute. 4. An agreement to pay a specified sum in the event of **breach of contract**, regardless of the **damages** actually sustained; i.e., a **penalty clause** incorporated in a contract not as compensation for a breach, but as punishment for default. *Compare* liquidated damages. 5. An additional payment for a privilege (for EXAMPLE, with respect to a loan, the privilege of paying the principal before the due date). *See* prepayment penalty. 6. An additional charge because of a delinquency

in making payment. The IRS imposes such a penalty on taxpayers who file late tax returns. *Note* that a penalty is not interest, and is usually assessed in addition to interest.
➤ sanction, sentence, forfeiture, castigation, retribution, punishment, consequence, reprisal.

penalty clause *n.* *See* penalty.

pendency [*pen* · den · see] *n.* The state of of being unconcluded, unfinished, unde-cided, or in suspense; **pending**.
➤ duration, continuance, interval, interim.

pendency of action [*ak* · shen] *n.* The status of a lawsuit from the time it is com-menced until its final determination. *See* lis pendens; notice of lis pendens; notice of pendency.

pendens [*pen* · denz] (*Latin*) *adj.* Means "pending." *See* lis pendens.

pendent [*pen* · dent] *adj.* 1. Not concluded; undecided; undetermined. 2. Hanging. 3. Supplemental.
➤ supplemental, adjunct, connecting, allied, ("the court has pendent jurisdiction over the party"); dangling, swinging, suspended.

pendent jurisdiction [joo · ris · *dik* · shen] *n.* The rule that, even though there is no **diversity of citizenship**, a federal court has the right to exercise **jurisdiction** over a state matter if it arises out of the same transaction as a matter already before the federal court. *See* before the court.

pendente lite [pen · *den* · tay lee · tay] (*Latin*) Means "while the lawsuit is pending." Refers to the status of a lawsuit, or the matters involved in a lawsuit, until the court has issued its **final judgment**.

pending [*pen* · ding] *adj.* Not concluded; undecided; in suspense. *See* pendency.
➤ not concluded, undecided, inconclusive, unresolved, approaching, prospective ("a pending action").

pending action [*ak* · shen] *n.* A term referring to a lawsuit that is pending. *See* pendency of action.

pending suit *n.* *See* pending action.

penetration [pen · e · *tray* · shen] *n.* 1. In connection with the crime of rape, contact between the genitals of the victim and the genitals of the perpetrator, however in-substantial. 2. Nonconsensual entry into

P

any part of a person's body. 3. The act of entering or invading.

➤ entering, invasion, encroachment, insertion, contact.

penitentiary [pen · i · *ten* · sher · ee] *n.* A prison; a place of confinement for persons convicted of **felonies**. A penitentiary is usually operated by the state or federal government, whereas a jail is usually maintained by local government.

➤ prison, jail, detention, cage, lock-up, joint, slammer.

Pennoyer rule [pen · *noy* · er] *n.* The rule that a court cannot render an **in personam judgment** against a party over whom it does not have **personal jurisdiction**.

pension [*pen* · shen] *n.* 1. A retirement benefit in the form of a periodic payment, usually monthly, made to a retired employee from a fund created by the employer's contributions, or by the joint contributions of the employer and employee, over the period the employee worked for the employer. *See* pension plan. 2. With respect to a former government employee or a retired member of the military, a regular allowance paid in consideration of the prior service.

➤ benefits, annuity, compensation, social security, support, reward ("A vested pension").

Pension Benefit Guaranty Corporation [*pen* · shen *ben* · e · fit gehr · en · tee kore · per · *ay* · shen] *n.* A **public corporation** of the United States government that, under certain circumstances and within certain limits, guarantees the payment of employer pension plans which terminate without sufficient **assets** to pay the promised benefits. *See also* Employee Retirement Income Security Act (ERISA).

pension fund *n.* A **fund** from which a **pension** is paid.

pension plan *n.* A plan through which an employer provides a pension for its employees' retirement. There are many types of pension plans. Some are funded solely by employer contributions; some are funded jointly by the employer and the employee. Most are regulated by the federal government under the **Employee Retirement Income Security Act**. All pension plans involve significant tax

implications. *See* qualified pension plan. Tax-deferred pension plans are also available to self-employed persons under certain circumstances. *See* Keogh Plan. *Also see* annuity; individual retirement account (IRA); retirement annuity; retirement plan.

pensive [*pen* · sive] *adj.* Thoughful; preoccupied; absorbed.

➤ thoughtful, reflective, rapt, deliberative, musing, absorbed, engrossed, dreamy ("Cory was in a pensive mood").

penumbra [pen · *num* · bra] *n.* A partially lighted area around an area of full shadow, e.g., the moon's penumbra during an eclipse.

➤ margin, shadow, shade, border, boundary, reflection.

penumbra doctrine *n.* The doctrine of **constitutional law** that the rights specifically guaranteed in the **Bill of Rights** have "penumbras" creating other rights that are not specifically enumerated. Thus, for EXAMPLE, **freedom of association** is more than the right to attend a meeting. **Privacy** is also an EXAMPLE of a **penumbra right**.

penumbra right *n.* *See* penumbra doctrine.

peonage [*pee* · en · ej] *n.* The status of a person who is forced, against his will, to work for a person to whom he is indebted. Peonage is a form of **involuntary servitude** and is prohibited by the **Thirteenth Amendment**. Forcing a person into peonage is also a crime. *Compare* slavery.

➤ slavery, servitude ("Many African-Americans have had to serve in peonage").

people [*pee* · pl] *n.* 1. The state; the nation. 2. The inhabitants of a state or nation. In some jurisdictions, criminal prosecutions are brought in the name of "the people" rather than in the name of the state. In such a state, a criminal case might, for EXAMPLE, be captioned *People v. William Brown*.

➤ citizens, population, mankind, community, general public ("We, the people").

peppercorn [*pep* · er · korn] *n.* A pepper berry. A term often used in contracts in past times to indicate that the **consideration** for the contract was merely a **nominal consideration**.

P

per *prefix, preposition (Latin) adv.* By; through; in; by means of; in accordance with; under. USAGE: "I will deliver the goods by July 1, per our contract."
➤ by, through, in, by means of, in accordance with, according to, under ("I will deliver the goods by July 1, per our contract").

per annum [*an* · num] (*Latin*) By the year; annually.

per anus [*ay* · nus] (*Latin*) Through the anus; by the anus. *See* penetration.

per autre vie [*oh* · tra vee] (*French*) Means "the life of another." *See autre vie*; estate per autre vie.

per capita [*kap* · i · ta] (*Latin*) Means "by the head"; by the individual. 1. For each person. USAGE: "**per capita income**"; "**per capita tax**." 2. A method of dividing or distributing an **estate** in which all persons who are equally related to the **decedent** share equally in the estate. EXAMPLE: Bill has two living children, Mary and Sam, and two grandchildren by Adam, a deceased child. If Bill's $300,000 estate is divided *per capita* among his heirs, Mary and Sam each receive $150,000 and Adam's children receive nothing. *Compare per stirpes.*

per capita income [*kap* · i · ta in · kum] The daily, weekly, or annual income of an individual person, as opposed, for EXAMPLE, to the total income of her household for the same period. *See per capita.*

per capita tax [*kap* · i · ta] A tax imposed on the basis of a **flat rate** per person. *See per capita.*

per contra [*kon* · tra] (*Latin*) *See contra.*

per curiam [*kyoo* · ree · am] (*Latin*) "By the court"; by the whole court. *See* per curiam opinion.

per curiam opinion [*kyoo* · ree · am o · *pin* · yen] An opinion, usually of an **appellate court**, in which the judges are all of one view and the legal question is sufficiently clear that a full written opinion is not required and a one- or two-paragraph opinion suffices. *See and compare* concurring opinion; dissenting opinion; majority opinion; minority opinion.

per diem [*dee* · em] (*Latin*) Meaning "by the day." 1. A term referring to a method of compensation in which a person is paid by the day. 2. A daily allowance paid to an employee or an **independent contractor** to cover his expenses (EXAMPLES: food; lodging) while working away from home. (USAGE: "The salary on my new job is excellent, and the company also pays mileage and a reasonable per diem.") Jurors also receive a per diem.

per os [ose] (*Latin*) Through the mouth; by mouth. *See* penetration.

per quod [kwode] (*Latin*) Whereby; by which; as a result of which. "*Per quod*" is sometimes used in **pleadings** in **tort** cases to introduce a **specification** of **damages** resulting from the tort that is the basis for the lawsuit. *See* actionable per quod; libel per quod; slander per quod.

per se [say] (*Latin*) By itself; in and of itself. Thus, for EXAMPLE, violation of an applicable statute (for instance, running a stop sign and hitting a car in the intersection) constitutes **negligence per se** (that is, negligence in and of itself), regardless of whether there is any other evidence of fault.

per stirpes [*ster* · peez] (*Latin*) Means "by the root"; according to **class**; by **representation**. *Per stirpes* describes the method of dividing or distributing an **estate** in which the heirs of a deceased heir share the portion of the estate that the deceased heir would have received had he lived. EXAMPLE: Bill has two living children, Mary and Sam, and two grandchildren by Adam, a deceased child. If Bill's $300,000 estate is divided *per stirpes* among his heirs, Mary and Sam each receive $100,000, and Adam's children each receive $50,000, sharing the $100,000 portion Adam would have received had he lived. *Compare per capita.*

per year Annually; **per annum**.

perceive [pur · *seev*] *v.* To recognize or comprehend.
➤ see, observe, apprehend, become aware of, note, notice, witness, understand.

percentage [pur · *sen* · tej] *n.* A part; a share; a portion.
➤ portion, share, commission, ratio, dividend. *Ant.* entirety.

percentage lease [per · *sen* · tej] *n.* A **lease** in which the rent is based, in whole or in part, upon a percentage of the sales made by the business occupying the leased premises.

P

percolate [*pur* · ke · layt] *v.* To filter or drain.
➤ filter, drain, seep, ooze, permeate, saturate, bubble, exude.

percolating waters [*per* · ke · lay · ting *waw* · terz] *n.* Waters that ooze, seep, or percolate through the ground under the surface without a definite channel. *Compare* ground water; natural watercourse; surface water.

peremptory [per · *emp* · ter · ee] *adj.* 1. Allowing no opportunity for challenge or contradiction; absolute. 2. Imperious; autocratic.
➤ unconditional, absolute, irreversible, binding, positive, unequivocal, axiomatic, total, unalterable; assertive, firm, necessary, obligatory, compulsory, authoritative, inflexible.

peremptory challenge [*chal* · enj] *n.* A challenge to a juror that a party may exercise without having to give a reason. *Compare* challenge for cause. *See* challenge to juror.

peremptory instruction [in · *struk* · shen] *n.* A **directed verdict**.

peremptory nonsuit [*non* · soot] *n.* A **judgment** rendered for the defendant upon the plaintiff's failure to establish a **prima facie case**. *See* nonsuit.

peremptory rule *n.* A **rule absolute**.

perfect [*per* · fekt] *adj.* 1. Complete; incontestable; perfected. 2. Flawless; free from error.
v. [per · *fekt*] 1. To complete; to fully perform; to execute. USAGE: "To perfect **title** to your property, you must **record** the deed." 2. To make perfect or without defect.
➤ *adj.* complete, incontestable, finished, whole, consummate, demonstrable, real; flawless, ideal, correct, precise, exact, excellent, superb, masterful.
v. finish, complete, consummate, execute, perform, fulfill, conclude, close ("to perfect title").

perfect title [*ty* · tel] *n.* Same as **clear title**. *See* perfecting title.

perfect trust *n.* An executed trust.

perfected [per · *fek* · ted] *adj.* 1. Completed; fully performed; executed. 2. Made perfect or without defect.
➤ finished, completed, executed, performed, finalized ("The will had to be perfected").

perfecting [per · *fek* · ting] *v.* 1. Completing; fully performing; executing. 2. Making perfect or without defect.

perfecting a security interest [se · *kyoo* · ri · tee *in* · trest] *n.* Under the **Uniform Commercial Code**, a method of protecting a **security interest** in **goods** against the claims of other creditors by filing a **financing statement** with the appropriate public officer (usually the **Secretary of State**). However, a security interest in **consumer goods** is perfected without such filing.

perfecting an appeal [a · *peel*] *n.* Completing all of the steps required by statute for obtaining **appellate court** review of a **judgment**.

perfecting bail *n.* The process of posting **bail**.

perfecting title [*ty* · tel] *n.* Taking all steps necessary to ensure the existence of **clear title**, including **recording** the **conveyance**.

perfection [per · *fek* · shen] *n.* 1. Excellence; flawlessness. 2. Completion. *See* perfecting.
➤ excellence, quality, superiority, accomplishment, attainment, flawlessness ("I strive for perfection"); realization, completion, consummation, fulfillment, attainment ("perfection of title").

perform [per · *form*] *v.* 1. In the language of the law, to completely fulfill an obligation, particularly under a contract. USAGE: "I'm not sure the court will find that Chris performed the contract, because delivery of the goods was a week late." *See* performance. 2. To do; to accomplish; to achieve; to produce.
➤ execute, fulfill, transact, accomplish, finish, do ("I will perform my duties to the best of my abilities"); enact, enforce, observe, respect ("perform a contract").

performance [per · *form* · ense] *n.* 1. The doing of that which is required by a contract at the time, place, and in the manner stipulated in the contract, that is, according to the terms of the contract. *See* nonperformance; part performance; partial performance; specific performance; substantial performance; substantial performance doctrine. 2. Fulfilling a duty in a manner that leaves nothing more to be done. 3. In **copyright**

P

law, publicly giving or presenting a play, musical work, dance, film, or the like.

➤ fulfillment, effort, production, work, skill, accomplishment, satisfaction, conclusion, achievement ("Her job performance was excellent"); presentation, showing, concert entertainment, exhibition ("Pilobolus's performance brought the audience to its feet!").

performance bond *n.* A **surety bond** which guarantees that the contractor will perform the contract; it usually provides that in the event of default the **surety** must either complete the contract or pay **liquidated damages** or a penalty in the amount of the bond. *See* indemnity bond; penal bond.

peril [*pehr* · il] *n.* 1. Under insurance law, exposure to **loss, risk, destruction**, or **injury**. 2. A hazard; a risk; a danger.

➤ risk, threat, menace, hazard, danger, pitfall.
Ant. safety, security.

perils of the lakes or rivers [*riv* · erz] *n. See* perils of the sea.

perils of the sea *n.* Accidents caused by circumstances that are not the result of human action and are not preventable or avoidable by human caution. (EXAMPLES: storms; lightning; typhoons; hurricanes.) This **maritime** law concept is also applicable to similar perils faced by ships on lakes and rivers.

period [*peer* · ee · ed] *n.* An interval of time; a point in time. "Period" is a word of flexible significance whose meaning usually depends upon the context in which it is used. It may mean any portion of time from, for EXAMPLE, a thousand days to one hour or less.

➤ span, interval, season, term, duration, cycle ("His period of tenure was 10 years").

periodic [peer · ee · *odd* · ik] *adj.* Occurring at regular intervals.

➤ intermittent, recurrent, systematic, cyclic, routine ("We have periodic job reviews").
Ant. constant, random.

periodic alimony [*al* · i · moh · nee] *n.* 1. **Alimony** paid less frequently than monthly. 2. **Lump-sum alimony** divided into a number of periodic payments.

periodic payments [*pay* · ments] *n.* Payments made at intervals. *See* installment payments.

periodic support [sup · *port*] *n. See* periodic alimony.

periodical [peer · ee · *odd* · i · kl] *adj.* Same as periodic.
n. A magazine or other publication published at regular intervals.

➤ *n.* magazine, publication, journal, newspaper, press.

perishable [*pehr* · ish · ebl] *adj.* Apt to spoil, decay, or deteriorate.

➤ decayable, decomposing, disappearing, destructible, unstable ("a perishable commodity").

perishable commodity [kem · *odd* · i · tee] *n. See* perishable goods.

perishable goods *n.* Goods or **commodities** that will spoil, decay, or deteriorate if they are not consumed or put to use within a short time. EXAMPLES: produce; meat; many medications; some chemicals.

perjure [*per* · jer] *v.* To make a false statement **under oath** or **affirmation**. *See* perjury.

➤ lie, misrepresent, deceive, trick ("Fear of the mob caused him to perjure himself").
Ant. confess, confirm.

perjurer [*per* · jer · er] *n.* A person who commits the crime of **perjury**.

perjury [*per* · jer · ee] *n.* Giving false testimony in a **judicial proceeding** or an **administrative proceeding**; lying under oath as to a **material fact**; swearing to the truth of anything one knows or believes to be false. Perjury is a crime. A person who makes a false **affirmation** is equally a **perjurer**. *Compare* false swearing. *See* subornation of perjury.

➤ misrepresentation, deceit, misstatement, dishonesty, false testimony, distortion ("The judge knew she was guilty of perjury").

perks *n. See* perquisites.

➤ perquisites, benefits, advantages, extras, pluses ("the perks make some mediocre jobs more tempting").

permanent [*per* · men · ent] *adj.* Enduring; irrevocable; continuing indefinitely, but not necessarily perpetually. *Compare* temporary.

➤ enduring, irrevocable, fixed, unending, constant, lasting ("permanent disability"). *Ant.* temporary, transient.

permanent abode [a · *bode*] *n.* A **permanent residence**; a home; a **domicile**. *See* abode.

permanent alimony [*al* · i · moh · nee] *n.* An allowance for **support** and **maintenance** that a court orders a spouse to pay the former spouse after divorce. Permanent alimony may also be ordered in the case of a **legal separation**. *Compare* temporary alimony.

permanent disability [dis · e · *bil* · i · tee] *n.* 1. A disability that will remain with a person throughout his lifetime. 2. A disability from which a person apparently will not recover; a disability that, in all probability, will continue indefinitely. *Compare* temporary disability. *See and compare* partial disability; total disability. *See* permanent disability.

permanent employment [em · *ploy* · ment] *n.* Employment for an indefinite period, which, under most circumstances, may be terminated at any time by either the employer or the employee. *Compare* temporary employment.

permanent injunction [in · *junk* · shen] *n.* An **injunction** granted after a **final hearing** on the merits, as distinguished from a **temporary injunction** granted to provide **temporary relief**. *Compare* ex parte injunction; temporary injunction; temporary restraining order.

permanent injury [*in* · jer · ee] *n.* An **injury** that causes **damage** that is likely to be lasting. A **personal injury** that is permanent may or may not cause **permanent disability**.

permanent nuisance [*new* · sense] *n.* A **nuisance** that, by its nature, will continue indefinitely. *Compare* temporary nuisance.

permanent residence [*rez* · i · dense] *n.* A **permanent abode**; a home; a **domicile**. *See* residence.

permanent resident alien [*rez* · i · dent *ale* · yen] *n.* *See* resident alien.

permanent separation [sep · e · *ray* · shen] *n.* 1. The status of a couple living apart,

having decided to end their marriage. 2. A **legal separation**.

permanent trespass [*tress* · pass] *n.* A **trespass** where the **injury** is continually renewed. EXAMPLE: Smith's cattle trespassing onto the Jones farm day after day, trampling and eating the crop. *See also* continuing trespass.

permission [per · *mish* · en] *n.* Leave; **license; sufferance**; authorization.

➤ leave, license, sufferance, authority, approval, consent, acceptance ("He has my permission to come in"). *Ant.* prohibition.

permission of court *n.* Same as **leave of court**.

permissive [per · *miss* · iv] *adj.* 1. Permitted; allowed; tolerated. *See* mandatory. 2. Lenient.

➤ permitted, allowed, sanctioned, tolerated ("a permissive counterclaim"); allowing, indulgent, free, tolerant ("a permissive parent").

permissive counterclaim [*koun* · ter · klaim] *n.* A **counterclaim** by a defendant against a plaintiff which does not arise out of the same transaction or occurrence that is the subject of the plaintiff's claim.

permissive joinder [*join* · der] *n.* The **joinder** as plaintiffs of all persons who claim they are entitled to **relief** arising out of the same transaction or occurrence. *See* class action.

permissive use *n.* The use of another person's premises with her consent.

permit [*per* · mit] *n.* A permission granted in writing (EXAMPLE: a building permit); a license.
v. [per · *mit*] 1. To give permission; to allow something to be done; to consent. 2. To **license**; to certify.

➤ *n.* permission, license, authorization, concession, privilege ("Serving alcohol requires a permit"). *Ant.* prohibition, denial.
v. admit, allow, authorize, endorse, concede ("Will you permit me to post this sign?"). *Ant.* deny, reject, forbid.

perpetrate [*per* · pe · trate] *v.* Engage in; commit; do. USAGE: "perpetrate a felony"; "perpetrate a fraud"; "perpetrate a hoax." *See* perpetration.

P

➤ commit, perform, cause, administer, execute, enact.
Ant. avoid.

perpetration [per · pe · *tray* · shen] *n.* The commission of a crime or **tort**; specifically, engaging in illegal, wrongful, or offensive conduct. USAGE: "A person who commits a **homicide** during the perpetration of a felony is guilty of **felony murder**."
➤ commission, enactment, doing, performance.

perpetrator [*per* · pe · tray · ter] *n.* A person who actually commits a criminal act, as distinguished from a person who **aids** or **abets** its commission. The slang term for perpetrator is "perp." *See* aiding and abetting.
➤ offender, criminal, felon, wrongdoer, lawbreaker ("The rapist was the perpetrator").
Ant. bystander, law-abiding citizen.

perpetual [per · *pet* · shoo · el] *adj.*
1. Continuous; without interruption.
2. Everlasting; eternal.
➤ continuous, everlasting, constant, ceaseless, recurrent ("perpetual succession").
Ant. temporary.

perpetual injunction [in · *junk* · shen] *n.* A **permanent injunction**; an injunction with no expiration date. *See* injunction.

perpetual lease *n.* A **lease** whose duration is for as long as the tenant complies with its terms.

perpetual succession [suk · *sesh* · en] *n.* The continuous and uninterrupted existence of a corporation, a concept having to do with the fact that a corporation (which is an **artificial person**) continues to exist even though its members (who are **natural persons**) cease to be members or cease to exist. *See* succession.

perpetuation of testimony
[per · pet · shoo · *ay* · shen of tess · ti · moh · nee] *n.* Preserving testimony for possible use in future litigation by taking a **deposition**. This process guards against the loss of a witness's testimony due to his death, unavailability for some other reason, or loss of memory.

perpetuities [per · pe · *tyoo* · i · teez] *n.* *See* rule against perpetuities.

perpetuity [per · pe · *tyoo* · i · tee] *n.*
1. Literally, something that lasts forever.
2. As used in the law of property, a

limitation of a contingent **future interest** in violation of the **rule against perpetuities**. *See* contingent estate.
➤ eternity, continuation, indefiniteness, forever.

perquisites [*per* · kwe · zits] *n.* Privileges or benefits, other than normal fringe benefits, that go with some jobs or positions, particularly high executive positions or high public office. (EXAMPLES: use of the company vacation retreat; a chauffeured government limousine.) Perquisites are commonly referred to as "perks." *Note* that "perquisites" are not "**prerequisites**."
➤ privileges, benefits, extras, perks, rewards, bonuses ("A company car is a perquisite of my job").

persist [pur · *sist*] *v.* To continue or linger.
➤ endure, persevere, prevail, linger, plug away, hold on, remain.

person [*per* · sen] *n.* 1. As the term is used in the law, either an individual or an organization; that is, either a human woman, man, or child (a **natural person**), or a **corporation** or other **artificial person**. Thus, depending upon the statutory or constitutional provision under consideration, a person may be, in addition to a human being or a corporation, a **partnership**, an **association**, a **municipality**, or a **government**, among other entities. Only persons possess legal rights. *People* whom the law recognizes as persons include aliens, illegitimate children, and minors. Although unborn children are not persons within the meaning of the law, rights nonetheless attach to the unborn. *See* life; personhood. *Also see* abortion; wrongful birth; wrongful pregnancy. 2. Also in the language of the law, a **party**. 3. The body of a human being. *See* larceny from the person.
➤ human, individual, customer, mortal ("Each man and woman is considered a person first"); corporation, party, association, partnership ("Legally, IBM is considered a person with certain rights").

persona [per · *soh* · na] (*Latin*) *n.* Person.

persona non grata [*grah* · ta] (*Latin*) *n.* A person who is unacceptable or unwelcome. This term is applied to a **diplomatic representative** when the country to which he is assigned refuses

P

to **accredit** him. However, it is also used in everyday language, for EXAMPLE, "she has been *persona non grata* at the country club ever since the New Year's Eve incident."

personal [*per* · sen · el] *adj.* 1. Pertaining to the person. 2. Limited to the person; not transferrable to anyone else. 3. Pertaining to personal property, as opposed to real property.
➤ intimate, private, confidential, special, individual ("Religious beliefs are personal"). *Ant.* public, universal.

personal action [*ak* · shen] *n.* 1. An **action** for the **recovery** of goods or **chattels**, or for **damages** for **breach of contract** or **personal injury**, as opposed to an action involving rights to real property. 2. An action that must be brought by the person injured or damaged, rather than by his **personal representative**.

personal assets [*ass* · ets] *n.* 1. The personal property, including money, of a **decedent** or a **bankrupt**, available through her **administrator, executor**, or **trustee** for the payment of debts. 2. One's own assets, as distinguished from the assets of one's business, the assets of one's spouse, or the like. *See* asset.

personal chattels [*chat* · elz] *n.* Property unrelated to land. (EXAMPLE: **movables**.) The term is used in contrast to **real chattels**.

personal contract [*kon* · trakt] *n.* 1. A contract relating to personal property. 2. A **personal service contract**. *See* contract.

personal covenant [*kov* · en · ent] *n.* A **covenant** that does not run with the land. *See* covenant running with the land; running with the land.

personal effects [e · *fekts*] *n.* Clothing, jewelry, ornaments, and other articles carried or worn upon the person. *See* effects.

personal execution [ek · se · *kyoo* · shen] *n. See* body execution; **capias**.

personal exemption [eg · *zemp* · shen] *n.* A taxpayer's exemption from income tax for himself and for each of his dependents who qualify under the **Internal Revenue Code**. The dollar amounts of such exemptions are specified in the Code. *See* exemption.

personal income tax [*in* · kum] *n.* The income tax imposed by federal, state, and

many local governments upon the income of **individuals**, as distinguished from the income tax imposed upon the income of **corporations, partnerships**, and **trusts**.

personal injury [*in* · je · ree] *n.* 1. As used in connection with **negligence** suits and workers' compensation actions, an **injury** to the body of a person. *See* personal tort. 2. In a broader sense, any violation or invasion of a **personal right**.

personal judgment [*juj* · ment] *n.* A **judgment in personam**.

personal jurisdiction [joo · ris · *dik* · shen] *n. See* jurisdiction in personam.

personal knowledge [*naw* · ledj] *n.* A person's direct knowledge, as distinguished from that which she attains at second or third hand or learns through **hearsay**. *Compare* imputed knowledge. *See* actual knowledge. *Also see* personally known to me.

personal liability [ly · e · *bil* · i · tee] *n.* **Liability** to satisfy a **judgment**, debt, or other obligation from one's **personal assets**. *Compare* corporate liability; limited liability acts. *See* shareholder's liability.

personal liberty [*lib* · er · tee] *n.* 1. Freedom from physical restraint; the ability to move about freely. 2. As guaranteed by the Constitution, personal freedom, including every form of individual prerogative that is not taken away by a valid law enacted for the common good. *See* liberty.

personal loan *n.* Money borrowed for personal use, as contrasted with a **consumer loan** or a **commercial loan**. *See* loan.

personal notice [*noh* · tiss] *n.* 1. **Actual notice**. 2. Notice given individually to the person concerned. *See* notice.

personal property [*prop* · er · tee] *n.* All property other than real property (EXAMPLES: money; goods; **chattels; movables**; a **chose in action; evidence of debt**), including **stock, bonds**, or a **mortgage**. Personal property may be further categorized as **corporeal property** (or **tangible property**) and **incorporeal property** (or **intangible property**).

personal recognizance [re · *kog* · ni · zense] *n.* Same as **own recognizance**.

personal representative [rep · re · *zen* · te · tiv] *n.* Ordinarily, the **executor** or **administrator** of a **decedent's**

P

estate, although the term may also include others (EXAMPLES: an **assignee**; a **trustee**; a **receiver**; a **guardian**; a **conservator**; a **next friend**) who have the responsibility to manage the property or affairs of a person who is unable to manage them for himself due to **incapacity, incompetency,** or **insolvency.**

personal rights *n.* The rights guaranteed in the **Bill of Rights.** *See* personal liberty.

personal security [se · *kyoo* · ri · tee] *n.* A debtor's promise to repay a debt, whether or not evidenced by a **note** or other instrument. As opposed to a debt for which **collateral** is **pledged** as **security,** personal security is the personal promise of the debtor. When a debtor gives her personal security, only her **personal assets** may be looked to by the creditor to satisfy the obligation in the event of default.

personal service [*ser* · viss] *n. See* personal service of process.

personal service contract [*ser* · viss *kon* · trakt] *n.* A contract for the furnishing of services by the **promisor** and only the promisor; that is, by no person other than the promisor. EXAMPLE: a writer's contract with a publisher to author a particular book. *See* personal contract.

personal service of process [*ser* · viss of *pross* · ess] *n.* Also referred to simply as **personal service;** the actual or direct delivery of **process** (EXAMPLES: a **writ**; a **summons**) to the person to whom it is directed or to someone authorized to receive it on her behalf; **actual service of process.** *Compare* constructive service of process; substituted service of process. *See* service of process.

personal tort *n.* A wrong against a person (EXAMPLES: an **assault**; a **rape**) or against a person's feelings or **reputation** (EXAMPLES: **libel; slander; malicious prosecution**). *See* personal injury. *Compare* crime, business tort.

personality [pur · sen · *al* · ih · tee] *n.* The sum total of a person's character and way of being. Note that "personality" is not "personalty."
➤ identity, character, makeup, uniqueness, nature, being, selfness ("an aberrant personality").

personally known to me [*per* · sen · e · lee] A common statement of identification appearing in the **certificate of acknowledgment** of a notary, which means that the notary is acquainted with the **affiant** or knows from competent facts (*see* competent evidence) that the affiant is who she says she is. *Compare* made known.

personalty [*per* · senl · tee] *n.* **Personal property.**
➤ property, assets, effects, holdings, investments, resources.

personam [per · *soh* · nam] *See in personam*; in personam action.

personhood [*per* · sen · hood] *n.* The condition, state, or status of being a **person.** "Personhood" is not, strictly speaking, a legal term. Rather, it is used in the field of **ethics** to refer to the status of a being that has moral rights even though, because it is not a "person" within the meaning of the law, it is without, or is substantially without, or may be without, legal rights in its own right. EXAMPLES: a fetus; a human being who is brain dead (*see* brain death). *However, see* life. *Also see* moral law.

persons needed for just adjudication [*nee* · ded for just a · joo · di · *kay* · shen] *n.* Under the **Federal Rules of Civil Procedure,** persons who must be **joined** as **parties** to an **action** for the court to grant "complete relief" to those who are already parties. *See* indispensable party; necessary party. *See also* joinder of parties.

persuade [pur · *swayd*] *v.* To cause someone to do something through the use of pleas, logic, or other methods.
➤ influence, motivate, induce, sway, urge, coax, cajole, compel, convert, exhort.

persuasive [pur · *sway* · siv] *adj.* Convincing; compelling.
➤ convincing, compelling, cogent, effective, irresistible ("a persuasive argument").

persuasive authority [per · *sway* · siv aw · *thaw* · ri · tee] *n.* **Authority** that is neither **binding authority** nor **precedent,** but which a court may use to support its decision if it chooses. EXAMPLES: a legal treatise; the decision of a court in a different jurisdiction.

pertinent [*per* · tin · ent] *adj.* Relevant; material; applicable; bearing upon the issues raised by the **pleadings**. *Compare* impertinent.
➤ relevant, pertaining, applicable, material, associated, suitable ("a pertinent objection"). *Ant.* irrelevant, immaterial.

peruse [pe · *ruze*] *v.* To examine or inspect; to look over.
➤ browse, scan, review, look over, explore, examine, inspect, study, peer into.

pessimism [*pess* · ih · mizm] *n.* A bleak outlook; gloom.
➤ hopelessness, dejection, cynicism, glumness, disconsolation, despondency, despair. *Ant.* optimism, hopefulness.

petit [*pet* · eet] (*French*) *adj.* Small; petty; little.
➤ small, petty, little. *Ant.* large, grand.
petit juror [*joo* · ror] *n.* A trial juror; a member of a **petit jury**.
petit jury [*joo* · ree] *n.* The jury in a **trial court**. *Compare* grand jury.
petit larceny [*lar* · sen · ee] *n.* Same as **petty larceny**.

petition [pe · *tish* · en] *n.* 1. A formal request in writing, addressed to a person or body in a position of authority (EXAMPLES: a city council; an administrative agency), signed by a number of persons or by one person. 2. The name given in some jurisdictions to a **complaint** or other **pleading** that alleges a **cause of action**. 3. An **application** made to a court *ex parte*. 4. A prayer; a request; an appeal. *v.* To request or appeal.
➤ *n.* appeal, request, plea, prayer, motion, application, demand ("The tenants circulated a petition demanding new carpeting"). *v.* plead, seek, solicit, ask, urge, entreat, apply for ("We petitioned the court for mercy").
petition in bankruptcy [*bank* · rupt · see] *n.* A document filed in a **bankruptcy court** initiating **bankruptcy proceedings**. *See* bankruptcy. *Also see* petitioning creditor.

petitioner [pe · *tish* · en · er] *n.* A person seeking **relief** by a **petition**.
➤ pleader, litigant, applicant, asker, supplicant ("The petitioner asked for relief"). *Ant.* respondent, defendant.

petitioning creditor [*kred* · it · er] *n.* A **creditor** who initiates **proceedings** against his debtor in a **bankruptcy court**. *See* bankruptcy proceedings; petition in bankruptcy.

pettifogger [*pet* · ee · fog · er] *n.* 1. A lawyer whose practice is of a petty character; a lawyer of little importance. 2. A person who squabbles or argues over unimportant details.
➤ wrongdoer, shyster, charlatan, cheater.

petty [*pet* · ee] *adj.* 1. Small; little. 2. Minor. 3. Small-minded; spiteful.
➤ small, minor, lower, subordinate, worthless, spiteful, bigoted.
petty average [*av* · e · rej] *n.* The necessary expenses laid out by the **master** of a ship. EXAMPLES: towing fees; docking fees.
petty cash *n.* A cash fund from which small or minor expenses are paid. *See* cash.
petty jury [*joo* · ree] *n.* Same as **petit jury**.
petty larceny [*lar* · sen · ee] *n.* **Larceny** in the taking of property of little value. The dollar value separating petty larceny from **grand larceny** varies from jurisdiction to jurisdiction; several hundred dollars is common. Petty larceny is a **misdemeanor**.
petty offense [o · *fense*] *n.* A minor criminal offense, usually tried before a justice of the peace or a **magistrate**. EXAMPLE: littering.

peyote [pay · *oh* · tee] *n.* A cactus plant which has hallucinogenic qualities. Same as **mescalin**.
➤ cactus, drug, mescaline, hallucinogen.

phase *n.* 1. A particular appearance or feature. 2. A period of time.
➤ facet, feature, part; period, term, tenure, span, state, epoch.

phobia [*fo* · bee · uh] *n.* Intense fear of an object or situation.
➤ fear, dread, abhorrence, terror, aversion, horror, loathing.

PHV Abbreviation of *pro hac vice*.

physical [*fiz* · i · kel] *adj.* 1. Pertaining to the body, as distinguished from the mind. *Compare* mental. 2. Pertaining to matter; pertaining to that which is **material, tangible**, or **corporeal**.

P

➤ tangible, material, real, concrete ("physical evidence"); bodily, earthly, fleshly, personal, nonspiritual ("My physical condition is excellent").
Ant. intangible; mental, spiritual.

physical cruelty [*kroo* · el · tee] *n.* As a ground for divorce, actual personal violence; physical treatment that endangers life, limb, and health and renders **cohabitation** unsafe.

physical depreciation [de · pree · shee · *ay* · shen] *n.* Reduction in the value of property due to age and wear.

physical disability [dis · e · *bil* · i · tee] *n.* A condition of the body resulting from accident, illness, or genetic defect that impairs the functioning of the body. *Compare* civil disability.

physical evidence [*ev* · i · dense] *n.* **Evidence** other than **testimony; demonstrative evidence**. *Also see* autoptic preference; real evidence.

physical fact *n.* A fact that can be perceived by the senses, i.e., by sight, hearing, touch, taste, or smell.

physical fact rule *n.* 1. The principle that the testimony of a witness that is contrary to **physical facts**, and to common observation and experience, has no value as evidence even though it is uncontradicted. 2. The principle that an **appellate court** is not bound to accept **findings of fact** that are inconsistent with well-known physical laws so basic as to properly be a subject of **judicial notice**. *See* physical impossibility.

physical force *n.* 1. As used in connection with assaults, synonymous with violence. 2. The power of the body as applied by a man or woman.

physical impossibility [im · poss · i · *bil* · i · tee] *n.* That which cannot be done or accomplished because it is contrary to the laws of nature and physical reality. *See* physical fact rule.

physical incapacity for marriage [in · ke · *pass* · i · tee for *mehr* · ej] *n.* The condition of a person who is unable because of physical defect to consummate his or her marriage. *See* consummation of marriage; impotence.

physical injury [*in* · je · ree] *n.* Harm to the body; **personal injury**.

physical possession [po · *zesh* · en] *n.* With respect to real property, being on the land and exercising **dominion** over it; physical occupancy. *See* possession. *Also see* occupancy.

physical violence [*vy* · o · lense] *n.* *See* physical force.

physician [fiz · *ish* · en] *n.* A person who is licensed to practice medicine.
➤ doctor, healer, M.D., medic.

physician-patient privilege [-pay · shent *priv* · i · lej] *n.* The rule that a physician cannot divulge what her patient tells her in connection with the patient's medical treatment without the patient's permission. This **privilege** extends to the physician's employees as well. In some states, an exception is made with respect to a psychiatrist or other psychotherapist who is told by her patient that he has committed a crime, or is about to. *See* privileged communication.

picket [*pik* · et] *n.* A person who engages in picketing.
v. To engage in picketing.
➤ *n.* demonstrator, protestor, striker, signholder, guard ("Mary was a picket in last week's strike").
v. patrol, march, protest, rally ("We picketed the erring employer's plant").

picketing [*pik* · e · ting] *n.* 1. In connection with a labor dispute, the presence of employees or others at an employer's place of business for the purpose of influencing other employees or prospective employees to refrain from working, or for the purpose of informing the public, customers, or suppliers of the dispute and inducing them not to do business with the employer. *See* mass picketing; peaceful picketing. 2. Similar activity by any group of people at any location for the purpose of protesting anything.

pickpocket [*pik* · pok · et] *n.* A thief who secretly steals money or other valuables from the pockets of her victims. It is a form of **larceny from the person**.
➤ thief, wrongdoer, sneak.

piecework [*peess* · werk] *n.* 1. Work compensated on the basis of the number of articles produced, as opposed, for instance, to work compensated by an hourly wage. 2. Work performed for a **jobber**.

P

piercing [*peerse* · ing] *adj.* Caustic; cutting; loud.

➤ biting, offensive, malicious, caustic, cutting, penetrating ("a piercing comment"); loud, noisy.

piercing the corporate veil [*peer* · sing the *kore* · pe · ret vale] *n.* Ignoring the corporate entity to reach or to proceed legally against the corporation's directors, officers, or managers directly and personally. Although a corporation's officers and directors are not normally liable for the acts of the corporation, the courts will hold them responsible for corporate acts if the purpose of organizing the corporation was to perpetrate **fraud** or if the corporation was a mere shell without substantial **assets** or **capital**. This judicial process is known as "piercing the corporate veil." *See and compare* limited liability; personal liability; shareholders' liability.

pilfer [*pil* · fer] *v.* To steal. *See* larceny; theft.
➤ steal, take, rob, snatch, deprive of ("He pilfered the gold").
Ant. restore, replace.

pilferage [*pil* · fer · ej] *n.* Stealing or **larceny**, particularly **petty larceny**.
➤ stealing, larceny, robbery, embezzlement ("The pilferage of the house was extensive").

pillage [*pil* · ej] *n.* The taking of property, particularly merchandise, by force or violence, usually by a mob; to plunder. *See* riot.
v. To take by force.
➤ *n.* piracy, plunder, robbery, thievery ("The pillage of the town by the gangsters was awful").
Ant. replacement, restoration.
v. destroy, devastate, ransack, ravage ("The bear pillaged our campsite").

pimp *n.* A person who obtains customers for a prostitute; a **panderer**.
v. To obtain customers for a prostitute; to **pander**.
➤ *n.* panderer, purveyor, procurer, madam, runner ("Prostitutes are often controlled by a pimp").
v. pander, hustle, procure ("His job was to pimp for my sister").

pimping [*pimp* · ing] *n.* Obtaining customers for a prostitute; **pandering**.
➤ pandering, hustling, procuring.

pinnacle [*pin* · uh · kul] *n.* The peak; the top point.
➤ peak, acme, apex, zenith, summit, top, culmination, apogee, tip.

pioneer [*py* · e · neer] *n.* One who first does something; an inventor, innovator, or developer.
➤ developer, explorer, inventor, harbinger ("a pioneer in the field of electronics").

pioneer patent [*py* · e · neer *pat* · ent] *n.* A **patent** in a new field; a totally new **device**; a **basis patent**.

piracy [*py* · re · see] *n.* 1. **Robbery** or acts of violence (EXAMPLES: plundering; **pillage**) on the high seas. *See also* air piracy. 2. A term for **infringement of copyright** or for using **literary property** without permission; plagiarism.
➤ robbery, stealing, plundering, larceny, pillage, plagiarism, infringement, appropriation ("Printing an article without the author's permission is piracy").

pirate [*py* · ret] *n.* A person who is guilty of piracy.
v. To steal.
➤ *n.* thief, wrongdoer, privateer, robber.
v. sack, seize, steal, plunder, despoil, loot, pillage.

PJ Abbreviation of **presiding judge** or **president judge**.

PL Abbreviation of **public laws** and **pamphlet laws**.

place *n.* An imprecise word whose meaning must be construed in the context in which it is used. It may denote, among other things, a site, a locality, a region, or a nation. *See locus in quo.*
v. 1. To set down. 2. To put in order. 3. To identify or recognize.
➤ *n.* location, vicinity, area, territory, locale ("I told him the place to meet"); rank, position, status, standing, grade ("His place was beneath the Queen"); habitat, location, residence, house, home; appointment, occupation, office, work, position.
v. locate, situate, spot, install; order, arrange, delegate, appoint, designate, name; identify, recognize, finger, peg, know.

place of abode [a · *bode*] *n.* A place where one lives permanently rather than temporarily; a residence; a **domicile**.

P

With respect to "place of abode" as it relates to **service of process**, *see* usual place of abode. *Also see* abode.

place of business [*biz* · ness] *n.* A place at which a person conducts her business or a place at which she is employed. With respect to "place of business" as it relates to **service of process**, *see* usual place of business.

place of contract [*kon* · trakt] *n.* The jurisdiction in which a contract is entered into. The laws of the state in which a contract is made determine its **construction** and validity.

place of delivery [de · *liv* · e · ree] *n.* The place where sold goods are to be delivered. Unless the buyer and seller agree otherwise, that place is the place of sale. *See* delivery.

place of employment [em · *ploy* · ment] *n.* The place where a person works or is employed. *See* safe working place.

placer claim [*pla* · ser] *n.* A mining claim covering a site located on **public land** in which the valuable mineral is not found in veins or lodes within the rock, but loose in the softer earth at or near the surface of the land.

plagiarism [*play* · jer · izm] *n.* 1. Stealing a person's ideas or copying or adapting his creative composition (for EXAMPLE, a short story, a musical score, or a painting) and passing it off as one's own. *See* piracy. 2. If the work is **copyrighted**, plagiarism is also **infringement of copyright**. However, fair use of copyrighted material is not plagiarism. *See* fair use doctrine.

➤ counterfeiting, falsification, fraud, copying, forgery, piracy.

plain *adj.* 1. Apparent; clear. 2. Common; commonplace; ordinary; usual. 3. Simple; unsophisticated. 4. Homely.

➤ apparent, clear, blatant, visible ("His handicap was plain"); common, commonplace, ordinary, usual ("She was so plain that no one noticed her in the crowd"); frank, clear, honest ("He made his opinions plain"). *Ant.* unclear; beautiful; cryptic.

plain error rule [*err* · er] *n.* The rule that **judicial error** that brings about a **miscarriage of justice** may be reviewed on appeal even though it was not brought to the court's attention during the trial of the case. *See* error. *See also* prejudicial error; reversible error.

plain meaning rule [*meen* · ing] *n.* 1. The rule that in interpreting a statute whose meaning is unclear, the courts will look to the "plain meaning" of its language to determine **legislative intent**. The plain meaning rule is in opposition to the **majority view** of statutory interpretation, which takes **legislative history** into account. 2. The rule that in interpreting a contract whose wording is unambiguous, the courts will follow the "plain meaning" of the words used. *See* four corners.

plain view doctrine [*dok* · trin] *n.* An exception to the **search warrant** requirement of the **Fourth Amendment**, which allows warrantless seizure of evidence observed in "plain view" by an officer from a place where she had a legal right to be.

plaintiff [*plain* · tif] *n.* A person who brings a lawsuit.

➤ complainant, accuser, suitor, petitioner, opponent, litigant.

plaintiff in error *n.* Same as **appellant**.

plan *n.* A method used to do something; a strategy; a system.
v. 1. To prepare in advance. 2. To intend or mean.

➤ *n.* strategy, course, agenda, method, pattern, system, intention, arrangement, design, projection.
v. arrange, design, orchestrate, organize, prepare, map, engineer, concoct, manage; intend, consider, contemplate, propose, envisage.

planned development [de · *vel* · ep · ment] *n.* Development of an area of land as a single unit according to a plan that calls for construction of both residences and commercial establishments, with provision also made for public buildings, parks, and the like. *See* developer; development.

plant patent [*pat* · ent] *n.* A **patent** granted on a manmade, multicellular living vegetable organism that does not exist in nature. *See also* animal patent.

plat *n.* A map of a tract of land, showing the boundaries of the streets, blocks, and numbered lots. A plat is also referred to as a "plat map" or a "plot."

P

➤ map, plan, chart, sketch, diagram ("We needed to see the plat of the city").

plat book *n.* An official book of plat maps. *See* plat.

plea [plee] *n.* 1. At **common law**, the response or responses that the defendant in a civil action was required to file to state a **defense** to a **complaint, petition, declaration**, or **bill in equity**. *See* pleading. *Also see* dilatory plea. 2. In criminal cases, a response required by law of a person formally accused of crime, specifically, either a **plea of guilty**, a **plea of nolo contendere**, or a **plea of not guilty**.

➤ appeal, petition, request, prayer ("Her plea was based on her innocence"); excuse, defense, argument, claim ("Joe's plea was insanity").

plea agreement [a · *gree* · ment] *n. See* plea bargain.

plea bargain [*barg* · in] *n.* An agreement between the prosecutor and a criminal defendant under which the accused agrees to plead guilty, usually to a lesser offense, in exchange for receiving a lighter sentence than he would likely have received had he been found guilty after trial on the original charge.

plea in abatement [a · *bate* · ment] *n.* Under **common law pleading**, a **dilatory plea** bringing to the court's attention some fact that defeats the plaintiff's **action** without destroying her **cause of action**. This plea is now made by **motion** under the **Federal Rules of Civil Procedure** and under most states' **rules of civil procedure**. *See* abatement of action. *Compare* plea in bar.

plea in bar *n.* Under **common law pleading**, a **dilatory plea** by the defendant designed to defeat the plaintiff's **action** absolutely and permanently. This plea is now made by **motion** under the **Federal Rules of Civil Procedure** and under most states' **rules of civil procedure**. *Compare* plea in abatement.

plea in confession and avoidance [ken · *fesh* · en and a · *void* · ense] *n.* Under **common law pleading**, a plea that admits the **cause of action** alleged by the plaintiff but avers some additional circumstance relieving the defendant of any obligation

to the plaintiff. This plea has been abolished by the **Federal Rules of Civil Procedure** and by most states' **rules of civil procedure**. *See* pleadings.

plea in discharge [*dis* · charj] *n.* Under **common law pleading**, a plea that admits the plaintiff's **cause of action** but avers that the defendant **satisfied** and **discharged** the plaintiff's claim. This plea has been abolished by the **Federal Rules of Civil Procedure** and by most states' **rules of civil procedure**.

plea of guilty [*gill* · tee] *n. See* guilty.

plea of insanity [in · *san* · i · tee] *n. See* insanity.

plea of nolo contendere [*no* · lo kon · *ten* · de · ray] *n. See* nolo contendere.

plea of not guilty [*gill* · tee] *n. See* not guilty.

plead [pleed] *v.* 1. To draft, **file**, and **serve** a **pleading**. 2. To ask, to beg, or to implore.

➤ prosecute, allege, argue, present ("to plead one's case in court"); ask, appeal, request, implore ("I plead for quiet from the children but seldom get it").

pleaded [*plee* · ded] *See* plead.

pleading [*plee* · ding] *n.* 1. *Singular* of **pleadings**. *See* pleadings. 2. The act of asking, begging, or imploring.

➤ allegation, answer, claim, complaint, statement, accusation, defense, denial.

pleadings [*plee* · dingz] *n.* Formal statements by the **parties** to an **action** setting forth their **claims** or **defenses**. EXAMPLES of pleadings include: a **complaint**; a **cross-complaint**; an **answer**; a **counterclaim**. The various kinds of pleadings, and the rules governing them, are set forth in detail in the **Federal Rules of Civil Procedure** and, with respect to pleading in state courts, by the **rules of civil procedure** of the several states. These rules of procedure abolished **common law pleading**. *See* alternative pleading; amendment of pleading; defective pleading; false pleading; frivolous pleading; judgment on the pleadings; responsive pleading; sham pleading; supplemental pleading.

plebiscite [*pleb* · i · site] *n.* A vote of the people on a proposed law or constitutional amendment; a **referendum**.

➤ vote, election, ballot, referendum, choice.

P

pled *n.* *See* plead.

pledge *n.* 1. A deposit or **bailment** of personal property, **tangible** or **intangible**, as **security** for a debt or other obligation. *Compare* hypothecation. *See* collateral; secured transaction 2. A promise; a vow.
v. to make a **pledge**. *See* pledge (*noun*).
➤ *n.* commitment, assurance, contract, promise, vow, deposit, bailment, pact, oath, guarantee.
Ant. denial.
v. guarantee, warrant, promise, assure, swear ("He pledged undying love to me").

pledgee [pled · *jee*] *n.* A person to whom personal property is **pledged**. *Compare* pledgor.

pledgor [pled · *jor*] *n.* A person who makes a **pledge** of personal property. *Compare* pledgee.

plenary [*plen* · e · ree] *adj.* Full; complete.
➤ full, complete, entire, total, whole ("plenary jurisdiction").
plenary action [*ak* · shen] *n.* A lawsuit in which the merits of the case are fully heard and determined, as distinguished from a **summary proceeding**.
plenary jurisdiction [joo · ris · *dik* · shen] *n.* A term referring to the court's **jurisdiction** over the **parties** as well as the subject matter of a lawsuit (*see* subject matter jurisdiction).
plenary power [*pow* · er] *n.* Power as broad as justice requires.

plenipotentiary
[plen · i · po · *ten* · shee · air · ee] *n.* A person who is fully empowered to act for another, particularly for a high-ranking official. EXAMPLE: a deputy mayor.
➤ agent, consul, delegate, emissary, spokesman, deputy, ambassador.

PLI Abbreviation of **Practising Law Institute**.

plight *n.* A predicament; a difficult or dangerous situation.
➤ adversity, difficulty, trouble, problem, predicament, position ("the plight of the elderly").

plot *n.* 1. Same as **plat**. 2. A plan or scheme to achieve some purpose, particularly a dishonest purpose. 3. The story line of a novel or other literary work.

v. To conspire; to plan or arrange.
➤ *n.* field, land, area; plan, scheme, conspiracy, trick, deception; story, design, events, scene, scenario ("Agatha Christie's plots are fun to read").
v. design, prepare, plan, scheme, outline, conspire ("She plotted her actions very carefully").

plottage [*plot* · ej] *n.* The additional value that two or more contiguous lots owned by the same person acquire by virtue of the fact that the larger property can be **improved** more valuably than the separate individual lots.

PLS Abbreviation of **professional legal secretary**.

plunder [*plun* · der] *n.* Property acquired by criminal acts, particularly by crimes involving force; booty.
v. To take property by force or violence; to pillage.
➤ *n.* loot, treasure, haul, spoils, booty ("The pirates' plunder was extensive").
v. pillage, loot, seize, pilfer, ruin, steal ("plunder the abandoned house").

plural [*ploo* · rel] *adj.* More than one.
➤ more than one, many, several, mass, multiple.
Ant. singular, one.
plural marriage [*mehr* · ej] *n.* **Bigamy, polygamy**, or **polyandry**.

plurality [ploo · *ral* · i · tee] *n.* 1. A **plurality vote**. 2. The excess of one number over another. 3. Any number greater than one. 4. The state of being numerous.
➤ majority, preponderancy, bulk, multitude.
plurality opinion [o · *pin* · yen] *n.* An **appellate court** opinion joined in by less than a majority of the justices, but by more justices than the number joining any other **concurring opinion**. *Compare* concurring opinion; dissenting opinion; majority opinion; minority opinion.
plurality vote *n.* In an election in which there are more than two candidates, the number of votes received by the leading candidate over the number received by the next candidate. Thus, for EXAMPLE, in a three-way election decided by plurality vote, in which 100,000 votes are cast, Green is the winner because he received 45,000 votes to Black's 35,000 and Brown's 20,000. *Compare* majority vote.

P

poaching [poh · ching] *v./n.* **Trespassing** upon land for the purpose of killing and taking game.
➤ trespassing, encroaching, hunting illegally, intruding, plundering ("He was poaching on my land").

pocket veto [pok · et *vee* · toh] *n.* The veto of a congressional **bill** by the president by retaining it ("keeping it in his pocket") until Congress is no longer in session, neither signing nor vetoing it. The effect of such inaction is to nullify the legislation without affirmatively vetoing it. The pocket veto is also available to governors under some state constitutions. *See* veto.
➤ nullification, inaction, veto.

POD account [a · *kount*] *n.* An account payable to a person, upon her request, during her lifetime and on her death to one or more named **payees**, or to one or more persons during their lifetimes and on the death of all of them to one or more named payees. "POD" is an abbreviation of **payable on death**. *See* multiparty account.

point *n.* 1. A **point of law**. 2. A matter **at issue**; an issue or question in controversy to be decided by a court. 3. A lending institution's charge or fee for making a mortgage; one point is equal to 1 percent of the loan amount. 4. With respect to stock, means dollar. USAGE: "My electric company stock went up two points today." 5. A point charged against a person's driving record. *See* point system. 6. A decimal point.
v. To aim.
➤ *n.* detail, thought, part, subject ("She made her point quite clearly"); dividend, fee, charge ("The buyer did not have to pay the points on the house").
v. aim, direct, lead, guide, head ("Joe's dog pointed him in the right direction").

point of law *n.* A **matter of law** or a **legal question** that is **at issue** in a lawsuit.

point reserved [re · *zervd*] *n.* A **point of law** decided by a court in the course of a trial, but only conditionally and subject to reargument.

point system [sis · tem] *n.* A system under which "points" are automatically charged against a driver's record for moving violations, and his license suspended upon the accumulation of a specified number of points.

points *n.* **Plural** of **point**. *See* point.

poison [poy · zen] *n.* A substance that can harm or kill.
v. To make impure or unclean.
➤ *n.* venom, contagion, harm, contaminant, toxicant ("She unknowingly drank the poison").
v. contaminate, pollute, destroy, infect, pervert, taint, undermine.

poison pill [poy · zen] *n.* A term for a strategy used by corporations to deter **hostile takeovers** by making the cost too high.

poisonous tree doctrine [poy · zen · ess tree dok · trin] *n.* *See* fruit of the poisonous tree doctrine.

police [po · *leess*] *n.* The law-enforcing department of a state or local government; the police department; the unit of government that has the duty of maintaining order, preventing and detecting crime, and making arrests. *See* law enforcement agency.
v. To patrol or guard.
➤ *n.* officer, detective, cop, law enforcement authority.
v. guard, patrol, watch, secure, oversee ("We depend on others to police our property").

police court *n.* A **municipal court** whose **jurisdiction** is confined to enforcing **municipal ordinances** and trying **petty offenses**.

police department [de · *part* · ment] *n.* *See* police.

police officer [*off* · i · ser] *n.* An **officer** of the police department; a "cop." *Also see* law enforcement officer; peace officer.
➤ cop, officer, detective.

police power [pow · er] *n.* 1. The power of government to make and enforce laws and regulations necessary to maintain and enhance the **public welfare** and to prevent individuals from violating the rights of others. 2. The **sovereignty** of each of the states of the United States that is not surrendered to the federal government under the Constitution. *See* Tenth Amendment.

policeman [po · *leess* · man] *n.* *See* police officer.

P

policewoman [po · *leess* · wu · man] *n. See* police officer.

policy [*pol* · i · see] *n.* 1. A course of action taken by a government in its own self-interest or in the interest of its citizens. *See* public policy. 2. A rule adopted by an organization as a matter of self-interest. USAGE: "It's against company policy." 3. An insurance policy. 4. A **numbers game**; a **policy game**.

➤ guidelines, goals, system, custom, plan, form ("public policy"); insurance; lottery, gambling, numbers.

policy game *n.* Same as **numbers game**.

policy of insurance [in · *shoor* · ense] *n.* Same as **insurance policy**. *See* insurance.

policyholder [*pol* · i · see · hole · der] *n.* The owner of an insurance policy. The policyholder is not always the **insured**. *Compare* beneficiary.

➤ customer, client, policy owner.

politic [*pol* · ih · tik] *adj.* 1. Characterized by shrewd awareness. 2. Wise or intelligent.

➤ clever, artful, shrewd, calculating, continued; prudent, thoughtful, cautious, sagacious.

political [po · *lit* · i · kel] *adj.* Relating to the administration or organization of government, to politics, or to a political party.

➤ civic, official, governmental, partisan.

political action committee [*ak* · shen ke · *mit* · ee] *n. See* PAC.

political activity [ak · *tiv* · it · ee] *n. See* Hatch Act.

political corporation [kore · per · *ay* · shen] *n.* A **municipal corporation** or **quasi corporation**.

political crime *n.* 1. An offense against the government. EXAMPLES: **treason; sedition**. 2. Violent activity in a political uprising, regardless of whether a specific offense is committed.

political liberty [*lib* · er · tee] *n. See* civil liberties.

political offense [o · *fense*] *n. See* political crime.

political office [*off* · iss] *n.* Any public office that is not protected under the **civil service system**.

political question [*kwes* · chen] *n.* A nonjudicial issue. The **political question doctrine** states that, under the Constitution, certain questions belong to the nonjudicial branches of the federal government to resolve. EXAMPLE: questions dealing with foreign affairs. *See* branch of government.

political question doctrine [*kwes* · chen dok · trin] *n. See* political question.

political subdivision [*sub* · di · vizh · en] *n.* A lesser political body of a state; i.e., a governmental unit established by the state. EXAMPLES: a county; a **municipality**; a **township**.

poll [pole] *n.* 1. A head. *See also* deed poll. 2. An individual among several persons. 3. A list of persons, particularly a list of jurors or of voters. 4. A sample of opinion. *See* poll (*verb*).

v. 1. To **examine** a **juror**. *See* polling the jury. 2. To sample the opinions of a limited number of people for the purpose of ascertaining, with respect to a larger body—a country or city, for EXAMPLE—what views are held by what percentage of the people in the community.

➤ *n.* list, register, census, figures, returns, questionnaire, referendum, vote, count.

v. ask, question, inquire, tabulate, count.

poll tax *n.* A **per capita tax** imposed upon each person living within a jurisdiction. Payment of a poll tax as a requirement for voting in federal or state elections is unconstitutional. *See* Twenty-fourth Amendment.

polling the jury [*pole* · ing the *joo* · ree] *n.* Individually examining the jurors who participated in a verdict to ascertain whether they unanimously support the verdict.

polls [poles] *n.* The place where voters vote in an election.

pollute [po · *loot*] *v.* To contaminate or corrupt.

➤ contaminate, adulterate, defile, tarnish, violate, taint, poison, stain.

pollution [po · *loo* · shen] *n.* Hazardous and toxic waste materials discharged into the water, ground, or atmosphere. *See* hazardous waste; toxic waste. *Also see* Environmental Protection Agency.

➤ poisoning, violation, corruption, deterioration.

Ant. purification, cleanliness.

polyandry [pol · ee · *an* · dree] *n.* The practice and offense of having several husbands. *Compare* polygamy. *See* bigamy; plural marriage.

P

➤ polygamy, plurality, bigamy.
Ant. monogamy.

polygamy [pol · *ig* · a · mee] *n.* The practice and offense of having several wives. *Compare* polyandry. *See* bigamy; plural marriage.

polygraph [*pol* · i · graf] *n.* Commonly called a lie detector, a machine for recording impulses caused by changes in a person's blood pressure, pulse, respiration, and perspiration while under questioning. The results, which are interpreted to indicate the truth or falsity of the answers given, are not admissible as evidence in many states, and in others may be admitted only in limited circumstances for limited purposes. Federal law prohibits employers from administering polygraph tests to employees or applicants for employment except in very restricted circumstances.

➤ examination, inspection, lie detector machine.

ponder [*pon* · der] *v.* To think over; to contemplate; to consider.

➤ consider, cogitate, weigh, reason, mull over, evaluate, digest ("to ponder the issues of the day").

pool *n.* 1. Any combination of persons engaged in a business or other commercial activity, each contributing to a common fund for the purpose of supplying **capital** to the enterprise. If such a combination is between competing manufacturers or suppliers, and is for the purpose of eliminating competition, it is a **combination in restraint of trade** and violates the federal **antitrust acts**. 2. The combined stakes contributed by a number of persons for the purpose of betting on an event (EXAMPLES: a horse race; a football game; the date on which a baby will be born), the winnings to be distributed among the successful bettors in proportion to the amounts they put in. *See* gambling; gambling contract. *v.* To combine.

➤ *n.* combination, agreement, monopoly, union, coalition ("Honest trade prevents illegal pools"); purse, reserve, jackpot ("the betting pool totaled $100").
v. unite, merge, blend, unify, ally ("Let's pool our resources").

pooling agreement [a · *gree* · ment] *n.* A contract made for the purpose of creating and carrying out a **pool**. Such a contract is legal if the pool is legal, and illegal if the pool is illegal.

poor *adj.* 1. Having little or no money. 2. Of lesser or inferior quality.

➤ destitute, indigent, insolvent, bankrupt; inadequate, inferior, dismal, pitiful, paltry, defective, low quality.

poor debtor's oath [*det* · erz] *n.* Same as **pauper's oath**.

poor man's oath *n.* Same as **pauper's oath**.

popular [*pop* · yoo · ler] *adj.*
1. Pertaining to the people or to "the common people." 2. Prevailing; fashionable; current; general. 3. Well liked.

➤ familiar, common, standard, ordinary, public, prevailing, fashionable, current, general, well-known, favorite, likeable, lovable, prominent.
Ant. unconventional; personal.

popular sense *n.* The meaning of a word or phrase according to contemporary usage, as opposed to its technical meaning. EXAMPLE: to a legislator, a "bill" may mean a proposed statute; to a layperson it may mean a statement of charges for merchandise purchased or services rendered.

pornographic [por · no · *graf* · ik] *adj.* A term referring to lewd and licentious portrayals of erotic behavior. Although "pornographic" and "obscene" are often used interchangeably, they are not synonyms. Offensive or disgusting conduct of any kind may constitute an **obscenity; pornography** is limited to written, graphic, or spoken depictions designed to cause sexual excitement. *See* obscene.

➤ graphic, carnal, lascivious, obscene, lewd, off-color.
Ant. pure, innocent.

pornography [por · *nog* · re · fee] *n.* That which is **pornographic**.

➤ debauchery, lust, graphic portrayal, erotica, smut, indecency, obscenity, vulgarity.

port *n.* A place on the seacoast or adjacent to **navigable waters** with facilities for loading and unloading cargo from vessels or for taking on passengers and allowing them to disembark. It is a place through which merchandise can be imported, from which it can be exported, and at which

P

duties may be paid. Under some uses of the term, "port" may also include "airport." *See* customs duties.

➤ harbor, dock, landing, boatyard, dockyard.

port authority [aw · *thaw* · ri · tee] *n.* An agency of state or local government with the power and responsibility to establish and maintain a port. In many localities, port authorities also operate airports, toll highways, toll bridges, and public transportation. *See also* transit authority.

port of entry [*en* · tree] *n.* 1. A port officially designated for collecting customs duties. 2. A port at which immigrants may enter the country.

portal-to-portal pay [*port* · el to *port* · el] *n.* A term applied to federal legislation that requires employers in some circumstances to pay employees for time spent traveling to their work site and preparing for work once they arrive.

portend [por · *tend*] *v.* To predict; to forewarn.

➤ forecast, predict, forewarn, herald, indicate, augur, announce.

portfolio [port · *foh* · lee · oh] *n.* 1. The total of **bonds**, stocks, and other securities owned by an investor or a financial institution. 2. A flat, portable case for carrying drawings, photographs, sheets of paper, and the like.

➤ investment, securities, funds, bonds ("I wish my portfolio was more diverse"); case, folder, briefcase ("the artist's portfolio").

portray [por · *tray*] *v.* To characterize or set forth.

➤ characterize, represent, reproduce, depict, convey, picture.

position [po · *sih* · shun] *n.* 1. A stand or point of view on an issue. 2. A situation. 3. One's business occupation.
v. To locate; to put in place.

➤ *n.* outlook, attitude, posture, bias, predilection ("his position on new taxes"); circumstance, plight, state, predicament ("in a difficult position"); job, duty, occupation, role, work, career ("the position of district attorney").
v. station, post, carry, arrange, array, put, locate.

positive [*paw* · zi · tiv] *adj.* 1. Determined by law; unquestionable. 2. Beyond all doubt; absolute; certain. 3. Definite; explicit. 4. Affirmative.

➤ definite, absolute, conclusive, certain ("She was positive about his guilt"); ordained, adopted, decreed, prescribed, legislated ("This law is positive, effective tomorrow"); happy, optimistic ("What a positive person!").

positive evidence [*ev* · i · dense] *n.* Evidence that an event occurred (EXAMPLE: eyewitness testimony which, if credited, proves a fact in issue), as distinguished from **negative evidence**, i.e., testimony that the witness did not see such a thing happen. *Compare* circumstantial evidence. *See* evidence.

positive fraud *n.* Same as **actual fraud**.

positive law *n.* Legislation, as opposed to **natural law** or **moral law**.

positive proof *n. See* positive evidence.

posse [*paw* · see] (*Latin*) *n.* Short for *posse comitatus*.

posse comitatus [*kom* · e · tot · us] *n.* Means "the power of the group." A body of individuals available to be assembled by a sheriff to assist him in maintaining order or making an arrest.

possess [poh · *zess*] *v.* To own or occupy; to have possession.

➤ occupy, acquire, gain, retain, obtain ("He wants to possess my land").

possessed [poh · *zest*] *past part.* 1. Having a **possessory interest** in property; having possession. 2. Having ownership of property. USAGE: "He died possessed of over 200 acres of land." 3. Obsessed; mentally ill; mad.

➤ demented, deranged, overtaken, crazed, obsessed, mad ("Mary thought he was possessed").

possession [poh · *zesh* · en] *n.* 1. Occupancy and **dominion** over property; a holding of land legally, by one's self (**actual possession**) or through another person such as a tenant (**constructive possession**). The holding may be by virtue of having **title** or an **estate** or **interest** of any kind. One need not have a residence on the land to be in actual possession of it. *See* adverse possession; constructive adverse possession; dispossession; exclusive possession;

P

interruption of possession; joint possession; naked possession; open and notorious possession; open possession; repossession; sole possession; unity of possession; writ of possession. 2. In the criminal law, an essential element of a number of crimes (EXAMPLES: possession of **burglary tools**; possession of a **controlled substance; receiving stolen goods**). A person cannot be guilty of criminal possession, however, without dominion and control over the **contraband**, and knowledge of its presence.

➤ dominion, proprietorship, ownership, holding, guardianship, keeping ("I have possession of my family's land"); goods, assets, valuables, belongings ("The thief had my possessions").

possession in fact *n.* **Actual possession**.

possession in law *n.* **Constructive possession**.

possessor [poh · *zess* · er] *n.* The person in possession.

➤ occupier, tenant, resident, dweller. *Ant.* nonresident.

possessory [poh · *zess* · e · ree] *adj.* Relating to or based upon being a possessor or being in possession.

    possessory action [*ak* · shen] *n.* An **action** brought to recover the **possession** of property, whether real property or personal property (EXAMPLES: **eviction; replevin**).

    possessory interest [*in* · trest] *n.* The right to possess property. Such a right may be based upon ownership, or it may arise from an **estate** or any other **interest** (a **tenancy**, for EXAMPLE).

    possessory lien [leen] *n.* A **lien** that entitles the creditor to possession of the property which is the subject of the lien.

    possessory right *n.* *See* possessory interest.

    possessory warrant [*war* · ent] *n.* **Summary process** which directs that the personal property which is the subject of the **warrant** be returned to the person from whom it was violently or fraudulently taken. *See* fraudulent.

possibiiity [poss · i · bil · i · tee] *n.* 1. That which may or may not happen; a **contingency**. The term may connote either a mere possibility (EXAMPLE: an **expectancy**), on the one hand, or a substantial possibility or likelihood, on the other. 2. That which is not contrary to nature and can be accomplished. *Compare* impossibility; probability.

➤ potential, hope, expectation, contingency, prospect, likelihood, circumstance, chance. *Ant.* certainty, fait accompli.

possibility of issue [*ish* · ew] *n.* *See* possibility of issue extinct.

possibility of issue extinct [*ish* · ew eks · *tinkt*] *n.* For the purpose of determining whether there is a violation of the **rule against perpetuities**, the possibility of **issue** is not considered extinct as long as a person lives. Thus, for the purpose of the rule, the courts have declined to fix an age beyond which a woman is deemed to be unable to bear children or a man is deemed incapable of fathering children. Accordingly, for EXAMPLE, a **remainder** to the children of a woman who has a **life estate** is not extinguished until her death, although she may be very old and childless. *See* fertile octogenarian rule.

possibility of reverter [re · *ver* · ter] *n.* A type of **future interest** that remains in a **grantor** when, by **grant** or **devise**, he has created an **estate** in **fee simple determinable** or **fee simple conditional**, the **fee** automatically reverting to him or his successors upon occurrence of the event by which the estate is **limited**. EXAMPLE: Sam conveys Blackacre to the school district with the condition that it should revert back to Sam or his **assigns** when the school district ceases to use the land for school purposes. In these circumstances, Sam owns a possibility of reverter. *See* reversion. *See also* limitation.

possible [*poss* · ih · bul] *adj.* Capable of being achieved; feasible.

➤ thinkable, plausible, viable, conceivable, believable, achievable, available ("A not guilty verdict is a possible, albeit unlikely, outcome").

post *n.* The place where a person performs her duty or job, particularly military duty. *v.* 1. To make entries in a ledger from entries previously made in a **book of original entry**. 2. To put a letter in the mail. 3. To keep oneself or another informed. USAGE:

P

"I will keep you posted concerning my job search." 4. To put up a notice so that its contents will become public information. *See* posted land. 5. To put up as, for EXAMPLE, to "post bail" or "post bond."

➤ *n.* camp, base, headquarters, lookout, position ("His post was at the front door"); support, column, doorpost, stake, brace ("The post under our treehouse fell down"). *v.* publish, announce, broadcast, report ("The school posts job offers"); advise, inform, brief, clue, notify ("The lookout will post us on strangers approaching").

post *prefix or adv.* (*Latin*) After; behind.
post facto [*fak* · toh] After the fact. *See ex post facto*; ex post facto law.
post hoc [hoke] After this; after this time.
post obit [*oh* · bit] After death.
post obit agreement [*oh* · bit a · *gree* · ment] *n.* An agreement under which a person borrows money and promises to repay a specified larger sum upon the death of a named person from whom he expects to inherit money or property. *See* expectancy.

postal [*post* · el] *adj.* Pertaining to the **Postal Service** or to services it provides; pertaining to the mail.
postal money order [*mun* · ee *or* · der] *n.* A **money order** issued by the **Postal Service**.
postal order [*or* · der] *n. See* postal money order.

Postal Service [*ser* · viss] *n.* An arm of the United States government that administers post offices and is responsible for delivering the mail. *See* postmaster; Postmaster General.

postconviction remedy [post · ken · *vik* · shen rem e · dee] *n.* A **writ of habeas corpus** or a **motion** filed by a prisoner, under a federal or state postconviction procedure act, seeking to **vacate**, set aside, or correct his sentence.

postdate [*post* · date] *n.* To put a later date on a check than the date on which it is actually written. *See* postdated check.

postdated check [*post* · day · ted] *n.* A check bearing a date later than the date on which it is actually written. Under the **Uniform Commercial Code**, the **payor bank** is free to pay a postdated check

unless the **drawer** has notified the bank of the postdating in accordance with the procedures established by the Code.

posted land [*post* · ed] *n.* Land on which a notice (EXAMPLES: "no trespassing"; "hunting prohibited"; "no swimming") is posted. *See* post.

posterity [*pawss* · terr · i · tee] *n.* 1. A person's descendants. 2. Future generations.
➤ future, family, heirs, breed, lineage, successors, succeeding generations.

posthumous [*poss* · che · mess] *adj.* After death.
➤ after death, delayed, late, post-orbit ("His book was posthumously published"). *Ant.* contemporary, present.
posthumous child *n.* A child born after the death of its father. *See* after-born child.
posthumous work *n.* 1. In **copyright** law, a creative work (EXAMPLES: a novel; a musical composition), the rights to which the author owned at the time of her death. 2. In the more general use of the term, a creative work published after the author's death.

posting [*post* · ing] *n. See* post.

postmaster [*post* · mas · ter] *n.* The title of the public official in charge of a local post office. *Compare* Postmaster General.

Postmaster General [*post* · mas · ter *jen* · e · rel] *n.* The head of the **Postal Service**. *Compare* postmaster.

postmortem [post · *mor* · tem] *adj.* After death.
postmortem examination [eg · zam · i · *nay* · shen] *n.* Same as autopsy.

postnuptial [post · *nup* · shel] *adj.* After marriage.
postnuptial agreement [a · *gree* · ment] *n.* A **marital agreement** entered into after marriage. *Compare* prenuptial agreement. *See also* property settlement.
postnuptial settlement [*setl* · ment] *n. See* postnuptial agreement.

postpone [post · *pone*] *v.* 1. To grant a **continuance**; to put off until a later date or time. 2. To place after in importance; to subordinate. 3. To defer; to delay.
➤ delay, defer, interrupt, wait, hesitate, suspend, shelve, reserve ("I wanted to

P

postpone the meeting"); subordinate, downgrade ("The payback was postponed until the first debt was paid").

postponement [post · *pone* · ment] *n.* 1. A **continuance**. 2. A **stay**. 3. A delay.
➤ delay, continuance, interruption, abeyance, stay, subordination.

postponement of lien [leen] *n.* The **subordination** of a **lien** to another lien that is entitled to **priority**.

posttrial [post · *try* · el] *adj.* Subsequent to trial. "Posttrial" is applied to any aspect of litigation occurring after the trial ends and **judgment** is **entered**. USAGE: "posttrial proceedings"; "**posttrial motions**"; "**posttrial diversion**."

posttrial discovery [dis · *kuv* · e · ree] *n.* **Discovery** conducted after **judgment** is **entered**, while an appeal is pending. EXAMPLE: a **deposition** taken for the purpose of perpetuating testimony. *See* perpetuation of testimony.

posttrial diversion [di · *ver* · zhen] *n.* *See* diversion program.

posttrial intervention [in · ter · *ven* · shen] *n.* *See* diversion program.

posttrial motions [*moh* · shenz] *n.* **Motions** filed after **judgment** is **entered**. EXAMPLES: a **motion for new trial**; a **motion to vacate judgment**.

posttrial remedies [*rem* · e · deez] *n.* *See* postconviction remedy; posttrial motions.

potential [po · *ten* · shel] *adj.* Capable of being or becoming; a term referring to that which is possible, but which is not actual. *n.* Possibility; capacity.
➤ *adj.* anticipated, expected, possible, likely, probable, apparent, imminent ("potential interest").
n. capacity, ability, aptitude, capability, talent, promise, potentiality, expectation, gift ("This woman's potential for excellence was obvious").
Ant. deficiency, lack.

potential existence [eg · *zis* · tense] *n.* An existence that is to come into being as a natural product of something that already exists. Things with only a "potential existence" may be the subject of a **sales agreement**. Thus, for EXAMPLE, a contract between Farmer Jones and the XYZ

Produce Company for next year's wheat crop is a valid contract.

poundage [*poun* · dej] *n.* 1. In some jurisdictions, a commission to which a sheriff is entitled for carrying out a **judicial sale**. The commission is calculated as a percentage of the price paid for the auctioned property. *See* public auction; public sale. 2. A fee paid by a person to retrieve an animal from the pound.

poverty [*pov* · ur · tee] *n.* Extreme need, especially financial; destitution.
➤ indigence, need, destitution, impoverishment, scarcity, lack, debt, depletion, insolvency, paucity.

poverty affidavit [*pov* · er · tee af · i · *day* · vit] *n.* *See* pauper's oath.

power [*pow* · er] *n.* 1. The ability to act or to do something; the capacity for action. Depending upon context, "power" may mean either legal, physical, or emotional ability or capacity. 2. Authority in the sense of a court's **jurisdiction** over a lawsuit. 3. The ability to bind another person, for EXAMPLE, the authority of an **agent**. 4. A **power of appointment**. 5. Physical force. *See* concurrent power; delegation of powers; enumerated powers; executive powers; express powers; governmental powers; implied powers; inherent power; judicial powers; legislative powers; police power; reserved powers; resulting power. *See also* authority; right.
➤ authority, potency, competency, potential, strength, might, force, endowment, brawn, muscle.
Ant. incompetency, weakness.

power coupled with an interest [*cup* · ld with an *in* · trest] *n.* 1. A **power of appointment** that includes an **interest** in the thing itself. *Compare* collateral power. 2. A power that gives an agent an interest in the subject of the **agency**. EXAMPLE: the power and interest of a **partner** in a business who is given the right to manage the business as **security** for loans he has made to the **partnership**.

power of alienation [ay · lee · e · *nay* · shen] *n.* The power to **convey** or otherwise to dispose of property.

P

power of appointment [a · *point* · ment] *n.* A power given by a person (the **grantor**) to another person (the **donee** or **grantee**) to select (**appoint**) a person or persons to receive an **estate** or to receive interest or income from an estate. A power of appointment may be given by deed or similar instrument, or by will. *See* beneficial power; collateral power; exclusive power of appointment; general power of appointment; limited power of appointment; naked power; nonexclusive power of appointment; objects of a power; power coupled with an interest; special power of appointment; testamentary power of appointment.

power of attorney [a · *tern* · ee] *n.* A written **instrument** by which a person appoints another as his agent or **attorney in fact** and confers upon her the authority to perform certain acts. A power of attorney may be "full" (a **general power of attorney**) or "limited" (a **special power of attorney**). The power to sell property without specifying which property, or to whom, is an EXAMPLE of a general power of attorney; the power to sell a particular piece of property to a particular person is an EXAMPLE of a special power of attorney. *See also* durable power of attorney.

power of eminent domain [*em* · i · nent do · *main*] *n. See* eminent domain.

power of sale *n.* A provision in a mortgage by which, in the event of default, the **mortgagee** is empowered to sell the mortgaged property without obtaining a **foreclosure decree** from a court.

power without interest [with · *thout in* · trest] *n.* Same as **collateral power**.

powwow *n.* A meeting; negotiations.
➤ meeting, discussion, conference, get-together.

pp. Abbreviation of "pages."

PPO Abbreviation of **preferred provider organization**.

practice [*prak* · tiss] *n.* 1. As opposed to **substantive law**, the legal rules by which a case is started, the **parties** brought into court, and the case tried either to **judgment** or earlier termination. The method for taking an appeal from a judgment is a matter of **appellate practice**. *See also* procedure.

2. The performing of any profession. EXAMPLES: the practice of law; the practice of medicine. 3. The customary way of operating; habit; custom. USAGE: "common practice." 4. Repetitive exercises or training to acquire or increase one's skill. USAGE: "violin practice."
v. 1. To follow or engage in a profession. USAGE: To "practice law"; to "practice medicine." 2. To engage in exercises or training for the purpose of increasing one's skill. USAGE: to "practice the piano." 3. To regularly engage in the rituals or requirements of a religion. USAGE: to "practice Judaism." 4. To habitually engage in a course of conduct for a reason or with an objective. USAGE: to "practice yoga."
➤ *n.* manner, method, rule, system, way, routine ("Night court was a general practice for Talbot City"); exercise, application, action, homework, training ("He needed more practice to be an expert in karate"); calling, business, vocation, employment, discipline, conduct ("the practice of law").
v. repeat, exercise, polish, hone ("practice his skills"); undertake, execute, perform, pursue ("We practice abstinence").

practice acts *n.* The **rules of civil procedure**, the **rules of criminal procedure**, and the **rules of court**.

practice of law *n.* The work of an attorney at law in the preparation of **pleadings** and other papers in connection with a lawsuit or other proceeding; the trial or management of such an **action** on behalf of clients before judges, courts, and administrative agencies; the preparation of legal **instruments** and documents of all kinds; and advising clients with respect to their legal rights and taking action for them in matters connected with the law.

practice of medicine [*med* · i · sin] *n.* The treatment of living things, particularly human beings, to prevent illness, heal injury or disease, and preserve health.

practise [*prak* · tiss] *n.* Same as **practice**.

Practising Law Institute [*prak* · ti · sing law in · sti · toot] *n.* An educational **institute** for lawyers. Its activities include conducting seminars designed to keep attorneys abreast of new developments in the law and publishing handbooks that provide

P

practical guidance to legal practitioners. The Institute is commonly referred to by its initials, **PLI**.

practitioner [prak · *tish* · e · ner] *n.* 1. A person who engages in the practice of a profession. 2. A person who practices the rituals or requirements of a religion. EXAMPLE: a Christian Science practitioner.
➤ worker, doer, performer, craftsperson, employer, laborer ("She was a practitioner of the law").

praecipe [*press* · i · pee] (*Latin*) *n.* A written request directed to the **clerk of court** to perform a **ministerial act**. EXAMPLE: a direction from a **judgment creditor** to issue a **writ of execution** to enforce a **judgment** previously **entered**.

praedial [*pree* · dee · al] *adj.* That which comes from the soil or out of the land. EXAMPLES: wheat; fruit; vegetables.

pragmatic [prag · *mat* · ik] *adj.* Practical; reasonable; efficient.
➤ reasonable, utilitarian, useful, practical ("a pragmatic solution").

prayer [*pray* · er] *n.* 1. Portion of a **bill in equity** or a **petition** that asks for **equitable relief** and specifies the relief sought. *See* demand for relief. 2. An appeal to God.
➤ petition, plea, motion, beseechment, appeal ("prayer for relief"); devotion, benediction, worship, adoration, thanksgiving ("prayer to God").

prayer for relief [re · *leef*] *n. See* demand for relief.

preamble [*pree* · ambl] *n.* A paragraph or clause at the beginning of a constitution, statute, or ordinance explaining the reasons for its enactment and the object or objects it seeks to accomplish.
➤ preface, introduction, opening, prologue ("preamble to the state constitution").

precarious [pre · *kare* · ee · us] *adj.* Uncertain; unstable; insecure; chancy; liable to end or be revoked.
➤ uncertain, unstable, insecure, dangerous, revocable ("precarious situation").

precarious right *n.* A right that is revocable at the will or **sufferance** of the person who granted it.

precatory [*prek* · a · tore · ee] *adj.* Pertaining to an entreaty or appeal; pertaining to words that express permission or a wish.
➤ suggestive, pleading, appealing, beseeching, imploring, wishing, prayerful, asking ("precatory language").
Ant. ordering.

precatory language [*lang* · wij] *n. See* precatory words.

precatory trust *n.* A **trust** created by words that express a wish or desire, but that are sufficiently mandatory that they may be construed as words of command or direction effective to create a valid trust (EXAMPLE: "I wish to create and **bequeath** a fund"). *See* precatory words.

precatory words *n.* Words of request, recommendation, or suggestion, or words that ordinarily signify a wish or desire (EXAMPLES: "I request"; "I expect"; "I hope"), but which, in an appropriate context, may be construed as words of direction or command. *See* precatory trust.

precedence [*press* · e · dense] *n.* The right, privilege, or status of preceding someone or something in time, rank, or order. USAGE: "A **first mortgage** takes precedence over a **second mortgage**." *See* preference; priority.
➤ priority, seniority, preference, lead, advantage.

precedent [*press* · e · dent] *adj.* Coming before; preceding. *See* condition precedent. *n.* 1. Prior decisions of the same court, or a higher court, which a judge must follow in deciding a subsequent case presenting similar facts and the same legal problem, even though different **parties** are involved and many years have elapsed. *See stare decisis. See also* binding authority. *Compare* authority; persuasive authority. 2. A point of reference; a standard; a model; a guide.
➤ *adj.* prior, earlier, previous, preexistent ("A precedent condition to getting a credit card is having good credit").
n. guide, model, standard, foundation ("*Roe v. Wade* is a precedent in abortion law").

precept [*pree* · sept] *n.* 1. A **warrant**; a **writ; process**; an order in writing from a person in authority. 2. A rule of moral or ethical conduct. *See* ethics.
➤ warrant, writ, order ("Sheriff Gomez ordered a precept"); code, rule, principle,

P

doctrine, axiom, action ("One of the precepts in court is respectful behavior").

precinct [*pree* · sinkt] *n.* 1. An **election district**. 2. The geographical area for which a given police station is responsible (a police precinct). 3. The geographical area of a **magistrate's** jurisdiction (a **magisterial district**). *See* jurisdiction.
➤ ward, section, province, parish, area, community, district.

precipe [*press* · i · pee] *n.* Same as *praecipe*.

precise [pre · *sise*] *adj.* Accurate; flawless.
➤ exact, accurate, literal, distinct, unerring, express, truthful, firm, particular, strict ("Look at the precise language of the contract").

preclusion [*pree* · *kloo* · zhen] *n.* The act of preventing.
➤ prevention, ban, forbidding, constrainment. *Ant.* facilitation, inclusion.

preclusion order [*or* · der] *n.* A court ruling prohibiting a **party** from introducing evidence that contravenes a **claim** or **defense** of his opponent in circumstances where that party failed to comply with **discovery** of facts bearing upon the same claim or defense.

precognition [pree · kog · *nish* · en] *n.* 1. The examination of a witness prior to trial of a case. *See* deposition; discovery. 2. Knowledge of an event that is yet to occur.
➤ examination, deposition, discovery; clairvoyance, foresight.

precondition [pree · ken · *dish* · en] *n.* A **condition precedent**.

precontract [*pree* · kon · trakt] *n.* A **contract** that a person has entered into which prevents him from entering into a second contract of the same nature.

predatory [*pred* · e · tore · ee] *adj.* Describes an animal or person who lives by robbing or taking from others.
➤ predative, preying, ravaging, thieving, hunting ("predatory behavior").

predatory pricing [*pry* · sing] *n.* Setting the prices one charges for one's goods or services at an extremely low level, usually below cost, to eliminate competition. This practice is a violation of the federal **antitrust acts**.

predecessor [*pred* · e · sess · er] *n.* 1. A person, corporation, or other organization that preceded its successor chronologically. 2. A person who precedes another in the same office.
➤ ancestor, forebear, forerunner, previous, prototype ("Seaboard Coastline is the predecessor of CSX Transportation").

predial [*pree* · di · al] *adj.* Same as **praedial**.

predicament [pre · *dik* · a · mint] *n.* A difficult situation; a problem.
➤ situation, circumstance, position, state, difficulty, crisis, dilemma, condition, jam, bind.

predict [pre · *dikt*] *v.* To anticipate; to foresee.
➤ forecast, portend, envision, foresee, promise, bode, prognosticate.

predilection [*pred* · ih · lek · shun] *n.* An affinity; a preference.
➤ penchant, leaning, proclivity, tendency, liking, proneness, partiality, bent, bias.

predisposition [pree · dis · pe · *zish* · en] *n.* Having a previous tendency or inclination. The **defense** of **entrapment** is not available to a defendant who had a "predisposition" to commit the crime; that is, it is not possible for the police to entrap a person who was inclined to commit the offense in the first place.
➤ willingness, inclination, proclivity, bias, leaning, proneness, tendency.

preempt [pree · *empt*] *v.* To take over, as if by right.
➤ assume, capture, occupy, preclude, usurp, arrogate.

preemption [pree · *emp* · shen] *n.* 1. The doctrine that once Congress has enacted legislation in a given field, a state may not enact a law inconsistent with the federal statute. Thus, for EXAMPLE, a state may not enact a **wage and hour law**, applicable to employers who are **in commerce**, that is inconsistent with the provisions of the **Fair Labor Standards Act**. A similar doctrine also governs the relationship between the state government and **local government**. *See also* occupancy of the field; supremacy clause. 2. The right granted by Congress to settle on certain **public land** on a "first come, first served" basis, and to acquire

P

title to the property. 3. The act of buying anything before or ahead of others. 4. The act of acquiring something before someone else acquires it.

➤ appropriation, substitution, usurpation, replacement, annexation ("preemption doctrine").

preemption doctrine [*dok* · trin] *n. See* preemption.

preemptive right [pree · *emp* · tiv] *n.* The right or privilege of a stockholder of a corporation to purchase shares of a **new issue** before persons who are not stockholders. This entitlement allows a shareholder to preserve her percentage of ownership (i.e., her **equity**) in the corporation.

preexisting condition clause [pree · eg · *zis* · ting ken · *dish* · en] *n.* A provision in a health insurance policy that excludes from coverage, for a specified period of time, medical conditions that existed when the insured purchased the policy. *See also* incontestability provision.

preexisting debt [pree · eg · *zis* · ting] *n.* Same as **antecedent debt**.

prefer [pree · *fer*] *v.* 1. To prosecute or proceed against. USAGE: "to prefer an indictment." 2. To like better; to favor.

➤ charge, proffer, file, lodge; like, choose, fancy, pick, espouse, advance, elevate, favor.

preference [*pref* · e · rense] *n.* 1. The act of a debtor in paying one or more of his creditors without paying the others. "Preference" is often confused with **priority**. However, a priority exists by **operation of law**; a preference is a transaction that, depending upon the circumstances, the law may consider **voidable**. *See* voidable preference. 2. Under the **Bankruptcy Code**, a transfer of property by an insolvent debtor to one or more creditors to the exclusion of others, enabling such creditors to obtain a greater percentage of their debt than other creditors of the same class. Such a transaction may constitute a **voidable preference** and be disallowed by the **trustee in bankruptcy**. *See* fraudulent preference. 3. The right of one person over other persons.

➤ partiality, election, advantage; priority, prejudice, promotion, upgrading, precedence.

Ant. even-handedness, equality.

preference shares *n.* Same as **preferred stock**.

preferential [pref · e · *ren* · shel] *adj.* Pertaining to a **preference**.

➤ favored, select, better, special, privileged, choice, first-rate ("preferential treatment"). *Ant.* inferior.

preferential assignment [a · *sine* · ment] *n.* An **assignment for the benefit of creditors** by which the **assignor** gives a **preference** to certain of her creditors; any **assignment** that prefers one creditor over another.

preferential debts *n.* Debts that, under the **Bankruptcy Code**, are payable before all other debts. EXAMPLE: wages owed employees.

preferential dividend [*div* · i · dend] *n.* Same as **preferred dividend**.

preferential shop *n.* Under a **collective bargaining agreement**, a place of employment where union members are given a preference over nonmembers with respect to hiring and other conditions of employment. *Compare* agency shop agreement; closed shop; open shop.

preferential tariff [*tehr* · if] *n.* An allowance given to a foreign country by permitting articles from that country to be imported upon payment of lesser **customs duties** than those charged other countries. *See* tariff.

preferential transfer [*tranz* · fer] *n. See* preference.

preferred [pre · *ferd*] *adj.* Having a **preference** or **priority**, especially with respect to the status of one's claim (EXAMPLES: a debt; a **lien**; a **judgment**) relative to the claims of other creditors.

➤ favorite, chosen, elected, picked, singled-out ("a preferred approach").

preferred creditor [*kred* · it · er] *n.* A **creditor** who is preferred. *Also see* preference.

preferred dividend [*div* · i · dend] *n.* A **dividend** paid on **preferred stock**.

preferred provider organization [pro · *vy* · der or · ge · ne · *zay* · shen] *n.* Commonly referred to by its initials, **PPO**; a group of doctors in private practice who have agreed to provide medical service at a discount price. *Compare* health maintenance organization.

preferred stock *n.* Corporate stock that is entitled to a priority over other **classes of stock**, usually **common stock**, in distribution of the profits of the corporation (i.e., **dividends**) and in distribution of the **assets** of the corporation in the event of **dissolution** or **liquidation**. *See* guaranteed stock.

preferred stockholder [*stok* · hole · der] *n.* A person who owns **preferred stock**. *See* stockholder.

prejudge [*pre* · judj] *v.* To make an assumption before receiving the facts.
➤ predetermine, presuppose, assume, presume, jump to a conclusion.

prejudice [*prej* · e · diss] *v.* To injure; to bias; to impair.
n. 1. Partiality; bias; preconceived opinion; an opinion formed before the facts are known or in disregard of the facts. 2. Detriment. *See and compare* dismissal without prejudice; dismissal with prejudice. *Also see* prejudicial.
➤ *v.* bias, sway, influence, predispose, spoil ("He tried to prejudice the jury"); injure, impair, harm, hurt, weaken, damage, destroy ("That admission really prejudiced his case").
n. bias, discrimination, bigotry, favoritism, racism, partisanship, partiality.

prejudice of judge *n.* Same as **bias of judge**. *See also* disqualified judge.

prejudice of juror [*joo* · rer] *n.* Same as **bias of juror**. *See also* disqualified juror.

prejudice of witness [*wit* · ness] *n. See* impeachment of witness.

prejudicial [prej · e · *dish* · el] *adj.* Detrimental to a party or person or to his interests. USAGE: "A **judgment** against Mr. Jones will be quite prejudicial to his financial health; he may have to file for bankruptcy." *See* prejudice.
➤ harmful, bigoted, bad, damaging, hurtful; reversible, appealable ("prejudicial error"). *Ant.* beneficial.

prejudicial error [*ehr* · er] *n.* **Reversible error; judicial error** that causes a **miscarriage of justice**.

prejudicial evidence [*ev* · i · dense] *n.* **Evidence** that is inadmissible because its only purpose is to prejudice the minds of the jury; evidence so likely to unfairly arouse the passions of the jury that its admission is **prejudicial error**.

preliminary [pre · *lim* · i · ner · ee] *adj.* Before; introductory; preparatory.
➤ preceding, initial, beginning, previous ("preliminary investigation").

preliminary examination [eg · zam · i · *nay* · shen] *n.* The **examination** that is the subject of a **preliminary hearing**.

preliminary hearing [*heer* · ing] *n.* A **hearing** to determine whether there is **probable cause** to formally accuse a person of a crime; that is, whether there is a reasonable basis for believing that a crime has been committed and for thinking the defendant committed it. If the judge concludes that the evidence is sufficient to hold the defendant for trial, and if the offense is a **bailable offense**, the court sets bail. If the judge concludes that the evidence is insufficient to bind the defendant over for trial, the defendant is discharged from custody. *See* binding over.

preliminary injunction [in · *junk* · shen] *n.* An **injunction** granted prior to a full hearing **on the merits**. Its purpose is to preserve the status quo until the final hearing. A **preliminary injunction** is also referred to as a **provisional injunction** or **temporary injunction**. *Compare* permanent injuction.

preliminary statement [*state* · ment] *n.* Same as **opening statement**.

premarital agreement [pree · *mehr* · i · tel a · gree · ment] *n. See* prenuptial agreement.

premeditate [pree · *med* · i · tate] *v.* To form an **intent**. *Also see* malice.
➤ prearrange, think out, scheme, plan, intend, contrive.

premeditated [pree · *med* · i · tay · ted] *adj.* Thought of beforehand; thought about for a space of time, however short.
➤ advised, careful, planned, contemplated, calculated, deliberate, intentional, malicious ("premeditated murder"). *Ant.* spontaneous, thoughtless.

P

premeditated malice [*mal* · iss] *n. See* malice aforethought.

premeditation [pree · med · i · *tay* · shen] *n.* Forethought; the act of thinking beforehand for any period of time, however brief. If a person had sufficient opportunity for premeditation before committing a criminal act, the law will **impute** an **intent** to commit the act. Premeditation is an essential element of **first degree murder**. *See also* malice aforethought.

➤ forethought, care, deliberation, malice, consideration ("A crime of passion usually isn't one of premeditation").
Ant. spontaneity.

premise [*prem* · iss] *n.* An assumption. In legal argument, a starting point from which conclusions may be drawn. *Singular* of **premises**. *See* premises.

➤ statement, belief, proposition, assumption, assertion, thesis, hypothesis ("Your premise is erroneous").

premises [*prem* · iss · ez] *n.* 1. In real estate law, land, including buildings or structures on the land. In this connection, "premises" may mean a unit as small as a single room. 2. That part of a deed, preceding the **habendum clause**, containing **recitals** of the **grantor's** reasons for making the conveyance, the names of the parties, and the **consideration** for the deed. 3. Part of a **bill in equity** setting forth the facts on which the plaintiff relies as grounds for **relief**. 4. A statement or proposition on which an argument or conclusion is based.

➤ grounds, property, dwelling, boundaries ("Protesters were dragged off the premises").

premium [*pree* · mee · yum] *n.* 1. Money paid an insurance company for an insurance policy. *See* insurance premium. *See also* earned premium; net premium; unearned premium. 2. Something given a purchaser in addition to the article, commodity, or service purchased. 3. A payment of rent in a lump sum, rather than periodic payments. 4. An amount paid above **par** because of demand. Thus, for EXAMPLE, with respect to **stock** or other securities, the "premium" is the amount by which its **market value** exceeds its **face value**. A **bond** which sells for more than its face value is called a **premium bond**. 5. A prize offered and given to a winner of a contest. 6. A bonus for doing something.
adj. Of high quality; selected.

➤ *n.* reward, gift, compensation; consideration, payment ("The premium on the car insurance is due").
adj. popular, scarce, choice, prime, excellent ("premium brand").

premium bond *n. See* premium.

premium earned *n.* Same as **earned premium**.

premium loan provision [pro · *vizh* · en] *n.* A provision in a life insurance policy stating that if the **insured** fails to pay a premium, the **insurer** may pay it on her behalf and charge it as a loan against the policy.

premium note *n.* A **promissory note** given to an insurance company for a premium due on an insurance policy.

prenatal injury [pree · *nay* · tel *in* · je · ree] *n.* An injury occurring to a child in the womb. *See* unborn child. *See* fetal alcohol syndrome.

prenuptial [pree · *nup* · shel] *adj.* Before marriage. *Compare* postnuptial.

prenuptial agreement [a · *gree* · ment] *n.* An agreement between a man and a woman who are about to be married, governing the financial and property arrangements between them in the event of divorce, death, or even during the marriage. Such an agreement may override obligations or rights provided by statute. Prenuptial agreements are also called **antenuptial agreements, antenuptial settlements**, or **premarital agreements**. *Compare* postnuptial agreement. *See* marital agreement.

prenuptial settlement [*stl* · ment] *n.* Same as **prenuptial agreement**.

prepaid [*pree* · paid] *adj.* Paid in advance. *See* prepayment.

prepaid legal services [*leeg* · el *ser* · viss] *n.* Similar to payments made to a **health maintenance organization** for medical services not yet required, a program that allows consumers to pay in advance for the services of attorneys or paralegals that they may require or desire in the future.

prepaid stock *n. See* paid-up stock.

preparation [prep · uh · *ray* · shun] *n.* Readiness; foundation.

P

➤ groundwork, readiness, readying, planning, provision, preliminary work, training, gestation.

prepayment [pree · *pay* · ment] *n./adj.* Payment of a debt or obligation before it is due.

    prepayment clause *n.* A clause in a mortgage or **note** that gives the borrower the right to pay the debt before it is due without a **prepayment penalty.**

    prepayment penalty [*pen* · el · tee] *n.* A **penalty** that a borrower must pay when he satisfies a debt before its due date, unless the **note** or mortgage contains a **prepayment clause.**

preponderance [pre · *pon* · der · ense] *n.* Superior in influence, importance, weight, or strength.

➤ majority, dominance, prevalence, plurality.

    preponderance of the evidence [*ev* · i · dense] *n.* The degree of proof required in most **civil actions.** It means "more likely than not"; that the greater weight and value of the credible evidence, taken as a whole, belongs to one side in a lawsuit rather than to the other side. In other words, the **party** whose evidence is more convincing has a "preponderance of the evidence" on its side and must, as a **matter of law**, prevail in the lawsuit because it has met its **burden of proof.** The expression "preponderance of the evidence" has nothing to do with the number of witnesses a party presents, only with the credibility and value of their testimony. *Compare* beyond a reasonable doubt; clear and convincing evidence. *See* weight of the evidence.

prerequisite [pre · *rek* · wiz · it] *n.* A pre-condition; that which is required beforehand. *Note* that "prerequisites" are not "**perquisites.**"

➤ precondition, requirement, necessity, essential condition, must, qualification.

prerogative [pre · *rog* · e · tiv] *n.* A special or exclusive right or privilege. Formerly, prerogatives were associated with persons of high status or rank. In modern times, the term more often relates to the exercise of governmental powers or to personal liberties.

➤ right, privilege, option, advantage, choice.

prerogative writs *n. See* extraordinary writs.

prescribe [pre · *skribe*] *v.* 1. To claim a right based upon use over a long period of time. *See* prescriptive easement. *See also* prescription. 2. To lay down a rule of conduct; to ordain; to impose an order or directive; to legislate. USAGE: "In this state, the law prescribes a two-week bow-and-arrow season for hunting deer." 3. To write a prescription, as a physician would.

➤ appoint, assign, choose, define, ordain, dictate.

prescription [pre · *skrip* · shen] *n.* 1. The acquisition of **title** by **adverse possession.** 2. The acquisition of an **easement** by an **adverse user** under a **claim of right** for the **prescriptive period.** 3. The acquisition of **incorporeal hereditaments** by an adverse user. 4. An order prepared by a physician directing a pharmacist to provide a drug to a patient, together with instructions for its use.

➤ claim, interest, right, license, permit, convention, custom, usage; charge, command, ordinance, rule.

prescriptive [pre · *skrip* · tiv] *adj.* Pertaining to or created by **prescription.**

➤ customary, settled, fixed, time-honored, accepted, recognized, traditional.

    prescriptive easement [*eez* · ment] *n.* An **easement** acquired by **prescription.**

    prescriptive period [*peer* · ee · ed] *n.* The period of time necessary to acquire a **prescriptive easement.**

presence [*prez* · ense] *n.* The fact of being at a particular place at a particular time. *See* present.

➤ being, occupancy, existence, attendance ("His presence gave me the chills"); appearance, demeanor, aura, air, behavior ("Her stately presence was intimidating"); closeness, nearness, proximity, vicinity ("The pit bull's presence was too close for comfort").

    presence of an officer [*off* · i · ser] *n.* An **arrest warrant** is not required if an offense is committed in the presence of the arresting officer. However, in the officer's "presence" does not necessarily mean right before her eyes; rather, the term refers to circumstances which give the officer

probable cause to believe that the person she arrests committed a crime. Such circumstances may be highly **circumstantial**. EXAMPLE: (an officer sees) a person running from the building in which the police have just discovered a corpse with a fresh and fatal wound.

presence of the accused [a · *kyoozd*] *n.* A term relating to a criminal defendant's right to be present at all stages of his trial. In some states, this requirement applies only to defendants accused of a **felony**.

presence of the court *n.* For the purpose of determining whether **contempt** has been committed, the term "court" means the judge, or the jury, or the witnesses, or any **officer of the court**, or any place where they are required to be to perform their duties. Thus an act that undermines the authority of the court and is directed to any of these individuals, or performed, for EXAMPLE, in the courtroom or the jury room, is an act done or performed "in the presence of the court." *See* criminal contempt; direct contempt.

presence of the defendant [de · *fen* · dent] *n. See* presence of the accused.

presence of the testator [*tes* · tay · tor] *n.* As it pertains to **attestation** of a will, the phrase "in the presence of the testator" is not limited to attestation within the **testator's** sight, but includes attestation by witnesses who the testator merely knows are present with her or nearby. EXAMPLES: witnesses who are in the next room; witnesses whom a blind testator can only hear.

present [*prez* · ent] *adj.* Current; existing; contemporary.
n. 1. A gift; a **gratuity**. 2. Being at a particular place at a particular time. *See* presence.
v. [pre · *zent*] 1. To make a gift or **gratuity**. 2. To submit an **item** (EXAMPLES: a **draft**; a check) for payment. *See* presented; presentment.
➤ *adj.* current, existing, contemporary, immediate, recent ("present danger"); in view, in attendance.
n. gift, gratuity, endowment, donation; existing time, here-and-now.
v. introduce, demonstrate, acquaint, submit ("The man presented his argument to me");

give, award, bestow, confer ("present the award"); accuse, incriminate, charge, cite ("present the indictment").

present danger [*dane* · jer] *n. See* clear and present danger.

present estate [es · *tate*] *n.* An **estate** that is **vested**, as opposed to a **future estate**. *See* vested estate.

present interest [*in* · trest] *n.* 1. An **interest** that is **vested**, as opposed to a **future interest**. *See* vested interest. 2. As used in connection with federal and state **gift taxes**, a present right to use or enjoy property one has received as a gift.

present memory refreshed [*mem* · er · ee re · *fresht*] *n.* Same as **present recollection revived**.

present recollection recorded [rek · e · *lek* · shen re · *kor* · ded] *n.* A term applied to the practice of permitting a witness to use a document to help remind him of a past event. As opposed to **past recollection recorded**, the witness's revived recollection of the past event (in the form of his testimony), not the contents of the document, is admitted into evidence. *Compare* present recollection revived; recorded past recollection.

present recollection revived [rek · e · *lek* · shen re · *vyvd*] *n.* The use by a witness of a writing or other object to refresh her recollection so she may testify to past events from present recollection. *Compare* past recollection recorded; present recollection recorded; recorded past recollection.

present value [*val* · yoo] *n.* The value of a thing under present circumstances, as distinguished from its value at some other time or its original value.

present worth *n.* The **commuted value** of money or property to be received in the future. *See* future interest. The law reduces **damages** for decreased **earning capacity** to their "present worth."

presented [pre · *zent* · ed] *adv./past part.* Submitted for payment. *See* presentment.
➤ submitted, given, done, accomplished.

presented for acceptance [ak · *sep* · tense] *See* presentment.

presented for payment [*pay* · ment] *See* presentment.

P

presentence hearing [pree · *sen* · tense *heer* · ing] *n.* Also referred to as a **sentencing hearing**; a proceeding during which the judge receives testimony and other material submitted by both the prosecutor and the defendant's attorney bearing upon the type and severity of the sentence to be ordered. *See* presentence investigation; sentencing guidelines.

presentence investigation [pree · *sen* · tense in · ves · ti · *gay* · shen] *n.* An **investigation** into the relevant aspects of a convicted defendant's background and life circumstances (for EXAMPLE, his education, his prior criminal record, his social history). It is conducted by a probation officer at the request of the court; the results are submitted at the **presentence hearing** to aid the judge in arriving at an appropriate sentence. See sentencing guidelines.

presenter [pre · *zen* · ter] *n.* Any person presenting an **item** (EXAMPLES: a **draft**; a check) for **payment**. *See* present; presentment.
➤ demonstrator, giver, donor, communicator, submittor.

presenting bank [pre · *zent* · ing] *n.* Any bank except a **payor bank**, presenting an **item** (EXAMPLES: a **draft**; a check). *See* present; presentment.

presentment [pre · *zent* · ment] *n.* 1. A formal accusation of the commission of a crime made by a grand jury on its **own motion**, as opposed to an **indictment**, which it returns based upon evidence presented to it by the prosecutor. 2. A demand to **accept** (*presentment for acceptance*) or to pay (*presentment for payment*) a **negotiable instrument**, made to the **drawee** by a person, usually the **payee** or **holder**, entitled to enforce the instrument. *See* acceptance; payment.
➤ accusation, presentation, production ("The grand jury gave a presentment to the defendant").

presents [*prez* · ents] *n.* A term commonly used in legal documents, meaning "this instrument." USAGE: "Know all men by these presents." *See* instrument. *Also see* know all men; these presents.
➤ instrument, document .

preservation [prez · er · *vay* · shun] *n.* The process of protecting somethng from harm or decay. USAGE: "The preservation of endangered species is essential for ecological balance."
➤ care, perpetuation, upkeep, protection, defense, guarding, saving, maintenance, shielding, conservation.

preserve [pre · *zerv*] *v.* 1. To care for, save, or maintain. USAGE: To preserve the evidence for examination. 2. To continue or uphold. USAGE: "to preserve a tradition."
➤ conserve, secure, nourish, maintain, aid, keep, uphold, protect, save.

preside [pre · *zide*] *v.* To exercise power; to exercise control over a group, an organization, or a meeting; to moderate; to chair.
➤ direct, control, oversee, chair, supervise, manage.
Ant. follow.

president [*prez* · i · dent] *n.* 1. In many countries, the title of the **chief executive officer**. 2. The title of the chief executive officer of most corporations, associations, and other organizations.
➤ chief, officer, head, director, official, title.
president judge *n.* The title in some states of the **chief judge** of a court having two or more judges. *Compare* presiding judge.

President of the United States [*prez* · i · dent of the yoo · *ny* · ted] *n.* The **chief executive officer** of the United States of America.

presidential electors [prez · i · *dent* · shel e · *lek* · terz] *n. See* electoral college.

presiding judge [pre · *zy* · ding] *n.* The judge who presides at a trial. *Compare* president judge.

press *n.* People who work in communication or journalism.
v. To push or force.
➤ *n.* media, journalists, reporters, correspondents, news writers.
v. crush, pressure, embrace, depress, squeeze.

pressure [*preh* · shur] *v.* To bother; to insist; to compel; to urge.
n. 1. Physical force or mass. 2. Demand; tension; urgency.

P

➤ *v.* compel, coerce, force, prod, plead, coax, cajole, beseech, push, solicit.

n. weight, load, mass, thrust, burden ("pressure per square inch"); difficulty, influence, strain, stress, tension, intensity, coercion ("testifying under tremendous pressure").

presume [pre · *zoom*] *v.* 1. To assume a thing to be a fact on the basis of human experience, reason, or facts in evidence, although the thing is not proven; to take for granted. 2. To take liberties; to be too forward. *See* presumption.

➤ assume, suppose, deduce, infer, believe ("We presumed that the innocent-looking young woman was the victim"); encroach, infringe, intrude, impose ("Because I was friendly to him, he presumed to touch me").

presumed [pre · *zoomd*] *adj./past part.* Assumed. *See* presume.

presumed intent [in · *tent*] *n.* The **intent** to commit the act is a necessary element of both a crime and a **tort**; it may be presumed or inferred from the fact that the act was knowingly and voluntarily committed. *See* infer; presume. *See also* criminal intent; *mens rea*.

presumed malice [*mal* · iss] *n.* Same as **malice in law**.

presumption [pre · *zump* · shen] *n.* 1. A rule of law that, on the basis of reason and human experience, accords **probative value** to specific facts in evidence or draws a particular inference as to the existence of a fact that is not actually known but which arises from other facts that are known or proven. A presumption is distinguished from an **inference** in that a judge or jury may or may not, as it chooses, infer that a thing is true, whereas a presumption *requires* the inference to be drawn. Some presumptions are **rebuttable**; others are **irrebuttable**. *See and compare* irrebuttable presumption; rebuttable presumption. *See* legal presumption; mixed presumption. 2. Unjustifiable boldness; behavior that is excessively forward.

➤ inference, probability, deduction, assumption, supposition; boldness, aggressiveness.

presumption of death *n.* The presumption that a person has died when she has been absent for a long period of time, usually seven years, in circumstances where her absence is unexplained and without apparent reason. *See* Enoch Arden statutes; seven years' absence.

presumption of fact *n.* A **rebuttable presumption**. *Compare* presumption of law.

presumption of innocence [*in* · o · sense] *n.* The presumption in a criminal case that the defendant is innocent until he is proven guilty. This presumption places upon the government the **burden of proof** of guilt.

presumption of law *n.* A presumption of law is not a true presumption; the term is more nearly synonymous with **inference**. *Compare* presumption of fact.

presumption of law and fact *n.* A **rebuttable presumption** containing elements of both a **presumption of fact** and a **presumption of law**; sometimes referred to as a **mixed presumption**.

presumption of legitimacy [le · *jit* · i · mes · ee] *n.* The presumption that a child born to a married woman is a legitimate child, that is, that her husband is the father of the child. *See also* presumption of paternity.

presumption of paternity [pa · *tern* · i · tee] *n.* The presumption that a married man is the father of a child born to his wife. *See also* presumption of legitimacy.

presumption of survivorship [ser · *vy* · ver · ship] *n.* In a jurisdiction without a **simultaneous death act**, a presumption that is applied when two people who have an **interest** in the same property, often a husband and wife, die in a **common disaster**. It requires that, absent evidence to the contrary, the younger, healthier person be deemed the survivor.

presumptive [pre · *zump* · tiv] *adj.* Grounded upon or based upon a **presumption**.

➤ inferred, assumed, apparent, likely, presumed, conjectured, probable ("presumptive evidence").

presumptive evidence [*ev* · i · dense] *n.* **Evidence** that the law regards as proof unless it is **rebutted; probable evidence**. EXAMPLE: **circumstantial evidence**. *See also* prima facie evidence.

P

presumptive heir *n.* Same as **heir presumptive**.

presumptive trust *n.* Same as **resulting trust**.

pretend [pree · *tend*] *v.* 1. To assert as true or real that which is false; to delude; to mislead. 2. To act; to play a part.

➤ affect, assume, fake, mislead, purport, imagine, feign, misrepresent; portray, represent, impersonate, mimic, act.

pretermitted [pree · ter · *mit* · ed] *adj.* Omitted; disregarded; overlooked; neglected.

pretermitted child *n.* A child of a **testator** who is omitted from the testator's will. Generally the right of such a child to share in the **decedent's estate** depends upon whether the omission was intentional or unintentional.

pretermitted heir *n.* *See* pretermitted child.

pretext [*pree* · tekts] *n.* An alleged reason; an excuse.

➤ claim, purpose, lie, justification, obfuscation, false motive, pretense, excuse, evasion, misrepresentation, fraud ("The policy was a pretext for discrimination").

pretrial [pree · *try* · el] *adj.* Prior to trial. "Pretrial" is applied to any aspect of litigation that occurs before the trial begins. USAGE: "pretrial proceedings"; "**pretrial motions**"; "**pretrial conference**."

pretrial conference [*kon* · fer · ense] *n.* A conference held between the judge and counsel for all **parties** prior to trial, for the purpose of facilitating disposition of the case by, among other actions, simplifying the **pleadings**, narrowing the issues, obtaining **stipulations** to avoid unnecessary proof, and limiting the number of witnesses.

pretrial discovery [dis · *kuv* · e · ree] *n.* *See* discovery.

pretrial diversion [di · *ver* · zhen] *n.* *See* diversion program.

pretrial intervention [in · ter · *ven* · shen] *n.* *See* diversion program.

pretrial motions [*moh* · shenz] *n.* **Motions** that may be filed prior to the commencement of a trial. EXAMPLES: a **motion to suppress**; a **motion to dismiss**.

pretrial orders [*or* · derz] *n.* An **order** resulting from a **pretrial conference**. It

controls the way the trial is conducted, although it may be modified by a subsequent order.

prevail [pre · *vale*] *v.* 1. To overcome; to succeed; to triumph; to win. 2. To be in general use; to be widespread; to be current.

➤ dominate, overcome, beat, succeed, persist; govern, control, exist, abound; persuade, inspire, motivate, woo, lure.

prevailing [pre · *vay* · ling] *adj.* 1. The act or fact of winning or overcoming. 2. The state or condition of being in general use, widespread, or current.

➤ overcoming, victorious, winning, dominant ("prevailing argument"); universal, majority, popular, fashionable, widespread, current ("prevailing opinion").

prevailing party [*par* · tee] *n.* The **party** who is successful or partially successful in a lawsuit; the party in whose favor **judgment** is entered. Under the **Federal Rules of Civil Procedure**, the prevailing party's costs are paid by the party who did not prevail.

prevailing rate *n.* The average wage received by those who are working at the same trade or occupation and in the same type of job.

prevailing wage *n.* *See* prevailing rate.

prevalent [*prev* · uh · lent] *adj.* Popular; extensive; comprehensive.

➤ accepted, accustomed, general, ordinary, customary, pandemic, prevailing ("the prevalent view").

prevent [pree · *vent*] *v.* To stop; to keep from happening.

➤ stop, avert, arrest, restrain, avoid, ward off, deter, halt, limit, restrict.

preventive [pre · *vent* · iv] *adj.* Serving to prevent; pertaining to that which prevents.

➤ precautionary, watchful, deterrent, restrictive, protective ("preventive measures").

preventive injunction [in · *junk* · shen] *n.* An **injunction** that commands the **party** against whom it is directed to refrain from doing a specified act, rather than an injunction requiring the performance of an act; a **restraining order**.

preventive justice [*jus* · tiss] *n.* A term applied to **relief** or to a **remedy** that attempts to prevent the occurrence of

breaches of the peace, such as domestic violence. EXAMPLES: a **peace bond**; a **protection order**; a **restraining order**.

preventive remedy [rem · e · dee] *n.* *See* preventive justice.

price *n.* 1. The amount charged or asked by a seller; the **consideration** furnished or to be furnished by a buyer. *See* fair market price; market price. *Also see* value. 2. The cost of something. In this sense, one can pay a nonmonetary price.

➤ consideration, value, compensation, fare, bill ("The price of the course is reasonable"); consequence, sacrifice, toll, penalty ("Sometimes freedom carries a high price").

price discrimination [dis · krim · i · nay · shen] *n.* Charging one customer more than another for the same article or service. Price discrimination violates the **antitrust acts** if its purpose is to eliminate competition.

price supports [sup · ports] *n.* *See* parity.

price-fixing [-fik · sing] *n.* The objective of an unlawful **combination in restraint of trade**, namely, the setting of prices by competing manufacturers or dealers in cooperation with each other. *See also* horizontal price-fixing; vertical price-fixing.

priest-penitent privilege [-pen · i · tent priv · 1 · lej] *n.* The rule that a priest cannot testify with respect to what a person tells him in confession. *Compare* attorney-client privilege. *See* privilege.

prima facie (*Latin*) [pry · muh fay · shee] *adj.* Means "at first sight." A term which, when used in reference to evidence, conveys the concept that, based upon its initial appearance, the evidence is adequate.

➤ adequate, satisfactory, legally sufficient; seemingly, ostensibly, presumably, on its face, apparently.

prima facie case *n.* A **cause of action** or **defense** that is sufficiently established by a party's evidence to justify a verdict in her favor, provided the other party does not **rebut** that evidence; a case supported by sufficient evidence to justify its submission to the **trier of fact** and the rendition of a compatible verdict.

prima facie evidence [ev · i · dense] *n.* **Evidence** that, if unexplained or uncontradicted, is sufficient to prove a particular fact; evidence that, if not rebutted, is sufficient to establish a **prima facie case**. *See also* presumptive evidence.

primarily liable [pry · mair · i · lee ly · ebl] *adv.* *See* primary liability.

primary [pry · mer · ee] *adj.* 1. Highest; main; principal. 2. Earliest; first; original; initial. 3. Basic. 4. Direct.
n. An intraparty election for a candidate.

➤ *adj.* best, principal, excellent, world-class ("His primary motive was love"); original, first, initial, earliest ("Her primary step in bettering herself was enrolling in school").

primary activity [ak · tiv · i · tee] *n.* **Concerted activity** against an employer by its employees or by the union representing them. EXAMPLES: a **boycott**; a strike; picketing. *Compare* secondary activity; secondary boycott; secondary picketing. *See also* primary boycott.

primary boycott [boy · kot] *n.* A **boycott** applied directly to a company, as opposed to a **secondary boycott**. *See* primary activity.

primary cause *n.* An **efficent cause**; a **proximate cause**.

primary conveyance [ken · vey · ense] *n.* Same as **original conveyance**.

primary election [e · lek · shen] *n.* An election conducted by a political party for the purpose of selecting candidates to be placed on the official ballot at the **general election**. A primary election is commonly referred to simply as a "primary."

primary evidence [ev · i · dense] *n.* The **best evidence** it is possible to **adduce** in a case in support of a particular fact. *Compare* secondary evidence.

primary jurisdiction [joo · ris · dik · shen] *n.* The power of a court to hear and determine a case brought before it. *See* primary jurisdiction doctrine.

primary jurisdiction doctrine [joo · ris · dik · shen dok · trin] *n.* The principle that the courts will not determine an **action** or question that is within the **jurisdiction** of an administrative agency until the matter has been brought before the agency and **adjudicated** by it.

primary liability [ly · e · bil · i · tee] *n.* The **liability** of a person who, by the terms

P

of the **instrument** he has executed, or because of some other **legal obligation** he has incurred, or by virtue of his legal relationship to an **injured party**, is absolutely required to make payment, satisfy the obligation, or assume full responsibility for the injury; the liability of a **maker** or **principal**, as distinguished from that of a **guarantor** or **indorser**. *Compare* secondary liability.

primary picketing [*pik · e · ting*] *n.* The picketing of an employer by its employees with whom it has a labor dispute, or by the labor organization representing them. *Compare* secondary activity; secondary picketing. *See* primary activity. *See also* primary boycott.

prime *adj.* 1. First; primary. 2. Principal; chief. 3. Leading; superior. 4. Best; best in quality.
 n. 1. The best time; the heyday. 2. Beginning; youth; spring.
 v. To prepare or get ready.
➤ *adj.* major, first, primary ("prime suspect in the case"); best, choice, highest, mature, peak ("a prime cut").
 n. height, maturity, peak ("in his prime"); start, youth, opening, springtime, dawn, puberty.
 v. educate, teach, brief, guide, rehearse, teach ("prime the witness").

prime contractor [*kon · trak · ter*] *n.* Same as **general contractor**. *Compare* subcontractor.

prime minister [*min · is · ter*] *n.* In many countries, the title of the head of the government. *See* minister.

prime rate *n.* The rate of interest a lending institution charges its customers for unsecured **short-term loans** if they have superior credit ratings. *See* unsecured.

primogeniture [*pry · mo · jen · e · cher*] *n.* 1. The status of being the firstborn child in a family. 2. A principle of the **common law**, no longer of much effect, that the eldest son has primary rights of inheritance.
➤ priority, firstborn, superior, heir, inheritance.

primordial [*prih · mor · dee · ul*] *adj.* Earliest; original.
➤ basic, elementary, fundamental, primeval, aboriginal, rudimentary, original, earliest, ancient.

principal [*prin · sipl*] *adj.* Of the first importance; in the first rank; chief; main.
 n. 1. The amount of money loaned or borrowed, as distinguished from interest accruing on the debt. 2. In an **agency relationship**, the person for whom the agent acts and from whom the agent receives her authority to act. *See* undisclosed principal. 3. The **corpus** of a **trust**. 4. The person for whose debt or default a **surety** is responsible under a contract of **suretyship**. 5. The person whose obligation is guaranteed by the **guarantor** under a contract of **guaranty**. 6. A *principal in the first degree* is a person who commits a crime, either in person or through an **innocent agent**; a *principal in the second degree* is a person who is present at the commission of a crime, giving aid and encouragement to the chief perpetrator. *See* aiding and abetting. *Compare* accessory before the fact. 7. The head of a school.
 Note that "principal" is not "**principle**."
➤ *adj.* chief, prime, first, strongest, key ("the principal contractor").
 n. investment, debt, assets, capital ("principal borrowed from Donald was $1,000"); administrator, chief, boss, director ("school principal"); party, accomplice, accessory, actor ("principals in the crime").

principal administration [*ad · min · is · tray · shen*] *n.* Same as **domiciliary administration**.

principal contractor [*kon · trak · ter*] *n.* Same as **general contractor** or **prime contractor**.

principal fact *n.* The main or chief fact at issue in a case.

principal office [*off · iss*] *n.* The main place of business of a corporation; its headquarters. *See* office.

principle [*prin · sipl*] *n.* A basic truth; a fundamental doctrine; a general rule; a belief that forms the foundation for an action, a point of view, or an argument; a law on which other laws are based. USAGE: "**Due process** is a fundamental principle of American constitutional law." *Note* that "principle" is not "**principal**."
➤ law, truth, standard, doctrine, axiom, rule.

prior [*pry* · er] *adj.* 1. Former; previous; preceding. 2. Having precedence, priority, or preference.

➤ preceding, earlier, previous, former, past ("Her prior criminal record was complicated"); primary, predominant, superior ("Mary's prior debts come before her new car debt").

prior adjudication [a · joo · di · *kay* · shen] *n.* A previous **judgment** in a case in which the same matter in dispute between the same **parties** was, or might have been, put at issue and tried. *See* adjudication. *Also see res judicata.*

prior conviction [ken · *vik* · shen] *n.* A previous conviction. A previous conviction for the same offense is a necessary element of **double jeopardy**. *See* conviction.

prior inconsistent statements [in · ken · *sis* · tent *state* · ments] *n.* Statements made by a witness prior to the trial in which she is testifying that are inconsistent with her present testimony may be admitted into evidence to **impeach** her testimony. Such statements are admissible hearsay. *See* impeachment of witness. *See also* quasi admission.

prior jeopardy [*jep* · er · dee] *n.* Same as **double jeopardy**.

prior lien [*leen*] *n. See* priority.

prior restraint [re · *straynt*] *n.* The imposition by the government, in advance of publication, of limits that prohibit or restrain speech or publication, as opposed to punishing persons for what they have actually said or written. *See* censorship.

prior testimony [tes · ti · *moh* · nee] *n.* When a witness has testified in a prior trial and, at the time of a later trial is unavailable because of death or **incompetency**, her former testimony is admissible in the later trial through a witness to her earlier testimony who can testify to it with substantial accuracy. This **exception to the hearsay rule** is available only when there is no transcript of the earlier testimony.

prior use principle [*prin* · sipl] *n.* The rule that property devoted to a **public use** is not subject to **condemnation** under the power of **eminent domain**.

priority [pry · *aw* · ri · tee] *n.* 1. The right to have one's claim against a **decedent's** estate satisfied out of the **assets** of the estate before other claimants. "Priority" is often erroneously confused with **preference**. A preference, however, may merely be **voidable**, whereas a priority exists by **operation of law** and is **mandatory**. 2. The superiority of one **lien** over another lien or liens, based upon the order of their filing. In addition, some liens have priority as a matter of **public policy**, regardless of their senority. EXAMPLE: a **tax lien**. 3. In **bankruptcy** law, the right of a **secured creditor** to receive **satisfaction** before an **unsecured creditor**. 4. The status of that which is earlier or previous in point of time, degree, or rank; precedence.

➤ lead, order, superiority, primacy, preference, precedence, right, seniority, rank.

prison [*priz* · en] *n.* A place of confinement for persons convicted of **felonies**, as opposed to jail, which is customarily a place of confinement for persons convicted of **misdemeanors**; a penitentiary.

➤ penitentiary, confinement, jail, house of detention, reformatory, guardhouse, pen, cell, facility.

prison breaking [*bray* · king] *n.* The crime committed by a person who uses force to leave lawful custody. *Compare* escape; rescue.

prisoner [*priz* · en · er] *n.* A person deprived of his liberty by virtue of a judicial order or other lawful process.

➤ convict, jailbird, detainee, felon, captive, wrongdoer, inmate, hostage.

privacy [*pry* · ve · see] *n.* As used in the law, a reference to the **right of privacy**. The right of privacy is the right to be left alone. It is a **penumbra right**. The right of privacy means, among other things, that a person's writings which are not intended for public consumption (EXAMPLES: a diary; personal letters) cannot be made public, that a person's photographs may not be publicly distributed, and that a person's private conversations may not be listened in on or recorded. It also means that personal information of the kind in the possession of, for EXAMPLE, the government, insurance companies, and credit bureaus may not be made public. The right to privacy, which is grounded in the Constitution,

P

is supported, and to some extent enforced, by federal and state **privacy acts**. *See* eavesdropping; invasion of privacy; wiretapping. A woman's right to an abortion is based upon her constitutional right of privacy. *See Roe v. Wade.*

➤ confidentiality, noninfringement, secrecy, solitude, concealment, isolation, quiet.

privacy acts *n. See* privacy.

private [*pry* · vet] *adj.* 1. Personal; subjective; **privileged**; confidential. 2. Exclusive; restricted. 3. Nonpublic. *n.* A person of the lowest rank in the United States Army and in the Marine Corps.

➤ *adj.* personal, subjective, privileged, confidential ("private information"); hidden, exclusive, restricted, discreet, concealed ("private getaway"). *Ant.* open; nonexclusive. *n.* GI, infantry, soldier, enlisted person.

private act *n. See* private statute.

private attorney [uh · *ter* · nee] *n.* In criminal practice, an attorney who has been retained by the defendant, as opposed to a defense attorney who has been appointed to handle the case.

private bill *n.* A legislative **bill** that relates to particular individuals or particular organizations, or to matters of purely local interest, and does not affect the community as a whole. *Compare* public bill. *See also* private statute.

private carrier [*kehr* · i · er] *n.* Same as **contract carrier**. *Compare* common carrier.

private college [*koll* · ej] *n.* A college supported by private funds or privately endowed. The fact that a private college also receives **public funds** does not make it a **public college**. *Compare* public college.

private corporation [kore · per · ay · shen] *n.* 1. An entity made up of individuals to which the government has granted a **charter**, so that it may have a legal existence separate from those individuals for the purpose of carrying on a private purpose (EXAMPLE: operating a business; operating a charity) under its own name. *Compare* public corporation. *See* corporation. *See also* business corporation; nonprofit corporation. 2. A **close corporation** or other **privately held** corporation, as distinguished

from a corporation whose stock is traded on a stock exchange.

private easement [*eez* · ment] *n.* An **easement** that confers a benefit upon certain individuals, as opposed to the public in general. *See* private way.

private foundation [foun · *day* · shen] *n.* A form of **charitable organization**, particularly one endowed with a large and permanent fund. *See* foundation.

private injury [*in* · jer · ee] *n. See* private wrong.

private international law [in · ter · *nash* · en · el] *n.* Another term for **conflict of laws**. *Also see* comity.

private law *n.* 1. The rules of conduct that govern activities occurring among or between persons, as opposed to the rules of conduct governing the relationship between persons and their government. *Compare* public law. *See* law. 2. A **private statute**.

private nuisance [*new* · sense] *n.* A **nuisance** that threatens **injury** to one or just a few persons; a nuisance that violates only **private rights** and produces **damages** to one or no more than a few persons. *Compare* public nuisance.

private offering [*off* · er · ing] *n.* An **offering** of **securities** to a limited number of persons.

private party [*par* · tee] *n.* A **party**, other than the government, to a lawsuit or a transaction.

private person [*per* · sen] *n.* A person who does not hold a public office.

private property [*prop* · er · tee] *n.* The property of a person, as distinguished from the property of the government or a governmental body.

private prosecutor [*pross* · e · kyoo · ter] *n.* An attorney who is not herself a **public officer** who is appointed to assist the government in the prosecution of a particular criminal case. *Compare* prosecuting attorney. *See* prosecutor. *Also see* special prosecutor.

private rights *n.* Rights that a person is entitled to exercise as an individual; **personal liberty; personal rights**. EXAMPLES: the **right of privacy**; the right to travel; the right to own property.

P

private road *n.* A road that a person maintains on his own premises for his own use and the use of his **licensees, invitees**, and guests. *Compare* public road. *See* private way.

private sale *n.* A sale carried out between a buyer and a seller, as opposed to a **public sale** held by **auction** upon **public notice**. *Compare* public sale.

private school *n.* A school operated by a private person, corporation, or religious organization. *See and compare* parochial school; public school.

private statute [*stat* · shoot] *n.* A **private bill** that has been enacted into law. *Compare* public statute.

private trust *n.* A **trust** created for a purpose other than a **public purpose** or **charitable purpose**.

private university [yoo · ni · *ver* · si · tee] *n. See* private college.

private waters [*waw* · terz] *n.* A body of water that is privately owned and completely subject to private control. *Compare* navigable waters.

private way *n.* A road or way intended for the use and benefit of one or more particular persons. EXAMPLE: a **private easement**. *Compare* public way. *See* right of way. *Also see* private road.

private wrong *n.* An infringement of a right belonging to an individual, as distinguished from violation of a duty to the nation, the state, or the community; a violation of a duty due one person by another, for the breach of which the law provides a **right of action**. EXAMPLES: a **tort**; a **breach of contract**; a **trespass**. *Compare* public wrong.

privateer [pry · ve · *teer*] *n.* A vessel owned and manned by private persons acting under a **commission** or **letters of marque** from a recognized government, equipped to plunder the vessels of the enemy of the country granting the commission. *See* letters of marque and reprisal.

privately held [*pry* · vet · lee] *adj.* 1. A term applied to property or other interests owned by individuals, as opposed to property owned by the government or the public. 2. A term referring to a group of related persons, or any other small group, who own or have an interest in something, as opposed to a large group whose members hold such interests. Thus, for EXAMPLE, a **close corporation** is referred to as "privately held"; a corporation whose stock is traded on a stock exchange is referred to as **publicly held**. *See and compare* private corporation; public corporation.

privies [*priv* · eez] *n.* Persons who are in **privity** with each other. *See* privy.

privilege [*priv* · i · lej] *n.* An **immunity**, exemption, right, or advantage possessed by an individual, a group of individuals, or a class of persons, which is not possessed by others and which exists by **operation of law** or by virtue of a **license, franchise, grant**, or other permission; an exemption from a burden. Some privileges are created to further **public policy** (EXAMPLES: **conditionally privileged communications**; the **newsman's privilege**; the **journalists' privilege**). Some privileges are created to promote the government's ability to govern (EXAMPLES: the **deliberative process privilege; executive privilege**; the **franking privilege**; the **informers' privilege**). *See also* state secrets privilege. **Privileged communications** are grounded in **privileged relationships** (EXAMPLES: the **attorney-client privilege**; the **marital communications privilege**; the **physician-patient privilege**). *Also see* confidentiality.

➤ right, due, allowance, advantage, immunity; liberty, license, entitlement, power, authorization.

privilege against self-incrimination [a · *genst* self-in · krim · i · *nay* · shen] *n.* The privilege of a person accused of a crime, under the **Fifth Amendment** as well as under the constitution of every state, not to be compelled to give self-incriminating testimony. *See* self-incrimination. *See also* incriminate; incrimination. A witness who testifies voluntarily waives the privilege.

privilege from arrest [a · *rest*] *n.* **Immunity** from arrest; immunity enjoyed by diplomatic representatives of foreign nations. *See* diplomatic immunity.

privilege tax *n.* A tax upon the privilege of pursuing an occupation or business.

privileged [*priv* · i · lejd] *adj.* Entitled to a **privilege**; possessing a privilege.

P

➤ protected, excused, immune, exempt, elite ("a privileged class"); confidential, secret, exceptional, top-secret ("privileged records").

privileged communication
[kem · yoon · i · *kay* · shen] *n.* A communication between persons in a **confidential relationship** or other **privileged relationship** (EXAMPLES: husband and wife; physician and patient; attorney and client). The contents of such communications may not be testified to in court unless the person possessing the privilege waives it. *See also* privilege.

privileged relationship
[re · *lay* · shen · ship] *n.* A relationship of a type such that communications between the parties to the relationship are protected by law against disclosure (i.e., are "privileged") unless the party whom the law protects waives the right to protection. *See* privileged communication. *Also see* privilege.

privileges and immunities
[im · *yoon* · i · teez] *n. See* privileges and immunities clause.

privileges and immunities clause
[im · *yoon* · i · teez] *n.* 1. Section 2 of Article IV of the Constitution, which provides that "[t]he citizens of each state shall be entitled to all privileges and immunities of citizens in the several states." *See* immunities. 2. The clause of the **Fourteenth Amendment** which provides that "[n]o state shall make or enforce any law which shall abridge the privileges or immunities of citizens of the United States ... ." These provisions represent a constitutional requirement that a state give out-of-state residents the same **fundamental rights** as it gives its own citizens. *See* full faith and credit.

privity [*priv* · i · tee] *n.* An identity of **interest** between persons, so that the **legal interest** of one person is measured by the same **legal right** as the other; continuity of interest; successive relationships to the same **rights of property**. EXAMPLES: **decedent** and **heir; intestate** and **administrator; testator** and **executor; grantor** and **grantee**.
➤ connection, relationship, link, tie, closeness ("privity of contract").

privity in law *n.* Same as **privity**.

privity of contract [*kon* · trakt] *n.* The legal relationship between the parties to a contract. In some circumstances, a party must be in privity of contract with another party in order to assert a claim.

privity of estate [es · *tate*] *n.* The connection between the **estate** of one person and the estate of another; a succession of rights in real property. EXAMPLE: a **lessor**, a **lessee**, and their **successors**.

privity of possession [po · *zesh* · en] *n.* A continuity of **actual possession**, as between prior, present, and subsequent occupants or users of real property . *See* adverse possession; adverse user.

privy [*priv* · ee] *n.* 1. A person who is in **privity** with another person. 2. An outside toilet.
adj. Secret; hidden.
➤ *adj.* secret, buried, concealed, confidential ("privy council").

prize *n.* A sum of money or an article given as a reward to the winner of a contest.
v. To value or regard highly.
➤ *n.* reward, winnings, premium, purse.
v. value, esteem, treasure, revere.

pro (*Latin*) *prefix, prep., adv.* For; on behalf of; in proportion to; as; by way of; in favor of.

pro bono [*bone* · oh] *See pro bono publico.*

pro bono publico [*bone* · oh *poob* · li · koh] Means "for the public good." An attorney who represents an indigent client free of charge is said to be representing her client *pro bono.*

pro forma [*form* · ah] Means "as a matter of form" or "for the sake of form." A pro forma financial statement is a **financial statement** setting forth hypothetical conclusions based upon hypothetical assumptions.

pro hac vice [hak vy · see] Means "for this occasion." An attorney who is not a member of the bar of a particular state may be admitted *pro hac vice* to try an individual case in that state.

pro rata [*rah* · ta] Means "in proportion to"; proportionately according to the share, interest, or liability of each person; in proportion to some specific rate, standard, or measure. *See* proportion; prorate.

pro rata clause [*rah* · ta] *n.* 1. A clause in an insurance policy providing that the

P

insurer shall not be liable for any greater proportion of any **loss** than the amount named in the policy bears to the total amount of insurance on the property. 2. A provision in an automobile liability insurance policy stating that if the insured has other insurance against a loss covered by the policy, the insurer shall not be liable for a greater proportion of such loss than the limit of liability stated in the policy bears to the total limit of liability of all insurance which the insured has against such loss. *See* limitation of liability.

pro rata contribution [*rah* · ta kon · tri · *byoo* · shen] *n.* Contribution among several **coobligors** so that no one of them is forced to bear more than her just share of the common obligation. *Note* that a *pro rata* contribution may well not be an equal contribution. *See* contribution.

pro rata distribution [*rah* · ta dis · tri · *byoo* · shen] *n.* A distribution of **assets** to creditors, in proportion to the size of their respective claims, when there are insufficient assets for the payment of all claims in full. *See* distribution.

pro se [say] Means "for one's self." Refers to appearing on one's own behalf in either a civil action or a criminal prosecution, rather than being represented by an attorney. *See* appear; appearance. *Also see* in person.

pro tanto [*tahn* · toh] Means "for so much"; for as far as it goes; to such as extent.

pro tem Short for *pro tempore*.

pro tempore [*tem* · po · re] Means "for the time" or "temporarily"; applied to an official who fills in temporarily during the absence of the regular official (EXAMPLE: a **pro tempore judge**).

pro tempore judge [*tem* · po · re] *n.* Also referred to as **judge pro tem** or simply as a *pro tem*, a temporary or substitute judge. A judge pro tempore is appointed for all or part of a **term of court** and, during that time, exercises all of the functions of a regular judge. *See pro tempore.*

probability [prob · e · *bil* · i · tee] *n.* A likelihood, but with some uncertainty as to whether what is likely will occur. To instruct a jury that they may act on "probabilities" means they may reach a verdict on proof less than **proof beyond a reasonable doubt**. *See* jury instructions.

➤ likelihood, chance, conceivability, prospect, odds, outlook, possibility, promise.

probable [*prob* · ebl] *adj.* 1. Likely to occur, but involving an element of uncertainty. 2. A term referring to circumstances in which the **weight of the evidence** is more on one side than on the other. *See* probability.

➤ likely, apparent, expected, credible, conceivable, reasonable.
Ant. implausible, unexpected.

probable cause *n.* A reasonable amount of suspicion, supported by circumstances sufficiently strong to justify a prudent and cautious person's belief that certain alleged facts are probably true. A judge may not issue a **search warrant** unless she is shown probable cause to believe there is evidence of crime on the premises. A police officer may not make an arrest without a **warrant** unless he has reasonable cause, based upon reliable information, to believe a crime has been or is being committed. *See* reasonable belief; reasonable cause.

probable cause hearing [*heer* · ing] *n.* Same as **preliminary hearing**.

probable consequence [*kon* · se · kwense] *n.* A result that is the reasonable rather than the extraordinary result of an act or occurrence. *See* natural and probable consequence.

probable evidence [*ev* · i · dense] *n.* Same as **presumptive evidence**.

probate [*proh* · bayt] *n.* 1. The judicial act whereby a will is **adjudicated** to be valid. 2. A term that describes the functions of the **probate court**, including the probate of wills and the supervision of the accounts and actions of **administrators** and **executors** of **decedents' estates**.
v. 1. To prove a will to be valid in **probate court**. 2. To submit to the **jurisdiction** of the probate court for any purpose. *See* probate jurisdiction.

➤ *n.* validation, adjudication, verification, confirmation ("to go through probate").
v. validate, authenticate, certify, establish, substantiate ("The court must probate this will").

P

probate code *n.* The body or system of law relating to **decedents' estates** and all other matters falling within **probate jurisdiction**.

probate court *n.* A court with **jurisdiction** to probate wills and to supervise the **administration** of **decedents' estates**. In some states, probate courts appoint **guardians** and supervise **guardianships**. In some states, probate court is called **orphans' court**; in others, **surrogate's court**.

probate duty *n.* Same as **estate tax**. *See also* probate tax.

probate estate [es · *tate*] *n.* The **estate** of a **decedent** subject to the **jurisdiction** of the **probate court**.

probate jurisdiction [joo · ris · *dik* · shen] *n.* Matters with respect to which a **probate court** has both the right and the duty to exercise its authority. *See* jurisdiction.

probate proceeding [pro · *seed* · ing] *n.* Any action or step taken in or by a **probate court** in connection with the disposition of a **decedent's estate**. *See* jurisdiction. *Also see* probate jurisdiction.

probate tax *n.* Same as **estate tax**. *See also* probate duty.

probation [pro · *bay* · shen] *n.* 1. A sentence that allows a person convicted of a crime to continue to live and work in the community while being supervised by a probation officer instead of being sent to prison. A person may also be sentenced to a term of probation to commence after the expiration of his prison term. 2. A period during which a person who holds a job, position, or license, who has failed to perform according to acceptable standards, must either conform to such standards or suffer termination or loss of the license. 3. A trial period during which a newly hired employee must demonstrate her suitability for the job, and during which she has fewer rights and benefits than permanent employees. *Compare* permanent employment.
➤ conditional release, test period, trial period, parole, furlough, exemption.

probation officer [*off* · i · ser] *n.* A person who, under the direction of the court, supervises **probationers**.

probationer [pro · *bay* · shen · er] *n.* A person who has been convicted of a crime and has been sentenced to a term of **probation**.

probative [*pro* · be · tiv] *adj.* Having a tendency to prove; serving to prove. USAGE: "Irrelevant evidence is not probative, which is the reason it's inadmissible." *See* probative evidence.
➤ evidentiary, demonstrative, probatory, empirical, contributing.

probative evidence [*ev* · i · dense] *n.* **Evidence** that tends to prove a fact.

probative facts *n.* **Evidentiary facts**; facts that tend to prove **ultimate facts**.

probative value [*val* · yoo] *n.* A term used to describe the relative benefit or importance to a party's case of some item of **probative evidence**. USAGE: "A confession normally has great probative value in a criminal case."

problem [*prob* · lum] *n.* 1. A bad situation; a predicament. 2. A puzzle; a question.
➤ concern, difficulty, trouble, obstacle, case, dilemma, enigma, quandary; mystery, enigma, conundrum, riddle, stumper.

procedendo [proh · se · *den* · doh] (*Latin*) *n.* An order issued by an **appellate court** directing an **inferior court** to proceed to **judgment** in a case pending before it, but not attempting to control the inferior court with respect to what its judgment should be.

procedural [pro · *seed* · jer · el] *adj.* Pertaining to **procedure**; according to procedure. *Compare* substantive.
➤ methodical, administrative, technical, mechanical.

procedural due process [*pross* · ess] *n.* In any **action** in which a person is entitled to **due process**, she is entitled to receive both procedural due process and **substantive due process**, both of which are grounded in the **Fifth Amendment** and the **Fourteenth Amendment**. The term procedural due process implies a **proceeding** in which a person has a full opportunity to protect her rights. *Compare* substantive due process.

procedural law *n.* The law governing the manner in which rights are enforced; the law prescribing the **procedure** to be followed in a case. Also called **adjective law**, procedural law dictates *how* rights are *presented* for interpretation and enforcement, as distinguished from **substantive law**, which *creates* legal rights. The **Federal Rules of Civil Procedure**, the **Federal Rules of Criminal Procedure**, and **rules of court** are EXAMPLES of procedural laws.

procedure [pro · *seed* · jer] *n.* 1. The means or method by which a court **adjudicates** cases (EXAMPLES: the **Federal Rules of Civil Procedure**; the **Federal Rules of Criminal Procedure; rules of court**), as distinguished from the **substantive law** by which it determines **legal rights**. *See* rules of civil procedure; rules of criminal procedure. *See also* practice. 2. A specific course of action; a particular method for doing something. EXAMPLE: a medical procedure.
➤ process, system, method, policy, routine, action, operation ("to use established procedures").

proceeding [pro · *seed* · ing] *n.* 1. In one sense, every **procedural** aspect of a lawsuit, from beginning to end, including all means or **process** by which a **party** is able to cause a court to act; a suit; an **action**. 2. In another sense, any procedural aspect of a lawsuit undertaken to enforce rights or achieve **redress**. EXAMPLE: a hearing on a **motion**. 3. A specific course of action. *See* administrative proceeding; adversarial proceeding; judicial proceeding; legal proceeding; special proceeding; summary proceeding; supplementary proceeding.
➤ undertaking, course, happening ("The divorce proceeding took longer than I thought"); records, minutes, report, account, transactions ("The proceedings from GALA are kept in a file").

proceedings [pro · *seed* · ingz] *n. Plural* of **proceeding**. *See* proceeding.

proceeds [*pro* · seedz] *n.* That which is received in exchange for something, either money or some other thing of value. USAGE: "I will pay the auctioneer from the proceeds of the auction."
➤ earnings, gains, profit, results, revenue.

process [*pross* · ess] *n.* 1. In a broad sense, all of the acts of a court from the beginning to the end of an **action** or **proceeding**; the means by which the law is applied and

carried out. 2. In a technical sense, the means of compelling a defendant to appear in court in a civil case. EXAMPLES: a **summons**; a **writ**; a **warrant**. 3. In a criminal case involving a **petty offense** or an **infraction** (EXAMPLES: littering; a traffic violation), the means of compelling a defendant to appear in court, used as an alternative to arrest (EXAMPLE: a **citation**). 4. In **patent** law, an act or series of acts performed upon matter to transform and reduce it to a different state or thing. 5. A method of producing something from raw material by applying additional elements or ingredients. 6. A series of actions or occurrences; a progressive transaction; a continuous operation. *See* abuse of process; actual service of process; constructive service of process; compulsory process; foreign service of process; malicious abuse of process; malicious use of process; mesne process; original process; personal service of process; service of process; substituted service of process; trustee process; void process.
v. To handle; to deal with. USAGE: "They did not have the time to process his application."
➤ *n.* method, sequence, procedure, proceeding, routine, strategy ("The legal process can be complicated"); subpoena, writ, citation, command.
v. alter, dispose, fulfill, handle, complete, prepare ("I will process the paperwork").

process of law *n. See* process. *See also* due process of law; service of process.

process patent [*pat* · ent] *n.* A **patent** for a **new and useful** method of producing something.

process server [*ser* · ver] *n.* A person authorized by the law or by the court to **serve** process. *See* service of process.

prochein ami [proh · *shen* ah · *mee*] (*French*) *n.* Same as **next friend**.

proclamation [prok · le · *may* · shen] *n.* An official announcement by the government.
➤ broadcast, announcement, decree, notification, publication, declaration ("A proclamation went out to all the world").

procrastinate [pro · *krass* · tih · nayt] *v.* To delay or put off doing.
➤ prolong, tarry, neglect, dally, dawdle, be neglectful, be dilatory, loaf, hesitate.

P

proctor [*prok* · ter] *n.* 1. A person who is appointed to manage another person's affairs; an **attorney in fact**; a **proxy**. 2. A member of a school's faculty or staff who supervises the taking of examinations. *v.* To administer or oversee.
➤ *n.* supervisor, proxy, delegate, monitor, representative, advocate, agent, vicar.
v. oversee, administer, direct, manage, monitor.

procuration [prok · yoo · *ray* · shen] *n.* 1. A **power of attorney**. 2. The act of appointing another person as one's **attorney in fact**. 3. The act of procuring. *See* procure.

procure [pro · *kyoor*] *v.* 1. To bring about; to make something happen; to obtain. 2. To **pander**; to pimp.
➤ instigate, effect, induce, initiate, pander, pimp; acquire, obtain, get, purchase.

procurement [pro · *kyoor* · ment] *n.* The act of making something happen or obtaining something.
➤ acquisition, buying, appropriation, gaining.
procurement contract [*kon* · trakt] *n.* A contract between the government and a manufacturer or supplier. Depending upon the regulations applicable to a given type of contract, **competitive bidding** may or may not be required. *See* letting a contract.

procurer [pro · *kyoor* · er] *n.* 1. A person who brings something about or makes it happen; a person who obtains something for someone. 2. A **panderer**; a pimp.
➤ panderer, pimp, parasite ("A prostitute sometimes uses a procurer").

procuring cause [pro · *kyoor* · ing] *n.* 1. The **efficient cause** of an occurrence. 2. The act that brings about a sale or similar transaction.

prod *v.* To urge; to motivate.
➤ encourage, incite, push, induce, goad, urge, entice, propel, provoke.

prodigal [*prod* · ih · gul] *adj.* Wasteful; excessive.
➤ extravagant, careless, squandering, wasteful, thriftless, lavish, improvident, profligate.

prodition [pro · *dish* · en] *n.* **Treason**.

produce [*pro* · dewss] *n.* Products of the farm, particularly those taken to market frequently. EXAMPLES: fruit; vegetables.

v. [pro · *dewss*] 1. To bring about; to bring forward. USAGE: "If the judge grants our **motion to compel discovery**, the defendant will have to produce his **books and records**." *See* production of documents. 2. To manufacture; to make. 3. To create.
➤ *n.* crop, harvest, yield, emblements, staples, fruit, vegetables.
v. exhibit, disclose, present, show ("to produce witnesses"); concoct, create, build, manufacture, construct, materialize ("He produced great diagrams").

producing cause [pro · *dewss* · ing] *n.* Same as **procuring cause**.

product [*prod* · ukt] *n.* 1. That which is produced. EXAMPLES: automobiles; carrots; movies. 2. That which results from a course of conduct. USAGE: "Successful litigation is the product of hard work and skill." 3. The number obtained upon multiplying one number by another.
➤ result, item, article, merchandise; handiwork, outcome, accomplishment, returns.
product liability [ly · e · *bil* · i · tee] *n.* The liability of a manufacturer or seller of an article for an injury caused to a person or to property by a defect in the article sold. A product liability suit is a **tort** action in which **strict liability** is imposed. The manufacturer or seller of a defective product may be liable to third parties (EXAMPLE: bystanders) as well as to purchasers, as **privity of contract** is not a requirement in a product liability case.

production [pro · *duk* · shen] *n.* 1. The act of making something happen or bringing something forward. 2. The act of manufacturing something. 3. The act of creating. 4. A performance, particularly of a play or musical.
➤ creation, construction, preparation, formation, execution; performance, presentation, spectacle, parade, extravaganza.
production of documents [*dok* · yoo · ments] *n. See* motion to compel discovery. *Also see* discovery.
production of goods for commerce [*kawm* · erss] *n.* The business activities of a manufacturer or handler of goods in **interstate commerce** are subject to regulation by the federal government. EXAMPLES of such regulation are the **Fair Labor**

Standards Act and the **Americans with Disabilities Act**. *See also* commerce clause; in commerce.

profanity [pro · *fan* · i · tee] *n.* Conduct or words that are blasphemous or vulgar. *See* blasphemy.

➤ desecration, immorality, cursing, blasphemy, irreverence, vituperation, vulgarity.

profession [pro · *fesh* · en] *n.* 1. An occupation that requires specialized, advanced education, training, and knowledge. EXAMPLES: accounting; law; medicine. 2. A statement or declaration, especially of religious faith or belief. 3. Any assertion or declaration.

➤ trade, avocation, business, career, occupation ("profession of medicine"); declaration, assertion, claim, allegation, testimony ("profession of faith").

professional [pro · *fesh* · en · el] *adj.* Pertaining to a profession or to a person who is a professional. *See* professional (*noun*). *n.* 1. A person who is engaged in a profession. 2. A person who pursues an activity for pay, as opposed to an amateur.

➤ *adj.* skilled, trained, unique, specialized, ethical, learned, adept ("to exhibit a professional demeanor"). *n.* specialist, authority, pro, superstar, practitioner, expert, master ("to treat opposing counsel as a professional").

professional association [a · so · see · *ay* · shen] *n.* 1. A group of persons who are associated for the purpose of practicing their profession in a group other than a **partnership** or a **professional corporation**. *See* association. 2. A group of people organized into a body for the purpose of advancing the interests of their profession. EXAMPLES: the **American Bar Association**; the **National Association of Legal Assistants**; the American Chiropractic Association.

professional conduct [kon · dukt] *n.* *See* Code of Judicial Conduct; Rules of Professional Conduct. *See also* ethics.

professional corporation [kore · per · *ay* · shen] *n.* A corporation formed for the purpose of practicing a profession (EXAMPLES: law; medicine; psychotherapy; dentistry) and to secure certain tax advantages. The members of a professional corporation remain personally liable (*see* personal liability) for **professional misconduct**. Professional corporations often identify themselves by the abbreviation **PC**. Thus, for EXAMPLE, a professional corporation composed of attorneys Jessica Smith and Sam Smith might be named "Smith & Smith, Esqs., PC." *See* corporation.

professional ethics [*eth* · iks] *n.* *See* ethics. *See also* Code of Judicial Conduct; Rules of Professional Conduct.

professional legal secretary [*leeg* · el sek · re · teh · ree] *n.* A person who has met the requirements for certification by the **National Association of Legal Secretaries**.

professional liability insurance *n.* Same as **malpractice insurance**.

professional misconduct [mis · *kon* · dukt] *n.* 1. **Malpractice**. 2. In the case of an attorney, violating the **disciplinary rules** of a jurisdiction in which he practices. *See also* Rules of Professional Conduct.

professional responsibility [res · pon · si · *bil* · i · tee] *n.* A general term referring to the duties and obligations of those in the legal field; legal ethics. *See* Code of Judicial Conduct; Rules of Professional Conduct. *See* **also** ethics.

proffer [*prof* · er] *n.* 1. An **offer of proof**. 2. An **offer**. 3. The act of producing or delivering the subject matter of an offer. EXAMPLES: money; goods. *v.* 1. To make an **offer of proof**. 2. To make an **offer**. 3. To produce or deliver that which is the subject of an offer. EXAMPLES: money; goods.

➤ *n.* offer, bid, suggestion, proposal. *v.* offer, bid, tender, suggest, adduce, advance, submit, propose ("He proffered proof of his heritage").

proficient [pro · *fish* · int] *adj.* Having knowledge or skill; competent; capable.

➤ capable, skilled, able, accomplished, competent, qualified, trained, talented, experienced ("a proficient trial attorney").

profit [*prof* · it] *n.* 1. The excess of **gross receipts** or **gross proceeds** over the cost or expenses of a transaction; the excess of receipts over expenditures. 2. Gain realized from the investment of **capital**. 3. For some purposes, the equivalent of income.

P

4. Gain; benefit. *See* gross profit; mesne profits; net profit; undistributed profits; undivided profits.

v. To gain or benefit; to realize an advantage.

➤ *n.* accumulation, acquisition, proceeds, gain, earnings ("the profit from the sale").

v. gain, capitalize, benefit, realize ("to profit from mistakes").

profit à prendre [*prof* · it a *prawn* · dra] (*French*) *n.* A right exercised by one person in the land (i.e., soil or water) of another, together with participation in the profits of the land or a right to take a portion of the produce of the land. EXAMPLES: the right to harvest timber; the right to mine coal; the right to fish. *See* timber lease; timber rights. *See also* easement in gross.

profit and loss statement [*state* · ment] *n.* A **financial statement** setting forth the income and costs of a business during a given period of time. If income exceeds cost, the difference (the "bottom line") is the business's profit for the period; if cost exceeds income, the difference is the business's loss. Frequently abbreviated as "P&L."

profit corporation [kore · per · *ay* · shen] *n.* A **corporation** organized for the purpose of realizing gain (i.e., earning profit) to be distributed among its shareholders; a **business corporation**. A corporation organized for profit-making purposes is often referred to as a **for-profit corporation**, as opposed to a **nonprofit corporation**.

profit-sharing plan [-share · ing] *n.* An arrangement or plan under which the employees participate in the profits of the company that employs them. There are various types of profit-sharing plans. Most are regulated by the federal government under the **Employee Retirement Income Security Act**. All profit-sharing plans involve significant tax implications.

profitable [*prof* · it · e · bul] *adj.* Lucrative; gainful.

➤ money-making, fruitful, viable, valuable, advantageous, remunerative, paying, lucrative, worthwhile, favorable ("a profitable venture").

profiteering [prof · i · *teer* · ing] *n.* Any practice that involves acquiring excessive profits by taking unfair advantage.

➤ graft, manipulation, racketeering ("Some oil companies have been guilty of profiteering").

profits [*prof* · its] *n.* *Plural* of **profit**. *See* profit.

profligate [*prof* · lih · git] *adj.* Immoral; depraved; wasteful.

➤ corrupt, evil, wicked, depraved, immoral, base, nefarious, vile, foul.

profound [pro · *fownd*] *adj.* Intellectually deep; thoughtful.

➤ deep, perceptive, philosophical, erudite, learned, thoughtful, astute, sagacious.

progeny [*proj* · e · nee] *n.* Children; descendants; offspring.

➤ children, descendants, offspring, lineage, family.

prognosis [prog · *no* · sis] *n.* Forecast; an educated guess as to what will happen in a given situation.

➤ forecast, estimate, outlook, conjecture, guess, belief, presumption.

program [*pro* · gram] *n.* 1. An agenda of things to be done. 2. The code for a piece of computer software.

v. To plan or organize.

➤ *n.* plan, outline, schedule, system, agenda, strategy, curriculum ("the program for the evening"); software, design, code ("a computer program").

v. arrange, schedule, docket, direct, design, outline, organize.

progress [*prog* · ress] *n.* Advancement; development.

v. [pro · *gres*] To move forward.

➤ *n.* development, achievement, growth, success, improvement, movement, betterment.

v. move, press on, advance, climb, forge ahead, make headway, proceed.

progressive [pro · *gress* · iv] *adj.* Liberal in thinking.

➤ liberal, forward-thinking, advanced, corrective, modern ("a progressive attitude").

progressive tax [pro · *gress* · iv] *n.* A **graduated tax**; a tax whose rate increases as the taxable income of the taxpayer increases. *Compare* regressive tax.

prohibit [pro · *hib* · it] *v.* To forbid; to prevent; to bar; to enjoin.

P

➤ prevent, forbid, restrain, constrain, inhibit ("intended to prohibit certain behavior").

prohibited [pro · *hib* · it · ed] *adj./adv.* Referring to that which is forbidden.

➤ forbidden, banned, barred, illegal, taboo ("Incest is prohibited behavior").

prohibited degrees of consanguinity [de · *greez* of kon · sang · *gwin* · i · tee] *n.* Those degrees of blood relationship in which intermarriage is prohibited. EXAMPLE: sister and brother. *See* consanguinity. *See also* blood relatives.

prohibition [pro · hi · bish · en] *n.* 1. A **remedy** whose purpose is to prevent an **inferior court** from exercising **jurisdiction** over matters with respect to which it has no authority, or from exceeding its jurisdiction in matters with respect to which it has authority. *See* writ of prohibition. 2. A word used in reference to the **Eighteenth Amendment**, and to the federal legislation enacted under that Amendment, which prohibited the manufacture, sale, and transportation of alcoholic beverages. The period during which alcoholic beverages were prohibited in the United States (1919–1933) is commonly referred to as the "Prohibition period" or simply as "Prohibition." The Eighteenth Amendment was repealed by the **Twenty-first Amendment**. 3. A ban; a bar; an interdiction. *See* interdict.

➤ prevention, suppression, outlawing, ban, barrier.
Ant. legalization.

prohibitory injunction [pro · *hib* · i · tore · ee in · *junk* · shen] *n.* Same as **preventive injunction**.

project [*proj* · ekt] *n.* A task; an undertaking. *v.* [pro · *jekt*] 1. To extend or hang out. 2. To launch or throw. 3. To forecast or predict.

➤ *n.* task, undertaking, pursuit, venture, deal, assignment, activity, program, plan. *v.* extend, protrude, jut, stick out; propel, thrust, eject, emit, impel; forecast, guess, estimate, contemplate, visualize.

prolix [pro · *lix*] *adj.* Wordy; verbose.
➤ boring, protracted, tedious, wordy, rambling, discursive, verbose.

promiscuous [pro · *miss* · kyoo · us] *adj.* Sexually active; sexually indiscriminate.

➤ immodest, carnal, wild, unchaste, free, casual, indiscriminate.
Ant. chaste, modest, prudish.

promise [*prom* · iss] *n.* 1. In contract law, an undertaking that binds the **promisor** to cause a future event to happen; an **offer** that, if supported by **consideration**, and if **accepted**, is a **contract**. 2. In contract law, an assurance that a thing will or will not be done. It gives the person to whom it is made the right to demand the **performance** or **nonperformance** of the thing if she acted in **reliance** and to her **detriment**. *See* promissory estoppel. 3. Under the **Uniform Commercial Code**, "a written undertaking to pay money signed by the person undertaking to pay." 4. A **pledge**; a **warrant**; a **covenant**; a contract. *See* breach of promise; illusory promise; implied promise; mutual promises; naked promise; new promise. *Also see* offer. *v.* To **pledge** oneself to **performance**; to **covenant**; to **warrant**; to vouch.

➤ *n.* oath, declaration, affirmation, vow, pledge, assurance, endorsement, covenant, hope, warrant ("I have her promise of loyalty").
v. affirm, warrant, bargain, swear, vow, pledge, covenant, vouch ("I promise I will do this for you").

promise of marriage [*mehr* · ej] *n.* A **breach of promise** to marry is **actionable** under the **heart balm statutes** of some states.

promise to pay *n. See* promise.

promise to pay the debt of another [a · *nuth* · er] *n.* An undertaking by a person not previously liable to **secure** or perform another person's obligation. The original debtor, however, continues to be liable. The **statute of frauds** requires that a promise to pay someone else's debt be made in writing.

promisee [prom · i · *see*] *n.* A person to whom a promise is made.

promisor [prom · i · *sore*] *n.* A person who makes a promise.

promissory [*prom* · i · sore · ee] *adj.* Containing a promise; implying a promise.

promissory estoppel [es · *top* · el] *n.* The principle that a **promisor** will be bound

P

to a promise (that is, **estopped** to deny the promise), even though it is without **consideration**, if she intended that the promise should be relied upon and it was in fact relied upon, and if a refusal to enforce the promise would result in an injustice. EXAMPLE: a general contractor whose successful bid for a contract to construct a house incorporates a supplier's bid to him may be entitled to hold the supplier to her bid on the theory of promissory estoppel. *See* estoppel. *Also see* reliance.

promissory note *n.* A written promise to pay a specific sum of money by a specified date or **on demand**. A promissory note is **negotiable** if, in addition, it is payable to the **order** of a named person or to **bearer**. *See* negotiable instrument.

promote [pro · *mote*] *v.* 1. To give a start to something. 2. To support; to contribute to growth.
➤ support, endorse, advertise, aid, advocate, foster.

promoter [pro · *mote* · er] *n.* 1. A person who organizes a business venture or is a major participant in organizing the venture. 2. A person who promotes anything.
➤ organizer, incorporator, planner; backer, patron, sponsor, advancer, supporter.

prompt *adj.* Punctual; expeditious; timely; on time. "Prompt" is a word with no precise legal meaning; rather, it takes its meaning from the context in which it is used.
v. To hint; to stimulate; to remind.
➤ *adj.* punctual, expeditious, timely, speedy, immediate ("prompt service").
Ant. slow, late, delayed.
v. advise, cue, evoke, help, guide, refresh, remind, incite, instigate ("He prompted me on my lines").

promptly [*prompt* · lee] *adv.* Punctually; expeditiously; timely; with **reasonable diligence** in the circumstances.
➤ punctually, expeditiously, timely, fast, rapidly.

promulgate [*pro* · mul · gate] *v.* 1. To publish, announce, or proclaim and, in particular, to give official notice of a public act, for EXAMPLE, the publication of an **executive order** in the *Internal Revenue Bulletin*. 2. To enact a law or issue a

regulation. USAGE: "The Labor Department will promulgate a regulation on this subject shortly."
➤ publish, announce, proclaim, broadcast, circulate, communicate.

promulgation [pro · mul · *gay* · shen] *n.* 1. The act of promulgating. *See* promulgate. 2. A public or official announcement. 3. A law that has been enacted or a regulation or other official order that has been issued.
➤ declaration, rule, proclamation, announcement, communication, decision, mandate.

prone *adj.* 1. Disposed or inclined to do something. 2. Positioned in a horizontal manner.
➤ apt, inclined, partial, tending, disposed, compliant, willing; flat, horizontal.

pronounce [pro · *nounss*] *v.* 1. To announce formally. USAGE: "The judge will pronounce sentence tomorrow." 2. To enunciate. USAGE: "I find some foreign words difficult to pronounce."
➤ pass, rule, decide, declare, announce, articulate, judge ("the judge will pronounce sentence on him"); speak, say, articulate, recite, deliver ("pronounce the word correctly").

proof *n.* 1. The effect of evidence; the establishment of a fact by evidence. 2. The conclusion reached after considering the evidence. *Compare* evidence. *See and compare* burden of going forward; burden of proof. *See* degree of proof; failure of proof; positive proof; standard of proof.
➤ establishment, certification, confirmation, evidence, authentication, verification, assurance ("Mario has proof of the crime").

proof beyond a reasonable doubt [be · *ond* a *reez* · en · ebl] *n.* *See* beyond a reasonable doubt.

proof of claim *n.* 1. In **bankruptcy**, a statement in writing, signed by a creditor, setting forth the amount owed and the basis of the claim. 2. A written claim for money owed, filed against a **decedent's estate** in **probate court**.

proof of loss *n.* A written statement of the dollar amount of a **loss** sustained, submitted by an insured. Proof of loss is a standard requirement of **casualty insurance** policies.

P

proof of publication [pub · li · *kay* · shen] *n.* An **affidavit** or certificate of publication made by a newspaper as proof that a given **legal notice** was published. *See* newspaper of general circulation.

proof of service [*ser* · viss] *n. See* return of service.

proof to a moral certainty [*ser* · ten · tee] *n. See* moral certainty.

propensity [pro · *pen* · sih · tee] *n.* An inclination or tendency.
➤ inclination, tendency, flair, leaning, penchant, proclivity.

proper [*prop* · er] *adj.* 1. Appropriate; fitting; suitable. 2. Correct; right; valid. 3. Respectable.
➤ appropriate, fitting, suitable, correct ("proper attire"); right, valid, dignified, respectable, formal ("He is a proper person"). *Ant.* inappropriate.

proper care *n.* Same as **due care**.

proper evidence [*ev* · i · dense] *n.* Same as **admissible evidence**.

proper parties [*par* · teez] *n.* Persons who are appropriate **parties** to an **action**, but who are not **necessary parties, indispensable parties**, or **persons needed for just adjudication**; parties who are appropriate parties for **joinder**. *See* joinder of parties.

property [*prop* · er · tee] *n.* 1. The **right** of a person to **possess, use, enjoy**, and **dispose** of a thing without restriction, i.e., not the material object itself, but a person's rights with respect to the object. 2. Ownership or **title**, either **legal** or **equitable**. *See* equitable title; legal title. 3. In the more common sense, **real property** and **personal property; tangible property** and **intangible property; corporeal property** and **incorporeal property**. 4. As employed in the **Fifth Amendment** and the **Fourteenth Amendment**, the right to acquire, possess, and dispose of things and objects. 5. Anything that can be owned. *See* community property; corporeal property; incorporeal property; intangible property; literary property; mislaid property; movable property; personal property; private property; public property; qualified property; real property; separate property; special property; tangible property. *See also* chattel.

➤ possessions, investments, holdings, capital ("his property at death"); characteristic, quality, attribute, trait ("a property of water"); land, real estate, realty, territory, acreage ("a beautiful piece of property").

property agreement [a · *gree* · ment] *n. See* property settlement.

property assessment [a · *sess* · ment] *n. See* assessment.

property settlement [*setl* · ment] *n.* 1. An agreement between husband and wife settling property rights between them as part of a divorce action. Court approval may or may not be required. 2. A **judgment** by a court in a divorce case determining the rights of the parties in **marital property**. See marital agreement; separation agreement.

property tax *n.* A tax on the ownership of property, real or personal, usually assessed in proportion to its value. *See* ad valorem tax; real estate tax. *See also* personal property; real property.

prophylactic [pro · fil · *ak* · tik] *adj.* Preventive; remedial.
n. A contraceptive; a condom.
➤ *adj.* preventive, protective, salutary ("a prophylactic measure").
n. condom, rubber, device, birth control, protection.

propinquity [pro · *ping* · kwih · tee] *n.* 1. Kinship; closeness in relationship. 2. Nearness in time.
➤ affiliation, kinship, relationship, connection, consanguinity; closeness, nearness, juxtaposition.

proponent [pro · *pone* · ent] *n.* A person who proposes or advocates something. EX-AMPLES: a person who offers a will for **probate**; a person who makes a **motion** at a meeting. *See* propound.
➤ advocate, backer, champion, supporter, defender, friend ("a proponent of the new bill").

proportion [pro · *pore* · shen] *n.* The comparative relation of one thing to another, especially to the relationship of a part to the whole. *See* pro rata; pro rata contribution; prorate.
➤ apportionment, measure, share, balance, relationship.

P

proportional representation
[pro · *pore* · shen · el rep · re · zen · *tay* · shen]
n. A system of election under which
minority points of view are guaranteed
representation in an elected body.

proportionate recovery clause
[pro · *pore* · shen · et re · *kuv* · e · ree] *n.*
Same as **pro rata clause**.

proposal [pro · *poze* · el] *n.* 1. An offer or
proposition. 2. A suggestion made to induce negotiations or to solicit offers from
others. *See* induce. 3. An offer of marriage.
➤ offer, suggestion, idea, motion, outline,
report, analysis, commentary.

proposition [prop · e · *zish* · en] *n.* 1. A
proposed law or **question** submitted to
the voters at an election. *See* referendum.
2. A proposal or offer. 3. A proposal made
to a person to engage in sexual relations.
4. A statement that supports or negates
something.
➤ suggestion, scheme, invitation, plan,
tender; theory, premise, assumption.
  proposition of law *n.* 1. A **point of law**.
  2. A legal principle. *See* principle.

propound [pro · *pound*] *v.* 1. To propose;
to offer. 2. To offer a will for **probate**.
See proponent.
➤ propose, offer, advance, explain, declaim.

proprietary [pro · *pry* · e · ter · ee] *adj.*
1. Pertaining to ownership. 2. Relating to
an **exclusive right**. *See* proprietor.
➤ exclusive, private, landed, private,
restrictive ("a proprietary interest").
  proprietary drug *n.* A drug that a drug
  company has the **exclusive right** to
  manufacture.
  proprietary function [*funk* · shen] *n.*
  A function of **local government** that it
  may or may not perform, at its discretion,
  as opposed to its **governmental duties.**
  Building a stadium is an EXAMPLE of a
  proprietary function; providing police
  and fire protection is an EXAMPLE of a
  governmental duty.
  proprietary interest [*in* · trest] *n.* An
  ownership interest. *See* interest.
  proprietary lease *n.* A **lease** between a
  cooperative apartment house association
  and a tenant that includes the right to occupy
  a specific apartment. *See* association.

proprietary rights *n.* The **rights** of an
owner.

proprietor [pro · *pry* · e · ter] *n.* An owner,
usually of a business. *See* proprietary; proprietorship. *See also* sole proprietorship.
➤ owner, holder, possessor, manager,
keeper, administrator, titleholder.

proprietorship [pro · *pry* · e · ter · ship] *n.*
A business owned by one person. Such a
business is often referred to as a **sole
proprietorship**.

prorate [pro · rate] *v.* To divide or
distribute proportionately; to allocate on a
pro rata basis. *See* allocation; proportion.
USAGE: "At the **closing** on our house on
June 30, the property taxes will be pro-
rated; we will pay the taxes for half of the
year and the seller will pay the balance."
➤ divide, shave, assess, distribute, allocate.

proscribed [pro · *skribed*] *adj.* Forbidden;
prohibited.
➤ forbidden, prohibited, censured,
denounced, excluded ("The proscribed
behavior is clearly specified").
Ant. welcome, allowed.

prosecute [*pross* · e · kyoot] *v.* 1. To
commence or **maintain** a **criminal action**.
USAGE: "The district attorney has announced
she will prosecute Lee for arson." 2. To
commence or maintain a **civil action**.
USAGE: "Sam insists he will prosecute his
libel action regardless of the cost." 3. To
pursue or carry forward an undertaking
that has been started. USAGE: "Leslie understands that, because her agent can't be with
her during the negotiations, it's up to her
to prosecute her own interests." *See*
prosecution.
➤ indict, litigate, sue, arraign ("She will prosecute this case"); persevere, conduct, direct,
execute, manage ("Leslie understands it's
up to her to prosecute her own interests").

prosecuting [*pross* · e · kyoo · ting] *adj.*
Relating or pertaining to a prosecution or
to a person who prosecutes.
  prosecuting attorney [a · *tern* · ee] *n.*
  A public official, elected or appointed, who
  conducts criminal prosecutions on behalf
  of his jurisdiction. *See* prosecutor.
  prosecuting witness [*wit* · ness] *n.* A
  person upon whose **complaint** a criminal

prosecution is begun and, generally speaking, the person on whose testimony it depends. Also called a complaining witness.

prosecution [pross · e · *kyoo* · shen] *n.* 1. A **criminal action** brought by the government. In this context, the government (or "**state**" or "**people**") is commonly referred to as "the prosecution." 2. The act of commencing or **maintaining** a criminal action. 3. The act of commencing or maintaining a **civil action**. 4. The act of pursuing or carrying forward an undertaking that has been started. *See* prosecute.
➤ litigation, trial, suit, proceedings, action; district attorney, state's attorney, government, state, people.

prosecutor [pross · e · kyoo · ter] *n.* 1. A public official, elected or appointed, who conducts criminal prosecutions on behalf of her jurisdiction. EXAMPLES: the **district attorney** of a county; the **attorney general** of a state; a **United States Attorney**. *See* prosecuting attorney. *See and compare* private prosecutor; public prosecutor. 2. A person who commences or **maintains** a **civil action**.
➤ public officer, district attorney, prosecuting attorney, solicitor, attorney general.

prosecutrix [pross · e · *kyoo* · trix] *n.* A rather outdated term for a woman who commences or maintains a lawsuit. *See* prosecutor. *Also see* prosecute.

prosequi [pross · e · kwee] (*Latin*) *See nolle prosequi.*

prospect [pros · pekt] *n.* 1. A possibility for the future. 2. An applicant, customer, or client.
➤ outlook, forecast, chance, likelihood ("the prospects for success"); recruit, candidate, client ("a highly regarded prospect").

prospective [pro · *spek* · tiv] *adj.* 1. Having to do with the future. 2. Anticipated; expected.
➤ anticipated, potential, expected, future, intended ("a prospective client").
  prospective damages [*dam* · e · jez] *n.* Same as **future damages.**
  prospective heir [air] *n.* An **heir apparent** or **heir presumptive**.
  prospective law *n. See* prospective statute.

prospective statute [*stat* · shoot] *n.* A statute that has no application to transactions that occurred, or rights that accrued, before it went into effect. *Compare* retrospective legislation.

prospector [*pross* · pek · ter] *n.* A person who explores an area for minerals or who works a mining claim for the purpose of assessing its worth.

prospectus [pro · *spek* · tus] *n.* A statement published by a corporation that provides information concerning stock or other securities it is offering for sale to the public. The contents of a prospectus are regulated by the **Securities Exchange Commission**. *See* registration statement.
➤ details, design, list, program, synopsis, statement, résumé ("CSX's prospectus is impressive").

prostitute [*pross* · ti · toot] *n.* A person who engages in prostitution.
  v. To sell oneself for sexual intercourse or for a low or unworthy purpose; to degrade oneself.
➤ *n.* whore, hooker, harlot, tart, call girl, rent boy.
  v. degrade, belittle, demean, taint, desecrate.

prostitution [pross · ti · *too* · shen] *n.* Engaging in sexual intercourse or other sexual activity for pay. A man as well as a woman may be a prostitute.
➤ sex for hire, debauchery, solicitation.

protagonist [pro · *tag* · uh · nist] *n.* The main character in a story.
➤ hero, principal character, leading agent.

protect [pro · *tekt*] *v.* To defend oneself, another, or a cause.
➤ secure, look after, take care of, preserve, safeguard, shield, conserve, immunize, support, guard.

protection *n.* 1. Money paid to racketeers to prevent violence against one's person or property. *See* racketeering. 2. Money paid to corrupt public officials, including police officers, by persons involved in crime so that their criminal activities will be ignored. 3. The act of keeping something or someone safe.
➤ custody, preservation, support, cover ("I needed his protection"); money, bribe,

P

racketeering ("Vera demanded protection from the shop owner if he didn't want the windows broken").

protection order [or · der] *n.* An **order** granted by a court in a **domestic relations** case, usually *ex parte*, restraining a spouse or partner from abusing or otherwise illegally interfering with the other spouse or partner or children in the household. *Note* that a "protection order" is not a "**protective order**." *See* restraining order. *See also* child abuse; spousal abuse.

protective [pro · *tek* · tiv] *adj.* That which provides protection.
➤ guarding, securing, careful, safeguarding, watchful ("protective custody").

protective custody [*kuss* · te · dee] *n.* **Custody** that is exercised for a person's own good. EXAMPLE: the confining of a **material witness** whose life has been threatened.

protective order [or · der] *n.* An **order of court** protecting a person from harassment by excessive **discovery, process**, or the like; it is requested by a **party** by means of a **motion for protective order**. *Note* that a "protective order" is not a "**protection order**."

protective tariff [*tehr* · iff] *n.* A **tariff** whose purpose is to discourage imports and, in so doing, to protect domestic industry from foreign competition.

protective trust *n.* A type of **spendthrift trust**.

protest [pro · test] *n.* 1. A formal declaration by a notary public that a specified **negotiable instrument** presented by the **holder** for **payment** or **acceptance** was refused, and giving the reasons for refusal. *See* dishonor; presentment. 2. The expression "**under protest**" means that the person receiving an article objects to accepting it in its present condition, that he accepts it only because circumstances require it, and that he reserves his right to **recover** the purchase price. 3. The procedure employed by a person who questions her liability (for EXAMPLE, to pay a tax in the amount **assessed**), thereby creating a basis for recovery of the amount paid. 4. A **remonstrance**. 5. An objection; an

exception. *See* note of protest; notice of protest; waiver of protest.
v. 1. To dissent or resist. 2. To affirm or assent.
➤ *n.* objection, resistance, revolt, demonstration, exception, defiance.
v. dissent, oppose, complain, object, challenge, dispute ("to protest the new policy"); affirm, assert, proclaim, allege, maintain, propound ("to protest her innocence").

prothonotary [pro · *thon* · noh · ter · ee] *n.* In some states, a **clerk of court**, particularly a chief clerk.
➤ clerk, official, officer ("Jim was a prothonotary of Cobb County Court").

protocol [*pro* · toh · koll] *n.* 1. A **memorandum** version of a contract or **treaty**, or of the minutes of a meeting. 2. Ceremonial etiquette governing official conduct toward heads of state and their **diplomatic representatives**.
➤ agreement, code, compact; custom, decorum, etiquette, courtesy.

provable [*proov* · uh · bul] *adj.* That which is capable of being proved or verified.
➤ incontestable, confirmable, indisputable, verifiable ("a provable claim").

prove *v.* To establish a fact by the required degree of evidence. *See* proof. *See also* degree of proof; standard of proof.
➤ establish, affirm, ascertain, attest, certify, explain, substantiate, verify, justify, show.

proved *adj.* Same as **proven**, but not as commonly used.

proven [*proo* · ven] *adj.* To have established a fact. "Proven" and "**proved**" have the same meaning, but proven is more commonplace. *See* prove.
➤ authentic, certified, established, settled, tested ("The test has been proven to be accurate").

proverbial [pro · *verb* · ee · el] *adj.* Traditional; commonly spoken of.
➤ well-known, familiar, commonplace, legendary, traditional ("the proverbial 'reasonable person'").

provide [pro · *vide*] *v.* 1. To supply. 2. To make preparations. 3. To determine or specify.
➤ supply, deliver, furnish, equip, feed, stock, sustain ("provide materials"); plan,

P

prepare, organize, ready ("provide for their arrival"); state, stipulate, require, postulate ("The contract provided for that contingency").

provided [pro · *vy* · ded] *past part.* 1. Upon condition. "Provided" is a word that creates a proviso or a provision. USAGE: "I leave my entire estate to my son Bill, provided he graduates from law school." 2. Arranged for, required, or specified in advance. USAGE: "She has provided for her children in her will." *See* provision.

provided by law *adj.* Required or made possible by law, usually by a statute.

provident [*prov* · ih · dent] *adj.* 1. Frugal; unwasteful. 2. Careful; judicious.
➤ frugal, careful, prudent, thrifty; circumspect, discerning, thoughtful, vigilant.

province [*prov* · inss] *n.* 1. A **political subdivision** in some countries, comparable to a state in the United States. USAGE: "Nova Scotia is a province of Canada." 2. A duty, function, or area of responsibility. USAGE: "Surgery is not within the province of a psychologist."
➤ district, county, division, zone, subdivision ("Nova Scotia is a province of Canada"); duty, function, expertise, authority, responsibility ("Surgery is not within the province of a psychologist").

provincial [pro · *vinch* · ul] *adj.* 1. Limited or unsophisticated. 2. Relating to the country; nonurban.
➤ narrow, limited, illiberal, insular, parochial ("a provincial attitude"); countrified, bucolic, pastoral, rustic ("a provincial setting").

provision [pro · *vizh* · en] *n.* 1. A clause in an **instrument** or statute dealing with a particular matter or subject. *See* proviso. 2. Money sent to the **drawee** of a **bill of exchange** by the **drawer** so that she can pay it when it is **presented**. 3. Arrangements made in advance.
➤ supplies, arrangement, foundation, stockpile ("He had provisions set up for the flood"); condition, clause, term, article, qualification ("per the provision in the will").

provisional [pro · *vizh* · en · el] *adj.* That which is merely temporary.
➤ contingent, tentative, conditional, limited ("the provisional government").

provisional injunction [in · *junk* · shen] *n.* A **preliminary injunction**.

provisional order [*or* · der] *n.* An **interlocutory order**.

provisional remedy [*rem* · e · dee] *n.* A **remedy** sought not as an **adjudication** of the **issues**, but as a means of preventing the **adverse party** from taking some action (EXAMPLE: transferring **assets**) that would defeat any **judgment** obtained in the case. A **writ of attachment** is an EXAMPLE of a provisional remedy, as is a **temporary injunction**.

proviso [pro · *vy* · zoh] *n.* A clause, provision, or stipulation in a deed, contract, or statute that imposes a condition, restriction, or limitation. *Compare* exception.
➤ clause, provision, condition, stipulation.

provocation [prov · e · *kay* · shen] *n.* Words or conduct that incite anger or passion or that cloud judgment and the ability to reason. A **homicide** that is the direct result of provoked anger and resentment is **manslaughter** rather than **murder** if, in the circumstances, the defendant's act was the act of a **reasonable person** and if the killing occurred in the **heat of passion**.
➤ incitement, stimulus, prompt, instigation, agitation, enragement, causation, incentive ("His provocation started the fight").

provocative [pro · *vok* · a · tiv] *adj.* 1. Exciting or stimulating, especially sexually. 2. Serving to draw or attract attention.
➤ alluring, titillating, arresting, ravishing, seductive, exciting; interesting, intriguing, influential, persuasive, thought-provoking.

provoke [pro · *voke*] *v.* To incite; to make angry. *See* provocation.
➤ incite, arouse, cause, prompt, goad, force, affront, upset, infuriate, irk ("Mike provoked the attack").
Ant. stop, block, calm.

proximate [*prok* · si · met] *adj.* Near; nearest; close; immediate.
➤ near, nearest, close, immediate, expected, following, connected.
Ant. remote, distant.

proximate cause *n.* As an element of liability in a **tort** case, that **cause** which,

P

unbroken by any **intervening cause**, produced the **injury**, and without which the result would not have occurred; the primary cause; the **efficient cause**. *Note* that the proximate cause of an injury is not necessarily the final cause or the act or omission nearest in time to the injury. *Compare* remote cause. *Also compare* immediate cause. *See* concurrent cause; legal cause; producing cause.

proximate consequences [kon · se · kwen · sez] *n.* See **proximate result**.

proximate damages [dam · e · jez] *n.* As opposed to **remote damages, damages** that may be recovered in a **tort** case, i.e., damages that are the direct result of the wrongful act. *Also see* direct damages.

proximate result [re · zult] *n.* A result (EXAMPLE: an **injury**) that is the direct consequence of a given act or omission. *See* proximate cause.

proximately [prok · si · met · lee] *adv.* Directly; effectively; immediately. *See* proximate.

proxy [prox · ee] *n.* 1. A person who holds an authorization to act in the place of another. 2. An authorization, usually in writing, under which one person acts for another. 3. Authority given in writing by one shareholder in a corporation to another shareholder to exercise her voting rights for her.
➤ representative, delegate, emissary, agent, broker ("Joe was my proxy at the meeting"); authorization, power ("I gave her my proxy").

proxy holder [hole · der] *n.* A person who holds another person's **proxy** and is therefore authorized to act in that person's place. *See* holder.

proxy marriage [mehr · ej] *n.* A marriage ceremony in which another person, or other persons, stand in for one or both of the parties. Proxy marriages are most common during wartime when either the bride or the groom, or both, are overseas in the military service.

proxy statement [state · ment] *n.* A statement sent to shareholders whose proxies are being solicited so that they may be voted at an upcoming stockholders' meeting. The statement, whose contents are regulated by the **Securities and Exchange Commission**, provides shareholders with the information necessary for them to decide whether to give their proxies.

prudence [proo · dense] *n.* The quality of being prudent.
➤ precaution, planning, diligence, wisdom. *Ant.* sloppiness, negligence.

prudent [proo · dent] *adj.* Sensible; cautious; exercising judgment. In the law of **negligence**, the words "prudent" and "cautious" are used interchangeably.
➤ sensible, cautious, reasonable, careful, sound, guarded. *Ant.* careless, reckless.

prudent man *n.* A **reasonable man, reasonable person**, or **ordinary prudent person**. Used in negligence law to describe the general standard of care owed to an individual. *See* reasonable man test. *Also see* prudent man rule.

prudent man rule *n.* A rule of **trust** law which declares that a **trustee** may make only such investments as a **prudent man** would make of his own property. *See* safe investment rule.

prudent person [per · sen] *n.* See reasonable man test.

prurient [proo · ree · ent] *adj.* Relating to a vulgar or debauched interest in sex or nudity.
➤ erotic, sexual, obscene, lewd, vulgar, carnal, ribald, lustful ("an appeal to prurient interests").

prurient interest [proo · ree · ent in · trest] *n.* Undue attention given to lewd, lascivious, or lustful things. *See* obscene; obscenity; pornographic; pornography.

PS Abbreviation of **public statute**.

PSC Abbreviation of **public service commission**.

psilocybin [sy · lo · sy · bin] *n.* A hallucinogenic drug, derived from a species of mushroom, that often produces temporary psychosis as a side effect. Psilocybin is a **controlled substance**; its possession, distribution, or sale is a criminal offense. *See* hallucinogen.

psychoactive [sy · ko · ak · tiv] *adj.* A word describing any drug that affects the mind.

P

psychoneurosis [sy · ko · new · *roh* · sis] *n.* Same as **neurosis**.

psychosis [sy · *koh* · sis] *n.* A mental disorder in which the personality is severely disordered. *Compare* neurosis. *See* insanity.
➤ mental disorder, illness, disease, insanity.

public [*pub* · lik] *adj.* Belonging to the entire community; that in which all members of the community may participate on an unrestricted basis.
n. 1. The people; all the people in a state, county, or town; the community as a whole. 2. Any portion of the entire community other than one, several, or a few.
➤ *adj.* unrestricted, accessible, common, communal, available, national ("U.S. parks are public areas").
n. people, community, citizenry, society.

public accommodation [a · kawm · e · *day* · shen] *n.* 1. A central term in the **Civil Rights Act of 1964**, which outlawed racial discrimination in "public accommodations" operating in **interstate commerce**. EXAMPLES: restaurants; hotels; bus stations. *See* Civil Rights Acts. *Also see* engaged in commerce. 2. Any place that serves the public.

public accountant [a · *koun* · tent] *n.* An accountant who has not been certified by the state to practice as a **certified public accountant**. The distinction between a public accountant and a certified public accountant is increasingly unimportant today, as almost every state requires newly graduated accountants to be certified.

public administrator [ad · *min* · is · tray · ter] *n.* A public official who administers the **estates** of **decedents** if no one else qualifies to act as a **personal representative**. *See* administrator.

public agency [*ay* · jen · see] *n.* An **administrative agency**.

public assistance [a · *sis* · tense] *n.* A term referring to **publicly funded** programs to assist the poor. (EXAMPLES: **AFDC; general relief**; food stamps; the **Legal Services Corporation**.) Public assistance is commonly referred to as welfare.
➤ welfare, charity, assistance, benevolence.

public attorney [a · *tern* · ee] *n.* An attorney at law.

public auction [*awk* · shen] *n.* A **public sale** to the highest bidder. *See* auction.

public authority [aw · *thaw* · ri · tee] *n.* 1. An agency created by government for the construction and operation of a **public work**. EXAMPLES: a **port authority**; a **housing authority**. 2. The authority of government.

public bill *n.* A legislative **bill** that affects the community at large. *Compare* private bill. *See* public law; public statute.

public body [*bod* · ee] *n.* 1. A **public corporation**. 2. Any governmental body.

public building [*bil* · ding] *n.* A building owned or leased by the government and used for a public purpose, for EXAMPLE, a courthouse or a post office.

public carrier [*kehr* · ee · er] *n.* Same as **common carrier**.

public charge *n.* A person who cannot support himself and must depend upon **public assistance**. *See* indigent.

public college [*koll* · ej] *n.* A college founded or supported almost exclusively by a state, county, or city. *Compare* private college.

public contract [*kon* · trakt] *n.* A contract for the construction of a **public improvement** or **public works**, or for the furnishing of supplies or services to a the government.

public convenience and necessity [ken · *veen* · ee · ense and ne · *sess* · i · tee] *n.* A statutory **condition precedent** in most states to the ability of the **public utility commission** to grant a **franchise** to a **public service corporation** to operate a **public utility**. As used in this phrase, "necessity" does not mean "indispensability," but implies only a public need; "convenience" here means that the public will be inconvenienced unless the franchise is granted.

public corporation [kore · per · *ay* · shen] *n.* 1. A **government corporation**. 2. A **municipal corporation**. 3. A corporation whose stock is traded on a stock exchange, as opposed to a **closely held corporation**. *See* corporation. *Compare* private corporation.

public debt *n.* 1. The total sum owed by a government, for EXAMPLE, a nation, a state,

P

or a town. 2. A **bond** or similar obligation of the government, for EXAMPLE, a **municipal bond** or a **treasury note**.

public defender [de · *fen* · der] *n.* An attorney appointed by the court to represent indigent persons in criminal cases. *Compare* private attorney.

public document [*dok* · yoo · ment] *n.* 1. Any document on file in a **public office** that the public has the right to inspect. *See* document. 2. Any document that is a **matter of record**. 3. Any publication printed by order of Congress or a state legislature. *See* public record.

public domain [do · *mane*] *n.* 1. Land owned by the United States or by a state. *See* Bureau of Land Management. 2. In **copyright** law, a literary composition or other work that has not been copyrighted or with respect to which the copyright has expired.

public drunkenness [*drunk* · en · ness] *n.* Same as **public intoxication**.

public easement [*eez* · ment] *n.* An **easement** that confers a benefit upon the public in general. *Compare* private easement.

public employee [em · *ploy* · ee] *n.* An employee of federal, state, or local government.

public figure [*fig* · yer] *n.* A person whose fame is such that the public has a legitimate interest in her or his activities. A public figure surrenders at least a part of the **right of privacy**. With respect to the law of **defamation**, the press is privileged to comment on public figures as long as such comment is without **malice** and is based upon the honest belief that what is said is true. *See* journalists' privilege.

public funds *n.* Money belonging to government. *See* publicly funded.

public health *n.* Public health, whose regulation is basic to a government's **police power**, includes concerns such a community sanitation standards, food inspection, and pollution control. Public health is a legitimate concern of government at all levels, whether federal, state, or local. *See* sanitary codes. *Also see* public safety.

public hearing [*heer* · ing] *n.* A **hearing** that is open to the public. *See* public trial.

public housing [*how* · zing] *n.* Housing subsidized by public funds and made available at low cost to people of limited means. Public housing is constructed and maintained by local **housing authorities**.

public improvement [im · *proov* · ment] *n.* An **improvement** planned or constructed by government for the use of the public. EXAMPLES: a library; a park; a power station.

public indecency [in · *dee* · sen · see] *n.* Lewd or lascivious conduct that is open to public view. EXAMPLE: **indecent exposure**.

public injury [*in* · je · ree] *n. See* public wrong.

public international law [in · ter · *nash* · en · el] *n.* The body of law that regulates questions of rights between nations, as opposed to **private international law**, which governs the rights of persons of one country in their dealings with persons of another country.

public intoxication [in · tok · si · *kay* · shen] *n.* The condition of being intoxicated in a public place.

public land *n.* Land that is in the **public domain**. *See* public property.

public law *n.* 1. Body of law dealing with the relationship between the people and their government, the relationship between agencies and branches of government, and the relationship between governments themselves. EXAMPLES: **criminal law; constitutional law; administrative law**. *Compare* private law. 2. A statute dealing with matters that concern the community as a whole. *Compare* private law. *See* law.

public laws *n.* Statutes, particularly **public statutes**. *See also* public law.

public liability insurance [ly · e · *bil* · i · tee in · *shoor* · ense] *n.* Same as **liability insurance**.

public money [*mun* · ee] *n.* Same as **public funds**.

public notice [*noh* · tiss] *n.* **Notice** given by means of posting in a **public place**, for EXAMPLE, a courthouse, or by publication in a **newspaper of general circulation**. *See* legal notice.

public nuisance [*new* · sense] *n.* An act or omission that adversely affects the safety, health, or morals of the public, or causes some substantial annoyance, inconvenience, or **injury** to the public. The "public" may,

P

for EXAMPLE, be everyone living along a polluted river; it may also simply be one's immediate neighbors. *See* nuisance. *Compare* private nuisance.

public offering [*off* · e · ring] *n.* *See* offering.

public office [*off* · iss] *n.* 1. An **office** whose duties, to some degree at least, consist of carrying out the **sovereign powers** of the state. The term is not synonymous with "public employment" because it does not apply to a position whose duties are merely clerical or **ministerial**; rather, it implies a position with responsibility to administer the law. 2. A place where the business of the public is carried out.

public officer [*off* · i · ser] *n.* A term that may appropriately be used interchangeably with **public official**, although it is not uncommon to limit its use to references to **police officers** or **officers of the court**.

public official [o · *fish* · el] *n.* A person who holds a **public office**, whether elected or appointed, and who carries out the functions of that office. The term includes public employees and thus contemplates, for EXAMPLE, a congressperson as well as a police officer, because both have duties relating to the **sovereign powers** of government which concern the public and which are assigned to them by law. The term does not, however, include all public employees, as it is not applicable to persons whose duties are purely **ministerial**. *See* public office; public officer.

public place *n.* A place commonly used by the general public or that the public has a right to use. EXAMPLES: a park; a street; a community swimming pool.

public policy [*pol* · i · see] *n.* A term referring to the concept that law should properly be created, interpreted, and applied in a manner that promotes the good and welfare of the people. To violate public policy means to act contrary to the norms and values of a society or community. If a contract violates public policy, it is void. *See* public welfare.

public property [*prop* · er · tee] *n.* Property belonging to the nation or a state, or to a **political subdivision** of a state, for EXAMPLE, a county, a city, or a town. *See* public land.

public prosecutor [*pross* · e · kyoo · ter] *n.* Same as **prosecuting attorney**.

public purpose [*per* · pes] *n.* A term describing that which is a recognized object of government, i.e., that which promotes the welfare of the community. Property used for a public purpose is exempt from taxation; similarly, property may be taken by **eminent domain** only if the taking is for a public purpose. *See* governmental purpose. *See also* condemnation.

public record [*rek* · erd] *n.* Any document or record that the law requires a public employee or public official to maintain as a **public document**. *See also* of record.

public road *n.* A road open to everyone. *Compare* private road; private way.

public safety *n.* By virtue of its **police power**, government may enact statutes or ordinances ensuring the safety of the public, including, for EXAMPLE, criminal statutes, traffic regulations, and building codes. *See* public health.

public sale *n.* A sale of property at auction, made after notice has been given to the public so that the public will have the opportunity to bid competitively. *Compare* private sale. *See* auction; public auction. *See also* foreclosure sale; judicial sale.

public school *n.* A school maintained by state, county, or **local government**, open to all on equal terms without the payment of tuition. Public schools are constructed, maintained, and staffed with public funds. *Compare* parochial school; private school.

public seal *n.* *See* official seal.

public securities [sek · *yoo* · ri · teez] *n.* **Bonds** or **notes** issued by a state, **local government**, or some other public body. *See* securities.

public service [*ser* · viss] *n.* 1. A term for utility service, for EXAMPLE, gas, electricity, or public transportation. Companies that provide such service under **franchise** from the government (usually, state or **local government**) are generally **private corporations** known as **public service corporations**. Public service corporations enjoy privileges not enjoyed by other citizens, chief among them freedom from competition. In turn, they are more closely regulated than most private businesses.

P

In every state, such regulation is carried out by a **public service commission** or **public utility commission**. *See also* public utility; quasi-public corporation. 2. A term for service rendered for or on behalf of the government.

public service commission [*ser* · viss ke · *mish* · en] *n.* A state agency to which the state legislature has delegated the power to regulate **public utilities**, including **rate making**.

public service company [*ser* · viss *kum* · pe · nee] *n.* Same as **public service corporation** or **public utility**.

public service corporation [*ser* · viss kore · per · *ay* · shen] *n.* A **private corporation** (sometimes referred to as a **quasi-public corporation**) that supplies a public service (EXAMPLES: electricity; gas; train service; telephone service; cable television) to the public. A public service corporation is also referred to as a **public utility**.

public statute [*stat* · shoot] *n.* A statute that affects the community as a whole; a **public law**. *Compare* private bill.

public trial [*try* · el] *n.* A trial that is not secret; a trial that the public may attend. A public trial is guaranteed by the **Sixth Amendment**. *See also* open court.

public trust *n.* 1. A **charitable trust**. 2. A **public office**.

public university [yoo · ni · *ver* · si · tee] *n. See* public college.

public use *n.* 1. The use of premises by the public at large, that is, the general public, rather than one person or a limited number of persons. 2. In **patent** law, any use of an invention other than a secret or experimental use. 3. For the purpose of the government's exercise of the power of **eminent domain**, "public use" means use of the property by the public after it is condemned, or by some portion of the public or some **public agency** on behalf of the public. See also condemnation.

public utility [yoo · *til* · i · tee] *n.* A corporation or business that renders a **public service**. *See* public service corporation.

public utility commission [yoo · *til* · i · tee ke · *mish* · en] *n.* In some states, the name for the **public service commission**.

public verdict [*ver* · dikt] *n.* A **verdict** delivered by the jury in **open court**.

public way *n.* A road, way, highway, or **public easement** intended for use or used by the public at large, as opposed to a **private way**. *See* right of way.

public welfare [*wel* · fare] *n.* The physical, economic, aesthetic, and spiritual interests of the community.

public works *n.* **Works** constructed by **public agencies** for public use. EXAMPLES: highways; public buildings; docks. *See also* public contract; public improvement.

public wrongs *n.* Violations of the duties owed to the whole community. EXAMPLES: crimes; **public nuisances**.

publication [pub · li · *kay* · shen] *n.* 1. A newspaper, magazine, or book. 2. The act of making something known to the public; the act of publishing. *See* publish. 3. The printing of a **legal notice** in a **newspaper of general circulation**. 4. A means of **service of process**, when authorized by statute. *See* service by publication. 5. With respect to **copyright** and the law of **literary property**, the act of making a writing, voice recording, musical score, or the like available to the public by sale or other form of distribution. 6. In the law of **libel** and **slander**, the act of communicating a **defamation** to a person or persons other than the person defamed. Publication is essential because, without it, there is no defamation.

▶ newspaper, book, magazine, brochure, leaflet, pamphlet ("a respected publication"); presentation, circulation, publishing, announcement, disclosure, discovery, notification, revelation ("publication in the newspaper").

publication of a forgery [*fore* · jer · ee] *n. See* uttering a forged instrument.

publication of process [*pross* · ess] *n. See* service by publication.

publication of summons [*sum* · enz] *n. See* service by publication.

publication of will *n.* A statement of intention made by a **testator**, on the occasion of the execution and **attestation** of her will, to the effect that the instrument does in fact represent her wishes with respect to the disposition of her **estate**.

P

publicly funded [*pub* · lik · lee *fun* · ded] *adj.* Funded or paid for with public money, that is, out of funds raised through taxes or by the sale of **public securities**. USAGE: "The library addition is a publicly funded project."

publicly held [*pub* · lik · lee] *adj.* 1. A phrase referring to corporations that, indirectly at least, are owned by the public. EXAMPLES: a **municipal corporation**; a **government corporation**. *See* public corporation. 2. A phrase referring to corporations whose stock is held by members of the public and is for sale to the public, generally through stock exchanges. *Compare* privately held.

publish [*pub* · lish] *v.* 1. To issue; to distribute; to disseminate; to circulate. 2. To communicate; to announce; to advertise. 3. To **utter**. *See* uttering a forged instrument. *Also see* publication.
➤ issue, distribute, disseminate, circulate ("publish a newspaper"); communicate, announce, advertise, spread ("publish an opinion").
Ant. suppress, inhibit.

publisher [*pub* · lish · er] *n.* A person who publishes something.

PUC Abbreviation of **public utility commission**.

puffery *See* puffing.

puffing [*puf* · ing] *v./n.* Exaggerating. A seller who "talks up" what he is selling by praising it is not guilty of **fraudulent misrepresentation** so long as he confines himself to his own opinion and does not misrepresent a **material fact**. Such salesmanship is "mere puffing."
➤ exaggerating, augmenting, boosting, hyping, pushing.

punishable [*pun* · ish · ebl] *adj.* Liable to punishment.
➤ indictable, chargeable, impeachable, culpable ("Her crime was punishable by a ten-year sentence").

punishment [*pun* · ish · ment] *n.* 1. The penalty for violating the law, which may include imprisonment, fine, or **forfeiture**. Punishment, in the legal sense, is imposed by a judge, either as a sentence in a criminal case or as a **civil penalty** in a civil action. *See* penalty. *See also* capital punishment;

corporal punishment; cruel and unusual punishment; infamous punishment. 2. The treatment of a person who breaks the rules, most commonly a child, by a parent or teacher.
➤ fine, penalty, chastisement, sentence, correction, infliction, deprivation, sanction.

punitive [*pyoon* · i · tiv] *adj.* Having to do with punishment.
➤ correctional, disciplinary, punishing, avenging, retributive ("Strong punitive measures will be sought").

punitive damages [*dam* · e · jez] *n.* **Damages** that are awarded over and above **compensatory damages** or **actual damages** because of the wanton, reckless, or malicious nature of the wrong done by the plaintiff. Such damages bear no relation to the plaintiff's actual **loss** and are often called **exemplary damages**, because their purpose is to make an example of the plaintiff to discourage others from engaging in the same kind of conduct in the future. *See also* treble damages.

punitive statute [*stat* · shoot] *n.* A statute that creates a **forfeiture** or imposes a penalty.

pur autre vie [per *oh* · tra vee] (*French*) *adj.* Same as *per autre vie*.

purchase [*per* · ches] *n.* 1. The transfer of property from one person to another for a **consideration**. *See* words of purchase. 2. Under the **Uniform Commercial Code**, any voluntary transaction creating an **interest** in property. Under this definition, which applies largely but not exclusively to personal property, a purchase includes a gift as well as a sale, discount, **negotiation, mortgage, pledge,** or **lien**. The term also applies to an **agreement of sale**. *See also* words of purchase.
v. 1. To buy; to acquire by purchase. *See* purchase (*noun*). 2. In a more technical and limited sense, to acquire **title** to land by means other than **descent**.
➤ *n.* acquisition, procurement, investment, property, asset ("My purchase was a valuable piece of art").
v. buy, obtain, acquire, earn, achieve, procure, attain.

purchase agreement [a · *gree* · ment] *n.* *Same as* agreement of sale.

P

purchase money [*mun* · ee] *n.* Money paid by a purchaser to a seller or vendor. It may be either the entire **consideration** in a lump sum, or it may be a downpayment (the balance being **secured** by a mortgage or a **security agreement**). *See* purchase money mortgage; purchase money security interest.

purchase money mortgage [*mun* · ee *more* · gej] *n.* 1. A **mortgage** executed by a purchaser of real property to **secure** her obligation to pay the purchase price. 2. With respect to personal property, *see* security agreement. *See also* purchase money security interest.

purchase money resulting trust [re · *zult* · ing] *n.* When one person pays money to another for real estate and directs that person to **convey** the land to the third person, a **resulting** trust is created for the benefit for the **payor**. In other words, in a circumstance where A pays the purchase price of land to B, and B, at A's direction, executes a deed to C, C is deemed, by **operation of law**, to hold the land as **trustee** for A. *See* trust.

purchase money security interest [*mun* · ee se · *kyoo* · ri · tee *in* · trest] *n.* A **security interest** created when a **security agreement** is executed by a purchaser of personal property. *Compare* purchase money mortgage.

purchase order [*or* · der] *n.* A document requesting a seller to sell specific items to a purchaser.

purchase price *n.* The agreed-upon price or **consideration** to be furnished by a buyer to a seller.

purchaser [*per* · ches · er] *n.* A person who acquires property by purchase. *See* bona fide purchaser; innocent purchaser.
➤ buyer, customer, client, owner, investor.

purchaser for value [*per* · ches · er for *val* · yoo] *n.* A purchaser who pays **valuable consideration**, as distinguished from **good consideration** or **nominal consideration**.

pure *adj.* 1. Untainted; unadulterated. 2. Unquestionable; definite.
➤ untainted, unadulterated, unquestionable, definite, clean, fresh, honest, uncontaminated ("pure water").

pure accident [*ak* · si · dent] *n.* An occurrence by chance; an occurrence in which no **negligence** is involved.

pure food laws *n. See* inspection laws. *Also see* Food and Drug Administration.

purge *v.* 1. To free oneself from guilt, particularly of **contempt**. 2. To cleanse something or oneself of an impurity.
➤ free, abolish, clarify, dismiss ("purge of guilt"); cleanse, excrete, unload, rid ("He purged the poison from his system").

purging contempt [*per* · jing kun · tempt] *n. See* purge.

purport [*per* · port] *n.* Meaning; general meaning; apparent meaning; import. *Compare* tenor.
v. [*per* · *port*] To convey or imply meaning; to profess.
➤ *n.* meaning, intention, significance, bearing, rationale ("purport of the lease"). *v.* claim, allege, pretend, pose ("He purports to be an expert").

purpose [*per* · pes] *n.* An aim; a plan; an intention; a goal; an objective.
➤ plan, intent, target, vision, goal, aim, objective ("The purpose of the course was education"); determination, will, persistence, tenacity ("She has a strong purpose in life").

purposely [*per* · pes · lee] *adv.* Intentionally; knowingly. *See* intentional.
➤ intentionally, knowingly, willfully, deliberately.

purpresture [per · *pres* · cher] *n.* An obstruction of or encroachment upon a highway, made without right or authorization.
➤ obstruction, encroachment.

purse *n.* 1. Something valuable offered by way of a prize for winning a contest. 2. A handbag.
➤ prize, kitty, gift, award, reward, contest ("The race's purse was substantial"); handbag, tote, bag, carry-all ("The thief snatched her purse").

purse snatching [*snat* · shing] *n.* A form of **larceny from the person**.

purser [*per* · ser] *n.* An officer of a ship who is in charge of the ship's accounts and who handles financial transactions with passengers; a **bursar**.
➤ officer, bursar.

P

pursuant to [per · *syoo* · ent] *adv.* Acting in a manner that carries something out; in conformity with; according to; following. USAGE: "Pursuant to your instructions [or "to our agreement," etc.], I have spoken with Ms. Smith."

pursue [per · *soo*] *v.* 1. To follow for the purpose of overtaking or apprehending. USAGE: "pursue a felon." 2. To attempt to bring about justice. USAGE: "pursue a complaint"; "pursue a **cause of action**." 3. To follow a profession or occupation. USAGE: "pursue a legal career."
➤ track, follow, search, trail ("pursue the criminal"); strive, aspire, work, struggle ("pursue success").

pursuit [per · *soot*] *n.* The act of pursuing. *See* pursue. *See also* fresh pursuit; hot pursuit.
➤ quest, chase, campaign, struggle ("pursuit of the truth").

pursuit of happiness [*hap* · i · ness] *n.* A phrase found in the Declaration of Independence, conveying the idea that a person has certain rights that are fundamental, **inalienable**, and **inherent**.

purview [*per* · vyoo] *n.* 1. The subject matter of a statute, as opposed to, for EXAMPLE, its **preamble**. 2. Scope; range.
➤ boundary, limit, jurisdiction, design, scope, range ("Interrogatories have to stay within a certain purview").

pusillanimous [pew · sil · *an* · ih · mus] *adj.* Lacking courage; cowardly.
➤ cowardly, dastardly, craven, recreant, poltroonish.

put *n.* An **option** to sell, particularly stock or other securities, or **commodities** at a stipulated price, on or before a specific future date or within a specified future period of time; more precisely, the privilege of delivering or not delivering something that has been sold. *Compare* call. *See also* futures; futures contract.
v. 1. To place. 2. To establish.
➤ *v.* place, deposit, position, establish, situate.

put in fear Intimidated. *Also see* intimidation. Putting a person "in fear" is an essential element of the crime of **robbery**. The term does not necessarily, however, imply any great degree of fright on the victim's part; it is sufficient if the words and gestures used by the robber create an uneasiness that would cause a **reasonable person** to part with property against her will.

put in issue [*ish* · oo] *See* at issue.

put option [*op* · shen] *n. See* put.

putative [*pyoo* · te · tiv] *adj.* Reputed; supposed; alleged.
➤ accepted, assumed, presumed, acknowledged, recognized ("putative father").

putative father [*fath* · ur] *n.* The man alleged to be the father of an illegitimate child.

putative marriage [*mehr* · ej] *n.* A marriage that, although invalid because of some **impediment** (EXAMPLE: impotence), was nonetheless entered into in good faith. *See* impediment to marriage.

putative spouse *n.* A person who is a party to a **putative marriage**.

puts *n. Plural* of **put**. *See* put.

pyramid sales [*peer* · e · mid] *n.* A scheme, often fraudulent, by which a person is induced to purchase something on the promise that he will be given a bonus, discount, or commission if he persuades others to make purchases as well. Such programs are illegal in many states.

pyramiding [*peer* · e · mid · ing] *n.* 1. Merging corporations in a complex form with a **holding company** at the top. *See* merger of corporations. 2. A method by which a person's stock ownership is increased by **underwriting** new stock purchases with the **margin** of the stock she already owns. *See* margin account; margin transaction.

P

q.v. An abbreviation of *quod vide*; a direction used in books, particularly reference books, to tell the reader that the word preceding it is used elsewhere in the book and is more fully explained there. In this dictionary, such referencing is accomplished by the use of boldface type.

QB Abbreviation of **Queen's Bench**.

qua *[kwah]* *(Latin)* *prep.* As; how; in the capacity of. USAGE: "*qua* **guardian**"; "*qua* **executor**."

quack *n.* 1. A person who pretends to have more knowledge or skill in a science or profession, especially medicine, than he has. 2. An incompetent physician.
➤ phony, incompetent, pretender, faker, sham, con man ("The doctor was a quack").

quaere *[kwee · ree]* *(Latin)* *n.* **Query**. The word *quaere* indicates a question. USAGE: "*Quaere:* Which Amendment to the Constitution abolished slavery in the United States?"

qualification *[kwaw · li · fi · kay · shen]* *n.* 1. A quality such as age, residency, or income that makes a person eligible for a given position or benefit, for EXAMPLE, holding public office, serving as a juror, appointment as the **administrator** of a **decedent's estate**, or receiving **public assistance**. 2. A **limitation**; a **condition** that limits. USAGE: "An **estate upon condition** is an EXAMPLE of an **estate** with a qualification." *See* qualified estate.
➤ standard, requisite, eligibility, ability, competence, capacity ("qualification to be president"); limitation, caveat, condition, restriction, stipulation, exception ("estate with a qualification").

qualification of voter *[voh · ter]* *n. See* qualified voter.

qualified *[kwaw · li · fide]* *adj.* 1. A term describing a thing (EXAMPLE: a **qualified pension plan**) or person (EXAMPLE: a **qualified voter**) who has the qualifications required for eligibility. *See* qualification. 2. Limited; conditioned; restricted. 3. Fit; able; suitable; competent.
➤ eligible, capable, worthy, proper, certified, knowledgeable ("qualified voter"); reserved, defined, narrowed, temporary ("qualified right of remitter"). *Ant.* unqualified; absolute.

qualified acceptance *[ak · sep · tense]* *n.* 1. In contract law, a **conditional acceptance** of an **offer**, that is, an **acceptance** that modifies the terms of the offer; in effect, a **counteroffer**. 2. In **negotiable instruments** law, an acceptance of a negotiable instrument that varies the effect of the instrument as originally drawn.

qualified elector *[e · lek · ter]* *n.* Same as **qualified voter**.

qualified estate *[es · tate]* *n.* Same as **estate upon condition** or **conditional estate**.

qualified fee *n.* Same as **conditional fee**. *See also* determinable fee.

qualified indorsement *[in · dorse · ment]* *n.* An **indorsement** that is **without recourse** to the **indorser**. *See* conditional indorsement; restrictive indorsement.

qualified interest *[in · trest]* *n.* An **interest** in property that is less than absolute. EXAMPLES: a **fee tail**; a **fee simple conditional**.

545

Q

qualified nuisance [*new* · sense] *n.* A **nuisance** created or maintained negligently rather than intentionally. *Compare* absolute nuisance.

qualified pension plan [*pen* · shen] *n.* A **pension plan** that meets certain requirements of the **Internal Revenue Code**, which ensures that the employer's contributions are not taxed to participating employees until the employees receive the benefits of the plan.

qualified privilege [*priv* · i · lej] *n. See* conditionally privileged communication.

qualified right *n.* A **right** that is limited, or that exists only to a certain extent or in certain circumstances. EXAMPLE: the rights of a tenant.

qualified stock option [*op* · shen] *n.* An **option** under which an employee of a corporation may buy stock in the corporation. Special tax considerations apply if the transaction is "qualified" under the **Internal Revenue Code**.

qualified voter [*voh* · ter] *n.* A person who meets the qualifications for voting; an **eligible voter**.

qualify [*kwaw* · li · fy] *v.* 1. To be ready, suitable, or authorized for something. 2. To limit or restrict. *See* qualification; qualified.
➤ authorize, certify, accredit, permit, prepare ("to qualify for the job"); restrict, limit, confine, control ("to qualify her statement").

qualifying [*kwah* · lih · fie · ing] *adj.* Modifying; limiting.
➤ limiting, extenuating, conditional, mitigating, modifying.

qualifying clause [*kwaw* · li · fy · ing] *n.* A provision in a contract, deed, will, or other instrument that contains a **condition**.

quality [*kwal* · ih · tee] *n.* 1. A high level of value. 2. Something distinctive or unique; a characteristic. 3. Degree of excellence.
➤ excellence, superiority, merit, ability, value, worth ("a person of quality"); attribute, characteristic, trait, feature ("She has an unusual quality"); nature, condition, endowment, condition, grade, caliber ("inferior quality of the material").

quandary [*kwan* · duh · ree] *n.* A delicate or perplexing situation; a predicament.
➤ dilemma, predicament, difficult situation, plight, problem, quagmire, impasse, bind.

quantity [*kwan* · tih · tee] *n.* The number or amount.
➤ amount, number, totality, multitude, aggregate, total.

quantum [*kwan* · tum] (*Latin*) *n.* "As much as"; how much.
quantum meruit [*mehr* · oo · it] *n.* Means "as much as is merited" or "as much as is deserved." The doctrine of *quantum meruit* makes a person liable to pay for services or goods that he accepts while knowing that the other party expects to be paid, even if there is no **express contract**. In such circumstances, the law creates an **implied contract** to avoid **unjust enrichment**. *See* quasi contract.

quarantine [*kwar* · en · teen] *n.* Isolation of persons or animals with contagious diseases, or animals, produce, or goods that carry pests, to prevent the spread of infectious disease. Under quarantine statutes and regulations, persons may be confined to their homes in appropriate circumstances, goods and commodities may be barred from entering the country or entering a state, and ships may be kept in port and prohibited from unloading for the period of the quarantine. *See* health laws.
➤ sequestration, confinement, seclusion, cordon, detachment, separation, division, isolation.
Ant. release.

quare [*kwah* · ray] (*Latin*) *adv.* Why; for what reason; on which account.
quare clausum fregit [*klawz* · em *free* · jit] *n.* Means "because he broke the **close**." *See* trespass quare clausum fregit.

quarter [*kwor* · ter] *n.* 1. One fourth of anything. 2. A section of a city or town. 3. Mercy; clemency.
v. 1. To assign soldiers living accommodations in private homes. The **Third Amendment** prohibits the quartering of troops without the owner's consent. 2. To cut the body of a convicted criminal into four parts. This practice prevailed in England in former times.
➤ *n.* division, farthing, fourth, semester, part, portion ("quarter of an hour"); zone, district, locality, point, precinct ("What quarter of town?"); clemency, favor, grace, leniency, mercy, pity ("to give quarter").

v. accommodate, board, billet, shelter, domiciliate, canton ("to quarter the soldiers"); cleave, cut, dismember, cut up ("draw and quarter").

quarter section [*sek* · shen] *n.* 1. A square piece of **public land** 160 acres in area, which is one-fourth of a **section** as laid out by **government survey**. *See* section. 2. Any tract of 160 acres.

quarterly [*kwor* · ter · lee] *adj./adv.* Every three months, or quarter-yearly.

quash *v.* To **suppress**; to **set aside**; to **vacate**; to **abrogate**. Thus, a **motion to quash indictment** is a **motion** that asks the court to suppress an **indictment** that is **defective**. Similarly, one may quash an **information** or quash a **subpoena**.
➤ suppress, abate, void, annul ("a motion to quash the indictment").
Ant. sanction, establish.

quasi [*kway* · zye] (*Latin*) *adj.* As if it were; resembling; relating to or having the character of.
➤ apparent, semi, near, virtual, partly nominal, resembling ("quasi-judicial").

quasi admission [ad · *mish* · en] *n.* An admission implied from the fact that a person has made inconsistent statements with respect to the same matter. *See* prior inconsistent statements.

quasi contract [*kon* · trakt] *n.* An obligation imposed by law to achieve **equity**, usually to prevent **unjust enrichment**. A quasi contract is a **legal fiction** that a contract exists where there has been no **express contract**. EXAMPLE: a contract implied on the theory of *quantum meruit*.

quasi corporation [kore · per · *ay* · shen] *n.* A **public corporation** (EXAMPLES: a **school district**; a **drainage district**) that has some functions or responsibilities of **local government**, but which is not itself a **municipal corporation**.

quasi crime *n.* Conduct that is not such as to make it subject to criminal prosecution, but for which **forfeiture** or a **penalty** may be imposed. EXAMPLES: a **qui tam action**; a *quo warranto* proceeding.

quasi delict [de · *likt*] *n.* A **tort** that involves no **malice**. EXAMPLE: an unintentional **trespass**. *See* delict.

quasi estoppel [es · *top* · el] *n.* Same as **estoppel in pais**.

quasi fee *n.* An **estate** gained by a wrongful act. *See* fee.

quasi in rem [rem] *See* in rem.

quasi in rem action [rem ak · shen] *n.* An **action** that **adjudicates** only the rights of the **parties** with respect to property, not the rights of all persons who might have an **interest** in the property. *See* judgment quasi in rem. *See and compare* in personam action; in rem action.

quasi-judicial [-joo · *dish* · el] *adj.* A term applied to the **adjudicatory** functions of an administrative agency, i.e., taking evidence and making **findings of fact** and **findings of law**. *See* judicial function.

quasi-judicial power [-joo · *dish* · el *pow* · er] *n.* The power exercised by **quasi-judicial** bodies such as administrative agencies. *See* judicial powers.

quasi-legislative [-*lej* · is · lay · tiv] *adj.* A term applied to the **legislative** functions of an administrative agency, for EXAMPLE, **rulemaking**. *See* legislative function.

quasi-legislative power [-*lej* · is · lay · tiv *pow* · er] *n.* The power exercised by an administrative agency when it performs a **quasi-legislative** function. *See* legislative powers.

quasi-municipal corporation [-myoo · *niss* · i · pel kore · per · *ay* shen] *n.* A **quasi corporation**.

quasi-public corporation [-*pub* · lik kore · per · *ay* · shen] *n.* A **public service corporation**.

Queen's (King's) Bench *n.* Short for Court of Queen's Bench, an English court with both **general jurisdiction** and **appellate jurisdiction**. Queen's Bench is important to Americans because it was the court that created much of the English **common law**, which forms the foundation of our law. When a king is on the throne, this court is called **King's Bench**.

quell *v.* 1. To reduce to submission; to defeat. 2. To appease or alleviate.
➤ crush, suppress, subdue, stifle, quash; calm, check, soothe, reduce, silence, mollify.
Ant. foment; aggravate.

Q

query [*kweer* · ee] *n./v.* The English word for the *Latin* **quaere**, meaning "question." *See quaere.*

➤ *n.* concern, doubt, dubiety, skepticism, problem, uncertainty ("a query as to how the funds were spent").
v. ask, cross-examine, audit, search, investigate, impugn, challenge ("to query the witness's trustworthiness").

question [*kwes* · chen] *n.* 1. A point in controversy; a matter at issue to be decided by a court. *See* judicial question. *See also* federal question. 2. A ballot question; a proposed law or other matter related to **public policy** that is submitted to the voters at an election. *See* referendum. *See also* political question. 3. Something that is asked. *See* hypothetical question; leading question.
v. 1. To scrutinize or doubt. 2. To ask questions of a witness on direct or cross-examination.

➤ *n.* point, proposal, theme, topic, hypothesis ("the question at hand"); query, inquiry, quiz, request, scrutiny ("answer the question"); doubt, controversy, uncertainty, misgiving, mystery, confusion, probability ("There was a question as to whether he told the truth").
v. scrutinize, test, enquire, inquire, interrogate, petition, solicit, cross-examine, ("to question the witness").

question of fact *n.* A question to be decided by the jury in a **trial by jury** or by the judge in a **bench trial**; that is, a question of what is the truth when the evidence is in conflict. *See* matter of fact.

question of law *n.* A question to be decided by the judge; that is, a question as to the appropriate law to be applied in a case, or its correct interpretation. *See* matter of law. *See also* judicial question.

qui [kwee] *(Latin)* *pron.* Who; which; what.
qui tam Who also.

qui tam action [*ak* · shen] *n.* An **action** brought by an informer under a statute which provides for such a suit and which also provides that one portion of the **recovery** goes to the informer and the other portion to the state. *See* relator.

quick *adj.* 1. Speedy; rapid; prompt. 2. Having or carrying life; pregnant. *See* quick with child.

➤ fast, speedy, fleet, express ("a quick runner"); smart, adept, clever, competent, intelligent, perceptive, shrewd ("a quick study").

quick assets [*ass* · ets] *n.* **Liquid assets**.

quick with child *n.* That point in a pregnancy at which the fetus becomes **viable**.

quid [kwid] *(Latin)* What.

quid pro quo [proh *kwoh*] Means "what for what" or, as it is more commonly used today, "this for that." Specifically, it means or refers to the **consideration** for a contract. USAGE: "I have agreed to withdraw my suit; the *quid pro quo* is that the defendant will give me $10,000 in full settlement and pay my court costs."

quiet [*kwy* · et] *adj.* 1. Being at rest. 2. Being free from disturbance or interference.
v. To pacify; to make tranquil; to calm. *See* quieting title.

➤ *adj.* collected, inactive, placid, sedate, sequestered, undisturbed ("to be quiet"); unmolested, pacific, tranquil, peaceful, untroubled ("quiet enjoyment"); low, muffled, reticent, taciturn, unspeaking, quiescent ("a quiet audience").
v. allay, mollify, squelch, pacify, make tranquil, calm ("to quiet the crowd").

quiet enjoyment [en · *joy* · ment] *n.* *See* covenant for quiet enjoyment.

quieting title [*kwy* · e · ting *ty* · tel] *v.* Bringing an **action to quiet title**, i.e., a lawsuit brought to remove a **cloud on the title** so that the plaintiff and those in **privity** with her may forever be free of claims against the property.

quirk *n.* A characteristic or odd mannerism.
➤ oddity, peculiarity, habit, eccentricity, mannerism.

quit *v.* 1. To vacate premises. *See* premises. *See also* notice to quit; quitclaim deed. 2. To voluntarily terminate one's employment. *See* voluntary quit. 3. To abandon; to leave; to get out.

➤ leave, retreat, vacate, abandon, evacuate, withdraw ("He quit the lease"); cease, end, resign, secede, discontinue, desist ("He quit painting").

quitclaim [*kwit* · klame] *v.* 1. To execute a **quitclaim deed**. 2. To release; to give something up or surrender it.

quitclaim deed [*kwit* · klame] *n.* A **deed** that **conveys** whatever **interest** the **grantor** has in a piece of real property, as distinguished from the more usual deed which conveys a **fee** and contains various **covenants**, particularly **title covenants**. A quitclaim deed is often referred to simply as a "quitclaim."

quittance [*kwit* · ense] *n.* A **release**.
➤ release, leaving, departure.

quixotic [kwik · *zot* · ic] *adj.* Foolishly impractical; resembling Don Quixote de la Mancha, a character created by Cervantes.
➤ visionary, fanciful, impractical, fantastic, chimerical.
Ant. practical, pragmatic.

quo [kwoh] *(Latin)* 1. What; at what place; where. 2. With what; by what.

quo warranto [wahr · *rahn* · toh] Means "by what authority." A **writ of quo warranto** is an **extraordinary writ** used to secure a judicial determination of whether a public officer is legally exercising his power, i.e., whether the law has granted his **office** the powers he is exercising.

quod [kwode] *(Latin)* Which; the point at which.

quod vide [*vee* · day] Means "which see" and is usually abbreviated *q.v. See q.v. Also see vide.*

quorum [*kwohr* · em] *n.* The number of members of a **body** (EXAMPLES: a legislature; a court, particularly an **appellate court**; a board of directors) who must be present for the body to be able to conduct business.

quota [*kwoh* · ta] *n.* 1. A proportional share or goal that each member of a group is asked or required to contribute or to achieve. 2. A proportional entitlement that is assigned to a person or group relative to a larger group to which it belongs, or that is assigned to anything relative to the whole. Thus, for EXAMPLE, an "immigrant quota" limits the number of immigrants from a given country and a "coffee quota" limits the amount of coffee that may be imported into the country. *See* proportion.
➤ percentage, share, quotient, allocation, ration, parcel, proportion.

quotation [kwo · *tay* · shen] *n.* 1. An exact rendition or presentation of previously written or spoken words. 2. A **market quotation**.
➤ quote, repetition, excerpt, report, citation, extract, selection.

quote [kwote] *v.* To repeat or cite exactly.
➤ cite, repeat, reiterate, reference, verify, restate, give word-for-word, adduce.

quotient [*kwoh* · shent] *n.* The number resulting from the division of one number by another.

quotient verdict [*ver* · dikt] *n.* In a **civil action**, a **verdict** reached by jurors by adding the total amount of money each would award and dividing that amount by the number of jurors. Such a verdict is illegal. *See also* chance verdict.

R A symbol for **registered trademark**, when enclosed within a circle: ®.

race *n.* An ethnic culture; a group of people of the same color and background.
v. To move or run quickly; to compete in speed.
➤ *n.* ancestry, ethnic group, people, culture, parentage.
v. hurry, dash, speed, sprint, tear, hustle, accelerate.

race acts *n. See* recording acts.

race-notice acts [-noh · tiss] *n. See* recording acts.

racial discrimination [*ray* · shel dis · krim · i · *nay* · shen] *n.* Discrimination against a person based upon his race. *See* Civil Rights Acts; Equal Employment Opportunity Commission (EEOC).

racism [*ray* · sizm] *n.* Bias against people because of their race; discrimination against people based upon their race. *See* racial discrimination.
➤ apartheid, bigotry, sectarianism, prejudice, bias.

racketeer [rak · e · *teer*] *n.* A gangster; a person engaged in criminal activity as a business. The term is often associated with organized crime. It suggests a person whose criminal enterprises involve the use of threats, coercion, intimidation, and violence, especially for purposes of **extortion** and **protection**.
➤ gangster, criminal, extortionist, miscreant, malefactor, pirate.

Racketeer Influenced and Corrupt Organizations Act [rak · e · *teer in* · floo · ensd and ker · *rupt* or · ge · ni · *zay* · shenz] *n.* A federal statute, commonly referred to as **RICO**, which criminalizes racketeering that affects **interstate commerce** or persons or businesses engaged in interstate commerce. *See* racketeering.

racketeering [rak · e · *teer* · ing] *n.* The criminal activity engaged in by a **racketeer**. Racketeering is an activity of members of organized crime.

radical [*rad* · ih · kal] *adj.* 1. Thorough; complete; fundamental. 2. Extreme; revolutionary.
n. A person who advocates significant or revolutionary change.
➤ *adj.* extreme, total, whole, thorough, profound, fundamental, vital ("Radical changes are needed"); militant, free-thinking, ultra-liberal, rebellious, uncompromising ("a radical idea").
n. rebel, agitator, leftist, subversive, revolutionary, fanatic, extremist.

radioimmunoassay
[ray · dee · oh · im · yoon · o · *ass* · ay] *n.* Often referred to as an **RIA**; a laboratory test used to identify the presence of **THC** in the blood or urine. *See* marijuana.

raffle [rafl] *n.* A **lottery** in which the prize is usually an item of merchandise, an all-expenses-paid vacation, or the like, with the players paying for their tickets and the winning ticket being chosen by chance.

R

➤ sweepstakes, drawing, lottery, disposition, wager, gaming.

raid *n.* A surprise attack; a sudden invasion. *v.* To invade or attack.

➤ *n.* attack, takeover, strike, arrest, assault, invasion.
v. attack, pillage, plunder, assault, rape, take over, ransack, despoil, devastate.

raiding [*ray* · ding] *n.* Attempting a corporate **takeover**.

railroad [*rail* · rode] *v.* 1. To rush something to completion very quickly. USAGE: "The treasurer attempted to railroad approval of the new budget." 2. To send a person to prison on a fictitious charge or without **due process**. USAGE: "He claims he was innocent and that he was railroaded." 3. To transport by rail.
n. A method of transportation by railway.

➤ *v.* push, goad, urge, intimidate, accelerate, speed, hasten, shove, press.

Railway Labor Act [*rail* · way *lay* · ber] *n.* A federal statute intended to produce settlement, through **mediation**, of labor disputes between railroad companies and their employees or the unions representing them.

raise *v.* 1. To create; to generate; to make; to produce. EXAMPLES: certain kinds of conduct create or "raise" a **presumption**; to make an issue is to "raise an issue"; to grow wheat is to "raise wheat." 2. To rear or bring up, e.g., to "raise children" or to "raise chickens." 3. To increase in size or amount. Thus, for EXAMPLE, an increase in pay is a "pay raise," a check whose amount is fraudulently increased is a "raised check," and taxes are increased to "raise revenue."
n. An increase in salary or position.

➤ *v.* activate, prompt, launch, evoke, kindle, instigate ("raise a presumption"); accede, hike, augment, increment, add, jump ("raise her salary"); rear, bring up ("raise children").
n. promotion, advance, jump, boost, addition, augmentation.

raise a check *See* raise.

raise a presumption [pre · *zump* · shen] *See* raise.

raise an issue [*ish* · ew] *See* raise.

raise revenue [*rev* · e · new] *See* raise.

rake-off [*rake*-off] *n.* A share in the proceeds of an illegal activity (EXAMPLE:

illegal gambling), or a share in a legal activity (EXAMPLE: a legitimate business) illegally acquired, for EXAMPLE, through **extortion**.

RAM 1. Abbreviation for **reverse annuity mortgage**. 2. Abbreviation for random access memory in computer terminology.

ransom [*ran* · sem] *n.* A price demanded or paid for the release of a captured person. *See* kidnapping; kidnapping for ransom.

➤ liberation, redemption, emancipation, deliverance, expiation ("$100,000 ransom").

rap sheet *n.* A list containing a person's arrest and conviction record, including dates, jurisdictions, and offenses. It is available to all law enforcement agencies. *See* NCIC.

rape *n.* Sexual intercourse with a woman by force or by putting her in fear or in circumstances in which she is unable to control her conduct or to resist (EXAMPLES: intoxication; unconsciousness). Under the **common law** definition of the crime, only a female can be raped and only a male can perpetrate the crime. In recent years, however, courts in several states have held that the rape statutes of their jurisdictions are gender-neutral and apply equally to perpetrators of either sex. *See* statutory rape. *See also* assault with intent to commit rape.
v. To commit rape.

➤ *n.* violation, assault, sexual assault, nonconsensual sex, defilement, seduction, abuse, defloration, despoilation.
v. molest, sexually assault, debauch, defile, ravish ("The woman was raped"); raid, sack, loot, pillage, ravage, desecrate, maltreat ("rape the museum's holdings").

rape shield laws *n. See* shield laws.

rapport [ra · *por*] *n.* An affinity; understanding; harmonious relations.

➤ accord, agreement, relationship, harmony, understanding, empathy, connection, intimacy ("Bud is generally able to establish great rapport with the jury").

rare *adj.* Uncommon; scarce; exceptional.

➤ uncommon, unique, precious, unusual, scarce, priceless, singular, noteworthy, special.
Ant. common, usual.

R

rasure [*ray* · zher] *n.* Erasing letters or words from a written **instrument** by scraping its surface. *Compare* obliteration.
➤ erasure, obliteration.

ratable [*ray* · tebl] *adj.* 1. Proportional. *See* proportion; *pro rata.* 2. That which may be estimated or **rated**. *See* rate.
  ratable property [*prop* · er · tee] *n.* Property that is capable of being **rated**, that is, **appraised** or **assessed** for purposes of taxation or insurance. *See* rate.

rate *n.* 1. A price or valuation. 2. A unit by which a computation is made, for EXAMPLE, the **rate of interest** or the **rate of exchange**. 3. The **mill rate** or **millage** on real property. 4. The charge by a **common carrier** for transporting persons or property. *See* Interstate Commerce Commission. 5. The charge by a **public utility** for its service. *See* public utility commission. *See also* confiscatory rate order; discount rate; flat rate; interest rate; legal rate of interest; prevailing rate; prime rate.
  v. 1. To estimate the value of something; to **appraise**. 2. To establish a charge or a fee.
➤ *n.* cost, payment, tariff, rent, assessment, quotation ("rate of payment"); clip, dash, measure, spurt, velocity, pace ("rate of speed").
  v. rank, appraise, quantify, prioritize, gauge ("rate the value of the house"); be accepted, be favorable, be worthy, deserve, merit, prosper ("to rate well").
  rate fixing [*fik* · sing] *n. See* rate making.
  rate making [*may* · king] *n.* The process engaged in by a **public service commission** in establishing a rate to be charged to the public for a **public service**.
  rate of exchange [eks · *chaynj*] *n.* 1. The rate at which the money of one country may be exchanged for the money of another, for EXAMPLE, the number of Japanese yen to be received for an American dollar. 2. The price at which a **foreign bill of exchange** can be purchased in the country in which it is **drawn**.
  rate of interest [in · trest] *n.* The charge made by a lender for the privilege of borrowing money; the interest rate. *See* interest.
  rate of return [re · *tern*] *n.* The return (i.e., profit or earnings) on an investment during a given period of time. *See* return.

ratification [rat · i · fi · *kay* · shen] *n.* The act of giving one's approval to a previous act, either one's own or someone else's, which, without such confirmation, would be nonbinding. A person may ratify a contract by expressly promising to be bound by it. Ratification may be implied from a person's conduct; it may also take place as a result of accepting the benefits of a transaction. Ratification is the confirmation of an act that has already been performed, as opposed to the authorization of an act that is yet to be performed.
➤ endorsement, certification, sanction, vindication, confirmation, corroboration, approbation.
  Ant. repudiation, rejection.
  ratification of treaty [*tree* · tee] *n.* Senate approval of a treaty. The Constitution requires ratification by the Senate of all **treaties** between the United States and foreign countries. Treaty ratification must be by a two-thirds vote.

ratify [*rat* · i · fy] *v.* To give approval; to confirm. *See* ratification.
➤ sanction, embrace, confirm, acquiesce, countersign, agree, affirm, authorize.
  Ant. repudiate.

ration [*ra* · shun] *n.* A portion or allotment of a limited supply.
➤ portion, allotment, part, share, quota, provision, dispensation.

rational [*rash* · en · el] *adj.* 1. Reasonable; capable of reasoning. 2. Sane. *Note* that "rational" is not "**rationale**."
➤ sensible, logical, cognitive, efficacious, pragmatic, commonsensical, reasonable.
  rational basis [*bay* · sis] *n.* A reasonable basis, under the law. The courts will not invalidate a statute or overrule an order of an administrative agency that has a "rational basis" in law. *Compare* arbitrary and capricious. *Compare* strict scrutiny test.
  rational doubt *n.* A **reasonable doubt**.

rationale [*rash* · en · *aal*] *n.* The reason or reasoning behind something. *Note* that "rationale" is not "**rational**."
➤ reason, cause, basis, justification, excuse, philosophy, motive.

ravish [*rav* · ish] *v.* 1. To rape. 2. To seize and carry away by force. 3. To captivate; to enthrall.

R

➤ abuse, defile, force, rape, violate, outrage ("He ravished the woman"); allure, captivate, enthrall, mesmerize, please, overjoy ("He was ravished by the colorful lights").

re [ray] *(Latin)* *See in re.*

reacquired stock [re · a · *kwired*] *n.* Same as **treasury stock**.

reaction [re · *ak* · shun] *n.* 1. Response. 2. Opposition.
➤ response, rejoinder, opinion, reply; opposition, resistance, disagreement.

ready [*red* · ee] *adj.* Prepared; available.
➤ prepared, completed, finished, available, primed, waiting.

ready, willing, and able [*red* · ee, *wil* · ing, and aybl] *adj./adv.* A phrase applied to a buyer who wants to make a purchase and who has the money or credit to do so.

reaffirm [re · uh · *firm*] *v.* repeat, restate, reiterate, accentuate, emphasize, insist.

real *adj.* 1. Pertaining to land or real estate. 2. Pertaining to the **corporeal** rather than the **incorporeal**. 3. Not fictitious or imagined.
➤ authentic, genuine, substantive, demonstrable, intrinsic, perceptible. *Ant.* spurious, fake.

real assets [*ass* · ets] *n.* Real estate; real property.

real chattels [*chat* · elz] *n.* 1. **Interests** in real estate less than **freehold**. EXAMPLES: an **estate for years**; a **leasehold**. 2. **Fixtures.** *Compare* personal chattels.

real contract [*kon* · trakt] *n.* 1. A **contract** involving something more than mutual promises, for EXAMPLE, a downpayment or a **pledge**. 2. A **real estate contract**.

real covenant [*kov* · e · nent] *n.* A **covenant** relating to land or to something attached to the land.

real defenses [de · *fen* · sez] *n.* Under the **Uniform Commercial Code**, the limited number of **defenses** that exist against a **holder in due course** of a **negotiable instrument**. These defenses are called "real defenses." **Fraud in the essence** is an EXAMPLE of a real defense.

real estate [es · *tate*] *n.* Real property.

real estate agent [es · *tate ay* · jent] *n.* An **agent** who, for a commission, finds a prospective buyer for real estate and negotiates on behalf of the seller and the prospective buyer to arrange the terms of the sale. *See* listing agreement.

real estate broker [es · *tate broh* · ker] *n.* *See* real estate agent.

real estate contract [es · *tate kon* · trakt] *n.* A **contract for sale of land**. *See also* installment land contract.

real estate investment trust [es · *tate* in · *vest* · ment] *n.* 1. A company that puts its **assets** into real estate investments and distributes the profits to its members. 2. An investment company that issues **shares** in itself and uses the proceeds from the sale of its stock to make other investments. *See* mutual fund.

real estate listing [es · *tate list* · ing] *n.* *See* listing agreement.

real estate tax [es · *tate*] *n.* A tax upon real estate based on its **assessed value**.

real evidence [*ev* · i · dense] *n.* **Physical evidence**, as opposed to testimony; **demonstrative evidence**. *See also* autoptic preference.

real injury [*in* · jer · ee] *n.* Same as **real wrong**.

real party in interest [*par* · tee in in · *trest*] *n.* 1. A **party** to an **action** who has an actual **interest** or stake in the controversy, as opposed to a **nominal party**; a person who will be directly affected by the outcome of litigation. A real party in interest is also referred to as a **party in interest**. 2. A person or party who has an interest in a transaction, as opposed to a **straw man** or **stranger**; an **interested person**.

real property [*prop* · er · tee] *n.* 1. Land, including things located on it or attached to it directly (EXAMPLE: buildings) or indirectly (EXAMPLE: **fixtures**); real estate. 2. In the technical sense, the **interest** a person has in land or her **rights** with respect to it. *Compare* personal property. *See* property.

real things *n.* *See* things real.

real wrong *n.* An **injury** to real property.

realize [*real* · ize] *v.* 1. Receive; cash in; obtain the benefit or burden of something, for EXAMPLE, an investment. USAGE: "She

R

will realize a profit on the sale and I will realize a loss." 2. Understand or comprehend. USAGE: "I realize my mistake."

➤ gain, earn, receive, make, acquire, obtain, win ("to realize a profit"); comprehend, perceive, fathom, discern, assimilate, grasp ("I realize my mistake").

realized [*real* · ized] *adj. See* realize.

realtor [*real* · ter] *n.* A real estate agent who is a member of the National Association of Realtors. The word "realtor" is a **collective mark** of the Association. *Note* that "realtor" is not "**relator.**"

➤ agent, broker.

realty [*real* · tee] *n.* Same as real property.

➤ property, real estate, land.

reapportionment [re · a · *por* · shen · ment] *n.* Changing the boundaries of **congressional districts** or other **legislative districts**. Reapportionment is undertaken periodically, generally after an increase or decrease in the population of a district, to ensure equality of representation. The Constitution requires that congressional reapportionment take place every 10 years. *See* apportionment; apportionment of representatives.

➤ reallotment, reclassification, rearrangement, redistribution, equalization.

reargument [re · *ar* · gyoo · ment] *n.* An additional opportunity to argue one or more points, granted by a **trial court**, an **appellate court**, or an administrative agency. *See* rehearing. *Compare* retrial.

reason [*ree* · zen] *n.* 1. The ability to think and reach conclusions. 2. Explanation; justification; motive; cause.
v. To discuss; to persuade with logic.

➤ *n.* insight, intelligence, comprehension, lucidity, perception ("to lose one's reason"); notion, motive, excuse ("For what reason?").
v. discuss, deliberate, think, explain, cogitate, deduce ("reason with him").

reasonable [*ree* · zen · ebl] *adj.* 1. Fair; equitable; just. 2. Rational; not **arbitrary** or **capricious**; sensible. 3. Appropriate; suitable. "Reasonable" is a term whose precise meaning depends upon the context in which it is used. *See* reasonable man test.

➤ fair, moderate, just, equitable, pragmatic, conscientious ("a reasonable amount of

money"); intelligent, practical, cerebral, logical, level-headed, tenable, sound, sensible, advisable ("a reasonable decision").

reasonable belief [be · *leef*] *n.* A belief based upon facts one honestly feels to be reliable. A judge cannot issue a **search warrant** unless she has a "reasonable belief" that a crime has been committed. *See* belief. *Also see* probable cause. *Compare* reasonable suspicion.

reasonable care *n.* Same as **due care** or **ordinary care**.

reasonable cause *n.* Same as **probable cause**.

reasonable compensation [kom · pen · *say* · shen] *n.* 1. In the context of the **taking** of property by **eminent domain**, **just compensation**. 2. With respect to the awarding of **damages**, a sum that fairly compensates a person for the **damage** done to him. *See* compensation.

reasonable diligence [*dil* · i · jense] *n.* Same as **due diligence** or **ordinary diligence**.

reasonable doubt *n. See* beyond a reasonable doubt.

reasonable force *n.* Force that is appropriate in the circumstances. A person is entitled to use "reasonable force" to defend herself or her property. *See* self-defense.

reasonable grounds *n. See* probable cause.

reasonable man *n. See* reasonable man test.

reasonable man standard *n. See* reasonable man test.

reasonable man test *n.* A standard for determining **negligence**, which asks: "What would a **reasonable person** have done in the same circumstances?" In short, it measures the failure to do that which a person of ordinary intelligence and judgment would have done in the circumstances, or the doing of that which a person of ordinary intelligence and judgment would not have done. *Compare* reasonable woman test.

reasonable notice [*noh* · tiss] *n.* Such **notice** as is fair and appropriate in the circumstances.

R

reasonable person [*per* · sen] *n. See* reasonable man test.

reasonable prudence [*proo* · dense] *n.* Same as **due care**, **ordinary care**, or **reasonable care**.

reasonable suspicion [suss · *pish* · un] *n.* Suspicion supported by facts. Reasonable suspicion is sufficient basis in law for a police officer to **stop and frisk** a suspect. *Compare* reasonable belief.

reasonable time *n.* A period of time that is appropriate in the circumstances.

reasonable use doctrine [*dok* · trin] *n.* The rule that one must make use of one's own property in a manner that does not deprive others of the lawful use and enjoyment of their property. Thus, for EXAMPLE, an **upper riparian owner** may use water as he wishes so long as he does not reduce the amount or quality of the water received by **lower riparian owners**.

reasonable woman test [*wuh* · man] *n.* In determining whether a woman has been a victim of **sexual harassment**, or exposed to a **hostile environment**, the standard used by the **EEOC** is whether a "reasonable woman" (as opposed to a "reasonable man") would find the conduct offensive. In other words, although a male supervisor might feel it perfectly acceptable to tell a woman who works for him that she has "great legs," the woman might reasonably find his remark unacceptable. *Compare* reasonable man test. *See* Equal Employment Opportunity Commission (EEOC); sex discrimination.

reasonably prudent man [*ree* · zen · eb · lee *proo* · dent] *n. See* reasonable man test.

reasonably prudent person [*per* · sen] *n. See* reasonable man test.

rebate [*ree* · bate] *n.* A refund, generally of a portion of the **consideration** previously given. A rebate is usually in the form of a discount or a deduction from the price of goods or services, given either as an inducement to make the purchase, as a form of reward for prompt payment, or as an adjustment because the goods or services are other than as **warranted**. *See* refund.
v. To give a **rebate**. *See* rebate (*noun*).

➤ *n.* abatement, discount, reimbursement, decrease, payback, kickback, reduction, refund, inducement.

rebellion [re · *bell* · yen] *n.* An armed **insurrection** against the government. *See* revolution.
➤ apostasy, heresy, dissent, revolution, uprising, strike, revolt.
Ant. submission.

rebuff [ree · *buf*] *v.* To turn away or ignore.
➤ ignore, slight, scorn, reprove, spurn, jilt, dismiss, insult.

rebut [re · *but*] *v.* To deny; to refute; to contradict; to **contravene**; to **traverse**. USAGE: "It is more difficult to rebut some **presumptions** than others." *See* rebuttable; rebuttal; rebuttal evidence; rebuttal of a presumption.
➤ deny, refute, contravene, rebuff, negate, dispute, contradict, retort, counterclaim, parry
Ant. substantiate.

rebuttable [re · *but* · ebl] *adj.* Capable of being rebutted. *See* rebut.
➤ negatable, refutable, inconclusive.

rebuttable presumption [pre · *zump* · shen] *n.* A **presumption** that is not conclusive and may be overcome or rebutted by evidence to the contrary. EXAMPLE: the **presumption of death** based upon **seven years' absence**. *Compare* irrebuttable presumption. *See* rebut.

rebuttal [re · *but* · el] *n.* 1. The stage in a trial or hearing at which a **party** introduces **rebuttal evidence**. It occurs after the opposite party has rested her case. 2. The act of rebutting. *See* rebut.
➤ retort, contradiction, counterargument, invalidation, upset, overthrow.
Ant. confirmation.

rebuttal evidence [*ev* · i · dense] *n.* **Evidence** introduced to explain, counteract, or disprove evidence introduced by the opposite party. *See* rebut; rebuttable.

rebuttal of a presumption [pre · *zump* · shen] *n.* The introduction of evidence that negates a **presumption**. *See* rebuttable presumption.

recall [re · *koll*] *n.* Return; withdrawal; dismissal.

R

v. 1. To call back; to **set aside**; to **vacate**. 2. To remove from office. *See* recall of a public officer.

➤ *n.* repudiation, rescission, withdrawal, dismissal, veto, reversal ("recall of the governor").
Ant. reinstatement, support.
v. remember, retrace, reminisce, recreate, evoke, place ("recall your wedding day").
Ant. forget.

recall of a judgment [*juj* · ment] *n.* The **setting aside** or **vacation** of a **judgment** by the court that issued it. *See* vacation of judgment.

recall of a public officer [*pub* · lik *off* · i · ser] *n.* A method of removing an elected public official from office by a vote of the people, usually at a special election requested by petition of a percentage of registered voters, as fixed by statute.

recall of a witness [*wit* · ness] *n.* The act of a **party**, with the permission of the court, in calling a witness for additional **examination** or **cross-examination** after he has already given testimony on **direct examination** or cross-examination. *See and compare* recross-examination; redirect examination.

recall of an order [*or* · der] *n.* *See* recall of a judgment.

recant [re · *kant*] *v.* To retract a previously made statement. USAGE: "He recanted his earlier testimony because it was untruthful."
➤ abjure, apostulate, disown, retract, disclaim, retract, abrogate.

recapitalization [re · kap · i · tel · i · *zay* · shen] *n.* A change in the **capitalization** of a corporation, especially in connection with a **reorganization**, usually by increasing or decreasing the number of shares of stock or by altering the value, **priority**, or **classes** of stock or other securities. *See* class of stock.

recaption [re · *kap* · shen] *n.* A **remedy** that involves taking possession of goods of which one has been wrongfully deprived. *See* reprisal.
➤ reprisal, repossession.

recapture [re · *kap* · cher] *n.* 1. In tax law, recovery by the **Internal Revenue Service** of a portion of the **accelerated** depreciation previously taken on property that has since been disposed of. 2. In tax law, recovery by the government of a portion of an **investment tax credit** previously claimed, after disposition has been made of the property for which credit was previously claimed. *See also* tax credit. 3. The act of capturing and returning an escaped prisoner to custody. 4. **Recaption** or **reprisal**. 5. The act of repossessing, recovering, or retaking anything.
v. To repossess or recover.
➤ *v.* restore, regain, repossess, countermand, rescue, liberate, recover, retake ("recapture the glory of the past").

receipt [re · *seet*] *n.* 1. An acknowledgment in writing that money or property has been received. 2. The act of receiving a delivery of property or a **tender** of money. *See* trust receipt; warehouse receipt. *See also* value received.
➤ admission, memo, slip, release, stub, proof of purchase ("Your receipt is in the bag with your purchase"); reception, acceptance, custody, acquisition, arrival ("in receipt of delivery"); cash flow, earnings, gain, revenue, returns, stream.

receipts [re · *seets*] *n.* 1. *Plural* of **receipt**. *See* receipt. 2. The money that a business enterprise takes in. *See* gross receipts.

receivable [re · *seev* · ebl] *n./adj.* An **account receivable**. *See* receivables.
➤ *adj.* due, owing, unpaid, outstanding, payable ("accounts receivable").

receivables [re · *seev* · eblz] *n.* *Plural* of **receivable**. **Accounts receivable** are often referred to simply as "receivables." *See* receivable.

receive [re · *seev*] *v.* To take into one's possession and control. *See* value received. *See also* receiver; receiving stolen goods.
➤ get, obtain, secure, acquire, procure, realize ("receive the goods"); allow, permit, accept, welcome, tolerate ("receive into evidence").

receiver [re · *seev* · er] *n.* A person appointed by the court to take custody of property in a **receivership**. *In the case of the assets or other property of an insolvent debtor*, whether an individual or corporation, the duty of a receiver is to preserve the **assets** for sale and distribution to the creditors.

R

In the case of assets or other property that is the subject of litigation, the duty of a receiver is to preserve the property or fund in litigation, receive its rent or profits, and apply or dispose of them as the court directs. Such a receiver is called a ***pendente lite*** receiver. If the property in dispute is a business, the receiver may have the additional responsibility of operating the business as a **going concern**.
➤ trustee, supervisor, administrator, depository, overseer, manager, collector.

receiver pendente lite [pen · *den* · tay lee · tay] *n. See* receiver.

receivership [re · *seev* · er · ship] *n.* A **proceeding** by which the property of an insolvent debtor, or property that is the subject of litigation, may be preserved and appropriately disposed of by a person known as a **receiver**, who is appointed and supervised by the court. A corporation as well as an individual may be "in receivership." *See* receiver.

receiving stolen goods [re · *seev* · ing *stoh* · len] *n.* Same as **receiving stolen property**.

receiving stolen property [re · *seev* · ing *stoh* · len *prop* · er · tee] *n.* Receiving property (*see* receive) with the knowledge that it is stolen property, and with fraudulent intent. *See* fraudulent. Although receiving stolen property is a crime separate and distinct from the crime of stealing the property (*see* larceny), if the theft was recent there is a **rebuttable presumption** that the theft was committed by the person in possession of the property.

recess [*ree* · sess] *n.* 1. A short break during a session of court. 2. A period when court is not in session because of an adjournment. *Compare* continuance. 3. A break or interval during a session of the legislature. *Compare* adjournment.
v. To take a break or stop the action.
➤ *n.* cessation, closure, hiatus, pause, rest, interregnum, respite, intermission ("a recess for the holidays").
Ant. continuation.
v. adjourn, pause, suspend, rest, stop, postpone, halt ("to recess until morning").

recidivism [re · *sid* · i · vizm] *n.* A term for the behavior of a **recidivist**.

recidivist [re · *sid* · i · vist] *n.* A **habitual criminal**; a **repeat offender**.
➤ habitual criminal, repeat offender, repeat criminal, incorrigible criminal, hardened criminal, outlaw, convict, reprobate.

reciprocal [re · *sip* · re · kel] *adj.* Mutual.
➤ mutual, bilateral, interdependent, corresponding, analogous, correlative.
Ant. independent, single.
reciprocal contract [kon · trakt] *n.* A **bilateral contract**.

Reciprocal Enforcement of Support Act *n.* A **Uniform Law** under which a person entitled to court-ordered support can initiate **proceedings** to enforce the order in the state where his or her spouse resides. The Act has been adopted in most states; it applies to child support as well as to spousal support. *See* nonsupport.

reciprocal promises [*prom* · iss · ez] *n.* **Mutual promises**.

reciprocal trusts *n.* Separate **trusts**, one being a trust that A creates for B, the other being a similar trust that B creates for A. A and B are usually husband and wife or members of the same family.

reciprocal wills *n.* **Wills** in which the **testators** name each other as beneficiaries. Reciprocal wills may or may not be **joint and mutual wills**.

reciprocity [ress · i · *pross* · i · tee] *n.* 1. A mutual exchange of privileges or advantages. 2. A short term for **reciprocity between states**. 3. Mutuality.
➤ cooperation, reciprocation, interchange, correspondence, quid pro quo, mutuality.
reciprocity agreement *n. See* reciprocity between states.

reciprocity between states [be · *tween*] *n.* A relationship between two states under which one state gives the citizens or residents of the other certain rights or privileges, with the understanding that its own citizens or residents shall enjoy similar rights or privileges in the other state. Reciprocity is not **comity**: comity exists between nations and the granting of it is discretionary; reciprocity is a term usually applied in connection with the states of the United States, and the granting of it is mandatory once a **reciprocity agreement** has been entered into or **reciprocity statutes** enacted.

reciprocity statute [*stat* · shoot] *n. See* reciprocity between states.

recision [ree · *sizh* · en] *n.* Same as **rescission**.

recital [re · *site* · el] *n.* 1. Sometimes referred to as a "whereas clause"; a statement in a will, deed, or other instrument giving the reason for the transaction. Thus, for EXAMPLE, a **family settlement agreement** might contain the following recital: "Whereas, the parties desire that the will of Samuel Smith be carried out and the estate distributed without the necessity of filing a formal account with the Court ..." 2. In a **pleading**, a statement introducing an **allegation**. 3. The act of relating facts in detail. 4. A musical performance, generally by one or two musicians, usually not of popular music.
➤ description, recitation, narration, summary, chronical, depiction ("the recitals of the will"); performance, concert ("The Sydeman recital received mixed reviews").

recite [re · *site*] *v.* 1. To make a **recital**. 2. To state in detail, whether verbally or in writing.
➤ declaim, enumerate, recapitulate, soliloquize, communicate, list, repeat.

reckless [*rek* · less] *adj.* 1. In one meaning, describes conduct demonstrating an indifference to consequences, particularly those involving danger to life or to the safety of others. 2. In another use, means **simple negligence** or the absence of **due care**.
➤ impulsive, unwary, careless, irresponsible, improvident, hasty, inattentive ("reckless driving").
Ant. circumspect, prudent.

reckless disregard [dis · re · *gard*] *n.* Synonymous with "recklessness." The law often applies this term to conduct that demonstrates an indifference to consequences and to the rights or safety of others. *See* reckless endangerment; reckless homicide.

reckless driving [dry · ving] *n.* Operating a motor vehicle under circumstances showing a reckless or willful and wanton disregard of the rights or safety of others. Reckless driving may be a **felony**, a **misdemeanor**, or a **traffic offense**, depending upon its gravity and other circumstances. *See* willful and wanton act.

reckless endangerment [en · *dane* · jer · ment] *n.* The crime of engaging in conduct that creates a substantial risk of death or serious bodily injury to another person. EXAMPLE: If a person standing nearby sees a cow grazing several yards from an approaching child and, without attempting to lure the animal away, kills it by discharging his rifle at close range, he may be guilty of reckless endangerment.

reckless homicide [*hom* · i · side] *n.* A form of **homicide**, usually **involuntary manslaughter**, involving death caused by some **willful and wanton act** (EXAMPLE: **driving while intoxicated**).

recklessness [*rek* · less · ness] *n.* Indifference to consequences; indifference to the safety and rights of others. Recklessness implies conduct amounting to more than **ordinary negligence**. *See* reckless.
➤ indifference, gross negligence, impulsiveness, negligence, precipitousness, impetuousness, irresponsibility.

reclaim [ree · *clame*] *v.* To get back; to recover.
➤ recover, reacquire, repossess, replevin, reestablish, rebuild ("her attempt to reclaim the property").

reclamation [rek · le · *may* · shen] *n.* 1. Making land fit for cultivation or development, for EXAMPLE, by draining swamps. 2. The retaking of property that one has abandoned, lost, or mislaid. 3. The act of reclaiming anything.
➤ retaking, repossession; restoration, reestablishment.

recognition [rek · eg · *nish* · en] *n.* 1. Ratification; confirmation; acknowledgment. 2. The act of acknowledging the validity of something. EXAMPLE: An employer who "grants recognition" to a union acknowledges that the union represents a majority of its employees and is entitled to represent them in **collective bargaining**. 3. The act of taking notice of something.
➤ perception, detection, remembrance, awareness, understanding, citation ("The phrase gained national recognition"); appreciation, honor, praise, approval, notice, credit, salute ("recognition for a job well done").

R

recognizance [re · *kog* · ni · zense] *n.* A person's obligation to the court to appear in court or to return to court to enter a plea or to stand trial in a criminal case. It may take the form of a **bail bond** or an **OR bond**. *See* own recognizance.

recognize [*rek* · eg · nize] *v.* 1. To identify. 2. To acknowledge or accept. *See* recognition.
➤ identify, remember, comprehend, discover, discern, recollect ("recognize the man"); accept, embrace, realize, uphold, validate, own ("recognize his task").

recollection [rek · e · *lek* · shen] *n.* The act of recalling something to mind. In the law of evidence, the term has extensive application in connection with the prompting of a witness's memory by means of memoranda or other writings made prior to the occasion of the witness's testimony. *See and compare* past recollection recorded; present recollection recorded; present recollection revived.
➤ recognition, memory, recall, consciousness, reminiscence, reconstruction, impression.

recommendatory words [rek · e · *men* · de · tore · ee] *n.* Same as **precatory words**.

recompense [*rek* · em · pense] *n.* A reward; compensation; remuneration.
➤ reward, compensation, remuneration, amends, emolument, expiation.

reconciliation [rek · en · sil · ee · *ay* · shen] *n.* The act of resolving differences. *In domestic relations law*, a resumption of **cohabitation** by spouses who have been living apart; *in construing a contract*, reading the contract so as to give effect to provisions that would otherwise be contradictory or conflicting; *in bookkeeping*, correcting one's records so that they agree with the bank statement.
➤ restoration, conciliation, rapprochement, concordance, propitiation, rapport, detente.

reconsideration [ree · ken · sid · e · *ray* · shen] *n.* Considering something again; thinking about something again or reviewing it. EXAMPLES: reconsideration by the legislature of a **bill** it previously declined to enact; reconsideration by an administrative agency of a determination it previously made.

reconstruct [ree · kon · *strukt*] *v.* 1. To reassemble or make a duplicate of. 2. To bring back or reestablish.
➤ duplicate, redo, recreate; restore, renovate, regenerate, refurbish.

reconveyance [ree · ken · *vey* · yense] *n.* A **conveyance** of **title** to real estate to a person who previously owned the property.

record [*rek* · erd] *n.* 1. A **memorial** that evidences something written, said, or done. EXAMPLES: a letter; a memorandum; a **book of account**; a dictation tape; a birth certificate. 2. A copy of a document or instrument (EXAMPLES: a deed; a mortgage) filed or deposited with a public officer (EXAMPLE: the **recorder of deeds**) to have it preserved as a **public record**. 3. An **official record**. 4. The act of **recording** or being **recorded**. *See* record (*verb*). *Also see* arrest record; books and records; business record; *Congressional Record*; court of record; court record; defective record; face of the record; matter of record; of record; official records; public record; record; sealing the record; title of record.
v. [re · *kord*] 1. To put in writing; to **memorialize**; to make a transcript. 2. To file or deposit a document or instrument (EXAMPLES: a deed; a mortgage) for recording. *See* record (*noun*). 3. To create or copy an audio or video recording on a tape or disk.
➤ *n.* account, annals, documentation, register, transcript, minutes, dossier, muster, enumeration ("record of the proceedings"); accomplishment, performance, reign, resume, reputation ("president's foreign policy record").
v. make note, transcribe, docket, document, register, calendar, chronicle, tabulate.

record date *n.* The date as of which a person must be registered as a stockholder on the corporate records to be entitled to receive a declared **dividend**. The record date is specified in the **declaration of dividend**.

record notice [*noh* · tiss] *n.* The **constructive notice** to **all the world** that occurs when a document or instrument (EXAMPLES: a deed; a mortgage) is recorded. *See also* legal notice.

record on appeal [a · *peel*] *n.* The papers a trial court transmits to the **appellate**

R

court, on the basis of which the appellate court decides the appeal. The record on appeal includes the **pleadings**, all **motions** made before the **trial court**, the **official transcript**, and the **judgment** or order appealed from.

record owner [*oh* · ner] *n.* 1. Also referred to as the **owner of record**; the person who has **title** to real estate according to the **public records**. *See* record title. 2. The person in whose name stock is registered on the records of the corporation that issued it. *See* corporate records.

record title [*ty* · tel] *n.* **Title** to real estate as evidenced by the **public records**, provable by a **title search** that establishes a regular **chain of title** down to the present **owner of record**.

recordation [rek · or · *day* · shen] *n.* The act of **recording** something. *See* record.

recorded [re · *kore* · ded] *adj. See* record.

recorded past recollection
[rek · e · *lek* · shen] *n.* A memorandum or other writing made at the time of occurrence of the events that are the subject of the writing. Such a document may be admissible as an **exception to the hearsay rule**. *See and compare* past recollection recorded; present recollection recorded; present recollection revived.

recorder [re · *kore* · der] *n.* 1. In some jurisdictions, a judge or **magistrate** of a **court of limited jurisdiction**. *See* recorder's court. 2. In some jurisdictions, a **public officer** with responsibility for **recording** instruments filed with her as **public records**. EXAMPLE: a **recorder of deeds**. *See* instruments.

➤ archivist, registrar, stenographer, historian, scribe, clerk, court reporter; judge, magistrate.

recorder of deeds *n.* A **public officer** in charge of the **recording** of deeds. *See* deeds. *See also* registrar of deeds.

recorder's court [re · *kore* · derz] *n.* A court in which the judge's title is "recorder." The **jurisdiction** of a recorder's court is generally the same as that of a **justice's court** or a **magistrate's court**.

recording [re · *kore* · ding] *n.* 1. The act of making a **record**. 2. A copy or a record of a transaction or of words, thoughts, sounds,

images, or the like. EXAMPLES: a transcript; a memorandum; a compact disc; a videotape.

➤ copy, record, memorandum, transcript, tape.

recording acts *n.* State statutes that provide for the recording of instruments, particularly those affecting **title** to real estate (EXAMPLES: a deed; a mortgage; a **tax lien**) and **security interests** in personal property (EXAMPLES: a **conditional sale contract**; a **security agreement**). There are several types of recording acts. In **notice act** states, an instrument that is not recorded is invalid with respect to a person who subsequently purchases the property who has no actual knowledge of the unrecorded transaction. In **race act** states, actual notice is immaterial because, in the event of conflicting claims of ownership, absolute priority is given to the first person who "wins the race to the courthouse" to record her instrument. **Race-notice acts**, which are in effect in some juridictions, combine various features of notice acts and race acts.

recording laws *n.* Same as **recording acts**.

recording statutes [*stat* · shoots] *n.* Same as **recording acts**.

records [re · kordz] *n. Plural* of **record**. *See* record.

records of corporation [*rek* · erdz of kore · per · *ay* · shen] *n. See* corporate records.

recount [re · *kownt*] *v.* To tell a story; to narrate.

➤ tell, narrate, impart, describe, detail, recapitulate, divulge, render ("recount the experience").

recoup [ree · *koop*] *v.* To regain; to get back what one has lost. *See* recoupment.

➤ regain, get back, redeem, remunerate, requite, satisfy, replevin, atone ("to recoup one's losses").

recoupment [ree · *koop* · ment] *n.* 1. In **pleading**, a reduction of a plaintiff's money claim as a result of a claim of the defendant arising out of the same transaction. More specifically, the right of a defendant to reduce the plaintiff's demand because the plaintiff has not fulfilled some obligation of the contract upon which she is suing.

Recoupment is achieved through a **counterclaim**. Recoupment should be distinguished from **setoff**, which involves **crossdemands** arising out of different transactions rather than out of the same transaction. 2. The act of getting back what one has lost.
➤ reduction, rebate, mitigation, offsetting.

recourse [ree · korse] *n.* 1. Resort by a creditor, **obligee**, or **holder** to a **surety**, **guarantor**, or **indorser** for payment after default by the principal debtor or primary **obligor**. *Compare* nonrecourse. *See and compare* without recourse; with recourse. 2. A seeking of aid or assistance.
➤ remedy, access, device, entreaty, asylum, option, refuge ("He was left without recourse").

recover [ree · *kuv* · er] *v.* 1. To obtain by litigation; to acquire as a result of a **judgment** or decree of court. 2. To get back what one has lost or surrendered; to recoup. 3. To get well after an illness.
➤ repossess, regain, reacquire, secure, replevy, collect ("to recover the lost treasure"); mend, revive, recuperate, rejuvenate, heal, rally ("to recover from battle wounds").

recoverable [ree · *kuv* · er · ebl] *adj.* Capable of being recovered or subject to recovery. *See* recover; recovery.

recovery [ree · *kuv* · er · ee] *n.* 1. In the broad sense, the effect of a **judgment** in favor of a person bringing a lawsuit, i.e, a validation of her rights. 2. In the more usual sense, the amount of **damages** or other **relief** awarded by a court in its judgment or order in favor of a plaintiff in a lawsuit. 3. The act of recovering. *See* recover.
➤ satisfaction, award, indemnification, restitution, redress, collection, repossession, reversion, procurement, retrieval, replevy; healing, convalescence, revival, restoration.

recrimination [re · krim · i · *nay* · shen] *n.* A **defense** in an **action** for divorce based upon misconduct by the plaintiff which would itself be grounds for divorce if the defendant had brought an action against the plaintiff.
➤ countercharge, retort, rejoinder, counterattack, reprisal, blame, retribution.

recross-examination [ree · kross eg · zam · i · *nay* · shen] *n.* Additional **cross-examination** of a witness following **redirect examination** of the witness.

rectify [rek · ti · fy] *v.* To make right; to correct; to modify; to **amend**.
➤ cure, attune, correct, modify, amend, calibrate, enumerate, revise, improve, square.

recusation [rek · yoo · *zay* · shun] *n.* The act of challenging a judge or a juror for prejudice or bias. *See* challenge to juror; disqualified judge. *Also see* recuse.

recuse [re · *kyooz*] *v.* To disqualify oneself from sitting as a judge in a case, either on the **motion** of a **party** or on the judge's **own motion**, usually because of bias or some **interest** in the outcome of the litigation. *See* bias of judge; disqualification; disqualified judge. *See also* recusation.
➤ disqualify, eliminate, challenge.

red tape *n.* Bureaucratic routine followed to trivial extremes. *See* bureaucracy.
➤ bureaucracy, paperwork, procedures, protocol, nonsense, triviality.

red-handed [han · ded] *adv.* A phrase applied to a person who is caught in the act of committing a crime or who is found with evidence of a crime on him. *See in flagrante delicto.*
➤ in the act, during commission, actively engaged ("He was caught red-handed").

redeem [re · *deem*] *v.* 1. To buy back; to pay off. 2. To recover something that has been **pledged**, or to recover **legal title** to it (EXAMPLES: a watch that was pawned; a home that was mortgaged), by satisfying the debt. *See* redemption. 3. To make up for a mistake or for a wrong done to someone.
➤ make good, satisfy, discharge, fulfill, acquit, perform ("redeem the note"); deliver, liberate, free, unbind, unchain, manumit ("redeem the prisoner").

redeemable [re · *deem* · ebl] *adj.* Capable of redemption; capable of being redeemed. *See* redeem.
    redeemable bond *n.* A **bond** that may be **called** for payment by the issuer before its **maturity**. *See also* callable bond.
    redeemable stock *n.* Stock that may be **called** for payment by the issuing corporation.

R

redelivery [ree · de · *liv* · e · ree] *n.* A second or subsequent delivery.
redelivery bond *n.* Same as **delivery bond**.

redemise [ree · de · *mize*] *n.* A second or subsequent **conveyance** of land previously **demised**.

redemption [re · *demp* · shun] *n.* 1. The recovery of **pledged** property by payment of what is due (EXAMPLE: paying off a mortgage) or by the performance of some other condition (EXAMPLE: appearing for trial, *see* bail; bail bond). 2. With respect to mortgaged property sold at **judicial sale**, the **statutory right** of a **mortgagor** or **lienor** to regain the property from the purchaser by satisfying the debt. *See* equity of redemption; right of redemption. *See also* foreclosure; foreclosure sale. 3. An issuer's repurchase of securities (EXAMPLES: stock; **bonds**; **notes**) by payment of their value to the **holder**. 4. Salvation from sin.
➤ restoration, repossession, indemnification, retrieval, discharge, rescue.
redemption of securities [se · *kyoor* · e · teez] *n.* *See* redeemable bond; redeemable stock.
redemption period [*peer* · ee · ed] *n.* The period of time during which a **mortgagor** or **lienor** may redeem property sold at **judicial sale**. *See* redemption.

redirect examination [ree · di · *rekt* eg · zam · i · *nay* · shen] *n.* The **examination** of a witness by the **party** who called her, after **cross-examination** by the other party. *Compare* recross-examination. *See* recall of a witness; rehabilitation.

rediscount [ree · *dis* · kount] *v.* The practice of a bank in **discounting commercial paper** that it has previously **discounted**. *See* discount. *See also* discount rate.
rediscount rate *n.* The legal rate at which **Federal Reserve Banks** can loan money to other banks in the **Federal Reserve System** on **commercial paper** that has previously been **discounted**. *See* discount; discount rate.

rediscounting [ree · *dis* · kount · ing] *n.* *See* rediscount.

redistricting [ree · *dis* · trik · ting] *n.* *See* reapportionment.

redlining [*red* · line · ing] *n.* 1. The refusal of a lending institution to enter into mortgages in neighborhoods it claims are deteriorating. Such a practice is often a pretext for racial discrimination and, as such, violates both federal and state statutes. 2. The editing of a document.
➤ discrimination, prejudice; editing, correction.

redraft [*ree* · draft] *n.* 1. The **drawing** of a new **bill of exchange** after **dishonor** of the original **draft**. 2. The preparation of a second draft of a document, for EXAMPLE, a will or a contract.

redraw [ree · *draw*] *v.* To **make** a **redraft** of a **bill of exchange**.

redress [ree · dress] *n.* Satisfaction with respect to an **injury** or other wrong. It may take the form of **damages** or **equitable relief**. *See also* remedy; reparation.
v. [ree · *dress*] To right a wrong; to rectify an abuse; to **remedy** an **injury**.
➤ *n.* indemnification, amends, compensation, propitiation, appeasement, acquittal.
v. adjust, amend, counter, check, mend, recompense, revise, rectify.
redress of grievances [*greev* · en · sez] *n.* *See* First Amendment.

reduce [ree · *doose*] *v.* To decrease or lessen.
➤ decrease, diminish, lessen, minimize, cut down, shorten, compress, attenuate.
Ant. increase, expand.

reductio ad absurdum [re · *duk* · tee · oh ahd ab · *ser* · dum] (*Latin*) *n.* Means "reduced to absurdity"; used to convey the idea that a given argument or point of view is invalid because it inevitably leads to a ridiculous conclusion.

reduction [re · *duk* · shen] *n.* 1. The act of diminishing, cutting back, or reducing. 2. Refining; extracting.
➤ decrease, limitation, abridgement, abatement, diminution, attenuation, mitigation.
Ant. increase, aggravation.
reduction into possession [po · *zesh* · en] *n.* Converting an **intangible** (EXAMPLE: a *right* to bring a lawsuit for possession of real property) into a **tangible** (EXAMPLE: **actual possession**).
reduction to possession [po · *zesh* · en] *n.* *See* reduction into possession.

R

reduction to practice [*prak · tiss*] *n.*
In **patent** law, completing the patenting
process by putting an invention to use or
into practice on a demonstration basis.

redundancy [re · *dun* · den · see] *n.*
Unnecessary repetition. A word referring
to irrelevant, immaterial, or superfluous
matter contained in a **pleading**. *See* immaterial allegations; impertinent matter.
Also see redundant.
➤ superfluity, duplication, profusion, surfeit,
tautology, pleonasm, reiteration, surplus,
excess.

redundant [re · *dun* · dent] *adj.*
Unnecessarily repetitive. *See* redundancy.
➤ superflous, needless, frivolous, expendable,
gratuitous, repetitive, repetitious, unrequired.

reentry [ree · *en* · tree] *n.* The resumption
of possession pursuant to a right reserved
when possession was parted with (EXAMPLE:
a landlord's taking possession of leased
premises upon termination of the lease).

reexchange [ree · eks · *chaynj*] *n.* The cost
incurred by a **holder** of a **bill of exchange**
as a result of **dishonor** of the bill in a foreign country. *See* foreign bill of exchange.

refer [re · *fer*] *v.* 1. To submit a case,
pursuant to court order, to a **referee** or
master. *Also see* auditor. 2. To direct
someone elsewhere for information or
assistance. *See* reference.
➤ accredit, allude, impute, interpolate,
exemplify, cite, commit, consign, introduce, recommend, transfer, turn over.

referee [ref · e · *ree*] *n.* 1. A person
appointed by a court to assist with certain
judicial functions in a specific case, usually
to try some or all of the issues and to report **findings of fact** to the court. *See also*
auditor; master. *Also see* refer; reference.
2. In many states, the title of the person who
hears and determines workers' compensation claims. *See* workers' compensation
insurance. 3. A person to whom something
is referred.
➤ adjudicator, arbiter, conciliator, master,
umpire, interceder.

referee in bankruptcy [*bank* · rupt · see]
n. The title formerly given to **bankruptcy
judges**.

referee in case of need *n.* A person
whose name is added to a **bill of exchange**
by the **drawer**, or by an **indorser**, as a
person to whom the **holder** may resort if
the bill is **dishonored**.

reference [*ref* · er · ense] *n.* 1. The act of
a court in submitting a case to a **referee**.
2. The act of the parties to a contract in
submitting a dispute under the contract to
arbitration. 3. A recommendation given
to a prospective employer, a lending institution, or the like, with respect to a person's
abilities, honesty, etc. 4. A person who
provides another person with a recommendation for employment, credit, or the like.
5. The act of referring or directing elsewhere. *See* incorporation by reference.
Also see refer.
➤ mention, referral, allusion, implication,
quotation, note ("in reference to Mrs.
Smith's Porsche"); endorsement, voucher,
commendation, statement, declaration,
affirmation ("a reference as to your good
work").

reference in case of need *n. See*
referee in case of need.

referendum [ref · e · *ren* · dum] *n.* Under
some state constitutions, the process by
which an **act of the legislature** or a
constitutional amendment is referred to
the voters at an election for their approval.
See proposition. *Also see* question.
➤ proposition, proposal, election, question,
mandate, plebiscite.

refinancing [ree · *fine* · an · sing] *n.* The
act of paying off an existing loan, or existing loans, with the proceeds of a new loan.

reform [re · *form*] *v.* 1. To correct; to make
better; to modify. 2. To change one's ways
for the better. *See* reformation.
n. A change; an improvement.
➤ *v.* cure, rectify, reconstitute, better, change,
ameliorate, regenerate, rework, transform.
Ant. deteriorate.
n. change, betterment, amelioration,
melioration.

reformation [ref · er · *may* · shun] *n.* 1. An
equitable remedy available to a party to
a contract provided she can prove that the
contract does not reflect the real agreement,
i.e., the actual intention, of the parties.
2. The act of reforming. *See* reform.

reformatory [re · *form* · e · tore · ee] *n.* A penal institution for juvenile offenders.

refresh [ree · *fresh*] *v.* To revive; to stimulate.

➤ revive, regenerate, strengthen, remind, prod, restore, awaken, prompt, stimulate ("refresh the witness's memory").

refreshing memory [ree · *fresh* · ing *mem* · e · ree] *n. See* past recollection recorded; present recollection recorded; present recollection revived.

refreshing recollection [ree · *fresh* · ing rek · e · *lek* · shen] *n. See* past recollection recorded; present recollection recorded; present recollection revived.

refund [*ree* · fund] *n.* A repayment; a rebate of all or a portion of a payment; the return of an overpayment.
v. [ree · *fund*] 1. To make or give a **refund.** *See* refund (*noun*). 2. To fund again; to finance again.
➤ *n.* acquittance, compensation, consolation, repayment, reimbursement, remuneration, retribution.
v. return, redeem, recompense, indemnify, relinquish, remit, remunerate.

refunding [ree · *fun* · ding] *n./adj.* 1. The act of making a refund. 2. The act of refinancing or of funding again. *See* fund.

refunding bonds *n.* The replacement of outstanding **bonds** with a **new issue**, an action undertaken by an issuer of bonds as a means of **refinancing.**

refusal [re · *fyoo* · zel] *n.* The denial of a request or demand. Although "refusal" usually implies that a demand has been made upon a person and that he has declined to comply, the word is frequently used in the law to mean the neglect of a **legal duty.** In this sense, the law sometimes uses "neglect" and "refusal" as synonymous terms. *See and compare* fail; failure; neglect; refuse.
➤ abnegation, declension, rejection, disavowal, enjoinment, veto, repudiation, dissent.

refuse [*ref* · yooss] *n.* That which is discarded or thrown away; trash; garbage.
v. [ree · *fyooz*] To reject; to deny or decline to comply with a request or demand. Although in their ordinary senses, the words "refuse" and "fail" are not synonymous, because a refusal, unlike a failure, involves an affirmative act, the law often treats the two terms as interchangeable. *Compare* fail; failure. *See* refusal.
➤ *n.* debris, rejectamenta, sediment, rubbish, excrement, trash, garbage. *Ant.* valuables.
v. object, decline, reject, abstain, deny, repudiate, renege, forbear ("I refuse to work for that man").
Ant. consent, agree.

refute [re · *fyoot*] *v.* To disprove; to deny; to contradict; to **rebut.**
➤ abnegate, contravene, negate, rebut, contradict, counter, deny, disprove ("to refute an allegation").

regents [*ree* · jents] *n. See* board of regents.

regime [re · *zheem*] *n.* The established authority or political system.
➤ rule, reign, administration, government, system, leadership.

register [*rej* · is · ter] *n.* 1. A book of records, particularly **official records** or **public records**; an official list; a **registry.** *See Federal Register.* 2. A **public officer** required by law to maintain certain public records. EXAMPLE: a **register of wills.** *See also* registrar.
v. 1. To enroll; to record. *See* registration. 2. To make an impression; to be comprehended.
➤ *n.* annals, archives, catalog, diary, ledger, roster, schedule ("Mark the date in the register").
v. enroll, enter, record, chronicle, schedule, inscribe ("to register for fall classes"); come home, get through, have an effect, impress, dawn, sink in, tell ("It finally registered what he was doing").

register of ships *n.* A register maintained by the customs authorities for the purpose of listing the nationality of merchant ships. *See* ship's papers.

register of wills *n.* The chief clerk of the **probate court** in some states.

registered [*rej* · is · terd] *adj.* Enrolled; recorded; made a matter of record.
➤ enrolled, recorded, certified, official ("registered securities").

registered bond *n. See* registered securities.

registered check *n.* A check purchased at a bank, drawn on bank funds that have been set aside to pay the check. *Compare* cashier's check; certified check. *See* check.

registered letter [*let* · er] *n. See* registered mail.

registered mail *n.* Mail whose delivery is insured by the **Postal Service**.

registered securities [sek · *yoor* · i · teez] *n.* **Bonds** or stock whose owner's name appears on the **instrument** and is also registered on the books of the corporation or governmental entity that issued them. Only the registered owner of **securities** may redeem them. *See* securities. *Also see* corporate records.

registered stock *n. See* registered securities.

registered trademark [*trade* · mark] *n. See* trademark.

registered voter [*voh* · ter] *n.* A person whose name is listed on the records where she resides as a person eligible to vote. Registered voter lists are often used to locate potential jurors. *See* eligible voter. *Also see* elector.

registrar [*rej* · is · trar] *n.* 1. A person whose duty it is to maintain a **register** or **registry**. EXAMPLE: a **registrar of deeds**. 2. A person employed by a college or university who is in charge of the enrollment of students.
➤ recorder, clerk, official.

registrar of deeds *n.* In some jurisdictions, the name given to a **recorder of deeds**.

registration [rej · is · *tray* · shen] *n.* The act of registering. *See* register.
➤ recording, reservation, inscription, enrollment, filing, listing.

registration of land titles [*ty* · telz] *n.* A system for the registration of **titles** to land, under which the name of the owner of land appears on a **certificate of title**. *See* Torrens title system.

registration of securities [se · *kyoor* · e · teez] *n.* 1. *See* registered securities. 2. A **registration statement**.

registration of trademark [*trade* · mark] *n. See* trademark.

registration of voters [*voh* · terz] *n. See* registered voter.

registration statement [*state* · ment] *n.* A document that must be filed with the **Securities and Exchange Commission** by a corporation that proposes to issue **securities** to the public. Its contents are similar to the contents of the **prospectus**.

registry [*rej* · is · tree] *n.* A list, book, or office for the registration or recording of documents as required by law.
➤ list, book, office.

regress [ree · *gress*] *v.* To move backward.
➤ deteriorate, wane, sink, return, relapse, retrogress.
Ant. advance, progress.

regressive tax [ree · *gress* · iv] *n.* A tax whose rate decreases as the taxable income of the taxpayer increases. *Compare* progressive tax.

regs *n.* A short form sometimes used in referring to government **regulations**. USAGE: "Our plan is illegal under the new regs issued by the Justice Department."
➤ regulations, rules, standards.

regular [*reg* · yoo · ler] *adj.* 1. Conforming to an established rule or to law or custom. 2. Consistent; following a fixed procedure or schedule. 3. Happening at uniform intervals. 4. Average; normal; routine; usual.
➤ normal, established, prevalent, traditional, orthodox, sanctioned ("the regular way of doing things"); even, exact, methodical, patterned, periodic, regulated ("at regular intervals").
Ant. unusual; sporadic.

regular course of business [*biz* · ness] *n.* For purposes of determining the applicability of the s**hopbook rule,** a term relating to a record made in the course of a normal commercial transaction at or within a reasonably short time of the transaction. *See* book of account; book of original entry. *See also* ordinary course of business.

regular deposit [de · *paw* · zit] *n.* Same as **special deposit**.

regular election [e · *lek* · shen] *n.* Same as **general election**. *Compare* special election.

regular employment [em · *ploy* · ment] *n.* 1. Employment for a definite and extended period of time. 2. Employment of a continuing nature. *Compare* casual employment; seasonal employment; temporary employment. *See* regular full-time employment.

regular full-time employment [em · *ploy* · ment] *n.* Regular employment that is also full-time. *See* full-time employment. *Compare* regular part-time employment.

regular indorsement [in · *dorse* · ment] *n.* Same as **indorsement**.

regular meeting [*mee* · ting] *n.* 1. A meeting of the board of directors or the stockholders of a corporation, held at a time and place provided by its **charter** or **by-laws,** or as required by statute. *See* annual meeting; stockholders' meeting. 2. A meeting of the **qualified voters** of a town, held at a time required by law. *See* town meeting.

regular on its face *n.* Refers to **process** when it proceeds from a court or other body having authority to issue it, is legal in form, and contains nothing to alert anyone that it is issued without authority. *See* face.

regular part-time employment [em · *ploy* · ment] *n.* Employment that is part-time. *See* part-time employment. *Compare* regular full-time employment.

regular process [*pross* · ess] *n. See* regular on its face.

regular session [*sesh* · en] *n.* A session of a legislature held during the ordinary period for the legislature to meet, as prescribed by law. *Compare* special session. *See* session.

regular term *n.* A **term of court** begun at the time required by law and ended no later than the time the law requires. *Compare* special term. *See* term.

regularly [*reg* · yoo · ler · lee] *adv.* Normally; routinely; usually.
➤ consistently, habitually, persistently, traditionally, customarily, usually. *Ant.* rarely, intermittently.

regularly employed [em · ploy] *See* regular employment.

regulate [*reg* · yoo · late] *v.* 1. To control; to direct; to govern; to engage in the act of regulation. *See* regulation. *Compare* deregulate. USAGE: "The Constitution gives

the federal government the power to regulate **interstate commerce.**" 2. To adjust. USAGE: "regulate the thermostat."
➤ direct, establish, govern, systematize, superintend, monitor.

regulation [reg · yoo · *lay* · shun] *n.* 1. The act of regulating. *See* regulate. 2. A rule having the **force of law,** promulgated by an administrative agency; the act of **rule-making.** *See* promulgate. 3. A rule of conduct established by a person or body in authority for the governance of those over whom they have authority.
➤ regimentation, conduct, arrangement, standardization, governance, modulation, coordination ("regulation of the fish's air flow"); canon, decree, directive, dictate, ordinance ("military regulations").

regulation charge *n.* A **license fee** or **privilege tax.**

regulation of commerce [*kawm* · erss] *n. See* interstate commerce.

regulations [reg · yoo · *lay* · shunz] *n.* *Plural* of **regulation.** *See* regulation.

regulatory [*reg* · yoo · le · tore · ee] *adj.* Pertaining to that which regulates; pertaining to the act of regulation. *See* regulation. *Also see* regulate.

regulatory agency [*ay* · jen · see] *n.* An **administrative agency** empowered to promulgate and enforce regulations. *See* regulation.

regulatory crime *n.* 1. A **strict liability crime.** EXAMPLE: discharging **hazardous waste.** 2. A **petty offense.** EXAMPLE: littering.

regulatory offense [o · *fense*] *n.* Same as **strict liability crime.**

rehab [*ree* · hab] *n./adj.* Short for **rehabilitation,** as in "rehab center" or "rehab program."

rehab center [*sen* · ter] *n.* Short for "rehabilitation center." *See* treatment program. *Also see* halfway house.

rehab program [*pro* · gram] *n.* Short for "rehabilitation program." *See* treatment program. *Also see* halfway house.

rehabilitate [ree · ha · *bil* · i · tate] *v.* 1. To correct; to restore. 2. To reestablish. 3. To heal; to cure. *See* rehabilitation.
➤ renovate, reconstruct, furbish, reintegrate, reinvigorate, rebuild; heal, cure.

rehabilitation [ree · ha · bil · i · *tay* · shun] *n.* 1. The act of restoring a sick person to health; the act of enhancing the abilities of a person with a disability. *See* vocational rehabilitation. 2. The act of restoring a drug addict or alcoholic to sobriety. *See* treatment program. 3. The act of reforming a criminal. 4. Restoring a witness's **credibility** after it has been **impeached** on **cross-examination**, i.e., the **rehabilitation of a witness**. 5. The act of restoring the financial position of a failing business by, for EXAMPLE, a **reorganization** (*see* corporate reorganization), a **composition with creditors**, or an **arrangement with creditors**.
➤ correction, renewal, indoctrination, convalescence, rejuvenation, renascence, salvation.

rehabilitation of a witness
[ree · ha · bil · i · *tay* · shun of a wit · ness] *n.* *See* rehabilitation.

rehearing [ree · *heer* · ing] *n.* A new **hearing** given a case by a court, **commission**, or **board** so that it may reconsider a previous action that may have been taken erroneously. *See* reconsideration. *See also* reargument; retrial.

reimburse [ree · im · *berss*] *v.* 1. To make a reimbursement; to repay. 2. To compensate for a **loss**; to **indemnify**.
➤ restore, repay, compensate, indemnify, rcquite, recompense.

reimbursement [ree · im · *berss* · ment] *n.* 1. The act of repaying or reimbursing. *See* reimburse; repay. 2. Compensation for a **loss**; **indemnification**.
➤ repayment, compensation, indemnification.

reinstate [ree · in · *state*] *v.* To restore a person or thing to a position or condition from which he or it has been removed; to effect a reinstatement.
➤ reconstitute, resuscitate, reinstall, reinvest, restore.

reinstatement [ree · in · *state* · ment] *n.* The act of restoring a person or thing to a position or condition from which she or it has been removed. EXAMPLES: rehiring an employee who has previously been fired; restoring coverage under an insurance policy that has lapsed for nonpayment.

➤ restoration, rehiring, readmittance ("The employee's reinstatement is effective immediately").

reinsurance [ree · in · *shoor* · ense] *n.* A contract between two insurance companies under which the second company (the **reinsurer**) insures the first company (the **insurer**) against **loss** due to policyholders' claims.

reinsurer [ree · in · *shoor* · er] *n.* An insurance company's insurance company. *See* reinsurance.

reject [re · *jekt*] *v.* 1. To decline; to disallow; to refuse; to refuse to grant; to refuse to receive. *See* rejection. 2. To throw away; to discard.
n. [*ree* · jekt] That which is cast aside.
➤ *v.* decline, despise, jettison, jilt, refuse, disaffirm, reprobate, rebuff ("to reject an appeal").
Ant. accept.
n. castaway, leftover, waste, castoff, outcast ("That auto part is a defective reject").

rejection [re · *jek* · shun] *n.* 1. Any act or word of an **offeree**, communicated to an **offeror**, conveying her refusal of an **offer**. *See* nonacceptance. 2. The act of rejecting.
➤ abandonment, disallowance, denial, snub, slight, proscription, abnegation, contempt, eviction, refusal, waiver.

rejoinder [re · *join* · der] *n.* 1. In **common law pleading**, a **pleading** by the defendant in response to the plaintiff's **replication**. 2. A reply; an answer; a retort.
➤ answer, response, defense, countercharge, reply.

relate [ree · *layt*] *v.* 1. To have a connection with; to pertain. 2. To give an account of.
➤ pertain, tie, interrelate, concern, correlate, affect, identify ("does it relate to the issue at hand?"); tell, impart, narrate, speak ("relate the story").

related [re · *lay* · ted] *adj.* A word referring to the connections between people, things, or events. *See* relation; relative.
➤ affiliated, cognate, connected, allied, consanguine, enmeshed, germane, leagued.

relation [re · *lay* · shun] *n.* 1. Broadly speaking, relatives by blood or **affinity**. *See* consanguinity; kin; relation by blood. 2. When used in a will, the term "relations" is generally construed to mean only **relations by blood**, i.e., those persons who could take from the **decedent** under the **intestate laws**. 3. Business, professional, or social connections. 4. Sexual relations. 5. The act of telling or relating a story or an account of some occurrence.

➤ relationship, rapport, connection, relevance, nexus, liaison, mutuality ("That has no relation to our topic"); relative, kin, family member ("He is one of our relations").

relation back *n.* A **legal fiction** that, in certain circumstances, considers an act to have been done on a date earlier than the date on which it was actually done. EXAMPLE: the principle that the date of final or actual delivery of an **instrument** held in **escrow** is the date on which it was originally deposited in escrow.

relation by affinity [a · *fin* · i · tee] *n.* *See* affinity.

relation by blood *n.* A person related to another through the blood of a **common ancestor**. *Compare* relation by affinity. *See* consanguinity; kin; next of kin.

relations [re · *lay* · shunz] *n.* *Plural* of **relation**. *See* relation.

relative [*rel* · e · tiv] *adj.* Dependent upon or considered with reference to something else. *Compare* absolute.
n. 1. A **relation by blood**. 2. A relation by blood or by **affinity**. *See* relation. 3. That which is dependent upon or to be considered with reference to something else. *Compare* absolute.

➤ *adj.* comparative, respective, dependent, analogous, reciprocal, referring, reliant ("That is relative to your point of view").
n. agnate, cognate, clansman, relation, kin, kindred ("We are blood relatives").

relative fact *n.* A fact that relates to another fact; a mere circumstance. *See* related; relation.

relative rights *n.* The **right** of one person considered in reference to the right of another. USAGE: "A driver's **right of way** is not an **absolute right**; it exists relative to the rights of other drivers on the road." *Compare* absolute right.

relatives [*rel* · e · tivz] *n.* *Plural* of **relative**. *See* relative.

relator [re · *lay* · tor] *n.* 1. A person on whose behalf an **ex rel. action** is brought by the state. 2. The informer in a **qui tam action**. *Note* that "relator" is not "**realtor**."

release [re · *leess*] *n.* 1. The act of giving up or **discharging** a claim or right to the person against whom the claim exists or against whom the right is enforceable. *See also* extinguishment. 2. A document or writing stating that a right or claim is given up or discharged. 3. Freedom from jail or prison.
v. 1. To give up or to **discharge** a claim or right to the person against whom the claim exists or against whom the right is enforceable. 2. To free from jail or prison.

➤ *n.* relinquishment, discharge, deliverance, indemnity, exoneration, amnesty ("sign a release"); freedom, liberation, discharge ("a release from prison").
v. discharge, let go, relinquish, emancipate, clear, deliver, exonerate, free, dismiss.

release deed *n.* A **quitclaim deed**, also referred to as a **deed of release**.

release of expectancy [eks · *pek* · ten · see] *n.* The **assignment** of an **expectancy**, either to the person from whom one has the expectancy or to another potential heir.

release on own recognizance [re · *kog* · ni · sense] *n.* *See* OR; own recognizance.

relevance [*rel* · e · vense] *n.* The state or condition of being relevant.

➤ materiality, pertinence, importance, applicability, significance.

relevancy [*rel* · e · ven · see] *n.* The logical relation between evidence offered and a fact to be established. Relevancy is required for evidence to be admissible. *See* offer; offer of proof. *Also see* pertinent; relevant.

relevant [*rel* · e · vent] *adj.* Pertinent; material. *See* material evidence; material fact; relevant evidence.

➤ pertinent, material, germane, on target, congruent, related, applicable, cognate ("relevant evidence").
Ant. irrelevant, unrelated.

relevant evidence [*ev* · i · dense] *n.* **Evidence** that proves or disproves a fact, or that tends to prove or disprove a fact. **Relevance** is the basic measure of the **admissibility** of evidence. *See* material evidence. *Also see* admissible evidence.

R

reliance [re · *ly* · ense] *n.* Trust; confidence; dependence. Intent to induce **reliance** is an essential element of **fraudulent misrepresentation**. It is also an essential element of **promissory estoppel**.
➤ trust, confidence, dependence, credence, credit, conviction.

reliction [re · *lik* · shun] *n.* An addition to land caused by the permanent withdrawal of water that previously covered it.

relief [re · *leef*] *n.* 1. A person's object in bringing a lawsuit; the function or purpose of a **remedy**. 2. **Public assistance**. 3. The lessening or alleviation of pain, oppression, or other distress.
➤ remedy, abatement, allayment, extrication, mollification, palliation, assuagement ("relief for damages inflicted"); welfare, aid, dole, handout, charity, care, ministry ("relief for the poor").

religion [re · *lij* · en] *n.* A system of belief and worship. The federal Constitution guarantees the right to freely practice the religion of one's choice. It also prohibits the involvement of government with a particular religion. *See* freedom of religion. *Also see* establishment clause; First Amendment.
➤ creed, faith, belief.

religious freedom [re · *lij* · ess *free* · dem] *n. See* freedom of religion.

religious liberty [re · *lij* · ess *lib* · er · tee] *n. See* freedom of religion.

religious use *n. See* charitable organization.

rem (*Latin*) *n.* Means "thing." *See in rem*; in rem action. *Also see res*.

remainder [re · *mane* · der] *n.* 1. An **estate** in land to take effect immediately after the expiration of a prior estate (known as the **particular estate**), created at the same time and by the same **instrument**. EXAMPLE (in a will): "I leave my land to Joe Jones for life, and after his death to Sarah Green and her heirs." The **interest** or **estate** of Sarah Green and her heirs is a remainder; Joe Jones's interest is a **life estate**. *Compare* reversion. *See* contingent remainder; cross-remainders; vested remainder. 2. A **residuary estate**. *See* rest, residue, and remainder. 3. That which is left over; the residue.

➤ balance, residue, surplus, excess, remains; estate, interest, property.

remainder estate [es · *tate*] *n.* A **remainder**.

remainderman [re · *mane* · der · man] *n.* A person entitled to receive a **remainder**.

remand [re · *mand*] *n.* The return of a case by an **appellate court** to the **trial court** for further **proceedings**, for a **new trial**, or for **entry of judgment** in accordance with an order of the appellate court.
v. To return or send back. A person convicted of a crime who has been released from custody pending the determination of her appeal is "remanded to custody" when her appeal is denied.
➤ *n.* return, reassignment.
v. return, recommit, reassign, send back.

remediable [re · *meed* · ee · ebl] *adj.* Capable of being remedied. *See* remedy.
➤ salvageable, amenable, inalleable, fixable.

remediable right *n.* A **right** for which there is an appropriate **remedy** either **in law** or **in equity**.

remedial [re · *meed* · ee · el] *adj.* 1. Providing a **remedy**. 2. Pertaining to remedy.
➤ corrective, medicinal, therapeutic, prophylatic, recuperative, beneficial, vulnerary, healing, reformative.

remedial action [*ak* · shen] *n.* An **action** for recovery of **compensatory damages** rather than **punitive damages**.

remedial laws *n.* 1. Body of law that provides a method for the enforcement of rights; the law of **practice**. EXAMPLE: the **Federal Rules of Civil Procedure** and the **judicial opinions** interpreting and applying them. 2. Laws that provide individuals or a class of persons with **remedies** in circumstances where existing law had either unfairly denied them **relief** or had provided inadequate relief.

remedial legislation [lej · is · *lay* · shun] *n.* **Legislation** that provides **relief** to a person or a class of persons to whom the law had previously either denied relief or had provided inadequate relief. *See* remedial laws.

remedial statute [*stat* · shoot] *n. See* remedial legislation.

remedy [*rem* · e · dee] *n.* The means by which a **right** is enforced, an **injury** is redressed, and **relief** is obtained. EXAMPLES: damages; an **injunction**; *habeas corpus*. *See* adequate remedy at law; administrative remedy; extraordinary remedies; inadequate remedy at law; legal remedy; provisional remedy.
  v. 1. To redress; to make right; to correct; to rectify. 2. To compensate; to **indemnify**; to **make whole**.
➤ *n.* antidote, countermeasure, pharmaceutical, physic, restorative ("a home remedy"); reparation, remediation, restitution, solution, redress, counteraction ("a legal remedy").
  v. alleviate, ameliorate, assuage, fix, heal, mollify, revive, mitigate ("to remedy the mistake").
  Ant. exacerbate.

remembrance [ree · *mem* · brants] *n.* 1. A memory; a recollection. 2. A gift; a testimonial.
➤ recollection, memory, recall, reconstruction; commemoration, tribute, testimonial, keepsake, celebration, memento.

reminder [ree · *mine* · der] *n.* 1. A warning; a notice. 2. A remembrance; a keepsake; a memento.
➤ memo, note, cue, hint, tickler, suggestion; souvenir, memorial, keepsake.

remise [re · *mize*] *v.* To give something up or to surrender it; to release; to **quitclaim**. *See* remission.
➤ give up, surrender, release, quitclaim.

remission [re · *mish* · en] *n.* 1. A **release**, **discharge**, or **extinguishment** of a debt. *See* extinguishment of debt. 2. A pardon; exoneration; forgiveness. 3. The lessening of a disease, usually temporarily.
➤ absolution, amnesty, discharge, exoneration, indulgence, reprieve, pardon ("the remission of the charges"); abatement, abeyance, diminution, ebb, reduction, relaxation, respite ("The disease has gone into remission").
  Ant. imposition; aggravation.

remit [re · *mit*] *v.* 1. To transmit or send something. USAGE: "Please remit payment in full." *See* remittance. 2. To pardon or forgive. USAGE: "The court has decided to remit your fine." 3. To **remise**. *See* remission.

➤ transmit, forward, disburse, proffer, consign, dispatch; alleviate, exonerate, modulate, rescind, reprieve, mitigate.
  Ant. retain; impose.

remittance [re · *mit* · ense] *n.* Money sent by one person to another, regardless of how it is transmitted (EXAMPLES: by mail; by telegraph) and regardless of its form (EXAMPLES: cash; check). *See* remit.

remittee [ree · mit · *tee*] *n.* A person to whom a **remittance** is made. *Compare* remitter.

remitter [ree · *mit* · er] *n.* A person who purchases a **remittance** (EXAMPLES: a **money order** or a **foreign bill of exchange**) to be sent to a **remittee**.

remittitur [ree · *mit* · i · ter] *n.* A reduction by the judge of the amount of a verdict because of the excessiveness of the award. *See* excessive damages.

  remittitur of record [*rek* · erd] *n.* The process by which an **appellate court** sends the **record** back to the **trial court** when it **remands** a case for further proceedings.

remittor [ree · *mit* · er] *n.* Same as **remitter**.

remonstrance [re · *mons* · trens] *n.* A protest or objection. "Remonstrance" is usually applied to a protest of something that has not yet occurred, i.e., something that is merely planned, for EXAMPLE, the proposed construction of a highway.
➤ protest, objection, disapproval, admonishment, warning, reprobation, castigation, criticism, exception.

remorse [ree · *morse*] *n.* Regret; shame; contrition.
➤ grief, regret, anguish, concern, sorrow, contrition, penitence, shame, guilt ("He showed no remorse").

remote [re · *mote*] *adj.* 1. Distant. The word "remote" may imply distance in time (months, minutes, seconds) or in space (miles, feet, inches); it may also imply separation between cause and consequence. *See and compare* remote cause; remote damages. 2. Slight; little; inconsequential.
➤ distant, sequestered, segregated, foreign, inaccessible ("remote reaches of the galaxy"); improbable, meager, imperceptible, small, inconsequential, negligible ("a remote chance").
  Ant. neighboring; substantial.

R

remote cause *n.* In the law of **negligence**, a speculative rather than a **proximate cause** of injury.

remote damages [*dam* · e · jez] *n.* **Damages** from an injury not occurring as a natural result of the wrong at issue; damages of an unusual or speculative nature. *Compare* direct damages; proximate damages.

removable [re · *move* · ebl] *adj.* A term describing a lawsuit that may be removed from a **state court** to a **federal court**. *See* removal; removal of case.

removal [re · *move* · el] *n.* 1. The moving of a person or thing. A person's "removal from the state" or "removal from the jurisdiction" means that she has taken up residence or acquired a new **domicile** in another state or another jurisdiction. 2. A firing, dismissal, or **recall** from public office. *See* removal for cause. 3. The removal of a lawsuit. *See* removal of case.
➤ relocation, transplantation, transference ("requires the removal of the jury"); elimination, eradication, extermination, excavation, abstraction ("removal of the stain"). *Ant.* installation; preservation.

removal for cause *n.* The dismissal of an officer from office, usually a public official from **public office**, for reasons the law recognizes as sufficient, for EXAMPLE, for **peculation**. *See* for cause; good cause; legal cause. *Also see* recall.

removal from office [*off* · iss] *n.* *See* removal for cause.

removal of case *n.* 1. In the usual sense, the transfer of a case from a **state court** to a **federal court**. 2. In the broad sense of the term, any transfer of a case from one court to another.

removal of cause *n.* Same as **removal of case**.

removal of cloud on the title [*ty* · tel] *n.* *See* cloud on the title; quieting title.

remove [ree · *move*] *v.* 1. To take away. 2. To change or transfer a case from one jurisdiction to another.
➤ eliminate, expunge, abolish, liquidate, eliminate, take away, exclude ("remove the trash"); transfer, change venue, relocate, switch, send, shift ("remove a case to federal court").

remuneration [re · myoo · ne · *ray* · shen] *n.* Compensation.
➤ compensation, pay, salary, reward.

render [*ren* · der] *v.* 1. To give; to furnish; to deliver; to make. USAGE: "**render a decision**." *See* render a verdict; render judgment. 2. To return; to give up something. USAGE: "render payment."
➤ state, deliver, convey, impute, proffer, administer ("render a decision"); cede, distribute, exchange, relinquish, tender ("render payment"); construe, paraphrase, transcribe, transliterate, ("render intelligible").

render a decision [de · *sizh* · en] *v.* A court or an administrative agency "renders a decision" when it issues or announces its conclusion in a case. *Compare* opinion. *See* decision.

render a verdict [*ver* · dikt] *v.* A jury "renders a verdict" when it agrees on a **verdict** and reports it to the judge.

render judgment [*juj* · ment] *v.* A judge "renders a judgment" when she announces or pronounces the **judgment** of the court, either in **open court** or in the form of a writing addressed to the **clerk of court**, i.e., when she makes a final determination in the case. Rendering of judgment, which is a **judicial act**, should not be confused with **entry of judgment**, which is a purely **ministerial act**.

rendezvous [*ron* · day · voo] *n.* Meeting; appointment.
v. To meet; to get together.
➤ *n.* appointment, meeting, encounter, engagement, get-together ("My rendezvous with MSH").
v. meet, gather, get together, convene, assemble ("Let's rendezvous at Mick's before the game").

rendition [*ren* · *dish* · en] *n.* 1. The act of rendering. *See* render. 2. A version or interpretation.
➤ arrangement, construction, transcription, interpretation, rendering, version ("my favorite rendition of that song").

rendition of decision [de · *sizh* · en] *n.* *See* render a decision.

rendition of judgment [*juj* · ment] *n.* *See* render judgment.

R

rendition of verdict [*ver* · dikt] *n. See* render a verdict.

renege [ree · *neg*] *v.* To go back on; to reject.
➤ quit, reverse, revoke, vacate, contradict, go back on, invalidate ("to renege on the deal").

renegotiation [ree · ne · go · she · *ay* · shun] *n.* Negotiation again. *See* negotiation. "Renegotiation" is always used in a context that assumes the existence of a contract whose terms the parties are willing to modify by negotiating again.

renew [re · *new*] *v.* To start again; to make new; to reestablish; to refresh; to revive.
➤ regenerate, recommence, revitalize, resuscitate, redress, revive, redeem. *Ant.* cancel, expire.

renewal [re · *new* · el] *n.* The act of renewing or reviving. *See* renew. *Also see* revive. A "renewal" involves the re-creation of a legal relationship rather than an extension of the existing relationship. Thus, for EXAMPLE, a *renewed contract* or a *renewal contract* is a new agreement, not merely a continuation of the original contract for an additional period of time.
➤ enhancement, continuation, salvage, salvation, reclamation, modernization. *Ant.* deterioration, elimination.
    renewal lease *n.* The creation of a new lease rather than an extension of an old lease. *Compare* extension of lease.
    renewal of lease *n.* Same as **renewal lease**.

renounce [re · *nounss*] *v.* To **waive**, particularly a right; to relinquish; to **disclaim**; to **abjure**. *See* renunciation.
➤ repudiate, disclaim, abdicate, deny, recant, disavow, waive, abjure.

rent *n.* 1. The **consideration** paid under a lease for the right to occupy. *See* abatement of rent; extinguishment of rent; ground rent; net rent. 2. The **royalty** or **return** received by a **lessor** under a **mining lease** or an **oil and gas lease**. *See* mining rent.
    v. 1. To occupy premises under a lease. 2. To **let** premises. 3. To **lease** anything.
➤ *n.* hire, lease, payment, rental, tariff ("Rent is $250 per month"); breach, discord, dissension, perforation, schism ("a large rent left between buyer and seller").
    v. lease, let, charter, farm out, engage, contract.

rent-a-judge *n.* A method of **alternative dispute resolution** in which the **parties** choose a third party to decide the dispute. If the parties so agree, the procedure followed in a rent-a-judge proceeding is similar to the procedure used in traditional trials, as opposed to more informal EXAMPLES of alternative dispute resolution such as **mini-trials** or **summary jury trials**.

rental [*rent* · el] *n.* Same as rent.
    rents and profits [*prof* · its] *n. See* rents, issues, and profits.
    rents, issues, and profits [*ish* · ewz and *prof* · its] *n.* Rent, **profits**, or other income from land, payable to the person in possession of the land (EXAMPLE: a **life tenant**) rather than to the owner of the land.

renunciation [re · nun · see · ay · shun] *n.* 1. In law, an act by which a person abandons or **waives** a right, but without transferring it to another. 2. The decision of a surviving spouse to take an **elective share** of the **estate** of the deceased spouse rather than accept the terms of the will. *See* election by spouse; renunciation of will. 3. Under the **Uniform Commercial Code**, the expressed willingness not to enforce an **instrument** by a person entitled to enforce it. 4. Withdrawal from criminal activity.
➤ abandonment, rejection, abdication, disavowal, disclaimer, forbearance ("the renunciation of the throne"). *Ant.* retention.
    renunciation by surviving spouse [ser · *vy* · ving] *n. See* renunciation of will.
    renunciation of will *n.* The rejection by a surviving spouse of the will of a deceased spouse in order, instead, to claim **dower** or an **elective share** of the **estate** of the deceased spouse. *See* election by spouse; renunciation of will.

renvoi [ron · *vwa*] (*French*) *n.* The doctrine in the field of **conflict of laws** that, in deciding the question before it, the court of the **forum** must take into account the **whole law** of the other jurisdiction, including its rules as to conflict of laws. The *renvoi doctrine* may thus result in the court of the forum, in the final analysis, being compelled to apply the **law of the forum**.

R

reopening a case [ree · *oh* · pen · ing] *v.* Permitting either **party** to present further evidence after both parties have rested. *See* rest.

reorganization [ree · or · ge · ni · *zay* · shun] *n.* The act of organizing anew.
➤ restructuring, overhaul, restoration, reconstitution, revision, conversion.
reorganization of corporation [kore · per · *ay* · shun] *n. See* corporate reorganization.

repair [re · *pare*] *n.* The act of restoring a thing to sound condition after decay, dilapidation, or partial destruction. *Compare* improvement. *See* good repair; necessary repairs; ordinary repairs.
v. 1. To restore to a sound condition that which is decayed, dilapidated, or partially destroyed. 2. To restore; to remedy; to correct.
➤ *n.* adjustment, improvement, reconstruction, substitution, replacement, overhaul ("a major repair").
v. fix, recondition, renovate, rejuvenate, rectify ("to repair a leaky faucet"); leave, retire, proceed, recur, refer, withdraw ("repair to bed").

reparable injury [*rep* · er · ebl *in* · jer · ee] *n.* An **injury** resulting in **loss** or **damage** that is purely pecuniary in nature and can be made whole by compensation in money. *Compare* irreparable injury. *See* make whole; pecuniary loss.

reparation [rep · e · *ray* · shun] *n.* 1. Compensation or **restitution** for an **injury**; **redress**. 2. Payments made to the victor by a country defeated in war, as compensation for losses caused by the war. 3. The act of making good or making amends for a wrong.
➤ adjustment, atonement, propitiation, expiation, indemnification, quittance.

repatriation [ree · pay · tree · *ay* · shun] *n.* 1. The return of a person to the country of her birth. 2. The return of a thing to the country of its origin.

repay [ree · *pay*] *v.* To pay back; to refund.
➤ accord, balance, compensate, indemnify, recompense, restore ("repay a debt"); avenge, vindicate, reciprocate, revenge, punish ("repay her evil deeds").

repeal [re · *peel*] *n.* **Abrogation**; **annulment**. The term "repeal" is usually associated with some action of government, for EXAMPLE, the repeal of statute. *Compare* amendment. *See* repeal of statute.
v. To **abrogate**; to **rescind**; to **annul**; to **recall**. *Compare* amend.
➤ *n.* abrogation, annulment, cancellation, nullification, rescindment, rescission, withdrawal.
v. abrogate, abolish, rescind, annul, recall, revoke.

repeal of statute [*stat* · shoot] *v.* The annulment of a statute by a later statute. When the later statute specifically terminates the effect of the earlier legislation, the process is known as **express repeal**. **Implied repeal** is the inferred repeal of a statute by a later enactment when the provisions of the old and the new are so conflicting that they cannot be harmonized.

repeat offender [re · *peet* o · *fen* · der] *n.* An **habitual criminal**. *See* habitual offender statutes. *See also* recidivist.

replace [ree · *plaiss*] *v.* To restore to a former condition; to provide an equivalent or substitute.
➤ compensate, reconstitute, duplicate, reinstate, supplant, supersede, subrogate, switch, swap, supplant.

replacement [ree · *plaiss* · ment] *n.* That which replaces another person or thing.
➤ equivalent, duplicate, reconstitution, replica, reconstruction, refund, reorganization.
replacement insurance [in · *shoor* · ense] *n. See* replacement value.
replacement value [*val* · yoo] *n.* In the context of an insurance **loss**, the cost of replacing insured property at its current value, as opposed to its original cost; that is, at what it costs now, not what it cost then.

replead [ree · *pleed*] *v.* To file a new **pleading**.

repleader [ree · *pleed* · er] *n.* Under **common law pleading**, an order by the court requiring the **parties** to file new **pleadings** from the point in the proceedings where faulty pleadings were first filed.

replevin [re · *plev* · in] *n.* 1. An **action** by which the owner of personal property taken or detained by another may recover possession of it. 2. The name of the **writ** issued by a court in an action of replevin authorizing the sheriff to seize the property that is the subject of the action pending the outcome of the litigation. *See* writ of replevin. *See* detinue. *See also* replevy; self-help; sequestration.

➤ acquisition, repossession, recovery, retrieval.

replevin bond *n.* A **bond** required of the plaintiff in an **action** of replevin. The bond is primarily for the defendant's protection if the plaintiff does not prevail in the action; it guarantees that the property will be returned to the defendant in the condition it was in when it was removed by the sheriff.

replevy [re · *plev* · ee] *v.* To secure the possession of personal property by **replevin**.

replication [rep · li · *kay* · shun] *n.* 1. In **common law pleading**, the plaintiff's **reply** to the defendant's **plea**. *Compare* rejoinder. 2. Reproduction; imitation.

➤ reproduction, copy, imitation, clone, model, photocopy.

reply [re · *ply*] *n.* 1. In **pleading**, the plaintiff's **answer** to the defendant's **setoff** or **counterclaim**. 2. A response; an answer. *v.* To respond to; to answer.

➤ *n.* rejoinder, replication, retort, refutation, retaliation, response, answer.
v. answer, counter, acknowledge, react, return.

reply brief *n.* A **brief** filed by the **appellant** in response to the points made by the **appellee** in his brief; a brief filed by the appellee in response to the points made by the appellant in her brief.

report [re · *port*] *n.* 1. A presentation of facts, sometimes in formal detail. EXAMPLES: a police report; a **master's report**; a **financial report**. 2. **Court reports**; **reporters**.
v. To relate information; in particular, to convey information to one's superior or supervisor.

➤ *n.* article, narration, chronicle, story, communiqué, tidings ("a report on the ozone hole"); rumor, suggestion, gossip, insinuation, hearsay, hint ("Reports tell us that the governor will run for president").
v. inform, circulate, disseminate, apprise, notify, divulge ("report your findings").

reported cases [*kay* · sez] *n.* A case which has been published. *See* court reports; reporters.

reporter [re · *port* · er] *n.* 1. *Singular* of reporters. 2. A **court reporter**. 3. A journalist.

➤ announcer, journalist, newscaster, correspondent, writer, interviewer.

reporters [re · *port* · erz] *n.* 1. **Court reports**, as well as official, published reports of cases decided by administrative agencies. 2. **Court reporters**.

reports [re · *ports*] *n.* 1. *Plural* of report. 2. Same as **reporters**.

repose statute [re · *poze stat* · shoot] *n.* *See* statutes of repose.

repossession [ree · po · *zesh* · en] *n.* 1. A **remedy** of the seller upon default by the buyer under a **conditional sale contract** or other **security agreement**. *See also* self-help. 2. A taking of possession by the owner of real estate after the occupant relinquishes possession or forfeits the right to possession. *See* reentry.

➤ recapture, restoration, retrieval, seizure, reacquisition, recovery.

represent [rep · re · *zent*] *v.* 1. To state something as a fact. USAGE: "I have represented the facts to you exactly as they occurred." *See* false representation; material representation. 2. To act for another, as an agent or attorney does; to stand in the place of another; to speak for another. USAGE: "I will be out of town, but my attorney will represent me at the meeting." *See and compare* attorney at law; attorney in fact. 3. To be symbolic of; to stand for. 4. To show; to depict; to portray. USAGE: "That portrait does not represent the mayor very flatteringly." *See* representation.

➤ evoke, portray, exemplify, imitate, indicate, signify, symbolize ("The sun in the painting represents God"); depict, delineate, outline, illustrate, narrate ("to represent the seriousness of the problem"); speak for, act for, replace, factor, act as attorney for ("to represent a client").

representation [rep · re · zen · *tay* · shen] *n.* 1. A statement of a fact, whether truthful or untruthful. *See* material representation. *See also* false representation; fraudulent

misrepresentation; misrepresentation.
2. The act of representing another. *See*
representation by counsel. 3. In the law of
fraud, words written or spoken with the
knowledge or belief that they are false, and
with the purpose of deceiving and inducing
action in reliance. *See* false representation;
fraudulent misrepresentation; material
representation; misrepresentation. 4. In
the law of insurance, a spoken or written
statement with respect to a **material fact**,
made by an applicant for coverage, which
is necessary for the insurance company to
decide whether to issue the policy and at
what premium. 5. In the law of **descent
and distribution**, a reference to the *per
stirpes* method of dividing a **decedent's
estate**, which involves distribution by
representation or by **class**. *Compare per
capita*. 6. A term referring to **derivative
actions** or other **class actions** in which a
limited number of plaintiffs bring a lawsuit as the representatives of a class of individuals. *See* representative action. *Also
see* represent. 7. A depiction, or the act of
depicting someone or something in visual
form. EXAMPLES: a painting; a sculpture.
➤ allegation, assertion, explanation,
depiction, account, description.

representation by counsel [*koun* · sel] *n.*
Having legal counsel; the act or fact of
being represented by an attorney in a lawsuit, a criminal prosecution, or any other
matter. *See* right to counsel. *See* counsel.

representation election [e · *lek* · shen] *n.*
An election conducted by the **National
Labor Relations Board** for the purpose
of determining whether a majority of an
employer's employees wish to be represented by the union or unions named on
the ballot for the purpose of **collective
bargaining**. *See* certification of
bargaining agent.

representative [rep · re · *zen* · te · tiv] *n.*
1. A person who acts on behalf of or
represents another, as an agent or attorney
does. 2. A **personal representative**.
EXAMPLES: a **trustee**; an **executor** or
administrator of a **decedent's** estate; a
conservator. *See* legal representative. 3. A
member of Congress, particularly of the
House of Representatives or of the **lower
house** of a state legislature.

adj. Typical; characteristic.
➤ *n.* assemblyman, commissioner,
congressperson, deputy, councilor,
delegate, proxy ("our representative in
Washington"); archetype, embodiment,
epitome, exemplar, personification,
specimen ("a representative of the group").
adj. adumbrative, delineative, depictive,
typical, typifying, evocative, exemplary,
prototypical, indicative, symbolic ("a
representative sample").

representative action [*ak* · shen] *n.* 1. A
derivative action. 2. Any **class action**.

representative capacity [ke · *pass* · i · tee]
n. The status a person occupies when she
acts on behalf of another person, and not
for herself personally. *See* capacity. *Also
see* as agent.

reprieve [re · *preev*] *n.* The postponement
of the carrying out of a sentence. A reprieve
is not a **commutation of sentence**; it is
merely a delay. *Compare* pardon. *See*
clemency.
➤ abatement, abeyance, clemency, deferment,
mitigation, palliation, remission.

reprimand [*rep* · ri · mand] *n.* A severe and
solemn rebuke or censure for disobedience
or wrongdoing.
v. To rebuke or chastise.
➤ *n.* admonishment, castigation, censure,
reprehension, chiding, lecture, warning,
reproval.
v. chastise, rebuke, reprove, admonish,
castigate, deprecate.

reprisal [re · *pry* · zel] *n.* 1. The seizure or
confiscation by one nation of the property
of another nation that has refused to pay
a debt owed to it or to repair some **injury**
done to it. 2. **Recaption**. 3. Retaliation; retribution. *See* letters of marque and reprisal.
➤ revenge, counterblow, requital, retribution,
vengeance.

reproduce [ree · pro · *dooss*] *v.* 1. To make
a copy of. 2. To make a child.
➤ copy, mimic, imitate; produce, beget, make,
generate, proliferate, sire, spawn, breed.

reproductive rights [ree · pro · *duk* · tiv] *n.*
A term often applied to a woman's right to
determine for herself whether to become
pregnant or to give birth. With respect to
specific reproductive rights, *see* embryo

transplantation; in vitro fertilization; *Roe v. Wade*; surrogate motherhood.

republic [re · *pub* · lik] *n.* A form of government that derives all its powers from the people and is administered by elected representatives who hold their offices for a limited period of time. *See* governmental powers.

republican form of government [re · *pub* · li · ken form of *guv* · ern · ment] *n. See* republic.

republication [ree · pub · li · *kay* · shun] *n.* 1. The **reinstatement** of a will that has been revoked. A will can be republished by **codicil**. 2. The publishing of anything more than once. *See* publication; publish.

repudiation [re · pyoo · dee · *ay* · shun] *n.* A denial of the validity of something; a denial of authority.
➤ denial, rejection, renunciation, repeal, retraction, nullification, spurning, disaffirmation.
Ant. acceptance, affirmation.
repudiation of contract [kon · trakt] *n.* The refusal to recognize the existence or validity of a **contract**; the renunciation of liability under a contract. *Compare* anticipatory breach.

repugnancy [re · *pug* · nen · see] *n.* 1. Inconsistency. In the language of the law, "repugnancy" is used in connection with contradictions or inconsistencies in a **pleading**, in the provisions of a statute, or in the clauses or paragraphs of a legal document, for EXAMPLE, a will, a deed, or a contract. *See* repugnant provisions. 2. In common usage, the state of being objectionable or disgusting.
➤ incompatibility, contradiction; unpleasantness, repulsiveness, obscenity, undesirability.

repugnant [ree · *pug* · nent] *adj.* 1. Arousing great dislike or contempt. 2. Contradictory.
➤ disgusting, foul, horrid, odious, noisome, hateful, contemptible, revolting ("repugnant behavior"); incompatible, inconsistent ("repugnant terms").

repugnant provisions [re · *pug* · nent pro · *vizh* · enz] *n.* Inconsistent provisions. A statute, a deed, a will, or a contract, for EXAMPLE, may contain repugnant provisions. *See* repugnancy.

reputation [rep · yoo · *tay* · shun] *n.* The regard in which a person is held in his community; not who a person is, but what people think or say about him. *Compare* character. *See* character evidence.
➤ acceptability, fame, infamy, notoriety, position, prominence, acclaim, distinction, standing, status, repute.

repute [re · *pyoot*] *n.* Reputation. *v.* To consider or believe.
➤ *v.* deem, assume, presume, suppose, judge, reckon, estimate.

reputed [re · *pyoot* · ed] *adj.* Said to be; publicly perceived as; **putative.** USAGE: "He is reputed to be a gangster."
➤ assumed, estimated, alleged, supposed.
reputed owner [*oh* · ner] *n.* A person who, by supposition or based upon outward appearances, seems to be the owner of the property in question.

request [re · *kwest*] *v.* To ask or express a wish for something. When used in a will, "request" is generally construed as **precatory language**, although, in some contexts, it has been held to be a mandatory term.
n. A desire; a petition; a plea.
➤ *v.* ask, desire, appeal, petition, plead, summon, urge, want, solicit, importune.
n. appeal, application, entreaty, inquiry, solicitation, requisition, motion, plea, prayer, want.
request for admission [ad · *mish* · en] *n.* Written statements concerning a case, directed to an **adverse party**, that she is required to admit or deny. Such admissions or denials will be treated by the court as having been established, and need not be proven at trial. *See* admission. *Also see* stipulation.
request for instructions [in · *struk* · shenz] *n.* A written request to the judge for **jury instructions**, made by either **party**, usually after both sides have rested. *See* rest.
request for proposal [pro · *poze* · el] *n.* When the government has funds available for a grant for a specific purpose, it is often required by law to solicit proposals (amounting to bids accompanied by **specifications**) from the general public. Such a solicitation is called a "request for proposal" or an **RFP.**

R

require [ree · *kwire*] *v.* 1. To direct or demand. 2. To need.

➤ order, command, compel, necessitate, obligate ("to require an appearance before the court"); need, crave, lack ("to require a great deal of attention").

requirement [ree · *kwire* · ment] *n.* An obligation; a mandatory condition.

➤ obligation, prerequisite, rule, regulation, commandment, fiat, provision, directive.

requirement contract [re · *kwire* · ment *kon* · trakt] *n.* A **contract** under which one party agrees to furnish the entire supply of specified goods or services required by the other party for a specified period of time, and the other party agrees to purchase his entire requirement from the first party exclusively. *See* entire output contract.

requisition [rek · wi · *zish* · en] *n.* 1. The **taking** of private property by the government. In this sense, the term usually applies to a governmental taking in an emergency situation, for EXAMPLE, to conduct military operations. 2. A demand or requirement, particularly one imposed by **authority**. 3. The act of demanding or requiring.

➤ appropriation, order, commandeering, request, summons, demand, application, petition, injunction.

res [reyz] (*Latin*) *n.* "The thing." The term "*res*," as used in the law, means, variously, a transaction, a matter, property held **in trust**, and property or status that is the subject of a lawsuit.

  res adjudicata [a · joo · di · *kay* · ta] *n.* Same as *res judicata*.

  res derelicta [deh · re · *lik* · ta] *n.* **Abandoned property**. The literal translation of the term is "derelict thing" (i.e., derelict property). *See* derelict.

  res gestae [*jess* · tee] *n.* "*Gestae*" means "acts" or "deeds." The term "*res gestae*" refers to acts or words through which a principal event "speaks"; that is, acts or words which, although incidental to the principal or litigated fact, tend to explain the transaction as a whole because they are closely connected to it in time and substance, and tend to be **credible** because they are spontaneous. For this reason, even though testimony concerning such acts or words is **hearsay**, it is admissible as an **exception to the hearsay rule.** EXAMPLE: In a murder prosecution, the testimony of the arresting officer, to the effect that, as she and the defendant struggled for the still-warm gun, the defendant stated he had just killed the victim, is admissible as a *res gestae* statement, even though it is hearsay. *See* excited utterance; spontaneous declaration; spontaneous exclamation; spontaneous statement; verbal acts rule.

  res ipsa loquitur [*ip* · sa *lo* · kwe · ter] *n.* Means "the thing speaks for itself." When an **instrumentality** (i.e., a **thing**) causes **injury**, an **inference** or **rebuttable presumption** arises that the injury was caused by the defendant's **negligence**, if the thing or instrumentality was under the exclusive control or management of the defendant and the occurrence was such as in the ordinary course of events would not have happened if the defendant had used **reasonable care.** EXAMPLE: The utility company may properly be held liable under the doctrine of *res ipsa loquitur* for a gas explosion that destroys a building in which its equipment is functioning imperfectly.

  res judicata [joo · di · *kay* · ta] *n.* Means "the thing (i.e., the **matter**) has been adjudicated"; the thing has been decided. The principle that a **final judgment** rendered **on the merits** by a **court of competent jurisdiction** is conclusive of the rights of the **parties** and is an absolute bar in all other **actions** based upon the same **claim**, **demand**, or **cause of action**. *Compare* collateral estoppel.

  res of the trust *n.* Property (EXAMPLES: land; cash; **securities**) that is the subject of a **trust**; the *corpus* of a **trust**; **trust property**.

  res publica [*pub* · lik · a] *n.* Literally means "public thing"; used in reference to **public property**. EXAMPLES: **public lands**; **public roads**; **public schools**.

resale [ree · sale] *n.* 1. A second sale, by a seller, of the same goods or property. Resale is a **remedy** of a seller who expressly reserves that right in the event of the buyer's default in payment. 2. A sale at retail following a purchase at wholesale.

rescind [ree · *sind*] *v.* To effect a **rescission**. Properly used, "rescind" means to annul a contract from the beginning, not merely to terminate the contract as to future transactions. *See* rescission.

➤ avoid, invalidate, reject, take back, abrogate, renege, counterorder, undo, disavow, annul.

rescission [ree · *sizh* · en] *n.* The **abrogation**, **annulment**, or cancellation of a contract by the act of a party. Rescission may occur by mutual consent of the parties, pursuant to a **condition** contained in the contract, or for **fraud**, **failure of consideration**, **material breach**, or **default**. It is also a remedy available to the parties by a **judgment** or decree of the court. More than mere termination, rescission restores the parties to the status quo existing before the contract was entered into.

➤ unmaking, termination, withdrawal, vitiation, voidance, extricating ("the rescission of the contract").

rescript [ree · *skript*] *n.* 1. A directive from a court to the **clerk of court** to **enter** a specific decree. 2. An order from an **appellate court** to a **trial court** to enter a specific decree. 3. A written statement by an appellate court of the reasons for its decision.

➤ directive, order, statement.

rescue [*ress* · kyoo] *n.* 1. The crime of **escape**. 2. The act of freeing or saving a person exposed to danger. *See* sudden emergency doctrine. *See also* last clear chance doctrine. 3. **Recaption**, **reprisal**, or **repossession**.

v. To save or help someone.

➤ *n.* deliverance, emancipation, succor, redemption, ransom, relief; recaption, reprisal, repossession.

Ant. abandonment.

v. save, redeem, ransom, deliver, extricate, protect, preserve, liberate.

Ant. injure, destroy.

rescue doctrine [*dok* · trin] *n.* Same as **good Samaritan doctrine**.

research [*ree* · surch] *n.* The collection of information about a subject.

v. To investigate the facts.

➤ *n.* investigation, scrutiny, study, inquiry, examination, analysis.

v. analyze, examine, probe, study, inspect, pursue, scrutinize.

reservation [rez · er · *vay* · shun] *n.* 1. The act of reserving. *See* reserve; reserved. 2. A **grant** of an **interest** in land back to the **grantor** from the **grantee**; i.e., the creation in the grantor of a *new* right from the property she has granted. Although the terms "reservation" and "**exception**" are often used interchangeably, they are distinguishable because, as opposed to a reservation, an exception withholds a right that would otherwise pass to the grantee. *See* exception in deed. 3. A large tract of public land set aside for a public purpose. EXAMPLES: an Indian reservation; a military reservation; a wildlife reservation.

➤ circumscription, hesitancy, provision, restriction, proviso ("have a reservation about attending the meeting"); bespeaking, limitation, restriction, retainment, booking ("reservation for a future date"); enclave, preserve, reserve, sanctuary, territory, tract ("Indian reservation").

reserve [re · *zerv*] *n.* 1. A fund or sum of money set aside for some special purpose. *See* contingency fund. 2. The **legal reserve** that a bank is required by law to maintain to guarantee that its depositors will be able to withdraw money as they wish. 3. In insurance law, money set aside by an insurance company in an amount adequate to meet all claims on its outstanding policies.

v. 1. To set aside, usually for a particular purpose. 2. To hold back or set apart for use in the future.

➤ *n.* supply, funds, accumulation, stock, resource, cache ("reserves to last a week"); detachment, rigidity, composure, condescension, inhibition, diffidence, reticence ("a cool reserve").

v. retain, withhold, preserve, amass, conserve, accrue ("reserve some funds").

reserve banks *n.* *See* Federal Reserve Banks; Federal Reserve System.

reserve clause *n.* A clause in the contracts of professional athletes, which provides that only the club for which the player presently plays has the right to trade him to another organization, and that he has no right to enter into his own agreement with another organization.

reserve fund *n.* *See* contingency fund.

Reserve Board [re · *zerv*] *n.* *See* Federal Reserve Board; Federal Reserve System.

Reserve System [re · *zerv*] *n.* *See* Federal Reserve System.

reserved [re · *zervd*] *adj./past part.* Set aside, usually for a particular purpose or for use in the future. *See* reserve.

➤ *adj.* retained, withheld, engaged, appropriated, preempted, restricted, taken ("this seat is reserved"); diffident, demure, misanthropic, sedate, shy, taciturn ("a reserved person").

reserved point *n.* Same as **point reserved**.

reserved powers [*pow* · erz] *n.* A term referring to Article X of the Constitution, which provides that the "powers not delegated to the United States by the Constitution, nor prohibited by it to the states, are reserved to the states respectively, or to the people."

reserved question [*kwes* · chen] *n.* 1. A term referring to a question of state law certified by a federal court. *See* certification of question. 2. Same as **point reserved**.

reserving a question [re · *zerv* · ing a *kwes* · chen] *n.* *See* point reserved.

reside [re · *zide*] *v.* To live or dwell in a place; to have a home, **abode**, or **residence**; to be a resident.

➤ abide, dwell, be intrinsic to, endure, occupy, tenant, populate, live.

residence [*rez* · i · dense] *n.* One's home; the place where a person lives with no present intention of moving. Although in a given context "residence" may have the same meaning as **domicile**, the terms are not synonymous, because, while a person may have many residences, she can have only one domicile. *Compare* legal residence.

➤ abode, address, domicile, inhabitancy, household, headquarters, home.

residency [*rez* · i · den · see] *n.* The status of being a resident or having a **residence**.

residency requirements [re · *kwire* · ments] *n.* The requirements imposed by states for eligibility for various benefits or opportunities (EXAMPLES: eligibility for **AFDC**; admission to a state college; the right to file a divorce action). Unduly restrictive residency requirements violate the **equal protection** and **due process** clauses of the Constitution.

resident *n.* One who resides in a place with no present intention of moving. Although a "resident" is not always a **domiciliary**, a domiciliary is always a resident. *Compare* nonresident. *See* residence.

adj. Living in a place; present.

➤ *n.* citizen, denizen, dweller, squatter, suburbanite, native, domiciliary.

adj. remaining, stationary, fixed, present, settled.

resident agent [*ay* · jent] *n.* A person residing in a state who is authorized by a **foreign corporation** to accept **service of process** on its behalf. *See* reside.

resident alien [*ale* · yen] *n.* An **alien** who has entered the United States with the intention of abandoning her foreign citizenship and of residing here.

residual [ree · *zid* · joo · el] *adj.* Leftover.

➤ surplus, remaining, excess, residue, spare, balance.

residuals [re · *zid* · joo · elz] *n.* Additional compensation paid to a writer or actor for the reuse, generally on television, of a film whose script she wrote or in which he appears as a performer.

➤ royalties, income.

residuary [re · *zid* · joo · e · ree] *adj.* Pertaining to the residue; pertaining to that which is left over.

➤ surplus, spare, remaining, leftover, outstanding, excess.

residuary bequest [be · *kwest*] *n.* A **bequest** by a **testator** of the remainder of her personal property.

residuary clause *n.* A clause in a will that disposes of the part of the **estate** that is left after all other **legacies** and **devises** have been paid and all claims against the estate are satisfied. Residuary clauses frequently contain the phrase "**rest, residue, and remainder**." USAGE: "All the rest, residue, and remainder of my property, both real and personal, I **devise and bequeath** to my friend Cris Garcia." *See* residuary estate.

residuary devise [de · *vize*] *n.* A **devise** by a **testator** of the remainder of his real property.

residuary estate [es · *tate*] *n.* The part of a **testator's** estate that remains after the payment of her debts and all of her **bequests** and **devises**.

residuary gift *n.* A **residuary bequest** or **residuary devise**.

residuary legacy [*leg* · e · see] *n.* A term which, correctly used, is synonymous with **residuary bequest**, although it is often loosely used to mean any **residuary gift**.

residue [*rez* · i · dew] *n.* That which is left over; that which remains; the remainder; the **residuum**. *See* rest, residue, and remainder.
➤ debris, dregs, excess, leavings, remnants, residuum, slag, remainder.

residue of estate *n.* *See* residuary estate.

residuum [re · *zid* · yoo · um] (*Latin*) *n.* The part that is left; something left over; the remainder; the residue. *See* residuary estate.

resignation [rez · ig · *nay* · shun] *n.* 1. The voluntary relinquishment of an office or position to which one has been appointed or elected. 2. Acceptance; nonresistance.
➤ abandonment, abdication, quitting, termination, yielding, divestment ("I received her resignation"); acquiescence, compliance, deference, docility, forbearing, fortitude ("resignation to the job he was assigned").

resist [ree · *zist*] *v.* To withstand or oppose.
➤ oppose, contest, disregard, retaliate, frustrate, dissent, obstruct, refuse, refrain.

resistance [ree · *zist* · ants] *n.* Opposition; noncompliance.
➤ protest, noncompliance, rebellion, defiance, opposition, contravention, rebuff, refusal, fighting.

resisting [re · *zis* · ting] *n.* The act of opposing or contesting.

resisting an officer [*off* · i · ser] *n.* The crime of obstructing, hindering, or otherwise interfering with a **public officer** in carrying out her duties. The offense may include resistance to arrest (*see* resisting arrest), but is broader in scope, including, for EXAMPLE, interfering with an **officer of the court** who is attempting to serve **process**. The resistance need not be violent. *See* service of process. *See also* obstructing process.

resisting arrest [a · *rest*] *n.* The crime of interfering with a police officer in making an arrest. *Compare* resisting an officer.

resolution [rez · e · *loo* · shun] *n.* 1. An expression of the opinion or the collective mind of a public body such as, for EXAMPLE, Congress, a state legislature, or a city council. Unlike a statute or ordinance, a resolution is not a law and does not have the effect of law. *See* joint resolution. 2. The settling of a dispute or the resolving of differences.
➤ determination, dedication, perseverance, purpose, sincerity, tenacity ("to have tremendous resolution to do a task"); declaration, exposition, presentation, settlement, solution, verdict ("the council's resolution").

Resolution Trust Corporation [rez · e · *loo* · shun trust kore · per · *ay* · shen] *n.* A federal agency responsible for managing and settling all cases involving **thrift institutions** whose accounts were previously insured by the **Federal Savings and Loan Insurance Corporation** and which have been or are in **receivership**. *See* Office of Thrift Supervision.

resort [re · *zort*] *n.* A place to which people go for relief of one sort or another. EXAMPLES: a **court of last resort**; a tennis resort.
v. 1. To have **recourse**; to turn to for aid or assistance. USAGE: "The world would be a safer place if nations resorted to the **International Court of Justice** rather than war to resolve their disputes." 2. To go to a place, particularly to go frequently; to frequent.
➤ *n.* camp, haven, holiday spot, spa, haunt, rendezvous, retreat, asylum ("vacation resort").
v. address, devote, recur, utilize, exercise, employ, try, turn to ("to resort to drastic measures").

resources [re · *sore* · sez] *n.* Means; the means of generating money. Although a person's "resources" may include his income, they are not limited to money in hand or in the bank; they also include credit as well as every **asset** that can be converted to money.
➤ wealth, property, possession, income, capital; ability, capacity, capability, facility.

respect [ree · *spekt*] *n.* The state of being esteemed; an expression of deference.
v. To admire, to hold in high regard.

➤ *n.* regard, recognition, esteem, favor, reverence, tribute.
v. regard, abide by, recognize, comply with, admire, value, esteem.

respond [ree · *spond*] *v.* To answer; to reply.

➤ answer, reply, plead, discuss, explain, counterclaim, parry.

respondeat superior [res · *pon* · dee · at soo · *peer* · ee · or] (*Latin*) *n.* Means "let the master respond." The doctrine under which liability is imposed upon an employer for the acts of its employees committed in the course and scope of their employment. Similarly, *respondeat superior* makes a **principal** liable for a **tort** committed by her **agent**, and a **master** responsible for the **negligence** of his **servant**. *See* borrowed servant rule. *See also* course of employment; scope of employment.

respondent [re · *spon* · dent] *n.* 1. The **party** against whom an appeal is taken to a higher court, i.e., the successful party in the lower court; the **appellee**. 2. The defendant in a suit **in equity**.

➤ defendant, appellee, accused, responding litigant.
Ant. petitioner, plaintiff.

responsible bidder [re · *spon* · sibl *bid* · er] *n.* A **bidder** in the **letting** of a **public contract** who has the financial responsibility, as well as the judgment, skill, and integrity, to complete the **public improvement** on which she is bidding. *See* letting a contract.

responsive [re · *spon* · siv] *adj.* 1. Making answer or reply. 2. Reacting easily or readily.

➤ reciprocal, reactive, sympathetic, receptive, sensitive, understanding.
Ant. unresponsive, uncooperative.

responsive pleading [*plee* · ding] *n.* A **pleading** that responds to another pleading. EXAMPLE: an **answer** to a **complaint**.

rest *n.* 1. The remainder or residue of something (as in "**rest, residue, and remainder**"). 2. Repose; leisure.
v. 1. To advise the court that one has offered all the evidence one intends to offer in the trial of a lawsuit. USAGE: "The prosecution rests." 2. To be quiet; to be in repose.

➤ *n.* cessation, intermission, interval, leisure, pause, quiescence, respite ("rest from the day's work"); balance, dregs, heel, remnant, residuum, superfluity ("Eat the rest of your food").
v. breathe, compose, relax, slumber, unwind ("rest your eyes"); end, finish, conclude ("The prosecution rests").

rest, residue, and remainder [*rez* · i · dew and re · *mane* · der] *n.* A phrase introducing the **residuary clause** of a will, disposing of the part of an **estate** that is left after all the **testator's** other **legacies** and **devises** have been paid. *See* residuary clause.

restatement [ree · *stayt* · ment] *n.* 1. A summary, paraphrase, or repetition of what was said. 2. One of the *Restatements of the Law*.

➤ review, summary, recapitulation, recital, iteration, abstract, digest ("Restatement of Torts").

Restatement of the Law [ree · *stayt* · ment] *n.* A series of volumes published by the **American Law Institute**, written by legal scholars, each volume or set of volumes covering a major field of the law (EXAMPLES: **torts**; **property**; **contracts**; **agency**). Each of the *Restatements* is, among other things, a statement of the law as it is generally interpreted and applied by the courts with respect to particular legal principles (EXAMPLES: the **rule against perpetuities**; **subrogation**; **attractive nuisance**).

restitution [res · ti · *tew* · shen] *n.* In both contract and **tort**, a **remedy** that restores the status quo. Restitution returns a person who has been wrongfully deprived of something to the position he occupied before the wrong occurred; it requires a defendant who has been unjustly enriched at the expense of the plaintiff to make the plaintiff whole, either, as may be appropriate, by returning property unjustly held, by reimbursing the plaintiff, or by paying compensation or **indemnification**. *See* unjust enrichment. *See also* make whole. In criminal law, restitution is sometimes made a **condition** of **probation** for persons convicted of certain types of crimes.

➤ compensation, repayment, amends, dues, recompense, reparation, squaring, remitter, redress ("to be required to pay restitution").

restrain [re · *strane*] *v.* 1. To prohibit; to limit. 2. To confine. A person or a thing may be restrained either temporarily or permanently. *See* restraining order. *See and compare* permanent injunction; temporary restraining order.
➤ arrest, circumscribe, constrain, fetter, govern, imprison, pinion, repress, bridle, curb, check.

restraining order [re · *strane* · ing *or* · der] *n.* An order of court equivalent to a **preliminary injunction** or a **temporary restraining order**. *Also see* protection order.

restraint [re · *straint*] *n.* 1. Limitation; prohibition. 2. Confinement. *See* unlawful restraint. 3. The act of keeping one's emotions or conduct under control.
➤ abstemiousness, coercion, curtailment, moderation, suppression, abridgement, limitation, prohibition, self-control.

restraint of marriage [*mehr* · ej] *n.* A provision in a will that denies a **testamentary gift** to a **legatee** or **devisee** who marries (an *absolute restraint*) or who marries a specified person or within a specified race or religion (a *partial restraint*). An absolute restraint is unenforceable. A partial restraint may or may not be enforceable, depending upon the nature of the restriction.

restraint of trade *n.* Contracts, **combinations**, and other practices interfering unreasonably with the production, supply, and pricing of goods, commodities, and services, with the objective of suppressing competition. *See* combination in restraint of trade.

restraint on alienation [ale · ee · e · *nay* · shen] *n.* A restriction in a deed that prohibits the **grantee** from selling the property (an *absolute restraint*) or from selling it under certain circumstances or to a specified class of buyers (a *partial* restraint). Most such provisions are unenforceable. *See* alienation. *See also* restrictive covenant.

restrict [re · *strikt*] *v.* To limit; to keep within limits.
➤ constrict, delimit, demarcate, modify, regulate, restrain, limit ("to restrict questions to relevant matters only").

restriction [re · *strik* · shun] *n.* A limitation. *See* limitation; limitation of estate.
➤ constriction, impediment, curb, contraction, obstruction, demarcation, reservation, stipulation, limitation.

restrictive [re · *strik* · tiv] *adj.* Tending to restrict or limit.
➤ restraining, prohibitive, obstructive, qualifying, controlled, exclusive.

restrictive covenant [*kov* · e · nent] *n.* 1. A **covenant** in a **deed** prohibiting or restricting the use of the property (EXAMPLE: the type, location, or size of buildings that can be constructed on it). A covenant prohibiting the sale of real property to persons of a particular race is unenforceable because it is an unconstitutional **restraint on alienation**. *See Shelley v. Kraemer.* 2. A **covenant not to sue**. 3. A covenant not to compete with one's former employer.

restrictive indorsement [in · *dorss* · ment] *n.* An **indorsement** limiting payment of a **negotiable instrument** to a particular person or otherwise prohibiting further **negotiation** of the instrument. *See also* conditional indorsement; qualified indorsement.

result [re · *zult*] *n.* 1. The **judgment** or decision in a lawsuit; the outcome of an **action**. 2. A consequence; that which has happened.
➤ upshot, decision, denouement, aftermath, eventuality, development, consequence, judgment.
Ant. cause.

resulting [re · *zult* · ing] *adj.* Following from; proceeding from; stemming from.
➤ concluding, emerging, consequent, emanating, ensuing, issuing.

resulting powers [*pow* · erz] *n.* The powers of the government of the United States that may be inferred from the totality of the powers expressly or impliedly granted to it by the Constitution. *See and compare* enumerated powers; implied power.

resulting trust *n.* A **trust** created by **operation of law** in circumstances where one person becomes **vested** with **legal title** but is obligated, as a matter of **equity**, to hold the title for the benefit of another person, even though there is no **fraud** and no declared intention to hold the property in trust. *Compare* constructive trust.

resurrect [*rez* · er · ekt] *v.* To bring back; to revive.
➤ rejuvenate, revitalize, revive, bring back, recondition, reinstate.

retail [*ree* · tale] *n.* Short for **retail sale**.
retail sale *n.* A sale to a customer for her own use rather than for resale. *Compare* wholesale.

retailer [*ree* · tale · er] *n.* A person engaged in the business of making retail sales of goods or merchandise. *Compare* wholesaler.
➤ businessperson, merchant, seller, dealer, entrepreneur.

retain [re · *tane*] *v.* 1. To hire or employ someone, particularly an attorney. *See* retainer. 2. To continue to hold; to keep.
➤ employ, hire, secure, commission, recruit, consult ("retain the lawyer's services"); maintain, secure, restrain, clutch, memorize, clench, absorb ("retain its freshness").

retainer [re · *tane* · er] *n.* 1. The act of hiring an attorney. 2. A preliminary fee paid to an attorney at the time she is retained, in order to secure her services. *See and compare* general retainer; special retainer. 3. In certain circumstances, the right of a person (EXAMPLE: an **executor**) who is rightfully in possession of funds belonging to a person who owes him money (EXAMPLE: money belonging to the **decedent's estate** that he is administering) to retain an amount sufficient to satisfy the obligation. *See* right of retainer.
➤ fee, contract, engagement fee, compensation, remuneration.

retaining lien [re · *tane* · ing leen] *n.* An **attorney's lien**.

retaliation [re · tal · ee · *ay* · shun] *n.* Getting even; reprisal.
➤ revenge, reprisal, recrimination, vengeance, requital, reciprocation.

retaliatory [re · *tal* · ee · e · tore · ee] *adj.* Having the characteristics of retaliation.
retaliatory eviction [ee · *vik* · shen] *n.* The **eviction** of a tenant because she complained to the landlord or took legal action with respect to a claimed breach of the lease by the landlord. Eviction for such a reason is illegal in many **jurisdictions**.
retaliatory statute [*stat* · shoot] *n.* A state statute whose purpose is to place the

same burdens or restrictions (EXAMPLES: taxes; **fees**; **penalties**) upon the citizens of other states as those states impose upon its citizens.

retire [re · *tire*] *v.* 1. To terminate one's employment and enter into retirement. *See* retirement annuity; retirement plan. 2. To withdraw **negotiable paper** from circulation. 3. To voluntarily pay or satisfy an **obligation**. *See* retirement.
➤ terminate, withdraw, quit, abdicate; redeem, reclaim; isolate, remove, seclude, retreat.

retirement [re · *tire* · ment] *n.* 1. A termination of employment or of one's occupation, usually based upon considerations such as advancing age or total years of service. Under certain circumstances, forced retirement based upon age may constitute illegal **age discrimination**. *See* Age Discrimination in Employment Act. 2. The withdrawal of **negotiable paper** from circulation. *See* retirement of securities. 3. Making final payment on an obligation such as a **bond** or stock.
retirement annuity [a · *new* · i · tee] *n.* A retirement benefit paid through **annuities**. *See* individual retirement account (IRA). *See also* annuity.
retirement benefit [*ben* · e · fit] *n.* A **benefit** paid under a **retirement plan**.
retirement of bond *n.* *See* retirement of securities.
retirement of securities [se · *kyoor* · i · teez] *n.* The **calling** and **redemption** of a **bond** by the corporation or other entity that issued it; the repurchase by a corporation of its own stock and the cancellation of the repurchased shares. *See* securities. *Also* see callable bond; redeemable stock.
retirement of stock *n.* *See* retirement of securities.
retirement plan *n.* A plan that provides for the payment of retirement benefits in the form of a pension or some similar arrangement. Thus, although an employer's pension plan is the retirement plan of choice for most people who have been employees, self-employed professionals might utilize a **Keogh Plan**, and others might use an **IRA**, as the primary means for subsidizing their retirement.

retraction [re · *trak* · shen] *n.* 1. A formal, published declaration taking back a **defamatory** statement. *See* defamation. 2. A withdrawal of anything.
➤ withdrawal, repudiation, abjuration, disavowal, denial.

retraxit [ree · *trak* · sit] (*Latin*) *n.* Means "he has withdrawn." A voluntary retraction by a plaintiff in **open court** of both his lawsuit and the grounds on which it is based. A *retraxit* causes a plaintiff to loss his **cause of action** forever.

retreat [re · *treat*] *v.* To withdraw; to draw back to a safe place.
n. 1. The process of withdrawing. 2. A place of safety.
➤ *v.* withdraw, disengage, pull back, reverse, flee, evacuate.
n. departure, ebb, evacuation, retirement, withdrawal ("a steady retreat from the field"); cloister, habitat, refuge, resort ("summer retreat").

retreat to the wall *n.* A term referring to the doctrine, in effect in some jurisdictions, that before a person is entitled to use **deadly force** in self-defense she must attempt to withdraw from the encounter by giving as much ground as possible.

retrial [*ree* · *try* · el] *n.* A **new trial** of a case that has been previously tried. *See* trial de novo. *See also* reargument; rehearing.

retroactive [ret · ro · *ak* · tiv] *adj.* Affecting things that are past; applying to a previous time; retrospective. *See* relation back.
➤ retrospective, ex post facto, relating back.
retroactive law *n.* *See* retrospective legislation.

retrospective [ret · ro · *spek* · tiv] *adj.* Retroactive.
retrospective law *n.* *See* retrospective legislation.
retrospective legislation [lej · is · lay · shun] *n.* Statutes that take away or impair **vested rights** acquired under existing laws, or create new duties or impose new **disabilities** with respect to transactions or events that have already passed. *Compare* prospective statute.
retrospective statute [*stat* · shoot] *n.* *See* retrospective legislation.

return [re · *tern*] *n.* 1. A coming back. 2. Profit or earnings. *See* fair return. 3. An official account, usually written, made by a **public officer** with respect to the manner in which she has carried out her official duties. A **return of service** is one EXAMPLE of such a return, although returns are made with respect to every form of **process**, including **attachments** ("a return of attachment") and **executions** ("a return of execution"). 4. A formal report or **indorsement** by a body charged with some public duty. EXAMPLES: a **no bill** or a **true bill** indorsement made by a grand jury on an **indictment**. *Also see* endorsement. 5. A formal accounting of a person's income, for EXAMPLE, a tax return.
v. 1. To come back; to bring back. 2. To yield a profit. 3. To render an official, usually written, account of the manner in which one (EXAMPLE: a sheriff) has carried out one's official duties. *See* return of service.
➤ *n.* profit, yield, inflation, appreciation, harvest, compensation ("a good return on investment").
v. replace, reinstate, deliver, reset, reinstall, reposition ("return it to its original position"); repeat, come back, resurrect, reoccur ("I have returned"); reciprocate, retaliate, requite, retort, refund, redress ("the fund returned a nice amount"); render, adjudicate, pronounce, hand down, publish, impart ("return a decision").

return day *n.* 1. The date specified in a **writ** or other **process** by which the defendant must respond to the process. *See* return of service. 2. The last day for a **return of process** to be made by the officer responsible for serving it.

return not found *n.* *See* not found.

return nulla bona [*null* · a *bone* · a] *n.* *See nulla bona.*

return of process [*pross* · ess] *n.* *See* return of service.

return of service [*ser* · viss] *n.* A short account in writing, made by an officer, with respect to the manner in which he has executed a **writ** or other **process** (EXAMPLES: a **summons**; a **warrant**). *See* service of process.

return on equity [*eq* · wi · tee] *n.* The relationship of the amount of annual earnings available, after all expenses are

R

paid, to the total value of the investment of all holders of **common stock**. *See* equity.

return on investment [in · *vest* · ment] *n. See* rate of return.

returnable [re · *tern* · ebl] *adj.* 1. That which is *required* to be returned. EXAMPLES: a **summons**; a **warrant**. *See* return. 2. More generally, *capable* of being returned.

Rev. St. An abbreviation of **revised statutes**.

Rev. Stat. An abbreviation of **revised statutes**.

reveal [ree · *veel*] *v.* To make publicly known; to disclose.
➤ confess, unearth, display, announce, affirm, disclose, uncover, publish, divulge, proclaim.

revenue [*rev* · e · new] *n.* 1. With respect to an individual or a corporation, **gross income** or **gross receipts** from property (i.e., rents), investments, or sales of products or services. 2. With respect to government, income derived from all sources (EXAMPLES: taxes; **duties**; fees).
➤ receipts, gross, proceeds, income, dividends, emolument, stipend.

revenue bill *n.* A **bill** that, when enacted into law, will **levy** taxes. Revenue bills for the support of the federal government must originate in the House of Representatives. *Compare* revenue law.

revenue bonds *n.* **Bonds** issued by a federal, state, or local governmental unit, often for the construction or maintenance of a particular **public improvement**, and payable solely from the revenues accruing from the operation of that project. EXAMPLE: **school bonds**.

revenue law *n.* A statute authorizing the **assessment** and collection of taxes for the support of the government.

revenue measure [*mezh* · er] *n. See* revenue law.

revenue rulings [*roo* · lingz] *n.* The conclusions of the IRS with respect to the interpretation and application of the **Internal Revenue Code**. Revenue rulings become the law with respect to the specific factual situations they describe. They generally arise from interpretations of the law issued by the IRS to taxpayers in **letter rulings**. Revenue rulings are published in the *Internal Revenue Bulletin*.

revenue stamps *n.* Stamps issued by the various states that must be placed on deeds and mortgages in order for them to be **recorded**. The cost of the stamps to be affixed to a given instrument is proportionate to the purchase price of the property. **Duty** or **excise tax** stamps affixed to bottled liquor and cigarettes are also EXAMPLES of revenue stamps.

reversal [re · *ver* · sel] *n.* 1. The act of an **appellate court** in **setting aside, annulling**, or **vacating** a **judgment** or order of a **lower court**. 2. The act of turning a thing or person around, or being turned around. *See* reverse.
➤ annulment, voiding, retraction, nullification, countermandment, invalidation, overturning ("The Supreme Court's reversal of an appellate court's ruling").

reverse [re · *verse*] *adj.* Opposite; contrary. *v.* To turn around or in an opposite direction.
➤ *adj.* opposite, contrary ("reverse discrimination").
v. overthrow, vacate, annul, nullify, transpose, disaffirm ("to reverse a prior decision").
Ant. affirm.

reverse annuity mortgage [a · *new* · i · tee more · gej] *n.* A type of **mortgage** under which the **equity** is distributed to the **mortgagor** periodically as a means of providing him with income. A reverse annuity mortgage (also called a **RAM**) is available only when the equity is substantial. It is paid off when the owner dies or the property is sold. *See* annuity.

reverse discrimination [dis · krim · i · *nay* · shen] *n.* A term arising out of the perception of some that certain of the **Civil Rights Acts**, particularly the **Civil Rights Act of 1964**, which were designed to correct the effects of discrimination against **minority** individuals, have had the effect of causing discrimination against members of the racial or other majority. *See* discrimination. *Also see* affirmative action.

reverse equity mortgage [*ek* · wi · tee more · gej] *n.* Same as **reverse annuity mortgage**.

reverse mortgage [*more* · gej] *n.* Same as **reverse annuity mortgage**.

R

reversed [re · *versed*] *adv./past part.* A term used in **appellate court** opinions to indicate that the court has **set aside** the **judgment** of the **trial court**.
➤ set aside, vacated, repealed, annulled, undone ("The trial court's ruling was reversed").

reversed and remanded [re · *man* · ded] *adv.* An expression used in **appellate court** opinions to indicate that the court has reversed the **judgment** of the **trial court** and that the case has been returned to the trial court for a **new trial**. *See* remand.

reversible error [re · *vers* · ibl *ehr* · er] *n.* **Prejudicial error**; **judicial error** that causes a **miscarriage of justice** and is therefore a basis for the **appellate court** to reverse the judgment of the court below.

reversion [re · *ver* · zhen] *n.* 1. A **future interest** in land to take effect in favor of the **grantor** of the land or his **heirs** after the termination of a prior **estate** he has **granted**; in other words, the returning of the property to the grantor or his heirs when the grant is over. (EXAMPLE: "I leave Blackacre to Joe Jones for life, and after his death to my heirs." The grantor's heirs have a **reversionary interest** in Blackacre, which will **vest** when Joe Jones dies; Joe Jones's interest is a **life estate**.) A reversion arises by **operation of law**. *Compare* remainder. 2. The interest or estate of an owner of land during the period of time for which he has granted his **possessory rights** to someone else. Thus, in the above EXAMPLE, the grantor and his heirs may also be said to have a reversionary interest in Blackacre during Joe Jones's life. A landlord's **interest** in premises that she has leased to a **tenant** is another EXAMPLE of a reversionary interest. *See* possessory interest.
➤ remainder, future interest, residue, estate, interest; return, throwback, retrogression, regression, turnaround.

reversionary [re · *ver* · zhen · e · ree] *adj.* Relating or pertaining to a **reversion** or **reversionary interest**.

reversionary interest [*in* · trest] *n.* A **future interest**, i.e., the right to the future enjoyment of a **reversion**.

reversioner [re · *ver* · zhen · er] *n.* A person with a **reversionary interest**.

revert [re · *vert*] *v.* 1. With respect to an **interest** in land, to come back to a former owner or her heirs at a future time. USAGE: "After Bill dies, the **life estate** in Blackacre that Sam granted to Bill will revert to Sam and, if Sam is also dead, it will revert to Sam's heirs." *See* reversion. 2. Turn backward.
➤ retreat, resume, deteriorate, relapse, retrogress, decay ("revert to old habits"); come back, return.

reverter [re · *ver* · ter] *n.* A **reversion**. *See* possibility of reverter.

review [re · *vyoo*] *n.* 1. The consideration by an **appellate court** of the decision of a lower court, the result of which may be either the affirmance, reversal, or modification of the decision. *See* appellate review; bill of review; judicial review; scope of review. 2. A reevaluation or reexamination of anything.
v. To evaluate or examine.
➤ *n.* analysis, inspection, reassessment, revision, scrutiny, retrospective, critique ("a review of the material").
v. consider, examine, contemplate, study, analyze, investigate, deliberate ("review a decision").

revise [re · *vize*] *v.* To modify, correct, rearrange, or update. *See* revised statutes.
➤ improve, rearrange, amend, alter, change, recalibrate, scrutinize, modify, update.

revised statutes [re · *vized stat* · shoots] *n.* The **official** statutes of a **jurisdiction**, collected, arranged, and published in a form that reflects the order in which they were enacted and, where such is the case, the order in which they were subsequently amended. Revised statutes are variously **cited** as **RS, Rev. Stat.**, or **Rev. St.** *See* statute.

revision [re · *vizh* · en] *n.* That which has been revised. *See* revise; revised statutes.
➤ alteration, modification, change, redraft, amendment, reappraisal.

revival [re · *vy* · vel] *n.* The act of restoring something to use, strength, or life.
➤ restoration, resurrection, revitalization, rebirth, awakening, invigoration.

revival of action [*ak* · shen] *n.* 1. The term for the substitution of a **personal representative** (EXAMPLES: an **executor**;

R

an **administrator**) as the plaintiff in place of the **decedent** who originally brought the **action** and has since died. *See* substitution of parties. 2. Certain actions that have been barred by the **statute of limitations** may be revived by some subsequent act or event (EXAMPLE: an action for nonpayment of a debt may be revived by an **acknowledgment** of the debt). *See* acknowledgment of debt.

revival of judgment [*juj* · ment] *n.* The act of giving new effect to a **dormant judgment** through new **process**.

revival of will *n.* The act of a **testator** in giving effect to a will she has previously revoked. Depending upon state law, this can be accomplished by reexecuting the will, by **republication**, or by revoking all wills made subsequent to the will she wishes to revive. *See* publication of will; revocation; revocation of will.

revive [re · *vive*] *v.* To restore to use, strength, or life. EXAMPLE: an **acknowledgment of debt** will revive a **cause of action** arising from a debt whose enforcement has been barred by the **statute of limitations**.
➤ animate, rekindle, invigorate, reanimate, resuscitate, reactivate, enliven, renew, restore, resurrect, revitalize.

revocable [*rev* · e · kebl] *adj.* That which can be **abrogated**, **annulled**, or withdrawn. *Compare* irrevocable. *See* revocation; revoke.
➤ reversible, retractible, voidable, cancellable.

revocable trust *n.* A **trust** in which the **settlor** does not give up the right to revoke. *Compare* irrevocable trust.

revocation [rev · e · *kay* · shen] *n.* A **nullification**, cancellation, or withdrawal of a power, privilege, or act.
➤ termination, elimination, disavowal, abrogation, defeasance, dissolution ("probation revocation").
Ant. confirmation, affirmation.

revocation hearing [*hear* · ing] *n.* The **due process hearing** required before the government can revoke a **privilege** it has previously granted. Thus, for EXAMPLE, neither parole nor probation may be revoked without **good cause** shown at a hearing at which the parolee or probationer has the opportunity to appear, to answer specific charges, and to examine witnesses. *See* revocation of license.

revocation of license [*ly* · sense] *n.* The cancellation of a license previously granted by a public body (EXAMPLES: a license granted by a town or city to sell alcoholic beverages; a driver's license issued by the state). Most licenses can be revoked only after a **revocation hearing**.

revocation of offer [*off* · er] *n.* The withdrawal of an **offer** by an **offeror** before it has been accepted. *See* offer and acceptance.

revocation of will *n.* The **annulment** of a **will**, in whole or in part, either by a later will, by disposing of property in a manner inconsistent with the provisions of the will, or by destroying or defacing the will. *Compare* revival of will.

revoke [re · *voke*] *v.* To withdraw, cancel, or **annul**; to make a revocation. *See* revocation.
➤ recall, annul, repudiate, ban, abrogate, expunge.

revolution [rev · e · *loo* · shen] *n.* 1. A radical and fundamental change in the political system of a government, often but not necessarily carried out with violence. *See and compare* insurrection; rebellion. 2. A circuit around something; a turn.
➤ anarchy, destruction, innovation, insubordination, metamorphosis, reformation, tumult ("American revolution"); circumvolution, gyration, cycle, rotation, whirl, pirouette ("revolution around the sun").

revolving [re · *vol* · ving] *adj.* A word used to convey the idea that a party will receive specified benefits on a regular basis (EXAMPLE: the extension of credit) so long as he performs specified acts on a regular basis (EXAMPLE: makes payments on account of the debt).

revolving charge account [a · *kount*] *n.* *See* open-end credit.

revolving credit [*kred* · it] *n.* *See* open-end credit.

revolving fund *n.* A **fund** or account established with the intention that all monies disbursed from it will be replaced or repaid. *See* disbursement.

reward [re · *ward*] *n.* Money or other compensation offered by the government, a corporation, or an individual for the performance of a special service (EXAMPLES: finding a lost child; giving information leading to the arrest of a criminal). A reward is payable in accordance with the terms of the offer.

➤ accolade, bonus, remuneration, award, prize, recompense, emolument, gratuity.

RFP Abbreviation of **request for proposal**.

RIA Abbreviation of **radioimmunoassay**.

RICO [*ree · ko*] Acronym for **Racketeer Influenced and Corrupt Organizations Act**.

rider [*ry · der*] *n.* 1. A sheet or sheets of paper, written or printed, attached to a document, that refer to the document in a manner which leaves no doubt of the parties' intention to incorporate it into the document. *See* incorporation by reference. Riders are most frequently used with insurance policies. 2. A new and often unrelated provision or measure added to a **bill** late in the legislative process, with the intention that it "ride" through. See log rolling. 3. A passenger.

➤ attachment, extension, insertion, supplement, addendum, codicil ("a rider to the bill").

right *adj.* 1. In accord with law, morality, and justice. 2. Correct; appropriate. 3. Principled.
n. 1. In the purely legal sense, a just or valid claim recognized or granted by the law and enforced by the law. (EXAMPLES: **marital rights**; **patent rights**; **stock rights**.) It is important to note that the law arms every **legal right** with a matching **legal remedy**. 2. In a more general sense, that which is morally and ethically proper. *See* ethics; moral. *See also* absolute right; Bill of Rights; civil rights; Civil Rights Acts; correlative rights; equitable right; exclusive right; legal right; natural right; private rights; qualified right; relative rights; riparian rights; vested right.

➤ *adj.* righteous, honorable, de jure, licit, sanctioned, punctilious ("do the right thing"); appropriate, accurate, precise, perfect, infallible, wholesome ("the right way to go").
n. claim, license, entitlement, liberty, heritage, certification ("right of remitter"); virtue, merit, righteousness, principle, probity, fidelity ("as a matter of right").

right and wrong test *n. See* M'Naghten rule.

right in action [*ak · shen*] *n.* Same as **chose in action**.

right in personam [per · *soh* · nam] *n.* A **right** against a person, as opposed to a right against a thing (i.e., a **right in rem**). *See in personam*; in personam action.

right in rem *n.* A **right** in or against a thing, as opposed to a right against a person (i.e., a **right in personam**). *See in rem*; in rem action.

right of action [*ak · shen*] *n.* The right to bring a suit in a particular case. *See* cause of action.

right of entry [*en · tree*] *n.* The right to possession of land. *Compare* right of reentry.

right of first refusal [re · *fyoo* · zel] *n.* A right to meet any other **offer**. A right of first refusal does not give the person who holds it the power to compel an unwilling owner to sell; rather, it requires the owner, when and if she decides to sell, to offer the property first to the person entitled to the right of first refusal. *Also see* option.

right of possession [po · *zesh* · en] *n.* A person's right to occupy and enjoy property. *See* occupant; enjoyment.

right of privacy [*pry* · ve · see] *n. See* privacy.

right of property [*prop* · er · tee] *n.* The right to freely use, enjoy, and dispose of property without restrictions other than those imposed by the law. *See* dispose; disposition; enjoyment; use.

right of redemption [re · *demp* · shen] *n. See* equity of redemption.

right of reentry [ree · *en* · tree] *n.* The right to repossess land. *Compare* right of entry. *See* repossession.

right of representation [rep · re · zen · *tay* · shun] *n. See* representation.

right of retainer [re · *tane* · er] *n.* The right of an **executor** or **administrator**, who is also a creditor of the **estate**, to retain sufficient funds to satisfy his claim out of the funds of the estate. *See* retainer.

right of subrogation [sub · ro · *gay* · shun] *n.* The right of a person to substitute one **party** for another and to give the substituted party the same rights and **remedies** as the party who has been replaced. *See* subrogation.

right of survivorship [ser · *vy* · ver · ship] *n.* In the case of a **joint tenancy** or a **tenancy by the entirety**, the entitlement of the surviving **tenant**, upon the death of the other, to hold in his or her own right whatever **estate** or **interest** both previously shared. *See* survivorship. *Compare* tenancy in common.

right of way *n.* 1. The right of a vehicle (EXAMPLES; a car; a boat; a train) to move forward without interruption in preference to another vehicle approaching from a different direction. Such a right is a **relative right**, not an **absolute right**. *See also* rules of the road. 2. The strip of land upon which railroad tracks are laid. 3. The right to pass over the land of another; an **easement**. *See and compare* private way; public way.

right to bear arms *n.* *See* Second Amendment.

right to counsel [*koun* · sel] *n.* The right of a person accused of a crime to have effective legal counsel for her defense, as guaranteed by the **Sixth Amendment**. *See* effective assistance of counsel. An **indigent defendant** has the right to have the court appoint an attorney to represent him. *See* assigned counsel.

right to die *n.* A term referring to the right of a person to determine what limits, if any, she wishes to impose with respect to efforts to prolong her life if she becomes gravely ill. *See* advance directive; chronic persistent vegetative state; healthcare proxy; living will.

right to life *n.* A term that is itself without meaning in the language of the law, but is commonly used to refer to the legal issues connected with abortion. *See Roe v. Wade.*

right to privacy [*pry* · ve · see] *n.* *See* privacy.

right to redeem [re · *deem*] *n.* *See* equity of redemption.

right to travel [trav · el] *n.* A **penumbra right** secured through the **equal protection clause** of the **Fourteenth Amendment**. The courts have held that a state violates the right to travel if it imposes unduly restrictive **residency requirements** upon eligibility for many of the forms of assistance it provides (EXAMPLES: **AFDC; public housing**).

right to work laws *n.* Statutes in many states prohibiting an employer and a union from entering into a **collective bargaining agreement** that compels a person to become a member of the union in order to be hired or to retain her job.

right, title, and interest [*ty* · tel and *in* · trest] *n.* A phrase sometimes used in legal **instruments** to indicate that a **grantee** is receiving whatever interest the **grantor** has in the property. EXAMPLE (in a **quitclaim deed**): "I hereby convey all of my right, title, and interest in Blackacre to Mary Brown."

rightful [*right* · ful] *adj.* Legal; legitimate. ➤ legal, legitimate, deserving, statutory, proper, just, lawful, true ("the rightful heir").

rights *n.* *Plural* of **right**. *See* right.

rigid [*rij* · id] *adj.* Stiff; severe; strict. ➤ stiff, inflexible, taut, tense, harsh, inelastic, precise, unbending, unalterable. *Ant.* loose, flexible.

rigor mortis [*rig* · er *mort* · iss] (*Latin*) *n.* Means "the stiffness of death." The phrase refers to the stiffening of the body that begins to occur shortly after death.

riot [*ry* · et] *n.* The acts of three or more persons assembled together who threaten to do injury to the persons or property of others, or who, by means of violence, actually do damage to others or their property. *See* unlawful assembly. *v.* To protest; to rebel or revolt. ➤ *n.* fight, brawl, fracus, donnybrook, affray, anarchism, brannigan, distemper ("A riot started over the voting policy"). *v.* fight, brawl, resist, oppose, rebel, pillage.

riparian [ry · *pare* · ee · en] *adj.* Belonging or relating to the bank of a river or stream. *Compare* littoral.

riparian land *n.* Land along the bank of a river or stream. Only land within the watershed of the river or stream is considered to be riparian.

riparian owner [*oh* · ner] *n.* A person who owns **riparian land**. *See and compare* lower riparian owner; upper riparian owner.

riparian proprietor [pro · *pry* · e · ter] *n.* Same as **riparian owner**.

riparian rights *n.* The rights of a **riparian owner**, i.e., the right to make reasonable use of a river or stream flowing through land she owns. EXAMPLES: fishing; boating; diverting the water in ways and in quantities (as for irrigation, drinking, etc.) that do not deprive **lower riparian owners**.

ripe *adj.* Fully matured; ready; fully developed.
➤ advanced, provident, complete, consummate, opportune, inclined, fully matured, ready, fully developed, mellow ("ripe fruit"); favorable, auspicious, ideal, suitable ("The conditions were ripe").

ripe for judgment [*juj* · ment] The status of an **action** in which every aspect of the **proceeding** that must be completed before **entry** of a **final judgment** has, in fact, been completed.

ripe for review [re · *vyoo*] The status of a case before the **lower court** that is at a point at which it may be appealed. *See* appealability.

ripeness doctrine [*ripe* · ness *dok* · trin] *n.* The doctrine that an administrative agency or a **trial court** will not hear or determine a case, and an **appellate court** will not entertain an appeal, unless an actual **case or controversy** exists. *See also* ripe for judgment; ripe for review.

rising of the court [*ry* · zing] *n.* The court's final adjournment on the last day of the **term of court**.

risk *n.* 1. In insurance law, the chance of **loss** or **injury**; the hazard or peril of loss that is protected by an insurance policy. EXAMPLES: fire; flood; sickness. *See* assumption of risk; risk of loss. 2. A gamble; a peril.
v. To expose to a danger or hazard.
➤ *n.* speculation, vulnerability, exposure, susceptibility, insecurity, gamble, peril ("Investing in that stock now is a big risk").
v. jeopardize, speculate, threaten, imperil, compromise, wager ("to risk it all").

risk arbitrage [*ar* · bi · trahzh] *n.* Purchasing the stock of a corporation that is the target of a **hostile takeover**, with the expectation that the takeover will increase the value of the stock. *See* arbitrage.

risk capital [*kap* · i · tel] *n.* Same as **venture capital**.

risk of loss *n.* The **risk** that a particular insurance policy covers.

risks of employment [em · *ploy* · ment] *n. See* ordinary risks of employment.

road *n. See* private road; public road; rules of the road.
➤ artery, way, asphalt, highway, boulevard, expressway, pavement, thoroughfare.

rob *v.* To commit the crime of **robbery**.
➤ abscond, bereave, defalcate, divest, pillage, steal.

robbery [*rob* · e · ree] *n.* The **felonious** taking of money or any thing of value from the **person** of another or from his presence, against his will, by force or by putting him in fear. *Compare* larceny; larceny from the person. *See* armed robbery.
➤ theft, holdup, piracy, commandeering, embezzlement, expropriation, abduction.

Roberts Rules of Order [*rob* · erts rules of *or* · der] *n.* A volume of **parliamentary rules** that have been adopted by many organizations and some legislatures for the purpose of governing the conduct of their meetings.

Roe v. Wade [roh vee wade] *n.* A 1973 **landmark decision** of the Supreme Court (410 U.S. 113) which held it **unconstitutional** for a state to criminalize abortions during the first three months of pregnancy under any circumstances, and **constitutional** for a state to do so during the second three months only if it has set standards for the conditions under which abortions are to be performed. The state is free to ban all abortions during the final trimester of pregnancy, except those performed to save the mother's life. The *Roe* decision is based upon the premise that, insofar as abortion is concerned, no **compelling state interest** outweighs a woman's **right of privacy**. *See* life.

rogatory letters [*roh* · ge · tore · ee] *n.* Same as **letters rogatory**.

role *n.* 1. Duty; function. 2. Impersonation or portrayal of a person or character.
➤ part, assignment, job, mission, position, work; act, performance, semblance, guise, show.

roll *n.* A **register**; an official record; a book of records. EXAMPLE: the **tax rolls**. *See also* judgment roll.
v. 1. To revolve or turn around. 2. A slang term meaning to rob a person who is drunk or helpless.
➤ *n.* annals, census, chronicle, master register, table, record ("the tax rolls"); cannonade, echo, ruffle.
v. bowl, circle, circumduct, elapse, furl, swathe, undulate; rock, rotate, flow, swirl, wrap.

rolling over [*role* · ing *oh* · ver] *n.* 1. The refinancing or renewal of a **note** that has reached **maturity**. 2. The reinvestment of funds in a different form of **security** or in a different type of investment.

room and board *n.* *See* boarder.

roomer [*room* · er] *n.* A person who lives in a rooming house. *Compare* boarder.
➤ boarder, tenant, occupant, lodger.

rooming house [*room* · ing] *n.* A house where bedrooms are furnished for a **consideration**, usually for limited periods of time such as a week or a month. *Compare* boarding house.
➤ boarding house, home, lodging, inn.

root *n.* Foundation; core.
➤ foundation, cause, reason, essence, nucleus, source, germ, base, origin ("the root of the problem").

root of title [*ty* · tel] *n.* The **conveyance** or **instrument** with which a **chain of title** begins.

ROR Abbreviation of **release on own recognizance**.

round lot *n.* The customary unit for a transaction involving the purchase or sale of **securities**; in the case of stock, 100 shares. *Compare* odd lot.

routine [roo · *teen*] *n.* The usual way of things; the norm.
adj. Habitual.
➤ *n.* procedure, pattern, habit, technique, practice, formula.
adj. habitual, established, customary, everyday, typical, standard, normal, repeated, ritual.

royalty [*roy* · el · tee] *n.* 1. **Consideration** paid for the right to use, manufacture, or sell something belonging to another (EXAMPLES: a **patented** item; **copyrighted** material; oil or gas), usually stated in the form of stipulated amounts of money per number of units used, manufactured, or sold, or a percentage of receipts. Thus, for EXAMPLE, an author might receive, in exchange for the copyright on her book, a royalty of 10 percent of the **net revenues** realized from the sale of the book. Royalties paid by the **lessee** to the **lessor** under an **oil and gas lease** or a **mineral lease** are also commonly in the form of a fractional interest in the oil, gas, or minerals produced or a flat sum per unit of output (EXAMPLE: dollars per ton of coal). When used in connection with a **license** under a patent, "royalty" means the compensation paid by the **licensee** to the **licensor**. 2. The status of a king, empress, princess, duke, or the like.
➤ consideration, compensation, pay, payments ("royalties from any publisher"); nobility, aristocracy, monarchy ("The ceremony was attended by royalty").

RS An abbreviation of **revised statutes**.

rule *n.* 1. That which is laid down by **authority** as a guide to conduct. 2. An order of a court or an administrative agency made in a particular **proceeding** with respect to the disposition of the case or some aspect of the case. 3. A regulation issued by an administrative agency. 4. A **rule of law**.
v. 1. To decide; to determine; to order. 2. To govern.
➤ *n.* ordinance, legislation, statute, code, norm, principle, decree, mandate, dictate, imperative ("rule of the game"); sovereignty, dominion, administration, leadership, authority, management ("rule of the king").
v. manage, administer, officiate, domineer, resolve, adjudicate, adjudge, establish, arbitrate, conclude ("rule on the issue"); manipulate, predominate, direct, command, oversee, preside over ("rule the country").

rule absolute [*ab* · so · loot] *n.* An order of court directing that a decree or order which had been conditional be made final. *Compare* decree nisi. *See* final order; final judgment.

rule against accumulations [a · *genst* a · kyoo · myoo · *lay* · shenz] *n.* A statutory provision in some states prohibiting a

R

trust from accumulating interest or income beyond a limited number of years. *See* accumulation trust.

rule against perpetuities [a · *genst* per · pet · *yoo* · i · teez] *n.* The **common law rule** that prohibits the creation of a **future interest** or a **future estate** that has the possibility of not **vesting** within 21 years, plus nine months, of some **life in being** at the time of creation of the interest. The rule, which is designed to prevent restrictions on the **power of alienation**, has been adopted in one form or another in every state of the United States. In the following EXAMPLE, the **devise** to the children of a deceased daughter is **void** because it violates the rule against perpetuities: "I leave Blackacre to my daughters, Mary and Beth, to be held **in trust** until they both obtain the age of 40; however, if either of my daughters should die without children who survive her, her share shall vest in my surviving daughter; but if my deceased daughter leaves surviving children, her share shall vest in those of her children who reach the age of 25 when their mother would have reached the age of 40 had she lived."

rule in Shelley's Case [*shel* · eez] *n.* Although this rule is no longer in effect, **life estates** and **remainders** now being recognized by the law, it deserves mention because of its historical importance. The rule is usually stated as follows: when a person takes a **freehold estate**, **legal** or **equitable**, under a deed, will, or other writing, and in the same instrument there is a **limitation** by way of remainder, either with or without the interposition of another estate, of an **interest** of the same legal or equitable quality, to his heirs or the **heirs of the body**, as a class of persons to take in succession from generation to generation, the limitation to the heirs entitles the ancestor to the whole estate.

rule in Wild's Case *n.* A rule of the law of **future interests**, established by the English **common law**, that is still applicable today in many states of the United States: a **devise** to a person and his children or **issue** creates a **fee tail** if such person has no issue at the time of the devise, but, if he does, he and his children take joint **life estates**.

rule nisi [*nie* · sie] *n.* *See* decree nisi.

rule of four *n.* An internal rule of the Supreme Court, which provides that a case will be reviewed by the Court if four justices wish it to be reviewed.

rule of law *n.* 1. A legal doctrine governing human conduct or the conduct of human affairs. EXAMPLES: the **last clear chance doctrine**; the **Miranda rule**; *cy pres*. Rules of law are often judge-made. *See* judge-made law. 2. A phrase referring to a society in which the conduct of its members is regulated by law rather than by the will or wishes of those in power. *See* presumption.

rule of presumption [pre · *zump* · shun] *n.* The rule under which a **presumption** arising from a certain fact or facts stands until proof to the contrary is introduced; in other words, a rule that shifts the **burden of proof** from one **party** to the other.

rule to show cause *n.* Same as **order to show cause**.

rules for lawyer discipline [*law* · yer *dis* · sip · lin] *n.* *See* disciplinary rules; professional responsibility; ethics.

rules of appellate procedure [a · *pel* · et pro · *see* · jer] *n.* A body of rules adopted in statutory form, with some variations, by most state legislatures and by Congress. These rules regulate the manner in which appeals to **appellate courts** are conducted in the jurisdictions that have adopted them. EXAMPLE: the **Federal Rules of Appellate Procedure**.

rules of civil procedure [*siv* · il pro · *see* · jer] *n.* A comprehensive set of rules that Congress and most state legislatures have enacted into law in one or another form. These rules govern **procedure** in **civil actions** in the jurisdictions that have adopted them. EXAMPLE: the **Federal Rules of Civil Procedure**.

rules of court *n.* Rules promulgated by the court, governing **procedure** or **practice** before it.

rules of criminal procedure [*krim* · i · nel pro · *see* · jer] *n.* A comprehensive set of rules enacted as statutes by Congress and most state legislatures, and varying from state to state in relatively few respects. These rules control **procedure** in criminal

R

prosecutions in the jurisdictions that have adopted them. EXAMPLE: the **Federal Rules of Criminal Procedure**.

rules of evidence [*ev · i · dense*] *n.* A body of rules enacted in statutory form, with some variations, by most state legislatures and by Congress. These rules control the **procedure** with respect to **evidence** in both civil cases and criminal prosecutions in the jurisdictions that have adopted them. EXAMPLE: the **Federal Rules of Evidence**.

rules of navigation [nav · i · *gay* · shun] *n.* A set of rules adopted by seagoing nations regulating the manner in which their vessels are to be operated on the open seas to avoid the risk of collision with each other. *See* navigation. *Compare* inland rules of navigation.

rules of practice [*prak* · tiss] *n.* Rules governing the **procedure** in a case, whether prescribed by statute or promulgated by the court. *See* rules of court; rules of procedure. *Also see* practice.

rules of procedure [pro · *see* · jer] *n.* *See* rules of civil procedure; rules of criminal procedure.

Rules of Professional Conduct [pro · *fesh* · en · el *kon* · dukt] *n.* Rules promulgated by the **American Bar Association** that detail an attorney's ethical obligations to her client, the courts, and opposing counsel. With variations, these rules have been adopted by most states and incorporated into their statutory codes of ethics. *See* ethics.

rules of the road *n.* *See* traffic regulations.

rulemaking [*rool* · may · king] *n.* The promulgation by an administrative agency of a **rule** having the force of law, i.e., a **regulation**. *See* quasi-legislative.

ruling [*roo* · ling] *n.* 1. A determination made by a judge or a **hearing officer** during the course of a trial or hearing. EXAMPLE: a determination with respect to the admissibility of particular evidence.

2. The final decision in a case, whether by a court or an administrative agency. 3. An interpretation by an administrative agency of a statute or regulation. EXAMPLE: a **determination letter**.
adj. Dominant; in power.
➤ *n.* decree, mandate, adjudication, order, pronouncement, resolution, verdict ("the judge's ruling").
adj. cardinal, central, controlling, dominant, guiding, reigning, sovereign ("the ruling class").

runaway shop [*run* · a · way] *n.* A shop, manufacturing plant, or other work site that an employer has relocated to avoid the unionization of its employees.

running [*run* · ing] *adj./n.* 1. Sustained; going on continuously. 2. Occurring in succession. 3. Passing; elapsing; going by. 4. Going along with; accompanying. 5. Moving fast. 6. Operating; being operated.
➤ *adj.* continuous, executing, incessant, perpetual, unbroken, unceasing ("a running joke").
n. administration, coordination, functioning, maintenance, oversight, superintendency ("the running of the store"); passing, elapsing ("running of the statute of limitations").

running account [a · *kount*] *n.* An **open account**.

running days *n.* Successive days; i.e., calendar days as opposed to **business days**.

running of the statute of limitations [*stat* · shoot of lim · i · *tay* · shenz] *n.* The passing of the period of time during which a person may bring an **action** as prescribed by the applicable **statute of limitations**. Once "the statute has run," the action is barred.

running with the land *n.* *See* covenant running with the land.

ruthless [*rooth* · les] *adj.* Heartless; mean; cruel.
➤ cruel, focused, draconian, treacherous, cold-blooded, merciless, ferocious, vicious.

S corporation [ess kore · per · *ay* · shen] *n.*
A **corporation** electing to be taxed under
Subchapter S of the **Internal Revenue
Code**. Its income is taxed to the share-
holders rather than at the corporate level.
Compare C corporation. *See* corporation.

S&L Abbreviation of **savings and loan
association**.

Sabbath [*sab* · eth] *n.* The day of each
week set aside for worship and rest. Most
Christian religions observe Sunday as the
Sabbath. *See* Sunday closing laws.
  Sabbath breaking [*brake* · ing] *n. See*
Sunday closing laws.

sabotage [*sab* · e · tahzh] *n.* 1. Intentional
acts of force or violence to the property
of an employer for the purpose of slowing
production, particularly in the context of a
labor dispute. 2. Any deliberate attempt to
reduce a manufacturer's productivity, motivated by a military or political objective.
➤ demolition, impairment, subversion,
treachery, treason, wrecking.

sadism [*say* · dizm] *n.* The act of obtaining
sexual satisfaction or other pleasure from
inflicting pain.
➤ cruelty, debauchery, deviation.

safe *adj.* Secure; protected; not in danger;
out of harm's way.
  n. A place where valuables are kept,
usually a heavily reinforced, locked metal
repository designed to resist burglary,
fire, and flood.
➤ *adj.* guarded, secure, covered, innocuous,
impregnable, unassailable, protected,
inpenetrable ("a safe place"); modest,

cautious, responsible, circumspect, timid
("a safe investor").
  n. chest, strongbox, depository, trunk,
case, locker.

safe deposit box [de · *pah* · zit] *n.* A
metal box with a double lock, kept in a
bank, used for the purpose of safely maintaining one's valuable papers and other
property, such as jewelry, or gold coins.

safe investment rule [in · *vest* · ment] *n.*
1. Same as **prudent man rule**. 2. A method
of calculating future earnings on the basis of
a theoretical return on low-risk investments.

safe place ordinances [*or* · di · nen · sez]
n. See safe place statutes.

safe place statutes [*stat* · shoots] *n.*
Statutes or ordinances that provide for the
safeness of places of **public accommodation**
by imposing strict obligations of maintenance and repair upon their owners. *See
also* safe working place.

safe working place [*wer* · king] *n.* A
term applied to the **standard of care**
required of an employer with respect to
preventing injury to employees; it neces-
sitates the exercise of that degree of care
practiced by prudent employers in similar
circumstances. *See* due care. This **common
law** standard has been supplemented by
the federal **Occupational Safety and
Health Act** and similar state statutes.

safekeeping [*safe* · keep · ing] *n.* Custody;
shelter.
➤ custody, conservation, supervision, shelter,
guardianship, auspices, trust, protective
custody.

S

said *adv./adj.* Aforesaid; previously mentioned; mentioned above.

sailor's will [*sale* · erz] *n. See* military will.

salable [*sale* · ebl] *adj.* Same as **merchantable**.
➤ merchantable, acceptable, needed, fashionable, staple, desirable.

salable value [*val* · yoo] *n.* The price for which an item will sell, i.e., its **market value**.

salary [*sal* · e · ree] *n.* As opposed to a wage, a fixed annual compensation paid to an employee on a periodic basis, for EXAMPLE, weekly or monthly.
➤ earnings, emolument, recompense, remuneration, stipend, wage, pay.

sale *n.* A transfer of **title** to property for money or its equivalent. Both real property and personal property (**tangible** as well as **intangible**) may be the subject of a sale. A sale may be **executory** or **executed**. A sale does not always result in an absolute transfer of title. (EXAMPLES of transactions that are not absolute include **conditional sale contracts** and **sales on approval**.) *See* agreement of sale; bargain and sale; bill of sale; bootstrap sale; bulk sale; cash sale; contract for sale of goods; execution sale; fire sale; foreclosure sale; gross sales; installment sale; judicial sale; memorandum sale; private sale; public sale; retail sale; sale on approval; sheriff's sale; short sale; tax sale; wash sale.
➤ exchange, trade, transaction, barter, vendition, reduction.

sale and leaseback [*leess* · bak] *n.* A sale to a purchaser who, as a part of the transaction, **leases** back to the seller the item that is the subject of the sale.

sale and return [re · *tern*] *n. See* sale or return.

sale as is *n. See* as is.

sale at auction [*awk* · shen] *n. See* auction.

sale by sample [*sam* · pl] *n.* When a sale is made on the basis of a **sample**, it creates an **express warranty** that the goods as a whole conform to the sample.

sale for taxes [*tak* · sez] *n. See* tax sale.

sale in gross *n. See* in gross.

sale of land *n. See* contract for sale of land.

sale on approval [a · *proov* · el] *n.* A sale in which the buyer has the right to reject the property as unsuitable to her needs if she gives timely notice of that fact.

sale or exchange [eks · *chaynj*] *n.* In tax law, a transaction that results in a **gain** or **loss**. *See* exchange.

sale or return [re · *tern*] *n.* A sale in which **title** to goods passes to the buyer, subject to reverting to the seller if the buyer decides to return the goods and does so according to the terms of the contract.

sale with all faults *n. See* all faults.

sales agreement [a · *gree* · ment] *n.* 1. A **contract for sale of goods** or a contract for the sale of other personal property. 2. A **contract for sale of land**.

sales contract [*kon* · trakt] *n.* Same as **sales agreement**.

sales tax *n.* A tax imposed by state or **local government** on retail sales. Sales taxes are based upon a percentage of the price of the goods or services sold.

salesperson [*saylz* · per · sen] *n.* A person whose job it is to sell things. The term is usually applied to an employee who makes sales for his employer or to an **independent contractor** or other agent who makes sales for his principal, but it applies equally to a person who sells his own product or services.
➤ clerk, seller, vendor, merchant, agent.

salient [*sail* · ee · ant] *adj.* Noticeable; important.
➤ outstanding, noticeable, prominent, conspicuous, pertinent, pronounced, striking, protruding.

salvage [*sal* · vej] *n.* 1. Property that remains after a **casualty** such as a fire or a flood. 2. The compensation paid to those who save a ship or its cargo from peril, or who recover a ship or its cargo after they have become a casualty because of some peril. 3. The act of saving something from peril or of retrieving what is left after it has been exposed to peril. 4. Scrap.
v. To save or rescue.

➤ *n.* remains, junk, debris, surplus, flotsam, residuum, salvation ("salvage from the crash").

v. recapture, save, retrieve, restore, rehabilitate, regenerate, ransom ("to salvage the ship").

salvage loss *n.* A **marine insurance** term meaning the extent of a **loss** as measured by the original value of the insured property less its value after it has been salvaged.

salvage value [*val* · yoo] *n.* The value something has as scrap; junk value.

same *adj.* 1. Alike in all respects; identical. 2. Of the identical kind.

➤ aforementioned, alike, comparable, compatible, equivalent, indistinguishable, likewise; changeless, consistent, invariable, perpetual, unaltered, uniform.

same evidence test [ev · i · denss] *n.* **Double jeopardy** prohibits a criminal defendant from being tried or convicted on two **indictments** if the evidence required to convict on the second indictment is the same as the evidence required to convict on the first.

same offense *n.* 1. For purposes of the **double jeopardy** provision of the **Fifth Amendment**, not simply an offense bearing the same name, but one arising from the same criminal transaction. 2. For purposes of sentencing under an **habitual offender statute**, an identical offense or a similar offense.

sample [*sam* · pl] *n.* An article or a portion taken from a large number or bulk that fairly represents the whole; a specimen. *See* sale by sample.

➤ constituent, element, exemplification, example, fragment, typification, specimen ("a fine sample of our product").

sanction [*sank* · shen] *n.* 1. Action taken by a tribunal, for EXAMPLE, a court or an administrative **board** or **commission**, by way of enforcing its **judgment**, decision, or order. EXAMPLES of sanctions include the imposition of a fine or a **penalty**, the seizure of property, and the revocation or suspension of a license. 2. The part of a statute that contains the penalty for violating the statute. 3. A punishment; a penalty. 4. Approval; support.

v. 1. To approve; to endorse; to authorize. 2. To punish; to penalize.

➤ *n.* acquiescence, allowance, endorsement, countenance, encouragement, ratification, sufferance ("the official sanction of Major League Baseball"); ban, boycott, decree, injunction, penalty, sentence, punishment ("unimposed sanctions").

v. concur, agree, authorize, support, validate, indorse, endorse, countenance ("The match was sanctioned by the IBF"); punish, ban, boycott ("The bar sanctioned the erring attorney").

sanctuary [*sank* · choo · er · ee] *n.* 1. A place where a person taking refuge is safe. 2. A place where wild animals are safe from those who hunt them. USAGE: "wildlife sanctuary." 3. A sacred place.

➤ altar, chancel, sanctum, holy place ("The service was held in the sanctuary"); asylum, cover, harborage, oasis, retreat, shelter ("sanctuary from the authorities"); asylum, preserve, park, refuge, reserve, shelter ("wildlife sanctuary").

sane *adj.* Of **sound mind**. *See* sanity.

➤ balanced, composed, judicious, moderate, competent, sagacious, sober.

sanitary [*san* · i · tare · ee] *adj.* Pertaining to the absence of conditions that cause infection or disease.

➤ healthful, hygienic, purified, salubrious, sanitive, sterile.

sanitary codes *n.* Ordinances or statutes that prescribe standards governing sanitary conditions for businesses and professions for which such regulation is required to ensure that the public health is maintained, for EXAMPLE, restaurants, meat packing plants, laboratories that handle human tissue, and doctors' offices. *See* inspection laws.

sanity [*san* · i · tee] *n.* The state or condition of a person who is of **sound mind**. *Compare* insanity.

➤ acumen, comprehension, judiciousness, lucidity, sagacity, saneness, soundness, competency, capacity.

sanity hearing [*heer* · ing] *n.* Same as **competency hearing**.

satisfaction [*sat* · is · *fak* · shen] *n.* 1. The **discharge** of an **obligation** by the payment of a debt. 2. The **performance** of a

S

S

contract according to its terms. 3. The act of satisfying. 4. A fulfillment of needs. *See* accord and satisfaction. *See also* satisfied; satisfy.

➤ payment, compensation, settlement, amends, atonement, indemnification ("satisfaction of a debt"); fulfillment, pleasure, contentment, felicity, gratification, realization ("satisfaction from helping others").

satisfaction contract [*kon* · trakt] *n.* A **contract** providing that the **performance** rendered by one party must be satisfactory to the other.

satisfaction of judgment [*juj* · ment] *n.* 1. The payment of a **judgment** in full. 2. A document (EXAMPLE: a **release**) stating that the judgment in question is paid or **satisfied**. *See* satisfied encumbrance.

satisfaction of mortgage [*more* · gej] *n.* The payment of a **mortgage** in full.

satisfaction piece *n.* A writing signed by both **parties** to a lawsuit, and intended for **recordation**, stating that they have resolved their dispute.

satisfactory [sat · is · *fak* · ter · ee] *adj.* Sufficient; adequate.

➤ adequate, sufficient, delighting, gratifying, competent, average ("a satisfactory, but not outstanding, cross-examination").

satisfactory evidence [*ev* · i · dense] *n.* Same as **satisfactory proof**.

satisfactory proof *n.* **Proof** that is **credible**.

satisfactory title [*ty* · tel] *n.* 1. **Title** to real estate that is satisfactory to the other party to the contract. *See* contract for sale of land. 2. **Marketable title**.

satisfied [*sat* · is · fide] *adj.* 1. Paid; having received **satisfaction**. 2. Content.

➤ paid, compensated; content, pleased, gratified.

satisfied encumbrance [em · *kum* · brense] *n.* A mortgage or other **lien** that has been paid in full. The term generally applies only to mortgages and liens **of record**. *See* satisfaction of judgment; satisfaction of mortgage. *See* encumbrance.

satisfy [*sat* · is · fy] *v.* 1. To make **satisfaction**; to pay off or pay in full. 2. To fulfill; to accommodate; to gratify.

➤ repay, reimburse, requite, fulfill, compensate, settle, annul ("satisfy a debt");

satiate, appease, gratify, assuage, indulge, amuse ("satisfy her every need"); convince, persuade, assure, reassure, answer ("satisfy the jury").

save *v.* 1. To exempt; to exclude; to reserve; to except. *See* save harmless. 2. To conserve; to accumulate. 3. To safeguard. 4. To rescue. *See* saving.

➤ rescue, salvage, preserve, safeguard, ransom, help, aid, shield, cover ("save from harm"); economize, retrench, accumulate, shelve, reserve, hoard ("save money").

save harmless [*harm* · less] *v.* Same as **hold harmless**.

save harmless agreement [*harm* · less a · *gree* · ment] *n.* Same as **hold harmless agreement**.

save harmless clause [*harm* · less] *n.* Same as **hold harmless clause**.

saving [*save* · ing] *adj.* 1. The act of exempting; excluding; reserving; excepting. EXAMPLE: a **saving clause**. 2. Conserving; accumulating. EXAMPLE: a **savings account**. *See* savings. 3. Safeguarding; rescuing. *See* save.

➤ exempting, excluding, reserving, excepting ("a saving clause"); conserving, accumulating ("a saving account").

saving clause *n.* 1. A clause in a statute stating that, in the event of a judicial determination that parts of the statute are **unconstitutional**, the valid portions of the act will be enforced. 2. In a statute that repeals a previous statute, a clause that **saves** existing rights granted by, or **pending actions** that arose under, the repealed statute. A saving clause is also referred to as a **severability clause**.

savings [*say* · vingz] *n.* That which one has accumulated or saved. *See* save; saving.

➤ resources, funds, capital, money, accumulations.

savings account [a · *kount*] *n.* A bank account on which interest is paid and against which a depositor may draw only a limited number of checks or none at all, being restricted instead to cash withdrawals. *Compare* checking account.

savings account trust [a · *kount*] *n.* A form of **Totten trust**.

savings and loan association (S&L)
[a · so · see · ay · shen] *n.* An organization of people cooperating by creating a common fund that may be loaned to members for the purpose of buying or building homes or purchasing land in order to build. Savings and loan associations are not **commercial banks** and in most jurisdictions they are not classified as **savings banks**, although in some states they are permitted to perform some banking functions. In recent years S&Ls have also become involved in commercial ventures unrelated to real estate. Savings and loan associations and **building and loan associations** are often referred to as **thrift institutions** or "thrifts."

savings bank *n.* A bank that pays interest on deposits. Historically, savings banks did not maintain checking accounts for their customers and did not permit depositors to draw checks on their savings accounts. The distinction between the services currently offered by savings banks and **commercial banks** has become increasingly blurred.

savings bank trust *n. See* savings account trust.

savings bond *n.* A **bond** issued by the United States, payable to a named **payee** in progressively larger amounts the longer it is held.

savings to suitors clause [soo · terz] *n.* A federal statutory provision requiring that federal law be applied in a suit involving **admiralty** matters, regardless of whether it is brought in state court or federal court.

Savings and Loan Insurance Corporation [say · vingz and loan in · shoor · ense kore · per · ay · shen] *See* Federal Savings and Loan Corporation.

SB Abbreviation of **Senate Bill**.

SBA Abbreviation of **Small Business Administration**.

scab *n.* A strike breaker.

scalper [skal · per] *n.* A person who engages in **scalping**.

scalping [skal · ping] *n.* 1. In the investment business, the practice of a small investor who makes a small profit from buying and quickly selling **securities**. 2. The practice of selling tickets, particularly tickets that are in demand (EXAMPLES: theater tickets; concert tickets; tickets to a football game), at prices higher than their official price.

scam *n.* A fraudulent deal.
➤ fraud, deception, trick, artifice, hoax.

scandal [skan · del] *n.* Gossip, including gossip that is **defamatory**. *See* slander.
➤ aspersion, belittlement, calumny, defamation, depreciation, ignominy, opprobrium, reproach, gossip, slander; outrage, outcry, fuss, furor, commotion.

scandalous [skan · del · ess] *adj.* Offensive; causing scandal.
➤ offensive, shocking, infamous, disgraceful, odious, impertinent ("a scandalous allegation").

scandalous matter [mat · er] *n.* **Matter** in a **complaint** or other **pleading** that is damaging to the reputation of the person to whom it refers. The court may order it to be stricken. *See* strike. *Also see* impertinent matter.

scarce *adj.* In short supply; insufficient; rare.
➤ scant, deficient, wanting, rare, limited, insufficient, unavailable.

scarcity *n.* A limited supply.
➤ paucity, dearth, lack, inadequacy, want, need.

scene *n.* The place of an occurrence.
➤ locality, location, place, surroundings, site, episode, act, setting.

schedule [sked · jool] *n.* 1. A page or a number of pages attached to a document (EXAMPLE: a tax return) listing additional details relating to the matter contained in the main document; an **inventory**. *See* appendix. 2. A list of times when certain events occur. EXAMPLE: a train schedule. 3. A list generally.
v. To arange events; to plan one's time.
➤ *n.* agenda, appointments, calendar, itinerary, registry, timetable ("the schedule for today").
v. organize, register, record; arrange, book, card, catalog ("to schedule an appointment").

schedule in bankruptcy [bank · rupt · see] *n.* A schedule filed by a **bankrupt** listing, among other things, all of his property, its value, his creditors, and the nature of their claims.

S

scheduled [*sked* · joold] *adj.* A term referring to information appearing on a schedule.

scheduled injuries [*in* · jer · eez] *n.* Under a **workers' compensation act**, injuries compensable in specified amounts, based upon the seriousness of the injury, regardless of whether the worker has been incapacitated or has suffered a loss of earning capacity. *See* compensable injury; loss of earning capacity.

scheduled property [*prop* · er · tee] *n.* Property that must be specifically listed on a schedule attached to the insurance policy; unless it is **listed**, the insurance company will not **indemnify** the insured.

scheme *n.* A plan; a systematic plan; a system. Although the word often carries with it the notion of a tricky or devious plan, it does not necessarily have that meaning; rather, its meaning depends upon the context in which it appears.
v. To plan; to arrange; to conspire.
➤ *n.* arrangement, plan, blueprint, codification, contrivance, presentation, strategy, tactics, theory, notion ("Aaron's scheme to make millions").
v. plan, arrange, plot, conspire, connive, machinate, design, devise.

scheme to defraud [de · frawd] *n.* A plan concocted for the purpose of perpetrating a **fraud**. *See* defraud. *Also see* fraudulent misrepresentation.

schism [*skiz* · im] *n.* A separation into different factions.
➤ break, rift, rupture, falling-out, difference, dissent, nonconformity, separation, division. *Ant.* union, coalition.

school *n.* A place of instruction or education. *See* parochial school; private school; public school.
v. To educate or train.
➤ *n.* academy, college, department, discipline, faculty, institute ("school of fine arts"); adherents, circle, class, clique, devotees, disciples ("school of followers"); belief, creed, faith, persuasion, outlook ("the old school").
v. advance, teach, coach, cultivate, indoctrinate, educate, discipline, prime ("school him in martial arts").

school board *n.* An elected body composed of a number of directors or commissioners whose duty it is to administer the **public schools** within a **school district**. *See* county board; intermediate units.

school bonds *n.* **Bonds** issued for the purpose of funding the construction of schools.

school district [*dis* · trikt] *n.* An administrative body created by the legislature for the purpose of administering the state's **public schools** within its **territorial limits**. School taxes are levied on a district basis and tend to vary from district to district. *See* district.

school taxes [*tak* · sez] *n.* Taxes levied exclusively for the purpose of financing the operation of the **public schools** and without regard to whether the taxpayer's children are enrolled in the public schools.

sci. fa. [*sye* · fah] (*Latin*) Abbreviation of *scire facias*. USAGE: Lawyers often use the term "*sci. fa.*" in referring to a **writ of scire facias**.

scienter [*see* · *en* · ter] (*Latin*) *n.* Knowledge, particularly **guilty knowledge**; i.e., knowledge a person has that, as a **matter of law**, will result in her liability or guilt. EXAMPLE: knowledge on the part of a person making a **fraudulent misrepresentation** that the representation is false. *See also mens rea.*
➤ knowledge, guilty knowledge, intent, purpose.

scintilla [sin · *til* · a] *n.* The tiniest particle; a mere trace.
➤ trifle, spark, trace, smidgen, iota, modicum, fleck, atom, grain.

scintilla of evidence [*ev* · i · dense] *n.* The slightest bit of evidence.

scintilla rule *n.* 1. The rule, rejected in most but not all jurisdictions, that a verdict cannot be directed in favor of a **party** if there is even a **scintilla of evidence** in favor of the other party; that is, if there is any evidence in favor of the other party, the case must be submitted to the jury. *See* directed verdict. 2. The rule that a **motion for summary judgment** cannot be granted if there is the slightest bit of evidence in favor of the opposing party.

scire facias [*sye* · ree *fay* · shee · ass] (*Latin*) *n.* Means "made known"; short for **writ of scire facias**. A *scire facias* is a writ based upon a **matter of record** (for EXAMPLE, a **judgment**) seeking some judicial action with respect to the thing that is of record (a **revival of judgment**, for EXAMPLE).

scope *n.* Range; an area of activity; the extent of a person's **authority**.
➤ range, breadth, latitude, ambit, purview, extension, zone, extent ("scope of authority").

scope of agency [*ay* · jen · see] *n.* The extent of the authority granted to an **agent** by her **principal**. *See* agency. *Also see* scope of authority.

scope of authority [aw · *thaw* · ri · tee] *n.* In the law of **agency**, the **authority** of an **agent**, conferred by his **principal**, for the performance of acts on behalf of the principal. The grant of authority by the principal need not be express; it may be implied from the acts of the principal, or the agent, or both. *See and compare* actual authority; express authority; implied agency.

scope of employment [em · *ploy* · ment] *n.* A phrase referring to activities carried out by an employee in doing the work assigned to him by his employer. Under the doctrine of *respondeat superior*, an employer is not liable for injury inflicted by an employee acting outside of the "scope of his employment." However, an employee's acts which are merely incidental to his regular duties, but are of benefit to the employer, are generally deemed to fall within the scope of his employment. *See also* course of employment. *Compare* frolic of his own.

scope of review [re · *vyoo*] *n.* A phrase referring to the nature and extent of the **jurisdiction** of an **appellate court** when reviewing the decision of a **lower court**, or the jurisdiction of any court when reviewing the decision of an administrative agency. The issues the reviewing tribunal may address, and the action it is entitled to take, are prescribed by state and federal constitutional and statutory provisions. *See* review.

scrawl *n.* 1. A mark or scroll made with a pen, intended to serve as a **seal**. 2. Illegible handwriting.
➤ doodle, scratch, scribble, squiggle, mark.

scrip *n.* A **certificate** of a right to receive something. In certain circumstances, instead of money, *governments* issue scrip that may be redeemed for money. *Corporations* issue scrip representing fractional shares of stock that, when accumulated in sufficient number, may be exchanged for stock. *Note* that "scrip" is not "**script**." *See* scrip dividend; share certificate.

scrip dividend [*div* · i · dend] *n.* A **certificate** issued by a corporation to its shareholders evidencing ownership of stock to be issued at a later date (a **stock dividend**) or evidencing a right to a **cash dividend** to be distributed later. *See* share certificate.

script *n.* 1. An original of a document or **instrument**, as opposed to a duplicate. 2. The manuscript of a play or a screenplay. *Note* that "script" is not "**scrip**."
➤ calligraphy, chirography, penmanship, longhand, characters ("Write the certificate in a nice script"); article, dialogue, lines, manuscript, scenario, text, typescript ("Stick to the lines in the script").

scrivener [*skriv* · ner] *n.* An outdated term for a person who drafts letters or documents for a living.
➤ writer, scribe, reporter, drafter.

scrivener's error *n.* A typographical or clerical mistake.

scroll [skrole] *n.* 1. A scrawl or mark intended as a **seal**. 2. A rolled-up document.

scrutinize [*skroo* · tih · nize] *v.* To examine or analyze carefully.
➤ examine, analyze, investigate, probe, review.

scrutiny [*skroo* · tih · nee] *n.* Examination or analysis.
➤ analysis, review, inquiry, examination, probe ("strict scrutiny").

seal *n.* An imprint made upon an **instrument** by a device such as an engraved metallic plate, or upon wax affixed to the instrument. The seal symbolizes authority or authenticity. Modern law does not commonly require that instruments be **under seal**. In instances where it does, the abbreviation "**LS**" is universally accepted as a legal seal. *See* corporate seal; official seal.
v. To close; to conclude; to consummate.

S

➤ *n.* emblem, logo, imprint, imprimatur, certification, authentication, trademark ("seal of the school").

v. close, cork, isolate, quarantine, segregate, plug ("seal the opening"); assure, authenticate, clinch, conclude, consummate, establish, ratify ("seal the deal").

sealed *adj.* 1. Having a seal affixed; **under seal**. 2. Closed; secured.

➤ closed, hidden, private, secured, occluded ("a sealed bid").

sealed and delivered [de · *liv* · erd] *adj.* *See* signed, sealed, and delivered.

sealed bid *n.* In connection with the **letting** of a **public contract**, a term describing the requirement that no bids be opened or their contents known until they are opened together on the same preannounced date.

sealed instrument [*in* · stroo · ment] *n.* An **instrument** to which one or both parties have affixed their seals as well as their signatures.

sealed record [*rek* · erd] *n.* *See* sealing the record.

sealed verdict [*ver* · dikt] *n.* A **verdict** reached by a jury during a recess of the court, signed by the jurors and placed in a sealed envelope, to be presented to the court when it reconvenes. *See* convene.

sealing the record [*see* · ling the *rek* · erd] *n.* The statutes of every state authorize judges, in their discretion, to limit access to, or to impound or "seal," the transcript and other court records in certain circumstances. EXAMPLES: criminal records regarding the possession of **controlled substances**; court papers relating to adoptions; court records specifying the terms of probation in criminal cases.

seaman's will [*see* · menz] *n.* *See* military will.

search *n.* 1. An inspection conducted by a law enforcement officer, acting under **legal authority**, of one's person, premises, or belongings for the purpose of discovering stolen, **contraband**, or illicit property as evidence of guilt, to be used in a criminal prosecution. *See* search and seizure. *Compare* seizure. 2. The right of a **belligerent** during wartime to inspect the merchant ship of a neutral nation. 3. A **title search**.

See blanket search warrant; custodial search; unreasonable search and seizure; warrantless search. *See also* exclusionary rule; Fourth Amendment; fruit of the poisonous tree doctrine; *Mapp v. Ohio*; McNabb-Mallory rule; plain view doctrine; probable cause.

v. To investigate; to look for evidence of criminal activity.

➤ *n.* prying, probe, inspection, scrutiny, pursuit, examination, perusal, inquisition, reconnaissance ("a search for stolen goods").

v. pry, probe, investigate, chase, scrutinize, examine, peruse, rummage ("search the premises").

search and seizure [*see* · zher] *n.* "**Unreasonable searches and seizures**" are prohibited by the **Fourth Amendment**. *See* unreasonable search and seizure.

search warrant [*war* · ent] *n.* An order in writing issued by a **magistrate** or other **judicial officer** and directed to a law enforcement officer, commanding her to search for and seize stolen, **contraband**, or illicit property, or other property evidencing the commission of a crime. *See* warrant.

search without warrant [with · *out war* · ent] *n.* *See* warrantless search.

season [*see* · zen] *n.* A time of the year. *See* open season.

v. 1. To acclimate or prepare. 2. To add flavor.

➤ *n.* division, interval, junction, occasion, opportunity, term ("season for football").

v. acclimate, accustom, anneal, inure, mature, temper, qualify ("seasoned with age"); color, enliven, lace, leaven, spice, add zest ("season the food").

seasonable [*see* · zen · ebl] *adj.* **Timely**; appropriate.

➤ timely, propitious, opportune, apposite, serviceable, felicitous, fortunate ("a seasonable acceptance is required").

seasonal employment [*see* · zen · el em · *ploy* · ment] *n.* Employment in occupations that can be carried on only in certain seasons or during fairly definite portions of the year. EXAMPLES: harvesting crops; working as a department store Santa Claus.

seat *n.* 1. A place where something is located. USAGE: "A state's capital is its

seat of government." 2. A place of power. USAGE: "It appears she will be reelected to her seat in Congress."

➤ chair, place, chesterfield, davenport, recliner, settee, stall ("There's a seat for you at the head of the table"); abode, axis, capital, cradle, polestar, source ("seat of government"); base, foundation, groundwork, seating, support ("seat of the building"); backside, breech, derriere, posterior, rear, behind, butt ("shot in the seat").

seat of government [guv · ern · ment] n. See seat.

seat on exchange [eks · chaynj] n. A term for membership in a **stock exchange** or **commodity exchange**. See exchange.

seated land [see · ted] n. Occupied or cultivated land; **improved land**.

SEC Abbreviation of **Securities and Exchange Commission**.

sec. Abbreviation of **section**.

secession [se · sesh · en] n. The act of withdrawing from membership in an organized group. Eleven southern states attempted secession from the United States at the time of the Civil War.

➤ withdrawal, separation, disaffiliation, resignation.

second [sek · end] adj. 1. Later in time than that which is first. 2. Lesser in rank, right, or importance. See junior.
n. 1. A short interval of time; 1/60 of a minute. 2. An assistant.
v. Support; encourage.

➤ adj. runner-up, next, alternate, consequent, resultant, subsequent ("second in line").
n. flash, instant, moment, split second ("just a second"); assistant, backer, double, exponent, supporter ("a second in the duel").
v. aid, approve, assist, encourage, support, endorse, promote ("second the motion").

Second Amendment [sek · end a · mend · ment] n. The Second Amendment to the Constitution provides: "A well regulated militia being necessary to the security of a free state, the right of the people to keep and bear arms shall not be infringed."

second degree crime [de · gree] n. See degrees of crime. Also see second degree murder.

second degree murder [de · gree mer · der] n. A **murder** that does not fall into the category of **first degree murder**; a murder committed with **intent to kill**, but without **premeditation** or **deliberation**. Compare voluntary manslaughter.

second look doctrine [dok · trin] n. In some jurisdictions, the name by which the **wait and see doctrine** is known.

second mortgage [more · gej] n. A **mortgage** that is **junior** to a **first mortgage**. See junior mortgage.

second-hand evidence [ev · i · dense] n. **Hearsay evidence**. Compare secondary evidence.

secondarily liable [sek · en · dare · i · lee ly · ebl] adv. See secondary liability.

secondary [sek · en · dare · ee] adj.
1. **Ancillary**; incidental; **remote**.
2. Derivative; stemming from.
3. Additional. Compare primary.

➤ auxiliary, consequential, subservient ("of secondary importance"); derivative, borrowed, consequent, eventual, proximate, resultant, subsidiary ("a secondary matter").

secondary activity [ak · tiv · i · tee] n. In labor law, activity designed to force an employer to meet a union's demands by coercing or otherwise illegally influencing its customers or suppliers not to do business with it. (EXAMPLES: a **secondary boycott**; **secondary picketing**.) Such activity is generally illegal under the **National Labor Relations Act**. Compare primary activity.

secondary authority [aw · thaw · ri · tee] n. As opposed to **case law**, which is **binding authority**, "secondary authority," which is merely **persuasive authority**, is not law itself but is simply commentary upon or a summary of the law. EXAMPLES of secondary authority include legal **treatises**, **law review** articles, legal encyclopedias, and paralegal dictionaries.

secondary boycott [boy · kot] n. A **boycott** applied by a union to **third persons** to cause them, against their will, not to patronize or otherwise deal with a company with whom the union has a dispute. A secondary boycott is one form of **secondary activity**. Compare primary boycott. See also secondary picketing.

S

secondary easement [*eez* · ment] *n.* An **easement** that is **appurtenant** or incident to the primary easement. *See* appurtenant easement.

secondary evidence [*ev* · i · dense] *n.* Evidence that is not the most reliable proof of a fact; that is, evidence that is not **primary evidence** or the **best evidence**. Secondary evidence is admissible in circumstances where it is not possible to produce the primary evidence. EXAMPLE: if an instrument or other writing relevant to a case has been lost, a witness may be permitted to testify orally to its contents. *Compare* primary evidence. *Also compare* second-hand evidence. *See* evidence. *Also see* best evidence rule.

secondary liability [ly · e · bil · i · tee] *n.* **Liability** that does not come about until the primary **obligor** fails to meet her **obligation**; the liability of a **guarantor** or **indorser** as distinguished from that of a **maker** or **principal**. *Compare* primary liability.

secondary picketing [*pik* · e · ting] *n.* **Picketing** a customer or supplier of a company with whom a union has a dispute, as opposed to picketing the company itself. Secondary picketing is one form of **secondary activity**. *Compare* primary picketing. *See also* secondary boycott.

secret [*see* · kret] *adj.* Undisclosed; hidden; that which is not communicated. *See* trade secret. *Also see* secrete.
n. Information that is confidential, priviliged, or kept hidden.
➤ *adj.* hidden, clandestine, covert, private, abstruse, conspiratorial, disguised ("a secret matter").
n. confidence, private affair, mystery, classified facts, privileged information ("It's a secret").

secret lien [leen] *n.* A **lien** that does not appear **of record**.

secret partnership [*part* · ner · ship] *n.* A **partnership** that includes at least one partner whose membership in the firm is not disclosed to the public.

Secret Service *n.* A division of the Treasury Department charged with, among its other duties, responsibility for protecting the president and vice president, detecting and arresting persons who commit crimes relating to currency and **securities**, and investigating and apprehending violators of laws pertaining to electronic fund transfers, credit card fraud, computer access fraud, and food stamps. *See* fraud.

secret trust *n.* An arrangement between a **testator** and a **legatee** under which the legatee agrees not to keep the property for herself, but to use it for the benefit of a third person.

secretary [*sek* · re · tare · ee] *n.* 1. A corporate officer, ordinarily with power to transact certain business on behalf of the corporation. 2. A **Secretary of State**. 3. A title given to cabinet officers in both state government and the federal government. EXAMPLES: the Secretary of Defense; the Secretary of Labor. 4. A person who handles correspondence and performs other functions in an office. With respect to legal secretaries, *see* National Association of Legal Secretaries (NALS).
➤ official, officer, director; clerk, assistant, typist.

secretary of corporation [kore · per · *ay* · shen] *n.* A corporate officer. *See* secretary.

Secretary of State [*sek* · re · tare · ee] *n.* 1. In many states, a public official whose duties include supervising and certifying the results of elections, monitoring compliance by corporations with certain legal requirements imposed upon them by the state, and accepting the filing of **financial statements** that give notice of the existence of a **security interest**. 2. In the federal government, the title of the cabinet officer who heads the Department of State and serves as a principal advisor to the president on foreign affairs.

secrete [se · *kreet*] *v.* 1. To conceal, particularly to hide a thing from law enforcement officers or to make it unavailable to **legal process**. 2. To give off a secretion.
➤ bury, cache, finesse, screen, hide, cover, seclude, veil ("secrete the information"); discharge, emit, emanate, extricate, extrude, perspire ("secrete sweat").

section [*sek* · shen] *n.* 1. A subdivision of a statute or **code**, sometimes of a **chapter**, often indicated by the symbol §. *Also see* title. 2. A **section of land**, i.e., a parcel of

land consisting of 640 acres as laid out by **government survey**. *See* quarter section.
v. To divide into parts; to partition.
➤ *n.* part, segment, component, subdivision ("a section of the class"); area, part, sector, neighborhood, locale, precinct, parcel ("this section of town"); classification, component, moiety.
v. divide, partition, allocate, sector, segment.

section number *n.* The number given a **section of land** laid out by **government survey**.

section of land *n. See* section.

secular [*sek* · yoo · ler] *adj.* Pertaining to things of the world, as distinguished from religious or spiritual things.
➤ nonreligious, lay, mundane, materialistic, worldly.
Ant. religious, sacred, holy.

secular business [*biz* · ness] *n.* A business or occupation that, under **Sunday closing laws**, may not be engaged in on Sunday.

secure [sek · *yoor*] *adj.* Safe; not exposed to danger; unlikely to fail; stable.
v. 1. To make certain of payment. 2. To give an assurance or a guaranty against a **risk** or hazard. 3. To safeguard; to protect. 4. To obtain. 5. To fasten. *See* secured; security.
➤ *adj.* safe, defended, guarded, immune, protected, riskless, unassailable.
v. assure, cover, defend, ensure, guarantee, screen, shield ("secure the debt"); adjust, anchor, bind, bolt, cement, fasten, moor, pinion, rivet ("secure the sail").

secured [se · kyoord] *adj.* 1. Made certain of payment; given **security**. 2. Guaranteed against a **risk** or peril. 3. Protected. 4. Obtained. 5. Fastened. *Compare* unsecured.
➤ guaranteed, protected, insured, sheltered ("a secured debt").

secured creditor [*kred* · it · er] *n.* A **creditor** who has **security** for her debt in the form of an **encumbrance** on property of the debtor. EXAMPLES: a **mortgagee**; a **lienee**. *Compare* unsecured creditor. *Also compare* general creditor.

secured debt *n.* A debt for which **security** or **collateral** has been given. *Compare* unsecured debt. *See* secured creditor.

secured loan *n.* A loan for which **security** or **collateral** has been given. *Compare* unsecured loan. *See* secured creditor.

secured party [*par* · tee] *n.* One who is a **holder** of a **security interest**.

secured transaction [tranz · *ak* · shen] *n.* A transaction that creates or provides for a **security interest** in personal property. EXAMPLE: a **secured loan**. *See* transaction.

securities [se · *kyoor* · i · teez] *n.*
1. Certificates that represent a right to share in the profits of a company or in the distribution of its **assets**, or in a debt owed by a company or by the government. (EXAMPLES: **stocks**; **bonds**; **notes** with **interest coupons**; any **registered security**.) What is and is not a "security" differs to some degree under different statutes, for EXAMPLE, the **securities acts**, the **Bankruptcy Code**, the **Uniform Commercial Code**, and the **Internal Revenue Code**. Generally speaking, however, under most legislation, a security is an **instrument** of a type commonly dealt in on **securities exchanges** or in similar markets and is commonly recognized as a means of investment. 2. *Plural* of **security**. *See* security. *Also see* certificated security; listed security; municipal securities; public securities; registered securities; uncertificated security; unlisted security.
➤ stocks, convertible debentures, negotiables, coupons, bills, warranties.

securities acts *n.* State and federal statutes regulating the issuance and sale of securities to the public. EXAMPLES: the **Securities Act of 1933**; the **Securities Exchange Act**; **blue sky laws**.

securities broker [*broh* · ker] *n.* A person employed in buying and selling securities for others. *See* broker; stockbroker.
➤ financial expert, agent, broker, financier, middleman.

securities exchange [eks · *chaynj*] *n.* A market for transactions in securities; a stock exchange.

securities offering [*off* · er · ing] *n. See* offering.

Securities Act of 1933 [se · *kyoor* · i · teez act of nine · teen · ther · tee · *three*] *n.* A federal statute regulating the issuance and sale of **securities** to the public, particularly

S

with respect to their **registration** (*see* registered securities) and with respect to providing information to prospective purchasers. The Act is administered by the **Securities and Exchange Commission**.

Securities and Exchange Commission [se · *kyoor* · i · teez and eks · *chaynj* kum · *ish* · en] *n.* The agency that administers and enforces federal statutes relating to **securities**, including the **Securities Act of 1933** and the **Securities Exchange Act**.

Securities Exchange Act [se · *kyoor* · i · teez eks · *chaynj*] *n.* The federal statute that empowers the **Securities and Exchange Commission** to regulate **securities exchanges**.

security [se · *kyoor* · i · tee] *n.* 1. *Singular* of **securities**. *See* securities. 2. **Collateral**; a **pledge** given to a creditor by a debtor for the payment of a debt or for the performance of an **obligation**. EXAMPLES: a **mortgage**; a **lien**; a deposit. *See* personal security. *See also* surety. 3. Protection; safety; assurance. *See* client security fund; internal security.
➤ warranty, bail, surety, escrow, collateral, debenture, assurance ("security for the mortgage"); safety, defense, strength, bulwark, fortification, stability, preservation, impregnability, immunity ("personal security").

security agreement [a · *gree* · ment] *n.* An agreement that creates or provides for a **security interest**.

security deposit [de · *pah* · zit] *n.* Money that a tenant deposits with a landlord as an assurance that he will abide by the terms of the lease and, in particular, as security for any damage he might do to the property. *See* deposit.

security for costs *n.* A **bond** given to the court by a plaintiff or by an **appellant** to guarantee the payment of **costs** if she is ordered by the court to pay the costs. Such security may also be given in the form of cash or property.

security interest [*in* · trest] *n.* 1. Under the **Uniform Commercial Code**, "an **interest** in personal property or **fixtures** which secures payment or performance of an obligation." *See* purchase money security interest. *See also* security agreement.

2. With respect to real property, a mortgage or other **lien**.

sedition [se · *dish* · en] *n.* 1. At **common law**, stirring up resistance to lawful authority, exciting discontent against the government, or attempting to promote public disorder, riot, or rebellion. 2. By federal statute, advocating the overthrow of the government by force or violence. *See* Smith Act; subversive activities.
➤ defiance, rebellion, mutiny, insubordination, apostasy, treachery, treason, infidelity.

seduce [se · *dooss*] *v.* 1. To persuade someone into an action. 2. To lure through false promises.
➤ lure, bewitch, tempt, allure, cajole; violate, abuse, defile, corrupt.

seduction [se · *duk* · shen] *n.* As used in the law, the act of inducing a person to have sexual relations, usually through some form of deception. Seduction is a criminal offense in some jurisdictions if it is accomplished by means of a promise of marriage. *See* criminal conversation; heart balm statutes.
➤ enticing, allure, temptation, delusion, misleading, coaxing, captivation.

sedulous [*sed* · yoo · lus] *adj.* Hardworking; diligent.
➤ diligent, industrious, hardworking, persevering, assiduous.

segregation [seg · re · *gay* · shen] *n.* 1. Often used as a short reference for racial segregation; the practice of separating people based upon religion, nationality, and, particularly, race or color, especially with respect to education and housing. This practice is **unconstitutional**. *See Brown v. Board of Education. See and compare* de facto segregation; de jure segregation. 2. The act of separating or dividing.
➤ classification, isolation, grouping, detachment, allocation, differentiation; bigotry, discrimination, prejudice, racial prejudice, ostracism, apartheid.

seisin [*see* · zin] *n.* The **possession** of a **freehold estate** by the owner. *See* seize. *See also* livery of seisin.
➤ possession, control, occupation, ownership, title ("equitable seisin").

seize *v.* 1. To take both **title** to and **possession** of land. A person who holds both is said to be "**seized**." *See* seisin. 2. To grab, grasp, or take possession of property or of a person. 3. To apprehend; to arrest. *See* seizure.

➤ sequester, sequestrate, capture, snatch, confiscate, mulct, pillage, plunder, appropriate, take.

seized *adj./past part. See* seize; seizure.

seizure [*see* · zher] *n.* 1. The taking of property into one's possession. In this context, the term is usually associated with the act of a law enforcement officer in seizing evidence or **contraband**, or in **attaching** property under a **writ**. A law enforcement officer violates the **Fourth Amendment** if he carries out an **unreasonable search and seizure**. *Compare* search. 2. The act of arresting a person. 3. A sudden attack brought on by disease.

➤ capture, confiscation, impoundment, annexation, expropriation, dispossession ("seizure of the money"); fit, paroxysms, stroke, attack, throe, spasm, visitation, crisis, spell ("convulsive seizure").

select [se · lekt] *adj.* 1. Chosen; selected. 2. Special; best; superior.
v. To choose; to single out.

➤ *adj.* excellent, elite, preferable, superior, culled, delicate, exquisite ("a select wine").
v. pick, cull, adopt, specify, choose, delimit, determine, discriminate, differentiate, except ("select a jury").

select committee [kum · it · ee] *n.* A special committee created for the purpose of looking into a specific matter or reporting on a specific **bill**. *Compare* standing committee. *See* legislative committee.

selective [se · lek · tiv] *adj.* Discriminating; discerning.

➤ particular, precise, discriminating, differentiating, choosy, picky, fussy, judicious.

selective enforcement [se · lek · tiv en · forss · ment] *n. See* selective prosecution.

selective prosecution [se · lek · tiv pross · e · kyoo · shen] *n.* A term applied to the state's failure to prosecute others who may be guilty of the same crime as the defendant. Selective prosecution may violate the **equal protection clause** of the **Fourteenth Amendment**. *See* prosecution.

Selective Service System [se · lek · tiv ser · viss sis · tem] *n.* An agency of the federal government that oversees registration for compulsory military service and selects those who are to be inducted into the armed forces. *See* induction.

selectmen [sel · ekt · men] *n.* In the New England states particularly, the title given to members of a town council or city council. The council itself is generally called a **board of selectmen**.

self *n.* Referring to the person.
➤ individual, person, being.

self-dealing [-*deel* · ing] *n.* With respect to a **fiduciary**, means acting in one's own interest rather than in the interest of the person to whom one owes a duty.

self-defense [-de · *fense*] *n.* The use of force to protect oneself from death or imminent bodily harm at the hands of an aggressor. A person may use only that amount of force reasonably necessary to protect himself against the peril with which he is threatened; thus, **deadly force** may be used in self-defense only against an aggressor who himself uses deadly force. *See* reasonable force.

self-employment tax [-em · *ploy* · ment] *n.* The social security tax paid by people who are self-employed. *See* Federal Insurance Contibutions Act (FICA).

self-executing [-ek · se · kyoo · ting] *adj.* Self-acting; going into effect without need of further action. For EXAMPLE: a **treaty** with a foreign country that is effective without requiring legislation to put it into action is a **self-executing treaty**; a constitutional amendment that takes effect without **enabling legislation** is a **self-executing constitutional provision**.

self-executing constitutional provision [-*ek* · se · kyoo · ting kon · sti · *too* · shen · el pro · *vizh* · en] *n. See* self-executing.

self-executing treaty [-*ek* · se · kyoo · ting tree · tee] *n. See* self-executing.

self-help *n.* Taking matters into one's own hands, i.e., obtaining a **remedy** without **recourse** to **legal process**. (EXAMPLE: under the **Uniform Commercial Code**, a

S

secured party has the right to take possession of the **collateral** in the event of default.) However, self-help is a doctrine of extremely limited application. *See also* necessity.

self-incrimination [-in · krim · i · *nay* · shen] *n.* Testimony, or any other act or statement, by which a person **incriminates** herself; i.e., implicates herself in the commission of a crime. *See* incrimination; privilege against self-incrimination.

self-insurance [-in · *shoor* · ense] *n.* Protecting one's property or business by establishing a fund out of which to pay for **losses** instead of purchasing insurance. Self-insurance is a means through which employers may provide workers' compensation and health coverage to their employees as an alternative to securing **workers' compensation insurance** and health insurance.

self-serving declaration [-*ser* · ving dek · le · *ray* · shen] *n.* A statement made out of court that is favorable to the interests of the person making the statement. A self-serving declaration is **hearsay** and is therefore inadmissible unless it falls within an **exception to the hearsay rule**.

sell *v.* To make a sale.
➤ peddle, vend, auction, trade, wholesale, traffic in, furnish, exchange, deal.

seller [*sell* · er] *n.* A person who sells property she owns; a person who contracts for the sale of property, real or personal; a **vendor**.
➤ agent, businessperson, retailer, merchant, dealer, peddler, shopkeeper, trader.

selling short [*sell* · ing] *n.* *See* short sale.

semblance [*sem* · blents] *n.* 1. Having a resemblance or similarity. 2. An aura; an appearance; the way something seems to be.
➤ closeness, similarity, likeness; air, appearance, identity, guise, look, form, pose, aura, atmosphere, pretense.

semiannual [sem · ee · *an* · yoo · el] *adj.* Occurring twice a year. *Compare* biannual.

Senate [*sen* · et] *n.* The **upper house** of Congress. Its 100 members, 2 from each state, are elected for 6-year terms; one-third of the Senate's members are elected every 2 years.

Senate Bill [*sen* · et] *n.* A legislative **bill** that originates in the Senate of the United States Congress or of a state legislature. Every such bill is assigned a number, preceded by the designation "**SB**." *Compare* House Bill. *Also see* act; statute.

senator [*sen* · et · er] *n.* A member of the United States Senate or of a state senate.
➤ representative, legislator, lawmaker.

send *v.* 1. To transmit or transfer; to deposit in the mail. *See* mailed. 2. To please or thrill.
➤ mail, post, transfer, transmit, freight, discharge, give, cast, convey, issue; delight, thrill, enrapture, excite, stir, please, turn on ("You send me").

senior [*seen* · yer] *adj.* 1. Of primary importance, rank, or right. *Compare* junior. 2. Longer in service. *See* seniority. *n.* The elder person(s) in a group.
➤ *adj.* superior, older, prior ("a senior interest"). *Ant.* junior. *n.* ancient, dean, doyen, doyenne, elder, matriarch, patriarch, pensioner, superior ("seniors of the group").

senior encumbrance [en · *kum* · brense] *n.* A mortgage or other **lien** that has greater **priority** in law than another mortgage or lien. *Compare* junior encumbrance. *See* encumbrance.

senior interest [*in* · trest] *n.* 1. An **interest** or **right** in property that is superior to another person's right in the same property. EXAMPLES: a **senior lien**; a **senior mortgage**. *Compare* junior.

senior lien [leen] *n.* A **lien** that is superior in **priority** to another lien. *Compare* junior lien.

senior mortgage [*more* · gej] *n.* A **mortgage** that is superior in **priority** to another mortgage. *See also* first mortgage. *Compare* junior mortgage.

seniority [see · *nyor* · i · tee] *n.* 1. In labor law, the principle that length of employment determines the order of layoffs, recall to work, promotions, and, frequently, rate of pay. 2. The status or state of being senior.
➤ tenure, longevity, longer service, station, rank, standing ("She was not laid off because of her seniority in the department").

S

sense *n.* 1. Judgment; discretion. 2. An impression or perception.

➤ intelligence, judgment, comprehension, prudence, reason, wisdom ("common sense"); instinct, perception, awareness, impression, apprehension, notion ("a sense of foreboding").

sensitive [*sen · si · tiv*] *adj.* 1. Thoughtful; perceptive. 2. Highly emotional; easily affected or disturbed.

➤ critical, mindful, discerning, perceptive, perspicacious, alert ("a sensitive rendition of that song"); susceptible, vulnerable, easily affected, touchy, impressionable, delicate, nervous, tender ("a sensitive person").

sentence [*sen · tense*] *n.* The **judgment** of the court in a criminal case. A criminal sentence constitutes the court's action with respect to the consequences to the defendant of having committed the crime of which she has been convicted. Generally, criminal sentences impose a punishment of imprisonment, probation, fine, or **forfeiture**, or some combination of these penalties. In some jurisdictions, **capital punishment** may be imposed in cases involving the commission of a **felony** of extreme gravity. In some states, depending upon the crime, the jury, rather than the judge, establishes the sentence. *See* accumulative sentences; concurrent sentences; consecutive sentences; cumulative sentences; determinate sentence; indeterminate sentence; merger of sentences; minimum sentence; presentence hearing; presentence investigation; split sentence; suspended sentence. *See also* sentencing; sentencing guidelines.
v. [*sen · tense*] To pronounce **sentence**. *See* sentence (*noun*).

➤ *n.* penalty, censure, condemnation, decision, dictum, pronouncement ("The sentence was severe").
v. penalize, commit, punish, fine, imprison, condemn, denounce ("sentence the prisoner").

sentencing [*sen · ten · sing*] *n.* The act of imposing a sentence.

➤ punishment, adjudication, penalty.

sentencing guidelines [*gide · lynz*] *n.* Because the existing sentencing system resulted in serious inconsistencies between the sentences imposed by federal judges, Congress passed the Sentencing Reform Act of 1984, which created a Sentencing Commission empowered to create binding guidelines establishing a range of **determinate sentences** for all federal offenses. *See* presentence hearing; presentence investigation.

sentencing hearing [*heer · ing*] *n. See* presentence hearing.

separability clause [sep · er · e · *bil* · i · tee] *n.* Same as **saving clause**.

separable [*sep* · e · rebl] *adj.* Severable; capable of being separated or divided.

➤ severable, divisible, detachable.

separable controversy [*kon* · tro · ver · see] *n.* In a lawsuit in which more than one **cause of action** is alleged, a cause of action that can be separated from the others and fully **adjudicated** separately. A lawsuit that includes a **removable** separable controversy may be removed in its entirety from **state court** to **federal court**. The federal court, in its discretion, may determine the case as a whole, or may **remand** to state court those portions of the action which were not independently removable. *See* controversy.

separate [*sep* · ret] *adj.* 1. Different. 2. Distinct; independent; unconnected; not a part of. 3. Unshared; lone; single. *v.* [*sep* · e · rate] To divide; to put in different places; to keep apart.

➤ *adj.* abstracted, apart, apportioned, disassociated, discrete, different, distinct, unconnected, isolated, severed ("a separate consideration").
v. break, divide, cleave, distinguish, dichotomize, detach, disentangle, sort, disjoint, dissever ("separate the copies").

separate action [*ak* · shen] *n.* Individual **actions** brought by different plaintiffs in connection with the same matter, as opposed to a **joint action** brought by the same individuals.

separate but equal doctrine [*ee* · kwel *dok* · trin] *n.* A doctrine overruled by ***Brown v. Board of Education***, under which the separation of the races in places of **public accommodation**, including public schools, had been held **constitutional**.

separate counts *n.* Two or more **counts**, charging separate offenses, contained in one **indictment** or **information**.

separate estate [es · *tate*] *n. See* separate property.

separate maintenance [*main* · ten · ense] *n.* Court-ordered support paid by one spouse to the other in circumstances where they are living apart but are not divorced. *See* maintenance.

separate property [*prop* · er · tee] *n.* With respect to married persons, property acquired by either of them before marriage and held separately during marriage. In **community property states**, property acquired by gift, **bequest**, **devise**, or inheritance during marriage, as well as property acquired before marriage. *Compare* marital property.

separate trials [*try* · elz] *n.* In criminal law, separate trials of each of several defendants accused of having jointly committed an offense.

separation [sep · e · *ray* · shen] *n.* 1. The status of a husband and wife who live separately. *See* divorce a mensa et thoro; divorce from bed and board; judicial separation; legal separation; limited divorce; living apart; permanent separation. 2. The state of being apart or coming apart.
➤ detachment, embarkation, disrelation, disassociation, partition, parting, sorting, rupture, uncompiling, disunion, alienation, cleavage.

separation agreement [a · *gree* · ment] *n.* An agreement between husband and wife who are about to divorce or to enter into a **legal separation**, settling property rights and other matters (EXAMPLES: **custody**; **child support**; **visitation**; **alimony**) between them. Separation agreements are subject to court approval. *See* property settlement. *Also see* marital agreement.

separation of powers [*pow* · erz] *n.* A fundamental principle of the Constitution, which gives exclusive power to the **legis-lative** branch to make the law, exclusive power to the **executive branch** to administer it, and exclusive power to the **judicial branch** to **enforce** it. The authors of the Constitution believed that the separation of powers would make abuse of power less likely.

separation of spouses [*spow* · sez] *n. See* separation; separation agreement.

separation of witnesses [*wit* · ness · ez] *n. See* sequestration of witnesses.

sequester [se · *kwest* · er] *v.* 1. To separate. *See* sequestration of witnesses. 2. To seize property. *See* sequestration. 3. To isolate oneself; to withdraw. USAGE: "I'm going to sequester myself in my study for the evening."
➤ cloister, confine, separate, insulate, secrete, segregate, withdraw, isolate ("sequester the jury"); attach, arrogate, confiscate, impound ("sequester assets").

sequestration [se · kwes · *tray* · shen] *n.* 1. A **writ** issued **in equity** under which property is taken into the possession of a court in order to assure obedience to a decree. 2. **Equitable relief** through a seizure of the **rents and profits** of real estate in order to preserve them during the pendency of an **action**. *See* pendency of action. 3. The act of **impounding** funds. *See* impound. 4. The **sequestration of witnesses**. 5. The sequestration of a jury. *See* sequestration of jury.
➤ attachment, appropriation, seizure ("the sequestration of property"); isolation, insulation, quarantine ("the sequestration of witnesses").

sequestration of jury [*joor* · ee] *n.* A court order prohibiting the members of a jury from having public contact, reading newspapers, watching television, or the like, while the trial is in progress and until they have delivered their verdict.

sequestration of witnesses [*wit* · ness · ez] *n.* The action of a court in barring the witnesses in a case from the courtroom until they are called to testify.

sergeant-at-arms [*sar* · jent-] *n.* An officer of a legislature, court, or other body whose duty is to keep order during meetings or sessions of the body.

serial [*seer* · ee · el] *adj.* Sequential; consecutive.
➤ continuous, periodical, successive, tabulated, scheduled, recurring ("serial killer"); sequential, consecutive.

serial bonds *n.* **Bonds** of a corporation or a municipality issued at the same time

S

but **redeemable** at different specified dates. *Compare* series bonds. *Also compare* term bonds.

serial note *n.* An **installment note**. *Compare* series of notes.

seriatim [see · ree · *ah* · tem] (*Latin*) *adj./adv.* Serially; in a series; one by one.

series [*seer* · eez] *n.* A sequence; a succession.
➤ cycle, regimen, progression, train, suit, circuit, routine, sequence, succession.

series bonds *n.* **Bonds** of a corporation or a municipality issued at different times and **redeemable** at different specified dates. *Compare* serial bonds. *Also compare* term bonds.

series of notes *n.* A group of **promissory notes** bearing different dates, but given in a series of transactions between the same parties over a period of time. *Compare* serial note.

serious [*seer* · ee · us] *adj.* 1. Severe; grave. 2. Significant; important; weighty. 3. Committed.
➤ genuine, earnest, definite, real, heartfelt, fervent; precarious, grim, grave, onerous, troublesome, alarming, critical.

serious and willful misconduct [*wil* · ful mis · *kon* · dukt] *n.* In the law of **workers' compensation**, the intentional doing of an act either with the knowledge that it is likely to result in serious injury or with a **wanton** and **reckless disregard** of its probable consequences. *Also see* willful misconduct.

serious bodily harm [*bod* · i · lee] *n.* *See* serious bodily injury.

serious bodily injury [*bod* · i · lee in · jer · ee] *n.* An **injury** that gives rise to a reasonable fear for the life of the person who has been injured.

serious illness [*ill* · ness] *n.* An illness that permanently or materially impairs, or is likely to permanently or materially impair, one's health. This term appears on life insurance application forms.

serious injury [*in* · jer · ee] *n.* *See* serious bodily injury.

serious misconduct [mis · *kon* · dukt] *n.* *See* serious and willful misconduct.

servant [*ser* · vent] *n.* 1. A somewhat outdated but sometimes still used term for employee. *See* master and servant. *See and compare* agent; employee; independent contractor. *See also* fellow servant. 2. A person employed to perform personal services for another. EXAMPLES: A maid; a butler; a cook.
➤ assistant, attendant, domestic, drudge, hireling, menial, minion, retainer.

serve *v.* 1. To effect **service** by delivering **process**. *See* service of process. 2. To perform a duty. USAGE: "serve in the military." 3. To be a servant.
➤ arrange, assist, deal, deliver, work, distribute, oblige, present, provision, succor.

service [*ser* · viss] *n.* 1. Work performed; labor. *See* service contract. 2. **Consortium**. *See* services of spouse. 3. The delivering of **process**; short for **service of process**. 4. Utility service. EXAMPLES: gas; electricity. *See* public service; public service corporation. 5. Military service. 6. Work performed; labor; employment. 7. The act of doing something helpful.
v. To maintain or repair.
➤ *n.* ceremony, formality, liturgy, observance, ritual ("Sunday service"); action, active duty, combat duty, fighting ("military time in service"); labor, employment, work ("community service"); notice, notification ("service by mail").
v. fix, check, inspect, repair, tune ("service the car").

service by mail *n.* In circumstances where permitted by statute, **service of process** by mailing a copy to the **party** to be served at his last known address or by mailing it to his attorney. *See* substituted service of process.

service by publication [pub · li · *kay* · shen] *n.* In circumstances where permitted by statute, **service of process** by publishing it in a newspaper. *See* newspaper of general circulation; legal notice.

service charge *n.* A fee charged for rendering a service. Thus, for EXAMPLE, banks charge a monthly service charge for the costs involved in "servicing" a depositor's account.

service contract [*kon* · trakt] *n.* In its most common usage, an agreement between

611

a seller and a consumer in which the seller agrees to maintain and repair the item sold. EXAMPLE: an agreement to service a washing machine.

service corporation [kore · per · *ay* · shen] *n.* See public service corporation.

service mark *n.* A **mark**, design, title, or motto used in the sale or advertising of services to identify the services and distinguish them from the services of others. A service mark is the property of its owner and, when registered under the Trademark Act, is reserved for the exclusive use of its owner. *Compare* trademark.

service of process [*pross* · ess] *n.* Delivery of a **summons**, **writ**, **complaint**, or other **process** to the opposite **party**, or other person entitled to receive it, in such manner as the law prescribes, whether by leaving a copy at her residence, by mailing a copy to her or her attorney, or by **publication**. See personal service of process; service by mail; service by publication; substituted service of process. *Also see* actual service of process; constructive service of process.

services [ser · viss · ez] *n. Plural* of **service**. *See* service.

services of spouse *n.* **Consortium.** *See* service.

servient [serv · ee · ent] *adj.* Subject to an **easement**. *See* servitude. *Compare* dominant.

servient estate [es · *tate*] *n.* Same as **servient tenement**. *Compare* dominant tenement.

servient tenement [*ten* · e · ment] *n.* Real property that is subject to an **easement** that benefits another piece of property, known as the **dominant tenement**. *See* tenement.

servitude [ser · ve · tyood] *n.* 1. The right of an owner of land to use the land of another for a particular purpose. EXAMPLE: an **easement**. *See* appurtenant easement. *See and compare* dominant tenement; servient tenement. 2. A state or condition in which one's personal liberty is controlled by someone else. *See* involuntary servitude.
➤ slavery, subjugation, oppression, serfdom, enthrallment, obedience, submission, vassalage.

session [*sesh* · en] *n.* 1. As opposed to a "term," the time when a court, legislature, or other body is actually meeting or sitting for the purpose of conducting its business. A court that is sitting, or a legislature that is meeting, is said to be **in session**. *See* term. *Also see* regular session; special session. 2. Synonymous with "term," i.e., the entire period during a particular year in which a court sits to conduct its business. *See* term.
➤ affair, assembly, concourse, discussion, hearing, huddle, conference, term.

session laws *n.* The collected statutes enacted during a session of a legislature. *Compare* annotated codes; revised statutes.

session of court *n.* *See* session.

session of the legislature [*lej* · is · lay · cher] *n.* *See* session.

set *adj.* Fixed or established.
n. A series of things of the same kind used together.
v. 1. To establish. 2. To put in place or in position. 3. To put on paper or record, i.e., to "set down."
➤ *adj.* agreed, appointed, concluded, stipulated ("a set price"); intended, inveterate, fixed, obstinate, immovable, rigid, situate ("set in her ways").
n. array, assemblage, class, clique, compendium, coterie, gaggle, organization, series, group ("a complete set").
v. affix, anchor, arrange, bestow, ensconce, lay, level ("set in stone"); allocate, allot, designate, stipulate, dictate, establish, impose, ordain ("set a price"); abet, begin, commence, foment, initiate, instigate, provoke ("set in motion").

set aside [a · *side*] *v.* To **vacate**, **annul**, **void**, or **reverse** a **judgment** or order of a court.

set for trial [*try* · el] *v.* To fix or establish a certain day on or after which the trial of a case will begin.

set forth *v.* To describe or to recite, particularly in a writing. USAGE: "The statute sets forth the elements of the offense."

set of exchange [eks · *chaynj*] *n.* A **foreign bill of exchange**, **drawn** in an identical series of exact copies, each executed and numbered, upon payment of any one of which the remaining copies become **void**.

set off *v.* 1. To reduce a **party's** claim for money by the amount of the claim of the other party to the transaction. *See* setoff. 2. To counterbalance.

➤ reduce, discount, counterbalance.

set out *v.* To recite or allege facts, particularly in a **pleading** or an **instrument** such as a deed. *See* recital.

set-aside [-a · *side*] *n.* That which is put aside (EXAMPLE: money) for a specific purpose.

setback lines [*set* · bak] *n. See* building lines.

setbacks [*set* · baks] *n.* Same as **setback lines**.

setoff [*set* · off] *n.* In **pleading**, a reduction of a plaintiff's **money claim** by virtue of a claim of the defendant arising out of a different transaction. Setoff is achieved through a **counterclaim**. Setoff should be distinguished from **recoupment**, which involves **cross-demands** arising out of the *same* transaction.

➤ reduction, mitigation, adjustment, offset.

setting aside [*set* · ing a · *side*] *n. See* set aside.

setting for trial [*set* · ing for *try* · el] *n. See* set for trial.

settle [setl] *v.* 1. To pay an account or bill. USAGE: "settle my account." *See* settled account. 2. To arrange or put in order. USAGE: "settle my affairs." 3. To resolve or adjust differences; to eliminate controversy. EXAMPLE: the settlement of a lawsuit. 4. To make a determination or a decision. USAGE: "settle the matter once and for all." 5. To reach an agreement. USAGE: "We settled upon Friday as the date for delivery of the merchandise." 6. To **liquidate**. USAGE: "settle the business." 7. To take up residence in a place. USAGE: "settle in Ohio." *See* settlement.

➤ resolve, accommodate, work out, mediate, reconcile, rectify, unravel ("settle the dispute"); allay, assure, pacify, quell, quieten, reassure, sedate, calm ("settle the children down"); abide, colonize, dwell, establish, reside, squat ("settle out West").

settled account [*set* · ld a · *kount*] *n.* An account that has been paid. *Compare* account stated.

settlement [*set* · el · ment] *n.* 1. The ending of a lawsuit by agreement. *See* out-of-court settlement. 2. A determination with respect to the correctness of an **open account** by the parties to the account; the adjustment of an account. *See* adjust. 3. A resolution of differences. *See* compromise and settlement; marriage settlement; property settlement. 4. With respect to a **decedent's estate**, the **final settlement**. 5. A **family settlement**.

➤ decision, adjustment, compensation, disposition, liquidation, remuneration, resolution, termination ("to reach a settlement"); colony, outpost, residence, reservation, hamlet, refuge ("the settlement near the river").

settlement option [*op* · shen] *n.* An **option** available under a life insurance policy, with respect to the method of payment. EXAMPLES: a lump-sum payment; periodic payments.

settlement statement [*state* · ment] *n.* A document, copies of which are distributed to both the seller and the buyer at a real estate **closing**, itemizing the costs connected with the transaction for which each is responsible.

settlor [set · *lor*] *n.* The creator of a **trust**; the person who **conveys** or transfers property to another (the **trustee**) to hold **in trust** for a third person (the **beneficiary**).

seven years' absence [*sev* · en years' *ab* · sence] *n. See* presumption of death. *See also* Enoch Arden statutes.

Seventeenth Amendment [sev · en · *teenth* a · *mend* · ment] *n.* An amendment to the Constitution that provides for direct popular election of United States Senators. Prior to this amendment, United States Senators were elected by the legislatures of their states.

Seventh Amendment [*sev* · enth a · *mend* · ment] *n.* The Seventh Amendment to the Constitution guarantees a jury trial in most **civil actions**.

sever [*sev* · er] *v.* 1. To separate **parties**, **actions**, or **claims**. *See* severance. 2. To separate; to disjoin; to divide; to split. 3. To terminate.

➤ bisect, carve, cleave, detach, disjoin, disunite, rend, slice, sunder ("sever a limb"); abandon, disjoin, dissolve, divide, separate, terminate ("sever ties").

severability [sev · er · e · bil · i · tee] *adj.* The quality of being severable. The quality of being susceptible to separation. *See* severance; severance of actions.

severability clause *n.* Same as **saving clause**.

severability of contract [kon · trakt] *n. See* severable contract.

severability of statute [stat · shoot] *n. See* severable statute.

severable [sev · er · ebl] *adj.* 1. Capable of being separated into independent legal rights or legal obligations. 2. Capable of being divided into separate parts.
➤ separable, divisible, apportionable, fissile, fissionable, detachable.

severable contract [kon · trakt] *n.* A **contract** the **consideration** for which may be construed as apportionable among separate promises contained within the contract, with the result that a breach of one promise is not a breach of the contract as a whole. *Compare* entire contract. *See* apportionment. *See also* breach of contract; breach of promise.

severable statute [stat · shoot] *n.* A statute that, when one or more of its provisions are declared **unconstitutional**, remains enforceable as to the remaining provisions. *See* saving clause.

several [sev · rel] *adj.* 1. Separate and distinct; severable; independent. *Compare* common; joint. *See* joint and several. 2. More than two, but less than a great many.
➤ certain, considerable, disparate, individual, numerous, proportionate ("several books on the subject"); separate, distinct, severable ("several liability").

several actions [ak · shenz] *n.* Separate lawsuits brought against two or more persons, each of whom are liable to the plaintiff as a result of the same transaction. *Compare* joint action. *See* action.

several inheritance [in · hehr · i · tense] *n.* An **inheritance** in which the heirs take as **tenants in common**. *See* take.

several liability [ly · e · bil · i · tee] *n.* As opposed to **joint liability** and **joint and several liability**, the separate, distinct, and individual **liability** of two or more persons to the same plaintiff.

severally [sev · rel · ee] *adv.* Distinctly; separately; apart from others.
➤ distinctly, separately, personally, apart from others ("severally liable").

severally liable [ly · ebl] *adj. See* several liability.

severalty [sev · rel · tee] *n.* 1. As the term relates to property, exclusive ownership by one person in his own right. *Compare* in common; jointly. *See* estate in severalty. 2. Separateness.

severance [sev · rense] *n.* 1. The separation, by judicial order, of **parties**, **actions**, or **claims**. *See* severance of actions. 2. The termination of a **joint tenancy**, particularly by converting it into a **tenancy in common**. 3. The act of detaching things affixed to the land (EXAMPLES: crops; minerals). 4. The act of severing, dividing, separating, or disjoining anything.
➤ separation, termination, partition, division.

severance of actions [ak · shenz] *n.* 1. A court-ordered division of a lawsuit into at least two independent suits. 2. A method by which a court grants separate trials to individual defendants in a **civil action**. *See* action.

severance pay *n.* A payment over and above salary or wages due, sometimes made by an employer to an employee when her employment is terminated. Severance pay is rarely paid when the termination is **for cause**.

severance tax *n.* An **ad valorem tax** on natural resources (EXAMPLES: timber; oil; natural gas) taken from the earth.

sewer district [soo · er dis · trikt] *n.* A **political subdivision** created by government for the purpose of establishing and maintaining sewers within a geographical area. *See* public corporation; quasi corporation.

sex *n.* 1. Intercourse; sexual union. 2. Male or female gender.
➤ intercourse, lust, reproduction, attraction; gender, masculinity, femininity.

sex discrimination [dis · krim · i · nay · shen] *n.* **Discrimination** against a person based upon gender. *See* Civil Rights Acts; Equal Employment Opportunity Commission (EEOC).

S

sexism [*sek* · sizm] *n.* Bias against people because of their gender; discrimination against people based upon their sex. *See* sex discrimination.
➤ bias, discrimination, chauvinism.

sexual [*sek* · shoo · el] *adj.* Of or relating to the sexes or the act of sex.
➤ prurient, erotic, carnal, indecent.

sexual assault [*sek* · shoo · el a · *sawlt*] *n.* *See* indecent assault.

sexual harassment [*sek* · shoo · el ha · *rass* · ment] *n.* A form of **sex discrimination**. Sexual harassment includes unwanted sexual attention from a supervisor. It also includes the toleration by an employer of sexual coercion or "hassling" in the workplace. *See* harassment; hostile environment. *See also* Civil Rights Acts; Equal Employment Opportunity Commission (EEOC).

sexual predator [*sek* · shoo · el *pred* · e · ter] *n.* The term used in some state statutes for a **sexually dangerous person**.

sexually dangerous person [*sek* · shoo · el · ee *dane* · jer · us] *n.* Under many state statutes, a person with a repeated history of sexual misconduct demonstrating an inability to control his sexual impulses or desires who is likely to attack other victims.

shall *v.* A word that the courts generally construe as mandatory rather than directory. Ordinarily it is the equivalent of "must." *Compare* may. *See and compare* directory provision; directory statute; mandatory provision; mandatory statute.

sham *adj.* False; pretended; **counterfeit**. *n.* A deception; a trick; a **fraud**.
➤ *adj.* artificial, counterfeit, adulterated, fictitious, substitute, feigned, false, pretended. *n.* burlesque, caricature, façade, deceit, fake, imitation, fraud, pretext.

sham pleading [*plee* · ding] *n.* Same as **false pleading**.

share *n.* 1. A share of corporate stock. *See* share of stock. 2. The portion or **interest** that a stockholder owns in a corporation, a **joint-stock** company, or any other venture. 3. The portion of a **decedent's estate** given to a particular beneficiary under a will or to which an heir is entitled in an **intestacy**. *See* distributive share. 4. The **elective share** or **statutory share** of a surviving spouse. 5. A portion of anything.
v. 1. To divide; to apportion. 2. To partake of with others.
➤ *n.* portion, allotment, contribution, ratio, percentage, quantum, pittance, need ("share of the business"); stock, security, asset ("corporate shares").
v. parcel out, partition, apportion, partake, divide, measure, mete, allot, assign ("to share the profits").

share and share alike [a · *like*] *v.* A phrase that, in a legal document (EXAMPLES: a will; a **trust indenture**), ordinarily indicates *per capita* distribution.

share certificate [ser · *tif* · i · ket] *n.* 1. A **stock certificate**. 2. A **warrant** or **certificate** issued by a corporation evidencing the right of its holder to receive a specified number of shares of stock in the corporation. *See* scrip.

share of stock *n.* A unit of **interest** in a corporation. A share of stock is the property of its owner (the **shareholder**) and represents a fractional interest in the property (i.e., the **assets**) of the corporation.

share warrant [*war* · ent] *n.* *See* share certificate.

shareholder [*share* · hole · der] *n.* Same as **stockholder**.
➤ stockholder, owner, investor.

shareholder's liability [ly · e · *bil* · i · tee] *n.* *See* stockholders' liability.

shave *v.* 1. To oppress by **extortion**. *See* oppression. 2. To overreach (*see* overreaching); to make a profit by taking unconscionable advantage of a person, particularly in the **discounting** of **negotiable instruments**. *See* unconscionable contract. 3. With respect to gambling, to induce a team to score fewer points than it might. 4. To cut away.
➤ oppress, overreach, cut away, skim, reduce, cheat.

Shelley v. Kraemer [*shel* · ee vee *kray* · mur] *n.* A 1948 decision of the Supreme Court (334 U.S. 1) which held that a state court violates the **Fourteenth Amendment** if it enforces a **restrictive covenant** under which property owners agree among themselves not to sell their property to persons of color. Such a **judgment** by a state court is an EXAMPLE of impermissible **state action**.

Shelley's Case [*shel* · eez] *n.* *See* rule in Shelley's Case.

shelter [*shel* · ter] *n.* 1. A place or building protecting one from the elements or from danger. 2. That which provides protection or benefit.
➤ sanctuary, care, cover, asylum, support, lodging ("shelter from the storm"); benefit, advantage, hedge, gain ("tax shelter").

shepardizing [*shep* · er · dy · zing] *v.* Using a **citator**.

sheriff [*sherr* · if] *n.* The chief law enforcement officer of a county. A sheriff's responsibilities include keeping the peace in the county and serving and enforcing process, both civil and criminal, issued by courts throughout the county and the state.
➤ police, official, marshal.

sheriff's deed *n.* A **deed** given by the sheriff to the purchaser of real estate at a **foreclosure sale** or **tax sale**. *See* sheriff's sale. *See also* execution sale; judicial sale.

sheriff's sale *n.* A sale of real estate carried out by the sheriff under a **foreclosure decree** or similar court order. A sheriff's sale is also referred to as an **execution sale**, **foreclosure sale**, or **judicial sale**.

Sherman Act [*sher* · men] *n.* A federal **antitrust act** that prohibits **combinations in restraint of trade**. *See* monopoly; price-fixing. *Also see* Clayton Act.

shield laws *n.* 1. Statutes that, in cases involving forcible sex crimes, prohibit the prosecution from introducing the victim's sexual history (especially alleged promiscuity or immorality) into evidence. 2. State statutes that, in some jurisdictions, make it a crime for the media to disclose the identity of the victim of rape or other forcible sexual assault. 3. Statutes that, in a few states, permit journalists to refuse to disclose information obtained in confidence and to refuse to disclose the identity of their confidential sources. *See* journalists' privilege.

shifting [*shif* · ting] *adj.* Changing position; varying; passing from one person to another.
➤ varying, wavering, vacillating, alternating, drifting, changing.

shifting income [*in* · kum] *v.* Moving income within a family from one person to another to decrease the total income taxes paid. *See* kiddie tax.

shifting risk *n.* In insurance law, a **risk** that increases or decreases as the property that is the subject of the policy is changed, as for EXAMPLE, is the case with inventory. *See* shifting stock. *See also* blanket policy; floater policy.

shifting stock *n.* The stock or inventory of a merchant that is reduced by sales and replenished by purchases on a daily basis.

shifting the burden of proof [*ber* · den] Moving the **burden of proof** from one side to the other during the course of a trial as the case progresses and evidence is introduced by one side and then the other. *See* prima facie case.

ship *n.* A vessel designed for transportation of goods or passengers over water.
v. 1. To deliver to a **carrier** for transportation. 2. To transport from one location to another.
➤ *n.* boat, freighter, vessel, yacht.
v. address, consign, direct, dispatch, embark, freight, transfer, deliver ("ship these goods").

ship's papers [*pay* · perz] *n.* Documents evidencing the registration of a ship, which the law requires the ship to carry as proof of her nationality and the nature of her cargo.

shipment [*ship* · ment] *n.* 1. The delivery of goods to a **carrier**. 2. The transportation of goods by a carrier. 3. Goods that are being transported by a carrier.
➤ delivery, cargo, goods, property.

shipper [*ship* · er] *n.* A person who ships goods to another. *See* consignor.
➤ carrier, transporter, consignor.

shipping [*ship* · ing] *n.* 1. The act of delivering goods to a **carrier** for transportation. 2. Ships. 3. The business of a person who ships, i.e., the shipping business.

shipping order [*or* · der] *n.* An order given to a **carrier** with respect to a shipment of goods, i.e., to whom they are to be delivered, the date of delivery, and the like. *See* bill of lading.

shipwreck [*ship* · rek] *n.* *See* wreck.

shirk *v.* To avoid responsibility; to neglect.
➤ evade, neglect, avoid, shun, dodge, duck, ignore.

shop right rule *n.* In **patent** law, the rule that an employee who perfects an invention during working hours with his employer's materials and tools must give his employer a right or **license** to use the invention without paying a **royalty**. **Title** to the invention, however, remains with the employee.

shop steward [*stew* · erd] *n.* In a factory or plant, an employee who is also an elected representative of the union, whose chief duties are to attempt to settle **grievances** filed by employees and to monitor the employer's compliance with the **collective bargaining agreement**.

shopbook [*shop* · book] *n.* The **book of account** or **account book** of a storekeeper or a business person.
shopbook rule *n.* An **exception to the hearsay rule** that allows a **book of original entry** to be admitted in evidence if the entries were made in the **regular course of business** at or about the time of each transaction and if they were the first permanent record of the transaction. *See* account book; book of account.

shoplifting [*shop* · lif · ting] *n.* **Larceny** of goods from a store or a shop.
➤ larceny, theft, stealing.

shore *n.* 1. With respect to **tidal waters**, the land adjacent to the water, lying between the **high water line** and the **low water line**. 2. With respect to **inland waters**, the land adjacent to the water.
v. To support; to reinforce.
➤ *n.* waterside, border, brim, littoral, margin, shingle, embankment ("down by the shore").
v. beef up, bolster, bulwark, buttress, strengthen, sustain, underpin, upbear ("shore up").
shore line *n.* The point at which the shore meets the water.

short *adj.* 1. Not having length. 2. Lacking funds. 3. In the language of the stock market, lacking in **securities** or **commodities**.
➤ succinct, laconic, terse, brief, concise, scanty, abridged ("short story"); small, truncated, stunted, dwarfish, diminutive, minuscule, bantam ("short person");
deficient, exiguous, inadequate, meager, needy, lacking, wanting ("short on funds").

short sale *n.* A sale of property, usually corporate stock or other securities, that the seller does not own but that she must acquire by the date agreed upon for delivery. In the case of stock, the customer does not actually produce the shares for delivery; the **broker** furnishes the stock, charges the customer the price of the furnished stock, and carries the account until the customer orders him to repurchase the stock, after which an adjustment is made between the broker and the customer on the difference between the selling and purchasing prices. *See* margin; margin account; margin transaction.

short summons [*sum* · enz] *n.* A **summons** that requires the defendant to **appear** and **answer** within a shorter time than the time usually required.

short swing profit [*prof* · it] *n.* A profit made on the sale of corporate stock held for less than six months. Such profits are generally available only to investors who possess **insider** information.

short weight *n.* The offense of selling merchandise on the basis of its weight and delivering a lesser weight.

short-term *adj.* Relating to a relatively brief period of time. *Compare* long-term.
short-term debt *n.* A debt due within one year. *Compare* long-term debt.
short-term financing [*fine* · an · sing] *n.* A **short-term loan**. *Compare* long-term financing.
short-term loan *n.* A loan with a term of less than one year.

show *n.* 1. A showing of something. 2. Public entertainment.
v. 1. To make apparent or clear by evidence. 2. To make apparent or clear by explanation or illustration.
➤ *n.* burlesque, carnival, entertainment, pageant, performance, presentation, spectacle ("to go to a show"); affectation, air, display, guise, illusion, ostentation, semblance ("to put on a show of happiness").
v. brandish, demonstrate, exhibit, flaunt, proffer, showcase ("to show the goods"); appear, demonstrate, evince, manifest, proclaim, reveal ("show remorse").

S

show cause *v.* To comply with an **order to show cause** by appearing before the court and presenting facts and legal arguments for the purpose of influencing the court not to take a certain action adverse to the **party** making the appearance. USAGE: "The judge required the union to show cause why the court should not issue an **injunction** against its picketing."

show cause order [*or · der*] *n.* Same as **order to show cause**. *Also see* decree nisi.

show up *v.* 1. To appear; to arrive. 2. To embarrass.
➤ arrive, attend, come, be visible, turn up; expose, embarrass, belittle, discredit.

show-up *n.* A police practice by which a witness to a crime confronts the suspect. Like a lineup, its purpose is to make an identification; unlike a lineup, it involves only the suspect and the witness.

shower [*shoh · er*] *n.* A person who, under the supervision of the court, escorts a jury to the scene of a crime or the site of an injury. *See* view.

shut-in royalty [*roy · el · tee*] *n.* A **royalty** paid by the **lessee** under an **oil and gas lease** to keep the lease in force when there is no production.

shyster [*shy · ster*] *n.* An unethical and unscrupulous lawyer.
➤ con man, charlatan, cheat, ripoff artist.

sick *adj.* Unhealthy; ill.
➤ unhealthy, unsound, miserable, distressed, perverted, infirm, weary, unwell, diseased.

sick leave *n.* A leave of absence granted to an employee because of illness or injury.

sidebar *n.* A term applied to a private discussion between the judge and the attorneys for the **parties** during the course of a trial. The conversation takes place at the **bench**, beyond the jury's hearing. USAGE: "I request a sidebar, Your Honor."

sight *n.* 1. The ability to see. 2. The act of seeing. 3. View.
➤ afterimage, appearance, perception, eyesight, ken, seeing ("to lose one's sight"); spectacle, display, exhibit, pageant, scene, show ("what a sight!").

sight draft *n.* A **bill of exchange** or **draft** payable upon **presentment** to the

drawee. It is the equivalent of a check that is **payable on demand**. *See* after sight; at sight.

sign *v.* 1. To affix one's name to an **instrument**; to **subscribe** in one's own handwriting; to execute a legal document. *Also see* signature. 2. To use sign language. *n.* 1. A mark or indication. 2. A public or commercial announcement.
➤ *v.* acknowledge, authorize, autograph, initial, inscribe, subscribe, witness ("sign on the dotted line"); beckon, express, flag, gesticulate, signalize, signify ("sign to him to walk this way").
n. indication, assurance, augury, divination, omen, foretoken, portent, presager ("sign of things to come"); board, billboard, placard, poster, bulletin, beacon, guidepost ("street sign").

signatory [*sig · ne · tore · ee*] *adj.* A person who signs an **instrument** or other document. A nation that has become a party to a **treaty** is a "signatory nation."

signature [*sig · ne · cher*] *n.* The name of a person as affixed by her, in her own handwriting, to an **instrument**, document, or other writing, or to any surface. A person's signature may also be affixed by **mark** or by a mechanical or photographic device that imprints a reproduction of the signature. A signature may be made on one's behalf by one's duly authorized **agent**. In some circumstances, a business's signature may be its **trademark**, **service mark**, or **collective mark**. *See* mark.
➤ autograph, endorsement, John Hancock, holograph.

signature by mark *n.* *See* mark; signature.

signature card *n.* A card given by a bank to a depositor for her signature. It is used by the bank to authenticate the signature on instruments (EXAMPLES: checks; withdrawal slips) purporting to have been executed by the depositor.

signed *adj.* Executed by the affixing of one's signature. *See* sign; signature.

signed, sealed, and delivered [*de · liv · erd*] *adj.* A phrase appearing in a notary's **certificate of acknowledgment**, which attests that the person who signed the document did so in the presence of the notary.

S

significance [sig · *nif* · ih · kants] *n.*
Meaning; importance.
➤ import, importance, value, relevance,
weight, substance, note, momentousness
("of great significance").

silence [*sy* · lense] *n.* Refraining from
speech; the absence of a response, whether
spoken, written, or otherwise. As a general
rule, silence does not amount to **assent**
or **acceptance** except when there is an
obligation to respond. *See* estoppel by
silence.
v. To make quiet.
➤ *n.* quiet, muteness, speechlessness,
quietude, reticence, timidity ("Silence is
required in the library").
v. still, hush, muzzle, nullify, quell, allay,
diminish, curb ("silence the crowd").
silence as assent [a · *sent*] *n. See* silence.

silent [*sy* · lent] *adj.* 1. Quiet; speechless.
2. Undisclosed; implied.
➤ quiet, reticent, reserved, uncommunicative,
uninformative ("The officer remained
silent"); undeclared, nonpublic, implied,
hidden, concealed ("a silent partner").
Ant. noisy, loud; disclosed.

silent partner [*sy* · lent *part* · ner] *n.* A
partner whose connection with the
partnership is unknown to the public
and who takes no part in the conduct of
the partnership business. A silent partner
who invests in the partnership and shares
in the profits is, by definition, a **limited
partner** as well.

similar [*sim* · i · ler] *adj.* Having a
resemblance to or being somewhat like.
Although "similar" generally means something less than an exact duplicate, it may,
depending upon the context in which it appears, mean "identical" or "exactly alike."
➤ like, cognate, analogous, collateral,
correlative, homogeneous, identical,
kindred.
similar sales *n.* A basis for establishing
the value of property. Thus, for EXAMPLE,
a **board of equalization**, in establishing
the value of a particular piece of real
estate for tax purposes, commonly bases
its **appraisal** on the sales prices of similar
properties in the same neighborhood in
the recent past.

simple [*sim* · pl] *adj.* 1. Not **aggravated**.
2. Not **under seal**. 3. Unmixed; pure. *See* fee
simple. 4. Easily understood; not complex.
➤ single, plain, ordinary, basic, fundamental,
unembellished, unmixed ("a simple book
of instructions"); uncomplicated, straightforward, uninvolved, manageable, unsophisticated, transparent ("a simple solution");
amateur, honest, trusting, naive, unpretentious, unsophisticated ("a simple person").
simple assault [a · *salt*] *n.* An **assault**
that does not involve **aggravating
circumstances**. EXAMPLE: a threat of force
unaccompanied by a **battery**. *Compare*
aggravated assault; assault and battery.
simple average [*av* · rej] *n.* Same as
particular average.
simple battery [*bat* · e · ree] *n.* A
battery that does not involve **serious
bodily injury**.
simple bond *n.* A **bond** containing no
penalty, under which the **obligor** binds
himself to pay a **sum certain** to a named
obligee either **on demand** or on a **day
certain**. *Compare* penal bond.
simple contract [*kon* · trakt] *n.* 1. A
parol contract. 2. At **common law**, any
contract not **under seal**. *See* contract.
simple interest [*in* · trest] *n.* **Interest**
computed on **principal** only, as opposed to
compound interest, which is interest computed on interest. *See* ordinary interest.
simple larceny [*lar* · sen · ee] *n.*
Larceny without violence.
simple negligence [*neg* · li · jense] *n.*
Ordinary **negligence**, as opposed to **gross
negligence**. *See* negligence.
simple obligation [ob · li · *gay* · shen]
n. An **obligation** that is **unconditional**.
Compare conditional obligation.
simple trust *n.* A straightforward
conveyance of property to one person
for the use of another, without further
specifications or directions.

simulated [*sim* · yoo · lay · ted] *adj.*
Imitated; pretended; counterfeited.
➤ imitated, pretended, practice, counterfeited,
feigned ("a simulated journey").
simulated sale *n.* A form of **fraudulent
conveyance** in which a fictitious or sham
sale, involving no **consideration**, is arranged
by the owner for the purpose of putting her
property beyond the reach of her creditors.

S

simultaneous [sy · mul · *tay* · nee · yes] *adj.* Occurring at the same time.
➤ contemporaneous, concurrent, synchronic, accompanying, contemporary, coexistent ("simultaneous events").

simultaneous death [sy · mul · *tay* · nee · yes] *n.* The death of two or more persons under circumstances in which it is impossible to determine who was the first to die or who was the last to survive. Most commonly, simultaneous death occurs in a **common disaster**.

simultaneous death acts *n.* State statutes providing that, when the **devolution** of **title** to property depends upon who died first, and there is insufficient evidence that the persons did not die simultaneously, the property of each shall be disposed of as if he had been the survivor. The Uniform Simultaneous Death Act is one of the **Uniform Laws**.

since *adv.* After. Generally, "since" refers to the time between the present and a past event.

sine [*see* · nay] (*Latin*) *adv.* Without.
sine die [*dee* · ay] Means "without day." An **adjournment sine die** is an adjournment without setting a time for another meeting or session.
sine qua non [kwa non] Means "without which it is not"; in other words, an indispensable requirement. USAGE: "A *corpus delicti* is the *sine qua non* of the crime of murder."

single [*sing* · gl] *adj.* 1. Individual; one only; standing alone. 2. Unmarried.
➤ distinguished, especial, exclusive, original, private, unique, unitary ("single most important issue"); bachelor, celibate, unmarried, mateless, unattached, companionless, unfetched ("single's bar").
single adultery [a · *dul* · te · ree] *n.* An **adultery** in which only one of the parties is a married person.
single creditor [*kred* · i · ter] *n.* A **creditor** having a **lien** upon only one fund or item of property belonging to the debtor.
single juror charge [*joor* · er] *n.* A **jury instruction** that if any member of the jury is not reasonably satisfied from the evidence that the plaintiff is entitled to recover against the defendant, the jury cannot return a verdict for the plaintiff.

single proprietorship [pro · *pry* · e · ter · ship] *n.* A **sole proprietorship**.

single publication rule [pub · li · *kay* · shun] *n.* The principle that a **cause of action** in **defamation**, or for **invasion of privacy**, arises from a single publication of a defamatory or invasive article in a newspaper or magazine. Although the number of lawsuits a plaintiff can bring does not multiply with the number of copies published, the extent of publication may be considered in awarding **damages**. *See* publication.

singular [*sing* · gyoo · lur] *adj.* Of or relating to a single instance; something considered by itself.
➤ different, distinct, exclusive, odd, eccentric, uncommon, unique, particular, unusual. *Ant.* common, usual.

sinking fund [*sing* · king] *n.* 1. A **fund** established by an issuer of **bonds**, usually a corporation or a **public body**, and invested in such a manner that the **accrued interest** will enable the issuer to **retire** the debt at **maturity**. *See* retirement of securities. 2. A fund created by taxes levied by government, which is appropriated for payment of the interest accruing on a **public debt** as well as for payment of the principal.

sit *v.* 1. To **preside** as a judge. *See* sitting; sitting of court. 2. To hold a session of a **governmental body**. USAGE: "The legislature does not sit until next month." 3. To be seated; to sit down.
➤ assemble, hold court, gather, convene, officiate, congregate, deliberate, reign ("A circuit court sits every day"); ensconce, install, lie, relax, remain, rest ("sit down").
sit-down strike *n.* A strike in which employees refuse to leave the plant and refuse to work. Sit-down strikes are illegal.

sitting [*sit* · ing] *n.* 1. The act of presiding as a judge. 2. The holding of a session by a **governmental body**. 3. The act of sitting down or being seated. *See* sit.
sitting en banc [on *bonk*] *See en banc*.
sitting in bank Same as **sitting en banc**.
sitting in camera [*kam* · e · ra] *See* in camera.
sitting of court *n.* A **session of court** or a **term of court**.

situated [*sit* · shoo · ay · ted] *adv.* Located; located physically. Personal property is "situated" wherever it happens to be at any given time.

situs [*site* · us] (*Latin*) *n.* Means "place" or "site." The place of the occurrence of an event or of the location of property. The term *situs*, as applied to personal property, may mean either its actual physical location or the location it is deemed to have by **operation of law**. Thus, for EXAMPLE, for purposes of taxation, the situs of personal property is generally held to be the state in which its owner is **domiciled**. *See in situ*.

Sixteenth Amendment [*siks* · teenth a · *mend* · ment] *n.* The amendment to the Constitution that gave the federal government the power to levy a graduated income tax. *See* graduated tax.

Sixth Amendment [a · *mend* · ment] *n.* An amendment to the Constitution that guarantees a criminal defendant the following civil rights: the right to a speedy and **public trial** by an **impartial jury**; the right to be informed of the nature of the accusation against her; the right to confront witnesses; the right to **subpoena** witnesses; the **right to counsel**. *See* speedy trial.

skeptical [*skep* · tih · kul] *adj.* Disbelieving; leery.
➤ doubting, mistrusting, incredulous, suspicious, scoffing, cynical, unbelieving, unconvinced.
Ant. credulous.

skill *n.* A talent or ability.
➤ aptitude, talent, expertise, intelligence, facility, proficiency, ability, mastery, prowess.

skilled *adj.* Having ability or proficiency.
➤ expert, qualified, talented, adept, able ("a skilled craftsman").

skilled witness [*wit* · nes] *n. See* expert witness.

skiptracing [*skip* · tray · sing] *n.* The location of missing or absent persons. Many firms offer services to locate delinquent debtors, missing spouses, heirs, witnesses, and the like.

SL Abbreviation of **session laws**.

slander [*slan* · der] *n.* A false and **malicious** oral statement tending to blacken a person's reputation or to damage her means of livelihood. *Compare* libel. *See* malice. *See also* defamation. *See and compare* slanderous per quod; slanderous per se.
v. To defame someone orally.
➤ *n.* defamation, slur, aspersion, calumny, vilification, denigration, vituperation ("slander of character").
v. discredit, impugn, belittle, defame, anathematize, denigrate, malign, degrade ("slander one's name").
Ant. praise.

slander of title [*ty* · tel] *n.* A false or malicious statement, oral or written, that brings into question a person's right or **title** to real or personal property, causing him **damage**.

slander per quod [kwode] *n. See* slanderous per quod.

slander per se [say] *n. See* slanderous per se.

slanderer [*slan* · der · er] *n.* A person who utters a **slander**.
➤ libelant, critic, tortfeasor, accuser.

slanderous [*slan* · der · us] *adj.* Containing or constituting **slander**; **defamatory**.
➤ defamatory, derogatory, vilifying, denigrating, accusatory, vituperative.

slanderous per quod [kwode] *adj.* A term referring to spoken words that are not **defamatory** in and of themselves and with respect to which, therefore, **injury** and **damages** must be proven. *Compare* slanderous per se. *See per quod. See also* actionable per quod; libelous per quod.

slanderous per se [say] *adj.* A term referring to spoken words that are **presumed** to be **defamatory** because they necessarily cause **injury** to the reputation of the person about whom they are spoken. (EXAMPLES: words that imply criminal conduct; words that could subject a person to professional disgrace; words that imply infection with a loathsome and communicable disease.) When words are slanderous per se, **actual damages** need not be proven. *Compare* slanderous per quod. *See per se. See also* actionable per se; libelous per se.

slavery [*slay* · ver · ee] *n.* A relationship in which one human being is owned by another; bondage. The **Thirteenth Amendment** outlawed slavery in the United States. *See* involuntary servitude; peonage.

S

➤ exploitation, captivity, enslavement, duress, subjugation, conquest, shackles, serfdom.

sleeping partner [*slee* · ping *part* · ner] *n.* Same as **silent partner**. *Also see* dormant partner.

slight *adj.* Minimal; inconsiderable.
n. An insult or show of disrespect.
➤ *adj.* insignificant, insubstantial, meager, minor, negligible, paltry, superficial ("a slight difference").
n. insult, disrespect, affront, discourtesy, disdain, indifference, neglect, rebuff ("a slight against someone").

slight care *n.* A very minimal degree of **care**; the least degree of care. *Compare* extraordinary care. *See* care.

slight diligence [*dil* · i · genss] *n.* A very minimal degree of **diligence**; the least degree of diligence. *See* diligence.

slight negligence [*neg* · li · jense] *n.* An absence of that degree of care expected of persons of extraordinary prudence. *See* negligence. *Also see* prudence.

slip opinion [o · *pin* · yen] *n.* A single judicial decision published shortly after it has been issued by the court and well before it is incorporated into a **reporter**.

slowdown [*sloh* · down] *n.* A **concerted** slowing down of production by employees for the purpose of inducing their employer to make concessions with respect to their **conditions of employment**.

SM Abbreviation for **service mark**.

small *adj.* 1. Tiny, slight. 2. Narrow-minded; petty. 3. Unimportant.
➤ little, tiny, short, minimal, scanty, paltry, diminutive ("a small amount"); petty, bigoted, parochial, selfish ("a small person"); minor, trivial, triffling, insignificant, negligible.

small business [*biz* · nes] *n.* In some areas of the law, "small businesses" receive incentives or privileges not available to larger enterprises. The **Small Business Administration**, for EXAMPLE, provides small businesses with special incentives for investment, and the **Internal Revenue Code** provides special tax allowances to **small business corporations** and their stockholders.

small business corporation [kore · per · *ay* · shen] *n.* See small business.

Small Business Administration [ad · min · is · *tray* · shen] *n.* A federal agency whose purpose is to make loans to **small businesses** to provide them with working capital and to help them finance construction and the purchase of equipment.

small claims court *n.* A **court of limited jurisdiction** for the litigation of small claims, that is, claims not exceeding a specified limited amount, which varies according to state statute. The purpose of small claims courts is to provide a forum for the prompt and inexpensive **adjudication** of small debt claims. Attorneys generally do not, and in many jurisdictions cannot, appear in small claims courts.

small loan acts *n.* State statutes regulating the activities of finance companies and other lending institutions that are in the business of making small loans.

smart money [*mun* · ee] *n.* 1. **Punitive damages**. 2. An **insider**; a person who has **insider information**.

Smith Act *n.* A federal statute that makes it unlawful to advocate the overthrow of the government by force. *See* sedition; subversive activities.

smuggling [*smug* · ling] *n.* The crime of covertly importing or exporting goods without paying **duty** or otherwise in violation of the law. *See* covert.
➤ bootlegging, exporting, pirating, pushing, running.

sober [*so* · bur] *adj.* 1. Not intoxicated; free of alcohol. 2. Rational or clear-headed. 3. Somber; sorrowful.
➤ rational, reasonable, moderate; somber, grave, serious.

sobriety [so · *bry* · e · tee] *n.* The state or condition of being sober, i.e., not intoxicated.

sobriety checkpoint [*chek* · point] *n.* A roadblock set up by the police at which motorists are given **field sobriety tests**. Courts have upheld the constitutionality of such stops in the absence of probable cause to stop or search a particular driver.

sobriety test *n.* *See* field sobriety test.

social [*so* · shel] *adj.* 1. Relating to **society**. 2. Relating to being sociable.

➤ societal, sociological, collective, communal, interdependent, common, human, civil.

social duty [*dew* · tee] *n.* A term referring to a person's duty to her community. A person's social duty is made up of both **legal obligations** and **moral obligations**.

social guest *n.* A person who receives the hospitality of another. *See* guest; invitee.

social insurance [in · *shoor* · ense] *n.* State and federal programs mandated by statute and designed to protect classes of persons within the society (EXAMPLES: unemployed or injured workers; the aged; persons with disabilities) from the adverse economic effects of their circumstances. EXAMPLES of social insurance include **social security (Old Age, Survivors' and Disability Insurance)**, **unemployment insurance**, **workers' compensation insurance**, **Medicare**, and **Medicaid**. *See* insurance.

social security [se · *kyoor* · i · tee] *n.* 1. The popular name for the benefits provided under the **Social Security Act**. 2. The popular name for the **Social Security Administration**.

Social Security Act [*so* · shel se · *kyoor* · i · tee] *n.* A federal statute providing for **Old Age, Survivors' and Disability Insurance**, i.e., **social security**, and establishing the **Social Security Administration**. *See* Social Security Administration.

Social Security Administration [*so* · shel se · *kyoor* · i · tee ad · min · is · *tray* · shen] *n.* The federal agency that administers the social security system. The primary programs administered by the agency are the benefits it pays to retired workers and their dependents, death and disability benefits, and **supplemental security income** or **SSI**. These programs are funded under the **Federal Insurance Contributions Act**, through involuntary contributions by employers, employees, and self-employed persons in the form of a tax on payroll and earnings. *See* social security; Social Security Act.

socialism [*so* · shel · izm] *n.* An economic system in which the state owns the means of production (manufacturing, agriculture, transportation) and in which, in theory, every citizen participates in production according to his ability. In fact, most socialist societies have incorporated various aspects of **capitalism** into their economic systems. A primary distinction between socialism and **communism** is that the former is generally democratic in greater or lesser degree, and the latter is almost universally totalitarian. *Compare* fascism.

society [so · *sy* · e · tee] *n.* 1. A **nation**, **state**, or other **community** or **body politic**. 2. An **association** organized and existing for the mutual benefit of its members and, usually, to pursue some patriotic, religious, charitable, or professional purpose; a **mutual benefit society**; sometimes a **benevolent corporation**. 3. A term sometimes used for **consortium**. 4. A social class composed of prominent, usually wealthy, people.

➤ association, group, civilization, commonwealth, fellowship, humanity ("today's society in America"); alliance, brotherhood, clique, coterie, fraternity, institute, league ("society of professional engineers"); aristocracy, elite, gentry, haut monde, quality, patriciate ("high society").

sodomy [*sod* · e · mee] *n.* A term whose definition varies from state to state, but which, at its broadest, criminalizes sexual relations between persons of the same sex, sexual contact *per anus* or *per os* between unmarried persons, and sexual intercourse with animals. Sodomy is also referred to as "the **crime against nature**" or **buggery**. *Also see* bestiality.

➤ bestiality, perversion, deviation, depravity, degeneration, anal intercourse.

soil bank *n.* A program under which the federal government pays farmers to take a portion of their crop land out of production and leave it fallow (put it in the "soil bank"). The program's purpose is to avoid the production of surplus commodities and to promote soil conservation.

sold *adj./past part. See* sale; sell.

soldier's will [*sole* · jerz] *n. See* military will.

Soldiers' and Sailors' Civil Relief Act [*sole* · jerz and *say* · lerz *siv* · il re · *leef*] *n.* A federal statute providing for a **stay** of any **civil action** brought against a person in the military service, unless, in the opinion of the court, the ability of the defendant to conduct a **defense** is not affected by the fact that he is in the service. See stay of action.

sole *adj.* Single; as one person only; not joint; exclusive.

➤ singular, single, unattached, alone, exclusive, solitary, particular, unconditional ("the sole heir").

sole actor doctrine [*ak* · ter *dok* · trin] *n.* The principle that knowledge possessed by an **agent** is **imputed** to her **principal**, even though the agent was acting adversely to the interests of her principal or acting fraudulently.

sole and unconditional ownership [un · ken · *dish* · en · el oh · ner · ship] *n. See* sole ownership; unconditional ownership.

sole custody [*kus* · te · dee] *n.* Exclusive **custody**. *Compare* divided custody; joint custody. *See* legal custody.

sole discretion [dis · *kresh* · en] *n.* A term signifying a grant of broad **discretion** to a **fiduciary**. USAGE: "as my **trustee**, in her sole discretion, may decide."

sole ownership [*oh* · ner · ship] *n.* Exclusive ownership. *See* unconditional ownership. *See also* sole proprietorship.

sole possession [po · *zesh* · en] *n.* Exclusive possession.

sole proprietorship [pro · *pry* · e · ter · ship] *n.* Ownership by one person, as opposed to ownership by more than one person, ownership by a corporation, ownership by a **partnership**, etc. *See* proprietorships; sole ownership. *Also see* feme sole trader.

sole source contract [*kon* · trakt] *n.* Government regulations requiring **competitive bidding** generally create an exception to that requirement when the item or service the government seeks to purchase is only available from a single responsible **vendor**, contractor, or other supplier.

solemn [*saw* · lem] *adj.* 1. Characterized by a formal ceremony or by formality. *See* form; formal. 2. Very earnest; highly serious.

➤ austere, deliberate, dignified, grave, serious, earnest, funereal, pensive, portentous ("solemn occasion"); ceremonial, devotional, dignified, hallowed, majestic, momentous, ostentatious ("solemn oath").

solemn oath *n.* An **oath** in which the **affiant** raises her arm or touches the Bible with her hand; a **corporal oath**.

solemnization of marriage [saw · lem · neh · *zay* · shen of *mehr* · ej] *n.* The performance of the marriage ceremony.

solemnize [*saw* · lem · nize] *v.* To perform a formal ceremony; to act with formality. *See* solemn; solemnization of marriage.

solicit [so · *liss* · it] *v.* 1. To commit the crime of **solicitation**. 2. To invite a business transaction. 3. To **pander**; to pimp; to procure. 4. To earnestly request; to ask; to plead for.

➤ accost, canvass, implore, inquire, postulate, request, query; pander, pimp, procure.

solicitation [so · liss · i · *tay* · shen] *n.* 1. The crime of encouraging or inciting a person to commit a crime. 2. The act of a prostitute in seeking clients; the act of a pimp. 3. Inviting a business transaction. 4. Earnestly requesting; asking; pleading for.

➤ petition, requisition, entreaty, demand, proposal, adjuration, plea.

solicitation of bribe *n.* The crime of offering to receive a **bribe**.

solicitor [so · *liss* · i · ter] *n.* 1. The title that many cities, towns, and departments or agencies of government give to their chief **law officer**. EXAMPLE: the **Solicitor General of the United States**. 2. In England, a person trained in the law who prepares briefs, drafts **pleadings** and legal **instruments**, and advises clients, but is limited with respect to the courts in which she may appear. *Compare* barrister. 3. A person who goes from person to person, or from house to house, seeking orders, subscriptions, contributions, and the like.

➤ lawyer, attorney, counsel, public attorney.

Solicitor General of the United States [so · *liss* · i · ter jen · e · rel of the yoo · *nite* · ed states] *n.* The Solicitor General is appointed by the president and has the authority to represent the United States in all **actions** in all state courts and federal courts, at both the **trial court** and **appellate court** level, including the Supreme Court. The Solicitor General works in close coordination with the **Attorney General of the United States**, who is the head of the Department of Justice.

solid waste [*sol* · id] *n.* Garbage and refuse, not including sewage. Sanitary landfills or "town dumps" are common disposal sites for solid waste. Landfills are regulated by federal and state statutes. *See* Environmental Protection Agency. *See also* hazardous waste; toxic waste.

solitary confinement [*sol* · i · tare · ee ken · *fine* · ment] *n.* A punishment for crime consisting of the complete or almost complete isolation of a prisoner from all other human contact.

solution [so · *loo* · shun] *n.* 1. An answer to a problem. 2. A mixture of liquids or liquid with other substances.

➤ answer, explanation, resolution; substance, compound, mixture, solvent, elixir, potion, blend.

solve *v.* To find a solution for a problem or question.

➤ resolve, untangle, answer, explain, fathom, understand, penetrate, unlock, decipher ("solve the mystery").

solvency [*sol* · ven · see] *n.* 1. The status of a person when his total **assets** are of sufficient value to pay his debts. 2. The ability of a person to pay her debts as they become due or in the **ordinary course of business**. *Compare* insolvency.

solvent [*sol* · vent] *adj.* The financial status of a person who is in a state of **solvency**. *Compare* insolvent.

➤ sound, financially stable, reliable, creditworthy, responsible, solid.

somnambulism [som · *nam* · byoo · lizm] *n.* A state or condition in which a person performs physical acts (EXAMPLES: walking; eating) while asleep. A person may not be legally responsible for acts committed while in a somnambulistic state.

Son of Sam laws *n.* State statutes that prohibit a convicted criminal from making a profit from a book or other written account of his crime. Such statutes are of doubtful constitutionality because they limit free expression. *See* First Amendment; freedom of expression.

sound *adj.* 1. Valid; sensible. 2. Healthy; free from disease or disability.
 v. 1. To make noise. 2. To pertain to or refer. *See* sounding.
 n. A noise or tone.

➤ *adj.* accurate, advisable, consequent, judicious, profound, sensible; authoritative, canonical, dependable, legal, solid, solvent, valid ("sound advice"); whole, healthy, sane ("sound mind").
 v. signal, babble, burst, chatter, crack, murmur, resound, reverberate ("sound the call"); pertain, refer, relate to, aim at ("This suit sounds in tort").
 n. noise, din, clamor, tone, vibration, intonation, music ("an insistent sound").

sound and disposing mind and memory [dis · *poze* · ing mind and mem · e · ree] *n.* **Testamentary capacity**. A **testator** is of sound and disposing mind and memory if at the time of making her will she has sufficient mental capacity to understand the nature of her act and, generally if not precisely, the nature and location of her property and the identity of those persons who are the natural objects of her bounty. *See* natural objects of bounty.

sound health *n.* In insurance law, a state of health marked by the absence of serious or significant disease. Good health, not perfect health.

sound mind *n.* A term referring to the mind of a person who is sane and mentally **competent**. *See* sound and disposing mind and memory.

sound title [*ty* · tel] *n.* A **marketable title**.

sounding [*soun* · ding] *v.* Having as a basis.

sounding in contract [*kon* · trakt] Arising out of a **breach of contract** or otherwise involving a **contract**. USAGE: "This lawsuit sounds in contract."

sounding in tort Arising out of a **tort**. USAGE: "This lawsuit sounds in tort."

source *n.* 1. The person or thing who originates something; the cause; the beginning. 2. An informant.

➤ root, foundation, cause, origin, initiator; informer, informant, stool pigeon.

sources of the law [*sore* · sez] *n.* The places from which the law, as applied by the courts and the **executive branch** of government, is derived. EXAMPLES: **constitutions**; **statutes**; **ordinances**; **custom and usage**.

sovereign [*sov · ren*] *n.* A ruler; a king; the government.

adj. Absolute; dominant; royal.

➤ *n.* monarch, queen, king, ruler, tyrant, head, czar, autocrat ("sovereign of the country").
adj. governing, absolute, imperial, authorized, independent, autonomous, dominant ("sovereign body").

sovereign immunity [im · *yoo* · neh · tee] *n.* The principle that the government—specifically, the United States or any state of the United States—is immune from suit except when it consents to be sued, as, for EXAMPLE, through a statute such as the **Federal Tort Claims Act**. *See* immunity.

sovereign nation [*nay* · shun] *n. See* sovereign state.

sovereign power [*pow* · er] *n.* The power to make and enforce laws to which everyone must conform.

sovereign right *n.* A right that the state alone, or its governmental agencies, can possess. *See* prerogative.

sovereign state *n.* A **body politic** or **state** in which **sovereignty** and control over all persons and things within its boundaries are exercised by means of an organized government; a state in which the laws of other states do not operate except by consent. The United States is both a sovereign state and a community of sovereign states.

sovereignty [*sov* · ren · ty] *n.* **Sovereign power**.

➤ self-rule, dominion, jurisdiction, autonomy, primacy, loyalty.

space *n.* 1. Room; expanse. 2. The size of an area through three dimensions: distance, area, and volume. 3. Outer space.

➤ distance, room, latitude; area, acreage, territory, footage, range.

speaking demurrer [*spee* · king de · *mer* · er] *n.* A **demurrer** that should be overruled because it introduces facts that do not appear in the **pleading** it attacks.

speaking motion [*spee* · king *moh* · shen] *n.* A **motion** that involves consideration of facts not alleged in the **pleadings**.

special [*spesh* · el] *adj.* 1. Particular; for a particular purpose. 2. Individual; distinctive. 3. Favored; select. 4. Unusual; extraordinary. 5. Limited.

➤ unique, limited, specific, noteworthy, extraordinary, idiosyncratic, distinct, distinctive, personal, generous, atypical, particular; favored, select, unusual, extraordinary.

special act *n.* Same as **special legislation**.

special administrator [ad · min · is · *tray* · ter] *n.* An **administrator** who administers some aspect of the **estate** of a **decedent**, as opposed to a **general administrator**, who administers the whole of the estate. *See* administration of estate.

special agent [*ay* · jent] *n.* An **agent** authorized to perform a particular or specific act connected with the business of her **principal**. *Compare* general agent.

special appearance [a · *peer* · ense] *n.* An **appearance** for the sole purpose of testing the **jurisdiction** of the court. A special appearance does not result in submission to the court's jurisdiction. *Compare* general appearance.

special assessment [a · *sess* · ment] *n.* An **assessment** imposed upon property within a limited geographical area for the purpose of paying for an **improvement** for the benefit of all property within the area (EXAMPLES: a public park; sewers). A special assessment is also referred to as a **local assessment** or a **local improvement assessment**.

special bailment [*bale* · ment] *n.* A **bailment** that affects the public interest and in which the law therefore imposes a stricter standard of liability upon the **bailee** than in an ordinary bailment. EXAMPLE: luggage given to a **common carrier** to be transported.

special bequest [be · *kwest*] *n.* Same as **specific bequest**.

special charge *n.* Same as **special instruction**.

special contract [*kon* · trakt] *n.* 1. A **contract under seal**; a **specialty**; a **specialty contract**. 2. A simple contract, as opposed to a complicated contract. 3. A unique contract. *See* simple contract.

special counsel [*koun* · sel] *n.* An attorney employed by the Attorney General of the United States, or the attorney general of a state, to assist in a particular case. *See* special prosecutor.

special court-martial [kort-mar · shel] *n. See* court-martial.

special damages [*dam* · e · jez] *n.* **Damages** that may be added to the **general damages** in a case, and arise from the particular or special circumstances of the case; the natural but not necessary result of a **tort**; damages arising naturally but not necessarily from a **breach of contract**.

special demurrer [de · *mer* · er] *n.* A **demurrer** directed to matters of **form** or **procedure** rather than to matters of **substance**. *Compare* general demurrer.

special deposit [de · *pah* · zit] *n.* A **deposit** of money in which the exact money, as opposed to a like sum, is to be returned to the depositor. *Compare* general deposit. *See* deposit.

special devise [de · *vize*] *n.* Same as **specific devise**.

special election [e · *lek* · shen] *n.* An election arising from some special need, such as filling a vacancy in office or the need to submit a **question** or **proposition** to the voters on an emergency basis. *Compare* general election.

special exception [ek · *sep* · shen] *n.* 1. An **exception** directed to a matter of **form** rather than **substance**. *Compare* general exception. *See* special demurrer. 2. In zoning law, a **special use**.

special execution [ek · se · *kyoo* · shen] *n.* An **execution** that specifies the particular property to be sold. *Compare* general execution.

special executor [eg · *zek* · yoo · ter] *n. See* special administrator. *Also see* executor.

special facts rule *n.* The rule that, when circumstances or facts make it inequitable for **corporate directors** to withhold information from a stockholder, a duty to disclose arises and concealment is **fraud**.

special finding [*fine* · ding] *n.* 1. A specific statement by a jury, or by a court sitting without a jury, of the **ultimate facts** to which the law is to be applied to determine the rights of the **parties**. *Compare* general finding. *See* special verdict. 2. A **finding** limited to a particular question. *Compare* general finding. *See* finding.

special grand jury [*joo* · ree] *n.* A grand jury summoned for the purpose of hearing a particular case. *See* grand jury.

special guaranty [*gah* · ren · tee] *n.* A **guaranty** limited to the person to whom it is offered. *Compare* general guaranty.

special indorsement [in · *dors* · ment] *n.* An **indorsement** that specifies the person to whom or to whose **order** the **instrument** is to be **payable**. *Compare* general indorsement.

special instruction [in · *struk* · shen] *n.* An **instruction** or **charge** to the jury on a particular point. *Compare* general instruction. *See* jury instructions.

special interrogatories [in · ter · *rahg* · eh · tore · eez] *n.* Written questions directed to a jury with a request for a **special verdict** or **special findings**. *See* interrogatories.

special jurisdiction [*joo* · ris · *dik* · shen] *n. See* court of limited jurisdiction.

special jury [*joo* · ree] *n.* A **struck jury**.

special law *n. See* special legislation.

special legacy [*leg* · e · see] *n.* Same as **specific legacy**.

special legislation [lej · is · *lay* · shen] *n.* A **private statute**. *Also see* private bill. *Compare* general law; public law.

special lien [leen] *n.* A **particular lien**. *Compare* general lien.

special master [*mas* · ter] *n.* A person appointed by the court to assist with certain judicial functions in a specific case. *Compare* standing master. *See* master.

special meeting [*mee* · ting] *n.* 1. A meeting of the directors or stockholders of a corporation, other than an **annual meeting** or a **regular meeting**. A special meeting is usually called for a particular purpose. 2. A meeting of the **qualified voters** of a town, other than a regular annual meeting. *See* town meeting.

special partner [*part* · ner] *n.* Same as **limited partner**. *Compare* general partner.

special partnership [*part* · ner · ship] *n.* Same as **limited partnership**. *Compare* general partnership.

special pleading [plee · ding] *n.* In **common law pleading**, a **pleading** required for the presentation of special matters of **defense**. EXAMPLE: a **plea in confession and avoidance**.

special power of appointment [*pow* · er of a · *point* · ment] *n.* Same as **limited power of appointment**.

special power of attorney [*pow* · er of a · *tern* · ee] *n.* *See* power of attorney.

special proceeding [pro · *seed* · ing] *n.* A **proceeding** in which one may obtain an **extraordinary remedy**. *See* proceeding.

special property [*prop* · er · tee] *n.* An **interest** in property that is less than full ownership. EXAMPLE: the interest of a **bailee** or **mortgagee**.

special prosecutor [*pross* · e · kyoo · ter] *n.* 1. **Special counsel** employed to assist the prosecuting attorney in the conduct of a criminal prosecution. 2. **Independent counsel** appointed to investigate and, if warranted, to prosecute high government officials. *See* independent counsel. *See also* private prosecutor.

special retainer [re · *tane* · er] *n.* The act of employing an attorney for a specific case. *Compare* general retainer. *See* retainer.

special session [*sesh* · en] *n.* Any **session** of a legislative body or court that is not a regular session or an adjournment of a regular session. *Compare* general session.

special statute [*stat* · shoot] *n.* *See* special legislation.

special term *n.* 1. As opposed to a regular term, a **term of court** scheduled at a time other than the customary time and held for the purpose of transacting some business out of the ordinary. 2. In some jurisdictions, a term of court set aside for the transaction of court business other than jury trials. *Compare* general term. *See* term.

special trust *n.* An **active trust**, as opposed to a **dry trust** or a **passive trust**. *See* trust.

special use *n.* In a zoning ordinance, a **special exception** to the limitations on use set forth in the ordinance. *See* use. *Also see* zoning.

special verdict [*ver* · dikt] *n.* A **verdict** making specific **findings of fact** in response to written questions. In a case in which a jury returns a special verdict, the court determines the case and makes a finding

of liability or nonliability on the basis of the facts the jury has found. *Compare* general verdict. *See* special finding.

special warranty [*war* · en · tee] *n.* In a deed, a **warranty** by which the **grantor** promises to protect the **grantee** and her heirs only against the claims of those claiming "by, through or under" her. *Compare* general warranty.

special warranty deed [*war* · en · tee] *n.* A **deed** that contains a **special warranty** rather than a **general warranty**. *See* warranty.

specialist [*speh* · shul · ist] *n.* One who has expertise in a particular area. *Compare* expert witness.

➤ master, expert, authority, skilled practitioner, scholar, virtuoso.

specialty *n.* A contract **under seal**, also referred to as a **special contract** or a **specialty contract**.

specialty contract [*kon* · trakt] *n.* *See* specialty.

specialty debt *n.* A **debt** that is acknowledged in a document **under seal**.

specie [*spee* · shee] *n.* 1. Gold or silver coins, as distinguished from paper money. 2. A term that, depending upon the context in which it appears, may mean either "of the same kind" or "exactly the same." *Note* that "specie" is not "species." *See in specie*.

specific [spe · *sif* · ik] *adj.* 1. Particular. 2. Limited.

➤ explicit, definite, distinctive, categorical, pertinent, relevant, circumscribed, particular, limited.

specific bequest [be · *kwest*] *n.* *See* specific legacy.

specific denial [de · *ny* · el] *n.* A denial by the defendant in her **answer** of a specific fact alleged by the plaintiff in his **complaint**. *Compare* general denial.

specific devise [de · *vize*] *n.* A **devise** of specific real estate. EXAMPLE: "I give and devise Blackacre to my son John." *Compare* general devise; specific legacy.

specific intent [in · *tent*] *n.* The **intent** to commit the very act with which the defendant has been charged. General **criminal intent** (*mens rea*) is an essential element of virtually all crimes. Specific intent is an additional requirement with respect to certain crimes; for EXAMPLE, **assault with intent to commit murder** is committed only if the reason the defendant assaulted the victim was that he intended to kill him. *See* assault.

specific legacy [*leg* · e · see] *n.* A **bequest** of specific personal property. EXAMPLE: "I bequeath my diamond tiara to my daughter Mary." *Compare* general legacy; specific devise.

specific performance [per · *form* · ense] *n.* 1. The **equitable remedy** of compelling **performance** of a contract, as distinguished from an action **at law** for **damages** for **breach of contract** due to nonperformance. Specific performance may be ordered in circumstances where damages are an inadequate remedy, for EXAMPLE, when a seller fails to perform a contract for the sale of land. *See* contract for sale of land. 2. The actual accomplishment of a contract by the party bound to fulfill it.

specification [spess · if · i · *kay* · shen] *n.* 1. A statement specifying or enumerating something in detail; an enumeration. 2. The doctrine under which **title** to personal property passes from its owner to a person who in good faith converts it into a completely different form. EXAMPLES: wheat into flour; rye into whiskey. 3. In a **court-martial**, the formal charge made against the defendant. 4. With respect to **patents**, a detailed written description of the invention filed with the application for a patent. 5. With respect to construction contracts and other contracts calling for the manufacture or production of something according to a plan, a statement in detail of the dimensions, materials, and the like.
➤ enumeration, designation, stipulation, termization, description, recital.

specifications [spess · if · i · *kay* · shenz] *n.* *Plural* of **specification**. *See* specification.

specificity [spess · i · *fiss* · i · tee] *n.* Detail; the state, condition, or quality of being specific; particularity.
➤ detail, particularity, precision, exactness ("to state with specificity").
Ant. vagueness.

spectrograph [spek · troh · graf] *n.* A machine that electronically maps the spectrum of sound waves, producing a

kind of "voice fingerprint" or "voiceprint." Some courts permit voice identification by this means. *See* voiceprinting.

speculation [spek · yoo · *lay* · shen] *n.* 1. The act of taking a risk, particularly in business, in the hope or expectation of achieving a gain, particularly in the form of profit. 2. Contemplation; meditation; reflection.
➤ belief, cerebration, contemplation, deliberation, guesswork, opinion ("speculation as to where the attack will be"); gamble, backing, flutter, hazard, plunge, venture, trading ("speculation on the market"); contemplation, meditation, reflection.

speculative [*spek* · yoo · le · tiv] *adj.* Involving an assumption of facts not yet proven to be true.
➤ theoretical, hypothetical, unproven, unconfirmed, suppositional, tentative, indefinite.

speculative damages [*spek* · yoo · le · tiv] *n.* **Damages** that have yet to occur and whose occurrence is doubtful. However, damages are not speculative merely because they cannot be computed with exactness. *See* future damages.

speech *n.* Oral expression; communication. *See* freedom of speech and of the press.
➤ articulation, communication, diction, dialogue, enunciation, expression, idiom ("strange speech pattern"); address, debate, disquisition, harangue, panegyric, parlance ("a long speech").

speedy trial [*spee* · dee *try* · el] *n.* A constitutional right of a criminal defendant under the **Sixth Amendment**; a trial scheduled and conducted according to fixed rules, free from capricious delays. The time within which a trial must commence is set by statute in every jurisdiction.

spendthrift [*spend* · thrift] *n.* A person who spends money recklessly.
➤ improvident, prodigal, profligate, wastrel.

spendthrift trust *n.* A **trust** that provides a fund for the maintenance of a spendthrift, protecting him against his own wastefulness and recklessness. A spendthrift trust prevents the **beneficiary** from voluntarily selling or conveying her entitlement and bars her interest from seizure by her creditors as well. *See and compare* involuntary alienation; voluntary alienation.

spin-off *n.* The **divesture** by a corporation of its stock in a **subsidiary corporation** that becomes a separate corporation. *Compare* split-off.

spirit [*spir* · it] *n.* 1. The soul or life force. 2. Intent; character.
➤ soul, character, energy, vigor, zeal, vitality, intent, psyche.

spirit of the law [*speer* · it] *n.* A phrase connoting an interpretation of a statute that emphasizes its intent rather than its exact or literal meaning. *Compare* letter of the law, strict construction.

spite fence *n.* A fence that is of no benefit to its owner, which she erects for the purpose of annoying her neighbor.

split *n.* A division into parts or factions; a difference; a disunion.
v. To break up; to divide; to separate.
adj. 1. Not unanimous. 2. Broken; torn; fractured.
➤ *n.* opening, breach, chasm, cleavage, cleft, cut, bisection, separation ("a split in one's pants"); division, alienation, discord, dissension, divergence, estrangement, fissure ("a split in the justices' opinions").
v. bifurcate, burst, dichotomize, dissever, isolate, sever ("to split up").
adj. divided, halved, splintered ("a split decision").

split decision [de · *sizh* · en] *n.* A **decision** to which one or more **dissenting opinions** are filed by a minority of justices; a decision involving a **majority opinion** and at least one **minority opinion**. *See* equally divided court.

split sentence [*sen* · tense] *n.* 1. A sentence in a criminal case that imposes both a fine and imprisonment, but suspends imprisonment although it enforces the fine. 2. A sentence that imposes imprisonment for a period of time, followed by probation or parole. *See* suspended sentence. *See* sentence.

split-off *n.* The creation by a corporation of a new corporation in an arrangement in which the stock of the new corporation is given to the stockholders of the original corporation who, in turn, transfer their

shares in the original corporation to the newly created corporation. *Compare* spin-off.

split-up *n.* A form of **split-off** in which two new corporations are created and the original corporation is liquidated. *See* liquidation. *Also see* spin-off.

splitting causes of action [*split* · ing kaw · zez of *ak* · shen] *n.* Bringing separate lawsuits based upon a single **cause of action**. (EXAMPLE: commencing successive suits for separate breaches of an **entire contract**.) Separate suits are permissible only if the causes of action are separable (EXAMPLE: successive lawsuits based upon separate breaches of a **severable contract**).

spoil *v.* 1. To ruin or hurt. 2. To decay. 3. To pillage or plunder. 4. To pamper or indulge.
➤ impair, harm, hurt, mutilate, ruin, wreck, botch, mess up ("spoil the party"); decay, decompose, sour, turn ("The fruit will spoil"); plunder, loot, despoil, ransack ("spoil the town"); coddle, pamper, indulge, baby ("to spoil a child").

spoils *n.* Possessions that are stolen or gained.
➤ takings, booty, haul, loot, prize, winnings.

spokesman [*spokes* · man] *n.* A person who speaks for another.
➤ voice, speaker, agent, delegate, messenger, mouthpiece, go-between, representative ("the spokesman for the White House").

spoliation [spo · lee · *ay* · shen] *n.* 1. Alteration of an **instrument** or other legal document (EXAMPLES: a **note**; will; deed) by a person who is not a **party** to it. 2. The intentional destruction of evidence. 3. The act of plundering or pillaging.
➤ alteration, destruction; plundering, pillaging.

sponsor [*spon* · ser] *n.* One who assumes responsibility for another or an event.
v. To stand up for or support a person or cause.
➤ *n.* patron, benefactor, backer, supporter, promoter, advocate.
v. endorse, finance, support, patronize, underwrite, back, promote.

spontaneous [spon · *tane* · ee · us] *adj.* Unrehearsed; impromptu; automatic; unpremeditated.
➤ casual, extemporaneous, impromptu, instinctive, irresistible, unavoidable, unpremeditated ("a spontaneous exclamation").

S

spontaneous declaration
[dek · le · *ray* · shen] *n.* Same as
spontaneous exclamation.

spontaneous exclamation
[eks · kle · *may* · shun] *n.* Words uttered
without thought. To be admissible as an
exception to the hearsay rule, an exclamation, declaration, or statement must have
been prompted by the stress of a shocking
or traumatic event and must have been
uttered at the moment the event occurred.
See res gestae.

spontaneous statement [*state* · ment] *n.*
Same as **spontaneous exclamation**.

spot sales *n.* A brokerage term for sales of
commodities or **securities** for immediate
delivery.

spot zoning [*zone* · ing] *n.* In zoning law,
classifying a property, or a number of
properties, in a manner that permits them
to be used for purposes incompatible with
the applicable zoning ordinance and inconsistent with the **uses** permitted in the
area as a whole. *See* zoning.

spousal [*spow* · zel] *adj.* Relating to a
spouse; relating to marriage.

spousal abuse [a · *byooss*] *n.* The
physical, sexual, verbal, or emotional abuse
of one spouse by the other. *See* abuse. *Also
see* protection order.

spousal immunity [im · *yoon* · i · tee] *n.*
See interspousal immunity.

spousal privilege [*priv* · i · lej] *n. See*
marital communications privilege.

spousal support [sup · *port*] *n. See*
nonsupport. *Also see* Reciprocal
Enforcement of Support Act.

spouse *n.* A husband or wife.
➤ wife, husband, mate, companion, partner.

springing use [*spring* · ing] *n.* A type of
future interest.

sprinkling trust [*sprink* · ling] *n.* A **trust**
whose income the **trustee** may distribute
among its **beneficiaries** as, when, and in
the amounts she chooses.

spurious [*spyure* · ee · es] *adj.* False; fake;
counterfeit.
➤ apocryphal, contrived, sham, bogus,
deceitful, feigned, illegitimate, simulated,
false, fake, counterfeit, unauthentic.

spy *n.* An undercover agent.
v. To secretly follow or watch another.
➤ *n.* informant, investigator, agent, sleuth,
snoop, secret agent.
v. observe, detect, view, watch, see, pry,
eavesdrop, snoop.

spying [*spy* · ing] *n.* 1. Obtaining or
transmitting defense information detrimental to the United States. 2. Secretly
listening in on the conversations or secretly
observing the activities of others. *See*
wiretapping. *Also see* eavesdropping;
peeping tom.

squatter [*skwatt* · er] *n.* A person who
occupies the real property of another with
no **claim of right**. *Compare* adverse
possession.

ss An abbreviation meaning "**to wit**" or
"namely," used most often in the caption
of **affidavits**, for EXAMPLE:

State of Illinois)
)
) ss:
)
County of Cook   )

SSI Abbreviation of **supplemental security
income**.

staff *n.* The employees of an organization.
➤ assistants, workers, associates, faculty,
crew, clerical staff, personnel.

stake *n.* 1. Money or other property put
up as a bet or wager. *See* stakeholder.
2. An **interest** in a business venture. 3. A
monument or marker used to establish a
boundary line.
v. To bet or risk.
➤ *n.* pale, paling, picket, post, spike, stone
("tent stake"); ante, chance, hazard, peril,
pledge, risk ("What are the stakes?"); claim,
concern, interest, involvement, prize, purse
("stake in a company").
v. bankroll, capitalize, finance, grubstake,
imperil, jeopardize, risk, venture ("to stake
everything").

stakeholder [*stake* · hole · der] *n.* 1. A
disinterested person who holds money or
property, the ownership of which is contested by two or more rival claimants, while
an **action** to **adjudicate** their respective
rights is pending. *See* interpleader. 2. A
person with whom money or property is

S

deposited pending the outcome of a bet or wager. *See* stake.

stale *adj.* 1. A word referring to **actions**, **claims**, or **demands** that are without legal effect because they have not been asserted in a timely manner. 2. Not fresh.
➤ unasserted, wasted, effete, withered, faded, untimely, stagnant ("stale claim").

stale check *n.* A **check** held for an unreasonable time before **indorsement** or presentation for payment. Under the **Uniform Commercial Code**, a bank is under no obligation to a customer to pay a check drawn on her checking account if it is presented more than six months after the date on which it is drawn.

stale claim *n.* A **claim** that has not been asserted for an unreasonable period of time and is therefore barred by the **statute of limitations** or subject to the **defense** of **laches**.

stalking [*staw* · king] *n.* The crime of willfully, maliciously, and repeatedly following or harassing another and making threats intended to put the person in imminent fear of death or serious bodily injury. *See* harassment.

stamp *n.* 1. A postal stamp. 2. A symbol or seal.
v. 1. To affix a stamp. 2. To trample; to pound one's feet.
➤ *n.* seal, certification, endorsement, attestation, sign, authentication, identification, hallmark, signature.

stamp tax *n.* The cost of **revenue stamps**.

stand *v.* 1. To endure ("stand trial"). 2. To leave the witness stand ("stand down"). 3. To remain firm ("stand on my testimony"). 4. To stay in position ("my objection stands"). 5. To set or place upright. See standing.
n. 1. A position or viewpoint. 2. The witness box in a courtroom.
➤ *v.* cock, dispose, erect, locate, mount, place, poise ("stand up"); be valid, continue, endure, fill, halt, hold, prevail, stay ("the decision stands").
n. angle, attitude, carriage, determination, bent, bias, view, slant, standpoint ("to take a stand on an issue"); board, booth, box, bracket, platform, station, post ("take the stand").

standard [*stan* · derd] *adj.* Normal; regular; uniform; ordinary; established; accepted. *n.* A benchmark or criterion used by the law to determine whether conduct is **reasonable**; a measure; a model. EXAMPLES: the **attractive nuisance doctrine**, the **M'Naghten rule**, the **reasonable man test**. *See* doctrine; rule; test.
➤ *adj.* regular, accepted, classic, customary, orthodox, regulation, normal, established ("standard deduction").
n. archetype, axiom, barometer, exemplar, gauge, median, principle ("standard for others"); banner, colors, emblem, ensign, figure, insignia, pennant ("The standard is always present at a military parade"); benchmark, criterion, measure ("the standard of care").

standard deduction [de · *duk* · shen] *n.* With respect to federal and state income taxes, taxpayers are given the option of taking a specified standard sum as a deduction from **adjusted gross income**, instead of itemizing their deductions. *Compare* itemized deduction. *See* deduction.

standard mortgage clause [*more* · gej] *n.* A **loss payable clause** in a fire insurance policy.

standard of care *n.* The standard by which **negligence** is determined in a particular situation. Although the **degree of care** the law requires is always the care that a **reasonable person** would exercise in similar circumstances, the applicable standard differs with the circumstances. For EXAMPLE, *see and compare* due care; extraordinary care; slight care; utmost care. *Also see* reasonable man test.

standard of need *n.* The standard by which a person's eligibility for **public assistance** is determined. *See also* means test.

standard of proof *n.* The kind, degree, or level of **proof** required in a particular case. For civil cases, the preponderance standard is used; in criminal cases, the state must prove its case beyond a reasonable doubt. For EXAMPLE, *see and compare* **clear and convincing** proof; proof **beyond a reasonable doubt**; proof by a **preponderance of evidence**.

standard weights and measures [*mezh* · erz] *n.* Standard weights and

S

sizes to which certain products and their containers must conform, as prescribed by statute or ordinance.

standing [*stan* · ding] *n.* 1. The position of a person with respect to his capacity to act in particular circumstances. Thus, for EXAMPLE, individuals vary with respect to their social standing, their standing in the community, their credit standing, their standing to sue, and so forth. *See* standing to sue. 2. Short for **standing to sue**. 3. The act of maintaining one's position. *See* standing mute. 4. The duration that a thing exists or the range of circumstances to which it applies. *See* standing committee; standing order. *Also see* stand.
  adj. That which is upright, continuing, or already established.
➤ *n.* position, cachet, consequence, dignity, eminence, repute ("The colonel's standing with the president").
  adj. continuing, permanent, existing, perpetual, regular, repeated ("standing army").

standing committee [kum · *it* · ee] *n.* A permanent **legislative committee**, as opposed to a **select committee**.

standing master [*mas* · ter] *n.* A **master** appointed to serve on an ongoing basis in any case in which a master may sit. EXAMPLE: a **master in chancery**. *Compare* special master.

standing mute *n.* The act of a defendant in a criminal case who refuses to enter a plea. The court will enter a plea of not guilty on behalf of a defendant who stands mute.

standing order [*or* · der] *n.* A **rule of court** that a court promulgates in the form of an **order**.

standing to sue *n.* The **legal capacity** to bring and to maintain a lawsuit. A person is without standing to sue unless some **interest** of hers has been adversely affected or unless she has been **injured** by the defendant. The term "standing to sue" is often shortened simply to "standing."

staple [*stay* · pl] *n.* 1. A commodity that is a product of the soil. EXAMPLES: wheat; corn; potato. 2. An item which is necessary or basic.
  adj. 1. Necessary; basic. 2. Usual or ordinary.
➤ *adj.* necessary, basic, essential, fundamental, important, predominant; standard.

stare decisis [*stahr* · ay de · *sy* · sis] (*Latin*) *n.* Means "standing by the decision." *Stare decisis* is the doctrine that judicial decisions stand as **precedents** for cases arising in the future. It is a fundamental policy of our law that, except in unusual circumstances, a court's determination on a point of law will be followed by courts of the same or lower rank in later cases presenting the same **legal issue**, even though different **parties** are involved and many years have elapsed. *See* authority. *See and compare* binding authority; persuasive authority.

start *n.* The beginning point.
  v. To begin or originate.
➤ *n.* origin, beginning, outset, opening, genesis, derivation.
  v. begin, originate, initiate, instigate.

stash *v.* To hide away; to conceal.
  n. A hidden supply.
➤ *v.* hide, store, hoard, cache, conceal, put.
  n. cache, loot, hoard.

state *adj.* 1. Pertaining to a state of the United States. 2. Pertaining to government generally.
  n. 1. A **body politic** or society of women and men united for the purpose of promoting their mutual safety through their combined strength, occupying a definite territory, and organized under one government; **people**, **territory**, and **government** considered in combination; a **nation**. *See* sovereign state. 2. A state of the United States. 3. The condition or status of a person or thing. *See* state of mind exception.
➤ *n.* accompaniment, capacity, character, circumstance, contingency, essential ("a state of flux"); cachet, ceremony, consequence, display, majesty, prestige; commonwealth, community, federation, kingdom, nation, republic, sovereignty ("controlled by the state").

state action [*ak* · shen] *n.* In **constitutional law**, action by state or local government, or conduct sanctioned by state or local authorities. Such action may violate a person's rights under the **Fourteenth Amendment**. Enforcement of a **restrictive covenant** by a **state court** is an EXAMPLE of state action. *See Shelley v. Kraemer*. *Also see* Civil Rights Acts.

state agency [*ay* · jen · see] *n.* A department, **commission**, **board**, or administrative agency of a state. *See* agency.

state auditor [*aw* · dit · er] *n.* A **state officer** whose duties involve overseeing the fiscal affairs of the state. *See* auditor.

state bank *n.* A bank **incorporated** under state statutes, as opposed to a **national bank**.

state constitution [kon · sti · *too* · shen] *n.* The **constitution** of a state, as opposed to the **Constitution of the United States**.

state courts *n.* Courts that form a state's judicial system, as opposed to **United States Courts**. *See also* county courts; municipal courts.

state government [*guv* · ern · ment] *n.* The government of a state, as opposed to the **federal government** or **local government**.

state law *n.* State statutes and local ordinances, and judicial decisions interpreting and applying them.

state legislature [*lej* · is · lay · cher] *n.* The **legislature** of a state, as opposed, for EXAMPLE, to Congress or to a city council.

state militia [mil · *ish* · a] *n. See* militia.

state of mind *n.* A person's mental processes, i.e., why she does what she does.

state of mind exception [ek · *sep* · shen] *n.* Testimony with respect to a person's out-of-court statement as to why he did what he did is admissible as an **exception to the hearsay rule**.

state officer [*off* · i · ser] *n.* A public official who holds a state **office**, whether elected or appointed. EXAMPLES: a governor; a **secretary of state**.

state police power [po · *leess pow* · er] *n.* A state's power to make and enforce laws. *See* police power.

state secrets privilege [*see* · krets *priv* · eh · lej] *n.* An absolute privilege enjoyed by the federal government permitting it to refuse to disclose evidence that might endanger national security. *See* privilege.

state statutes [*stat* · shoots] *n.* Statutes enacted by **state legislatures**, as opposed to statutes enacted by Congress.

state's attorney [a · *tern* · ee] *n.* An attorney who represents the state in criminal prosecutions. EXAMPLES: an **attorney general** or his deputy; a **district attorney**; a **prosecuting attorney**.

state's evidence [*ev* · i · dense] *n.* In a criminal prosecution, testimony that **incriminates** the witness or others as participants in the crime. Such testimony is generally given in exchange for some form of **immunity** or in hope of a lighter sentence. USAGE: "He decided to turn state's evidence."

stated [*stay* · ted] *adj.* 1. Declared; expressed. 2. Agreed; settled. 3. Official.
➤ decided, ordained, defined, ascertained, stipulated, mandated, declared, expressed; agreed, settled, official.

stated account [a · *kount*] *n.* Same as **account stated**.

stated capital [*ka* · pi · tel] *n.* The total of the **par values** of all shares of stock that a corporation has issued, plus the total **consideration** paid for its **no-par stock**. *See* capital stock.

stated case *n.* Same as **agreed case**.

stated meeting [*mee* · ting] *n.* Same as **regular meeting**.

stated term *n.* Same as **regular term**.

stated value [*val* · yoo] *n.* Same as **par value**.

statement [*state* · ment] *n.* An **allegation** or **declaration**, or a recital of facts, either in writing or orally. *See* annual statement; false statement; financial statement; opening statement; prior inconsistent statements; registration statement; voluntary statement.
➤ acknowledgement, affidavit, allegation, description, dictum, manifesto, testimony, deposition, proclamation, utterance, vocalization ("statement on the record"); affidavit, audit, bill, budget, charge, invoice, reckoning ("monthly bank statement").

statement of affairs [a · *fairz*] *n.* In **bankruptcy** law, a document that the **bankrupt** must file providing her creditors and the **trustee** with information concerning her financial affairs. *See* trustee in bankruptcy.

S

statement of claim *n.* The **pleading** of a **demand** or **claim** in a **complaint**.

statement of defense [de · *fense*] *n.* The **pleading** of an **affirmative defense** in an **answer**.

statim [*stay* · tem] (*Latin*) *adv.* Immediately. Often abbreviated or shortened to "stat."

status [*stat* · iss] *n.* 1. The position of a person or thing in relation to the law. EXAMPLE: A person who is under 18 has the status of a minor and, as such, lacks the **legal capacity** to contract. 2. A person's position in relation to his community; his rank in society. 3. The condition, shape, or state a person or thing is in.
➤ rank, cachet, position, dignity, merit, mode, prominence.

status crime *n.* A crime based solely on a person's condition in life or his lifestyle, i.e., a crime based solely on his status. (EXAMPLE: **vagrancy**.) Status crimes are of dubious **constitutionality**.

status quo [kwoh] *n.* The existing state of affairs; things as they are. USAGE: "**Precedent** is a doctrine that supports the status quo."

statute [*stat* · shoot] *n.* A law enacted by a legislature; an **act**. *Compare* bill. *Also compare* constitution; judge-made law; ordinance; regulation. *See* criminal statute; declaratory statute; expository statute; penal statute; private statute; public statute; punitive statute; revised statutes.
➤ law, bill, act, canon, edict, ordinance, precept, mandate, enactment.

statute of frauds *n.* A statute, existing in one or another form in every state, that requires certain classes of contracts to be in writing and signed by the parties. Its purpose is to prevent fraud or reduce the opportunities for fraud. A contract to guarantee the debt of another is an EXAMPLE of an agreement that the statute of frauds requires to be in writing.

statute of uses [*yooss* · ez] *n.* An early English statute now a part of the **common law** of almost every state of the United States; its most significant effect was the validation of **executory interests**.

statute of wills *n.* An early English statute that first established a person's right to **devise** real property.

statutes at large *n.* An official publication of the federal government, issued after each session of Congress, which includes all statutes enacted by the Congress and all congressional **resolutions** and **treaties**, as well as presidential proclamations and proposed or ratified amendments to the Constitution.

statutes of distribution [dis · trib · *yoo* · shen] *n.* **Intestate laws**.

statutes of limitations [lim · i · *tay* · shenz] *n.* Federal and state statutes prescribing the maximum period of time during which various types of civil actions and criminal prosecutions can be brought after the occurrence of the **injury** or the offense. *See* limitation of action; tolling the statute.

statutes of mortmain [*mort* · mane] *n.* *See* mortmain statutes.

statutes of repose [re · *poze*] *n.* Unlike **statutes of limitations**, statutes of repose establish a maximum period of time in which an action can be brought, whether or not there has been an **injury**. Statutes of repose relate only to **civil actions**.

statutory [*stat* · shoo · tore · ee] *adj.* Created or existing by virtue of a statute.
➤ legal, lawful, sanctioned, authorized, legislative.

statutory benefits [*ben* · e · fits] *n.* Benefits granted under a **statute**. The term is most commonly applied to benefits paid under **social insurance** statutes, for EXAMPLE, **veterans' benefits**, **unemployment compensation**, or **social security**. *See* benefits.

statutory bond *n.* A **bond** required by **statute**.

statutory construction [kun · *struk* · shen] *n.* Determining the meaning of a **statute**. *See* construction. *Also see* interpretation.

statutory crimes *n.* **Crimes** created by **statute**. *Compare* common law crimes.

statutory dedication [ded · i · *kay* · shen] *n.* *See* dedication by plat.

statutory foreclosure [for · *kloh* · zher] *n.* **Foreclosure** of a mortgage carried out pursuant to a **power of sale** as authorized by **statute**.

statutory law *n.* **Law** that is promulgated by **statute**, as opposed to law that is promulgated by the judiciary, i.e., a decision of the court. *Compare* case law; common law; judge-made law.

statutory lien [leen] *n.* 1. A **lien** created by **statute** for a situation where no **right of lien** existed at **common law**. 2. A lien existing under the common law and restated by statute. *Compare* common law lien.

statutory penalty [pen · el · tee] *n.* A **penalty** imposed by **statute** in either a civil action or a criminal prosecution. *See* penalty.

statutory period [peer · ee · ed] *n.* The period of time during which a given civil action or criminal prosecution may be filed under the applicable **statute of limitations**. *See also* statutes of repose.

statutory rape *n.* Sexual intercourse with a female under the **age of consent**, with or without her consent. *Compare* rape.

statutory right *n.* A **right** granted by **statute**.

statutory share *n.* *See* elective share.

stay *n.* 1. A postponement or suspension of an **action** or **proceeding**. 2. The act of a court in granting a stay. *See* injunction; restraining order; supersedeas.
v. To put a stop to further proceedings, usually temporarily; to restrain; to hold back; to suspend.
➤ *n.* deferment, halt, remission, reprieve, standstill, suspension ("stay of execution"); brace, underpinning, buttress, reinforcement, truss, stanchion ("a supporting stay").
v. abide, continue, dally, linger, loiter, sojourn, remain, hover ("stay here"); adjourn, arrest, hinder, postpone, intermit, obstruct, suspend ("stay the execution").

stay of action [ak · shen] *n.* The suspension of **proceedings** in a case by order of court until the occurrence of some act that is necessary for the **action** to continue; a form of **injunction** issued by the court on a temporary basis against further proceedings.

stay of execution [ek · se · kyoo · shun] *n.* 1. An order issued by the court blocking or temporarily suspending **execution** on a **judgment**. It may be granted for various reasons, including to give the defendant additional time in which to satisfy the judgment or to give **security** for the debt, or to permit the defendant to appeal. 2. An order issued by a court temporarily blocking the carrying out of the death penalty while an appeal is pending.

stay of proceedings [pro · see · dingz] *n.* *See* stay of action.

stay on appeal [a · peel] *n.* *See* stay of execution.

stay statutes [stat · shoots] *n.* State statutes that temporarily suspend **foreclosures** or **executions** on certain types of debts for limited periods of time. *See* moratorium.

steal *v.* 1. To commit **larceny**. 2. In a broader sense, to take something to which one is not entitled, whatever the means (whether, for EXAMPLE, by **embezzlement**, **fraud**, or outright **robbery**). *See* theft. *Also see* stolen.
➤ abduct, appropriate, cozen, divert, pillage, purloin ("to steal money"); creep, flit, glide, insinuate, skulk, slip ("to steal away for a weekend").

stealing child [steel · ing] *n.* *See* child stealing.

stealth *n.* Acting in a secretive manner. As used in an **indictment** or **information** accusing a person of taking property "by stealth," the word connotes lack of knowledge on the victim's part.

stealthy *adj.* Characterized by a quiet, covert, or secretive manner.
➤ covert, clandestine, secretive, shifty, sly, underhanded.

stellar [stel · lur] *adj.* 1. Excellent; outstanding. 2. Relating to the stars.
➤ eminent, main, outstanding, principal, paramount, distinguished; astral, starry, sidereal, starlike.

stenographic notes [sten · o · graf · ik] *n.* The **court reporter's** notes, taken in shorthand or on a shorthand machine, of the testimony in a case, the questions asked witnesses by counsel, objections by counsel, rulings or other statements by the court, and the like. A court reporter may also record a **proceeding** by electronic means, usually by simultaneously dictating (or "voice writing") the proceedings onto a magnetic tape. *See* record; transcript.

step *n.* Movement or action toward a goal.
➤ advance, achievement, move, procedure, degree, rung, progression, act, action ("a step in the right direction").

S

step-child *n.* A son or daughter of one's spouse by a former spouse. Step-children do not inherit from their step-parents under the **intestate laws**; however, they cease to be step-children if they are adopted by their step-father or step-mother.

step-parent [*-pare* · ent] *n.* A wife, in her relationship to her spouse's child by a former marriage; a husband, in his relationship to his spouse's child by a former marriage. *See* step-child.

sterile [*ste* · ril] *adj.* 1. Incapable of bearing children. 2. Clean; sanitary.

➤ barren, bare, fallow, effete, impotent, unprolific; clean, hygenic, sanitary, germ-free, disinfected, antiseptic.

sterility [ste · *ril* · i · tee] *n.* The inability of a man or woman to produce offspring. *Note* that sterility is not **impotence**. *See* sterilization.

sterilization [ste · ril · i · *zay* · shen] *n.* 1. The act by which a person, male or female, is rendered unable to produce offspring. *Compare* castration. *See* sterility. 2. The process by which something is rendered germ-free.

steward [*stew* · erd] *n. See* shop steward.

stillborn child [*stil* · born] *n.* A child who is dead when born.

stipulate [*stip* · yoo · late] *v.* 1. To enter into a **stipulation**. 2. To mandate; to require; to impose a condition. USAGE: "If you are hired, I will stipulate the terms of your employment."

➤ agree, covenant, designate, particularize, specificate, mandate, require, impose.

stipulated damages [*stip* · yoo · lay · ted] *n.* Same as **liquidated damages**.

stipulation [stip · yoo · *lay* · shen] *n.* 1. An agreement by the **parties** to a lawsuit with respect to certain uncontested facts. A stipulation avoids the need to present evidence regarding the matters it covers; it is entered into to save time and expense. 2. Any agreement, admission, or concession voluntarily made by the parties to a lawsuit. 3. A mandate; a requirement; a condition. *See* agreed case.

➤ agreement, circumscription, designation, precondition, engagement, requirement, reservation, admission, concession; mandate, requirement, condition.

stirpes [*ster* · peez] (*Latin*) *n. See per stirpes.*

stock *n.* 1. The **shares of stock** or **stock certificates** issued by a corporation or a **joint-stock company**. 2. **Shares** in a corporation or a joint-stock company owned by shareholders; put another way, the sum of all the rights and duties of the shareholders. 3. The **capital** of a corporation. 4. **Stock in trade**. 5. **Stock of descent**. 6. Livestock. *See* assessable stock; authorized capital stock; blue chip stock; bonus stock; capital stock; common stock; convertible stock; guaranteed stock; nonvoting stock; no-par stock; outstanding stock; paid-up stock; preferred stock; redeemable stock; registered stock; subscribed stock; treasury stock; unissued stock; voting stock; watered stock.

adj. Commonplace; typical.

v. To accumulate; to provide or supply.

➤ *n.* merchandise, array, assets, cache, commodities, reservoir, store, supply ("large stock"); animals, beasts, domestic animals, flock, fowl, horses, livestock ("Our stock is at 20 head"); background, breed, clan, extraction, forebears, parentage, pedigree ("from good stock"); assets, blue chips, bonds, capital, convertible paper, share ("stock in the company").

adj. commonplace, banal, conventional, customary, boilerplate, overused, traditional ("a stock answer").

v. accumulate, amass, equip, furnish, gather, provision ("to stock up").

stock assessment [a · *sess* · ment] *n.* A demand made by a corporation that its stockholders contribute funds for the purpose of replacing a loss of **capital**. Stock assessments are levied in proportion to the number of shares a stockholder owns. *See* assessable stock; assessment. *Also see* contribution.

stock association [a · so · see · *ay* · shen] *n.* Same as **joint-stock company**.

stock certificate [ser · *tif* · i · ket] *n.* An **instrument** issued by a corporation stating that the person named is the owner of a designated number of shares of its stock. *See* certificate. *Also see* share certificate.

stock company [*kum* · pe · nee] *n.* A corporation or **joint-stock company**. *Compare* mutual company. *Also see* stock insurance company.

S

stock corporation [kore · per · *ay* · shen] *n.* A **stock company**.

stock dividend [*div* · i · dend] *n.* A **dividend** paid by a corporation in the stock of the corporation. *Compare* cash dividend.

stock exchange [eks · *chaynj*] *n.* *See* exchange.

stock in trade *n.* 1. The goods a merchant has for sale. 2. Raw materials, work in process, or materials used or consumed in a business. It is said that a lawyer's time and advice are her stock in trade. *See* inventory.

stock insurance company [in · shoor · ense *kum* · pe · nee] *n.* An **insurance company** organized and operating as a corporation rather than as a **mutual insurance company**.

stock issue [*ish* · ew] *n.* All of the stock issued by a corporation or **governmental entity** at a given point in time. *See* new issue.

stock manipulation [men · ip · yoo · *lay* · shen] *n.* Artificially raising or lowering the **market price** of **securities** by setting up sham sales or sham purchases.

stock market [*mar* · ket] *n.* A market where **securities** are bought and sold. EXAMPLES: a **stock exchange**; the **over-the-counter market**.

stock of descent [de · sent] *n.* The ancestor with whom a **line of descent** begins. *See* descent.

stock option [*op* · shen] *n.* An **option** to purchase or to sell stock at a designated price within a specified period of time.

stock redemption [re · *demp* · shen] *n.* The act of a corporation in buying its stock back from its shareholders. *See* redemption. *Also see* redeemable stock.

stock rights *n.* **Preemptive rights**.

stock split *n.* The act of a corporation in replacing some or all of its **outstanding stock** with a greater number of shares of lesser value.

stock subscription [sub · *skrip* · shen] *n.* *See* subscribed stock.

stock transfer [*trans* · fer] *n.* The process of transferring the ownership of corporate stock. *See* transfer agent.

stock transfer agent [*trans* · fer *ay* · jent] *n.* *See* transfer agent.

stock transfer tax [*trans* · fer] *n.* *See* transfer tax.

stock warrant [*war* · ent] *n.* *See* share certificate.

stockbroker [*stok* · bro · ker] *n.* A person employed in buying and selling **stock** for others. *See* broker; securities broker.
➤ broker, securities broker, agent.

stockholder [*stok* · hole · der] *n.* The owner of one or more **shares of stock** in a corporation or a **joint-stock company**; a person who appears on the books of a corporation as the owner of one or more shares of its stock. The terms "stockholder" and "shareholder" are used interchangeably.
➤ investor, owner, shareholder.

stockholders' derivative action [*stok* · hole · derz de · *riv* · e · tiv ak · shen] *n.* *See* derivative action.

stockholders' liability [*stok* · hole · derz ly · e · *bil* · i · tee] *n.* 1. The **personal liability** of stockholders for the debts of the corporation. 2. The obligation of stockholders to pay for **stock** they own but for which they have not yet paid. *See* paid-up stock.

stockholders' meeting [*stok* · hole · derz *mee* · ting] *n.* A meeting of the stockholders of a corporation called for the purpose of electing directors or transacting other business requiring the consent of the stockholders. *See* annual meeting; regular meeting.

stockholders' representative action [*stok* · hole · derz rep · re · *zen* · te · tiv ak · shen] *n.* *See* representative action.

stolen [*stoh* · len] *adj.* 1. Obtained by **larceny**. 2. Obtained by any form of theft. *See* steal.

stolen goods *n.* *See* receiving stolen goods.

stolen property [*prop* · er · tee] *n.* *See* receiving stolen property.

stop *n.* 1. An arrest; a police officer's action in halting a person's freedom of action, even briefly. 2. A place for stopping. EXAMPLE: a bus stop.
v. 1. To halt; to cease movement; to come to an end. 2. To halt something; to prevent movement; to obstruct.

➤ *n.* barricade, block, check, control, cutoff, stoppage, layoff ("work stop"); destination, sojourn, station, termination ("reach one's stop on the train route").

v. cease, close, desist, discontinue, finish, pause, end, tarry ("stop working"); arrest, bar, congest, hinder, restrain, repress, stall, suspend ("stop and frisk").

stop and frisk *n.* The detaining of a person briefly by a police officer and "patting him down" with the purpose of ascertaining if he is carrying a **concealed weapon**. **Fourth Amendment** rights are not violated if the officer has a **reasonable suspicion** that the person is armed and dangerous. *See* search and seizure.

stop order [*or* · der] *n.* A direction given by a customer to a broker that he should buy or sell specified stock if it reaches a certain price. USAGE: "Joan placed a stop order with her broker to sell her shares at 30."

stop-loss order [*or* · der] *n.* Same as **stop order**.

stop-loss provision [pro · *vizh* · en] *n.* A provision in an insurance policy, particularly health insurance, that binds the insurance carrier to reimburse the insured dollar for dollar after she has incurred expenses in excess of a specified amount (the "stop-loss point").

stop-payment order [-*pay* · ment *or* · der] *n.* A notice from the **drawer** of a check to the **payor bank** or **drawee** that it is not to pay the check.

stoppage [*stop* · ej] *n.* The act of stopping; the state or condition of being stopped. *See* stop.

➤ abeyance, blockage, check, closure, cutoff, deduction, hindrance, interruption.

stoppage in transit [*tran* · zit] *n.* A right that a seller of goods on credit has to retake them while they are in the possession of a **carrier** or other intermediary, upon discovering that the buyer is insolvent.

stoppage of work *n.* Same as **work stoppage**.

stopping payment [*stop* · ing *pay* · ment] *n.* *See* stop-payment order.

storage [*store* · ej] *n.* 1. The act of storing. *See* store. 2. A place in which things are stored. EXAMPLE: a warehouse. *See and compare* dead storage; live storage.

➤ accumulation, storing, saving, collection, stockpiling.

store *n.* A place where merchandise or other goods are sold.

v. 1. To put in a place (EXAMPLE: a warehouse) for safekeeping. 2. To lay away. *See* layaway. 3. To accumulate. USAGE: to "store up."

➤ *n.* arsenal, bank, cache, conservatory, depository, depot, pantry ("take supplies to the store").

v. accumulate, amass, hoard, stockpile, treasure ("store for later use").

story [*stor* · ee] *n.* 1. A lie; a fabrication. 2. An account; a telling.

➤ lie, deceit, fabrication, concoction, distortion, fantasy, myth, prevarication; narrative, recounting, account, tale, article, report, version, description.

straddle [*strad* · dl] *n.* A transaction that is a combination of both a **put** and a **call**, in which a person protects himself against both a rise and a fall of the price of a stock or a **commodity** by obtaining **options** both to purchase and to sell.

straight *adj.* 1. Authentic or dependable. 2. Marked by free expression; honesty. 3. Having a surface without curves or bends. 4. Heterosexual.

➤ genuine, reliable; direct, frank, bold; uncurved, linear, level; heterosexual, normal, non-gay.

straight life *n.* *See* straight life insurance.

straight life insurance [in · *shoor* · ense] *n.* **Life insurance** in which the **cash surrender value** of the policy increases as the insured makes premium payments throughout her lifetime. Straight life insurance is also referred to as **whole life insurance** or **ordinary life insurance**. *Compare* term insurance.

straight-line depreciation [de · pree · shee · *ay* · shen] *n.* In income tax law, a method of depreciating an **asset** at an even pace by subtracting its estimated **salvage value** from its cost and dividing the remainder by the number of years of its estimated **useful life**. *Compare* accelerated depreciation. *See* depreciation.

stranger [*strane* · jer] *n.* 1. A person who is not a **party** to the transaction; a person

S

who has no **interest** in the transaction; a **third party** or **third person**. *Compare* privy. 2. A person who is unknown to another.

➤ foreigner, newcomer, disinterested party, bystander, immigrant, interloper.

strategy [*strat · e · gee*] *n.* A plan of action.

➤ approach, plan, course, tactics, means, system, method, proposed action ("an effective litigation strategy").

straw man *n.* A person who appears as the **record owner** of real estate, but who in fact holds the **title** for another; a **dummy**. *Compare* interested person; real party in interest.

street *n.* A public road in a city, town, or village.

➤ artery, road, avenue, boulevard, byway, passage, terrace, thoroughfare.

stress *n.* 1. Excessive pressure or tension. 2. Emphasis.

v. To emphasize.

➤ *n.* strain, exertion, anxiety, burden, pressure, tension, demand ("the stress of the job"); emphasis, importance, accent, weight.

v. accent, emphasize, accentuate, point out, repeat, spotlight.

strict *adj.* Narrow; literal; restrictive.

➤ austere, dictatorial, despotic, exacting, stringent, puritanical, adamant ("strict parents"); complete, faithful, meticulous, precise, restrictive, scrupulous, utter, veracious ("strict regimen"); literal, narrow ("strict construction").

strict construction [*kun · struk · shen*] *n.* As opposed to a **broad construction**, a narrow or literal **construction** of written material, for EXAMPLE, a contract or a statute. *See and compare* letter of the law; spirit of the law. *Also see* interpretation.

strict constructionist [*kun · struk · shen · ist*] *n. See* original intent.

strict foreclosure [*for · kloh · zher*] *n.* The **foreclosure** of a mortgage without a sale of the property. Strict foreclosure is accomplished by a court order requiring payment of the debt within a specific time and further providing that, upon failure to make timely payment, **title** to the mortgaged property shall **vest** in the **mortgagee**.

strict liability [*ly · e · bil · i · tee*] *n.* Liability for an injury whether or not there is fault or **negligence**; **absolute liability**. The law imposes strict liability in **product liability** cases.

strict liability crimes [*ly · e · bil · i · tee*] *n.* Crimes or offenses in which *mens rea* or **criminal intent** is not an element. Such offenses include **regulatory crimes**, **petty offenses**, and **infractions**.

strict scrutiny test [*skrew · ten · ee*] *n.* A term the Supreme Court uses to describe the rigorous level of **judicial review** to be applied in determining the **constitutionality** of legislation that restricts a **fundamental right** or legislation based upon a **suspect classification**.

strictly [*strikt · lee*] *adj.* 1. Narrowly; restrictively. 2. Exclusively.

strictly construed [*kun · stroohd*] *adv./adj. See* strict construction.

strike *n.* A concerted stoppage of work by a group of employees for the purpose of attempting to compel their employer to comply with a demand or demands they have made.

v. 1. To act together with other employees in refusing to work; to engage in a strike. *See* strike (*noun*). 2. To eliminate; to expunge; to delete. *See* struck jury. In **pleading**, a **motion to strike** is the procedural device for challenging a pleading containing **scandalous** or **impertinent matter** or **immaterial allegations**, as well as **sham pleadings** or **defective pleadings**. *See* impertinent matter; scandalous matter. 3. To administer a blow; to assault.

➤ *n.* stoppage, revolt, walkout, dispute, boycott.

v. hit, bang, beat, chastise, clobber, impel, pummel, punch ("to strike one's spouse"); achieve, attain, come across, effect, encounter, seize, take ("to strike gold"); arbitrate, mediate, mutiny, resist, revolt, slow down ("to strike from work"); be plausible, carry, have semblance, impress, influence, inspire ("to strike someone as being smart"); eliminate, disqualify, dismiss ("to strike a juror").

strike breaker [*brake · er*] *n.* A person who takes the job of an employee who is on strike.

strike off *n.* A term used in connection with **striking a pleading**. *See* strike. *Also see* struck off.

striking [*strike* · ing] *adj.* Beautiful; arresting.
v. Disallowing; undoing. *See* strike.
➤ *adj.* arresting, astonishing, compelling, dazzling, forcible, impressive ("a striking presence").

striking a jury [*strike* · ing a *joor* · ee] *See* struck jury.

striking a pleading [*strike* · ing a *plee* · ding] *See* strike.

strong hand *n. See* with strong hand.

struck jury [*joor* · ee] *n.* 1. Sometimes called a **special jury**, a jury **impaneled** for a particular case, and not from the regular **jury panel**. 2. A jury drawn by the exercise of "strikes," each **party** being entitled to delete a certain number of names from a list prepared by a **jury commissioner** or other official.

struck off *adv./adj.* The completion of the sale of an article at auction by the acceptance of a bid. Property is said to be "struck off" or "**knocked down**" when the auctioneer, by her hammer or otherwise, indicates to the bidder that his bid is accepted.

structural alteration [*struk* · cher · el all · te · *ray* · shen] *n.* An alteration so substantial in nature that it creates a different thing. The term is usually applied to buildings. *See* alteration.

study [*stuh* · dee] *v.* To read in detail; to research.
➤ review, read, reflect on, learn, investigate, observe, explore, analyze.

style *n.* 1. **Caption** or heading; the caption of a case. 2. Class; category. 3. Fashion.
v. To make a caption; to fashion. USAGE: "how is the case styled?" means "how is the case captioned?"
➤ *n.* appearance, bearing, behavior, carriage, genre, idiosyncrasy, trend ("today's style").
v. address, caption, heading, call, denominate, designate.

sua sponte [*soo* · ah *spon* · tay] (*Latin*) *adj./adv. See* own motion.

suable [*soo* · ebl] *adj.* Capable of being sued. *See* sue.

sub *combining form* or *prefix* (*Latin*) *prep.* Under; subordinate to.
sub judice [*joo* · dee · say] Before the court for consideration and determination.
sub rosa [*roh* · zah] Secretly; privately; covertly.

subagent [*sub* · ay · jent] *n.* The **agent** of an agent.

Subchapter C corporation [*sub* · chap · ter see kore · per · *ay* · shen] *n. See* C corporation.

Subchapter S corporation [*sub* · chap · ter ess kore · per · *ay* · shen] *n. See* S corporation.

subcontract [*sub* · kon · trakt] *n.* An arrangement in which a person (the **principal contractor**) who has entered into a contract with another person to do something for that person (EXAMPLE: a contractor who has agreed to build a house for a property owner) enters into a separate contract with a third person (called a **subcontractor**) under which the third person agrees to perform some part of the work. *See also* general contractor; prime contractor.

subcontractor [sub · *kon* · trak · ter] *n.* A person who takes a portion of a contract from the **principal contractor**; a person who, by **subcontract**, agrees with the original contractor to perform some part of her original obligation for her. *Compare* general contractor; prime contractor.

subdivide [*sub* · di · vide] *v.* To again divide something that has already been divided. EXAMPLE: to divide a tract of land into lots for development or **improvement**. *See* subdivision.

subdivision [*sub* · di · vizh · en] *n.* 1. An area set aside for land development that has been divided into building lots. 2. The act of redividing something that has already been divided. *See* subdivide. *See also* political subdivision.
➤ class, community, area, development, group, subclass, subsidiary.

subdue [sub · *doo*] *v.* To keep under control; to defeat or quiet.
➤ beat, conquer, suppress, quell, quiet, silence, tame, curb, calm, humble.

S

subjacent support [sub · *jay* · sent sup · *port*] *n.* The right of a landowner to have his land supported by the earth that lies under it. A landowner has a duty not to alter her land (by excavation, for EXAMPLE) in a way that deprives the adjoining landowners of subjacent support for their land. *Compare* lateral support.

subject [*sub* · jekt] *n.* 1. A citizen; a person who enjoys the protection of the **sovereign power** of a nation or state. 2. A topic; a subject matter. *See* subject to.
v. [sub · *jekt*] 1. To make liable to, vulnerable to, or exposed to. 2. To bring under control; to bring under the authority of.
adj. Prone to; vulnerable to.
➤ *n.* topic, affair, discussion, material, proposal, problem, question ("stay on the subject"); case, client, customer, dependent, liege, patient, vassal ("the king's subject").
subject matter [*mat* · er] *n.* That which is the subject of a lawsuit, statute, contract, **trust**, etc. *See* subject matter jurisdiction.
subject matter jurisdiction [*mat* · er joo · ris · *dik* · shen] *n.* The **jurisdiction** of a court to hear and determine the type of case before it. EXAMPLE: the jurisdiction of a **family court** to try cases involving matters of **family law**. *Compare* personal jurisdiction.

subject to [*sub* · jekt] *adj./adv.* 1. Exposed to; vulnerable to; liable to. 2. Dependent upon; subordinate.
➤ accountable, captive, dependent, collateral, contingent, exposed, vulnerable, obedient, prone ("subject to allergy attacks").

sublease [*sub* · leess] *n.* A **lease** by a **lessee** of an **interest** in premises he occupies, or has a right to occupy, under a lease from the landlord. The subleased interest must be of shorter duration than the original lease; if it is for the entire term of the lease, it is, in law, an **assignment**.

sublessee [sub · less · *ee*] *n.* The **lessee** under a **sublease**.

sublessor [sub · less · *or*] *n.* A person who is at one and the same time the **lessor** under a **sublease** and the **lessee** or tenant under the principal lease. *See* lease.

sublet [*sub* · let] *v.* To enter into a **sublease**.
➤ lease, rent, take over.

submission [sub · *mish* · en] *n.* 1. The act of referring a matter, or agreeing to refer a matter, for determination by a court or other tribunal. 2. The act or state of surrendering, complying, or being obedient.
➤ compliance, acquiescence, defeat, humility, pliability, tractability, surrender.
submission to arbitration [ar · bi · *tray* · shen] *n.* Resort to **arbitration** for the resolution or determination of a controversy.
submission to jury [*joor* · ee] *n.* The act of a judge in giving a case to the jury for deliberation. *See* deliberate. *See also* final submission; jury instructions.

submit [sub · mit] *v.* 1. To refer for a decision. 2. To surrender; to comply; to obey. 3. To propose; to suggest. *See* submission.
➤ abide, surrender, accede, acquiesce, capitulate, indulge, succumb, tolerate, refer, present, propose, suggest ("submit issues for your consideration").

subordinate [sub · *or* · din · et] *adj.* Of lesser rank, status, or priority.
n. An underling; an assistant.
v. [sub · *or* · din · ate] To place in a lower position; to make inferior in rank, status, or priority.
➤ *adj.* auxiliary, ancillary, secondary, subalternate, subsidiary, unequal ("The captain is a subordinate officer to the general").
n. aide, assistant, attendant, inferior, junior, underling, second ("to be a subordinate to one's boss").
subordinate body [bod · ee] *n.* An entity that is under the control of another entity. EXAMPLE: a local union in its relationship to the international union that chartered it.
subordinate lien [leen] *n.* Same as **junior lien**.
subordination [sub · or · di · *nay* · shen] *n.* 1. The process of prioritizing interests. 2. Submission; subservience; surrender.
subordination agreement [a · *gree* · ment] *n.* An agreement by which a person agrees that his **security interest** in a specified piece of property shall have less **priority** than other **liens** or **interests**.
subordination clause *n. See* subordination agreement.

suborn [sub · *orn*] *v.* To engage in **subornation**.

subornation [sub · or · *nay* · shen] *n.* The crime of persuading or inducing another person to commit a crime.

subornation of perjury [*per* · jer · ee] *n.* The crime of persuading or inducing another person to commit the crime of **perjury**.

subpena [sub · *peen* · ah] *n.* Same as **subpoena**.

subpoena [sub · *peen* · ah] *n.* A command in the form of written **process** requiring a witness to come to court to testify; short for **subpoena ad testificandum**.
  v. To issue or **serve** a **subpoena**. *See* subpoena (*noun*).
➤ *n.* order, command, mandate, citation, summons, writ, call, directive ("to serve a subpoena").
  v. order, command, summon, beckon, demand ("to subpoena the other party in the case").

subpoena ad testificandum [ahd *tes* · te · fe · *kan* · dem] *n.* The *Latin* term *ad testificandum* means "testify under penalty." A subpoena ad testificadum is a subpoena to testify. *Compare* subpoena duces tecum.

subpoena duces tecum [*doo* · ses *tee* · kum] *n.* The *Latin* term *duces tecum* means "bring with you under penalty." A subpoena duces tecum is a written command requiring a witness to come to court to testify and at that time to produce for use as evidence the papers, documents, books, or records listed in the subpoena.

subrogation [sub · ro · *gay* · shen] *n.* The substitution of one person for another with respect to a claim or right against a third person; the principle that when a person has been required to pay a debt that should have been paid by another person, she becomes entitled to all of the **remedies** that the creditor originally possessed with respect to the debtor. (EXAMPLE: After the insurance company that insures Lloyd's car **indemnifies** him for the damage done to his car by Mary's negligence, the insurance company has the same **cause of action** against Mary as Lloyd originally had.) Subrogation is sometimes referred to as **substitution**.

➤ displacement, substitution, transfer, transference, exchange, switch, supplanting.

subrogee [sub · ro · *zhee*] *n.* A person who acquires the rights of another person by **subrogation**.

subrogor [sub · ro · *zhor*] *n.* A person whose rights are acquired by another person through **subrogation**.

subscribe [sub · *skribe*] *v.* 1. To sign; literally, to "sign under" one's name at the end of a document. 2. To agree to take and to pay for, for EXAMPLE, a newspaper or corporate stock. *See* subscribed stock; subscription. 3. To sanction; to approve of.
➤ buy, endorse, enroll, register, ("subscribe to the magazine"); accede, adhere, advocate, consent, endorse, favor, sanction, sign ("to subscribe to a school of thought").

subscribed [sub · *skribed*] *adv.* 1. Signed. 2. Agreed to take and pay for. 3. Approved of; sanctioned.
➤ signed, approved of, sanctioned.

subscribed and sworn to before me [be · *fore*] A phrase appearing in a notary's **certificate of acknowledgement**, which **attests** that the document was sworn to in the presence of the notary. *See* jurat.

subscribed stock *n.* **Stock** that a stockholder has agreed to purchase. *See* subscribe; subscription; subscription contract.

subscriber [sub · *skribe* · er] *n.* A person who has subscribed to something. *See* subscribe; subscribed stock; subscription; subscription contract.

subscription [sub · *skrip* · shen] *n.* 1. A signature, particularly at the end of a document. 2. The act of signing one's name. 3. An agreement to take and pay for something. *See* subscribe; subscribed stock; subscription contract.
➤ enrollment, acceptance, registration; endorsement, confirmation, signature.

subscription contract [kon · trakt] *n.* An agreement to subscribe, for EXAMPLE, to corporate stock or to a newspaper. *See* subscribe; subscribed stock.

subscription rights *n.* The right of a shareholder to buy additional stock in the corporation. *See also* preemptive right.

subsequent [*sub* · se · kwent] *adj.* Coming after, whether in time, place, rank, order, or priority; following.
➤ succeeding, ensuing, sequential, trailing, eventual, proximate.
Ant. prior, preceding.
subsequent condition [kun · *dish* · en] *n. See* condition subsequent.
subsequent negligence [*neg* · li · jense] *n.* When a person has put himself in danger, the **negligence** of another person in failing to remove him from harm's way.

subsidiary [sub · *sid* · ee · er · ee] *adj.* Of secondary importance; subordinate; auxiliary.
n. 1. That which is subordinate or secondary to something else. 2. Short for **subsidiary corporation**.
➤ *adj.* secondary, subordinate, auxiliary, adjurant, collateral, tributory.
subsidiary corporation
[kore · per · ay · shen] *n.* A **corporation** controlled by another corporation, known as the **parent company**, which owns all or a majority of its stock. *See* wholly owned subsidiary.

subsidize [*sub* · si · dize] *v.* To provide a **subsidy**.
➤ bankroll, contribute, endow, finance, promote, sponsor, support, underwrite.

subsidy [*sub* · si · dee] *n.* A grant of money by the government to a private person or organization in furtherance of the **public welfare** or of some public purpose. EXAMPLE: **agricultural price supports (parity)**.
➤ grant, alimony, bequest, allowance, gift, gratuity, indemnity, pension, subsidization.

subsist [sub · *sist*] *v.* To survive; to live; to keep going.
➤ continue, endure, persist, survive, last, live, remain, endure, get by.

subsistence [sub · *sis* · tense] *n.* 1. Support. 2. A means of support, for EXAMPLE, **alimony**.
➤ affluence, competence, income, livelihood, necessities, provision, ration, support, allowance.

substance [*sub* · stense] *n.* 1. The meaning of a thing; the essential nature of a thing, as opposed to its appearance or its form; the opposite of **procedure**. 2. A term for drugs, including alcohol, abused by persons suffering from chemical dependency; that is, persons involved in substance abuse. *See* alcoholism; drug addiction. 3. Matter.
➤ actuality, concreteness, reality, corpus, fabric, person, staple ("analyze an unknown substance"); effect, essentiality, focus, import, innards, marrow, quintessence ("the substance of an argument"); wealth, affluence, assets, estate, fortune, means, resources ("a person of substance").

substantial [sub · *stan* · shel] *adj.* 1. Having worth or value. 2. Having substance. 3. Considerable.
➤ abundant, consequential, durable, extraordinary, heavyweight, plentiful ("a substantial supply"); actual, concrete, existent, physical, righteous, sensible, tangible ("substantial problem"); affluent, comfortable, easy, opulent, prosperous, solvent.

substantial compliance [kum · *ply* · ense] *n. See* substantial performance.

substantial evidence [*ev* · i · dense] *n.* **Evidence** that a **reasonable person** would accept as adequate to support the conclusion or conclusions drawn from it; evidence beyond a **scintilla**.

substantial evidence rule [*ev* · i · dense] *n.* The rule that a court will uphold a decision or ruling of an administrative agency if it is supported by **substantial evidence**. *See* evidence.

substantial justice [*juss* · tis] *n.* Substantial justice is done if the court's **judgment** is based upon the applicable principles of **substantive law**, notwithstanding the fact that the court may have made technical errors.

substantial performance [per · form · ense] *n.* **Performance** of a contract that, although not full performance, is in good faith and in compliance with the contract except for minor deviations. *Compare* part performance.

substantial performance doctrine [per · *form* · ense dok · trin] *n.* The doctrine that there is **adequate consideration** to support a contract if there has been **substantial performance** of the contract.

substantial right *n.* Same as **substantive right**.

S

substantiate [sub · *stan* · chee · ayt] *v.* To establish the truth of something through proof or evidence.
➤ corroborate, prove, verify, attest, affirm, uphold, validate ("to substantiate an assertion").

substantive [*sub* · sten · tiv] *adj.* Real; essential; pertaining to substantive law.
substantive due process [*pross* · ess] *n.* A right grounded in the **Fifth Amendment** and the **Fourteenth Amendment**. The very essence of those amendments, as they relate to substantive due process, is the concept that the government may not act **arbitrarily** or **capriciously** in making, interpreting, or enforcing the law. A person is entitled to both substantive due process and **procedural due process**.
substantive evidence [*ev* · i · dense] *n.* **Evidence** that is **offered** for the purpose of proving a fact, as opposed to **corroborating evidence** or evidence that is introduced to **impeach** a witness.
substantive law *n.* Area of the law that defines right conduct, as opposed to **procedural law**, which governs the process by which rights are **adjudicated**. *Compare* procedural law.
substantive right *n.* A right that is essential to achieving justice, as opposed to a right that is purely **procedural** in nature. *See* right. *Also see* fundamental right.

substitute [*sub* · sti · tewt] *n.* A person or thing that stands in the place of another person or thing; a replacement.
v. To replace a person or thing with another.
adj. Replacement; alternate.
➤ *n.* alternate, auxiliary, backup, delegate, proxy, surrogate, expedient.
v. exchange, replace, supersede, swap, supplant, fill in for.
adj. vicarious, provisional, alternative, replacement ("a substitute teacher").

substituted [*sub* · sti · tew · ted] *adj.* Pertaining to a person or a thing that stands in the place of another person or thing.
substituted administrator [ad · *min* · is · tray · ter] *n.* An **administrator DBN**.
substituted executor [eg · *zek* · yoo · tor] *n.* A person named in a will to act as **executor** in the event the first person named cannot serve or refuses to serve.

substituted party [*par* · tee] *n.* *See* substitution of parties.
substituted service [*ser* · viss] *n.* *See* substituted service of process.
substituted service of process [*ser* · viss of *pross* · ess] *n.* Generally referred to as **constructive service** or **constructive service of process**; **service** by any method other than **personal service** (EXAMPLES: **service by mail**; **service by publication**). *Compare* actual service of process; personal service of process.

substitution [sub · sti · *tew* · shen] *n.* 1. The replacement of one person or one thing in the place of another person or thing. 2. **Subrogation**.
➤ change, replacement.
substitution by will *n.* The effect of a clause in a will in which the **testator** provides for the replacement of a deceased **beneficiary** by another person or persons, rather than allowing the **interest** of the deceased beneficiary to be shared with other beneficiaries or to become a part of the **remainder** of the **estate**.
substitution of parties [*par* · teez] *n.* 1. A change of **parties** by replacing the original plaintiff or defendant with a new plaintiff or defendant. 2. A **revival of action**.

substitutional [sub · sti · *tew* · shen · el] *adj.* Same as **substitutionary**.

substitutionary [sub · sti · *tew* · shen · er · ee] *adj.* Pertaining to a substitute or a substitution.
substitutionary executor [eg · *zek* · yoo · tor] *n.* *See* substituted executor.
substitutionary gift *n.* *See* substitution by will.

subversive [sub · *ver* · siv] *n.* A radical or rebellious person.
adj. Rebellious; insurgent.
➤ *n.* insurgent, revolutionary, radical, defiant.
adj. revolutionary, radical, undermining, destructive, riotous, seditious.

subversive activities [sub · *ver* · siv ak · *tiv* · i · teez] *n.* Advocating the overthrow of the government by force. *See* sedition; Smith Act.

subvert [sub · *vert*] *v.* To undermine; to rebel against.
➤ defeat, undo, topple, disestablish, dismantle, extinguish, extirpate, rebel, destroy, overturn.

S

succeed [suk · *seed*] *v.* 1. To achieve a goal. 2. To accede or follow. *See* succession.
➤ accomplish, achieve, acquire, earn, conquer, master ("succeed in finishing the race"); accede, assume, ensue, follow, postdate, inherit, replace ("succeed to the throne").

successful party [suk · *sess* · ful *par* · tee] *n.* Same as **prevailing party**.

succession [suk · *sesh* · en] *n.* 1. The passing of the property of a **decedent** by will or by inheritance (**intestate succession**), as opposed to taking **title** by deed, **grant**, gift, or contract. *See* hereditary succession; intestate succession; vacant succession. 2. Succeeding to the rights of another. EXAMPLE: in the law of corporations, **perpetual succession**. 3. Following and taking the place of another. EXAMPLE: succession in office, as when one office-holder takes the place of another who has retired, died, or not been reelected.

succession duty [*dew* · tee] *n.* Same as **inheritance tax**.

succession tax *n.* Same as **inheritance tax**.

successor [suk · *sess* · er] *n.* 1. A person who follows another in **interest**; a **successor in interest**. USAGE: "An heir is a successor to her ancestor's interest in the property she inherits." 2. A person who assumes a public office after it has been vacated by the previous officeholder. 3. A corporation that acquires the rights of another corporation through **amalgamation**, **merger**, or **consolidation**.
➤ heir, substitute, recipient, donee, grantee, beneficiary.

successor in interest [*in* · trest] *n.* A subsequent owner of rights or property previously owned by someone else. *See* interest; successors.

successors [suk · *sess* · erz] *n.* *Plural* of **successor**. A term in a contract indicating that the contract is **assignable**.

successors and assigns [a · *synz*] *n.* A phrase used in contracts for the purpose of conferring the benefits and obligations of the agreement upon the **successors in interest** of either of the parties. *See* assigns.

succinct [suk · sinkt] *adj.* To the point; brief.

➤ brief, concise, terse, laconic, compact, pithy, curt.
Ant. verbose, wordy, prolix.

sudden [*sud* · en] *adj.* Unexpected; surprising; immediate.
➤ instant, immediate, unexpected, unanticipated, unplanned, abrupt, unannounced, impetuous.
Ant. planned.

sudden emergency doctrine [*sud* · en e · *mer* · jen · see *dok* · trin] *n.* The principle that a person who is placed in a position of sudden emergency, not created by his own **negligence**, will not be held responsible if he fails to act with the **degree of care** that the law would have required of him had he had sufficient time for thought and reflection.

sudden passion [*pash* · en] *n.* *See* heat of passion.

sue *v.* To file a lawsuit.
➤ accuse, appeal, beseech, litigate, plead, prosecute, claim.

sue out *v.* To obtain a **writ** or other **process** from a court.

suffer [*suf* · er] *v.* 1. To authorize or consent to an action or course of conduct, generally by nonresistance, with knowledge that it is taking place or that it will take place; to tolerate; to accept. Thus, for EXAMPLE, a plaintiff "suffers a **nonsuit**" when he agrees to a court order dismissing his case. *See* sufferance. 2. To experience physical or emotional pain or distress.
➤ ache, agonize, brave, deteriorate, droop, hurt, languish, sicken, writhe ("suffer great pain"); abide, accept, acquiesce, countenance, indulge, sustain ("suffer the consequences").

sufferance [*suf* · er · ense] *n.* Consent to, approval, or tolerance of an action or course of conduct with knowledge that it is taking place or will take place. *See* suffer.

suffering [*suf* · er · ing] *n.* Anguish; pain. *See* pain and suffering. *See also* suffer; sufferance.
➤ adversity, anguish, affliction, discomfort, dolor, martyrdom.

sufficient [suf · *fish* · ent] *adj.* Adequate; enough; as much as is needed.
➤ enough, acceptable, ample, aplenty, commensurable, competent, copious, adequate.

sufficient cause *n.* 1. **Probable cause**. 2. **Good cause**.

sufficient consideration [ken · sid · e · *ray* · shen] *n.* **Adequate consideration**; **legal consideration**.

sufficient evidence [*ev* · i · dense] *n.* 1. **Evidence** that will satisfy an unprejudiced mind of the truth. 2. Enough evidence in law to support a verdict. *See* weight of the evidence. *Compare* conclusive evidence; insufficient evidence.

suffrage [*suf* · rej] *n.* 1. The right to vote. 2. The act of voting.

sui [*soo* · ee] (*Latin*) *prep.* One's own self; itself.

sui generis [*jen* · e · ris] "Of its own kind"; unique.

sui juris [*joor* · is] A phrase literally meaning "of his own right"; applied to a person who has **legal capacity** and is without **legal disability**.

suicide [*soo* · i · side] *n.* The act of killing oneself. Although suicide is not a crime, in some jurisdictions an attempted suicide is a criminal offense, as is **aiding and abetting** or being an **accessory before the fact** to suicide. *Also see* attempt.
➤ self-destruction, death, hara kiri, seppuku.

suit *n.* A lawsuit; an **action**, either an **action at law** or an **equitable action**, but, as the term is generally used, not a criminal prosecution. *See also* legal action.
v. To please; to satisfy.
➤ *n.* case, cause, litigation, proceeding, trial ("a suit in court").
v. accord, agree, befit, beseem, conform, correspond, match ("It suits me just fine").

suit in equity [*ek* · wi · tee] *n. See* equitable action.

suitor [*soo* · ter] *n.* 1. A **plaintiff**; a **petitioner**. 2. A male who romantically pursues a female.
➤ litigant, petitioner, plaintiff, party; admirer, boyfriend, wooer, date, pursuer.

sum *n.* 1. An amount or quantity of money. 2. The result of adding numbers.
➤ aggregate, amount, body, bulk, entirety, integral, total, synopsis.

sum certain [*ser* · ten] *n.* A definite, fixed, or stated amount of money. To be **negotiable**, an **instrument** must be payable in a **fixed amount**, i.e., payable in a specific amount or a "sum certain." The fact that a **negotiable instrument** or other obligation includes interest or similar charges does not make the sum owed any less certain, so long as the total amount owed is capable of calculation. *See* sum payable.

sum payable [*pay* · ebl] *n.* The amount due or to be paid under a **bill**, **note**, or contract.

summarily [sum · *ehr* · i · ly] *adv.* 1. Without the customary legal formalities. *See* summary. 2. Quickly; expeditiously.
➤ arbitrarily, expeditiously, forthwith, immediately, peremptorily, promptly, quickly.

summary [*sum* · e · ree] *adj.* Short; concise; brief; reduced to few or relatively few words. *n.* That which is short, concise, or brief; that which is reduced to a few words or to relatively few words. EXAMPLES: an **abstract of title**; the **headnote** to a **reported case**.
➤ *adj.* short, concise, brief, cursory, laconic, succinct.
n. abbreviation, abridgment, abstract, compendium, epitome, essence, headnote, precise, prospectus, sketch ("a summary of the speech").

summary conviction [kun · *vik* · shen] *n.* Conviction by a **court of limited jurisdiction**, for EXAMPLE, by a **magistrate's court** or a **police court**. *See* conviction.

summary court-martial [-*mar* · shel] *n. See* court-martial.

summary judgment [*juj* · ment] *n.* A method of disposing of an **action** without further **proceedings**. Under the **Federal Rules of Civil Procedure**, and the **rules of civil procedure** of many states, a **party** against whom a **claim**, **counterclaim**, or **cross-claim** is asserted, or against whom a **declaratory judgment** is sought, may file a **motion for summary judgment** seeking **judgment** in her favor if there is no genuine issue as to any **material fact**. *See* motion.

summary jurisdiction [joo · ris · *dik* · shen] *n.* The **jurisdiction** exercised by a court that conducts a **summary proceeding**.

summary jury trial (SJT) [*joor* · ee *try* · el] *n.* A court-ordered form of **alternative dispute resolution** sometimes used by the federal courts in complex

S

cases that would otherwise require a lengthy jury trial. An SJT is a kind of nonbinding capsule trial that allows the parties to obtain the thoughts of jurors with respect to the merits of the case. The facts are presented in simplified form to a reduced jury, questions of admissibility of evidence are decided with the judge in advance, and counsel interview the jurors after the verdict. Although the verdict is nonbinding, the parties may agree to be bound by it, or they may settle the case based upon the reactions of the jurors. *Compare* mini-trial.

summary proceeding [pro · *seed* · ing] *n.* A **proceeding** in which a case is disposed of or a trial is conducted in a prompt and simple manner without a jury and without many of the ordinary requirements (such as **complaint**, **summons**, **indictment**, or **information**). EXAMPLES: a **contempt proceeding**; trial before a **magistrate** or a justice of the peace; trial in a **small claims court**.

summary process [*pross* · ess] *n.* A course of action or **process** that is undertaken lawfully, but without resort to the courts. EXAMPLES: a **possessory warrant**; the **recaption** of goods.

summary remedy [*rem* · e · dee] *n.* In a **civil action**, a **remedy** obtainable in a **summary proceeding**.

summary trial [*try* · el] *n. See* summary proceeding.

summation [sum · *ay* · shen] *n.* The closing argument or final argument made by counsel for each of the **parties** in a case.
➤ summary, recapitulation, closing argument, final argument, summing-up.

summing up [*sum* · ing] *n. See* summation.

summon [sum · en] *v.* 1. To issue a **summons**. 2. To call or require a person or a group of people to appear or to obey some other command. EXAMPLE: to "summon a grand jury" means to appoint or to convene a grand jury. 3. To call up; to call upon. USAGE: "I will summon my courage."
➤ arouse, call, assemble, beckon, cite, petition, mobilize, muster.

summons [*sum* · enz] *n.* 1. In a civil case, the **process** by which an **action** is commenced and the defendant is brought

within the **jurisdiction** of the court. 2. In a criminal case involving a **petty offense** or an **infraction** (EXAMPLE: a traffic offense), process (EXAMPLE: a **citation**) issued for the purpose of compelling the defendant to appear in court. In such a case, a summons is used as an alternative to arrest.
➤ citation, mandate, process, notification, command, direction.

Sunday [*sun* · day] *n.* The first day of the week; the Christian Sabbath.

Sunday closing laws [*kloh* · zing] *n.* Statutes and ordinances prohibiting commerce or public entertainment on Sunday. These laws are sometimes referred to as **blue laws**.

sunset law [*sun* · set] *n.* A statute that includes a provision requiring the statute to expire by a specified date unless the legislature votes for its continued existence.

sunshine law [*sun* · shine] *n.* State and federal statutes requiring that meetings of administrative agencies be open to the public.

suo nomine [*soo* · oh *noh* · mi · nee] (*Latin*) *adj./adv.* Means "in his own name."

supercilious [soo · per · *sil* · ee · us] *adj.* Characterized by an arrogant or condescending attitude.
➤ arrogant, haughty, patronizing, lofty, disdainful, pompous, prideful, egotistical, scornful.

superficial [soo · per · *fish* · al] *adj.* 1. Without depth; cursory. 2. Concerned only with the obvious; shallow.
➤ cursory, hasty, surface, perfunctory ("a superficial examination of the room"); shallow, unthinking, empty, flimsy, depthless, empty ("a superficial person").

superfluous [su · *per* · flew · us] *adj.* Unnecessary; irrelevant.
➤ excessive, unnecessary, irrelevant, dispensible, inessential, redundant, extra. *Ant.* essential, necessary.

Superfund [*soo* · per · fund] *n.* A fund created by federal statute to be used in locating and cleaning up hazardous waste sites.

superior [soo · *peer* · ee · er] *adj.* Of higher rank or importance; more important. *n.* A higher rankng person.

➤ *adj.* excellent, better, sterling, eminent, marvelous, nonpareil, distinguished, inimitable ("superior quality"); sanctimonious, snobby, lordly, arrogant, vainglorious, patronizing ("a superior attitude").
n. director, senior, principal, commander, master, leader, foreman ("my superior at work").

superior court *n.* 1. In some jurisdictions, the title given **trial courts**. 2. In some jurisdictions, the title of **intermediate appellate courts**. *Also see* inferior court.

superior lien [leen] *n.* A **senior lien**; a **prior lien**. *Compare* inferior lien. *See* lien.

supersede [soo · per · *seed*] *v.* To put one thing into effect in place of another; to replace one person in power with another. *See* superseding cause.
➤ supplant, abandon, annul, desert, replace, discard, outmode, suspend, void.

supersedeas [soo · per · *see* · dee · es] *n.* A court order or **writ** that **stays** the power of a **lower court** to **execute** on its **judgment** or decree. An appeal from a **trial court** to an **appellate court** automatically serves as a supersedeas of the trial court's judgment. *See* stay of action; stay of execution.

superseding cause [soo · per · *seed* · ing] *n.* Same as **intervening cause**.

supervening [soo · per · *veen* · ing] *adj.* Additional; over and above; subsequent.
➤ additional, subsequent, new, independent.

supervening cause *n.* In the law of **negligence**, a new or additional event that occurs subsequent to the original negligence and becomes the **proximate cause** of injury. *Also see* intervening cause.

supervening negligence [*neg* · li · jense] *n.* The **negligence** of a defendant who is held liable under the **last clear chance doctrine**; the negligence of a defendant whose conduct is the **supervening cause** of an injury.

supervision [soo · per · *viz* · en] *n.* The management or control of people or projects.
➤ guidance, control, care, administration, management, charge, leadership.

supervisor [*soo* · per · vy · zer] *n.* 1. Under the **National Labor Relations Act**, a person who has the authority to hire, transfer, suspend, lay off, recall, promote, discharge, assign, reward, or discipline other employees, or the responsibility to direct them or to adjust their **grievances**, or to effectively recommend such action. 2. A member of a **board of supervisors**.
➤ administrator, caretaker, boss, curator, superintendent, inspector, director.

supplant [suh · *plant*] *v.* To displace or take over.
➤ replace, displace, dismiss, supersede, eject, drive out, substitute, take the place of.

supplemental [sup · le · *men* · tel] *adj.* Added to make up a deficiency or deficit; additional.
➤ supplementary, additional, incidental, extraneous, further.

supplemental act *n.* A statute enacted to improve an existing statute by adding something, without changing the original text.

supplemental affidavit [af · i · *day* · vit] *n.* An **affidavit** that adds something to a previously given affidavit.

supplemental complaint [kum · *plaint*] *n.* A **complaint** that **pleads** matters occurring after the filing of the original complaint. *Compare* amendment of complaint.

supplemental pleading [*plee* · ding] *n.* A **pleading** that contains matter occurring after the filing of the original pleading. EXAMPLE: a complaint alleging **new matter**.

supplemental security income (SSI) [se · *kyoor* · i · tee *in* · kum] *n.* A program administered by the **Social Security Administration**, which provides a minimum monthly income to persons who are at least 65 years old, blind, or disabled as defined by Social Security regulations, and who have **gross income** and **assets** below a specified level.

supplemental unemployment benefits program [un · em · *ploy* · ment ben · e · fits *pro* · gram] *n.* Another term for **extended benefits program**.

supplementary [sup · le · *men* · ter · ee] *adj.* Supplemental.

supplementary proceeding [pro · *see* · ding] *n.* A **proceeding** for the enforcement of a **judgment**, separate

S

from the proceeding in which the judgment was rendered, for the purpose of ascertaining the location of the debtor's property and other relevant information. *See* turnover order.

supply [suh · *ply*] *v.* To make available for use; to furnish.
n. Quantities of goods for sale; amounts held for use.
➤ *v.* equip, provide, stock, deliver, bestow, endow, furnish, contribute, dispense.
n. amount, hoard, cache, provisions, number, quantity, surplus.

support [sup · *ort*] *n.* 1. That which provides a person with subsistence, **maintenance**, or sustenance (food, clothing, shelter, medicine, and other **necessaries**), or the means to purchase them (money or its equivalent). *See* nonsupport. 2. The right of a landowner to support for his land in its natural state from the land adjoining or underlying it. *See and compare* lateral support; subjacent support. 3. That which provides a foundation or basis. USAGE: "in support of my argument"; a "**supporting affidavit**." 4. That which sustains. USAGE: "emotional support"; "support the cause of freedom."
v. To provide funds or other means of **maintenance** of a person; to provide **support**. *See* support (*noun*).
➤ *n.* abutment, backing, collar, flotation, fulcrum, pillar, reinforcement ("Good supports hold the building up"); aid, assistance, encouragement, succor, patronage, sustenance, loyalty ("to give support to an upset person"); alienation, alimony, maintenance, provision, responsibility, sustenance ("child support").
v. bolster, buttress, embed, reinforce, undergird ("The beam supports the ceiling"); bankroll, encourage, maintain, nourish, stiffen, underwrite ("His parents still support him"); abet, assist, countenance, justify, substantiate, uphold, verify ("support her claim").

supporting [sup · *ort* · ing] *adj.* That which supports.
supporting affidavit [af · i · *day* · vit] *n.* An **affidavit** filed in support of a petition or other **application** made to a court. A **motion for summary judgment** and a petition for a **preliminary injunction** are EXAMPLES of applications that may require supporting affidavits. *See* moving papers; supporting papers.

supporting papers [*pay* · perz] *n.* **Affidavits** or other documents (EXAMPLE: a **memorandum of law**) filed in support of a **motion, petition, application**, or the like. *See* moving papers.

suppress [sup · *press*] *v.* 1. To exclude illegally obtained evidence by means of a **motion to suppress**. *See* suppression hearing; suppression of evidence. 2. To restrain; to conceal; to prevent. 3. To put down by force.
➤ annihilate, censor, muffle, overthrow, quench, spike ("to suppress rebellion"); restrain, conceal, exclude ("suppress the evidence").

suppression [sup · *presh* · en] *n.* 1. **Suppression of evidence**. 2. The act of restraining, concealing, or preventing. 3. Subduing by force. *See* suppress.
➤ control, concealment, inhibition, restraint.

suppression hearing [*heer* · ing] *n.* A **hearing** held in advance of trial in which a criminal defendant who, having filed a **motion to suppress**, presents facts and arguments to persuade the court that evidence the prosecution will use against her has been illegally seized and is therefore inadmissible. *See* suppression of evidence. *See also* exclusionary rule.

suppression of evidence [*ev* · i · dense] *n.* 1. The **relief** obtained by a criminal defendant in whose favor a court has granted a **motion to suppress**. *See* suppression hearing. 2. The crime of destroying evidence or refusing to testify in a criminal **proceeding**. 3. The deliberate failure or refusal of the prosecution to disclose evidence favorable to the defendant.

supra [*soo* · pra] (*Latin*) *adv.* Above; above mentioned. *Supra* is used in legal writing when the author refers to an **authority** that she has also **cited** at an earlier point in the work. EXAMPLE: If at footnote 40 of her brief the author has cited "Children and Young Persons Act, 1969," she might, at footnote 61, refer to that citation as follows: "See *supra* note 40." *Compare id.*; *infra.*
➤ above-mentioned, foregoing.

supremacy [soo · *prem* · e · see] *n.* The condition of possessing the highest power or authority.
➤ mastery, leadership, superiority, preeminence, excellence, dominance.

supremacy clause [soo · *prem* · e · see] *n.* The provision in Article VI of the Constitution that "this Constitution and the laws of the United States . . . shall be the supreme law of the land, and the judges in every state shall be bound thereby."

supreme court [soo · *preem*] *n.* 1. The United States Supreme Court. The United States Supreme Court is the highest court in the federal court system. It is established by the Constitution and has both **original jurisdiction** and **appellate jurisdiction**. 2. In most states, the highest **appellate court** of the state. 3. In some states, a **trial court**. *See* court of general jurisdiction.

Supreme Court of the United States [soo · *preem* court of the yoo · *ny* · ted] *n.* *See* supreme court.

surcharge [*ser* · charj] *n.* 1. A **surtax**. 2. An additional amount added to the usual charge. 3. The act of holding a **guardian** or other **fiduciary** responsible for money or property lost or not earned because of a breach of his fiduciary duty. 4. To disprove an **account stated** by demonstrating a failure to include an item that should have been included.
v. To impose a **surcharge**. *See* surcharge (*noun*).
➤ *n.* surtax, fee, penalty.

surety [*shoor* · e · tee] *n.* A person who promises to pay the debt or to satisfy the obligation of another person (the **principal**). As opposed to the obligation of a **guarantor**, the obligation of a surety is both **primary** and **absolute**; that is, it does not depend upon a default by the principal.
➤ sponsor, backer, indemnitor, insurer, cosigner, bondsman, signatory, voucher.

surety bond *n.* A **bond** that **secures** the performance of an **obligation**; for EXAMPLE, the obligation to appear in court for trial (a **bail bond**) or the obligation to fulfill a construction contract (a **performance bond**). *Also see* suretyship bond.

surety company [*kum* · pe · nee] *n.* A company engaged in the business of acting as a surety or **guarantor**.

suretyship [*shoor* · e · tee · ship] *n.* The contractual relationship between a **surety**, her **principal**, and a **creditor**.

suretyship bond *n.* 1. The agreement between a **surety**, a **principal**, and a **creditor**. 2. The **instrument** evidencing the agreement between a surety, a principal, and a creditor and binding the principal to the creditor.

suretyship contract [*kon* · trakt] *n.* Same as **suretyship bond**.

surface [*ser* · fiss] *n.* The exterior; the covering. As used in deeds and other conveyances, a rather elastic term, depending upon the property that is the subject of the deed, the intention of the parties, and the business venture involved. EXAMPLES of purposes for which the "surface" of land is conveyed include agricultural uses, mining, the right to use water, and the right to extract oil or gas.
adj. Relating to the exterior appearance.
v. To rise or emerge.
➤ *n.* covering, expanse, exterior, periphery, superficiality, superficies, veneer ("the surface of the space shuttle").
adj. apparent, covering, depthless, exterior, shallow, superficial ("surface paint").
v. appear, arise, emerge, materialize, transpire ("The body surfaced in the lake").

surface water [*waw* · ter] *n.* Water derived from falling rain or melting snow, or rising to the surface in springs and spread out over the surface of the ground. *Compare* natural watercourse. *Also compare* ground water; percolating waters.

surfeit [*sur* · fit] *n.* An abundance.
➤ excess, abundance, profusion, oversupply, surplus, glut.

surname [*ser* · name] *n.* A person's last name; the family name.
➤ last name, family name.

surpass [*ser* · *pass*] *v.* To go beyond.
➤ beat, exceed, outrank, prevail, outshine ("to surpass one's mentor").

surplus [*ser* · plus] *n.* That which is not needed or that which is left over, especially the remainder of a particular fund or money set aside for a particular purpose. *See* accumulated surplus; capital surplus; earned surplus.

adj. Extra; unnecessary.

➤ *n.* balance, overage, overflow, plethora, residue, surfeit ("The grocery store has a surplus of meat products").

adj. superfluent, supernumery, extra, unused, excess, spare ("surplus material").

surplusage [*ser · plus · ej*] *n.* 1. Matter included in a **pleading** that is **irrelevant**, **immaterial**, or **redundant**. *See* motion to strike; strike. 2. Words in an **instrument** that are unnecessary and add nothing to its legal effect. 3. That which is extra; surplus.

➤ surplus, redundancy, irrelevance, immateriality, verbosity, extraneous material.

surprise [*ser · prize*] *n.* The unexpected; by unexpected means. 1. A **party** to a lawsuit who, unexpectedly and through no fault or neglect of his own, is taken unawares by an action of the opposite party may be entitled to a **new trial** if, without a new trial, he would be deprived of **substantial justice**. 2. A party may **impeach** her own witness with **prior inconsistent statements** if the witness's testimony takes her by surprise.

v. To astonish or amaze someone, especially with something unexpected.

➤ *n.* amazement, bewilderment, fortune, precipitance, wonder, marvel, awe.

v. amaze, astound, discomfit, discover, flabbergast, petrify, stagger ("to surprise someone").

surrebuttal [*ser · re · but · el*] *n.* Evidence offered in response to a defendant's **rebuttal**.

surrender [*ser · en · der*] *v.* To give up; to give back; to give back possession; to yield. *Compare* abandonment.

n. 1. The yielding of an **estate** to the person who owns the **reversionary interest** or the **remainder** (EXAMPLES: a **life estate**; an **estate for years**). 2. The **discharging** of liability on an instrument (EXAMPLES: a check; a **note**) by surrendering the instrument, i.e., by delivering it to its **maker** with the intention of releasing her from liability. 3. Giving oneself up. USAGE: "his surrender to the police."

➤ *v.* abandon, capitulate, give up, consign, knuckle under, relinquish, renounce ("to surrender the army").

n. abandonment, abdication, acquiescence, capitulation, sedition, relenting ("the army's surrender").

surrender value [*val · yoo*] *n.* Same as **cash surrender value**.

surreptitious [*sur · ep · tish · us*] *adj.* Secret; hidden; covert.

➤ secret, furtive, covert, stealthy, sly, clandestine, underhand.

surrogate [*ser · e · get*] *n.* 1. In some states, the title of a judge who presides in **probate court**. 2. A person who acts for another.

➤ alternate, substitute, agent, vicarious, actor, delegate, recourse, proxy, stand-in ("surrogate mother").

surrogate motherhood [*muth · er · hood*] *n.* The status of a woman who "hosts" the fertilized egg of another woman in her womb or who is artificially inseminated with the sperm of a man who is married to someone else and to whom (with his wife) she has agreed to assign her parental rights if the child is delivered. *See also* embryo transplantation; in vitro fertilization.

surrogate motherhood agreement [*muth · er · hood a · gree · ment*] *n. See* surrogate motherhood.

surrogate's court [*ser · e · gets*] *n.* In some states, the name of **probate court**.

surtax [*ser · taks*] *n.* An additional tax imposed on income or property that has already been taxed. *See* surcharge.

surveillance [*ser · vale · ense*] *n.* Observation, especially by the police, of persons suspected of criminal activities. However, surveillance may also be conducted by private detectives and others, and may include the observation of activities that are perfectly legal. Wiretapping is one form of surveillance. *Also see* eavesdropping.

➤ observation, bugging, control, direction, examination, scrutiny, supervision, vigil, eavesdropping, wiretapping.

survey [*ser · vay*] *n.* 1. The method by which the boundaries of land are determined. *See* government survey. 2. A map, **plat**, or other document reflecting a surveyor's determination of the boundary or boundaries of land. 3. An examination or inspection. 4. A poll; a study; a canvass. *v.* [ser · *vey*] 1. To determine the boundaries of land. 2. To examine or to look something over in detail.

➤ *n.* analysis, study, audit, outline, scan, review, précis, syllabus ("a survey of the history of western civilization").
v. appraise, assay, canvass, measure, prospect, reconnoiter, scrutinize, superintend ("to survey the land").

survival [ser · *vy* · vel] *n.* 1. Continuing in existence. 2. Staying alive.
➤ sustenance, staying, lasting, leftover, durability, vestige, relic.

survival action [*ak* · shen] *n.* With respect to a **personal injury**, a **right of action** that continues to exist after the death of the person who has been injured. *Compare* wrongful death statutes. *See* survival statutes.

survival statutes [*stat* · shoots] *n.* Statutes that provide for the survival of a **cause of action** even though the **party** who had the right to bring the action, or who brought it, has died. *Compare* survival action. *Also see* wrongful death statutes.

survive [ser · *vyve*] *v.* To continue in existence.
➤ last, live, hang on, endure.

surviving [ser · *vy* · ving] *adj.* Continuing in life; continuing in existence. *See* survival.

surviving spouse *n.* A widow or widower. Generally speaking, the surviving spouse has the option of taking under the will of his or her deceased spouse or of taking an **elective share**. *See* election by spouse; election under will.

survivor [ser · *vy* · ver] *n.* A person who outlives another person or lives beyond a designated date or a designated occurrence. *See* surviving spouse; survivorship. *See also* presumption of survivorship.
➤ widow, widower, orphan, descendant, heir, beneficiary.

survivorship [ser · *vy* · ver · ship] *n.* The fact of being a survivor, that is, of outliving another person or persons. *See* presumption of survivorship; right of survivorship.

survivorship annuity [a · *nyoo* · i · tee] *n.* An **annuity** for the joint lives of two persons, usually a husband and wife, and then for the life of the survivor.

suspect [*sus* · pekt] *adj.* Suspicious; under suspicion.
n. [*sus* · pekt] A person who is suspected of having committed a crime.
v. [sus · *pekt*] 1. To have a suspicion of someone's guilt. *Also see* reasonable suspicion. 2. To believe something, as opposed to being able to prove it.

➤ *adj.* doubtable, dubious, incredible, questionable, suspicious, unclear ("suspect origins").
n. accused, alleged criminal, defendant ("to interrogate the suspect").
v. distrust, conceive, disbelieve, mistrust, presume, speculate, surmise ("to suspect someone of murder").

suspect class *n.* *See* suspect classification.
suspect classification
[klas · i · fi · *kay* · shen] *n.* Legislation that grants or restricts rights or privileges on the basis of membership in a particular group, for EXAMPLE, race or religion. Such legislation frequently violates the **equal protection clause** of the **Fourteenth Amendment** and the **due process clause** of the **Fifth Amendment**.

suspend [sus · *pend*] *v.* 1. To interrupt; to temporarily adjourn or discontinue. USAGE: "The committee has suspended its deliberations until next week." 2. To temporarily remove from office or from employment. USAGE: "The mayor has the right to suspend the chief of police for **good cause**." 3. To temporarily withdraw a privilege. USAGE: "If I am arrested for speeding once more, the state will suspend my driver's license." *See* suspended; suspension.

➤ append, dangle, sling, swing, attach, hang down ("to suspend a banner from the ceiling"); adjourn, discontinue, intermit, put off, procrastinate, retard, postpone, eliminate ("The committee has suspended its deliberations"); withdraw, revoke ("suspend his license").

suspended [sus · *pen* · ded] *adj.* Temporarily inactive or temporarily not effective.
➤ tabled, discontinued, deferred, shelved, withheld, delayed, put off ("a suspended license").

suspended sentence [*sen* · tense] *n.* A **sentence** imposed after conviction of a crime, the carrying out of which is **stayed**. *See* split sentence.

suspense [sus · *pense*] *n.* A state of inactivity or uncertainty.
➤ anxiety, uncertainty, dilemma, expectation, impatience, perplexity, tension.

suspension [sus · *pen* · shen] *n.* 1. Temporary interruption, or discontinuance. 2. The temporary removal of an officeholder from office or an employee from employment. 3. The temporary withdrawal of a privilege, particularly a license. *See* suspend; suspended.
➤ delay, abeyance, adjournment, cessation, deferment, intermission, latency, interruption; removal, withdrawal.

suspicion [sus · *pish* · en] *n.* Surmising the existence of something without a factual basis. *See* reasonable suspicion.
➤ cynicism, incredulity, qualm, belief, surmise, wariness ("on suspicion of murder").

sustain [sus · *tane*] *v.* 1. To uphold. USAGE: "The court decided to sustain, rather than invalidate, the statute." "The court decided to sustain, rather than overrule, the objection of counsel." 2. To endure; to undergo.
➤ approve, bolster, continue, uphold, nourish, nurse, prolong ("sustain the lower court's ruling"); endure, abide, brook, digest, encounter, tolerate, undergo ("sustain one's faith through the experience").

swear *v.* 1. To administer an **oath**; to put a person **under oath**. 2. To take an oath; to put oneself under oath. 3. To curse; to take the name of God in vain. *Compare* affirm; affirmation. *See* false swearing.
➤ affirm, attest, vow, avow, depose, maintain, testify ("swear to tell the truth"); bedamn, blaspheme, curse, cuss, execrate, imprecate ("to swear out of anger").
swear in *v.* To administer the **oath of office** to a person appointed or elected to that office.

sweating [*swet* · ing] *n.* Another term for the **third degree**.

sweatshop [*swet* · shop] *n.* A shop or business establishment in which the labor laws are disregarded by the employer,

and the employees work long hours for extremely low wages.

sweetheart contract [*sweet* · hart] *n.* A **collective bargaining agreement** unscrupulously entered into between an employer and a union, which provides for substandard working conditions and wages well below the **prevailing rate**.

Swift v. Tyson [*tie* · son] *n.* An 1842 landmark decision of the Supreme Court (41 U.S. 1) which decided that, in **diversity of citizenship** cases, the federal courts have the right to apply the "general" law of commerce even if it is different from the law of the state and even if no **federal question** is presented.

swindle [*swin* · dul] *v.* To cheat or defraud someone intentionally.
➤ cheat, defraud, misrepresent, con, deceive, exploit.

swindling [*swin* · dling] *n.* Acquiring anything of value by means of deceit or **fraudulent misrepresentation**; cheating.

sworn *adj.* **Verified**; stated **under oath**. *See* swear.
➤ verified, stated under oath, certified ("a sworn statement").
sworn statement [*state* · ment] *n.* A declaration made or **testimony** given **under oath**; an **affidavit**. *Compare* unsworn statement.
sworn to *adj.* Refers to a statement made or declaration given **under oath**.

syllabus [*sil* · a · bus] *n.* 1. The **headnote** of a **reported case**. 2. A summary outline of a course of study.
➤ headnote, outline, brief, abstract, summary; course plan, lesson plan.

symbol [*sim* · bul] *n.* An indication or manifestation.
➤ mark, note, indication, trademark, emblem, manifestation, sign.

symbolic [sim · *bahl* · ik] *adj.* Representative.
➤ suggestive, illustrative, denotative, figurative, constructive ("That examination was symbolic of his approach to litigation").

symbolic delivery [sim · *bahl* · lik de · *liv* · e · ree] *n.* With respect to the transfer of **title** to property that cannot be physically delivered (EXAMPLES: land;

S

a building), or cannot readily be physically delivered (EXAMPLE: the contents of a warehouse), the **delivery**, instead, of a token representing the property (EXAMPLES: the delivery of a key to the building being sold or to the warehouse in whch the goods being sold are stored). *Compare* actual delivery; constructive delivery.

sympathy strike [*sim* · peth · ee] *n.* A strike in support of a strike against another employer. A sympathy strike is an EXAMPLE of **secondary activity**. *Also see* secondary boycott.

syndicalism [*sin* · dik · e · lizm] *n.* A doctrine that advocates **aiding and abetting** crime, sabotage, and terrorism as a means of causing a political change in which industry would no longer be privately owned but, instead, would be publicly owned. Syndicalism is sometimes referred to as **criminal syndicalism**.

syndicate [*sin* · dik · et] *n.* An association of individuals formed for the purpose of conducting and carrying out a business transaction, usually financial in nature, in which the members have a mutual interest.

v. [*sin* · di · kate] To form a **syndicate**; to engage in **syndication**.

➤ *n.* association, board, cartel, chamber, committee, conglomerate, organization.

syndication [sin · di · *kay* · shen] *n.* The act of forming a **syndicate**.

synopsis [sin · *op* · sis] *n.* A summary or outline.

➤ review, summation, brief, outline, summary, abstract ("just give me a synopsis, not the detailed story").

synthesize [*sin* · thih · size] *v.* To combine or incorporate.

➤ integrate, harmonize, coordinate, combine, unify, interrelate.

system [*sis* · tem] *n.* A method or procedure.

➤ program, strategy, technique, means, method, design, procedure ("to use a proven system").

systematic [sis · te · *mat* · ik] *adj.* Characterized by a deliberate, organized approach.

➤ regular, deliberate, organized, careful, precise, efficient ("to be systematic in one's thinking").

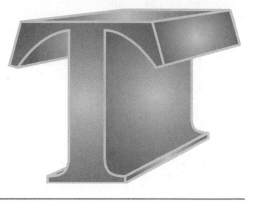

10-K *n.* The annual report that the **Securities and Exchange Commission** requires of **publicly held** corporations.

tabloid [*tab* · loyd] *n.* A newspaper.
➤ newspaper, journal, press ("I read it in the tabloid").

tacit [*tass* · it] *adj.* Silent; not expressed; implied.
➤ silent, implied, allusive, assumed, inarticulate, inferred, undeclared, unstated.
 tacit admission [ad · *mish* · en] *n.* An **admission** implied from a person's silence. With respect to *silence as assent, see* silence.

taciturn [*tass* · ih · turn] *adj.* Uncommunicative; quiet; reserved.
➤ reserved, untalkative, reticent, laconic, quiet, restrained, brusque.
 Ant. loud, talkative.

tacking [*takk* · ing] *n.* 1. With respect to acquiring **title** to real property by **adverse possession**, a doctrine that permits a person who is in possession of the property to add her period of possession to that of a prior adverse possessor in order to establish continuous possession for the period required by the applicable statute. 2. Adding the period of time that a plaintiff was under one **civil disability** (EXAMPLE: **infancy**) to a period of succeeding disability (EXAMPLE: **insanity**) for the purpose of determining whether the **statute of limitations** has run against his **cause of action**. 3. Joining **liens**. Under some circumstances, a creditor having two liens of different **priorities** may **join** them so as to gain priority over the intervening lien of a third person.

Taft-Hartley Act [-*hart* · lee] *n. See* National Labor Relations Act.

tail estate [es · *tate*] *n. See* fee tail.
 tail female [*fee* · male] *n. See* fee tail female.
 tail male *n. See* fee tail male.

taint *v.* To contaminate; to tarnish.
➤ poison, pollute, spoil, blemish, adulterate, befoul, pervert, tarnish, debase, defile.

take *v.* 1. To receive possession or to receive **title**. Thus, for EXAMPLE, a person who receives property either under a will or by **intestacy**, or by buying it, is said to "take" the property; similarly, the heirs of a **decedent** "take" *per stirpes* or *per capita*. 2. To acquire; to obtain; to receive; to attain; to claim. In this meaning, "take" may refer to obtaining things by either legal or illegal means. For EXAMPLE, to take illegally is to commit **larceny** or some other form of theft, while EXAMPLES of noncriminal applications of the word include "take a **default judgment**" (meaning "obtain a default judgment"), "take testimony" (meaning receive the testimony of witness), "take the stand" (meaning enter the witness stand), "take up" (meaning pay or discharge an obligation), and "take the Fifth" (meaning claim the protection of the **Fifth Amendment**). 3. To appropriate property for public use; to effect a **taking**. *See* taking. 4. To make happen. EXAMPLE: to "put into effect." *n.* The gain; the proceeds.
➤ *v.* abduct, arrest, attain, clutch, entrap, overtake, seize ("to take an item"); abduct, approach, annex, rob, confiscate, purloin, seize ("to take jewelry from a store");

T

accept, accommodate, bear, suffer, weather, undergo ("take the pain"); devour, feed, drink, inhale, ingest, eat ("take the medicine").
n. cut, gate, proceeds, receipts, revenue ("the take from the robbery").

take for public use [*pub* · lik] *v. See* take; taking.

take-home pay *n.* An employee's wages or salary, less deductions for withholding taxes, **FICA**, health insurance, and the like.

takeover [*take* · o · ver] *n.* The act of gaining control of something. In corporation law, the term relates to taking over the management of a company, usually by another company. Such a takeover may be either voluntary or involuntary. *See and compare* friendly takeover; hostile takeover.
➤ merger, consolidation, purchase, deal, buyout.

taking [*tay* · king] *n.* 1. The act of the government in appropriating private property for public use through the exercise of the power of **eminent domain**. Most commonly, a taking is associated with **condemnation**, the legal process by which government appropriates or takes title to property. However, governmental action less than outright physical appropriation which affects rights is also, in law, a taking. EXAMPLE: the sound of aircraft landing at and departing from a public airport which interferes with egg production at a nearby poultry farm. *See also* expropriation. 2. A **taking from the person**. *See* take. 3. In criminal law, laying hold of, seizing, or grasping. *See* larceny. 4. The act of obtaining anything.
➤ dispossession, seizure, appropriation.

taking by eminent domain [*em* · i · nent do · mane] *n. See* taking.

taking case from jury [*joor* · ee] *v.* Directing a verdict. *See* directed verdict.

taking for public use [*pub* · lik] *n. See* taking.

taking from the person [*per* · sen] *n.* An element of **larceny from the person**. *See* taking. *Also see* larceny.

talesman [*tailz* · man] *n.* A juror **summoned** from among bystanders in the courthouse.

tam (*Latin*) *See qui tam*; qui tam action.

tamper [*tam* · per] *v.* 1. To interfere with; to alter. 2. To bribe or fix; to engage in corrupt practices. *See* tampering.
➤ interfere, alter, diversify, interpose, interlope, manipulate; corrupt, fix, influence, lubricate, manipulate, rig.

tampering [*tam* · per · ing] *n.* Altering; meddling; making uninvited changes. The word does not necessarily imply criminal conduct. However, *tampering with evidence* (altering evidence), *tampering with a jury* (attempting to influence jurors other than through evidence admitted in a court of law), *tampering with a witness* (attempting to influence a witness's testimony), or *tampering with consumer products* (adulteration of food, medicine, etc.) are EXAMPLES of criminal tampering.
➤ altering, meddling, adulteration, interference.

tangible [*tan* · jibl] *adj.* Having physical or material substance; **corporeal**. *Compare* intangible.
➤ appreciable, corporeal, touchable, material, detectable, discernable, incarnate, manifest.

tangible asset [*ass* · et] *n.* **Tangible property** that has value. *Compare* intangible asset. *See* asset.

tangible property [*prop* · er · tee] *n.* Property, real or personal, that has physical substance; property that can be physically possessed. EXAMPLES: real estate; automobiles; jewelry. *Compare* intangible property.

tangible value [*val* · yoo] *n.* The worth of **tangible property**.

target [*tar* · get] *n.* 1. The object of an attack. EXAMPLE: an abused child is a *target of abuse*. 2. The goal or objective of an undertaking. EXAMPLES: a corporation that is the object of a **hostile takeover** is a *target company*; a person who is the subject of a criminal investigation is the *target of the investigation*.
➤ ambition, destination, function, intention, objective, goal, purpose ("deficit targets"); byword, game, prey, quarry, victim ("target of our jokes").

tariff [*tahr* · if] *n.* 1. A list published by the government setting forth the various amounts of **duty** it imposes on various articles of import or export. *See* protective

tariff. 2. The duties themselves. 3. The published list of the rates charged by **common carriers**, as approved by the **Interstate Commerce Commission** or a state's **public service commission**.
➤ assessment, tax, duty, fee, charge, excise, impost, rate, toll.

tariff preference [*pref* · rense] *n. See* preferential tariff.

tawdry [*taw* · dree] *adj.* Cheap; gaudy; vulgar.
➤ cheap, common, crass, crude, shoddy, shabby, sleazy, vulgar, gaudy, tacky, inelegant.

tax *n.* An involuntary charge imposed by government (whether national, state, or local, or any of their **political subdivisions**) upon individuals, corporations, or **trusts**, or their income or property, to provide revenue for the support of the government. Taxes may be imposed on, among other things, sales, gifts, and **estates**, and may be called, among other things, **imposts**, **duties**, **excises**, **levies**, and **assessments**. EXAMPLES of different types of taxes include: **ad valorem tax**, **capital gains tax**, **estate tax**, **excise tax**, **export tax**, **franchise tax**, **gift tax**, **income tax**, **inheritance taxes**, **intangibles tax**, **luxury tax**, **occupation tax**, **payroll tax**, **privilege tax**, **property tax**, **sales tax**, **school taxes**, and **transfer tax**. *See also* back taxes; capitation tax; death taxes; declaration of estimated tax; direct tax; equalization of taxes; graduated tax; indirect tax; investment tax credit; kiddie tax; local tax; personal income tax; poll tax; progressive tax; real estate tax; regressive tax; self-employment tax; surtax; withholding tax.
v. 1. To assess a tax. 2. To burden or weigh heavily on. 3. To accuse.
➤ *n.* levy, assessment, tribute, impost, exaction, imposition, capitulation, tithe ("a graduated tax").
v. assess, levy, exact, collect, require; burden, oppress, overload, deplete, enervate, wear down, encumber, weigh, task ("to tax my patience"); arraign, censure, criminate, impeach, impute, inculpate, reproach ("to tax one's credibility").

tax assessor [a · *sess* · er] *n. See* assessor.

tax audit [*aw* · dit] *n.* An examination by the IRS of a taxpayer's **books and records** to determine the accuracy of his income tax return. *See and compare* field audit; office audit.

tax avoidance [a · *void* · ense] *n.* A legal method of lessening one's tax burden, for EXAMPLE, by taking advantage of all legal deductions. *Compare* tax evasion.

tax benefit rule [*ben* · e · fit] *n.* The rule that the recovery by a taxpayer of any item deducted on her income tax return for a prior year is taxable in the year of recovery.

tax bracket [*brak* · et] *n.* A taxpayer's tax rate category. "Tax bracket" is synonymous with **tax rate**, and is based upon the amount of the taxpayer's **taxable income**.

tax certificate [ser · *tif* · i · ket] *n.* A **certificate** furnished to a person who buys property at a **tax sale**; it evidences his ownership of the property pending the expiration of the **redemption period**. *See* tax deed.

tax collector [ke · *lek* · ter] *n.* A public official appointed or elected to collect taxes. Generally speaking, the position of tax collector is **ministerial** in nature.

tax credit [*kred* · it] *n.* A **credit** that reduces the amount of income tax owed by a taxpayer, as opposed to a **deduction**, which merely reduces a taxpayer's **taxable income**. *Also see* exemption.

tax deduction [de · *duk* · shen] *n. See* deduction.

tax deed *n.* A **deed** evidencing the **conveyance** of **title** to land sold at a **tax sale** for the nonpayment of taxes. *See* tax certificate.

tax district [*dis* · trikt] *n.* A state, or an administrative district or **political subdivision** within a state (EXAMPLES: a county; a city; a town; a school district; a **sewer district**), upon whose inhabitants a particular tax is **levied** and collected. *See* district.

tax evasion [e · *vay* · zhen] *n.* **Willfully** avoiding payment of taxes legally due, for EXAMPLE, fraudulently concealing or understating one's income. Tax evasion is also referred to as **tax fraud**, and is a **felony**. *Compare* tax avoidance.

tax exemption [eg · *zemp* · shen] *n.* 1. Freedom from the obligation to pay taxes. 2. A **personal exemption** under the

T

Internal Revenue Code. *See* exemption. *Compare* tax deduction.

tax fraud *n.* The crime of **tax evasion**. Tax evasion which is intentional but not **willful** is **civil fraud**. *See* fraud.

tax lien [leen] *n.* A **statutory lien** that exists on the property of every taxpayer, allowing the property to be sold for the payment of taxes when payment is in default. *See* lien.

tax list *n.* Same as **tax rolls**.

tax rate *n.* The rate established by statute for the payment of a tax. Taxes may be computed on a **flat rate** or a **graduated** rate, among others. *See* tax bracket. *See and compare* graduated tax; progressive tax; regressive tax.

tax return [re · *tern*] *n.* 1. A formal accounting that every person who has income is required to make to the government every **tax year**; the form on which a taxpayer reports his **taxable income** annually and on the basis of which he pays his income tax. 2. Independent of income, any formal accounting required by law to be made to any taxing authority with respect to property, gifts, **estates**, sales, or the like. *See* return. *Also see* amended return; declaration of estimated tax; joint return.

tax rolls *n.* An official list of all property located within a **tax district**, with the **assessed value** and the name of the owner of each property.

tax sale *n.* A **judicial sale** of a delinquent taxpayer's property.

tax title [*ty* · tel] *n.* The **title** acquired by the purchaser at a **tax sale**. *See* tax certificate; tax deed.

tax year *n.* A taxpayer's 12-month accounting period; the period covered by her tax return. A taxpayer's tax year may be a calendar year or a **fiscal year**.

tax-exempt income [-eg · *zemt in* · kum] *n.* **Income** which is **exempt** from income tax; nontaxable income. EXAMPLE: interest on **municipal bonds** is exempt from federal income tax.

tax-exempt organization [-eg · *zemt* or · gan · i · *zay* · shen] *n.* An organization that, because of its religious, educational, or other charitable purpose, is exempt from taxation. EXAMPLES: a **charitable**

corporation; a **charitable trust**. *See* charitable organization.

Tax Court *n.* A federal court that hears and determines cases involving deficiencies or overpayments in income taxes, **estate taxes**, and **gift taxes** as determined by the IRS.

taxable [*tak* · sebl] *adj.* Subject to tax; liable to taxation.
➤ liable to taxation, assessible, chargeable, exactable ("a taxable gift").

taxable costs *n.* *See* taxation of costs.

taxable estate [es · *tate*] *n.* For purposes of **estate tax** or **inheritance tax**, the value of the **decedent's estate** less the deductions allowed by law; a decedent's **net estate**.

taxable gift *n.* *See* gift tax.

taxable income [*in* · kum] *n.* With respect to liability for federal income tax: in the case of an individual, **adjusted gross income**, less itemized deductions, or the **standard deduction** plus **personal exemptions**; in the case of a corporation, **gross income** less deductions.

taxable year *n.* *See* tax year.

taxation [tak · *say* · shen] *n.* The act or process of **levying, assessing**, and collecting taxes; the act of taxing. *See* tax. *Also see* double taxation.

taxation of costs *n.* A term referring to the process by which the **costs** of an **action** are determined and charged to the party against whom costs have been awarded by the court. *See* court costs.

taxing [*tak* · sing] *n.* The act or process of **levying, assessing**, and collecting a tax; taxation.
adj. Difficult or trying.
➤ *adj.* difficult, trying, effortful ("a taxing attempt to finish").

taxing district [*dis* · trikt] *n.* *See* tax district.

taxing power *n.* The power of government to **levy, assess**, and collect taxes.

taxpayer [*taks* · pay · er] *n.* A person who is under a legal obligation to pay a tax; a person who has paid a tax.
➤ individual, citizen, person.

taxpayer suit *n.* An **action** brought by a taxpayer to restrain the unlawful expenditure of **public funds**.

teacher [*tee* · cher] *n.* One who teaches or instructs.

➤ instructor, professor, educator, master, mentor, academician, guide.

technical [*tek* · nikl] *adj.* 1. Involved in detail or in **form** rather than in a principle or in **substance**. 2. Pertaining to a specific science, art, or profession.

➤ skilled, specialized, scientific, vocational, technological, particularized, esoteric, abstruse ("a technical field"); immaterial, clerical, insubstantial, without prejudice ("a technical error").

technical battery [*bat* · ter · ee] *n.* A physician whose treatment exceeds the scope of the patient's consent is guilty of a technical battery. *See* battery.

technical error [*ehr* · er] *n.* **Error** that is not **material**; error committed by the court in the course of a trial, but which is **without prejudice** to the **party** who complains of it; **harmless error**. *Compare* prejudicial error. *See* judicial error.

technicality [tek · nih · *kal* · ih · tee] *n.* A detail; an unimportant matter.

➤ detail, minor point, trifle, triviality, fine point ("overturned on a technicality").

teller [*tel* · er] *n.* 1. In a bank, a clerk who transacts business with customers, receiving, counting, and paying out money. 2. An election officer who counts votes. 3. One who tells a story.

➤ clerk, cashier, bank employee; narrator, raconteur, reporter, chronicler.

temporary [*tem* · pe · rer · ee] *adj.* Lasting only for a limited time. *Compare* permanent.

➤ fading, limited, provisional, momentary, evanescent, ephemeral, elusive, pro tempore.

temporary administrator [ad · *min* · is · tray · ter] *n.* An **administrator** of a **decedent's estate** who is appointed pending the appointment of a permanent administrator.

temporary alimony [*al* · i · moh · nee] *n.* Court-ordered **alimony** paid while a divorce action is pending. Temporary alimony is also referred to as **alimony pendente lite**. *Compare* permanent alimony.

temporary disability [dis · e · *bil* · i · tee] *n.* 1. A disability from which a person will recover. 2. With respect to **workers' compensation**, a condition that exists until the injured employee is as nearly restored as the permanent character of her injuries will permit. *Compare* permanent disability. *See* disability.

temporary employment [em · *ploy* · ment] *n.* Employment for a specific and limited period of time, as opposed to permanent employment or **employment at will**.

temporary injunction [in · *junk* · shen] *n.* A **preliminary injunction**. *Compare* permanent injunction; perpetual injunction. *See also* temporary restraining order.

temporary insanity [in · *san* · i · tee] *n.* A derangement of the mind that is of limited duration. *See* insanity.

temporary nuisance [*new* · sense] *n.* A **nuisance** that, by its nature, can be remedied.

temporary receiver [re · *seev* · er] *n.* A **receiver** who is appointed pending the appointment of a permanent receiver.

temporary relief [re · *leef*] *n.* **Relief** granted by a court that is designed to be effective for a limited period of time; the type of relief provided by a **preliminary injunction** or a **temporary restraining order**.

temporary restraining order (TRO) [re · *strane* · ing *or* · der] *n.* Under the **Federal Rules of Civil Procedure**, **injunctive relief** that the court is empowered to grant, without notice to the opposite **party** and pending a hearing on the merits, upon a showing that failure to do so will result in "immediate and irreparable injury, loss, or damage." **TROs** are similarly available under state **rules of civil procedure**.

tenancy [*ten* · en · see] *n.* 1. The right to **hold** and occupy realty or personalty by virtue of owning an **interest** in it. 2. Possession of realty under a lease; the relationship existing between a landlord or lessor and a tenant or lessee. *See* cotenancy; joint tenancy. 3. A term for the interest a tenant has under a lease.

➤ holding, leasing, occupancy, residence, rental.

T

tenancy at sufferance [*suf* · rense] *n.* The tenancy of a person who continues in possession after her **right of possession** has ended; the tenancy of a **holdover tenant**. *Compare* tenancy at will. *See* sufferance.

tenancy at will *n.* A tenancy that continues only as long as both parties wish it to, i.e., "at the will of" the parties. The duration of such a tenancy is uncertain and indefinite. *See* at will; will. *Compare* tenancy at sufferance.

tenancy by the entirety [en · *ty* · re · tee] *n.* A form of **joint tenancy** in an **estate in land** or in personal property that exists between husband and wife by virtue of the fact that they are husband and wife. As with a conventional joint tenancy, a tenancy by the entirety is a tenancy with **right of survivorship**. "Tenancy," in this context, means ownership of the jointly held **estate** or **interest**, whether, for EXAMPLE, it is a **fee simple estate**, a **life estate**, a savings account, or the like. *Compare* tenancy in common. *See* entirety. *Also see* estate by the entirety.

tenancy for life *n.* A **life estate**.

tenancy for years *n.* A tenancy under a lease or other contract for the period of a year or for a stated number of years.

tenancy from month to month *n.* 1. A tenancy in which no definite term is agreed upon and the rate is so much per month; i.e., a tenancy under a **month to month lease**. *See* month to month tenancy. 2. A **tenancy at will**. 3. The tenancy of a **holdover tenant**, i.e., a **tenancy at sufferance**. *Compare* tenancy from year to year.

tenancy from year to year *n.* A tenancy in which no definite term is agreed upon and the rate is so much per year. A tenancy from year to year may also be a **tenancy at sufferance** or a **tenancy at will**. *Compare* tenancy from month to month.

tenancy in common [*kahm* · en] *n.* A tenancy in which two or more persons own an **undivided interest** in an **estate in land**, for EXAMPLE, in a **fee simple estate** or a **life estate**, or in personal property, for EXAMPLE, in a savings account. As opposed to **joint tenants**, **tenants in common** have no **right of survivorship**; when a tenant in common dies, her interest passes to her heirs rather than to her cotenant or cotenants.

Also compare tenancy by the entirety. *See* in common.

tenant [*ten* · ent] *n.* 1. A person who **holds** or possesses realty or personalty by virtue of owning an **interest** in it. 2. A person who occupies realty under a lease with a landlord; a lessee. *See* tenancy.

➤ lessee, occupier, renter, boarder, leaseholder, inhabitant, roomer.

tenant at sufferance [*suf* · rense] *n.* *See* tenancy at sufferance.

tenant at will *n.* *See* tenancy at will.

tenant for life *n.* *See* life estate; life tenant.

tenant for years *n.* *See* tenancy for years.

tenant from month to month *n.* *See* tenancy from month to month. *Also see* month to month lease.

tenant from year to year *n.* *See* tenancy from year to year.

tenantable [*ten* · nen · tebl] *adj.* Premises that are **habitable**.

tenants by the entirety [en · *tire* · e · tee] *n.* *See* tenancy by the entirety.

tenants in common [*kahm* · en] *n.* Two or more owners of property under a **tenancy in common**.

tender [*ten* · der] *n.* 1. Money offered in payment of a debt or in satisfaction of an obligation. 2. Money or any other thing of value that is proffered for any reason. 3. Money; **legal tender**. 4. A **tender of performance**.
v. 1. To offer money in payment of a debt or in satisfaction of an obligation. 2. To proffer money or any other thing of value for any reason.
adj. 1. Affectionate; loving. 2. Fragile. 3. Painful and sore. 4. Young; inexperienced.

➤ *n.* payment, offer.
v. advance, offer, give, pay, submit.
adj. caring, affectionate, benevolent; delicate, fragile, weak, vulnerable; painful, sore, aching, inflamed; young, inexperienced, youthful, vernal.

tender of delivery [de · *liv* · e · ree] *n.* Under the **Uniform Commercial Code**, an **offer** coupled with a present ability to fulfill all the conditions of the contract, followed by actual performance if the other party shows that he is ready to proceed.

tender of performance [per · *form* · ense] *n.* An offer to **perform** a contract according to its terms, the effect of which is to place the other party in default if she unjustifiably refuses it. *See* performance.

tender offer [*off* · er] *n.* An attempt by a corporation to acquire a controlling interest in another corporation by offering to purchase a specified number of shares of its stock at a specified price per share.

tender years *n.* A term used to describe minors, particularly when they are very young. USAGE: "a child of tender years."

tenement [*ten* · e · ment] *n.* 1. An **interest** or **estate** in a **freehold** or in the **rents, issues, and profits** or other **incorporeal hereditaments** arising from a freehold. 2. Slum rental housing.
➤ slum housing, rental housing, apartment building, dwelling.

tenet [*ten* · et] *n.* A belief or principle.
➤ doctrine, belief, principle, creed, presumption, rule, canon, maxim, thesis.

tenor [*ten* · er] *n.* 1. In the language of law, the exact words or the very words. USAGE: the "tenor of a contract" or the "tenor of a deed" means the "terms of the contract" or the "terms of the deed." 2. In ordinary English, not just what is said, but what is meant by what is said; the general meaning; the purport. 3. A musical range between alto and bass.
➤ meaning, current, direction, terms, evolution, inclination, substance, purport, tendency ("the tenor of a note or deed").

tentative [*ten* · tuh · tiv] *adj.* 1. Indefinite; temporary. 2. Uncertain.
➤ provisional, conditional, negotiable, exploratory; cautious, doubtful, hesitant, wavering.

tentative trust [*ten* · tet · iv] *n.* *See* Totten trust.

Tenth Amendment [a · *mend* · ment] *n.* An amendment to the Constitution which provides that the powers not delegated to the federal government by the Constitution are reserved to the states or to the people.

tenure [*ten* · yer] *n.* 1. Under medieval English **common law**, the system under which lands or **tenements** were **held**. 2. The act of **holding** or possessing something.

Thus, for EXAMPLE, the term during which a public official holds office is her *tenure of office* and a university professor who is given a permanent appointment to the faculty is *tenured faculty*.
➤ administration, term, incumbency, occupancy, proprietorship, residence.

term *n.* 1. A portion of an agreement relating to a particular matter, for EXAMPLE, price, quantity, or delivery date. *See* terms. 2. An expression or word, especially one that has a particular meaning in a particular science or profession, i.e., a **term of art**. 3. A period of time; the duration of something. *See* term of lease; term of office. 4. The period during which a court sits, i.e., a **term of court**. 5. The period during which an **estate** (EXAMPLES: a **life estate**; an **estate for years**) is to be **held**.
➤ interval, tenure, session, incumbency, semester, cycle ("the president's term in office"); appellation, article, caption, nomenclature, terminology, vocable ("term of art"); limit, boundary, culmination, fruition, limitation, confine.

term annuity [a · *new* · i · tee] *n.* *See* annuity.

term bonds *n.* **Bonds** issued at one time, all of which fall due at one time. *Compare* serial bonds; series bonds.

term for years *n.* An **estate** that terminates after a specified number of years; an **estate for years**.

term insurance [in · *shoor* · ense] *n.* *See* term life insurance.

term life *n.* *See* term life insurance.

term life insurance [in · *shoor* · ense] *n.* **Life insurance** that provides protection only for a stated number of years and has no **cash surrender value**. *Compare* ordinary life insurance; straight life insurance; whole life insurance. *See* decreasing term insurance.

term loan *n.* As opposed to a **demand loan**, a loan with a specified due date.

term of art *n.* Technical words; words or expressions that have a particular meaning in a particular science or profession.

term of court *n.* The entire period during which a court sits to conduct its business during a particular year. *Compare* session. *See* general term; regular term; special term.

T

T

term of lease *n.* The period during which a **lease** is in effect.

term of office [*off* · iss] *n.* A fixed period of time during which an office-holder is entitled by law to hold a given office. *See* tenure.

term of years *n.* A period of years. USAGE: "The court sentences you to serve a term of 10 years' confinement in prison."

term policy [*pahl* · li · see] *n. See* term insurance.

terminable [*term* · in · ebl] *adj.* That which may be terminated; that which is subject to termination.
➤ defeasible, limitable, finite, conditional ("a terminable interest").

terminable interest [*in* · trest] *n.* An **interest** in property that ends with the death of the person who holds the interest or upon the happening of some named event.

termination [term · i · *nay* · shen] *n.* 1. An end of something in time. 2. The act of bringing an end to something. USAGE: "The termination of a contract or a lease is very different from its **expiration**." *Also see* cancellation. 3. The ending of an employment relationship. Although, strictly speaking, an employee may terminate her employment by resigning, the word "termination" usually refers to the dismissal of the employee by the employer.
➤ abortion, ending, consequence, cessation, desistance, finale, outcome, terminus, cancellation.

terminus [*ter* · me · nus] *n.* 1. A boundary; a limit; an ending point. 2. The point at which a railroad line or bus line ends.
➤ boundary, limit, ending point.

terms *n. Plural* of **term.** "Terms" or **"terms and conditions,"** as applied to an agreement or other legal relationships, may mean specific conditions (EXAMPLES: price; quantity; delivery date) or more generic rights existing under the agreement or in the relationship (EXAMPLES: the right to **rescind**; the right to **subrogate**). USAGE: "the terms of the contract"; "the **terms of the trust.**"
➤ conditions, provisions, details ("terms of the deed").

terms and conditions [kun · *dish* · enz] *n. See* terms.

terms of the trust *n. See* terms.

territorial [tehr · i · *tore* · ee · el] *adj.* 1. Pertaining to territory; based upon territory. EXAMPLE: **territorial jurisdiction**. 2. Pertaining or belonging to a **territory** of the United States, for EXAMPLE, Guam or the Virgin Islands.

territorial jurisdiction [joor · is · *dik* · shen] *n.* 1. The limits of the geographical boundaries over which a government has **jurisdiction**. 2. The limits of the geographical boundaries of a district within which a judge has jurisdiction. *See* judicial districts.

territorial limits [*lim* · its] *n. See* territorial jurisdiction.

territorial waters [*waw* · terz] *n.* Waters that fall under the **sovereignty** of a nation either because they are **inland waters** of the nation or because they are its **coastal waters**. *See* twelve-mile limit.

territory [*tehr* · i · tore · ee] *n.* 1. A geographical region or area over which a nation exercises **sovereignty** but whose inhabitants do not enjoy political, social, or legal parity with the inhabitants of other regions or areas that are **constitutional** components of the nation. With respect to the United States, for EXAMPLE, Guam or the Virgin Islands as opposed to New York, California, or Texas. *Also see* commonwealth. 2. Any geographical area. EXAMPLE: a salesperson's territory.
➤ area, boundary, nation, commonwealth, mandate, neighborhood, province, sector, enclave.

terrorism [*tare* · or · iz · em] *n.* The process of using fear or violence to achieve the goals of an individual, group, or government.
➤ coercion, duress, cruelty, inhumanity.

terroristic threats [tare · or · *iss* · tik] *n.* The crime of threatening to commit a crime of violence in order to frighten or intimidate someone, or in order to cause serious public inconvenience (EXAMPLES: causing the evacuation of a building or a subway). *See* intimidation; threat.

test *n.* 1. A standard or means used for determining or assessing something.

EXAMPLES: an **evidential breath test**; the **minimum contacts test**; a **means test**. 2. An examination.

v. To give or make a test or examination. *See* test (*noun*).

➤ *n.* examination, assessment, confirmation, elimination, evaluation, check, inspection, trial, investigation.

v. examine, analyze, experiment, investigate, evaluate, question, appraise, inquire ("to test one's knowledge").

test case *n.* An **action** brought for the purpose of establishing the law on an important point. A test case is not a **moot case**.

test oath *n.* A **loyalty oath**.

testacy [*tes* · te · see] *n.* The status of the **estate** or property of a person who dies without leaving a valid will. *Compare* intestacy. *See* testate.

testament [*tes* · te · ment] *n.* 1. A will. The terms "testament," "**will**," "**last will**," and "**last will and testament**" are synonymous. 2. A declaration of faith, belief, or principle.

➤ attestation, colloquy, covenant, demonstration, statement, exemplification, testimonial, will, last will.

testamentary [tes · te · *men* · ter · ee] *adj.* Pertaining to a will; pertaining to a **testament**. *See* letters testamentary.

testamentary capacity [ke · *pass* · i · tee] *n.* The mental capacity of a **testator**, at the time of making her will, to be able to understand the nature of her act and, generally if not precisely, the nature and location of her property and the identity of those persons who are the natural objects of her bounty. *See* capacity. *See also* natural objects of bounty; sound and disposing mind and memory.

testamentary class *n.* Persons included under a general description in a will, who bear a certain relationship to the **testator** and have a common relationship with each other. EXAMPLES: "my nephews and nieces"; "my college classmates who survive me." *See* class.

testamentary disposition [dis · pe · *zish* · en] *n.* The **disposition** of property by deed, will, gift, or otherwise, in such a manner that it does not take effect

until the **grantor** dies. *See* testamentary instrument.

testamentary gift *n.* 1. A **gift** that is the subject of a **testamentary disposition**. 2. A generic term for a **legacy**, **bequest**, or **devise**.

testamentary instrument [*in* · stroo · ment] *n.* An **instrument** whose language clearly indicates that its author intended to make a **disposition** of his property, or some of his property, to be effective upon his death. A will is an EXAMPLE of a testamentary instrument.

testamentary intent [in · *tent*] *n.* For a court to admit a will to **probate**, it must determine that the **testator** intended the instrument to be her **last will**.

testamentary power of appointment [*pow* · er of a · *point* · ment] *n.* A **power of appointment** that the **donee** has the power to exercise only upon his death through his will.

testamentary trust *n.* A **trust** created by will. *Compare* inter vivos trust.

testate [*tes* · tate] *adj.* Pertaining to a person, or to the property of a person, who dies leaving a valid will. *Compare* intestate. *See* testacy.

n. 1. A person who dies leaving a valid will. 2. The status of a person who dies leaving a valid will. *Compare* intestate.

testate estate [es · *tate*] *n.* The **estate** of a person who dies leaving a valid will.

testate succession [suk · *sesh* · en] *n.* Taking property under a will rather than by inheritance. *Compare* intestate succession. *See* succession.

testator [*tes* · tay · ter] *n.* A person who dies leaving a valid will.

testify [*tes* · ti · fy] *v.* To give testimony **under oath** or **affirmation** as a witness in a **proceeding**.

➤ affirm, announce, corroborate, depose, evince, swear, warrant, declare, attest.

testimonium clause [tes · ti · *moh* · nee · um] *n.* A clause at the end of a deed, which recites that the parties have "set their hands and seals" to the deed on the date specified. *See* attestation clause.

testimony [*tes* · ti · moh · nee] *n.* The words of a witness given **under oath** or

affirmation in a **proceeding**. See expert testimony; negative testimony.

➤ affidavit, attestation, corroboration, demonstration, evidence, substantiation, assertion, deposition.

THC *n.* Abbreviation of tetrahydrocannabinol; a hallucinogenic derivative of marijuana that produces a feeling of euphoria in humans. Temporary **psychosis** is a frequent side effect. THC is a **controlled substance**; its possession, distribution, or sale is a criminal offense. The presence of THC in the blood or urine is detectable by **radioimmunoassay**. *See* hallucinogen.

theft *n.* 1. **Larceny.** 2. In a broader sense, taking something to which one is not entitled, whatever the means (for EXAMPLE, whether by **embezzlement**, **extortion**, **fraud**, or outright **robbery**); stealing. *See* steal. *Also see* auto theft.

➤ stealing, annexation, deprivation, embezzlement, peculation, pilferage, purloining, rapacity, larceny, seizure.

theft by deception [de · sep · shen] *n.* The crime of obtaining money or other property by deceit or **fraudulent misrepresentation**.

theft insurance [in · shoor · ense] *n.* Insurance against **risk of loss** by theft.

theocracy [thee · ahk · re · see] *n.* A government that recognizes God as its ruler.

theory [theer · ee] *n.* A set of propositions that explain an event or an occurrence.

➤ hypothesis, approach, assumption, codification, guesswork, philosophy, postulate, principle, idea.

theory of the case *n.* The principle on which a **cause of action** is based; the theory that translates the facts in a case into legal concepts.

thereafter [thair · af · ter] *adv.* After a specified event.

➤ afterward, thereby, somewhat, generally, nigh, roughly.

thereby [thair · by] *adv.* By reason of; by virtue of; because of.

➤ by reason of, by virtue of, because of.

therefor [thair · for] *adv.* For it; for them. *Note* that "therefor" is not "**therefore**."

therefore [thair · for] *adv.* Consequently; accordingly; wherefore. *Note* that "therefore" is not "**therefor**."

therein [thair · in] *adv.* In that place.

thereupon [thair · e · pawn] *adv.* Without delay or lapse of time.

these presents [prez · ents] *n.* Formal words for "this **instrument**." *See* presents.

thief *n.* A person who commits theft.

➤ pirate, robber, embezzler, defrauder, pilferer, purloiner, kleptomaniac, criminal, peculator, outlaw, lawbreaker.

thing *n.* 1. That which is felt or experienced. 2. An act or deed. 3. A fixation; an obsession. *Singular* of **things**. *See* things.

➤ apparatus, commodity, corporeality, instrument, phenomenon, substance ("What is that thing?"); accomplishment, deed, episode, obligation, occasion, phenomenon, proceeding ("to do the thing"); attitude, craze, fad, fetish, fixation, crush, mania ("to have a thing for someone").

things *n.* 1. **Corporeal**, **tangible**, or inanimate objects that are or may be the subject of property rights. EXAMPLES: realty (**things real**); personalty (**things personal**). 2. **Incorporeal** or **intangible** property in which one has or may have an **incorporeal right**. EXAMPLE: **things in action**. 3. Subjects of abstract thought or imagination. USAGE: "things of wonder."

things in action [ak · shen] *n.* Same as **choses in action**.

things of value [val · yoo] *n.* Things having a monetary value. With respect to the law of **larceny**, any **tangible** things which the law recognizes as being property. With respect to gambling, any things that entice a person to gamble.

things personal [per · sen · el] *n.* Goods, money, and all other **movables**.

things real *n.* **Immovables**, i.e., land, **hereditaments**, and **tenements**.

third *adj.* 1. In the language of the law, a reference to the one-third portion of the **estate** of a deceased spouse to which the surviving spouse is entitled by **operation of law**. *See* elective share. *Also see* dower. 2. In the language of the law, a reference to a party or person who is a **stranger** to a transaction. *See* third party; third person. 3. That which comes between second and fourth in priority. EXAMPLE: a **third mortgage**.

third degree [de · *gree*] *n.* The practice of conducting a police interrogation of a suspect in an abusive manner designed to coerce information, a procedure prohibited by the **Miranda rule**. *See* sweating.
➤ interrogation, examination, inquiry, inquest, prolonged questioning.

third mortgage [*more* · gej] *n.* A **mortgage** that is junior in **priority** to both a **first mortgage** and a **second mortgage**.

third party [*par* · tee] *n.* 1. A person who is not a **party** to an agreement, **instrument**, or transaction, but who may have an **interest** in the transaction. *See* interested person. *Compare* stranger. 2. A person or **party**, other than the original plaintiff or defendant, who is brought into an **action**. *See* third-party action; third-party practice. *Also see* real party in interest; third person.

third person [*per* · sen] *n.* As the term is used in the law, either a person who has an **interest** in a transaction or an **action** (i.e., a **party** or a **third party**), or, simply, an uninvolved person (i.e., a bystander). *See and compare* interested person; real party in interest; stranger.

third-party action [*-par* · tee *ak* · shen] *n.* An **action** by which a defendant in a lawsuit brings into the lawsuit a **third person**, alleging that she is liable to him with respect to the **cause of action** the plaintiff has asserted against him.

third-party beneficiary [*-par* · tee ben · e · *fish* · er · ee] *n.* The intended **beneficiary** of a contract made between two other persons. As opposed to an **incidental beneficiary**, a third-party beneficiary may sue to enforce such a contract. *See* third-party beneficiary contract.

third-party beneficiary contract [*-par* · tee ben · e · *fish* · er · ee kon · trakt] *n.* A **contract** made for the benefit of a third person. *See* third-party beneficiary.

third-party check [*-par* · tee] *n.* A **check** that the **payee** has **indorsed** to a **third person**.

third-party claim [*-par* · tee] *n.* 1. A **claim** to property held under an

attachment as the property of the defendant in a lawsuit, made by a person who is not a **party** to the **action**. 2. A claim set forth in a **third-party complaint**.

third-party complaint [*-par* · tee kum · *plaint*] *n.* A **complaint** filed by the defendant in a lawsuit against a **third person** whom he seeks to bring into the **action** because of that person's alleged liability to the defendant. *See* third-party action.

third-party practice [*-par* · tee prak · tiss] *n.* The process and procedure by which a defendant in a lawsuit brings into the lawsuit a **third person**, alleging that she is liable to him with respect to the **cause of action** the plaintiff has asserted against him. *See* practice.

Third Amendment [therd a · *mend* · ment] *n.* An amendment to the Constitution forbidding the **quartering** of soldiers in any house in peacetime without the consent of the owner, and during time of war only in the manner prescribed by law.

Thirteenth Amendment [ther · *teenth* a · *mend* · ment] *n.* The amendment to the Constitution that abolished slavery and **involuntary servitude**.

threat *n.* Words or conduct intended to intimidate; a means of duress. A "threat" is a declaration of intention to **injure** a person by committing an unlawful act, whereas **intimidation** is the act of making a person fearful by such a declaration. *See* terroristic threat.
➤ warning, rattling, intimidation, imminence, fulmination, impendence, menace, blackmail, omen.

threat by mail *n.* The federal offense of using the mails to transmit threatening matter.

three-judge court *n.* Federal statutes require a **panel** of three judges to hear and determine certain types of cases, for EXAMPLE, certain **actions** arising under several of the **Civil Rights Acts**.

three-mile limit [*-lim* · it] *n. See* twelve-mile limit.

thrift institution [in · sti · *too* · shen] *n.* Also simply called a "thrift"; a **savings and loan association** or a **building and loan association**.

T

through *adv./adj./prep.* A word whose exact meaning depends upon the context in which it is used. Its several meanings include "from end to end," "by way of," "by means of," and "because of."
➤ *adv.* complete, concluded, over, terminated, done ("to be through with something"). *adj.* constant, nonstop, opened, rapid, regular, unbroken ("through street"). *prep.* by the agency of, via, on account of, as a consequence of, in the name of, as the agent of ("through the power invested in me"); about, clear, in and out, into, throughout, past, around, straight ("through the door").

through bill of lading [*lay* · ding] *n.* A **bill of lading** used when goods are transported by several connecting **carriers**.

through rate *n.* The total rate for a shipment of goods that involves several connecting **carriers**.

thwart *v.* To stifle; to inhibit.
➤ defeat, stifle, stop, impede, interrupt, obstruct, avert.

ticket [*tik* · et] *n.* 1. A document evidencing a right under a contract. EXAMPLES: a theater ticket (a right to attend); a railroad ticket (a right to ride). 2. With respect to an election, the list of candidates of a particular political party. 3. A traffic citation.
➤ admission, badge, board, card, pass, credential, document, license, receipt.

tidal waters [*ty* · del *waw* · terz] *n.* Waters in which the tide ebbs and flows; waters that rise and fall with the tides of the sea. *See* tide.

tide *n.* The twice-daily rising and falling of the ocean due to the gravitational influence of the moon and sun. *See* high tide; low tide; mean high tide; mean low tide.
➤ course, direction, ebb, flow, flux, torrent, vortex, wave.

tidelands [*tide* · landz] *n.* Land that lies between the lines of the **mean high tide** and the **mean low tide**; land that is alternately covered and uncovered by the rise and fall of the tide.

timber lease [*tim* · ber] *n.* A contract that grants the right to harvest lumber and to remove it from the premises.

timber rights [*tim* · ber] *n.* A *profit à prendre* to harvest lumber and to remove it from the premises.

time *n.* 1. The period that exists between events. *See* enlargement of time; reasonable time. 2. The point at which something is to take place, takes place, or took place. 3. A period in history.
➤ age, allotment, day, duration, interval, juncture, tempo ("time of day"); break, chance, occasion, peak, shot, show ("Now is the time").

time bill *n.* Same as **time draft**.

time certificate [ser · *tif* · i · ket] *n.* *See* certificate.

time deposit [de · *pah* · zit] *n.* A bank deposit that must remain **on deposit** for a stated period of time, and can only be withdrawn before that time by paying a penalty. EXAMPLE: a **certificate of deposit**. *Compare* demand deposit. *See* deposit.

time draft *n.* A **draft** payable at a fixed or determinable future time.

time immemorial [im · mem · *or* · ee · el] *n.* A time **beyond legal memory**. *See* legal memory. *Also see* immemorial.

time is of the essence [*ess* · ense] *n.* Phrase in a contract clause providing that performance (EXAMPLE: delivery of the goods) by or within the time specified is essential and that failure to do so is a **breach of contract**. *See* essence.

time note *n.* A **note** payable at a fixed or determinable future time. *Compare* demand note.

time of legal memory [*leeg* · el *mem* · e · ree] *n.* *See* legal memory.

time paper [*pay* · per] *n.* **Commercial paper** payable at a time stated in the instrument or at a determinable future time. EXAMPLES: a **time draft**; a **time note**. *Compare* demand paper.

time-price *n.* A term referrring to the difference in price that may legally be charged for an item purchased for cash and the same item purchased on credit. The cost of credit is always higher.

timely [*time* · lee] *adj.* Within the time required by contract or prescribed by statute and, in the absence of a stated time, within a **reasonable time**.

➤ appropriate, auspicious, convenient, opportune, propitious, toward ("timely request"). *Ant.* late, inappropriate.

timeshare [*time* · share] *n.* The ownership or rental of property, often a **condominium** and usually for vacation purposes, on a joint basis with others, allowing each of the participants to occupy the premises separately on a rotating basis for a limited period of time (a month, for EXAMPLE).

tipstaff [*tip* · staf] *n.* A **bailiff**.

title [*ty* · tel] *n.* 1. The rights of an owner with respect to property, real or personal, i.e., **possession** and the **right of possession**. *See* abstract of title; action to quiet title; chain of title; clear title; cloud on the title; covenants for title; cover of title; defective title; equitable title; examination of title; good title; legal title; marketable title; merchantable title; muniment of title; paper title; paramount title; perfect title; quieting title; record title; root of title; tax title; Torrens title system; unity of title; unmarketable title; warranty of title; worthier title doctrine. 2. A document that evidences the rights of an owner; i.e., ownership rights. EXAMPLES: in the case of real property, a deed; in the case of personal property, a **bill of sale**. *See* certificate of title; document of title. 3. The name by which something is known or called. EXAMPLES: a **trademark**; a **service mark**; the **title of an action**; the **title of a statute**; the title of a book or a movie. *See* caption; mark. 4. The status, rank, position, or office by which a person is known. EXAMPLES: "mayor"; "admiral"; "princess"; "professor"; "doctor." 5. A subdivision or section of a statute or **code** similar to a **chapter**.
v. To label or name something.
➤ *n.* appellation, banner, caption, headline, description, rubric ("title of a book"); brand, cognomen, epithet, decoration, honorific, pseudonym ("title of honor"); authority, claim, commission, holding, entitlement ("clear title to the land").
v. baptize, christen, denominate, designate, dub, entitle, label, style, term ("to title the book").

title by accession [ak · *sesh* · en] *n. See* accession.

title by adverse possession [*ad* · verse po · *zesh* · en] *n. See* adverse possession.

title by descent [de · *sent*] *n.* Title acquired by will or by **intestate succession**. *See* descent.

title by prescription [pre · *skrip* · shen] *n. See* prescription. *Also see* adverse possession.

title company [*kum* · pen · ee] *n.* A company that conducts **title searches** and sells **title insurance**. For all practical purposes, a title company is the same as a **title guaranty company**.

title covenants [*kov* · e · nents] *n.* **Covenants** normally inserted in **conveyances** to protect the purchaser against receiving from the seller title that is inadequate or insufficient. EXAMPLES: a **covenant for further assurance**; a **covenant for quiet enjoyment**; a **covenant of warranty**; a **covenant of seisin**.

title deed *n.* A **deed** that conveys **legal title**.

title document [*dok* · yoo · ment] *n. See* document of title.

title guaranty company [*gehr* · en · tee *kum* · pen · ee] *n.* A company that conducts **title searches** and insures or guarantees titles to real estate. For all practical purposes, a title guaranty company is the same as a **title company**. *See* title insurance.

title insurance [in · *shoor* · ense] *n.* An insurance policy in which the **insurer** agrees to **indemnify** the purchaser of realty, or the **mortgagee**, against **loss** due to **defective title**.

title of a statute [*stat* · shoot] *n.* The heading of a statute, setting forth the name by which it is to be known as well as the subject to which it relates.

title of an action [*ak* · shen] *n.* The name or **style** of a case; the way in which a given case or **action** is captioned. EXAMPLE: *Smith v. Jones. See* caption.

title of record [*rek* · erd] *n. See* record title.

title opinion [o · *pin* · yen] *n.* A **legal opinion** with respect to the condition or status of title to real estate. It is required by a **title company** in order to issue **title insurance**.

title registration [rej · is · *tray* · shen] *n. See* Torrens title system.

title search *n.* An examination of all documents **of record** relating to the status or condition of the title to a given piece of real estate (including deeds reflecting past ownership and outstanding mortgages and other **liens**) in order to verify title.

title state *n. See* mortgage.

title theory state [*theer* · ee] *n. See* mortgage.

Title VII [*ty* · tel *sev* · en] *n.* The section of the **Civil Rights Act of 1964** dealing with discrimination in employment. *See* Civil Rights Acts.

TM *n.* 1. Abbreviation of **trademark**. 2. Abbreviation of Transcendental Meditation.

to *prep.* 1. Until. Although "to" is generally defined as a word of exclusion, it has been held to be a word of inclusion when that is the intention of the parties or the **legislative intent**. Thus, for EXAMPLE, "January 1 to January 10" is generally construed to mean "January 1 *until* January 10," unless the clear indication is that "January 1 *through* January 10" is what was meant. 2. Toward. 3. Into.

to have and to hold *See* habendum clause.

to indemnify and save harmless [in · *dem* · ni · fy and save *harm* · less] *See* hold harmless clause.

to wit That is to say; namely.

token [*toh* · ken] *n.* 1. A coin-like piece of metal or plastic, purchased with money and used in place of money for bus fare, subway fare, arcade game machines, etc. 2. A symbol or demonstration of intention or good faith. 3. A symbol; a **mark**. EXAMPLE: **earnest money**.

➤ badge, clue, symbol, mark, indicia, keepsake, manifestation, memento, sample.

tolerance [*tol* · er · ents] *n.* Patience; understanding; broad-mindedness.

➤ patience, compassion, understanding, abiding, endurance, capacity, freedom from prejudice, ability to withstand, fortitude, liberalism, sensitivity.

tolerate [*tol* · er · ayt] *v.* To allow; to put up with.

➤ accept, endure, forbear, allow, abide, suffer, submit to, stand, indulge ("to tolerate difficult circumstances").

toll *n.* A charge for the use of something, generally a public facility, for EXAMPLE, a turnpike, a bridge, or telephone service. *v.* 1. To interrupt or suspend. *See* tolling the statute. 2. To sound a bell.

➤ *n.* assessment, charge, customs, duty, exaction, impost, levy ("pay the toll"); casualties, cost, expense, inroad, losses, penalty ("the hurricane's death toll"). *v.* announce, ring, chime, knell, peal, signal ("Toll the good news"); interrupt, suspend ("Toll the statute of limitations").

tolling the statute [*toh* · ling the *stat* · shoot] *n.* A term referring to circumstances that, by **operation of law**, suspend or interrupt the running of the **statute of limitations**; for EXAMPLE, the period of time during which an accused has fled the jurisdiction to avoid prosecution (*see* flight to avoid prosecution) or the period during which a plaintiff is under a **civil disability**.

tonnage [*tun* · ej] *n.* 1. The capacity of a cargo ship, calculated in tons. 2. **Tonnage duty**.

tonnage duty [*dew* · tee] A tax levied on a ship, based upon its tonnage.

tonnage tax Same as **tonnage duty**.

tontine insurance [tahn · *teen* in · *shoor* · ense] *n.* An arrangement in which equal sums of money are contributed by a number of persons to a "pot" or "kitty," and the total sum is awarded to the participant who outlives the others.

tontine policy [tahn · *teen pah* · li · see] *n.* A **life insurance** arrangement in which a number of persons contribute to a common fund and, at the end of a specified period, those who are still alive and who have kept their policies in force share in the **benefit**.

Torrens title system [*tore* · enz *ty* · tel *sis* · tem] *n.* A system for the **registration of titles** to land, which exists in several states. Under the Torrens system, a **title search** is rendered unnecessary as a means of verifying title because the name of the owner of the land appears on a **certificate of title** that is **conclusive evidence** of ownership.

tort *n.* A **wrong** involving a **breach of duty** and resulting in an **injury** to the person or property of another. A tort is distinguished

from a **breach of contract** in that a tort is a violation of a **duty** established by law, whereas a breach of contract results from a failure to meet an obligation created by the agreement of the parties. Although the same act may be both a crime and a tort, the crime is an offense against the public which is prosecuted by the state in a **criminal action**; the tort is a **private wrong** that must be pursued by the injured party in a **civil action**. *See* Federal Tort Claims Act; intentional tort; maritime tort; joint tort; joint tortfeasors, personal tort.
➤ wrong, civil wrong, violation, breach of duty.

tortfeasor [*tort* · fee · zer] *n.* A person who commits a **tort**. *See* joint tortfeasors.
➤ wrongdoer, defendant.

tortious [*tore* · shus] *adj.* 1. Involving a **tort**; wrongful. 2. Pertaining to a tort.
tortious interference with contract [in · ter · *feer* · ense with *kon* · trakt] *n.* *See* malicious interference with contract.

torture [*tore* · cher] *n.* The infliction of severe pain as a means of coercing a confession, extracting information, or breaking a person's spirit. Torture is also engaged in as a form of sadism.
v. To inflict pain in order to gain information.
➤ *n.* agony, distress, dolor, excruciation, impalement, martyrdom.
v. hurt, maim, agonize, excruciate, inflict pain, punish.

total [*toh* · tel] *n./adj.* Comprising the whole of a thing; the entire quantity or amount; complete; utter.
v. To add together; to calculate.
➤ *n.* aggregate, all, budget, entirety, gross, quantum, sum ("the sum total").
adj. absolute, comprehensive, consummate, integral, plenary, totalitarian ("the total amount").
v. add, calculate, comprise, number, reckon, summate, totalize, tote ("total the invoice").
total disability [dis · e · bil · i · tee] *n.* A **disability** that renders a person substantially unable to perform his normal work or substantially destroys his earning capacity. The fact that the person may be able to perform light work does not prevent a **finding** of total disability. *Compare*

partial disability. *See* permanent disability; temporary disability.

total loss *n.* As the term is used in fire insurance, the complete destruction of the insured property by fire so that nothing of value remains of it, as distinguished from a **partial loss**. *See* actual loss; casualty loss; loss.

totalitarianism [to · tal · i · *tair* · ee · en · izm] *n.* A political system in which the ruling group maintains absolute control of the government and suppresses all dissent or opposition.
➤ oppression, coercion, tyranny, control.

Totten trust [*tot* · en] *n.* A **trust** created by a bank deposit which a person makes with his money in his own name as **trustee** for another person. Such a trust is also called a **tentative trust** because it is revocable **at will** until the depositor dies or completes the gift in his lifetime by some unequivocal act or declaration (EXAMPLE: delivery of the **passbook** to the **beneficiary**). *See* revocable trust.

town *n.* 1. In legal terms, a word whose meaning varies from state to state. In general terms, a town is a form of **municipal corporation** that is smaller than a city and larger than a village. In some parts of the country, however, a town is synonymous with a **township** and is a **political subdivision** of a county. In others (the New England states, for EXAMPLE), it is itself the primary governmental unit within the geographical limits of the state. 2. In popular terms, a small urban community, as distinguished from the countryside that surrounds it.
➤ city, community, borough, hamlet, metropolis, village, municipality, township.
town council [*koun* · sil] *n.* The **legislative council** of a town.

town meeting [*mee* · ting] *n.* In the New England states, a **regular meeting** or a **special meeting** of the citizens of a town, held for the purpose of deciding matters relating to the public business (EXAMPLES: levying taxes; making **appropriations**).

township [*toun* · ship] *n.* 1. A **political subdivision** in some states. 2. As laid out

T

by **government survey**, a tract of land six miles square.

toxic [*tok* · sik] *adj.* Poisonous; containing toxins.
➤ poison, polluted, hazardous, infectious, poisonous, septic, virulent.

toxic waste [*tok* · sik] *n.* Poisonous material discharged into the environment, often by industrial facilities. The discharging of toxic waste is prohibited or regulated by both federal and state legislation. *See* Environmental Protection Agency. *Also see* hazardous waste; pollution; solid waste.

toxicology [tok · si · *kahl* · e · jee] *n.* The branch of medicine involving the study of poisons and their effect upon the body.

tract *n.* 1. A lot or **parcel** of land. 2. A leaflet.
➤ lot, district, expanse, extent, parcel, spread, stretch; leaflet, pamphlet.

tract index [*in* · deks] *n.* An **index** of records (EXAMPLES: deeds; mortgages; **liens**) according to the tracts or **parcels** of land to which they pertain. *Compare* grantor-grantee indexes.

trade *n.* 1. Buying and selling; commerce. 2. Exchange or barter. 3. Any occupation or business carried on in order to make a living.
v. To engage in commerce; to exchange goods or money.
➤ *n.* barter, commerce, enterprise, interchange, merchantry, transaction, truck ("world trade"); art, avocation, business, employment, handicraft, pursuit ("business trade").
v. exchange, buy, barter, deal, sell, transact, traffic, do business.

trade acceptance [ak · *sep* · tense] *n.* A form of **commercial paper**, i.e., a **draft** or **bill of exchange**, **drawn** by the seller on the purchaser of goods sold, and **accepted** by the purchaser, the purpose of the transaction being to enable the seller to raise money on the paper before it is due under the terms of the sale. *See* acceptance.

trade association [a · so · see · *ay* · shen] *n.* A number of businesses, usually in the same field or industry, joined together for the purpose of sharing ideas and promoting their common interests, for EXAMPLE, lobbying or setting industry-wide standards. *See* association.

trade commission [ke · *mish* · en] *n.* *See* Federal Trade Commission.

trade fixtures [*fiks* · cherz] *n.* Articles attached to leased premises by the tenant to aid him in carrying on his trade or business. (EXAMPLES: counters; shelves; display cases.) Unlike residential fixtures, the tenant is free to remove trade fixtures upon termination or expiration of the lease. *See* fixtures.

trade libel [*ly* · bel] *n.* A **libel** that **defames** the goods or products a person produces in her business or occupation, as opposed to a libel against the person herself. *See* defamation.

trade name *n.* The name under which a company does business. The **goodwill** of a company includes its trade name. *Compare* trademark.

trade secret [*see* · kret] *n.* Confidential information concerning an industrial process or the way in which a business is conducted. Trade secrets are of special value to a business and are the property of the business.

trade union [*yoon* · yen] *n.* A labor union; a union.

trade usage [*yoo* · sej] *n.* Under the **Uniform Commercial Code**, "Any practice or method of dealing having such regularity of observance in a place, vocation, or trade as to justify an expectation that it will be observed with respect to the transaction in question." Trade usage is also referred to as **usage of trade**. *See* usage. *Also see* custom.

trademark [*trade* · mark] *n.* A **mark**, design, title, logo, or motto used in the sale or advertising of products to identify them and distinguish them from the products of others. A trademark is the property of its owner and, when registered under the Trademark Act, is reserved for the exclusive use of its owner. *Compare* service mark. *Also compare* trade name. *See* collective mark.
➤ logo, brand, identification, mark, design, initials, logotype, stamp.

trading [*tray* · ding] *adj.* Commercial; mercantile; business.
➤ commercial, mercantile, business ("a trading company").

trading company [*kum* · pe · nee] *n.* A company, either a **trading corporation** or a **trading partnership**, whose chief business is buying and selling.

trading corporation [kore · per · *ay* · shen] *n. See* trading company.

trading partnership [*part* · ner · ship] *n. See* trading company.

trading stamps *n.* Stamps that a retailer gives as a premium to customers when they purchase goods. The value and number of stamps given is directly proportionate to the value of the purchase. The stamps are redeemable for selected "gifts," which are usually other goods.

trading with the enemy [*en* · e · mee] *n.* The crime of carrying on commercial relations with the enemy during time of war.

traditional [tra · *dish* · ih · nal] *adj.* Regularly or commonly done; conventional.
➤ usual, customary, common, accepted, longstanding, conventional, fixed.

traffic [*traf* · ik] *n.* 1. The passing of goods or commodities from one person to another in exchange for money or other goods; buying and selling; commerce; trade. 2. Goods or commodities that are passed from one person to another in exchange for money or other goods or commodities. 3. The movement of vehicles on the streets or highways. *v.* To pass goods or commodities from one person to another in exchange for money or other goods, particularly **contraband**. USAGE: "People who traffic in cocaine will be arrested."
➤ *n.* movement, freight, gridlock, passengers, flow, vehicles ("heavy traffic on the roads"); barter, communion, familiarity, intimacy, intercourse, merchantry ("business traffic"); passing, transfer, dealings, sale, exchange ("traffic of goods"). *v.* barter, contact, deal, interact, sell, buy, interface, network ("to traffic drugs").

traffic citation [sy · *tay* · shen] *n. See* citation.

traffic offense [o · *fense*] *n.* A violation of **traffic regulations**.

traffic regulations [reg · yoo · *lay* · shenz] *n.* State statutes and local ordinances that establish the relative rights and duties of operators of vehicles using the public roads.

traffic violation [vy · e · *lay* · shen] *n.* A **traffic offense**.

trafficking [*traf* · ik · ing] *n. See* traffic.

traitor [*tray* · ter] *n.* A person who has committed **treason**.
➤ betrayer, informer, turncoat, deserter, conspirator, Judas, apostate, quisling.

transacting business [tranz · *ak* · ting *biz* · nes] *n.* **Doing business**.

transaction [tranz · *ak* · shen] *n.* 1. The doing or carrying on of some business between two or more persons; business dealings. EXAMPLES: a sale; an auction; a **liquidation**; a **foreclosure**. *See* arm's-length transaction; margin transaction; secured transaction. 2. Any act or series of acts involving more than one person. It is in this sense that a **burglary**, for EXAMPLE, is properly referred to as a "criminal transaction," and that, for EXAMPLE, the **Federal Rules of Civil Procedure** require that a **compulsory counterclaim** be filed when a defendant's claim arises out of the "same transaction" as the plaintiff's. 3. Something that has taken place. When used in this sense, however, "transactions" are to be distinguished from "occurrences" or "events," as the latter do not necessarily involve consent or knowledge.
➤ action, activity, convention, negotiation, occurrence, purchase, business, dealing.

transactional immunity [tranz · *ak* · shen · el im · *yoon* · i · tee] *n.* A guaranty given a person that if he testifies against others he will not be prosecuted for his own involvement in the crime (i.e., the "criminal transaction") to which his testimony relates. *Compare* use immunity. *See* immunity; transaction. *Also see* immunity from prosecution.

transcend [tran · *send*] *v.* To go beyond; to surpass.
➤ exceed, go beyond, surmount, prevail, outrank, outshine, rise above, transform.

transcript [*tran* · skript] *n.* A typewritten copy of the court reporter's stenographic notes of a trial, i.e., a **record** of the **proceedings**. *See* stenographic notes.
➤ copy, record, writing.

T

transcript of the record [*rek* · erd] *n.* The complete **record** of a case as furnished to the **appellate court** when an appeal is taken.

transfer [*trans* · fer] *n.* 1. Placing property in the hands of another; passing property from the ownership or possession of one person to the ownership or possession of another, whether by the act of the parties or by **operation of law**. (EXAMPLES: a **conveyance**; a **deed**; a **mortgage**; a **bill of sale**; a **payment**; an **indorsement**; a **pledge**; a **lien**; an **encumbrance**; a **gift**; **security**; an **assignment**.) "Transfer of ownership" and "transfer of **title**" are synonymous terms. 2. The **instrument** or document by which ownership or possession is passed from one person to another. 3. The act of moving anything from one place or person to another.
v. [*tranz* · fer] To move, pass, or **convey** something from one person to another and, particularly, to shift **title** or possession of property.
➤ *n.* alteration, convention, deportation, relegation, passing, transference ("The transfer of power is complete").
v. assign, delegate, express, carry, relegate, tote ("to transfer title to someone").

transfer agent [*ay* · jent] *n.* A person or company that acts on behalf of a corporation in carrying out the transfer of its stock from one owner to another and **registering** the **transaction** on the corporate records. *See* registration of securities; stock transfer.

transfer in contemplation of death [kon · tem · *play* · shen] *n.* A transfer of property, motivated by the thought of impending death. *See* contemplation of death. *See and compare* gift causa mortis; inter vivos gift.

transfer of case *n.* The transfer of a case from one court to another. *See* removal of case.

transfer of cause *n.* Same as **transfer of case**.

transfer payments [*pay* · ments] *n.* Government payments that are neither **earned income** nor income from investments; **entitlement** payments (EXAMPLES: **AFDC**; social security; unemployment compensation benefits).

transfer tax *n.* A tax on the transfer of property by **succession**, whether under a will or by **intestate succession**. The tendency is to refer to a state tax on succession as a "transfer tax" and the federal tax as an **estate tax**.

transferable [tranz · *fer* · ebl] *adj.* That which may be the subject of a **transfer**; that which may be transferred.
➤ negotiable, assignable, transmissible ("a transferable lease").

transferee [tranz · fer · *ee*] *n.* A person to whom a **transfer** is made. *Compare* transferor.

transferor [tranz · fer · *or*] *n.* A person who makes a **transfer**. *Compare* transferee.

transferred intent [tranz · *ferd* in · *tent*] *n.* The doctrine that if a defendant who intends to **injure** (for EXAMPLE, to **assault** or **murder**) one person unintentionally harms another, the **intent** is transferred to the person who is unintentionally harmed. This doctrine permits the defendant to be prosecuted as if she had intended to harm the person injured.

Transfers to Minors Act [*trans* · ferz to *my* · nerz] *n.* One of the **uniform laws**, adopted in various forms in most states. It allows most kinds of property, real or personal, **tangible** or **intangible**, to be made the subject of a **transfer** to a **custodian** for the **benefit** of a minor. In most states, the Uniform Transfer to Minors Act superseded the **Uniform Gifts to Minors Act**, which covered only gifts of money and **securities**.

transform [*tranz* · form] *v.* To change in a fundamental way.
➤ convert, reconstruct, alter, modify, redo, restyle, revamp, revolutionize.

transgression [tranz · *gress* · shun] *n.* A violation; a wrong; an offense.
➤ crime, breach, wrong, wrongdoing, misconduct, misbehavior, infringement, violation.

transgressive trust [tranz · *gress* · iv] *n.* A **trust** that violates the **rule against perpetuities**.

transhipment [tran · *ship* · ment] *n.* Same as **transshipment**.

transit [*tran* · zit] *n.* 1. The act or fact of passing through. USAGE: "Will the goods you are shipping to me be insured while they are in transit?" 2. **Conveyance** or a means of conveyance.

➤ carriage, conveyance, infiltration, permeation, transference, passing.

transit authority [aw · *thah* · ri · tee] *n.* An agency of state or local government with the power to establish and maintain bus lines, subways, etc. *See* authority. *Also see* port authority.

transition [tran · *zih* · shun] *n.* A change; a conversion.

➤ movement, passing, break, change, conversion, shift, growth, development ("the transition from military to civilian life").

transitory [*tran* · zi · tore · ee] *adj.* 1. Not permanent. 2. Passing.

➤ fleeting, ephemeral, passing, evanescent, fugacious.
Ant. permanent, enduring.

transitory action [*ak* · shen] *n.* An **action** that can be brought in any jurisdiction where the defendant can be **served** with **process**, as opposed to a **local action**, which can be brought only where the **cause of action** arose. *See and compare* in personam action; in rem action.

transmit [trans · *mit*] *v.* To send; to communicate.

➤ deliver, dispatch, send, ship, communicate, transport, issue, impart ("to transmit the message").

transshipment [tranz · *ship* · ment] *n.* Moving cargo out of one ship or other means of transportation and into another.

trauma [*trouw* · ma] *n.* 1. An injury or wound to the body caused by physical impact. 2. An experience or a number of experiences that cause emotional injury.

➤ agony, anguish, collapse, derangement, upheaval, upset, injury.

traumatic [trouw · *mat* · ik] *adj.* Pertaining to trauma; caused by trauma.

➤ upsetting, stressful, injurious.

traveler's check [*trav* · lerz] *n.* An **instrument**, usually one of a set, purchased from a bank or other financial institution and similar in many respects to a **cashier's check**. Traveler's checks must be signed by the purchaser at the time of purchase and countersigned when cashed.

traverse [*trav* · ers] *adj.* Denying; contradicting; crossing.
v. [tra · *verse*] 1. With respect to **pleading**, to deny or contest an **allegation** of fact contained in the opposite party's pleading. 2. To deny or contradict generally. 3. To cross or to go across.

➤ *adj.* denying, contradicting, crossing.
v. bisect, cross, negotiate, peregrinate, ply, range, transverse ("traverse the desert"); balk, contest, contravene, disaffirm, frustrate, gainsay ("traverse the lower court's opinion").

traverse jury *n.* A **petit jury**.

treason [*tree* · zen] *n.* The act of transferring one's allegiance from one's own country to the enemy, and giving the enemy **aid and comfort**. *See* misprision of treason.

➤ crime, deceit, duplicity, faithlessness, perfidy, sedition.

treasure-trove [*trezh* · er-] *n.* Money, or gold or silver coin, plate, or bullion found buried in the earth or concealed in a house or other private place, and whose owner is unknown.

treasurer [*trezh* · er · er] *n.* A corporate officer or an officer of government whose duties are to collect, manage, and pay out funds.

➤ corporate officer, officer, controller, accountant.

treasury [*trezh* · er · ee] *n.* 1. The accumulated funds of a government, for EXAMPLE, of a nation, state, or city. 2. A place for the safekeeping of funds. 3. A **department of government** responsible for collecting, managing, and disbursing public funds. *See* Treasury.

➤ archive, bursar, cache, coffer, repository, vault.

Treasury bill *n.* *See* Treasury securities.
Treasury bond *n.* *See* Treasury securities.
Treasury certificate [ser · *tif* · i · ket] *n.* *See* Treasury securities.
Treasury note *n.* *See* Treasury securities.
Treasury securities [se · *kyoor* · i · teez] *n.* A term applied to the various types of **securities** issued by the United States of

T

T

America, including **Treasury bills**, **Treasury bonds**, **Treasury certificates**, and **Treasury notes**. These **obligations** have different investment implications, inasmuch as they are for terms of varying length, and interest is calculated and paid differently on each of them. *See and compare* bill; bond; certificate of deposit; note. Although **treasury stock** is a corporate obligation, not an obligation of the United States, is also referred to as a "treasury security."

Treasury shares *n. See* treasury stock.

treasury stock *n.* **Corporate stock** that has been issued to shareholders and paid for in full, and has later been repurchased or otherwise reacquired by the corporation.

Treasury warrant [*war* · ent] *n. See* warrant.

Treasury [*trezh* · er · ee] *n.* Short for the Department of the Treasury; the treasury of the United States. *See* treasury.

treatise [*tree* · tiss] *n.* A book that discusses, in depth, important principles in some area of human activity or interest, for EXAMPLE, law or medicine.
➤ argument, commentary, disquisition, dissertation, pamphlet, tractate, work, book.

treatment [*treet* · ment] *n.* 1. Medical care. 2. An approach to or handling of a matter.
➤ cure, therapy, medication, regimen; angle, conduct, approach, manner, mode, method.

treatment program [*treet* · ment *pro* · gram] *n.* A program for the treatment and rehabilitation of drug addicts and alcoholics. Some treatment programs are residential; some are nonresidential. *See* halfway house; rehab; rehab program.

treaty [*tree* · tee] *n.* A formal written agreement between two or more nations with respect to matters of common concern (EXAMPLES: trade; **extradition**; fishing rights). The Constitution requires **ratification**, by a two-thirds vote of the Senate, of all treaties between the United States and foreign countries. *Compare* convention.
➤ accord, alliance, concordance, entente, negotiation, settlement, understanding.

treaty power [*pow* · er] *n.* The power to enter into treaties with foreign nations

which the Constitution gives the president, acting with the advice and consent of the Senate and with the concurrence of two-thirds of its members. *See* ratification of treaty.

treble damages [trebl *dam* · e · jez] *n.* **Damages** in triple the amount of the damages actually incurred. Treble damages are a form of **punitive damages** or **exemplary damages** authorized by statute in some circumstances if warranted by the severity of the violation or the seriousness of the wrong. *Compare* actual damages; compensatory damages.

trespass [*tress* · pas] *n.* 1. An unauthorized entry or intrusion on the real property of another. *See* continuing trespass; criminal trespass; joint trespass; permanent trespass. 2. In the widest sense of the term, any offense against the laws of society or **natural law**; any **wrong**; any violation of law. 3. An **action at common law** for the **recovery** of **damages** for **injury** resulting from the use or application of force. *See* trespass on the case; trespass quare clausum fregit; trespass vi et armis. *Also see* forcible trespass. 4. Any misdeed, act of wrongdoing, or sin.
v. To infringe or transgress.
➤ *n.* breach, contravention, entry, encroachment, iniquity, misdemeanor, obtrusion, poaching.
v. infringe upon, invade, poach, interlope, violate, offend.

trespass on the case *n.* A **common law action** for the redress of a **tort**; the forerunner of a **negligence** action.

trespass quare clausum fregit [*kwah* · reh *klaw* · zem *free* · jit] *n. Quare clausum fregit* is *Latin* for "because he broke the **close**." *See* close. Trespass quare clausum fregit was the **remedy** at **common law** for the **recovery** of **damages** for wrongful intrusion upon the real property of another.

trespass vi et armis [vee et *ar* · mis] *n.* The *Latin* phrase *vi et armis* means "by force and arms." Trespass vi et armis was the **remedy** at **common law** for **damages** inflicted as the result of the use of force.

trespasser [*tress* · pas · er] *n.* Broadly, a person who commits a **trespass**. Most commonly, however, the term is applied to a person who enters the land of another without an invitation to do so and whose presence is not **suffered**. *Compare* invitee; licensee.

➤ intruder, invader, transgressor, offender.

triable [*try* · ebl] *adj.* Capable of being tried. *See* try.

trial [*try* · el] *n.* 1. A hearing or determination by a court of the issues existing between the **parties** to an **action**; an examination by a **court of competent jurisdiction**, according to the law of the land, of the facts or law at issue in either a **civil case** or a **criminal prosecution**, for the purpose of **adjudicating** the matters in controversy. *See* bench trial; bifurcated trial; fair and impartial trial; judge trial; jury trial; mini-trial; mistrial; new trial; nonjury trial; public trial; separate trials; speedy trial; summary jury trial. 2. The process by which a thing is tested or verified. USAGE: "trial and error." *See* trial balance. *adj.* Experimental; in the process of being used or tested.

➤ *n.* analysis, audition, endeavor, probation, struggle, venture ("a trial of my abilities"); action, citation, hearing, litigation, prosecution, suit ("trial by jury"); adversity, affliction, bane, irritance, plague, rigor, tribulation ("trial in my life").
adj. exploratory, pilot, test, preliminary, provisional, tentative ("a trial run").

trial balance [*bal* · ense] *n.* A bookkeeping term for a statement of the debit and credit balances of all the accounts in a business's **general ledger** for a given period.

trial by court *n.* *See* trial by the court.

trial by jury [*joor* · ee] *n.* A trial in which the jurors are the judges of the facts and the court is the judge of the law. Trial by jury is guaranteed in all criminal cases by the **Sixth Amendment**, and in most civil cases by the **Seventh Amendment**. *Compare* trial by the court. *Also compare* bench trial; judge trial; nonjury trial. *Also see* jury trial.

trial by ordeal [or · *deel*] *n.* An ancient method of criminal trial based upon the belief that if a person was innocent, God would save him from death or injury when he was subjected to an **ordeal**. *See* ordeal.

trial by the court *n.* A trial held before a judge sitting without a jury. A trial by the judge alone is also referred to as a **judge trial**, a **bench trial**, or a **nonjury trial**. *Compare* trial by jury.

trial calendar [*kal* · en · der] *n.* A list of cases awaiting trial. *See* calendar.

trial court *n.* A court that hears and determines a case initially, as opposed to an **appellate court**; a **court of general jurisdiction**. *Also see* court of original jurisdiction.

trial de novo [deh *noh* · voh] *n.* A **new trial**, a **retrial**, or a trial on appeal from a **justice's court** or a **magistrate's court** to a **court of general jurisdiction**. A trial de novo is a trial in which the matter is tried again as if it had not been heard before and as if no decision had previously been rendered. *See de novo.*

trial docket [*dok* · et] *n.* Same as **trial calendar**. *See* docket.

trial examiner [eg · *zam* · i · ner] *n.* A term used in some circumstances for an **administrative law judge** or a **hearing examiner**.

trial judge *n.* The judge who presides at the trial of a case.

trial jury [*joor* · ee] *n.* A **jury** for the trial of a case, as distinguished from a **grand jury**.

trial list *n.* Same as **trial calendar**.

tribal lands [*try* · bel] *n.* *See* Indian lands.

tribe *n.* An ethnic group; a race or type of people. *See* Indian tribe.

➤ association, caste, division, horde, society, race, group, family.

tribunal [try · *byoon* · el] *n.* A **body** that sits in judgment. In its most common application, "tribunal" is synonymous with "court." However, the term also encompasses administrative **boards** or **commissions** (administrative tribunals) and **legislative committees** (legislative tribunals).

➤ court, board, commission, panel, committee, bench, chancery, judiciary.

trick *n.* 1. A scheme; a devious plan. *See* larceny by fraud or deception; larceny by trick. 2. A prostitute's customer or an act of prostitution.

➤ ambush, artifice, circumvention, distortion, imposition, scheme, intrigue, maneuver ("a magic trick"); accomplishment, frolic, gamble, lark, sport, stunt ("a nasty trick"); ability, command, craft, key, device, facility, gift ("the trick to something").

trier of fact [*try* · er] *n.* In a **nonjury trial**, the judge; in a **jury trial**, the jury.

trimester [try · *mes* · ter] *n.* 1. A period of three months. 2. One of three periods of time of equal duration.

trite *adj.* Commonplace; unoriginal; well-worn.

➤ ordinary, common, overused, banal, hackneyed, prosaic, stale, platitudinous, stock, clichéd, commonplace ("a trite saying").

trivial [*triv* · ee · ul] *adj.* Small; unimportant.

➤ unimportant, meaningless, petty, small, inconsequential, negligible, nugatory, trifling.

TRO Abbreviation of **temporary restraining order**.

trouble [*trub* · el] *n.* Difficulty or misfortune.

➤ hardship, difficulty, adversity, distress, catastrophe, misfortune, trial, tribulation, problem, affliction.

trover [*troh* · ver] *n.* The **action at common law** for the **recovery** of **damages** for the **wrongful conversion** of personal property.

➤ return, reparation, compensation, redress, requital, recoupment, satisfaction, recompense.

truancy [*troo* · en · see] *n.* The act of a person of school age in willfully avoiding attendance at school.

➤ absence, delinquency.

true *adj./adv.* 1. In accord with fact; in accordance with the actual state of things. 2. Real; genuine. 3. Honest; sincere. 4. Accurate.

➤ *adj.* accurate, appropriate, authentic, indubitable, legitimate, undeniable, unfeigned ("A true Picasso"); allegiant, conscientious, devoted, dutiful, liege, loyal, staunch ("a true friend").
adv. correctly, perfectly, precisely, unerring, veraciously, veritable ("The shot was true").

true bill *n.* An **indorsement** that a **grand jury** enters on a **bill of indictment** when it **indicts** a criminal defendant. *Compare* no bill; not a true bill.

true copy [*kop* · ee] *n.* An exact copy of a document or **instrument**.

true value [*val* · yoo] *n.* *See* fair market value.

true verdict [*ver* · dikt] *n.* As opposed to a **chance verdict** or a **quotient verdict**, a **verdict** reached in circumstances where each juror has exercised his or her best judgment, guided by the law and the evidence.

trust *n.* 1. A **fiduciary relationship** involving a **trustee** who holds **trust property** for the benefit or use of a **beneficiary**. Property of any description or type (real, personal, **tangible**, **intangible**, etc.) may properly be the subject of a trust. The trustee holds **legal title** to the **trust property** (also called the *res* or *corpus* of the trust); the beneficiary holds **equitable title**. A trust is generally established through a **trust instrument**, such as a **deed of trust** or a will, by a person (known as the **settlor**) who wishes the beneficiary to receive the benefit of the property but not outright ownership. A trust may, however, also be created by **operation of law** (EXAMPLES: a **constructive trust**; a **resulting trust**; an **implied trust**). There are many types of trusts; EXAMPLES include **spendthrift trusts**, **Claflin trusts**, **Totten trusts**, **inter vivos trusts**, **Massachusetts trusts**, and **revocable trusts**. 2. Although not every fiduciary relationship is a trust in the technical sense of the term, every fiduciary relationship, and every **confidential relationship**, is a relationship "of trust," that is, a relationship in which one person has, or has a right to have, faith or trust in another's honesty or integrity. *See* trust fund; trust fund doctrine. 3. In antitrust law, a number of companies acting together to form a **monopoly** or otherwise acting as a **combination in restraint of trade**. *See* antitrust acts.

Also see accumulation trust; active trust; blind trust; breach of trust; business trust; cestui que trust; charitable trust; common law trust; community trust; declaration of trust; deed of trust; direct trust; directory

T

trust; dry trust; executed trust; express trust; honorary trust; indestructible trust; instrumental trust; insurance trust; investment trust; involuntary trust; irrevocable trust; land trust; life insurance trust; living trust; ministerial trust; nominal trust; nominee trust; oral trust; passive trust; perpetual trust; precatory trust; private trust; public trust; purchase money resulting trust; reciprocal trusts; savings account trust; secret trust; simple trust; sprinkling trust; testamentary trust; Totten trust; transgressive trust; unitrust; voting trust. *v.* 1. To give to another for safekeeping. 2. To believe in; to depend upon.

➤ *n.* assurance, certainty, certitude, dependence, positiveness, reliance ("the trust you have in your parents"); account, charge, duty, guardianship, liability, obligation ("in trust for"); bunch, cartel, combine, conglomerate, crowd, multinational, outfit, syndicate ("a corporate trust"). *v.* advance, aid, command, consign, delegate, store, transfer ("to trust a keepsake to someone"); have faith in, place reliance on, lean on, rely on, confide in, count on ("Trust your friend").

trust account [a · *kount*] *n.* A bank account created by a depositor for the benefit of a person or persons other than the depositor. The money in a trust account may not be commingled with other funds of the depositor or of the bank. An **IOLTA** account, in which attorneys deposit their clients' funds, is an EXAMPLE of one type of trust account. *See* multiparty account; special deposit.

trust company [*kum* · pen · ee] *n.* A bank or other financial institution whose business includes serving as a **trustee** of **trust estates** and an **executor** of wills.

trust de son tort *n.* *See* trustee de son tort.

trust deed *n.* *See* deed of trust.

trust deposit [de · *pah* · zit] *n.* A deposit made to a **trust account**.

trust estate [es · *tate*] *n.* Phrase sometimes used to mean the property held by the **trustee** for the benefit of the **beneficiary**, and sometimes used to mean the **interest** that the beneficiary has in the property.

trust ex maleficio [eks mal · e · *fish* · ee · oh] *n.* *See* trustee ex maleficio.

trust fund *n.* 1. A fund held **in trust** by a **trust company** or other **trustee**. *See* trust funds. 2. A fund that, although not held in trust in the technical sense, is held under a relationship "of trust" which gives one the legal right to impose certain obligations upon the holder of the funds. For an EXAMPLE of such a circumstance, *see* trust fund doctrine.

trust fund doctrine [*dok* · trin] *n.* The principle that the property of an **insolvent** corporation must be used to pay the debts of the corporation before any of its **assets** are distributed among the stockholders; in other words, the doctrine that the assets of a corporation are a trust fund for the benefit of its creditors.

trust funds *n.* Money held in a **trust account**. *See* trust fund.

trust indenture [in · *dent* · sher] *n.* An **instrument** stating the terms and conditions of a trust, for EXAMPLE, the trust created by a corporation as **security** for a **bond issue**. *See* indenture. *Also see* terms of the trust.

trust instrument [*in* · stroo · ment] *n.* A document in which a trust is created. EXAMPLE: a **deed of trust**; a will. *See* declaration of trust.

trust inter vivos [*in* · ter *vy* · vose] *n.* *See* inter vivos trust.

trust officer [*off* · i · ser] *n.* An **officer** of a financial institution who manages **trust funds**.

trust property [*prop* · er · tee] *n.* Property that is the subject of a trust. It is also referred to as the **trust res**, the **res of the trust**, or the *corpus* of the trust.

trust receipt [re · *seet*] *n.* An older form of **security agreement** by which a bank or finance company protected itself for money or credit which it advanced to a dealer for the purchase of goods. The bank received **title** from the manufacturer and took a statement from the dealer that she held the goods **in trust** for the bank. The transaction contemplated that the dealer would sell the goods to a consumer and repay the bank and that the consumer would obtain **clear title**.

trust res *n.* **Trust property**; the *corpus* of a **trust**; property that is the subject of a trust.

T

trustee [trust · *ee*] *n.* 1. The person who holds the **legal title** to **trust property** for the benefit of the **beneficiary** of the **trust**, with such powers and subject to such duties as are imposed by the **terms of the trust** and the law. 2. In some jurisdictions, the title of certain public officials, for EXAMPLE, the members of the board of directors of a public college or university.
➤ guardian, fiduciary, custodian.

trustee ad litem [*ly* · tem] *n.* A trustee appointed by the court, as opposed to a trustee appointed in a **trust instrument**. *See ad litem.*

trustee de son tort *n.* A person whom the law deems to be a trustee by virtue of his wrongdoing with respect to property over which he has control; the trustee of a **constructive trust**.

trustee ex maleficio [mal · e · *fish* · ee · oh] *n.* A person who is deemed to be a trustee by **operation of law** because, without the right to do so, he has taken possession of, or assumed the management of, the property of another; the trustee of a **constructive trust**.

trustee in bankruptcy [*bank* · rupt · see] *n.* A person appointed by a **bankruptcy court** to collect any amounts owed the debtor, sell the debtor's property, and distribute the proceeds among the creditors.

trustee process [*pross* · ess] *n.* In some jurisdictions, a **remedy** similar to **garnishment**.

truth *n.* That which is actual or real; that which is factual; that which is a fact or which is based upon facts; that which is accurate.
➤ accuracy, certainty, factualism, legitimacy, rectitude, truism ("a known truth"); authenticity, candor, dedication, dutifulness, openness, verity ("truth in advertising").

truth in lending acts [*len* · ding] *n. See* consumer credit protection acts.

try *v.* 1. To hear and determine a case judicially by means of a trial. USAGE: to "try a case." 2. To attempt.
➤ aspire, contend, essay, go after, propose, speculate, venture ("to try to play"); appraise, check, evaluate, sample, scrutinize, taste ("Try some broccoli"); agonize, crucify, imitate, martyr, plague, test, tax, torture ("try one's patience"); adjudge, arbitrate, examine, hear, judge, referee ("to try in court").

turning state's evidence [*tern* · ing state's *ev* · i · dense] *n.* The act of a witness in a criminal case in giving testimony that **incriminates** her or others in the crime. *See* state's evidence.

turnkey contract [*tern* · kee kon · trakt] *n.* 1. An expression of the construction industry, meaning a contract in which the contractor agrees to produce a building that will be fully ready for occupancy when the contractor finishes work. 2. In the oil industry, an undertaking by the driller of an oil well to furnish everything required to place a well in production and turn it over ready to start the oil running into the storage tanks.

turnover order [*tern* · o · ver *or* · der] *n.* An **order** rendered in a **supplementary proceeding** requiring a **judgment debtor** to turn over property identified in the proceeding, to satisfy the judgment against him.

turntable doctrine [*tern* · taybl dok · trin] *n.* Another term for **attractive nuisance doctrine**.

turpitude [*terp* · i · tewd] *n. See* moral turpitude.
➤ corruption, depravity, wrong, delinquency.

Twelfth Amendment [a · *mend* · ment] *n.* An amendment to the Constitution that prescribes the manner of choosing a president and vice president.

twelve-mile limit [*lim* · it] *n.* The outer boundaries of the **territorial waters** of the United States and most other nations, which are designated the "twelve-mile limit" because they extend 12 miles off shore. Until 1988, the United States had adopted a **three-mile limit**. *See also* territorial jurisdiction.

Twentieth Amendment [*twen* · tee · eth a · *mend* · ment] *n.* An amendment to the Constitution that set January 3 as the beginning date of the **congressional term** and January 20 as the date for the inauguration of the president and the vice president. These dates were six and eight weeks earlier, respectively, than they had previously been, and had the effect of eliminating the brief (or "**lame duck**") session of Congress that formerly began shortly after the November elections and lasted no later than February. The Twentieth Amendment is commonly referred to as the "Lame Duck Amendment."

Twenty-first Amendment [twen · tee-*ferst* a · *mend* · ment] *n.* An amendment to the Constitution that repealed the **Eighteenth Amendment** and ended Prohibition. *See* prohibition.

Twenty-fourth Amendment [twen · tee-*forth* a · *mend* · ment] *n.* An amendment to the Constitution barring the government, state or federal, from disqualifying any citizen from voting in an election for federal office because she failed to pay a **poll tax** or any other tax.

Twenty-second Amendment [twen · tee-*sek* · end a · *mend* · ment] *n.* An amendment to the Constitution that prohibits a person from being elected president more than twice.

Twenty-sixth Amendment [twen · tee-*siksth* a · *mend* · ment] *n.* An amendment to the Constitution that granted 18-year-olds the right to vote in federal and state elections.

Twenty-third Amendment [twen · tee-*therd* a · *mend* · ment] *n.* An amendment to the Constitution giving residents of Washington, D.C., the right to vote for president and vice president.

twice in jeopardy [*jep* · er · dee] *n. See* double jeopardy; prior jeopardy.

two-dismissal rule [-dis · *miss* · el] *n.* The rule in some jurisdictions that a notice of **voluntary dismissal** of an **action** acts as a bar to bringing the action again if the plaintiff previously filed a voluntary dismissal of an earlier action based upon the same claim. In other words, to put it simply, the plaintiff is entitled to change his mind more than once, but not more than twice. *See* notice of dismissal. *Also see* dismissal with prejudice.

two-issue rule [-*ish* · ew] *n.* The rule in some jurisdictions that if a judge commits **prejudicial error** in **charging** the jury on one of two or more separate issues in a case, the verdict will not be **set aside** if the charge to the jury on at least one of the issues was free from error. *See* jury instructions.

two-witness rule [-*wit* · nes] *n.* The rule in some jurisdictions that in certain types of criminal cases (EXAMPLES: **perjury**; **capital cases**), two witnesses, or one witness and **corroborating evidence**, are required to prove the crime.

typical [*tip* · ih · kal] *adj.* Usual; commonplace.
➤ common, prevailing, popular, usual, stereotyped, regular, recurrent, model, conforming, prosaic, customary.

T

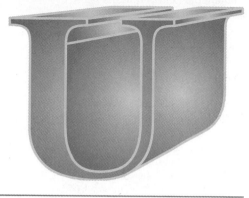

ubiquitous [yoo · *bik* · kwih · tus] *adj.*
Ever-present.
➤ omnipresent, pervasive, universal,
everywhere.

UCC Abbreviation of **Uniform Commercial Code**.

ukase [*yoo* · kase] *n.* An order, decree, or proclamation.

ulterior [ul · *teer* · ee · ur] *adj.* Secret; hidden.
➤ hidden, veiled, unseen, undisclosed, undivulged, obscure, secret ("ulterior motives").

ultimate [*ul* · ti · met] *adj.* 1. Final; last. 2. Farthest; furthest. 3. Maximum.
➤ capping, conclusive, decisive, last, farthest, furthermost, ("the ultimate try"); maximum, paramount, preeminent, superlative, surpassing, transcendent, unequalable ("the ultimate sacrifice"); absolute, categorical, elemental, empyreal, empyrean, transcendental ("the ultimate rule").
    ultimate facts *n.* The facts in a case upon which liability is determined or based. *Compare* ultimate issue.
    ultimate issue [*ish* · ew] *n.* The **legal question** or **legal issue** that determines liability in a case. *Compare* ultimate facts.

ultra [*ul* · tra] (*Latin*) *adj./adv.* Beyond; outside of; more than; in excess of.
➤ beyond, outside of, more than, in excess of ("an ultra vires act").
    ultra vires [*vee* · rayz] Means "beyond the power." A term that the law applies to a contract, transaction, or other act of a corporation which is beyond those powers enumerated or implied in its **articles of**

incorporation, **charter**, or **by-laws**. *See and compare* enumerated powers; implied power.
    ultra vires act [*vy* · reez] *n.* *See ultra vires*.

umbrella policy [um · *brel* · a *pah* · li · see] *n.* An insurance policy that provides coverage over and above the liability limitations of the insured's basic **liability insurance** policies. *See* limitations of liability.

umpire [*um* · pire] *n.* 1. A person chosen to decide an **arbitration** case when the **arbitrators** are deadlocked. *See* arbitration panel. 2. An official in baseball, tennis, and other sports, who rules on plays.
➤ adjudicator, arbitrator, assessor, compromiser, mediator, negotiator, proprietor, referee.

UN Abbreviation of **United Nations**.

unadjusted [un · a · *just* · ed] *adj.* Uncertain in amount; not settled or agreed upon. USAGE: "unadjusted debt"; "unadjusted claim." *See* claims adjuster.
➤ uncertain, unsettled, pending ("an unadjusted claim").

unadulterated [un · uh · *dul* · ter · ay · ted] *adj.* Pure; clean; natural.
➤ pure, genuine, unmixed, uncorrupted, undiluted.

unaffected [un · uh · *fek* · ted] *adj.* 1. Sincere; honest. 2. Indifferent; unmoved.
➤ sincere, frank, honest, open, straightforward, natural, unpretentious ("an unaffected manner"); unaltered, unstirred, indifferent, untouched, unmoved, unchanged ("unaffected by his plea").

unalienable [un · *ale* · yen · ebl] *adj.* Same as **inalienable**.

unambiguous [un · am · *big* · yoo · us] *adj.* Clear; evident.
➤ clear, lucid, obvious, precise, articulate, explicit, evident, sure, certain ("The message was unambiguous").

unanimous [yoo · *nan* · i · muss] *adj.* Complete approval or concurrence; the concurrence of everyone.
➤ accepted, collective, communal, complete, undisputed, unified.
    unanimous decision [de · *sizh* · en] *n.* A **decision** in which all of the judges or justices hearing the case concur. *Compare* concurring opinion; dissenting opinion; majority opinion; minority opinion.
    unanimous verdict [*ver* · dikt] *n.* A **verdict** in which all the jurors concur.

unattested instrument [un · a · *test* · ed in · stroo · ment] *n.* An **instrument** that does not have the signatures of **attesting** or **subscribing** witnesses. *See* attest; attestation; subscribe.

unauthorized [un · *aw* · ther · ized] *adj.* Done without authority or right.
➤ illegal, illegitimate, unapproved, unofficial, unwarranted, wrongful.
    unauthorized practice of law [*prak* · tiss] *n.* Engaging in the practice of law without the license required by law.
    unauthorized use of a motor vehicle [*mo* · ter *vee* · hikl] *n. See* joyriding.

unavailability [un · e · vale · e · *bil* · i · tee] *n.* Generally speaking, a witness is deemed to be "unavailable" within the meaning of statutes relating to the admissibility of **prior testimony** or **hearsay evidence** if she is deceased, insane, or beyond the reach of the court's **process**. *See also* perpetuation of testimony.

unavoidable [un · e · *void* · ebl] *adj.* That which cannot be prevented; that which is inevitable.
➤ certain, compulsory, inductable, inevasible, obligatory, necessary, inevitable.
    unavoidable accident [*ak* · si · dent] *n.* An **inevitable accident**; an **inescapable peril**; an occurrence that could not reasonably have been foreseen or prevented.

unavoidable casualty [*kazh* · you · al · tee] *n.* An occurrence or accident that is beyond human foresight or control. *See* casualty.

unavoidable cause *n.* In the law of **negligence**, a **cause** that could not have been avoided by the exercise of **due diligence** and foresight; an accidental cause. *See* accidental injury.

unbelievable [un · bee · *leev* · uh · bul] *adj.*
1. Beyond belief or imagination.
2. Untrustworthy.
➤ incredible, inconceivable, staggering, unthinkable, awesome; dubious, distrusted, questionable, unlikely.

unbiased [un · *bi* · assed] *adj.* Fair; not partial; not prejudiced.
➤ fair, impartial, open, neutral, just, detached, independent, nonpartisan, nonprejudiced, unslanted, objective.

unborn child [*un* · born] *n.* A child in its mother's womb, i.e., a fetus that has become **viable**. *See* viable child.

uncertain [un · *sert* · in] *adj.* Doubtful; changeable.
➤ disputable, contestable, obscure, indeterminate, vague, tentative, unconfirmed, suspect, untrustworthy, precarious.

uncertificated security
[un · ser · *tif* · i · kay · ted se · *kyoo* · ri · tee] *n.* A **Uniform Commercial Code** term for a "share . . . or other interest in property of or an enterprise of the issuer" that is not evidenced by an **instrument**, for EXAMPLE, a **share** in a corporation that is **registered** on the **books** of the corporation but is not represented by a **stock certificate**. *Compare* certificated security. *See* registered securities; security.

unclean hands doctrine [*un* · kleen hands *dok* · trin] *n. See* clean hands doctrine.

uncollected funds [un · ke · *lek* · ted] *n.* Money that a depositor's bank credits to her account on the basis of checks she has deposited, which are **drawn** to her **order** on other banks but have not yet been **collected**. *See* collection.

unconditional [un · ken · *dish* · en · el] *adj.* Without conditions; without restrictions; absolute.

➤ actual, decisive, genuine, indubitable, unconstrained, unequivocal, absolute, certain.

unconditional ownership [oh · ner · ship] *n.* **Title** that is not limited or restricted by any condition.

unconscionability [un · kon · shen · e · bil · i · tee] *n.* The state or condition of being **unconscionable**.

unconscionable [un · *kon* · shen · ebl] *adj.* Morally offensive, reprehensible, or repugnant. An **unconscionable contract** is a contract in which a dominant party has taken unfair advantage of a weaker party, who has little or no bargaining power, and has imposed terms and conditions that are unreasonable and one-sided. A court may refuse to enforce an unconscionable contract. What is or is not "unconscionable" often depends upon the contract's commercial setting. *See* adhesion contract; overreaching contract.

➤ excessive, preposterous, exorbitant, unscrupulous, inexcusable, unequal, grossly unfair.

unconscionable bargain [barg · en] *n.* *See* unconscionable.

unconscionable contract [kon · trakt] *n.* *See* unconscionable.

unconstitutional [un · kon · sti · too · shen · el] *adj.* 1. In conflict with the Constitution of the United States. 2. In conflict with a **constitution**. 3. Not grounded in or based upon the Constitution or a constitution. *Compare* constitutional.

➤ illegal, impermissible, unenforceable.

unconstitutional statute [stat · shoot] *n.* A statute that is unenforceable because it violates the Constitution.

unconstitutionally vague [un · kon · sti · too · shen · el · ee] *adj.* A term applied to a statute that is held to be **unconstitutional** because it is too vague, i.e., because it violates the **vagueness doctrine**.

uncontested [un · kun · test · ed] *adj.* Not disputed; unopposed; not defended against; not litigated. USAGE: "uncontested divorce"; "uncontested claim." *Compare* contested.

➤ not disputed, unopposed, consensual, accepted, admitted, unchallenged.

uncontrollable impulse [un · ken · trol · ebl im · pulse] *n.* *See* irresistible impulse.

undecided [un · dee · side · ed] *adj.* 1. Not yet adjudicated. 2. Not sure or definite.

➤ open, pending, unsettled; dubious, doubting, tentative, indefinite, vacillating, wavering.

undeniable [un · dee · ny · uh · bul] *adj.* Proven; definite; unquestioned.

➤ certain, clear, pelling, proven, established, unquestionable, uncontrovertable, evident, firm ("an undeniable truth").

under [un · der] *adv./prep.* 1. Inferior; lesser; subordinate. 2. Below; beneath, lower. 3. Subject to. 4 Subjected to; controlled by.

➤ beneath, concealed by, down, inferior, nether, amenable, belonging, collateral, governed, obeying, subsequent, subservient.

under and subject to [sub · jekt] A provision in a **conveyance** of mortgaged property indicating that the **grant** is **subject to** the mortgage.

under color of law [kull · er] An action taken "under color of law" is an action which is based on an apparent legal right. *See* color; color of law.

under oath A term referring to a **sworn statement** or to a declaration or testimony that is **sworn to**. *See* oath.

under protest [pro · test] *See* protest.

under seal With **seal** affixed.

under the influence [in · floo · ense] *See* driving under the influence; driving while intoxicated.

undercapitalized [un · der · kap · i · tel · ized] *adj.* A term used to describe a business with insufficient **capital** to function as a **going concern**.

underinsured motorist clause [un · der · in · shoord moh · ter · ist] *n.* Sometimes an owner or operator of an automobile legally responsible for an accident does not have sufficient insurance to cover the **damages** resulting from the injury he has caused. An automobile insurance policy with underinsured motorist coverage **indemnifies** persons injured or killed as the result of an accident caused by someone who has insufficient insurance if the persons harmed are legally entitled to **recover** from the owner or the operator of the underinsured vehicle. *Compare* uninsured motorist clause.

U

underlease [*un · der · leess*] *n. See* sublease.

undersheriff [*un · der · sherr · iff*] *n.* A deputy sheriff. *See* sheriff. *Also see* deputy.

undersigned [*un · der · sined*] *n.* The person whose name is signed, or the persons whose names are signed, at the end of a document; i.e., the **subscriber** or subscribers.
➤ signatory, subscriber, signer, attestant.

understand [*un · der · stand*] *v.* 1. To comprehend. 2. To think or believe.
➤ appreciate, know, recognize, realize, discern, deduce; suppose, conclude, gather, conceive, deduce.

understanding [*un · der · stan · ding*] *n.* 1. An agreement, or a **stipulation** or provision in an agreement. USAGE: "We arrived at an understanding after quite a few hours of bargaining." *See* memorandum of understanding. 2. The mental quality of prehending something. USAGE: "This textbook added a lot to my understanding of constitutional law." *adj.* Tolerant; compassionate.
➤ *n.* acumen, apperception, decipherment, penetration, perspicacity, savvy ("the students' understanding of the material"); acceptance, conception, estimation, judgment, perception, significancy, viewpoint ("Her understanding is that she will be paid"); accord, agreement, concord, deal, harmony ("an understanding for the purchase of the house"). *adj.* passionate, discerning, empathetic, generous, sensitive, perceptive ("an understanding woman").

undertaking [*un · der · tay · king*] *n.* 1. In a contract, a promise by one of the parties. *Compare* mutual promises. 2. A person's written obligation. EXAMPLES: a **note**; a **draft**. 3. Any promise or **pledge**. 4. Any venture, particularly a business venture. 5. Any endeavor. 6. The business of a funeral director.
➤ adventure, business, engagement, outfit, operation.

undertenant [*un · der · ten · ent*] *n.* A tenant under a **sublease** or an **underlease**.

underwrite [*un · der · rite*] *v.* 1. To guarantee **capital** for a business venture. *See* guarantee. 2. In the case of an insurance company, to insure a policyholder against a **risk of loss**; i.e., to insure or to issue an insurance policy. 3. With respect to a **public offering** of **securities**, an agreement by an **underwriter** (i.e., an *underwriting contract*) to purchase the remainder of a **stock issue** or **bond issue** not purchased by the public. *See* offering.
➤ accede, approve, guarantee, countersign, initial, sanction, subsidize.

underwriter [*un · der · ry · ter*] *n.* A person or firm that **underwrites** some activity or venture. *See also* underwriting.

underwriting [*un · der · ry · ting*] *n.* The act of a business or a person who **underwrites** some activity or venture. *See also* underwriter.

undisclosed [*un · dis · klozed*] *adj.* Not revealed; hidden.
➤ unrevealed, hidden, clandestine, deceptive ("an undisclosed principal").
undisclosed agency [*ay · jen · see*] *n.* A situation where a person who is in fact an **agent** for another deals with a third person as if he were the **principal**, the fact that he is an agent being unknown or hidden.
undisclosed assets [*ass · ets*] *n.* **Assets** of a **bankrupt** or other debtor that she does not reveal to her creditors.
undisclosed principal [*prin · sipl*] *n.* The unrevealed **principal** in a situation involving an **undisclosed agency**.

undisputed [*un · dis · pyoo · ted*] *adj.* Recognized as true.
➤ unquestioned, absolute, accepted, undoubted, positive ("an undisputed point").

undistributed profits [*un · dis · trib · yoo · ted prof · its*] *n. See* undivided profits.

undivided [*un · di · vy · ded*] *adj.* 1. Not distributed. *See* distribution. 2. Not separated.
➤ absorbed, circumspect, concentrated, engrossed, minute, unanimous, united, vigilant, wholehearted ("undivided attention").
undivided interest [*in · trest*] *n.* A fractional **interest** in property, for EXAMPLE, the nature of the **title** held by a **tenant in common**, a **joint tenant**, or by **tenants by the entirety**.

undivided profits [*prof* · its] *n.* Profits of a corporation that have not been distributed as **dividends** or retained as **surplus**. *See* profit. *Also see* earned surplus.

undivided right *n. See* undivided interest.

undivided title [*ty* · tel] *n. See* undivided interest.

undue [un · dew] *adj.* Excessive; extreme.
➤ excess, exorbitant, disproportionate, inappropriate, extreme ("undue burden").

undue influence [un · dew in · flew · ense] *n.* Inappropriate pressure exerted on a person for the purpose of causing him to substitute his will for the will or wishes of another. Undue influence is a form of coercion to which the aged or infirm are particularly vulnerable, especially at the hands of a person whom they feel they have reason to trust, for EXAMPLE, a clergyman or an attorney.

unearned [un · ernd] *adj.* 1. Not worked for. 2. Undeserved; unmerited.
➤ gratuitous, unprovoked, excessive, groundless, arbitrary, unfair, undeserved, unmerited.

unearned income [in · kum] *n.* Income from property or from an investment (EXAMPLES: interest; **dividends**), as distinguished from incomereceived from one's employment. *Compare* earned income.

unearned premium [*pree* · mee · um] *n.* Portion of an insurance premium payment relating to coverage for a period that has not yet occurred, as opposed to a period for which the **carrier** is presently responsible. EXAMPLE: With respect to a $500 premium paid for a year's fire insurance, after six months the unearned premium is approximately $250; at that point the **earned premium** is also approximately $250. *See* earned premium. *Also see* premium.

unemployed [un · em · *ployd*] *adj.* Without a job; without work.
➤ jobless, idle, inactive.

unemployment [un · em · *ploy* · ment] *n.* A term usually applied to the state or status of being involuntarily unemployed.

unemployment compensation [kom · pen · *say* · shen] *n.* Short for **unemployment compensation benefits** or **unemployment insurance**.

unemployment compensation acts [kom · pen · *say* · shen] *n.* State statutes that provide for the payment of benefits to persons who are unemployed through no fault of their own. An employee who, for EXAMPLE, has voluntarily left her employment, or has been discharged for **willful misconduct,** is ineligible to receive **unemployment compensation benefits**. Unemployment compensation is a form of **social insurance**. *See* availability for work. *See also* extended benefits program.

unemployment compensation benefits [kom · pen · *say* · shen ben · e · fits] *n. See* unemployment compensation acts.

unemployment insurance [in · *shoor* · ense] *n. See* unemployment compensation acts.

unenforceable [un · en · *forss* · ebl] *adj.* That which cannot be put into effect or carried out. USAGE: "unenforceable contract"; "unenforceable judgment." *Compare* enforceable.
➤ void, illegal, without effect.

unequal [un · *e* · kwal] *adj.* 1. Not balanced or fair. 2. Different.
➤ biased, partial, unfair, prejudiced, one-sided; unalike, distant, mismatched, disparate.

unequivocal [un · e · *kwiv* · ekl] *adj.* Certain; not doubtful; clear; unambiguous.
➤ absolute, categorical, incontestible, indubitable, manifest, palpable, certain, clear, unambiguous.

unessential [un · e · *sen* · shul] *adj.* Extra; unnecessary.
➤ needless, secondary, irrelevant, superfluous, incidental, collateral.

unethical [un · *eth* · ikl] *adj.* Not ethical; lacking **ethics**.
➤ corrupt, disreputable, immoral, unprofessional, prohibited, mercenary, underhanded, unprincipled, unscrupulous, improper.

unfair [un · *fare*] *adj.* 1. Unreasonable; undue. 2. Unethical. 3. **Unconscionable**.
➤ arbitrary, bigoted, biased, discriminatory, illegal, immoral, iniquitous, partisan, unreasonable, unethical.

unfair comment [*kom* · ent] *n.* As opposed to **fair comment**, dishonest or

U

U

malicious media comment on matters of public interest.

unfair competition [kom · pe · *tish* · en] *n.* In business, the use or imitation of another firm's name, **mark**, logo, design, or title for the purpose of creating confusion in the public mind and inducing the public to believe that a competitor's business or product is one's own. Such practices are illegal. *Compare* fair competition.

unfair labor practice [*lay* · ber *prak* · tiss] *n.* An action by either a union or an employer in violation of the **National Labor Relations Act** or similar state statutes. EXAMPLES: firing an employee because she joins a union; **secondary picketing**.

unfair labor practice strike [*lay* · ber *prak* · tiss] *n.* A strike for the purpose of protesting or of inducing an employer to refrain from **unfair labor practices**.

unfair methods of competition [*meth* · edz of kom · pe · *tish* · en] *n.* A doctrine used by the **Federal Trade Commission** to restrain methods of competition that are not illegal under the more narrow **common law** principle of **unfair competition**.

unfair trade practices [*prak* · tiss · ez] *n. See* unfair competition; unfair methods of competition.

unfavorable [un · *fave* · er · uh · bul] *adj.* Negative; critical.
➤ adverse, hostile, inopportune, bad, ominous ("an unfavorable opinion").

unified bar [*yoon* · i · fide] *n.* Same as **integrated bar**.

uniform [*yoon* · i · form] *adj.* Consistent in pattern; unchanging; without variation; conforming to a standard.
  n. Required dress; an outfit.
➤ *adj.* consistent, compatible, habitual, homogeneous, equal, even, identical, constant, undeviating, conventional ("Uniform Code of Military Justice").
  n. attire, costume, dress, garb, habit, khaki, livery, regalia ("nurse's uniform").

Uniform Acts [*yoon* · i · form] *n. See* Uniform Laws.

Uniform Code of Military Justice [*yoon* · i · form code of *mil* · i · tare · ee *juss* · tis] *n. See* Code of Military Justice.

Uniform Commercial Code [*yoon* · i · form ke · *mersh* · el] *n.* One of the **Uniform Laws**, which has been adopted in much the same form in every state. It governs most aspects of commercial transactions, including **sales**, **leases**, **negotiable instruments**, **deposits** and **collections**, **letters of credit**, **bulk sales**, **warehouse receipts**, **bills of lading** and other **documents of title**, **investment securities**, and **secured transactions**. *See* commercial law.

Uniform Enforcement of Foreign Judgments Act [*yoon* · i · form en · *forss* · ment of *for* · en *juj* · ments] *n. See* Enforcement of Foreign Judgments Act.

Uniform Laws [*yoon* · i · form] *n.* Model legislation prepared and proposed jointly by the **American Law Institute** and the **Commission on Uniform State Laws**, the purpose of which is to promote uniformity throughout the country with respect to statutes governing significant areas of the law. Many Uniform Laws are adopted by many, most, or all of the states, with variations from state to state. The **Uniform Commercial Code**, the **Uniform Reciprocal Enforcement of Support Act**, the **Uniform Transfers to Minors Act**, and the **Model Penal Code** are EXAMPLES of Uniform Laws.

Uniform Reciprocal Enforcement of Support Act [*yoon* · i · form re · *sip* · re · kel en · *forss* · ment of *sup* · port] *n. See* Reciprocal Enforcement of Support Acts.

Uniform State Laws [*yoon* · i · form] *n. See* Uniform Laws.

Uniform Transfers to Minors Act [*trans* · ferz to *my* · nerz] *n. See* Transfers to Minors Act.

unilateral [yoon · i · *lat* · er · el] *adj.* 1. Affecting the interests of only one party or one side. 2. One-sided; having only one side. *Compare* bilateral.
➤ lone, singular, independent, one-sided, unaided, single.

unilateral contract [kon · trakt] *n.* A **contract** in which there is a promise on one side only, the **consideration** being an act or something other than another promise. In other words, a unilateral contract is an **offer** that is **accepted** not by another promise, but by **performance**. EX-AMPLE: the Acme Ball Bearing Company promises Sam that if he buys advertising material from Acme he will be the sole Chicago distributor of Acme's ball bearings. *Compare* bilateral contract.

unilateral mistake [mis · *take*] *n.* A misconception by one, but not both, **parties** to a contract with respect to the terms of the contract. *Compare* mutual mistake. *See* mistake.

unimproved land [un · im · *proovd*] *n.* Land that has not been improved. *See* improved land.

unincorporated [un · in · *kore* · per · ay · ted] *adj.* Not **incorporated**.

unincorporated association [a · so · see · *ay* · shen] *n.* *See* association.

uninsured motorist clause [*un* · in · shoord *mo* · ter · ist] *n.* An automobile insurance policy with uninsured motorist coverage **indemnifies** persons injured or killed as the result of an accident caused by someone who has no insurance if the persons harmed are legally entitled to **recover** from the owner or operator of the uninsured vehicle. *Compare* underinsured motorist clause.

union [*yoon* · yen] *n.* 1. A labor union. *See* company union; craft union; industrial union; local union; union shop vertical union. 2. A **federation**. 3. A term used to refer to the United States of America. USAGE: "the Union, now and forever." 4. Any joining together of persons or groups. EXAMPLE: a credit union.
➤ abutment, centralization, merger, conciliation, intercourse, melding, unison ("the union of two railroads"); alliance, brotherhood, coalition, guild, federation, syndicate ("trade union").

union certification [ser · tif · i · *kay* · shen] *n.* *See* certification of bargaining agent.

union contract [*kon* · trakt] *n.* *See* collective bargaining agreement.

unissued stock [un · *ish* · ewd] *n.* **Corporate stock** that has been authorized but is not **outstanding**. *See* authorized capital stock; outstanding stock.

unit [*yoon* · it] *n.* One single thing or person.
➤ assemblage, bunch, complement, detachment, entirety, system ("the entire unit"); block, part, item, compound, constituent, fraction, integer, sequent ("the refrigerator's cooling unit").

unit ownership acts [*oh* · ner · ship] *n.* State statutes dealing with **condominium** ownership.

unit price *n.* A method of setting the price for goods on the basis of volume or weight rather than by the item. EXAMPLES: by the pound as opposed to by the box; by the quart as opposed to by the jar.

unit rule *n.* A method of determining the value of **securities** by multiplying the total number of **shares** to be valued by the sale price of one such share on a **stock exchange**.

unit-price contract [*kon* · trakt] *n.* A **contract** in which price varies according to the type of article or service provided, as opposed to an overall contract price.

unite [yoo · *nite*] *v.* To bring together.
➤ join, link, connect, blend, concur, coalesce, combine, cement.

united [yoo · ny · ted] *adj.* Combined; collective.
➤ joint, cooperative, conjoint, affiliated, associated, federal, allied, unanimous, linked.

United Nations [yoo · ny · ted nay · shenz] *n.* An organization created by the nations of the world to deal with international matters, and, in particular, to prevent war. Its related concerns and activities are economic, social, cultural, educational, medical, and nutritional in nature.

United States [yoo · ny · ted] *n.* 1. The federal government. 2. A **sovereign nation** or **sovereign state** called the "United States." 3. The territory over which this sovereign nation called the "United States" exercises **sovereign power**.
adj. Federal, national sovereign.

United States Attorney [a · *tern* · ee] *n.* The public official appointed by the president, one for each **judicial district** of the United States. It is the United States Attorney's responsibility to bring all

U

federal criminal prosecutions and all civil actions affecting the interests of the United States which are within the jurisdiction of her or his judicial district.

United States Attorney General [a · *tern* · ee *jen* · e · rel] *n. See* Attorney General of the United States.

United States bills *n. See* Treasury.

United States bonds *n. See* Treasury.

United States certificates [ser · *tif* · i · kets] *n. See* Treasury.

United States Claims Court *n. See* Claims Court.

United States Code *n.* The official **codification** of the statutes enacted by Congress. *See also* revised statutes.

United States Code Annotated [*an* · o · tay · ted] *n.* The **annotated** version of the **United States Code**. *See* annotated statutes; annotation.

United States Commissioner [kum · *ish* · en · er] *n. See* commissioner.

United States Constitution [kon · sti · *too* · shen] *n. See* Constitution of the United States.

United States Court of Military Appeals [*mil* · i · tare · ee a · *peelz*] *n. See* Court of Military Appeals.

United States Courts *n.* The courts upon which the judicial power of the United States is conferred by the Constitution; i.e., the **federal courts**, as opposed to **state courts**. The United States Courts include the **United States Supreme Court**, the **Courts of Appeals of the United States**, the **District Courts of the United States**, the **Claims Court**, the **Tax Court**, and the **bankruptcy courts**.

United States Courts of Appeals [a · *peelz*] *n. See* Courts of Appeals of the United States.

United States District Courts [*dis* · trikt] *n. See* District Courts of the United States.

United States Magistrate [*maj* · is · trate] *n. See* magistrate.

United States Marshal [*mar* · shel] *n. See* marshal.

United States notes *n. See* Treasury.

United States of America [a · *merr* · i · ka] *n. See* United States.

United States Reports [re · *ports*] *n.* The official **court reports** of the decisions and opinions of the Supreme Court of the United States. *Also see* reporters.

United States Statutes at Large [*stat* · shoots] *n. See* statutes at large.

United States Supreme Court [soo · *preem*] *n. See* Supreme Court of the United States.

unitrust [*yoon* · i · trust] *n.* Under the **Internal Revenue Code**, a **trust** that, in accordance with IRS regulations, annually pays its **beneficiary** a specified percentage of the **fair market value** of all the property in the trust.

unity [*yoon* · i · tee] *n.* 1. Oneness; togetherness. The essential elements of a **joint tenancy** are **unity of interest, unity of possession, unity of time**, and **unity of title**. 2. Agreement; accord; harmony.
➤ alliance, coadunation, confederation, consensus, homogeneity, rapport, solidarity.

unity of interest [*in* · trest] *n.* One of the elements of a **joint tenancy**; the requirement that the **interests** of the **tenants** must be equal in duration and quantity. *See* unity.

unity of possession [po · *zesh* · en] *n.* One of the elements of a **joint tenancy**; the requirement that each of the **tenants** have the **undivided right** to possess the entire property; that is, that no one of them have the right to sole possession of any part. *See* undivided interest. *Also see* unity.

unity of time *n.* One of the elements of a **joint tenancy**; the requirement that the tenancies begin at the same time. *See* tenancies; unity.

unity of title [*ty* · tel] *n.* One of the elements of a **joint tenancy**; the requirement that each of the **estates** must be created by the same **grant** or **conveyance**. *See* unity.

universal [yoon · i · *ver* · sel] *adj.* Not limited; pertaining to all.
➤ accepted, worldwide, global, catholic, empyrean, mundane, planetary, ubiquitous, total, usual.

universal agent [*ay* · jent] *n.* An **agent** who is authorized to do everything her **principal** is entitled to delegate.

U

universal partnership [*part* · ner · ship] *n.* A **partnership** in which the individual **partners** have agreed to contribute everything they own.

unjust [un · *just*] *adj.* Unfair; contrary to justice; not just.

➤ biased, inequitable, partisan, undeserved, unmerited, unrighteous, unfair ("an unjust law").

unjust enrichment [en · *rich* · ment] *n.* The **equitable** doctrine that a person who unjustly receives property, money, or other benefits that belong to another may not retain them and is obligated to return them. The **remedy** of **restitution** is based upon the principle that **equity** will not permit unjust enrichment. EXAMPLE: Sam promises to convey Blackacre to Robin if Robin builds a house and barn on the property; Robin builds the house and barn, but Sam refuses to convey Blackacre to Robin. Because Sam has been unjustly enriched, a court will order him to pay Robin for the **improvement** of his property.

unlawful [un · *law* · ful] *adj.* Illegal; illicit; contrary to law; not permitted by law; not done in the manner required by law. *Compare* lawful.

➤ actionable, banned, illegal, illicit, nefarious, taboo ("unlawful activity").

unlawful act *n.* An act done in violation of law.

unlawful arrest [a · *rest*] *n. See* false arrest; false imprisonment.

unlawful assembly [a · *sem* · blee] *n.* The acts of three or more persons assembled together with the intention of doing violent injury to the persons or property of others. *Compare* riot. *See* assembly.

unlawful detainer [de · *tane* · er] *n.* Remaining in possession of real property after one's right to do so no longer exists. EXAMPLE: the act of a tenant who refuses to leave his apartment after his lease has expired. *See* detainer; ejectment.

unlawful entry [en · tree] *n.* Going upon the property of another without right or authority; a **trespass**. *See* entry. *Also see* burglary.

unlawful picketing [*pik* · e · ting] *n.* Picketing that gives untruthful information, is violent, or otherwise violates the law

(EXAMPLE: **secondary picketing**). *Compare* peaceful picketing.

unlawful restraint [re · *straint*] *n.* The act of restraining a person's freedom of movement without the right or authority to do so. *See also* restraint of trade.

unlawful search *n. See* unreasonable search; unreasonable search and seizure.

unliquidated [un · *lik* · wid · ay · ted] *adj.* 1. Unpaid; not **satisfied**; not **discharged**. 2. Unsettled or uncertain as to amount; not agreed upon. *Compare* liquidated.

➤ unpaid, not satisfied, not discharged; unsettled, uncertain.

unliquidated claim *n.* A **claim** whose existence or amount is not agreed upon by the parties; a claim whose amount cannot be determined by applying rules of law or by mathematical calculation. *Compare* liquidated claim.

unliquidated damages [*dam* · e · jez] *n.* **Damages** whose amount is not agreed upon by the parties or which cannot be determined by applying the rules of law or by mathematical calculation. *Compare* liquidated damages.

unliquidated debt *n.* A **debt** that has not been paid or about which there is uncertainty as to how much is due. *Compare* liquidated debt.

unliquidated demand [de · *mand*] *n. See* unliquidated claim.

unlisted security [un · *list* · ed se · *kyoor* · i · tee] *n.* Shares of stock or other **securities** not listed on a stock exchange. *Compare* listed security.

unmarketable title [un · *mark* · et · ebl *ty* · tel] *n.* **Title** that a person of **reasonable prudence** and intelligence would not accept, or would not be willing to pay **fair market value** for, because it is not sufficiently **clear**. *See* clear title. *Compare* marketable title.

unmarried [un · *mahr* · eed] *adj.* 1. Not presently married. 2. In some contexts, never married.

➤ celibate, eligible, single, uncoupled.

unnatural [un · *nat* · sher · el] *adj.* Contrary to nature.

➤ aberrant, concocted, synthetic, contrived, imitation, perverted, theatrical, unorthodox.

U

U

unnatural act *n.* *See* unnatural sexual intercourse.

unnatural sexual intercourse [*sek* · shoo · el *in* · ter · korss] *n.* A **crime against nature**. EXAMPLES: **sodomy**; **buggery**; **bestiality**.

unnecessary [un · *ness* · e · ser · ee] *adj.* Inessential; not required.
➤ gratuitous, unneeded, unearned, immaterial, surplus, excess, needless, profuse, wanton.

unnecessary hardship [un · *ness* · e · sare · ee hard · ship] *n.* In zoning law, a term referring to a restriction on the use of land that deprives the owner of any practical economic application for his property with no proportionate advantage to other properties in the neighborhood. Such a circumstance may warrant the granting of a **variance**.

unprecedented [un · *press* · e · den · ted] *adj.* 1. Without **precedent**. 2. Unusual; new; original.
➤ aberrant, anomalous, eccentric, outlandish, unique, unusual, new, original ("an unprecedented decision").

unprofessional [un · pro · *fesh* · en · el] *adj.* Characterized by inefficiency or negligence.
➤ amateurish, unethical, dishonest, immoral, illegal, incompetent, inadequate ("his unprofessional behavior").

unprofessional conduct [un · pro · *fesh* · en · el *kon* · dukt] *n.* *See* Rules of Professional Conduct. *Also see* malpractice.

unreasonable [un · *reez* · en · ebl] *adj.* Not reasonable. *See* reasonable.
➤ absurd, biased, headstrong, invalid, quirky, senseless, unreasoned ("an unreasonable boss"); absonant, exorbitant, inordinate, unconscionable, unrightful, unwarranted, wrongful ("unreasonable punishment").

unreasonable restraint of trade [re · *straint*] *n.* *See* restraint of trade. *Also see* combination in restraint of trade.

unreasonable restraint on alienation [re · *straint* on ale · ee · e · *nay* · shen] *n.* A **restraint on alienation** that is unenforceable because it violates the law or **public policy**.

unreasonable search *n.* *See* unreasonable search and seizure.

unreasonable search and seizure [*see* · zher] *n.* The **Fourth Amendment** prohibits the police and other agents of government from conducting "unreasonable searches and seizures." This means that, with limited exceptions (EXAMPLE: in connection with a lawful arrest), one's home can be searched only if a **warrant** is issued authorizing the search; further, the warrant must be based upon **probable cause**. *See* exclusionary rule; search; seizure.

unrelated business income [*un* · re · lay · ted *biz* · nes *in* · kum] *n.* Income of a **tax-exempt organization** derived from a trade or business not substantially related to the organizational purpose on which the **tax exemption** is based. (EXAMPLE: income generated by a tax-exempt religious organization from a hotel operated for profit on the site of a conference center owned by the organization.) Such income is taxable.

unrelated offenses [*un* · re · lay · ted o · *fensez*] *n.* Crimes unconnected to each other but committed by the same person.

unresponsive [un · ree · *spon* · siv] *adj.* Elusive; evasive; aloof.
➤ evasive, aloof, passive, taciturn, phlegmatic ("The witness remained unresponsive").

unresponsive answer [*un* · res · pon · siv *an* · ser] *n.* An answer by a witness that ignores or evades the questions asked.

unrestricted [un · re · *strik* · ted] *adj.* Without restrictions; without conditions; without limitations.
➤ unlimited, open, limitless, comprehensive, boundless, uncontrolled.

unruly [un · *rule* · ee] *adj.* Hard to control; undisciplined; wild.
➤ wild, uncontrolled, disobedient, contrary, irrepressible, obstinate.

unsatisfactory [un · sat · iss · *fak* · tuh · ree] *adj.* Inadequate; not acceptable.
➤ deficient, poor, insufficient, unfit, unacceptable, disapproved, inadequate, inferior ("in unsatisfactory condition").

unsecured [un · se · *kyoord*] *adj.* A term describing debts or obligations for which no **security** has been given. *Compare* secured.

unsecured creditor [*kred* · i · ter] *n.* A **creditor** who has received no **security**

(EXAMPLE: a mortgage). *Compare* secured creditor.

unsecured debt *n.* A **debt** for which no **security** has been given. *Compare* secured debt. *See* unsecured creditor.

unsecured loan *n.* A **loan** for which no **security** or **collateral** has been given. *Compare* secured loan.

unsettled [un · *set* · uld] *adj.* 1. Open to change. 2. Upset; nervous.

➤ open, indefinite, uncertain, changeable ("unsettled terms"); nervous, agitated, unsteady, upset, disturbed ("unsettled stomach").

unsolicited [un · so · *liss* · ih · ted] *adj.* Unasked for; voluntary.

➤ free, offered, uninvited, unwelcome, gratuitous, unwanted, unrequested ("unsolicited advice").

unsound [un · sownd] *adj.* 1. Incorrect. 2. Weak; not well.

➤ fallacious, erroneous, deficient; frail, sick, infirm, fragile, ill, unsteady.

unsound mind [un · sound] *n.* A term referring to the mind of a person who is not mentally **competent**. It relates to the person's ability to transact business or to manage her **estate**. *Compare* sound mind.

unsworn statement [un · sworn *state* · ment] *n.* A declaration or statement, written or oral, which is not made **under oath**. *Compare* sworn statement.

untenantable [un · *ten* · ent · ebl] *adj.* A phrase used to describe leased premises that are unfit for occupancy. *Compare* habitable.

➤ unfit, uninhabitable, run down.

until [un · *til*] *prep.* To. "Until" is generally interpreted as a word of exclusion. Thus, for EXAMPLE, "June 1 until June 10" is generally construed to mean "June 1 *to* June 10," unless the clear indication is that "June 1 *through* June 10" is what was meant.

➤ before, continuously, prior to, up to, up till.

untrue [un · *troo*] *adj.* 1. False. 2. Inaccurate.

➤ apocryphal, counterfactual, wrong, deceitful, delusive, false, inaccurate, erroneous, prevaricating.

unusual [un · *yoozh* · oo · ul] *adj.* Different; not ordinary.

➤ notable, different, unorthodox, alien, original, atypical, striking, bizarre, distinctive.

Ant. typical, normal.

unvalued policy [un · *val* · yood] *n.* An insurance policy in which the value of the insured property is not stated in the policy, but is to be determined at the time a **loss** occurs. *Compare* valued policy.

unveil [un · *vale*] *v.* To expose; to divulge.

➤ divulge, bare, uncloak, show, present, display, expose.

unwritten [un · *rit* · en] *adj.* Oral.

➤ oral, implied, customary, nuncupative, traditional, parol ("unwritten law").

unwritten law [*un* · rit · en] *n.* Rules and principles that the courts enforce as **law** even though they are not found in statutes. EXAMPLES: **custom**; **trade usage**. *Compare* written law.

uphold [up · *hold*] *v.* To sustain; to affirm.

➤ affirm, sustain, endorse, corroborate, bolster, support, stand by ("to uphold the law").

upkeep [*up* · keep] *n.* Maintenance.

➤ budget, conservation, expenditure, preservation, sustenance, subsistence, maintenance.

upon [up · *on*] *prep.* On.

upon information and belief [in · fer · *may* · shen and be · *leef*] A term used by a **declarant** to indicate that his statement is not intended as a statement of fact, but merely what he believes to be the fact or has been informed is the fact. *See* information and belief.

upon sight Same as **at sight**.

upon trial [*try* · el] At trial; at the time of trial; when the case is tried; when the case was tried. *See* trial.

upper house [*up* · er] *n.* The Senate of the Congress of the United States or of any **bicameral** legislature. *Compare* lower house. *See* state legislature. *Also see* legislature.

upper riparian owner [*up* · er ry · *pair* · e · en *oh* · ner] *n.* A **riparian owner** who owns land upstream from a **lower riparian owner**.

upset [up · *set*] *v.* 1. To bother or unsettle. 2. To defeat or overturn.
adj. Disturbed; bothered.
➤ *v.* disturb, fluster, bother, agitate, enrage; reverse, quash, overturn, overthrow.
adj. troubled, unsettled, confused, shocked, distressed.

upset price [*up* · set] *n.* A price set by the court in a **foreclosure sale** below which the property may not be sold.

urban [*er* · ben] *adj.* Pertaining to the city, as opposed to the country.
➤ city, citified, civil, municipal, nonrural. *Ant.* rural.

urban easement [*eez* · ment] *n.* The right of properties located on city streets to receive light and air without obstruction by adjoining buildings. *See* easement. *Also see* ancient lights; easement of light and air.

urban redevelopment [ree · de · vel · ep · ment] *n.* Planned redevelopment, for all types of uses (EXAMPLES: housing; public transportation; retail stores; parks), of areas of a city that have become economically depressed and blighted.

urban renewal [re · *new* · el] *n. See* urban redevelopment.

urban servitude [*ser* · vi · tewd] *n.* Same as **urban easement**.

urge *v.* To encourage; to promote.
n. A strong desire.
➤ *v.* beg, persuade, prompt, propel, coax, beseech, rouse, impel, instigate.
n. longing, lust, desire, fancy, yearning, yen.

US Abbreviation of **United States**.

usage [*yoo* · sej] *n.* A uniform course of conduct in a particular business or occupation; a customary practice. Usage gives rise to **custom**; indeed, in the language of the law "**custom and usage**" is commonly a single term. *See also* trade usage.
➤ acceptance, convention, habitude, mode, routine, custom, practice.

usage of trade *n. See* trade usage.

usance [*yoos* · ense] *n.* The customary time allowed for the payment of **bills of exchange** or **drafts**.

USC Abbreviation of **United States Code**.

USCA Abbreviation of **United States Code Annotated**; abbreviation of **United States Courts of Appeals**.

USDC Abbreviation of **United States District Courts**.

use [yooss] *n.* 1. The **enjoyment** of real property by occupying it or by otherwise putting it to use. *See* beneficial use. 2. The benefit of or profit from lands in the possession of another who holds them for the **beneficiary**, i.e., a form of **passive trust**. *See* statute of uses. 3. The right granted by a **patent**. *See* fair use doctrine. 4. In zoning law, a right granted a property owner under a zoning ordinance to utilize her property in a specified manner for a specific purpose. *See* conditional use permit; conforming use; nonconforming use; special use. 5. The act of utilizing something; the act of putting something to use.
v. [yooz] 1. To utilize. To make use of. 2. To exploit.
➤ *n.* adoption, applicability, convenience, exertion, mileage, relevance; benefit, profit, right.
v. accept, exercise, handle, practice, relate, run, utilize.

use and benefit [*ben* · e · fit] *n.* A common term in deeds and other conveyances of land, which simply means "**benefit**."

use immunity [im · *yoon* · i · tee] *n.* A guaranty given a person that if he testifies against others, his testimony will not be used against him if he is prosecuted for his involvement in the crime. *Compare* transactional immunity. *See* immunity; immunity from prosecution.

use tax *n.* A form of **sales tax** on personal property purchased outside the state, imposed by a state to prevent residents from making purchases outside the state in order to avoid paying the state's sales tax.

useful [*yooss* · ful] *adj.* 1. To be **patentable** an invention must be **new and useful**. An invention is "useful" if it is capable of performing the functions for which it was intended and its use is not contrary to law, morality, or **public policy**. 2. Beneficial. 3. Serviceable.

➤ advantageous, commodious, functional, pragmatic, salutary, utile, beneficial, serviceable.

useful life *n.* With respect to income tax, the period of time over which business property may be depreciated. *See* depreciation.

user [yoo · zer] *n.* 1. Use; the actual exercise or enjoyment of a right. EXAMPLE: possession of property. 2. The right to use. 3. A person who uses property without a legal right to do so, for EXAMPLE, an **adverse user**. 4. Generally, a person who uses something. EXAMPLE: a drug addict is a user of narcotics or, simply, a "user."

➤ party, person, customer, consumer, possessor; addict, druggie, junkie.

using the mails to defraud [yoo · zing the mailz to de · frawd] *n. See* mail fraud.

usual [yoo · zhoo · el] *adj.* Accustomed; ordinary; occurring in the ordinary course of events.

➤ chronic, current, familiar, material, prevalent, accustomed, ordinary, typical, normal.

usual course of business [biz · nes] *n. See* regular course of business. *See also* ordinary course of business.

usual covenants [kov · en · ents] *n.* Same as **title covenants**.

usual place of abode [a · bode] *n.* The place where a person customarily lives; a residence; a **domicile**. State statutes normally authorize **personal service of process** by leaving a copy of the **process** at the person's **place of abode** or his "usual place of abode." *See* abode.

usual place of business [biz · nes] *n.* The place where a person is employed or customarily conducts her usual business. The statutes of some jurisdictions authorize **personal service of process** by leaving a copy of the **process** at the person's **place of business** or her "usual place of business."

usufruct [yoo · zyoo · frukt] *n.* The right to the **use**, **enjoyment**, or **profits** of another's property.

usurious [yoo · zhoor · ee · us] *adj.* Constituting or engaging in **usury**.

➤ excessive, predatory, exorbitant, avaricious, greedy, stingy.

usurious contract *n.* A **contract** in which the rate of interest exceeds the rate permitted by law. *See* usury.

usurpation [yoo · ser · pay · shen] *n.* The exercise or seizure of a position of authority without right and, in particular, exercising the powers of a public office without **color of right**.

➤ seizure, preemption, assumption, intrusion, deprivation.

usury [yoo · zher · ee] *n.* Charging a rate of interest that exceeds the rate permitted by law.

➤ excessive interest, overcharge, cheating.

utility [yoo · til · i · tee] *n.* 1. To be **patentable**, an invention must have "utility." *See also* new and useful; useful. 2. Short for "public utility." 3. Usefulness.

➤ adequacy, usefulness, benefit, practicality, relevance, service.

utility patent [pat · ent] *n.* The most common type of **patent**, granted on the basis that the invention is of benefit to society. *Compare* design patent; improvement patent.

utmost care [ut · most] *n.* Same as **highest degree of care**.

utter [ut · er] *v.* 1. To put counterfeit money or forged checks into circulation. *See* forgery; uttering a forged instrument. 2. To express, either orally or in writing; to publish. USAGE: "he didn't utter a sound"; "she didn't utter a word."
adj. Complete; total.

➤ *v.* forge, counterfeit; affirm, announce, chime, exclaim, put forth, modulate, pronounce ("to utter a noise").
adj. complete, absolute, outright, thorough, total, unmitigated, unqualified ("the utter truth").

uttering a forged instrument [ut · er · ing a forged in · stroo · ment] *n.* Tendering an **instrument** that is **forged**, with knowledge that it is forged and with the intent to **defraud**.

ux. [uks] *n.* Abbreviation of *uxor, Latin* for wife. Older legal documents commonly referred to a man and his wife as, for EXAMPLE, "Samuel Johnson *et ux.*" *See et ux.*

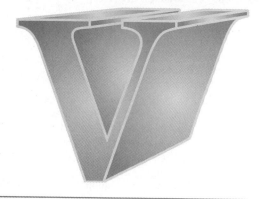

v. Abbreviation of *versus, Latin* for "against." This abbreviation is used in the **caption** of a case and indicates who is suing whom. (EXAMPLE: *Smith v. Jones* means that Smith is suing Jones.) Although *vs.* is also used as an abbreviation for *versus, v.* is preferred.

VA Abbreviation of **Veterans Administration**.

VA mortgage [*more* · gej] *n. See* Veterans Administration.

vacancy [*vay* · ken · see] *n.* An opening.
➤ void, opening, space, position, situation, opportunity, job, room, lodging.

vacancy in office [*vay* · ken · see in *off* · iss] *n.* A term referring to an **office**, whether public or corporate, that is unoccupied (i.e., without an **incumbent**), either because it is newly created, or because of the death or resignation of the incumbent, or because of his removal from office. *See* corporate officers; public office.

vacant [*vay* · kant] *adj.* 1. Empty; unoccupied. 2. Expressionless; blank.
➤ empty, unoccupied, available, untaken, deserted, uninhabited; blank, foolish, vapid, vacuous, silly, stupid, inane.

vacant succession [*vay* · kent suk · *sesh* · en] *n.* An inheritance that no one claims and the **lawful heirs** of which are unknown. *See* succession.

vacate [*vay* · kate] *v.* 1. As applied to a **judgment**, decree, or other order of a court, to **annul**, **set aside**, **void**, or cancel. *See* vacation of judgment. 2. As applied to land or premises, to **quit**, depart, or leave.

➤ abrogate, quash, rescind, reverse, revoke ("vacate a judgement"); quit, depart, leave ("vacate the premises").
Ant. institute; inhabit.

vacation [vay · *kay* · shen] *n.* 1. An **annulment** of a prior act, order, or decision; the act of **vacating**. *See* vacate. 2. A period of freedom from work, school, or other customary daily activities.
➤ break, holiday, intermission, layoff, recess, respite, sabbatical.

vacation of judgment [*juj* · ment] *n.* Under most state **rules of civil procedure**, **relief** from a **final judgment** or order may be granted, and the judgment or order set aside, if it was based upon or issued by mistake, **surprise**, **excusable neglect**, **fraud**, **misrepresentation**, or unintentional error. *See* judgment.

vagrancy [*vay* · gren · see] *n.* At **common law**, the offense of wandering about or going from place to place with no **visible means of support**. State statutes or municipal ordinances that incorporate this standard are **unconstitutional** for **vagueness**. *See* vagueness doctrine. Therefore, **vagrancy laws** are drafted so as to apply to or prohibit specific conduct such as panhandling, public intoxication, or the like. Still, such statutes and ordinances are often of dubious constitutionality because they tend to be overbroad and to create **status crimes**. *See* overbreadth doctrine.
➤ drifting, wayfaring, roaming, gallivanting, hoboism, roving, homelessness, vagabondage.

vagrancy laws *n. See* vagrancy.

V

vagrant [*vay* · grent] *n.* One who engages in **vagrancy**.
➤ wanderer, nomad, tramp, vagabond, hobo, homeless person.

vague *adj.* Not definite; not clear; general.
➤ unclear, obscure, ambiguous, indefinite, imprecise, indistinct, undefined.
Ant. precise.

vagueness [*vayg* · nes] *n.* Uncertainty; indefiniteness; ambiguity.
➤ obscurity, fuzziness, obfuscation, dimness, dubiousness, inexactness, opaqueness, inconstancy.

vagueness doctrine [*dok* · trin] *n.* The rule of **constitutional law** that a statute, particularly a criminal statute, that does not reasonably put a person on notice as to what it is he may not do, or what he is required to do, violates **due process** and is therefore unconstitutional. *See* overbreadth doctrine.

valid [*val* · id] *adj.* 1. Effective; sufficient in law; legal; lawful; not **void**; in effect. USAGE: "valid contract"; "valid marriage"; "valid **defense**." 2. Permissible, legitimate. 3. Convincing; persuasive. *Compare* invalid.
➤ attested, authentic, compelling, irrefutable, proven, substantial ("a valid transcript"); effective, legal, lawful ("valid contract"); convincing, powerful, well-founded ("a valid argument").

validate [*val* · i · date] *v.* To permit; to approve; to confirm; to certify.
➤ authenticate, corroborate, endorse, justify, legalize, sanction, permit, approve, confirm.

validation [val · i · *day* · shen] *n.* 1. The act of giving **legal effect** to something; **legalization**. *Also see* legalize. 2. The act or fact of confirming, approving, permitting, or certifying.

validity [ve · *lid* · i · tee] *n.* The state or condition of being effective or valid.
➤ genuineness, cogency, efficacy, grounds, legality, potency ("to question the validity of a law").

valuable [*val* · yoo · ebl] *adj.* 1. Having monetary value, **market value**, or some other value. 2. Having considerable monetary value or worth. 3. Esteemed; meritorious; deserving.

➤ esteemed, meritorious, fine, treasured, select, deserving ("a valuable addition"); sufficient, adequate ("valuable consideration").

valuable consideration [kun · sid · e · *ray* · shen] *n.* **Consideration** that, in law, is sufficient to support a contract. Such consideration may be in money, in something having monetary value, in the **release** of a right or the compromise of a demand, or in **mutual promises**. *Compare* good consideration; inadequate consideration. *See* adequate consideration; fair consideration.

valuable papers [*pay* · perz] *n.* Papers that a person has in some way indicated are worthy of preservation, for EXAMPLE, the papers a person keeps in a safe deposit box.

valuation [val · yoo · *ay* · shen] *n.* 1. The price set upon something; the estimated worth of a thing; **assessed value**. 2. The act of establishing or estimating the value of a thing.
➤ price, worth, value.

value [*val* · yoo] *n.* 1. Monetary worth. For EXAMPLE, *see* cash value; face value; fair market value; par value; surrender value. 2. The worth of a thing in money, material, services, or other things for which it may be exchanged. *See* medium of exchange. 3. Estimated worth. *See* assessed value; valuation. 4. **Valuable consideration**; **adequate consideration**; **fair consideration**; **legal consideration**. *See* for value; holder for value; purchaser for value. *See also* actual book value; cash surrender value; cash value; commuted value; fair cash value; fair value; going concern value; intrinsic value; present value; stated value; true value.
➤ worth, appraisal, assessment, equivalent, price, expense, rate ("the value of the house"); bearing, connotation, denotation, esteem, importance, merit ("the value of doing it this way").

value added tax (VAT) [*ad* · ed] *n.* An **excise tax** imposed on the worth of a thing which each stage of processing or production adds to its value, its effect on the consumer being essentially the same as a **sales tax**.

value received [re · *seevd*] *n.* As used in a written instrument (EXAMPLE: a **promissory note**), the words "for value received" indicate that **legal consideration** has been given for the instrument.

value rule *n.* A **measure of damages** in an **action** for **breach of contract**, particularly an action brought by a homeowner against a builder; i.e., the difference between the value of the house as constructed and the house as it should have been constructed.

valued policy [*pol* · i · see] *n.* An insurance policy in which the value of the insured property is specifically stated in the policy. *Compare* unvalued policy.

vandalism [*van* · del · izm] *n.* Willful or malicious injury to or destruction of property; wanton and willful acts intended to injure, damage, or destroy property.
➤ destruction, mischief, ruination.

variable [*vair* · ee · ebl] *adj.* Changeable; capable of being changed.
➤ capricious, fickle, changeable, fluctuating, protean, temperamental, vacillating. *Ant.* fixed, certain.

variable annuity [a · *new* · i · tee] *n.* An **annuity** in which the amount the **annuitant** receives is not fixed but varies according to the degree of success of the investments made by the insurance company issuing the **annuity policy**.

variable rate mortgage [*more* · gej] *n.* Another term for an **adjustable rate mortgage**.

variance [*var* · ee · ense] *n.* 1. In zoning law, an exception from the strict application of a zoning ordinance, granted to relieve a property owner of unnecessary hardship. A variance allows the landowner to use the land in a manner that the law would not otherwise permit. 2. In **pleading**, an inconsistency between the **allegations** of a **complaint** or an **indictment** and the evidence offered at trial. A **fatal variance** will result in the dismissal of an **action** or the reversal of a conviction.
➤ inconsistency, conflict, discord, disunity, fluctuation, mutation.

VAT [vat] *n.* Acronym for **value added tax**.

vehicle [vee · *ik* · ul] *n.* 1. An automobile or other mode of transportation. 2. An agent or medium; a means to achieving a result.
➤ car, carrier, transportation, auto, automobile; agency, instrumentality, method, means, agent, expedient.

vehicular homicide [vee · *hik* · yoo · ler *hom* · i · side] *n.* A form of **negligent homicide** in which the death of a person is caused by the negligent, reckless, or unlawful operation of a motor vehicle.

veil *n.* A disguise; a covering.
v. To hide.
➤ *n.* screen, shelter, mask, shroud, camouflage, concealment, façade, mantilla.
v. disguise, mask, obscure, shroud, shield, conceal.

vendee [ven · *dee*] *n.* Buyer; purchaser. *Compare* vendor.

vendor [ven · *dor*] *n.* Seller. *Compare* vendee.
➤ businessperson, dealer, hawker, merchant, seller, peddler.

vendor's lien [ven · *dorz* leen] *n.* 1. The **lien** of a seller of real estate, which permits him to retain **title** until the **purchase money** is paid. 2. The **common law lien** a seller of goods has for the unpaid portion of the purchase price in circumstances where she is still in possession of the goods.

venire [vee · *nee* · ree] *n.* A **jury panel**.

venireman [vee · *nee* · ree · men] *n.* A member of a **jury panel**; a prospective juror.

venture [ven · cher] *n.* An undertaking; an enterprise, particularly a business enterprise. *See* joint venture.
v. To try; to take a chance.
➤ *n.* gamble, adventure, endeavor, essay, hazard, jeopardy, stake ("a risky venture"). *v.* hazard, chance, dare, assay, grope, attempt, operate, speculate, defy, endanger ("to venture out").

venture capital [*kap* · i · tel] *n.* **Capital** invested in a business enterprise, particularly a new enterprise; **risk capital**.

venue [ven · yoo] *n.* The county or **judicial district** in which a case is to be tried. In civil cases, venue may be based on where the events giving rise to the **cause of action**

V

699

V

took place or where the **parties** live or work. The venue of a criminal prosecution is the place where the crime was committed. Venue is distinguishable from **jurisdiction** because it is an issue only if jurisdiction already exists and because, unlike jurisdiction, it can be waived or changed by consent of the parties.

➤ county, district, zone, area, neighborhood, place of jurisdiction.

veracity [ve · *rass* · i · tee] *n.* Truthfulness.
➤ actuality, exactitude, genuineness, impartiality, precision, rectitude, truthfulness.

verbal [*ver* · bel] *adj.* 1. By word of mouth; spoken; as opposed to written; oral. *See* parol. 2. Pertaining to words, whether spoken or written.
➤ spoken, expressed, lingual, oral, rhetorical, stated, unwritten.

verbal acts *n.* Words which, in and of themselves, have legal consequences. EXAMPLE: The words "Lee is a thief" are a **defamation** if they are untrue.

verbal acts rule *n.* The rule that **verbal acts** are not **hearsay** because they are not offered to prove the truth of what was said.

verbal contract [*kon* · trakt] *n.* A **parol contract**; an **oral contract**.

verbal will *n.* An **oral will**; a **nuncupative will**.

verbatim [ver · *bay* · tim] *adj.* Word for word.
➤ accurately, directly, literally, precisely ("a verbatim transcript").

verbatim transcript [*tranz* · kript] *n.* A **transcript** that contains the exact words of the witnesses, the judge, counsel, and the other participants in a trial.

verdict [*ver* · dikt] *n.* The final decision of a jury concerning **questions of fact** submitted to it by the court for determination in the trial of a case. A **guilty verdict** can be returned in a criminal case only if it is the unanimous decision of the jurors. In a civil case, the jury may be required to return either a **general verdict** or a **special verdict**. *See also* chance verdict; compromise verdict; directed verdict; judgment notwithstanding the verdict; not guilty verdict; partial verdict; public verdict; quotient verdict; sealed verdict.

➤ adjudication, arbitration, conclusion, decision, decree, finding.

verdict against the evidence [a · *genst* the *ev* · i · dense] *n.* A verdict that is contrary to the **evidence**, or to the **weight of the evidence**, or that is not supported by **sufficient evidence**.

verdict by lot *n.* Same as **chance verdict**.

verdict contrary to law [*kon* · trare · ee] *n.* The verdict of a jury that has failed to follow the **instructions** of the judge with respect to **matters of law**. *See* jury instructions.

verdict of guilty [*gil* · tee] *n.* *See* guilty verdict.

verdict of not guilty [*gil* · tee] *n.* *See* not guilty verdict.

verification [vehr · i · fi · *kay* · shen] *n.* A **sworn statement** certifying the truth of the facts recited in an **instrument** or document. Thus, for EXAMPLE, a **verified complaint** is a **pleading** accompanied by an **affidavit** stating that the facts set forth in the complaint are true. *See also* authentication.
➤ confirmation, proof, evidence, corroboration, authentication.

verified [*vehr* · i · fide] *adj.* **Sworn**; **sworn to**; stated **under oath**.
➤ sworn, sworn to, authenticated, confirmed, corroborated.

verified complaint [kem · *plaint*] *n.* *See* verification.

verify [*vehr* · i · fy] *v.* 1. To **certify** the accuracy or truth of a statement **under oath**; to make a **verification**. 2. To establish the accuracy or truth of anything, whether or not by oath.
➤ attest, authenticate, confirm, debunk, document, justify, establish, certify; swear, declare, state, avow.

verisimilitude [*ver* · ih · sih · mil · ih · tyood] *n.* A likeness or similarity; authenticity.
➤ likeness, similarity, semblance; authenticity, credibility, plausibility.

versus [*ver* · ses] (*Latin*) *adv.* "Against." Its abbreviations, *v.* or *vs.*, are used in the **caption** of a case to indicate who is suing whom. EXAMPLE: *Smith v. Jones* (or *Smith vs. Jones*) means that Smith is suing Jones.

vertical [*ver* · ti · kel] *adj.* Perpendicular or at right angles to the ground; standing upright.
➤ upright, cocked, erect, perpendicular, plumb, sheer, upward.

vertical agreement [a · *gree* · ment] *n.* An agreement between a manufacturer and its dealers or distributors, the purpose of which is to control the price at which the manufacturer's product is sold to consumers. *Compare* horizontal agreement.

vertical integration [in · teg · *ray* · shen] *n.* *See* vertical merger.

vertical merger [*mer* · jer] *n.* A **merger** of two companies, one of which manufactures the product that the other buys from it and, in turn, sells to consumers. Depending upon the circumstances, a vertical merger may also be a **vertical restraint of trade.** *Compare* horizontal merger.

vertical price-fixing [-*fik* · sing] *n.* **Price-fixing** in **restraint of trade** under a **vertical agreement.** *Compare* horizontal price-fixing.

vertical restraint of trade [re · *straint*] *n.* **Restraint of trade** carried out under a **vertical agreement.** *Compare* horizontal restraint of trade.

vertical union [*yoon* · yen] *n.* Same as **industrial union.**

very [*vehr* · ee] *adv.* To a high degree.
➤ extremely, greatly, unusually, uncommonly, exceptionally.

very high degree of care [*vehr* · ee high de · *gree*] *n.* In the law of **negligence,** the **degree of care** that would be exercised by an extremely careful person in similar circumstances.

vest *v.* To give an immediate fixed right of present or future **enjoyment.** USAGE: "I will worry less about the future when my pension vests a year from now." *See* vested; vested pension.
➤ authorize, bestow, confer, empower, endow, pertain.

vested [*vest* · ed] *adj.* 1. That which cannot be taken away; **indefeasible.** 2. Absolute; definite; established; fixed.
➤ accrued, absolute, irrevocable, inalienable, immutable, inviolable, unconditional, definite, established, fixed ("a vested estate").

vested devise [de · *vize*] *n.* A **devise** that is **absolute** and **unconditional,** although it may be payable at a future time.

vested estate [es · *tate*] *n.* An **interest** in real property that is **absolute, unconditional,** and **indefeasible**; an **estate** that is not **contingent** or **expectant.** A vested estate provides a certain and fixed right of present or future **enjoyment**; it may be **conveyed** or **assigned** in the present even though it involves a **future interest.**

vested gift *n.* A gift that **vests** immediately, even though its **enjoyment** may be postponed.

vested in interest [*in* · trest] *n.* An **estate** is vested in interest when there is a present right of future **enjoyment.** *Compare* vested in possession. *See* vested estate.

vested in possession [poh · *zesh* · en] *n.* An **estate** is vested in possession when there is a right of present **enjoyment.** *Compare* vested in interest. *See* vested estate.

vested interest [*in* · trest] *n.* 1. As applied to real property, used interchangeably with **vested estate.** *Also see* interest. 2. In ordinary speech, a special interest. USAGE: "Farmers have a vested interest in price supports."

vested legacy [*leg* · e · see] *n.* A **legacy** that is **absolute** and **unconditional,** although it may be payable at a future time.

vested pension [*pen* · shen] *n.* A **pension** that cannot be taken away, regardless of what the employer or the employee does. Note, however, that a pension may vest either fully or partially. *See* Employee Retirement Income Security Act (ERISA).

vested remainder [re · *mane* · der] *n.* A **remainder estate** in real or personal property that is certain because the person or persons who are to inherit it exist or are identified at the time the will is written, and because their right to inherit is not contingent upon the occurrence of some future event. EXAMPLE: "I leave Blackacre to Bill Brown for as long as he lives and, after he dies, to his daughter, Bonnie Brown, and her heirs." Bonnie Brown and her heirs are the owners of a vested remainder. *See* contingent remainder.

vested right *n.* An **absolute right** that has been granted, or has accrued, and

V

V

cannot be taken away. EXAMPLE: one's right to a **vested pension**.

veteran [*vet* · ren] *n.* 1. A former member of the armed services. Generally, the term is applied only to those who received an honorable discharge. 2. A person who has had a great deal of experience at anything. USAGE: "a veteran trial lawyer."
adj. Experienced; seasoned.
➤ *n.* expert, past master, professional, trooper, master ("a trial court veteran"). *adj.* adept, disciplined, exercised, expert, hardened, inured ("a veteran ballplayer").

veterans' benefits [*ben* · e · fits] *n.* *See* Veterans Administration.

veterans' preference [*pref* · rense] *n.* Statutes, both federal and state, giving priority to veterans, particularly with respect to hiring and seniority.

Veterans Administration [*vet* · er · enz ad · min · is · *tray* · shen] *n.* Commonly referred to as the **VA**; the federal agency that administers federal statutes providing for the welfare of military veterans and their dependents. **Veterans' benefits** include medical and hospital care, disability payments, and insured mortgage loans at low rates of interest.

veto [*vee* · toh] *n.* The refusal of the **executive officer** of government (EXAMPLES: the president; a governor) to approve a **bill** passed by the legislature (EXAMPLES: Congress; a state legislature). A **veto** by the executive nullifies the bill unless the legislature is able to override the veto by the constitutionally required number of votes. In the case of a presidential veto, the requirement is two-thirds of the members of both houses of Congress. *See* line item veto; pocket veto.
v. To refuse permission; to reject.
➤ *n.* ban, declination, denial, interdiction, nonconsent, prohibition ("the president's veto").
v. ban, decline, deny, discountenance, forbid, interdict ("to veto the idea").

veto power [*pow* · er] *n.* The constitutional power of the **executive officer** of government to veto a legislative act.

vexatious [vek · *say* · shes] *adj.* Troublesome; annoying; harassing. *See* harassment.

➤ afflicting, disturbing, pesky, provoking, troublesome; annoying, harassing ("vexatious litigation").

vexatious litigation [lit · i · *gay* · shen] *n.* **Litigation** for the purpose of harassing and annoying an opponent, rather than for the purpose of **adjudicating** rights; a **frivolous suit**. *See also* malicious abuse of process.

vexatious refusal to pay [re · *fyooz* · el] *n.* A phrase that describes an insurance company's bad faith refusal to pay a claim.

vexatious suit *n.* *See* vexatious litigation.

viability [vy · e · *bil* · i · tee] *n.* 1. The ability of a fetus to live outside of its mother's womb. *See* viable child. 2. The ability of anything to exist.

viable [vy · ebl] *adj.* Capable of living; in the case of humans, a fetus that has reached a stage of development sufficient to permit it to live outside of the womb is described as "viable" and is referred to as a **viable fetus** or a **viable child**.
➤ applicable, doable, feasible, operable, usable, workable.

viable child *n.* In most jurisdictions, a **right of action** exists for a **personal injury** done to a "viable child" (*see* viable), and a viable child is a **person** under most states' **wrongful death statutes**.

viable fetus [*fee* · tes] *n.* *See* viable; viable child.

vicarious [vy · *kehr* · ee · us] *adj.* Done or experienced through another.
➤ commissioned, delegated, deputed, empathetic, surrogate, pretended, indirect, second-hand ("a vicarious thrill").

vicarious liability [ly · e · *bil* · i · tee] *n.* **Liability** imposed upon a person because of the act or omission of another. EXAMPLES: the liability of an employer for the conduct of its employees; the liability of a **principal** for the conduct of her **agent**. *See respondeat superior*.

vice *n.* 1. Evil, sinful, or immoral conduct. Thus, a police department's "vice squad" enforces laws prohibiting **pandering** and prostitution. 2. An imperfection or a bad habit. USAGE: "Chocolate is my vice."

adj. A title applied to a person who is empowered to take the place of another. EXAMPLE: a vice president.

➤ *n.* carnality, debasement, debauchery, iniquity, licentiousness, malignance ("Smoking is a vice"); blemish, demerit, fault, foible, imperfection, shortcoming ("Working too hard is my vice").
adj. second, assistant.

vicinity [vi · *sin* · i · tee] *n.* A nearby place. It is a relative term because, in the country, 15 miles away may be "in the vicinity," whereas, in the city, 15 blocks away may not.

➤ district, environs, locality, nearness, precinct, propinquity, purloins.

vicious [*vish* · es] *adj.* Corrupt, wrong; hateful.

➤ dangerous, bad, corrupt, cruel, hateful, malicious, violent, wicked ("vicious lies").

vicious animal [*vish* · ess *an* · i · mel] *n.*
1. An animal that is dangerous by nature.
2. A domestic animal with a known tendency for injuring people.

victim [*vik* · tem] *n.* A person against whom a crime, **tort**, or other wrong has been committed.

➤ target, complainant, aggrieved, prey, sufferer, injured party.

victim impact statement [*im* · pakt *state* · ment] *n.* At the time of sentencing, a statement made to the court concerning the effect the crime has had on the victim or on the victim's family.

victimless crime [*vik* · tem · less] *n.* A term applied to a crime that has no victim. EXAMPLES: prostitution; **sodomy** involving consenting adults.

victualer [*vit* · ler] *n.* A person who sells food for consumption on the premises. In some jurisdictions, a person who has been granted a license to operate a restaurant is known as a "licensed victualer."

vide [*vee* · day] (*Latin*) *v.* See; refer to. For EXAMPLE, *quod vide* or its abbreviation, *q.v.*, means "which see" and is a direction used in reference books to tell the reader that the preceding word is used elsewhere in the book.

videlicet [vee · de · *ly* · sit] (*Latin*) *prep.* That is to say; namely; **to wit**. In **pleading**, a term used to particularize a general statement or to explain a vague **allegation**. It is commonly abbreviated "*viz.*"

view *n.* 1. An **urban easement** that gives a person the right to an unobstructed vista from her windows. *See* urban servitude. *See also* ancient lights; easement of light and air. 2. An inspection by a judge or jurors of the scene of a crime or the site of an **injury**. *See* shower; viewer. 3. Sight. *See* plain view doctrine. 4. Opinion, i.e., point of view.
v. to look at; to inspect.

➤ *n.* appearance, aspect, glimpse, illustration, vista, prospect, spectacle, stretch ("The view from the window was wonderful"); analysis, audit, contemplation, display, inspection, scrutiny; attitude, concept, deduction, judgment, notion, opinion, persuasion ("to have a view on abortion").
v. consider, descry, behold, examine, observe, perceive, discern, spy, explore ("to view the murder scene").

viewer [*vyoo* · er] *n.* A member of a **body** or **commission** appointed by the court to inspect a site for a specific purpose (EXAMPLES: making a **property assessment**; locating a new highway) and to report its findings to the court.

➤ witness, eyewitness, bystander, observer, watcher.

village [*vil* · ej] *n.* A word whose meaning varies from state to state. In most states, it simply means a small community with residences and, sometimes, businesses clustered together; in other states, it means a **municipal corporation** smaller than, or no larger than, a town.

➤ center, crossroads, hamlet, town, suburb, community.

vinculo matrimonii [*vin* · kyoo · loh mat · ri · *moh* · ni · eye] (*Latin*) *n./adj.* Means "bonds of marriage." *See* divorce a vinculo matrimonii.

vindicate [*vin* · di · kate] *v.* To clear of blame or doubt.

➤ absolve, exculpate, acquit, release, justify, pardon, excuse, clear.

V

vindictive damages [vin · *dik* · tiv *dam* · e · jez] *n.* Same as **exemplary damages** or **punitive damages**.

violate [*vy* · o · late] *v.* 1. To disobey; to infringe. USAGE: "violate the law." 2. To ravish or rape. 3. To treat someone dishonorably or disrespectfully. *See* violation.
➤ breach, disobey, encroach, resist ("violate the law"); abuse, befoul, defile, deflower, desecrate, invade, profane ("to violate the sanctity of marriage").

violation [vy · o · *lay* · shen] *n.* 1. The act of breaking the law; an infringement of the law; a violation of the law. 2. Sometimes used as a synonym for an **infraction**. 3. The act of ravishing or raping. 4. Treating someone dishonorably or disrespectfully.
➤ abuse, contravention, illegality, misdemeanor, transgression ("a violation of the law"); assault, defacement, destruction, dishonor, pollution, profanation, rapine, ruin, sacrilege ("a violation of the sanctity of marriage").
violation of law *n.* *See* violation.

violence [vy · o · lense] *n.* Unjustified physical force applied with the intention to **injure** or **damage**. *See* violent.
➤ brutality, constraint, fierceness, sharpness, storminess, terrorism, aggressiveness, savagery, assault, fury, eruption.

violent [vy · o · lent] *adj.* Acting with unjustified physical force. *See* violence.
➤ savage, brutal, coercive, berserk, demonic, hysterical, murderous, potent ("a violent crime"); acute, devastating, immoderate, outrageous, painful, terrible ("a violent seizure").
violent death *n.* As used in the law, death caused by an **instrumentality** or **agency** external to the deceased, i.e., death from other than natural causes.

vir [veer] (*Latin*) *n.* A man; a husband.

virtual [*ver* · choo · el] *adj.* Almost; near.
➤ constructive, essential, implicit, implied, indirect, potential ("virtual reality").
virtual adoption [a · *dop* · shen] *n.* Same as **equitable adoption**.
virtual representation [rep · re · zen · *tay* · shen] *n.* The principle under which members of a **class** are deemed to be represented in a lawsuit by one of the class, although the members themselves are not named as **parties**; in effect, a **class action**. *See* representation.

virtue [*ver* · choo] *n.* 1. Moral excellence. 2. Chastity. 3. Effect; power; efficacy. *See* by virtue of.
➤ character, ethicality, innocence, morality, respectability, uprightness; effect, power, efficacy.

visa [*vee* · za] *n.* A stamp affixed to a passport by an official of a country one wishes to visit. It is a recognition of the validity of the passport and approval to enter the country.
➤ permission, indorsement, certification.

visible [*viz* · ih · bul] *adj.* Able to be seen; perceptible.
➤ perceptible, clear, apparent, noticeable, blatant, plain, manifest, conspicuous.

visible means of support [*viz* · ibl means of sup · *port*] *n.* A standard for determining **vagrancy**. It means circumstances from which it may be presumed that a person is able to support himself or to obtain support. Having a job, receiving **unemployment compensation benefits**, or the fact that one lives with a spouse who is employed are EXAMPLES of visible means of support.

visitation [viz · i · *tay* · shen] *n.* 1. Short for **visitation rights**, i.e., the right of a divorced parent who does not have custody of his child to visit the child at such times and places as the court may order. 2. An official visit made for the purpose of investigating or supervising. EXAMPLE: the visit of a welfare worker to the home of an **AFDC** recipient.
visitation rights *n.* *See* visitation.

visitor [*viz* · i · ter] *n.* A person who enters premises at the invitation of the occupant, whether for business or social purposes. *See* business invitee.
➤ caller, guest, habitué, inspector, invitee, transient, visitant.

vital [vy · tel] *adj.* 1. Essential. 2. Alive.
➤ essential, basic, necessary, required, principal, material, significant ("vital to our case"); living, breathing, animate, live ("vital signs").

V

vital statistics [*vy* · tel ste · *tiss* · tiks] *n.*
Statistics maintained by government, commonly by state health departments, pertaining to births, deaths, and marriages, as well as to matters of health and disease.

vitiate [*vish* · ee · ate] *v.* To invalidate; to nullify; to **void**.
➤ invalidate, nullify, void, abrogate, quash, annul, revoke, abate.

viz. (*Latin*) *prep.* Abbreviation of *videlicet*, meaning "that is to say"; namely; **to wit**.

vocation [vo · *kay* · shen] *n.* A trade, profession, or occupation, as opposed to a hobby.
➤ career, employment, métier, occupation, trade, profession, pursuit, work.

vocational rehabilitation
[vo · *kay* · shen · el re · hab · il · i · *tay* · shen] *n.* Training that restores physical, mental, or emotional health and, with it, earning capacity, to persons disabled by injury, sickness, or other trauma. Most states have vocational rehabilitation departments or bureaus that supervise and fund such activities. *See* rehabilitation.

voiceprinting [*voiss* · prin · ting] *n.* A process by which, using a **spectograph**, a "map" or "print" may be made of a person's voice which distinguishes it from all other voices, as a person's fingerprints distinguish her from everyone else. Many courts allow voiceprints to be used as a means of identification in circumstances where identification can be made by voice.

void *adj.* **Null**; without **legal effect**. Although, strictly speaking, a transaction that is void is a transaction that, in law, never happened, the words "void", "void and of no effect," and "**null and void**," are often used in statutes and in other legal documents, such as deeds, mortgages, and leases, to mean merely **voidable**, that is, capable of being avoided. *Compare* voidable.
n. An empty space. USAGE: "The rocket was fired into the void."
v. To invalidate; to **nullify**. USAGE: "Did the court void its order?"
➤ *adj.* abandoned, barren, bereft, deprived, empty, tenantless ("a void area in space"); nullified, avoided, fruitless, ineffectual, unenforceable, unnotified ("a void check").

n. blank, cavity, hollow, nihility, nullity, space, vacuity ("a void in space").
v. clear, discharge, dispose, evacuate, relieve, vacate ("to void a container"); abnegate, annul, invalidate, launder, sanitize, trim, vacate ("to void a check").

void contract [*kon* · trakt] *n.* A **contract** that creates no **legal rights**; the equivalent of no contract at all. *Compare* voidable contract.

void judgment [*juj* · ment] *n.* A **judgment** that has no **legal effect**; a judgment that binds no one. EXAMPLE: a judgment rendered by a court lacking **jurisdiction**. *Compare* voidable judgment.

void marriage [*mehr* · ej] *n.* A marriage absolutely prohibited by law. EXAMPLE: marriage with a person who is not **of age**. *Compare* voidable marriage.

void process [*pross* · ess] *n.* **Process** issued by a court that has no power to issue it.

voidable [*void* · ebl] *adj.* Avoidable; subject to **disaffirmance**; **defective** but valid unless **disaffirmed** by the person entitled to disaffirm. *Compare* void.
➤ avoidable, reversible, revokable, nullifiable ("a voidable contract").

voidable contract [*kon* · trakt] *n.* A **contract** that may be avoided or **disaffirmed** by one of the parties because it is **defective**, for EXAMPLE, a contract induced by **fraud** (*see* fraud in the inducement) or a contract with a minor. *Compare* void contract.

voidable judgment [*juj* · ment] *n.* A **judgment** that is erroneous and is therefore subject to being **reversed** or **vacated**. *Compare* void judgment.

voidable marriage [*mehr* · ej] *n.* A marriage that is prohibited by law but can only be dissolved by **annulment**. EXAMPLE: a **bigamous** marriage. *Compare* void marriage. *See* annulment of marriage.

voidable preference [*pref* · rense] *n.* Under the **Bankruptcy Code**, a **preference** is voidable if it takes place within a specified number of days before the filing of the **petition in bankruptcy** and if it allows the creditor to obtain more than she would have received from the **bankruptcy court**.

V

V

voiding [*void* · ing] *n.* 1. The act of declaring **void** that which is **voidable**. 2. Emptying.

voir dire [vwar deer] (*French*) *n./adj.* Means "look speak." *See* voir dire examination.

voir dire examination [eg · zam · i · *nay* · shen] *n.* **Examination** of a potential juror for the purpose of determining whether she is qualified and acceptable to act as a juror in the case. A prospective juror who a **party** decides is unqualified or unacceptable may be **challenged for cause** or may be the subject of a **peremptory challenge**.

volenti non fit injuria [voh · *len* · tee non fit in · *joor* · ee · ah] (*Latin*) *n.* Means "there is no injury if there is consent." The legal maxim that a person is not **injured** in the eyes of the law if he consented to the act in question or was willing that it should occur. It is the concept upon which the principle of **voluntary assumption of risk** is based.

voluntary [*vol* · en · ter · ee] *adj.* A word applied to an act freely done out of choice, not brought about by coercion, duress, or accident.
➤ uncoerced, elective, gratuitous, unimpelled, volitional, chosen.
Ant. mandatory, forced.

voluntary abandonment [a · *ban* · dcn · ment] *n.* Voluntarily leaving one's spouse. The voluntary **abandonment** of one's spouse gives the abandoned spouse grounds for divorce. *See also* desertion.

voluntary alienation [ale · yen · *ay* · shen] *n.* The act of voluntarily transferring **title** to property. *Compare* involuntary alienation. *See* alienation.

voluntary assignment [a · *sine* · ment] *n.* An **assignment for the benefit of creditors** which a debtor makes voluntarily, as opposed to an involuntary assignment in a **bankruptcy proceeding**. *See* assignment.

voluntary assumption of risk [a · *sump* · shen] *n.* *See* assumption of risk.

voluntary bankruptcy [*bank* · rupt · see] *n.* A **bankruptcy** that the debtor himself initiates, as opposed to an **involuntary bankruptcy**.

voluntary bar *n.* A bar from which attorneys may resign without losing the privilege of practicing law; a **bar association**. *Compare* integrated bar.

voluntary commitment [ku · *mit* · ment] *n.* The process by which a person suffering from a mental illness is admitted of his own free will to a mental institution and retained for diagnosis and treatment. *Compare* involuntary commitment.

voluntary confession [kun · *fesh* · en] *n.* A **confession** given of her own free will by a criminal defendant. A criminal defendant's voluntary confession is admissible as evidence against her. *Compare* involuntary confession.

voluntary conveyance [kun · *vey* · ense] *n.* *See* voluntary deed.

voluntary deed *n.* A **deed** or other conveyance for which no **valuable consideration** is given. EXAMPLE: a deed made in **voluntary settlement**. *Compare* involuntary conveyance.

voluntary discontinuance [dis · kun · *tin* · yoo · ense] *n.* Same as a **discontinuance**, as every discontinuance is voluntary. *Compare* involuntary discontinuance.

voluntary dismissal [dis · *miss* · el] *n.* The **dismissal** of a lawsuit at the plaintiff's request; the **discontinuance** of an **action**. *Compare* involuntary dismissal.

voluntary domicile [*dom* · i · sile] *n.* Same as **domicile of choice**.

voluntary intoxication [in · tok · si · *kay* · shen] *n.* Self-induced intoxication, as opposed to **involuntary intoxication**. Only involuntary intoxication is an **affirmative defense** to a criminal charge.

voluntary manslaughter [*man* · slaw · ter] *n.* A **homicide** committed with the **intent to kill**, but without **deliberation, premeditation**, or **malice**; i.e., a homicide committed with **provocation** or in the **heat of passion**. *Compare* involuntary manslaughter. *See* manslaughter.

voluntary nonsuit [*non* · sute] *n.* *See* nonsuit.

voluntary payment [*pay* · ment] *n.* A payment made willingly and without objection, as opposed to a payment made for the purpose of avoiding **legal process**.

voluntary quit *n.* Under **unemployment compensation acts**, an employee who leaves her employment by choice. Such an employee is a "voluntary quit" and is therefore ineligible for **unemployment compensation benefits**.

voluntary settlement [*setl* · ment] *n.* A **settlement** that requires no **consideration** other than **love and affection**. EXAMPLE: a **family settlement**.

voluntary statement [*state* · ment] *n.* *See* voluntary confession.

voluntary trust *n.* A **trust** in which the **trustee** consents to perform trust duties, as opposed to an **involuntary trust** or **constructive trust**, which is imposed by **operation of law**.

volunteer [vol · en · *teer*] *n.* 1. A person who, without either a moral or legal duty to do so, pays the debt or **discharges** the **obligation** of another. A person who discharges an obligation to which he is a **party**, or pays a debt in which he has an **interest**, is not a volunteer. *See* mere volunteer; officious intermeddler. 2. A person who works for another, without compensation, of his own free will. 3. A person who enlists in the armed services of her own volition, not under the threat of being drafted.
v. To offer one's services without compensation.
➤ *n.* unpaid worker, charity worker, gratuitous worker, good samaritan ("a Red Cross volunteer").
v. step forward, present oneself, submit, put forward, donate, supply ("to volunteer for the mission").

vote *n.* 1. The choice expressed by a voter in an election, with respect either to candidates or to a **proposition**. 2. The point of view of a legislator with respect to a **bill** submitted to the legislature for approval. 3. The total number of votes cast at an election. *See* majority vote; one person, one vote rule; plurality vote.
v. To cast a ballot in an election.
➤ *n.* ballot, preference, suffrage, franchise, say, plebiscite, election ("the presidential vote").

v. choose, confer, declare, determine, enact, judge, opt, pronounce ("to vote for the governor").

voter [*voh* · ter] *n.* 1. A person who expresses her choice in an election. 2. A person who is legally entitled to vote. *See* eligible voter; qualification of voter; qualified voter; registered voter; registration of voters.
➤ citizen, participant, elector.

voting [*voh* · ting] *n./adj.* Pertaining to the vote or the right to vote.

voting rights *n.* *See* voting stock. *Also see* Voting Rights Act of 1965.

voting stock *n.* Corporate stock, usually **common stock**, that carries with it the right to vote on certain matters affecting the corporation, including the membership of the board of directors. *Compare* nonvoting stock.

voting trust *n.* An agreement under which the owners of **voting stock** transfer the right to vote their **shares** to a **trustee**, retaining all other rights, including the right to receive **dividends**.

Voting Rights Act of 1965 [*voh* · ting] *n.* *See* Civil Rights Acts.

vouch *v.* 1. To **warrant**. 2. To affirm the truth of a statement. 3. To give assurance of another's honesty or ability.
➤ substantiate, certify, authenticate, warrant, underwrite, document, affirm.

voucher [*vouch* · er] *n.* 1. A receipt or other evidence of payment, showing the date, amount, and purpose of a payment. 2. A writing that authorizes the disbursement of money.
➤ receipt, release, acknowledgment.

vow *n.* A promise.
v. To promise; to swear.
➤ *n.* promise, word, affirmation, convenant, pledge, oath.
v. declare, promise, pledge, swear, testify, covenant, affirm.

voyeur [vwoy · *er*] *n.* A person who obtains sexual gratification by observing sexual acts. A **peeping tom** is a voyeur.
➤ peeping tom, snooper, eavesdropper, visual rapist.

V

vs. *adv.* Abbreviation of **versus**, *Latin* for "against." Although the abbreviation **v.** is preferred, *vs.* is also used in case **captions** to indicate who is suing whom. EXAMPLE: *Smith vs. Jones* means that Smith is suing Jones.

vulnerable [*vul* · ner · uh · bul] *adj.* Unguarded; open to attack, either physical or mental.
➤ dependent, defenseless, unprotected, accessible, emotional.

V

waffle [*waf* · ful] *v.* To be indecisive; to flip-flop on issues.

➤ hedge, flounder, bobble, grope ("He waffled on various points, like a typical politician").

wage *n.* Compensation or earnings paid to employees, whether by the hour or by some other period of time, or by the job or piece. *See* piecework. Wages include all remuneration paid for personal services, including commissions, bonuses, and **gratuities**, and, under the **Fair Labor Standards Act**, includes board and lodging as well. In one sense, the term "wage" includes salary; in other uses, the term "salary" is reserved for the remuneration paid to executives, professionals, or supervisors, usually on a weekly, biweekly, monthly, or semimonthly basis. *Compare* salary. *See* minimum wage laws; prevailing wage.

v. To conduct or carry on.

➤ *n.* allowance, compensation, emolument, payment, salary, stipend ("daily wage").
v. carry out, conduct, do, fulfill, make, prosecute, pursue ("to wage a war").

wage and hour acts *n.* Federal and state statutes establishing the minimum wage that may be paid to employees and the number of hours they may work. The **Fair Labor Standards Act** is the federal wage and hour act. *See* hours of labor; minimum wage laws.

wage and hour laws *n.* Same as **wage and hour acts**.

wage assignment [a · *sine* · ment] *n.* An **assignment** of one's wages, usually to a creditor for the payment of a debt or **judgment**.

wage earner's plan [*ern* · erz] *n.* Under **Chapter 13** of the **Bankruptcy Code**, a debtor who is a wage earner and who files a repayment plan acceptable to his creditors and the court will be given additional time in which to meet his obligations.

wager [*way* · jer] *n.* An activity in which money or property is risked against the occurrence of chance or upon the outcome of an uncertain event; i.e., a bet.
v. To bet.

➤ *n.* action, challenge, gamble, bet, parlay, stake, venture ("a wager on the game").
v. bet, chance, hazard, lay, pledge, risk ("to wager on the football game").

wager policy [*pol* · i · see] *n.* Same as **gambling policy**.

wagering contract [*way* · jer · ing *kon* · trakt] *n.* Same as **gambling contract**.

wages [*way* · jez] *n. Plural* of **wage**. *See* wage.

Wagner Act [*wag* · ner] *n. See* National Labor Relations Act.

wait and see doctrine [*dok* · trin] *n.* A rule followed in some states, under which the determination as to whether the **grant** of a **future interest** violates the **rule against perpetuities** is made at the time of the occurrence of the uncertain event upon which the future interest depends, rather than at the time the grant is made. In some jurisdictions, this principle is known as the **second look doctrine**.

waiting period [*way* · ting *peer* · ee · ed] *n.*
1. A period of time immediately after an injury, for which **workers' compensation** is not payable. 2. A period of time following the effective date of health insurance, during which coverage is not applicable or during which a **preexisting condition clause** is in effect.

waive *v.* To voluntarily relinquish or renounce a right one knows one has and could have enforced. *See* waiver.
➤ abandon, cede, defer, forgo, postpone, prorogue, resign, suspend, relinquish ("to waive a preliminary hearing").

waiver [*way* · ver] *n.* The intentional relinquishment or renunciation of a **right, claim**, or **privilege** a person knows he has. *See and compare* express waiver; implied waiver.
➤ abandonment, abdication, forgoing, refusal, relinquishment, renunciation.

  waiver by election [e · *lek* · shen] *n.* A **defense** that arises when a plaintiff who has sought two **remedies** which are inconsistent with each other waives one of them by choosing the other. *See* election; election of remedies.

  waiver of exemption [eg · *zemp* · shen] *n.* The voluntary relinquishment by a debtor of her statutory right to retain a portion of her property free from the claims of her creditors. Such a waiver usually takes the form of a provision in a **note**, lease, or other agreement. *See* exemption; exemption statutes.

  waiver of immunity [im · *yoon* · i · tee] *n.* A witness who testifies voluntarily waives her **privilege against self-incrimination**. *See* immunity.

  waiver of protest [*proh* · test] *n.* The relinquishment by a party of his right to have a **draft** or check **protested** upon nonpayment. *See* protest.

  waiver of tort *n.* The relinquishment by a plaintiff of his right to sue in **tort** by electing to sue in contract in a case where both **remedies** are available to him. *See* waiver by election.

walkout [*wawk* · out] *n.* Same as **strike**.
➤ strike, protest, work stoppage, picket.

want *n.* The absence of something needed or desired.
v. 1. To desire; to wish for. 2. To have need of. 3. To be needy. To lack.
➤ *n.* desire, appetite, craving, fancy, hankering, necessity ("the want of food"); absence, dearth, lack, exigency, impoverishment, paucity ("for want of water").
v. ache, aspire, choose, covet, desire, lust ("to want a new car"); be deficient, be insufficient, be without, miss, require, starve ("to want for water in the desert").

want of consideration [kun · sid · e · *ray* · shen] *n.* Total absence of **consideration** for a contract. *Compare* failure of consideration.

want of jurisdiction [joor · is · *dik* · shen] *n.* With respect to a court, the absence of authority to hear and determine a case; in other words, lack of power over the **parties**, the subject matter, or the property involved in the dispute. *See* jurisdiction.

want of prosecution [pross · e · *kyoo* · shen] *n.* Lacking evidence or witnesses necessary to prosecute a case. USAGE: "to dismiss for want of prosecution." *See* failure to prosecute.

wanton [*want* · en] *adj.* 1. Reckless; careless; undisciplined; aimless; recklessly indifferent to the rights or safety of others. 2. Malicious; willful. 3. Lewd; lascivious. *n.* A profligate person.
➤ *adj.* extravagant, lustful, dissipated, promiscuous, unconscionable, unprincipled ("wanton need"); cruel, malicious, gratuitous, groundless, malevolent, perverse ("wanton misconduct"); capricious, fanciful, heedless, intemperate, lavish, reckless, volatile, whimsical ("wanton disregard for human life").
n. debauchee, libertine, pampered person, prostitute, rake, spoiled person.

wanton misconduct [mis · *kon* · dukt] *n.* An act or failure to act performed with knowledge that injury is likely to result, and with reckless disregard for the consequences.

wanton negligence [*neg* · li · jense] *n.* Conduct that evidences a total lack of care for the safety of others and complete indifference to consequences. *See* negligence.

W

wanton omission [o · *mish* · en] *n.* The failure to perform an act with knowledge that such omission is likely to result in injury.

war *n.* Armed conflict; combat.

➤ combat, battle, conflict, hostility, fight, feud, strife, struggle.

war power [*pow* · er] *n.* On occasion, the constitutional power of Congress to declare war is in conflict with the president's constitutional control of the armed forces and his authority to make foreign policy. This conflict is, to some degree, reduced by the *War Powers Act,* which limits the number of days the president can commit U.S. troops abroad without congressional authorization.

ward *n.* 1. An administrative division of a city or town. 2. A person placed under **guardianship** because he is unable to manage his own affairs. (EXAMPLES: a **minor**; an **incompetent person**.) Such a person is often referred to as a **ward of the court**. *See* conservator; guardian.

➤ district, canton, diocese, division, parish, quarter ("city ward"); charge, client, dependent, godchild, guardianship, minor, orphan ("The bachelor supports his young ward").

ward of the court *n.* *See* ward.

warden [*ward* · en] *n.* The superintendent of a prison; a keeper; a guard.

➤ administrator, caretaker, curator, deacon, guardian, skipper, superintendent.

warehouse [*ware* · house] *n.* A building used for the storage of goods.

➤ depository, distribution center, establishment, storehouse, stockroom, store.

warehouse receipt [re · *seet*] *n.* A receipt for goods issued by a person engaged in the business of storing goods. It is a **document of title**.

warehouseman [*ware* · house · men] *n.* A person engaged in the business of storing goods.

warehouseman's lien [*ware* · house · menz leen] *n.* The right of a **warehouseman** to retain possession of goods stored with her until the storage charges are paid. *See* lien.

warning [*worn* · ing] *n.* Notice; indication.

➤ notice, alert, foreboding, admonition, caution, augury, notification, portent ("to receive warning of an impending attack").

warrant [*war* · ent] *n.* 1. A form of **process** issued by a court. EXAMPLES: an **arrest warrant**; a **search warrant**. *See also* bench warrant; possessory warrant. 2. A certificate issued by a corporation evidencing the right of its holder to receive a specified number of shares of stock in the corporation; i.e., a **stock warrant** or **share warrant**. *See* share certificate. 3. A **draft** on the treasury of a city or town, issued by its governing body (EXAMPLE: a **city council**; a town council), ordering that a particular payment be made; a **treasury warrant**. 4. Notice of a **town meeting**. *v.* 1. To guarantee that a thing is as it is declared to be or as it seems to be. 2. To give assurance that **title** to real property is **good title**. 3. To assure; to promise.

➤ *n.* authorization, authentication, permit, license, shingle, subpoena ("a warrant for his arrest").

v. guarantee, authorize, affirm, empower, endorse, permit, assure, promise, stipulate ("to warrant that delivery will be made on time").

warrant of arrest [a · *rest*] *n.* *See* arrest warrant.

warrant of attorney [a · *tern* · ee] *n.* A form of **power of attorney** designating and authorizing an **attorney in fact** for the **confession of judgment**.

warrantless [*war* · ent · less] *adj.* Without a **warrant**.

warrantless arrest [a · *rest*] *n.* The arrest of a person without an **arrest warrant**. A police officer may make such an arrest if a crime is committed in her presence or if she has a **reasonable belief** that a crime has been committed.

warrantless search *n.* The arrest of a person without a **search warrant**. A police officer may make such a search if it is made in connection with a **lawful arrest**. Otherwise, a warrant must be obtained. *See* Fourth Amendment; search and seizure.

warranty [*war* · en · tee] *n.* 1. Generally, an agreement to be responsible for all **damages** arising from the falsity of a statement or the failure of an assurance. 2. With respect to a **contract for sale of goods**, a promise, either express or **implied by law**, with respect to the fitness or

W

W

merchantability of the article that is the subject of the contract. *See and compare* express warranty; implied warranty; implied warranty of fitness for a particular purpose; implied warranty of merchantability. *See also* full warranty; limited warranty. 3. The **covenants** made by a **grantor** in a **warranty deed**. *See also* construction warranty; homeowners warranty. 4. The term "warranty" in an insurance policy usually constitutes an assurance by the insured of the existence of specified circumstances on which coverage depends, as well as an assurance that those circumstances will continue to exist.
➤ assurance, bail, bond, certificate, covenant, guarantee, pledge, assurance, obligation.

warranty deed *n.* A **deed** that contains **title covenants**. *See and compare* general warranty; special warranty.

warranty of fitness [*fit* · ness] *n. See* implied warranty of fitness for a particular purpose. *See also* implied warranty.

warranty of fitness for a particular purpose [*fit* · ness for a per · *tik* · yoo · ler *per* · pes] *n. See* implied warranty of fitness for a particular purpose. *See also* implied warranty.

warranty of habitability [hab · it · e · *bil* · i · tee] *n.* 1. A warranty **implied by law** that leased premises are fit to occupy. *See* habitability. *Also see* habitable; habitable repair. 2. A **construction warranty**.

warranty of merchantability [mer · chent · e · *bil* · i · tee] *n. See* implied warranty of merchantability. *Also see* implied warranty.

warranty of title [*ty* · tel] *n.* With respect to the sale of goods, a warranty by the seller, **implied by law**, that she has **title** to the goods.

wash sale *n.* An illegal method of manipulating stock prices by quickly buying and selling the same stock to create the impression of activity and thereby attract investors.

waste *n.* 1. The destruction, misuse, alteration, or neglect of premises by the person **in possession**, to the detriment of another's **interest** in the property. EXAMPLE: a tenant's polluting of a pond on leased land. *See* nul waste. 2. The failure to

conserve generally. EXAMPLE: a loss of **assets** or the diminution of a **decedent's estate** due to mismanagement by the **executor**. 3. That which is left over, useless, or even dangerous. EXAMPLES: **hazardous waste; solid waste; toxic waste**.
v. 1. To dwindle; to dissipate. 2. To ruin or destroy.
➤ *n.* decay, desolation, disuse, improvidence, misapplication, squandering ("a waste of time"); badlands, barrens, brush, jungle, solitude, tundra ("a waste of desert land"); debris, dregs, excess, leavings, leftovers, rummage, scrap ("the pile of waste").
v. atrophy, corrode, debilitate, decline, emaciate, gnaw, misemploy, prodigalize, thin ("to waste away"); depreciate, devastate, desolate, despoil, pillage, rape ("to waste the village").

wasting [*waste* · ing] *v.* 1. Consuming needlessly or uselessly. 2. Being gradually consumed.

wasting assets [*ass* · ets] *n.* **Assets** that are subject to depletion; i.e., to being consumed by harvesting or production. EXAMPLES: timber; oil; natural gas; mineral deposits. *See* depletion allowance.

wasting property [*prop* · er · tee] *n.* Property that is rendered valueless by the passage of time or that is consumed by use. EXAMPLES: **copyrights**; manufacturing equipment; mineral deposits.

wasting trust *n.* 1. A **trust** in which the **trust property** is **wasting property**. 2. A trust in which the **trustee** is authorized to use the **principal** to provide income to the **beneficiaries**.

watch *v.* 1. To look at; to observe. 2. To guard or protect.
➤ observe, witness, see, discern, notice, glimpse, behold ("to watch a ballgame"); patrol, tend, protect, attend to ("to watch over the compound").

water [*waw* · ter] *n. See* ground water; high water line; high water mark; inland waters; navigable waters; nonnavigable waters; percolating waters; private waters; surface water; territorial waters; tidal waters.

water district [*dis* · trikt] *n.* A territorial division created by government for the purpose of providing the public with a water supply. *See* public corporation; quasi corporation. *Compare* drainage district; sewer district.

water rights *n.* An **easement** for the use of water or for the right to use another's premises to transport water over or through.

watercourse [*waw · ter · corse*] *n.* A river or other stream or channel for water. It may be either a **natural watercourse** or a manmade stream or artificial channel.

watered stock [*waw · terd*] *n.* **Shares of stock** issued by a corporation as **paid-up stock** but which have in fact been issued without any **consideration** or for **inadequate consideration** (for EXAMPLE, in exchange for property or services that were deliberately overvalued).

waters of the United States [*yoo · ny · ted*] *See* inland waters; territorial waters.

watershed [*waw · ter · shed*] *n.* An area drained by a particular river or stream.

way *n.* 1. A method or approach. 2. A passage or a right to pass over the land of another. *See* private way; public way; right of way.
➤ action, approach, method, contrivance, expedient, manners, modus, scheme ("Which way will we do this?"); access, admittance, alternative, boulevard, entrance, path ("the way to the back room"); aspect, behavior, custom, detail, fashion, fettle, proxis ("That's just her way").

way of necessity [*ne · sess · i · tee*] *n.* A type of **easement of access**. In circumstances where the **conveyance** of a part of a tract of land results in either the part conveyed or the part retained being shut off from access to a public road, an **implied easement** is created to provide a road or way to the outside world.

waybill [*way · bil*] *n.* A document generated by a **carrier**, listing and describing all of the goods in a particular shipment, together with shipping and delivery instructions.

ways *n.* Manner; method; means.

ways and means committee [*kum · it · ee*] *n.* A **legislative committee** whose responsibility is to study and propose methods for raising revenue for the support of the government.

weapon [*wep · en*] *n.* Any device used to destroy, defeat, or injure an enemy; an instrument of offensive or defensive combat. *See* deadly weapon.
➤ arms, armament, artillery, firearm, cudgel, explosive, gun, rifle, pistol, heat.

wear and tear *n.* The gradual deterioration of premises as a result of normal use, lapse of time, the weather, and the like. USAGE: "A landlord is not entitled to use the tenant's **security deposit** to pay for damage resulting from ordinary wear and tear."

wedlock [*wed · lok*] *n.* The state of being married; marriage.
➤ marriage, matrimony, connubiality, union.

week *n.* 1. A period of any seven consecutive days. 2. A period of seven consecutive days beginning with Sunday and ending with Saturday.

weight *n.* 1. As it concerns evidence, the importance or effect of evidence. *See* weight of the evidence. 2. The heaviness of a person or a thing, commonly expressed in pounds and ounces. *See and compare* gross weight; net weight.
➤ adiposity, mass, ballast, density, gross, ponderosity ("to be beyond one's ideal weight"); anchor, ballast, counterpoise, pendulum, plumb, sandbag ("The scale's weight was too light"); access, authority, clout, credit, efficacy, force ("to give weight to a pressing matter"); burden, duty, encumbrance, incubus, onus, oppression ("to carry emotional weight").

weight of the evidence [*ev · i · dense*] *n.* The total effect of all of the **evidence** in a case. The **party** who has the "weight of the evidence" on his side must, as a **matter of law**, prevail in a lawsuit. The "weight of the evidence" has nothing to do with the amount of evidence the party presents, only with whether that evidence is convincing. *See* preponderance of the evidence.

welfare [*wel · fare*] *n.* 1. A common term for **public assistance** programs that aid the poor. EXAMPLES: **general relief; AFDC.** 2. In a broader sense, the good of the people; the public welfare.
➤ aid, relief, dole, assistance; prosperity, happiness, success, benefit, profit, felicity, affluence, relief, assistance, financial aid.

W

W

wetlands [*wet* · landz] *n.* Areas of land that consistently have wet soil. (EXAMPLES: swamps; marshes.) Wetlands are protected by **federal statute** because they are breeding and nesting grounds for fish, birds, and other wildlife.

Wharton Rule [*whar* · ten] *n.* Same as **concert of action rule**.

when *adv.* At what time. Sometimes "when" is used instead of "if" to indicate a condition or a contingency.

whereas [where · *az*] *adv.* An introductory word used in formal documents, meaning "when in fact."

whereby [where · *by*] *adv.* A word that often appears in a **complaint**, meaning "by means of which."

wherefore [*where* · for] *adv.* A word that often introduces the **prayer** at the end of a **complaint**, meaning "for this reason."

whiplash [*whip* · lash] *n.* The term used to describe a **personal injury** to the neck. Whiplash commonly occurs when the car in which the victim is riding is struck in the rear, the impact throwing her head violently backwards.

whistleblower acts [*whissl* · bloh · wer] *n.* Federal and state statutes protecting employees who disclose safety violations and related illegal conduct engaged in by their employers.

white collar crime [*koll* · er] *n.* A phrase describing nonviolent crimes of the sort committed by executives, bankers, accountants, and others who are regularly involved with large sums of money. EXAMPLES: **embezzlement**, tax fraud; violations of the **antitrust acts**.

white knight *n.* A corporation that is the target of a **hostile takeover** often solicits another corporation (the "white knight") to merge with it in order to convert the hostile takeover to a **friendly takeover**.

white slavery [*slay* · ver · ee] *n.* A term sometimes used for the transportation of women and girls across state or national boundaries for immoral purposes, in violation of the **Mann Act**.

Whiteacre [*white* · aykr] *n.* Like Blackacre, the name of a hypothetical tract of land,

often used in teaching the law of real property or **future interests**. *Also see* Blackacre.

whole *n./adj.* 1. Undivided; all of something; the entire amount. 2. Healthy; sound; not disabled.

➤ *n.* aggregate, assemblage, complex, integral, quantum, supply ("the group as a whole").
adj. accomplished, consummate, exhaustive, integral, plenary, unabbreviated ("the whole pizza"); cured, fit, healed, hearty, recovered, robust, sound ("to be a whole person again").

whole law *n.* All of a country's laws, including its statutes and judicial decisions governing **conflict of laws**. *See renvoi.*

whole life *n.* *See* whole life insurance.

whole life insurance [in · *shoor* · ense] *n.* **Straight life insurance** or **ordinary life insurance**, as opposed to **term life insurance** or **group insurance**.

wholesale [*hole* · sale] *adj.* 1. A sale by a manufacturer to a retailer, **jobber**, or dealer, for resale, as opposed to a sale directly to the consumer. 2. Thorough; complete.

➤ bulk, complete, extensive, general, indiscriminate, sweeping ("wholesale changes").

wholesale dealer [*deel* · er] *n.* Same as **wholesaler**.

wholesale price *n.* The price paid to a wholesaler by a retailer, as opposed to the higher price which the retailer charges the consumer.

wholesaler [*hole* · say · ler] *n.* A person who sells goods at wholesale, as opposed to retail. *Compare* retailer.

wholly [*hole* · ee] *adv.* Entirely; totally; completely.

➤ altogether, comprehensively, outright, perfectly, quite, roundly, utterly ("wholly committed").

wholly destroyed [de · *stroyd*] *adv. See* total loss.

wholly disabled [dis · *aybld*] *adv. See* total disability.

wholly owned subsidiary [sub · *sid* · ee · air · ee] *n.* A **subsidiary corporation** that is totally owned, as opposed to merely controlled, by its **parent company**.

widow [*wid* · oh] *n.* A woman whose husband has died and who has not remarried.

widow's allowance [*wid* · ohz a · *louw* · ense] *n.* Same as **elective share**.

widow's election [*wid* · ohz e · *lek* · shen] *n. See* election by spouse; election under the will.

widower [*wid* · oh · wer] *n.* A man whose wife has died and who has not remarried.

widower's allowance [*wid* · oh · werz a · *louw* · ense] *n.* Same as **elective share**.

widower's election [*wid* · oh · werz e · *lek* · shen] *n. See* election by spouse; election under the will.

Wild's Case *n. See* rule in Wild's Case.

wildcat strike [*wild* · kat] *n.* A strike that is not authorized by the union representing the strikers.

will *n.* 1. An **instrument** by which a person (the **testator**) makes a disposition of her property, to take effect after her death. A will is **ambulatory** and **revocable** during the testator's lifetime. *See* double wills; holographic will; joint and mutual wills; joint will; last will; living will; military will; mutual wills; nuncupative will; oral will; reciprocal wills; renunciation of will; revocation of will. 2. Conscious choice; volition; wish; desire. USAGE: "Mary must give up the house any time the owner tells her to because she only has an **estate at will**." *See* at will. *See also* tenancy at will. *v.* 1. To cause to happen. 2. To give to someone in a will.
➤ *n.* aim, appetite, decisiveness, liking, purpose, temperament ("free will"); bequest, bestowal, declaration, disposition, estate, legacy ("last will and testament"). *v.* authorize, bid, command, decree, effect, enjoin, request ("to will that something occur"); bequest, confer, devise, legate, probate ("to will an estate to someone").

will contest [*kon* · test] *n.* The challenging of provisions in a will. *See* contest.

willful [*wil* · ful] *adj.* 1. Intentional; having a bad purpose, evil intent, or **malice**. 2. Intentional or deliberate, but not necessarily with malice. 3. Voluntary, as distinguished from accidental. 4. Stubborn; obstinate; inflexible.
➤ adamant, bullheaded, contumacious, factional, intransigent, refractory, conscious, deliberate, designed, planned, intentional, premeditated, studied ("willful violation of the law").

willful and malicious injury [ma · *lish* · ess *in* · jer · ee] *n.* An **injury** to a person or property inflicted intentionally and deliberately, without cause and with no regard for the legal rights of the injured party.

willful and wanton act [*want* · en] *n.* 1. An act or conduct that the perpetrator knows or should know is likely to result in **injury**, but about which he is indifferent. EXAMPLE: **reckless driving**. 2. A deliberate and intentional **wrong**.

willful and wanton misconduct [*want* · en mis · *kon* · dukt] *n. See* willful and wanton act.

willful and wanton negligence [*want* · en *neg* · li · jense] *n. See* willful negligence.

willful misconduct [mis · *kon* · dukt] *n.* Under state **unemployment compensation acts**, an employee who is fired for engaging in "willful misconduct" (deliberate disregard of his employer's interests, work rules, safety standards, etc.) is ineligible to receive unemployment compensation benefits.

willful neglect [neg · *lekt*] *n.* The deliberate or intentional failure of a person to perform a duty to others as required by law. EXAMPLES of such duties include: the duty of a parent to care for a child (*see* child neglect) in some circumstances; the duty of a spouse to provide care to his or her partner (*see* nonsupport); the obligation of a public official to perform a duty required by virtue of her office (*see* neglect of duty).

willful negligence [*neg* · li · jense] *n.* **Reckless disregard** of a person's safety, evidenced by the failure to exercise **ordinary care** to prevent **injury** after discovering an **imminent peril**. *See* negligence.

willful violation [vy · o · *lay* · shen] *n.* A deliberate failure to comply with the law.

willfully [*wil* · ful · ee] *adv.* 1. Intentionally and maliciously. 2. Intentionally but not

W

W

maliciously. 3. Voluntarily. 4. Stubbornly. *See* willful.

➤ knowingly, intentionally, deliberately, voluntarily, consciously.

winding up [*wine* · ding] *n.* The **dissolution** or **liquidation** of a corporation or a partnership.

wirefraud [*wire* · frawd] *n.* The use of interstate telephone or telegraph lines to perpetrate a **fraud**. Wirefraud is a federal crime. *See also* mail fraud.

wiretapping [*wire* · tap · ing] *n.* Listening in on a telephone conversation, or intercepting a telegraph message, by "tapping" the wires. Wiretapping is illegal unless authorized by a court for law enforcement purposes.

➤ spying, eavesdropping.

wish *v.* To desire; to want. "Wish" is a **precatory word**. For the effect of "wish" in creating a **trust**, *see* precatory trust.
n. A hope; a desire.

➤ *v.* aspire, entreat, hanker, prefer, request, solicit ("to wish for a new car").
n. ambition, inclination, invocation, preference, urge, yearning, aspiration, yen, hope ("a wish for the future").

with *prep.* 1. Close to; near to; in the company of. 2. In addition to.
with all faults A clause in a **contract for sale of goods** indicating that the article is taken by the purchaser "as is."
with interest [*in* · trest] Bearing **interest**. *See* interest-bearing.
with prejudice [*prej* · e · diss] A phrase applied to actions or words that have harmful consequences. *Compare* without prejudice. *See* prejudice. *Also see* dismissal with prejudice.
with recourse [*ree* · corss] An **indorsement** by which the **indorser** remains liable for payment of the **negotiable instrument**. *Compare* without recourse. *See* recourse.
with strong hand A phrase used in statutes and **pleadings** in reference to a forcible entry upon real property.

withdrawal [*with* · *draw* · el] *n.* The act of drawing back from, taking back, or removing. EXAMPLES: **withdrawal from**

criminal activity; withdrawal of funds from a savings account.

➤ abandonment, abdication, abjuration, exodus, relinquishment, rescission, secession, drawing back ("withdrawal from conspiracy").
withdrawal from conspiracy [kun · *spihr* · e · see] *n.* Termination of participation in a **conspiracy**. A **conspirator** who withdraws from a conspiracy before it is carried out may avoid criminal liability if she discloses the conspiracy to law enforcement authorities.
withdrawal from criminal activity [*krim* · i · nel ak · *tiv* · i · tee] *n.* Termination of criminal activity before it is committed. A person is not liable for prosecution for the criminal activity of others with whom he is involved if, before the crime is committed, he both discontinues his participation in the crime and attempts to prevent it.
withdrawal of charges [*char* · jez] *n. See nolle prosequi.*

withhold [with · *hold*] *v.* To keep back; to suppress.

➤ retain, keep, suppress, repress, deny, limit, impede.
Ant. relinquish, give.

withholding [with · *hole* · ding] *n./adj.*
1. Short for **withholding tax**. 2. Retaining that which belongs to another.
withholding tax *n.* Federal and state income tax and **FICA** contributions deducted by an employer from the pay of employees and remitted by the employer to the government.

within [with · *in*] *adv.* In; into; inside.

➤ in, indoors, inner, interior, not beyond, not over.
within the course of employment [em · *ploy* · ment] *See* course of employment.
within the meaning of the law [*meen* · ing] As set forth or described in a statute or as otherwise prohibited or permitted by law.
within the scope of employment [em · *ploy* · ment] *See* scope of employment.

without [with · *out*] *adv.* 1. Lacking. 2. On the outside; beyond.

➤ after, beyond, externally, out, outdoors, outwardly; lacking.

without benefit of clergy [*ben* · e · fit of *kler* · jee] A phrase sometimes applied to a man and a woman who **cohabit** without having been married.

without day *See sine die.*

without issue [*ish* · ew] *See* die without issue.

without notice [*noh* · tiss] To be a **holder in due course** or a **holder in good faith** of a **negotiable instrument**, the **holder** must have taken the instrument without **notice of dishonor** or of any other **claim** or **defense** against it.

without prejudice [*prej* · e · diss] A phrase applied to actions or words that do not have harmful consequences. *See* prejudice. *Also see* dismissal without prejudice. *Compare* with prejudice.

without recourse [*ree* · corss] An **indorsement** that relieves the **indorser** from liability for the payment of a **negotiable instrument**. *Compare* with recourse. *See* recourse.

witness [*wit* · nes] *n.* 1. A person who testifies or gives evidence before a court or at an **administrative hearing** with respect to something she has observed or of which she has knowledge. *See* adverse witness; competent witness; expert witness; eyewitness; hostile witness; lay witness; material witness; prosecuting witness. 2. A person who is asked to be present at a transaction (for EXAMPLE, the signing of a contract) in order to **attest** that it took place. *See* attestation. *v.* 1. To see or observe. 2. To **attest**; to act as an observer for the purpose of attesting. ➤ *n.* attestant, attestor, eyewitness, signatory, testifier, viewer ("a witness to the murder"). *v.* attend, behold, be present, look on, make note, perceive ("to witness a will"); testify, authenticate, affirm, corroborate, indicate, observe.

witness against oneself [a · *genst* won · *self*] *See* self-incrimination.

witness fees *n.* Fees paid to witnesses for their attendance at court. Witness fees are commonly included as taxable costs. *See* court costs; taxation of costs.

witness my hand and seal A formal phrase appearing in an **attestation clause** or **testimonium clause**.

witness tampering [*tam* · per · ing] *n.* Improper interaction with a witness, usually involving pressure to change the witness's testimony. *See* tampering.

witnessing part [*wit* · nes · ing] *n.* The **attestation clause** in a will, contract, or other formal document.

wittingly [*wit* · ing · lee] *adv.* Intentionally; knowingly; by design.

word *n.* 1. "Word" or "words," as most often used in legal language, mean technical words or expressions with particular significance in the language of the law, i.e., **words of art** or **terms of art**. EXAMPLES: **words of limitation; words of negotiability; words of purchase**. 2. Speech sounds that are the basis of language. 3. A promise. USAGE: "He kept his word." ➤ chat, colloquy, confabulation, conversation, discussion, talk ("to have a word with someone"); account, adage, directive, declaration, hearsay, proverb, remark ("the word from the White House"); concept, morpheme, phrase, term, usage, utterance, vocable ("our word in the English language"); behest, charge, decree, dictate, injunction, mandate ("give the word"); affirmation, assertion, engagement, guarantee, promise, parole, plight ("to give one's word").

words actionable per se [*ak* · shen · ebl per say] *n. See* actionable per se; libelous per se; *per se*; slanderous per se.

words of art *n. See* term of art.

words of limitation [lim · i · *tay* · shen] *n.* Words in a **devise** or other **grant** that determine the nature or duration of an **estate**. EXAMPLE: In a grant of Blackacre "to Mary Ellen for life," the words "for life" are words of limitation. *Compare* words of purchase. *See* limitation; limitation of estate.

words of negotiability [neg · oh · sheb · il · i · tee] *n.* Words in an **instrument** that make it **negotiable**. EXAMPLES: "pay to **bearer**"; "pay to **order**"; "payable **on demand**."

words of purchase [*per* · ches] *n.* Words in a will or other **grant** that **convey** or give an **estate in land**. EXAMPLE: In a grant of Blackacre "to Mary Ellen for life, and after her death to her heirs," the words that ultimately give the estate to Mary Ellen's

W

heirs (i.e., "to her heirs") are "words of purchase." *Compare* words of limitation. *See* purchase.

work *n.* 1. Any form of physical or mental exertion, or both combined, for the purpose of attaining some object other than recreation. 2. Employment. See availability for work.
   v. 1. Labor; toil. 2. A person's business or occupation. 3. A creation or achievement.
➤ *n.* manual labor, effort, toil, struggle, travail, drudgery ("sweatshop work"); endeavor, pursuit, attempt, discipline, métier ("a person's choice of work"); creation, composition, deed, feat, fruit, invention, handiwork ("work of art").
   v. toil, sweat, practice, endeavor, drudge, slave.

work of necessity [ne · *sess* · i · tee] *n.* Activities that are exempt from **Sunday closing laws** because the legislature considers them to be necessary activities.

work product [*prod* · ukt] *n.* Material prepared by counsel in preparing for the trial of a case. EXAMPLES: notes; memoranda; sketches.

work product rule [*prod* · ukt] *n.* The rule that an attorney's **work product** is not subject to **discovery**.

work release [re · *leess*] *n.* Programs that permit prisoners to be employed in the community during the day, returning to the correctional facility at night.

work stoppage [*stop* · ej] *n.* A strike.

work week *n.* *See* hours of labor.

worker [*wer* · ker] *n.* 1. A person who does work. 2. A person who is employed.
➤ artisan, breadwinner, employee, laborer, toiler, trader.

workers' compensation [*wer* · kerz kom · pen · *say* · shen] *n.* Short for **workers' compensation acts** or **workers' compensation insurance**.

workers' compensation acts [*wer* · kerz kom · pen · *say* · shen] *n.* State statutes that provide for the payment of **compensation** to employees injured in their employment or, in case of death, to their dependents. Benefits are paid under such acts whether or not the employer was **negligent**; payment is made in accordance with predetermined schedules based

generally upon the loss or impairment of earning capacity. *See* scheduled injuries. Workers' compensation laws eliminate **defenses** such as **assumption of risk, contributory negligence**, and **fellow servant**. Workers' compensation systems are funded through employer contributions to a common fund, through commercially purchased insurance, or both. **Occupational diseases** are compensable under these acts as well. *See also* Federal Employees' Liability Act (FELA).

workers' compensation insurance [*wer* · kerz kom · pen · *say* · shen in · *shoor* · ense] *n.* *See* workers' compensation acts.

working [*wer* · king] *adj.* 1. Bringing about results; functioning; operating. 2. Pertaining to work.
   n. The act of doing work.
➤ *adj.* active, occupied, alive, dynamic, engaged, laboring, moving.

working capital [*wer* · king] *n.* A company's **liquid assets** or **current funds; current assets** less **current liabilities**.

working papers [*pay* · perz] *n.* 1. In some states, an official document certifying that its holder is of working age as established by law. *See* of age. 2. A lawyer's **work product** is sometimes referred to as her "working papers."

workmanlike manner [*werk* · men · like *man* · er] *n.* A term applied to work done competently or skillfully.

works *n.* 1. A factory; a manufacturing establishment. 2. A structure of any sort, especially one used by the public or that has a public purpose. *See* public works. 3. Drug paraphernalia, particularly hypodermic syringes.
➤ factory, mill, foundry, workshop, plant, assembly.

world *n.* 1. The planet Earth. 2. The human race. 3. A person's environment or experience.
➤ planet, globe, earth, microcosm, nature, sphere, terrain ("in the entire world"); class, division, everybody, group, humankind, man, race, realm ("The whole world comes together"); ambience,

W

atmosphere, business, domain, kingdom, memory ("in his own little world").

worldly goods [*werld* · lee] *n.* The property one leaves behind when he dies. The term, in a will, includes both real property and personal property.

worth *n.* 1. In the law, the monetary value of a thing. 2. Importance; merit.
➤ assistance, avail, caliber, desirability, merit, significance, value, importance.

worthier title doctrine [*wer* · thee · er *ty* · tel *dok* · trin] *n.* 1. The **common law rule** that when an heir is given by **devise** the same **interest** she would receive by **descent**, she takes by descent, not by devise, descent being regarded as the better or "worthier" **title**. 2. In some states, the rule is applied to **inter vivos transfers** of real property so as to prevent the **grantor** from creating a **remainder** in his heirs, the **presumption** being that he intended to create a **reversionary interest**.

worthless [*werth* · les] *adj.* Having no worth; of no value or use.
➤ abandoned, barren, bogus, despicable, mediocre, unessential, unimportant, valueless.
Ant. valuable, important.

worthless check *n.* A **check** drawn on **insufficient funds**.

worthless stock *n.* **Stock** in a corporation whose **assets** are less than its **liabilities**.

wreck *n.* 1. A ship that, because of damage done to it, is not navigable or is unable to continue its voyage without repairs exceeding half its value. 2. Goods washed ashore after a shipwreck or as a result of having been thrown overboard in an effort to save the ship; **jetsam**.
v. To tear down; to damage or destroy; to cause serious injury to anything.
➤ *n.* collapse, debacle, debris, derelict, founder, litter, relic ("The 50-year-old car is a wreck").
v. batter, decimate, devastate, founder, impair, ravage, sabotage ("to wreck the car").

writ *n.* A written order issued by a court directing the person to whom it is

addressed to do a specified act. Writs may be addressed to an **officer of the court** (EXAMPLE: a **writ of attachment**), to an **inferior court** (EXAMPLE: a **writ of certiorari**), to a **board** (EXAMPLE: a **writ of prohibition**), to a corporation (EXAMPLE: a **writ of mandamus**), or to an individual (EXAMPLE: a **summons**), among others. Writs are also issued by authorities other than courts. EXAMPLES: a **commission** issued by the governor to a public official; a **citation** issued to a violator by a police officer. *See* alias writ; alternative writ; executed writ; extraordinary writs; ordinary writ; prerogative writ.
➤ command, decree, document, replevin, subpoena, summons, warrant.

writ of assistance [a · *sis* · tense] *n.* A **judicial writ** similar to a **writ of possession**, issued to secure the possession of land after **title** or the **right of possession** has been determined by the court.

writ of attachment [a · *tach* · ment] *n.* A writ ordering an **attachment**. See attachment.

writ of capias [*kay* · pee · es] *n. See capias.*

writ of certiorari [ser · sho · *rare* · ee] *n. See certiorari.*

writ of coram nobis [*kor* · em *no* · bis] *n. See coram nobis.*

writ of coram vobis [*kor* · em *vo* · bis] *n. See coram vobis.*

writ of ejectment [ee · *jekt* · ment] *n.* The **judicial writ** issued in an **action** of **ejectment**. *See* ejectment.

writ of entry [*en* · tree] *n. See* entry.

writ of error [*err* · er] *n.* A formal order issued by an **appellate court**, directed to the **lower court**, ordering it to transfer the **record** for review and for the correction of **errors of law** that the **appellant** alleges were committed by the lower court. *See* error, judicial error.

writ of error coram nobis [*err* · er *kor* · em *no* · bis] *n.* Same as **writ of coram nobis**.

writ of error coram vobis [*err* · er *kor* · em *vo* · bis] *n.* Same as **writ of coram vobis**.

writ of execution [ek · se · *kyoo* · shen] *n. See* execution.

W

writ of fieri facias [*fie* · e · ree *fay* · shee · ass] *n.* *See fieri facias.*

writ of habeas corpus [*hay* · bee · ess *kore* · pus] *n.* *See habeas corpus.*

writ of mandamus [man · *day* · mus] *n.* *See mandamus.*

writ of ne exeat [nay *eks* · ee · at] *n.* *See ne exeat.*

writ of possession [po · *zesh* · en] *n.* A **judicial writ** used to enforce a **judgment** to recover the **possession** of real property. *See* possession.

writ of prohibition [pro · hi · *bish* · en] *n.* A **writ** issued by a **higher court** directing a **lower court** not to take a certain action, i.e., prohibiting it from attempting to exercise **jurisdiction** in a matter in which it has no jurisdiction. *See* prohibition.

writ of quo warranto [kwoh wah · *rahn* · toh] *n.* *See quo warranto.*

writ of replevin [re · *plev* · in] *n.* **Process** issued in an **action** of **replevin**. *See* replevin.

writ of scire facias [*sye* · ree *fay* · shee · ass] *n.* *See scire facias.*

writ of supersedeas [soo · per · *see* · dee · es] *n.* *See supersedeas.*

write-in candidate [*kan* · di · date] *n.* A candidate for election whose name is not on the ballot but who campaigns to have people vote for her by writing her name on the ballot.

write-off *n.* Elimination of an item as an **asset** or reducing its value on the **books** to reflect its actual loss of value. **Bad debts**, for EXAMPLE, are generally "written off." A write-off is also referred to as a **charge-off**.

writing [*write* · ing] *n.* 1. An **instrument**. EXAMPLES: a contract; a deed; a **negotiable instrument**. 2. Any document. 3. Anything that is written. The **Uniform Commercial Code** defines "**written**" or "writing" to include "printing, typewriting, or any other intentional reduction [of words] to tangible form." 4. Handwriting. 5. The expression of ideas by visible letters, numbers, or other symbols.
➤ autograph, calligraphy, handwriting, hieroglyphics, print, scribble ("His writing is difficult to read"); article, discourse, dissertation, document, literature, opus

("His writing on disease prevention is informative").

writing obligatory [ob · *lig* · e · tore · ee] *n.* A **bond**.

written [*writ* · en] *adj.* Expressed in writing. *Compare* oral; parol.

written contract [*kon* · trakt] *n.* A **contract** in writing, as distinguished from an **oral contract** or **parol contract**.

written instrument [*in* · stroo · ment] *n.* *See* writing.

written law *n.* The law as contained in statutes, ordinances, constitutions, and **treaties**. *Compare* unwritten law.

wrong *n.* 1. The invasion or infringement of a **legal right**. A "wrong" implies an **injury** to another's person or property. The law creates a **remedy** for every wrong and, accordingly, every wrong is the basis of a **cause of action**. 2. The violation of a moral principle. *See* principle.
adj. 1. Illegal. 2. False or mistaken.
➤ *n.* blunder, immorality, omission, trespass, abuse, malfeasance, infringement ("to commit a wrong against society").
adj. lawless, corrupt, detestable, delinquent, illegitimate, vicious ("a wrong act towards another"); incorrect, false, mistaken, imprecise, erroneous, fallacious ("a wrong assumption").

wrongdoer [*rong* · doo · er] *n.* A person who commits a **wrong**; a **tortfeasor**.
➤ lawbreaker, tortfeasor, transgressor, offender, convict, villain, criminal.

wrongful [*rong* · ful] *adj.* 1. Unlawful; illegal. 2. Harmful; damaging. 3. Unfair; not **equitable**. 4. Immoral.
➤ evil, blameworthy, dishonest, improper, unethical, unlawful, illegal, harmful, damaging, unfair, inequitable, immoral.

wrongful abstraction [ab · *strak* · shen] *n.* An unauthorized and illegal taking or withholding of funds or **securities**, and their **appropriation** to the taker's benefit.

wrongful act *n.* Any act that is an infringement of the rights of another to his **damage**, unless done in the exercise of an equal or superior right. "Wrongful acts" include not only acts that are **negligent**, but **willful, wanton, reckless**, and **criminal acts** as well.

W

wrongful birth *n.* When an unsound child is born to parents who decided not to prevent or terminate the pregnancy because of erroneous medical advice, or because of medical advice not offered that should have been, the birth may, in some jurisdictions, be the basis for a wrongful birth **action**. *See* medical malpractice.

wrongful conception [kun · *sep* · shun] *n.* When a child is born as the result of a **negligently** performed sterilization of either the father or the mother, the birth may, in some jurisdictions, be the basis of an **action** for wrongful conception.

wrongful conduct [*kon* · dukt] *n. See* wrongful act.

wrongful conversion [ken · *ver* · zhen] *n.* Same as **conversion**.

wrongful death *n.* A death that results from a **wrongful act**.

wrongful death action [*ak* · shen] *n.* An **action** arising under a **wrongful death statute**.

wrongful death acts *n. See* wrongful death statutes.

wrongful death statutes [*stat* · shoots] *n.* State statutes that allow the **personal representative** of the **decedent** to bring an **action** on behalf of the decedent's statutory **beneficiaries** (EXAMPLES: spouse; children) if the decedent's death was the result of the defendant's **wrongful act**.

wrongful discharge [*dis* · charj] *n.* The discharge or termination of an employee in violation of law. *See* discharge.

wrongful life *n. See* wrongful birth; wrongful conception.

wrongful pregnancy [*preg* · nan · see] *n. See* wrongful conception.

wrongful termination [term · i · *nay* · shen] *n. See* wrongful discharge.

wrongfully [*rong* · ful · lee] *adv.* Unlawfully; illegally; harmfully; unfairly; immorally. *See* wrongful.

W

X

x A symbol or **mark** made by an illiterate or disabled person as a substitute for a complete signature. Such a mark is a valid signature when witnessed as required by statute.

x-ray *n.* A picture of the inside of a body or thing.
➤ radiograph, picture, skiagraph, fluoroscope, encephalogram.

Y

yard *n.* An area around a structure; a lawn.
➤ lawn, garden, courtyard, grounds, enclosure.

yarn *n.* 1. Fiber used for knitting. 2. A story; a tall tale.
➤ fiber, thread, wool; story, tall tale, narrative, anecdote, alibi, fable, line.

year *n.* Unless another meaning is specifically expressed, a calendar year of 365 days, or 366 days in a leap year, as opposed to any period of 365 consecutive days. *Compare* civil year. *See* fiscal year; tax year. *See also* estate for years; seven years' absence; tenancy for years; tenancy from year to year; term of years.
➤ period, cycle, span, epoch, age.
  year and a day *n.* The rule in prosecutions for **homicide**, in many jurisdictions, that if death does not occur within a year and a day after the occurrence of the **wrongful act**, it will be **presumed** that death resulted from some other cause.

yearn *v.* To want or desire strongly.
➤ dream, long, thirst, want, chafe, ache, hunger.

yellow-dog contract [*yel* · oh dog *kon* · trakt] *n.* An employment contract in which an employee agrees that he will not join a union. Such contracts are illegal.

yield *n.* 1. The return or profit on an investment. USAGE: "These bonds yielded a 4 percent return last year." 2. The amount of a crop grown on a specified area of land, usually calculated by the bushel or the pound.
  v. 1. To surrender; to submit; to give up; to relinquish. 2. To produce, specifically to produce a return on an investment; to return, to generate; to bring in.
➤ *n.* crop, earnings, harvest, revenue, takings, turnout ("The year's yield was good").
  v. accrue, allow, discharge, tender, give, turn out ("The fields will yield crops"); abandon, break, capitulate, cede, relax, relent ("to yield to demands"); accede, surrender, acquiesce, admit, concede ("to yield in battle").

youngster [*yung* · stir] *n.* A person before the age of maturity; a child.
➤ youth, minor, child, juvenile, junior, student, pupil.

youth *n.* 1. A child. 2. The early part of life.
➤ child, minor, youngster; childhood, innocence, salad days, minority, inexperience.

youthful [*yooth* · ful] *adj.* Characterized by youth; young; like a child.
➤ juvenile, adolescent, inexperienced, childlike.

youthful offender [*yooth* · ful o · *fen* · der] *n.* Same as **juvenile offender**.

Z

zeal *n.* Passion; enthusiasm.

➤ vigor, determination, passion, conviction, purpose, enthusiasm.

zealous [*zell* · es] *adj.* Characterized by enthusiasm and fervent dedication.

➤ diligent, earnest, active, ardent, committed, impassioned.

zealous witness [*zell* · es *wit* · nes] *n.* A witness who is overly eager to be of service to the **party** who called her, to the point of bending the truth.

zenith [*zee* · nith] *n.* The top; The highest point.

➤ apex, top, pinnacle, peak, acme, crest, culmination, climax.
Ant. nadir, bottom.

zone *n.* 1. An area or district created by a **zoning board** in accordance with **zoning regulations**. 2. A distinct area that is unlike the surrounding areas.
v. To engage in **zoning**.

➤ *n.* area, belt, circuit, district, realm, territory, tract, sector.

zone of employment [em · *ploy* · ment] *n.* For the purpose of an employer's liability under **workers' compensation acts**, the areas surrounding or near an employee's work station.

zoning [*zone* · ing] *n.* The creation and application of structural, size, and use restrictions imposed upon the owners of real estate within districts or zones in accordance with **zoning regulations** or ordinances. Although authorized by state statutes, zoning is generally legislated and regulated by **local government**. Zoning is a form of **land use regulation** and is generally of two types: regulations having to do with structural and architectural design; and regulations specifying the use(s) to which designated districts may be put, for EXAMPLE, commercial, industrial, residential, or agricultural. *See and compare* cluster zoning; spot zoning.

zoning board *n.* An administrative agency of a **municipality** that administers **zoning regulations** or ordinances.

zoning commission [kum · *ish* · en] *n. See* zoning board.

zoning map *n.* A map showing the **zones** established by a zoning law.

zoning regulations [reg · yoo · *lay* · shenz] *n. See* zoning.

zoom *v.* To move quickly.

➤ dart, dash, speed, tear, rip, hurtle, rocket, shoot, whip.

zygote [*zy* · goat] *n.* 1. The cell created when an ovum is fertilized by sperm, i.e., a fertilized egg. 2. The developing individual created by fertilization. In the law, zygotes are of particular significance in **actions** involving the custody of frozen human embryos.

APPENDIX

The Constitution of the United States of America

We the People of the United States, in Order to form a more perfect Union, establish Justice, insure domestic Tranquility, provide for the common defence, promote the general Welfare, and secure the Blessings of Liberty to ourselves and our Posterity, do ordain and establish this Constitution for the United States of America.

ARTICLE I

Section 1 All legislative Powers herein granted shall be vested in a Congress of the United States, which shall consist of a Senate and House of Representatives.

Section 2 (1) The House of Representatives shall be composed of Members chosen every second Year by the People of the several States, and the Electors in each State shall have the Qualifications requisite for Electors of the most numerous Branch of the State Legislature.

(2) No Person shall be a Representative who shall not have attained to the age of twenty-five Years, and been seven Years a Citizen of the United States, and who shall not, when elected, be an Inhabitant of that State in which he shall be chosen.

(3) Representatives and direct Taxes shall be apportioned among the several States which may be included within this Union, according to their respective Numbers, which shall be determined by adding to the whole Number of free Persons, including those bound to Service for a Term of Years, and excluding Indians not taxed, three fifths of all other Persons. The actual Enumeration shall be made within three Years after the first Meeting of the Congress of the United States, and within every subsequent Term of ten Years, in such Manner as they shall by Law direct. The Number of Representatives shall not exceed one for every thirty Thousand, but each State shall have at Least one Representative; and until such enumeration shall be made, the State of New Hampshire shall be entitled to chuse three, Massachusetts eight, Rhode Island and Providence Plantations one, Connecticut five, New York six, New Jersey four, Pennsylvania eight, Delaware one, Maryland six, Virginia ten, North Carolina five, South Carolina five, and Georgia three.

(4) When vacancies happen in the Representation from any State, the Executive Authority thereof shall issue Writs of Election to fill such Vacancies.

(5) The House of Representatives shall chuse their Speaker and other Officers; and shall have the sole Power of Impeachment.

Section 3 (1) The Senate of the United States shall be composed of two Senators from each State, chosen by the Legislature thereof, for six Years; and each Senator shall have one Vote.

(2) Immediately after they shall be assembled in Consequence of the first Election, they shall be divided as equally as may be into three Classes. The Seats of the Senators of the first Class shall be vacated at the Expiration of the second Year, of the second Class at the Expiration of the fourth Year, and of the third Class at the Expiration of the sixth Year, so that one third may be chosen every

second Year; and if Vacancies happen by Resignation, or otherwise, during the Recess of the Legislature of any State, the Executive thereof may make temporary Appointments until the next Meeting of the Legislature, which shall then fill such Vacancies.

(3) No Person shall be a Senator who shall not have attained to the Age of thirty Years, and been nine Years a Citizen of the United States, and who shall not, when elected, be an Inhabitant of that State for which he shall be chosen.

(4) The Vice President of the United States shall be President of the Senate, but shall have no Vote, unless they be equally divided.

(5) The Senate shall chuse their other Officers, and also a President pro tempore, in the Absence of the Vice President, or when he shall exercise the Office of the President of the United States.

(6) The Senate shall have the sole Power to try all Impeachments. When sitting for that Purpose, they shall be on Oath or Affirmation. When the President of the United States is tried, the Chief Justice shall preside: And no Person shall be convicted without the Concurrence of two thirds of the Members present.

(7) Judgment in Cases of Impeachment shall not extend further than to removal from Office, and disqualification to hold and enjoy any Office of honor, Trust or Profit under the United States: but the Party convicted shall nevertheless be liable and subject to Indictment, Trial, Judgment and Punishment, according to Law.

Section 4 (1) The Times, Places and Manner of holding Elections for Senators and Representatives, shall be prescribed in each State by the Legislature thereof; but the Congress may at any time by Law make or alter such Regulations, except as to the Places of chusing Senators.

(2) The Congress shall assemble at least once in every Year, and such Meeting shall be on the first Monday in December, unless they shall by Law appoint a different Day.

Section 5 (1) Each House shall be the Judge of the Elections, Returns and Qualifications of its own Members, and a Majority of each shall constitute a Quorum to do Business;

but a smaller Number may adjourn from day to day, and may be authorized to compel the Attendance of absent Members, in such Manner, and under such Penalties as each House may provide.

(2) Each House may determine the Rules of its Proceedings, punish its Members for disorderly Behaviour, and, with the Concurrence of two thirds, expel a Member.

(3) Each House shall keep a Journal of its Proceedings, and from time to time publish the same, excepting such Parts as may in their Judgment require Secrecy; and the Yeas and Nays of the Members of either House on any question shall, at the Desire of one fifth of those Present, be entered on the Journal.

(4) Neither House, during the Session of Congress, shall, without the Consent of the other, adjourn for more than three days, nor to any other Place than that in which the two Houses shall be sitting.

Section 6 (1) The Senators and Representatives shall receive a Compensation for their Services, to be ascertained by Law, and paid out of the Treasury of the United States. They shall in all Cases, except Treason, Felony and Breach of the Peace, be privileged from Arrest during their Attendance at the Session of their respective Houses, and in going to and returning from the same; and for any Speech or Debate in either House, they shall not be questioned in any other Place.

(2) No Senator or Representative shall, during the Time for which he was elected, be appointed to any civil Office under the authority of the United States, which shall have been created, or the Emoluments whereof shall have been encreased during such time; and no Person holding any Office under the United States, shall be a Member of either House during his Continuance in Office.

Section 7 (1) All Bills for raising Revenue shall originate in the House of Representatives; but the Senate may propose or concur with Amendments as on other Bills.

(2) Every Bill which shall have passed the House of Representatives and the Senate, shall, before it become a Law, be presented to the President of the United States; If he approve he shall sign it, but if not he shall return it, with his Objections to that House

in which it shall have originated, who shall enter the Objections at large on their Journal, and proceed to reconsider it. If after such Reconsideration two thirds of that House shall agree to pass the Bill, it shall be sent, together with the Objections, to the other House, by which it shall likewise be reconsidered, and if approved by two thirds of that House, it shall become a law. But in all such Cases the Votes of both Houses shall be determined by Yeas and Nays, and the Names of the Persons voting for and against the Bill shall be entered on the Journal of each House respectively. If any Bill shall not be returned by the President within ten Days (Sunday excepted) after it shall have been presented to him, the Same shall be a Law, in like Manner as if he had signed it, unless the Congress by their Adjournment prevent its Return, in which Case it shall not be a Law.

(3) Every Order, Resolution, or Vote to which the Concurrence of the Senate and House of Representatives may be necessary (except on a question of Adjournment) shall be presented to the President of the United States; and before the Same shall take Effect, shall be approved by him, or being disapproved by him, shall be repassed by two thirds of the Senate and House of Representatives, according to the Rules and Limitations prescribed in the Case of a Bill.

Section 8 (1) The Congress shall have Power To lay and collect Taxes, Duties, Imposts and Excises, to pay the Debts and provide for the common Defence and general Welfare of the United States; but all Duties, Imposts and Excises shall be uniform throughout the United States;

(2) To borrow Money on the credit of the United States;

(3) To regulate Commerce with foreign Nations, and among the several States, and with the Indian Tribes;

(4) To establish an uniform Rule of Naturalization, and uniform Laws on the subject of Bankruptcies throughout the United States;

(5) To coin Money, regulate the Value thereof, and of foreign Coin, and to fix the Standard of Weights and Measures;

(6) To provide for the Punishment of counterfeiting the Securities and current Coin of the United States;

(7) To establish Post Offices and post Roads;

(8) To promote the Progress of Science and useful Arts, by securing for limited Times to Authors and Inventors the exclusive Right to their respective Writings and Discoveries;

(9) To constitute Tribunals inferior to the supreme Court;

(10) To define and punish Piracies and Felonies committed on the high Seas, and Offenses against the Law of Nations;

(11) To declare War, grant Letters of Marque and Reprisal, and make Rules concerning Captures on Land and Water;

(12) To raise and support Armies, but no Appropriation of Money to that Use shall be for a longer Term than two Years;

(13) To provide and maintain a Navy;

(14) To make Rules for the Government and Regulation of the land and naval Forces;

(15) To provide for calling forth the Militia to execute the Laws of the Union, suppress Insurrections and repel Invasions;

(16) To provide for organizing, arming, and disciplining, the Militia, and for governing such Part of them as may be employed in the Service of the United States, reserving to the States respectively, the Appointment of the Officers, and the Authority of training the Militia according to the discipline prescribed by Congress;

(17) To exercise exclusive Legislation in all Cases whatsoever, over such District (not exceeding ten Miles square) as may, by Cession of particular States, and the Acceptance of Congress, become the Seat of the Government of the United States, and to exercise like Authority over all Places purchased by the Consent of the Legislature of the State in which the Same shall be, for the Erection of Forts, Magazines, Arsenals, dock-Yards, and other needful Buildings;—And

(18) To make all Laws which shall be necessary and proper for carrying into Execution the foregoing Powers, and all other Powers vested by this Constitution in the Government of the United States, or in any Department or Officer thereof.

Section 9 (1) The Migration or Importation of such Persons as any of the States now existing shall think proper to admit, shall not be prohibited by the Congress prior to the Year one thousand eight hundred and eight, but a Tax or Duty may be imposed on such Importation, not exceeding ten dollars for each Person.

(2) The Privilege of the Writ of Habeas Corpus shall not be suspended unless when in Cases of Rebellion or Invasion the public Safety may require it.

(3) No Bill of Attainder or ex post facto Law shall be passed.

(4) No Capitation, or other direct, Tax shall be laid, unless in Proportion to the Census or Enumeration herein before directed to be taken.

(5) No Tax or Duty shall be laid on Articles exported from any State.

(6) No Preference shall be given by any Regulation of Commerce or Revenue to the Ports of one State over those of another; nor shall Vessels bound to, or from, one State, be obliged to enter, clear or pay Duties in another.

(7) No Money shall be drawn from the Treasury, but in Consequence of Appropriations made by Law; and a regular Statement and Account of the Receipts and Expenditures of all public Money shall be published from time to time.

(8) No Title of Nobility shall be granted by the United States: And no Person holding any Office of Profit or Trust under them, shall, without the Consent of the Congress, accept of any present, Emolument, Office, or Title, of any kind whatever, from any King, Prince or foreign State.

Section 10 (1) No State shall enter into any Treaty, Alliance, or Confederation; grant Letters of Marque and Reprisal; coin Money; emit Bills of Credit; make any Thing but gold and silver Coin a Tender in Payment of Debts; pass any Bill of Attainder, ex post facto Law, or Law impairing the Obligation of Contracts, or grant any Title of Nobility.

(2) No State shall, without the Consent of Congress, lay any Imposts or Duties on Imports or Exports, except what may be absolutely necessary for executing its inspection Laws: and the net Produce of all Duties and Imposts, laid by any State on Imports or Exports, shall be for the Use of the Treasury of the United States; and all such Laws shall be subject to the Revision and Controul of the Congress.

(3) No State shall, without the Consent of Congress, lay any Duty of Tonnage, keep Troops, or Ships of War in time of Peace, enter into any Agreement or Compact with another State, or with a foreign Power, or engage in War, unless actually invaded, or in such imminent Danger as will not admit of Delay.

ARTICLE II

Section 1 (1) The executive Power shall be vested in a President of the United States of America. He shall hold his Office during the Term of four Years, and, together with the Vice President, chosen for the same Term, be elected, as follows:

(2) Each State shall appoint, in such Manner as the Legislature thereof may direct, a Number of Electors, equal to the whole Number of Senators and Representatives to which the State may be entitled in the Congress: but no Senator or Representative, or Person holding an Office of Trust or Profit under the United States, shall be appointed an Elector.

The Electors shall meet in their respective States, and vote by Ballot for two Persons, of whom one at least shall not be an Inhabitant of the same State with themselves. And they shall make a List of all the Persons voted for, and of the Number of Votes for each; which List they shall sign and certify, and transmit sealed to the Seat of the Government of the United States, directed to the President of the Senate. The President of the Senate shall, in the presence of the Senate and House of Representatives, open all the Certificates, and the Votes shall then be counted. The Person having the greatest Number of Votes shall be the President, if such Number be a Majority of the whole Number of Electors appointed; and if there be more than one who have such Majority, and have an equal Number of Votes, then the House of Representatives shall immediately chuse by Ballot one of them for President; and if no Person have a Majority, then from the five highest on the List the said House shall in like Manner chuse the President. But in chusing the President, the Votes shall be taken by States, the Representation from each State having one Vote; a quorum for this Purpose shall consist of a Member or Members from two thirds of the States, and a Majority of all the States shall be necessary to a Choice. In every Case, after the Choice of the President, the Person having the greatest Number of Votes of the Electors shall be the Vice President. But if there should remain two or more who have equal Votes, the Senate shall chuse from them by Ballot the Vice President.

(3) The Congress may determine the Time of chusing the Electors, and the Day on which they shall give their Votes; which Day shall be the same throughout the United States.

(4) No Person except a natural born Citizen, or a Citizen of the United States, at the time of the Adoption of this Constitution, shall be eligible to the Office of President; neither shall any Person be eligible to that Office who shall not have attained to the Age of thirty five Years, and been fourteen Years a Resident within the United States.

(5) In Case of the Removal of the President from Office, or of his Death, Resignation, or Inability to discharge the Powers and Duties of the said Office, the Same shall devolve on the Vice President, and the Congress may by Law provide for the Case of Removal, Death, Resignation or Inability, both of the President and Vice President, declaring what Officer shall then act as President, and such Officer shall act accordingly, until the Disability be removed, or a President shall be elected.

(6) The President shall, at stated Times, receive for his Services, a Compensation, which shall neither be increased nor diminished during the Period for which he shall have been elected, and he shall not receive within that Period any other Emolument from the United States, or any of them.

(7) Before he enter on the Execution of his Office, he shall take the following Oath or Affirmation:—"I do solemnly swear (or affirm) that I will faithfully execute the Office of President of the United States, and will to the best of my Ability, preserve, protect and defend the Constitution of the United States."

Section 2 (1) The President shall be Commander in Chief of the Army and Navy of the United States, and of the Militia of the several States, when called into the actual Service of the United States; he may require

the Opinion, in writing, of the principal Officer in each of the executive Departments, upon any Subject relating to the Duties of their respective Offices, and he shall have Power to grant Reprieves and Pardons for Offenses against the United States, except in Cases of Impeachment.

(2) He shall have Power, by and with the Advice and Consent of the Senate, to make Treaties, provided two thirds of the Senators present concur; and he shall nominate, and by and with the Advice and Consent of the Senate, shall appoint Ambassadors, other public Ministers and Consuls, Judges of the supreme Court, and all other Officers of the United States, whose Appointments are not herein otherwise provided for, and which shall be established by Law: but the Congress may by Law vest the Appointment of such inferior Officers, as they think proper, in the President alone, in the Courts of Law, or in the Heads of Departments.

(3) The President shall have Power to fill up all Vacancies that may happen during the Recess of the Senate, by granting Commissions which shall expire at the End of their next Session.

Section 3 He shall from time to time give to the Congress Information of the State of the Union, and recommend to their Consideration such Measures as he shall judge necessary and expedient; he may, on extraordinary Occasions, convene both Houses, or either of them, and in Case of Disagreement between them, with Respect to the Time of Adjournment, he may adjourn them to such Time as he shall think proper; he shall receive Ambassadors and other public Ministers; he shall take Care that the Laws be faithfully executed, and shall Commission all the Officers of the United States.

Section 4 The President, Vice President and all Civil Officers of the United States, shall be removed from Office on Impeachment for, and Conviction of, Treason, Bribery, or other high Crimes and Misdemeanors.

ARTICLE III

Section 1 The judicial Power of the United States, shall be vested in one supreme Court, and in such inferior Courts as the Congress may from time to time ordain and establish.

The Judges, both of the supreme and inferior Courts, shall hold their Offices during good Behaviour, and shall, at stated Times, receive for their Services, a Compensation, which shall not be diminished during their Continuance in Office.

Section 2 (1) The judicial Power shall extend to all Cases, in Law and Equity, arising under this Constitution, the Laws of the United States, and Treaties made, or which shall be made, under their Authority;—to all Cases affecting Ambassadors, other public Ministers and Consuls;—to all Cases of admiralty and maritime Jurisdiction;—to Controversies to which the United States shall be a party;—to Controversies between two or more States;—between a State and Citizens of another State;—between Citizens of different States;—between Citizens of the same State claiming Lands under Grants of different States, and between a State, or the Citizens thereof, and foreign States, Citizens or Subjects.

(2) In all Cases affecting Ambassadors, other public Ministers and Consuls, and those in which a State shall be Party, the supreme Court shall have original Jurisdiction. In all the other Cases before mentioned, the supreme Court shall have appellate Jurisdiction, both as to Law and Fact, with such Exceptions, and under such Regulations as the Congress shall make.

(3) The Trial of all Crimes, except in Cases of Impeachment, shall be by Jury; and such Trial shall be held in the State where the said Crimes shall have been committed; but when not committed within any State, the Trial shall be at such Place or Places as the Congress may by Law have directed.

Section 3 (1) Treason against the United States, shall consist only in levying War against them, or in adhering to their Enemies, giving them Aid and Comfort. No Person shall be convicted of Treason unless on the Testimony of two Witnesses to the same overt Act, or on Confession in open Court.

(2) The Congress shall have Power to declare the Punishment of Treason, but no Attainder of Treason shall work Corruption of Blood, or Forfeiture except during the Life of the Person attainted.

ARTICLE IV

Section 1 Full Faith and Credit shall be given in each State to the public Acts, Records, and judicial Proceedings of every other State. And the Congress may by general Laws prescribe the Manner in which such Acts, Records and Proceedings shall be proved, and the Effect thereof.

Section 2 (1) The Citizens of each State shall be entitled to all privileges and Immunities of Citizens in the several States.

(2) A Person charged in any State with Treason, Felony, or other Crime, who shall flee from Justice, and be found in another State, shall on Demand of the executive Authority of the State from which he fled, be delivered up, to be removed to the State having Jurisdiction of the Crime.

(3) No Person held to Service of Labour in one State, under the Laws thereof, escaping into another, shall, in Consequence of any Law or Regulation therein, be discharged from such Service or Labour, but shall be delivered up on Claim of the Party to whom such Service or Labour may be due.

Section 3 (1) New States may be admitted by the Congress into this Union; but no new State shall be formed or erected within the Jurisdiction of any other State; nor any State be formed by the Junction of two or more States, or Parts of States, without the Consent of the Legislatures of the States concerned as well as of the Congress.

(2) The Congress shall have power to dispose of and make all needful Rules and Regulations respecting the Territory or other Property belonging to the United States; and nothing in this Constitution shall be so construed as to Prejudice any Claims of the United States, or of any particular State.

Section 4 The United States shall guarantee to every State in this Union a Republican Form of Government, and shall protect each of them against Invasion; and on Application of the Legislature, or of the Executive (when the Legislature cannot be convened) against domestic Violence.

ARTICLE V

The Congress, whenever two thirds of both Houses shall deem it necessary, shall propose Amendments to this Constitution, or, on the Application of the Legislatures of two thirds of the several States, shall call a Convention for proposing Amendments, which, in either Case, shall be valid to all Intents and Purposes, as Part of this Constitution, when ratified by the Legislatures of three fourths of the several States, or by Conventions in three fourths thereof, as the one or the other Mode of Ratification may be proposed by the Congress; Provided that no Amendment which may be made prior to the Year One thousand eight hundred and eight shall in any Manner affect the first and fourth Clauses in the Ninth Section of the first Article; and that no State, without its Consent, shall be deprived of its equal Suffrage in the Senate.

ARTICLE VI

(1) All Debts contracted and Engagements entered into, before the Adoption of this Constitution, shall be as valid against the United States under this Constitution, as under the Confederation.

(2) This Constitution, and the Laws of the United States which shall be made in Pursuance thereof; and all Treaties made, or which shall be made, under the Authority of the United States, shall be the supreme Law of the Land; and the Judges in every State shall be bound thereby, any Thing in the Constitution or Laws of any State to the Contrary notwithstanding.

(3) The Senators and Representatives before mentioned, and the Members of the several State Legislatures, and all executive and judicial Officers, both of the United States and of the several States, shall be bound by Oath or Affirmation, to support this Constitution; but no religious Test shall ever be required as a Qualification to any Office or public Trust under the United States.

ARTICLE VII

The Ratification of the Conventions of nine States, shall be sufficient for the Establishment of this Constitution between the States so ratifying the Same.

ARTICLES IN ADDITION TO, AND AMENDMENT OF, THE CONSTITUTION OF THE UNITED STATES OF AMERICA, PROPOSED BY CONGRESS, AND

RATIFIED BY THE SEVERAL STATES, PURSUANT TO THE FIFTH ARTICLE OF THE ORIGINAL CONSTITUTION

AMENDMENT I (1791)

Congress shall make no law respecting an establishment of religion, or prohibiting the free exercise thereof; or abridging the freedom of speech, or of the press; or the right of the people peaceably to assemble, and to petition the Government for a redress of grievances.

AMENDMENT II (1791)

A well regulated Militia, being necessary to the security of a free state, the right of the people to keep and bear Arms, shall not be infringed.

AMENDMENT III (1791)

No Soldier shall, in time of peace be quartered in any house, without the consent of the Owner, nor in time of war, but in a manner to be prescribed by law.

AMENDMENT IV (1791)

The right of the people to be secure in their persons, houses, papers, and effects, against unreasonable searches and seizures, shall not be violated, and no Warrants shall issue, but upon probable cause, supported by Oath or affirmation, and particularly describing the place to be searched, and the persons or things to be seized.

AMENDMENT V (1791)

No person shall be held to answer for a capital, or otherwise infamous crime, unless on a presentment or indictment of a Grand Jury, except in cases arising in the land or naval forces, or in the Militia, when in actual service in time of War or public danger; nor shall any person be subject for the same offence to be twice put in jeopardy of life or limb; nor shall be compelled in any criminal case to be a witness against himself, nor be deprived of life, liberty, or property, without due process of law; nor shall private property be taken for public use, without just compensation.

AMENDMENT VI (1791)

In all criminal prosecutions, the accused shall enjoy the right to a speedy and public trial, by an impartial jury of the State and district wherein the crime shall have been committed, which district shall have been previously ascertained by law, and to be informed of the nature and cause of the accusation; to be confronted with the witnesses against him; to have compulsory process for obtaining witnesses in his favor, and to have the Assistance of Counsel for his defence.

AMENDMENT VII (1791)

In Suits at common law, where the value in controversy shall exceed twenty dollars, the right of trial by jury shall be preserved, and no fact tried by a jury, shall be otherwise re-examined in any Court of the United States, than according to the rules of the common law.

AMENDMENT VIII (1791)

Excessive bail shall not be required, nor excessive fines imposed, nor cruel and unusual punishments inflicted.

AMENDMENT IX (1791)

The enumeration in the Constitution, of certain rights, shall not be construed to deny or disparage others retained by the people.

AMENDMENT X (1791)

The powers not delegated to the United States by the Constitution, nor prohibited by it to the States, are reserved to the States respectively, or to the people.

AMENDMENT XI (1798)

The Judicial power of the United States shall not be construed to extend to any suit in law or equity, commenced or prosecuted against one of the United States by Citizens of another State, or by Citizens or Subjects of any Foreign State.

AMENDMENT XII (1804)

The Electors shall meet in their respective states and vote by ballot for President and Vice-President, one of whom, at least, shall not be an inhabitant of the same state with themselves; they shall name in their ballots the person voted for as President, and in distinct ballots the person voted for as Vice-President, and they shall make distinct lists of all persons voted for as President, and of all persons voted for as Vice-President, and of the number of votes for each, which lists they shall sign and certify, and transmit sealed to the seat of the government of the United States, directed to the President of the Senate;—The President of the Senate shall, in the presence of the Senate and House of Representatives, open all the certificates and the votes shall then be counted;—The person having the greatest number of votes for President, shall be the President, if such number be a majority of the whole number of Electors appointed; and if no person have such majority, then from the persons having the highest numbers not exceeding three on the list of those voted for as President, the House of Representatives shall choose immediately, by ballot, the President. But in choosing the President, the votes shall be taken by states, the representation from each state having one vote; a quorum for this purpose shall consist of a member or members from two-thirds of the states, and a majority of all the states shall be necessary to a choice. And if the House of Representatives shall not choose a President whenever the right of choice shall devolve upon them, before the fourth day of March next following, then the Vice-President shall act as President, as in the case of the death or other constitutional disability of the President—The person having the greatest number of votes as Vice-President, shall be the Vice-President, if such number be a majority of the whole number of Electors appointed, and if no person have a majority, then from the two highest numbers on the list, the Senate shall choose the Vice-President; A quorum for the purpose shall consist of two-thirds of the whole number of Senators, and a majority of the whole number shall be necessary to a choice. But no person constitutionally ineligible to the office of President shall be eligible to that of Vice-President of the United States.

AMENDMENT XIII (1865)

Section 1 Neither slavery nor involuntary servitude, except as a punishment for crime whereof the party shall have been duly convicted, shall exist within the United States, or any place subject to their jurisdiction.

Section 2 Congress shall have power to enforce this article by appropriate legislation.

AMENDMENT XIV (1868)

Section 1 All persons born or naturalized in the United States and subject to the jurisdiction thereof, are citizens of the United States and of the State wherein they reside. No State shall make or enforce any law which shall abridge the privileges or immunities of citizens of the United States; nor shall any State deprive any person of life, liberty, or property, without due process of law; nor deny to any person within its jurisdiction the equal protection of the laws.

Section 2 Representatives shall be apportioned among the several States according to their respective numbers, counting the whole number of persons in each State, excluding Indians not taxed. But when the right to vote at any election for the choice of electors for President and Vice-President of the United States, Representatives in Congress, the Executive and Judicial officers of a State, or the members of the Legislature thereof, is denied to any of the male inhabitants of such State, being twenty-one years of age, and citizens of the United States, or in any way abridged, except for participation in rebellion, or other crime, the basis of representation therein shall be reduced in the proportion which the number of such male citizens shall bear to the whole number of male citizens twenty-one years of age in such State.

Section 3 No person shall be a Senator or Representative in Congress, or elector of President and Vice-President, or hold any office, civil or military, under the United States, or under any State, who, having previously taken an oath, as a member of Congress, or as an officer of the United States, or as a member of any State legislature, or as an executive or judicial officer of any State, to support the Constitution of the United States, shall have engaged in insurrection or rebellion against the same, or given aid or comfort to the enemies thereof. But Congress may by a vote of two-thirds of each House, remove such disability.

Section 4 The validity of the public debt of the United States, authorized by law, including debts incurred for payment of pensions and bounties for services in suppressing insurrection or rebellion, shall not be questioned. But neither the United States nor any State shall assume or pay any debt or obligation incurred in aid of insurrection or rebellion against the United States, or any claim for the loss or emancipation of any slave; but all such debts, obligations and claims shall be held illegal and void.

Section 5 The Congress shall have power to enforce, by appropriate legislation, the provisions of this article.

AMENDMENT XV (1870)

Section 1 The right of citizens of the United States to vote shall not be denied or abridged by the United States or by any State on account of race, color, or previous condition of servitude.

Section 2 The Congress shall have power to enforce this article by appropriate legislation.

AMENDMENT XVI (1913)

The Congress shall have power to lay and collect taxes on incomes, from whatever source derived, without apportionment among the several States, and without regard to any census or enumeration.

AMENDMENT XVII (1913)

The Senate of the United States shall be composed of two Senators from each State, elected by the people thereof, for six years; and each Senator shall have one vote. The electors in each State shall have the qualifications requisite for electors of the most numerous branch of the State legislatures.

When vacancies happen in the representation of any State in the Senate, the executive authority of such State shall issue writs of election to fill such vacancies: *Provided,* That the legislature of any State may empower the executive thereof to make temporary appointments until the people fill the vacancies by election as the legislature may direct.

This amendment shall not be so construed as to affect the election or term of any Senator chosen before it becomes valid as part of the Constitution.

AMENDMENT XVIII (1919)

Section 1 After one year from the ratification of this article the manufacture, sale, or transportation of intoxicating liquors within, the importation thereof into, or the exportation thereof from the United States and all territory subject to the jurisdiction thereof for beverage purposes is hereby prohibited.

Section 2 The Congress and the several States shall have concurrent power to enforce this article by appropriate legislation.

Section 3 This article shall be inoperative unless it shall have been ratified as an amendment to the Constitution by the legislatures of the several States, as provided in the Constitution, within seven years from the date of the submission hereof to the States by the Congress.

AMENDMENT XIX (1920)

The right of citizens of the United States to vote shall not be denied or abridged by the United States or by any State on account of sex.

Congress shall have power to enforce this article by appropriate legislation.

AMENDMENT XX (1933)

Section 1 The terms of the President and Vice President shall end at noon on the 20th day of January, and the terms of Senators and Representatives at noon on the 3d day of January, of the years in which such terms would have ended if this article had not been ratified; and the terms of their successors shall then begin.

Section 2 The Congress shall assemble at least once in every year, and such meeting shall begin at noon on the 3d day of January, unless they shall by law appoint a different day.

Section 3 If, at the time fixed for the beginning of the term of the President, the President elect shall have died, the Vice President elect shall become President. If a President shall not have been chosen before the time fixed for the beginning of his term, or if the President elect shall have failed to qualify, then the Vice President elect shall act as President until a President shall have qualified; and the Congress may by law provide for the case wherein neither a President elect nor a Vice President elect shall have qualified, declaring who shall then act as President, or the manner in which one who is to act shall be selected, and such person shall act accordingly until a President or Vice President shall have qualified.

Section 4 The Congress may by law provide for the case of the death of any of the persons from whom the House of Representatives may choose a President whenever the right of choice shall have devolved upon them, and for the case of the death of any of the persons from whom the Senate may choose a Vice President whenever the right of choice shall have devolved upon them.

Section 5 Sections 1 and 2 shall take effect on the 15th day of October following the ratification of this article.

Section 6 This article shall be inoperative unless it shall have been ratified as an amendment to the Constitution by the legislatures of three-fourths of the several States within seven years from the date of its submission.

AMENDMENT XXI (1933)

Section 1 The eighteenth article of amendment to the Constitution of the United States is hereby repealed.

Section 2 The transportation or importation into any State, Territory or possession of the United States for delivery or use therein of intoxicating liquors, in violation of the laws thereof, is hereby prohibited.

Section 3 This article shall be inoperative unless it shall have been ratified as an amendment to the Constitution by conventions in the several States, as provided in the Constitution, within seven years from the date of the submission hereof to the States by the Congress.

AMENDMENT XXII (1951)

Section 1 No person shall be elected to the office of the President more than twice, and no person who has held the office of President, or acted as President, for more than two years of a term to which some other person was elected President shall be elected to the office of the President more than once. But this Article shall not apply to any person holding the office of President when this Article was proposed by the Congress, and shall not prevent any person who may be holding the office of President, or acting as President, during the term within which this Article becomes operative from holding the office of President or acting as President during the remainder of such term.

Section 2 This Article shall be inoperative unless it shall have been ratified as an amendment to the Constitution by the legislatures of three-fourths of the several States within seven years from the date of its submission to the States by the Congress.

AMENDMENT XXIII (1961)

Section 1 The District constituting the seat of Government of the United States shall appoint in such manner as the Congress may direct:

A number of electors of President and Vice President equal to the whole number of Senators and Representatives in Congress to which the District would be entitled if it were a State, but in no event more than the least populous State; they shall be in addition to those appointed by the States, but they shall be considered, for the purposes of the election of President and Vice President, to be electors appointed by a State; and they shall meet in the District and perform such duties as provided by the twelfth article of amendment.

Section 2 The Congress shall have power to enforce this article by appropriate legislation.

AMENDMENT XXIV (1964)

Section 1 The right of citizens of the United States to vote in any primary or other election for President or Vice President, for electors for President or Vice President, or for Senator or Representative in Congress, shall not be denied or abridged by the United States or any State by reason of failure to pay any poll tax or other tax.

Section 2 The Congress shall have power to enforce this article by appropriate legislation.

AMENDMENT XXV (1967)

Section 1 In case of the removal of the President from office or of his death or resignation, the Vice President shall become President.

Section 2 Whenever there is a vacancy in the office of the Vice President, the President shall nominate a Vice President who shall take office upon confirmation by a majority vote of both Houses of Congress.

Section 3 Whenever the President transmits to the President pro tempore of the Senate and the Speaker of the House of Representatives his written declaration that he is unable to discharge the powers and duties of his office, and until he transmits to them a written declaration to the contrary, such powers and duties shall be discharged by the Vice President as Acting President.

Section 4 Whenever the Vice President and a majority of either the principal officers of the executive departments or of such other body as Congress may by law provide, transmit to the President pro tempore of the Senate and the Speaker of the House of Representatives their written declaration that the President is unable to discharge the powers and duties of his office, the Vice President shall immediately assume the powers and duties of the office as Acting President.

Thereafter, when the President transmits to the President pro tempore of the Senate and the Speaker of the House of Representatives his written declaration that no inability exists, he shall resume the powers and duties of his office unless the Vice President and a majority of either the principal officers of the executive department or of such other body as Congress may by law provide, transmit within four days to the President pro tempore of the Senate and the Speaker of the House of Representatives their written declaration that the President is unable to discharge the powers and duties of his office. Thereupon Congress shall decide the issue, assembling within forty-eight hours for that purpose if not in session. If the Congress, within twenty-one days after receipt of the latter written declaration, or, if Congress is not in session, within twenty-one days after Congress is required to assemble, determines by two-thirds vote of both Houses that the President is unable to discharge the powers and duties of his office, the Vice President shall continue to discharge the same as Acting President; otherwise, the President shall resume the powers and duties of his office.

AMENDMENT XXVI (1971)

Section 1 The right of citizens of the United States, who are eighteen years of age or older, to vote shall not be denied or abridged by the United States or by any State on account of age.

Section 2 The Congress shall have power to enforce this article by appropriate legislation.

AMENDMENT XXVII (1992)

No law varying the compensation for the services of the senators and representatives shall take effect, until an election of representatives shall have intervened.